Sixth Edition

ECONOMICS
PRIVATE MARKETS AND PUBLIC CHOICE

THE ADDISON-WESLEY SERIES IN ECONOMICS

SIXTH EDITION

ECONOMICS

Private Markets and Public Choice

Robert B. Ekelund, Jr.
Auburn University

Robert D. Tollison
University of Mississippi

WITH INTERNET RESOURCES PROVIDED BY

Audrey B. Davidson
University of Louisville

AND

Barry Haworth
University of Louisville

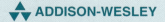

ADDISON-WESLEY

An imprint of Addison Wesley Longman, Inc.

Reading, Massachusetts • Menlo Park, California • New York • Harlow, England
Don Mills, Ontario • Sydney • Mexico City • Madrid • Amsterdam

Executive Editor: Denise J. Clinton
Senior Sponsoring Editor: Andrea Shaw
Senior Project Manager: Mary Clare McEwing
Supplements Editor: Deborah Kiernan
Senior Production Supervisor: Juliet Silveri
Cover Design: Regina Hagen
Marketing Manager: Amy Cronin
Composition, Illustration, and Packaging Services: Electronic Publishing Services Inc., NYC
Text Design: Electronic Publishing Services Inc., NYC, and Regina Hagen
Print Buyer: Tim McDonald
Printer: R.R. Donnelley & Sons Company

Library of Congress Cataloging-in-Publication Data.

Ekelund, Robert B. (Robert Burton), 1940-
Economics : private markets and public choice / Robert B. Ekelund, Jr., Robert D.
Tollison.--6th ed.
    p.   cm.
Includes index.
ISBN- 0-201-65752-X
1. Economics.   I. Tollison, Robert D.   II. Title.
HB171.5 .E47 2000   99-052895
330--dc21

2 3 4 5 6 7 8 9 10—DOW—03020100

**In Memory of Tim Fowler,
Chuck Maurice,
and Margaret O'Donnell-Whitlock,
and for those who loved them
RBE**

**For Anna
RDT**

CONTENTS

CHAPTER 3

PRIVATE MARKETS AND PRICES: LAWS OF DEMAND AND SUPPLY 51

CHAPTER 4

DEMAND AND SUPPLY: PROPERTY, MARKETS, AND PUBLIC CHOICE 83

PART 2 THE ARCHITECTURE OF PRIVATE MARKETS 113

CHAPTER 5 ELASTICITY 115

CHAPTER 8   COMPETITIVE MARKETS

PART 3   INPUT MARKETS   295

CHAPTER 12   COMPETITIVE LABOR MARKETS   297

CHAPTER 21   ## CLASSICAL MACROECONOMIC THEORY   525

CHAPTER 22   ## KEYNESIAN MACROECONOMICS   547

CHAPTER 23   **AGGREGATE DEMAND AND AGGREGATE SUPPLY 581**

CHAPTER 24   **FISCAL POLICY AND THE SUPPLY SIDE: USING THE TOOLS 603**

CHAPTER 25   **TAXES, DEFICITS, AND THE DEBT   623**

PART 6   MONEY   649

CHAPTER 26   **MONEY, BANKING, AND THE FEDERAL RESERVE   651**

PREFACE

Economic issues dominate the world we live in, affecting our perceptions about ourselves and our futures. Like it or not, we are faced with economic issues on television, in newspapers, in the voting booth, in career choice, and perhaps most significantly, in balancing our checkbooks every month! For example, after four decades of budget deficits, what should the federal government do with the unexpected surplus—pay off national debt, provide tax cuts, or fund more of its own spending? Can we expect the children of our generation to be better off than our generation or that of our parents? Do federally guaranteed entitlements—such as Medicare, Social Security, and welfare—have a future? Will international trade agreements, such as the North American Free Trade Association (NAFTA) or the General Agreement on Tariffs and Trade (GATT), have a positive or negative impact on the economic well-being of Americans? Should government mandate a Patients' Bill of Rights for HMOs if it will contribute to higher premiums and less affordable insurance for more people?

A solid foundation in economics helps us answer such questions. In this sixth edition of our introduction to economics, we again present economic ideas in a policy-real-world context that students—both those who continue the study of economics and those for whom this is the first and last class—can master and understand. Since our approach stresses the relationship between theory and policy, the technical presentations in this book are concise and straightforward. We rely heavily on examples to illustrate abstract theory, and describe graphs and graphical relationships in patient detail.

Our approach to economic study is "market oriented." It stresses that, in general, society's welfare is maximized when markets are used to allocate resources to their most desired private uses. Our approach goes further, however, to show (as early as the first chapter) how our public choices working through a political process can have a number of effects, not all of them desirable from the perspective of society. Democratic politics (as we make clear in Chapter 4) and interest groups may actually reduce society's welfare. In short, our approach to basic economics is underscored by the integration of politics and markets and is illustrated by the complete title of our book—*Economics: Private Markets and Public Choice.*

The sixth edition again covers both microeconomics and macroeconomics in clear and student-friendly prose with:

- Renewed emphasis on the use of markets to solve the basic economic problems created by scarcity;
- New and interesting examples of how economic and political markets interact and affect economic efficiency;
- Coverage of recent and continuing global events, including the Asian financial crisis and the advent of the euro as a common currency for Europe;
- Clear analysis of important domestic policies and proposals relating to such issues as tax reform, health insurance, welfare reform, poverty and deregulation; and
- Targeted, but streamlined discussions of theory and policy in a shorter presentation than that of the fifth edition (now 31 rather than 32 chapters).

CHANGES IN THE SIXTH EDITION

The overarching aims for the sixth edition have been to streamline the material for the typical principles course and to continue to enliven and enrich the material for students approaching economics for the first time. Among the main changes in the sixth edition are the following:

- *New material on the economics of information,* such as the problem of asymmetric information.
- *New, broadened discussion of environmental economics* and approaches to market failures such as pollution, overfishing, endangered species, and finite natural resources. We frame the discussion of renewable and nonrenewable resources in terms of the familiar concepts of supply and demand.
- *Tightening of the exposition of microeconomics,* including the subsuming of material on the firm into the chapter on costs.
- *A wealth of new applications.* About half the Focus Boxes and lengthier end-of-chapter Applications are new to the sixth edition. These features spotlight the applicability of a economic theory to real-world situations and scenarios. Among the many new topics and questions explored are whether Social Security protects the poor, how the Microsoft case can be viewed as monopoly or competitors' envy, what the repercussions of the Telecommunications Act of 1996 might be, how the "economics of Doomsday" has been part of environmental economics since the beginning of recorded history, what caused the economic boom of the 1990s, whether budget surpluses mean less government or not, whether work is obsolete, and how the Asian financial crisis evolved.
- *The addition of Internet exercises to each chapter.* These exercises get students "working with the Web" in ways that help them see the relevance of the chapter material to all sorts of issues and situations—economic, political, and personal.

ENDURING THEMES

The public choice theme (present in all previous editions) continues in the sixth edition. In spite of the proposed public choice emphasis of other texts, we have found that the critical issue of how politics affects markets it not integrated into discussions of standard economic issues. In our book we provide this coverage in both the micro and macro halves of our presentation. In addition to carrying two full chapters dealing with public choice (Chapters 4 and 18), we provide in-text and "application-style" examples integrating public choice with discussion of basic economic issues. Thus, the student is introduced to such issues as how laws against scalping affect the revenue of public agencies (Chapter 3); the relationship between politics and excise taxes (Chapter 5); why voting is rational (Chapter 6); jury conscription (Chapter 7); campus parking politics (Chapter 8); the U.S. postal monopoly (Chapter 9); bid rigging (Chapter 11); the American Medical Association (Chapter 13); patients' rights (Chapter 15); airline deregulation (Chapter 16); the underground economy (Chapter 21); the economics of budget surpluses (Chapter 25); central bank independence (Chapter 27); budget balance rules (Chapter 28); and property rights and economic growth (Chapter 29).

There is an ongoing emphasis on the importance of all trade, including international trade. The principles of specialization, opportunity cost, and trade run throughout the book and are explicitly introduced to the student in Chapter 2, which explains the role of free trade associations such as NAFTA in producing greater economic welfare and integrates international trade and interest group considerations right from the beginning. The emphasis on the importance of international trade and markets is carried throughout the text. See, for example, discussions of how the macroeconomy is related to international trade in Chapter 24 and discussions of property rights arrangements and their relation to growth in China, Korea, and other nations in Chapter 29.

ORGANIZATION

Microeconomics The organization of *Economics: Private Markets and Public Choice* follows the popular micro-macro format. The microeconomics portion of the book is divided into four parts, consisting of 18 chapters:

Part One—The Power of Economic Thinking

Part Two—The Architecture of Private Markets

Part Three—Input Markets

Part Four—Applied Microeconomics and Public Choice

The object of our presentation of microeconomics is again to focus on an intuitive and carefully graded exposition of basic economic principles. The fundamental issues of supply and demand, elasticity, competitive and non-competitive markets, and input pricing are given this treatment right along with the topics that have become "standard" text material only recently (such as game theory in Chapter 11). In addition, we have attempted to include important and topical microeconomic issues, including free trade (Chapter 3), interest groups (Chapter 4), teen smoking (Chapter 5), agricultural policy and the Freedom to Farm Act (Chapter 8 Appendix), the U.S. postal monopoly (Chapter 9), advertising (Chapter 10), cartels (Chapter 11), regional wage differences (Chapter 12), labor unions (Chapter 18), entrepreneurship (Chapter 14), Social Security and health care reform (Chapter 15), antitrust policy (Chapter 16), deregulation (Chapter 16), environmental issues and finite resources (Chapter 17), expenditures and public goods (Chapter 17), and, of course, public choice (Chapter 18).

We have made two basic changes in the microeconomics presentation. Chapter 7 of this edition (on the firm and production costs) is now a combination of the previous Chapters 7 and 8, which treated these topics separately. The new Chapter 7 more effectively integrates the theory of the firm with the theory of costs. We have also expanded Chapter 17 into a full-scale presentation of environmental economics and issues in recognition of this increasingly important area.

Macroeconomics Our macroeconomics presentation is provided in three parts:

Part Five—The Fundamentals of Macroeconomics

Part Six—Money

Part Seven—Macroeconomic Policy and Economic Growth

We have found that many books attempting to provide an "orderly" and simple presentation of macroeconomic theory actually do the opposite. Students taking the "macro half" of principles of economics who are barely conversant with supply and demand are overwhelmed by "three-sector equilibrium" models of macroeconomic theory with short-run/long-run aggregate supply distinctions. We take a different approach—one that presents a smooth, logical, and historical transition from classical economics (Chapter 21) to Keynesian economics (Chapter 22) to aggregate demand and supply (Chapter 23). Our remaining chapters in macroeconomics then develop macroeconomic and monetary policies in the context of this progression (Chapters 24-27). This logical approach permits instructors to spend as much time emphasizing their own views of "key issues" as they wish while maintaining an orderly approach to macroeconomic theory. Those desiring to elongate the discussion of macroeconomic policies and their relation to U.S. and global growth may then go on to Chapters 28 and 29.

The presentation of macroeconomics continues to be historically based, with a logical, smooth progression from classical to Keynesian to modern macroeconomics. While most texts today tend to "hide" the nature of Keynes's contributions, we do not. Keynes appears as a major figure whose influence continues to be felt in contemporary debates about macroeconomic theory and policy. To understand modern macroeconomics, the student must understand both classical and Keynesian ideas. Our presentation enables this understanding.

We also present a streamlined approach to monetary theory and policy with updates of recent developments in Chapters 26 and 27. Modern views of monetary and fiscal policy are presented in Chapter 28, while Chapter 29 reviews the theory and evidence about what factors are related to more rapid economic growth and development across countries.

The Global Economy   Part Eight—International Trade and the Global Economy—includes Chapters 30 and 31, which are devoted to issues relating to international trade and finance, including recent major events such as the Asian financial crisis and the arrival of a common European currency, the euro. A number of instructors have told us that they prefer to teach these issues as a special unit or topic. These chapters have been streamlined and completely updated for that purpose. However, international trade issues and their relation to our economy and well-being are an integral part of our entire book. Our view is that these issues are not separate from trade issues in general. We therefore begin, in Chapter 2, with matters of specialization, comparative advantage, and trade from an international perspective. These ideas and applications are then carried throughout the book.

PEDAGOGICAL FEATURES

We have incorporated a number of learning tools for students to aid understanding and retention of material.

- Each chapter opens with an overview of the topics covered and a bulleted list of chapter objectives.
- Figures are drawn with consistent use of color, helping students understand key concepts and the direction and magnitude of changes in economic behavior.
- Key concepts and terms are boldfaced when first mentioned in the text, with definitions appearing in the margin.
- Reader-friendly Focus boxes—at least one per chapter—provide interpretations and perspectives on critical or illustrative ideas or policies mentioned in the text. Many of the Focus features are new to the sixth edition. New examples from the microeconomics half of the book include: "Price Floors Cost You More than Peanuts" (Chapter 3); "Shipping Live Prisoners to Australia" (Chapter 4); "Politicians Are Demanded and Supplied" (Chapter 4); "Elasticity and Your World" (Chapter 5); "All You Can Eat Pizza" (Chapter 6); "Going Into Business for Your-

self" (Chapter 7); "Going Into Business With Others" (Chapter 7); "Big Business—The Corporation" (Chapter 7); "Let Your Fingers Do the Walking: Information in Markets" (Chapter 10); "The American Medical Association as a Union" (Chapter 13); "Services Pay and the Restructuring of the American Economy" (Chapter 13); "Who Pays the Bill for Patients' Rights?" (Chapter 15); "The Microsoft Case: Is It Monopoly or Is It Envy?" (Chapter 16); "The Economics of Doomsday" (Chapter 17); "The Kyoto Treaty: Who Benefits from Global Warming?" (Chapter 17); "Can You Buy an Election?" (Chapter 18); and "Economics of the Birds and the Bees" (Chapter 18). New examples from the macroeconomics portion of *Economics* include: "The Boom of the 1990s: Is the Business Cycle Dead?" (Chapter 19); "Business Investment Leads the 1990s Boom" (Chapter 20); "'Other Things' Also Matter: Technology and Growth in the Twenty-First Century" (Chapter 21); "Fat Chance for Flat Taxes" (Chapter 25); "From Truman to Clinton: 50 Years of Price Changes" (Chapter 27); "Deflation: Malignant or Benign?" (Chapter 27); "When Surpluses Are Really Deficits" (Chapter 28); "Is Work Obsolete?" (Chapter 29); "Is There a 'Star Wars' in Our Future?" (Chapter 29); and "The Euro: Europe's New Money" (Chapter 31).

- Applications of key text material are again included in our presentation. These are in-depth discussions of issues or policies brought up in the text. New applications include: "How Economics Prepares You for Life and Work" (Chapter 1); "AIDS and Reduced Production Possibilities in Africa" (Chapter 2); "Opportunity Cost, 'Scalping', and Full Price: Waiting for Van Gogh" (Chapter 3); "The Draft, Jury Duty, and Conscripted 'Public Service': Opportunity Cost and You" (Chapter 7); "Do You Having a Hunting License?: The Full Price of Parking on Campus" (Chapter 8); "Does Social Security Protect the Poor?" (Chapter 15); "The Telecommunications Act of 1996: Good Intentions Meet Market Realities" (Chapter 16); "From Outhouse to Penthouse: First Recession, the Boom, Boom, Boom in the 1990s" (Chapter 23); "Do Budget Surpluses Mean Less Government?" (Chapter 25); "Modernizing Financial Services" (Chapter 26); "Are Growth and Freedom Related?" (Chapter 29); and "The Asian Economic Crisis"(Chapter 31).

- Every chapter contains a concluding summary of the major ideas and concepts of the chapter, a list of key terms, questions for review and discussion, and, where applicable, problems for the student to solve.

- "Working with the Web" exercises, designed to give students research experience on the Internet, are new to this edition.

- Point/Counterpoint features containing biographies of great economists, past and present, along with their contrasting ideas, conclude each book part.

- A glossary of terms is provided at the back of the book, together with a useful and thorough index.

PRINT SUPPLEMENTS

The *Study Guide* by John Keith Watson of the University of Southwestern Louisiana is a comprehensive learning package containing chapter overviews; learning objectives; helpful hints; fill-in, true/false, multiple-choice, and short-answer questions; and "Something to Think About" segments.

The *Instructor's Resource Manual* by John Keith Watson of the University of Southwestern Louisiana is coordinated with the text and contains chapter overviews and outlines, learning objectives, answers to text questions, extra problems and essays with solutions, "One Step Further" segments, and suggestions for additional readings.

The *Test Bank* by John Thompson of Louisiana State University contains over 3,400 multiple-choice questions coded by level of difficulty. Ten percent of the questions are new to this edition and are identified with a marginal icon.

SOFTWARE SUPPLEMENTS

The *Instructor's Resource CD-ROM (Instructor's Resource Disk)* contains a Power-Point presentation, electronic Word files of the Instructor's Manual and Test Bank, and a Computerized Test Bank in TestGen-EQ 3.0.

The PowerPoint presentation contains all of the art from the book and is available in Macintosh and Windows formats. Those who have PowerPoint software can easily edit these slides to fit their individual teaching approaches. Those who do not have the software can still view the presentation through the PowerPoint Viewer provided on the disk.

TestGen-EQ 3.0, a computerized test generator that allows you to construct tests by choosing questions from the test bank, is available in Macintosh and Windows versions. If desired, test questions can be viewed on the screen, edited, saved, and printed. Instructors can also add or create their own questions.

ACKNOWLEDGMENTS

No book of this size and structure could be developed without the help of friends, colleagues, friendly critics, not-so-friendly critics, and editors. This book, both in its former editions and in the new sixth edition, is no exception. We gratefully acknowledge the following colleagues, friends, users, and students (past and present) whose generosity and advice fill these pages: John Allen, Gary Anderson, Leonardo Auernheimer, Andy Barnett, Raymond Battalio, Randy Beard, Richard Beil, Don Boudreaux, the late Katherine Boudreaux, Bill Biret, Butch Browning, Steve Caudill, Roy Cordato, Mark Crain, Elynor Davis, Charles DeLorme, David Gay, Kathie Gilbert, Cary Heath, Bob Hebert, Elmer Holt, Justin Issacs, John Jackson, Dave Kaserman, Roger Koppel, Dave Laband, Dwight Lee, Bobby McCormick, the late Charles Maurice, Francois Melese, the late Margaret O'Donnell, Karen Palasek, Chris Paul, Phil Porter, Ed Price, Morgan Reynolds, Richard Saba, Tom Saving, Bill Shughart, John Sophocles, Chris Thomas, Henry Thompson, Marc Ulrich, John Wells, and David Whitten. For special help and assistance we want to thank Roy Gilbert of Texas A&M University, Rand Ressler of the University of Southwestern Louisiana, and Bill Biret of Trinity University. John Thompson of Louisiana State University has offered valuable advice and provided an excellent and streamlined *Test Bank* for the sixth edition.

Several individuals deserve very special gratitude for helping us improve the quality and direction of *Economics* in both this edition and previous ones: Frank Adams, Troy State University; Richard Ault, Auburn University; Rob Blackstock, Auburn University; Audrey Davidson, University of Louisville; Paula Gant, Duke Energy; Rand Ressler, University of Southwestern Louisiana; David Saurman, San Jose State University; Keith Watson, University of Southwestern Louisiana; and Mark Thornton, Columbus State University.

Past and present graduate assistants—many of whom are now professors and productive contributors to economic research—were of help with all six editions of *Economics:* Manisha Perrera, Bharat Vijayan, Brian Goff, Ladd Jones, Cassandra Copeland, Dan Berry, George Ford, Elmer Holt, Yvan Kelly, Paul Gentle, Dwight Nystrom, Shawn Rittenour, Ken Somppi, John Thompson, Jim Tillery, Marc Ulrich, Deborah Walker, Doug Walker, and Biff Woodruff. Of special help in this sixth edition was Mark Thornton, Columbus State University.

We are grateful to Andrea Shaw and (in this and earlier editions) to Denise Clinton for unflagging support for our book. Most of all, however, we wish to sincerely thank Mary Clare McEwing, Senior Project Manager for the sixth edition, for her humor, intelligent criticism, good taste, and hard work in guiding our work. It could not have been done without her.

Official reviewers for this edition were Audrey Davidson, University of Louisville; Edward Flaherty, College of Charleston; Tom Means, San Jose State University; Ernest Morgan, College of The Albermarle; Mark Perry, University of Michigan; and Rand Ressler, University of Southwestern Louisiana.

Official reviewers and contributors for the earlier editions were Douglas K. Agbetsiafa, Indiana University; Ralph E. Ancil, Southwestern Missouri State University; Robert A. Baade, Lake Forest College; Dean Baim, Pepperdine University; Richard O. Beil, Jr., Auburn University; J. Lloyd Blackwell, IV, University of North Dakota; Robert Carbaugh, Central Washington University; Albert Celoza, Phoenix College; John Dennis Chasse, State University of New York-Brockport; George Shih-Fan Chu, University of Nevada at Reno; Paul A. Cleveland, University of Central Florida; Cheryl Cohen, Millikin University; Barbara Craig, Oberlin College; Robert D. Crofts, Salem State College; Steve Cunningham, University of Connecticut; William W. Davis, Western Kentucky University; David Denslow, University of Florida; Carl E. Enomoto, New Mexico State University; Donald H. Farness, Oregon State University; Arthur A. Fleisher III, Metropolitan State College of Denver; Andrew W. Foshee, McNeese State University; Robert Gillette, Texas A&M University; Richard F. Gleisner, St. Cloud State University; Jack Goddard, Northeastern State University; Anthony Greco, University of Southwestern Louisiana; Carole A. Green, University of South Florida; William B. Green, Sam Houston State University; Edward Greenberg, Washington University; Anthony O. Gyapong, Wayne State University; Jan M. Hansen, University of Wisconsin-Eau Claire; Cary Heath, University of Southwestern Louisiana; Steven C. Hine, State University of New York-Binghamton; George Hoffer, Virginia Commonwealth University; James H. Holcomb, Jr., University of Texas-El Paso; John B. Horowitz, Ball State University; Arthur Kartman, San Diego State University; Philip King, San Francisco State University; Gary F. Langer, Roosevelt University; Stephen E. Lile, Western Kentucky University; David MacPherson, Florida State University; Marvin S. Margolis, Millersville University; Lawrence W. Martin, Michigan State University; Warren Matthews, Texas A&M University; James N. McGowen, Jr., Belleview Area College; Mary Ann Meiners, Middle Tennessee State University; Charles C. Milliken, Siena Heights College; Khan Mohabbat, Northern Illinois University; Dan Myers, Western Kentucky University; Emmanuel Nnadozie, Northeast Missouri State University; Edd Noell, Westmont College; Terry Olsen; Don Owen, Ottawa University; Elliot Parker, University of Nevada at Reno; Ken Patterson, Oregon State University; Gerald Pelovsky, College of the Sequoias; Steven C. Pitts, Houston Community College; J. M. Pogodzinski, San Jose State University; Munir Quddus, University of Southern Indiana; Farhad Rassekh, University of Hartford; Rand Ressler, University of Southwestern Louisiana; Doralia Reynolds, Seward County Community College; Peter Rupert, West Virginia University; Carlos E. Santiago, State University of New York-Albany; Gerald W. Sazama, University of Connecticut; Phil Sorenson, Florida State University; Chaitram J. Talele, Columbia State Community College; Steven G. Thorpe, University of Colorado at Boulder; H. Bruce Throckmorton, Tennessee Technological

University; Abraham Usumang, Bowling Green State University; James VanBeck, Blinn College-College Station Campus; John Wakemann-Linn, Williams College; Harold Warren, East Tennessee State University; Walter J. Wessells, North Carolina State University; Darrell Young, University of Texas-Austin; and Mahmood Yousefi, University of Northern Iowa.

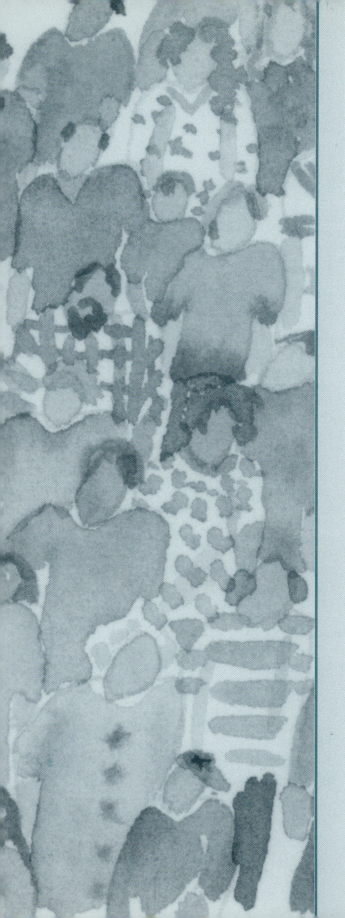

PART ONE

The Power of Economic Thinking

Economics in Perspective

E conomics is the general study of human behavior in most, if not all, of its manifestations. As such, it offers a way of thinking about how the world works and a framework for making choices and decisions of all kinds. These choices may be private choices about such issues as how much you should invest in higher education, or they may be public choices about which candidate to vote for or which public policy is most desirable. Close study of economics gives us a new perspective on a wide variety of human activities and institutions. When you finish Chapter 1 you should understand

- how individuals, societies, and nations solve the pervasive economic problem caused by scarce resources and unlimited wants.
- the functions of prices and how they act as signals to producers, consumers, and governments in any economy.
- how individuals actually make economic decisions.
- how economics gives insight into human behavior regarding the private and public choices that individuals make.

WHAT ECONOMICS IS

Economics is a social science—the oldest and best developed of the social sciences. As such, it studies human behavior in relation to three basic questions about an economy: What **goods** and **services** are produced? How are goods and services produced? For whom are goods and services produced?

3

Goods
All tangible things that satisfy people's wants and desires.

Services
All forms of intangible but useful activities that are valued by people.

Resources
Those things used to produce goods and services. These include land, machines, energy, and human labor and ingenuity. Resources are also called factors of production.

Scarcity
The condition whereby the resources, goods, and services available to individuals and society are limited relative to the wants and desires for them.

For at least 200 years, economists have tried to analyze how individuals and societies answer these questions. Communism, for example, appeared to be a viable answer to the questions *what, how,* and *for whom* in many countries throughout much of the twentieth century, but today it has largely been abandoned in favor of capitalism, free markets, and limited government.

Economics, particularly the study of markets, has much to say about the link between the amount of government economic control and personal freedom and democracy. The insistent questions—What? How? and For whom? —must be asked; for at least two centuries, economists have tried to analyze how individuals and societies answer them.

Economics: A Working Definition

A common thread runs through all definitions of economics. Each definition emphasizes the inescapable fact that **resources**—the wherewithal to produce goods and services—are not available in limitless quantities and that people and societies, with their unlimited desires for goods and services, must make some hard choices about what to do with the resources that are available. Our working definition of economics may be expressed as follows:

> Economics is the study of how individuals, experiencing virtually limitless wants, choose to allocate scarce resources to best satisfy their wants.

Unlimited wants, scarcity, and the choices they force on us are thus the key elements in understanding economics.

The Economic Condition: Scarcity

What, exactly, is **scarcity**? More to the point, what are scarce resources? As individuals and as a society, we cannot get all of what we want because the amount of available resources is limited. The role of the economist and of economics in general is to explain how we can make the most of this problem of scarcity—how to get as much as we can of what we want.

The most important problem in economics is that while the wants of individuals and societies must be satisfied by limited resources, the wants themselves are not limited; they are endless. We are never satisfied with what we have. Individuals will forever be lured by more tempting foods, more cleverly engineered computers, more up-to-date fashions. We also desire safer highways, more national security, greater Social Security benefits, or more cancer research. Problems of scarcity and unlimited wants—economics itself—apply to all nations, regardless of political, social, and religious orientation. Moslems, Jews, and Christians all face the eternal problem of satisfying limitless wants with limited means. Methods of dealing with scarcity, of course, differ from society to society, depending on cultural differences and on particular endowments of resources within political boundaries, but the fundamental problem is the same everywhere and at all times.

Scarcity affects both private and public choices. We must choose virtually every day among items that we commonly purchase, such as food, transportation, and clothing, and we surely cannot have all of the things that we would like to have. How about a new Mercedes? And in our public choices as well, scarcity dictates that we must choose. Do we want to support candidates who want to spend more resources on public programs or less? How about increased space missions?

**Economic goods
and services**

Goods and services that
are scarce.

Costs

An implication of scarcity; the
necessary sacrifices associated
with making any choice.

All scarce goods—from television to chlorinated water—are called **economic goods**. Their scarcity leads to **costs**. While it is customary to associate cost with the money price of goods, economists define cost as the value of the good or activity given up in place of the good or activity actually chosen. Since all unlimited wants cannot be met with scarce resources, individuals have to make choices—between, for instance, more steaks and more computer games. Public choices have to be made between safer highways and more accurate missiles. Cost is, therefore, the direct result of the scarcity of resources. Scarcity of resources means that individuals, both in their public and private choices, must endure the costs of acquiring more of any good or service. That cost is the value of the good or activity given up in place of the good chosen.

Think for a moment about that scarce resource time. Being absolutely limited in supply for each of us, time—or rather, the use of time—bears a definite cost. No college student, certainly, has escaped being confronted with economic decisions arising from the need to allocate this costly resource. (See the Focus "Scarcity, Economizing, and the College Student's Time.")

Free goods and services

Things that are available
in sufficient amounts and
provide all that people want
at zero cost.

You may feel that some things are not scarce and that some things—such as love, sunshine, and water—are free. In economic terms, **free goods and services** are goods that are available in sufficient amounts to satisfy all possible demands. But are many things truly free? Surface water is usually unfit for drinking except in areas far from human habitation. Water suitable for drinking must be raised to the

FOCUS

Scarcity, Economizing, and the College Student's Time

College students know the principle of scarcity all too well. Indeed, a successful student needs an ability to make sound and efficient economic decisions not only in the case of scarce monetary resources but in the allocation of scarce time resources as well. Time is a valuable resource to all human beings, but it exists in finite quantities of 24 hours a day, 168 hours a week, and (approximately) 720 hours a month.

Every student knows that he or she cannot have and do everything and that economic decisions, whether they are recognized as such or not, must be made every day. A student's time often must be allocated over a day or a week. A weekend trip to an out-of-town football game must be "paid for" not only in monetary terms but also in less time to work on the English paper due on Wednesday. The end of a term always necessitates economizing: Given the limited time available, should an additional two hours be directed to chemistry or art history? Actual choices will depend on perceived net gain or potential net gain from the array of alternatives.

College students are not alone, of course. For anyone, the choice may be between attending a rock concert or a Bach organ recital. We may have chosen a career in acting or dance instead of law or computer programming. A retiree may choose to return to the classroom rather than to spend time fishing or playing bridge. Economizing—maximizing the value of monetary or time resources under conditions of scarcity—forms the foundation of human behavior. Students, workers, politicians, philanthropists, business executives—all must make choices, and an analysis of these choices forms the basis of the social science of economics.

surface from deep wells or piped from reservoirs and treatment plants, operations involving resources that are scarce even when water itself is not. Scarcity of winter sun in the North leads many people to seek costly winter vacations in the snowbird states. And if you think love is free. . . .

Scarce Resources and Economic Problems

Human resources
All forms of labor and skill used to produce goods and services.

Nonhuman resources
All resources other than human resources, such as machines and land.

There are basically two categories of scarce resources: human resources and nonhuman resources. **Human resources** encompass all types of labor, including specialized forms of labor such as management or entrepreneurship. **Nonhuman resources** include land, natural resources such as minerals and water, and capital.

Examples of human resources abound. By definition, all human resources apply talent and energy to produce goods and services. The cook at the Chicken Shack, the hairstylist at the Mad Hacker, the chief executive of a computer firm, and the assembly-line worker at a General Motors plant all represent human resources. Obviously, labor includes a huge variety of skills, both general and precise. Knowledge, or know-how, is also part of human resources. Economists are interested not only in the scarcity of labor but in its quality. The quality of human resources can be enhanced through investments in education and training.

Economists view *entrepreneurship* as a special form of labor. An entrepreneur is a person who perceives profitable opportunities and who combines resources to produce goods or services. Entrepreneurs attempt to move resources from lower- to higher-valued uses in the economy and take the risk that they can make profits by doing so. Inventors, such as Thomas Edison, are good examples of entrepreneurs. *Management*, a second special form of labor, guides and oversees the process by which separate resources are turned into goods or services.

Human resources utilize nonhuman things such as land, minerals, and natural resources to produce goods and services. A commercial lot in Manhattan, a farm acre in Iowa, a coal deposit in Pennsylvania, a uranium mine in South Dakota, and a timber stand in Oregon are all scarce nonhuman resources. New deposits of minerals can be discovered, forests can be replanted, and agricultural land can be reclaimed from swamps. But at any one time, the available supply of nonhuman resources is limited.

Capital, another category of nonhuman resources, comprises all machines, implements, and buildings used to produce goods and services either directly or indirectly. A surgeon's scalpel, a factory, an electric generator, and an artist's brush are all used to produce goods and services and, thus, are considered to be capital goods.

Many different forms of capital may be needed to produce a single economic good. With a wheat harvesting machine, a South Dakota farmer can reap a huge crop. But the wheat must also be milled into flour and transported from South Dakota to bakeries in, say, California. Once the wheat has arrived, bakeries must utilize brick or convection ovens to produce bread. The harvesting and milling machines, the railroad, and the baker's ovens are all capital goods, created to increase the amount of final production.

Capital—and the resources used to produce it—is scarce. To create capital, we must sacrifice consumer goods and services because the production of capital takes time away from the production of goods that can be consumed in the present. Societies and individuals must therefore choose between immediate consumption and future consumption. That choice is crucial to economic growth and ultimate economic well-being.

Other Factors Affecting Resources and Growth

Quantities of human and nonhuman resources are only one prerequisite for economic growth and well-being in an economy. The institutional framework of an economy, such as the nature of its legal system and its form of government, is also critical for economic growth and development, as are factors such as technology and information. Consider, first, the nature of technology and information.

Technology and information assist resource utilization in a modern, functioning economy. **Technology,** in general, is composed of know-how, inventions, and innovations that help us get more from scarce resources. An improvement in technology implies that we can produce more from a given amount of resources. Existing technology is the outcome of many inventions, some of which were the invention of new resources—such as aluminum and hybrid plants. All inventions that increase the productivity of labor and capital can be considered improvements in technology. Innovation is the application of technology to the production of goods and services. Technology, then, helps make other resources less scarce.

Information is a scarce and costly ingredient in the economic process. The acquisition of information for economic decision making has never been free. In the nineteenth and early twentieth centuries, businesses hired armies of bookkeepers to provide sufficient information for managers to make decisions. The development of the digital computer in the mid-twentieth century made the storage and retrieval of information less costly. Technology has progressed so rapidly that the quantity of information that could be stored in a warehouse-sized computer in 1950 can now be placed on a chip the size of a fingernail. Information, then, helps us economize on the use of scarce resources.

Resources, both human and nonhuman, never operate in a vacuum; they always exist in some real-world setting that includes government, a legal system, and a structure of property rights. **Property rights** are those rules that establish and govern the ownership and control of resources. Property rights are established by laws developed within a society's traditions and social relations. **Institutions** are the sum total of the traditions, mores, laws, and governmental structures of an economy. Institutions in the United States include the Constitution and the laws of the states. Some of these institutions restrict and define the rights to own and use resources. Others enhance the flow of resources among individuals and states. The U.S. Constitution, for example, guarantees the free movement of resources from state to state.

These institutions represent a type of capital that is the result of public choices that citizens and leaders in a society make. We live in a world filled with many governments representing many different institutional structures. Some countries are blessed with huge quantities of land and natural resources but still do not manage to achieve economic growth and development beyond the barest minimum. Prior to the 1980s, China's communist government directed almost all human and nonhuman resources from the highest levels of bureaucracy. Despite China's huge resource base, these institutions reduced the country's ability to achieve economic development. More recently, and in spite of periodic political repression, the Chinese government has tentatively embraced some elements of a Western-style free market system, in which some areas of the economy, such as agriculture, are given over to self-interested production, distribution, and exchange. However slowly, Western institutions and technology are being adopted in China because they have

Technology
Knowledge of production methods associated with producing a particular good.

Information
A costly but necessary input in the process of economic exchange and growth.

Property rights
Any legal and/or enforceable rights to the use of resources of any kind.

Institutions
The sum total of the traditions, mores, laws, and governmental structures of an economy.

encouraged a more efficient use of human and nonhuman resources in producing goods and services.

When property rights are not assigned to scarce resources, the resources tend to be wasted. The old adage "What is owned by all, is cared for by none" means the failure to legally assign property rights to specific resources will ensure that the resources will not be utilized in the most efficient fashion. Most Western economists believe that private rights over property—combined with free and unregulated private markets for human and nonhuman resources—are essential to economic growth in any nation. The success stories of relatively free and unrestricted economies such as Hong Kong, Taiwan, and Singapore—each endowed with very modest quantities of resources—are often presented as evidence that noninterventionist institutions contribute greatly to economic development. The lesson to be learned from these cases is that institutions—especially the form of government and the nature of controls over resources and resource utilization—are keys to productivity and economic growth in any society.

When it comes to material goods, most people throughout history have believed that more is better than less. Accordingly, economic growth has been defined as *more* housing, *more* food, *more* health care, *more* leisure, *more* of everything. Growth, however, may be defined to include the attainment of less tangible environmental goals as well as an increase in the output of physical goods and services. Today, some people prefer the kinds of "goods" associated with a simpler, safer, and cleaner life for society. The acquisition of these goods also requires public decisions and public choices about the expenditure of scarce resources.

Scarcity of resources and scarcity of imagination in designing institutions to facilitate resource use are at the heart of all economic problems. Resources can be augmented over time; indeed, we are much better off materially than our grandparents, and our grandparents were better off than their grandparents. At any one time, however, individuals and societies cannot get all of what they want. Given scarcity, individuals and societies must make choices, and a primary role of economists is to analyze scarcity and the process of choosing.

KEY PRINCIPLES OF ECONOMIC THINKING

All economists share certain ways of thinking. These perspectives, which form the core of the science of economics, appear many times throughout this book. A look at these economic perspectives in simple, commonsense language should convince you that economics and economic reasoning are closely related to the private and public decisions you make every day.

Accounting costs
Actual money expenditures associated with any activity; out-of-pocket costs.

Explicit costs
Accounting costs.

Implicit costs
Nonpecuniary costs associated with the consumption of a good or service.

Resources and Activities Cost More than You Think

What does it cost you to take a skiing weekend in the mountains or to make a trip to the beach during spring break? Your reply might include the costs of gasoline, auto depreciation, airfare, lift tickets, food, drink, entertainment, and a motel room. These money expenditures are called **accounting costs,** or explicit money costs.

Economists define *costs* more broadly than accountants do. In addition to the **explicit** (money) **costs** considered by accountants, economists consider additional **implicit costs** associated with an action. In the case of a ski trip, an economist would recognize that an additional implicit cost of a ski weekend is the forgone opportunity of using the time in its next most valuable use when all viable alternatives are considered. For example, if the student who goes skiing would otherwise have spent the weekend working at a part-time job, an implicit cost of skiing is the income that would otherwise have been earned, if working is the highest-valued alternative. Therefore, the full economic cost of the ski weekend—the **opportunity cost**—equals the explicit money costs (that money does have an alternative use) plus the implicit costs of forgone income.

Opportunity cost
The highest-valued alternative forgone in making any choice.

Such opportunity costs also exist for public choices. Use of government lands in Wyoming and Montana as national forests entails a cost. Through lease or purchase, these lands could be used as a source of oil, minerals, and timber. Such use would contribute to society's well-being, but park land serves the recreational needs of society as well. Whatever public choices we make for the use of land will imply a cost in economic terms. An opportunity must be forgone when the land is used in either manner.

A favorite saying of economists is "There is no such thing as a free lunch." The first fundamental principle of economics is that most things in life come at the opportunity cost of something forgone. They are never free. In economics, opportunity cost is the true measure of the costs of anything.

Economic Behavior Is Rational

A second fundamental principle of economics is that people behave according to **rational self-interest.** Economists focus on a particular view of human behavior—that of *homo economicus* (economic man or woman). Economists argue that human behavior is predictably based on a person's weighing the costs and benefits of decisions. Simply stated, individuals pursue their goals, whether public or private in nature, in a purposeful fashion. A student will choose to eat lunch at the local health-food restaurant rather than the fast-food cafeteria on campus if the perceived personal benefits of doing so—eating nutritious food in a pleasant atmosphere, say—outweigh the perceived costs, such as longer lines and a greater distance to be walked.

Rational self-interest
The view of human behavior espoused by economists. Given circumstances and preferences, people weigh the costs and benefits of choices in order to do the best they can for themselves.

The view of the individual espoused by economists has always been subject to misinterpretation. When economists say that humans are self-interested, they do not mean that other aspects of human behavior and motivation are unimportant or irrelevant. Altruistic or charitable behavior, for example, is perfectly compatible with *homo economicus*. If a person values altruism, then an act that benefits others will carry personal benefits and will therefore be in that person's self-interest. Economists simply maintain that people consider the costs and benefits of their decisions and act in their own self-interest.

No economist would deny that love, charity, and justice are important aspects of human behavior. Economists have merely advanced the simple but powerful proposition that, given personal tastes, values, and social philosophy, rational self-interest is a better guide to predicting behavior than any other assumption about why people act as they do.

The economist's view of the rational self-interested individual applies not only to economic behavior, but also to other realms of behavior. Economics as a social science includes observations of what people, motivated by self-interest, actually do. Politicians maximize their self-interest by wooing voters to elect and reelect them. Even activities such as dating, marriage, and divorce have been analyzed using the self-interest assumption! After more than 200 years of economic theorizing, self-interest remains a most powerful predictor of human behavior.

Choices Are Made at the Margin

Margin

The difference between costs or benefits in an existing situation and after a proposed change.

Economists are typically concerned with decisions made at the **margin**—the additional costs or benefits of a specific change in the current situation. An individual consumer, for example, does not spend his or her entire budget solely on food, cassette tapes, or weekends at the beach. Consumers purchase hundreds of goods and services. Their choice to purchase or not purchase additional units of any one good is based on the additional (or marginal) satisfaction that that single unit would bring to them.

Marginal analysis

Looking at changes in the costs and benefits of a change from the status quo to a proposed new situation. These marginal changes in the costs and benefits are the basis for rational economic choice.

Marginal analysis is a method of finding the optimal, or most desirable, level of any activity—how much coffee to drink, how much bread to produce, and so on. In an economic sense, every activity we undertake involves both benefits and costs, so an optimal level of an activity is the point at which the activity's total benefits outweigh its costs by the greatest amount.

Students make marginal decisions all the time, whether studying for exams, purchasing a new sweater, or voting. Clearly, additional study for a mathematics examination will improve the grade you receive. But doing your best will not mean devoting all available time to the project. The total gain in terms of grade achieved will rise, but the total costs due to the opportunity cost of time will rise also. Additional hours spent studying math may require forgone activities such as work, sleep, studying history, or even recreation. The rational student will stop studying for an examination when the marginal benefits from another hour of study equal the marginal costs of study. Beyond this point, additional study hours would likely raise the exam grade by a few more points, but the additional study would not be worth the additional cost in terms of other activities given up. The net benefits of studying math (net benefits = total benefits − total costs) are always maximized where the marginal benefits equal the marginal costs. It is the same for all choices that individuals make, even highly complex ones such as voting, buying a house, and so on.

Prices Are Signals to Producers and Consumers

Consumers decide what is to be produced—TVs, automobiles, public parks —with the scarce resources in our society. Economists say that consumers transmit their desires through **markets,** which are simply arrangements where buyers and sellers exchange goods or services for money. In a market economy **prices** are the essential signals that tell producers and resource suppliers what and how much to produce. Take, for example, a fairly new product, the compact disc (CD) player.

Market

A collection of buyers and sellers exchanging resources, goods, or services.

Prices

The market-established opportunity costs of goods and services obtained through exchange.

What happened when consumers suddenly wanted more CD players than cassette decks or turntables in their homes and automobiles? Consumers expressed this desire by buying many more CD players and leaving cassette decks and turntables to gather dust on store shelves. Meanwhile, the relative unavailability of CD players caused their price to rise, because, temporarily, there were insufficient resources and production to meet the new demand. Manufacturers observed the increased sales and rising prices and realized that producing more CD players would be profitable. They reacted by producing more players, which meant ordering more electronics and circuitry and plastics, and hiring more labor and machinery. Higher prices for integrated circuits, fabricated metals, and wiring gave producers in Silicon Valley and other resource suppliers a signal to supply more of their inputs and services. Why did they do it? Because higher prices mean greater profitability to resource suppliers as well. Resources were diverted to CD players as both demand for and production of cassette decks and turntables declined.

Consumers also view prices as signals that help them decide what, and how much, to buy. Prices are both a mechanism that signals the degree of scarcity of goods and services to consumers and an allocator of the available quantities of goods and services among consumers.

Prices serve two basic functions in an economy. They serve to determine how much and what goods and services are produced by producers. They also serve to allocate available commodities among different consumers and competing end uses.

Public Choices Are Different from Private Choices

Private choice

Any choice made through private markets.

Public choice

The economic analysis of political decision making, politics, and the democratic process.

Individuals make private and public choices. Their **private choices** are made through markets, and involve the supply and demand of cars, housing, and other private goods. **Public choices** are also made by that individual with respect to the things that he or she wants government to do. How much should we spend on national defense versus national parks, for example?

The individuals who make public choices are the *same* individuals who make private choices. We thus make the same assumption about their behavior—that is, they act in their self-interest, broadly defined as before, when they make public choices.

What is different about public choices is that the setting or constraints that affect public choices are different from those that affect private choices. Public decisions in democracies are made by voting, and voting does not work in the same way as markets. To understand how voting and the market differ is to study public choice. This is the study of the behavior of self-interested political actors—voters, politicians, bureaucrats, regulators, judges—as they go about their "ordinary" business of governing. Economics is concerned with both private and public choices and how they are made, and with the consequences of allocating resources through markets and voting.

Economists Do Not Decide Who Gets What

Economists study poverty and wealth, but as economists they have no unique knowledge to make judgment about how rich people should be or how much poverty (if any) is tolerable. Economists basically explain that the economic value of all individuals—expressed as their income—is determined by the relative desires for their services and by the relative scarcity of their talents and abilities.

Most products and services—such as food and vacations—are allocated to those with the greatest desire and ability to pay for them. Our ability to pay is determined by the economic value of our own particular services or resources in the marketplace. This value depends on our education, on-the-job training, health, luck, inheritance, and a host of other factors.

The distribution of publicly provided goods and services—such as highways and bridges and space weapons—is conducted by governments through the filter of politics and voting. Ultimately, therefore, decisions on how public resources are to be distributed are made by voter choices. In government, as in the workings of the market, the chief role of economists is not to say who should get what, but to describe and analyze the process—the costs, benefits, and incentives—through which the distribution of all products and services takes place.

Money Is Helpful, but Not Too Much

Barter
Direct exchange of one good or service for another without the use of money.

Economists also place a special significance on the role of money in our lives. The trade of goods for goods, called **barter,** will not work in any economy that completes billions of transactions every day. Barter may have been sufficient in primitive societies where few things were produced and traded, but as the number of commodities grew, the cost of transacting by barter grew enormously. Low-cost trade demanded a double coincidence of wants—you had to demand the corn I produced at the same time and place that I demanded the baskets you produced. A common denominator, acceptable to all, developed within economic societies to reduce the costs and inconveniences of barter. That common denominator is **money,** which serves as a medium of exchange.

Money
A generally accepted medium of exchange.

Money is not limited to coins and paper dollars. Throughout history many things—shells, feathers, paper, gold, and cattle, for instance—have served as money. The important point to economists is that money, whatever it is, reduces the costs associated with barter and increases specialization and trade. At the same time, economists are concerned that money should not be available in such quantities as to become unacceptable and valueless to people who produce, buy, and sell. For society, at least, huge increases in the money supply may be too much of a good thing.

Inflation
A sustained increase in the general level of prices; inflation reduces the purchasing power of money.

When the quantity of money increases beyond its use as a means of making transactions, confidence in the medium of exchange and its value (in terms of the quantity of goods and services a unit of it can purchase) deteriorates. Economists call this phenomenon **inflation.** Inflation was a fact of American life during the 1970s, and it is a persistent element in nations around the world, as in the republics of the former Soviet Union. Inflation, if left untamed, can result in the collapse of entire economies, with reversion to primitive barter conditions. Economists therefore are very concerned with the relation between the production and trade of goods and the quantity of money available to facilitate these crucial activities.

Voters Choose the Role of Government— The Economist Analyzes

In a functioning democratic system, society chooses an economic role for government by electing politicians. In general, that role has included such activities as taxation for and provision of collective goods such as national defense, highways, and education; the regulation of monopoly; pollution control; control of the money supply; and alleviation of poverty through welfare programs. In its economic role of taxing and spending, government can affect economic factors such as inflation, the degree of unemployment, economic growth, and international trade.

Economists have always been concerned with the effects of government activity in these areas. In the United States, economists are in the thick of government policy-making. Since 1946 an official Council of Economic Advisers has been appointed by the president to aid in the formulation and implementation of economic policy. Almost every agency of government employs economists to provide analysis in their areas of expertise.

In their role as advisers, economists primarily evaluate, from the perspective of economic theory or analysis, the effects of proposals or, more correctly, of changes in economic policies. Economists are not confined to giving advice on specific issues such as the Social Security program or the effects of advertising regulation by the Federal Trade Commission. Larger issues are within economists' purview as well. Predicting the effects of government taxing and spending policies on employment, interest rates, and inflation is a very large part of economists' role. As such, economists are concerned with economic stabilization.

Despite economists' influence, however, the economic role of government is ultimately decided by voters in periodic elections. Economists evaluate the implications of government's economic policies. They do not make ultimate decisions about what the government should do.

THE ROLE OF THEORY IN ECONOMICS

Economists organize their thoughts about human behavior and its results through models. Economists, like all scientists, construct models to isolate specific phenomena for study. Constructing a **model** requires assumptions and abstractions from the real world.

Model
A simplified abstraction of the real world that approximates reality and makes problems easier to analyze; also called a theory.

Economists must *abstract* from extraneous factors to isolate and understand some other factor because, as one economist has put it, people's minds are limited and nature's riddles are complex. Economists must assume that the extraneous factors are constant—that "other things are equal"[1]—or that, if altered, they would have a predictable effect on the relations or model under consideration. Humanity has never progressed very far in understanding anything—be it chemistry, astronomy, or economics—without abstracting from many factors that are not central to a given problem. *Thus, all economic models are of necessity abstractions. Good models, those that perform and predict well, use relevant factors; poor models do not.*

An economic model (or, essentially the same thing, a theory) can be expressed in verbal, graphical, or mathematical form. Sometimes verbal explanation is sufficient, but graphs or algebra often serve as convenient shorthand means of expressing models. Economics is like other sciences in this regard. A complicated chemical or physical process can be described in words, but it is more convenient to use mathematics. All methods of expressing models will be used in this book, but we rely primarily on words and graphs. The appendix to this chapter explains how to read and interpret graphs.

Since a complex world is the economist's workshop, economic theory cannot always be tested in the way chemical or physical theories can. The accuracy of economics is like that of meteorology. Total accuracy is not within the meteorologist's abilities.

In economics, the problem of imperfect conditions for testing is a limitation to theory, but theory is essential nonetheless. Nothing can substitute for the usefulness of theory in organizing our thoughts about the real world and in describing the regularities of economic behavior.

THE ROLE OF ECONOMICS AND ECONOMISTS

Economics—and its practice by economists—permeates society. University-trained economists wear many hats and perform diverse roles within the profession. Most economists specialize in some area of particular concern. Some economists work as researchers in think tanks, such as the Hoover Institution at Stanford University or the Brookings Institution in Washington, D.C. Others serve as corporate

---

[1]The Latin phrase *ceteris paribus*, meaning "other things being equal," is common economic shorthand for this assumption about human behavior.

forecasters for private businesses. Every conceivable area of the economy—health, energy, agriculture, research on the role of particular technologies—is part of the research program of these economists. Many economists don policy hats and advise federal, state, and local governments on a huge variety of matters—including budgets, taxes, government spending, and policies toward business. Last, but not least, economists teach economics. In virtually every college and university in America, economists perpetuate their field by teaching undergraduate and graduate courses and conducting research. Since 1969, a Nobel Prize has been awarded in economics, underlining the special prestige of the discipline as a social science. The Nobel Prize has been awarded to an impressive number of economists at American universities (How and in what manner economics may be of value to you is explored in the Application at the end of this chapter, "How Economics Prepares You for Life and Work").

Positive and Normative Economics

Positive economics

Observations, explanations, or predictions about economic life; scientific economics.

Economics is primarily a positive rather than a normative science. **Positive economics** describes what is or predicts what will be under certain circumstances, whereas **normative economics** entails value judgments about what should be. For the most part, economists confine themselves to positive statements. This does not mean that economists as individuals act always as pure scientists. They most certainly do arrive at normative positions based on their own personal values in addition to their positive analyses.

Normative economics

Value judgments based on moral principles or preferences about how economic life should be.

Consider U.S. welfare programs. To say that additional tax dollars should be spent on welfare would involve a normative (or value) judgment on the part of economists. Once society has decided to spend more on welfare, however, economists can make positive statements about the effects of such spending. Or economists may observe the welfare system and analyze how the system could work more efficiently in achieving its goals. In other words, economic analysis can show, once society has decided on a welfare system and on some dollar amount to be devoted to welfare, how alternative systems of welfare distribution would alter the effectiveness of the program.

Microeconomics and Macroeconomics

Microeconomics

Analysis of the behavior of individual decision-making units, including individuals, households, and business firms.

The first half of this book concerns what economists call microeconomics, while the second half deals with macroeconomics. **Microeconomics,** like microbiology, concerns the components of a system. Just as a frog is made up of individual cells of various kinds, individual sales and purchases of commodities from potatoes to health care are the stuff of which the whole economy is composed. Microeconomists are thus concerned with individual markets and with the determination of relative prices within those markets. Supply and demand for individual goods, services, and factors of production are the subject matter of microeconomics. Microeconomists address questions such as the following: Will the use of larger quantities of solar energy reduce the total energy bill of Americans? Will an increased tax on cigarettes increase or decrease federal revenues from the tax? Will the quality and quantity of nursing services in the state of Wyoming be changed by the licensing of nursing in that state?

Macroeconomics

Analysis of the behavior of an economy as a whole.

Macroeconomics is the study of the economy as a whole. The overall price level, inflation rate, international exchange rates, unemployment rate, economic growth rate, and interest rate are issues of concern to macroeconomists. Macro-

Gross domestic product (GDP)

A measure of the final goods and services produced by a country with resources located within that country.

Gross national product (GNP)

The value, measured at market prices, of all final goods and services produced in an economy in one year.

economists analyze how these crucial quantities are determined and how and why they change. The most common measures of macroeconomic well-being are **gross domestic product (GDP)** and **gross national product (GNP).**

Some issues contain elements of both microeconomics and macroeconomics—for instance, a proposed U.S. tariff on Japanese auto imports. Microeconomists would be interested in the effects of the tariff on auto prices, on the American auto industry, and on the quantity of cars bought by U.S. consumers. Macroeconomists would be primarily interested in the effects of the tariff on economic growth, employment, international trade, the balance of payments, and total spending.

Let's Get to Work

Economics, like meteorology, is an inexact science, and it is likely to remain so. But economic theory and prediction provide extremely important insights into numerous issues that touch our lives. And the science of choice and scarcity is constantly being improved from both theoretical and empirical perspectives. The well-established power of economic thinking is the result of 200 years of such continuing improvements. Sound understanding of the principles of economic thinking will improve your understanding of the world.

APPLICATION

How Economics Prepares You for Life and Work

Economics is a way of thinking about all kinds of events. More precisely, economics prepares you to think about all behavior—particularly about how consumers' and producers' behavior is influenced by certain events (changes in prices, changes in interest rates, new government regulations, marriage rules, and so on). Even more particularly, it is a method for organizing your thoughts based on a long-tested theory about human behavior—self-interest.

The principle that individuals act rationally and in their own self-interest has far-reaching implications. After some necessary technical training regarding the working out of this principle, you will learn the how and why of many things: why the value of some goods and services rise and fall—why, for example, Picassos, gym memberships, tech stocks, and avocados vary in price over time. You will, with some creativity and basic economic tools, be able to pinpoint areas where new products and market innovations may be expected, such as fast foods, talking books, pool cleaning equipment, and audio-visual communications facilities and equipment. You will come to understand why information and time are considered valuable commodities. Economics even extends into sociological areas—helping you to understand law, marriage, divorce, and child bearing and rearing. (Indeed, economics is one of the most popular preparations for the study of law.)

Your education in economics (especially as a college major) thus prepares you for employment in a wide variety of jobs, from policy-oriented work with foundations and trade associations to technically oriented work with public utility commissions and private firms. Virtually every large corporation in America, as well as numerous medium-sized firms, employs economists to help make appropriate pricing decisions for their products, to evaluate the impact of government regulations, and to forecast future demand and supply conditions and product innovations within their industry. Trade organizations, representing small firms, also make much use of economists.

Public sector agencies at the federal, state, and local levels hire economists to monitor performance of the economy, to assess the desirability and impact of regulations, and to contribute to ongoing discussions of policy formation. Nonprofit groups such as hospitals, community foundations, charitable organizations, and schools employ economists as well.

After all is said and done, economics is important because it provides an essential means of thinking about the world and your place in it. Economics is not like accounting or physics in that it does not provide specific work skills. But unlike management or marketing, there *is* a widely accepted body of knowledge attached to economics. Further, and perhaps most importantly, you will be entirely flexible in the workplace armed with a good understanding of economics. The days of having only one or two jobs throughout a lifetime are gone forever. Learning to construct and manipulate a web page or a spreadsheet is a specific (and important) skill. Learning to adapt to a changing business or personal environment—*what*, in effect, to put on a spreadsheet or the computer and how to analyze it—is even more important. The flexibility that economic understanding provides will help you make wise business and personal choices for a lifetime.

QUESTION

Can you name any trade or occupation over the next fifty years that will escape the necessity of learning economics, as defined in this chapter?

SUMMARY

1. Economics is basically concerned with three questions: What goods and services are produced? How are goods and services produced? For whom are goods and services produced?

2. Economics is the study of how individuals make private and public choices to allocate scarce resources given unlimited wants.

3. Scarce resources include human and nonhuman resources as well as time, institutions, and technology. Human resources consist of labor, including entrepreneurship and management. Nonhuman resources include land and all natural resources, technology, information, and capital.

4. All scarce resources bear an opportunity cost. This means that individuals forgo other opportunities whenever scarce resources are used to produce specific goods and services.

5. Economic behavior is rational. Human beings are assumed to behave predictably by weighing the costs and benefits of their decisions and their potential actions.

6. Economic choices are made at the margin—that is, they take into account the additional costs or benefits of a change in the current situation. Prices are the signal that indicates individual choices for goods and services as well as the relative scarcity of the resources necessary to produce the goods and services.

7. Private and public choices are made by the same persons, but public choices are made by voting while private choices are made in markets.

8. The study of prices of individual products and inputs is called *microeconomics*, and the study of inflation, unemployment, economic growth, and related problems is called *macroeconomics*.

9. Economics is a science. It predicts much economic behavior and provides insight into a large number of important problems.

KEY TERMS

goods
services
resources
scarcity
economic goods and services
costs
free goods and services
human resources
nonhuman resources
technology
information
property rights

institutions
accounting costs
explicit costs
implicit costs
opportunity cost
rational self-interest
margin
marginal analysis
market
prices
private choice
public choice

barter
money
inflation
model
positive economics
normative economics
microeconomics
macroeconomics
gross domestic product (GDP)
gross national product (GNP)

QUESTIONS FOR REVIEW AND DISCUSSION

1. What problem creates the foundation of economic analysis? Is this problem restricted to the poor?

2. Can wants be satisfied with existing resources?

3. What are resources? How is the resource capital different from the resources land and labor?

4. What is the difference between behaving in one's self-interest and behaving selfishly?

5. What functions do prices have in the economy?

6. You have already paid your tuition. What does it cost you, at the margin, to attend your afternoon economics class on Friday? On Tuesday? (Remember: The margin refers to the additional cost of attending one additional class.)

7. Is air a free good? Is clean air a free good? Is cleaner air a free good?

8. Why do economists abstract from reality when formulating theories? Does this imply that their theories have no relevance in the real world?

9. "The distribution of income in the United States is not fair." What type of statement is this? Can "fair" be used to describe something without being normative?

10. To what extent can we say that economics is an accurate science?

11. John gives an annual contribution of $500 to his church. By doing so, he is acting in his own self-interest. Explain.

12. Would you expect a discussion of the Great Depression of the 1930s to be covered in a macroeconomics class or a microeconomics class?

WORKING WITH THE WEB

1. The impact of economics throughout history has been significant. While you have not yet been introduced to many of the famous economists throughout history, you will be learning about them throughout the course. To get a quick introduction to the scope of economic thought and its contributors, go to http://www.frbsf.org/econedu/curriculum/great/frames.html. Once there, take a tour of this site by clicking on the links on the right-hand side of the page (Contents). After reading the material, you are ready for the Treasure Hunt. Click on the link "play the treasure

hunt" and answer the questions here to test your understanding of the scope of economics. You can either submit your answers or simply choose "Complete" to finish the game.

2. The Application in Chapter 1, "How Economics Prepares You for Life and Work," discusses the role of economics in everyday life. It discusses how economics can help you understand not only business–related issues, but also sociological issues such as marriage and divorce! In 1992, the Nobel Prize in economics was awarded to Gary Becker, an economist at the University of Chicago. Go to http://nobelprizes.com/nobel/economics/1992a.html and click on the link "Chicago's Becker Wins Nobel Prize." Briefly explain how Becker's ideas correspond with sociological issues.

Working
With
Graphs

A P P E N D I X

Economists frequently use graphs to demonstrate economic theories or models. This appendix explains how graphs are constructed and how they can illustrate economic relations in simplified form. By understanding the mechanics and usefulness of graphs, you will find it much easier to grasp the economic concepts presented in this book.

THE PURPOSE OF GRAPHS

Most graphs in this book are simply pictures showing the relation between economic variables, such as the price of a good and the quantity of the good that people are willing to purchase. There are many such pairs of variables in economics: the costs of production and the level of output, the rate of inflation and the level of unemployment, the interest rate and the supply of capital goods, for example. Graphs are the most concise means of expressing the variety of relations that exist between such variables.

Many of the graphs in this book use the Cartesian coordinate system, which consists of points plotted on a grid formed by the intersection of two perpendicular lines. See Figure 1.1. The horizontal line is the **x-axis,** and the vertical line is the **y-axis.** The intersection of the two lines is the point 0, called the *origin.* Above the origin on the vertical axis, all values are positive. Below the origin on the vertical axis, all values are negative. Values to the right of the origin

are positive on the horizontal axis; values to the left are negative. The economic variables we use in this book are usually positive; that is, to plot economic relations we will usually use the upper-right portion, or quadrant, of a graph such as the one in Figure 1.2.

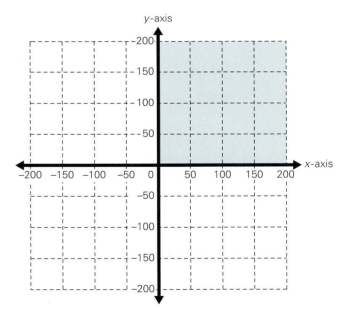

FIGURE 1.1

A Grid for Plotting Graphs
Any pair of numerical values can be plotted on this grid. The upper-right quadrant, shaded here, is the portion of the graph most often used in economics.

19

FIGURE 1.2

A Simple Line (or Linear) Graph

Curve *AE* shows the essential relation between two sets of variables: the number of words memorized and the number of minutes spent memorizing. The relation is positive; as the variable on the *x*-axis increases or decreases, the variable on the *y*-axis increases or decreases, respectively. A positive relation is shown by an upward-sloping line tracing the intersection of each pair of variables.

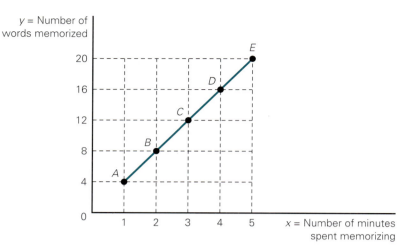

HOW TO DRAW A GRAPH

Suppose you wish to graph the relation between two variables. Variable *y* is the number of words memorized, and variable *x* is the number of minutes spent memorizing words. Table 1.1 presents a set, or schedule, of hypothetical data for these two variables.

We can plot the data from Table 1.1 on a graph using points in the upper-right quadrant formed by the *x*-axis and the *y*-axis. See Figure 1.2. The variable, number of words memorized, is measured along the *y*-axis and is considered the *y* value. The variable, number of minutes spent memorizing, is measured along the *x*-axis and is the *x* value. From the data in Table 1.1 we see that each increase of 1 minute of memorizing resulted in 4 more memorized words. The graph in Figure 1.2 illustrates this relation.

The points marked as large dots in Figure 1.2 represent pairs of variables. Point *A* represents the pair on the first line of Table 1.1: 4 words and 1 minute.

Point *B* represents 8 words and 2 minutes, and so on. When we connect the points, we have a straight line running upward and to the right of the origin. Lines showing the intersection of *x* and *y* values on a graph are referred to as **curves** in this book, whether they are straight or curved lines.

Curves show two types of relations between variables: positive and negative. The relation between the *x* and *y* values in Figure 1.2 is positive: As the *x* value increases, so does the *y* value. (Or, as the x value decreases, the y value decreases as well. Either way, the relation is positive.) On a graph, a **positive, or direct, relation** is shown by a curve that slopes upward and to the right of the origin. In a **negative, or inverse, relation,** the two variables change in opposite directions. An increase in *y* is paired with a decrease in *x*. Or a decrease in *x* is paired with an increase in *y*. Figure 1.3 shows a negative, or inverse, relation on a graph. The curve for a negative relation slopes downward from left to right—the opposite of a positive relation.

TABLE 1.1

Schedule of Hypothetical Data

Number of Words Memorized (*y*)	Number of Minutes Spent Memorizing (*x*)
4	1
8	2
12	3
16	4
20	5

General Relations

Throughout this book, some graphs display general relations rather than specific relations. A general relation does not depend on particular numerical values of variables, as was the case in Figure 1.2. For example, the relation between the number of calories a person consumes per week and that person's weight (other things being equal) is positive. This suggests an upward-sloping line, as shown in Figure 1.4a, with calories on the *x*-axis and weight on the *y*-axis. Figure 1.4a represents a general relation, so it does not need numerical values on either axis. It does not specify the

FIGURE 1.3

A Negative Relation Between Two Variables

As the price of a cup of coffee increases, the number of cups drunk each day decreases. When variables move in opposite directions, their relation is negative, or inverse. Negative relations are shown by a curve that slopes downward and to the right of the origin.

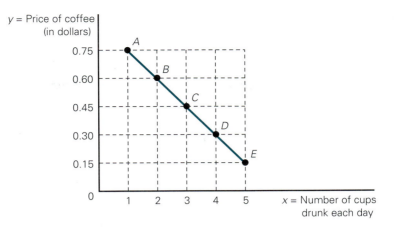

particular number of calories required to maintain a particular body weight; it simply shows that an increase in the number of calories consumed increases body weight. Figure 1.4b shows an inverse relation between body weight and the amount of exercise per week, again a general relation. Sometimes two variables are not related. Figure 1.4c shows that a person's weight is independent of a neighbor's caloric intake. Thankfully, no matter how much your neighbor eats, it has no effect on your weight.

At this point you should be able to construct a graph showing simple relations. For example, graph the relation between the weight of a car and the miles per gallon it achieves or between the length of the line at the school cafeteria and the time of day. If the relationship between any two variables you select is represented by a straight line, it is said to be a **linear relation.** A linear relationship means that for every unit change (increase or decrease) in one of the variables (the weight of a car), the other variable (miles per gallon of gasoline) changes (increases or decreases) by some fixed amount.

Nonlinear Relations

Often, relations between two variables are not the simple linear relationships depicted in Figures 1.2, 1.3,

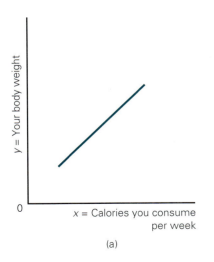

(a)

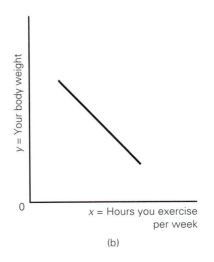

(b)

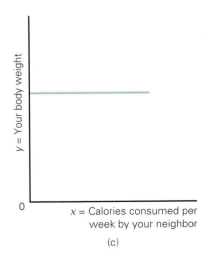

(c)

FIGURE 1.4

General Graphical Relations

General relations are (a) positive, (b) inverse, or (c) independent. General relations are not measured numerically on the *y*- or *x*-axis.

and 1.4. For example, unlike in Figure 1.2, where each additional minute spent studying enables one to memorize 4 additional words, it may be that the number of additional words memorized changes as the number of minutes changes. Such a **nonlinear relation** is depicted in Figure 1.5. There, 1 minute of studying enables a student to memorize 6 words, but 2 minutes of studying enables a student to memorize only 11 words—the second minute adds only 5 additional words to the total. Additional minutes of studying beyond 2 lead to even smaller increases in the total number of words memorized. Therefore, there is a positive relationship between the two variables, but the relationship is *nonlinear.*

Occasionally, nonlinear relations are more complex than the one depicted in Figure 1.5 and do not fall into the simple categories of positive or negative. A U-shaped curve, as graphed in Figure 1.6, shows that the *x* value is at first inversely related to the *y*

value and then positively related. After some critical value, x^*, the *y* value begins to rise as the *x* value increases. The *y*-axis in this example might represent the probability of having an accident on an interstate highway, and the *x*-axis might show the miles per hour at which a car travels. To avoid accidents, x^* is the optimal, or "best" speed. Driving at speeds lower than x^* increases the probability of an accident, but rates faster than x^* mph also increase the chances of an accident.

SLOPE OF THE CURVE

In graphical analysis, the amount by which the *y* value increases or decreases as the result of an increase or decrease in the *x* value is the *slope* of the curve. The slope of the curve is an important concept in economics. Much economic analysis studies the margin of

FIGURE 1.5

A Nonlinear Graph

Curve *AE* shows the nonlinear relation between the number of minutes spent studying and the number of words memorized.

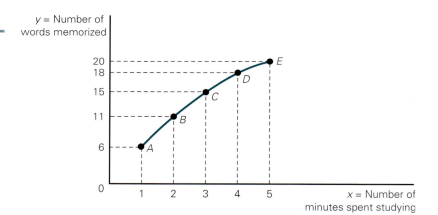

FIGURE 1.6

A U-shaped Curve

Some relations yield a U shape. Variables along the x- and y-axes are inversely related at first, but after some critical value, here shown as x^*, they become positively related. Naturally curves may also be bow-shaped with relations reversed.

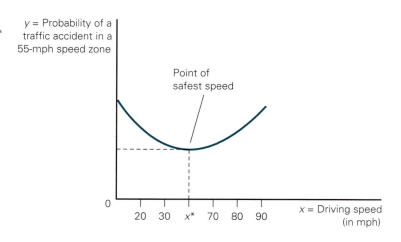

change in a variable or in a relation between variables, and the slope of a curve measures the marginal rate of change. In Figure 1.2, for example, every change in the x value—every increase of 1 minute—is associated with an increase of 4 words memorized. The slope of the curve in Figure 1.2 is the rate of change. Economists express the concept "change in" with the symbol Δ. So in Figure 1.2 the slope of the line AE is $\Delta y/\Delta x = 4/1 = 4$.

For the straight-line curves in Figures 1.2 and 1.3 the slope is constant. Along most curves, however, the slope is not constant. In Figure 1.6, an increase in driving speed from 55 to 60 mph will increase the probability of an accident only slightly, but an increase from 60 to 65 mph would increase the probability by a greater amount. Not only does the probability increase for each mile-per-hour increase in driving speed, but it increases by a progressively greater amount. This indicates that the slope not only is positive but also is increasing.

The slope of a curved line is different at every point along the line. To find the slope of a curved line at a particular point, draw a straight line tangent to the curve. (A tangent touches the curve at one point without crossing the curve.) Consider point A in Figure 1.7. The slope at A on the curved line is equal to the slope of the straight line tangent to the curved line. Dividing the change in the y variable (Δy) by the change in the x variable (Δx) yields the slope at A. In Figure 1.7, every change in x from 0 to 1, 1 to 2, and so on, results in a change in y along the curve. At point A, $\Delta y = 4$ on the tangent line. So $\Delta y/\Delta x = -4/1 = -4$. At lower points along the curve, such as B, the curve is flatter—that is, less steep. The line tangent at B has a slope of -1. As we move from point A to point B, equal increases in x result in smaller and smaller decreases in y. In other words, the *rate* at which y falls decreases as x increases along this particular curve.

Other relations lead to different slopes and different changes in the slope along the curve. Along the curve in Figure 1.8, not only does the y value increase as the x value increases, but the slope increases as the x value increases. For equal increases in the x value, the incremental changes in the y value become larger.

Interpreting the essential concepts illustrated in graphs is a necessary part of learning economic principles. Should you encounter difficulty in interpreting any of the graphs in later chapters, a brief review of this appendix will prove helpful.

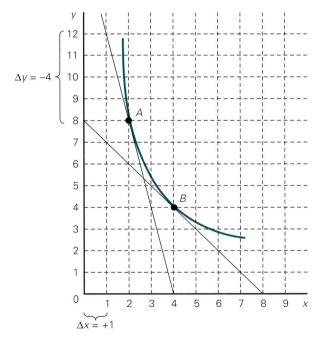

FIGURE 1.7

Slope Along a Curve
The slope of a curve at a particular point is the slope of a straight line tangent to the curve at that point.

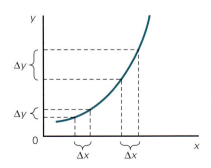

FIGURE 1.8

A Curve with an Increasing Slope
As the x variable increases, the change in the y variable increases.

SUMMARY

1. Graphs are a concise expression of economic models, or theories. Graphs usually show the relation between two variables, such as price and quantity.

2. Linear graphs are drawn with two perpendicular lines, called axes. The *x*-axis is a horizontal line. Variables measured along the *x*-axis are called *x* values. The *y*-axis is a vertical line. Variables along it are called y values.

3. Lines showing the correlation between *x* and *y* values are called curves. An upward-sloping curve indicates a positive, or direct, relation between variables: As the *x* value increases or decreases, the *y* value increases or decreases. A downward-sloping curve indicates a negative, or inverse, relation between variables: As the *x* value increases, the *y* value decreases, and vice versa.

4. Relations between variables may be specific or general. Specific relations are based on numerical quantities measured on either the *x*- or *y*-axis or both. General relations are not based on specific numerical quantities.

5. Relations between two variables can be either linear (straight lines) or nonlinear (curved lines).

6. Variables can be both positively and negatively related over certain ranges. In such complex relations, a curve is either bow-shaped or U-shaped.

7. The slope of a curve measures the ratio of change in the *y* value to change in the *x* value, expressed as $\Delta y/\Delta x$. Along a straight-line curve, the slope is constant. Along a curved line, the slope is different at every point.

KEY TERMS

x-axis, *y*-axis
curve
positive (direct) relation

negative (inverse) relation
linear relation
nonlinear relation

slope

QUESTIONS FOR REVIEW AND DISCUSSION

1. Explain how the slope of a line tells you whether the relation between the two variables illustrated is direct or inverse. If you drew a line illustrating your score on a history test as you study more hours, what would its slope be?

2. Plot the following points on a graph with X on the horizontal axis and Y on the vertical axis. Connect the dots to show the relation between X and Y.

	X	Y
A	0	2
B	2	4
C	4	8
D	6	14
E	8	22

What is the slope of the line between points A and B? What is the slope between C and D? Is this a straight line?

3. Curves can be represented in algebraic form by an equation. For example, the points along a certain line can be demonstrated by the equation

$$Y = 10 - 2X.$$

The value of Y can be found by inserting different values of X and solving the equation for Y.

Some of the values of Y for different values of X are shown in the following table. Fill in the blanks by solving the equation for the value of Y for each value of X given.

X	Y
0	10
2	6
4	—
6	—
8	—
10	—
12	—

Draw this set of points on a graph. Does this show a direct or inverse relation between X and Y? What is the slope of this line between the first and second points? Between the second and third? Is this a straight line?

4. If you measured body weight on the horizontal axis and the probability of dying of heart disease on the vertical axis, what would be the slope of a curve that showed the relation between these two variables?

Opportunity Cost, Specialization, and Trade

The essence of the economic problem is how to get as much value as we can from limited and costly resources. To do so, we constantly make choices. Economists emphasize that decisions to use scarce resources bear an **opportunity cost**. The opportunity cost of a decision is the next most preferred or next-best alternative to a good or activity that one must forgo in order to obtain some other good. Economists have developed tools for expressing that choice and opportunity costs are central to all decisions. After reading Chapter 2 you should understand

- the role of specialization and trade for individuals and societies.
- how individuals actually make decisions given that they are always costly.
- how specialization and trade increase quantities of output for parties who exchange goods and services.
- how exchange, transaction costs, and certain public choices to erect barriers to trade reduce the benefits from specialization and trade.

SPECIALIZATION AND TRADE: A FEATURE OF ALL SOCIETIES

Specialization refers to a situation in which the tasks associated with the production of a product or service are divided—and sometimes subdivided—and performed by many different individuals to increase the total production of the good or service. Virtually all known peoples have engaged in specialization and trade, and theories and principles related to specialization and trade have been part of economists' tool kits for more than 200 years. Adam Smith (1723–1790), the Scottish philosopher and recognized founder

27

Opportunity cost
The highest-valued alternative forgone in making any choice.

Specialization
An economic entity producing only one good or service, or the performance of a single task in a production process by an individual.

Division of labor
Individual specialization in separate tasks involved with a production process; the result of specialization.

of economics, published his great work *An Inquiry into the Nature and Causes of the Wealth of Nations* in 1776 (a year of declarations). It formally established the science of what we now call economics. (For more information about Adam Smith, see Point/Counterpoint, pp. 109–111.)

At the very core of economics, according to Smith, is the ability of individuals and societies to deal with the facts of scarcity through specialization and trade. When tasks are divided, permitting each individual to concentrate on a single element in the production of a good, output increases over what it would be if each individual produced the entire good. Specialization and the **division of labor** lead to increased output. As a result, people became more dependent on one another for all goods. We may work in an automobile plant, for example, but we still want eggs for breakfast. Think of any organization and try to list the number of distinct divisions of labor in it. Think of a larger factory, a steel mill, a football team, a fraternity, a church. Specialization exists in almost everything we do. (See the Focus "Economic Specialization in Everyday Life: Marriage and Roommate Selection" for illustrations.)

FOCUS

Economic Specialization in Everyday Life: Marriage and Roommate Selection

Specialization and trade have increased economic welfare and human progress from the very beginning of time. These gains have depended on the diverse talents of individuals as well as the different resources of great nations. Consider two examples that do not often come to mind when considering the economic principles of specialization: the selection of a marriage partner and selection of a roommate.

Although relationships like marriage have many bases—love, security, and so on—one of them is surely economic. The greatest gains from trade occur when individuals (or countries) with widely differing skills or resources trade. In a society in which males and females acquire widely different skills, the incentive to marry is quite strong. If, as in primitive society, women do not know how to hunt or fish and men cannot prepare food or make clothing, the gains to both partners in a marriage relationship are immense. In fact, survival outside of a marriage-type relationship may be impossible. In such societies, nearly everyone would marry, and individuals would abandon a marriage relationship only to enter another one. In societies where men and women acquire similar skills, the gains from exchange between marriage partners are much smaller. Individuals, therefore, have a weaker incentive to marry or to remain married. The slowing marriage rate and the growing divorce rate in Western societies in recent decades may partly be attributed to greater occupational equality. As the incomes of women rise (and the opportunity cost of child rearing), a lower birth rate may be expected. Specialization may even be reversed, with men taking more active roles in raising children. "Mr. Mom" may become more common due to economic specialization and trade.

Roommate selection, an activity perhaps closer to your experience, also takes place, in part, on the basis of economic specialization and trade. Students room together to save money, but they also do so, in part, because of the gains from specialization and trade. Communal arrangements ranging from fraternities and sororities to clubs and study groups work best when the participants have tradable skills. Ideally, then, one roommate would be an excellent cook, say, while another roommate would be an expert carpenter, and yet another would be adept at yard work. Even if individuals' skill levels are pretty much the same, trade is still profitable when roommates' tastes and preferences for specific jobs differ and trade is possible. Problems and disputes arise most often between roommates when trade agreements or "contracts" are not enforceable. You may do the cooking, but can you "force" your roommate to clean up the kitchen—assuming you both agreed she would?

The benefits of specialization and trade are not just of academic interest, nor do they pertain only to trade in goods and services between nations such as Japan and the United States. As workers, club members, marriage partners, roommates, or friends, these principles affect us every day.

All modern nations, states, firms, and individuals specialize in the production of economic goods and services, in varying degrees. The individual, the most basic economic entity, specializes to the greatest extent. Your teacher for this course specializes in economic research and teaching. Other people specialize in mechanical engineering services or in breeding thoroughbred racehorses. Some businesses produce only one product, whereas others offer a multitude. One very critical point must be made about all specialization and trade—it is as significant as having more and better resources or improved production techniques. Specialization and division of labor lead to increased output without any additional resources. The gains from specializing in and exchanging goods and services are, in effect, equivalent to acquiring or developing additional natural resources or capital.

OPPORTUNITY COST AND PRODUCTION POSSIBILITIES: INDIVIDUALS AND SOCIETY MUST CHOOSE

Imagine a society in which the following things are true:

1. Only two goods are produced;
2. Supplies of resources are fixed; and
3. Technology is held constant, and no economic growth occurs.

Our hypothetical (theoretical) society can produce cheeseburgers and/or automobiles. Note that it is an example of an economic model where signifying assumptions are used to abstract from nonessential aspects of the problem.

    Given the state of technology and assuming that the society uses all its resources, the society could produce either 100 million cheeseburgers or 16 million automobiles (see Table 2.1). Or the society may choose to devote some of its resources to producing cheeseburgers and some to producing automobiles. These choices, called society's *production possibilities,* are listed *A–E* in Table 2.1. From this information a production possibilities curve can be constructed (see Figure 2.1). A production possibilities curve depicts the alternatives open to society for the production of two goods, given full utilization of all existing resources, human and nonhuman, and an existing state of technology at some point in time. When resources are fully employed, moreover, society is said to be producing on its **production possibilities frontier**.

    At choice *A* in Figure 2.1, society produces 100 million cheeseburgers and no automobiles, whereas at choice *E* society uses all its resources in automobile

Production possibilities frontier

The curve that graphs all the possible combinations of two goods that an economy can produce given the available technology, the amount of productive resources available, and the full utilization of these resources.

TABLE 2.1

Society Decides: Cheeseburgers or Automobiles

Society must choose among many alternative combinations of goods to produce. The cost of one good is the lost production of other goods.

Choice	Cheeseburgers (millions)	Automobiles (millions)
A	100	0
B	90	4
C	75	8
D	50	12
E	0	16

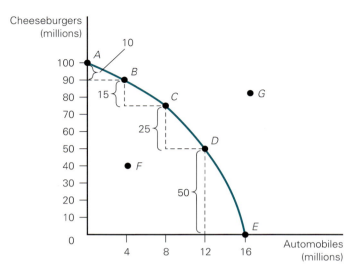

FIGURE 2.1

Production Possibilities Curve

As more and more automobiles are produced, the opportunity cost per automobile increases. The opportunity cost of producing the first 4 million automobiles is 10 million cheeseburgers. The opportunity cost of producing the next 4 million automobiles is an additional 15 million cheeseburgers, and so on.

production. Choices in between, with some of both commodities produced, are shown at points *B, C,* and *D.* Continuous choices of all other possible combinations are shown along the curve; resources are assumed to be fully employed at all points on the curve. The curve therefore shows all of the possibilities for the production of automobiles and cheeseburgers, assuming resources are fully employed at present or at some given point in time. Points such as *G* lie beyond the production possibilities frontier. The country's resources and technology do not permit it to produce at points, such as *G,* that lie outside the frontier.

The Law of Increasing Costs

There is an opportunity cost for society in any choice between producing cheeseburgers and automobiles.

Consider a society that produces nothing but cheeseburgers, choice *A* in Figure 2.1. The opportunity cost of that choice is that no automobiles can be produced. A move to choice B, representing a movement of some resources from cheeseburger production to automobile production, means a sacrifice of 10 million cheeseburgers, but society gains 4 million automobiles. Thus the opportunity cost of producing the first 4 million automobiles is 10 million cheeseburgers. To get the second 4 million automobiles, however, a larger quantity of cheeseburgers must be given up—15 million. Thus as society becomes more specialized in production of either automobiles or cheeseburgers, the opportunity cost per unit of the good rises. This effect is called the **law of increasing costs**.

Law of increasing costs

As more scarce resources are used to produce additional units of one good, production of another good falls by larger and larger amounts.

Why does the law of increasing costs hold? Resources, training, and talents are not all alike and are not perfectly adaptable to alternative uses. Capital suited to cattle raising or dairy farming is not equally suited to steel making or automobile manufacturing, and vice versa. Cowboys and farmers are not equally adept at the manufacture of seat covers for automobiles or metal fabricating without additional training. The most-suited human and nonhuman resources are moved into production first, but as production of a good increases and becomes more specialized, less-adaptable resources must be used to produce it. The costs of producing additional units of the good rise because larger amounts of these increasingly less-adaptable resources are required to produce each successive unit. This means that greater quantities of another good do not get produced and must therefore be sacrificed in the process.

The law of increasing costs always applies when resources are fully employed. When there is a degree of **unemployment of resources,** however—such as a certain amount of land lying idle—society finds itself producing at a point within the production possibilities curve. Point *F* in Figure 2.2 represents such a situation. From point *F* to the curve, additional cheeseburgers or automobiles can be produced without any increase in opportunity costs until resources become fully employed. The production possibilities curve is thus referred to as a *frontier* because it represents full employment of resources. Full employment means that society is realizing its maximum output potential.

This society (or the individuals in it) must choose the level of cheeseburger and automobile production that it prefers. Such a choice involves trade-offs among the alternative possibility. To have more cheeseburgers means having fewer automobiles. Choices are made at the margin and balanced accordingly. If individuals want to increase automobiles from 8 to 12 million in Figure 2.1, the opportunity cost is 25 million cheeseburgers. The final outcome will depend on how individuals weigh the costs and benefits of these **choices at the margin**. Remember: When we say "society," we mean the individuals who make up that society. Societies do not make decisions, individuals make decisions.

Unemployment of resources

A situation in which some human and/or nonhuman resources that can be used in production are not utilized.

Choices at the margin

Decisions based on the additional benefits and costs of small changes in a particular activity.

WHY THE PRODUCTION POSSIBILITIES FRONTIER SHIFTS

If we keep in mind the meaning and assumptions of the production possibilities frontier, we will also understand that an increase or decrease in society's human or nonhuman resources can shift society's output potential. An understanding of such changes is central to an understanding of economic growth—or the lack of it.

The Shifting Frontier

The production possibilities frontier can shift leftward or rightward in response to any change in the quantity of human resources, any change in the quantity of nonhuman resources, or any change in technology. Changes in these factors, which we previously assumed to be constant, shift the production possibilities frontier.

In Figure 2.2, a general change in productivity, technology, or resource supply is assumed. An increase in the quantity of labor (through a simple growth in population), for example, shifts the entire production possibilities frontier rightward from PP_1 to PP_2. Suppose society now chooses the cheeseburger/automobile combination A_1. More of both goods are produced and consumed as a result of the technological improvement. But society faces new trade-offs once it is producing on its new frontier. Opportunity costs arise again in resource utilization, just as they did at combination A on production possibility curve PP_1. Society cannot escape scarcity, yet it can improve its production possibilities through growth in technology, quantity of human or nonhuman resources, or resource productivity.

Economic Growth: How Economies Progress

We can understand the nature of economic growth with the aid of the production possibilities curve model. The key to economic growth in society is related to the growth or change in capital stock and other crucial resources.

FIGURE 2.2

Shifting the Production Possibilities Frontier

A general increase in technology or resource supply shifts the entire production possibilities curve outward.

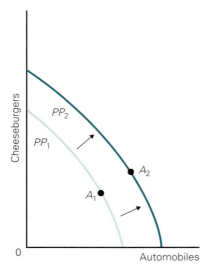

Capital stock

The amount of nonhuman resources available in the economy. These include tools, land, machinery, equipment, and so on.

The creation of **capital stock** (a supply of items used to produce other items) takes time and bears an opportunity cost in present consumption. The benefits of creating capital, however, are in increased amounts of future consumption. In other words, forming new capital stock requires that people save—that is, abstain from consuming in the present. When investment in capital stocks results from this saving, capital formation and growth occur. The formation of capital goods—tools, tractors, computers and so on—requires a redirection of resources from consumption of goods to production of capital goods. The opportunity cost of acquiring capital is thus consumption goods forgone, but the reward for society is an increase in future productive capacity in consumption goods, capital goods, or both.

We can illustrate this phenomenon with the production possibilities curve. Figure 2.3 shows two production possibilities frontiers that contrast capital goods production (the vertical axis) with consumption goods production (the horizontal axis) for two hypothetical societies with initially similar production possibilities curves. Consider society A's choice of consumption and capital goods in 2000, represented by point E_A in Figure 2.3a. Clearly, society A devotes a larger proportion of its resources to capital goods production than to consumption goods production. Saving (abstaining from current consumption), investing, and capital formation are all high in that society. The payoff for society A will come later, say in 2010, with vastly enlarged productive capacity, designated by the shift of the production possibilities curve to PP_{2010} in Figure 2.3a.

Economic growth

A permanent increase in the productive capacity of the economy.

Society B chooses to use almost all of its resources in 2000 for consumption goods, with only a small quantity of resources devoted to capital goods, a combination represented by point E_B in Figure 2.3b. The consequence of this choice is low economic growth over the following decade. By 2010, the production possibilities of that society have grown by only a small amount, as curve PP_{2010} in Figure 2.3b indicates. Thus **economic growth** in the future is largely determined by current decisions about production. Technological changes are important factors in the progress of society, but to take advantage of technology, society must sacrifice some present consumption. With reductions in human or nonhuman resources, societies can actually regress. After World War II, for example, the production possibilities of Germany

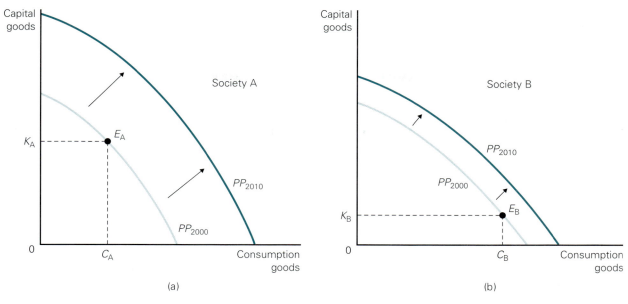

(a)   (b)

FIGURE 2.3

Growth Choices on the Production Possibilities Curve

(a) By producing more capital goods, K_A in 2000, society A can produce more consumption goods in the future than (b) society B, which produces only K_B capital goods in 2000.

and Japan were virtually smashed, leading to a massive shift to the left of their relevant production possibilities curves. Production possibilities may be reduced by other kinds of disastrous events as well. See the Application at the end of this chapter, "AIDS and Reduced Production Possibilities in Africa," for example.

And keep in mind something we have not addressed so far. We have discussed trade-offs and opportunity costs, but we have not told you how individuals make private choices or public choices about these tradeoffs. In short, where on the production possibilities curve does one end up or choose to be? Individuals make these choices in both private and public settings, and we will explore how they do this throughout the rest of the book.

In addition to making choices between consumption now and later, both individuals and societies can increase their output by specializing in and trading, or exchanging, goods and services. The manner in which both individuals and societies specialize is related to an important principle—the law of comparative advantage.

COMPARATIVE ADVANTAGE

While Adam Smith developed the fundamentals underlying specialization and trade, it was left to his English followers, David Ricardo (1772–1823) and Robert Torrens (1780–1864), to develop the critically important principle of specialization—the theory of comparative advantage. Comparative advantage (and its relation to specialization and trade) is best understood with a simple, hypothetical example. Table 2.2 describes three combinations of silver and lumber production for two different countries, Canada and Mexico. The production possibilities information in Table 2.2 is represented graphically in Figure 2.4. The production possibilities curves of Figure 2.4 do not look exactly like the production possibilities curves we have discussed so far. For simplicity, we have temporarily assumed that the law of increasing costs does not hold in the two countries—at least not where lumber and silver production are concerned. Instead, we assume that in each country both silver and lumber production are subject to constant opportunity costs of production. This means that the production possibilities curves are straight lines instead of curves.

Table 2.2 indicates that production of the first 30,000 ounces of silver in Canada means 300,000 board-feet of lumber do not get produced. Moving from point *A* to point *B* on Canada's production possibilities curve reduces the production of lumber from 1 million to 700,000 board-feet. In such a move, each additional ounce of silver produced has an opportunity cost of 10 board-feet of lumber. If Canada is producing 30,000 ounces of silver and shifts productive resources from the lumber industry to produce 70,000 more ounces of silver (for a total of 100,000 ounces), lumber production drops by 700,000 board-feet. Each additional ounce of silver produced has a constant opportunity cost of 10 board-feet of unproduced lumber, regardless of how many ounces of silver are already being produced.

Marginal opportunity production cost

The number of units of one good that do not get produced when one additional unit of another good is produced.

The same information may be expressed in a different manner. In Canada, the additional cost, or **marginal opportunity production cost,** of 1 board-foot of lumber is constant and equal to 1/10 of an ounce of silver. Silver and lumber production in Mexico are also subject to constant (marginal opportunity) production costs. For each additional ounce of silver produced, only 1 board-foot of lumber goes unproduced. The marginal opportunity cost of producing 1 ounce of silver in Mexico, 1 board-foot of lumber, is less than it is in Canada, where it is equal to 10 board-feet of lumber. Mexico is said to possess a comparative advantage over Canada in producing silver. A comparative advantage exists because the marginal opportunity cost of producing an ounce of silver in Mexico (1 board-foot of lumber) is less than it is in Canada (10 board-feet). So, any locale with a lower marginal opportunity cost of producing a good possesses a comparative advantage over some other locale in producing that good.

TABLE 2.2

Production Possibilities in Canada and Mexico

Canada has a comparative advantage in lumber. If Canada were to move to producing combination *A* instead of *B*, 300,000 board-feet of lumber could be had at an opportunity cost of 30,000 ounces of silver. Each board-foot of lumber has a marginal opportunity cost ¹/₁₀ of an ounce of silver going unproduced. If Mexico were to move from *B* to *A*, 40,000 more ounces of silver could be had at an opportunity cost of 40,000 board-feet of lumber. Each ounce of silver costs Mexico 1 board-foot of lumber. Conversely, Mexico has a comparative advantage in producing silver. In Canada an extra ounce of silver costs 10 board-feet of lumber.

	CANADA'S PRODUCTION POSSIBILITIES			MEXICO'S PRODUCTION POSSIBILITIES		
	A	*B*	*C*	*A*	*B*	*C*
Silver (ounces)	0	30,000	100,000	0	40,000	80,000
Lumber (board-feet)	1,000,000	700,000	0	80,000	40,000	0

FIGURE 2.4

Canada's and Mexico's Production Possibilities Curves

Both countries agree that each 1000 ounces of silver trades for 5000 board-feet of lumber, or a board-foot of lumber for 1/5 of an ounce of silver. Each agrees to trade on these terms because obtaining a good through trade is less costly than obtaining the good by producing it at home. After specialization and trade, each country will consume combination *D*, a combination that lies beyond each country's production possibilities curve.

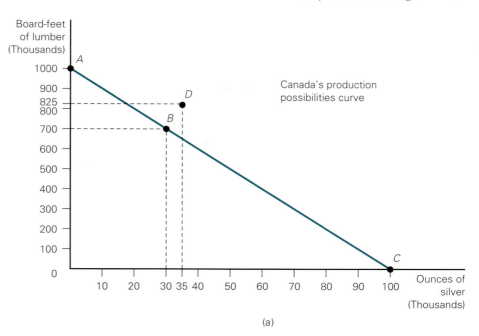

(a)

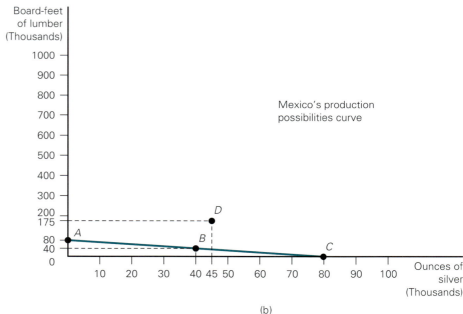

(b)

Canada has a comparative advantage over Mexico in lumber production, as indicated in Table 2.2. Canada can produce lumber at a lower marginal opportunity cost (1/10 of an ounce of silver) than can Mexico (1 ounce of silver). If Canada has a comparative advantage in lumber production, this necessarily means that Mexico has a **comparative advantage** in silver production. One ounce of silver costs Mexico only 1 board-foot of lumber, whereas in Canada the cost is 10 board-feet. Each country has a comparative production advantage over the other, but in a different good.

Comparative advantage

An economic entity's ability to produce a good at a lower marginal opportunity production cost than some other entity.

Suppose that both Mexico and Canada are initially self-sufficient in silver and lumber. That is, each country produces and consumes some of both goods and does not trade with the other nation. Specifically, suppose that both countries produce and consume the combination of silver and lumber labeled *B* in Table 2.2 and Figure 2.4. We assume that combination *B* represents the most desirable consumption combination for both Canada and Mexico that is attainable from self-production.

How might Mexicans and Canadians be made better off economically? Excluding economic growth, residents of each country could improve their economic situation through specialization and trade. Each could specialize in producing the good for which that locale has a comparative advantage and then trade some of its output for the other good. The residents could consume more of both goods or more of one good and the same quantity of the other good.

Specialization

Suppose that Mexico and Canada happen to hire the same economic consultant to help them improve their respective economic fortunes. After a study of each economy, the consultant brings representatives of both countries together and suggests a plan that will leave each better off economically: Specialize according to comparative advantage and trade with each other.

The benefits of specialization and trade are shown in Tables 2.3 and 2.4, and Figure 2.5. Table 2.3a shows the situation in each country before specialization and trade occur. Specifically, it reproduces combination *B* from each locale's production possibilities curves shown in Figures 2.4a and 2.4b. Combination *B*, recall, is assumed to be the most desirable consumption combination for each country. Also shown in Table 2.3a is the sum total of both countries' production and consumption of each good. It is assumed that Canada and Mexico constitute the "world."

TABLE 2.3A

Canada and Mexico Before Specialization and Trade
The amounts actually produced and thus consumed in Canada and Mexico are the combinations labeled *B* in Table 2.2. Amounts of each good for the "world" are the sums of the two countries' production.

	Canada Produces and Consumes	+	Mexico Produces and Consumes	=	World Produces and Consumes
Silver (ounces)	30,000		40,000		70,000
Lumber (board-feet)	700,000		40,000		740,000

TABLE 2.3B

Canada and Mexico After Specialization, but Before Trade
Specialization in production according to comparative advantage yields a world gain in the output of both goods.

	Canada Produces	+	Mexico Produces	=	World Produces	World Gains
Silver (ounces)	0		80,000		80,000	+10,000
Lumber (board-feet)	1,000,000		0		1,000,000	+260,000

FIGURE 2.5

The Trade Between Canada and Mexico

Canada and Mexico agree that each ounce of silver trades for 5 board-feet of lumber, or a board-foot of lumber trades for 1/5 of an ounce of silver. Each agrees to trade on these terms because obtaining a good through trade is less costly than obtaining it by producing it at home.

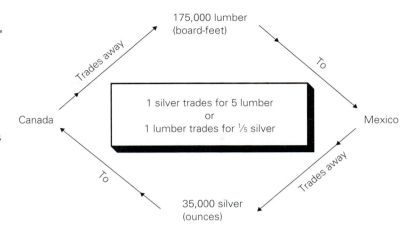

Table 2.3b depicts the production situation in each country, and, therefore, the world, after Canada and Mexico have specialized in production according to comparative advantage. After specialization, total world output of silver is 10,000 ounces greater than it was at combination B on the production possibilities curve in Figure 2.4. World production of lumber has also increased. It is 260,000 board-feet more than before specialization. The world is better off economically (more of both goods), but we have yet to show that each individual country is made better off as a result of specialization according to comparative advantage. There is one more step to the process, that of trade.

Trade: The Fruits of Specialization

Our consultant realizes that neither Canada nor Mexico would voluntarily agree to an exchange that would leave them worse off (than before trade). For voluntary exchange to take place, each nation must end up better off economically. With this in mind, the consultant proposes that Canada trade 175,000 board-feet of lumber to Mexico in exchange for 35,000 ounces of silver, or 5 board-feet of lumber for each ounce of silver. The Canadians would agree to this trade since domestic production of the 35,000 ounces of silver would cost them 10 board-feet of lumber each, for a total of 350,000 board-feet. This exchange allows the Canadians to obtain silver from the Mexicans more cheaply than it costs to produce it themselves.

The Mexicans would also agree to the proposed trade. Each board-foot of lumber costs them 1 ounce of silver to produce, but the proposed trade allows them to obtain each board-foot for 1/5 of an ounce of silver. The trade with Canada enables Mexico to obtain 175,000 board-feet of lumber for 35,000 ounces of silver. The opportunity cost to Mexico of producing 175,000 board-feet of lumber would be 175,000 ounces of silver. It is less costly for Mexico to obtain lumber through trade than through self-production. This trade is depicted in Figure 2.5.

The number of board-feet of lumber that trade for an ounce of silver is called the **terms of trade.** The terms of trade is really a price that is not measured in terms of either country's money. In this example, Canada pays Mexico 5 board-feet of lumber for each ounce of silver. Mexico pays 1/5 ounce of silver for each board-foot of lumber. The terms of trade is a price that defines the number of units of one good that exchange for one unit of some other good. The terms of trade will always fall somewhere between the marginal opportunity production costs of a given good in each of the two countries. In this case, an ounce of silver has an opportunity cost

Terms of trade

The number of units of one good that exchange in the market for one unit of some other good. Although not expressed in terms of money, it is a price nonetheless.

of 10 board-feet of lumber in Canada and 1 board-foot of lumber in Mexico, so the terms of trade will be at least 1 board-foot of lumber for 1 ounce of silver and at most 10 board-feet of lumber for 1 ounce of silver. Terms of trade outside these limits would cause trade to be counter to the interests of citizens in one of the countries—for instance, Canadians would be better off producing their own silver than paying more than 10 board-feet per ounce for Mexican silver.

Table 2.4 summarizes the economic positions of Canada and Mexico after specializing in production and trading. Most important, both countries end up with more of both goods to consume than before trade. Canada consumes 125,000 more board-feet of lumber than it did initially; Mexico, an additional 135,000 board-feet. Both enjoy 5000 more ounces of silver than in the period before specialization and trade. In Figures 2.3a and 2.3b, both countries are consuming combination D—combinations of goods that lie beyond the respective production possibilities curves. Without specialization and trade, these combinations could only be attained through economic growth. It is as if additional resource quantities of silver and lumber were actually created through specialized production and division of labor. Residents in each country are better off economically. Specialization according to comparative advantage and trade has led to increased living standards in both parts of the world.

Factors Explaining Comparative Advantage

There are basically two reasons that a locale would have a comparative advantage over some other locale in producing any given good relative to other goods—differences in technology or differences in the quantities of productive inputs in the two locales. Relative differences in production technologies of the goods in the two locales can lead to a comparative advantage for each locale. Certain institutional factors can also affect both the level of technology utilized and costs. One country may impose minimum wage laws on employers. Another may contain effective environmental laws that create different costs to producers.

Alternatively, if production technologies are identical in both locales, an abundance of the productive resources used in producing lumber in Canada compared

TABLE 2.4

Canada and Mexico After Specialization and Trade
Specialization in production according to comparative advantage and trading yields a world gain and a gain for each country.

			CANADA		
	Produces	**Trades For (+) Away (−)**	**Consumes After Trade**	**Produced and Consumed Before Trade**	**Gains from Trade**
Silver (ounces)	0	+35,000	35,000	30,000	+5,000
Lumber (board-feet)	1,000,000	−175,000	825,000	700,000	+125,000
			MEXICO		
	Produces	**Trades For (+) Away (−)**	**Consumes After Trade**	**Produced and Consumed Before Trade**	**Gains from Trade**
Silver (ounces)	80,000	−35,000	45,000	40,000	+5,000
Lumber (board-feet)	0	+175,000	175,000	40,000	+135,000

with Mexico's amounts of these resources could exist. This would give Canada a comparative advantage in lumber. Patterns of comparative advantage may, of course, shift over time with either natural or artificially induced changes in resource prices and supplies or with changes in technology.

Consider another aspect of the situation in Mexico and Canada. Table 2.2 indicates that Canada has the ability to produce more lumber in absolute terms than Mexico if each country produces only lumber (1 million board-feet versus 80,000 board-feet). Canada also has the capacity to produce absolutely more silver (100,000 ounces versus 80,000 ounces) than Mexico. Canada has what economists call an absolute advantage in production of both goods. That is, Canada can specialize in silver production and simply produce more silver than Mexico. The same holds for lumber production. Any time a country can specialize in producing a good and produce absolutely more of it than some other country, the first country has an absolute advantage over the second. An absolute advantage can arise because of technological factors or because one country possesses a larger quantity of productive resources. Although Canada has an absolute advantage in producing both goods, it has a comparative advantage only in lumber. Mexico has an absolute disadvantage in both goods, but it still can produce silver at a lower marginal opportunity cost than Canada. Both countries still benefit from specialization and trade according to comparative advantage.

It is important to understand the simplification attached to the preceding discussion of comparative advantage. Differences in marginal opportunity costs explain comparative advantages, but the economic system does not actually require an "economic consultant" to tell countries (or businesses or individuals) about the potential gains from specialization and trade. Relative scarcities based on differences in marginal opportunity costs are transmitted to producers and consumers through the price system. Prices "inform" producers and consumers about what, how much, and when to supply and consume millions of goods and services. The details of how prices are formed through the interaction of supply and demand are reserved for Chapter 3. Nonetheless, it is useful to remember that prices, not hypothetical economic consultants, "discover," signal, and reflect the comparative advantages that exist between nations, businesses, and individuals.

Exchange Costs

The model of comparative advantage and trade—along with all other economic models—is a simplification of reality. A number of important assumptions hide behind our simple discussions. But there are also costs to the process of exchange that must be accounted for when calculating the benefits of specialization and trade. We classify these **exchange costs** as transaction costs, transportation costs, and artificial barriers to trade.

Exchange costs

The opportunity costs of the resources used in making trades; includes transaction costs, transportation costs, and artificial barriers to trade.

Transaction costs

The opportunity costs of the resources directly associated with trade; includes time costs, brokers' fees, and so on.

Transaction Costs   Transaction costs are all the resource costs (including time-associated costs) incurred because of exchange. Transaction costs occur every time goods and services are traded, whether exchanges are simple (purchase of a pack of gum) or complex (a long-term negotiated contract with many contingencies). Here's a simple example: Gwen goes to the supermarket to purchase a pound of coffee. What are the costs of the transaction? Gasoline and auto depreciation must be considered as resource costs, of course, but the principal cost is the opportunity cost of Gwen's time. Gwen might have spent this time working or playing tennis instead of grocery shopping. Gwen's wage rate might then serve as her opportunity cost. If the shopping trip takes 30 minutes and if Gwen's wage rate is $15 an hour, the time part of her transaction costs is $7.50.

In this simple case the contracting and negotiating are instantaneous—Gwen simply gives the money to the checkout person, takes her coffee, and the transaction is complete. In other, more complex exchanges—such as the purchase of a house, a car, or a major appliance or the negotiation of a long-term labor contract—contracting and negotiating costs can be substantial. Think of the time and other resource costs associated with long-term supply contracts such as U.S. arms deals with allies or negotiations for ammonia plants in China. Every detail must be studied, formulated, and then spelled out.

The important point is that transaction costs include resources used by each party to the exchange. The higher the resource costs, the lower the benefit that comes from specialization and trade. Institutions—new legal arrangements, new marketing techniques, new methods of selling—have emerged, and are continually emerging, to reduce all forms of transaction costs. Gwen could have purchased coffee at a convenience store nearer to her house. The price of the coffee might have been somewhat higher, but Gwen's time costs, and therefore her total transaction costs, would have been lower. In a broader sense, laws about contracts, and law itself, are means by which transaction costs are reduced. The invention of money and the development of various forms of money and financial instruments are responses to transaction costs associated with barter and more primitive means of exchange.

In addition to money, intermediaries such as wholesalers and advertisers developed over the ages to facilitate exchange. The creative marketing of goods and services from bazaars to discount stores to media advertising has increased consumer information and thus reduced the costs of making transactions. Intermediaries have lowered transaction costs by decreasing the risk of exchange. The production of some goods entails some risk and uncertainty on the part of buyers and sellers. Planting wheat in the spring for sale in the fall obviously entails some uncertainty about what prices will be at harvest. Intermediaries-speculators who deal in futures provide sellers and buyers assurance of prices in the future. This type of intermediaries makes profits on the miscalculations of buyers and sellers but reduces uncertainty and thereby increases trade and specialization.

Transportation costs

The value of resources used in the transportation of goods that finalize any trade.

Transportation Costs   Transportation costs, resource costs associated with the physical transport of products from place to place, are also an impediment to trade. The higher these resource costs are, the lower the benefits from specialization and trade.

We did not include transportation costs in our initial examples of comparative advantage with Canada and Mexico. Let's do so now. Suppose that transportation costs associated with the trade amounted to 10,000 board-feet of lumber to each country. Even after paying these transportation costs, Canada and Mexico still enjoy more lumber than they did before specializing and trading (see Table 2.4). However, if transportation costs were high enough, possible advantages to specialization and trade could be wiped out completely. Cheaper transportation costs permit more trade and open up opportunities for new forms of and increases in specialization. The invention of the railroad in the nineteenth century, the spread of the automobile and the truck, and the dawning of air freight transport in the twentieth century were all boons to specialization and increased output.

Artificial barriers to trade

Restrictions created by the government that inhibit or prevent trade; includes import quotas and tariffs.

Artificial Barriers to Trade   The final impediments to specialization and trade are government-imposed restrictions such as tariffs, quotas, and outright prohibi-

Tariff
A tax or levy on imported goods.

Quota
A restriction or limit on the quantity of an imported good.

tions on the import or export of goods. **Tariffs** are taxes or levies on imported goods. **Quotas** are quantity limitations on imports of products purchased from abroad. Such impositions, known as artificial barriers, either reduce or eliminate the benefits of specialization and trade.

Governments always have reasons for these restrictions, but the reasons must be closely scrutinized because the benefits from international and domestic specialization and trade are potentially huge for all consumers. Artificial barriers have the power to reduce economic welfare by reducing or eliminating the benefits of specialization according to the law of comparative advantage.

The possible effects of restrictions on trade can be seen in the growing volume of trade between Japan and the United States in commodities such as TVs, automobiles, stereo equipment, and musical instruments. Special-interest groups—such as American autoworkers and manufacturers—have lobbied for import tariffs and other trade restrictions to protect their own interests, which include increased demand for American-made products and therefore increased domestic production. Government-enforced tariffs make Japanese goods more expensive, however, causing a reduction in the general well-being of Americans. Artificial restrictions on trade, whatever their purpose, reduce the advantages of specialization and trade. As a matter of economic principle, therefore, most economists generally advocate free trade over any type of trade restriction. Further, any institution or mechanism that reduces the costs of exchange usually gets the support of economists because greater specialization permits better utilization of scarce resources. Specialization, in other words, helps us get more of what we want, given a limited amount of resources.

Tariffs, Trade, and Trade Zones   In both the modern and ancient worlds, trade and specialization take place when countries agree to special trade arrangements. Fine details of free trade zones differ, but the basic idea is that certain nations agree to have free trade with each other while continuing to have trade barriers—tariffs or quotas, for example, against other countries. Currently the best known, but by no means the only, free trade association affecting the United States is the North American Free Trade Association, or NAFTA. It is composed of the countries of Mexico, Canada, and the United States. NAFTA went into

Mexican workers assembling shoes at a plant in Guadalajara, Mexico.

effect on January 1, 1994, creating the largest free trade association in the world and affecting more than 360 million consumers. (See Focus: "Free Trade Associations, Past and Present" for details about these important international trade organizations.) We will have more to say about such associations in this book, but a simple example will help you understand how tariffs and trade agreements affect the quantity and directions of trade. Consider a simple example of computer trade between three countries, the United States, Mexico, and Taiwan.

Table 2.5 illustrates several points concerning real-world patterns of trade. It shows the potential effects of a free trade zone on Mexican consumers. Assume that Mexico, the United States, and Taiwan are all able to produce computers, and that computers are subject to a Mexican tariff rate of 40 percent. The Mexican pro-

FOCUS

Free Trade Associations, Past and Present

Economic unions, taking advantage of the principles of specialization and trade, have been common since ancient Greek and Roman times and even before. As such, the North American Free Trade Agreement is only one of the latest in a long list of arrangements for economic gain. All unions—for economic betterment and growth, for defense, or for any political purpose—presuppose that mutual gain can be had by enacting policies that are beneficial to all parties. However, the extent of the union may vary from full political and economic unification, where separate countries may in fact become one, to far less extensive agreements on tariffs and other trade restrictions.

The prototype for a popular form of modern union was the Zollverein or customs union of the last century. The name was given by the Prussians to a union established in 1833 to set uniform tariffs among separate German states (initially comprising Hesse Cassel, Hesse Darmstadt, Bavaria, and Wurtemberg) and the rest of the world. The agreement specified no tariffs or trade restrictions among these states. The Zollverein was the nineteenth-century model for many other unions.

These nineteenth-century agreements provided models for contemporary trade blocs in North America and Western Europe. The most famous economic union in the post–World War II period was the European Economic Community or Common Market, which formed the basis for the European Union (EU) of today. The EU is the most important present-day regional trading bloc, and there are fifteen member countries (Belgium, France, Luxembourg, Germany, Italy, the Netherlands, Denmark, Ireland, the United Kingdom, Greece, Spain, Portugal, Austria, Finland, and Sweden.) In 1999 the euro became the common currency of eleven European countries, with an initial value set at 1 euro = $1.16. It is used for all official and interbank transactions plus securities quotations and transactions. National currencies still exist for *private* transactions. On January 1, 2002, euro coins and bank notes will be introduced to replace all national coins and notes. The union will make trade within Europe as regulation-free among the countries of Europe as it is between the states of Massachusetts and New Hampshire. Eventually, all tariff and nontariff barriers will fall to zero and the EC will, after the NAFTA countries, become the largest and most populous trading area of the world.

Many unanswered questions accompany this new-world scenario of "competing Zollvereins." Not to be minimized is the potential for dissolution of any trade bloc from internal disagreements and dissension. For example, the debate over the net benefits of NAFTA within the United States did not end with its passage in January 1994. Financial problems in Mexico, U.S. loans to bolster Mexico's currency, and the (inevitable) adjustments in domestic employment in some fields have led to much dissension in the political arena.

TABLE 2.5

Example of Potential Effects of a Free Trade Zone on Mexican Computer Consumers

Producer of Computers	Domestic Price of Computers		
	MEXICO'S TARIFF RATES ON COMPUTERS		
	0%	**20%**	**40%**
Mexico	$2000	$2000	$2000
U.S. before NAFTA	$1800	$2160	$2520
U.S. after NAFTA	$1800	$1800	$1800
Taiwan	$1600	$1920	$2240

ducers can make a computer for $2000 and do not pay a tariff. U.S. producers can make a computer for $1800. With a 40 percent tariff, their price is $2520 in the Mexican market. Taiwanese producers can make a computer for $1600 and, under the same tariff rate, their price is $2240 in the Mexican market. Mexican firms emerge, as a result of the 40 percent tariff, as the low-cost producers in their domestic market and supply the entire market demand; thus, there is no international trade.

Now consider the trade-creating effects of the North American Free Trade Agreement (NAFTA). The fundamental premise behind NAFTA is the creation of a free trade zone (no tariffs) between Mexico, the U.S. and Canada only. In other words, the agreement establishes a system of preferential treatment for particular trading partners. If Mexican tariff rates on imported computers are 20 percent, the United States will emerge as the low-cost producers ($1800) following the implementation of the Agreement. This result emerges from tariff-free trade between the United States and Mexico while trade in computers between Mexico and Taiwan would still be subject to a 20 percent tariff and, thus, a higher price ($1920). In this example, NAFTA's creation of a free trade zone diverts trade from the low-cost producer, Taiwan, to a relatively higher-cost producer, the United States.

Notice that only when tariff rates are 0 percent between all three countries will an efficient pattern of production and trade result with the low-cost producer, Taiwan, supplying the Mexican (and the American) market. Trade diversion is not a problem for the member nations, but from a global perspective trade diversion results in inefficient production, because the more efficient producer loses sales to a less efficient producer. Thus a key feature in the debate over free trade zones is the debate over whether the free trade zone results more in trade creation or more in trade diversion. But economists are almost uniform in their support of free trade and would almost unanimously support a worldwide reduction in tariff and nontariff barriers to trade. For the United States, there are many benefits from the creation of free trade zones such as NAFTA. One is the reduction in the prices of imports to U.S. consumers because of reduced tariffs. Another benefit is the increased efficiency of production and the increased competition that comes from a larger market. Some estimate that after the ten- or fifteen-year phase-in period, NAFTA could yield additional trade of $1 to $2 trillion. But there will be winners and losers as free trade becomes a reality between the United States, Mexico, and Canada. Over the fifteen or so years of adjustments, in 2010, some U.S. business owners and employees of those businesses that cannot compete with Mexican and Canadian producers will lose. Some business owners will lose their investments, and some workers will lose their jobs. Some textile firms, for example, will lose their production facilities to Mexico since labor is cheaper there.

Economists argue that the *net effects* of tariff reduction through free trade associations and other means is positive. But even if economists condemn tariffs and quotas, they also recognize how individuals in their public choices may be able to convince government to pass a tariff. Think of it. The benefits of the tariff to a domestic industry may be highly concentrated on the workers and owners in the industry. New trade agreements that lower tariffs and quotas ordinarily create jobs and destroy other jobs. The costs of the tariff in terms of higher prices and costs are spread across the general public so that they may not even notice the effects. Government decision makers respond to this concentrated benefit–diffused cost condition by "supplying" a tariff to the industry. We will have a great deal more to say about this process later in this book. The point is that government can and often does override comparative advantage in order to respond to political pressures for protection.

Real-World Patterns of Trade   The previous sections suggest that trade occurs between two countries when the countries have differences in opportunity costs of producing various goods (i.e., when comparative advantages exist), when transaction costs and transportation costs are small, and when the countries promote free trade. Real-world evidence reported in Table 2.6 and Figure 2.6 supports these arguments. For example, Canada is the leading trade partner of the United States. Transportation costs between the two countries are very low, and the two countries have one of the freest trade relationships in the world. In contrast, the United States trades substantially less with the United Kingdom and other European

---

TABLE 2.6

Leading Trading Partners of the United States
In terms of exports, Canada is the biggest customer of the United States. In terms of imports, Canada is also the biggest supplier of the United States.

Country	Value of U.S. Imports (billions)	Value of U.S. Exports (billions)
All countries, total	$870.6	$689.2
Canada	168.2	151.8
Japan	121.7	65.6
Germany	39.0	24.5
United Kingdom	32.7	36.4
Mexico	86.0	71.4
France	20.6	16.0
South Korea	23.2	25.1
Hong Kong	10.3	15.1
Singapore	20.1	17.7

Source: U.S. Bureau of the Census, *Statistical Abstract of the United States,* 1998 (Washington, D.C.: U.S. Government Printing Office), pp. 801–804.

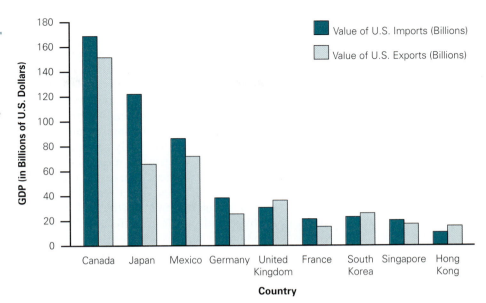

FIGURE 2.6

Leading Trading Partners of the United States

In terms of both import and export values, the greatest amount of trade takes place between Canada, Mexico, and Japan. These high values are best explained by comparative advantage.

nations because their trade policies are more restrictive and transportation costs are much greater than those for trade with Canada.

Other factors explain the relative importance of foreign trade in the economies of different nations. Foreign trade is relatively more important to the Hong Kong and Singapore economies than to the German or Canadian economies, although it is quantitatively less important in trade with the United States. Geography and transport costs are part of the explanation, but the resource endowments (or lack thereof) is another principal explanation for larger volumes of trade. Further, nations pursuing less restrictive trade policies may, other things being equal, be expected to engage in more foreign trade.

The tremendous volume of trade between the United States and other nations is best explained by strong comparative advantages. Because the types of productive resources found in the countries differ greatly, certain goods that have high opportunity costs elsewhere have low costs in the United States, and vice versa. A huge trade volume, therefore, exists between nations of the world despite transportation costs and the fact that many nations pursue policies to restrict trade. The gains to specialization and trade are enormous, no less between nations as between individuals and all other trading units.

APPLICATION

AIDS and Reduced Production Possibilities in Africa

Almost everyone is familiar with the devastating toll the AIDS (autoimmune deficiency syndrome) epidemic has taken on individuals, families, and communities. In light of the huge number of personal tragedies resulting from the disease, it is unsurprising that the societal impact of AIDS has received relatively little attention. However, it is important not to overlook the extent to which the AIDS crisis could wreak havoc with the economies of certain developing nations, particularly those in sub-Saharan Africa.

More than a decade ago (in 1987) the World Health Organization estimated that about two and a half million adults in Africa were infected with human immunodeficiency virus (HIV), the pathogen that causes AIDS. By 1990 that figure had tripled for many countries. Now, as the millennium is crossed, the infection rate in most central African nations exceeds 10 percent, and several have rates well above 15 percent. (By contrast, less than 1 percent of American adults are thought to be infected.) Unlike many other diseases, which primarily affect the very young or the old, AIDS has its greatest impact on people between the ages of twenty and forty. In economies dominated by agriculture and light industry, these are the most economically productive years of a person's life. Another characteristic of AIDS in African nations is that incidence rates are approximately the same for men and women. As a result, many children are losing both parents to AIDS at a very early age and there is a high incidence of mother-to-child (intrauterine) transmissions. Further, although many new drugs (protease inhibitors) have had significant effects in slowing or, in some cases, preventing the development of the virus in developed countries, such medicines are costly and less available in developing countries. The result is that because AIDS affects all socioeconomic groups, the ranks of the political and entrepreneurial leaders of many African nations are being thinned.

In the late 1980s, experts believed that AIDS would reduce population growth rates throughout Africa by as much as 3.5 percent per year. They further predicted that certain African nations could find particular populations devastated. These dire and economically significant predictions have been borne out. The 1998 Revision of the World Population Estimates and Projects of the United Nations reveal a devastating mortality toll. One in four adults are infected with HIV in Botswana. Life expectancy at birth in Botswana is anticipated to fall from 61 years in 1990–1995 to 41 years by 2000–2005. Based on these projections, Botswana's population may be 23 percent smaller in 2025 than it would have been without the AIDS epidemic. The pre-AIDS life expectancy in Zimbabwe of 65 years sank to

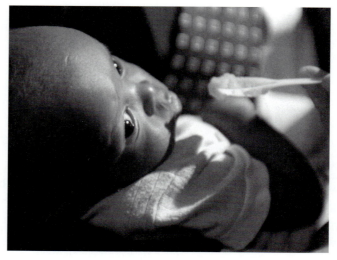

The human tragedies of the AIDS virus in Africa are accompanied by a reduction in production possibilities.

FIGURE 2.7

Production Possibilities and AIDS in Africa

A loss in labor resources caused by AIDS shifts the production possibilities curve toward the origin. A higher percentage of resources must be devoted to consumption goods after the crisis.

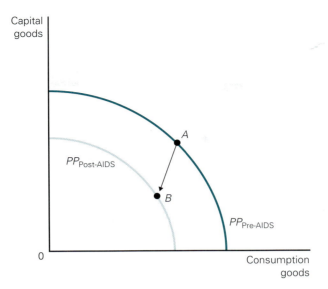

39 in the post-AIDS period. Such reductions are similar in countries such as Malawi, Kenya, Uganda and the Ivory Coast.

Figure 2.7 shows what happens to a nation's production possibilities curve when a large percentage of the nation's working population is decimated. Note that these plunging life expectancies do not eliminate the trade-off between consumption goods and capital goods. Because labor has been cheap and plentiful relative to other resources in central African nations, agricultural methods have been oriented to the large, untrained labor supply. A scarcity of labor caused by the AIDS epidemic in a particular country would mean that that country would have to devote a larger proportion of its resources to consumption goods in order to survive (point *B* in Figure 2.7). In other words, labor-saving technology would be employed to economize on scarce labor inputs.

The development of an AIDS vaccine, the deployment of life-extending drugs, or the implementation of more effective AIDS education would prevent a reduction in the output potential of the developing countries of central Africa. Still, the AIDS crisis provides convincing evidence that disease can create reduced production possibilities even in modern societies.

QUESTION

How do you think the following catastrophic events would affect the production possibilities curve? A hurricane that kills hundreds of thousands in a small developing country? A war that devastates both population and machinery and buildings? A drug that eradicates all infectious diseases?

Sources: Information for this discussion was drawn from Ken Sidey, "AIDS Reshapes African's Future," *Christianity Today* 34 (October 22, 1990), p. 47; Gary W. Shannon, Gerald F. Pyle, and Rashid L. Bashshur, *The Geography of AIDS: Origins and Course of the Epidemic* (New York: The Guilford Press, 1991); and the United Nations, *Revisions of the World Population Estimates and Projections*, Department of Economic and Social Affairs, Population Division, 1998.

SUMMARY

1. Economic choices, both for the individual and for society, always involve an opportunity cost.

2. Opportunity cost is the highest-valued alternative forgone in the decision to engage in a particular activity.

3. The law of increasing costs means that as more of one good is produced by a society, the opportunity costs of obtaining additional units of that commodity rise. The increase in cost is the result of resources becoming less adaptable as production becomes more specialized.

4. Specialization—the division of tasks to produce goods and services—takes place in all known societies. The principles of specialization are thus related to the decisions all societies and economic organizations face in trying to overcome the basic problem of scarcity.

5. The production possibilities curve shows the possible quantities of two goods that could be produced given the state of technology and society's scarce resources.

6. Changes in technology or increases (or decreases) in the amount of resources cause rightward (or leftward) movements in the production possibilities frontier.

7. Greater quantities of output can be obtained with society's scarce resources when people specialize and trade. Trade takes place according to the principle of comparative advantage.

8. Trade can take place between two individuals or economic entities even if one of the entities is more efficient at producing all goods. All that is required is that each entity be relatively more efficient than the other in some production.

9. Transaction costs, transportation costs, and artificial trade barriers such as tariffs and quotas reduce the benefits obtainable from specialization and trade.

KEY TERMS

opportunity cost
specialization
division of labor
production possibilities frontier
law of increasing costs
unemployment of resources
choices at the margin

capital stock
economic growth
marginal opportunity production
   cost
comparative advantage
terms of trade
exchange costs

transaction costs
transportation costs
artificial barriers to trade
tariff
quota

QUESTIONS FOR REVIEW AND DISCUSSION

1. What did reading this chapter cost you? Did you include the price of the book? What will reading the next chapter cost? Does that include the price of the book?

2. Do government-sponsored financial aid programs for college students influence the amount of education produced? Do these programs shift the production possibilities curve?

3. What does a movement along the production possibilities frontier suggest? What does a point inside the curve suggest?

4. A subsidy to farmers who purchase combines and tractors increases the production of this farm machinery. Does this cause an increase in the production possibilities curve or just a movement along the curve? Can subsidies cause economic growth?

5. Why would a country with an absolute advantage in the production of all goods be willing to trade with other countries?

6. Alpha can produce 60 bottles of wine or 40 pounds of cheese. Beta can produce 90 bottles of wine or 30 pounds of cheese. Both have constant

costs of production. Draw their production possibilities curves. What is Alpha's cost of 1 bottle of wine? What is Beta's cost of 1 pound of cheese? If they trade, who should specialize in cheese?

7. What are the costs of going to college? Does the marginal benefit outweigh the marginal cost?

8. Is the lost present consumption associated with the production of capital goods worth the benefit of the new capital?

9. Does Japan have an absolute advantage over the United States in the production of televisions and stereo equipment, or is it just a comparative advantage?

10. Who is hurt by and who benefits from an import quota on foreign beef?

11. How does the cost of purchasing a loaf of bread at a supermarket compare with the cost of purchasing a loaf of bread at a convenience store?

12. What is the law of increasing costs, and why does it hold?

13. When the gains from specialization and trade are assessed, exchange costs must be considered. What are these costs?

14. If the United States opened its border with Mexico and lowered all tariffs and quotas, what would happen to the production possibilities frontier of the United States?

PROBLEMS

1. Countries A and B both produce golf balls and golf clubs. The table shows what each country can produce at full employment.

	A		B
Golf Balls	Golf Clubs	Golf Balls	Golf Clubs
1200	0	900	0
1000	50	750	25
800	100	600	50
600	150	450	75
400	200	300	100
200	250	150	125
0	300	0	150

a. Graph the production possibilities curve of each country.
b. Do both production functions exhibit constant costs?
c. Who has the absolute advantage in both golf ball and golf club production?
d. Who has the comparative advantage in the production of golf balls?
e. Who has the comparative advantage in the production of golf clubs?

2. Consider the following data concerning the production possibilities of the countries Alpha and Beta.

ALPHA		BETA	
x	y	x	y
0	20	0	60
20	15	10	45
40	10	20	30
60	5	30	15
80	0	40	0

a. Which commodity, X or Y, does Alpha have a comparative advantage in producing?
b. Where does Beta's comparative advantage lie?
c. Show the results in a graph.

3. Consider the following production possibilities for the United States and France for two commodities, steel and concrete:

	United States	France
Steel	100 tons	25 tons
Concrete	200 tons	100 tons

a. Which country has the comparative advantage in the production of concrete? Carefully explain why you believe your answer to be correct.
b. What would be the "loss" if both countries became self-sufficient and did not exchange?

WORKING WITH THE WEB

1. The theories of specialization and division of labor are at work in many careers. Go to the web site http://sports.yahoo.com/mlb/players/ and scroll through the players whose last name begins with A–D. How do the concepts of specialization and division of labor apply to the lives of these major league baseball players?

2. Consider trade that exists between the United States and Canada as well as the United States and China, where both Canada and China produce and export household furniture (wood and upholstered) as well as cutlery to the United States.

   First, go to http://www.ita.doc.gov/ocg/imp2511.htm and look at the statistics for both countries (Canada and China) in 1998 regarding the level of household furniture imported by the United States (measured in dollars). Next, go to http://www.ita.doc.gov/ocg/imp3421.htm and do the same comparison for each country in 1998 for U.S. imports of cutlery. If Canada and China were to decide to only manufacture one of these two types of products (and assuming each faces similar marginal opportunity production costs), which country has a comparative advantage in the production of household furniture and which country should produce cutlery? Why?

C H A P T E R

3

Private Markets and Prices: Laws of Demand and Supply

S imple specialization began to take place in primitive cultures as individuals recognized unique abilities in themselves and in others. As we have seen, increasing specialization led to organized markets where people bought and sold goods, to the use of money, and to increasingly large groups of buyers and sellers. Economists define these organized markets—such as bazaars, the stock exchange, or Saks Fifth Avenue—as places or circumstances that bring together demanders (buyers) and suppliers (sellers) of any goods or services. After reading Chapter 3 you should understand

- the motivations of demanders and suppliers in the exchange of goods and services in markets.
- how and why some goods and services get produced and sold at certain prices while other items are not produced or sold at all.
- what happens to demand and supply when governments or other agencies institute price or rent controls.
- that the full price we pay for goods and services includes the money price and such things as time and the other costs involved in a transaction.

AN OVERVIEW OF THE PRICE SYSTEM

In the familiar economic transactions of everyday life, we enter markets where buyers and sellers congregate to buy and sell a great variety of products and services. The typical American supermarket sells thousands of products, and as we wander through the store we can view a price system in action. In the produce section, for instance, quantities and prices of fruits and vegetables depend on the quantities consumers want and on the season. Early crops usually bring in the highest prices. Watermelon may sell for more than $2 per pound in March but only $0.15 per pound by the Fourth of July.

What determines who will get the early melons or how they will be rationed among those who want them? Why are prices and quantities constantly rising and falling for millions of goods and services in our economy? How do new products find their way to places where buyers and sellers congregate? The answers are simple. In a market society, the self-interest of consumers and producers, of households and businesses, determines who gets what and how much. To paraphrase Adam Smith, it is not to the benevolence of the butcher and the baker that we owe our dinner but to their self-interest. The primary way that consumers and producers express their self-interest is through the economic laws of supply and demand. Sticking a price tag on a product does not imply price-setting power, as anyone who has run a garage sale knows. In a market system, demand and supply determine prices, and prices are the essential pieces of information on which consumers, households, businesses, and resource suppliers make decisions. High melon prices in March will encourage suppliers and discourage demanders, whereas low prices in July will encourage demanders and discourage suppliers. Before investigating the mechanics of these laws of supply and demand, we consider a simple overview of the price system.

As market participants, households and businesses play dual roles. Businesses supply final output of products and services—rock concerts, bananas, hair stylings—but also must hire or demand resources to produce the outputs. Households demand rock concerts, bananas, and hair stylings for final consumption. But they also supply labor and entrepreneurial ability, as well as quantities of land and capital to earn income for the purchase of products and services.

The Circular Flow of Products and Resources

Products market
The forces created by buyers and sellers that establish the prices and quantities exchanged of goods and services.

As Figure 3.1 shows, businesses and households are interconnected by the **products** (outputs) **market** and by the **resources** (inputs) **market**. Each market depends on the other; they are linked by the prices of outputs and inputs. The particular mix of goods and services exchanged in the products market depends on consumer demands in that market plus the cost and availability of necessary resources. Similarly, the particular mix of resources available at any one time or through time is determined by what households are demanding—subject also to the availability of the resources. If land suitable for banana growing is available, it is most likely to be sold for banana plantations if households are demanding a lot of bananas, thereby making it possible for banana growers to pay landowners for their land.

Resources market
The forces created by buyers and sellers that establish the prices and quantities exchanged of resources such as land, labor services, and capital.

Prices are the impulses of information that make the entire system of input and output markets operate. The prices formed in both product and resource markets reflect the relative desires of consumer-demanders for particular goods and services as well as the relative scarcity of the resources required to produce them. The very fact that a product or service bears a price means that scarcity exists. Supply and demand in all markets is at the core of scarcity and, therefore, of economics.

Money price
The dollar price that sellers receive from buyers; a price expressed in terms of money, not in terms of an amount of another good.

Full Versus Money Prices

A distinction must be made about prices resulting from the forces of supply and demand: There is a difference between the **money price** of a product or service

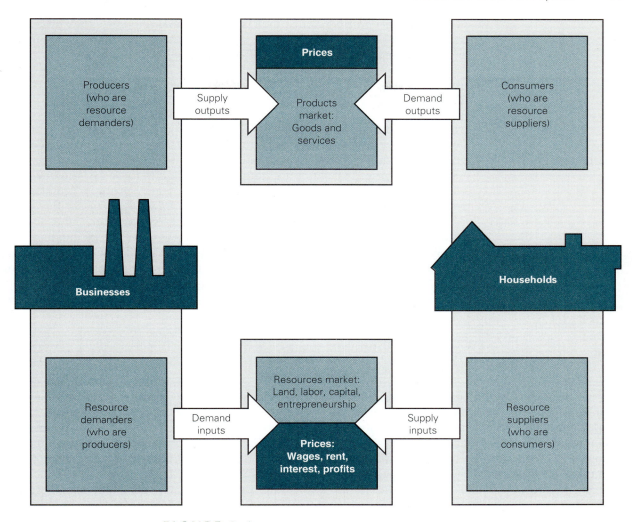

FIGURE 3.1

The Product and Resource Markets: A Circular Flow

Businesses play a dual role in the market economy: They are the suppliers of goods and services as well as the demanders of resources. Households also have a dual role. They are both demanders of goods and services and suppliers of resources.

Full price

The total opportunity cost to an individual of obtaining a good; includes money price and all other costs, such as transportation costs or waiting costs.

and the **full price**. Consider the money price of a haircut for which the customer pays $12.50 in cash. Is this the full price of a haircut?

Money price is often not the only cost to consumers. In the case of a haircut, we must account for the time spent traveling to and from the salon, the time spent waiting, and the time spent with the hairdresser. Time is a scarce resource, and it bears an opportunity cost. Time costs are often estimated in terms of the wage rate forgone, the leisure time forgone, or, generally, as the opportunity cost of the consumer's next-best alternative. Thus the full price of a haircut or any other good or service includes the price in money terms plus any other resource costs required in the purchase of the commodity. (See the Focus "Full Price and a New Orleans Restaurant.") Prices as interpreted in the simple model of demand and supply of this chapter are to be regarded as full prices.

THE LAW OF DEMAND

Relative price

The price ratio or "trade-off" in consumption between one product (or service) and another product (or service) or between one good and other goods taken as a whole.

The concept of demand is intuitive. The notion that the amount of goods sold depends on the prices charged seems to "just make sense." The amount of any one good bought during a sale, for example, depends on the **relative price** of the good on sale—the price in relation to the price of some other good or of goods as a whole. The actual money price of the good in isolation does not determine what we purchase. If the relative price of a particular pair of shoes declines—that is, the item is put "on sale"—the price has fallen relative to other shoes, shirts, or camcorders. Intuitively, we understand that more of these shoes will be purchased.

What determines how much of any good or service—camcorders, compact discs, or hair styling—consumers will purchase during some period of time? Econ-

FOCUS

Full Price and a New Orleans Restaurant

New Orleans is considered a restaurant town by gourmets. Restaurants such as Le Ruth's, Antoine's, Brennan's, and Commander's Palace consistently offer some of the best cuisine to be found anywhere. One of our favorite French Quarter restaurants, however, is Galatoire's. Galatoire's has earned a reputation for producing some of the highest-quality meals in the city. Menu prices, however, have remained low relative to other famous establishments over the past several decades.

Have both menu prices and full prices remained low at Galatoire's? If not, why not? Finally, what evidence might be offered for a real price increase? How would an economist view the matter?

The economist would focus on elements in the full price of a meal at Galatoire's. The restaurant has not enlarged its classic physical plant over the years but, over time, longer and longer lines form outside the door during the day and evening. Galatoire's, unlike most of its competition, does not take reservations and has only recently begun accepting credit cards. Moreover, Galatoire's enforces a dress code—ties or coats for men (evenings and all day on Sundays) and, until a few years ago, dresses (no pants) for women.

All these factors would tend to increase the full price of dining at Galatoire's. There are opportu-

nity costs to waiting for a table (time is a scarce resource); the time and resources spent dressing for dinner are also applicable to the full price. The length of the line at the restaurant can also make the real price higher or lower than anticipated, although diners can form hunches about when the line is apt to be shortest.

These additional costs mean that the full price exceeds the money price printed on the menu. However, the economist must calculate all benefits as well as all costs associated with purchasing products or services. Consider the possibility that some customers get positive benefits from dressing for dinner and from being surrounded by those similarly attired. Others may value the prestige or satisfaction of dining at the legendary restaurant. Such factors would tend to increase the benefits to these consumers. The full price paid for a meal at Galatoire's varies among consumers, depending on opportunity cost. However, all consumers marginally balance the perceived costs of buying products and services with the perceived benefits associated with consumption. When price or price formation is discussed in this book, it is therefore the full price, not the nominal or money price, that is being considered.

Law of demand

The price of a product or service and the amount purchased are inversely related. If price rises, then quantity demanded falls; if price falls, quantity demanded increases, all other things held constant.

Quantity demanded

The amount of any good or service consumers are willing and able to purchase at all various prices.

Demand curve

A graphical representation of the quantities of a product that people are willing and able to purchase at all possible prices.

omists have answered that question for hundreds of years in the same manner—by formulating a general rule, or law, of demand. The **law of demand** states that, other things being equal or constant, the quantity demanded of any good or service increases as the price of the good or service declines. In other words, **quantity demanded** is inversely related to the price of the good or service in question.

The relation between price and quantity demanded is a fact of everyday experience. The reaction of individuals and groups to two-for-the-price-of-one sales, cut-rate airline tickets, and other bargains is common proof that quantities demanded increase as prices decrease. Likewise, gas price hikes will lower the quantity of gasoline demanded. The formalization of the inverse relation between price and quantity demanded is called a law because economists believe it is a general rule for all consumers in all markets. Imagine a graphical representation of the law of demand—called a **demand curve**—for two consumers.

The Individual's Demand Schedule and Demand Curve

Suppose that we observe the behavior of Dave and Marcia over one month. These two music lovers own compact disc players and are willing and able to purchase, or demand, CDs. To determine Dave's and Marcia's demand for CDs, we need only vary the price of discs over the month, assuming that all other factors affecting their decisions remain constant, and observe the quantities of CDs they would demand at the various prices. This information is summarized in Table 3.1.

Table 3.1 shows a range of CD prices available to Marcia and Dave over the one-month period and the quantities (numbers) of discs that each would purchase, all other things being equal. Given factors such as their income and the availability of other forms of entertainment, neither person would choose to purchase even a

TABLE 3.1

Two Consumers' Demand Schedules

While individuals' demand schedules may differ, they do not violate the law of demand. For both people, the quantity demanded increases as the price falls.

Price of Compact Discs (dollars)	QUANTITY DEMANDED (PER MONTH)	
	Dave	Marcia
20	0	0
19	1	0
18	2	0
17	3	1
16	4	2
15	5	3
14	6	4
13	7	5
12	8	6
11	9	7
10	10	8

Fast-food restaurants reduce the full cost of meals by saving time for college students.

single CD at $20 per disc. Dave, however, would buy one CD per month at $19 and two at $18. Marcia would not buy her first CD until the price was $17. Each would purchase more discs as the price falls. Thus, Dave's and Marcia's CD-buying habits conform to the law of demand.

We obtain the individuals' demand curves by plotting or transferring the information from Table 3.1 to the graphs in Figure 3.2. The prices of CDs are given on the vertical axis of each graph, and the quantities of CDs demanded per month are given on the horizontal axis. The various combinations of price and quantity from Table 3.1 are plotted on the graphs. Each demand curve is then drawn as the line connecting those combinations of price and quantity. For both Dave and Marcia, the demand curve slopes downward and to the right (a negative slope), indicating an increase in quantity demanded as the price declines and a decrease in quantity demanded as the price rises.

Factors Affecting the Individual's Demand Curve

In addition to the price of a good or service, there are dozens, perhaps hundreds, of other factors and circumstances affecting a person's decision to buy or not to buy. These **factors affecting demand** include income, the price of related goods, price expectations, income expectations, tastes, the number of consumers, and time.

Factors affecting demand

Anything other than price, such as consumer income and preferences, that determines the amount of a product or service that consumers are willing and able to purchase.

Holding Factors Other Than Price Constant To isolate the effect of price on quantity demanded, essential factors must be held constant. We want to know what quantity of CDs Dave and Marcia would choose to purchase in a month at various possible prices, given that other factors affecting their decision do not change. This condition is called *ceteris paribus* ("other things being equal") by economists. It is essential to the development of any economic theory or model dealing with real-world events since all events cannot be controlled. Economists hold factors such as income and the price of related goods constant when constructing a demand schedule or curve. This does not mean that these factors cannot change, but if they do change, the demand schedule or curve must be adjusted to account for them.

Ceteris paribus

The Latin phrase for "all other things held constant."

Changes in Demand Versus Changes in Quantity Demanded A simple but crucial distinction exists between a change in Dave's or Marcia's demand for CDs and a **change in quantity demanded** of CDs for Dave or Marcia. Other things being equal, a change in the price of CDs will change the quantity demanded of CDs, as we have seen. Figures 3.3 and 3.4 illustrate an increase and a decrease in quantity demanded, respectively. The graphs illustrate a movement along a single demand curve, indicating that factors like buyers' incomes and preferences are held constant. Figure 3.3 shows that a decrease in the price of discs leads to an increase in the quantity demanded. Figure 3.4 shows that an increase in the price of discs reduces the

Change in quantity demanded

A change in the amount of a good a consumer is willing and able to purchase that is caused by a change in the price of the good or service.

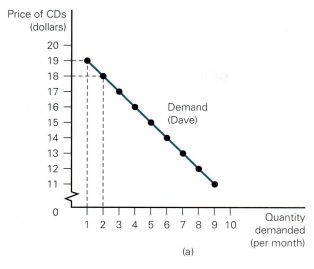

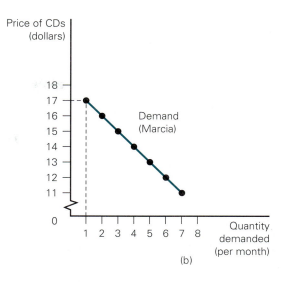

(a)   (b)

FIGURE 3.2

Demand Curves for Two Consumers

A consumer's demand for a product is the quantity that he or she is willing to purchase at each price. The demand curve is downward sloping for both Dave (a) and Marcia (b). As the price falls, the quantity demanded increases; and as the price rises, the quantity demanded decreases.

Change in demand

A shift of the entire demand curve to the right or left

quantity demanded. A change in any factor other than the price will shift the entire demand curve to the right or left. Economists call this a **change in demand**. An increase in demand is shown as the rightward shift of the entire demand curve in Figure 3.5. A decrease in demand, shown in Figure 3.6, is a leftward shift of the entire demand curve.

Change in Income   Marcia's or Dave's income may change, and such a change would necessitate a redrawing of the entire demand curve for CDs. For most goods,

FIGURE 3.3

Increase in Quantity Demanded

Holding Marcia's demand constant, a decrease in the price of CDs from $14 to $13 will lead to an increase in the quantity of CDs demanded from 4 to 5 per month.

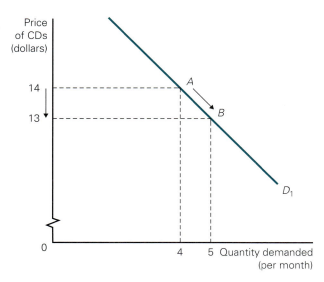

a rise in income means an increase in demand. For instance, if Marcia's income increases from $1500 to $2000 a month, she will demand more CDs at every price because she can afford more. Figure 3.5 shows that, given a new, higher income, Marcia's demand curve shifts to the right for every price of CDs. When demand increases, quantity demanded increases at every price.

Although the theory that rising income means greater demand for goods holds true for most goods, it does not apply to all goods. Economists distinguish between normal goods and inferior goods. **Normal goods** are those products and services for which demand increases (decreases) with increases (decreases) in income; the demand for **inferior goods** actually decreases (increases) with increases (decreases) in consumers' income. Joe's demand for Honda automobiles may decrease as his income increases; a Honda automobile is an inferior good to him. Beth purchases

Normal good

A good that a consumer chooses to purchase in smaller (larger) amounts as income falls (rises).

Inferior good

A good that a consumer chooses to purchase in smaller quantities as income rises or in larger amounts as income falls.

FIGURE 3.4

Decrease in Quantity Demanded

Holding Marcia's demand constant, an increase in the price of the CDs from $14 to $16 will cause Marcia to decrease the quantity of CDs demanded from 4 to 2 per month.

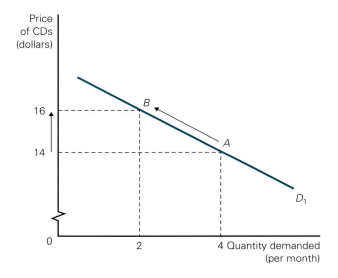

FIGURE 3.5

Increase in Demand

A change in any factors affecting demand causes a shift to the right or left in the demand curve. In this case, Marcia's income increases, causing an increase in her quantities demanded for CDs at every price. The demand curve shifts to the right. At a price of $14 per disc, Marcia previously would purchase 4 CDs, but given her increased income, she would now purchase 8 CDs.

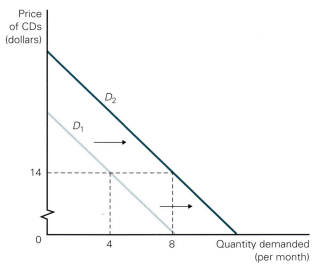

less Haagen-Dazs vanilla ice cream as her income falls, indicating that Haagen-Dazs ice cream is a normal good for her.

The terms *normal* and *inferior* contain no implications about intrinsic quality or about absolute standards of goodness or badness. Indeed, a good or service that is normal for one consumer in a given income range may be inferior for another consumer in the same income range. It is even possible for a good to be normal for an individual consumer at certain levels of income and inferior at other levels. As one's income rises, for example, hamburgers or compact cars may change from normal to inferior. We will discuss this distinction in more detail later, but it is important for now to note that a change in income will produce a shift in the demand curve.

Prices of Related Goods   Suppose that the price of a good closely related to CDs—such as cassette tapes or CD players—changes during the month for which Dave's and Marcia's demand curves are drawn. What happens? Clearly, one of the assumptions about other things being equal has changed, and the demand curve will shift right or left depending on the direction of the price change and on whether the closely related good is a **substitute** for or a **complement** to the product under consideration.

Suppose that other forms of entertainment can substitute for CDs in Dave's or Marcia's budgets. If ticket prices for movies or tape prices decline during the month, the demand curve for CDs for both consumers would shift to the left; that is, the demand for CDs would decline. For every price of CDs, the quantity demanded would be lower. This shift is represented in Figure 3.6. If the price of a substitute good increased during the month, the demand for CDs would increase.

If the price of a good or service complementary to CDs rises or falls, the demand curve for CDs would shift. Such a complementary good or service might be compact disc players for home or auto. If the price of the complement increases, the demand for CDs would decrease (shift left). If the price of the complement decreases, demand for CDs would increase (shift right).

Other Factors Shifting the Demand Curve   A number of factors other than income and the price of related goods can cause a shift in the demand curve. Among

Substitutes

Products that are related such that an increase in the price of one will increase the demand for the other or a decrease in the price of one will decrease the demand for the other.

Complements

Products that are related such that an increase in the price of one will decrease the demand for the other or a decrease in the price of one will increase the demand for the other.

FIGURE 3.6

Decrease in Demand

A leftward shift of the demand curve indicates a decrease in demand. In this case, the price of a substitute good decreased, causing Dave to demand fewer discs at every price. The demand curve shifts to the left. Before the price change in the substitute good, Dave would purchase 5 CDs at $15 each, but given the change in the substitute good's price, he would purchase only 2 CDs at $15 each.

these are consumers' price and income expectations and consumers' tastes. If the price of CDs or the income of consumers is expected to change in the near future, the demand for CDs during the month will be altered. Marcia may discover during the month that she will receive an inheritance. The basis under which her original demand curve was derived changes because she anticipates a change in income. Or back-to-school CD sales might be announced for August during the middle of July, causing a decrease in demand during July. Likewise, any alteration in the time period under examination—changing from a month to a day, week, or year—will alter the construction of the demand curve. A purchase of four pizzas per month at a price of $6.95 each would be represented differently than a weekly consumption of one pizza. A change in the time period requires a redrawing of the demand curve. Also held constant is the quality of the good or service. Changing the amount of ice in a 10-ounce soft drink, for example, will alter the quality of the drink. The change in quality will alter quantity demanded at any price.

Reviewing the Law of Demand

The demand curve expresses an inverse relation between the price of a good and the quantity of the good demanded, assuming that a number of factors affecting demand are held constant. As price rises, quantity demanded falls; as price falls, quantity demanded rises. When any of the other factors affecting demand change, we must reevaluate the demand schedule and curve.

Economists predict that individuals (and collections of individuals), all things being equal, will purchase more of any commodity or service as its price falls. To verify this prediction, the individuals in question do not even have to be fully aware of their behavior; they need only act in the predicted manner. Individuals' response to sales of any kind—they buy more when price declines—is evidence that a general and predictable law of demand exists. That law is a fundamental tool of economists' analyses of real-world events.

From Individual to Market Demand

Market demand

The total amount consumers are willing and able to purchase of a product at all possible prices, obtained by summing the quantities demanded at each price over all buyers.

While an individual's demand curve is sometimes of interest, economists most often focus on the **market demand** for some product, service, or input such as automobiles, intercontinental transport, or farm labor. Market demand schedules are simply the summation of all individual demand schedules at alternative prices for any good or service. An increase in the number of consumers increases the market demand curve, and a reduction decreases market demand. The key is to add up the quantities demanded by all consumers at alternative prices for the good or service in question.

We can use the CD demand example to understand market demand. We constructed individual demand schedules for Dave and Marcia by varying the price and observing the quantities of discs that they would buy at those prices, other things being equal. To determine the market demand schedule, we simply observe the behavior of all other consumers in the same market situation.

Table 3.2 begins with the data on Dave's and Marcia's demand from Table 3.1. The table also contains a summary of quantity demanded for all other consumers at every price and, finally, the total quantity demanded for all consumers, or the total market demand. At a price of $20 no one, including Dave and Marcia, wants to buy CDs. At a slightly lower price, $19 per disc, Marcia does not choose to buy, but Dave and 39 other consumers buy 1 disc. The total market demand is, therefore, 40 discs at a price of $19. (Note that actual numbers of discs sold to all con-

TABLE 3.2

Market Demand Schedule
The total market demand for a product is found by summing the quantities demanded by all consumers at every price.

	QUANTITY DEMANDED (PER MONTH)			
Price of CDs (dollars)	Dave	Marcia	All Other Consumers	Total Market Quantity Demanded
20	0	0	0	0
19	1	0	39	40
18	2	0	78	80
17	3	1	116	120
16	4	2	154	160
15	5	3	192	200
14	6	4	230	240
13	7	5	268	280
12	8	6	306	320
11	9	7	344	360
10	10	8	382	400

sumers would be much higher. We use low numbers for simplicity. The important point is that the market demand schedule for CDs or any other privately produced product or service is constructed in precisely this manner.)

The market demand schedules can be represented graphically as market demand curves (see Figure 3.7). Dave's and Marcia's demand curves are repeated from Figure 3.2. The demand of all other consumers, taken from Table 3.2, is plotted in Figure 3.7c. The total market demand, shown in Figure 3.7d, is simply the horizontal addition of the demand curves of Figures 3.7a, 3.7b, and 3.7c.

As in the case of individual demand curves, the market demand curve is downward sloping (negatively sloped) and drawn under the assumption that all factors other than the price of CDs remain constant. If the incomes of consumers change, or the price of goods or services closely related to CDs is altered, the market demand would shift right or left, as in the case of individuals' demand curves. Economists must focus closely on these related factors in any real-world application. Changes in the demand for any product—compact cars, energy, crude oil—will be closely related to factors such as income changes and the price of substitutes and complements.

The important concept of market demand summarizes only half of the factors determining and affecting prices. Like the cutting blades of a pair of scissors, two sets of factors—demand and supply—simultaneously determine price.

Law of supply
The price of a product or service and the amount that producers are willing and able to offer for sale are positively related. If price rises, then quantity supplied rises; if price decreases, then quantity supplied decreases.

THE LAW OF SUPPLY AND FIRM SUPPLY

The **law of supply** states that, other things being equal, firms and industries will produce and offer to sell greater quantities of a product or service as the price of that product or service rises. There is a direct relationship between price and

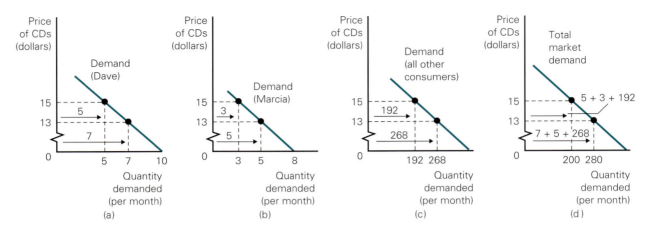

FIGURE 3.7

Market Demand Curve

The total market demand curve for a product is obtained by summing the points on all the individual demand curves horizontally. This is accomplished by selecting prices and summing the quantities demanded by all individuals to obtain the total quantity demanded at each price.

Quantity supplied

The amount of any good or service that producers are willing and able to produce and sell at some specific price.

Supply curve

A graphical representation of the quantities of a product or service that producers are willing and able to sell at all possible prices.

quantity supplied: As price rises, **quantity supplied** increases; as price falls, quantity supplied decreases. The assumption of other things being equal is invoked, as in the case of demand, so that the important relation between price and quantity supplied may be specified exactly. This relation, called a **supply curve**, shows the quantities of any good that firms would be willing and able to supply at alternative prices over a specified time period.

The method for constructing an individual firm's (and the market's) supply schedule is identical to the method we used for individual and market demand. All factors affecting supply except the price of the good or service are held constant. The price of the good or service is varied and the quantities that the firm or the industry will supply are specified.

To see how the supply curve is drawn, we turn to the supply side of CDs. Suppose that there are a number of firms supplying CDs in a given geographic area and that the output per month of two typical firms (Oranges Inc. and Joe's Audio) and all other firms combined is as shown in Table 3.3. The supply schedules of Oranges Inc. and Joe's Audio are given in the table by the combination of price and quantity supplied. That is, given alternative prices of CDs and the assumption that all other things are equal, Oranges Inc. and Joe's Audio specify the quantity of CDs that they would be willing to supply during a one-month period. At a price of $20 per disc, Oranges Inc. would be willing and able to supply 24 discs, but if the price falls to $13 per CD, Oranges Inc. will supply only 3 discs.

As in the case of demand schedules, the information from supply schedules can be graphically expressed as supply curves (see Figure 3.8). The individual supply curves for Oranges Inc. and Joe's Audio conform to the law of supply—other things being equal, as price rises, the quantity supplied increases and as price falls, quantity supplied decreases. Note that the supply curve for the individual firm slopes upward and to the right. This is because the marginal opportunity cost of

TABLE 3.3

Individual Firm and Market Supply Schedules

Individual firms' supply schedules follow the law of supply: As the price of the product increases, the quantity supplied increases. The total market supply is obtained by summing the quantities supplied by all firms at every price.

	QUANTITY SUPPLIED (PER MONTH)			
Price of CDs (dollars)	Oranges Inc.	Joe's Audio	All Other Firms	Total Market Quantity Supplied
20	24	16	410	450
19	21	14	365	400
18	18	12	320	350
17	15	10	275	300
16	12	8	230	250
15	9	6	185	200
14	6	4	140	150
13	3	2	95	100
12	0	0	50	50
11	0	0	0	0
10	0	0	0	0

resources used for increased CD production rises as more discs are produced. As more CDs are produced, less-adaptable resources are drawn into disc production. To increase the quantity of CDs supplied, a firm may have to enlarge its quarters by buying and converting buildings formerly used for other purposes, incur the costs of hiring and training workers who have never made CDs before, and perhaps redesign its product to use alternative materials as original materials become more scarce. These increases in marginal costs may make it unprofitable for the firm to supply more CDs unless the price of CDs rises.

Changes in Quantity Supplied and Shifts in the Supply Curve

Change in quantity supplied
A change in the amount of a good a producer is willing and able to produce and sell that is caused by a change in the price of the good or service.

As in the case of demand, a change in price will cause a **change in quantity supplied**, indicated by a movement along a given supply curve, and a change in any other factor will cause **a change in supply**, indicated by a shift in the supply curve either right or left. An increase in price will increase the quantity supplied, but a decrease in price will reduce the quantity supplied. The supply curve is positively sloped—upward and to the right—and, as we saw, the demand curve is negatively sloped—downward and to the right. When **factors affecting supply**—that is, factors other than the price of the good—change, the whole supply curve shifts.

Change in supply
A shift of the entire supply curve to the right or left.

Factors affecting supply
Anything other than price, such as technology or input costs, that determines the amount of a product or service that sellers are willing and able to offer for sale.

Changes in Cost of Production   The most important influence on the position of the supply curve is the cost of producing a good or service. The price of resources—labor, land, capital, managerial skills—may change, as may technology or production or marketing techniques peculiar to the product. Any improvement in

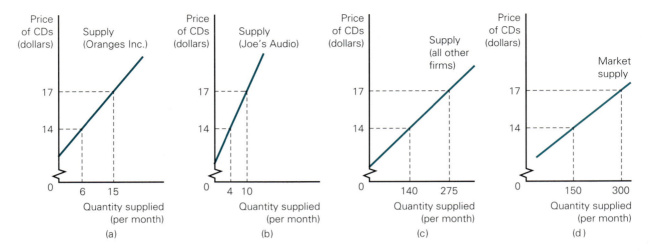

FIGURE 3.8

Market Supply Curves

The market supply curve of a product is obtained by summing the quantities that will be supplied by the two individual firms and by all other firms at every price. For example, at a price of $17 the total quantity supplied is 300 (15 + 10 + 275).

technology or any reduction in input prices would increase supply; that is, it would shift the supply curve to the right. More is supplied at each price.

   Suppose that the price of plastic materials used in compact disc construction falls or that the wages of salespeople available to CD stores decline. As the production or sales costs to firms producing and selling CDs decline, the quantity supplied increases and the supply curve shifts to the right for every price of CDs. An increase in supply is shown in Figure 3.9a. At price P_0, the firm was willing to sup-

FIGURE 3.9

A Shift in the Supply Curve

As factors other than price change, the supply curve shifts. When input costs fall, the quantity supplied increases from Q_0 to Q_1 at the price P_0, shifting the supply curve to the right from S_0 to S_1. An increase in input costs causes a decrease in quantity supplied from Q_0 to Q_2 and the supply curve shifts to the left, from S_0 to S_2.

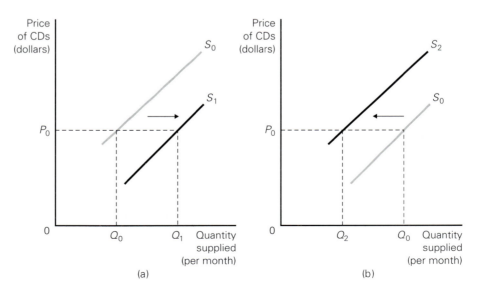

ply quantity Q_0 of discs when the supply curve was S_0. After the firm (and all other firms) experiences a reduction in costs, the supply curve shifts rightward to S_1, indicating a willingness to supply a quantity Q_1 at price P_0. An improvement in production or sales techniques or a reduction in the price of some resource shifts the supply curve to the right. An increase in any input cost shifts the supply curve to the left, as shown in Figure 3.9b.

Other Determinants of Supply   Factors other than cost of production changes can affect the location of the supply curve. One such factor is changes in producer-seller price expectations. The supply curve, like the demand curve, is drawn for a certain time period. If expectations of future prices change drastically in a market—for example, prices of the good or service are expected to rise suddenly—suppliers would withhold current production from the market in anticipation of higher prices. The current supply would be reduced, causing the supply curve to shift to the left, as in Figure 3.9b.

One other factor deserves mention. The supply curve is drawn for a given time period. A change in the time period (from one month to one week or one year) will alter the dimensions of the supply curve; it must be redrawn if the time period changes.

Market Supply

Market supply

The total amount producers are willing and able to offer for sale of a product at all possible prices, obtained by summing the quantities supplied at each price over all producers.

Market supply is the addition of all firms' quantities supplied for every price. If the number of firms in a given market increases or decreases, the supply curve would increase or decrease accordingly because the market supply curve is constructed by adding all the supply curves of individual firms. The market supply of CDs represented by the price-quantity combinations of the first and last columns of Table 3.3 is plotted in Figure 3.8d. The market supply curve is obtained by plotting the total quantities of CDs that would be produced and sold at every price during the time period. Note that market supply is simply the horizontal summation of all of the individual supply curves. For example, at a price of $14, quantity supplied would be 6, 4, and 140 units of CDs, respectively, from the three suppliers depicted in Table 3.3 and Figure 3.8. Thus the market supply of CDs at a price of $14 is $6 + 4 + 140 = 150$.

The market supply curve is positively sloped—that is, total quantity supplied increases with increases in price—because the real marginal opportunity cost of CD production rises as more discs are produced. Resources become more costly as more and more inputs are diverted from other activities into CD production.

MARKET EQUILIBRIUM PRICE AND OUTPUT

Market

The interaction of buyers and sellers producing and buying goods and services. Prices tend toward equality in a market through the continuous exchange between suppliers and demanders.

We now put the concepts of supply and demand together to understand how market forces work to establish a particular price and output. A **market** is any area in which demand and supply prices of products or services tend toward equality through the continuous interactions of buyers and sellers. Competitive (self-interested) forces of both buyers and sellers guarantee this result. All other things being equal, a buyer of dog food will always choose the seller with the lowest price, whereas a seller will choose if possible to sell at higher prices. Buyers will not pay more than price plus transportation costs, and sellers will not take less. There will always be a tendency to one price.

Perfect market

A market in which there are enough buyers and sellers that no single buyer or seller can influence price.

In a **perfect market**, both buyers and sellers are numerous enough that no single buyer or seller can influence price. In addition, buyers and sellers are free to enter or exit the market at any time. In this case of perfect competition, no single seller sells enough of the commodity and no buyer buys enough of the product or service to influence price or quantity. Each party to exchange has complete information. In a perfect market the **law of one price** holds: After the market forces of supply and demand, of buyers and sellers, are at rest or in equilibrium, a single price for a commodity (accounting for transportation and other costs) will prevail. If a single price did not prevail, someone could get rich by buying low and selling at a higher price, thereby driving prices to equality. The self-interested, competitive forces of buyers and sellers acting through supply and demand guarantee this important result.

Law of one price
In perfect markets, the market forces of supply and demand produce a single, equilibrium price for a good or service.

The Mechanics of Price Determination

Price and output are determined in a market by the simple combination of the concepts of supply and demand already developed in this chapter.

Tabular Analysis of Supply and Demand   Table 3.4 combines the data on the market supply and demand for compact discs and contrasts the quantities supplied and quantities demanded at various prices. The numbers used in Table 3.4 come from Tables 3.2 (market demand for CDs) and 3.3 (market supply of CDs). The principles discussed here apply to supply and demand functions in any market.

Consider a price of $20 for CDs in Table 3.4. At the relatively high price of $20, the quantity of discs supplied would be 450 while quantity demanded would be zero. That is, suppliers would be encouraged to supply a large number of CDs at $20, but consumers would be discouraged from buying CDs at that high price. If a price of $20 prevailed in this market, even momentarily, a **surplus** of 450 CDs would exist and would remain unsold on the sellers' shelves.

Surplus
The amount by which quantity supplied exceeds quantity demanded at a price above the equilibrium price.

TABLE 3.4

Market Supply and Demand
The equilibrium price is established when quantity supplied and quantity demanded are equal. Prices above equilibrium result in surpluses; prices below equilibrium result in shortages.

Price (dollars)	Quantity of CDs Supplied (per month)	Quantity of CDs Demanded (per month)	Surplus (+) or Shortage (−)
20	450	0	450 (+)
19	400	40	360 (+)
18	350	80	270 (+)
17	300	120	180 (+)
16	250	160	90 (+)
15	200	200	0
14	150	240	90 (−)
13	100	280	180 (−)
12	50	320	270 (−)
11	0	360	360 (−)
10	0	400	400 (−)

These unsold inventories of CDs would create a competition among sellers to rid themselves of the unsold discs. In this competition sellers would progressively lower the price. Consider Table 3.4 and assume that the price is lowered to $17. At $17 the quantity supplied of discs is 300, while the quantity demanded is 120—a surplus of 180. Only when the price falls to $15 per CD is there no surplus in the market.

Now consider a relatively low price: $13 per CD. As the hypothetical data of Table 3.4 tell us, the quantity demanded of CDs at $13 would far exceed the quantity that sellers would willingly sell or produce. There would be a **shortage** of 180 CDs—that is, 280 minus 100. Clearly some potential buyers would be unable to buy CDs if CD prices remained at $13. However, some buyers would be willing to pay more than $13 per CD rather than go without music. These buyers would bid CD prices up—offer to pay higher prices—in an attempt to obtain the product.

As the price bid by buyers rises toward $15, sellers will be encouraged to offer more CDs for sale; simultaneously, some buyers will be discouraged (will buy fewer CDs) or drop out of the market. For instance, at a price of $14 per disc, sellers would sell 150 CDs while buyers would demand 240, creating a shortage of 90 CDs. The shortage would not be eliminated until the price reached $15.

Equilibrium price in this market is $15; equilibrium quantity is 200 compact discs supplied and demanded. At this price, there is neither a shortage nor a surplus. A price of $15 and a quantity of 200 is the only price–output combination that can prevail when this market is in equilibrium—that is, where quantity demanded equals quantity supplied. The very existence of shortages or surpluses in markets means prices have not adjusted to the self-interest of buyers and sellers. Equilibrium means "at rest." In economic terms, equilibrium is that price–output combination in a market from which there is no tendency on the part of buyers and sellers to change. It is the price–output combination that clears the market. The free competition of buyers and sellers leads to this result.

Graphical Representation of Supply and Demand   The most common and useful method of analyzing the interaction of supply and demand is with graphs. Figure 3.10 displays the information of Table 3.4 in a graph that combines the market demand curve of Figure 3.7d with the market supply curve of Figure 3.8d.

The interpretation of Figure 3.10 is identical to the interpretation of Table 3.4, but the point of equilibrium is pictured graphically. Equilibrium price and quantity for CDs is established at the intersection of the market supply and demand curves. The point where they cross is labeled *E* for *equilibrium*. At equilibrium, both demanders and suppliers of CDs are mutually satisfied. Any price higher than $15 causes a surplus of CDs; that is, a higher price eliminates some demanders and includes more suppliers. Any price below $15 eliminates some suppliers and includes more demanders, resulting in a shortage of CDs.

The theory of supply and demand is one of the most useful abstractions from the world of events that is available to economists. Here we will discuss a few of the implications of supply and demand for society and for public policy.

Price Rationing

Prices, which are formed through the interaction of supply and demand, are **rationing** devices. Scarce resources are channeled to those who can produce a desired product in the least costly fashion for the demanders who most desire the product. Another way of saying this is that resources flow to their most highly

---

Shortage
The amount by which quantity demanded exceeds quantity supplied at a price below the equilibrium price.

Equilibrium price
The price at which quantity demanded is equal to quantity supplied; other things being equal, there is no tendency for this price to change.

Rationing
The allocation of goods among consumers with the use of prices. The equilibrium price rations the limited amount of a good produced by the most willing and able suppliers, or sellers, to the most willing and able demanders, or buyers.

FIGURE 3.10

Equilibrium Price and Quantity
The equilibrium price is established at the point where the demand and supply curves intersect. At this price, quantity demanded equals quantity supplied. At prices below equilibrium, the quantity demanded exceeds the quantity supplied, and the price is bid upward. At prices above equilibrium, the quantity supplied exceeds the quantity demanded, and the price is bid downward.

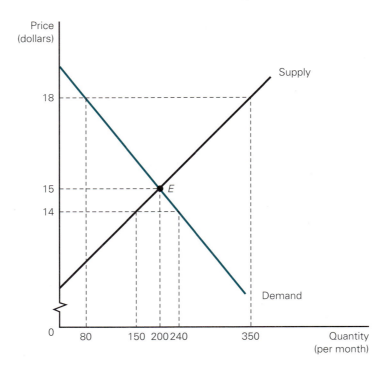

valued uses. Consider our hypothetical market for compact discs again. Suppliers who are able and willing to produce or sell CDs at a cost below $15 (including a profit) are "successful" in that their discs will be purchased. Demanders who are willing and able to purchase CDs at a price at or above $15 are the successful buyers of CDs. Only the most able sellers and buyers of CDs are successful in this market. High-cost producers (above $15) and buyers with a low preference for CDs (below $15) are eliminated from the market. CDs and all other goods are rationed by a price system—by the free interplay of supply and demand. In such a theoretical system no conscious attempt is made by any organization (such as government) to allocate scarce resources on the basis of factors such as presumed need, eye color, morals, skin color, or ideas of justice. As such, the market system plays no favorites. A price-rationing system ensures that only the most able suppliers and demanders participate in markets. All consumption decisions are made by individuals themselves.

Effects on Price and Quantity of Shifts in Supply or Demand

Both individual and market supply and demand functions are constructed by assuming that other things are equal. What happens if other things do not remain equal?

Demand Shifts   Any change in a factor other than the price of a good will shift the curve left or right. (Remember the difference between a change in demand, which is caused by a change in other factors, and a change in quantity demanded, which is caused by a change in price.) When demand changes, equilibrium price and quantity move in the same direction.

FIGURE 3.11

Shifts in the Demand Curve

(a) An increase in demand from D_0 to D_1 will increase equilibrium price and equilibrium quantity. (b) A decrease in demand from D_0 to D_1 will decrease both equilibrium price and quantity.

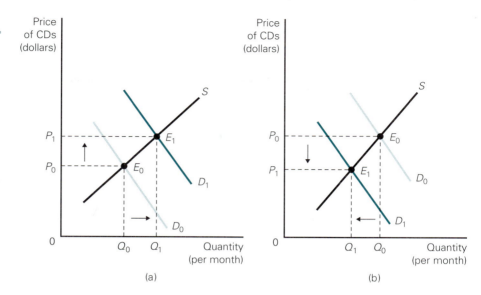

(a)

(b)

These facts can be seen graphically in Figure 3.11. Factors causing an increase in demand will have the effects on price and quantity shown in Figure 3.11a. An increase in demand shifts the whole demand curve rightward from D_0 to D_1. A shortage appears at price P_0. All the self-interested market forces that we discussed earlier now come into play. Demanders bid price up to P_1, where additional quantities are supplied by firms and where a new equilibrium, E_1, is established. Thus, an increase in demand has the effect of increasing the equilibrium price and the quantity of the product demanded and supplied. A decrease in demand causes the demand curve to shift leftward (Figure 3.11b). This has the effect of reducing equilibrium price and quantity demanded.

Supply Shifts   Any increase or decrease in a factor such as resource prices or price expectations will cause increases or decreases in the whole supply schedule. Effects of such changes are shown graphically in Figure 3.12.

Figure 3.12a shows the effects on price and quantity of an increase (rightward shift) in the supply schedule. At price P_0 a surplus is created and self-interested competitive firms and buyers bid price down to P_1. Note, however, that while equilibrium price decreases, equilibrium quantity increases from Q_0 to Q_1. A price decline from P_0 to P_1 means that an additional quantity of the product or service will be demanded by consumers. Figure 3.12b shows the effects on price and quantity of a factor that decreases the supply curve (shifts it leftward). A decrease in supply has quantity-decreasing (from Q_0 to Q_1) but price-increasing (P_0 to P_1) effects, as Figure 3.12b shows. With supply shifts, unlike demand shifts, equilibrium price and quantity change in opposite directions.

Shifts in Both Supply and Demand   In the previous two sections, we have examined the effects of shifts in either the demand curve or the supply curve. We now consider the effects of simultaneous shifts in both curves. If both curves shift simultaneously, changes in both equilibrium price and quantity are possible, but the direction of

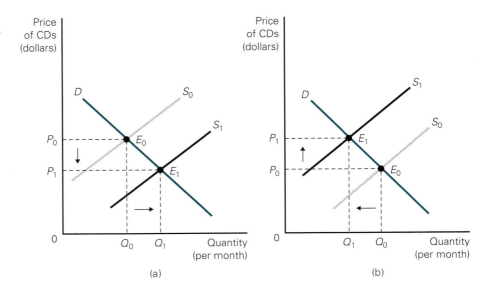

FIGURE 3.12

Shifts in the Supply Curve

(a) An increase in supply from S_0 to S_1 will lower the equilibrium price and increase the equilibrium quantity. (b) A decrease in supply from S_0 to S_1 will increase the equilibrium price and lower the equilibrium quantity.

change for only one of the two can be predicted. To see why this is true, we turn to a new example. Each of the three parts of Figure 3.13 shows the initial positions of demand (D_0) and supply (S_0) of U.S. wheat. The initial equilibrium price in each part is P_0. An increase in the number of U.S. farmers who grow wheat would cause the supply curve in each part to shift from S_0 to S_1. If demand for wheat remained unchanged, the increase in supply would unambiguously lead to a decline in the equi-

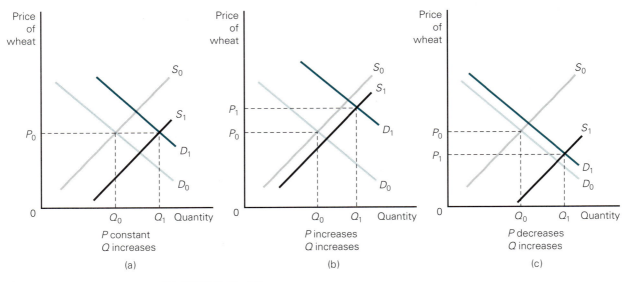

FIGURE 3.13

Simultaneous Demand and Supply Increases

An increase in demand and supply will result in an increase in equilibrium quantity, but could cause an increase, a decrease, or no change in equilibrium price. Thus, the price change is said to be indeterminate.

librium price to some level below P_0. Suppose, however, that during the same time period that supply increases, Russia arranges to purchase a large amount of U.S. wheat, which leads to increased demand. In each part of Figure 3.13, the increase in demand is depicted as a shift from D_0 to D_1. The new equilibrium points occur where D_1 intersects S_1. Comparing each new equilibrium with each old one reveals that the equilibrium quantity has increased in each case. Since both increases in demand and increases in supply lead to higher equilibrium quantities, simultaneous increases in supply and demand also lead to higher equilibrium quantities. However, it is impossible to predict what will happen to the equilibrium price when both supply and demand increase. The increase in demand will raise the equilibrium price, but the increase in supply will lower it. The final result depends on the relative size of the change. As shown in Figure 3.13b, the equilibrium price will increase if the increase in demand is greater than the increase in supply. The equilibrium price will decrease, however, if the increase in demand is smaller than the increase in supply (see Figure 3.13c). Figure 3.13a shows that no change at all in the equilibrium price occurs when supply and demand increase by the same amount.

Because both decreases in demand and decreases in supply tend to lower equilibrium quantities, simultaneous decreases in supply and demand will also lead to lower equilibrium quantities. As is true with simultaneous increases in supply and demand, the effect of simultaneous decreases in supply and demand on equilibrium price depends on the sizes of the changes.

Suppose an increased demand for U.S. wheat occurs simultaneously with a decreased supply of U.S. wheat—perhaps due to a drought in the Midwest or a rise in the price of inputs used in wheat production. The decrease in supply is shown in each part of Figure 3.14 as a shift from S_0 to S_1; the increase in demand is shown

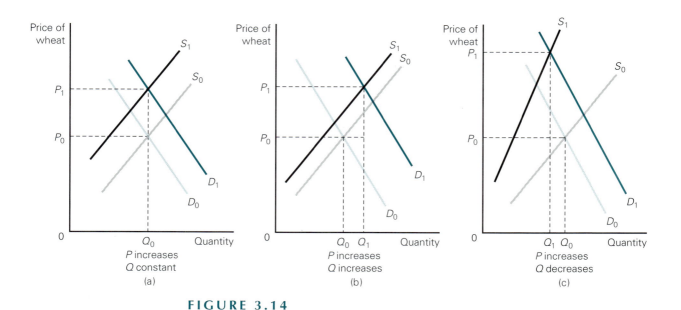

FIGURE 3.14

A Simultaneous Increase in Demand and Decrease in Supply
An increase in demand and a decrease in supply will always produce an increase in equilibrium price. Quantity change, however, will depend on the relative sizes of the shifts.

as a shift from D_0 to D_1. Since an increase in demand (with no change in supply) will always have a price-increasing effect and a decrease in supply (with no change in demand) will always have a price-increasing effect, equilibrium price will always rise with increased demand and decreased supply. However, the equilibrium quantity may remain constant (Figure 3.14a), rise (Figure 3.14b), or fall (Figure 3.14c), depending on the relative sizes of the shifts. If the decrease in supply is large relative to the increase in demand, equilibrium output declines; if the decrease in supply is small relative to the demand increase, equilibrium output increases.[1]

SIMPLE SUPPLY AND DEMAND ANALYSIS: OTHER CONSIDERATIONS

Many real-world events—new entrants into markets, oil price increases, new computer technology—can be analyzed using the simple laws of supply and demand. Some seemingly unrelated events also affect supply and demand. The theory of supply and demand is one of the most powerful tools the economist has to analyze the real world. It is important to understand some limitations and some possible applications and extensions of the simple mechanics described in this chapter.

Price Controls and Public Choice

As we have seen, a major effect of the free interplay of supply and demand is the rationing of scarce goods by a system of prices. One of the best ways to understand price rationing and its usefulness is to examine what happens when government intervenes with regulation in freely functioning markets. One such intervention into the natural functioning of supply and demand is called a **price control**. Rent controls, price controls, agricultural price supports, usury laws (controls on interest rates), and numerous other policies are examples of such tinkering in free markets. Simple supply and demand analysis provides the basis for an initial discussion of the rationing of goods and services by non-price means. For an example relating shortages, full price and supply and demand see the Application entitled "Opportunity Cost, 'Scalping,' and Full Price: Waiting for Van Gogh" at the conclusion to this chapter.

Price control

The setting, by government, of a price in a market different from the equilibrium price.

Price ceiling

A form of regulation in which a maximum legal price is established by government above which exchange between buyers and sellers is illegal.

Price Ceilings and Price Floors   Imagine a hypothetical market for wheat. The market demand and supply curves are depicted in Figure 3.15. Without government interference, the equilibrium price of $7 per bushel would be reached with 12 million bushels of wheat being bought and sold each month. Government officials could become concerned about the high price of food and impose a **price ceiling** of, say, $5 per bushel. The government is declaring that wheat can be sold only at prices of $5 per bushel or less. While the intent of the legislation is to enable buyers to obtain all the wheat they want at a lower price, Figure 3.15 shows that at the ceiling price of $5 per bushel, the number of bushels that buyers would like to buy (14 million bushels) exceeds the quantity that sellers are willing to sell (9 million bushels) by 5 million bushels. In other words, at the $5 price, there will be a shortage of wheat equal to 5 million bushels. Clearly, the desires of buyers and sellers are not synchronized at that price. Wheat buyers who cannot obtain desired quantities of wheat will offer to pay more than $5 per bushel (in some cases even more than $7 per bushel) rather than go without.

---

[1]Note that it is also possible for demand decreases to be accompanied by supply increases. In such cases, the equilibrium price declines. The change in the equilibrium quantity, if any, will be determined by the relative sizes of the supply and demand shifts.

To prevent the price from rising above legal levels, the government must engage in potentially costly enforcement activities. If the government succeeds in preventing illegal price increases, some other means will be used to determine which buyers get wheat. Any number of allocation plans could be used. Sellers could make the wheat available on a first-come, first-served basis, in which case long lines of consumers would form. Consumers could buy wheat at a reduced dollar price, but they would also pay with their time. Alternatively, the government could impose rationing so that each consumer is restricted to buying a fraction (nine-fourteenths) of their desired quantity of wheat. Other possibilities would be for government to establish priority schemes, with some consumers being permitted to buy and others being denied that opportunity. At any price below the equilibrium level there is an insufficient amount of wheat to meet demand, and some non-price rationing scheme must be used to determine who does and does not obtain wheat.

Alternatively, given the same circumstances, government officials might decide that the equilibrium price of $7 per bushel is too low to assure prosperity to wheat growers. They might decide to keep the price of wheat up by imposing a **price floor**—a minimum legal price of perhaps $9 per bushel—on the sale of wheat. Figure 3.16 shows that at $9 per bushel, the quantity supplied of wheat (16 million bushels)

Price floor

A form of regulation in which a minimum legal price is established by government below which exchange between buyers and sellers is illegal.

FIGURE 3.15

A Shortage Caused by a Price Ceiling

When the price of wheat is not allowed to rise above $5 per bushel, quantity demanded exceeds quantity supplied, creating a shortage of wheat.

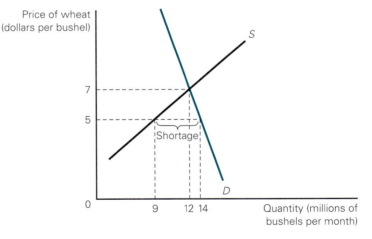

FIGURE 3.16

A Surplus Caused by a Price Floor

When a price floor above equilibrium price is placed on any commodity, quantity supplied exceeds quantity demanded, creating a surplus of wheat.

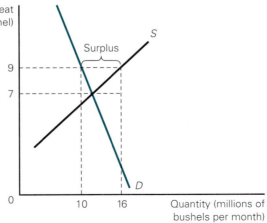

Milk price floors and subsidies established by dairy interests in Congress have long kept the price of milk above its equilibrium level in the United States.

exceeds the quantity demanded (10 million bushels) by 6 million bushels. In this case, a surplus of wheat of 6 million bushels exists. Wheat producers would find it difficult to locate buyers at the legal price, and they would have an incentive to reduce the price (in the absence of government enforcement). With effective enforcement, only 10 million bushels will be purchased at $9 per bushel; the government would be forced to use taxpayers' money to buy the surplus and put it into storage. At any price above the equilibrium level, government must have a program to deal with the predicted surplus of product. Price floors are also costly for consumers; for an example, see Focus "Price Floors Cost You More Than Peanuts."

Price Controls and Quality Changes   An additional implication of price controls is interesting and relevant to understanding the competitive market process. We have assumed in the foregoing that the quality of goods and services produced remains the same when price controls are established. This is not generally the case.

Price ceilings also may be avoided through quality changes. New York, Washington, D.C., Los Angeles, and a host of other U.S. cities impose rent controls on apartments and other rental housing. This means that the rental price of these apartments is fixed by law. While such price controls are often enacted to "protect" low-income families, quality changes may often mean lower quality to these groups over time. In some cases, available housing goes to upper-income and well-connected individuals rather than to the poor. When landlord-owners cannot by law raise rents as the demand for housing increases or as the cost of supplying housing rises, equilibrium rents rise above the controlled ones. If these rates are adequately enforced, the available housing will be rationed to housing demanders as a result of the shortage. Since some of the demanders will be willing to pay higher prices than the controlled rate for the lower available quantity of housing, black markets (extralegal markets) may develop. Illegal side payments to landlords, known as "key money," are common in rent-controlled cities.

Another possibility exists, however. If controls are effectively enforced and illegal side payments to landlords are prohibited, landlords have little incentive to

FOCUS

Price Floors Cost You More than Peanuts

Price floors have undoubtedly affected you. The U.S. government has supported prices of products such as milk, cheese, and peanuts for many years, and the purchase and storage programs (supported by your tax dollars) have been costly. Other nations have done the same. Trade disputes or "wars" have often broken out for these reasons. But more directly, you, the consumer, are paying more for milk and peanut butter than if quantity demanded were allowed to equal quantity supplied (see Figure 3.16).

As a taxpayer you pay for these subsidies, but as a consumer you pay as well. Suppose, for example, that the price floors on only three subsidized commodities—dairy products, sugar, and peanuts—costs you $5 per week. (Note that you also pay higher prices for all commodities and foodstuffs

that *use* these ingredients.) This price floor "tax" may seem a relatively small amount, but small amounts add up. The addition to the prices of the goods you buy is approximately $250 *per year* and over a seventy-year lifetime, $17,500. If you were able to save this money each year over a lifetime, beginning at birth and ending at seventy years old, you would have some real money. Given a real (or inflation adjusted) interest rate of 10 percent, you would have $2,000,000 (almost exactly) for retirement.[a] That ain't peanuts!

[a]Introductory business math texts demonstrate that the sum (S) of an annuity of R dollars per period at interest rate i for n years is $S = R\{1/i[1 + i)^n - 1]\}$. Using $R = \$250$, $i = 0.10$, and $n = 70$ in the above example yields the almost unbelievable figure of $2,000,000. Of course, a real or inflation adjusted rate of 10 percent may be high, but a real rate of only 5 percent would provide you with about half a million dollars at seventy years old.

FIGURE 3.16

A Surplus Caused by a Price Floor

When a price floor above equilibrium price is placed on any commodity, quantity supplied exceeds quantity demanded, creating a surplus of wheat.

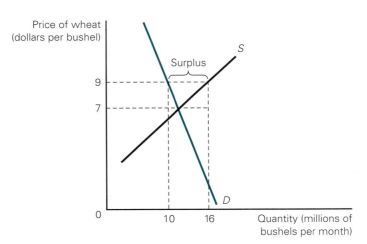

maintain rental property. Excess demand for apartments at the controlled price makes it possible to obtain tenants even if the unit deteriorates. Regulations that prevent prices from adjusting to equilibrium levels cause predictable changes in quality. Experience with rent controls in cities as diverse as New York City; Lisbon, Portugal; and Berkeley, California, shows that such programs produce low prices, substandard housing, and the allocation of rent-controlled housing to the well connected and well-to-do. Markets can clear at very low prices if quality can be reduced to a sufficiently low level. This type of nonprice competition has thwarted the best intentions of many regulators to provide better housing to low-income renters.

APPLICATION

Opportunity Cost, "Scalping," and Full Price: Waiting for Van Gogh

Matters relating to opportunity cost, full price, and supply and demand fill our daily lives, although we seldom stop to think of the mechanics of these central principles of economics. Our time is, as the French say, "money" and we have this scarce resource only twenty-four hours a day. Standing in line—at the grocery, at the movie theater, or waiting at the doctor's office—carries an opportunity cost. The opportunity cost of standing in line is our highest-valued alternative to, for example, working, sleeping later, or playing tennis. (Note that the highest-valued alternative does not have to be lost income from missed work time.) In general, however, the lower our income, the lower our opportunity cost of time. The fact that line-standing turns into a profession in many big cities is proof positive that such time has value. We can (and many do) pay individuals to stand in line for some items. In many cases, such transactions between people who have high value of time and those who will stand in line for a fee are perfectly legal.

In other cases, line-standing to obtain tickets for some event and the reselling of the ticket (called scalping) is restricted by law. Ticket scalping is often declared illegal by cities or other entities (if they catch you, that is). Football tickets, tickets to rock concerts, and passes to major art exhibits are all examples. Why, do you think, opportunities for scalping arise? Scalping arises from the policy of agencies or governments to keep the prices of goods or services low *despite the conditions of supply and demand*.

Consider a real-world example. Every year in major cities of the world, so-called blockbuster art exhibits come to city museums. Rembrandt, Vermeer, Cezanne, Degas, and many others are regularly represented in the great museums of the United States. In late 1998 a great exhibit of the works of Vincent Van Gogh hit the United States, first appearing at the National Gallery in Washington, D.C. That exhibit, lent from the Van Gogh Museum in Amsterdam, was provided "free" to the public. That is to say that tickets were free in nominal terms as described by Figure 3.17.

Consider Figure 3.17. Demanders, as described in this chapter, desire tickets depending on their price. At a money nominal or price of zero, Van Gogh lovers

FIGURE 3.17

Excess Demand at "Zero Price"

When quantity demanded (*OA*) exceeds quantity supplied (*OB*) and tickets are distributed "free," "scalping" often results.

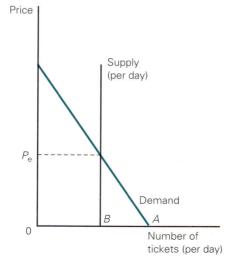

Lines form and full costs rise for tickets to see the Van Gogh exhibit at the National Gallery in Washington, D.C.

would demand an average quantity *A* of tickets to the exhibit per day. Unfortunately, the gallery can only accommodate *B* patrons per day (2050 same-day tickets). This means that at a zero money price, quantity demanded of tickets exceeds quantity supplied by some amount *AB*.

Fans may initially have favored the policy of free tickets, but lines got much longer, at times forming at midnight for the next day's tickets. Clearly, the full price, that includes time cost, was not zero. To those Van Gogh fans who valued time highly, the price of a ticket to see the exhibit was high indeed.

Enter the scalper. As you can see from the demand curve in Figure 3.17, there are Van Gogh lovers who would be willing to pay high prices for the exhibit. Some would be willing to pay—dearly—to avoid the long wait in line. Scalpers with lower time values were therefore able to sell tickets for prices ranging from $75 to $100 (and more). Clearly, there are winners and losers from this policy. We might sympathize with the losing Van Gogh fans who either must stand in line or pay high nominal prices for tickets of scalpers who were also willing to stand in line. Further, there are those who simply do not approve of the practice of scalping. But there are clear winners as well. Those paying scalped prices reveal that they value a Van Gogh ticket more than they value the dollars they pay. Scalpers obviously value the money more than the ticket.

It is the failure to price tickets to accommodate limited space that almost guarantees scalping in the first place. In other words, there are important effects when the laws of supply and demand are ignored. The National Gallery, by forgoing an entrance fee, misses out on millions of dollars in revenue. Such revenue could be used to expand facilities, among other projects. Laws, moreover, are costly to enforce, and private or semisecret transactions are seldom capable of being monitored to any degree. Finally, it is unclear why laws against scalping should be used to profit one group while hurting another.

QUESTION

Suppose your football, basketball, or baseball team makes it to the finals and that the final game is played at your school's field or stadium. Further, assume that tickets are sold out well in advance. What evidence could be gathered to show that quantity demanded exceeded quantity supplied at the ticket price charged by your school's athletic department?

Source: Some of the material for this discussion was drawn from "Perspective: Waiting for Van Gogh," *Investor's Business Daily* (October 30, 1998), p. A7.

SUMMARY

1. The extension of specialization from earlier societies is the modern market society, where individuals and collections of individuals buy and sell—demand and supply—millions of products and services.

2. Demand can be expressed as a schedule or curve showing the quantities of goods or services that individuals are willing and able to purchase at various prices over some period of time, all other factors remaining constant.

3. Supply can be expressed as a schedule or curve showing the quantities that individuals or businesses are willing and able to sell at different prices over a period of time, other factors remaining constant.

4. Equilibrium prices and quantities are established for any good or service when quantity supplied equals quantity demanded. In equilibrium, there is no tendency for price to change.

5. A change in the price of a good or service changes the quantity demanded or quantity supplied along a given demand or supply curve. A change in demand or supply occurs when some factor other than price is altered. When these factors change, the demand or the supply curve shifts to the right or left, either raising or lowering equilibrium price and quantity.

6. Simultaneous shifts of the supply and demand curves have predictable effects on either equilibrium price or equilibrium quantity, but not on both.

7. The market system, through supply and demand, rations scarce resources and limited quantities of

goods and services among those most willing and able to pay for them. Products and services, moreover, appear and disappear in response to the market system of supply and demand.

8. Price controls instituted by governments tend to create shortages or surpluses of products. Market forces usually result in some form of rationing other than price rationing under such circumstances.

KEY TERMS

products market
resources market
money price
full price
relative price
law of demand
quantity demanded
demand curve
factors affecting demand
ceteris paribus
change in quantity demanded
change in demand

normal good
inferior good
substitutes
complements
market demand
law of supply
quantity supplied
supply curve
change in quantity supplied
change in supply
factors affecting supply
market supply

market
perfect market
law of one price
surplus
shortage
equilibrium price
rationing
price control
price ceiling
price floor

QUESTIONS FOR REVIEW AND DISCUSSION

1. What happens to demand for a product if the price of that product falls? What happens to the quantity demanded?

2. What happens to the supply of coal if the wages of coal miners increase?

3. If income falls, what happens to the demand for potatoes? Are potatoes inferior goods?

4. If price is above equilibrium, what forces it down? If it is below equilibrium, what forces it up?

5. What is a shortage? What causes a shortage? How is a shortage eliminated?

6. If the demand for compact disc players increases, explain the process by which the market increases the production of CD players. What are the costs of CD players?

7. A price ceiling on crude oil has an effect on the amount of crude oil produced. With this in mind,

explain what happens to the supply of gasoline if there is a price ceiling on crude oil.

8. What happens to the supply of hamburgers at fast-food restaurants if the minimum wage is increased?

9. What is the full price of seeing a movie? Is it the same for everyone?

10. "Lately the price of gold keeps going up and up, and people keep buying more and more. The demand for gold must be upward sloping." Does this statement contain an analytical error?

11. What are price controls? When is a price floor imposed? What are some of the consequences of price controls?

12. Do the actions of self-interested coalitions of voters working through the political process help explain price controls? How? Can you think of an example?

13. What happens to the demand for pizza if the price of hamburgers increases? What happens to the demand curve for pizza? What are the effects on the equilibrium price and quantity of pizza?

14. If the price of sugar doubles, what will happen to the supply of regular (nondiet) colas? How will this affect the equilibrium price and quantity of regular colas?

15. Given the scenario in question 14, what will happen to the demand for diet colas? (Hint: Diet and regular colas are substitutes. What effect will this have on equilibrium price and quantity of diet colas?)

16. Suppose that a big football or basketball game or a rock concert is a sellout on your campus at some given ticket price and that the quantity demanded far exceeds the quantity of tickets supplied at that price. "Scalping" results. Explain it on the basis of supply and demand.

PROBLEMS

1. Use the data in the table to answer the following.
   a. Graph the supply and demand curves.
   b. What is the equilibrium price?
   c. What is the equilibrium quantity?
   d. At what price does a shortage of 280 exist?
   e. At a price of $19, how much of a surplus exists?

Price	Quantity Demanded (per month)	Quantity Supplied (per month)
$0	400	0
3	340	60
5	300	100
8	240	160
10	200	200
13	140	260
16	80	320
19	20	380

2. Disasters have a way of highlighting economic problems. Consider the hurricane that devastated South Florida in 1992. As Hurricane Andrew approached, the people of South Florida rushed to buy batteries, canned food, and other provisions. Afterward, a number of commodities, including ice, became extremely scarce. Assume that the price of ice was $50 per bag on the day after the storm and answer the following questions given the supply and demand schedule.
   a. What is the result of a price ceiling on ice at $30 per bag? Does $30 represent the full price of ice?
   b. If the mayor of Homestead, Florida, sets the minimum price of ice at $60 per bag, what type of price control is this?
   c. What is the impact on quantities traded at a controlled price of $60 per bag?
   d. Draw a graph of the price ceiling at $30 and indicate the shortage.

Price	Quantity Demanded (per month)	Quantity Supplied (per month)
$20	1600	250
30	1400	500
40	1200	750
50	1000	1000
60	800	1250
70	600	1500

Working With the Web

1. Suppose you decide it is time to buy a new polo shirt, and you are trying to decide whether to buy the interlock polo from L. L. Bean or Land's End. First, go to www.llbean.com and click on the "Product Guide." Next, click on Casual Clothing (Men's). Scroll down to "Shirts" and then find the interlock polo shirt. As of this writing, the current price for the L. L. Bean all cotton solid shirt is $18.50.

   Now go to www.landsend.com and under "Shop Our Store" select "Men's Casual." Next, find Interlock Polos and select solid short–sleeve. Here you see that the price of the regular short sleeve polo is $23.50.

   a. Assuming the shirts at L. L. Bean and Land's End are substitutes, if the price of the L. L. Bean polo rises, what do you expect to happen to both L. L. Bean's and Land's End's demand curves?

   b. What is the "demand shifter" at work here?

2. Everyone consumes water, and some consume more than others. We typically have tap water in our homes, yet bottled water has moved from being a fad to a staple for many consumers; it has become a multibillion dollar industry. To find out why so many people are consuming bottled water, go to http://www.bottledwaterweb.com/indus.html.

   a. In 1981, what was the level of bottled water consumption relative to all U.S. Liquid Consumption Trends?

   b. What was the level of consumption in 1997, and what was the growth rate of bottled water consumption in 1997?

   c. What do the statistics reveal about changes in the demand for bottled water?

   d. What factors are contributing to the change in demand?

4

Demand And Supply: Property, Markets, and Public Choice

The present chapter extends your knowledge of supply and demand to show how government or "the public sector" interacts with and affects private markets. Clearly, a role for government is critical in such areas as protecting property and establishing a rule of law. These institutions provide the very framework for free market functioning. Yet another concept—the idea of why economists believe free and competitive markets to be "efficient"—should be mastered before turning to the possible reasons that markets might "fail" or, alternatively, that additional roles might be provided for government. The political context of how decisions get made in the public sector will also help you understand the role and functions of government.

There are obviously many ramifications of government actions in the private economy and we will consider many examples later in this book. But after mastering this chapter you should understand:

- the basic institutions that facilitate a market system.
- the nature and efficiency of competitive markets.
- why markets might not function in a competitive fashion, thereby providing a role for government.
- some reasons that public choices (through voting and politics) differ from market choices in affecting the supply of goods and services to people.
- how efficiency might be affected by transfers and regulations granted in political markets.

INSTITUTIONS ARE "RULES OF THE GAME" THAT FACILITATE MARKETS

Economic system

The part of the social system determining what, how, and for whom goods and services are produced.

Pure capitalism

An economic system in which most resources are owned, and most relevant decisions are made, by private individuals.

Pure communism

An economic system in which most productive resources, both human and nonhuman, are publicly owned.

Socialism

An economic system in which most nonhuman productive resources are owned by the state.

Economic efficiency

The allocation of resources that allows maximum benefit to be achieved at minimum cost.

All exchange takes place within the context of some economic system. An **economic system** is the particular form of social arrangements through which the "what to produce," "how to produce" and "for whom to produce" questions are answered. The economic system of any given country is based on the institutions surrounding property ownership, incentives, and decision making that underlie all economic activity in that country.

Systems differ among countries. The extremes are **pure capitalism** and **pure communism**, with **socialism** in between. A society organized along the lines of pure capitalism is one in which government economic control is minimal. Under pure capitalism, most resources are privately owned and government's role in the economy is pretty much limited to protecting and enforcing private property rights and to providing national defense and other public goods. Common ownership of both human and nonhuman resources, at the other extreme, typifies pure communism. Socialism, in between these two extremes, is a system in which the state owns most nonhuman productive resources and makes production decisions by planning the economy's output. In reality, of course, all systems that we observe in the world today are "mixed" with elements of each other. The initial "rush to capitalism" in the Russian Republics (after the breakup of the Soviet Union) and in Eastern European countries such as Poland is being rethought, with some communist politicians (if not the system) making a resurgence. Institutions—such as enforceable property rights—must exist to support capitalism, and such institutions have been lacking in many parts of Eastern Europe and Russia.

Institutions are therefore the key to understanding the conditions and incentives under which exchange takes place. **Economic efficiency**—producing goods and services at lowest cost and exchanging goods so as to maximize the advantage of all traders—can be discussed only under some given set of institutions. The basic economic "questions" of every society are answerable only under the legal rules that determine rights, ownership, and obligations. The forms of legal institutions regarding contracts, property rights, and their enforcement are central to the attainment of high or low economic efficiency. They guide production, exchange, and consumption in all economies.

Different societies, in past and present, have created different institutions for the *ownership* and *use* of property, including goods and money. A capitalist economy relies primarily on market forces and the profit motive for production, distribution, and consumption of goods and services. Capitalism is characterized by individual ownership of property, free enterprise, open competition, and (ideally) a minimal role for government. Let us consider each of these features briefly.

Property Rights and Contracts

We exchange property every day. Billions of exchanges—contracts between exchanging parties—take place in the United States alone. Explicitly or implicitly, we make a contract when we supply or demand labor. On the New York Stock Exchange, an average of 700 million shares of stock are traded daily. A purchase of cat food at the supermarket is as much a contract as the agreement by a New Jersey electrical utility to buy a five-year supply of coal from a Montana mine. Throughout the world, in stock and commodity markets, bazaars, shopping centers, and resource markets, literally trillions of contracts are made every day. Property, a bundle of rights, is transferred through contracts in all cases.

Private property

Property that an individual (as opposed to a government) holds the right to control.

In the U.S. economy the individual's right to own and dispose of property is regarded as basic. In a system of **private property**, the individual (as opposed to government) holds the right to control property. The individual receives the benefits and must pay the costs associated with the use of her property. Property here takes on a wide definition. It includes both physical property (such as houses and computers) and intellectual or intangible property. For example, the ownership of poems, songs, and books by their authors is protected by copyright laws. Inventions are protected by patents. The formal legal apparatus set up to protect such rights may even make a distinction between property and property rights. Rental of a carpet cleaner from U-Rent-Um gives the renter certain property rights over the cleaner but not ownership of the property itself. In all societies, rights to use property are limited. For example, the Environmental Protection Agency has used its legislatively derived power to limit the rights of businesses to pollute air and water and has established worker protection standards (such as those limiting the use of asbestos) that restrict individuals' free use of property. The real key to understanding the importance of property rights is their link to economic incentives.

Property Rights and Economic Incentives

When we consider the operation of large economies like those of the United States, Japan, Poland, or Russia, we can see how overwhelmingly complex it is to solve basic economic problems. To attain efficiency, decision makers must have

Individuals, such as reggae artist Ziggy Marley, have rights to their own intellectual property, such as songs, in a market system.

the incentive to make correct economic decisions. That incentive is governed by the legal institutions surrounding property rights. To put the matter more clearly, the assignment of property rights is the key to economic efficiency. The manner in which property rights are assigned, moreover, often has enormous implications for economic and social incentives and the ultimate welfare of people. (For a good example, see the Focus: "Shipping *Live* Prisoners to Australia.")

FOCUS

Shipping *Live* Prisoners to Australia

Legal changes, legislation and administration of rules and regulation may all be used to direct and channel incentives to achieve economic and social ends. In other words, given the costs and benefits of doing so, buyers and sellers in markets will find it profitable to make contracts and contract terms ever more perfect in terms of incentives and outcomes. A famous historical example drives this point home. One of the greatest reformers of nineteenth-century England (akin to modern-day consumer activist Ralph Nader) was Sir Edwin Chadwick (1800–1890).[a] Chadwick once devised a plan for reducing the mortality of British criminals transported to Australia. He noted that the British government paid a flat fee to a ship's captain for each convict who boarded from a British port. The captains quickly discovered that they could maximize their profits by packing on as many prisoners as could be carried without endangering the ship and by minimizing expenditures on prisoner food, drink, and hygiene en route to the colony. The survival rates stood at 40 percent under this incentive system. Humanitarians were outraged at the state of affairs. After a quick assess-

ment of the program, Chadwick changed the payment system so that the ship's captain received a fee for each *live* convict that *disembarked* in Australia. Soon the survival rate increased to 98 percent. The rule change gave ship's captains incentives to protect the health of the convicts. A new contract arrangement rearranged incentives and created an identity of interest between the public interest (that is, the health and safety of the prisoners) and private interests (that is, the profit of the shipper). Similarly, the design of modern-day contracts in the purely private sector to transfer property rights works toward ever more efficient results—that is, toward more efficient use of scarce resources in producing goods and services of highest value to consumers and society.

---

[a]See Edwin Chadwick, "Opening Address," *Journal of the Royal Statistical Society of London* 25 (1862), p. 12. Chadwick was also a pioneer contributor to the economics of crime, the courts, sanitation, and the public supply of utilities and other services. These and a number of other examples are discussed in Robert B. Ekelund, Jr., and Robert F. Hebert, *A History of Economic Theory and Method*, 4th ed. (New York: McGraw-Hill, 1997).

The basic point concerning property and incentives is simple: When property, such as a meadow or whales or owls, is communally owned, no one can exclude others from its use. All members of the community regard the use of the meadow, whales, or owls as "free" and of zero opportunity cost. A rush will be on to exploit the resource, because the marginal opportunity cost and the price of using it is virtually zero. Maximum demand (at a zero price) leads to overutilization and ultimately ruination of the resources. Here private incentives (to get there first and to get as much as one can) conflict with socially desirable incentives (to conserve the resource). This so-called "tragedy of the commons," that is to say, of common property, exists today in the problems generated by common property resources such as fisheries, endangered species, and ill-defined water rights (see the discussion of "externalities" later in the chapter).

Private property, on the other hand, where each individual is permitted to own or exchange property rights as she sees fit, is the key to economic efficiency. You bear the full costs of your decision to use or trade property, but you also receive the full benefits that might result from your decision. Without some guarantees that property rights will be protected, there would be little incentive to accumulate capital stock and, therefore, to grow economically. Without government guarantees of rights to property, individuals would have to protect their own property at high personal cost. Indeed, the higher opportunity costs of individual protection as one's property accumulates makes the collective enforcement of property rights through police, courts, and prisons less costly than the total costs of such enforcement to individuals acting separately (such as through the use of mercenaries or posses). In other words, the protection of property rights of citizens is naturally (in economic efficiency terms) a major function of government.

Private Competitive Markets

Free enterprise

Economic freedom to produce and sell or purchase and consume goods without government intervention.

Contracting and the exchange of property rights takes place within private competitive markets. American capitalism approximates these conditions. Free competition or **free enterprise** is a primary feature of this world. It is the freedom to pursue one's economic self-interest, with few or no governmental restraints or subsidies and where resources may be combined by businesspeople to produce goods and services for profit. Businesses, consumers, laborers and input owners of all types are free to produce, purchase, and exchange property rights to any good or service provided that their activity does not infringe on others' rights. Individuals are of course constrained by the rule of law concerning the use of property—you cannot drive your auto on the sidewalk, for example. (Bear in mind that participants are also not free of the constraints of limited resources and unlimited wants.)

Within these limits, however, the American economic system is characterized by free competitive markets. This means that, as implied above, property rights are well-defined, enforceable, and tradable. But **competition** implies two other important conditions: There is no collusion among consumers or any other market participants (such as laborers), and all transactors are able to freely enter or exit the market. The self-interested behavior of buyers and sellers will tend to keep the prices of goods and services at a competitive level—that is, at the costs of producing the good or service plus a normal profit for the entrepreneur—when these conditions are met.

Competition

A market which functions under two conditions—no collusion among sellers or buyers (which occurs with a large number of buyers and sellers) and freedom to enter and exit the market. Competition results in prices equal to the costs of production plus a normal profit for sellers.

Under the discipline of private competitive markets, noncollusion means that each seller and each buyer makes decisions about their willingness and ability to sell or buy that are completely independent of the decisions of other sellers or consumers. While this condition does not require large numbers of buyers and sellers, the existence of large numbers virtually guarantees that no individual buyer or seller can affect the market price of a product or service. Many millions of individuals purchase canned soup, for example, but not one buyer purchases enough to affect the market price of the soup. Likewise, the existence of competing suppliers means that no individual seller can acquire enough power to alter the market for his or her gain. Sellers of canned soup are numerous enough that no one seller can affect the price of soup by altering the market.

Firms must also be free to enter and leave markets in response to profit opportunities or actual losses. But bankruptcies and business failures are expected consequences of a competitive system (yes, failure of some is an essential feature of competition). New fast-food restaurants open every day in anticipation of profits. Airlines declare bankruptcy and leave the industry—a sure sign of losses. Competition requires that entry and exit into business be free and unregulated.

Actually, coordination of the billions of individual decisions involved in competition is an interconnected system of prices for inputs and outputs that is so complex that no individual or computer can fully comprehend it. We began to study the intricacies of the price system in Chapter 3. Supply and demand explains much about how resources are "efficiently" allocated between the production of CDs, chiropractic services, and home computers. However, we must be able to explain exactly what is meant by economic efficiency.

WHY ARE PRIVATE COMPETITIVE MARKETS EFFICIENT?

Clearly, the protection of private property and a legal system that protects the assignment of property rights are key factors in permitting markets to function. Noncollusive behavior and freedom of entry and exit from the market are two others. Other institutions, some of them provided by government, are critical as well. As we have seen, the provision of a stable money supply and the freedom to use resources in any way we please underlies free competitive markets. These and other factors define what we mean by competitive markets, but why should economists (or anyone else) champion private competitive markets? We must return to the principles of supply and demand learned in Chapter 3 in order to understand why private markets are considered "efficient" by economists.

Demanders Value Goods

Markets are the means through which individuals—self-interested demanders and suppliers—help relieve the problems brought on by the scarcity of resources. Economic efficiency means that total value is, in general, maximized in that goods are produced at least cost. And those who "want" the goods the "most" get them. Let us see how "value" is calculated and recorded by demanders.

Any demand curve—for an individual or for a whole market—may be given two different but equivalent interpretations. As you learned in Chapter 3, the demand curve indicates the specific amount of some good or service that consumers are both willing and able to purchase *at a given price* per unit of time (of course, holding all other factors affecting demand constant). Market demand is

FIGURE 4.1

Demand and Marginal Private Benefit Curve

The market demand curve represents the value consumers as a whole place on marginal units of the good. The total value of any quantity produced is the area under the demand or marginal private benefit curve from zero up to that quantity. The difference between what consumers would be willing to pay for the good or service and what they actually pay is called *consumers' surplus*.

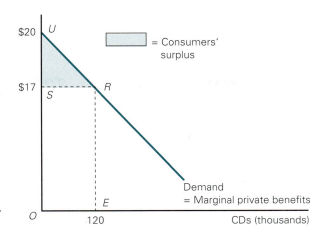

Marginal private benefit curve

A curve, equivalent to a demand curve, which represents the value that consumers place on marginal units of the good or service.

simply the summation of the quantities demanded by all consumers of the good or service at each price.

A demand curve, under certain conditions, may also measure the value that consumers place on a good because it expresses what they are willing and able to sacrifice to obtain it.[1] Consider Figure 4.1, which shows the market demand (taken from Table 3.4) for a competitively produced product—compact discs (CDs). The amount in terms of price that CD demanders are willing to sacrifice in order to obtain discs in Figure 4.1 is a measure of value. Specifically, the demand curve is equivalent to a **marginal private benefit curve**—which represents the value consumers place on the last (marginal) disc under consideration.

Continuing the numerical example from Chapter 3 (see Table 3.4), we may say that the value consumers place on the marginal disc—the 120th disc per month— is $17. The value that consumers would place on fewer discs per month, say the 40th, is $19. Looking at the areas under the demand curve, it is clear that the total expenditure is the quantity purchased times the price of discs (when each unit of discs is purchased at the same price). If the price of a disc, in Figure 4.1, was actually $17, consumers would buy 120 of them. Their total expenditure would be $17 times 120 or $2040. (In our example, we are keeping numbers simple—a more realistic demand would simply multiply consumers and expenditure by 1000.)

Clearly the figure—$2040—represents consumer expenditures on discs. But does it represent value to consumers? The answer is no! The total valuation of the 120 discs is higher than the $2040 that disc consumers must pay to get them. In fact, consumers are willing and able to pay a good deal more for a given quantity of most goods and services rather than not get these goods or services at all.

---

[1]This interpretation holds if we assume that consumers are buying a good or service that does not have any external or "third-party" effects, such as would take place if, for example, secondhand smoke had to be accounted for in the consumption of cigarettes. We consider the relevance of these external effects later in the chapter.

Total consumer valuation

The total amount that consumers are willing to pay for a given quantity of a good or service rather than go without it.

Consumers' surplus

The difference between what consumers are willing to pay for a given quantity of a good or service (the total consumer valuation) and what they have to pay (their total expenditure).

Total consumer valuation is the total amount consumers in the market are willing and able to pay for a given quantity of a good or service rather than go without it. This total value may be shown graphically as the area under the demand/marginal valuation curve from zero quantity (0) out to the quantity under consideration (in this case 120 discs).

In effect, most consumers get a real bargain because they are willing and able to pay more for discs than they must pay for discs. This is *value received but not paid for* by consumers in association with a purchase. For more than a century and a half, economists have known about this surplus and by consensus call it *consumers' surplus*. **Consumers' surplus** is defined as the total valuation consumers place on a given quantity of a good or service minus the total cost or expenditure of obtaining the good or service in exchange. If the market demand curve for discs is the one identified in Chapter 3 (in Table 3.3), total expenditures on discs at a price of $17 is $2040, but consumers get a surplus of the shaded area when they consume 120 of them—this is, the amount they would have spent less what they actually had to spend for 120 discs. The actual value of the surplus going to consumers may also be calculated—it is $180.[2] It is also equal to the shaded area of Figure 4.1 (triangle *SUR*). In general these surpluses exist in all markets for all goods and services—for airline travel, for broccoli, and for school tuition. Thus, the total valuation of consumers (area *OURE* in Figure 4.1) consists of two parts—total expenditures on the good or service (area *OSRE*) and consumers' surplus (area *SUR*). It is the total that consumers would be willing and able to pay for any good or service.

Supply, Costs, and Value

Recall now our definition of *supply* from Chapter 3. A so-called "law of supply" is the assumption we make concerning the behavior of producers or sellers of some good or service. A seller will be willing and able to sell or produce a larger quantity of a good or service at a higher rather than at a lower price, given all other factors that influence his decision (the *ceteris paribus* assumption). Conversely, any producer or seller would be willing and able to produce and sell smaller quantities of a good or service at a lower price than at a higher price, given all other factors affecting the decision (the *ceteris paribus* assumption again). Other things being equal, as price rises, the quantity supplied of a good or service increases and, as price declines, the quantity supplied decreases. A supply curve, recall, is obtained by summing up the quantities supplied at each price over all producers. A market supply curve, such as the one for compact discs in Figure 4.2, can be thought of as a collection of price and quantity supplied combinations of many individual suppliers. At a price of $13 dollars per disc, suppliers will be willing to put 100 discs per month on the market.

There are other ways to view the supply curve that are correct and equivalent to that above. The market supply curve indicates the minimum price (per unit or per disc in our case) that sellers will be willing and able to receive in order to get them to produce and sell the units of the good or service under consideration. Sell-

---

[2]The actual amount of consumers' surplus in dollars may be calculated in the following manner. Note from Table 3.4 that all consumers of discs disappear at a price of $20 per disc. The (shaded) area of Figure 4.1—consumers' surplus—is half a rectangle (that is, a triangle). The rectangle is calculated by the difference between the price consumers must pay ($17) and the price that eliminates consumption of discs altogether ($20) or $3 multiplied by the quantity consumed at a price of $17 or 120 discs. That value is $360 (the rectangle) and half of that—the consumers' surplus—is $180.

FIGURE 4.2

Supply and Marginal Private Costs

Market supply represents the marginal private cost curve showing the opportunity cost of producing additional units of the good or service. The total cost of producing any quantity of the good is equal to the area under the supply curve up to that point (that is, the alternative uses of opportunity cost in terms of resources forgone). Total receipts of sellers less this total cost results in a "producers' surplus" associated with the production of many goods.

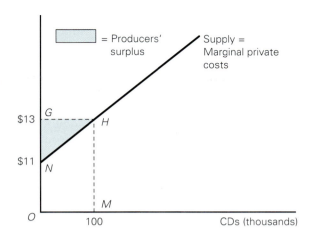

Marginal private cost curve

A curve showing the marginal or additional cost to society—the opportunity cost of scarce resources—of producing additional units of a good or service.

ers must receive $13 at a minimum in order to get them to sell 100 discs per month in the example above. We must now recall *why* this is so. Under competitive conditions, the supply curve (for any individual seller) is also the marginal cost of the inputs or resources used to produce the discs. These costs are, as we noted in Chapter 3, the marginal opportunity costs associated with any given amount of discs produced. As the quantities of discs produced rises, resources that are less and less adaptable to disc production must be drawn into use, producers must enlarge facilities and hire and train workers who have not produced CDs before, and marginal costs may be expected to rise. The opportunity cost of using resources in disc production rises and the rising supply curve reflects this fact. The production of more discs by sellers may become unprofitable if the market price of discs does not rise. When the production of a good or service (discs) does not create third-party or external effects (discussed below), the marginal or additional cost to society is the opportunity cost of the scarce resources used to produce discs. We may call the supply curve the **marginal private cost** curve of producing discs for society.

These points about supply may be illustrated with Figure 4.2. Consider again the price of $13 for discs. At this price 100 discs are produced. The total revenue of all disc sellers is simply the quantity sold times the price, and when the price of discs is $13, total revenue is $1,300 or area *OGHM* in Figure 4.2. But these total revenues are not equivalent to total cost. Total costs are the opportunity costs of all of the productive resources used up in the production process. The total opportunity cost is the sum of all of the marginal opportunity costs of producing 100 discs. Graphically, it is the area under the supply or marginal private cost curve from 0 quantity up to the quantity under consideration. It is, in Figure 4.2, equal to $1,200 or to area *ONHM*.[3]

---

[3]Note that in Figure 4.2, the total cost of producing 100 discs can be calculated by dividing up the area under the supply curve into two portions—a rectangle with a height of $11 and base of 100 units plus a right triangle with a height of $2 ($13 minus $11) and base of 100. The money amount of producers' surplus is the area formed by the triangle *GHN* in Figure 4.2. Since the area of the triangle is one-half the area of the rectangle found by multiplying the base (100 units) times the height ($2), the amount of producers' surplus in the example shown in Figure 4.2 is $100.

Producers' surplus
The difference between the total revenue to producers from selling a given quantity of a good or service and the total cost to them and to society of using the scarce resources in that particular production.

The difference between total revenue of the producers and the total cost to them (and to society) is called **producers' surplus**. (In dollar terms, producer surplus is $100 in Figure 4.2.) The concept, analogous in some respects to consumers' surplus, is expressed from the point of view of the factors of production that are employed in producing and supplying a good or service (discs in our case). It is the payment received by a factor of production over and above the minimum payment just necessary to induce the factor into the particular use (producing discs). The producers' surplus is equal to the total revenue of the disc sellers minus the total opportunity cost of all of the scarce resources used in producing 100 discs. Through the exchange process, the total revenue of disc sellers is distributed among all of the factors used in making discs. The total revenue of the disc sellers thus represents the total payments to the factors of production in association with producing and selling 100 discs.

Just like consumers, then, most producers receive a surplus from supplying production in the marketplace. The marginal producer who produces the last CD in Figure 4.2 just covers his or her opportunity cost of production, which is obviously $13. Every other producer along the supply curve form N to H earns a producer surplus given by the difference that they are actually paid, $13, and their opportunity cost as read off the supply curve. The first resources committed to the production of CDs are the most adaptable or lowest cost, and they therefore earn large producer surpluses. These lower-cost producers earn a producer surplus up to GN, or $2, in Figure 4.2.

And it should be kept in mind that both consumers' and producers' surplus represents wealth and wealth creation in the price system. Consumers' surplus in Figure 4.1 was $180, and producers' surplus in Figure 4.2 is $100. *This represents wealth that accrues to consumers and producers as a result of their market interactions.* The market system works to maximize the total of these surpluses and, what is the same thing, produces what economists call economic efficiency.

Competitive Equilibrium and Economic Efficiency

The efficiency of competitive markets may be analyzed with these simple tools. Recall from earlier in this chapter that competitive markets required certain conditions. They were that property rights were well defined, enforced, and tradable; that sellers or buyers were not able to collude or to have an effect on the market-clearing price (large numbers of buyers and sellers tend to guarantee this); and that any firm willing and able to become a seller can enter the market without entry barriers. Under these conditions, which we assume hold in the production, sale, and purchase of compact discs, the market will be efficient! Figure 4.3 tells us what is meant by this concept.

Figure 4.3 (as in Figure 3.10) shows the market-clearing price for compact discs. At $15 the market clears—that is, the quantity supplied (per month) of discs is 200 and the quantity demanded (per month) is 200. Alternatively, the quantity exchanged in the market is the amount that sellers produce (200 discs) and the amount that consumers buy at the market clearing price (200 discs). This is what is meant when we say "the market clears." In the case described in Figure 4.3, market equilibrium under competitive conditions means that just the right amount of

FIGURE 4.3

Allocative Economic Efficiency

The "market clears" where supply and demand (or marginal private benefit curve and marginal private cost curve) intersect. This means that the total net value of the good or service is maximized. At this point, the *sum* of consumers' and producers' surplus is maximized.

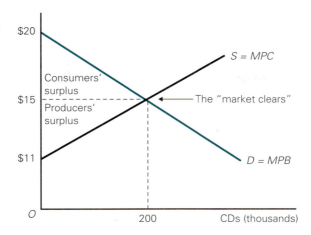

discs—not too many or too few—are produced. Competitive markets, under the conditions described, are said to result in *allocative efficiency*. Those individuals who most demand the product get it at a price that exactly represents society's opportunity cost of resources in producing it. All but the very last consumers value discs higher than the equilibrium price of $15, and only the very last consumer(s) pay the marginal opportunity cost of producing discs in terms of resources given up by society to produce discs.

The market clearance of Figure 4.3 is also critical to understanding economic efficiency. *Economic efficiency* means that, under competitive conditions, the net value of society's scarce resources is maximized. The *total value* produced by 200 discs to society (with reference to Figure 4.3) is equal to the area under the demand curve from 0 discs produced to 200. We may call that area the *total social value of consuming the scarce resources*. After subtracting the *total social cost* of using the scarce resource to produce discs—equal to the area under the supply curve from 0 to 200 discs—we arrive at the net social value of the scarce resource. If there are no third party effects, that is, if consuming or producing discs does not produce costs or benefits that are not borne by consumers or producers—a competitive market creates a maximum of *net* social value. This means that society's resources have been allocated in efficient fashion. The sum of consumers' surplus and factor or producers' surplus is maximized when net social value is maximized under competition.[4] Any attempt by producers or consumers to get a greater share of the surplus—such as through the political process—may result in a reduction in the sum of the total surplus produced (i.e., less consumers' + producers' surplus). We will soon see how this might well happen in the context of a democratic political system.

---

[4]In numerical terms, the net social value may be found by combining the procedures discussed in notes 2 and 3. You may verify that consumers actually pay $3,000 for discs, but that they would have been willing to pay $3,500 so that consumer surplus is $500. Sellers of discs receive $3,000 for 200 units (what the consumers actually pay), but of this $400 is producer surplus. Therefore, the total net value of disc production to society is $900.

THE ROLE OF GOVERNMENT

Government has always played a critical role in the economies of all nations current and historical. We have seen, at the beginning of this chapter, how one fundamental and essential role of government is to set the "rules of the game" for the economy. This means that, through government, a legal framework for the definition and enforcement of private property rights is established. Competitive markets function within these rules. But what if competitive markets fail to provide a maximum of total value to society; that is, what if society's assumed goal of maximizing the net social value of resources (described above) is not achieved? How might this **market failure** happen and what, if anything, can be done about it? Consider some possible market failures.

Market failure
A situation in which the socially optimal (most economically efficient) amount of a good or service does not get produced by the private market; usually stems from unclear property rights assignment.

The Environment, Externalities, and Market Failure

The failure of markets to provide maximum economic efficiency is most often related to problems with property and the definition of rights over property. Owners of private property are free to hold, trade, or exchange rights, and they bear the full costs and benefits of their actions. Market failure most often occurs when the rights over resources are either ill-defined or not defined at all. These so-called common property resources, such as air, whales, underground pools of oil, and the atmosphere belong in specific quantities to no one. But when they belong to no one, no individual has an interest in conserving them. Indeed, self-interest and the goals of society often conflict, so that individuals in the pursuit of their own self-interest damage the resource, sometimes irreparably, for society as a whole. You do not have to reach far to understand these cases—the "save the whale" and other endangered species campaigns or the "global warming problem" arising from the burning of fossil fuels are well known. For obvious reasons, these are called environmental problems.

Markets may fail for other reasons, but these failures are most often related to ill-defined or nonexistent property rights. The active pursuit of self-interest by one person may impose costs or benefits on others. There might be, in other words, third-party effects from consuming or producing particular products. **Externalities**, therefore, are the costs and benefits of somebody's behavior or activity that that particular individual does not bear. Well-known examples come to mind. Secondhand smoke might injure people who do not do the smoking. A factory emits smoke or waste products to the detriment of the population in the area or downstream. Automobile exhaust creates smog for the population generally, especially in congested urban areas. Other examples are your roommate's loud stereo, airport noise, or obnoxious perfume or cologne worn by the student sitting next to you.

Externalities
Benefits or costs of an individual's activity that the individual does not receive or bear.

But externalities may be positive as well as negative. Your neighbor may maintain a beautiful yard or garden, all of which pleases you and improves the value of your own property. This benefit—a positive externality—is (ordinarily) not compensated for by paying the neighbor for the benefits you receive. Small-pox vaccinations or flu shots provide other examples. The presence of externalities means that the marginal private costs or benefits of actions do not always

Vaccinations against communicable disease constitute a positive externality—others are protected when you protect yourself.

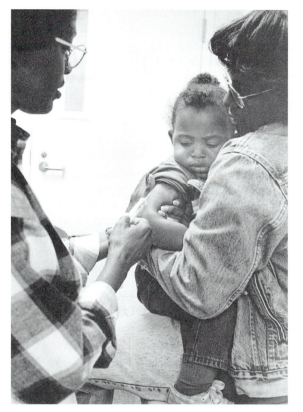

equal the marginal social costs or benefits of consumer or producer behavior on the part of the whole society. This divergence between self-interest and society's overall welfare would have the effect of causing adjustments in the "efficiency" arguments developed in the preceding discussion in this chapter. When marginal social costs exceed marginal private costs, unfettered private competitive markets produce too much of a good or service. When, however, marginal social benefits from some consumption (a beautiful garden or a polio vaccination) exceed marginal private benefits, too little of a good or service is produced. Economic efficiency might be achieved in these cases, but some nonmarket adjustments might be necessary.

Obviously, a wise and efficient government would identify and address each of these situations. But there are enormous problems involved in identifying and addressing externalities on the part of government. Not all problems should be addressed. If the cost of adding noise control devices on airplanes landing at some specific airport exceeds the collective value that homeowners around the airport place on noise reduction or elimination, the costs of eliminating the externality would exceed the benefit and it would be "uneconomic" to proceed. Determining just what these costs and benefits are is, of course, a very difficult problem to begin with in particular situations.

Once relevant externalities have been identified, there are a number of approaches that might be taken, some of them involving government, some not. In general, when the costs of bargaining and transacting between the parties to an externality are low, simply assigning property rights to one or the other parties to the externality may do the trick. If smokers and "relevant" nonsmokers are able to freely transact with one another, a private solution may be possible. Other cases are far more difficult to handle and demand other solutions. Water rights or rights to whales can hardly be assigned to individuals. Governments therefore often resort to taxing or subsidizing externalities in order to "correct" "inefficient" markets. Another well-known solution is to use administrative regulations of all kinds to address negative externalities. The Environmental Protection Agency, administered by the federal government, is an example of a regulatory approach to externalities. Indeed, many kinds of policies, including the sale of "rights to pollute" with proceeds going to reducing the effects of pollution, have been and are being tried. All of these solutions are partial in effect and, sometimes to the detriment of all parties, must be filtered through a political process. We will have more to say concerning this critical matter later in this book. For now, however, it is useful to remember that there is a positive role for government in addressing externalities, be it through the definition and enforcement of property rights or through more direct means.

Public Goods and Market Failure

Public good
A good such that, once produced, one individual's consumption of the good does not reduce or exclude the ability of other individuals to consume the good.

Another and somewhat more obvious role for government is in the provision of public goods—goods that would not or could not be provided through free competitive markets. Public goods are another kind of "market failure." What economists call **public goods** are those which, once produced, cannot reduce or impede the ability of others to consume the good regardless of whether consumers are willing to pay or not. The most widely acknowledged public good is national defense. Why should I provide national defense (in the right amounts) if you and everybody else in society can "free ride" on my provision? If I could exclude you from receiving the benefits of my provision, I could charge you for "units" of defense (missile protection, jet carriers). But I cannot exclude you from protection and you have no incentive to reveal how much national defense you "demand." So, it is not in a private individual's self-interest to pay for defense. More specifically, your consumption of national defense does not compete with mine; we both "consume" each unit of defense that is provided. Since defense is necessary to protect the property of all individuals in society, a role for government is created.

The failure or inability to assign property rights has led to specie endangerment, inlcuding certain members of the wolf family.

Conceptually, the case of national defense is easily understood. Not so for many other candidates. Are lighthouses public goods? Would they not be produced at all or in the right numbers if not provided by governments? (It is a historical fact that many were created and maintained privately.) What about circuses or outdoor rock performances? Does one individual's consumption compete with or complement another's consumption at an outdoor Lauryn Hill concert? These are difficult questions that await some answers later in this book.

One issue concerning the provision of public goods is worth noting at the outset. Just as it is difficult to determine costs and benefits in assessing the extent of "externalities," it is just as perplexing to determine, through a political process, how much of a public good would be "value maximizing" for society. Many smaller countries of the world have, for example, been "free riders" on U.S. investments in national defense. Further, certain features of the political process to be discussed later in this chapter bring into question the efficiency of national defense expenditures. What is indisputable, however, is that the government's provision of public goods, especially national defense, is a justifiable role for government.

Antitrust and Monopoly Regulation

Several other important problems in markets, in addition to externalities and public goods, have been put forward as justifying a role for government in markets. All of these reasons collapse into one—the existence of significant monopoly power. Monopoly (a single firm's control of a market) or oligopoly (the control of a market by a small number of firms) has justified government control over property rights through direct regulation of the activities of firms (over, for example, electric, water, or communications utilities) or by enforcing a set of "rules" with which firms must comply at the risk of civil and criminal penalties (antitrust regulations).

Antitrust policies
Regulations established by laws and government agencies that attempt to preserve business competition.

Industry regulation has included, since the early decades of this century, **antitrust policies** prohibiting price discrimination, collusion among producers, and deceptive advertising practices all passed in an attempt to restore competition where it no longer existed. Even earlier, however, economists and politicians believed that government had a role whenever competition could not exist, perhaps because of economies of large-scale production, or what economists call natural monopolies. Such monopolies are created when each seller can produce more and more output at lower and lower costs. Eventually it becomes profitable for only one seller to supply the total quantity demanded of a good, thereby creating a monopoly. Federal, state, and local governments undertook the regulation—not the ownership or operation—of transportation, communications, energy, and many other industries that were regarded as natural monopolies. Government regulation, in this view, was regarded as a substitute for competition or state ownership where viable competition could not exist because of industry production and cost conditions.

Some economists have strongly disputed this view and question the existence of large-scale economies (natural monopoly) in many of these regulated industries. Some economists believe, with some justification, that regulation of prices and profits must fail, either because regulation has been ineffective or because these industries are more competitive than previously thought. For example, since the early 1980s there has been significant deregulation affecting airlines, long-distance communications, and trucking. Questions have been raised concerning the self-interested supply of regulation by politicians combined with the self-interested demand for regulation by firms and industries. Do industries and other interest groups use the government regulatory apparatus for their own benefit? Should broad new areas of industry regulation, such as in telecommunications and public utilities, be reduced or eliminated? These and many other questions concerning the expanded role of government are in hot debate, and a firm foundation in economic theory will help you in providing answers to them.

PUBLIC CHOICE—THE RELATION BETWEEN POLITICS AND ECONOMIC EFFICIENCY

We live in a democracy with a particular set of political institutions. These include majority voting, the existence of political parties, a federal system or a hierarchy of representative governments, a huge administrative bureaucracy, and organized interests of all kinds. Public choice, as noted in Chapter 1, is the analysis of the political sector based on the economic notion that self-interest guides public decision makers (voters, politicians, bureaucrats) as well as private decision makers (consumers, sellers, and market intermediaries). Obviously, the individual who buys a new automobile is the same individual who votes, so that political and economic decision makers are often one and the same person. Importantly, however, there are different institutions and constraints facing economic markets—the decision to buy a car—and political markets—the decision to vote or the decision to sponsor legislation as a politician.

A fundamental question that we answer later in this book is whether political processes are themselves efficient at reflecting the true preferences of voters. But political decisions also have enormous implications for the efficiency of private markets. Environmental regulations may benefit some firms at the expense of others. Entry restrictions in certain professions may be designed to benefit a few workers at the expense of many. Tariffs on imported sugar or peanuts may raise their price to consumers in order to benefit a few favored domestic producers. We must therefore understand a few basic reasons (a) why political markets do not work the same way that economic markets do, and (b) how special interests tend to dominate the political process, often reducing economic efficiency in the process.

Political Versus Economic Markets

There are numerous differences between political and economic markets, although both are guided by *self-interested* behavior. Individuals make decisions in private markets in which *all* costs and benefits are borne by the decision maker. Suppose you decide to make an investment in a high-tech stock or in some rental property. If the stock or property fails to earn a competitive return, *you* will bear the full costs of your actions. Likewise, if the investment proves to be a bonanza, *you* receive the full benefits.

This complete internalization of costs and benefits does not take place in political markets. The politician does not bear the full economic consequences of his decisions and has poor incentives to control costs. Politicians cannot personally recoup any savings they make for the public and they are only weakly controlled by voters when high costs are incurred.

Logrolling
The exchange of votes by legislators, usually in order to gain support for particular legislation.

The self-interest of politicians also explains an enormous amount of activity within legislatures. The phenomenon of vote-trading or **logrolling**, where you vote for my courthouse and I'll vote for your water reclamation project, is clearly understood by most of the voting public. (*Why* voters let it go on is a question we pose presently.) While economists generally regard exchange as efficient, logrolling in a political context may not be efficient behavior. Since politicians represent particular geographic areas and since politicians face a re-election constraint (two years for U.S. House of Representatives, six years for U.S. Senate), bringing the "pork" back home improves reelection prospects. The problem is that logrolling is not generally efficient in reflecting the preferences of voters on national issues. Rather, it redistributes income toward certain regions and industries and generally does not lead to a more productive economy. We, as collective Americans, get more dams, military bases, and special-interest tax "reform" bills than we want. The political system, in short, tends to produce economic inefficiency. This occurs, even though politicians are in a "market" not unlike IBM stock, computer chips, or diapers—see the Focus, "Politicians Are Demanded and Supplied."

Why Are Voters "Myopic"?

Clearly, the electorate is not made up only of fools or idiots. Why do they "let" politicians pursue their own self-interest at the expense of the common good expressed as the will and preferences of the people? It is because there are substantial and critical differences in the private market and the political market that facilitate logrolling and other noneffiency producing political behavior.

When you buy a second car, you buy only a second car. When you vote for your local congressional representative, you vote not for a single issue, but for a whole package of issues or a platform that she represents. We say that the consumer

FOCUS

Politicians are Demanded and Supplied

People who pursue (supply) a career in politics must, if they are rational, expect to achieve a higher level of satisfaction from a political career than from their alternatives. The rewards from supplying a political career include (but are not limited to) salary and benefits, the perks of office, the utility from being in a position of power, and the satisfaction of helping others. Those who seek the rewards of a life in politics must first be elected and then reelected to maintain this career path. Election (and then reelection) will be uppermost in their minds.

In a democracy such as ours, the individual citizen's role is indirect, with the voter usually restricted to selecting who will make the final decision on the many questions that come before the government. The problem is to determine which politicians to support (demand). The self-interest

of voters implies that they will select the candidates who support legislation that promotes their interests (both financial and nonfinancial). Individuals vote for the candidates who are closest to their own position on the "issues." An issue that is near and dear to the hearts of everyone is their source of income. Those earning their income in an industry (for example, defense, agriculture, housing, or automobile) will tend to vote for politicians who support that industry.

This process by which politicians seek and attain elective office bears a striking resemblance to the model of supply and demand. Politicians demand votes and need a majority of the votes to ensure election or reelection. Voters supply votes to the politicians who meet their "price," where the voter's price is a position on the issues.

makes marginal choices in the private market, but only all-or-none decisions in the political market. Another point is that voting is irregular when compared to shopping in the marketplace. That feature of political markets makes it difficult to alter your "consumption" of policies and candidates. You can fairly quickly change grocery stores when you find inferior vegetables at one of your local markets, but it is more difficult to change elected officials.

Perhaps the greatest problems occurring in political markets stem from the fact that voters have weak incentives to inform themselves on the particular political choices their representatives are making. Do you really know or care how your representative feels about or votes on providing a new federally sponsored park in northern Oregon? Voters have few incentives to gather information concerning their public choices, whereas they have strong incentives to acquire information concerning market choices. The costs of staying informed on the hundreds (even thousands) of decisions made by all of your representatives is enormous. Therefore, as a rational voter—one calculating the direct costs and benefits of your representative's decisions—you stay rationally uninformed or rationally ignorant. This does not mean that voters are stupid or that they "don't care about government." Rational ignorance simply means that the costs of being fully informed on each and every decision made are prohibitively high. The pro rata share of the costs and benefits of so many of these decisions—the new Oregon park—are so low to individual voters that they are not concerned with how politicians vote in such cases. When you decide to buy some private good, such as a health club membership, a new swimsuit or a plate of Asian food, you do so with direct "dollar votes." Whether or not a formal contract exists— it might for the membership but might not for the dinner or the swimsuit—property rights are directly traded in your purchase. You give rights over a certain amount of money, and you obtain property rights over the good or service you have purchased. You incur the costs of the exchange and obtain all the benefits of the new property rights.

This is not the case for public choices. Public choices, like private choices, are self-interested, but differ in important aspects. Political decision makers do not bear the full costs of their decision, nor do they reap all of the benefits. They cannot capitalize on decisions and have no incentives to control costs. Such is the case for many student governments at colleges and universities across the country. You pay a fee for student government activities—akin to a tax—and you vote for representatives. How do the results of student government activities differ from your private market participation?

First, allocations for funding student groups are made by your representatives and committees composed thereof, but there is no reason to believe that such funding will accurately or even closely reflect your preferences. Who gets the money will depend on who can muster the strongest coalitions within the student government. On some campuses, Panhellenic (fraternity and sorority) interests will dominate. On others, athletic interests or the Society of Student Engineers or even minority group clubs will win larger allocations. Allocations, in other words, will be made on the basis of interest groups and the coalitions they form. You may want to add new journals to the school library or to expand aerobics classes in the student union with the fees collected, but your preferences might not be recognized.

Then there is the familiar problem of voter or student apathy. You may be so busy with classes, activities, or a job that you remain rationally ignorant of exactly what the student government is actually doing or what the candidates are like in the first place. Even if you were *acutely* interested in the outcomes of the political process at your university, it would be exceedingly costly to monitor your representatives once they are elected. And, since most office holders in student governments are only around for one or two years, it is highly unlikely that "turning the rascals out" would be a viable or effective option. You cannot change student representatives as you can brands of fast-food hamburgers. In these senses, therefore, you are a captive (at least temporarily) of a political process not unlike that established for democratically elected officials at all levels of government.

Interest Groups Tend to Dominate

Since voters are rationally uninformed, they present serious difficulties for politicians. Naturally, elections do tend to generate some information for representatives, but that information is seldom direct. Inasmuch as individual voters are rationally ignorant of voting on particular issues, politicians are uncertain about voter preferences. But some individuals and, particularly, blocs of voters—called **interest groups**—are clearly interested in particular outcomes.

Interest groups
Collections of individuals with one or more common characteristics, such as occupation, who seek collectively to affect legislation or government policy so as to benefit members of the group.

Coalitions of particular interests—businesses surrounding the proposed Oregon park—are in a prime position to put pressure on politicians to vote their way. Politicians, ever mindful of promised votes, campaign contributions, and other perks, are all too eager to supply legislation. (See the Application at the end of this chapter: "Why Are There So Many Restaurants and Golf Courses in State Capital Cities?" for some insight into this issue.) Special-interest legislation at all levels of government—local, state, and federal—is therefore explained as the result of rational self interest on the part of voters at large (who are rationally ignorant), coalitions of particular interest groups directly affected by legislation, and by politicians who, in *their* own self-interest, want to be reelected. The problem, and it is a big problem, is that the demand and supply of such legislation within the political process reduces the economic efficiency of markets and thwarts the general will and preferences of the electorate. Let us see how with an example.

INTEREST GROUPS AND WEALTH TRANSFERS: THE CASE OF BARBERS AND COSMETOLOGISTS

The behavior of interest groups explains much in the political arena. Concentrated interests on the part of particular groups of individuals—as against the wider public interest—are represented by lobbyists in all political venues. Lobbyists and political action committees (PACs) for particular groups cover every conceivable interest at one level of government or another. Examples include real estate, physicians (the American Medical Association), defense industries, teachers, postal workers, banking and financial institutions, textiles, petroleum, labor unions, and virtually any other interest for which legislation or regulation can affect economic benefits or costs in a positive or negative fashion. To see how interest groups affect government policy, consider the process by which a statewide group of barbers might organize to advance their interests. (We conclude this discussion with some real-world data on how hair styling fees are affected by state regulations.)

The most fundamental problem that barbers (or hair stylists or health professionals) face is how to get organized. Specifically, each barber has incentives to stay outside the interest group, for if the interest group is successful in, say, obtaining higher prices for haircuts, a free-riding barber—one who does not pay dues to the barbers' association—can benefit without incurring any costs. Free-riding behavior makes the formation of interest groups difficult, but by no means impossible. For such reasons, interest groups seek ways to limit the benefits of their activities to members only.

Assume that the barbers organize. The group's representatives go to the state legislature and seek a legally sanctioned barbers' monopoly. The purpose of this monopoly (actually a cartel or interest group) is to protect barbers from new competition by erecting barriers to entry into barbering, thereby allowing barbers to raise the price of a haircut above competitive levels—that is, above costs in terms of resources used in providing a haircut. In other words, the barbers petition the state government to raise their wealth at the expense of haircut consumers. Put another way, they are demanders of a wealth transfer from the state.

Who are the potential suppliers of wealth transfers? The "suppliers" are those—in this case, consumers of the barbers' product—who do not find it worthwhile to organize and to resist having their wealth taken away by the barbers. This is an unusual concept of supply, but it is a supply curve nonetheless. The attitude that will prevail among suppliers of a wealth transfer is that it would cost them more to protest the barbers' proposal than any benefits they would derive from protesting. For example, the average consumer might spend $100 to defeat the barbers' proposal, the net result of which would save $10 in haircut costs. Why spend $100 to save $10?

This example describes a "demand" and a "supply" of wealth transfers in the case of barbers. How does the market for wealth transfers work? Politicians are brokers in this market and in the market for legislation generally. The politician's job is to pair demanders and suppliers of wealth transfers. If they transfer too much or too little wealth, they will be replaced at the next election by more efficient politician-brokers.

The outcome for the barbers may be shown (in Figure 4.4) as an extension of our discussion on the meaning of competitive economic efficiency earlier in the chapter. The barbers start out as a purely competitive industry, producing Q_c haircuts per year at a price of P_c. When their interest group forms, they persuade the legislature to grant them special cartel status. This persuasion is not very difficult because the consumers who are harmed by the cartel do not find it worthwhile to protest to the legislators. The barbers are the only ones to be heard, and perhaps by putting their arguments for a cartel in public-interest terms ("higher prices mean higher quality," "barbers must be licensed to ensure an orderly marketplace," and so on), they carry the day with the legislature.

Legislators, for their part, assess the costs and benefits of creating a barber cartel. In Figure 4.4, the barbers seek $P_m A B P_c$ in cartel profits at the expense of

FIGURE 4.4

How an Interest Group's Demands Are Met

P_c is the competitive price that the barbering industry charges per haircut, and P_m is the price established by the group after it is granted protected (cartel) status through the political process. After the cartel is formed, it stands to gain P_mABP_c in profit from consumers of haircuts. This transfer is from consumer surplus to profits, but society also loses a net amount ACB in welfare.

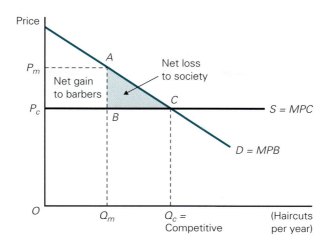

consumers' welfare. (We assume, for simplicity and not unreasonably, that barbering services are produced at constant opportunity cost of resources and that the supply curve lies flat at the competitive price.) This means that an amount of consumer surplus (P_mABP_c) is transferred to barbers as profits. Area ACB represents a net welfare loss to consumers due to the legal monopoly supplied by legislators. The per capita gains to barbers, who are a relatively small number of producers, exceed the per capita costs to the more numerous haircut consumers. The result: The legislature passes a law giving the barbers a cartel (and, perhaps, the barbers make campaign contributions to the legislators who supported their cartel bill). *The net value of society's resources is not maximized because of the transfer.*

There is actual evidence that state regulation of hair stylists has produced this result. A recent study of cosmetology regulation in the fifty states has shown that a variety of restrictions, on entry into the market, including educational, age, and training restrictions have had the effect of increasing the price of hair style services across the United States.[5] The greater the degree to which the cosmetology profession in a particular state has attained political power and influence, the greater the benefit to the profession in the state and the greater the cost to consumers of these services. Even a modest average increase in price due to restrictions—say 50 to 75 cents per hair style—will reduce consumer surplus by an enormous amount—possibly by several billion dollars per year—over all consumers. *The moral*: An industry does not have to be vital to health or national defense to seek transfers in this case from consumers to suppliers of barbering and cosmetological services—through the political process.

[5]See A. Frank Adams, III, Robert B. Ekelund, Jr., and John D. Jackson, "Occupational Licensing of a Competitive Industry: The Case of Cosmetology" (Manuscript: Auburn University, 1999).

Legal licensing granted through the political process transfers gains to barbers and cosmetologists from consumers along with a net loss to society.

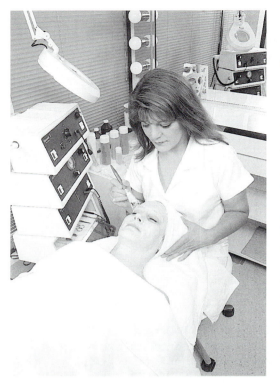

Our discussion of barbers concerns a particular kind of restriction. Interest groups do not always work as producers versus consumers. Technically, any group can organize and act as an interest group, and we find that interest groups represent many overlapping segments of society. There are labor unions; women's rights groups; religious groups; trade associations; and organizations for doctors, nurses, and all health professionals, for lawyers, hunters, environmentalists, and farmers. Moreover, not all of these groups are small. Many large groups, such as farmers, are effectively organized as an interest group. The fundamental point is that you can begin to explain why a certain law is passed if you try to answer two questions: Who wins? and Who loses?

Another critical point is that the particular features of political markets—at least in a representative democracy—permit sanctioned and legal transfers of wealth from one group to another. Almost every policy you can think of has this effect. While transfers are not so important to the economists, overall economic efficiency—the maximization of the net value of all of society's resources—is of great concern. The differences between private markets and public choice practically guarantees that overall economic efficiency will not be attained.

Clearly, markets are excellent institutions through which to allocate resources. Markets, along with institutions such as private property and free contracting described in this chapter, give people in society the goods they value most. Indeed, they do this most of the time. When market activity creates third-party effects such as pollution or other externalities, government may step in to attempt to alleviate problems. In general, however, markets underlie wealth creation and wealth creation is about making society better off.

Market functioning, however, takes place in the context of democratic political institutions in a world of "public choice." When left alone, markets are unconcerned with "welfare triangles." But when politics and interest groups enter the picture, as we have seen in this chapter, society's wealth may be redistributed and the triangles under supply and demand curves become important. They showed, for example, how the barbers were able to increase their wealth at the general expense of the net wealth of society. When political participation in the economy is considered, the economist's emphasis turns from efficiency to distribution. Our discussion of public choices revealed that democracy and its institutions create the possibilities for losses through redistributions. This does not mean that democracy must be done away with or significantly altered, however. Democracy remains the best conceivable system in a world of imperfections.

APPLICATION

Why Are There So Many Restaurants and Golf Courses in State Capital Cities?

It is obvious that a lot of effective lobbying takes place. It would be difficult otherwise to explain many local, state, or federal allocations and subsidies, such as water subsidies in the West or inland waterways in the South. How much activity takes place is another question. If politicians are self-interested, as modern public-choice economists believe, they will always make policy with an eye to reelection and enrichment. Because the direct transfer of money for votes is fairly easy to detect, politicians must rely on other kinds of transfers and perquisites. Interest groups are often able to deliver blocs of votes, as mentioned in the text, or to finance campaigns by a variety of means. Most proposed reform focuses on changing methods of campaign finance.

But there are numerous other ways to pay off politicians for economic interventions that benefit special interests. For example, it would be a rare representative or senator specializing in banking or transportation legislation who did not have opportunities to work for the industry he or she regulated after retiring from politics. Family members or business partners and associates of the politician, moreover, may be in a position to accept payoffs.

Distortions (payoffs?) may take many other forms. Although most of the attention has been fixed on cash and other bribes, many forms of in-kind transfers (that is, not in money) are in fact used. Overt cash bribes attract attention and invite regulation, but lobbying efforts may be indirect, as when trips, fancy (or not-so-fancy) meals, transportation or limo services, employment of relatives or business associates, or golf rounds are provided for legislators.

Recent research into in-kind perquisites of state politicians has produced convincing results. When allowance is made for per capita income and other key variables, state capital cities have been shown to contain a larger per-capita percentage of sit-down (non–fast food) restaurants than paired, randomly chosen same-state cities with similar income characteristics.[a] The bigger the budget of the state (the more opportunities for profit-seeking transfers by special interests) and the more full-time lobbyists in the state, other things equal, the more restaurants the city has. The same goes for golf courses.

What are the costs of such lobbying by special interests? First, there is the cost to society of skewing regulations and goods toward concentrated interests and not to the public interest as discussed in this chapter. But there is a direct cost as well. In the sample of forty-seven state capitals, there are a total of 9,635 additional restaurants for the capital cities solely because of their political status as capital cities. A lower-bound estimate of resource distortion from restaurant payoffs is suggested by multiplying 9,635 times the average start-up cost per restaurant. Then there are also 286 additional golf courses to consider.

There are many forms of political payoffs from special interests. More hidden in-kind payoffs may be expected where functions and funding are shifted away from the federal level and to cities and states. Cruder, lower-cost forms of payoffs may be expected where the gains from special treatment are lower. In smaller communities, lunch at McDonald's or Wendy's or a weekend fishing vacation may do the trick. Whatever the case, such special-interest legislation and regulation will likely have negative benefits for voter-consumer-taxpayers at large.

---

[a]See Franklin G. Mixon, Jr., David N. Laband and Robert B. Ekelund, Jr., "Rent Seeking and Hidden In-Kind Resource Distortion: Some Empirical Evidence," *Public Choice* 78 (1994), pp. 171–185.

These negative benefits from lobbying may of course be resisted by the electorate at large. Voters at any level of government might demand lobbying restrictions by special interests, limits to campaign spending, and so on. In 1996, for example, the U.S. Congress placed a "gift ban" on its own members in response to criticisms from the media and the electorate. The "exemptions" that Congress passed along with the ban were interesting, however. Free meals are OK, it seems, if interest groups invite a "large group" to dine. And both major parties supported a total exemption on gift and party giving at the Republican and Democratic National Conventions held in August of 1996! At the federal level, moreover, "payoffs" continue to entail far more restaurant meals and golf games. Attempts to pass legislation that would curb campaign contributions at the federal level have not been successful. Despite a number of initiatives on the part of federal legislators and in spite of demands of consumer and other groups, the momentum for change has not enflamed voters. Without voter activism, self-interested U.S. Representatives and Senators, along with their state counterparts, have little incentive to limit campaign contributions and other payoffs that affect votes on critical economic and social issues. Those politicians who favor limits to campaign contributions have not been particularly successful in convincing their parties of the wisdom of that policy, and voter apathy continues into the new millennium.

QUESTION

How can you explain the proliferation of sit-down restaurants and golf courses in state capitals?

SUMMARY

1. All economies are characterized by institutions—the "rules of the game"—that shape and guide economic activity.

2. A key capitalist institution is private property. Private property, protected and enforced by government, permits and facilitates efficient contracting between individuals. It also encourages private incentives for long-term planning and investment, which promotes economic growth.

3. Private competitive markets exist when individuals are free to buy and sell resources, enter or exit business, and produce and consume goods and services with little or no government intervention.

4. Free and private competitive markets, in which there are no third-party effects to exchange, produce allocative efficiency. Such economic efficiency occurs at quantities where the demand curve or (what is the same thing) the marginal private benefit curve intersects the supply or marginal private cost curve. In different terms, maximum economic efficiency occurs where total net benefits are maximized, that is, where the difference between total value and total cost for producing some good or service is the greatest. Allocative efficiency is also (and equivalently) achieved when the sum of producer and consumer surplus is maximized.

5. Government's role in the economy, besides setting the institutional "rules of the game," is to address problems when markets and private exchange fails to produce allocative economic efficiency. Failures might occur when third-party effects, such as externalities, are created through market exchange or when property rights are difficult or impossible to define. Water pollution, factory smoke, and noise around airports are possible examples of this phenomenon.

6. The provision of public goods such as national defense provide another rationale for the role of government. Once produced, a public good is provided at little or no cost to all.

7. The government also institutes industry regulation through the regulation of business practices and through anti-monopoly regulation (called *antitrust laws*).

8. Public choice is the study of political markets—how self-interested individuals and groups of voters, politicians, and bureaucrats guide public decision making. Organized interest groups are often able to use the political process to transfer wealth. Unorganized and myopic voters permit transfers as they remain "rationally uninformed" or "rationally ignorant" when the cost of being informed is high and the *pro rata* cost of the political decision is low.

KEY TERMS

economic system
pure capitalism
pure communism
socialism
economic efficiency
private property
free enterprise

competition
marginal private benefit curve
total consumer valuation
consumers' surplus
marginal private cost curve
producers' surplus
market failure

externalities
public good
antitrust policies
logrolling
interest groups

QUESTIONS FOR REVIEW AND DISCUSSION

1. What is *capitalism* and what does it have to do with property rights and economic freedom?

2. What, exactly, is an *institution?* How do institutions help solve the basic economic "questions" in capitalist societies?

3. What is private property? What is common property? How do incentives differ under such systems?

4. What are the conditions underlying private competitive markets? Why is "noncollusion" a necessary condition for the existence of free competition in markets?

5. What is a marginal private benefit curve, and why is it equivalent to a demand curve for a good or service? What is a marginal private cost curve, and why is it equivalent to a supply curve for a good or service?

6. Explain clearly why economic efficiency (without third-party effects) occurs when the marginal private benefits from producing a good equal the marginal private costs of producing that good. Is this equivalent to saying that economic efficiency occurs when the *sum* of producer and consumer surplus is maximized? Why?

7. What are some of the roles of government in the U.S. economy?

8. What is an "externality"? Does cigar smoking on a crowded bus create an externality? Explain.

9. What is a public good? Explain whether or not the following items fit the definition of a public good: national defense, education, cable television.

10. Explain some of the differences between private choices and public choices. Why is a "vote" for a hamburger different from your vote for your congressional representative or city councilmember?

11. Are voters "myopic" or shortsighted in permitting politicians to pursue their own interests? What does it mean to be "rationally uninformed" or "rationally ignorant"?

12. Explain the process by which special interests might be able to take over the political apparatus for their own gain and against economic efficiency or the "general welfare."

13. How might you explain the desires for "campaign finance reform" on the part of the voters and the (successful) resistance on the part of the politicians to such reforms?

WORKING WITH THE WEB

1. As explained in this chapter of the text, economic efficiency in a market system depends on the assignment of property rights. There is some debate surrounding the question of who holds the property rights of Leonardo Da Vinci's famous painting, *The Last Supper*. Go to www.mises.org and select "Daily Articles." Next, select June 1999 and select the article "Who Owns Art?" Read the article. What is the nature of the property rights dispute, and what is Machan's point?

2. The dominance of interest groups is pervasive in contemporary society. Ekelund and Tollison discuss the role of interest groups and their attempts to influence legislation as well as the role of lobbyists and PACs. Go to http://www.opensecrets.org/lobbyists/98lookup.htm. Select "Agriculture" in the industry overview search box. For January–June 1998 (or the current year), what was the level of spending on lobbying in the agriculture industry? Return to the search page and select "Health." For the same period, what was the total lobbyist spending for the health industry? Return to the search page once more and select "Other" for the industry. Here, note the level of spending on education for the same six-month period in 1998 is $14,007,762. Using the theory of interest groups presented in the text, why do you think the level of spending in both the agriculture and health industries far outweighs the level of lobbyist spending in education? Is such spending efficient from a market perspective?

Adam Smith

POINT

Karl Marx

Adam Smith and Karl Marx: Markets and Society

COUNTERPOINT

Adam Smith, one of the most important figures in the history of economics, actually began his career as a lecturer in moral philosophy at Scotland's Glasgow College in 1751. Moral philosophy in Smith's time encompassed a wide range of topics, including natural theology, ethics, jurisprudence, and economics. In 1776, Smith published *An Inquiry into the Nature and Causes of the Wealth of Nations,* known usually by the shorter title *Wealth of Nations.* The book won much attention from scholars of the day, and it brought together most of what was then known about the workings of the market system.

Smith was born in Kirkcaldy on the east coast of Scotland in 1723 and lived most of his life in his native country. Although known for his brilliant lectures (and for his many eccentricities), Smith did not devote his entire career to teaching. In 1778, he accepted a well-paying job as commissioner of Scottish customs, a post at which he remained until his death in 1790.

Karl Marx "looked like a revolutionary," writes Robert Heilbroner in *The Worldly Philosophers.* "He was stocky and powerfully built and rather glowering in expression with a formidable beard. He was not an orderly man; his home was a dusty mass of papers piled in careless disarray in the midst of which Marx himself, slovenly dressed, padded about in an eye-stinging haze of tobacco smoke."[a]

Marx wrote in response to the miseries of the European working class during the Industrial Revolution of the late eighteenth and nineteenth centuries. Coauthor with Friedrich Engels of the *Communist Manifesto,* which predicted the inevitable downfall of capitalism and the triumph of communism, Marx spent most of his life in difficult circumstances. His activities as a radical in the communist movement caused his exile from his native Germany as well as from Belgium and France. In 1849, a year after the publication of the *Manifesto,* he settled in London, where he and his family survived through the benevolence of Engels and where Marx researched and wrote *Das Kapital,* a theory and history of capitalism and its ills. Marx died in 1883 in London.

The "Invisible Hand"

Smith's views of the free-market system are summarized in a passage from the *Wealth of Nations,* in which

---

[a]Robert L. Heilbroner, *The Wordly Philosophers* (New York: Simon and Schuster, 1953), p. 131.

he writes that individuals pursuing their own self-interest are "led by an invisible hand to promote an end which was no part of [their] intention."[b] Smith believed that by freely exchanging goods and services across markets, individuals contribute to the public good—the aggregate wealth of society—even though they act from purely self-interested motives. In other words, markets cause individuals to benefit others when they intend only to benefit themselves.

To Smith, voluntary market exchange coordinated the decisions of consumers and producers and generated economic progress. Producers compete with one another to satisfy consumers with the most appropriate and cheapest goods and services, simply because they maximize their profits by doing so. Markets coordinate supply and demand by way of the price system. Consumers express their preferences in their decisions about what to buy; producers attract customers by producing goods at the least cost. In this system of coordination without command, individuals pursuing their own interests are led "as if by an invisible hand" to mesh their interests with those of other individuals trading across markets.

Smith was not opposed to government, but argued that its proper role in society was to provide a legal framework—police and courts—within which the market could operate, as well as to provide certain other services (including national defense, highways, and education) that the market itself would either not supply or would tend to supply in inadequate amounts. Smith also felt that government should provide welfare services for the poor. But he strongly believed that government could best assist the market economy achieve growth by stepping out of the way—that is, by not regulating and by not granting monopoly privileges to favored groups.

In Smith's view, income was distributed in a market economy by the production of wealth. An individual's income was a strict function of the value of his or her output. Smith did not feel that income inequality by itself was unfair, because he believed that anyone can increase his or her income in a free market by serving the consumers in a new, better, or faster way.

The "Anarchy of Production"

In *Das Kapital*, Karl Marx argued that Smith's writing represented merely the interests of the ruling capitalist class. To Marx, the market process was a system of exploitation by which owners of capital robbed their employees by paying them wages less than the worth of their labor (a situation he termed the *alienation of labor*).

The alternative social system that Marx thought would eliminate this exploitation and at the same time greatly increase the efficiency of production was a "general organization of the labor of society. . .[that] would turn all society into one immense factory."[c] He viewed the market economy as one of general disorganization. Its main feature was "the anarchy of production," where producers overproduced and consumers were forced to accept goods they neither wanted nor needed.

In Marx's view, Smith's "invisible hand" was a euphemism for describing the economic system in which "chance and caprice have full play in distributing the producers and their means of production among the various branches of industry…[T]he division of labour within the society [the theme of much of Smith's *Wealth of Nations*] brings into contact independent commodity-producers, who acknowledge no other authority but that of competition, of the coercion exerted by the pressure of their mutual interests…[T]he same bourgeois mind which praises division of labour in the workshop [as a conscious organization that increases productivity] denounces with equal vigour every conscious attempt to socially control and regulate the process of production."[d] Only the central planning of economic activity by society (government), which owned all means of production, could coordinate the needs of consumers and producers and eliminate the wastefulness of capitalism. To Marx, it was nonsense to describe the market as organized economic activity, because there was no organizer. Coordination of economic activity requires conscious, centralized control.

---

[b]Adam Smith, *An Inquiry into the Nature and Causes of the Wealth of Nations,* ed. Edwin Cannan (1776; reprint, New York: Modern Library, 1937), p. 423.

[c]Karl Marx, *Das Kapital,* ed. Max Eastman (1867; reprint, New York: Modern Library, 1932), p. 83.
[d]Marx, *Das Kapital,* p. 83.

While Smith described the emerging market economy of his day and offered reforms, Marx offered a vision of economic organization that did not exist at the time he wrote but that he maintained was the inevitable wave of the future. In a sense he was proven correct. Followers of the teachings of Marx and his admirer Lenin (who filled in many details of what a central planning system would look like in practice) imposed avowedly Marxist-socialist, centrally planned economies on many countries, including Russia and China, in the first half of the twentieth century. However, without exception, the centrally planned economies seemed to function poorly—providing low per capita income and poor rates of economic growth—relative to the modern versions of the capitalist economies whose central principle of market organization was so clearly seen by Smith.

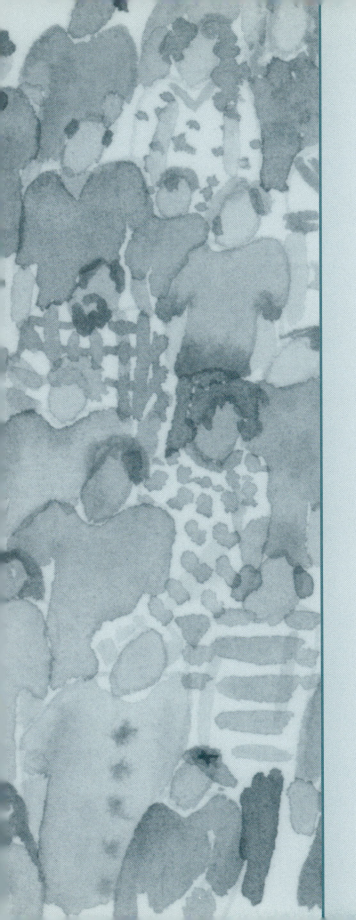

PART TWO

The Architecture of Private Markets

2

Elasticity

S tudying the laws of supply and demand helps economists organize their thoughts about real-world problems. But it is not enough to understand that an inverse relation exists between price and quantity demanded or that a decrease in supply causes price to rise in a market. For supply and demand theory to explain and predict economic events, economists must be able to say how much the quantity demanded or supplied of a product will change after a price change. The laws of supply and demand tell us nothing about how responsive quantity demanded or quantity supplied is to a price change. But if, for example, you owned a fast-food restaurant, you would be very interested to know how responsive your customers would be to a hamburger price discount. The law of demand tells you that you would sell more hamburgers, but it does not tell you how many more. Or, if you worked for a legislator and she asked you how an excise tax increase would affect cigarette smoking (and how much revenue the tax would raise), you would have to find out how responsive cigarette sales would be to the proposed tax.

Economics does provide a means of determining how many more (or less) goods and services will be bought when prices or other factors change: the application of the concept of **elasticity**. When you finish Chapter 5 you should understand

- the idea of elasticity and how elasticity is measured.
- how to apply the idea of elasticity to economic events.
- what factors determine elasticity of demand and supply.
- how time affects the elasticity of demand.

Elasticity

A measure of the relative responsiveness of one variable to a change in another variable; the percentage change in a dependent variable divided by the percentage change in the independent variable.

THE CONCEPT OF ELASTICITY

You are contemplating two business alternatives: buying a gourmet delicatessen or opening a new travel agency. Best estimates tell you that consumers' incomes are expected to rise by 5 percent per year over the next eight years. On these grounds, which business should you enter? By what percent will an increase in consumers' incomes increase the amounts of gourmet foods purchased compared with the amounts of travel and leisure services consumed?

To answer these questions we must gauge the relative responsiveness of decision makers—consumers—to changes in price or income, or the elasticity. Elasticity is calculated as the ratio of the percent change in some effect (quantity demanded of a good or service) to the percent change in the cause (price change, income change, or any other change). You should keep in mind that while elasticity most often relates changes in demand to changes in price or income, the calculation may be applied to *any* cause-and-effect relationship. Elasticity is *always* a percent change divided by a percent change, resulting in a number that is independent of any absolute change in a cause or an effect.

PRICE ELASTICITY OF DEMAND

Elasticity, as the examples of fast food or excise taxes suggest, is a general and wide-ranging concept with many applications. The most common and important applications relate to the demand curve.

Formulation of Price Elasticity of Demand

Price elasticity of demand

A measure of buyers' relative responsiveness to a price change; the percentage change in quantity demanded divided by the percentage change in price.

The formal measurement of demand elasticity, like the generalized concept itself, is simple and straightforward. **Price elasticity of demand** is the percent change in quantity demanded divided by the percent change in price:

$$\varepsilon_d \; = \; \text{price elasticity of demand coefficient} \; = \; \frac{\% \text{ change in quantity demanded}}{\% \text{ change in price}}.$$

Price elasticity of demand is expressed as a number. In actual calculation, the demand elasticity coefficient will always be negative, owing to the inverse relation between price and quantity demanded (the law of demand). If price goes up, quantity demanded for a good or service goes down, and vice versa. Unless otherwise noted, this point is irrelevant to the interpretation of elasticity. We will accordingly eliminate use of a negative sign before the demand elasticity coefficient. If, for example, a 10 percent reduction in the price of jogging shoes causes a 15 percent increase in the quantity of jogging shoes demanded, then the ratio, called the **demand elasticity coefficient**, ε_d, is

Demand elasticity coefficient

The numerical representation of the price elasticity of demand:
$\varepsilon_d = (\Delta Q/Q) \div (\Delta P/P)$.

$$\frac{15\%}{10\%} = 1.5.$$

This elasticity coefficient or ratio, 1.5, and the percent changes in price and quantity demanded from which it was calculated are independent of the absolute prices and quantities of jogging shoes. If a 10 percent rise in the price of jogging shoes causes a 2 percent decline in sales, the price elasticity coefficient is calculated in the same way:

$$\frac{2\%}{10\%} = 0.2.$$

The price elasticity of demand coefficient (or, more simply put, the demand elasticity coefficient) always measures consumers' responsiveness, in terms of purchases, to a percent change in price.

Elastic, Inelastic, and Unit Elastic Demand

Elastic demand

A situation in which buyers are relatively responsive to price changes; the percent change in quantity demanded is greater than the percent change in price: $\varepsilon_d > 1$.

Unit elasticity of demand

A condition where the percent change in quantity demanded is equal to the percent change in price: $\varepsilon_d = 1$.

Inelastic demand

A situation in which buyers are relatively unresponsive to price changes; the percent change in quantity demanded is less than the percent change in price: $\varepsilon_d < 1$.

The size of the elasticity coefficient is important because it measures the relative consumer responsiveness to price changes. If the number obtained from the elasticity calculation is greater than 1.0, we say that demand is **elastic**; the percent change in quantity demanded is greater than the percent change in price. The larger the demand elasticity coefficient is above 1.0, the more elastic demand is said to be. (*Remember*: Price elasticity of demand measures the *relative* response of quantity demanded to a price change, the percent change in quantity demanded caused by some percent change in price.)

Unit elasticity of demand means that the elasticity coefficient equals 1. In this case, a given percent change in price is exactly matched by the percent change in quantity demanded. If, for example, a 2 percent increase in the price of candy bars causes a 2 percent reduction in purchases, demand would be of unit elasticity. The same would be said if an 8 percent decrease in the price of Volkswagens caused an 8 percent increase in quantity demanded.

An **inelastic demand** coefficient is a number less than 1, meaning that a percent change in quantity demanded is less than the percent change in price that caused the change in quantity. If the price of salt increases by 5 percent and the quantity demanded decreases by 2.5 percent, the demand elasticity coefficient would be 0.5, placing it in the inelastic category.

The various categories of price elasticity of demand can be shown with demand curves. Figure 5.1 depicts three responses to a 20 percent increase in pizza prices over a given time period in a small college town. In Figure 5.1a, a 20 percent increase in price causes a 5 percent reduction in quantity demanded. This means that pizza consumers are not very responsive to a change in price; since $\varepsilon_d = 0.25$, which is less than 1, demand is inelastic. In Figure 5.1b, a 20 percent increase in pizza price reduces pizza consumption by exactly 20 percent, meaning that demand is of unit elasticity: $\varepsilon_d = 1$. Figure 5.1c shows an elastic demand—a 20 percent price increase causes a 50 percent reduction in the quantity of pizzas demanded, so $\varepsilon_d = 2.5$ (greater than 1).

The elasticity of two special forms of the demand curve is also of interest in analyzing economic problems. Figure 5.2 shows a completely inelastic curve and a completely elastic demand curve. Total or complete price inelasticity means that consumers are not responsive at all to price changes, a condition that is seldom met in the real world. Increases or decreases in price leave quantity demanded unchanged—the demand curve is vertical, as in Figure 5.2a. One might think of the demand for addictive drugs—at least for certain price ranges and certain levels of use—as being completely inelastic. The price elasticity of demand coefficient is zero along such a curve: $\varepsilon_d = 0$.

A completely elastic demand curve is shown in Figure 5.2b. Individual businesses in competitive markets view the demand for their products as totally elastic. In a competitive market, producers are so numerous that they are unable

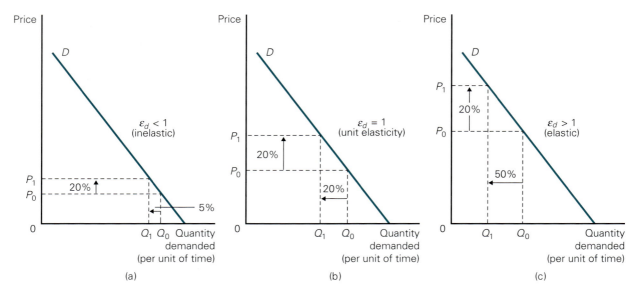

FIGURE 5.1

Price Elasticity of Demand

(a) The percent reduction in quantity demanded (from Q_0 to Q_1, 5%) is less than the per-cent increase in price (from P_0 to P_1, 20%). Demand is inelastic: $\varepsilon_d < 1$. (b) The percent reduction in quantity demanded equals the percent increase in price. Demand is unit elastic: $\varepsilon_d = 1$. (c) The percent reduction in quantity demanded is larger than the percent increase in price. Demand is elastic: $\varepsilon_d > 1$. The same relations hold for reductions in price or increases in quantity demanded.

to affect prices. The huge number of wheat farmers in the United States, for example, prohibits a single small producer from affecting the market price by altering production. If the wheat farmer raises his or her price by even a small amount, buyers will not purchase any of the farmer's production. Buyers can get all the wheat they want at the (lower) prevailing market price. In these com-petitive circumstances, a single wheat farmer faces an infinitely elastic demand curve ($\varepsilon_d = \varepsilon$). Quantity demanded is supersensitive to price increases. The farmer can sell as much or as little as he or she desires at the market price, but none at any higher price.

Elasticity Along the Demand Curve

Every negatively sloped demand curve will, in general, contain portions that are elastic, unit elastic, and inelastic. The elasticity coefficient will vary along straight (linear) and curving (nonlinear) demand curves. To verify this fact, consider the simple elasticity equation once more:

$$\varepsilon_d = \frac{\% \text{ change in quantity demanded}}{\% \text{ change in price}}.$$

FIGURE 5.2

Demand Curves May Be Totally Inelastic or Totally Elastic

(a) Quantity demanded is unresponsive to price changes (totally inelastic). (b) Quantity demanded is completely responsive to price changes (totally elastic); a small increase in price will cause quantity demanded to disappear. Perfectly competitive suppliers view the demand for their output as totally elastic.

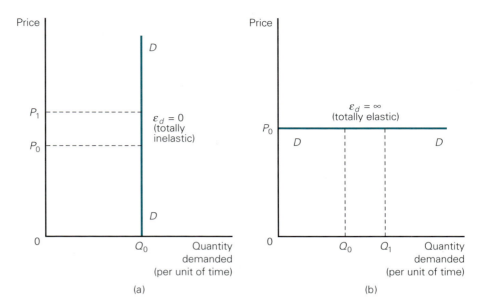

In the numerator, the percent change in quantity demanded is determined by dividing the change in quantity demanded by the initial quantity demanded. In the denominator, the percent change in price is determined by dividing the change in price by the initial price. This can be represented algebraically as follows:

$$\varepsilon_d = \frac{\Delta Q/Q}{\Delta P/P},$$

where Q stands for quantity and P stands for price. (The symbol Δ means "the change in.") The simple elasticity equation can also be written this way:

$$\varepsilon_d = \frac{\Delta Q}{Q} \times \frac{P}{\Delta P}.$$

The change in quantity demanded (ΔQ) can be written $Q_2 - Q_1$, where Q_2 is the new quantity demanded and Q_1 is the initial quantity demanded. Similarly, the change in price can be written $P_2 - P_1$, where P_2 is the new price and P_1 is the initial price. Therefore, substituting $Q_2 - Q_1$ for ΔQ and $P_2 - P_1$ for ΔP in the last equation yields

$$\varepsilon_d = \frac{Q_2 - Q_1}{Q_1} \times \frac{P_1}{P_2 - P_1}.$$

This is the form of the simple elasticity equation that we will use to make actual calculations.

Table 5.1 and Figure 5.3 show the market demand function—or price-quantity pairs—that constitutes the demand schedule for paperback books. Suppose that the price of paperbacks declines from $7 to $6. Quantity demanded would increase from 120 to 160 paperbacks. How would elasticity be calculated?

TABLE 5.1

Market Demand Schedule for Paperback Books

Price of Paperback Books (dollars)	Quantity Demanded (per month)
10	0
9	40
8	80
7	120
6	160
5	200
4	240
3	280
2	320
1	360

Returning to our simple formula, we can calculate the elasticity across this price range as follows:

$$\varepsilon_d = \frac{Q_2 - Q_1}{Q_1} \times \frac{P_1}{P_2 - P_1}$$

$$= \frac{160 - 120}{120} \times \frac{\$7.00}{\$6.00 - \$7.00}$$

$$= \frac{40}{120} \times \frac{7.00}{-1.00}$$

$$= -2.33.$$

The elasticity coefficient is −2.33, which means that demand is elastic over this range of prices. Consumers are responsive to a price reduction from $7 to $6.

Now assume that paperbacks are selling at $4 and that the price is reduced to $3:

$$\varepsilon_d = \frac{Q_2 - Q_1}{Q_1} \times \frac{P_1}{P_2 - P_1}$$

$$= \frac{280 - 240}{240} \times \frac{\$4.00}{\$3.00 - \$4.00}$$

$$= -0.67.$$

The coefficient indicates that demand is inelastic for a decline in price over the price range from $4 to $3. Consumers are far more responsive to a one-dollar price reduction from $7 to $6 than they are to a one-dollar price reduction from $4 to $3.[1]

The fact that elasticity changes at different points along demand curves suggests another important difficulty in accurately calculating elasticity. Since elasticity varies at all points along the demand curve, it also varies along the arc—for

---

[1] Note that the elasticity coefficient is always a negative number. In subsequent calculations we drop the negative sign as being understood.

FIGURE 5.3

Differing Elasticities Along a Market Demand Curve

The elasticity of demand is different between various points along a downward-sloping demand curve. If prices fall by $1 between A and B, demand is elastic. If prices fall by $1 between C and D, demand is inelastic.

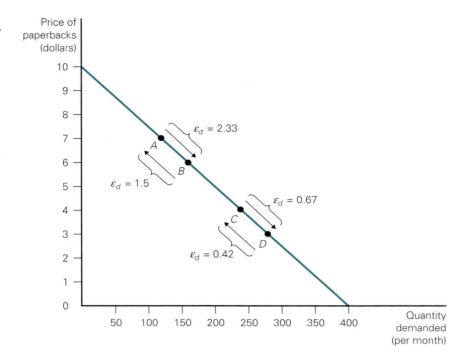

Arc elasticity

A measure of the average elasticity between two points on the demand curve.

example, along length AB or CD in Figure 5.3. As shown in Figure 5.3, we will even get a different elasticity coefficient for a price *increase* from $3 to $4 (0.42) than we will get for a price *decrease* from $4 to $3 (0.67).

One compromise solution to the problem of determining the exact elasticity of demand over such a price range is to find the **arc elasticity**, or the average elasticity within the arc between two price–quantity combinations. To calculate the arc elasticity in the $3 to $4 price range for paperbacks, the prices $3 and $4 and the quantities 240 and 280 are given equal weight. To express the formula algebraically, we can let Q_0 represent one quantity and Q_1 represent the other quantity. The price at Q_1 is P_1; the price at Q_0 is P_0. The average elasticity of their relation can then be calculated as follows:

$$\varepsilon_d = \frac{Q_1 - Q_0}{(Q_1 + Q_0)/2} \div \frac{P_1 - P_0}{(P_1 + P_0)/2}$$

$$= \frac{Q_1 - Q_0}{Q_1 + Q_0} \times \frac{P_1 + P_0}{P_1 - P_0}$$

$$= \frac{280 - 240}{280 + 240} \times \frac{\$3.00 + \$4.00}{\$3.00 - \$4.00}$$

$$= 0.53.$$

The average elasticity coefficient is *naturally* between the coefficients calculated for a price increase and for a price decrease.

Relation of Demand Elasticity to Expenditures and Receipts

It is often necessary to estimate the effect of a proposed increase or decrease in price on total revenue—how much, for instance, a fast-food chain will make (or lose) by offering a half-price sale on hamburgers. Estimates of elasticity from previous experience can make such projections possible. Or, if the price change and consumer response have already occurred, we can look at what happened to determine the elasticity of demand by examining either what customers have spent for a good or what businesses have received for it.

Common sense tells us that an industry's revenues are the same as consumers' expenditures for the industry's product. The number of items bought by all consumers multiplied by the price paid for each item is the same as the number of items sold by all producers multiplied by the average price charged for the items. Elasticity, therefore, is related both to **total expenditures** of customers and to **total revenues**, or receipts, of businesses.

To understand how elasticity is related to consumer expenditures, we consider the case of a single customer's purchases of paperback books. Let's call our consumer Anna. Table 5.2 shows Anna's demand and total expenditures (quantity times price) for paperbacks, and Figure 5.4 displays her demand curve with the associated elasticities. Anna's total expenditures on paperbacks begin to rise as the price of paperbacks falls below $10. As the price falls to $9, $7, and $5, Anna's quantity demanded *and* total expenditures on paperbacks rise. For decreases in price, if elasticity is greater than 1, total expenditures will increase. Why? When demand is elas-

Total expenditures

The total amount spent by consumers on a good or service; calculated as equilibrium price times equilibrium quantity.

Total revenues

Total receipts of businesses; always equal to total expenditures by consumers.

TABLE 5.2

Elasticity and Consumer Expenditures

The average elasticity of demand is greater at higher prices and falls as price falls. At the midpoint (near $5), the elasticity is equal to 1 and total expenditures are at a maximum.

Price of Paperbacks (dollars)	Quantity Demanded (per month)	Total Expenditure	Average Elasticity of Demand
10	0	0	
			} ··············· 19
9	1	9	
			} ··············· 5.66
8	2	16	
			} ··············· 3
7	3	21	
			} ··············· 1.85
6	4	24	
			} ··············· 1.22
5	5	25	
			} ··············· 0.81
4	6	24	
			} ··············· 0.53
3	7	21	
			} ··············· 0.33
2	8	16	
			} ··············· 0.17
1	9	9	
			} ··············· 0.05
0	10	0	

FIGURE 5.4

An Individual's Elasticity of Demand

The elasticity of demand varies along a downward-sloping demand curve. As price falls, the elasticity falls.

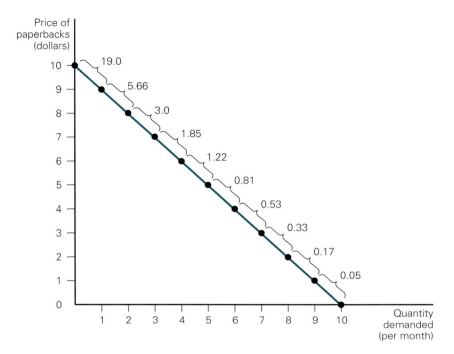

tic, the percent change in quantity demanded dominates (is larger than) the percent change in price. But as price is reduced below $5, Anna's total expenditures begin to decline, even though her consumption of paperbacks continues to increase. In the price range in which demand is inelastic (a coefficient of less than 1), total expenditures decrease as price falls. Here the percent decline in price dominates the percent increase in quantity, and total expenditures fall. *In other words, prices and total expenditures change in the same direction if demand is inelastic.*

The same relation between price and total expenditures is found when prices increase. If demand is inelastic, expenditures rise as prices increase from some low level, say $2, to a new level or over a range. If demand is elastic for that price range, total expenditures actually fall as prices increase. At some price–quantity combination, demand is unit elastic ($\varepsilon_d = 1$). For Anna in Figure 5.4, unit elasticity of demand occurs around $5, when her total expenditures for paperbacks will remain constant whether price is increasing or decreasing by some miniscule amount. At this point Anna's expenditures are at a maximum, as shown in Table 5.2.

If total expenditures are known, the relations between the direction of the price changes and total expenditures can be used as an informal method for determining elasticity, though not of calculating elasticity coefficients. The relations between the direction of the price change, the elasticity, and total expenditures (or revenues) are summarized in Figure 5.5. As the price falls from P_1, where consumption of the good is zero, to P_2, the midpoint on the demand curve, demand is elastic; total expenditures and, therefore, total receipts are rising. At P_2, price elasticity of demand is unitary, and total receipts and expenditures remain constant as the price rises or falls around this price. As the price falls below price P_2 (where quantity Q_2 is demanded), the demand elasticity coefficient falls below 1. Below P_2, total expenditures and receipts fall and demand is inelastic, becoming more inelastic as the price approaches zero.

FIGURE 5.5

Total Expenditures and Total Receipts Along a Demand Curve

As the price falls ($P\downarrow$) along the demand curve, both total receipts (TR) and total expenditures (TE) rise, indicating that elasticity is greater than 1. At the point of unit elasticity, TE and TR remain constant. As the price falls from the midpoint, TE and TR decline owing to inelasticity of demand. Rising price ($P\uparrow$) has the opposite effects on expenditures and receipts.

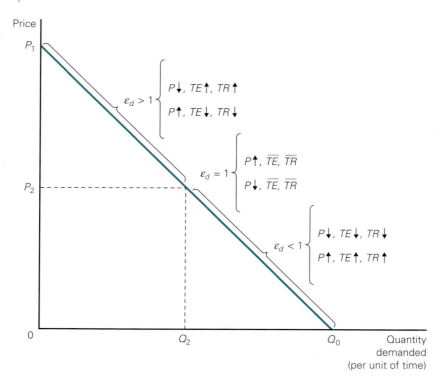

Armed only with this information, you are now in a position to teach yourself a simple economic lesson. Suppose you owned the business or product represented by the demand curve in Figure 5.5. Assuming you have no costs of production, what price would you set? Clearly, if you are interested in maximizing your revenues, you would set price at P_2, because that is the point where total expenditures on the product are greatest. In this simple case, elasticity is a useful guide to rational behavior.

The major point to remember is that elasticity varies along any ordinary demand curve. It makes no sense to say, for instance, that salt is an inelastically demanded commodity without reference to some price range. The demand for salt may be elastic over some price range and inelastic over another. In the next section we consider what makes the demand elasticity coefficient greater than, equal to, or less than 1 and what factors determine consumer responses to price changes. (See the Focus "How to Tell Who Your Friends Are" for an application of elasticity.)

DETERMINANTS OF PRICE ELASTICITY OF DEMAND

There are three major determinants of price elasticity: (1) the number and availability of substitutes, (2) the size and importance of the item in the consumer's budget, and (3) the time period involved. Since all three factors interact, the condition of other things being equal must be invoked to determine the specific effect of any one factor.

FOCUS

How to Tell Who Your Friends Are

Elasticity is a general measure of the responsiveness of one thing relative to another. The concept of elasticity is more than an intellectual device to examine strictly economic data, however. It has many practical applications, including, among others, providing a means of classifying relationships.

Friendship can be interpreted from an economic perspective. A "good friend" is someone who has a low price elasticity of demand for your companionship. In other words, the person in question desires your company pretty much independently of what it costs him or her. You can raise the "price" of your friendship to a friend by behaving badly—being late for dates, being loud and obnoxious, grinding your teeth, not keeping your word, lying, and so on. But your friend will not desert you at the higher "price." The demand for your friendship is inelastic; consumption of your friendship does not change much when its price rises.

Other people will not pass the friendship test. Their demand for your companionship will be very elastic. If things get even slightly more difficult, they will desert you. Perhaps there are larger numbers of substitutes for your friendship available.

Figure 5.6 illustrates this phenomenon. The "price of friendship" on the vertical axis is what it costs an individual to be your friend—Are you easy to get along with? Are you fun? Are you a good conversationalist? Are you trustworthy? Higher or rising prices mean that being your friend becomes more costly in terms of your behavior. The quantity of friendship on the horizontal axis may be thought of as the amount of time you spend with a friend. The two demand curves in Figure 5.6 illustrate two types of behavior. The steeper demand curve D_F is relatively less elastic than D_{NF} (NF = no friend). Demand curve D_F represents the behavior of someone who is a "true friend." At high prices or low, that person has a fairly constant desire to be around you. Demand curve D_{NF} proxies a "fickle friend." At a slightly higher price (suppose you get sick), the demand for your company is radically reduced. Friendship is an inelastic demand curve for you; a relatively higher elasticity of demand implies a weaker concern.

Think of your own personal relationships. Do you know of people who have a high elasticity of demand for you? How does their behavior indicate this—missed phone calls, only call when they need something, always insisting on doing what they want to do? And what about your good friends? Need we say more? Indeed, is not "love" a relatively inelastic demand curve?

FIGURE 5.6

Demand Curves for Friendship

Good friends express demand curves of relatively lesser elasticity for your friendship. Poorer friends show more elasticity of demand.

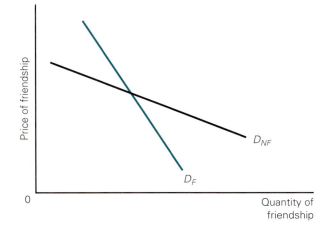

Number and Availability of Substitutes

By far the most important predictor of demand elasticity is the ability of consumers to find good substitute products. If the price of one brand of toothpaste rises, many consumers may respond by switching to a different brand. This substitution will happen only when alternatives are available.

Food is a vital commodity—everyone must eat. Elasticity of demand for nutrients in general is probably very low over relevant price ranges. For most of us, there is no substitute for food. But it is possible to substitute between kinds of food. While the demand for food as a whole tends to be inelastic, the consumer may substitute between broad food groups such as meat and seafood and also between foods within the broad groups. Consumers of meat, for instance, have a wide choice of substitutes, such as chicken, beef, pork, duck, quail, or alligator. Consumers are far more sensitive to changes in the price of beef when other substitutes are available. Elasticity of demand for meat itself is lower than that for *kinds* of meat over the same price ranges.

What about the elasticity of demand for beef versus beef products such as hamburger, sirloin steak, oxtails, and so on? The consumer can substitute among beef products. When the price of sirloin rises relative to that for hamburger, the consumer can substitute hamburger for sirloin. The elasticity of demand for hamburger is therefore higher than the elasticity of demand for meat. By now, the general rule should be apparent: The broader the product or service group, the lower the elasticity, because there are fewer possibilities for substitution. We expect the elasticity of demand for Budweiser beer to be more elastic than the demand for beer, just as the demand for a Ford or Mercedes-Benz is more elastic than the demand for automobiles. Ordinarily, the wider the selection and substitutability of similar products and services, the larger the elasticity of demand for those products.

The Importance of Being Unimportant

The size of the total expenditure within the consumer's budget is another determinant of elasticity. Ordinarily, the smaller the item in the consumer's budget, the less elastic the consumer's demand for the item will be over some price ranges. A salt user may be insensitive to price increases in salt simply because expenses for salt are a small part of his or her budget. If the price of salt were to rise too high, the user might substitute alternatives, such as artificial salt or lemon juice. Thus, in calculating elasticity it is important to analyze both substitutability and the size of the item in the consumer's budget.

The condition of other things being equal aids our understanding of elasticity determinants. Given some constant degree of substitutability, the more unimportant the commodity is to a consumer—that is, the smaller the item in the consumer's budget—the lower demand elasticity will be. This indicates that tastes, substitutability, and importance of the commodity in the consumer's budget must all be examined in gauging the demand elasticity of products over given price ranges.

Time and Elasticity of Demand

Time is the final factor affecting the elasticity of demand. We alluded to this at the beginning of the chapter, but now we expand on the effects of time.

Let's assume a local market for tennis rackets is represented in Figure 5.7. (For simplicity, we may neglect the supply function.) Assume that the initial price is P_0

FIGURE 5.7

Elasticity of Demand over Time

As time goes by, a given price change (ΔP) may be associated with larger and larger changes in quantity demanded (ΔQ). Since the percent change in quantity demanded grows over time, the elasticity of demand grows as well.

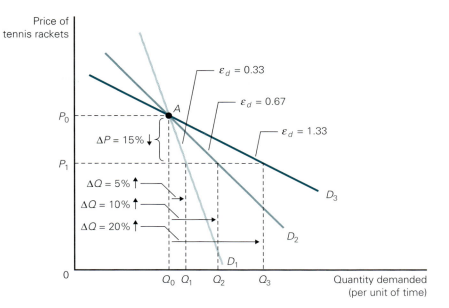

and the initial quantity demanded is Q_0. What happens to elasticity of demand over time if tennis rackets go on sale—that is, if the price falls to P_1 per unit, a 15 percent decline?

The answer depends on how long it takes for consumers and potential consumers to adjust to the new price. If the sale is totally unpublicized, there may be no immediate reaction to the new price. As consumers gain information, however, demand increases. Thus, we may think of the demand curve as rotating around a point (A in Figure 5.7) as news of the sale becomes more widespread. Greater quantities (Q_1, Q_2, and so on) will be sold *through time* at the new lower price. For the given price change, the elasticity of demand will be different at different times—that is, it will depend on whether it is calculated on the first day of the sale ($\varepsilon_d = 0.33$) or one week ($\varepsilon_d = 0.67$) or one month later ($\varepsilon_d = 1.33$). Percent changes in quantity demanded are greater as time passes, meaning that the demand elasticity coefficient is larger and larger (up to some limit). The general rule holds: Given quality and consumer preferences, elasticity of demand increases the longer any given price change is in effect.

The time period of adjustment is a crucial factor in calculating or estimating all types of actual elasticities. Not only do tastes, substitutability, and size within the consumer's budget affect elasticity, but the ability of consumers to recognize and adjust to changes also plays an important part.

OTHER APPLICATIONS OF ELASTICITY OF DEMAND

The concept of elasticity is not restricted to price elasticity of demand. In general, we can calculate an elasticity of any dependent variable (effect) to a change in any independent variable (cause). We will briefly consider two other important applications of this versatile and useful economic concept: income elasticity of demand and cross elasticity of demand.

Income Elasticity of Demand

As you will recall from Chapter 3, a consumer's income is an important determinant of the demand for goods and services. It is often very informative to inquire about consumers' **income elasticity of demand**. Producers of all kinds are interested in the magnitude of consumption changes as incomes rise or in consumption habits within various income groups. Budget data compiled by the government and other sources can be used to calculate recent and historical trends in changing consumption patterns as incomes change.

The mechanics of income elasticity of demand are identical to those involved in the calculation of price elasticity; only the independent variable changes. With price held constant, income elasticity is the percent change in quantity demanded resulting from (divided by) a given percent change in income. It is expressed as ε_y, with Y representing income:

$$\varepsilon_y = \frac{\% \text{ change in consumption of a good}}{\% \text{ change in income}} = \frac{\Delta Q}{Q} \div \frac{\Delta Y}{Y}$$

or

$$\varepsilon_y = \frac{Q_2 - Q_1}{Q_1} \div \frac{Y_2 - Y_1}{Y_1}.$$

The income elasticity coefficient, ε_y, may be positive or negative, depending on whether the good is normal or inferior. (Recall from Chapter 3 that a good is normal if an increase in income results in greater consumption and inferior if an increase in income results in a reduction in product consumption.) When applying the income elasticity formula, if ε_y is greater than zero, the good is normal; if ε_y is less than zero, the good is inferior.

If the elasticity coefficient ε_y is greater than 1, demand (or consumption) is said to be income elastic; if ε_y is less than 1, the product is income inelastic; and if ε_y equals 1, the good is unit elastic. Suppose that income in the United States rose by 10 percent in 2000 and that the quantity of new automobiles consumed over the year increased by 8 percent. (New automobiles are a normal good; their consumption increases along with the increase in income.) The simple computation for income elasticity is

$$\varepsilon_y = \frac{8\%}{10\%} = 0.8.$$

The income elasticity of demand for automobiles in this hypothetical calculation is less than 1 but greater than zero. What does this mean for the auto industry? Other things being equal (such as price and tastes), the demand for automobiles will rise, but at a slower pace than income. In this example, cars are a normal good, but are income inelastic. This fact is important to groups such as auto manufacturers, investors, boat dealers, and airlines.

Income elasticity for a particular good may be determined for any individual consumer or for consumers as a group. The practical importance of this calculation is undeniable. An individual deciding between opening a gourmet food shop and a travel agency during a period of rapidly rising income would be very interested to know, for example, that income elasticity for gourmet foods is perhaps 0.2, while the same coefficient for Mediterranean vacations is 6.2. However, to achieve accuracy in actual use, all other factors, such as substitutability and the price of the product, must be kept constant. If these factors vary, as they often do in the real

FOCUS

Elasticity and Your World

The concept of elasticity is critically important in everyday decisions taken by businesses, politicians, and you. Elasticity is not some abstract issue. It becomes important almost every time the question of "how much" is asked. Consider the following examples:

Politicians acting through some state or federal legislature decide to crack down on teen smoking. The law of supply, which we developed in Chapters 3 and 4, tells us that new taxes will raise the price of cigarettes, and the law of demand tells us that this increase in prices causes a reduction in all smoking, including teen smoking. If the purpose of the tax is to reduce teen smoking, it is important to know whether teen smoking will fall by a large or a small amount from the tax. (Since cigarette smoking competes with other goods, including illegal substances like marijuana, it would also be interesting to know whether such other items will be substituted for cigarettes.) If demand is highly elastic with respect to an increase in price, the policy goal of reduced teen smoking will be achieved. If not, the tax might raise revenue, but it will not achieve the desired objective.

Or consider this; you are contemplating two business alternatives: buying a gourmet delicatessen or opening a new travel agency. Best estimates tell you that consumers' incomes are expected to rise by 5 percent per year over the next eight years. On these grounds, which business should you enter? By what percent will an increase in consumers' incomes increase the amounts of gourmet foods purchased compared with the amounts of travel and leisure services consumed?

To answer these questions, the relative responsiveness of decision makers and consumers to changes in prices or income must be gauged. *Exact* measurements are not possible when estimating the *future* effects of price or income changes. Economists can, however, make calculations based on past experience in particular markets. If such estimates remain reliable, that is, if conditions do not change significantly, these calculations may be used to predict quantity changes caused by changes in price or income in the future. Large firms that develop pricing strategies often employ economists to do just that. The success of given policies of politicians and businesses thus depend on elasticity—on "how much" of a change may be expected, given some particular change in price or income.

---

world, their impact on consumption must be determined and integrated into the analysis. Some real world applications of elasticity concepts are discussed in the Focus "Elasticity and Your World."

Cross Elasticity of Demand

Cross elasticity of demand reveals the responsiveness of the quantity demanded of one good to a change in the price of another good. As such, a cross elasticity coefficient can define either substitute or complementary products or services. In more general terms, cross elasticity is an extremely useful economic tool for identifying groups of products whose demand functions are related. Cross elasticity is

Cross elasticity of demand
Measures buyers' relative responsiveness to a change in the price of one good in terms of the change in the quantity demanded of another good; the percent change in the quantity demanded of one good divided by the percent change in the price of another good.

calculated as the ratio of the percentage change in the quantity demanded of one good, A, to the percentage change in the price of another good, B, or

$$\varepsilon_c = \frac{\Delta Q_A}{Q_A} \div \frac{\Delta P_B}{P_B}.$$

Substitutes

Two goods whose cross elasticity of demand is positive; $\varepsilon_c > 0$.

If the price of one good rises and, other things being equal, the quantity demanded of another good increases, those products are **substitutes**. If Dorothy's demand for Bayer aspirin rises 85 percent following a 10 percent rise in the price of Bufferin, her cross elasticity of demand for aspirin is +8.5. The coefficient of cross elasticity of demand is calculated thus:

$$\varepsilon_c = \frac{\% \text{ change in the quantity demanded for Bayer}}{\% \text{ change in the price of Bufferin}} = \frac{85\%}{10\%} = 8.5.$$

For substitute commodities, the cross elasticity coefficient is positive because an increase in the price of one good causes an increase in the quantity demanded of the other. The larger the elasticity coefficient (in absolute terms), the more substitutable the products or services are.

Complements

Two goods whose cross elasticity of demand is negative; $\varepsilon_c < 0$.

Some items are complements in consumption—bacon and eggs; gasoline and automobiles; light bulbs, lamps, and electricity. Two goods are **complements** when an increase in the price of one results in a decrease in the quantity demanded of the other. A negative number is obtained for the cross elasticity coefficient for complementary goods because the increase in the price of one is always associated with a decrease in the quantity demanded for the other.

In calculating cross elasticity, therefore, a positive sign indicates that goods are substitutes and a negative sign indicates that they are complements. The absolute size of the coefficient, moreover, tells us the degree of substitutability or complementarity. A coefficient of −28.0 indicates a greater degree of complementarity than one of −4.0, for example.

ELASTICITY OF SUPPLY

Elasticity of supply

A measure of producers' or workers' relative responsiveness to price or wage changes; the percent change in quantity supplied divided by the percent change in the price or wage rate.

The versatile concept of elasticity, applied thus far only to demand, can also be applied to problems related to supply. **Elasticity of supply** is the degree of responsiveness of a supplier of goods or services to changes in the price the supplier receives for those goods or services.

A price elasticity of supply coefficient can be mechanically calculated in the same manner as all other elasticities. To determine the relation between a change in quantity supplied and a change in price, the following simple formula, which we studied earlier in the chapter in the discussion of price elasticity of demand, can be applied:

$$\varepsilon_s = \frac{\% \text{ change in the quantity supplied}}{\% \text{ change in price}}$$

$$= \frac{\Delta Q_s}{Q_s} \div \frac{\Delta P}{P},$$

$$= \frac{\Delta Q_s}{Q_s} \times \frac{P}{\Delta P},$$

or

$$\varepsilon_s = \frac{Q_2 - Q_1}{Q_1} \times \frac{P_1}{P_2 - P_1}.$$

Such a simple coefficient or some more elaborate "average elasticity" can be calculated for any supply curve at any instant in time, just as it can be for the elasticity of demand.

Time and Elasticity of Supply: Maryland Crab Fishing

An extremely important issue concerns the time dimension over which the economist calculates supply elasticities. To illustrate, consider a crab fisherman from Chesapeake Bay who daily brings in a catch and offers it for sale. The supply curve for crabs on any given day would be totally inelastic. On any given day, the quantity supplied of crabs would be completely unresponsive to price changes.

How, then, does the market establish a price? Price is determined by the interaction of supply and demand. If the demand for crabs on some particular day happens to be D_0 in Figure 5.8, price will settle at P_c and the entire quantity of crabs (a commodity that we assume, unrealistically, is not storable) will be sold.

Now suppose there is a change in consumers' taste. Maryland crabs become more desirable, and the demand curve shifts permanently to D_1. The fisherman's good fortune is revealed when his usual catch of Q_0 crabs brings a higher price P_0. How will the fisherman respond? If the price P_0 is higher than his average production costs, meaning a higher-than-normal profit, the fisherman will adjust by shifting available resources into crab fishing as soon as possible. If he has idle boats or nets and if there is plenty of labor available, all will be put to use. The act of producing more crabs takes time because resources are not instantly adaptable to crab fishing.

During ensuing days, weeks, or months, more crabs will be offered for sale per day, resulting in a more elastic supply curve for crabs. Such a supply curve over the initial adjustment period may look like S_1 in Figure 5.8. The price may temporarily fall to P_1 given that the demand for crabs remains stationary at D_1. Comparing the quantity Q_1 sold at price P_1 with the previous quantity of crabs sold, Q_0, shows us that over some adjustment period the supply curve for crabs is not completely inelastic but that quantity supplied is responsive to the initial price change.

If price P_1 is still abnormally profitable, the fisherman will continue to shift resources into crab production by purchasing new boats and equipment and by training new workers. Again, such activity takes time, but the effect will be to increase crab supply (perhaps to S_2). The end result in the crab market will depend on the adaptability and availability of resources for crab fishing and on the cost of producing new inputs. But the general rule is that elasticity of supply will tend to increase over time. The full impact of economic policy changes—levying taxes on industries, for example—often hinges on the elasticity of supply over time.

The concept of elasticity is not just related to the private choices of individuals; it is

The elasticity of supply increases through time with an increase in the demand for crabs.

FIGURE 5.8

Time and Elasticity of Supply

If the demand for crabs shifts from D_0 to D_1, then price rises quickly to P_0. As time goes by and crab fishermen are able to adjust inputs, the price begins to fall to P_1. After a long period of time and all adjustments are made to the increased demand, price falls to P_2. Over time, elasticity of supply increases.

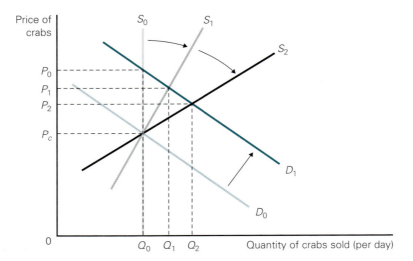

related to important public choices that individuals must make as well. Should we raise taxes or lower taxes, should we charge higher fees to go to public parks and museums, should we subsidize the arts and agriculture? These are but a few of the public choices that we must make that can be better understood by application of the concept of elasticity. In the Application, "Cigarettes, Elasticity, and Public Choice: The Effects of an Excise Tax," we provide an example of just such a situation.

APPLICATION

Cigarettes, Elasticity, and Public Choice: The Effects of an Excise Tax

An excise tax is a simple per-unit tax on the sale of a particular item. Tax collectors determine the amount of the taxable good sold by a retail or wholesale firm and require that the firm pay the amount of the tax times the quantity sold. Whatever the object taxed, an excise tax will have important effects on both demanders and suppliers, depending on elasticities of demand and supply. Consider a well-known excise or "sin" tax—the tax on cigarettes. For many years, particular interest groups within the voting public have found such a tax extremely appealing both as a revenue device and as a means of restricting "sinful" or undesirable behavior.

The equilibrium effects of an excise tax on cigarettes are shown in Figure 5.9. The hypothetical supply and demand curves for cigarettes before the excise tax are S_1 and D. The equilibrium price, E_1, is \$1.75 per pack and the quantity is 50 million packs per day. The effect of a 30-cent-per-pack excise tax can be shown by shifting the supply curve vertically upward by 30 cents to S_2. For each quantity along S_2, the price at which producers were willing to offer that quantity has now increased by 30 cents.

The new equilibrium quantity, E_2, is lower, at 40 million. This change occurs because buyers respond to price changes; their elasticity of demand for cigarettes is greater than zero. As the excise tax puts upward pressure on the price, a smaller quantity is demanded. The posttax equilibrium price to consumers, P_c, is \$1.90.

FIGURE 5.9

Effect of an Excise Tax on Cigarettes

When a 30-cent excise tax is added to the price of a pack of cigarettes, the entire supply curve for cigarettes shifts from S_1 to S_2. At the new equilibrium price, $1.90, the elasticity of demand is greater than zero; specifically, consumers will reduce their consumption of cigarettes by 10 million packs, and total tax revenues will equal 40 million times the tax. The shaded area represents government tax revenues, the 30-cent excise tax per pack multiplied by the number of packs of cigarettes sold after the tax is imposed.

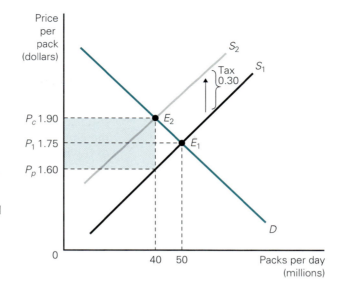

From this price, producers must pay the 30-cent excise tax and receive the net price, P_p, of $1.60 per pack.

The total revenues received by the government from the tax may not be as great as some politicians expected. Before the tax was instituted, the quantity bought was 50 million. A simple multiplication of 30 cents times 50 million would yield an overestimate of tax revenues. The actual tax revenues were 30 cents times 40 million, the new equilibrium quantity. For any excise tax the elasticity of supply and demand must be taken into account before a projection is made for tax revenues.

The elasticities of supply and demand also determine the relative burden of the excise tax. Who actually pays the tax—producers or consumers—is shown by the change in price to the buyers and sellers. In this example, the price to consumers increased 15 cents and the net price to producers fell 15 cents. Here the burden is shared equally by consumers and producers, but this is not necessarily the case.

If demand had been relatively less elastic, then price would have increased more to consumers than it fell to producers. If supply had been less elastic, more of the burden would have shifted back to the producers.

To summarize the effects of an excise tax: The lower the elasticity of demand, the greater the price increase or tax burden to consumers. The lower the elasticity of supply, the greater the net price decrease or burden to the producers.

QUESTION

Why are federal and state taxes on alcoholic beverages so prevalent? If "moral objections" to such beverages are the reason for raising excise taxes, do you believe that the taxes have had the desired effects? Why or why not?

SUMMARY

1. Elasticity is the ratio of the percent change in effect to the percent change in some cause. If changes in quantity demanded (the effect) are caused by changes in price, elasticity of demand is the percent change in quantity demanded divided by the percent change in price. This ratio is called the demand elasticity coefficient (ε_d).

2. A demand elasticity coefficient greater than 1 means that consumers are responsive to price changes; demand is elastic. When $\varepsilon_d = 1$, demand is unit elastic. When ε_d is less than 1, consumers are not very responsive to price changes; demand is said to be inelastic.

3. Elasticity can also be derived (in a general, shorthand manner) by examining total expenditures (or total revenues) as price rises or falls. If total expenditures rise (fall) as price rises (falls), ε_d is less than 1. If total expenditures remain constant as price rises or falls, $\varepsilon_d = 1$. If total expenditures fall (rise) as price rises (falls), the demand elasticity coefficient is greater than 1—that is, it is elastic.

4. There are three major determinants of demand elasticity: (1) the number and availability of substitutes; (2) the size and importance of the item in the consumer's budget; and (3) the time period over which the coefficient is calculated.

5. Other applications of the elasticity concept are the relation between income changes and changes in quantity demanded (income elasticity of demand) and between price changes for one good and changes in quantity demanded for another complementary or substitute good (cross elasticity of demand between two goods).

6. Time is at the center of most important economic calculations, including elasticity. A general rule regarding time and elasticity is that the elasticity of demand and supply increases with the time that a change (in price, for instance) is in effect.

KEY TERMS

elasticity
price elasticity of demand
demand elasticity coefficient
elastic demand
unit elasticity of demand

inelastic demand
arc elasticity
total expenditures
total revenues
income elasticity of demand

cross elasticity of demand
substitutes
complements
elasticity of supply

QUESTIONS FOR REVIEW AND DISCUSSION

1. The formula for elasticity is

$$\frac{\%\Delta Q_d}{\%\Delta P} = \frac{\Delta Q_d / Q}{\Delta P / P} = \frac{\Delta Q_d}{Q} \times \frac{P}{\Delta P}.$$

Using this formula, calculate the elasticity of demand for a product when the price changes from $1 to $1.50, $2 to $2.50, $3 to $3.75, and the change in quantity demanded is 15 to 10, 25 to 5, 50 to 30, respectively. (Hint: Remember that ΔQ is equal to $Q_2 - Q_1$ and that ΔP is equal to $P_2 - P_1$.)

2. What are the three determinants of consumers' sensitivity to a change in price? Do these always work in the same direction?

3. Is it feasible to talk about *an* elasticity all along a single demand or supply curve? Why or why not?

4. Given that a price change remains in effect over a period of time, will elasticity increase or decrease? Why?

5. What is meant by cross elasticity? How is it algebraically different from elasticity of supply and elasticity of demand, which we calculated earlier?

6. What do cross elasticities indicate about relations between two goods?

7. What might reports about a link between aspirin consumption and heart attacks do to the elasticity of demand for aspirin?

8. Is the demand elasticity coefficient for large industrial consumers of electricity larger or smaller than that for residential users? If electric companies lower the price to both groups, would total revenues from each group change in the same direction?

9. Suppose a friend has an allowance of $25 per week. She spends all of her weekly income on banana splits. What is her income elasticity of demand for banana splits?

10. A college town pizza parlor decides to offer a back-to-school two-for-one special, in effect cutting the price of pizza in half. More pizzas will be sold according to the law of demand. Will the total receipts of the parlor increase, decrease, or remain the same if pizza consumption increases by 30 percent? By 80 percent?

11. What type of price elasticity of demand is likely for a casual user of drugs such as cocaine or heroin as opposed to a dependent user? If the enforcement of prohibitions on these drugs is increased, what will happen to the extent of the changes in price and quantity demanded for the casual user?

12. What would you expect to be more price elastic— a year's membership at a fitness club or a month's membership at the same club?

PROBLEMS

1. Consider the following figure.

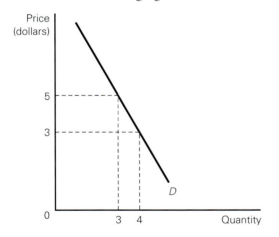

a. Compute the price elasticity of demand for a change in price from $5 to $3.

b. Is the resulting value elastic, inelastic, or unit elastic?

c. Will the firm's total revenue rise or fall from such a price change?

2. The Sunrise Pet Store sells cats and dogs. During July, the price of each cat was $15. In August, the price increased to $20. The store sold 23 dogs in July and 35 dogs in August. Calculate the cross elasticity of demand. Are cats and dogs substitutes? Explain.

3. Sometimes societal problems are attacked without full considerations of elasticity. Politicians and sociologists often argue, for example, that the price of cigarettes should be raised through taxation to reduce or prevent teen smoking. Suppose cigarette taxes increase and that demand is found to be elastic, i.e., smoking is reduced among teens. Given that substitutes clearly exist for ordinary cigarettes among teens, comment on the possible effects of the tax as social policy.

WORKING WITH THE WEB

1. Suppose you are in the market to buy a new car and are considering your options. Go to www.autobytel.com and select "new cars." Next, click on the link for Sport Utility Vehicles and take a look at the number of vehicles available under this heading (there are several!). For a typical consumer (i.e., not brand loyal), do you expect the price elasticity of demand to be more or less elastic for a Ford Expedition or for a Sport Utility Vehicle in general? Why?

2. Go to ftp://ftp.bls.gov/pub/special.requests/ce/-msa/y9697/norteast.txt. This will bring you to Table 21, "Selected northeastern metropolitan statistical areas: Average annual expenditures and characteristics, Consumer Expenditure Survey, 1996–1997." Compare the income before taxes for consumers in Boston and Pittsburgh.

   a. What are these incomes in these two cities for this year?

   b. Now, find the average annual expenditure on alcoholic beverages in the two cities.

   Now go to ftp://ftp.bls.gov/pub/special.-requests/ce/msa/y9495/norteast.txt and find the same information for 1994–1995.

   c. What was the income before taxes in Boston and Pittsburgh in this year?

   d. Now find the average annual expenditure on alcoholic beverages in the two cities for 1994–1995.

   For simplicity, assume the level of expenditure represents units (quantity) rather than dollars. For example, in 1994–1995, alcoholic beverage expenditure in Boston was $487. Assume that this is 487 units of alcohol (where units could be tons, crates, etc.).

   e. Calculate the (point) income elasticity of demand for alcoholic beverages in each city, assuming the initial level of income and quantity of alcoholic beverage consumption is reported in 1994–1995.

   f. What type of good is alcohol to the average consumer in each city?

The Logic
Of Consumer
Choice
And
Demand

We have seen in Chapters 3, 4, and 5 that the law of demand is an accurate and useful generalization about human behavior. Other things being equal, individuals will consume more of a good when its price is lower. In this chapter we examine why individuals increase their purchases of a good or service when its price falls. The heart of the analysis involves how consumers deal with the problem of scarcity. In other words, given that a consumer has a fixed budget or income, how does he or she allocate the budget among goods and services to obtain the most satisfaction from consumption? When you finish Chapter 6 you should understand

- how consumers affix value to goods and services in the marketplace.
- how scarcity affects individual behavior.
- how the economic theory of consumer behavior explains the law of demand.
- how marginal utility explains consumer behavior.

This chapter analyzes consumer choice in terms of marginal utility; in an appendix at the end of the chapter, the same analysis is cast in terms of indifference curves. Both approaches to the analysis of individual choice-making behavior are useful and introduce new tools and insights with which to study economic behavior.

UTILITY AND MARGINAL UTILITY

Why do we demand anything at all? The obvious answer is that we get satisfaction or pleasure from consuming goods and services. A vacation at the beach, a ticket to the big game,

Utility

A measure of the satisfaction that the consumption of goods or services yields an individual.

dinner at a fine restaurant—all give us pleasure. Economists call this pleasure or satisfaction **utility**. Economics, unlike psychology, does not provide any answers to questions such as why some people prefer red shirts to blue shirts or why so many people like chocolate. Economics analyzes the results of people's preferences—the observations that people will demand or pay for those things that give them utility.

Although economics cannot offer an answer to questions such as why people like chocolate, economics is interested in the intensity of consumer desires for goods. Why will individuals pay $3.50 for a magazine and $1000 for a vacation at the beach? In other words, why is the intensity of demand, as reflected in the prices people are willing to pay, greater for some goods than for others? Economists address questions like these with the aid of the **principle of diminishing marginal utility**. This principle is a simple proposition: As people consume a good in greater and greater quantities, eventually they get less and less extra utility from that good.

Principle of diminishing marginal utility

The more of a good or service being consumed, the smaller is the marginal utility obtained by consuming one additional unit of the good or service, all other factors equal.

Although the utility derived by a consumer from some good—shoes, books, raspberries—depends on many factors, such as past experience, education, and psychological traits that we may not be able to explain, the principle of diminishing marginal utility allows us to predict certain bounds for consumption behavior. Other things being equal, an individual will not be willing to pay more for an additional unit of good than what was paid for the last unit. Sooner or later, as the amount consumed increases, the consumer will be willing to pay even less for an additional unit because of diminishing marginal utility.

The principle of diminishing marginal utility is based on common sense. At lunch you might be ravenously hungry as a result of having skipped breakfast. The satisfaction, or utility, you get from eating the first hamburger in the cafeteria would likely be great. But after one burger, or certainly after two or three, the additional satisfaction you experience from an additional hamburger must decline. The amount of money that you would be willing to pay for additional burgers— amounts that reflect their **marginal utility** for you—would also decline.

Marginal utility

The amount by which total utility changes when consumption of a good or service changes by one unit; calculated by dividing the change in total utility by the change in quantity consumed.

Some given time period of consumption also must be specified in order for the principle of diminishing marginal utility to be relevant to behavior. Why, for example, do vending machine sellers of soft drinks and foods use costly and elaborate procedures to prevent buyers from stealing, while newspaper sellers usually permit the purchaser to take as many papers as he or she wants after the first is purchased?[1] It is because the marginal utility of the second or third candy bar, sandwich, or soft drink does not diminish much or at all after the first is consumed if the consumer paces his or her consumption of them through time. The additional utility you get from the fifth soft drink or prepackaged sandwich is clearly less if all are consumed over the period of an hour. However, packages of peanuts and diet drinks can be saved for later consumption. The utility of a daily newspaper, once read, is ordinarily used up immediately. The marginal utility of a second daily paper is low or zero, and vendors do not ordinarily use up costly resources in order to prevent you from taking three or four papers after paying for one. More "honesty" is therefore expected among paper buyers than would be expected from consumers of other products from vending machines, and the theory of diminishing marginal utility explains why.

---

[1]The example is suggested by the delightful mystery novel by Marshall Jevons (the nom de plume of economists William Briet and Kenneth Elzinga) in *The Fatal Equilibrium* (Cambridge, Mass.: MIT Press, 1985), pp. 113–114. We highly recommend this book and the latest in the series titled *A Deadly Indifference* (New York: Carrol & Graf Publishers, Inc., 1995). These mysteries, featuring economist-sleuth Henry Spearman, use marginal utility and a variety of other basic economic concepts to solve a series of murders.

TABLE 6.1

Total Utility and Marginal Utility
The umbrella consumer buys and uses between 1 and 5 umbrellas. The satisfaction the consumer gains from the umbrellas is measured in imaginary units called *utils*. Total utility increases as the consumer adds more umbrellas to his or her stock, but marginal utility—the satisfaction associated with each additional umbrella—decreases.

Umbrellas Acquired	Total Utility (utils)	Marginal Utility (extra utils per umbrella)
1	6	6
2	11	5
3	15	4
4	18	3
5	20	2

Total utility
The total amount of satisfaction derived from consuming any given quantity of a good or service.

The principle of diminishing marginal utility can be numerically and graphically illustrated. Most people use umbrellas as shields from rain and sun. Unfortunately, umbrellas are items that are easily misplaced or lost; in addition, they are sometimes not available when we need them. Many of us, therefore, own more than one umbrella, although the first umbrella we own obviously yields us the most satisfaction, since, without it, we would go unprotected from the elements. Consider the data in Table 6.1 and Figure 6.1. Table 6.1 indicates the relation between the number of umbrellas a consumer owns, the **total utility** the consumer derives from umbrellas, and the marginal utility of each additional umbrella to the consumer. For convenience, economists construct imaginary units called *utils* with which to measure quantities of utility derived by the umbrella consumer. Note that as the number of umbrellas owned increases, total utility—a measure of the total satisfaction gained from the entire amount consumed—increases, but at a decreasing rate. Marginal utility—the satisfaction gained by the consumer from each additional umbrella—declines as the consumer acquires additional umbrellas.

In Figure 6.1a, the dotted step lines measure the total utility generated by the consumption of umbrellas. A smooth curve has been drawn through the steps to show that a positive relation exists between units of consumption and total utility. Notice that as consumption increases, total utility increases—but at a decreasing rate. The downward-sloping curve in Figure 6.1b shows the corresponding marginal utility associated with each umbrella acquired. As more umbrellas are consumed, the marginal utility of each additional umbrella declines.

CONSUMER EQUILIBRIUM: DIMINISHING MARGINAL UTILITY AT WORK

If the principle of diminishing marginal utility applies only to a consumer's choices regarding umbrellas, then it is not very useful. To be useful, the concept of diminishing marginal utility must help us explain behavior in a world in which many different goods are consumed.

FIGURE 6.1

FIGURE 6.1

Total Utility and Marginal Utility

(a) Total utility increases, but at a decreasing rate, as more and more umbrellas are added to the consumer's stock.

(b) Marginal utility declines with each additional umbrella.

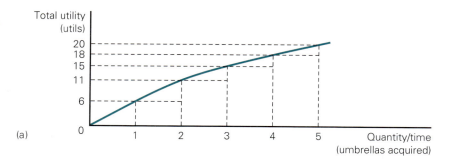

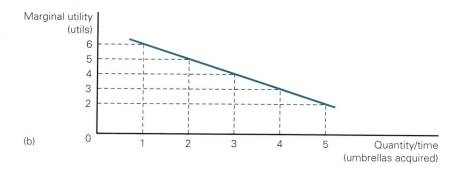

Basic Assumptions

To use diminishing marginal utility to understand consumer behavior, four concepts of consumer behavior need to hold.

1. Each consumer desires many goods, and no one good is so precious that it will be consumed to the exclusion of all other goods. Moreover, goods can be substituted for one another as alternative means of yielding satisfaction. For example, the consumer good of exercise can be satisfied by jogging, playing basketball, hiking, swimming, or a number of other activities. Dinner offers a variety of choices—steak, chicken, pizza, and so on.

2. Consumers pay prices for the things they want. For the purposes of the following analysis, it is convenient to assume that consumers pay fixed, constant prices for the things they choose to buy. Each good carries a given price, no matter how much is bought or where it is bought.

3. Consumers cannot afford everything they want. They have a budget or income constraint that forces them to limit their consumption and to make choices about what they will consume.

4. Consumers seek the most satisfaction they can get from spending their limited funds for consumption. Consumers are not irrational. They make conscious, purposeful choices designed to increase their well-being. This does not mean that consumers do not make mistakes or sometimes make impulsive purchases that they later regret. By gaining experience over time as they deal in goods and services, consumers try to get the most possible satisfaction from their limited budgets given their past experience. (See the Focus "Menus and

Marginal utility explains why college students will pay a bundle for a beach vacation and much less for a magazine or a soft drink.

Marginal Utility: 'Save Room for Dessert!'" for an explanation of how restaurant menus help increase your total utility from dining.)

Balancing Choices Among Goods

Armed with these concepts, we can better understand the behavior of consumers in the real world. To see how diminishing marginal utility works in a practical setting, assume that you—a consumer—are deciding how much of two goods to choose: movies and concerts. For each additional dollar you spend on movies, you experience an increase in utility. Simultaneously, you forgo the utility you could have experienced by spending the dollar on concerts. Because you seek to maximize the satisfaction you get from your consumption expenditures (concept number 4), you will spend your additional dollar on the good that yields you the largest increase in utility—that is, the good with the greatest marginal utility for you.

According to the principle of diminishing marginal utility, whether the utility of one good is greater than the other depends on the amount of each good consumed. If, during a month, you have already attended a large number of concerts but have seen relatively few movies, the marginal utility of concerts will tend to be low and that of movies high for you. You are therefore more likely to spend an additional dollar on movies than on concerts.

In this simple world of two goods, you will continue to spend additional dollars on movies until the marginal utility you receive from an additional dollar spent on movies is equal to the marginal utility of an additional dollar spent on concerts. This process of reaching equality in the two marginal utilities per dollar occurs naturally because the marginal utility of movies declines relative to the marginal utility

FOCUS

Menus and Marginal Utility: "Save Room for Dessert!"

Individuals make choices of all kinds every day. Consumers will demand, and suppliers have profit incentives to supply, choices in the forms that increase total utility.

Consider the typical restaurant menu, which is usually posted or presented individually to customers. However they are used, one function of menus is to serve as a device that limits diminishing marginal utility and increases the total utility *of any given meal.*[a] The typical menu is divided into appetizers, soups, salads, entrees (often subdivided into more specific categories of meat, seafood, pasta, vegetarian delights, and the like), and desserts. We all pick and choose the kind and variety of foods we eat so that excesses among the early courses do not diminish the marginal utility of later courses and so that the total utility of the whole meal is as great as possible. A huge quantity of onion soup will ordinarily provide less total utility than a cup of soup combined with a small salad and a modest entree.

---

[a]Another important function of menus is to convey information regarding the prices of each offering. The prices do affect the choice process, but our concern here is with other dimensions of the diner's choice.

Many variations and extensions of the menu exist. In some French and American restaurants, a *de gustation* menu is offered. This menu typically offers very small quantities of many dishes to thrill the palate of diners seeking higher total and less diminishing marginal utility. Cafeterias post the entire menu at the beginning of the queue and (for reasons related to diminishing marginal utility) usually present desserts early in the line. To say that "you haven't saved room for dessert" usually refers less to the capacity of your stomach than to the total utility-maximizing choices made about the range of offerings on a menu. How many times have we "regretted" total consumption levels at a menuless meal when our favorite dessert arrives, its identity previously unannounced?

Menus are devices that provide information to consumers about the availability of specific items. But a menu also enables an individual diner to plan his or her meal so as to maximize total utility from eating at any particular time. It also reminds us that the expression "variety is the spice of life" applies to the principle of diminishing marginal utility.

---

of concerts as you attend more movies. When the marginal utility per dollar of consuming the two goods is equal, you have maximized the total utility of your purchases, subject to the resources you have to spend. In other words, at the point of equality of marginal utility per last dollar spent, you will have no incentive to alter the pattern of your choices between concerts and movies. This condition of balance in consumer purchases, from which there is no tendency to change, is called **consumer equilibrium**.

Consumer equilibrium

A situation in which a consumer chooses quantities of goods that maximize total utility given a budget constraint; equilibrium implies that the per dollar marginal utility obtained from the last unit of each good consumed is equal for all goods.

How do economists take the differing goods—as well as their differing marginal utilities—into account? Note that consumer equilibrium occurs where the marginal utility of a dollar's worth of concerts is equal to the marginal utility of a dollar's worth of movies. To accommodate the differing goods, the following equation is used to describe the condition of consumer equilibrium:

$$\frac{\text{Marginal utility of concerts}}{\text{Price of concerts}} = \frac{\text{Marginal utility of movies}}{\text{Price of movies}}.$$

Equilibrium is reached when the marginal utility of the last concert attended divided by the price of a concert is equal to the marginal utility of the last movie seen divided by the price of a movie.

This equation is just a representation of consumer equilibrium. To see what it means, assume that concerts cost \$12 and movies cost \$6, and that you, the consumer, are initially not in equilibrium. This means that the above equation does not hold for you—that is,

$$\frac{\text{Marginal utility of concerts}}{\$12} \neq \frac{\text{Marginal utility of movies}}{\$6}.$$

Suppose that you begin by buying a movie ticket because its marginal utility per dollar to you is initially higher than that of concerts.

$$\frac{\text{Marginal utility of movies}}{\$6} > \frac{\text{Marginal utility of concerts}}{\$12}.$$

As you attend more movies, the marginal utility of an additional movie seen declines relative to the marginal utility of an additional concert attended. At each point you are trying to get the most possible satisfaction from your expenditures on the two goods—you are balancing the marginal utility of spending a dollar toward an additional movie against the marginal utility of spending a dollar on another concert.

At the end of the process, as the ratio of the marginal utility of movies to the price of movies declines relative to the ratio of the marginal utility of concerts to the price of concerts, equality between the two ratios is reached. Consumer equilibrium is restored at the point where additional movies seen add 2 times as much utility as a concert. Put another way, you will adjust your consumption of the two goods until the marginal utility of a dollar's worth of movies is equal to the marginal utility of a dollar's worth of concerts. This is what the equation of consumer equilibrium means and how it is reached by a consumer.

The Budget Constraint and Consumer Equilibrium

Consider a more specific example of how a consumer maximizes utility in the everyday world. Assume that a student consumer, Keith, is trying to allocate his (hypothetical) food budget on two goods—macaroni and cheese, and pizza—over some given time period. Call macaroni and cheese product X, pizza product Y, and Keith's relative preferences for macaroni and cheese versus pizza MU_x and MU_y, respectively. It is clear from Table 6.2 that Keith prefers pizza to macaroni and cheese. The marginal utility of the first unit of pizza consumed brings Keith 80 utils, whereas the first box of macaroni and cheese yields only 50. Likewise, for every successive unit from the first to the sixth of the two meals consumed, Keith's utility preference is for pizza over macaroni and cheese. How, then, do we explain why individuals always buy combinations of goods in order to maximize their utility? What rule do we apply to Keith's consumer behavior to explain how choices are actually made? The rule is simple: *Consumers will always balance the consumption of all of the various goods purchased so as to maximize utility given their respective budget constraints.*

Knowing that Keith prefers pizza to macaroni and cheese is not enough to explain the decisions he makes. Many of us would say that we would prefer (have a higher preference for) a Maserati or a Porsche to a Ford or a Hyundai. Most of us do not buy high-priced sports cars, however, when our utilities are adjusted for the relative prices of these two categories of automobiles and when our incomes

TABLE 6.2

A Consumer's Utility Maximization

Keith, a consumer with preferences for two goods, chooses a utility-maximizing combination of macaroni and cheese and pizzas by equating the "adjusted" marginal utilities of the two goods under an income constraint. When his income is $34, he buys 2 boxes of macaroni and cheese and 3 pizzas.

Units of Product	PRODUCT X: MACARONI AND CHEESE (BOXES) PRICE: $2 PER BOX		PRODUCT Y: PIZZAS (12-INCH) PRICE: $10 PER PIZZA	
	(1) Marginal Utility (utils)	(2) Marginal Utility (per dollar's worth)	(3) Marginal Utility (utils)	(4) Marginal Utility (per dollar's worth)
First	50	25	80	8
Second	8	4	50	5
Third	4	2	40	4
Fourth	2	1	20	2
Fifth	0	0	10	1
Sixth	−2	−1	0	0
Seventh	−10	−5	−40	−4

are considered. Thus, the marginal utilities of *all* goods consumed must be adjusted by the prices of those goods before we can explain the choices consumers make.

Price adjustments are made to the marginal utilities of macaroni and cheese and pizza in columns (2) and (4) of Table 6.2. If we assume that the price of macaroni and cheese is $2 per box and pizzas are $10 each, the marginal utilities per dollar's worth of the two goods may be readily calculated. For the first unit of macaroni and cheese, for example, the marginal utility per dollar's worth, or MU_x/P_x, is equal to 25 (50/$2). For the first unit of pizza, the marginal utility per dollar's worth, or MU_y/P_y, is equal to 8, or 80 divided by $10. Just as in the case of movies and concerts, consumers will attempt to balance these "adjusted" marginal utilities to maximize satisfaction given their income or budget constraint. Consider Keith's choices. As soon as he has an income of $2 per time period, he will buy a box of macaroni and cheese. Why? Because the marginal utility per dollar's worth of this item is greater than that of the first unit of pizza.

As Keith's budget or income constraint becomes less stringent, his consumption pattern changes, as Table 6.2 shows. Suppose that his budget rises to $12 over the time period. Table 6.2 tells us that he will buy the first unit of pizza in preference to more macaroni and cheese. The first unit of pizza would add 8 utils per dollar to his total utility, whereas the second unit of macaroni and cheese would add only 4 utils per dollar to his satisfaction. To maximize satisfaction, Keith will buy the first pizza with the additional $10 in income.

When his budget rises to $34 for these two products, Keith is in equilibrium when he buys 2 units of product X (macaroni and cheese) and 3 units of product Y (pizza). To see why, let Keith simply shop for the highest marginal utility per dollar. He first buys X (25), then Y (8), then another X (5), and then another X (4) and another Y (4). At this point, Keith has spent all his money ($34) on 3 pizzas ($30) and 2 boxes of macaroni and cheese ($4).

To look at Keith's behavior in another way, simply calculate the total utility that Keith receives. His total satisfaction on good X will be 58 utils (50 + 8), and the total utility obtained from good Y will be 170 (80 + 50 + 40), for a total of 228 utils of satisfaction. With $34 Keith could buy other possible combinations of products, such as 7 boxes of macaroni and cheese and 2 pizzas, but this purchase would yield a lower total satisfaction (52 utils on X and 130 on Y, for a total of 182 utils). Keith is looking for the *utility-maximizing combination*, and that is always found where the marginal utilities per dollar's worth of the two (or more) goods or services are equal. In terms of the simple problem considered in Table 6.2, equilibrium occurs when the dollar-adjusted marginal utilities of the items purchased are equal:

$$\frac{MU_{\text{Macaroni and cheese}}}{P_{\text{Macaroni and cheese}}} = \frac{MU_{\text{Pizza}}}{P_{\text{Pizza}}},$$

or

$$\frac{8}{\$2} = \frac{40}{\$10}.$$

All of us, moreover, are subject to a budget constraint. In Keith's case, the income constraint is assumed to be $34; the sum of the total expenditures for both items must equal that amount.

$$P_{\text{Mac}} \times Q_{\text{Mac}} + P_{\text{Pizza}} \times Q_{\text{Pizza}} = \$34,$$

$$\$2 \times 2 + \$10 \times 3 = \$34.$$

Here we assume that Keith, the consumer, expends all of his income on macaroni and cheese and pizza. This assumption is a simplification, since any consumer typically purchases hundreds or even thousands of goods and saves and borrows, as well. Some of these complications are treated below, but the same principles of utility maximization always apply. Symbolically, the equilibrium conditions for maximum consumer satisfaction may be stated

$$\frac{MU_X}{P_X} = \frac{MU_Y}{P_Y}.$$

This equilibrium condition for maximum consumer satisfaction is always subject to a budget constraint, or

$$P_X X + P_Y Y = \text{Income}.$$

Another interesting aspect of the consumer equilibrium described above is that Keith or any consumer will never knowingly consume a unit of any good or service that brings him or her *negative* marginal utility. Even if Keith's budget constraint permitted him to purchase 7 boxes of macaroni and cheese and 7 pizzas over the time period, he would never do so. Even if both of the commodities were *free*, Keith would never consume more than 5 boxes of macaroni and cheese and 6 pizzas. The purchase of units of goods giving negative marginal utilities will reduce the total utility produced by these consumptions. The last two boxes of macaroni and cheese would reduce total utility by 12 utils, and the last pizza would cause it to decline by 40 utils. No rational consumer would spend scarce resources to reduce utility.

Consumers Maximize Satisfaction Among Thousands of Goods

The two-good examples for entertainment and for food consumption are simplifications of consumers' actual choices among thousands of goods and services. We consume not only food and entertainment, but such items as electricity, medical services, music lessons, and cable television. To express the general condition of consumer equilibrium, the two-good equation may be expanded, with N denoting the total number of goods and services consumed. If $X, Y, Z,...,N$ are goods in the consumer's budget; $MU_X, MU_Y, MU_Z,...,MU_N$ are the marginal utilities of these goods and services; and $P_X, P_Y, P_Z,...,P_N$ represent the corresponding prices of these goods and services, then the equilibrium equation for maximum consumer satisfaction is

$$\frac{MU_X}{P_X} = \frac{MU_Y}{P_Y} = \frac{MU_Z}{P_Z} = \cdots = \frac{MU_N}{P_N}.$$

The only numbers we have to put in the consumer equilibrium equation are the prices of the goods. We do not know—or need to know—what the subjective marginal utilities of the consumer are. The important point about the equation is that it is a proposition about individual behavior. It outlines how consumers will achieve balance or equilibrium in allocating their incomes among goods and services. In a sense, consumers assign their own utility numbers and arrange their patterns of consumption to achieve equilibrium; that is, they buy less of one good in order to buy more of another. Consumers solve the equation for themselves as an expression of their rational choices.

Consumers will equate the "adjusted" marginal utilities in the consumer equilibrium equation subject to an income constraint; in other words, the sum of all expenditures made on each item in the budget equals total income:

$$P_X X + P_Y Y + P_Z Z + \cdots + P_N N = \text{Income}.$$

In the budget constraint equation, prices of all the various goods and services as well as the consumer's income must be supplied, reminding us that utility is maximized only under an individual's budget limitations. The individual can only maximize satisfaction subject to given prices (of macaroni and cheese and pizzas, in Keith's case) and to income. The explanation given here of the rational consumer's behavior states that the individual always acts to maximize his or her satisfaction or utility—whatever that may be to any individual—given the economic environment. That environment always includes the prices of individual goods and services and the consumer's income.

Consumer Rationality and a Famous Riddle: Marginal Utility and Smith's Diamond–Water Paradox

Diamond–Water paradox
Adam Smith's belief that water and diamonds did not follow the same theory of value—a paradox confusing total and marginal utility that is unlocked by the principle of diminishing marginal utility.

Is consumer choice always rational? In describing the famous **diamond–water paradox**, Adam Smith pondered what seemed to be an irrational willingness of consumers to spend vast sums of money on "useless" goods like diamonds:

> Things which have the greatest value in use frequently have little or no value in exchange; and on the contrary, those which have the greatest value in exchange have frequently little or no value in use. Nothing is more useful than water; but it will scarce purchase anything, scarce anything can be had in exchange for it. A

diamond, on the contrary, has scarce any value in use; but a very great quantity of other goods may frequently be had in exchange for it.[2]

Water is useful but cheap; diamonds are not useful but expensive. This seems paradoxical. But using the principle of diminishing marginal utility, what errors can we find in Smith's reasoning about the paradox?

First, Smith failed to grasp the importance of the relative scarcity of a commodity in determining its value in use, or marginal utility. He compared a single diamond with the total supply of water. Had he compared the marginal utility of a single diamond with a single gallon of water, no other water being available, the paradox would have disappeared, for the scarce water would be considered quite valuable. As economic theorists later discovered, water commands little in exchange because its supply is so abundant relative to the intensity of consumer desire for it. Diamonds are scarce relative to consumer desires and therefore command much in exchange. There is no diamond–water paradox when one focuses on the value of the marginal unit of supply to the consumer. Water is plentiful and cheap; diamonds are scarce and expensive.

Second, Smith makes a personal judgment of utility when he suggests that diamonds have no value in use. Many wearers and investors in diamonds would disagree on this point. Within reason, modern utility theory does not allow judgments to be made that some preferences are good and others are bad.

A third point, related to the first, is that Smith's value paradox failed to distinguish between marginal and total utility. Assume for a moment that the marginal utilities of water and diamonds are identical, as in Figure 6.2. Figure 6.2 shows that the marginal utility of each good declines as units of each increase. For any given number of units (numbers of diamonds or gallons of water), the marginal

---

[2]Adam Smith, *An Inquiry into the Nature and Causes of the Wealth of Nations,* ed. Edwin Cannan (1776; reprint, New York: Modern Library, 1937), p. 28.

FIGURE 6.2

The Diamond–Water Paradox

When relative scarcity is considered, the marginal utility of diamonds is greater (when supply is given) than the marginal utility of water. This valuation is not incompatible with the total utility of water being greater than the total utility of diamonds.

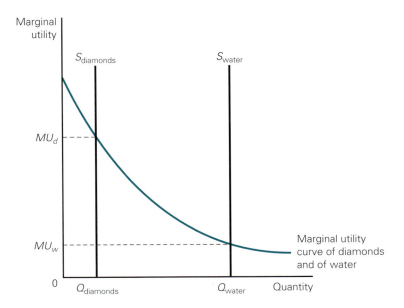

and total utility would be the same. Under ordinary circumstances, diamonds are more scarce than water, which means that the supply curve for water is to the right of the supply curve for diamonds. Thus the marginal utility of diamonds is greater than the marginal utility of water. However, the total utility of water—represented by the area up to Q_{water} under the marginal utility curve in Figure 6.2—is greater than that of diamonds. (Return to Figure 6.1 and the related discussion earlier in this chapter for further explanation of this point.)

Of course, Adam Smith did not have modern utility theory available to him when he wrote his statement. Indeed, it was in trying to resolve this simple paradox that modern utility theory was developed by economists in the nineteenth century in France. The principle of diminishing marginal utility, developed many years after Smith's writings, helps us understand the rationality behind such choices. Intuitively, a rational consumer will always equate the marginal benefits to the marginal cost of his or her actions. This rationality applies to all kinds of human behavior, including various public choices the individual has to make. (For an example related to public choice, see the Application "Is It Rational to Vote?" at the conclusion of this chapter.)

FROM DIMINISHING MARGINAL UTILITY TO THE LAW OF DEMAND

The marginal utility equation helps us understand the relation between diminishing marginal utility and the law of demand. Assume that you, the consumer, are in equilibrium with movies priced at $6 and concerts priced at $12. The equation of consumer equilibrium then looks like this:

$$\frac{MU_{\text{movies}}}{\$6} = \frac{MU_{\text{concerts}}}{\$12}.$$

If the price of concerts falls to $6, this equality will be upset. The resulting disequilibrium will be temporary, however, for you will act to restore equality by attending more concerts. As you attend more concerts, the principle of diminishing marginal utility tells us that the marginal utility of concerts for you will fall. When the marginal utility of concerts has fallen by the same proportion that their price has fallen, consumer equilibrium will be restored.

Note the relation of this behavior to the law of demand. Because the price has been reduced, you will attend more concerts until a dollar's worth of concerts generates no more utility for you than a dollar's worth of movies—or anything else. The law of demand says that consumers will respond to a fall in the relative price of a good by purchasing more of that good. Diminishing marginal utility thus provides a behavioral basis for the law of demand. When price falls, consumption increases until consumer equilibrium is again established. Indeed, the marginal utility curve may, under certain circumstances, be associated with the demand curve. For such an example and for an understanding of how different pricing arrangements on the part of entrepreneurs could alter your consumption, see the Focus "'All You Can Eat' Pizza."

Substitution effect
The change in the quantity demanded of a good that results only from a change in the relative price of the good.

The Substitution Effect and Income Effect

Consumers' tendency to buy more of a good when its price drops in relation to the price of other goods is called the **substitution effect**. The relatively cheaper good is

FOCUS

"All You Can Eat" Pizza

One of the most popular foods served on and off campus at colleges and universities is that wonderful American invention, pizza. (It is actually a variation on traditional Italian cuisine, but only an American could invent taco pizza on pita bread.) There are a number of ways to order pizza other than a whole pie—by the slice or "all you can eat" are common. However it is ordered, the laws of marginal utility and costs apply. Consider the marginal utility–demand curve for pizza shown in Figure 6.3. Each person's curve will differ, of course, but assume that the one depicted in the graph is yours. The number of slices of pizza is depicted on the quantity axis (horizontal) and the price per slice on the vertical axis in Figure 6.3.

All other things equal, how much pizza will you consume at one time (dinner today)? A look at the figure shows that the answer will depend on your utility for pizza versus the cost to you. In particular, you will equate the marginal utility of pizza consumed (which diminishes with quantity like all other goods) and the cost to you of the pizza. Clearly, that cost will vary depending on *how* pizza is offered.

Suppose there are two pizzerias in your town, one offering pizza by the slice and the other "all you can eat." Assume that the pizza is of the same quality at both restaurants. At the first restaurant, pizza is offered at $1 a slice. From the figure, you will buy four pieces by the slice. Why? Because that is where your marginal utility for pizza equals the (marginal) cost of $1 to you. As the figure shows, the fifth slice has marginal utility (value), but it is not worth the extra dollar you would have to pay.

Now consider the "all-you-can-eat" restaurant. When you pay a fixed sum for the "all-you-

---

FIGURE 6.3

Marginal Utility and Demand for Pizza

At a price of $1 per slice, this consumer buys 4 slices. At an all-you-can-eat buffet, however, the consumer drives her marginal utility to zero by consuming five slices.

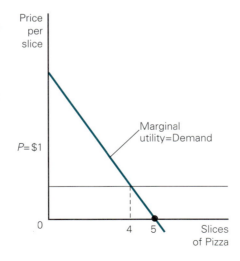

continued

continued

can-eat" dining alternative, the additional or marginal cost of an additional slice is, in effect, zero to you. Note that from Figure 6.3, you will eat 5 pieces of pizza in equilibrium. Small wonder that at such restaurants, sharing food and doggie bags are not allowed and that you have the strong temptation to eat "too much." Naturally the restaurant that you will choose will be the one giving you the greatest overall utility (consumer) surplus.

substituted for other now relatively more expensive goods. Concerts are substituted for movies when the price of concerts drops. To be precise, the substitution effect refers to that portion of the increase or decrease in quantity demanded of a good that is the direct result of its change in price relative to the price of other goods.

Price, however, is not the only relevant factor affecting the quantity demanded of a good. Changes in income will also tend to shift the demand curve for goods, as we saw in Chapter 3. The larger an individual's income, the more he or she will demand of most goods.[3] Other things being equal (primarily the prices of other goods remaining the same), the fall in price of a particular good will raise the **real income**, or buying power, of the individual consumer even where nominal income remains constant. This change in real income means that the consumer can buy more of all goods under the same budget constraint as before. This **income effect** can be stated more technically: It is that portion of the change in the quantity demanded of a good that occurs because of the change in the individual's real income that resulted from a price change.

Real income

The buying power of a consumer's budget; determined by the consumer's money income and the prices of goods and services.

Income effect

The change in the quantity demanded of a good that results from a change in real income.

Marginal Utility and the Law of Demand

The principle of diminishing marginal utility and the law of demand are thus closely related. A price change leads to a change in quantity demanded, which is composed of a substitution effect and an income effect. When the price of a good falls relative to the prices of other goods, the principle of diminishing marginal utility, acting by means of the substitution effect, tends to increase the quantity of the good that the consumer demands. The income effect is a separate and distinct influence that generally reinforces the substitution effect; that is, the income effect tends to increase the quantity demanded of the good whose price has fallen. Though there are cases where the income effect can pull in the opposite direction from the substitution effect, economists generally predict that the strength of the substitution effect will outweigh the strength of the income effect, leading to an increase in the quantity demanded of a good whose relative price has fallen.

Sometimes people claim that they have found exceptions to the law of demand, but the exceptions turn out, on close examination, to be based on simple mistakes in reasoning. For example, sometimes a fall in price of a good seems to result in a decline in the quantity demanded of that good. A department store may actually

---

[3]Increases or decreases in quantity demanded as a result of an increase in income will depend upon whether the good in question is normal or inferior. Goods for which consumption increases as the consumer's income rises, such as medical care, are called normal goods. When the consumption of a good falls with increases in income, we say that such goods are inferior goods. Used cars may be an example of an inferior good. See Chapter 3 for a discussion of these terms.

sell less furniture after it lowers furniture prices. If we look more closely at such cases, we may find that, in the calculations of consumers, the relative price of furniture has not fallen. Consumers may judge that the store is phasing out its furniture department and, as a result, expect that furniture prices will soon be even lower. Often what appears to be an exception to the law of demand is actually a confusion between a change in demand and a change in quantity demanded (see Chapter 3). This is the law of demand in action—relative and not absolute prices matter to consumers.

One more of the many possible examples of an apparent, but not real, exception of the law of demand is the case of a "prestige" good. The demand for caviar, for example, is sometimes said to be much higher as an expensive item than it would be if its price per pound were comparable to, say, tuna fish. The high price of caviar is said to actually increase the quantity demanded of caviar, contrary to the law of demand. But this notion is confused. Would the quantity demanded of caviar continue to increase as the price rose to $1000, $10,000, or $1 million per pound? It would not. Although prestige goods are usually expensive goods, they do not defy the law of demand. If they did, we would see their prices rise without limit, which does not happen.

SOME PITFALLS TO AVOID

The principles of diminishing marginal utility and marginal utility analysis are useful constructs for analyzing individual behavior. As we have seen, they help explain individual choice behavior and offer a richer understanding of the law of demand. In using this analysis, however, some fairly common misunderstandings must be avoided.

1. The individual wishing to maximize utility is motivated by personal self-interests, but the principle says nothing about what those interests may be. They may be based on purely selfish, greedy goals or on humanitarian concern for others. Marginal utility analysis does not specify the goals or desires of individuals; it is useful only in understanding and analyzing individual behavior once those goals have been specified.

2. Only individuals make economic decisions. When we refer to a government agency, a corporation, or a snorkeling club as making a decision, we are only using a figure of speech. Take away the individual members who make up these organizations, and nothing is left to make a decision.

3. Economics is concerned with the effects of scarcity on the lives of people. It does not address the issue of human needs. A need is not an object that can be measured in a way that everyone can agree on (like the size of a desk or the height of a building). Needs are subjective, just like love, justice, and honor. Economics is neutral with respect to subjective judgments.

4. Marginal utility analysis is an explanation, not a description, of individual choice behavior. Economists do not claim that individual consumers actually calculate marginal utility trade-offs before they go shopping. Indeed, most consumers, if asked, would probably deny that they behave in the way that marginal utility analysis suggests they do. The proof is obviously in the pudding. Individuals behave so as to generate the same outcomes they would produce if they actually did calculate and equate marginal utilities. Marginal utility analysis explains the outcomes we observe rather than describing the mental process involved.

APPLICATION

Is It Rational to Vote?

You decide to vote in a presidential election. Typically, you will be joined by more than 60 million other people. Your vote therefore has only 1/60,000,000 worth of influence on the outcome of the election, and it is, of course, filtered through the Electoral College process in the United States.

We also know that voting is not costless. To make a trip to the polling place, voters must pay for transportation, take time off from work or leisure, and so forth. Moreover, prior registration often means another trip to the voter registration office. Thus, voting is not free—it clearly places opportunity costs on the voter.

Suppose, in a radical simplification, that all these opportunity costs equal $1; that is, it costs you $1 to vote. Given that you are 1 out of 60 million voters who vote and that it costs you $1 to vote, what must your vote be worth to you to make it rational for you to go to the polls on election day? Since you have only a tiny effect on the election, the outcome would have to have an enormous impact on you to make it worth your while to vote. This concept can be represented algebraically by the formula

$$\frac{1}{60,000,000} \times \text{ benefits } = \$1,$$

which gives the large value of $60 million in benefits to you to justify the cost of voting. In terms of this analysis, it is hardly reasonable to expect the outcome of any given election to be worth $60 million to the average voter. Therefore, no one should vote, and democracy should fall on its face.

Yet herein lies a paradox. A great number of people do vote, and the question is, why? Economics provides a simple explanation for the conditions under which it is rational to vote. Obviously, voters are smarter than to view themselves as only 1 vote out of 60 million. They have identified—before the election and during the campaign—with parties (Democratic, Republican, Socialist, Libertarian, and so forth) and individual candidates, and they will make their own estimates of the prospects of the candidates in the election.

Economics says that voters will behave in terms of the marginal utility and marginal cost of voting. Notice that the above example was stated in terms of the average influence of a voter on the election. The fact that the average influence of any one voter is low does not tell us anything about his or her marginal influence on the election. (As we stress repeatedly, the distinction between *average* and *marginal* is a crucial one in economics.) While we cannot directly measure the marginal influence of a voter in an election, we can indirectly gauge the marginal benefit from voting. The marginal influence of a vote will be greater the closer the election is predicted to be. Your vote counts for more in a close election than in a lopsided election. Therefore, economic theory leads to the following prediction: Voting turnout will be positively related to the expected closeness of the election. In other words, voter turnout will be heavier the closer the election is expected to be.

Marginal benefits (broadly construed to include *all* benefits) and marginal costs explain why individuals vote in all elections, including campus elections.

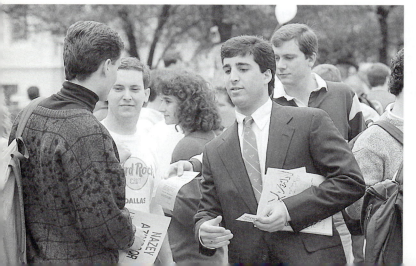

So the simple economic proposition that individuals behave according to marginal cost and marginal benefit provides an explanation for the conditions under which voting is rational. This is not to argue that the only reason people vote is to obtain narrow personal benefits. Benefits can be construed in a wide variety of ways, such as patriotic duty, citizenship, support for an ideological cause, voting for a friend, and so forth. The point is not what the benefits are but that, depending on the closeness of the election, these benefits are likely to be higher or lower relative to costs. Thus, if your friend is running for Congress, you are more likely to vote if he or she is in a tight contest than if your friend is a shoo-in.

QUESTION

Logically, how should each of the following situations affect voter turnout on election day?

a. Rain

b. An international crisis

c. A close race

d. Television coverage

SUMMARY

1. As individuals, we demand goods and services because the consumption of such things gives us utility, or satisfaction.

2. The principle of diminishing marginal utility says that the more we consume of a good, the less utility we get from consuming additional amounts of that good.

3. Consumer equilibrium occurs when individuals obtain the most possible utility from their limited budgets. Their respective consumption patterns are in balance, and they cannot increase total utility by altering the way they allocate their given budgets among goods.

4. In equation form, consumer equilibrium for N goods (the total number of goods and services that a consumer chooses from) is

$$\frac{MU_X}{P_X} = \frac{MU_Y}{P_Y} = \frac{MU_Z}{P_Z} = \cdots = \frac{MU_N}{P_N}.$$

In other words, the ratios of marginal utility to price are equal among all the goods a consumer

purchases. The consumer's purchases, however, are always limited by a budget constraint:

$$P_X X + P_Y Y + P_Z Z + \cdots + P_N N = \text{Income}.$$

5. The principle of diminishing marginal utility underlies the law of demand. In the first equation in number 4, if the price of good X falls, the equality of the marginal utility ratios is upset. To restore equality, the consumer will consume more of the good that has fallen in price, driving its marginal utility down proportionately to its fall in price. This is equivalent to the type of behavior predicted by the law of demand. Other things being equal, more of a good is consumed when its price falls.

6. The increase in consumption of a good when its price falls is caused by two effects. More is consumed because the price of the good has fallen relative to the prices of other goods. This is called the *substitution effect*. In addition, more is consumed because the consumer has more real income owing to the fall in price. This is called the *income effect*.

7. Generally, the substitution and income effects taken together lead to increased consumption of a good when its price falls.

8. The law of demand is a widespread empirical regularity. We observe its action everywhere. Supposed exceptions to the law are usually misapplications or misunderstandings of basic economic principles.

9. Marginal utility analysis explains the observed patterns of consumers in making their consumption choices.

KEY TERMS

utility

principle of diminishing marginal utility

marginal utility

total utility

consumer equilibrium

diamond-water paradox

substitution effect

real income

income effect

QUESTIONS FOR REVIEW AND DISCUSSION

1. What is meant by *utility*? How do you measure utility?

2. Define *marginal utility*.

3. What are the four basic assumptions about consumer preference?

4. Express consumer equilibrium algebraically in terms of marginal utility. Explain what your expression means in words.

5. "I love seafood so much that I could never get enough of it." Why would an economist disagree with this statement? Could there ever be a time when the person making this statement might actually receive negative utility from consuming more seafood? Give your answer in a graph and in words.

6. Explain the difference between substitution effects and income effects.

7. Oil is essential to the economic life of the nation. Our machines and homes cannot run without it. Yet a quart of oil is cheaper than a ticket to the Super Bowl. How can oil be so precious and yet so cheap? Resolve this oil–Super Bowl paradox.

8. Two economists are walking past the local Porsche dealer's showroom. One says, "I really want one of those Porsche 968s." The other says, "Obviously not." Who is right, and why?

9. In order to maximize total utility, the following must be true: $MU_X/P_X = MU_Y/P_Y = \ldots = MU_N/P_N$, where $X, Y, \ldots, N$ denote different goods and services consumed. Explain.

10. If Juan likes eclairs better than doughnuts, then for any given level of income, he will always purchase fewer doughnuts than eclairs. Do you agree or disagree? Explain.

11. Ocean cruises are becoming cheaper and more popular as vacation choices. The price of a cruise typically includes all food but not drinks (including colas but excluding water and tea) for the voyage. Analyze this practice from the standpoint of marginal utility.

PROBLEMS

1. Let the following table represent the total utility you receive from consuming chocolate chip cookies and glasses of milk. Calculate the marginal utilities.

Number of Cookies	Total Utility	Marginal Utility	Number of Glasses of Milk	Total Utility	Marginal Utility
1	14	———	1	10	———
2	26	———	2	18	———
3	36	———	3	24	———
4	44	———	4	28	———
5	48	———	5	28	———
6	48	———	6	27	———
7	44	———	7	24	———

2. Suppose you visit a friend's house whose family's policy is "all-you-can-eat-and-drink." According to the table, how many cookies and how many glasses of milk will you consume?

3. Suppose the price of cookies at a cookie shop in the mall is 25 cents each, and the price of milk is 50 cents per glass. Using your answers in problem 1, calculate the marginal utility per dollar to you at these prices.

Cookies	MU/$	Glasses	MU/$
1	———	1	———
2	———	2	———
3	———	3	———
4	———	4	———
5	———	5	———
6	———	6	———
7	———	7	———

4. If you only had $2.25 to spend, would you buy 4 cookies and 2 glasses of milk at the prices charged? Why or why not?

5. If you had $4, how many cookies and glasses of milk would you buy? If you had $7.25, how many of each would you buy?

WORKING WITH THE WEB

1. Suppose you love fine chocolates, especially Godiva chocolates. Go to the Godiva web site's chocolate guide at http://www.godiva.com/godiva-/store/chocguide.asp and click the link for Truffles. After looking over the selection of truffles, you realize that ordering the 12 ounce deluxe assortment of truffles, which can be viewed with its description at http://www.godiva.com/godiva-/store/product.asp?id=9, will give you 81 utils of satisfaction. This box of truffles has a price of $27. You are also considering buying some assortment of milk chocolates, and the 11 ounce All Milk Assortment box, described at http://www.godiva.-com/godiva/store/product.asp?id=5, seems like it will satisfy your chocolate craving and will provide 48 utils of satisfaction. This box of chocolates is priced at $24.

Suppose you buy and consume a box of each selection of chocolates given the information above.
a. Are you in equilibrium? If yes, how do you know? If not, why not and what should you do to move toward equilibrium?
b. Why does your decision move you toward equilibrium?

2. Assume your uncle Bob has told you he will buy you a new car for your graduation present, so you decide to start shopping now. Return once again to www.autobytel.com and select the "research" link. Assume the car of your dreams is a Porsche 911. Select the "Porsche" link on the research page. The 1999 Cabriolet Convertible 2 door has a base MSRP of $74,460. Since this is the car of your dreams, let us assume that this car will allow you to achieve the highest level of satisfaction subject to your budget constraint. Now, let's assume you've told your uncle Bob what your choice in cars actually is; he tells you it is out of the question due to the high price tag and limits you to a car priced at $35,000 or less.

   a. Graphically, what happens when your uncle Bob reduces your spending limit?

   b. If you select an alternative automobile at the lower spending level, what does this suggest about your level of satisfaction subject to your budget constraint?

   c. Are you in consumer equilibrium?

Indifference Curve Analysis[a]

A P P E N D I X

Suppose that we want to determine how a consumer feels about consuming various combinations of two goods, such as mystery and science fiction (SF) novels. One approach would be to ask the person how much utility she gets from consuming 4 mystery novels and 9 SF novels per year. She would perhaps answer, "50 utils." This would not be a very helpful answer because we do not know how much 50 utils represents to this person.

A second approach would be to observe how the individual chooses among various combinations of mysteries and SF books over a specified period of time, such as a year. We could then see, through her **revealed preferences**, how she ranks the various combinations. For example, does she prefer a combination of 4 mysteries and 9 SFs to a combination of 9 mysteries and 4 SFs? That is, when offered a choice of the two combinations, does she choose one over the other? Proceeding in this way, we are more likely to derive useful information about preferences. This type of approach yields the concept of an indifference curve.

INDIFFERENCE CURVES

Indifference curves are based on the concept of **indifference sets**. Indifference sets can be easily illustrated.

[a]We present indifference curve analysis in an appendix because it is not necessary to know the technique to understand any of the basic points about economics presented in this book. Indifference curve analysis is, however, an integral part of more advanced courses in economics, and many students who plan to do more work in economics will want to learn the technique.

Suppose that four possible combinations of two goods confront an individual—say, four possible combinations of quantities per year of mystery and science fiction novels. Four combinations are given in Table 6.3. Assume that the consumer, through her revealed behavior, obtains the same total utility from consuming 10 mysteries and 3 SFs as she would from consuming 7 mystery novels and 5 science fiction novels, and so on through the table. Each combination is equivalent to the others in terms of the total utility yielded to the consumer. For example, if we compare combinations *C* and *D*, an additional mystery in

TABLE 6.3

Combinations of Novels Yielding Equal Total Utility
The data represent the consumer's observed behavior. The consumer derives as much satisfaction from consuming combination *A*, 10 mystery novels and 3 SF novels per year, as she does from consuming combination *D*, 4 mystery novels and 9 SF novels. The total utility of each combination, *A, B, C,* and *D,* is the same.

| | NOVELS PER YEAR | |
| | Mystery | Science Fiction |
Combination		
A	10	3
B	7	5
C	5	7
D	4	9

combination *C* exactly makes up for the utility lost by consuming 2 fewer science fiction novels. The consumer reveals herself to be indifferent among these various combinations of the two goods; each combination yields the same level of total utility to her. An indifference set, then, is all combinations of the two goods among which the consumer is indifferent.

With this information about the individual's evaluation of the combinations, we can draw an indifference curve, as in Figure 6.4. Each point on the graph represents a combination of mystery and science fiction novels per year. The points representing combinations *A* through *D* are shown on the graph. These points and points in between them are joined by a smooth curve because they are members of an indifference set. The curve is the indifference curve, a curve made up of points that are all members of a particular indifference set. Any point on the indifference curve is equally preferred to any other by the consumer; all yield the same level of total utility.

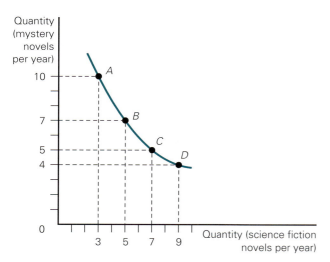

FIGURE 6.4

An Indifference Curve

This indifference curve is based on the data in Table 6.3. The curve shows the various combinations of mystery and science fiction novels among which the consumer is indifferent. The marginal rate of substitution of one good for the other is given by the slope of the indifference curve. The indifference curve is usually convex, which means that its slope decreases from left to right along the curve. The decreasing marginal rate of substitution is due to the principle of diminishing marginal utility.

CHARACTERISTICS OF INDIFFERENCE CURVES

Indifference curves have certain characteristics designed to show established regularities in the patterns of consumer preferences. Five of these characteristics are of interest to us.

1. Indifference curves slope downward from left to right. This negative slope is the only one possible if the principles of consumer choice are not to be violated. An upward-sloping curve would imply that the consumer was indifferent over the choice between a combination with less of both goods and another with more of both goods. The assumption that consumers always prefer more of a good to less requires that indifference curves slope downward from left to right.

2. The absolute value of the slope of the indifference curve at any point is equal to the ratio of the marginal utility of the good on the horizontal axis to the marginal utility of the good on the vertical axis. In Figure 6.4, the slope of the indifference curve between A and B is about −1.5, or simply 1.5 in absolute value. This absolute value tells us that in the area of combinations A and B, the marginal utility of SF novels is approximately one and one-half times that of mysteries. In this region, about 3 mysteries can be substituted for 2 SFs without lowering the consumer's total utility. For this reason, the slope of the indifference curve is called the **marginal rate of substitution**—in this case, substitution of science fiction for mystery novels. The marginal rate of substitution tells us the rate at which one good can be substituted for another without gain or loss in utility.

3. Indifference curves are drawn to be convex: The slope of an indifference curve decreases as one moves downward to the right along the curve. This convexity reflects diminishing marginal utility. As the quantity consumed of one of the goods increases, the marginal utility of that good declines. Hence, the ratio of the marginal utilities—the slope of the indifference curve—cannot be the same all along the curve. The slope must decrease as we move farther down and to the right because the quantity of science fiction novels consumed is increasing and their marginal utility is

therefore decreasing, whereas the quantity of mystery novels is decreasing and the marginal utility of mysteries is therefore increasing.

In Figure 6.4, the marginal rate of substitution of SFs for mysteries falls from 1.5 between points *A* and *B* to 0.5 between points *C* and *D*. As more science fiction novels are consumed, their marginal utility (measured by how many mystery novels the consumer is willing to give up per year in order to get an additional science fiction novel while remaining on the same indifference curve) falls. Fewer mysteries are consumed, and their marginal utility rises. Between *A* and *B*, the consumer is indifferent between 3 more mysteries and 2 less science fiction novels per year. Between *C* and *D*, fortified with more SFs, the consumer is indifferent between 1 additional mystery and 2 fewer SFs. With the consumption of more SFs, the marginal utility of mystery novels has risen and the marginal utility of science fiction novels has declined.

4. A point representing any assortment of consumption alternatives will always be on some indifference curve. Figure 6.5 presents a graph of combinations of bacon and eggs. We can select a point on the graph—such as A, representing 10 eggs and 1 bacon strip, or D, representing 9 bacon strips and 1 egg—and that point will have a corresponding indifference curve through it showing other bacon and egg combinations that generate the same level of total utility for the consumer. We can see from the graph that this particular consumer is indifferent among 10 eggs and 1 bacon strip *(A)*, 5 eggs and 4 bacon strips *(B)*, and 3 eggs and 8 bacon strips *(C)* per week.

Moreover, we know that the consumer will prefer any point on the *ABC* indifference curve, I_1, to any point on the *FED* indifference curve, I_2, because points on I_1 contain more of both goods than do points on I_2. The farther from the origin the indifference curve lies, the higher the level of utility the individual will experience.

We can draw as many indifference curves on the graph as there are indifference sets confronting the consumer. However many we draw—two or two hundred—the resulting graph is termed an **indifference map**.

5. Indifference curves never cross. The reason for this is **transitivity of preferences**, which simply

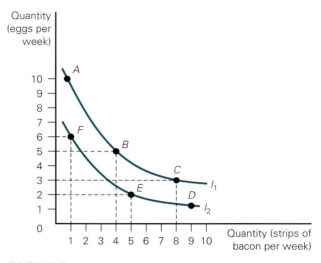

FIGURE 6.5

An Indifference Map

This consumer indifference map illustrates combinations of bacon and eggs. Any point on the graph will be associated with an indifference curve. Since a large number of indifference curves can be placed on the graph, it is called an indifference map. Indifference curves that are farther from the origin, such as I_1, represent higher levels of utility for the consumer because greater quantities of both goods are consumed.

means that if an individual prefers carrots to squash and squash to artichokes, he or she will also prefer carrots to artichokes. Indifference curves that cross would violate this assumption. Figure 6.6 illustrates this point.

In this graph two indifference curves do cross. The point where they cross (point *A*) lies on both indifference curves, I_1 and I_2. Since, by definition, all points along one indifference curve are equally preferred by the individual, the consumer will be indifferent among choices *A*, *B*, and *C* on I_1 and *A*, *D*, and *E* on I_2. This implies that the consumer is indifferent among all these points. But we see that this is impossible—if the consumer were indifferent between point *B* on I_1 and point *D* on I_2, this would mean that having more of both bacon and eggs (point *B*) made him or her no better off than having less of both (point *D*). Other things being equal, consumers always prefer more to less, so indifference curves cannot intersect

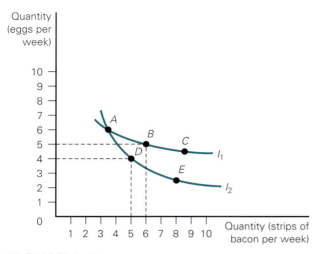

FIGURE 6.6

Indifference Curves Cannot Cross

Because preferences are transitive, point *A* cannot lie on two different indifference curves. If it did, the consumer would be indifferent among the combinations of bacon and eggs at point *B* with higher quantities of both, and point *D* with lower quantities of both.

without implying a type of irrationality that we do not observe in the real world.

THE BUDGET CONSTRAINT

Although we know that an individual consumer prefers a point on an indifference curve that is farther from the origin to a point on an indifference curve that is closer to the origin, this knowledge does not enable us to establish which indifference curve represents the best an individual can achieve with a limited budget. We can solve this problem by introducing a budget constraint, represented on the graph by a budget line.

In Figure 6.7a, we have assumed that the prices of two goods—apples and oranges—are the same: $1 per pound. If the consumer has a weekly budget of $10, the budget line will be a straight line running from the $10 level of apples (on the vertical axis) to the $10 level of oranges (on the horizontal axis). This line simply reflects the fact that the consumer can allocate his budget between apples and oranges in any way he sees

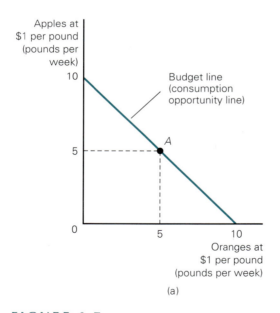

(a)

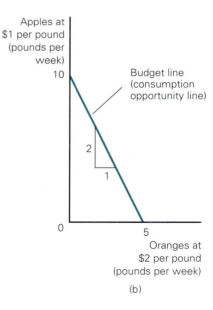

(b)

FIGURE 6.7

Budget Constraint

The budget line, or consumption opportunity line, depends on the relative prices of the two goods. The absolute value of the slope of the budget line is the ratio of the price of the good on the horizontal axis to the price of the good on the vertical axis. (a) The budget line represents all possible combinations of apples and oranges at $1 per pound each within a budget constraint of $10 per week. The absolute value of the slope of the line is 1. (b) The budget line, still with the budget constraint of $10 per week, has changed to reflect an increase in the price of oranges to $2 per pound. The absolute value of the slope of the line is 2.

fit—$10 on apples and zero on oranges, $10 on oranges and zero on apples, or any other combination that adds up to $10, such as point A: $5 for each.

How does a change in price affect the budget line? Figure 6.7b shows that the individual's budget remains the same ($10) but that the relative prices of the two goods have changed. While the price of apples remains at $1 a pound, the price of oranges has risen to $2 a pound. Although the consumer can still allocate his entire income to the purchase of either apples or oranges, $10 spent on apples would purchase 10 pounds of apples, while the same amount spent on oranges would yield only 5 pounds of oranges.

The budget line is thus drawn to reflect any combination of prices for the two goods. The absolute value of the slope of the budget line is equal to the ratio of the price of the good on the horizontal axis to the price of the good on the vertical axis. As illustrated in Figure 6.7b, where the price of oranges is $2 a pound and the price of apples $1 a pound, the absolute value of the slope is 2.

CONSUMER EQUILIBRIUM WITH INDIFFERENCE CURVES

The combination of an individual's indifference curves and budget line allows us to represent consumer equilibrium in a way that is equivalent to the method of marginal utility analysis. This alternative method is illustrated in Figure 6.8, which combines the budget line from Figure 6.7b with a set of indifference curves.

We can see that the consumer represented here will prefer point C to point F, because C lies on a higher indifference curve. She will also prefer point A to point C. All three of these points are actual opportunities confronting the consumer; she can afford them, given her budget constraint. Other things being equal, she would prefer point G to point A. However, point G is beyond the limit of her budget line. The best point she can achieve—the point on the highest indifference curve that can be reached within her budget constraint—is point A. This point represents consumer equilibrium—the combination yielding maximum utility from a given budget.

At A, the relevant indifference curve is exactly tangent to the budget line. This means that the slope of the budget line is equal to the slope of the indifference curve. We therefore know that in equilibrium the ratio of the marginal utility of the good on the horizontal axis (oranges) to the marginal utility of the good on the vertical axis (apples), indicated by the slope of the indifference curve, is equal to the ratio of the price of oranges to the price of apples, indicated by the slope of the budget line. Or, expressed somewhat differently,

$$\frac{\text{Marginal utility of oranges}}{\text{Marginal utility of apples}} = \frac{\text{Price of oranges}}{\text{Price of apples}}.$$

With terms rearranged, this formula is exactly the same result we arrived at earlier in the chapter when

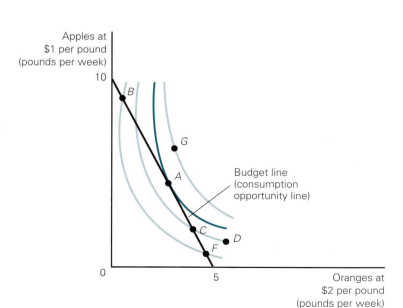

FIGURE 6.8

Determining Consumer Equilibrium with Indifference Curves

The consumer attains maximum satisfaction at point A, where the budget, or consumption opportunity, line is tangent to the highest possible indifference curve. At A the slope of the indifference curve, or the ratio of the marginal utilities of the two goods, is equal to the slope of the budget line, or the ratio of the prices of the two goods. This relation reflects the same condition for consumer equilibrium as that suggested by marginal utility analysis.

FIGURE 6.9

Indifference Curves and the Law of Demand

As the price of oranges falls from $2 a pound to $1 a pound, the budget line rotates to the right from B_1 to B_2. The consumer reaches a higher level of utility by attaining the highest indifference curve, I_2 rather than I_1, possible. As the price of oranges falls, the consumer purchases a larger quantity; O_2 is larger than O_1. This is precisely what the law of demand predicts—that, other things being equal, quantity demanded varies inversely with price.

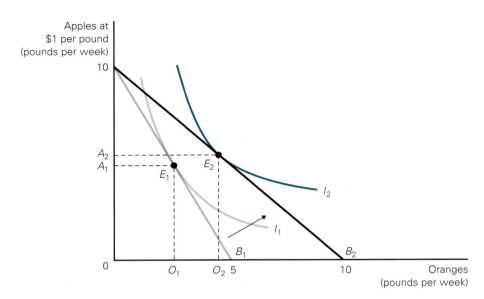

we discussed consumer equilibrium in marginal utility terms without the aid of indifference curves; that is, the preceding equation is equivalent to

$$\frac{\text{Marginal utility of oranges}}{\text{Price of oranges}} = \frac{\text{Marginal utility of apples}}{\text{Price of apples}}.$$

The two approaches thus yield the same predictions about consumer behavior.

INDIFFERENCE CURVES AND THE LAW OF DEMAND

Indifference curve analysis also can be used to demonstrate the law of demand. A demand curve can be derived by first allowing the price of a good to change, then finding the new equilibrium quantity of the good, and, finally, graphing the new and old price/equilibrium quantity combinations. Figures 6.9 and 6.10 together show how this is accomplished. Budget line B_1 is drawn by assuming that the price of oranges is $2 per pound and the price of apples is $1 per pound. Given these prices, and the consumer's income, the equilibrium quantity of oranges and apples for this consumer is shown as E_1 in Figure 6.8. Point E_1 is where indifference curve I_1 is tangent to budget line B_1. The consumer buys quantity O_1 of oranges per week when the price of oranges is $2 per pound.

If we allow the price of oranges to fall from $2 per pound to $1 per pound, the budget line rotates outward to line B_2. Indifference curve I_2, which is tangent to the new budget line at point E_2, lies farther from the origin than indifference curve I_1. This indicates that the lower price of one good leads to an increase in total utility. As Figure 6.9 shows, the lower price of oranges results in a larger quantity of oranges purchased, O_2.

By taking some of the information from Figure 6.9 and transferring it to Figure 6.10, the consumer's demand curve for oranges can be plotted. Figure 6.10 shows that at a price of oranges equal to $2 per pound, the consumer will purchase quantity O_1 of oranges per week. This information has come from the beginning situation in Figure 6.9, where the initial price of oranges was $2 per pound, the budget line was B_1, and the equilibrium quantity of apples and oranges consumed was E_1.

Figure 6.9 also shows that when oranges are priced at $1 per pound, the consumer will buy quantity O_2 of oranges per week. This information came from budget line B_2, where the price of oranges is $1 per pound and equilibrium quantity is E_2. The smooth line connecting the two points in Figure 6.10, labeled D_{oranges}, is the consumer's demand curve for oranges. It is downward sloping, indicating that the lower the price of oranges, other things being equal, the larger will be the amount of oranges purchased per week. The consumer equilibrium obtained through

FIGURE 6.10

The Demand Curve for Oranges

The consumer's equilibrium quantity of oranges consumed increases from O_1 to O_2 if the price of oranges falls from $2 to $1 per pound. The demand curve for oranges is downward sloping.

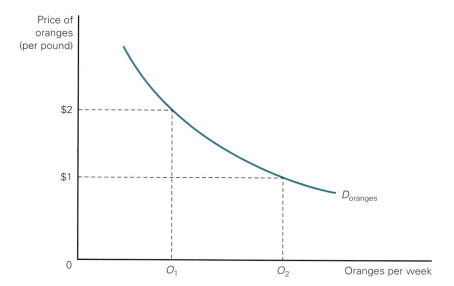

indifference curve analysis thus yields the type of demand curve predicted by the law of demand.

SUBSTITUTION AND INCOME EFFECTS

This chapter discussed the two reasons that consumers buy more of a good when its price falls, or that demand curves are downward sloping. When a good's price falls, the good becomes relatively less expensive in comparison with other goods. Other goods become relatively more expensive when this happens. As a result, consumers tend to substitute relatively less expensive goods for relatively more expensive goods in their purchases. This is what we referred to as the substitution effect.

However, when the price of only one good falls, the total buying power of the consumer's budget increases. This rise in what economists call real income induces the consumer to buy more of any given good. The increase in consumption of a good due to the consumer's increased buying power (which, in turn, is due to a drop in some good's price) was called the income effect.

The substitution and income effects of a change in the price of oranges can be depicted graphically by using a graph similar to Figure 6.9. Parts of Figure 6.9 have been reproduced in Figure 6.11. Combination

E_1 on indifference curve I_1 is the initial combination of apples and oranges consumed when apples are $1 per pound and oranges are $2 per pound. Combination E_2 and budget line B_2 are also the same in both figures. Figure 6.11 ignores the effects on apple consumption in order to concentrate on the two effects on orange consumption.

Both Figures 6.9 and 6.11 show that when the price of oranges falls from $2 to $1 per pound, the equilibrium quantity of oranges consumed rises from O_1 to O_2. However, Figure 6.11 shows how much of this increased orange consumption is due to the substitution effect (the amount O_S minus O_1) and how much to the income effect (O_2 minus O_S). To see why these amounts are the substitution and income effects, we need to apply the formula for consumer equilibrium.

Consider point E_1 in both Figures 6.9 and 6.11. Combination E_1 is the initial amounts of the goods consumed. For this to be a point of consumer equilibrium, we know that

$$\frac{\text{Marginal utility of oranges}}{\text{Marginal utility of apples}} = \frac{\$2}{\$1} = \frac{\text{Price of oranges}}{\text{Price of apples}}.$$

At point E_1 in each figure, the ratio of the marginal utilities, given by the slope of I_1 at point E_1, equals the ratio of prices, given by the slope of the budget line. The substitution effect conceptually measures by how

FIGURE 6.11

Substitution and Income Effects

When the price of oranges is $2 per pound, O_1 pounds of oranges are consumed per week. When the price of oranges falls to $1 per pound, two things happen. The consumer substitutes oranges for apples because oranges have become relatively cheaper. Orange consumption changes from O_1 to O_S due to the substitution effect. The buying power of the fixed budget also rises. Orange consumption rises from O_S to O_2 due to the income effect.

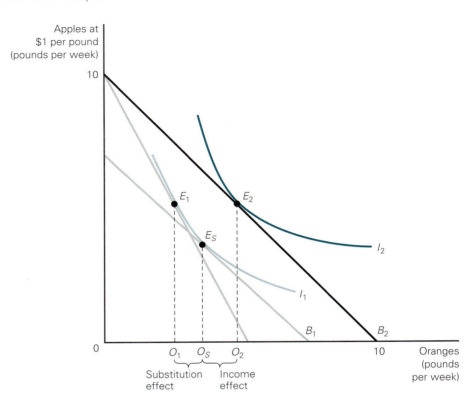

much consumption of a good would change if the consumer's real income remained unchanged when a price changes. This is accomplished by finding a combination of goods on the *original indifference curve* I_1 that would be chosen by the consumer if the ratio of the prices were $1/$1 instead of $2/$1. This combination of goods, E_S in Figure 6.11, yields the consumer the same level of total utility as does combination E_1. Keeping total utility constant is the economist's way of hypothetically preventing a change in real income when a price changes. At combination E_S in Figure 6.11, the ratio of the marginal utilities (the slope of the indifference curve) is equal to the new price ratio, $1/$1. Conceptually holding real income, or total utility, constant, this consumer would buy amount O_S pounds of oranges if the price of oranges were to fall to $1 per pound. The substitution effect of a drop in the price of oranges is then measured as O_S minus O_1 pounds of oranges.

We know, however, that when one price decreases, the buying power of the consumer's budget increases. Figures 6.9 and 6.11 both show the consumer buying combination E_2 (O_2 pounds of oranges) after all is said and done. Both figures also indicate that the consumer's total utility has increased as a result of the

price decrease. This increased total utility results from the increased buying power of the budget, which in turn is caused by the price decrease. The change in orange consumption per week due to the budget's larger buying power is measured as O_2 minus O_S pounds of oranges in Figure 6.11. This is the income effect of the decrease in the price of oranges. It is that part of the increased consumption of oranges that is not explained by the substitution effect.

The sum of the substitution effect (O_S minus O_1) and the income effect (O_2 minus O_S) equals the total effect (O_2 minus O_1) on orange consumption of a fall in the price of oranges. This is so because the single price change affects the consumer's environment in two ways. It alters the relative price of one good compared to another. This induces the consumer to substitute one good for another in consumption—the substitution effect. It also changes the budget's purchasing power, allowing the consumer to buy more (in the case of a price decrease) of the good and thus increasing the consumer's total utility. While we could never actually see these two effects separately (we can only observe the total effect in the real world), they nonetheless exist and are important in explaining consumer behavior.

SUMMARY

1. The method of indifference curves is an alternative way to study the process of individual choice and consumer equilibrium. It is based on the idea of observing how an individual chooses among consumption alternatives.

2. An indifference set is a group of consumption alternatives that yield the same total utility to the consumer.

3. An indifference curve is a graphical representation of an indifference set. Each point on the curve represents the same total utility to the consumer.

4. Indifference curves have negative slopes, are convex, and do not intersect.

5. The slope of an indifference curve is called the marginal rate of substitution of one good for another.

6. There is an indifference curve associated with any combination of goods selected by the consumer. An indifference map consists of a set of possible indifference curves of the consumer.

7. The budget line shows the relative prices of the goods an individual consumes and the amounts of the goods that he or she can consume without spending beyond the budget constraint.

8. In the indifference curve approach, consumer equilibrium occurs at the point where the consumer's budget line is tangent to the highest possible indifference curve. This condition is the same as that derived for consumer equilibrium using marginal utility analysis—namely, $MU_x/P_x = MU_Y/P_Y$.

9. The indifference curve technique can be used to show that the quantity consumed of a good is inversely related to its price—in other words, the law of demand.

10. In terms of indifference curves, the substitution effect shows how a change in a good's relative price affects consumption of the good. The income effect shows the impact on consumption of a change in the consumer's real purchasing power.

KEY TERMS

revealed preference
indifference map
indifference set

transitivity of preferences
indifference curve
budget constraint

marginal rate of
substitution

QUESTIONS FOR REVIEW AND DISCUSSION

1. Explain why indifference curves cannot intersect.

2. What is the relation between the principle of diminishing marginal utility and the marginal rate of substitution?

3. Suppose that the consumer feels that each combination of X and Y in the following table yields the same total utility. What comment would you make about the individual's choice process?

	GOODS	
Combinations	X	Y
A	10	7
B	15	8
C	20	9
D	25	10
E	30	11

4. What are the characteristics of indifference curves? What is the rationale for each characteristic? What would be the consequences of violating each of these characteristics?

5. How does the indifference curve approach show that consumer demand curves are negatively sloped? Explain.

6. Suppose that the price of oranges increases rather than decreases in Figure 6.10. Using indifference curve analysis, show the income and substitution effects of this price increase.

PROBLEM

Figure 6.12 shows three hypothetical indifference curves for Jill. Points A, B, C, and D represent different combinations of compact discs and movies.

1. Which combination represents the lowest level of satisfaction for Jill?

2. Which combination represents the highest level?

3. Is Jill indifferent about any of the combinations? If so, which combinations?

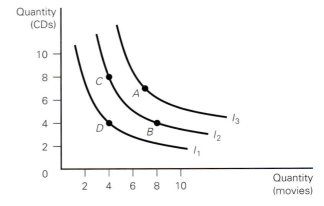

FIGURE 6.12

The Firm
and Costs
of Production

All profit-oriented business firms are alike in one basic sense: Firms purchase inputs in resource markets and use these inputs to produce a product or service, which is then sold to consumers. The fact that inputs to a production process are not free—that they carry an opportunity cost—leads to the concept of production costs.

In this chapter we develop the concept of production costs from the perspective of the economist. When you complete Chapter 7 you should understand

- The nature of product in a firm.
- How production costs are actually a form of opportunity costs.
- How an accountant's out-of-pocket costs may sometimes differ from an economist's measure of opportunity cost.
- How costs of production influence a firm's behavior.
- How the various types of costs relate to both business decision making and to the function of the market.

THE NATURE OF THE FIRM

We are now at the point in our study of microeconomics where the concept of the business **firm** comes into play. We will discuss the cost curves of a firm, and we will discuss competitive firms and monopoly firms. Before we do so, however, we briefly present an economic depiction of a firm.

Firm
An economic institution that purchases, organizes, and assembles resources to produce goods and services.

Firms occupy a critical role in a market economy. In fact, there are over 17 million business firms in the United States, ranging in size from the small corner grocery store owned by one individual to the immense multinational corporations owned by millions of stockholders.

In broad terms, the economic function of a business firm is to combine scarce resources (factors of production) to produce goods and services demanded by consumers. Firms that perform this function well make profits and survive; firms that perform this function poorly experience losses and fail. This brief definition of a firm, however, touches only the surface of the matter. To understand the role of firms in a market economy, we need to explore how a firm organizes resources.

HOW MARKETS AND FIRMS COORDINATE RESOURCES

Market coordination
The process that directs the flow of resources into the production of goods and services through the price signaling mechanism.

Basically, there are two methods of economic coordination in a market economy: market coordination and firm coordination. **Market coordination** is what we have studied so far in this book. It is the use of the price system to provide incentives to suppliers and demanders, to produce and consume goods and services in the appropriate amounts. Market coordination refers to the myriad daily economic activities that are guided by the "invisible hand" of the market. Our study of demand and supply is the study of how the market coordinates activities.

Not all activities in a modern economy are coordinated by the market, however. Part of the division of labor is carried out within firms. Automobile assembly-line workers do not sell their output directly in a market. Rather, they supply labor to the auto company, which employs managers to direct and coordinate the uses of their labor within the firm. **Firm coordination** is a productive process that depends on managerial rather than market direction.

Firm coordination
The process that directs the flow of resources into the production of a particular good or service through the forces of management organization within the firm.

The distinction between market and firm coordination is not absolute. Resource allocation within the firm is not really outside the price system, although it might superficially look that way. Decision making in the firm is centralized and performed by **managers**. Managers transfer and allocate resources within the firm in ways that are efficient given the prices for equivalent resources on the market. The manager's decision to transfer a quantity of a particular resource within the firm is based on prices, even though resources are not actually bought and sold within the firm.

Manager
An individual who organizes and monitors resources within a firm to produce a good or service.

If market and firm coordination are so similar, what accounts for the existence of firms? In actuality, much production is undertaken by independent individuals, and it is common for individual demanders to contract with individual suppliers for particular goods and services. For example, Saks Fifth Avenue, Tiffany's, and Neiman-Marcus contract with individual artists and artisans for many of their wares. Many publishers hire work out to freelance editors and artists rather than having all editorial services performed by in-house staff. It is often cheaper or more efficient to do so. Economic coordination between contracting individuals in such cases is achieved directly through the operation of the price system. So an interesting question arises: Why is all production not undertaken by freelance individual operators? In other words, why will an owner of capital goods hire employees for long periods of time instead of contracting out for the performance of specific tasks as they arise?

Ronald H. Coase was the first economist to pose and answer this important question. His answer was simple and profound: Firms exist when they are the least costly form of economic coordination; their size is determined by what is most efficient (least costly) for production.[1] (Coase won the Nobel Prize in economics in 1991, partly for his work on the theory of the firm.) We do not use the market to organize all production because it is not costless to use markets. Using the market necessitates finding out what prices are, negotiating and enforcing contractual agreements with suppliers, going to court when promises are not kept, paying transaction costs, and engaging in various other costly and resource-using activities. For these reasons, not all production in a market economy is coordinated through market exchange. It costs less in many cases to organize production in a firm where resource allocation is directed and coordinated by managers.

In firm production, the inside of the firm will be run by managerial coordination; the firm will deal with the outside world through market coordination. Which activities the firm chooses to organize internally will be related to the cost of organizing the same activities through market exchange. Automobile manufacturers can buy tires in a contractual arrangement with tire companies, or they can make their own tires. The relative costs of these alternatives will determine how the auto company gets its tires.

Firms exist in a market economy because they represent a least-cost means of organizing production. However, firms will not grow without limit, because at some point the marginal cost of organizing a task within the firm will exceed the marginal cost of organizing the same task through market contracting. This limit on firm size will evolve naturally because the managerial cost of organizing and keeping track of inside production rises along with the number of tasks the firm undertakes. There will be a natural division of production in an economy between firms and markets, determined by the relative costs of producing goods and services in each way. Limits on firm size have created a variety of types of business in our economy. The three Focus boxes within this chapter provide discussion of the principal kinds of firms that have emerged, from the most popular type, the single proprietorship (see the Focus "Going Into Business for Yourself" on p. 170), to the partnership ("Going Into Business With Others" on p. 178) to the type of organization that supports the very largest firms in our economy ("Big Business—The Corporation" on p. 185).

COSTS IN A BUSINESS FIRM

Consumers have unlimited wants, but resources to satisfy their wants are limited. Costs of production in a firm arise from the fact that resources have alternative uses. The same resources that are used to produce a good to satisfy consumers' demands can also be used to produce other goods. For resources to be drawn into the production of a particular good, they must be bid away from other uses. Production of a newspaper might require, among other things, that wood pulp be turned into newsprint rather than notebook paper, that photographers be enticed to work as photojournalists rather than as portrait photographers, and that youngsters be hired to distribute newspapers rather than earn money by babysitting or mowing lawns. The expenditures representing the opportunity costs necessary to do all of these things are called **opportunity costs of production**. Costs of production are therefore the value of resources in their next-best uses.

Opportunity costs of production
The opportunity costs of resources used to produce goods and services.

[1]Ronald H. Coase, "The Nature of the Firm," *Economics* (November 1937), pp. 386–405.

FOCUS

Going into Business for Yourself

Most people dream of going into business at one time or another in their lives. Hundreds of thousands of individuals go into (and out of) business every year. That form of business organization is called a proprietorship. A proprietorship is a firm that has a single owner who is liable—or legally responsible—for all the debts of the firm—a condition termed unlimited liability. The sole proprietor has unlimited liability in the legal sense that if the firm goes bankrupt, the proprietor's personal as well as business property can be used to settle the firm's outstanding debts.

More often than not, the sole proprietor also works in the firm as a manager and a laborer. Thus, most single-owner firms are small. Many small retail establishments, such as restaurants and men's clothing, dress, or antique shops, are organized as proprietorships.

The primary advantage of the proprietorship is that it allows the small businessperson to have direct control of the firm and its activities. It is up to the sole proprietor to decide how much effort to expend in producing output. In other words, the sole proprietor can be his or her own boss.

The primary disadvantage of the proprietorship is that the welfare of the firm and the liabiltiy for its activities largely rests on one person. The typical sole proprietor is the chief stockholder, chief executive officer, and chief cook and bottle washer for the firm. Since there are only twenty-four hours in a day, the sole proprietor faces problems in attending to the many different aspects of the business. Some say that the happiest two days in your life are the day you go into business "for yourself" and the day you get out!

Nevertheless, proprietorships are the dominant form of business organization in the American economy. They accounted for more than 75 percent of all businesses in 1998, but generated only 7 percent or so in revenues. But individual inventiveness sometimes pays off, and dreams of success do come true. It seems safe to conclude that this form of business enterprise will continue to be popular in the twenty-first century.

Explicit and Implicit Costs

The opportunity costs of production include both explicit and implicit costs. Take, for example, a small, owner-operated dry cleaning firm organized as a sole proprietorship. The dry cleaner has to purchase labor, cleaning fluids, hat blocks, bagging machines, insurance, accounting and legal services, advertising, and so on to produce dry cleaning services. The costs of these resources are called **accounting costs**, or explicit costs. They are so named because they are quite visible; they are the wages and bills the sole proprietor must pay to conduct business.

The firm does not make explicit payments for all the resources it uses to produce dry cleaning services. The owner of the firm may not include a wage for his own services. Omitting his salary from calculations, however, does not mean that the owner's services are free. They carry an **implicit cost**, valued by what the owner

Accounting costs
Payments a firm actually makes to resource suppliers; out-of-pocket costs or explicit costs.

Implicit costs
The opportunity costs of resources used in production for which no explicit payments are made.

could have done with his time instead of working in the firm. Implicit costs are the opportunity costs of resources owned by the firm. They are called *implicit costs* because they do not involve contractual payments.

Opportunity cost of capital
The return that could be received from the next-best alternative investment.

The main implicit cost is the **opportunity cost of capital**. Individuals who invest in firms expect to earn a normal rate of return on their investment. For instance, they could have placed their capital in money market certificates and earned perhaps a 6 percent rate of return. In this case, the 6 percent rate of return represents the opportunity cost of capital invested in business ventures. Unless investors earn at least the opportunity cost of capital, they will not continue to invest in a business.

Total cost of production
The total opportunity cost of all resources used in production; the sum of all explicit and implicit production costs.

The **total cost of production** is the sum of explicit and implicit costs. Total cost is the value of all the alternative opportunities forgone as a result of production of a particular good or service.

The Nature of Economic Costs

Opportunity cost is a forward-looking concept. Opportunity costs are incurred when the decision maker decides about the future use of resources; they are the expected costs of possible alternatives available to an owner.

Historical costs
Costs measured by the cost of a resource at the time the resource was purchased.

Sunk costs
Previously incurred, irretrievable costs of a currently owned resource.

In contrast, accounting costs are **historical costs**, or costs that have been incurred in the past. While historical costs can be useful in estimating economic costs, historical costs look backward; opportunity costs look forward. Historical costs are poor guides to opportunity costs. Consider the case of **sunk costs**, which are closely related to historical costs. Current sunk costs are the difference between the initial cost—which exists prior to a commitment to a given investment or project—and the value that can be recovered after commitment to the given investment or project. Sunk costs are the irretrievable part of any fixed or historical investment.

For better or worse, certain portions of earlier decisions cannot be reversed. Economists consider certain of the costs of previous decisions—the sunk costs—to be irrelevant to current decisions. Suppose that you buy a farm in Vermont for $300,000 and spend an additional $200,000 refurbishing the old farmhouse, which you plan to operate as a bed and breakfast. After a year you realize that your location prevents you from profitably remaining in business. If you decide to sell, should your asking price be dictated by your having spent $500,000 on the property?

The answer is no. A portion of the $500,000 in costs you have already incurred is a sunk cost. Some of the alterations you made may have no value if the property is to be put to a use other than serving as a bed and breakfast—in fact, some changes may actually reduce the property's value for other uses. You must realize that some of your costs cannot be recaptured. Some of the money you invested is gone forever. It may be that we have to learn this the hard way—from experience. However, viewed rationally, current decisions should be based on current or expected costs and benefits of future actions, not on sunk costs and past benefits.

The general irrelevance of sunk costs is critically important for many economic decisions—some of them personal decisions. Indeed, the old adage "never cry over spilt milk" has a firm foundation in economic logic. A college athlete may skip her senior year to turn professional. Three years of studying, attending class, and other costs should be ignored when deciding whether to choose the degree or a million-dollar salary. Opportunity costs of all kinds affect our lives. Government policies, such as the draft, serving on juries, or being required to provide "public service," often have a direct effect on individuals' opportunity costs. (See the Application at the end of this chapter, "The Draft, Jury Duty, and Conscripted 'Public Service': Opportunity Cost and You" for a discussion of how these policies might affect you.)

Economic Profits Versus Accounting Profits

Economic profit

The amount by which total revenues exceed total opportunity cost.

Businesspeople must compare their total costs with their total revenues (all the money they take in) to determine whether they are making a profit. **Economic profit** is the difference between total revenue and total opportunity cost. It exists when the revenue of the firm more than covers all of its costs, explicit and implicit. Economic loss results when revenue does not cover the total opportunity cost. A firm's economic profit is said to be zero when its total revenue equals its total cost. Zero economic profit does not mean that the firm is not viable or about to cease operating. It means that the firm is covering all the costs of its operations and that the owners and investors are making a normal rate of return on their investment.

Since accounting costs do not usually include implicit costs—such as the value of the sole proprietor's time or the opportunity cost of capital invested in the firm—accounting costs are an understatement of the opportunity costs of production. **Accounting profits** will generally be higher than economic profits because economic profits are calculated after taking both explicit and implicit costs into account.

Accounting profit

The amount by which total revenues exceed total accounting, or explicit, costs.

Private Costs and Social Costs

Private costs

The opportunity costs of production that are borne, or paid, by producers.

We have so far discussed a world of **private costs**, in which the firm pays a market price for the resources it uses in production. The dry cleaner's costs of production were private costs, equal to the sum of explicit and implicit costs. The key aspect of the concept of private costs is that someone is responsible for them; that is, someone pays for the use of the resources. The owner of the dry cleaning firm incurs both explicit and implicit costs in business, and he incurred these costs to engage in business.

But what if the dry cleaner dumps used cleaning fluid into the town lake adjacent to his plant? In doing so, he is using the lake as a resource in his dry cleaning business—as a place to dispose of a by-product of his production process—but he pays nothing for the use of the lake as a dumping site. No one owns the lake for purposes of dumping, and it is therefore unpriced for this use. The private costs of the dry cleaner thus do not reflect the full costs of his operation. The cost of the use of the lake is not reflected in the dry cleaner's costs of production. Such a cost is called an **external cost** because the cost is borne by someone other than the owner of the firm.

External costs

The opportunity costs of production that are not borne, or paid, by producers.

Social costs

The opportunity costs of all resources used in the production of goods and services; the sum of private and external costs.

When external costs arise from a firm's activities—such as polluting the air or water—the private costs of the firm are lower than its **social costs**. The total cost to society of the firm's production includes the firm's input costs and the costs of using common property or other resources not owned by the firm, such as the town lake.

In Chapter 17 we further analyze external costs, including ways in which society can make public choices about problems arising from external costs. The important point here is that private costs of production do not always reflect the full opportunity costs of production; the use of unpriced resources, such as the environment, may also carry a hidden cost to society.

ECONOMIC TIME

Variable input
A factor of production whose level of usage may be changed in the short run.

Fixed input
A factor of production whose level of usage cannot be changed in the short run.

Short run
An amount of time insufficient to allow the usage of all inputs to vary.

Long run
An amount of time sufficiently long that all input usage levels can be varied.

The passage of time is fundamental to the theory of costs. Economic time is not the same thing as calendar time. To the economist analyzing costs, the firm's time constraints are defined by its ability to adjust its operations in light of a changing marketplace. If the demand for the firm's product decreases, for example, the firm must adjust production to the lower level of demand. Perhaps some of its resources can be immediately and easily varied to adapt to the changed circumstances. In the face of declining or increasing sales, an automobile firm can reduce or increase its orders of steel and fabric. Inputs whose purchase and use can be altered quickly are called **variable inputs**. The auto firm with declining sales cannot immediately sell its excess plants and equipment or its inventory. Such resources are called **fixed inputs**; a reduction or increase in their use takes considerably more time to arrange.

There are two primary categories of economic time: the short run and the long run. The **short run** is a period in which some inputs remain fixed. In the long run, all inputs can be varied. In the **long run**, the auto firm can make fewer cars not only by buying less steel but also by reducing the number of plants and the amount of equipment and labor it uses for car production. The time it takes to vary all inputs is different for different industries. In some cases, it may take only a month, in others a year, and in still others ten years.

SHORT-RUN COSTS: AN INTRODUCTION

In the short run, some of the firm's inputs are fixed and others are variable. Building on this distinction, the short-run theory of costs emphasizes two categories of costs—fixed and variable.

Fixed Costs and Variable Costs

Fixed costs
The costs of inputs that cannot be varied in the short run.

Variable costs
The costs of inputs whose usage levels can be changed in the short run. Variable costs change as output changes.

Total costs
All the costs of a firm's operations; total variable costs plus total fixed costs.

Average fixed cost
Total fixed costs divided by the level of output.

A **fixed cost** does not change as the firm's output level changes. Whether the firm produces more or less, it will pay the same for such things as fire insurance, local property taxes, and other costs that are independent of its output level. Fixed costs exist even at a zero rate of output. Perhaps the most important fixed cost is the opportunity cost of the firm's capital equipment and plant—that is, the next-best alternative use of these resources. This cost exists even when the plant is not operating. The only way to avoid fixed costs is to shut down and go out of business, an event that can occur only in the long run. Total fixed costs (*TFC*) equal the price of fixed inputs multiplied by the quantity of fixed inputs employed.

Variable costs are costs that change as the output level of a firm changes. When the firm reduces its level of production, it will use fewer raw materials and perhaps will lay off workers. Consequently, its variable costs of production will decline. Variable costs are expenditures on inputs that can be varied in short-run use. Total variable costs (*TVC*) equal the price of variable inputs multiplied by the quantity of variable inputs employed. **Total cost** (*TC*) is the sum of total fixed and total variable costs.

It is useful to determine how the cost of producing output changes in the short run as the level of output is increased or decreased. The fixed cost per unit is called **average fixed cost** (*AFC*) and is found by dividing the total fixed cost (*TFC*) by

TABLE 7.1

Short-Run Cost Relations

Terms	Symbols	Definition
Average fixed cost = Total fixed cost ÷ Output	$AFC = TFC/q$	A fixed cost does not vary with output. Average fixed cost per unit declines as output rises.
Average variable cost = Total variable cost ÷ Output	$AVC = TVC/q$	Average variable cost exhibits a U-shaped pattern as output increases.
Average total cost = Total cost ÷ Output = Average fixed cost + Average variable cost	$ATC = TC/q$ $ATC = AFC + AVC$	Total cost is the sum of fixed and variable costs. Average total cost also forms a U-shaped curve when graphed from very low to very high output levels.
Marginal cost = Change in total cost ÷ Change in output	$MC = \Delta TC/\Delta q$	Marginal cost first falls and then rises as the short-run capacity of a firm's fixed plant is approached.

the firm's total output of the good (referred to as q throughout this chapter). Since total fixed costs are the same at all levels of output, AFC will decline continuously as output increases. This relation is defined in Table 7.1 and shown graphically in Figure 7.1a. Symbolically, average fixed cost is expressed

$$AFC = \frac{TFC}{q}.$$

Average variable cost
Total variable costs divided by the level of output.

Average variable cost *(AVC)* is found by dividing total variable cost *(TVC)* by the firm's output. It is also drawn in Figure 7.1a and defined in Table 7.1. Average variable cost ordinarily has a U shape and may be expressed in the formula

$$AVC = \frac{TVC}{q}.$$

Average total cost
Total costs divided by the level of output.

Average total cost *(ATC)* is total cost divided by total output. Average total cost also can be found by adding average fixed costs and average variable costs. Thus, in Figure 7.1a, the ATC curve is shown as the vertical sum of the AFC and AVC curves. Average total cost is sometimes referred to as unit cost, and it is total cost (fixed plus variable) divided by the firm's output:

$$ATC = \frac{TC}{q}.$$

Although the average total cost curve provides useful information, economic decisions are made at the margin. In considering a change in the level of production, firms must determine the marginal cost of the change.

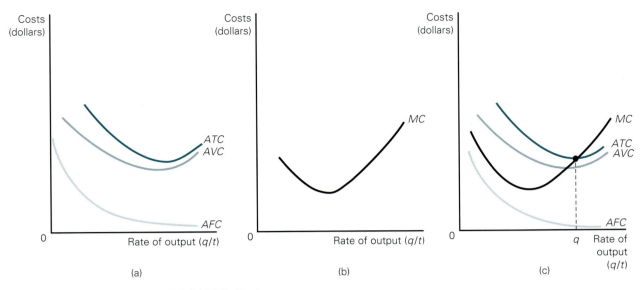

(a)   (b)   (c)

FIGURE 7.1

Short-Run Cost Curves of the Firm
(a) The behavior of average fixed cost *(AFC)*, average variable cost *(AVC)*, and average total cost *(ATC)* as output changes. *ATC* is the vertical sum of *AVC* and *AFC*. (b) The behavior of the firm's marginal costs *(MC)* as output increases. *MC* ultimately rises as the short-run capacity limit of the firm is approached. (c) All the short-run cost curves. Notice in particular the U shape of the *ATC* curve. *ATC* is high where the firm's plant is underutilized at low rates of output or overutilized at high rates of output. The rate of output is measured per unit of time.

Marginal cost

The additional cost of producing one more unit of output; the change in total cost divided by the change in output.

Marginal cost *(MC)* is the cost of producing each additional unit of output; it is found by dividing the change in total cost by the change in output. Symbolically, marginal cost may be expressed

$$MC = \frac{\Delta TC}{\Delta q}.$$

The result of such calculations is a marginal cost curve, shown in Figure 7.1b. As output rises, marginal cost declines, reaches a minimum, then rises—because it becomes increasingly hard to produce additional output in a **fixed plant**. Extra workers needed to produce additional output begin to get in each other's way; inefficiencies proliferate as workers must take turns using machines; storage room becomes filled; and so on.

Fixed plant

A given amount of equipment and size of production facilities with which the firm can use variable inputs in the short run.

Figure 7.1c brings all the short-run cost curves together. Notice that the *ATC* curve is U-shaped. At low levels of output a firm does not utilize its fixed plant and equipment very effectively. The firm does not produce enough relative to the fixed costs for its plant, causing the average total cost to be high. At high levels of output the inefficiencies of overloading the existing operation cause marginal costs to rise, raising the average total cost. These two effects combine to yield a U-shaped average total cost curve. Either low or high utilization of a fixed plant leads to high average total cost. The minimum point on the *ATC* curve, *q*, represents the lowest average total cost—the lowest cost per unit for producing the good. The *MC* curve crosses both the *AVC* and the *ATC* at their minimum. Table 7.1 provides a short-hand reference to all these concepts. We will return to these concepts below and explain them in more detail.

Diminishing Returns

Law of diminishing marginal returns

A situation in which adding more and more of a variable input to a fixed plant results in smaller and smaller amounts of additional output produced.

The behavior and shape of the short-run marginal cost and average total cost curves can be understood more completely with the **law of diminishing marginal returns**. The law of diminishing marginal returns states that as additional units of a variable input are combined with a fixed amount of other resources, the amount of additional output produced will start to decline beyond some point. The returns—additional output—that result from using more and more of the variable input will ultimately diminish.

Though the language sounds formidable, the law of diminishing marginal returns is little more than formalized common sense. Suppose that the dry cleaner in our previous example has a plant of a given size that we will view as his fixed input. He begins operations by adding workers one at a time and observes what happens to the resulting output of dry cleaning. The first few additional workers are very useful. One specializes in cleaning, another in pressing, another in bagging, and so on. The output of dry cleaning increases as the laborers are added. But the process cannot go on forever. At some point the output provided by one additional laborer will begin to diminish because capacity of the existing physical plant will be reached.

The law of diminishing marginal returns is a fact of nature. Imagine how the world would work if it were not true: All of the world's dry cleaning could be done in a single plant. And if diminishing returns did not exist in agriculture, all of the world's food could be grown on a fixed plot of land, say an acre.

The law of diminishing marginal returns can be illustrated numerically and graphically. A standard example comes from agriculture; we experiment by adding laborers to a fixed plot of land and observe what happens to output. To isolate the effect of adding additional workers (the variable input), we keep all inputs except labor fixed and assume that agricultural technology does not change.

Table 7.2 is a numerical analysis of the results of such an experiment. The first column shows the amount of the variable input—labor—that is used in combination with the fixed input—land. The simplified numbers for **total product** and **marginal product** represent real measures of output, such as tons of soybeans grown per year.

Total product

The total amount of output produced.

Marginal product

The additional output produced by employing one additional unit of a variable input.

Marginal product is the change in total product caused by the addition of each additional worker, or

$$MP = \frac{\text{change in output}}{\text{change in quantity of variable input}}.$$

At first, as workers (the variable input) are added, total product, or output, expands rapidly. The first three workers show increasing marginal products (10, 12, and 14 extra tons of soybeans with the addition of each worker). Diminishing marginal returns set in, however, with the addition of the fourth worker. That is, the marginal product of the fourth worker is 13 tons, down from the 14-ton marginal prod-

TABLE 7.2

Law of Diminishing Marginal Returns

If units of a variable input (labor) are added one at a time to a production process with a fixed plant (growing soybeans with no change in technology on a fixed plot of land), the total product, marginal product, and average product all increase at first. But as more workers are added, they begin to get in each other's way. Total output gained by adding more workers begins to decline, as predicted by the law of diminishing marginal returns.

Variable Input (units of labor)	Total Product (tons per year)	Marginal Product (tons per year)	Average Product (tons per year)
0	0		0
		} · · · · · · · · · · · · · · 10	
1	10		10.00
		} · · · · · · · · · · · · · 12	
2	22		11.00
		} · · · · · · · · · · · · · 14	
3	36		12.00
		} · · · · · · · · · · · · · 13	
4	49		12.25
		} · · · · · · · · · · · · · 11	
5	60		12.00
		} · · · · · · · · · · · · · 10	
6	70		11.67
		} · · · · · · · · · · · · · 5	
7	75		10.71
		} · · · · · · · · · · · · · 3	
8	78		9.75
		} · · · · · · · · · · · · -2	
9	76		8.44
		} · · · · · · · · · · · · -6	
10	70		7.00

uct gained by adding the third worker. Marginal product continues to decline as additional workers are added to the plot of land. This agrees with our earlier definition of the law of diminishing marginal returns: As additional units of a variable input are added to a fixed amount of other resources, beyond some point the amount of additional output produced will start to decline. In fact, the addition of the ninth and tenth workers leads to reductions in total product. Marginal product in these cases is negative, meaning that the addition of these workers actually reduces output. It becomes more and more difficult to obtain increases in output from the fixed plot of land by adding workers. At some point the workers simply get in each other's way.

Average product

Total output divided by the number of units of the variable input used to produce the total output; output produced per unit of variable input used.

The last column in the table introduces the concept of **average product**, which is total product divided by the number of units of the variable input, or

$$AP = \frac{q}{\text{quantity of variable input}} .$$

The average product is the average output per worker. Average product increases as long as it is less than marginal product. Thus, average product increases through

FOCUS

"Going into Business with Others"—The Partnership

A partnership is an extended form of the proprietorship (see the Focus on "Going Into Business for Yourself" earlier in this chapter). Rather than actually "going into business for yourself," a partnership has two or more co-owners and so involves "going into business with others." The partners, who are team members, share financing of capital investments and, in return, residual claims to the firm's profits. Jointly, they manage the firm, organize team production, and monitor one another's behavior to control shirking. A partnership is a form well suited to lines of team production that involve creative or intellectual skills.

The partnership also has certain limitations. Individual partners cannot sell their share of the partnership without the approval of the other partners. Moreover, each partner is considered legally liable for all the debts incurred by the partnership up to the full extent of the individual partner's wealth—a condition called joint unlimited liability. Because of these limitations, partnerships are usually small and are found in businesses where monitoring of production by a manager is difficult.

A law firm is an example of team production in action. Most law firms are organized as legal partnerships. Each partner's liability does not end with the size of the partner's investment in the firm; it extends to the limit of each partner's personal assets. In the event of bankruptcy, creditors can attach the personal assets of the partners to settle claims against the firm.

What does this unlimited liability mean economically? Partners will be most careful about how they conduct their business. In particular, they will screen candidates for partners in the firm very carefully. A young lawyer is first given an associate status in the firm and must learn and compete with other young associates to become a partner after five or six years. This screening and training process is clearly motivated by the unlimited liability condition—the cost of making a mistake in the selection of a partner can be very high.

A law firm is a little society of profit sharers when organized as a partnership. A lawyer is engaged in what might be loosely called "artistic production." How do you know if your legal partner is working on a case when he or she is staring out the window or walking down the street? An external observer cannot tell whether the lawyer is goofing off or considering a new legal angle on a case. Making the lawyer a partner with shared responsibilities in the firm and a share of the firm's profits is a way to make sure that the lawyer devotes his or her time to cases and not to shirking. Thus, one rationale for the partnership is to promote efficient behavior by artistic producers such as lawyers, accountants, architects, and commercial artists. While partnerships constitute a small percentage of firms and business revenues in the U.S. economy, many important services are organized in this manner.

the addition of the fourth worker. The marginal product of the fifth worker is 11, which is less than the average product for five workers, and beyond this point the average product falls.

Figure 7.2 graphically illustrates the law of diminishing marginal returns with the data from Table 7.2. Figure 7.2a illustrates the total product curve. Total product increases rapidly at first, as the marginal product of the first three workers

FIGURE 7.2

Total, Average, and Marginal Product Curves

(a) Total product curve, plotting the data from Table 7.2. (b) Average product and marginal product curves. Marginal product is the rate of change of the total product curve. The area of diminishing marginal returns begins when marginal product starts to decline. Average product rises when marginal product is greater than average product, and it falls when marginal product is less than average product.

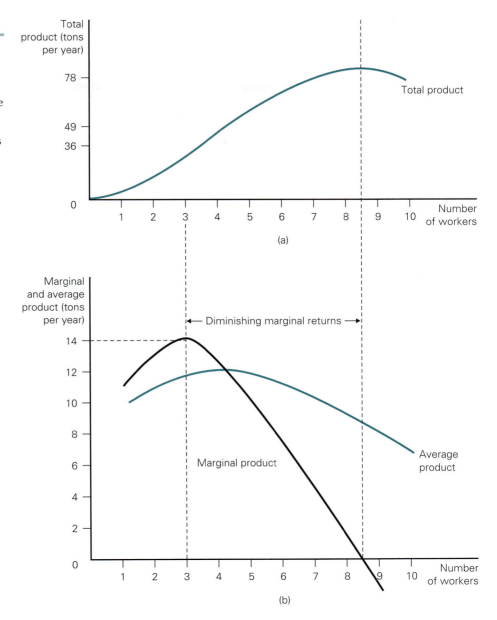

(a)

(b)

increases. Diminishing returns set in with the fourth worker, and thereafter the total product increases less rapidly. Beyond eight workers, the total product curve turns down and starts to decline. The maximum total product is reached with eight workers. The marginal product and average product curves are shown in Figure 7.2b. The marginal product curve is simply the slope of the total product curve. It rises to a maximum at three workers and then declines as diminishing returns set in. Eventually, it becomes negative past eight workers, indicating that total product is decreasing. The average product curve rises when marginal product is greater than average product, and it declines when marginal product is less than average product.

How can the law of diminishing marginal returns be applied to economic decision making? Consider the thinking of the farmer who owns the plot of land in this experiment. How many workers will he or she choose to hire? Before the area of diminishing marginal returns is reached, additional workers have an increasing marginal product. The farmer will add these workers and will go no further in hiring than the point where the marginal product falls to zero. Even if labor were free, the farmer would not go beyond this point because there would be so many workers on the land that the marginal product of an additional worker would be negative and the total product would decline. This implies that it is rational for the farmer to operate somewhere in the area of diminishing marginal returns.

Precisely how many workers will maximize profits? The answer depends on the cost of the workers (and on the productivity and prices of other inputs). Assume that each worker is paid a wage rate equivalent to 4 units of output. The farmer will compare the marginal product of each worker with the wage rate. The fourth worker adds 13 units of output and costs the farmer the equivalent of only 4 units. In fact, the marginal product of the first seven workers exceeds their wage rate. However, the marginal product of the eighth worker is 3 units of output, which is less than the wage rate. The rational farmer will therefore hire seven workers. This is the law of diminishing marginal returns in action. It points the farmer toward the rational utilization of factors of production.

Diminishing Marginal Returns and Short-Run Costs

What does the law of diminishing marginal returns imply about the behavior of the firm's short-run cost curves? Once diminishing marginal returns set in, more and more of the variable input—in our example, labor—is needed to expand output by an additional unit. If the price of the variable input is fixed, the firm's marginal costs will rise as a reflection of diminishing returns. Adding more workers to the plot of land at a fixed wage rate eventually leads to both diminishing returns and rising marginal costs. These are two ways of looking at the same thing. To argue that marginal returns are diminishing is to argue that marginal costs are rising: As the quantity of variable inputs increases, marginal product (and output) rises and then falls. This means that as output rises, marginal cost falls and then rises.

Table 7.3 presents a numerical illustration of how the law of diminishing marginal returns affects a firm's short-run costs. Columns (2), (3), and (4) show how total costs behave as output increases in the short run, and columns (5), (6), and (7) show the behavior of the corresponding average cost concepts.

In this example, we keep the numbers low for simplicity. Total fixed cost is constant at $10 per day; average fixed cost per unit is the total fixed cost divided by output. Fixed costs must be paid in the short run whether the firm operates or not. The level of average fixed cost falls continuously as output is increased. For the first unit produced, for example, both total fixed cost and average fixed cost are $10. Total fixed cost remains at $10 for the second unit, but average fixed cost falls to $5 per unit. As business grows, average fixed cost falls.

Remember, total variable cost is the sum of the firm's expenditures on variable inputs. As Table 7.3 shows, in order to produce more output, more must be spent on variable inputs. It takes an additional expenditure of $1.60 on variable inputs to expand output from 0 to 1 unit, but an additional expenditure of only $1.45 to expand output from 1 to 2 units. The increases in total variable cost get progressively smaller as output is expanded to 9 units; after 9 units the increases grow progressively larger. Since average variable cost is the total variable cost divided by output, it first declines and then rises at the tenth unit of output.

TABLE 7.3

Short-Run Cost Data for a Firm

The various concepts of short-run costs are expressed in both total and average terms. Columns (1) through (4) present the firm's total cost data; columns (5) through (8) present the cost data in marginal and average terms. Notice especially that short-run marginal cost ultimately rises because of the law of diminishing marginal returns.

(1) Output (units)	(2) Total Fixed Cost	(3) Total Variable Cost	(4) Total Cost (2) + (3)	(5) Average Fixed Cost (2) ÷ (1)	(6) Average Variable Cost (3) ÷ (1)	(7) Average Total Cost (4) ÷ (1)	(8) Marginal Cost Δ(4) ÷ Δ(1)[a]
0	$10.00	$0.00	$10.00	$—	$—	$—	$—
1	10.00	1.60	11.60	10.00	1.60	11.60	1.60
2	10.00	3.05	13.05	5.00	1.53	6.53	1.45
3	10.00	4.40	14.40	3.33	1.47	4.80	1.35
4	10.00	5.70	15.70	2.50	1.43	3.93	1.30
5	10.00	6.90	16.90	2.00	1.38	3.38	1.20
6	10.00	8.00	18.00	1.67	1.33	3.00	1.10
7	10.00	9.00	19.00	1.43	1.29	2.71	1.00
8	10.00	9.90	19.90	1.25	1.24	2.49	0.90
9	10.00	10.20	20.20	1.11	1.13	2.24	0.30
10	10.00	10.85	20.85	1.00	1.09	2.09	0.65
11	10.00	12.15	22.15	0.91	1.10	2.01	1.30
12	10.00	13.65	23.65	0.83	1.14	1.97	1.50
13	10.00	15.40	25.40	0.77	1.18	1.95	1.75
14	10.00	17.80	27.80	0.71	1.27	1.99	2.40
15	10.00	21.05	31.05	0.67	1.40	2.07	3.25
16	10.00	25.30	35.30	0.63	1.58	2.21	4.25
17	10.00	30.65	40.65	0.59	1.80	2.39	5.35
18	10.00	37.20	47.20	0.56	2.07	2.62	6.55
19	10.00	45.00	55.00	0.53	2.37	2.89	7.80
20	10.00	54.30	64.30	0.50	2.72	3.22	9.30

[a]Δ means "the change in."

Total cost is the sum of total fixed and total variable costs. Average total cost is the sum of average variable and average fixed costs, or total cost divided by output. Average total cost, like average variable cost, is U-shaped. Since the influence of declining average fixed cost is less and less as output rises, the average total cost curve takes on the U shape of the average variable cost curve.

Marginal cost, shown in column (8), is the change in total cost that results from producing one additional unit of output. The behavior of marginal cost reflects the law of diminishing marginal returns. In this example, marginal cost falls through the production of the ninth unit of output and rises thereafter. The rising portion of the marginal cost schedule reflects diminishing marginal returns from additions of the variable input.

The data in Table 7.3 are plotted in Figure 7.3, which graphically demonstrates the behavior of short-run cost curves. Figure 7.3a illustrates the concepts of total cost, and Figure 7.3b presents the corresponding average and marginal cost concepts. In Figure 7.3b, *MC* intersects *AVC* and *ATC* at their minimum points; marginal cost bears a definite relation to average variable cost and average total cost. In the case of average total cost, marginal cost lies below average total cost when average total cost is falling and above average total cost when average total cost is rising. Marginal cost is equal to average total cost when average total cost is at a minimum. In Table 7.3, this occurs between the thirteenth and fourteenth units of output. At lower levels of output, the *MC* values in column (8) are less than the *ATC* values in column (7). *ATC* therefore declines. At higher levels of output—in this case, 14 and over—the *MC* values are greater than the *ATC* values, and *ATC* rises. The same analysis holds for the relationship between *MC* and *AVC*. Here, *MC* becomes greater than *AVC* at 11 units of output.

This type of relation holds for marginal-average series in general. If a baseball player is batting .400 and goes 3 for 4 today (.750), his batting average rises because the marginal figure (.750) lies above the average (.400). If he goes 1 for 4 today (.250), his average falls because the marginal figure (.250) lies below the average (.400). An example can be found closer to home. Suppose that your average grade in economics to date is 85. If you score 90 on your next exam, your average will rise. If you score 80, it will fall. When the marginal figure is above the average, it pulls the average figure up, and vice versa. This same relation holds for average total cost and marginal cost, which both Table 7.3 and Figure 7.3 verify.

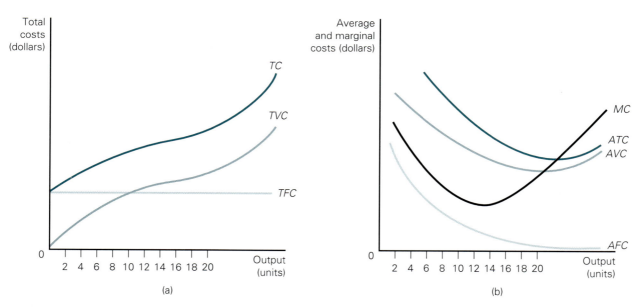

(a)

(b)

FIGURE 7.3

Short-Run Cost Curves

(a) Total cost data plotted from Table 7.3. (b) Average cost and marginal cost data. Notice the U-shaped average total cost curve. At low levels of output, *ATC* is high because *AFC* is high, and the firm does not utilize its fixed plant efficiently. At high levels of output, *ATC* is high because *MC* is high as the firm approaches the capacity limit of its plant.

In sum, the firm's short-run cost curves show the influence of the law of diminishing marginal returns. First, the firm has certain fixed costs that are independent of the level of output. These costs correspond to what the firm must pay for fixed inputs, and they must be paid whether or not the firm operates. Second, assuming the price of the variable inputs is constant, marginal costs reflect the behavior of the marginal product of the variable input. As output rises, marginal costs first decline because marginal product is increasing and it requires less and less of the variable input to produce additional units of output. At some point, however, diminishing marginal returns set in, and it takes more and more of the variable input to produce additional units of output. When this happens, marginal costs start to rise. Third, marginal cost will eventually rise above average variable cost and average total cost, causing these costs to rise as well, which results in U-shaped average variable and average total cost curves.

LONG-RUN COSTS

In the short run, some inputs are fixed and cannot be varied. These fixed inputs generally are characterized as a physical plant that cannot be altered in size in the short run. Short-run costs therefore show the relation of costs to output for a given plant. In the long run, however, all inputs are variable, including plant size. As economic time lengthens and the contracts that define fixed inputs can be renegotiated, a firm owner can adjust all parts of his or her operation. In fact, the scale of a firm's operations can be adjusted to best fit the economic circumstances that prevail in the long run; an owner can choose to arrange the organization in the best possible way to do business. Stated in terms of plant size, the owner will seek the plant size that minimizes long-run costs of producing the profit-maximizing output.

Adjusting Plant Size

Long-run average total cost
The lowest per unit cost of producing any level of output when the usage of all inputs can be varied.

The choice of plant size affects production costs. To determine the optimum long-run plant size, we introduce a new concept: **long-run average total cost** (*LRATC*). This measure shows the lowest-cost plant for producing each level of output when the firm can choose among all possible plant sizes. In fact, the number of possible plant sizes is unlimited. The owner sees the world of possibilities in terms of a long-run average total cost (or planning) curve such as that drawn in Figure 7.4. The long-run average total cost curve is smoothly continuous and allows us to see the full sweep of a firm owner's possibilities. On its downward course, the long-run average total cost curve is tangent to each short-run average total cost curve *before* the point of minimum cost for each given plant size. On its upward course it touches each short-run average total cost curve *past* the point of minimum cost. Only at the bottom of the long-run U shape do the minimum points of the long-run and short-run average total cost curves coincide. In effect, the long-run average total cost curve is an envelope of short-run average total cost curves.

Long-run marginal cost curve
The additional cost of producing an additional unit of output when all inputs, including plant size, can be varied.

Figure 7.4 also contains the firm's **long-run marginal cost curve**, *LRMC*. It is similar to the short-run marginal cost curve in that it shows the additional cost arising from producing an additional unit of output. However, the long-run marginal cost curve depicts the change in total cost associated with a one-unit expansion in output when all inputs can be varied. Expansions in output in the long run are accomplished not only by increases in labor (variable) inputs but also by changing the scale of operations, or the plant size. Thus long-run marginal cost measures *all* additional costs of changing output. Notice that the *LRMC* curve intersects the

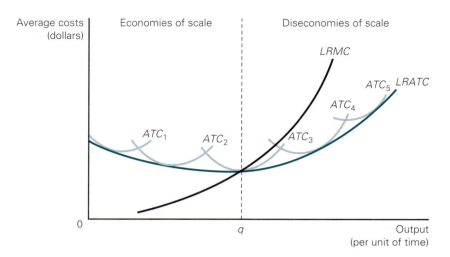

FIGURE 7.4

Long-Run Average Total Cost and Marginal Cost Curves

LRATC is the planning curve of the firm owner. It shows how plant size can be adjusted in the long run when all inputs are variable. The plant size shown at *q* represents the lowest possible unit cost of production in the long run. Economies of scale prevail before *q* on the curve, and diseconomies of scale prevail past *q*. *LRMC* is the long-run marginal cost curve. It shows the additional cost of producing output under the condition that all inputs can be varied.

LRATC curve where the *LRATC* curve reaches a minimum. At output levels greater than *q* in Figure 7.5, *LRMC* is greater than *LRATC*, which implies that *LRATC* must be rising. Just the opposite is true at output levels less than *q* in Figure 7.4. The most preferred operating rate in Figure 7.4 is clearly at *q* when *LRATC* is at a minimum. Think of it this way — if you dropped a marble into the *LRATC* bowl, where would it come to rest?

Economies and Diseconomies of Scale

Why does long-run average total cost have a U shape, falling to *q* and rising thereafter? The answer involves two new concepts: economies and diseconomies of scale.

Economies of scale

A situation in which long-run unit costs *(LRATC)* decline as plant size increases.

The initial falling portion of the *LRATC* curve is due to **economies of scale**. To a certain point, long-run unit costs of production fall as output increases and the firm gets larger. There are a number of reasons that a larger firm might have lower unit costs: (1) A larger operation means that more specialized processes are possible in the firm. Individual workers can concentrate on and become more proficient at more narrowly defined tasks, and machines can be specially tailored to individual processes. (2) As the firm grows larger and produces more, workers and managers gain valuable experience in production processes, learning by doing. Since workers and managers of a larger firm produce more output, they acquire more experience. Such experience can lead to lower unit costs. (3) Large firms can take advantage of mass production techniques, which require large setup costs. Setup costs are most economical when they are spread over a large amount of output. Production techniques such as the assembly line used by large automobile manufacturers would result in very high unit costs if used by a small producer of specialized cars.

Diseconomies of scale

A situation in which, beyond a point, the long-run average total cost of producing output increases as plant size increases.

The fact that the *LRATC* curve rises after *q* is due to **diseconomies of scale**. In this range of outputs, the firm has become too large for its owner to control effectively. Managers do not have the monitoring technology to hold costs down in a very large firm, and bureaucratic inefficiencies creep in. If such bureaucratic problems did not exist, firms would be much larger. Large firms will reorganize, spin off component parts, hire new managers, and seek ways to avoid diseconomies of scale.

FOCUS

Big Business: The Corporation

Big businesses, such as Microsoft, General Motors, or Motorola, are all corporations. Although corporations are the smallest category of business organization in the United States (about 20 percent in 1998), they account for *90 percent* of buiness revenues. Thus, most businesses engaged in large-scale production and marketing are corporations.

There are enormous advantages to the corporate form. In a corporation, ownership is divided into equal parts called shares of stock. If any stockholder dies or sells out to a new owner, the existence of the business organization is not terminated or endangered as it is in a proprietorship or a partnership (see the previous Focus boxes in this chapter). For this reason, the corporation is said to possess the features of continuity and share transferability. Share transferability is the most economically important feature of the corporation; in fact, share transferability is one reason for the origin of the corporation. It allows owners and managers to specialize, thereby increasing efficiency and profitability in the firm. Large amounts of capital can be accumulated, because small investors can get into the act with a minimum of risk.

Another feature of the corporation that distinguishes it from other forms of business organization is limited liability. Corporate shareholders are responsible for the debts or liabilities of the corporation only to the extent that they have invested in it. This characteristic sharply contrasts with sole owners or partners, who are legally responsible for the firm's debts up to the amount of their entire personal wealth. The amount of direct investment in corporations is therefore increased as a result of the limited liability involved.

Not all observers see the corporation as the goose that lays the golden egg. Critics of the modern corporation often claim that it is inefficient because ownership and control are separated: Shareholders are the owners of the firm, but the control of the firm is vested in professional managers. While shareholders are interested in profits and higher stock values, managers *might* pursue different objectives. Managers may want to be "captains of industry," have job security, or occupy plush corporate headquarters. They may not be faithful agents of the stockholders, in other words.

This problem is not insurmountable, however. Corporate shareholders are not held in bondage by the corporation's management—the shareholder can sell shares at any time. When the corporation becomes inefficient due to bad management, stock values tend to fall, leaving the business ripe for corporate takeovers or stockholder rebellion (in which management is replaced). Further, the incentives for efficiency may be instilled in management by requirements that management own (or take as compensation) stock in the company. Self-interest, in this case as in all others, is a powerful motive for profit-maximizing behavior on the part of the manager.

Other Shapes of the Long-Run Average Total Cost Curve

The *LRATC* curve in Figure 7.4 shows a unique ideal plant size at q. There is only one minimum point on this U-shaped curve. This means that there is a small range of plant sizes that are efficient in a particular industry, and plant sizes in the industry will tend to cluster at the level of q. The fact that most discount department stores are approximately the same size illustrates this point.

Figure 7.5 shows two other possible shapes the *LRATC* curve can take. Figure 7.5a illustrates **constant returns to scale**. In certain industries an initial range of economies of scale prevails up to a minimum efficient size of q_1. Beyond q_1, a wide variation in firm size is possible without a discernible difference in unit costs. Small firms and large firms can operate with the same unit costs over this range of outputs. This flat portion of the *LRATC* curve shows constant returns, or the same unit costs, for a range of output levels from q_1 to q_2. Beyond q_2, diseconomies

Constant returns to scale
As plant size either increases or decreases, long-run average total cost does not change.

FIGURE 7.5

Alternative *LRATC* Curves

Not all *LRATC* curves are U-shaped. (a) Constant returns to scale. The lowest possible production costs per unit exist within a large range between output levels q_1 and q_2. Both small and large firms can have the same long-run unit costs between q_1 and q_2. (b) Increasing returns to scale. The more output the firm produces, the lower its long-run average total cost.

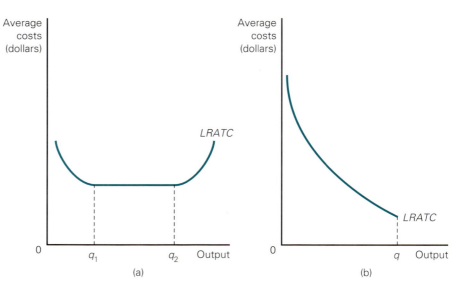

of scale begin. This is apparently a very common *LRATC* curve in the real world because we observe both small and large firms surviving—even prospering—side by side in such industries as publishing and textiles.

Figure 7.5b shows an *LRATC* curve that exhibits economies of scale over its whole range; this is called **increasing returns to scale**. In such cases, the larger the firm, the lower its costs. This type of *LRATC* curve is perhaps representative of such industries as utilities and telephone service. Large firms may be more efficient in the provision of these services. Where one large firm prevails in a marketplace, some form of regulatory control over the pricing power of the firm may be required.

Increasing returns to scale

As plant size increases, long-run average total cost decreases.

SHIFTS IN COST CURVES

Our analysis of cost curves has been based on the familiar *ceteris paribus*, or other things constant, assumption. In other words, we held certain factors constant in the discussion of short-run and long-run costs. What factors did we hold constant, and how do they affect cost curves?

Resource prices have been held constant. If resource prices rise or fall, the firm's cost curves will rise or fall by a corresponding amount. If the price of gasoline falls, the cost curves of a trucking firm fall; this is illustrated by the fall from ATC_1 and MC_1 to ATC_2 and MC_2 in Figure 7.6.

Taxes and government regulation have been held constant. If government increases the excise tax on gasoline, the trucking firm's cost curves will rise. In fact, the average and marginal costs of the trucking firm will rise by the amount of the tax. Similarly, if government imposes more stringent highway weight limits for trucks, the costs of trucking firms will increase.

Technological change has been held constant. Advances in technology make it possible to produce goods and services at lower costs. The invention of the diesel engine, which is more durable and less expensive to operate than the conventional gasoline engine, shifted the cost curves of trucking firms downward. Trucking services can now be produced with fewer resources because of this technological improvement. Such changes obviously affect the cost curves of firms.

FIGURE 7.6

The Effect of a Decrease in Resource Prices on Costs

As resource prices decrease, the cost curves of the firm fall from ATC_1 and MC_1 to ATC_2 and MC_2. If resource prices increased, the cost curves of the firm would rise.

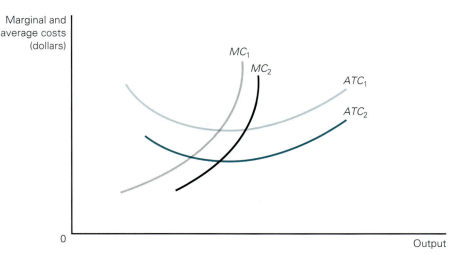

COSTS AND SUPPLY DECISIONS

Costs help explain the supply or output decisions of firms. Firms compare their expected costs and expected revenues in deciding how much output to produce. In the short run, the relevant comparison is between marginal cost and expected revenue. If the latter exceeds the former, the firm will supply additional units of output. In the long run the owner of a firm decides whether to enter an industry or to expand output within an industry by comparing long-run marginal cost with additional expected revenue. Again, if additional expected revenue exceeds long-run marginal cost, the firm enters or increases production, and industry output is expanded. There is a critical link between firm costs and the supply curve in a competitive industry; we examine this link in the next chapter.

APPLICATION

The Draft, Jury Duty, and Conscripted "Public Service": Opportunity Cost and You

The establishment of an all-volunteer army in the United States and in many other nations was based on the concept of opportunity costs. That is, to induce people (likely of your age) to volunteer for military service, the U.S. Government offered them benefits comparable to those they would receive in civilian careers.

Assume that you have a civilian job (before or after going to college) and that economics is your only consideration. If the government can offer you a package including salary, room and board, education (technical training or educational subsidies after serving) clothing, health care, and travel opportunities equal to or greater than your opportunity cost, then you would sign up. That very thing has happened in the post-Vietnam era.

If the opportunity cost to new recruits is not balanced by the army's offer, people will not volunteer in sufficient numbers. In this case, the government returns to the draft to meet its quota for national defense (as was argued for by some during the Kosovo-Albanian crisis). Such forced conscription can be viewed as a tax— "the draft tax." The draft tax is equal to what an individual could have earned as a civilian minus any compensation he or she gets from serving in the military. If

Much of the full costs of the jury system are borne by jurors themselves.

a man or woman earns $25,000 as a civilian but the military pays only $10,000 (including the value of benefits such as food and shelter), the draft tax is $15,000. This financial cost (where only money wages matter) would understate the real opportunity cost of a draft to you if you strongly prefer to work as a civilian no matter what the pay for military service is.

The draft is not the only example of "conscript labor." (A conscript is someone who is forced, by law and the threat of punishment, to provide labor services.) An American example (since the all-volunteer army) is the justice system's method of selecting jurors. Jurors are in fact paid a nominal sum, but this payment usually falls short of the costs of jury duty. Opportunity cost tells us why. If juror "pay" was more than the full costs of jury duty to individuals, people would volunteer their services and conscription would not be necessary.

Jurors are only one of a number of necessary inputs to the justice system of the United States. Judges, attorneys, court reporters, and courtrooms are also vital ingredients. Jurors (along with defendants and witnesses) are different in that they are not paid their opportunity costs. Other inputs participate voluntarily, however, indicating that their total compensation (money and nonmoney) is at least equal to their opportunity cost—that is, to their return in their next-best alternative.

An important thing to note about the draft and the jury system is that conscription does not reduce the cost or supply any product or service (national defense or justice): conscription merely shifts the costs of production from one group to another. Clearly, the economic costs of jury duty are the alternative value of jurors' time. These costs would be explicit under an all-volunteer system. An all-volunteer jury system, like an all-volunteer army, would attract participants by bidding them away from other activities. (Note that these would not have to be wage-earning activities—you might prefer to play tennis.) Under the conscript system, only part of the costs are explicit—the jury fees. You, the juror, pay the remainder of the costs. The conscription of jurors shifts some of the costs of the judicial system from taxpayers to conscripts. An all-volunteer jury would make all costs explicit. We would then know the exact cost of the U.S. system of justice.[a] Informed decisions are difficult when some of the costs of decisions are hidden.

Periodically, other forms of conscription are entertained. Compulsory public service by the youth of America has been proposed in one form or another. A popular proposal makes some form of public service, either military or civilian, a prerequisite for college aid programs. Others would make such service necessary for college admission, and other forms would make compulsory service universal. Instillation of "citizenship" is the rationale for most of these proposals. Missing in the arguments for mandatory public service, as in other forms of conscription such as the draft, is the fact that such programs represent a shift in taxation from older Americans to a "public service tax" on the young.

[a]Economists have attempted to estimate the full costs of the jury system; see, for example, D. L. Martin, "The Economics of Jury Conscription," *Journal of Political Economy*, 1972.

SUMMARY

1. Costs result from the fact that resources have alternative uses. An opportunity cost is the value of resources in their next-best use.

2. Explicit costs are like accounting costs; they are the bills that the firm must pay for the use of inputs. Implicit costs are the opportunity costs of resources owned by the firm. The total cost of production is the sum of explicit and implicit costs.

3. Economic or opportunity costs are the expected future costs of forgoing alternative uses of resources. Accounting or historical costs are costs that have been incurred in the past. Sunk costs are irretrievable historical costs and are not relevant to present decisions.

4. Private costs are payments by the firm for the use of inputs. External costs arise when the firm uses an input without paying for its services. The sum of private and external costs is social cost.

5. The short run is a period of economic time when some of the firm's inputs are fixed. The long run is a period over which all inputs, including the size of the firm's plant, can be varied.

6. The law of diminishing marginal returns states that when adding units of a variable input to a fixed amount of other resources, beyond some point the resulting additions to output will start to decline.

7. The law of diminishing marginal returns implies that the marginal cost curve of the firm will ultimately rise. As the firm adds more variable inputs to its fixed plant, diminishing marginal returns set in at some point, and marginal cost will start to rise as the firm approaches its short-run capacity.

8. Short-run costs are (a) fixed costs—costs that do not vary with the firm's output; (b) variable costs—the costs of purchasing variable inputs; (c) total costs—the sum of fixed and variable costs; and (d) marginal costs—the change in total cost with respect to a change in output. These costs can be expressed in total or average (unit) terms. The short-run average total cost curve is U-shaped. When marginal cost is below average total cost, the latter falls. When it is above average total cost, the latter rises.

9. Long-run average total cost shows the lowest-cost plant for producing output when the firm can choose among all possible plant sizes. It is the planning curve of the firm; it helps the firm pick the right plant size for long-run production.

10. Long-run marginal cost is the additional cost associated with producing an additional unit of output when all inputs can be varied. It measures additional costs arising from producing more output not only with more labor but also by altering plant size.

11. A U-shaped long-run average total cost curve results from economies and diseconomies of scale. Economies of scale cause long-run unit costs to fall, and diseconomies of scale cause long-run unit costs to rise as output is expanded.

12. Other shapes of the long-run average total cost curve are possible. Most important, the long-run average total cost curve can have a flat range with constant returns to scale, or it can be downward sloping over its entire range, reflecting a condition called increasing returns to scale.

KEY TERMS

opportunity costs of production
accounting costs
implicit costs
opportunity cost of capital
total cost of production
historical costs
sunk costs
economic profit

accounting profit
private costs
external costs
social costs
variable input
fixed input
short run
long run

fixed costs
variable costs
total costs
average fixed cost
average variable cost
average total cost
marginal cost
fixed plant

law of diminishing marginal
   returns
total product
marginal product
average product

long-run average total cost
long-run marginal cost
economies of scale
diseconomies of scale
constant returns to scale

increasing returns to scale
firm
market coordination
firm coordination

QUESTIONS FOR REVIEW AND DISCUSSION

1. Compare and contrast limited liability and unlimited liability. Which of them characterizes (a) a sole proprietorship, (b) a partnership, (c) a corporation?

2. What are the major advantages and disadvantages of the corporation as a form of business organization?

3. What is the difference between market coordination of resources and firm coordination?

4. Explain the difference between explicit and implicit costs.

5. State and explain the law of diminishing marginal returns.

6. What is the definition of marginal cost? How is it linked to the law of diminishing marginal returns?

7. Define economies and diseconomies of scale, and give an example of each.

8. How long is the long run? How does it compare to the short run?

9. When is the marginal cost curve below the average total cost curve? When is it above the average total cost curve?

10. An engineering student invests in obtaining an engineering degree. Let us say that the degree cost $50,000 in opportunity costs. Five years later, the engineer decides to become an artist. Is the $50,000 investment in the engineering degree relevant to the decision to become an artist?

11. Derive the long-run cost model using the short-run model. Be sure to include short-run average total cost *(ATC)*, marginal cost *(MC)*, and long-run average total cost *(LRATC)*. Where is the single most preferred operating position in the long-run model?

12. Suppose that the long-run average total cost curve in an industry exhibits increasing returns to scale. How will firms compete in such an industry? Will there be many suppliers in the industry in the long run?

13. Having spent $145,000 opening an exclusive dress shop, Judy realizes that her location is poor, causing her to lose money. In deciding whether to close the store or continue doing business at a loss, should she take the $145,000 into consideration? What term do economists use for this sum?

14. A business spends $20,000 on land, $50,000 on equipment, and $312,000 on salaries. What is the total cost of production for this business?

PROBLEMS

1. Use the table to answer the questions.
   a. What is the average total cost of producing 4 units of output?
   b. What is the total cost of producing 3 units of output?
   c. What is the marginal cost of producing the third unit?

Units of Output	Total Fixed Cost	Total Variable Cost
1	$1000	$300
2	1000	550
3	1000	900
4	1000	1400
5	1000	2050

2. Complete the following table.

Q	FC	VC	TC	MC	AFC	AVC	ATC
1	240	50	290	50	240	50	290
2	240	—	330	—	—	45	—
3	—	110	—	20	—	—	—
4	—	—	—	—	60	—	100
5	—	—	480	—	—	—	—

WORKING WITH THE WEB

1. First, be sure you have read the Application: "The Draft, Jury Duty, and Conscripted 'Public Service': Opportunity Cost and You" in this chapter. After reading it, go to www.mises.org and select (on the left-hand side) the link "daily articles." Next, select the link June 1999 and scroll down until you see the article "Jury Duty." In this article, Armentano reinforces the position described in your text regarding jury duty as a form of conscripted labor.
   a. What does Armentano advocate as a solution to mandatory jury duty and on what grounds? Explain.
   b. What are the potential objections to Armentano's free market system for jury duty? What are Armentano's solutions to the objections? Explain.

2. By now you should recognize that labor is a significant cost of production for most firms. In the short run, typically the firm will vary labor to increase output when capital is fixed. Eventually, this will create diminishing marginal returns for the firm. Consider some broad (by sector) measures of productivity in the U.S. economy.
   Go to http://www.bls.gov/news.release/prod2.t01.htm and look at Table 1, "Business Sector: Productivity, hourly compensation, unit labor costs, and prices, seasonally adjusted."
   a. Which column measures the productivity of workers?
   b. What is the level of productivity for workers for the year 1997?
   Next, go to http://www.bls.gov/news.release/prod2.t03.htm and look at Table 3, "Manufacturing Sector: Productivity, hourly compensation, unit labor costs, and prices, seasonally adjusted."
   c. What is the level of productivity for workers for the year 1997?
   d. Which sector (Business or Manufacturing) reports a higher level of productivity per worker in 1997?
   e. Assume that the difference in productivity in the two sectors is attributable to the fact that diminishing returns begins with fewer workers employed in the business sector than in the manufacturing sector. *Ceteris paribus* (including wages held constant in each sector), how will the marginal product and marginal cost curves in the Business and Manufacturing sectors differ?

Competitive Markets

Competition exists in virtually every aspect of life. Students compete for grades, animals compete for habitat, sports teams compete for championships, government agencies compete for budget appropriations, firms compete for customers. In each case, scarcity causes the competition. Funds available to support government agencies are limited; defense and social agencies therefore compete for scarce budget dollars. Likewise, there can be only one World Series champion; major league baseball teams therefore compete for this scarce distinction. If resources were freely available, there would be no competition. Everyone could have all they wanted of whatever they wanted.

This chapter introduces the economist's model of firm and industry behavior under pure competition (a market with many buyers and sellers, with sellers producing nearly identical products). It is the first of five chapters that analyze the impact of industry structure on price and output. Four chapters look at models of industry behavior: pure competition, monopoly, monopolistic competition, oligopoly, and cartels. The fifth relates industry structure to government policies. In this chapter we discuss the usefulness of the abstract model of pure competition and its relevance for real-world problems. After reading Chapter 8 you should understand

- the difference between competition as a dynamic process and the economist's static model of a competitive market.
- the principles underlying the behavior of competitive firms in both the short run and the long run.
- the nature of the supply curve of a perfectly competitive firm.
- how economic profits (or losses) motivate competitive firms to expand, contract, or go out of business.

THE PROCESS OF COMPETITION

Naturally, most people think of competition as the process of competition or the conduct of competitors. Seen in this way, the important question in determining whether firms are competing with one another is whether they are exhibiting rivalrous, competitive behavior. Do they compete hard for customers? Do they try to outperform one another? Do they use a variety of methods—persuasive advertising, a carefully chosen location, and attractive price—to win and keep customers? Do they seek the best managerial talent available? Are they forward-looking and innovative? Do they seek to eliminate waste and inefficiency? The list could go on, but the point is clear: Competition is normally thought of as a process of rivalry among firms.

This process of rivalry leads to better and less expensive products for consumers. Business firms compete to make profits, but the competitive process actually forces firms to meet consumer demands at the lowest possible level of profit. As Adam Smith observed more than 200 years ago, firms' self-interest is harnessed by the competitive process to promote the general well-being of society:

> It is not from the benevolence of the butcher, the brewer, or the baker, that we expect our dinner, but from their regard for their own interest. We address ourselves, not to their humanity but to their self-love, and never talk to them of our own necessities but of their advantages.[1]

The process of competition channels the pursuit of individual self-interest to socially beneficial outcomes, and for this reason economists put the study of the competitive process at the heart of their science.

The process of competition takes place in an uncertain world. Individuals have to make conjectures as they make resource commitments for the future. Some conjectures will turn out to be correct, and individuals who forecast correctly will prosper. Individuals whose conjectures turn out not to be correct will not fare so well in the future. The concept of competition as a process of rivalry under uncertain conditions is especially important for understanding entrepreneurial behavior in the economy.

PURE COMPETITION

Pure competition is an abstract model of the competitive process that emphasizes the importance of industry structure. In particular, it stresses the number of independent producers in an industry. The model of pure competition is a useful abstraction that, interpreted carefully, can help us understand the competitive behavior of producers in real-world industries.

Market
The interaction of buyers and sellers for the purpose of making transactions.

The model of pure competition is based on the concept of a **market**. As you will recall, market prices are subject to the laws of demand and supply, and within a market the price of a good or service will tend toward a single value. Buyers at point x will not pay more for a commodity than the price at point y plus transportation costs. Buyers at point y will not pay more for a commodity than the price at point x plus transportation costs. Price deviations will quickly be spotted by buyers, restoring the market's tendency to one price. Suppose that the price at point y

---

[1]Adam Smith, *An Inquiry in the Nature and Causes of the Wealth of Nations,* ed. Edwin Cannan (1776; reprint, New York: Modern Library, 1937), p. 14.

fell below the price at point x plus transportation costs. What would happen? Buyers would shift their purchases from point x to point y, decreasing demand and lowering price at point x and increasing demand and raising price at point y. This shift of buyers would restore the tendency to a single price.

The behavior of sellers in a market is equally predictable. In fact, one way to determine if two commodities are in the same market is to find out whether price reductions or increases for the commodity in one area are matched by price reductions or increases in other areas, after accounting for transportation costs. If the price of gasoline goes down in Atlanta because of a gas war, does it also go down in Savannah? In Chicago? In Seattle? In other words, do sellers in other areas of the country respond with competitive price reductions? To the extent that they do, we can delineate the market for gasoline from the tendency of all sellers to adjust prices in the same direction. Perhaps there is an Atlanta–Savannah gasoline market, but there is not an Atlanta–Seattle market.

Building on this concept of a market, we can define four conditions that characterize a **purely competitive market**.

Purely competitive market

The interaction of a large number of buyers and sellers under the condition that entry and exit are not restricted.

Homogeneous product

A good or service for which the consumer is indifferent as to which firm produces it; each firm's product is a perfect substitute for other firms' products in the eyes of the consumer.

Perfect information

A situation that arises when information about prices and products is costless to obtain; complete knowledge about the market.

1. Firms in a purely competitive market sell a **homogeneous product;** that is, they sell identical or nearly identical products that are perfectly substitutable for one another and all have access to the same level of productive technology. This means that advertising does not exist in a purely competitive market. Why would one firm want to advertise the advantages of its product if it cannot be distinguished by consumers from the products produced by a large number of competing firms?

2. A large number of independent buyers and sellers exists in a purely competitive market. Moreover, the large number of buyers and sellers ensures that the purchases or sales of any one buyer or seller will not affect the market price. Each buyer and seller is small relative to the total market for the commodity and exerts no perceptible influence on the market.

3. There are no barriers to entry or exit in a purely competitive market. Features of economic life such as control of an essential raw material by one or a few firms do not exist under pure competition.

4. A perfectly competitive market also offers **perfect information** to buyers and sellers. Everybody in the market has equal, free access to information about the location and price of a product. This assumption provides the basis for a single price to prevail in a perfectly competitive market. Buyers and sellers are constantly informed about price differences and act in turn to drive industry price to a single value. (The Focus "The Economics of Information: Searching for the Best Deal" shows how economists think about the process of acquiring information when it is not free.)

These four conditions are the assumptions on which the theory of pure or perfect competition is based. The assumptions may seem unrealistic. Products, for example, are rarely homogeneous. But the strict realism of the assumptions is not the point of this model. The point is the empirical relevance of the model. Does it explain behavior in real-world markets? As we will see, the purely competitive model helps us analyze important actual markets and industries such as the stock market and agriculture. Moreover, the purely competitive model gives us an analytical framework for what might be loosely described as the ideal working of an economy. In this sense the model provides a benchmark against which other industry models, such as pure monopoly, can be compared.

FOCUS

The Economics of Information: Searching for the Best Deal

The model of perfect competition is based on several key assumptions. One is that information about the price of products and services is free. Consumers are immediately aware at zero cost of any price differences in a given market for a given product. By acting to buy low and sell high, they will drive price in the market to a single value. One price for a product will prevail when a perfectly competitive market is in equilibrium.

We live, of course, in a more complex world. Information—about prices, quality, or anything else—is rarely free. It is an economic good that is costly to produce and to obtain.

Figure 8.1 illustrates the economics of information. The *MC* curve represents the marginal cost to the consumer of searching for a lower price for some product or service. Additional search is typically more and more costly, so *MC* rises to the right. If you are in the market for a used car, for example, the marginal cost of search might be the costs of visiting and negotiating with one or more used car dealers. Moreover, the level of the *MC* curve will vary across goods. It will be low, for example, when shopping for clothes by mail-order catalogue. It will be high, for example, when searching for a wedding dress.

The *MB* curve represents the marginal benefit to the consumer of searching for a lower price. As

you check the prices of more and more sellers, the prospect of finding a lower price from the next seller declines, and so *MB* declines to the right. The marginal benefits of additional search also will vary across markets. When the value of the product is large (for example, consumer durables—houses, refrigerators, cars), it will pay the consumer to search more for a lower price. However, it will not pay the consumer to search widely for a lower price of toothpicks. Ordinarily, the larger proportion that the item is in the consumer's budget, the greater is the benefit of longer search.

The consumer will search until the *MC* of search equals the *MB* of search. This is the point of optimal or efficient search, depicted by point *E* in Figure 8.1. At levels of marginal cost and benefit before point *E*, the extra benefits of more search exceed the extra costs. After point *E*, marginal costs of search exceed the marginal benefits. Point *E* represents the correct or equilibrium amount of search for a given consumer (for a particular good). Consumers will employ such search procedures in an intuitive, instinctive manner. Since point *E* will not be the same for all consumers (for all products), the fact that information about prices is costly to produce and to obtain means that in most markets there will be a dispersion of final transaction prices and not a single price for a product at all locations.

FIGURE 8.1
—————————————

Marginal Costs and Marginal Benefits from Search

Consumers, without free information about the prices or qualities of products or services, will spend resources to discover these attributes until the marginal benefit just equals the marginal cost of search.

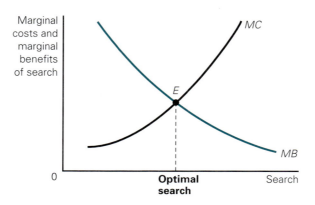

THE PURELY COMPETITIVE FIRM AND INDUSTRY IN THE SHORT RUN

How do firms behave within a purely competitive industry? We focus first on the purely competitive firm's decisions about how much output to supply in the short run—that is, over a period of time when it cannot adjust its plant size.

The Purely Competitive Firm as a Price Taker

Price taker

An individual seller who faces a single market price and is able to sell as much as desired at that price.

In a purely competitive market, an individual firm cannot influence the market price for its good or service by increasing or decreasing its output. Because each seller is only a small part of the total market, its actions have no perceptible influence on the market. The competitive firm is called a **price taker**: It must accept the going market price for its product. The farmer, for example, does not negotiate over the price of his wheat with the operator of the grain elevator. He either sells at the posted price or stores his wheat for a future sale.

The Demand Curve of the Competitive Firm

Figure 8.2a shows the demand curve (d) facing a Virginia peanut producer, and Figure 8.2b shows the world market demand (D) and supply (S) curves for peanuts. The demand curve of the Virginia producer is perfectly elastic with respect to the price of peanuts; it is drawn as a flat line at the level of market price (P). A perfectly elastic demand curve means that the firm can sell all it wants to sell at the prevailing market price. If it tried to sell its output at a slightly higher price, demand for its product would vanish because buyers can purchase peanuts at the lower price in whatever quantities they choose. If the firm is trying to maximize its profits, it has no reason to sell its product for less than the market price.

The scale for price is the same in both parts of Figure 8.2. They obviously are not the same for quantity because of the Virginia producer's minuscule proportion of world output. Keep this in mind as you interpret the diagrams in this chapter. Always check to see whether the horizontal axis represents *firm* or *industry* quantity. Capital Q will be used to represent industry output; small q will represent individual firm output.

To summarize: Every firm in a purely competitive industry is a price taker and faces a demand curve such as that of the Virginia peanuts producer in Figure 8.2a. And every purely competitive firm produces a tiny proportion of industry output.

Short-Run Profit Maximization by the Purely Competitive Firm

Profits

The amount by which total revenue exceeds total opportunity cost of production.

The purely competitive firm is a price taker and faces a given price represented by a perfectly elastic demand curve. Under these circumstances how does the firm decide how much to produce? The simple answer is that the firm compares the costs and benefits of producing additional units of output. As long as the added revenues from producing another unit of output exceed the added costs, the firm will expand its output. By following this rule, the firm is led to maximize its **profits** in the short run.

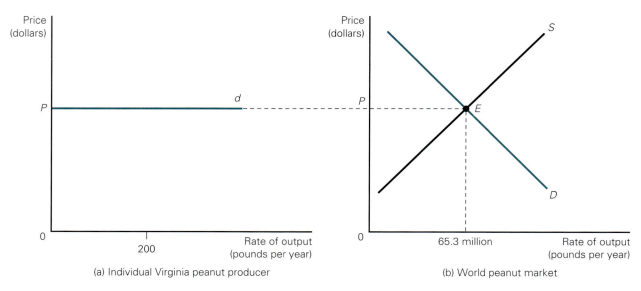

(a) Individual Virginia peanut producer (b) World peanut market

FIGURE 8.2

Firm and Industry Demand in a Purely Competitive Market

In a purely competitive industry, demand for an individual firm's product is perfectly elastic. The perfectly elastic demand curve facing the individual Virginia peanut producer is shown in (a) at the level of P, which is also the equilibrium price for the world market in (b) at an output of 65.3 million pounds per year. Note that the scale for price is the same for both the individual producer and the world market but that the scale for quantity is much different for the two.

The added cost of producing an additional unit of output is the marginal cost. We know from our analysis in Chapter 7 that the short-run marginal cost curve of a firm will eventually rise. This is due to the law of diminishing marginal returns, which comes into play as the firm uses its fixed plant more intensively in the short run.

Marginal revenue

The change in total revenue resulting from the sale of one additional unit of output; the change in total revenue divided by the change in output.

The extra revenue from producing an additional unit of output is **marginal revenue** *(MR)*. Simply, marginal revenue is the addition to total revenue from the production of one more unit of output, or

$$MR = \frac{\text{change in total revenue}}{\text{change in output}}.$$

In a purely competitive market, the denominator is 1—a one-unit increase in output—and the numerator is always the market price (*P*) because the demand curve facing the competitive firm is perfectly elastic. Therefore, marginal revenue equals market price, *MR = P*, for the purely competitive firm.

The purely competitive firm will decide how much to produce in the short run by comparing marginal cost with marginal revenue. To maximize its profits, the firm will produce additional units of output until marginal cost and marginal revenue are equal. Figure 8.3 illustrates this process.

The firm's perfectly elastic demand curve (*d*) in Figure 8.3a is drawn at the level of market price (*P*) from Figure 8.3b. As we have just seen, *d* is also the marginal revenue curve for the firm. Revenue will increase by the market price each time output increases by one unit. In other words, *MR = P*. We have also drawn the marginal cost (*MC*) and average total cost (*ATC*) curves of the firm.

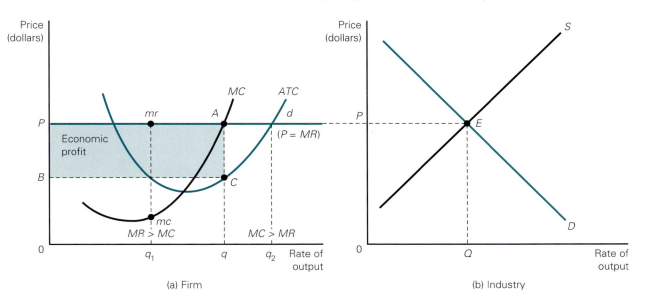

(a) Firm   (b) Industry

FIGURE 8.3

Short-Run Output Choice and Profit Maximization

(a) The short-run choice of output confronting the individual firm. At rates of output less than q, additional production adds more to revenue than to cost. Beyond q, additional production addes more to cost than to revenue. Therefore, the purely competitive firm will produce at q. At this rate of output the firm earns an economic profit equal to the difference between total revenues and total costs: $PAq0 - BCq0 = PACB$. (b) Prevailing market conditions in the industry.

The owners of the firm want to make as much money as possible, so their problem is to find the level of production or output that yields the largest profit. Suppose that the firm is producing peanuts by the pound. The firm presently produces a certain quantity q_1. Should the owners expand their level of production? The answer is yes because additional pounds of peanuts add more to revenue than to costs. In other words, marginal revenue exceeds marginal cost at q_1, as you can see by comparing points mr and mc at quantity q_1. Since the owners want to maximize their profits, they will expand output beyond q_1 as far as q.

Suppose instead that the owners are operating at an output q_2. What will their profit-maximizing reaction be in this case? At this level of production, an additional unit of output adds more to cost than it adds to revenue. That is, marginal cost exceeds marginal revenue. The rational profit-maximizing response of the owners will be to lower production. Through a process of trial and error, they find that their best level of output is q. At a market price of P, they can do no better for profits than to produce q pounds of peanuts. The short-run equilibrium level of production for the purely competitive firm is therefore defined by the condition $P = MC$. Since we know that price and marginal revenue are the same for the purely competitive firm, we can also write $P = MR = MC$.

Total revenue

The total money receipts of a firm from selling its product; calculated as market price multiplied by the amount of output sold; the dollar value of sales.

Using the average total cost curve in Figure 8.3, we can see exactly how well the peanut firm fares by producing at level q. The total revenue of the firm equals its sales, which are the level of output q, times the price P for the output. **Total revenue** at q therefore equals Pq, represented by the rectangular area $PAq0$ in Figure 8.3a. Total cost is the level of average total cost (C) times the level of output q. Total cost

Peanut farmers must adjust to the many conditions that affect the demand and supply of their products, including weather.

at output q thus equals Cq, represented by $BCq0$. Total revenue exceeds total cost in this case: $PAq0 - BCq0 = PACB$. This firm's short-run economic profit is shown by area $PACB$, the return in excess of the total opportunity cost of production.

In the real world, businesspeople do not spend a lot of time trying to draw marginal cost and marginal revenue curves for their firms. Moreover, they operate in an uncertain environment where future costs and prices cannot be known with certainty. Despite these considerations, however, the $P = MR = MC$ rule for profit maximization has predictive power. It is a rule based on common sense. If additional production promises to add more to revenue than to cost, most businesses will try to increase their production. If additional units will probably add more to cost than to revenue, most businesses will cut back production. Such behavior leads to the $P = MR = MC$ result even when businesspeople may know nothing about the economic rule involved.

A Numerical Illustration of Profit Maximization

Another way to understand how the choice of output levels allows a competitive firm to maximize profits is to examine the specific costs and revenues at each level of production. Table 8.1 presents a numerical schedule for the peanut firm. The

TABLE 8.1

Profit Maximization for a Purely Competitive Firm

This numerical schedule of the costs and revenues the peanut firm faces at each level of output provides data for determining the profit-maximizing rate of output. Marginal revenue equals marginal cost when the firm produces 14 pounds per day, and profit is maximized at $5.80 per day.

(1) Rate of Output (pounds/day)	(2) Price = Marginal Revenue	(3) Marginal Cost	(4) Total Revenue (1) × (2)	(5) Total Cost	(6) Profit (4) − (5)
6	$2.40	$1.10	$14.40	$18.00	$−3.60
7	2.40	1.00	16.80	19.00	−2.20
8	2.40	0.90	19.20	19.90	−0.70
9	2.40	0.30	21.60	20.20	1.40
10	2.40	0.65	24.00	20.85	3.15
11	2.40	1.30	26.40	22.15	4.25
12	2.40	1.50	28.80	23.65	5.15
13	2.40	1.75	31.20	25.40	5.80
14	2.40	2.40	33.60	27.80	5.80
15	2.40	3.25	36.00	31.05	4.95
16	2.40	4.25	38.40	35.30	3.10
17	2.40	5.35	40.80	40.65	0.15
18	2.40	6.55	43.20	47.20	−4.00

firm's output level is given in column (1). Column (2) shows that the firm confronts an unvarying market price of $2.40 per pound for its output. Price equals marginal revenue ($P = MR$) because this is a purely competitive firm. The marginal cost and total cost data in columns (3) and (5) are taken from Table 7.3, where these cost concepts were introduced and discussed. Total revenue in column (4) is the sales of the firm, or price times output: column (1) × column (2). Profit, in column (6), is the difference between total revenue and total cost, or column (4) − column (5)

There are two methods by which the firm will choose a rate of output to maximize profits. Suppose, with reference to Table 8.1, that managers do not actually draw the cost curves of the firm, as most real businesses do not. Instead, they operate the firm under a simple rule: Produce and sell output until profits begin to decrease. Examine column (6) in Table 8.1, which measures the firm's profits (total revenue minus total cost) from producing and selling various amounts of output. At a low rate of output, 8 units per day and under, profits are negative; that is, the firm is suffering losses. But as the firm expands output beyond 8 units, losses decline. This is the same thing as saying that profits are rising in this range.

When the firm produces the ninth unit of output, profits become positive ($1.40 per day). Profits continue to rise as the firm expands output up to 13 units per day, at which point profits are $5.80 per day. When the firm produces the fourteenth unit of output, profits level off at $5.80. With the firm's production rule of producing and selling output as long as profits do not fall, we know that at least 14 units of output will be produced.

If the firm were to continue to expand output, profits would decrease. The production of 15 pounds instead of 14 would yield the firm a profit of $4.95 rather than $5.80. If the firm produced 18 pounds of peanuts, it would again suffer a loss, this time equal to $4. As output expands beyond 14 units, profits decline and eventually turn to losses.

The simple decision to stop production when profits begin to decrease leads the firm to produce a rate of output, 14 units per day in Table 8.1, that maximizes profits for the firm. By comparing the total revenue and the total cost of producing and selling additional amounts of output, the firm will choose to produce that rate of output that maximizes profits.[2]

Figure 8.4a illustrates the total revenue–total cost approach to maximizing profits. The figure graphs columns (4) and (5) with respect to the output of the firm. The maximum profits possible in the short run occur where the total revenue line (TR) exceeds the total cost curve (TC) by the largest vertical difference. As Table 8.1 indicates, this takes place at a sale of 14 pounds of peanuts per day.

The second way to find the profit-maximizing rate of output using the numerical schedule in Table 8.1 is to compare marginal revenue and marginal cost,

---

[2]Even though profits are maximum ($5.80) at both 13 and 14 units of output, the marginal condition for maximum profit $MC = MR$ is true only at 14 units of production.

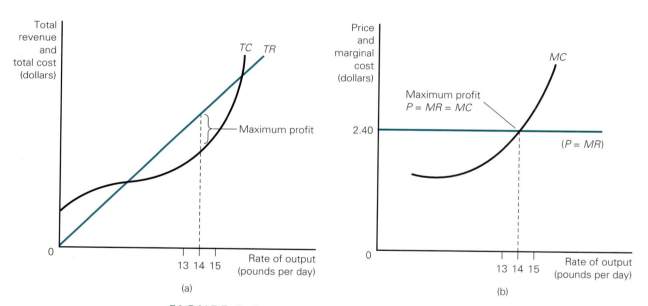

FIGURE 8.4

Profit-Maximizing Output for a Purely Competitive Firm

(a) Total revenue–total cost approach to profit maximization. The profit-maximizing rate of output occurs when the vertical distance between total revenue and total cost is greatest. (b) Marginal revenue–marginal cost approach. Profit maximization occurs where price, or marginal revenue (which are identical for the purely competitive firm), equals marginal cost ($P = MR = MC$). Both approaches result in the same profit-maximizing rate of output.

columns (2) and (3). As long as marginal revenue is greater than marginal cost, it pays to produce additional units of output. Clearly, marginal revenue ($2.40) is greater than marginal cost up to and including an output of 14 pounds of peanuts. This means that the point of maximum profit occurs at 14 pounds per day. The firm will cease producing additional peanuts after 14 pounds, since the marginal cost of producing the next pound is $3.25 and the marginal revenue is only $2.40. Units of output beyond 14 add more to costs than to revenue; that is, they cause profits to decline. Both the total revenue–total cost and the marginal revenue–marginal cost approaches yield the same answer for the profit-maximizing rate of output.

Figure 8.4b illustrates the marginal revenue–marginal cost approach. Again, note the equivalence of the two approaches by comparing the optimal rate of output, at 14 pounds of peanuts per day, in both graphs.

Economic Losses and Shutdowns

What will the firm do if the short-run situation changes for the worse? What if, for example, demand for peanuts declines because the government publishes an adverse report on the health consequences of eating too many peanuts? In this case, the market demand curve for peanuts will decrease, as shown in Figure 8.5b, shifting to the left from D_0 to D_1. This results in a price reduction in the peanuts market, causing

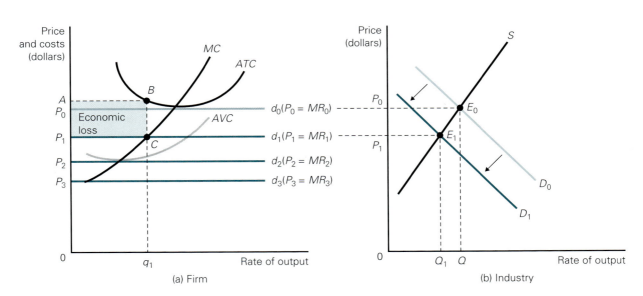

(a) Firm   (b) Industry

FIGURE 8.5

Short-Run Loss Minimization

(a) Firm's response to economic losses caused by (b) decreased industry demand from D_0 to D_1 and a price drop from P_0 to P_1. At P_1, the firm will minimize losses by continuing to operate in the short run because it covers all of its variable costs and some of its fixed costs by operating. At P_2, the firm may either operate, covering its variable costs, or shut down, eliminating its variable costs. At P_3, the firm will shut down in the short run because the price is too low to cover even its variable costs. It minimizes losses by shutting down and paying only its fixed costs, which must be paid whether the firm operates or not.

the market price confronting the firm to fall from P_0 to P_1. The firm's situation is shown in Figure 8.5a. Note that the average variable cost curve (AVC) has been added because it is now an important consideration.

We see in Figure 8.5a that the firm incurs an economic loss because the new market price, P_1, is below its average total cost curve. The firm's revenues are not sufficient to cover its total costs, and it therefore loses money on its operations. What will the firm do in the face of an economic loss? The firm has two options in the short run.

If it expects the adverse effect on sales to be short-lived, the firm can continue to operate in the face of short-run losses. While the price remains depressed at P_1, the firm can minimize losses by following the same rule it followed to maximize profits: It determines the output level at which price is equal to marginal cost and lowers production to that level, q_1 in the figure. Total cost at an output of q_1 is ABq_10, and total revenue is P_1Cq_10. The firm therefore incurs an economic loss equal to the difference between the two: $ABCP_1$. Why might the firm continue to operate in this case while making a loss? It covers all of its variable costs and some of its fixed costs at a price of P_1. If the firm stopped operating, it would still have to pay its fixed costs. These payments must be made whether or not the firm operates. By continuing to operate at price P_1, the firm earns *something* toward the payment of its fixed costs and pays all of its variable costs. Another way to understand this point is to compare the average fixed and average variable costs of producing q_1 rate of output. At q_1, the vertical distance between the average total cost curve and the average variable cost curve is average fixed cost. Figure 8.5a shows that the losses per unit of output incurred by producing q_1, the vertical distance BC, are less than average fixed cost. If the firm shuts down, its losses would equal fixed costs. It therefore "pays" the firm to stay in business in that its losses are lower than if the firm were to shut down.

Suppose, however, that the market price for peanuts continues to fall in the industry, say to P_3. At P_3, the firm does not take in enough revenue to cover even its variable costs of production. The loss-minimizing policy for the firm at this point is to cease operations. By shutting down, the firm is ensured of having to pay only its fixed costs. If it tried to operate at a price below its average variable cost, such as P_3, it would not only have to pay its fixed costs but also would incur a deficit in its average variable cost account. The loss-minimizing policy for the firm is to proceed with a **shutdown** when the price falls below its AVC curve.

Shutdown

A loss-minimizing procedure in which the firm stops production to eliminate all variable costs, although it must still pay fixed costs.

Suppose that the market price falls to point P_2, where it is just equal to the minimum AVC. What can the firm do in this case? Either operating or shutting down is a reasonable option. If it operates, it can cover its variable costs but none of its fixed costs. If it shuts down, it still must pay its fixed costs. Other things being equal, the firm should be indifferent about whether it operates in the short run under these conditions.

Keep in mind that we are discussing *short-run* policies for the firm. The short run is a period of time in which fixed inputs cannot be varied. Given that fixed costs must be paid, the firm's objective in the short run, when price falls below ATC and losses begin, is to minimize its losses. The firm's long-run adjustment will depend on what it expects to happen to prices and costs in the industry. If it expects prices to rise, the firm may shut down temporarily, keep its plant intact, and plan to reopen at some time in the future. Indeed, the firm may use the shutdown period to reorganize in an effort to have lower costs when production begins again. If the firm expects price to remain so depressed in the industry that losses are likely to continue into the future, it may act to sell off its plant and equipment and go out of business.

Supply Curve of a Purely Competitive Firm

The previous considerations help us understand a competitive firm's willingness to supply product as the market price changes, even when it declines. We saw in Chapter 3 that a supply curve shows the relation between the quantity supplied of a good and its price, other things being equal. What is the supply curve of a purely competitive firm in the short run? We answer the question in Figure 8.6.

We have drawn the firm's marginal cost curve and average variable cost curve and a series of different price levels that the firm faces from a competitive market. We know that the general profit-maximizing rule for the competitive firm is to operate at the level of output at which $P = MR = MC$. We also know that the loss-minimizing rule for the firm is to shut down when price falls below the minimum average variable cost. With these two facts, we can derive a supply curve for the competitive firm.

We know that the firm will not produce at a price such as P_0 in Figure 8.6. Since P_0 is below the minimum AVC, the firm will shut down and produce no output at that price. (Notice that no output corresponding to P_0 is given along the horizontal axis.) This decision of the firm applies at any price below P_1, which is the point of minimum AVC. At P_1, the firm will just cover its variable costs and will be economically indifferent about whether it operates. We show the firm producing q_1 units of output at the price P_1. At prices above P_1, the firm will operate in the short run and produce at the output level at which $P = MR = MC$. We show two such cases, at P_2 and P_3. In other words, the firm responds to changes in price above P_1 by producing output along its marginal cost curve. The marginal cost curve of the purely competitive firm above the point of minimum average variable cost is its **short-run firm supply curve**; it shows the relation between price and quantity supplied in a period of time when the firm's plant size is fixed.

Short-run firm supply curve

That portion of a firm's marginal cost curve above the minimum point on the average variable cost curve.

FIGURE 8.6

Short-Run Supply Curve of the Purely Competitive Firm

The short-run supply curve of the purely competitive firm is its marginal cost curve (MC) above the point of minimum average variable cost. The firm will not operate below P_1 because it cannot cover its variable costs of production. Above P_1, the firm produces where $P = MR = MC$.

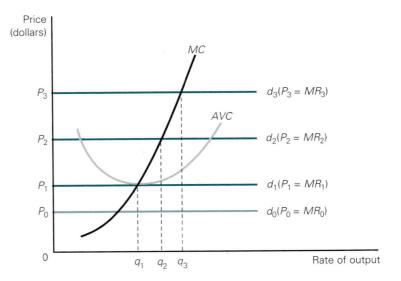

From Firm to Industry Supply

Short-run industry supply curve

The horizontal sum of all existing firms' short-run supply curves.

It is a simple step from the competitive firm's short-run supply curve to the short-run industry supply curve. The **short-run industry supply curve** is the horizontal sum of the individual firms' marginal cost schedules above their points of minimum average variable cost. This process is illustrated in Figure 8.7.

For simplicity, assume that the industry consists of two firms producing peanuts. At a price of P_0, firm A produces 3 pounds of peanuts per day and firm B produces 2 pounds; at these outputs, $P = MR = MC$ for each firm. In each case, P_0 is above the firm's minimum AVC. This point on the industry supply curve is 5 pounds per day at a price of P_0. That is, 5 pounds is the horizontal sum of 3 and 2 pounds of peanuts produced by the two firms. If price rises to P_1, the firms expand production, to 5 and 4 pounds, respectively, along their MC curves. The corresponding point for the industry is at 9 pounds of peanuts. Other points on the short-run industry supply curve (S_{SR}) are obtained in the same manner. The short-run supply curve of a competitive industry is the horizontal sum of all the individual firms' marginal cost curves above their respective points of minimum average variable cost.

Three points should be kept in mind about this discussion. First, a purely competitive industry encompasses many independent producers; the two-firm model used to illustrate the derivation of the industry supply schedule is an abstraction. In a real case of pure competition, thousands of marginal cost curves would have to be summed horizontally. Second, our analysis is conducted in the economic time

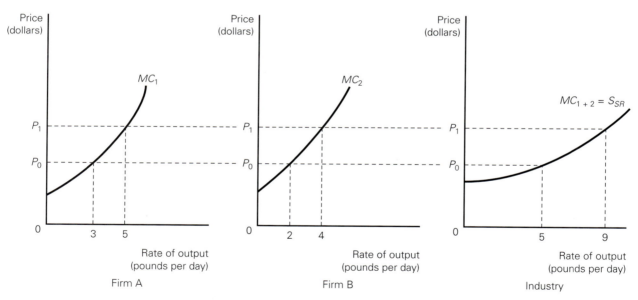

FIGURE 8.7

From Firm to Industry Supply Curves

The short-run supply curve of a competitive industry is the horizontal sum of individual firms' marginal cost curves above their respective points of minimum average variable cost. At price P_0, firm A supplies 3 units (pounds of peanuts) of output, and firm B supplies 2 units. Market supply is 5 units at P_0. Other points on the industry supply curve, such as $5 + 4 = 9$ units at P_1 are derived in the same way.

frame of the short run, in which firms adjust to price changes within the limits imposed by their fixed plant sizes. Third, the intersection of the industry demand curve and the short-run market supply curve determines the market price for the industry. Both firm and industry are in short-run equilibrium. The firm produces at a level where $P = MR = MC$ for its fixed plant, and industry demand equals industry supply. These two conditions define a short-run equilibrium for the purely competitive model.

THE PURELY COMPETITIVE FIRM AND INDUSTRY IN THE LONG RUN

The long run is a period of economic time during which firms can select the lowest-cost plant to produce their output and firms can enter and exit the industry. The result of these adjustments by firms in the face of economic profits and losses is to move the industry toward long-run equilibrium.

Equilibrium in the Long Run

Long-run competitive equilibrium

A market situation in which economic profits are zero for all firms; each firm produces output at minimum average total cost.

Zero economic profits

A condition in which total revenue equals total opportunity cost of production. Firms earn a normal rate of return and $P = MR = LRMC = LRATC$.

Long-run competitive equilibrium occurs when two conditions are met: (1) quantity demanded equals quantity supplied in the market and (2) firms in the industry are making a normal rate of return on their investments, a situation called **zero economic profits.**

Positive economic profits are returns above and beyond the total (explicit plus implicit) costs to the owner of or investor in a firm. They are returns above the opportunity cost of the owner's capital investment in the firm; that is, they are above the normal return that an owner could expect to make on an investment of some other form, such as a money market certificate. Positive economic profits therefore attract the notice of other investors. They are a signal that prods others to try to capture above-normal returns by entering the industry. Economic profits also lead firms already in the industry to seek to expand their scale of operations. Both cases will result in an increase in output in the industry. This causes the short-run industry supply curve to increase and the market price to fall, erasing economic profits and returning the rate of return in the industry to a normal level. This level is referred to as zero economic profits; investors do make an accounting profit, but they make no more than what their money would have earned through the prevailing rate of return on any other investment.

If firms in the industry are making economic losses, the opposite situation holds. Firms will cut back operations, and some firms will leave the industry. The short-run industry supply curve decreases, causing the market price to rise and restoring a normal rate of return to surviving firms.

A long-run equilibrium state for a purely competitive industry is depicted in Figure 8.8. The two conditions for this equilibrium are illustrated in the diagram: (1) quantity demanded equals quantity supplied at the industry level of output, and (2) price just equals the minimum average total cost of the firm. In other words, each firm earns a normal rate of return on its investment in the industry. Notice also that in a long-run equilibrium situation, the market price of output equals long-run marginal cost. Thus the price consumers pay for the good or service just equals the additional cost of producing the good or service.

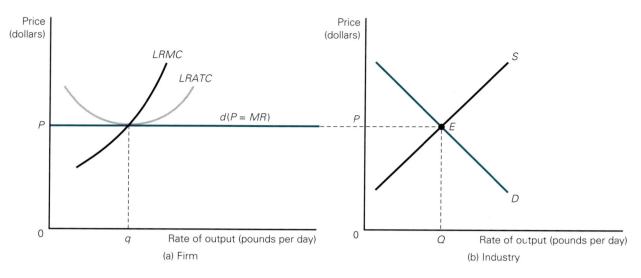

(a) Firm

(b) Industry

FIGURE 8.8

The Purely Competitive Industry in Long-Run Equilibrium

In a long-run equilibrium, two conditions are met: (a) the competitive firm earns zero economic profit, or a normal rate of return, and (b) at the equilibrium market price, industry quantity demanded equals industry quantity supplied. Market price is exactly equal to minimum long-run average total cost. The market price of the good also equals the long-run marginal cost of producing the good.

The Adjustment Process: Establishing Equilibrium

Establishment of equilibrium is a continual process in the purely competitive industry. (The Appendix to this chapter discusses how this process of adjustment takes place in agriculture.) To see how the position of long-run equilibrium is reached, consider a condition of long-run equilibrium in the peanut industry, which is depicted in Figure 8.9.

Increase In Demand Now imagine that peanuts are not only given a clean bill of health by government researchers but also are praised as a cure for the common cold by a prominent scientist. The industry demand curve for peanuts suddenly shifts to the right, as shown in Figure 8.9b, raising the market price to P_1 from the previous equilibrium price P_0.

At first, individual firms in the industry (Figure 8.9a) adjust to the higher price P_1 by expanding output from q_0 to q_1 within their fixed plant sizes—that is, along their *SRMC* curves. This increase in firms' output is reflected at the industry level (Figure 8.9b) by the movement along S_0 as price rises from P_0 to P_1. Industry output thus initially rises from Q_0 to Q_1. However, P_1 is above the firm's *SRATC*, so firms in the industry are earning positive economic profits. Other firms will therefore be attracted to the industry. The effect of this adjustment will be to shift the market supply curve to the right, from S_0 to S_1. Eventually, long-run equilibrium is restored at the original price P_0, where firms again earn a normal rate of return. In the process, industry output has further expanded, from Q_1 to Q_2. The economy now produces and consumes more peanuts. In this case, larger industry production is accomplished with a larger number of firms, each operating at the plant size depicted by *SRATC* in Figure 8.9a.

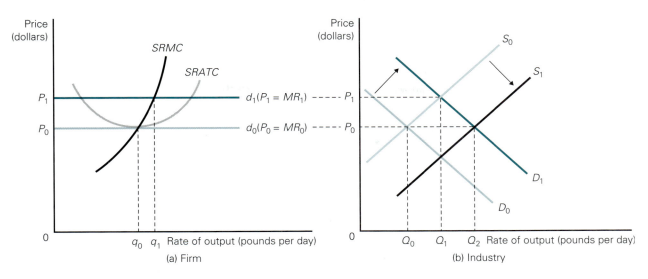

FIGURE 8.9

Industry Adjustments to Long-Run Equilibrium: An Increase in Market Demand
Demand increases from D_0 to D_1 in the industry, and price rises from P_0 to P_1 (b). As demand and price rise, firms now earn profits in excess of their average total costs (a). The opportunity for higher-than-normal profits induces entry by new firms. As this expansion of output takes place, the industry supply curve shifts to the right until a normal rate of return and the original price P_0 are restored in the industry.

Two points should be noted about this process. First, the long-run adjustment process in this example returned price to the original level of minimum average total cost—that is, to the previously prevailing price P_0. This is a special case of long-run adjustment in an industry in which the prices of resources used in the industry do not change when industry output is expanded.

Second, entry can take place from both without and within the industry. Entry from without is the entry of new firms. Entry from within is the expansion of old firms. Entry from within can take place only if there is a range of long-run firm sizes consistent with minimum-cost production. If the long-run average total cost curve of firms in the industry were U-shaped, only one firm size would offer lowest cost in the long run. When this is the case, entry takes place entirely by new firms. The existing firms will not expand their scale of operations because they are already operating with the lowest-cost plant size.

Decrease In Demand   Whereas economic profits lead to the expansion of output in an industry, economic losses lead to a contraction of industry output. Figure 8.10b illustrates a reduction in industry demand from D_0 to D_1. At the resulting lower price of P_1, firms incur economic losses because P_1 is less than firms' average total cost (Figure 8.10a). In the short run, the output of individual firms is reduced, depicted by movement down the $SRMC$ curve, or firms shut down if P_1 is less than their minimum average variable cost. The short-run drop in production by individual firms causes quantity supplied in the industry to fall to Q_1 along S_0. In the long run, some firms will leave the industry by going out of business. The decrease in the number of firms in the industry causes the industry supply curve to shift to the left, from S_0 to S_1. This causes a decrease in total market output from

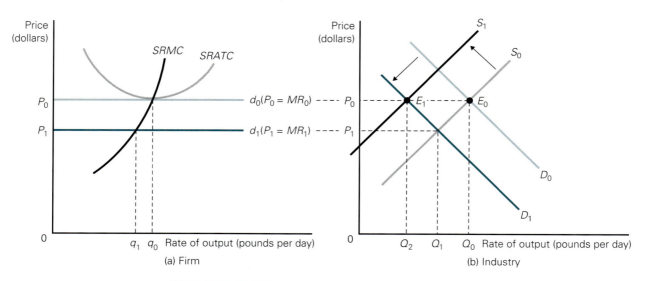

FIGURE 8.10

Industry Adjustments to Long-Run Equilibrium: A Decrease in Market Demand
Industry demand declines from D_0 to D_1, and market price falls from P_0 to P_1 (b). At P_1 firms incur economic losses and cut back production to $q1$ (a). Industry output falls to Q_1. Losses cause some firms to leave the industry. The overall decline in production shifts the industry supply curve to the left, from S_0 to S_1, thus restoring the original price P_0 and a normal rate of return to firms that remain in the industry.

Q_1 to Q_2 and puts pressure on the industry price to rise. Ultimately, price will rise enough to restore the original price P_0 and a normal rate of return to firms in the industry. Here again, the size of each firm producing output is the same initially and after the long-run industry adjustments to the decrease in demand have taken place. Lower industry output is produced by a smaller number of firms, each operating a plant size represented by *SRATC* in Figure 8.10a.

What are some of the uses of these analyses? First, they depict the desirable effects of competition on the use and allocation of resources. Signals to producers about what consumers want are sent through the market system, and producers respond by adjusting and supplying what consumers want in a way that minimizes the cost of production. (For an application of the competitive model, see the Application "Do You Have a 'Hunting License?': The Full Price of Parking on Campus" at the end of this chapter.) Second, the model generates testable propositions, such as the assertion that excess returns should promote entry in a competitive market, from both without and within. An indirect way to test for the presence of a competitive market is to see if excess returns or the presence of positive economic profits leads to an expansion of output in the industry, or if a decline in output follows economic losses.

Long-run industry supply
The quantities of a product that all firms in an industry are willing and able to offer for sale at various prices when the number of firms and the scale of operations of each firm are allowed to adjust.

The Long-Run Industry Supply Curve

The **long-run industry supply** curve represents the quantities of a product that all firms in the industry will be willing to supply at alternative prices in the long run— that is, during a period long enough for entry into and exit out of the industry to occur and for firms to adjust their plant sizes to the lowest-cost level. The long-run supply curve reflects what happens to the prices of inputs as the output of an industry is increased or decreased. In our example of long-run equilibrium, depicted in Figures 8.9 and 8.10, price returned to its original level after first rising or falling with a rise or fall in demand. As we noted, this is a special case that does not always apply because the costs of inputs may change as industry output changes. There are three possibilities related to input costs: They may remain constant, increase, or decrease, depending on the nature of the industry.

Constant Cost In Figures 8.9 and 8.10, long-run adjustments led to the restoration of the original price in the industry (P_0). In the first case, the size of the industry expanded, and in the second case, the size of the industry contracted. In both cases, price returned to the level of P_0 as entry and exit and adjustments by firms in the industry took place.

Figures 8.9 and 8.10 are examples of a **constant-cost industry**, an industry in which expansions or contractions of industry output have no impact on input prices or costs of production. The long-run industry supply (LRS) curve in this case is perfectly elastic—a flat, straight line at the level of the long-run equilibrium price in the industry, as shown in Figure 8.11. Notice that the curve is derived by connecting points E_0 and E_1, the points where long-run industry demand intersects supply—that is, points of long-run equilibrium.

Constant cost is most likely to occur in industries where the resources used in industry production are a small proportion of the total demand for the resources in the economy. Take, for example, the toothpick industry. A major expansion, say a tripling, of the output of toothpicks would probably not have much impact on the price of wood used in the industry because far more wood is consumed in other uses, such as building materials, paper, and firewood. The cost of wood to toothpick producers would therefore remain the same as the industry expanded.

Increasing Cost In an **increasing-cost industry**, expansions of industry output lead to higher input prices and therefore higher costs of production for individual firms. This type of industry exhibits the common slope of the long-run industry supply curve because the expansion of most industries puts upward pressure on costs in the industry. An increase in the demand for chicken meat will cause the

Constant-cost industry

An industry in which the minimum $LRATC$ of production does not change as the number of firms in the industry changes; expansion (contraction) of the number of firms does not bid up (down) input prices; long-run industry supply is horizontal.

Increasing-cost industry

An industry in which the expansion (contraction) of the number of firms bids up (down) input prices; minimum $LRATC$ of production changes as the number of firms in the industry changes; long-run industry supply is upward sloping to the right.

FIGURE 8.11

Long-Run Price in a Constant-Cost Industry

The long-run industry supply curve *(LRS)* for a constant-cost industry is horizontal at the level of the market price. Expansions in industry output do not change resource costs to individual firms.

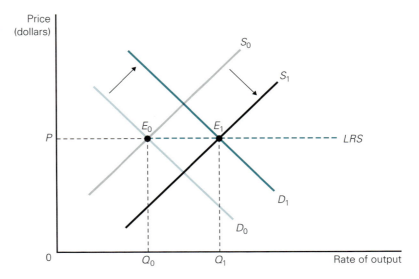

prices of chicken feed, farm land, and chicken coops to rise. An increase in the demand for newspapers will lead to higher prices for paper, printers, reporters, and so on. These increases in cost lead to a higher long-run price for the goods produced. To obtain more of these goods, consumers must pay higher prices in the long run in order to attract additional resources into their production.

The effects of industry expansion on price and supply in an increasing-cost industry are shown in Figure 8.12. Initially, the firm and industry are in equilibrium at E_0, with a market price of P_0. Demand increases, the market demand curve shifts to the right from D_0 to D_1, and price rises initially to P_1. Entry into the industry and increased production are encouraged by the higher price, with the additional entry represented by a shift in the supply curve from S_0 to S_1. As production expands, however, resource costs to producers in the industry rise, causing the individual firms' cost curves to shift upward. Thus, as entry takes place, price falls from its height at P_1, and costs to producers rise until a new equilibrium is reached at E_1. This new equilibrium price is higher than the initial equilibrium price of P_0. Connecting the two equilibrium points at E_0 and E_1 yields the long-run industry supply curve. The long-run industry supply curve in an increasing-cost industry slopes upward to the right because additional resources needed to produce additional output in such an industry come at higher costs.

Decreasing-cost industry

An industry in which the long-run industry supply is downward-sloping; expansion (contraction) of the number of firms bids down (up) input prices; minimum $LRATC$ of production falls as the number of firms in the industry increases.

Decreasing Cost   In a **decreasing-cost industry**, expansion of industry output leads to lower input prices and lower costs for individual firms and hence to a lower long-run market price for the product. This is an unusual type of long-run industry supply, but a decreasing-cost industry is logically possible. As the clothing industry expands, for example, the costs of certain inputs may fall. Producers of cutting and sewing machines may experience economies of scale, leading to lower prices for their machines. Hence, it is possible for the long-run supply curve of clothing producers to exhibit the decreasing-cost phenomenon.

FIGURE 8.12

Long-Run Price Changes in an Increasing-Cost Industry

Expansions of industry output in response to higher demand D_1 and resulting higher price P_1 lead to higher resource costs facing individual producers in the industry. Equilibrium is reached at P_2 as costs to producers rise and price falls from P_1 to P_2. The long-run industry supply curve (LRS) for an increasing-cost industry, determined by connecting equilibrium points E_0 and E_1, slopes upward to the right.

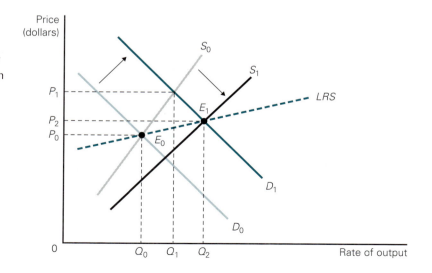

PURE COMPETITION AND ECONOMIC EFFICIENCY

The model of a purely competitive market is often used by economists as a benchmark or ideal against which other models of market structure are compared. This point will be more obvious in Chapter 9, where we discuss the market structure of pure monopoly. But we first need to understand in what sense the operation of the purely competitive market represents an ideal outcome in the economy and in what sense the model is only an ideal.

The Competitive Market and Resource Allocation

Pure competition produces what most economists would agree is an ideal or optimal resource allocation. Purely competitive allocation of resources is optimal or best in two fundamental senses.

Productive efficiency

A condition in which total industry output is produced at the lowest possible opportunity cost of resources.

First, a competitive industry minimizes the resource costs of producing output. In effect, competition forces firms to produce their output at the minimum long-run average total cost and at a price just sufficient to cover that cost. This **productive efficiency** can be seen in long-run equilibrium in competitive firms, which produce at the point where $P = LRATC = LRMC$. It is the minimum possible opportunity cost of producing the good or service. Consumers benefit because they get the goods they desire at the lowest possible cost. This is so because market equilibrium price equals minimum long-run average cost of production. Inefficient, high-cost firms will incur economic losses and will be driven from competitive markets. Surviving will be firms who can provide industry output at the lowest cost.

Allocative efficiency

A situation in which the socially optimal amount of a good or service is produced in an industry; the socially optimal amount depends on the tastes and preferences of society and on the opportunity cost of the resources used to produce the good or service.

Second, a competitive market also results in **allocative efficiency**. Allocative efficiency exists when the price paid by consumers for one more, or the last, unit of a good or service just equals the cost of the resources that produce the additional, or last, unit of the good or service. It is the socially optimal output of the good or service. In a competitive market, consumer demands are met as long as consumers are willing to pay a price for the production of an additional unit of output equal to the cost of the additional resources required to produce the additional output. In competitive markets, resources flow to their most highly valued uses, resulting in allocative efficiency. As noted in Chapter 4, the equation of supply and demand in competitive equilibrium produces a maximum net value to society of using scarce resources to produce a product. Competitive equilibrium also creates the maximization of the sum of consumer and producer surplus in the process of allocating resources to their most highly valued uses. Collectively, this means that market competition—in the absence of "third-party effects" in the use of resources—creates allocative efficiency and it is what economists mean when they say that "competition is efficient."

This situation is expressed in the now familiar condition $P = LRMC$. Price reflects the desire of consumers for additional units of a good. Long-run marginal cost represents the opportunity cost of the resources necessary to produce an additional unit of the good. If P is greater than $LRMC$, consumers will pay more for additional units of production than the cost to produce them. When this is the case, resources in the economy will be reallocated from other uses considered less valuable by consumers. If a chicken farmer, for instance, finds that consumers will now pay more for the relatively scarce rooster hackle feathers prized for fly-fishing than they will pay for relatively abundant chicken meat, the farmer will shift the use of some chicken coops, chicken feed, and farmhands from production of meat birds to production of roosters bred for hackle feathers.

If P is less than $LRMC$, consumers will pay less for additional units of production than the cost to produce them. Resources will be reallocated out of such production. If the price for hackle feathers is less than the cost, then fewer hackle feathers will be available for fly-fishing. If P equals $LRMC$, resource allocation is ideal in the sense that the things consumers want are produced by competitive firms in the exact quantities and combination (of feathers and food, for instance) that consumers desire and at the lowest cost.

This discussion should sound familiar. In Chapter 4 we pointed out why the intersection of supply and demand curves and the equilibrium price in a competitive market were so important in economics. We have now come full circle to establish this fact in greater detail. Long-run competitive equilibrium represents the best that society can do in producing and consuming goods and services. This condition ensures that products are produced at least cost and that individuals obtain the goods they want. As discussed in Chapter 4, such a process maximizes the sum of consumers' and producers' surplus in an economy. This is as good as it gets in economics.

The competitive model is really Adam Smith's concept of the "invisible hand" at work. Acting in their self-interest, consumers and producers create a mutually beneficial outcome. Looking out for their own interests, producers seek to maximize profits, and yet in a competitive market the result is that consumers' desires are met in the most efficient way possible. Consumers demand the goods and services they want, but competitive producers balance those demands against other demands for other goods and services. An incredibly complex process of consumer demand and producer response is put in motion by the behavior of each individual in heeding his or her own interest. No central planner is required, and yet a result emerges that is ideal.

Perfect competition may not be perfect in every sense, however. While a purely competitive world leads to an ideal resource allocation, it might not lead to an ideal distribution of income among people. Equity will conflict sometimes with the achievement of economic efficiency. In other words, competitive solutions will not always result in equitable solutions (or what is considered equitable in law or by society). Also, while pure competition accommodates consumers' preferences, these preferences themselves may not conform to anyone's image of the ideal state of human existence. Individuals are free to buy and sell as they see fit. If consumers want gadgets rather than great books, they are free to make this choice. Further, the model of perfect competition assumes that there are no "third-party" effects—social costs or externalities being inflicted on others by the competitive firms. This issue is addressed in more detail in Chapter 17. Finally, as we have noted earlier (see, for example, the Focus "The Economics of Information: Searching for the best Deal"), information is a costly "good" like running shoes or a steak. Information is seldom perfect, as the basic competitive model assumes it to be. Sometimes, the parties to an exchange have different information. This may cause problems in particular markets, such as those for used cars or other consumer durables. However, the competitive market provides some relief even in these cases (see, for example, the Focus "Don't Buy a 'Lemon': Information Problems and You").

FOCUS

Don't Buy a "Lemon": Information Problems and You

Suppose that you, a college student of somewhat limited means, are in the market for a used pickup truck. Your local newspaper runs the ad shown below, which catches your eye. This is exactly the kind of vehicle you want, so you call to inquire about the price. The price you are quoted over the phone is $2,000 lower than the price listed in a used car "bluebook." Instead of being ecstatic, however, you are suspicious.

> 1997 Ford Ranger, blk, 4WD, a/c,
> AM/FM/cass., showroom condition
> Call 555-1238 after 5 P.M.

Many products are sold in a used or "secondary" market under competitive conditions. When you manage to pay less than the going rate for many of these products, such as a bicycle or an exercise machine, you believe you are getting a great deal. This is not necessarily the case for used cars or other durable goods (washing machines and television sets, for example), because with "complicated" products of high replacement costs, you must be particularly careful about getting a "lemon," or a product of substandard quality.

In addition to asking price, the age of a car—or any other consumer durable such as a refrigerator or dryer—is a factor when you are trying to determine whether a seller is attempting to unload a lemon. While people have all sorts of reasons for wanting to sell their cars—even relatively new cars—most people hold off until they have put many thousands of miles on a car or until the car is several years old. (Some would sell a year-old refrigerator because it is the wrong color, however.) You would probably be suspicious of a car that is "too new" as you would a car that is "too good" a deal. In fact, you are probably willing to pay a high price for a high-quality used car. While this price would certainly be acceptable to the seller, the competitive market might not facilitate such trades.

The problem is one of "asymmetric," or one-sided, information. Used car sellers tend to know the quality of the cars while buyers do not. If, for some given grade or model of car or refrigerator, there is an excess supply at an above-equilibrium price, price will tend to fall (some sellers will take less). But this very market mechanism that *lowers* price makes you even more suspicious that the car or other consumer durable is a lemon. Demand declines causing price to fall further, and you become even more suspicious, and so on....

Many transactions do in fact take place every day in used car and other secondary markets. Some buyers' and sellers' assessments will overlap. More importantly, the competitive market works at least partially to solve the information problems relating to such trades. Used car warranties offered by sellers, independent garages that will provide assessments, and reputations of new car dealers (who also sell used cars) are several ways to provide assurances of quality. Markets where "lemons" might exist may not function perfectly, but there are competitive forces at work to ensure that efficient, utility-producing trades will become more likely under such circumstances.

Competition in the Real World

Many critics argue that in the real world it is nearly impossible to find examples of perfectly competitive markets. To them, evidence that products sold by rival firms are not homogeneous, that prices charged by these firms are not identical, or that buyers are not perfectly informed proves the competitive model is not applicable.

Defenders of the competitive model, in turn, argue that the competitive model can explain real-world behavior in a variety of markets. To them, the assumption of homogeneous products is not essential.

The market for student apartments is one in which we can readily contrast the two conflicting points of view. As any student who has shopped for an apartment knows, the units are not homogeneous, and prices are not uniform. Should one infer from these real-world facts that the market for apartments is not competitive?

Advocates of free markets would argue that use of the competitive model in this case is quite appropriate. Instead of viewing apartment units as goods being bought and sold, imagine a market for some intangible good called housing services. Although a unit of housing services cannot be defined exactly, each apartment can be viewed as giving some quantity of services to its tenant. Luxury units in prime locations have a large number of units of housing services; substandard units in undesirable locations have a small quantity of housing services. In the rental housing market there are many students who are buyers of housing services, and many landlords who sell housing services.

From this perspective, the disparity in rental prices among apartment units is entirely consistent with the theory of perfect competition. If a particular apartment is perceived to be twice as good as another unit (yielding twice the quantity of housing services), we would expect the first apartment to rent for twice as much. The two units are physically quite different and have different locations, but the apartment owners still compete with each other. Although student tenants have imperfect information about apartment prices, students do have an incentive to acquire such information. The real-world alternative to perfect information is some information—not complete ignorance. The assumption of complete information is not totally unrealistic.

Price differences among auto dealers or among gasoline stations also can be reconciled with the competitive model. In each case, sellers are competing for the sale of services to buyers, so price differences may only reflect differences in the units of service provided to customers.

In the real world, owners of competitive firms are faced with constantly changing conditions: fluctuating prices for their products, new government regulations, natural disasters. To put it another way, entrepreneurs must operate in a world of risk and uncertainty.

The concept of risk involves aspects of the economic environment that, to some extent, can be predicted. The fact that risks are predictable implies that they are known. Fires and natural disasters, for example, are known risks involved in business ownership. When entrepreneurs take steps to protect themselves from known risks—for example, by purchasing insurance—they incur costs. These costs become a part of the firm's long-run marginal and average costs.

Uncertainty is distinct from risk in that uncertain events cannot be predicted. Pure uncertainty refers to events with no known probabilities—the announcement of an invention that will decrease (or increase) a firm's sales, for example. Therefore, competitive entrepreneurs cannot protect themselves from uncertainty by buying insurance. Entrepreneurs simply must live with uncertainty. The lucky ones will profit from uncertain events, and the unlucky ones will suffer a loss.

Neither risk nor uncertainty undermines the usefulness of the competitive model. As we have seen, risk can be treated as a cost of doing business in the competitive marketplace. And uncertainty brings out the best instincts in competitive entrepreneurs.

It should be obvious that the competitive model can be used to analyze markets even if all the underlying assumptions are not met. However, economists have developed alternatives to the competitive model to analyze the behavior of firms in industries comprising a single firm or only a few large firms. Economists have also developed useful models for examining forms of nonprice competition in markets that are not easily explained by the competitive model. The following three chapters develop several of the alternative models.

APPLICATION

Do You Have a "Hunting License?": The Full Price of Parking on Campus

A common problem at most universities—especially those in an urban setting—is parking. Universities, colleges, and public facilities must somehow allocate parking spaces among competing demanders. Space for parking, to the dismay of faculty and students, is grossly inadequate at most universities. Many devices are used to restrict campus parking to the available number of spaces. Parking stickers are commonly assigned with some kind of "pecking order" designed for faculty (chaired scholars, deans, assistant professors) and students (undergraduate students, graduate students). In many cases, however, without "reserved" spaces, stickers are no more than hunting licenses.

Problems are often compounded by universities who, often to please particular constituencies, invoke standards of "justice" in doling out the limited number of places. A popular standard that is usually devised by a faculty committee is to keep parking fees "low" in the interests of justice. A response to low prices and a means of reducing demand for spaces would be to schedule classes at all hours of the day and night, but this would run afoul of certain campus constituencies. Campus bureaucrats, faculty, and students would be up in arms. Another (and more

Valuable student and faculty time is spent "hunting" for a parking space on campus.

popular) means of allocating the spaces is to raise *implicit* prices of parking to faculty and students by imposing stiff fines for parking violations.

The typical problems may be viewed with the aid of Figure 8.13. In Figure 8.13 some homogeneous demand for campus parking is assumed (faculty, students, and administrators are lumped together in the demand curve). Full price, which includes not only the nominal sticker price of parking but the time spent in finding a parking space as well, is depicted on the vertical axis. The number of spaces is given on the horizontal axis. The supply of parking spaces is assumed to be limited to Q_s. The average price of stickers (hunting licenses) is P_s, a low nominal price set by the faculty committee in the interests of "fairness" or "justice." The result is an excess demand of $Q_d - Q_s$ or HG at price P_s.

What is the result of this low nominal or dollar price for parking? Clearly, ever-vigilant campus police, armed with tickets representing high fines, could reduce the demand to Q_s. This would, however, be at the cost of reduced utility and increased fine payments to those who require parking. This means that the implicit price of a parking sticker rises. If the system described in Figure 8.13 remains in place, students and faculty will be forced to hunt for a parking place at popular class times during the day. The costs to you will vary with the class time of day (how long you have to hunt) and with the value of time to you as an individual. Normally, this full price (the money or sticker price plus the value of time spent) will be greater for full professors (eminent scholars) than for assistant professors (they generally earn less income). For all individuals, however, these "hunting" costs form part of the full price of parking on campus. The result is that the full price rations the scarce number of spaces for students and faculty, but at higher costs—the time costs—not collected by anyone. The full price charged equals $P_s + t$, where t is the opportunity cost of search time for a parking space.

Competitive markets, even with spaces limited to Q_s in the short run, could come to the rescue. One solution would be to auction off spaces to faculty and students alike. Spaces would go to the highest bidders who may be well-heeled freshmen or wealthy sorority members. This would undoubtedly cause "outrage" among faculty, administrators, and less wealthy students. But the university would be richer (up to the amount of $0AFQ_s$) and would, in the long run, be able to build new parking facilities. Another solution is to randomly allocate the limited parking spaces at

FIGURE 8.13

The Campus Hunting License

The graph demonstrates some of the problems associated with campus parking when the nominal sticker price is P_s and quantity demanded of parking spaces (Q_d) exceeds the quantity supplied (Q_s).

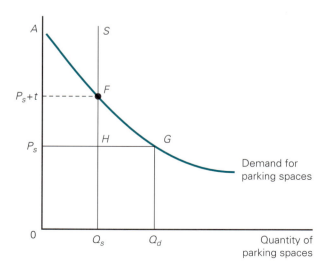

the sticker price (P_s in Figure 8.13) and to let faculty and students freely trade (buy and sell) their stickers. Those who valued them more would enrich those who valued stickers less. An amount P_sAG would be transferred. Thus, competition could be used to allocate the scarce spaces $0Q_s$. Mandatory imposition of "just" prices by the university, it must be noted, does not mean that a competitive market does not work. It does mean that more costly solutions are imposed on the market. Think about this the next time that you spend valuable time hunting for a parking space.

SUMMARY

1. Economists study competition in two basic senses: as a rivalrous, natural process among competitors and as an abstract concept described by the model of a purely competitive market.

2. A purely competitive market is characterized by many buyers and many sellers, a homogeneous product, no barriers to entry or exit by firms, and free information. Examples of this type of market include the stock market and agricultural markets.

3. The purely competitive firm is a price taker: the firm is so small in relation to the total market for its product that its output has no influence on the prevailing market price. The demand curve facing the purely competitive firm is perfectly elastic at the level of the prevailing market price.

4. Marginal revenue is the change in total revenue caused by an increase in output. Since the purely competitive firm faces a perfectly elastic demand curve, each unit is sold at the prevailing market price. Thus, marginal revenue is equal to market price for the pure competitor.

5. In the short run, the pure competitor decides how much output to produce by setting marginal cost equal to market price. If price is above the average total cost, the firm earns an economic profit in the short run. If price is below the minimum average variable cost, the firm will shut down in the short run to minimize its losses.

6. The supply curve of a purely competitive firm is its marginal cost curve above the point of minimum average variable cost. The supply curve of a purely competitive industry in the short run is the horizontal sum of individual firms' marginal cost curves above their respective points of minimum average variable cost.

7. Short-run equilibrium for the purely competitive firm and industry occurs when the quantity supplied and quantity demanded are equal in the market and each firm is producing at the level where $P = MR = SRMC$.

8. In the long run, firms in a purely competitive industry can enter and exit the industry and seek the optimal plant size in which to produce their output. The presence of positive economic profits leads to entry and expansion in the industry, and economic losses lead to the opposite.

9. Long-run equilibrium in a purely competitive industry results when firms in the industry earn zero economic profits and industry demand and supply are equal. In the long run, the purely competitive firm's position is such that price equals long-run marginal cost equals long-run average total cost: $P = LRMC = LRATC$.

10. The long-run industry supply curve in a purely competitive industry reflects what happens to firm costs as industry output expands or contracts. In a constant-cost industry, resource prices and firm costs are unchanged by industry expansion, and the long-run industry supply curve is perfectly elastic. An increasing-cost industry experiences rising costs as industry output expands; the long-run industry supply curve slopes upward to the right. In a decreasing-cost industry, resource prices fall as industry output expands, and the long-run industry supply curve slopes downward to the right.

11. The working of the purely competitive model represents a benchmark against which the working of the economy can be measured. In this model, resources flow to their most highly valued uses, and output is produced at the lowest cost in terms of resources used. In the real world, entrepreneurs face risk and uncertainty and the competitive model has useful applicability.

KEY TERMS

market
purely competitive market
homogeneous product
perfect information
price taker
profits
marginal revenue

total revenue
shutdown
short-run firm supply curve
short-run industry supply curve
long-run competitive equilibrium
zero economic profits
long-run industry supply

constant-cost industry
increasing-cost industry
decreasing-cost industry
productive efficiency
allocative efficiency

QUESTIONS FOR REVIEW AND DISCUSSION

1. What is a market? What is a purely competitive market?

2. Why are price and marginal revenue the same thing for a purely competitive firm?

3. What is the supply curve of a purely competitive firm? Of a purely competitive industry?

4. Describe the adjustment process between points of long-run equilibrium in an increasing-cost industry.

5. Suppose that the news media report the contamination of oyster fisheries in the coastal waters off the eastern United States. The news creates a decrease in demand for oysters. If oyster production is a constant-cost industry, describe the adjustment to the new equilibrium using graphical analysis.

6. Suppose that a competitive firm is earning economic profits because its owner has figured out a way to lower the costs of production. Since the

source of the reduced costs is known only to the owner, how can entry take place? Should such information be proprietary (belong to the owner), or should the owner be required to tell potential competitors the reason for the lower costs?

7. Which of the following markets could be analyzed with the competitive model: (a) automobiles; (b) Swiss cheese; (c) blue jeans; (d) cheeseburgers; (e) trash collection; (f) television news; (g) janitorial services?

8. How long will a firm in a competitive industry endure economic losses before it leaves the industry? In your answer, assume that price is above minimum *SRAVC* but below *SRATC*.

9. Suppose that a perfectly competitive industry is in long-run equilibrium. In an effort to make a profit, could a firm in this industry raise the price of its product? Why or why not?

PROBLEMS

1. The following data and the graph at right pertain to a competitive firm.

Output	MC	MR	TR	TC	Profit
1	5.00	9.00	9.00	10.00	− 1.00
2	4.10	9.00	18.00	14.10	3.90
3	4.25	9.00	27.00	18.35	8.65
4	4.67	9.00	36.00	23.02	12.98
5	5.50	9.00	45.00	28.52	16.48
6	6.60	9.00	54.00	35.12	18.88
7	7.66	9.00	63.00	42.78	20.22
8	9.00	9.00	72.00	51.78	20.22
9	10.75	9.00	81.00	62.53	18.47
10	12.50	9.00	90.00	75.03	14.97

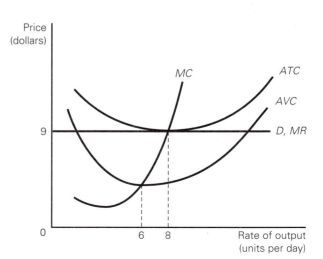

a. How much output should this competitive firm produce?

b. What will be the firm's profit at its profit-maximizing rate of output?

c. Why can't the firm charge a long-run price of $10?

2. Suppose that a cancer researcher finds that eating a large amount of turkey every day virtually eliminates your chances of getting a certain kind of cancer. Assuming that the market for turkey is perfectly competitive (for both inputs and outputs), construct figures and show what you would expect to occur in the short and long run for each of the following.

a. the industry demand for turkeys

b. profits of turkey producers

c. profits of beef producers

d. wages for experienced turkey science researchers

e. the price of turkey

3. Take any item of common consumption—for example, premium gasoline or a particular textbook that you require, and sample sellers' prices in your college town or campus area. You will likely find that prices are not homogeneous among sellers. How do you explain the differences in price? Does the variability in prices suggest that the market is not "competitive"?

WORKING WITH THE WEB

1. You have now learned about the problem of asymmetric information from the Focus "Don't Buy a 'Lemon': Information Problems and You." To consider how the problem of asymmetric information applies to you, go to www.ebay.com and select the link for "Collectibles." Scroll down and find the link for Lunchboxes and select "metal." Assuming you are a collector of metal lunchboxes, scroll through the available items up for auction. You will notice that some sellers provide pictures and descriptions, while other sellers do not provide pictures. For example, today there are two *Munsters* lunchboxes available—one for $20 and one for $12. The $20 item provides a picture while the $12 item does not. Look for a similar situation and click on the links to examine the lunchbox descriptions (and picture).

a. Assuming the descriptions are very similar and that the prices are comparable (as in the above example), which lunchbox would you select?

b. How does asymmetric information apply to your situation?

2. Parking on campus is typically a problem, as described in the Application "Do You Have a 'Hunting License': The Full Price of Parking on Campus" in this chapter. Some of the possible remedies suggested to help solve the parking problem were to have reserved spaces, auction the spaces to the highest bidder, or have a random distribution of spaces. Let's see if any of these remedies are put into action on a college campus. First, go to http://www.louisville.edu/admin/dps/parking/permit.htm and look at the permit options and fees.

A Red (reserved) space is available only to faculty and staff, and there are a limited number of reserved spaces. This is the most expensive permit and the permit holder is assigned a numbered, reserved space (until 5:00 P.M.). Since the University of Louisville is largely a commuter campus, the most common permit for students is the Green permit. Faculty, staff, and graduate assistants can also purchase a Blue permit. Holders of a Red permit are also permitted to park in the Blue or Green lots. Both the Green and Blue permits are "licenses to hunt." Blue parking lots tend to have closer proximity to campus buildings than Green lots. Red lots tend to be closest to campus buildings. Clearly, faculty and staff have the most choice, as they can select any of the three options. Students have the least choice, since they can only purchase the Green permit.

a. Has the University of Louisville done anything to remedy the problem of "hunting" for a space?

b. Why do faculty and staff have more options than students in choosing a permit? Is this fair from an economic perspective?

The Economics
of Agriculture
in the United States:
Toward a Market Approach

A P P E N D I X

When economists are asked to provide real-world examples of perfectly competitive markets, agricultural examples are usually among the first mentioned. There is a good reason for this. First, the total number of farms in the United States is huge—currently about 2.2 million. In addition, the number of competing producers within each segment is also quite large; for example, there are about 30,000 poultry producers and about 165,000 dairy farmers in this country. Therefore, the competitive model, which assumes a large number of competing producers of homogeneous products, is entirely appropriate for analyzing agricultural markets. Although economists consider competitive markets to be models of efficiency, agricultural markets continue to experience many economic difficulties. Year-to-year income instability has plagued the nation's farmers. Poverty on the farm continues, with many farmers forced out of business each year despite numerous government assistance programs.

Some indication of the farm problem may be seen in Table 8.2, which shows the number of farms, the acreage in farming, and the average (acre size) per farm between 1980 and 1996. (The annual change in the number of farms is from the immediate preceding year.) Clearly, the number of U.S. farms has declined precipitously—by almost 400,000 farms—with most of the reductions in the 1980s but with a reduction in almost 100,000 farms in the 1990s. Interestingly, the total number of acres farmed has declined, while the average size of the American farm has undergone an upward trend. This means, in part, that a high rate of new technology is being experienced in U.S. agriculture, but technology is not the whole story. What is the underlying explanation for these phenomena? By applying some of the economic principles we have covered in the text to this point, we can gain insight into these problems. Further, the problems found in the U.S. farming sector help to explain the market-oriented approach of the new programs of the 1990s and the prospect for farming in the twenty-first century.

GOVERNMENT ATTEMPTS TO SOLVE BASIC AGRICULTURAL PROBLEMS

Since the 1930s, the federal government has implemented thousands of assistance programs aimed at reducing price instability or subsidizing the incomes of American farmers. Among them were programs to directly support agricultural prices, restrict production, promote consumption, and subsidize exports and restrict imports. All the programs fall into one of two categories. In the first category are programs that attempt to alter the demand or supply curves of farm products while allowing markets to clear at equilibrium prices. In the second type of program, the government regulates farm prices with direct price supports but does not attempt to manipulate demand or supply.

TABLE 8.2

Number and Acreage of U.S. Farms, 1980–1996

	FARMS		LAND IN FARMS	
Year	Number (1,000)	Annual Change (1,000)	Total (mil. acres)	Average per farm (acres)
1980	2,440	3	1,039	426
1985	2,293	−41	1,012	441
1987	2,213	−37	999	451
1988	2,201	−12	994	452
1989	2,175	−26	991	456
1990	2,146	−29	987	460
1991	2,117	−29	982	464
1992	2,108	−9	979	464
1993	2,083	−25	976	469
1994	2,065	−18	973	471
1995	2,072	7	972	469
1996	2,063	−9	968	469

Source: Statistical Abstract of the United States 1997 (Washington, D.C.: U.S. Government Printing Office), p.668.

Note: Over the past twenty years, the number of farms has declined steadily while the amount of land in farming has also declined. The steady increase in farm production has taken place on larger farms (on average).

Agricultural Programs That Manipulate Demand And Supply

Since both demand and supply of agricultural products tend to be inelastic with respect to price, relatively small shifts in either curve can affect incomes. Therefore, government policies that increase demand for farm products lead to large price increases and to huge increases in farmers' incomes. In Figure 8.14a, an increase in demand from D_0 to D_1 for apples causes the equilibrium price to rise from 10 cents per pound to 15 cents per pound and the equilibrium quantity to rise from 6 to 8 billion pounds per year. Such a shift would cause the receipts of apple producers to double from $600 million to $1.2 billion. Over the years, the federal government has implemented a number of policies that have affected demand in this way, including the school lunch and breakfast programs, food stamp programs, and export subsidy programs.

Programs that restrict the supply of agricultural products have similar effects on farmers' incomes.

Figure 8.14b shows that a decrease in supply from S_0 to S_1 will cause the price to rise from 10 cents per pound to 16 cents per pound and will increase the receipts of apple growers from $600 million to $880 million per year (5,500,000,000 × $0.16 = $880,000,000). Over the years, the federal government has implemented acreage restriction programs that limit the number of acres farmers can use for production of certain crops; land retirement programs that pay farmers to withdraw land from production; and conservation programs that subsidize farmers to plant cover crops in place of cash crops to improve soil fertility. The federal government has also, at times, restricted imports of agricultural products. Assuming that supply curve S_0 in Figure 8.14b includes apples produced by foreign growers, programs that restrict apple imports will also increase incomes of domestic apple growers.

Each of these programs has increased incomes of domestic farmers; however, the programs have done little to stabilize farm incomes. In fact, when programs

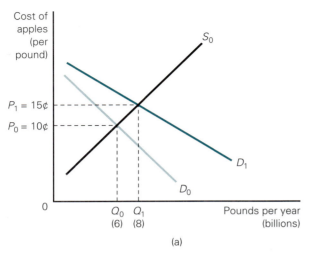

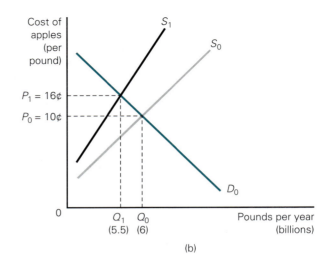

(a)

(b)

FIGURE 8.14

The Economic Consequences of Government Programs That Shift Demand or Supply

(a) Government subsidy programs that increase demand cause price and quantity to rise.
(b) Government programs that restrict supply cause price to rise but quantity to fall. If demand is inelastic, farmers' incomes will rise.

are changed from year to year, the effect can be a destabilization of farm prices.

Agricultural Programs That Regulate Prices

In addition to the various government programs designed to affect demand and supply of certain agricultural products, the government has also implemented two general types of programs that directly control prices. The first is a standard price support program. Under this program, the government sets a minimum price for a commodity and agrees to buy the commodity at that price.

Figure 8.15 shows the effect of setting a minimum price on wheat at $7.50 per bushel. When the government offers to buy wheat at $7.50 per bushel, growers will be unwilling to sell in private markets at any price below $7.50. As a consequence, growers will harvest 3.25 billion bushels but will sell only 2.25 billion bushels at $7.50 per bushel. The federal government must then buy the surplus 1 billion bushels of wheat at a price of $7.50 per bushel for a total cost of $7.5 billion. Farmers' incomes will go up, but consumers

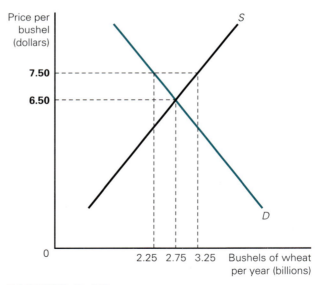

FIGURE 8.15

The Economic Effects of a Price Support Program

A government support price of $7.50 per bushel will lead to a wheat surplus of 1 billion bushels, which the government is forced to purchase.

FIGURE 8.16

The Economic Effects of a Target Price Program

A target price of $7.50 per bushel causes wheat farmers to harvest 3.25 billion bushels, which they sell for $5.50 per bushel. The government pays $2.00 per bushel to farmers to raise the price to the target level.

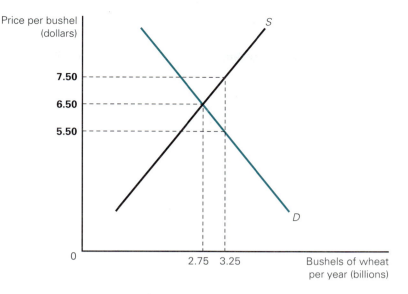

will pay higher food prices and higher taxes to provide the required subsidy. Having purchased the surplus wheat, the government must also determine what to do with it. It would do no good to sell the wheat—this would decrease the amount of wheat that could be sold privately at $7.50 per bushel and increase the surplus the government had to purchase. Instead, the alternatives are storing the wheat (and paying to do so), destroying it, or giving it away (to buyers who would not under any circumstances purchase American wheat).

Figure 8.15 illustrates how a direct price support program can become costly to finance. Increased supply due to improved technology leads to larger surpluses and greater government costs. Therefore, price support programs have usually been accompanied by programs to limit supply. In this way, the price can be kept at the support level without causing large surpluses.

In recent years the Department of Agriculture has phased out the simple price support system. Under the newer system, the government set a target price for affected commodities and agreed to make up the difference between the farmer's selling price and the target price. Figure 8.16 illustrates the operation of target prices, using demand and supply curves identical to those in Figure 8.15. If the government sets the target price at $7.50 per bushel, producers will supply 3.25 billion bushels. They would be willing to supply this

quantity because with the government subsidy included, the price they will receive is $7.50 per bushel. As the graph shows, producers will be able to sell that quantity at a price of $5.50 per bushel. Therefore, the government must pay a subsidy of $2 per bushel (the difference between $7.50 and $5.50) for each of the 3.25 billion bushels. The total subsidy cost of this program will be $6.5 billion.

The government, at least partially, has replaced traditional price supports with target prices for several reasons. One reason is that a given level of income can be generated with lower government subsidies. The subsidies in Figures 8.15 and 8.16 produce equal incomes to farmers, but the target price subsidy saves taxpayers $1 billion. In addition, the target price program keeps prices down for consumers and makes it easier for agricultural output to be sold abroad. And target prices require less expensive storage and wasteful destruction of surpluses.

THE MOVE TO MARKETS IN AGRICULTURE

Despite the use of target pricing in the subsidization of the farm sector, enormous problems and misallocations remained in the first half of the 1990s. Political pressures developed over the issues raised by subsidies and target pricing, with farmers often

Sales of farm equipment due to farm bankruptcies are common in some parts of the U.S.

supporting different sides of the issues. The maintenance of grain and other large "reserve programs" and acreage allotments on particular crops were not eliminated under target pricing—only lessened. Political pressures developed on all sides of the issue as farm problems grew. The results of almost seventy years of government involvement in agriculture, when combined with the rate of technological change over that period, have been disastrous for many farmers. Consider some of the problems.

Government's Impact On Agriculture: An Assessment

Table 8.3 shows the extent of subsidy spending on various types of farms. Clearly, larger farms receive the lion's share of the farm subsidy. In real 1995 dollars, subsidies reached a high in 1988 of the years considered and, in recent years, they have declined on average. But the data are deceptive: Many government programs (particularly those that manipulate supply

TABLE 8.3

Government Payments to Farms of Various Sizes
Government subsidies for various size farms are shown below. The average dollar payment has been converted to 1995 dollars for easy comparison.

	AVERAGE PAYMENT PER FARM			
Amount of Farm Sales	**1975**	**1980**	**1988**	**1992**
Less than $20,000	$343	$190	$1,188	$383
$20,000 to $39,999	$1,261	$913	$7,378	$2,992
$40,000 to $99,999	$2,065	$2,050	$14,534	$6,425
$100,000 to $500,000	$3,555	$3,377	$30,941	$16,136
Greater than $500,000	$14,711	$6,749	$52,448	$26,764

Source: Statistical Abstract of the United States 1984, 1990, and 1994 (Washington, D.C.: U.S. Government Printing Office, 1997).

and demand and support the price of products) make no direct government payments to farmers. Despite massive government expenditures, the woes of American farmers continue. Farm debt has increased from $53 billion in 1970 to more than $140 billion today, and farm foreclosures and auctions have become weekly events in many regions.

Critics of U.S. farm policy argue that government subsidies are in fact responsible for many of these problems. With unrestricted competition, gains in productivity would create only short-run problems for farmers. As fewer farmers were needed, competitive forces would drive some out of business. In the long run, surviving farms would earn a normal profit. Government subsidy programs, however, have encouraged farmers to continue despite economic losses. While these programs have reduced the risks of farming and ensure an overabundance of agricultural products for consumers, they also contribute to long-run problems. For example, when drought conditions struck much of the United States in 1986 and again in 1988, the government provided emergency assistance even to farmers who had not purchased government-subsidized crop insurance. The same was true when the Mississippi River inundated huge quantities of midwestern farm land in the early 1990s. Rather than encouraging farmers to remain in an unprofitable industry, government reeducation and retraining programs could be instituted to encourage farmers to leave the industry. Such a policy would eliminate losses and the need for government income support programs.

The Freedom to Farm Act of 1996

The low income of farmers has been the legacy of improved productivity, low short-run elasticities of supply and demand, and, indirectly, government subsidy programs. Government support of farmers is very much a product of the social problems—hunger and malnourishment, in particular—of the 1930s. These conditions do not exist in the 1990s. This fact plus the huge cost of the farm program ($40 billion of taxpayers' money over five years prior to 1995) has led to attempted reforms. These reforms touch some, but certainly not all, commodities heretofore subsidized.

The Freedom to Farm Act, signed by President Clinton in April 1996, took a new and more "market-oriented" approach to the subsidization of American agriculture. At a price tag of $47 billion for seven years, the new approach eliminates target pricing and acreage allotments on many products. Over the seven years farmers have received a subsidy regardless of market prices. The bill covers rice, corn, soybeans, wheat, and other crops.

As usual, there are both winners and losers from the new legislation. Many farmers will welcome the flexibility of being able to plant what they want. Consumers may notice some small fluctuation in the price of groceries as the free market takes over (on average only about 20 percent of the price of farm products at the supermarket is the actual return to farmers). Taxpayers will, if all goes as planned, begin to find relief as the direct subsidy is phased out over time. But the truth is that

Floods and other natural disasters have profound impacts on agricultural production and prices.

political pressures mean that only *part* of agriculture will be opened up to market forces. The "Freedom to Farm" provision failed to eliminate price support programs for such items as tobacco, sugar, and peanuts. Huge (and unseen) subsidies in the form of import tariffs and quotas also protect many items, such as sugar, from foreign competition. Milk marketing regulations continue to add as much as 40 cents to the price of a gallon of milk. Lobbying efforts for some commodities appear to be too strong for many politicians to resist.

In the summer of 1999, drought conditions again plagued the eastern and midwestern farming areas of the United States. The plight of farmers became political fodder for politicians at the federal level, who got into a bidding war producing subsidies in the range of $8 billion. These subsidies, whatever their humanitarian value, will have the effect of maintaining and encouraging farm production and lowering farm prices over time.

Whether farm support programs will continue into the twenty-first century is debatable. Proponents argue that the loss of the small farmer would eliminate an American tradition and would create other social and economic problems, such as urban overcrowding and higher unemployment. Opponents believe that we have too many farmers and that this oversupply is and has long been an unnecessary burden on taxpayers. The fate of government subsidy programs, like other considerations of equity, will be dealt with through the political process.

Monopoly: The Firm As Industry

I n a purely competitive market, each firm's production is such a small proportion of industry output that a single firm has no influence on the market price. As we have seen, the competitive firm is a price taker. The opposite extreme to a purely competitive firm is a pure monopoly: a single seller in an industry. The pure monopoly, in fact, is an industry. It alone faces the industry demand curve for its output, and it can affect market price by changing the amount of output that it produces. For this reason, we refer to the pure monopoly firm as a **price searcher**: It must seek the price that maximizes its profits. The ability of the pure monopoly firm to affect market price is not absolute, however. Even a single seller in an industry is subject to competitive pressures from the makers of substitute products. When you finish Chapter 9 you should know

- how barriers to market entry can create monopoly power.
- the principles underlying the economist's (static) model of monopoly behavior, including how the monopolist makes profits or sustains losses.
- how, under specific circumstances, monopolists can charge different prices to different consumer groups for the same product or service.
- the costs of monopoly power to the economy.
- the pros and cons of monopoly as a market structure.

Price searcher
A firm that is able to choose a profit-maximizing price from a range of prices rather than have price imposed by market conditions and competition; such a firm faces a downward-sloping demand curve.

Pure monopoly
An industry in which a single firm produces a product that has no close substitutes and in which entry of new firms cannot occur.

WHAT IS A MONOPOLY?

A **pure monopoly** is an industry composed of a single seller of a product with no close substitutes and with high barriers to entry. This definition seems clear, but we must use some care in applying it.

Examples of pure monopoly in the sense of a single seller in an industry are rare. In sixteenth- through eighteenth-century Europe, monarchs granted monopoly rights to individuals for a variety of productive undertakings. These were pure monopolies because each was given the exclusive right to run an entire industry. For example, the king of England created only one English East India Company, which was empowered with a monopoly over the trade with India. This monopoly power was manifested in the high prices the East India Company charged for the goods it brought back from India and sold in England. (See the Focus "Mercantilism and the Sale of Monopoly Rights" for a more detailed discussion of such historical monopolies.)

Even in these historical cases of monopoly, the monopoly was usually granted to a group of merchants. These monopolies were therefore not technically a single seller; rather, they were a group of sellers acting as a single seller. This is a

FOCUS

Mercantilism and the Sale of Monopoly Rights

Mercantilism refers to the form of economic organization that dominated Western Europe from roughly 1500 to 1776. The English, French, and Spanish economies of the time were typical mercantile economies. They were characterized by monarchies in which a king or queen represented the central government. As practiced by these monarchs, mercantilism involved widespread and detailed regulation of the economy. More often than not, this regulation took the form of creating monopoly rights for favored individuals. The mercantile economies therefore came to be characterized by the existence of pure monopolies in such diverse areas as brewing, mining, trading, playing cards, and so on, endlessly.

The creation and protection of these monopoly rights had a clear purpose—to raise revenue for the "needs" of the sovereign. Such needs included the expenses of the king's court and the resources needed to fight foreign wars. In other words, the monarchies sold monopoly rights to raise revenues.

Why did sovereigns use monopolies rather than taxes for revenue? Fundamentally, tax collection was a relatively inefficient means to raise revenue for the central state because the costs of monitoring and controlling tax evasion were high. Barter and nonmarket production were widespread in the agricultural economy of the times; moreover, commercial record keeping was not highly developed. Tax collection was therefore a difficult and unattractive alternative as a source of revenue.

The granting of monopoly rights as a means to raise revenue did not have the same deficiencies as taxation. Most important, competition among potential monopolists revealed to the state authorities the worth of such privileges. There were no problems of evasion or guessing at taxable values in this case. Those who wanted the monopoly right would come to the king or queen and make an offer for the right. The potential monopolists were buying the agreement of the ruler to protect and enforce the monopoly privileges that he or she granted.

Thus, pure monopoly had a prominent place in economic history because of its effectiveness at raising revenue for the state. As the state's power to tax has increased in modern times, this revenue-raising role of monopolies has diminished.

broader meaning of monopoly. In fact, we typically observe monopoly in the real world in groups of sellers acting together. Such associations of sellers are called cartels. The analysis of pure monopoly presented in this chapter is relevant to cartels, but pure monopolies and cartels are not the same. A group of sellers must somehow organize to form a cartel agreement; the single pure monopolist faces no such organizational problem. In this chapter, we discuss pure monopoly in the sense of a single seller facing the industry demand curve. In Chapter 11, we return to the cartel problem and see what extra elements have to be added to monopoly theory to account for cartel behavior.

A second problem in applying the definition of monopoly concerns the criterion that there be no close substitutes. All products exhibit some degree of substitutability. The monopolist's isolation from competition from substitute products is therefore a matter of degree. Consider electricity, usually sold by firms holding local monopolies on its distribution. Are there good substitutes for electricity? The answer depends on what the electricity is used for. If it is used for lighting services in residential homes, the few possible alternatives—such as candles and oil lamps—are not very good substitutes for the convenience of electric lighting. If it is used for heating, however, the range of substitute products is greater. The wood stove, oil, and natural gas industries are competitors with the electric utility company in the market for home heating. The degree of substitutability for the monopolist's product is an important determinant of monopoly behavior. Where there are close substitutes, the monopolist cannot substantially raise prices without losing sales. Where there are no close substitutes, the monopolist has more power to raise prices.

A third consideration in defining monopolies is high barriers to new entry by potential competitors, the basic source of a pure monopoly. There are several types of barriers to new competition: legal barriers, economies of scale, and control of an essential resource.

Legal Barriers to Entry

Sometimes the power of government is used to determine which industry or firm is to produce certain goods and services. Such **legal barriers to entry** take several forms.

First, it may be necessary to obtain a **public franchise** to operate in an industry. Franchises are granted by government for a variety of undertakings. The U.S. Postal Service, for example, has an exclusive franchise to deliver first-class mail. (See the Application "Technology, Economics, and the Postal Monopoly" at the end of this chapter.) Similar arrangements for food and gasoline service are made along toll roads such as the New Jersey Turnpike. The essence of an exclusive public franchise is that a monopoly is created; competitors are legally prohibited from entering franchised markets.

Second, in many industries and occupations a **government license** is required to operate. In most states a license is required to practice architecture, dentistry, embalming, law, nursing, medicine, or veterinary medicine; to dispense drugs; and to teach. At the federal level, a license is required from the Federal Communications Commission to operate a radio or television station. If you want to operate a trucking firm that carries goods across state lines, you must obtain a license from the Interstate Commerce Commission. Licensing therefore creates a type of monopoly right by restricting the ability of firms to enter certain industries and occupations.

Third, a **patent** grants an inventor a monopoly over a product or process for 20 years in the United States. The patent prohibits others from producing the

Legal barriers to entry
Government actions that prohibit other firms or individuals from producing particular products or entering particular occupations or industries; such barriers take the form of legal franchises, licenses, and patents.

Public franchise
A firm or industry's exclusive, government-granted right to produce and sell a good or service.

Government license
A legal right granted by state, local, or federal governments to enter an occupation or industry.

Patent
A monopoly right granted by government to an inventor for a product or process; valid for twenty years in the United States.

patented product and thereby confers a limited-term monopoly on the inventor. The purpose of a patent is to encourage innovation by allowing inventors to reap the exclusive fruits of their inventions for a period of time. Yet a patent also establishes a legal monopoly right. In effect, the social benefit of innovation is traded off against the possible social costs of monopoly. (See the Focus "Patents: The Inventor's Monopoly" later in the chapter.)

Economies of Scale and Natural Monopoly

In some industries, low unit costs may be achieved only through large-scale production. Such economies of scale put potential entrants at a disadvantage. To be able to compete effectively in the industry, a new firm has to enter on a large scale, which can be costly and risky. The effect is to deter entry.

Natural monopoly
A monopoly in which the relation between industry demand and cost structure makes it possible for only one firm to exist in the industry.

In a **natural monopoly**, economies of scale are so pronounced that only a single firm can survive in the industry. In such a case, government enacts some sort of regulatory scheme to control the natural monopoly. Public utilities such as natural gas, water, and electricity distribution are examples of natural monopolies that are regulated. The regulation of natural monopoly is discussed in more detail in Chapter 16.

A firm may own all of an essential resource in an industry, in which case new entry is barred because potential entrants cannot gain access to the essential resource. The De Beers Company of South Africa, for example, controls 80 percent of the world's diamond supply. (For more on the De Beers cartel, see the Application at the end of Chapter 11.) This makes the company a virtual monopolist in the diamond market.

MONOPOLY PRICE AND OUTPUT IN THE SHORT RUN

The theory of monopoly can be applied to a large number of situations in the economy. These range from the behavior of government-created monopolies to natural monopolies, patent rights, and diamond companies. Moreover, virtually every firm has some control over the prices it charges. The degree of control varies with the type of market in which the firm sells, but the fact that the firm can choose its prices makes the concept of the monopoly firm as price searcher relevant to understanding firm behavior in general.

The monopoly firm, like the competitive firm, faces both long- and short-run production and pricing decisions. In this section we explore the concept of price searching, and we examine how the monopoly firm decides how much output to produce and what price to charge in the short run.

The Monopolist's Demand Curve

The demand curve of the pure monopolist is fundamentally different from that of the pure competitor. The purely competitive firm is a price taker; it accepts market price as given but can sell as much as it wants at the prevailing market price because demand for its product is perfectly elastic. The monopoly firm faces a downward-sloping market demand curve and must find the price that maximizes its profits. This means that to sell more, the monopolist must lower price. The monopoly firm therefore confronts the problem of finding the best price–output combination. For this reason, we say that the monopolist is a price searcher.

Figure 9.1 illustrates the difference in the demand curves facing price takers and price searchers: The former is perfectly elastic, while the latter slopes downward. How elastic is the price searcher's demand curve? Economic theory does not give us a single answer to this question. Recall from Chapter 5 that the degree of elasticity along a demand curve depends on a number of variables, including the price and the number of close substitutes for the monopolist's product. Even though monopolists are synonymous with the industries they occupy, they are not immune to competition from producers of substitute products. The cheaper and more numerous these substitutes are, the more elastic the monopolist's demand curve will be. And the more elastic a monopolist's demand curve, the less valuable is its monopoly position in setting prices. Figure 9.1b represents the demand curves for two monopoly industries. The demand curves for these two industries, D_1 and D_2, both slope downward, but D_1 is more inelastic than D_2 at price P_m because the latter monopoly faces stiffer competition from substitutes.

For this reason, a monopoly in tuna fishing, for example, would not be a tremendously valuable monopoly right. While tuna is a unique product, significant price increases for tuna would cause consumers to switch to other protein sources, such as chicken or beef. A monopoly over crude oil production, however, where consumers have few viable consumption alternatives in the short run, has proved to be tremendously valuable, as the price-raising success of OPEC in the 1970s testifies.

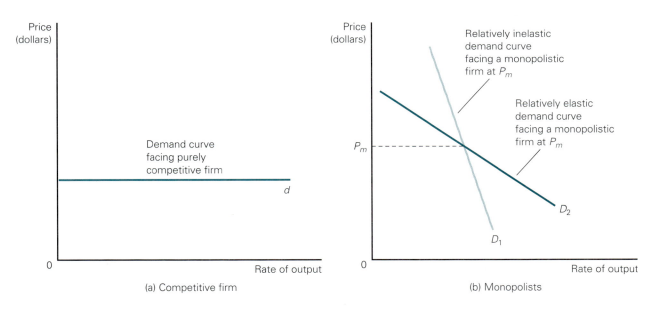

(a) Competitive firm   (b) Monopolists

FIGURE 9.1

Demand Curves for Competitive and Monopoly Firms

(a) A perfectly elastic demand curve *d* facing a purely competitive firm. This firm is a price taker: It can sell all of its product that it wants at the prevailing market price.
(b) Two market demand curves facing different monopolists. The firm facing demand curve D_1 has more leeway than the firm facing curve D_2 in choosing price–output combinations because consumers cannot easily find substitutes for the former's product. But both monopolies are price searchers. They face downward-sloping demand curves; to sell more, they must lower price.

The basic point to remember about the demand curve facing the monopolist is that it is downward-sloping. The monopoly firm must lower price to sell more and must search for the best, or profit-maximizing, level of output. The concept of marginal revenue will help the monopolist to answer the question: Does the revenue gained by selling more at a lower price exceed the revenue lost by lowering the price?

The Monopolist's Revenues

Suppose that you are the owner of a monopoly. You have discovered a special kind of rock on your land that, when split, reveals a natural hologram. The mysterious beauty of these rocks is highly appealing to rock collectors and gift purchasers. If your aim is to earn the maximum profit from the production and sale of the rocks, how do you decide what price to charge for them?

By trial and error—for you have no previous experience on which to base your pricing decision—you find that the revenues, costs, and profits you encounter at different prices vary considerably, as illustrated in Table 9.1. Columns (1) and (2) show the decreasing prices you must charge to sell increasing numbers of rocks. Together, columns (1) and (2) represent the market demand curve for hologram rocks, of which you are the sole seller. Your total revenue per day (also known as sales) is column (1) × column (2), or price × quantity.

Marginal revenue

The change in total revenue arising from a one-unit change in output; the change in total revenue divided by the change in output.

Marginal revenue (*MR*) is the change in total revenue brought about by a change in output, or $\Delta TR/\Delta Q$. In Table 9.1, column (4) reflects the change in column (3) each time you lower price and produce an additional rock. In Chapter 8, we saw that for the purely competitive firm, *MR* was equal to price because the firm did not have to lower its price to sell additional units of output (see Table 8.1, p. 201). However, as Table 9.1 here shows, *MR* is not equal to price for you as a monopoly firm, except for the very first unit you sell, because you face a downward-sloping demand curve. When you cut your price, as for example from $22 to $21, two conflicting influences affect your total revenues. You gain additional revenue from the additional units you sell at the lower price. In this case, you sell one more rock for $21. But because the price reduction also applies to output that you were previously able to sell at a higher price, in effect you *lose* revenue on these units. In other words, the three rocks per day you could previously sell at $22 are now priced at $21, a reduction of $3 from your total revenues. Your marginal revenue is therefore $21 − $3 = $18 in this case.

When demand is downward-sloping, *MR* ($18) is less than price ($21) by the amount of the revenue lost on units that would have sold at the higher price. For price searchers, marginal revenue is less than price ($P > MR$) because of the need to lower price to sell additional units of output.

Figure 9.2 provides another way of looking at the fact that marginal revenue is always lower than price for the monopoly firm. At a price of P_1, total revenue is $P_1 \times Q_1$. At a price of P_2, total revenue is $P_2 \times Q_2$. Marginal revenue is the difference between these two total revenue rectangles. To see its components more clearly, consider what happens when price is cut from P_1 to P_2. First, additional revenue is generated by the sale of extra units at the lower price. This additional revenue is indicated by the shaded rectangular area CBQ_2Q_1. Second, there is a loss of revenue on units previously sold for P_1 but now sold for P_2. This loss is represented by the shaded area P_1ACP_2. Thus, the marginal revenue derived from a price reduction by the monopolist is less than the new price charged. Except for the first unit of output, the *MR* curve of the monopolist therefore lies below or

TABLE 9.1

Revenues, Costs, and Profits for the Pure Monopolist

These data are for the hologram rock monopolist. Columns (1) and (2) show the components of the demand curve facing the firm. Column (3) gives total revenue, or sales. Column (4) is the important concept of marginal revenue, which is the change in total revenue divided by the change in output. Columns (5) and (6) are the cost data. Maximum profits in column (7) occur where marginal cost equals marginal revenue, at 6 units of output per day.

(1) Rate of Output (units per day)	(2) Price (per unit)	(3) Total Revenue (per day) (1) × (2)	(4) Marginal Revenue $\Delta TR \div \Delta Q$	(5) Total Cost (per day)	(6) Marginal Cost	(7) Profit (per day) (3) − (5)
0	—	—		$40.00		−$40.00
			}······· $24.00		}······· $10.00	
1	$24.00	$24.00		50.00		−26.00
			}········· 22.00		}········· 8.00	
2	23.00	46.00		58.00		−12.00
			}········· 20.00		}········· 7.00	
3	22.00	66.00		65.00		1.00
			}········· 18.00		}········ 10.00	
4	21.00	84.00		75.00		9.00
			}········ 16.00		}········ 12.00	
5	20.00	100.00		87.00		13.00
			}········· 14.00		}········ 13.00	
6	19.00	114.00		100.00		14.00
			}········· 12.00		}········ 15.00	
7	18.00	126.00		115.00		11.00
			}········ 10.00		}········ 20.00	
8	17.00	136.00		135.00		1.00
			}········· 3.50		}········ 25.00	
9	15.50	139.50		160.00		−20.50
			}········· 0.50		}········ 30.00	
10	14.00	140.00		190.00		−50.00

FIGURE 9.2

The Dual Effects of a Price Reduction on Total Reveues

When the monopoly firm lowers price, it gains revenue from the additional output sold, Q_1 to Q_2, and loses revenue on the output previously sold at price P_1 and now sold at a lower price, P_2. The net effect is a marginal revenue curve that lies below and inside the demand curve.

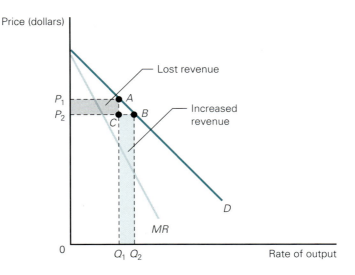

inside the demand curve. Even though the monopoly firm faces no direct competition, it still must search for its best price.

Total Revenue, Marginal Revenue, and Elasticity of Demand

The demand curve facing the monopoly firm shows the amount of output that can be sold at different prices. It also shows how the firm's revenues vary as price and output are changed. By observing this, we can learn something about the elasticity of the monopolist's demand curve over various ranges. Figure 9.3 illustrates the relation between total revenue, marginal revenue, and the elasticity of the monopolist's demand curve at various points. Suppose that we are joint owners of a firm with a monopoly on Gas-Saver, a unique additive that doubles gas mileage if one can is added to each tankful of gas. If we conduct a pricing experiment along our demand curve, we can observe its effects on our revenues. We start with a high price of $12 per can and lower it gradually to $6. At $12, we will not sell any of the stuff, for consumers know that a can will cost them more than the gas they save. As we lower the price toward $6, we sell more and more.

Figure 9.3b shows what happens to our total revenue as the price falls. Over the range of sales up to 30 cans per day, our total revenue rises. In Figure 9.3a, this rise is reflected by the positive marginal revenue. A demand curve is elastic when price reductions cause total revenue to rise. Thus, our demand curve is elastic up to the level of 30 units of output and a price of $6. Beyond 30 units of out-

FIGURE 9.3

Changes in Elasticity of Demand and Total Revenue as Price Changes

The elasticity of the monopolist's demand curve is linked to the behavior of total revenue as price changes. In the elastic ($\varepsilon_d > 1$) portion of the demand curve, price reductions cause total revenue to rise. When demand is unit elastic ($\varepsilon_d = 1$), price reductions leave total revenue unchanged. When demand is inelastic ($\varepsilon_d < 1$), price reductions lead to a fall in total revenue. The point of unit elasticity in part (a), beyond which marginal revenue becomes negative—30 cans per day—is also the point in part (b) at which total revenue stops rising and starts declining.

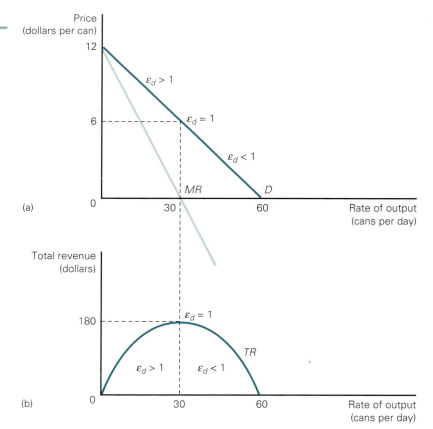

put, however, we observe that as we further lower our price, our total revenue falls, and our marginal revenue is negative. This drop means that we have reached the inelastic portion of our monopoly demand curve. Here, price reductions cause our sales to decline.

The regions of our Gas-Saver demand curve that are elastic and inelastic are labeled $\varepsilon_d > 1$ and $\varepsilon_d < 1$, respectively, in Figure 9.3. (ε_d is the symbol for price elasticity of demand.) The point labeled $\varepsilon_d = 1$ is where the demand curve is unit elastic. This point occurs where marginal revenue equals zero and where total revenue is at a maximum. It is the dividing line between the elastic and inelastic portions of the monopolist's demand curve. The link between MR and elasticity of demand can be stated thus: MR goes from positive to negative as demand goes from elastic to inelastic.

With this simple model, we can begin to discuss the rational pricing strategy of the monopolist. Suppose that our Gas-Saver monopoly firm has no costs of production so that profits are equal to total revenue. What price should we set to maximize our revenue? Figure 9.3b clearly illustrates that we can do no better than to be at the top of the total revenue curve. At this point, we reach our total maximum revenue: $180 per day. Reading vertically up to Figure 9.3a, you can see that to earn this maximum total revenue, we should produce 30 cans of Gas-Saver per day and sell them for $6 each. The profit-maximizing monopolist with no costs of production will set price along the demand curve where demand is unit elastic, or equal to 1. A monopoly firm will never operate along the inelastic portion of its demand curve because marginal revenue is negative along this portion. Increases in output and reductions in price actually cause total revenue to fall.

This simple analysis helps us understand the pricing behavior of any firm facing a downward-sloping demand curve. Such firms will not set price in the inelastic part of their demand curve because they can earn more revenue by raising price. This result and the discussion of this section are based on the properties of a straight-line, or linear, demand curve.

Short-Run Price and Output of the Monopolist

Although for simplicity we did not consider costs in the previous discussion, we introduce them now, because all firms incur costs of production. The fact that the monopolist possesses a monopoly in the output market says nothing about its position in input markets. In this respect the monopoly firm is like the competitive firm; it is one of many buyers of inputs. The cost curves of the monopolist therefore resemble those of the competitive firm.

By combining cost concepts with the revenue concepts of monopoly, we can analyze the choice of the best, or profit-maximizing, rate of output and price for the monopoly firm in the short run. To maximize profits, the monopolist follows the same rule that the competitive firm follows—it sets marginal cost equal to marginal revenue. The logic is identical in both cases. If MR is greater than MC, it pays to produce additional units of output because they add more to revenues than to costs. If MR is less than MC, it pays to reduce production because extra output adds more to costs than to revenues. The monopolist will therefore do best by producing at the output level where MC equals MR.

Look back at the cost and profit data in Table 9.1 for the hologram rock monopoly to check the viability of this rule for profit maximization. Comparing marginal revenue in column (4) with marginal cost in column (6), we see that the first 6 rocks produced per day add more to revenue than to costs; that is, $MR > MC$

over this range of outputs. The sixth unit of output adds $14 to revenues and $13 to costs. It pays to produce that sixth unit. Producing the seventh rock, however, has a marginal cost of $15 and a marginal revenue of $12. The firm would be losing money if it increased operations to 7 rocks a day. The maximum profit occurs at a rate of output of 6 rocks per day and a price of $19 for each. The profitability of this decision is recorded in column (7), which is the difference in total revenue from column (3) and total cost from column (5). The maximum daily profit of $14 occurs when 6 rocks are produced, the point at which MR equals MC.

The same point is illustrated graphically in Figure 9.4, where a monopoly's marginal cost curve is combined with its demand and marginal revenue curves. To determine the profit-maximizing rate of output, the monopolist would find the point along the horizontal axis where $MR = MC$—in this case Q_m. For outputs less than Q_m, $MR > MC$, and it pays the monopolist to expand production. In this area, extra units of output add more to revenue than to cost. For outputs greater than Q_m, it pays the firm to reduce output. At Q_m, $MR = MC$, and the firm can do no better than produce this output. Profits are maximized at Q_m.

The monopolist sets a price for Q_m units of output by reading the market value of this output off the demand curve at a point directly above the point where $MR = MC$. In other words, the price for this output is read off the demand curve by drawing a straight line from the intersection of MR and MC to the demand curve and over to the price axis, as shown by the dashed lines in the figure. Price is not set where $MR = MC$ on the marginal revenue curve; it is set by reference to the demand curve. In Figure 9.4, P_m is the **profit-maximizing price**.

Profit-maximizing price
The price associated with the quantity sold at which the difference between total revenue and total cost is greatest; the price associated with the quantity sold at which marginal revenue equals marginal cost.

Monopoly Profits

Figure 9.4 shows how the monopolist applies the $MR = MC$ rule and also depicts the level of profits the monopoly earns. To discuss monopoly profits we add the monopolist's average total cost curve to the analysis.

The monopolist sets $MR = MC$, selling Q_m units at a price of P_m. Just as in the case of the purely competitive firm, the monopolist's profits are determined with

---

FIGURE 9.4

Monopoly Profits
At point B, the monopoly firm would just cover its average total cost. But since it holds a monopoly, it can charge price P_m, creating economic profits equal to $AB \times Q_m$, represented by the area P_mABC. In other words, P_mABC is equal to total revenue, P_mAQ_m0, minus total costs, CBQ_m0.

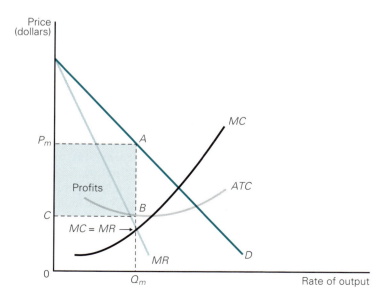

respect to the average total cost curve. At point B, the monopolist would just cover its average total cost. But its monopoly position and the demand for its product allow it to set price at P_m on its demand curve, creating economic profits in excess of its costs. In Figure 9.4, these profits are given by the shaded area P_mABC, or the amount by which total revenue, the area P_mAQ_m0, exceeds the total cost of producing Q_m, the area CBQ_m0. Another way to look at monopoly profits in such a graph is to say that the monopolist makes AB profits per unit of output, where $AB \times Q_m = P_mABC$.

This is a profitable monopoly. These returns are in excess of the total costs of the firm, which means that they are above the opportunity cost of the monopolist's capital investment. Were this a purely competitive firm, these excess returns would stimulate new entry and expansion in the industry. Remember, however, that this is a pure monopoly. Entry cannot occur here, by definition. So, unlike the profits of the competitive firm, which ultimately are restored to a normal rate of return by entry, the profits of the monopolist will persist in the long run.

Not all monopolies make monopoly profits. Some lose money. Such a case is graphed in Figure 9.5. In this case, demand is not sufficient to cover the average total cost of the monopolist at the level of output where $MR = MC$. Total revenue at Q_m is represented by P_mCQ_m0; total cost is represented by the larger area ABQ_m0. Total cost exceeds total revenue by the amount of the shaded area, $ABCP_m$. This monopolist makes an economic loss in the short run. As long as P_m is high enough to cover the monopolist's variable costs, the monopoly will continue to operate in the short run if it expects market conditions for its product to improve. Over time, however, if the losses depicted in Figure 9.5 persist, the monopolist will cease operations and go out of business. The investment in the monopoly firm is not earning a normal rate of return, and by closing down, the firm is free to move its investment where it can earn higher rates of return.

It may seem curious that monopolists should make losses, but this is a very real phenomenon. Many holders of patents, for example, never market their products because there is no demand for them. The fact that one has a monopoly does not automatically make it a valuable monopoly.

FIGURE 9.5

An Unprofitable Monopoly

Not all monopolies make profits. This monopoly makes BC losses per unit of output because demand for its product is not sufficient to cover its average total costs. Its total revenue at Q_m is represented by P_mCQ_m0, and its total cost by ABQ_m0. Therefore, its total losses are represented by the shaded area, $ABCP_m$. If the situation does not improve in the long run, this monopoly will go out of business.

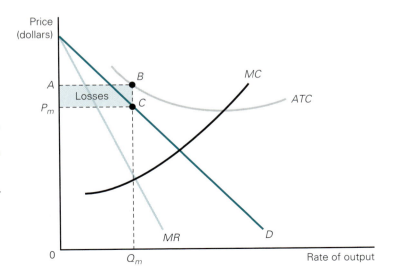

Comparing the Monopoly Firm and the Purely Competitive Firm

Before we move on to long-run considerations for the monopolist, we note two important differences between the monopoly firm and the purely competitive firm. First, in a pure monopoly no distinction is made between the firm and industry. The pure monopoly is the industry, so there is no room for a separate theory of industry versus firm behavior, such as the one we presented for pure competition.

Second, recall that the marginal cost curve of a competitive firm (above the point of minimum average variable cost) is its supply curve because the firm sets marginal cost equal to price to maximize profits. Its pricing behavior traces out a relation between quantity supplied and price. No such relation exists for pure monopoly. The monopolist controls the quantity of output produced and sets $MR = MC$, but MR does not equal price for the monopolist. Because the monopolist does not set MC equal to price, no unique relation exists between MC and price in the case of pure monopoly. To know what the monopolist will produce at a given price, we need to know more than the firm's MC; we need to know the shape and position of its demand and marginal revenue curves as well. The lesson is simply that the monopolist does not have a supply curve—that is, a unique relation between the amount it produces and the price.

PURE MONOPOLY IN THE LONG RUN

Like all firms, the pure monopolist must face the long run, the period of economic time over which the firm can vary all of its inputs and enter or exit the industry. The long run for the pure monopolist is not analogous to the long run for a purely competitive firm and industry. Certain adjustments take place, but entry and other efficiency-enhancing adjustments do not occur. Monopoly and its effects persist in long-run equilibrium.

Entry and Exit

A pure monopoly may not be profitable and, hence, may leave the industry. Exit is a distinct possibility. Entry is not. By definition, high and prohibitive barriers to entry exist with monopoly; entry by new firms is barred. Long-run adjustments in the form of competitive entry do not take place in the case of the monopoly. Monopoly profits therefore persist in the long run.

Adjustments to Scale

The monopoly firm can adjust its scale of operations in the long run. Given that it makes a profit, the monopolist can seek to produce the profit-maximizing rate of output in the most efficient plant for that level of output. This plant size, however, will not generally be the most efficient plant size overall, as it was in the purely competitive model in long-run equilibrium. Typically, the monopoly will produce output in the long run with a higher-cost plant size than will a competitive industry.

PRICE DISCRIMINATION

In our discussion of monopoly theory so far, the profit-maximizing monopoly has charged a single price for its product. Each customer who buys the product pays the same price. Under certain conditions, however, a monopoly can make more money by charging different customers different prices for its product. For example, movie theaters and airlines often charge lower prices to children and senior citizens than to others, and utilities charge different rates for electricity to businesses and residences. This method of pricing is called **price discrimination**.

Two points should be kept in mind as we discuss price discrimination. First, price differences that reflect cost differences do *not* constitute price discrimination. For example, large buyers (those purchasing more goods) are often charged less per unit for some goods than are small buyers. The general reason for this difference is that selling costs per unit are lower when dealing with the large buyer. Each sale may require the same paperwork, but the paperwork cost is lower per unit of sales for the large buyer. The lower price charged to the large buyer is not the result of price discrimination; it reflects the seller's different costs of serving the two customers. Second, equality of prices across buyers does not necessarily imply the absence of price discrimination because the costs of supplying the buyers may be different. Price discrimination is illegal under the Robinson–Patman Act (1936), which is enforced by the Federal Trade Commission.

When Can Price Discrimination Exist?

Price discrimination can occur only under certain conditions. First, the firm must have monopoly power and face a downward-sloping demand curve for its output. In other words, the firm must be a price setter, not a price taker. A price taker cannot charge different prices to different customers because the price it charges is determined by the prevailing market price, over which it has no influence. Second, the monopolist's buyers must fall into at least two clearly and easily identifiable groups of customers who have different elasticities of demand for the product. Third, the separation of buyers is crucial. Without the ability to separate buyers, the seller will not be able to keep buyers who are charged a low price from reselling the product to buyers who are charged a high price. Such behavior (normally called *arbitrage*) would undermine a price discrimination scheme and lead to a single price for the monopolist's product. The identification and separation of groups of consumers must be possible at low cost to make price discrimination worthwhile for the firm.

A Model of Price Discrimination

Figure 9.6 shows how a monopolist can gain from price discrimination. There are two groups of customers for the monopolist's product. The demand of buyers in market A is relatively more elastic than the demand of buyers in market B at a given price.

Two points are crucial in understanding the analysis in Figure 9.6. First, the marginal cost to the monopolist of supplying both markets is the same. The best way to think about this condition is to assume that the output sold to each market is produced in the same plant. *MC* is thus at the same level in both market A and market B. Second, to maximize profits, the monopolist sets marginal cost equal to marginal revenue in each market.

Following the $MC = MR$ rule in this case, the monopoly firm sets $MC = MR$ in both markets. In market A this leads to a price of P_1; in market B it leads to a price of P_2. The buyers in market B with the less elastic demand are charged a higher price than the buyers in market A ($P_2 > P_1$). These are the profit-maximizing prices in the two markets. The monopolist benefits from price discrimination to the degree

Price discrimination

The practice of charging one buyer or group of buyers a different price than that charged to others. The price difference is not due to differences in the cost of supplying the two groups.

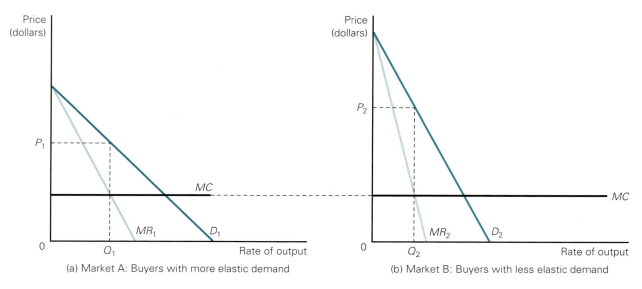

(a) Market A: Buyers with more elastic demand   (b) Market B: Buyers with less elastic demand

FIGURE 9.6

Price Discrimination

The figures demonstrate a case of price discrimination for the same product in two markets. Consumers in market A have a relatively more elastic demand than those in market B. The profit-maximizing monopolist confronts market A consumers with a lower price. That is, $P_1 < P_2$. For a price discrimination scheme to be viable, the monopolist must prevent buyers in market A from reselling its product to buyers in market B.

that its profits go up relative to what they would be if it sold its output at a single price to all buyers.

The monopolist must be able to keep the two markets separate to sustain a price discrimination scheme. Otherwise, buyers in market A could profitably resell the product to buyers in market B. In 1984 Apple Computer Inc. offered to sell all students at selected universities its then-new Macintosh computer for less than half of the full price being charged to other customers. Students and profiteers immediately saw the potential for profit in reselling the computers to nonstudents at marked-up but still below-retail prices. Newspaper ads hooked up students wishing to sell the cut-rate Macintoshes with nonstudents desiring to buy Macintoshes.

The seller who wants to practice price discrimination must therefore be able to distinguish and separate customers on the basis of their elasticity of demand. Moreover, the seller must be able to perform this feat without a large expenditure of resources. Thus, most real-world price discrimination schemes are based on general characteristics of customers, such as age, education, income, and sex. For example, children and older people are often charged lower prices for certain products because their age is thought to indicate that they have more elastic demand for these products.

A subtle factor that provides a basis for price discrimination is differences in the opportunity cost of time among customers. The practice of giving discount coupons for grocery purchases, for example, allows sellers to separate buyers into elastic and inelastic demand categories. Buyers in the inelastic demand category will not take the time and trouble to collect coupons and redeem them. These are customers who place a relatively high value on their time. They value other uses of their time and do not want to clip coupons. Buyers in the elastic demand group place a lower value on their time and will take the time to clip coupons and convert them into lower prices at the store. Sellers use coupons to separate buyers into classes and charge them different prices based on their different elasticities of demand.

A huge number of examples of ongoing cases of discrimination may be found in all areas of life. Many examples of price discrimination can be found on college and university campuses. Most publicly funded institutions charge different tuition rates to in-state and out-of-state students, even though the marginal cost of educating each type of student is the same. The students separate themselves into two groups when they complete the institution's application form and give their addresses. An in-state student cannot transfer registration in a class to an out-of-state student. Thus, no arbitrage can take place. Other things being equal, this pricing behavior will reap the institution larger tuition revenues than would the practice of charging one price to all students. For other examples, see the Focus "Are You a Victim of Price Discrimination on Campus?"

FOCUS

"Are You a Victim of Price Discrimination on Campus?"

Many examples of price discrimination can be found on college and university campuses. As mentioned in the text, most publicly funded schools charge different rates to in-state and out-of-state students. But there are a number of other methods of practicing price discrimination against students.

Consider the academic scholarship. Students with better academic credentials (high school GPA, SAT or ACT scores, and so on) generally find themselves with a larger number of schools to which they are accepted. The number of close substitutes they have for any particular institution is larger. This implies that their price elasticity of demand for a particular institution is relatively greater and that they will be charged a lower tuition than their less-adept fellow students. The college or university lowers price to them through the granting of a scholarship. Again, the institution of higher education is seen to be a practiced price discriminator.

Many university bookstores offer faculty members a small discount (usually 5 to 15 percent) on their purchases that is not given to students. This is

but another example of price discrimination. Resale of bookstore items from faculty to students is discouraged not only by college regulations, but also by the faculty member's opportunity cost of time. With such small discounts, most teachers find the profit from buying at a discount and reselling to students at a price below the student price not worth the time and effort. The two markets are separated at low cost in that faculty must usually present their ID cards to obtain the discount. In this market, faculty members are the relatively elastic demanders because of the number of alternative suppliers that are available to them. The students' relatively low elasticity is also probably due to the fact that many students live on campus, which makes substitutes for college-run bookstores more difficult to patronize. (Internet purchase of textbooks may disturb this relationship over time.) Whatever the reasons, price discrimination at the college bookstore implies larger bookstore revenues than if faculty and students both paid the same price for bookstore items.

Services of all kinds, in particular, are ripe areas for the practice of discrimination because services are ordinarily nontransferable from one consumer to another.[1] Whatever the source of discrimination, its desirability or lack thereof is closely related to the question of whether monopoly is good or bad for economic efficiency.

THE CASE AGAINST MONOPOLY

Monopoly is generally viewed as bad for the economy in comparison with the good expected from a competitive organization of markets. Critics base their indictment of monopoly on arguments that monopolies are lacking in both efficiency and equity, or fairness. After considering arguments against monopoly, we will examine the theory that monopolies provide certain social benefits that may offset their social costs.

The Welfare Loss Resulting from Monopoly Power

Contrived scarcity

A situation in which a monopoly produces an output below what a competitive industry would produce; the contrived scarcity results in price and profits above competitive levels.

The main efficiency argument against monopoly is that this market structure leads to **contrived scarcity**—that is, that a monopoly withholds output from the market to maximize its profits. The monopolist not only sets price where $MC = MR$, but where $P > MR$. At the profit-maximizing output for the monopolist, price therefore exceeds marginal cost. In the case of pure competition, price reflects the marginal benefit that consumers place on additional production, and marginal cost reflects the economic cost of the resources necessary for additional production. When price is greater than marginal cost, this is a signal to producers to increase output. The monopoly firm will not do so, because this approach is not consistent with maximizing its profits. Given market demand and the cost curves, the monopolist will produce a smaller quantity of output than would a competitive industry. So we say that the monopolist causes a contrived scarcity, a condition in which the monopoly's product is short in supply and high in price. For example, the gasoline crisis of the 1970s was a contrived scarcity put into effect by the OPEC cartel. The price of gasoline rose as the supply of oil was reduced.

A contrived scarcity is a social cost to the economy. Its nature and magnitude can be estimated with an economic model that contrasts the effects of monopoly and competition in a given market, as shown in Figure 9.7.

Figure 9.7 shows the industry demand and supply functions, D and S, for some commodity, say, cranberry juice. There are no economies of scale in this industry. The average total cost of producing cranberry juice is the same at all levels of output. This is a constant-cost industry with a flat long-run supply curve, along which $MC = ATC$.

Suppose that the industry is organized competitively, with many producers of cranberry juice. Long-run industry equilibrium is established at E, where industry demand and supply are equal. The juice output of the various firms is priced accord-

[1]Professional services such as those for physicians or lawyers are often used to illustrate the possibilities of discrimination between low and high income demanders. Organ transplants are an especially interesting and timely example: See Andy H. Barnett, T. Randolph Beard and David L. Kaserman, "The Medical Community's Opposition to Organ Markets: Ethics or Economics?" *The Review of Industrial Organization* (December 1993), pp. 669–678.

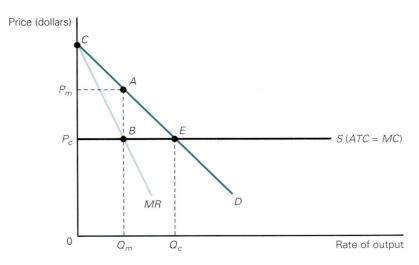

FIGURE 9.7

Welfare Loss Due to Monopoly Power

This graph illustrates the hypothetical case of converting a competitive industry into a monopoly. Consumer surplus at price P_c and output Q_c in a constant-cost industry is represented by CEP_c. When the industry becomes a monopoly, it cuts back output to Q_m, resulting in a decreased consumer surplus of CAP_m and monopoly profits of P_mABP_c. The welfare loss to the economy—that is, the amount of real income that does not reappear for anyone after the monopoly is formed—is represented by AEB. The area of monopoly profits can be considered a transfer from consumers to the monopolist.

ing to the marginal cost of producers along the industry supply curve and according to the wishes of the consumers along the demand curve. In other words, price is equal to the long-run marginal cost of production.

At the competitive price–output combination, P_c and Q_c, how much surplus do consumers receive? They are willing to pay the amounts given by the demand curve, but they pay only P_c. They thus receive a surplus of real income, in this case represented by the large area above the industry supply curve and below the industry demand curve, or CEP_c. This triangle represents the concept of consumer surplus: the amount that consumers would be willing to pay over what they actually pay for a commodity.

Now suppose that the cranberry juice industry is turned over to a single seller, a monopolist. As a result, the monopolist restricts juice output to Q_m (contrived scarcity) and raises price to P_m to maximize its monopoly profits. What has happened to the level of consumer surplus in this market? The consumer surplus before monopoly is given by CEP_c, but consumer surplus after monopoly is only CAP_m. The difference in these two areas is the trapezoid P_mAEP_c.

The area P_mAEP_c is made up of two components. First we consider the rectangle P_mABP_c, depicting monopoly profits, to represent a transfer from consumers to the monopolist. In other words, these dollars do not leave the economy: They are taken out of the pockets of consumers and put into the pocket of the monopolist. The triangle AEB is left over. Who gets the real income represented by this triangle? No one—it simply vanishes when the monopoly is formed. This triangle is therefore called the **welfare loss due to monopoly**, or the *deadweight loss*. It is a cost to the economy because it does not reappear as income to anyone.[2]

Production Costs of a Monopoly

Recall from our earlier discussion that the typical monopoly firm, after long-run adjustment, does not produce at the point of minimum long-run average total cost. In other words, the monopoly firm does not produce its output in the most efficient plant size in the long run. We learned in Chapter 8 that the competitive firm was compelled by competition to produce at the point of minimum long-run average total cost. By comparison, the monopoly produces its output inefficiently, resulting in another social cost of the monopoly relative to the competitive outcome.

Monopoly and the Distribution of Income

In addition to the potential efficiency cost arguments against monopoly—welfare loss and inefficient costs of production—there is an equity argument. The creation of a monopoly transfers wealth from consumers to the monopolist. In Figure 9.7, this transfer is represented by the area of monopoly profits, P_mABP_c. The average consumer gets poorer; the monopolist gets richer. Most people would regard this transfer to the monopolist as unfair.

In sum, pure monopoly compares unfavorably with pure or perfect competition. The pure monopolist ignores social costs by producing less output at a higher price and by producing that output inefficiently. Coupled with concerns about the fairness of monopoly profits, this is the case against monopoly.

THE CASE FOR MONOPOLY

We have seen that monopoly leads to economic inefficiency compared with a purely competitive organization of the economy. The monopolist essentially produces too little output at too high a price ($P > MC$). This type of inefficiency, called **static inefficiency**, can be seen as a social cost of monopoly given that other things are equal.

What if other things are not equal? Specifically, what if the monopoly produces more new ideas and products than the competitive firm? If this is the case, there may be an offsetting **dynamic efficiency** that makes monopoly a desirable form of market organization. One way to look at these counterforces is that the static inefficiency caused by monopoly pushes the economy inside its production possibilities frontier. This loss of production is the cost of monopoly power. But the dynamic efficiency of monopoly pushes the production possibilities curve out-

---

Welfare loss due to monopoly
The consumers' surplus lost by consumers and not gained by the monopolist that results from a monopoly producing a less-than-competitive amount of output and charging a greater-than-competitive price; also called deadweight cost.

Static inefficiency
A condition associated with the welfare loss due to the presence of a monopoly. The loss can be summarized as the production of too little output sold at too high a price.

Dynamic efficiency
A condition summarized in the idea that monopolies may, over time, be more innovative and efficient than competitive firms at developing new products and new production techniques.

---

[2]Economist Gordon Tullock has argued that the monopoly profits rectangle, P_mAPB_c, can also represent a social cost of monopoly power if these profits are wasted in lobbying to procure a monopoly right or privilege. See Gordon Tullock, "The Welfare Costs of Tariffs, Monopolies, and Theft," *Western Economic Journal* 5 (June 1967), pp. 224–232.

ward over time, potentially swamping the short-run costs of monopoly power. In other words, monopoly has costs and benefits for the economy, and the benefits (dynamic efficiency) may outweigh the costs (static inefficiency).

This view of the potential efficiency of large-scale, monopolistic enterprise was put forth by Joseph Schumpeter.[3] He stressed the advantages of the ability of large firms to finance large research laboratories and hire thousands of scientists. While these firms with well-known, productive research labs—such as Du Pont, AT&T, and IBM—are not typically pure monopolies, they usually are large firms with dominant positions within their industries.

To Schumpeter, the traditional theory that competition spurred innovation seemed wrong. Small competitive firms were at a disadvantage in the innovation process because they could not afford large-scale research. Large firms were the key to innovation and success in the industrial order.

In Schumpeter's theory, the innovative monopolist did not possess a perennial advantage in the marketplace. He believed that innovation would proceed apace, and no one large firm would have more than a transitory monopoly in the face of a constant supply of new ideas and innovations by other large firms. The monopoly that any one large firm achieved by being creative was short-lived.

Studies of the source of major inventions indicate that a surprisingly large number of innovations have come from the backyard shops of independent inventors. John Jewkes, David Sawers, and Richard Stillerman found, for example, that more than half of sixty-nine important inventions were produced by individual academics or by individuals unaffiliated with any research organization.[4] Among these inventions were air conditioning, the Polaroid Land camera, the helicopter, and xerography. Much invention is individually inspired and created in small-scale, personal labs and workshops. Industrial creativity thus seems to stem from something other than firm size alone. (For more on the returns to invention, see the Focus "Patents: The Inventor's Monopoly.")

Evidence suggests that Schumpeter's vision of the economy is not entirely accurate. But, then, neither is the vision that pure competition is best for the economy. Innovation springs from many sources, from the backyard or basement lab of the inventor to the lab of the large industrial company. Diversity produces innovation—better yet, *individuals* produce innovation, whether they work in their own workshops or a large firm. Perhaps the most typical scenario is that an individual or small firm comes up with a new idea, and a large firm provides the vehicle by which the idea is realized.

Finally, what kind of balance is struck between the costs and benefits of monopoly? It is hard to generalize on this issue. In filling out a report card on firms, the best approach is to be pragmatic. Does the firm possess monopoly power? If so, can we judge how large this power is and how much it costs the economy? Does monopoly power carry with it some redeeming merit such as increased innovation? These are not easy questions to answer or to weigh in the balance, but they are the types of issues that must be confronted if the costs and benefits of monopoly are to be understood and its model applied intelligently.

---

[3]Joseph A. Schumpeter, *Capitalism, Socialism, and Democracy* (New York: Harper, 1942).
[4]John Jewkes, David Sawers, and Richard Stillerman, *The Sources of Invention* (New York: St. Martin's, 1959).

FOCUS

Patents: The Inventor's Monopoly

A patent is an exclusive right given to an inventor for his or her invention. In other words, a patent is a monopoly right given to the inventor for the invention. In general, economists complain about the costs of monopoly because they believe that the same industry could be organized competitively. A new patent monopoly grant for 20 years presents a different problem. That is, the purpose of the patent system is to encourage invention. The issue is not monopoly versus competition but, more fundamentally, invention versus no (or little) invention. Is the world better off with the invention, even though it is monopolized for 20 years? In other words, what are the costs and benefits of a patent?

Consider the simple case, depicted in Figure 9.8, of a new consumer product with a positive demand, such as a camera utilizing a new exposure process. The costs of the patent monopoly are simply the deadweight costs of monopoly as discussed in this chapter. These are measured by the area

BCD in Figure 9.8. Area BCD is the lost consumers' surplus from the 20-year patent monopoly. This cost must be assessed carefully in the context of an invention, however.

Obviously, the incentive to the inventor to reveal his or her new product and to market it resides in the monopoly profits that he or she hopes to capture as a result. These are given by the area P_mBDP_c. These profits are a transfer from consumers to the inventor, and as such, they represent neither a cost nor a benefit of the patent system.

What are the benefits of the patent system? First, there is the increase in consumer well-being brought about immediately by a desirable invention. This is measured by the area ABP_m. This area of consumers' surplus would not have existed without the new product. In 20 years, the patent monopoly ends, and a second source of benefits arises: The price of cameras will fall to a competitive level, such as P_c, and consumers will reap the

FIGURE 9.8

A Camera Patent Monopoly

An inventor's patent confers a temporary monopoly on the holder. Price of the patented good is P_m, in contrast to the competitive price P_c. Consumers' surplus of BCD is the temporary loss due to the patent.

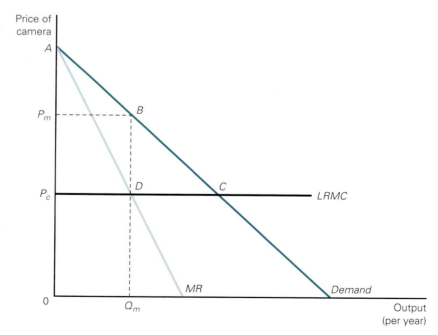

continued

continued

benefits of the camera at a lower price. Thus the patent system generates benefits in the amount ABP_m now and in the amount of an additional BCD in 20 years. Consumers also receive a transfer from the monopolist in 20 years in the amount of P_mBDP_c.

In sum, the theory of monopoly helps us to assess the costs and benefits of the patent system. The costs are BCD for 20 years. The benefits are ABP_m forever plus BCD forever after 20 years. P_mBDP_c is a trans-

fer to the inventor from consumers of his or her product, which he or she gives back to consumers after 20 years. In the end, the patent system creates goods and services and technologies that did not previously exist. It also underscores the importance of property rights to ideas as a source of economic growth and progress.[a]

---

[a]Readers interested in additional information on patents, trademarks and copyrights are directed to the U.S. Patent and Trademark Office web site at www.uspto.gov.

APPLICATION

Technology, Economics, and the Postal Monopoly

The postal monopoly has been criticized since it began operating under federal protection in 1775, but the criticism has intensified over the past two decades. The cost of mailing a one-ounce first-class letter has risen by 800 percent since 1958—twice as fast as the increase in the general price level (see Table 9.2). While the Constitution gives Congress the power to "establish post offices and post roads," it does not require postal service to be a monopoly or to be a government monopoly. Congress placed piecemeal restrictions on private carriage of mail throughout the nineteenth century. Since 1872, with the elimination of the Pony Express, only government employees can legally deliver a letter. The monopoly applies to first-class mail but not to second-class mail (newspapers and magazines), third-class mail (direct-mail advertising), or to parcels (fourth-class mail). The U.S. Post Office became the independent Postal Service in 1970 and retained the right to define a letter, which includes bills, receipts, and other business documents.

In this chapter's terms, the Postal Service is a nonprofit monopoly with the power to price-discriminate among customers. Since it is not permitted to retain profits, the Postal Service has little incentive to hold costs down or to improve the quality of service. Recall that price discrimination often accompanies monopoly

TABLE 9.2

Postal Rates, 1919–2000

Between 1958 and 1999, the cost of mailing a one-ounce first-class letter increased by 725 percent. Given technological changes, such as electronic banking and inexpensive facsimile transmitting (fax) machines, critics are questioning the necessity of a government monopoly on the delivery of first-class mail.

1919—2 cents	1981—18 cents
1958—4 cents	1981—20 cents
1963—5 cents	1985—22 cents
1968—6 cents	1988—25 cents
1971—8 cents	1991—29 cents
1975—10 cents	1995—32 cents
1975—13 cents	1999—33 cents
1978—15 cents	

and takes place when rates are not based on differences in costs of providing service. Equal rates are discriminatory when the costs of provision differ. This is the kind of price discrimination practiced when the Postal Service charges the same price to deliver a first-class letter from New York to Hawaii as it does to deliver the same letter across town, because costs are lower in the latter case. In effect, the price of a first-class stamp enables the Postal Service to internally subsidize distant customers and customers in small towns and isolated locales at the expense of urban, local, and business consumers.

The Postal Service also engages in price discrimination in pricing first-class mail compared with other classes. The Postal Service exploits its monopoly on first-class mail by pricing well above its marginal and average costs. It is then able to price lower classes of mail below cost by using profits from first-class mail to cover these losses. In this way it succeeds in extending its first-class monopoly to other classes of mail.

Criticism of the Postal Service is not limited to its rate structure. Despite rapid increases in postal rates since 1970, service has continued to deteriorate. Twice-a-day delivery has been halted, and most door-to-door delivery for businesses and multifamily dwellings has been abandoned. Many post offices have been closed, and many remaining offices no longer provide Saturday window service. Despite the adoption of ZIP codes, mail delivery is slower than it has been in years.

According to critics, privatization or repeal of the laws giving the Postal Service a monopoly is the only way to obtain rational, cost-based, and efficient service. Technological change poses threats to any monopoly, and the Postal Service is no exception. In 1974, the Postal Service's failure to develop an innovative way to transport parcels created the United Parcel Service (UPS). By introducing mechanization and containerization, UPS reduced both breakage and costs. Despite the Postal Service's attempts to learn from UPS's success, UPS remains a viable competitor in the area of parcel service. Other private commercial carriers developed in the 1960s and 1970s—these specializing in the rapid and reliable carriage of commercial documents. Despite past threats of legal action by the Postal Service, firms such as Federal Express and Emery Air Freight now openly and freely compete for overnight service. The Postal Service's "Express Mail" overnight service, despite a lower and subsidized price, has not been successful in eliminating private services. Lower-quality service—specifically, fewer cities covered and fewer services offered—is one reason for the lack of success.

Rapidly developing electronic and computer technology promises to offer serious competition for both the Postal Service and private overnight services. Banks, increasingly, are offering electronic bill-paying services. Offered at a price below that for stamps, envelopes, and checks, electronic bill-paying services provide stiff competition, especially for first-class mail. Yet more troubling to the Postal Service and overnight carriers is the remarkable increase in the use of facsimile transmitting (fax) machines and computer e-mail. Virtually unheard of when they sold for almost $4500 in the early 1980s, fax machines now cost, on average, less than $300 and are considered standard office technology, as are computers and e-mail.

Critics of the postal monopoly estimate that open competition for postal customers in all classes of mail could save $10 billion annually. While it is difficult to predict the exact form of the market with no postal monopoly, many economists, politicians, and observers argue that competition should be given a try.

Internet e-mail services, along with falling computer prices, are providing viable competition for traditional postal services.

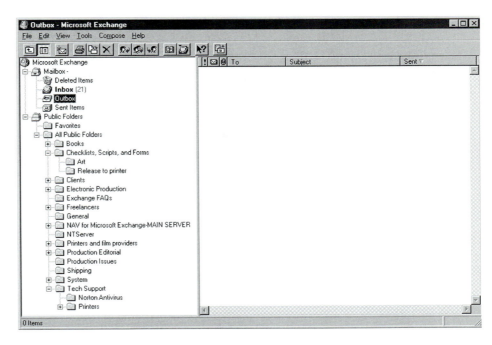

QUESTIONS

In what way does the Postal Service currently engage in price discrimination? How does the absence of competition facilitate slow mail delivery and high postal rates?

Sources: For more details, see James C. Miller III, "End the Postal Monopoly," *Cato Journal* (Spring/Summer 1985), pp. 149–155; James Bovard, "The Slow Death of the U.S. Postal Service," *Policy Analysis*, Cato Institute (April 3, 1988); and "Banks Hope to Stamp Out Paying by Check," *USA Today* (April 27, 1990).

SUMMARY

1. A pure monopoly is a single seller of a product for which there are no close substitutes in a market characterized by high barriers to new entry.

2. The monopoly firm faces the industry demand curve. When it lowers price, it must accept a lower price for all units previously sold for a higher price. The total revenue at the lower price minus the total revenue at the higher price is equal to the marginal revenue of the monopoly firm. For the monopoly, marginal revenue is less than price.

3. The monopoly selects an output to produce by setting marginal cost equal to marginal revenue. Since marginal revenue is less than price, the monopoly firm sets prices along its demand curve where price is greater than marginal cost.

4. Not all monopolies make profits. In the short run it is possible for the monopoly to incur a loss. If the loss persists in the long run, the monopoly will go out of business.

5. In the long run the monopoly firm can adjust its plant size. Normally, however, the monopoly does not operate at the point of minimum long-run average total cost.

6. Price discrimination requires that a seller be a monopoly firm, be able to separate buyers on the basis of their elasticities of demand, and be able to prevent buyers in the low-price market from reselling to buyers in the high-price market.

7. Where buyers can be separated into two classes, the monopoly firm will set marginal cost, which is

the same in both markets, equal to marginal revenue in each market. This is the definition of price discrimination—price differences that do not reflect cost differences.

8. There are two potential efficiency costs of monopoly: the welfare loss due to monopoly power—the deadweight cost—which is the lost consumer surplus caused by monopoly, and the degree to which the monopoly firm has higher costs of production than the competitive firm.

9. Monopoly affects the distribution of income. Monopoly transfers wealth from consumers to the monopolist.

10. A potential advantage of monopoly is that large firms may be more effective developers of new products. The monopoly or large firm might thus possess a dynamic advantage over a small, competitive firm.

KEY WORDS

price searcher
pure monopoly
legal barriers to entry
public franchise
government license

patent
natural monopoly
marginal revenue
profit-maximizing price
price discrimination

contrived scarcity
welfare loss due to monopoly
static inefficiency
dynamic efficiency

QUESTIONS FOR REVIEW AND DISCUSSION

1. What is a barrier to entry? Why is it important in the definition of monopoly?

2. Depict the short-run equilibrium of a pure monopolist. Can the monopoly firm make a loss? If so, diagram what the loss situation for the monopoly might look like.

3. What conditions need to be met before a monopolist can price-discriminate?

4. What are the efficiency costs of monopoly? What is a potential benefit of a monopoly firm?

5. Insurance companies offer lower rates for life insurance to individuals who do not smoke and who jog. Is this an example of price discrimination? Why or why not?

6. If entry is not possible with pure monopoly, how can the monopoly sell its monopoly right?

7. Monopolies and large firms are sometimes blamed for rising prices. Does the theory of monopoly presented in this chapter imply that prices under monopoly will rise quickly or will be high? Explain.

8. Would a license to operate a taxicab in your hometown constitute a monopoly restriction? Why or why not?

9. Suppose that you have invented a new and far more efficient means of converting salt water to drinkable water and that you have just received a patent on the process. As a student of economics, how would you justify such a restriction?

PROBLEMS

1. Use the figure to answer the following questions.

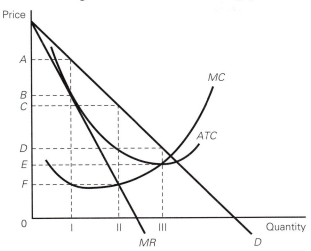

a. At what price and quantity will the monopolist operate?
b. Do monopolists produce more or less than competitive firms?
c. If the demand curve crosses the horizontal-axis when $Q = 500$, what does Q equal when the marginal revenue curve crosses the horizontal axis?

2. Owners of major league baseball teams are effectively monopolists in the sale of tickets in their franchise area (for example, Chicago or New York City). However, many of them price tickets such that there is excess capacity (unsold seats) for most games. Is it wise for them to pursue such a pricing policy? Use a figure to explain your answer.

WORKING WITH THE WEB

1. Patents are a source of monopoly power for many corporations in the United States. Because the holder of a patent holds a monopoly right for twenty years, patents are a great motivator for firms to invest in research and development. To get an idea of the impact of patents in U.S. business, go to http://www.uspto.gov/web/offices/ac/ido/oeip/taf/reports.htm#asgstc and scroll down to the section "By Patenting Organization," where single-year reports of the "Top 10 or 11 Patenting Organizations" are available for viewing. First, select 1998 and view the top 10 organizations in 1998 in terms of the number of patents awarded to the organization. The previous year is listed on the right-hand side and the current year on the left-hand side.
   a. Which organizations are newcomers to the top 10 list in 1998?
   b. Which public organization fell off the list in 1998, and how long had it been on the list?
   c. As of 1998, how long has IBM maintained the number one position in patents among the top 10 organizations?
   d. When IBM started its run in the top position, what organization did it displace from the number one spot? (You will have to look at other years to determine the answer to this question.)

2. This chapter introduces you to the economics of price discrimination. From the examples discussed in the text, you are probably aware of several instances of price discrimination, some of which might affect you. To examine price discrimination on campus, first go to http://www.bowdoin.edu/cwis/admissions/tuition.html and examine the tuition and fees charged per year at Bowdoin College. Next, take a look at Bowdoin's policy on financial aid at http://www.bowdoin.edu/cwis/admissions/finaid.html.
   a. Does Bowdoin engage in price discrimination between in-state and out-of-state students? Why or why not?
   b. If Bowdoin does not discriminate by residency, how might it practice price discrimination among its student body via the awarding of financial aid?
   c. How are the demanders of financial aid separated, and how do you think arbitrage is prevented?

Monopolistic Competition and Advertising

U ntil the 1930s, microeconomic theory analyzed only two basic market structures: pure competition and pure monopoly. These structures are, of course, opposite extremes. With pure competition, prices tend to equal costs in the long run and consumers' economic welfare is theoretically maximized, whereas the pure monopolist may restrict output, raise prices, and capture economic profits. In the 1930s, two economists, E. H. Chamberlin of Harvard University and Joan Robinson of Cambridge University, wrote books developing models of market structures that did not fit the mold of either pure competition or pure monopoly. Both Robinson and Chamberlin emphasized that the real world was characterized by market structures that did not easily fit into existing economic theory.

All models of firms and markets other than the extremes of pure competition and pure monopoly are called theories of **imperfect competition**. The word *imperfect* means that not all the conditions for pure competition are met.

Some imperfectly competitive markets contain large numbers of sellers (as in pure competition) selling slightly different products (unlike pure competition). These are monopolistically competitive markets.

Other structures are composed of small numbers of competing sellers who recognize that their actions affect one another's sales, prices, and profits. Under these circumstances, firms may engage—or try to engage—in various forms of combination or collusion. Such associations are called oligopoly or cartel market structures. They are closer in economic results to pure monopoly than to pure competition. The spectrum of market structures, therefore, runs from pure competition to monopolistic competition to oligopoly and cartels to pure monopoly.

Imperfect competition
Market models, such as oligopoly, cartels, monopoly, and monopolistic competition, in which individual sellers' actions influence price.

Because real-world markets seldom fit into the neat categories of competition or monopoly, it is important to develop more realistic models. The economist, moreover, must assess the effects of these real-world market structures on consumers' and producers' welfare and on economic efficiency in general. We begin with monopolistic competition, the economic model closest to pure competition. After reading Chapter 10 you should understand

- the characteristics of monopolistic competition as a model of how firms behave when many sellers are selling different products or services.
- advertising's role in differentiating products.
- how economically efficient monopolistically competitive markets are when compared with pure competition and pure monopoly.
- how monopolistic competition can be useful as a model of a firm's behavior.

MONOPOLISTIC COMPETITION

In his search for more realistic models of firms and markets, E. H. Chamberlin developed a model close but not equivalent to pure competition. Since the model contained some monopolistic elements, Chamberlin labeled this theory "monopolistic competition."

Characteristics of Monopolistic Competition

Monopolistic competition
A market model with freedom of entry and exit and firms producing similar but differentiated products.

Monopolistic competition is a market structure in which a large number of sellers sell similar but slightly different products and in which no barriers to entry or exit exist. Advertising is a principal tool for differentiating products within monopolistic competition.

Large Number Of Sellers   Monopolistic competition, like pure competition, is characterized by a large number of competing sellers. The effect of large numbers is the same in both cases: Collusion to fix prices or other kinds of cooperation is costly—so costly that it ordinarily does not occur. The presence of many sellers is a competitive element in monopolistic competition. Unlike pure competitors, however, monopolistic competitors are not always price takers because of another characteristic—product differentiation.

Differentiated product
A product with features that make it distinct, in consumers' eyes, from close substitutes.

Nonprice competition
Any means other than pricing decisions that firms use to sell output.

Product Differentiation   Competitive sellers sell a homogeneous or identical product, such as corn. Monopolistic competitors sell products that are highly similar but not identical. Products may be distinguished by brand names, location, services, even differences merely perceived by the consumer. Because the monopolistic competitor is selling a slightly **differentiated product**, the firm will have a degree of control over price, unlike the competitive firm. Product differentiation is an example of **nonprice competition**, a term commonly used to refer to any action other than price cuts taken by a competitor to increase demand for its product.

There are many varieties of nonprice competition. One is differences created in the products themselves. Consumers shopping for personal computers can choose among many firms' products, each differing slightly in hardware, software, styling, sturdiness, and user-friendly or state-of-the-art appeal. Sometimes, distinctions between brands are more illusory than real. Although aspirin is essentially a homogeneous product, monopolistically competitive firms produce it under many different brand names—Bayer, Excedrin, Bufferin, and so on—often at very different prices. The reason for the different prices for aspirin is that each brand is differentiated in consumers' minds, often through advertising or some other form of sales effort. Consumers who are convinced that brands actually differ will have some allegiance to a particular brand. This brand allegiance permits the seller to set price, within limits.

Location may also differentiate a seller's products. There may be ten Exxon gas stations within a city, alike in every respect, including the gasoline they sell. The gas stations each occupy a different location, however, and thus are free to set different prices. The Exxon station near the interstate might charge a higher price than the station downtown because travelers in a hurry are willing to pay more.

Service is another form of nonprice competition. Physically identical products may be offered for sale in supermarkets at identical money prices. However, one store may be untidy, another may employ rude cashiers, and still another may suffer chronically slow-moving checkout lines. Markets with well-swept aisles, neat shelves, automated checkout, and friendly clerks will have differentiated their products by the services they offer.

Subtle product differentiation, whether by packaging, service, location, or any other variable, is a common fact of life, but the degree of substitutability among such products is high. While demand is highly elastic under monopolistic competition, it is not infinitely elastic, as in perfect competition. A sudden tenfold increase in the price of one brand of aspirin would send buyers scurrying for substitutes. The monopolistically competitive firm, in other words, like the firm in pure competition, is primarily a price taker. It has a small and limited degree of control over price, however, stemming from its ability to differentiate its individual product from those of its many competitors. This limited control over price is the monopoly element in these markets.

No Barriers To Entry   Just as with competitive markets, entry into and exit from the monopolistically competitive market is open. Although monopolistic competition shares the free-entry conditions of perfectly competitive markets, entry is not costless in either market structure. Free entry means that there is no government regulation over entry and that essential raw materials are not controlled by one or a few firms. There are resource costs and commitments in opening any business: hiring labor, investing capital in fixed items such as buildings, training or hiring managers, and so forth.

In addition to the start-up costs of entering any new business, entry into monopolistically competitive markets entails the cost of introducing a new product. New product development and market entry through advertising and other sales efforts constitute a cost that the competitive firm does not face. A farmer's entry into the winter wheat market, for example, will not involve a sales or advertising campaign, whereas entry into the deodorant or restaurant market will. Product differentiation is simply part of the cost of entry under monopolistic competition. Entry is nonetheless assumed to be free, and in this characteristic, monopolistic competition is very much like perfect competition. Firms in this industry should expect to earn a normal rate of return in the long run.

Advertising and Monopolistic Competition

The keystone of monopolistic competition is product differentiation and advertising. Advertising, in fact, helps create product differentiation, giving individual firms some control over the product price. How does advertising affect the demand for products, and what is the economic assessment of such activity?

The Importance Of Advertising   With the general characteristics of the monopolistically competitive structure in mind, we examine a typical firm's demand curve and assess the impact of **advertising** on it. The existence of nonprice competition coupled with a high degree of substitutability means that the firm's demand curve, while highly elastic, is downward sloping. Such a demand curve is drawn in Figure 10.1 for a hypothetical antacid product, Relief. The demand curve for Relief approximates that of a competitive firm, but it is downward sloping because Relief is not the same product as competitors Tums, Rolaids, Mylanta, and Maalox.

Advertising

Any communication or information that firms offer consumers to increase demand for a product.

As with the pure monopoly firm, the monopolistically competitive firm's marginal revenue curve lies below its demand curve, and for the same reason: Additional units can be sold only at a lower price. The main difference between a monopoly firm and a monopolistic competitor is that the monopoly firm sells a unique product—one with no close substitutes—while substitutes abound for the monopolistic competitor's product.

How elastic or inelastic will the demand curve be for Relief? The answer will depend on the size and intensity of consumer preferences for Relief, given the range and price of substitutes. Naturally, the firm will be interested in increasing the size of its market and in intensifying consumers' preferences for its product. The firm accomplishes these goals through product advertising. Advertising is essential to the introduction of new products in monopolistic competition and to the manipulation or management of demand for existing products.

Advertising is a variable under the monopolistically competitive firm's control, within the limits imposed by its advertising budget. The firm in monopolistic competition will seek, along with all firms who advertise, to equate the addition to revenue from the final dollar spent on advertising to the marginal addition to cost from the advertising. Firms seeking to enter markets will often spend large amounts of money to introduce their products. But whether the firm is an established competitor or a new entrant, the purpose of advertising is the same: to increase demand and lower the elasticity of demand for the firm's product.

In Figure 10.2, demand curve $d_0 d_0$ depicts a monopolistically competitive firm's demand curve. The hoped-for effect of increased advertising is a shift rightward in the position of the demand schedule $d_1 d_1$ and a reduction in the elasticity of the

FIGURE 10.1

Demand Curve Facing Monopolistically Competitive Firm

The demand curve for the monopolistic competitor slopes downward because the firm sells a product differentiated from its competitors. The marginal revenue curve lies below the demand curve because additional units can be sold only at a lower price.

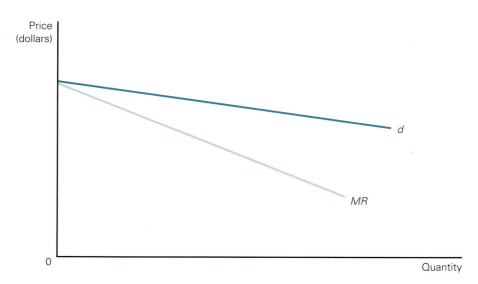

FIGURE 10.2

The Effects of Advertising on the Firm's Demand Curve

The firm advertising its product hopes to shift its demand curve to the right and to reduce its elasticity at a given price. In doing so, the firm tries to intensify demand for the product by distinguishing it in the minds of buyers.

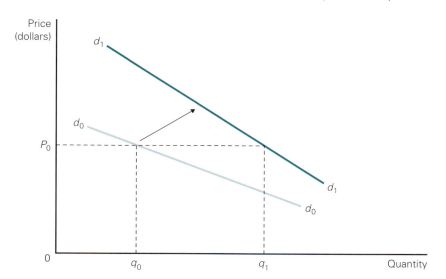

curve at a given price. Thus advertising is intended not only to increase demand but to intensify demand by differentiating the good or service in consumers' minds so that the firm can raise the product's price. If the advertisements for Relief are able to convince consumers that the product is "easier to swallow," "has no unwanted side effects," and the like, demand becomes more inelastic (less substitutable), and consumers are willing to pay more for it.

The Pros And Cons Of Advertising   Few subjects in economics have been debated as vigorously as advertising. Critics argue that ads are tasteless and wasteful assaults on consumers' senses. Since the products of monopolistically competitive firms are close substitutes, actual differences between the products of competing producers, if any, may be difficult to discern. Advertising creates perceived differences among similar goods and allocates demand among firms that produce products that are

Advertising takes on different forms in different media: it is often a blend of persuasion and information.

fundamentally alike. Some economists, then, view advertising as a squandering of society's resources on a costly exercise by which rival firms divide total sales.

Another criticism of advertising is that advertising expenditures raise both the costs of producing goods and services and the prices consumers pay. The resources used in advertising have opportunity costs, which means that the firm that advertises will bear higher costs and charge higher prices than the firm that does not advertise. And, of course, it should be kept in mind that there are various types of advertising. Some ads are designed to be persuasive, while others are designed to be informative. Generally, persuasive advertising has been the target of the critics of advertising.

Defenders of advertising deny that advertising is wasteful. They argue that advertising provides consumers with valuable information concerning the existence, characteristics, and location of goods and services. Such information reduces consumers' search costs and thereby reduces the full price that consumers pay. (See the Focus "Let Your Fingers Do the Walking: Information in Markets.")

Defenders of advertising also deny that advertising systematically leads to higher prices. While advertising is costly, it has two price-reducing effects. Since advertising can increase sales, advertising enables some firms to take advantage of economies of scale and produce output at a lower average total cost. Advertising also provides firms with a means of entry into markets and product lines. Without the ability to advertise, the process whereby new firms enter a market and compete away profits is short-circuited. The Focus "Advertising, Interest Groups, and the Price of Eyeglasses" examines the impact of advertising on prices in a specific market.

FOCUS

Let Your Fingers Do the Walking: Information in Markets

Entrepreneurs and sellers do not provide information willy-nilly. Market activity is rational, and sellers do not go to the expense of advertising their wares at random. Advertising, after all, is a key form of information provision. We would expect that advertising for high-value, infrequently purchased goods (for example, wedding dresses, travel agencies, carpet cleaning) would contain a higher proportion of information about quality than would advertising for low-value, frequently purchased goods (chewing gum, restaurants, photo finishing). The loss to us of making a mistake at a fast food restaurant is, after all, much lower than that resulting from the purchase of poor quality furniture. We will, therefore, demand more information about the latter kind of good.

Is this logic borne out in a traditional advertising outlet like the Yellow Pages? Two studies tested the proposition that the supply of product quality signals in advertisement increases with a rise in the expected marginal return to customers utilizing the Yellow Pages.[a] Sellers offering goods that were infrequently purchased (and/or of high value) placed ads that were far more informative (statistically) concerning quality (e.g., mention of certification or licensing) than were the ads placed by sellers of others kinds of goods. These studies found, further, that the proportions of informative ads rose in highly mobile cities (e.g., college or tourist towns) relative to cities with more sedentary populations. In short, advertising is both demanded and supplied as information connected to the purchase of goods and services of all types.

[a]See David N. Laband, "Advertising as Information: An Empirical Note," *Review of Economics and Statistics* 68 (1986), pp. 517–21; and Robert B. Ekelund, Jr., Frank G. Mixon, Jr., and Rand W. Ressler, "Advertising and Information: An Empirical Study of Search, Experience and Credence Goods," *Journal of Economic Studies* 22 (1995), pp. 33–43.

FOCUS

Advertising, Interest Groups, and the Price of Eyeglasses

The issue of advertising's effect on prices is an empirical (or statistical) issue. Economic theory suggests that two different effects on prices can exist. Since advertising requires scarce resources, it adds to the cost of producing output. In this sense, advertising would tend to cause prices to be higher than otherwise. But advertising also can be viewed as a tool of competition and as one vehicle businesses use to enter markets and product lines. From this perspective, advertising would exert price-lowering effects. Whether advertising raises or lowers price cannot be resolved through economic theory alone. The answer must be found by looking at actual markets and data.

In trying to gauge the effect of advertising on prices, economist Lee Benham considered the effect that a prohibition, or ban, on advertising has on prices. In the 1960s (and today still) a number of states had severe legal restrictions and outright prohibitions on the advertising of eyeglasses and eye examinations by physicians and optometrists. Other states had few or no restrictions on such advertising. Benham argued that the different states provided a good laboratory for the economic study of the relationship between advertising and prices. After adjusting for such factors as family income, sex, and customer age, any difference in prices paid in the two different types of states could be reasonably attributed to advertising (or the lack of it).

Some of Benham's findings are presented in Table 10.1. (Benham used prices during 1963. We have converted his results to 1998 dollars for easy comparison.) Table 10.1 contains average price differences for both glasses and glasses plus an eye exam between states with wide-ranging advertising restrictions and states with essentially no advertising prohibitions. The results suggest that the price-lowering effects of advertising dominate in the eyewear market.

Although Benham's study made no attempt to adjust for quality, it suggests empirical support for the proposition that advertising is a part of the competitive process. The prevention of advertising appears to have made prices higher than they would have been had advertising been allowed in the market.

State advertising restrictions are of course the product of interest group politics. Where groups (such as optometrists or physicians) are able to pass laws restricting advertising, returns as well as prices may be assumed to be higher than if advertising is not restricted. Rationales—such as ethics or consumer protection—are often used in order to quell opposition to price-increasing restrictions. But whatever the reason, such restrictions are price increasing and welfare diminishing in effect.

Source: Lee Benham, "The Effect of Advertising on the Price of Eyeglasses," *Journal of Law and Economics* 15 (October 1972), pp. 337–352.

TABLE 10.1

Advertising Restrictions and the Price of Eyeglasses

Average prices in states with severe advertising restrictions to prices in states with few, if any, legal advertising restraints. These prices, originally measured in 1963, have been converted to their 1998 equivalents.

	States With Restrictions	States Without Restrictions	Average Price Difference	Average Percentage Difference
Eyeglasses	$177.53	141.52	36.01	20%
Eyeglasses plus exam	$220.08	199.34	20.73	10%

Source: Lee Benham, "The Effect of Advertising on the Price of Eyeglasses," *Journal of Law and Economics* 15 (October 1972), p. 342, updated by authors.

Short-Run and Long-Run Equilibrium Under Monopolistic Competition

Now that we have defined the overall conditions for monopolistic competition, we can discuss how firms set prices. The firm in monopolistic competition has some control over price, but its control differs in the short and the long run.

Short-Run Equilibrium Monopolistically competitive firms, like firms in all other market structures, always equate marginal cost to marginal revenue to maximize profits. In the short run, the firm may enjoy economic profits or endure losses.

Figure 10.3 gives a firm's short-run cost curves, demand curve, and marginal revenue curve. MC intersects, or is equal to, MR at quantity q_0. The firm produces that quantity and sets price P_0 for q_0 units of output. At this price and quantity, the firm will earn economic profits. These profits are calculated by multiplying price times quantity sold ($P_0 \times q_0$) to get the firm's total receipts, and then subtracting the total cost of q_0 units, $ATC_0 \times q_0$. Profits to the firm are shown in the shaded area of the figure. Although the firm's demand curve is highly elastic (due to the large number of substitutes), it is still negatively sloped because, under monopolistic competition, products are differentiated through advertising and other forms of nonprice competition.[1] So far, this analysis is identical to that for the simple monopolist in Chapter 9.

The monopolistic competitor does have one advantage over the pure competitor in the short run: the ability to manipulate demand through advertising and intensified product differentiation. Optimum advertising outlay for the firm occurs when one dollar of additional selling costs adds exactly one dollar to the firm's receipts. In this sense, the cost of advertising is treated like the cost of any other input, such as capital or labor.

Long-Run Equilibrium: The Tangency Solution Long-run equilibrium for the firm in monopolistically competitive markets may take a number of forms. One of

---

[1]Like firms in all other markets structures, monopolistically competitive firms do not always make a profit.

FIGURE 10.3

Short-Run Profits for the Monopolistically Competitive Firm

The firm earns short-run profits. It sets price P_0 for q_0 units of output. Its profits are the difference between its revenue ($P_0 \times q_0$) and its costs ($ATC_0 \times q_0$).

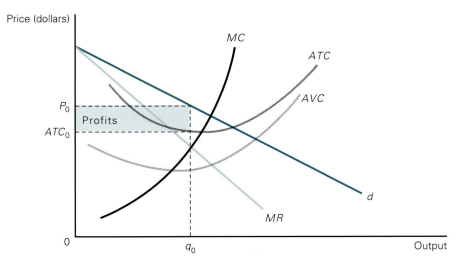

Tangency Solution
A long-run equilibrium situation in which the firm's downward-sloping demand curve is tangent to its *LRATC* curve; zero economic profits are earned.

them, described by E. H. Chamberlin, is the **tangency solution**, wherein the firm ends up making zero economic profits; that is, it simply breaks even.

Consider the situation of the firm in Figure 10.3. In short-run equilibrium, the firm is making economic profits. Just as in the case of pure competition, in the long-run entry and exit and other adjustments take place in the monopolistically competitive industry. In Figure 10.3 the economic profits of the monopolistic competitor send a signal that excess returns are present in this "industry." Hence, entrepreneurs will seek to enter the industry with similar but slightly differentiated products. As these entrepreneurs take away sales from the firm in Figure 10.3, its demand curve will shift to the left, reflecting the increased number of firms selling a similar product.

Figure 10.4 shows where the process comes to rest or equilibrium. Finally, demand curve *d* becomes tangent to the long-run average total cost function *LRATC* (thus the term *tangency solution* to describe this case). At point *E* in Figure 10.4, all firms will produce q_2 units of output and charge price P_1 per unit. Quantities above this amount and prices below P_1 would force firms out of business. Quantities less than q_0 and prices higher than P_1 would provoke the entry of new rivals. Under these circumstances, a stable equilibrium characterized by zero economic profits for all firms is generated.

The model described in Figure 10.4 reflects but one set of behavioral assumptions among many possibilities. Its value is considerable, however, because it describes a tendency to zero economic profits. Additionally, the tangency model of monopolistic competition provides a convenient benchmark for a comparison of the attributes and economic effects of pure competition and those of monopolistic competition.

Does Monopolistic Competition Waste Resources?

A charge commonly leveled at monopolistic competition—unrelated to the alleged wastes of advertising—is that the tangency solution requires (1) underallocation of resources in production or (2) generation of excess capacity and prices higher than minimum long-run unit costs of production. This portrayal of monopolistic competition is possible when it is compared with the long-run competitive model.

FIGURE 10.4

The Tangency Solution
When all firms lower price from P_0 to P_1, the monopolistically competitive firm's demand curve shifts leftward. In final equilibrium *E*, the point of tangency with the *LRATC* curve, all firms break even.

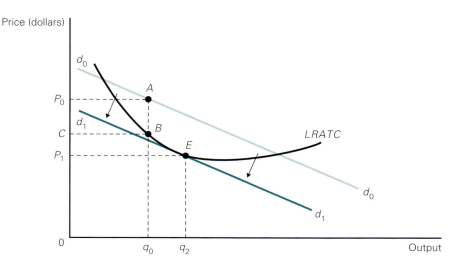

Monopolistic Competition Versus Pure Competition   Long-run equilibrium in the perfectly competitive model, discussed in Chapter 8, results in the following three conditions:

1. Price = long-run marginal costs;
2. Price = minimum long-run average total costs; and
3. Total revenue = total costs.

The first condition means that the consumer's marginal sacrifice (price) just equals the marginal opportunity cost of producing the last unit of a product or service consumed. The second condition means that consumers are getting the product at the lowest price at which the product can be produced. The third conclusion means that no competitive firm earns more than a normal profit in the long run. Firms are price takers under competition. Freedom of entry guarantees normal profits in the long run.

Consider, with the aid of Figure 10.5, how monopolistic competition compares to pure competition in these respects. Figure 10.5a shows the demand curve $P_c d_c$ and the short-run and long-run average cost curves for the typical firm in pure competition. Both long-run and short-run costs are tangent to the perfectly elastic demand curve for the firms in competition. Quantity q_c is produced at price P_c, which equals long-run (and short-run) marginal cost. Figure 10.5b shows the downward-sloping demand curve d_m of a monopolistically competitive firm in a tangency solution with the firm's long-run average cost curve. Given that the firms'

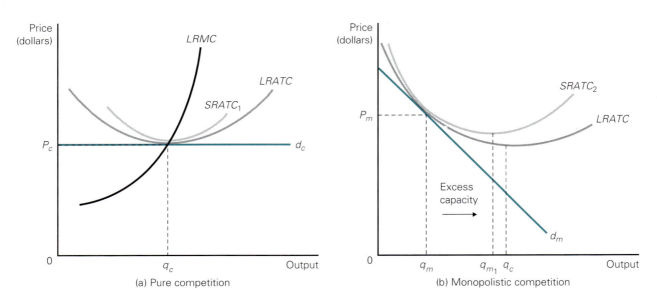

(a) Pure competition   (b) Monopolistic competition

FIGURE 10.5

A Comparison of Pure Competition and Monopolistic Competition

In a technical sense, the monopolistically competitive firm (b) charges a higher price, P_m, than the purely competitive firm (a), P_c. The monopolistically competitive firm sets output at q_m to maximize profits, but the most efficient use of its plant would be an output of q_{m1}. The firm therefore produces with excess capacity, or underutilization of its scale of plant.

cost curves are identical under both market structures, how do they compare in terms of economic efficiency?

As Figure 10.5 shows, monopolistic competition has the following features:

1. Price > long-run marginal costs;
2. Price > minimum long-run average costs; and
3. Total revenue = total costs.

We can put the first point slightly differently: The additional sacrifice (price) that consumers are willing to make for an additional unit of the good is greater than the marginal opportunity cost of producing that additional unit. So resources are underallocated in the production of goods by monopolistically competitive firms, just as they usually are by pure monopolies.

Notice also that consumers pay more for goods produced under conditions of monopolistic competition than they do when goods are supplied by perfect competitors. The fact that P_m in Figure 10.5b is greater than P_c in Figure 10.5a means that price is higher and output is lower under monopolistic competition than under pure competition. Consumers are not paying the lowest possible unit cost. However, like perfect competitors, monopolistic competitors do not earn economic profits because a tangency solution means that total revenues equal total costs to the firm (or, alternatively, that the firm's average cost equals its average revenue).

Excess capacity

A situation in which industry output is not produced at minimum average total cost. The output actually produced is less than the output that would minimize average total cost.

Critics of monopolistic competition raise still another issue: **Excess capacity** is generated under the monopolistically competitive market structure. This criticism ordinarily holds for any less-than-perfectly competitive market. To understand what excess capacity means, consider Figure 10.5 again. The $LRATC$ function is called an envelope curve because it is composed of a series of tangencies of points on the short-run average total cost curves (see Figure 7.5 on p. 186). The short-run curves $SRATC_1$ and $SRATC_2$ drawn in Figure 10.5 are two such curves. To utilize fully any scale of plant or to produce at an optimum rate of output in the short run, the existing scale of plant or existing resources invested must be used at the lowest average cost of production. For the monopolistically competitive firm depicted in Figure 10.5b, the output corresponding to that lowest short-run average total cost of production is q_{m_1}, not q_m, the profit-maximizing quantity the firm has chosen. From society's point of view, the firm producing at q_m is wasting, or underutilizing, resources. Excess capacity is the unused capacity of the scale of plant that the firm has built. From the firm's perspective, however, the scale of plant represented by $SRATC_2$ is perfect, or optimal, in that it produces the quantity q_m more cheaply than any other scale of plant could. Thus, critics argue that monopolistic competition creates excess capacity as well as the long-run resource inefficiencies outlined above.

A Defense Of Monopolistic Competition   Is monopolistic competition as inefficient as the critics say? In assessing this issue we must be careful to distinguish between pure **economic efficiency** and **economic welfare**. Economic efficiency means that resources are properly allocated (at minimum cost for a given output) from the firm's perspective. Pure economic welfare is the value that society places on goods and services consumed. Chamberlin argued that the monopolistically competitive market structure is not wasteful in either sense because product differentiation creates variety and extends the array of consumers' choices.

If price is established close to but not at minimum long-run average total cost, some inefficiency might exist with monopolistic competition, but consider what

Economic efficiency

The allocation of resources that allows maximum benefit to be achieved at minimum cost.

Economic welfare

The value society places on goods and services consumed.

consumers get in return: varied products and a vastly expanded number of products and services from which to choose. If this variety is socially valued, advertising and product differentiation are not necessarily wasteful. Such differentiation, summed across all consumers, means that monopolistic competition may increase social welfare. A society that produces only white shirts may be efficient in a technical sense, but the repeated purchase of other colors of shirts at higher prices means that consumers are willing to pay for differentiation.

Depending on a given consumer's preferences, excess capacity may be either a cost or a benefit. Resource costs other than money are involved in the purchase of goods. Time, for example, is an important cost for some consumers. Since excess capacity reduces the time cost of making purchases, it reduces consumption costs. For consumers who place a high value on time, excess capacity is likely to be beneficial. For example, in cities where cab fares are relatively high, cabs typically line up in front of hotels and airports. Business executives who place a high value on their time are willing to pay a high dollar price rather than wait for a less expensive means of transportation. For them, excess capacity is clearly beneficial. In contrast, consumers who place a low value on their time will choose to pay lower money prices but higher time prices by taking public transportation or the hotel van.

How Useful Is the Theory of Monopolistic Competition?

When models of monopolistic competition and pure competition are subjected to real-world observation, is there a dime's worth of difference between them? How useful, in other words, is the model of monopolistic competition?

If the demand curve is very elastic when products are differentiated, the model of monopolistic competition is a close approximation of pure competition. Thus, a study of markets with differentiated products and rapid and free entry of substitutes is a study of what is usually called competition. Indeed, it is the rapid entry of new products and new brands that has often been the target of criticisms of competitive markets (see the Application "What's in a Brand Name? The Consumer Chooses"). With the ready emergence of substitutes, the adjective in *monopolistic competition* may be downplayed. Firms' ability to set prices is critically restricted by such entry and even by potential entry. Viewed in this light, the model of monopolistic competition, with its emphasis on product differentiation and other forms of nonprice competition, is of great value in helping us understand how dynamic real-world markets function, change, or thrive.

APPLICATION

What's in a Brand Name? The Consumer Chooses

Elaborate and seemingly bewildering displays of products greet the consumer at the modern American supermarket. And that is nothing compared with the new consumer goods we hear about daily on TV and in computer ads, newspapers, and magazines. Thousands of products are sold and thousands more are introduced every year. In any single year, massive quantities of new brands, new flavors, new sizes, new ways to sell products, or other variations on established brands are introduced by business entrepreneurs. How many new brands of chips or cold remedies came onto the market last year? The answer may be "hundreds."

Brand "variations" in type or quality are most common. You may now purchase spaghetti sauce plain, with green peppers, "Cajun style," with three different kinds of cheeses, with beef, with pepperoni, and in a host of other variations. Critics of the market system blast such product proliferation as unnecessary, costly, and of little value to the consumer or to the economy. This criticism is often primarily directed toward monopolistic competition. However, such criticism basically represents a misunderstanding of how the market system works to contribute to economic efficiency and to maximize the sum of producer and consumer surplus.

Big consumer-product-oriented companies such as Procter & Gamble, Johnson & Johnson, or Kraft Foods have every incentive to maintain "market share" and profitability for company stockholders by differentiating their products. The question is: Does such differentiation increase consumer welfare? The answer is (in the vast majority of cases) a resounding yes! This is especially so in markets characterized by repeat purchases and monopolistic competition.

Most product differentiation or quality variations do not come free to consumers and are offered only at added cost. Most often, the "plain" or "classic" variety remains available. The subjective evaluation of the consumer concerning the new product or variety will turn on whether the change (improvement?) in utility terms and in terms of how much "extra" the customer is willing to pay is sufficient to overcome the additional charge for the product or service. If it is, the consumer buys and her dollar votes encourage such variety. If not, the producer/seller discontinues the new brand (think of the Edsel automobile and the host of products that "don't make it" each year). Moreover, successful innovations in product or packaging—such as new computer software—are immediately imitated by other producers.

What critics of innovation and differentiation seem to misunderstand is that the market system, in responding to the particular demands of consumers and groups of consumers, is creating greater welfare for consumers. If there is no increase in utility, consumers will not buy a new product at a higher price. The ideal (perhaps) would be the ultimate in product differentiation—that each and every consumer gets exactly the product or service he or she wants. Because of resource scarcity and opportunity cost, this is not possible. The truth is, however, that the

A market system has provided an enormous range of choice for athletic shoes (of all kinds and descriptions), as it has for so many goods and services. This has led to a charge of "brand proliferation" from critics of free markets.

market system that allows trial, error, and fishing by producers and sellers for new variations or products to entice consumers comes closest to the ideal. Restrictions on this system are more likely to harm consumers than to help them.

QUESTION

Some politicians, economists, and media persons argue that brand proliferation by large corporations merely confuses people and is therefore not a benefit to the consumer. Do you agree? Why or why not?

SUMMARY

1. Monopolistic competition is a market structure that contains a large number of firms. Each firm sells a product that is similar to but slightly differentiated from the products of other firms in the industry. Freedom of entry and exit exists in this model.

2. Advertising is a means by which firms distinguish their products and attempt to increase demand for them. Advertising and other forms of nonprice competition characterize monopolistic competition.

3. In the long run, a tangency between the firm's demand curve and its long-run average cost exists under monopolistic competition. If this tangency

occurs, then the firm produces a rate of output less than the rate associated with minimum average total cost—that is, excess capacity exists.

4. The excess capacity that exists in a monopolistically competitive market may have value. A large variety of differentiated products offers consumers a wider variety of choice than they have in a purely competitive market, where firms sell a homogeneous product.

5. The long-run equilibrium of the monopolistically competitive firm is similar to a competitive firm in that its price is equal to its average cost. It is similar to a monopolist in that its price is greater than its marginal cost.

KEY TERMS

imperfect competition	nonprice competition	excess capacity
monopolistic competition	advertising	economic efficiency
differentiated product	tangency solution	economic welfare

QUESTIONS FOR REVIEW AND DISCUSSION

1. Select two products or services that you regularly consume. Are these goods produced under monopolistically competitive conditions? What information must you have before giving a definite answer to this question?

2. What, exactly, is the role of product differentiation and advertising in monopolistic competition?

3. How many forms of competition can you name and analyze in addition to price competition? How is location a factor in competition?

4. Suppose that Pepsi is the best-selling soft drink in the market. Is it wasteful for Pepsi to continue to advertise on a large scale? Give reasons for your answer.

5. Suppose you are moving to a new town and must find an apartment. What benefits do you receive from apartment advertisements? What costs do you incur?

6. What is the tangency solution to the market model of monopolistic competition? Are half-empty airplanes on the New York–San Francisco route definite evidence of excess capacity and economic waste? Give reasons for your answer.

7. Compare the results of long-run equilibrium in pure competition and monopolistic competition from the standpoint of both economic efficiency and welfare.

8. Which of the following is more realistic, the model of perfect competition or the model of monopolistic competition?

WORKING WITH THE WEB

1. One of the characteristics of monopolistic competition is that firms differentiate their products in an attempt to capture more market share. An example of a monopolistically competitive industry is cereal. There are relatively few manufacturers, yet there are over one hundred different boxes of cereal on the shelves of your local supermarket. The two top manufacturers of ready-to-eat cereal are Kellogg's and General Mills.

   Go to http://www.kelloggs.com/corphq/products/index. html and look at the ready-to-eat cereals that Kellogg's sells. Next, do the same for General Mills by viewing its ready-to-eat cereals at http://www.generalmills.com/products/prodlist. asp?id=1.

   a. Which company is more diversified in terms of the number of different cereals it manufactures?

   b. Both Kellogg's and General Mills are publicly held corporations. To compare the dividend per share in each corporation, first go to http://www.kelloggs.com/corphq/financial/index.html and scroll down to the table titled "Per Common Share." Under the second column, cash dividends, what is the level of dividends per share in 1998? How does this compare with the dividends per share at General Mills in 1998? (Go to http://www.generalmills.com/financial/dividend and scroll down until you see the table containing the Fiscal Year and its associated dividend per share.)

   c. How might you explain the difference that exists in dividends per share in these two corporations in light of product differentiation?

2. The extent of advertising in monopolistically competitive industries is greater than in competitive industries. One source of advertising, as discussed in this chapter, is the Yellow Pages. Go to http://yellowpages.excite.com/bus and choose the option that allows you to search by category. In the search box, type "restaurants" (without the quotes). For "Search Area," select "City only" and in the search box, type in Auburn, AL.

   a. How many restaurant categories are there in Auburn (click on the "+" next to restaurants)?

   b. Enter a new search area—Washington, DC. How many restaurant categories are advertised in Washington? How do you explain the difference in the extent of Yellow Page advertisements in Washington relative to Auburn?

CHAPTER 11

Few Competitors: Game Theory, Oligopoly, And Cartels

Where sellers of a particular product or service are few in number, the market is called an **oligopoly**. Beer, automobiles, cigarettes, steel, and aluminum are just some of the products of oligopoly markets. The key element in these markets composed of small numbers of competing sellers is that each seller recognizes that his or her actions have an impact on the other sellers' sales, prices, and profits. The fate of any one competitor is linked to the actions of each of the other competitors in the market; further, each competitor recognizes that this is the case. Economists call this condition **mutual interdependence**. Under such oligopoly conditions, firms may, for survival or profit, try to engage in various forms of combination or collusion.

A **cartel** is a formal or informal alliance among producers to restrict competition and to achieve some or all of the gains of monopoly. Such a structure may be closer in economic results to pure monopoly than to pure competition. While an oligopoly refers to an industry with a few sellers, a cartel can exist in any industry, depending on the difficulty of forming a collusive agreement among producers.

This chapter focuses on those market structures in which mutual interdependence is a factor in the functioning of the market and is recognized as such. When you finish reading Chapter 11 you should understand

- the implications of game theory for explaining mutual dependence and for the behavior of oligopoly firms and cartels.
- the conditions under which collusion may be expected when large competitors are few.
- how strategic behavior is important in understanding oligopoly market structures.
- the nature of legal and illegal cartels in U.S. and world markets.

Oligopoly
Market models characterized by a few firms producing either homogeneous or differentiated products, with entry of new firms very difficult or prevented.

Mutual interdependence
A relation among firms in which the decisions and actions of one firm have a significant impact on the decisions, actions, and profits of other firms.

Cartel
An alliance of firms that act collusively to reduce output and increase price in an industry in order to increase profits.

Game theory
A theory involving decision making in an atmosphere of mutual interdependence and imperfect information.

GAME THEORY AND MUTUAL INTERDEPENDENCE

Game theory is a tool that can be used in the analysis of strategic behavior between competing entities, such as the United States and the former Soviet Union.[1] In economics, game theory permits us to focus on the central feature of oligopoly—mutual interdependence—and the principles behind the strategies of firms in markets where the number of firms is small. First, we consider the matter of mutual interdependence more closely.

Mutual Interdependence in the Economic World

The key to the existence of oligopoly is that mutual interdependence develops among a small number of sellers. Mutual interdependence is a relation among firms such that what one firm does with its price, product, or advertising budget directly affects other firms in the market, and vice versa. For example, if Chrysler Corporation introduces two new types of automobiles or if the company increases its overall advertising budget by a significant percentage, sales of General Motors, Ford, and foreign automobile manufacturers will be directly affected. These oligopolistic competitors know that their sales and profits are affected by Chrysler's actions and are likely to react accordingly. Firms therefore devote resources to keeping track of their competitors' actions.

Recall that a firm under pure or perfect competition simply takes the market price as a given and produces accordingly and the pure monopoly has no direct competition to worry about. This is not the case with oligopolists. When competitors recognize mutual interdependence, each firm will base its market decisions (on price, product innovation, and advertising) at least partially on what it thinks its rivals will do. Because of the uncertainty facing sellers in oligopoly markets, mutual interdependence can lead to a variety of outcomes. The outcome of any action an oligopoly firm takes depends on the responses—both actual and assumed—of rival firms.

Game Theory: A Basis for Small-Numbers Behavior

The basic problem facing oligopolies should be familiar to everyone; we all find ourselves in situations of mutual interdependence every day. Anyone who has ever played competitive games of any sort—tennis, blackjack, bridge—will immediately recognize the problem. Our actions are interdependent when playing games because our actions affect other players' behavior, and our own behavior is conditioned by what we expect other players' reactions to our own behavior to be. Suppose that you and Joan have a weekly tennis match. Respectful of your powerful serve, Joan has learned to stand well behind the baseline when receiving. This position allows her to return an increasingly high percentage of your serves. Noticing this, you decide to surprise her with a shallow slicing serve. If you serve this way consistently, Joan will likely change her behavior. Joan's actions and yours are

---

[1]See John von Neumann and Oskar Morgenstern, *Theory of Games and Economic Behavior* (Princeton: Princeton University Press, 1944), the classic work applying game theory to economic analysis. Data for and discussion of several of the games considered in this chapter are taken, with permission, from Richard O. Beil, Jr., *Collusion in Experimental Oligopoly Markets* (Unpublished doctoral dissertation, Texas A&M University, 1988).

clearly interdependent—and recognized to be so. Game theory is the formalization of the effects of mutual interdependence on strategy.

The Prisoner's Dilemma As A Basis For Game Theory   An intriguing basis for game theory as applied to economic rivalry is called the prisoner's dilemma. The **prisoner's dilemma** originated in a story told by mathematician A. W. Tucker. It involves two criminals (here, Butch Cassidy and the Sundance Kid) and their likely behavior after capture. Suppose that the police have captured Butch and Sundance. Further, suppose that the police have sufficient evidence to convict both of lesser crimes but suspect that Butch and Sundance have committed more serious offenses that are punishable by lengthier stays in jail. The police separate the prisoners and attempt to obtain confessions. Butch and Sundance each know that (1) if one confesses, the confessor will receive a light sentence and the other will receive a more severe sentence; (2) if neither confesses, both will receive the modest penalty that goes with the lesser crime; (3) if both confess, both will receive a sentence that, while severe, is short of the sentence that would be given to each individual if he did not confess and the other did.

The decisions facing Butch and Sundance are organized in Figure 11.1, which represents the prisoner's dilemma by arranging the "payoffs" (in this case, punishments in years in jail) faced by the two decision makers. (Figure 11.1 is the *payoff table* for this situation.) The potential number of years of incarceration for Sundance is shown on the left side of each individual block, or quadrant, and the potential time served for Butch is shown on the right side. The police will try to get Butch and Sundance to testify against each other. If Butch confesses but Sundance does not confess, Sundance gets 12 years in prison to Butch's 1 year. Similarly, if Sundance confesses to the greater crime and Butch holds out, Sundance serves only 1 year in jail and Butch serves 12. If both refuse to confess, each receives 3 years, but if both confess, they each serve 7 years.

What is the most likely outcome of this "game" of strategy between Butch and Sundance? The outcome depends on the presumptions that each makes about the other's behavior. We may reasonably assume (1) that both Butch Cassidy and the Sundance Kid want to minimize their time in jail and (2) that neither is concerned about the cost his decision imposes on the other. Given these two assumptions, the

Prisoner's dilemma

A scenario that illustrates the mutual interdependence of decision making; the basis for game theory.

FIGURE 11.1

Butch Cassidy and the Sundance Kid Face the Prisoner's Dilemma

If Butch and Sundance want to minimize their time in jail, the prisoner's dilemma leads both of them to confess. Each receives a 7-year sentence.

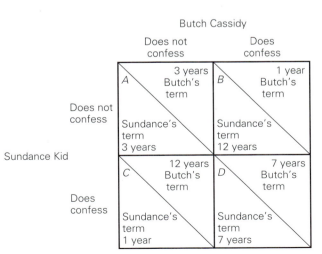

The best choice for Butch Cassidy and the Sundance Kid is for neither to confess to wrongdoing.

Dominant solution

A situation in game theory in which each player has the same best choice no matter what course of action other players may choose.

solution to the game is for *both* Butch and Sundance to confess. Look at Figure 11.1 and consider the potential years served. What is Sundance's best strategy? If Butch confesses, Sundance gets 7 years if he confesses too, but *12 years if he doesn't.* If Butch does not confess, Sundance gets 1 year if he confesses and 3 years if he does not confess. Sundance is better off confessing. Given that Sundance cannot know Butch's decision, and can in no way influence that decision, a confession is the only way for Sundance to ensure a lesser jail term for himself. A look at Figure 11.1 will verify that the same is true for Butch; the best choice for each criminal is to confess and serve 7 years. (If the two could communicate, however, and if each could hold the other to his word, the best choice for both Butch and Sundance would be to not confess.) In the terminology of game theory, the choices offered to Butch and Sundance have a **dominant solution**: Each player has the same best choice, no matter what strategy the other player chooses. In the game represented by Figure 11.1, the dominant solution is to confess.

The Prisoner's Dilemma As Economic Game   The prisoner's dilemma can be directly related to economic behavior. Contests offered by fast-food chains can be viewed within the context of simple game theory. A contest increases the restaurants' production costs (prizes, promotion fees, and so on) and at the same time tends to reduce profits. Yet contests are often offered by firms acting in their own self-interest. Their reasoning is illustrated in Figure 11.2, in which profits to the restaurant chains replace the time in prison spent by Butch Cassidy and the Sundance Kid. Here, the two fast-food chains are trying to maximize their profits, represented by the dollar figures in the boxes.

From the industry's standpoint, the best decision for both firms is represented in box *A* of Figure 11.2. Industry profits total $120 million in box *A* ($65 million for Wendy's and $55 million for Burger King), as opposed to $100 million in boxes *B* and *C* and $90 million in box *D*. Yet box *A* does not represent the individual profit-maximizing choice for either firm separately. If Burger King offers a contest and Wendy's does not (box *B*), Burger King's profits are $70 million, up $15 million. If Burger King offers a contest and Wendy's does likewise, Burger King's profits will be only $40 million (box *D*). But if Burger King does not offer a contest and Wendy's does, Burger King's profits will drop to $30 million (box *C*). Wendy's management considers its own set of options and reaches a similar conclusion: namely, that acting independently, Wendy's will always be better off giving customers a contest to play. If each chain makes a decision that tends to maximize its individual profits, both will introduce contests and together earn smaller profits ($90 million) than they would have earned in the absence of contest offerings by both ($120 million).

The dilemma for Burger King and Wendy's is this: Both parties would be better off if they could communicate and stay in box *A*; but firms cannot legally com-

FIGURE 11.2

The Prisoner's Dilemma and Fast-Food Contests

Various possible combinations exist when Wendy's and Burger King try to maximize profits by deciding whether to offer contests. Profits for the firm's decisions are given in millions of dollars. The best choice for the industry as a whole is box *A*, where neither firm offers a contest. The best profit-maximizing option for each individually is to offer a contest.

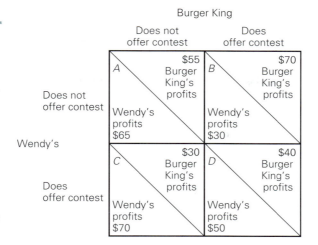

municate because of the fear that they might talk about more than contests—that is, that they would collude or cooperate to raise prices, an activity that would be a violation of federal antitrust laws. Therefore, the best option for each firm acting alone is box *D*.

One-Shot Versus Infinite-Series Games   Two keys to the actual outcome of such "games" in real-world situations are (1) the conjecture made about rivals' responses and (2) the time frame over which combatants work out their responses and strategies. The two games presented in Figures 11.1 and 11.2 are one-shot games; in each case, each party has just one chance to make the best decision. If these games were played repeatedly, perhaps both parties in each game—both Sundance *and* Butch and Wendy's *and* Burger King—would eventually decide to do what's best for both. Butch and Sundance might eventually get to box *A* in Figure 11.1, with each serving three years; Burger King and Wendy's might eventually get to box *A* in Figure 11.2, with neither offering contests. Such **tacit collusive solutions**—or outcomes without specific, formal agreement—exist when, over an indefinite period of time, firms recognize that their own interests will best be served when joint or combined profits are maximized.

When the time horizon facing two rivals is finite—that is, when the game has a known end point—the outcome is shaped by the principle of **backward induction**. Backward induction results from an incentive to cheat in the last period of the game.

Suppose Wendy's and Burger King's contest "game" will last three "periods." If the two firms have been in box *A* of Figure 11.2 for two periods, it would be in either Burger King's or Wendy's best interest to **cheat** in the third and final period. Why? To do so would mean bigger profits for the cheater—*but only if the other does not cheat.* If you think your rival will cheat in the third period, then you have an incentive to get there first—to cheat in the second period. If you think your rival will cheat in the second period, then you will cheat in the first period. The collusive, or joint profit-maximizing, solution tends to break down when the end period of the game is known. Each player has an incentive to cheat *before* the joint profit-maximizing solution has a chance to get off the ground; the outcome in such a case is identical to the outcome of a one-shot game.

Tacit collusive solution
A possible outcome in game theory when, given an indefinite time horizon and no formal communication, rivals recognize that it is in their best interest to act so that joint profits are maximized.

Backward induction
The incentive each player has to cheat in the last period of the game; exists because there are no future periods left to play in which possible consequences from cheating could occur.

Cheat
To violate a collusive agreement; cheating may result in an increase in short-run economic profits to the firm that cheats, followed by zero economic profits in the long run.

OLIGOPOLY

As noted previously, industries with a few sellers or with a few large sellers and a large number of fringe competitors are characteristic of the modern marketplace. Oligopolies may sell homogeneous products such as steel or differentiated products such as automobiles or soft drinks. The simple principles of game theory tell us that pricing decisions by oligopolistic firms are much more complex than for firms in monopolistic or monopolistically competitive markets. Unlike other types of firms, oligopolistic firms find it extremely difficult to estimate their demand curves. If Ford is considering a 5 percent increase in prices, there is no reliable way of estimating sales at that higher price without knowing the price response of other firms like General Motors or Toyota. Before turning to some specific models of oligopoly, we consider another characteristic of all oligopolies: barriers to entry.

Barriers to Entry

Market power

A situation in which an established firm has influence over price and profit levels due to barriers impeding the entry of rival firms.

Oligopoly firms are normally thought to possess a large degree of **market power**. Subject to the reactions of competitors and to the ability of new competitors to enter the market, oligopoly firms are able to set prices and make economic profits, much like pure monopolists. But how does a firm achieve market power in the oligopoly market structure?

The source of the market power of oligopolists, as in any market structure, is barriers to entry. The pure monopolist is the sole supplier of a product because of barriers to entry into its industry. In any locality, for instance, there is ordinarily no close substitute for cable TV or residential power service, and there are legal barriers to firms wishing to enter these markets. If entry were free in these markets, new competitors would be attracted by higher-than-competitive prices, and excess profits would be eroded. Entry barriers are likewise essential to the maintenance of market power by oligopolists.

For an oligopoly, an entry barrier is a cost that confronts a potential entrant into the industry but does not affect the incumbent firms. There are both natural and artificial entry barriers in an oligopoly market.

Natural Barriers   Economies of scale are an example of a natural barrier to entry. The economies of large-scale production and distribution mean that long-run average costs decline as output grows. Minimum average cost is not reached until the firm is producing a huge proportion of the total industry output. Economies of scale in the U.S. automobile industry, for example, have promoted the presence of a few firms in the long run—far fewer than the hundreds of automobile manufacturers in existence at the beginning of the twentieth century. There are other natural entry barriers, including high fixed costs, high risk, scarce managerial talent, personal technological knowledge, and high capital costs.

Great care must be used in interpreting natural entry barriers, because most of these barriers reflect the different efficiencies of firms in producing output. Society benefits when firms achieve economies of scale, produce with the best technology, and allocate scarce managerial talent carefully. If a natural force like economies of scale leads to the possibility of market power, then the firm may be subject to antitrust prosecution. This means that the firm may be subject to laws enforced by the Federal Trade Commission and the Justice Department, which limit or eliminate anticompetitive practices.

Artificial Barriers   Government restrictions—patents, government regulations, licensing, tariffs, quotas, and other government actions—constitute artificial barriers to entry for oligopolists. Such restrictions are fairly self-evident, but consider some examples.

Government-sponsored import tariffs on foreign automobiles or steel are an example of government restrictions that encourage and protect oligopolies. Government-sponsored and -enforced cartels or legal agreements to collude—in such industries as railroads, ocean transportation, communications, TV, and radio—are another example of an artificial barrier to entry. Cartel arrangements legalized through regulation are probably the most important artificial barriers to entry established by government. The basic point is that oligopoly theory rests on the concept of barriers to entry, both natural and artificial.

Models of Oligopoly Pricing

Like other firms, oligopolies seek to maximize their profits. To do so, however, the oligopolist can pursue many different strategies because firms can compete on a number of bases—product development, prices, advertising budgets, and so on—and can form a whole spectrum of opinions about how rivals will react. Many theories of oligopoly based on price or nonprice competition have been developed. We present some of the standard models used by economists to analyze oligopolistic markets.

Game Theory And Oligopoly Behavior   While game theory becomes extremely complex in models involving more than two competitors or complicated strategies, simple models provide many insights into the problems of small-numbers competition. Unlike monopoly, where a firm's fortunes are largely dependent on the firm's behavior, game theory reveals an oligopoly firm's profits, prices, and output to be the result of mutually interdependent behavior. Further, game theory shows how mutual interdependence creates incentives to collude, as well as contradictory incentives to cheat on collusive agreements.

The Cournot–Nash Model   A slightly more complex model than those presented in Figures 11.1 and 11.2 can add to our understanding of strategic behavior in oligopolistic markets. The principles underlying our discussion were first put forth in 1838 by the French economist Augustin Cournot (1801–1877), and they were extended by mathematician John Nash in the 1950s. These principles are called the **Cournot–Nash solution** in game theory.[2]

Cournot–Nash solution
The likely outcome of a one-shot game or a game with a known end point; in this case, both firms cheat, thus bringing profits below the joint profit-maximizing level.

Suppose that two competitors—for example, Sony and Motorola—are considering three marketing or advertising strategies for the sale of high-resolution television sets. As shown in the payoff table in Figure 11.3, these three marketing strategies are labeled X, Y, and Z, giving Sony and Motorola nine possible combinations of choices, with the profits given in the nine individual boxes. If, for example, Sony chooses strategy Z and Motorola chooses X, profits to Sony are $544 million and Motorola's profits are $220 million.

The same basic solutions apply to the three-choice game as to the two-choice games described previously. The addition of an intermediate solution, however, helps us understand some other possible features of small-numbers behavior. As

[2]John Nash, along with two other developers of game theory John Harsanyi and Reinhard Selten, won the Nobel Prize in Economics for this work in 1994.

FIGURE 11.3

Sony and Motorola Caught in the Prisoner's Dilemma

In an "infinite" or many-period game, we expect Sony and Motorola to arrive at the joint profit-maximizing, or tacit collusive, solution (X, X). In a one-shot game or in one with a known end point, the Cournot–Nash solution (Z, Z) is most likely. (Payoffs are expressed in millions of dollars.)

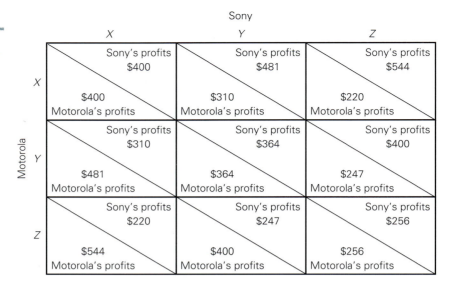

in simpler games, a one-shot or single play of the strategies open to Sony and Motorola will produce the prisoner's dilemma and result in the Cournot–Nash solution (Z, Z), where each earns profits of $256 million. When the time frame becomes infinite, we expect the tacit collusive arrangement (X, X) to emerge, where the rivals each earn $400 million in profits. The same is generally true when the competitive game is finite, provided that neither competitor knows the end point. Even when these competitive games are considered infinite or of unknown duration, there is still room for strategic behavior, due to the mutually interdependent nature of the competition.

Cheating appears as strategic behavior in most games. A close look at Figure 11.3 reveals that even if Sony and Motorola reach their joint profit-maximizing strategies (X, X), there is room for short-term profits from cheating by either party. Suppose that Sony continues "playing" the joint profit-maximizing marketing strategy, X, but that Motorola begins to employ strategy Y or Z. Sony's profits decline to $310 million or $220 million, while Motorola *raises* its returns from $400 million to $481 million or $544 million. Examination of Figure 11.3 tells us that Sony has a similar incentive to cheat on the tacit agreement with Motorola. In the real world, some cheating may be difficult to detect, but in this simple two-firm game any cheating is detected immediately by the victim's reduced profits.

One safeguard against cheating on the tacit collusive solution is to punish the offender. If Motorola moved to "cheating" strategy Y, Sony could immediately move to strategy Z, thereby restoring its returns to $400 million and reducing those of Motorola from $481 million to $247 million. Should Sony continue with strategy Z, Motorola could do no better than to also shift to strategy Z. We can easily verify that the Cournot–Nash solution (Z, Z) is the likely result once cheating begins.

Signals between game players are common in many games. As the dynamics of this game reveal, Motorola will be punished for cheating, but Sony's profits also fall with the movement to the Cournot–Nash solution. If the length of the game is infinite, or even just sufficiently long, cooperation and the re-establishment of the collusive solution is the most likely result. Either party, Sony or Motorola, *may* signal the other that it would like to return to collusion from the (Z, Z) level of profits.

Either may do so by moving to another strategy for a few periods, taking temporary losses, and giving its rival gains for those periods. Having been the first to cheat, if Motorola initiated this behavior, the move would be considered *repentance*. Such temporary losses may be a relatively small sacrifice if the joint profit-maximization, or collusive, solution can be maintained (or restored) over the long run.

These simple principles of games are more than just theory. They help explain a good deal of the maneuvering that actually occurs among firms. Clearly, it would be in the interests of businesses selling similar products to collude and to reach the joint profit-maximizing level of returns. But as the complexities of game theory tell us, such collusion is far less likely as the number of sellers increases. Successful collusion with little or no cheating is also less expected when firms compete in a large number of areas—for example, service, product qualities, and advertising. As games grow more complex—that is, accommodate a larger number of participants and items upon which competition is based—the possibilities for collusive behavior are drastically reduced. Simple game theory, including the prisoner's dilemma or Cournot–Nash game, is nevertheless of great value in helping economists understand the dynamics of competition and market processes.

Dominant-Firm Model   Many industries consist of one or a few large firms and many smaller rivals. Examples are the airlines, steel manufacturers, and the personal computer industry. Pricing in such a market is often characterized by **price leadership**, which means that there is an unwritten agreement that the largest firm sets pricing policy for the industry. When the largest firm announces that it is raising its price by 5 percent, the other firms in the industry follow suit (and usually on the same day!). This unwritten code of industry conduct is one way to solve problems of interdependent pricing.

The largest firm is not always the price leader; sometimes the price leader is the most respected firm in the industry or the firm, called a "barometric" firm, that best reflects average cost, demand, and other conditions in the industry. And sometimes the role of price leader shifts among firms. Jones-Laughlin, though not the

Price leadership
A market where a single firm sets industry price, with the remaining firms charging what the price leader charges. Industry price changes are initiated by the leader.

In many cases when competitors are in close proximity, the conditions for a competitive "game" (and for collusion) are set up. "Price wars" sometimes take place between competing gas stations that locate close to one another.

largest firm in the market, was for years the steel industry's price leader, whereas General Motors, clearly the dominant firm, provided a similar role for the automobile industry.

Oligopolists With Differentiated Products   Just as there are many cases of pure oligopoly, there are many cases in which few sellers supply differentiated products. Under such conditions, oligopolists may compete with each other and perhaps try to bar new entrants through nonprice means, such as advertising and quality variations, or through pricing strategies. Note that not all nonprice competition by oligopolists promotes efficiency in the economy. Our discussion of fast-food contests with regard to game theory illustrates how this sort of competition can lead to wasteful results.

Advertising   In oligopoly, as in monopolistic competition, advertising is used by rival firms to increase demand for their products (shift demand curves rightward and make them more inelastic) through the creation of brand loyalty and product identity. Heavy advertising by a few large firms is often held to be an entry barrier to new competition. The argument is that new firms cannot enter because they cannot afford the heavy advertising expenses necessary to establish a presence in the market.

Quality Variations   Quality variation and product development are other familiar methods of nonprice competition by oligopolists. Oligopolists, like monopolistic competitors, will alter products to increase their demand curves and to make demand more "intense" and inelastic in consumers' minds. Adding new colors to toothpaste, more or less chrome to automobiles, and more service to airline travel are familiar attempts to differentiate products and services.

Limit pricing
A pricing policy consisting of temporarily setting a price lower than the short-run profit-maximizing price in order to deter entry and maximize profits in the long run.

Limit Pricing   In oligopoly industries with a differentiated product, incumbent firms may seek to deter potential competition by limit pricing. **Limit pricing** is the incumbent's practice of reducing price as much as necessary to limit entry.

Imagine a situation in which a new firm wants to enter an industry. Since other firms' products have already been differentiated, the new firm will have to incur heavy advertising expenses to become competitive with incumbent firms assumed to be earning positive economic profits. If a new entrant is successful in its bid for a share of the market, its sales will come at the expense of the incumbent firms. To block this challenge, an incumbent firm may lower price and increase output in response to the threat of entry, voluntarily (if temporarily) reducing its profits. In general, the incumbent firm could set a price (or threaten to set a price) at which entry would not be worthwhile for any potential rival.

We are talking about oligopolistic behavior. The potential entrant must make an estimate of what the incumbent firm will do in the face of entry. If the incumbent firm practices or even threatens limit pricing, entry may not be feasible. Indeed, the most rational thing for the incumbent firm to do is to keep price at profitable levels and at the same time make it clear to potential entrants that it will lower price and increase output if they enter.

CARTEL MODELS

To this point in our discussion of oligopolies, we have assumed that competitor firms will not openly cooperate to set prices. But what if firms do openly cooperate? This question brings us to the topic of cartels.

Cartels and oligopolies are close cousins. The distinguishing feature of a cartel is an explicit (verbal or written) agreement among firms to restrict output in order to raise price and to achieve monopoly power over a market.

Characteristics of Cartels

Normally cartels are supported by agreements that restrict and segment output among markets. Cartel agreements may be legal or illegal. In countries with antitrust laws, including the United States, cartels are illegal, but they sometimes operate covertly. An illegal cartel rests on private, collusive agreements that are out of sight of the antitrust authorities. In the 1960s, certain U.S. firms made a secret agreement to fix the prices of electrical generators sold to municipalities; this illegal collusion was discovered and prosecuted under antitrust laws, with the guilty firms paying damages. (See the Focus "Bid Rigging: Cartels in Action.") Beyond the threat and reality of antitrust prosecution, such secret arrangements may tend to fall apart on their own. Reasons for the fragile nature of cartels will be discussed

FOCUS

Bid Rigging: Cartels in Action

All levels of government in the United States purchase many goods and services from private suppliers. At the federal level, the Department of Defense purchases cars, ammunition, and other products from private companies; state governments purchase paper, pencils, and road paving services from private contractors; and local governments buy milk for schoolchildren and services from water and sewer contractors. These are just a few of the many purchases that are made by government.

The process by which government typically purchases goods and services from private contractors is called sealed bidding. A road contractor, for example, will work up a bid or price for a road paving job, seal it, and submit it to the state highway department. Each road contractor submits his or her bid independently of other bidders. An official at the highway department then opens the sealed bids and awards the contract to the lowest bidder.

For the most part, the sealed bidding process works well, promoting the efficient, low-cost supply of services to government—as long as there is no bid rigging. Unfortunately, the provision of government services by private contractors has tended to encourage anti-competitive behavior. Bid rigging occurs when independent contractors get together and agree not to compete on their bids. Meeting at a restaurant, for example, the contractors might decide to "assign" job X to company A, job Y to company B, and so on. The contractors do not bid aggressively for jobs that have been assigned to someone else, guaranteeing that each company gets "its" job or a high bid. Since the bids are opened and read in public, all of the bidders can easily know if their bid conspiracy is being followed.

Obviously, bid rigging is a cartel or conspiracy in restraint of trade. By agreeing not to compete, firms earn cartel or monopoly profits. The result for taxpayers is higher prices for public services and, therefore, higher taxes.

During the 1980s and early 1990s, federal and state antitrust officials across the country uncovered numerous bid rigging schemes in such areas as road paving, water and sewer construction, and the sale of milk to school districts. The conspiracies were uncovered and the conspirators were prosecuted. Many executives of companies who participated in bid rigging were fined and sent to jail. The vigilance of the antitrust authorities thus served to save taxpayers money by ensuring the provision of basic government services at the lowest cost.

later in the chapter, but most are related to the incentives for some members to cheat on the agreement.

A legal cartel is supported by a law limiting entry and restricting competition among members. Such cartels may be made legitimate by the legal and political organization of an industry—communications, electrical distribution, and railroads, for example—under the umbrella of government regulation restricting competition and allowing price fixing. Or cartels may be made legitimate by legislation granting exceptions to antitrust statutes. Such is the case for some exporters, labor unions, and farm organizations.

Legal status does not protect such cartels from breaking down in the long run. Technology and competition have all but destroyed the railroad cartel in the United States enforced by the Interstate Commerce Commission since the late nineteenth century. OPEC (the Organization of Petroleum Exporting Countries) was unable to maintain its full cartel status, not because it was illegal within the participating countries, but because of the lack of adequate enforcement and the unwillingness of certain nations, notably Saudi Arabia, to meet the terms demanded by other members. The Colombian coffee cartel of the 1960s broke down for similar reasons, and the De Beers diamond cartel had some shaky times in the early 1980s. Thus, both legal and illegal cartels tend to be fragile, although cartel agreements enforced by law and the government are less so.

Cartel Formation

Assume for the sake of simplicity that cartels do not violate any law and that we are analyzing a case in which the cartel is to be privately enforced by the cartel members and not by government. The first problem facing any potential cartel or association of sellers is how to get organized. In this respect the cartel is no different from any other group. The usual problem in getting any group to do anything can be roughly summarized as "passing the buck." If somebody else forms the cartel or takes the lead in restricting output, other members can generally enjoy the benefits of the cartel without bearing any of the costs of organization. This behavior is called *free riding.*

Of course, if everybody in the cartel were a free rider, the cartel would never be formed. All potential members would hold back and expect to benefit from the organizational efforts of others. Suffice it to say that a cartel has to get organized. Someone has to get the individual suppliers in the industry together and hammer out an agreement to restrict output in order to raise price. The details of this feat are not simple. Which firms will reduce output and by how much? How will the resulting cartel profits be shared? How will deviations from cartel policies be monitored and enforced?

These and other questions are difficult for the cartel manager to answer and for cartel members to reach agreement on. The problem becomes more pronounced the more firms there are in the industry. As a rule, smaller groups are easier to organize than larger groups.

The Cartel in Action

Figure 11.4 illustrates how a cartel operates. Imagine that orange juice producers try to form a cartel. Initially, the orange juice industry is competitively organized. Orange juice industry demand and supply intersect to yield price P. Industry output is Q.

FIGURE 11.4

Organizing a Competitive Industry into a Cartel

Price rises from P to P_c as the cartel is formed and output is cut back from Q to Q_c. In the extreme case, the cartel price, P_c, is equivalent to the monopoly price.

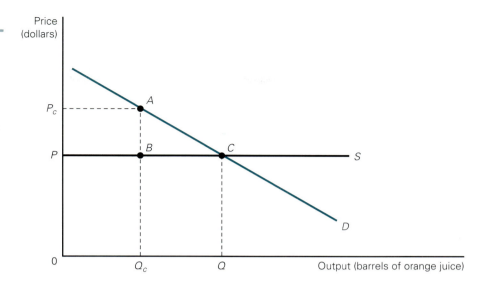

A cartel manager emerges and strikes an agreement among the competitive producers to cut back production from the industry's Q to Q_c and to raise price from P to P_c. Cartel output Q_c will ordinarily not be equivalent to the output a pure monopolist would select. Why? In an industry such as orange juice production, with a relatively large number of suppliers, the costs of eliminating all competitive behavior—the costs of enforcing the cartel agreement against free riders—would be too high. Some competitive behavior will remain. Cartel price will therefore tend to be lower than the profit-maximizing price of a pure monopolist.

The incentive to form cartels is nevertheless clear. Cartel members who were previously earning a competitive rate of return in a competitive industry now earn an agreed-upon portion of $P_c ABP$—an equal share of cartel profits.

Cartel Enforcement

Holding the cartel together is not easy. Once the cartel has been organized, has restricted output, and has raised price to P_c, what is the position of the individual orange juice firm in the cartel? If an individual firm in the cartel lowers its price slightly below P_c, it will face a very elastic demand curve for its output. Buyers will prefer the lower price and will switch their purchases to the lower-priced firm. The fact that individual firms in a cartel can significantly increase their sales and profits by secretly lowering their price puts tremendous pressure on the cartel to fall apart. Given that individual firms have a large incentive to cheat on the agreement, cartels must give careful consideration to the matter of **cartel enforcement** from the outset.

Of course, to expect the price cutter's profits to hold up in the long run is unrealistic. Other firms would easily discover what was going on because they would suffer a drastic loss of sales. If they responded in kind with price reductions, the result would be that the initial price cutter would not experience an increase in sales and profits for long. Further spates of secret price cuts and price competition would lead to a return to competitive equilibrium.

Recognizing these possibilities, the individual firm in the cartel must form an estimate of what it can reasonably expect to gain from secret price reductions and

Cartel enforcement

Attempts by members of the cartel to prevent other members from cheating and thus destroying economic profit potential.

compare this estimate with its share of cartel profits. A cartel will not be stable if the former amount is larger than the latter.

The general case in which a firm might expect to gain by secret price cutting is illustrated in Figure 11.5. Cartel equilibrium is at price P_c and output q_c, represented by E_c. D/n represents the prorated firm demand curve, where n is the number of firms in the industry. The gains to an individual cartel member from secretly cutting price are represented by d_i; d_i is more elastic than D/n. With the more elastic d_i curve, price increases would cause a sharp drop in sales, but price reductions cause a sharp gain in sales and profits at the expense of other cartel members. The gains of a secret price cut to P_s are traced out by d_i below P_c.

The key to cartel enforcement is now apparent. Means must be found to make d_i approximate D/n. Perfect cartel enforcement exists when each cartel member knows that secret price cuts are not possible and will be matched by other members. In this case, the prorated demand curve, D/n, is the relevant demand curve. If a firm cuts price, it will immediately be matched by other cartel members. There is thus no gain to cutting price. Movements will be along the prorated firm demand curve, D/n. Where it is costly to detect secret price cuts, a demand curve like d_i will confront each cartel member. Each firm's decision about whether or not to cheat will depend on the expected profits from cheating relative to the expected profits from staying in the cartel. In general, we can gauge the effectiveness of cartel enforcement by the degree to which the cartel is able to make the cheating demand curve d_i coincide with the prorated firm demand curve D/n. That is, how good is the cartel at detecting cheating?

Cartels will spend resources to control the incentive to cheat. Historically, many devices have been used. (See the Application "Diamonds, the De Beers Cartel, and the Russian Threat" at the conclusion of this chapter for a famous example.) Perhaps the most effective device is a common sales agency for the cartel. All production is sold through the agency, and individual producers do not negotiate sales for themselves. Cheating is not a viable strategy under such a condition. Producers pro-

FIGURE 11.5

Cheating in a Cartel

P_c is the agreed-upon cartel price at cartel output q_c. E_c is therefore the cartel equilibrium. If secret price cuts cannot be detected, the cheating firm will face the more elastic demand curve, d_i, and can gain from cheating on the agreement. If such behavior can be detected, movements will be along D/n, the prorated firm demand curve. The degree to which d_i diverges from D/n reflects the efficiency of the cartel enforcement system.

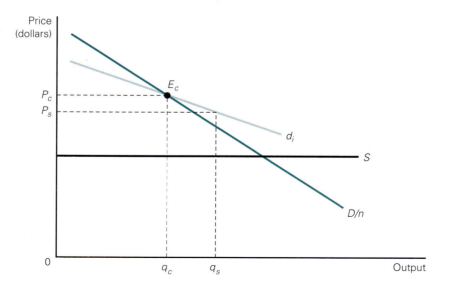

duce their allotted quotas, and the sales agency markets the agreed-upon cartel output (q_c). Exclusive sales territories and customer lists are other ways to control incentives to cheat on the cartel price. For example, exclusive territories are a way to divide markets, making intrusions by other cartel members easy to spot.

Why Cartels May or May Not Succeed

Collusive cartel agreements are more likely to occur under some circumstances than others. We offer now a menu of factors thought to be conducive to cartel-like behavior. Our list is not meant to be exhaustive—just illustrative of the types of economic conditions associated with a great likelihood of cartel activity.

1. A cartel is easier to form among a smaller number of sellers than a larger number.
2. It is easier to reach a cartel agreement when members produce a homogeneous product; sellers do not have to worry that their competitors will secure bigger market shares through advertising.
3. Collusion is more likely in stagnant or decaying industries. In this case low profits stimulate the demand for collusion.
4. The costs of collusion are reduced when there are many small buyers. Large buyers have a clear incentive and the power to seek to undermine collusion among sellers. In effect, large buyers make cheating on the cartel price very worthwhile to individual sellers.
5. Low turnover among buyers makes collusion easier. If sellers cheat on the cartel agreement, frequent turnover of buyers makes it difficult to detect who is cheating.

At this point, one fact should be clear: Private collusive agreements are hard to sustain. The incentive to cheat on such agreements is very strong, as game theory suggests, and cartels therefore tend to be unstable. Moreover, where antitrust law prevails, cartels must operate on the sly to avoid law enforcement; this secrecy further reduces their ability to control cheating.

FROM COMPETITION TO MONOPOLY: THE SPECTRUM REVISITED

We are now in a position to take an overview of the economic characteristics and welfare effects of market structures from pure competition (Chapter 8) to pure monopoly (Chapter 9) to those in between (Chapters 10 and 11). Table 11.1 organizes the long-run economic tendencies and conclusions of the various structures we have examined.

The table distinguishes the five market structures by number of sellers, barriers to entry, product characteristics, and long-run market tendencies. The number of sellers ranges from many under competition and monopolistic competition to one in the case of pure monopoly. Significant entry barriers characterize oligopolies, cartels, and monopolies. Oligopolies and cartels are characterized by the sale of *either* homogeneous or differentiated products, unlike the purely or monopolistically competitive structures. Pure monopolies sell unique products.

TABLE 11.1

Characteristics and Consequences of Market Structures

When static market structures are considered, only pure competition yields an efficient and welfare-maximizing allocation of resources. Resources are underallocated to the production of goods and services under all other structures from the consumers' perspective.

Type of Market Structure	Number of Sellers	Barriers to Entry	Type of Product	Long-Run Market Tendencies
Pure competition	Many	No	Homogeneous	$P = MC$ $P = ATC$
Monopolistic competition	Many	No	Differentiated	$P > MC$ $P = ATC$
Oligopoly	Few	Yes	Homogeneous or differentiated	$P > MC$ $P > ATC$
Cartels	Relatively few, acting as one	Yes	Homogeneous or differentiated	$P > MC$ $P > ATC$
Pure monopoly	One	Yes	Unique	$P > MC$ $P > ATC$

Most important, Table 11.1 provides a category—long-run market tendencies—that gives us some insight into the consumer and economic welfare created under these alternative structures. As the table reveals, price tends to equal long-run average total cost in only two of the structures—pure and monopolistic competition. Price, moreover, tends to equal long-run marginal cost only in the purely competitive market structure. What does this mean in terms of consumers' economic welfare?

An important concept introduced in Chapter 4 aids us in interpreting the effects of market structure on social welfare. In Chapter 4, we introduced the concept of consumers' surplus, defined as the difference between the amount of money that consumers would be willing to pay for a quantity of a good and the amount that they actually pay for the good.

Figure 11.6 shows what happens to consumers' surplus for a given hypothetical market—personal computer software—if the market is organized along monopolistic rather than competitive lines. The industry demand curve for this market has the usual negative slope, but the industry has a flat supply curve in this simplified conception. In other words, this is a constant-cost industry, in which additional output may be produced at a constant average cost that is also equal to marginal cost. The supply curve is simply a flat line.

To verify what happens to consumers' surplus under the different market structures represented in Figure 11.6, look again at the long-run market tendencies of the various models in Table 11.1. As we saw in Chapter 4 and Chapter 8, if the computer software industry is purely competitive, it will be producing an output of q_c at price P_c, which is the lowest possible price because it is equal to both the average cost and the marginal cost of production. In this situation, consumers enjoy a surplus represented by ACP_c. In contrast, price exceeds both average cost and marginal cost in the market models of oligopoly, cartels, and pure monopoly. Economic profits are therefore captured at the expense of consumers in these markets. In Figure 11.6, P_m and q_m represent the effects of a market structure on the monop-

FIGURE 11.6

The Effects of Competitive versus Monopolistic Markets

In contrasting the higher price and lower quantity (P_m and q_m) produced under a monopolistic market structure with the lower price and higher quantity (P_c and q_c) theoretically possible in a purely competitive situation, ACP_c represents the area of consumer surplus. This is real income available to anyone who can capture it. Under competition, it goes to consumers. Under monopoly, cartels, and oligopolies, part of it (P_mBFP_c) typically goes to producers and part (BCF) is lost to society.

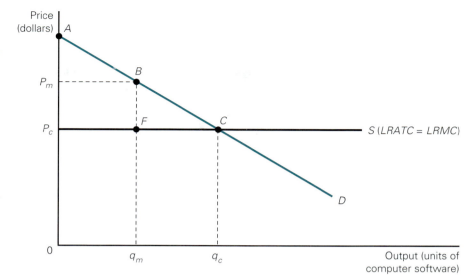

oly end of the spectrum; the area P_mBFP_c is redirected from consumers' surplus to producers' profits. In addition, society must also pay a deadweight loss (the area BCF in Figure 11.6) because price exceeds cost. This deadweight or social loss due to monopoly power or the power of cartels and oligopolies causes economists to criticize such structures.

As we have seen, monopolistic competition is something of a special case. Under monopolistic competition, there is a long-run tendency for price to equal average total cost, although price does not equal marginal cost when economies of scale are considered. The benefits of differentiated products—a greater range of choices—also exist in this structure. But the only unambiguously welfare-maximizing structure is that of pure competition. Only pure competition maximizes society's welfare by maximizing consumers' surplus.

This, of course, is a simple restatement of the discussion in Chapter 4. And it should be kept in mind that the model can fail to maximize economic welfare when monopoly power, externalities, and public goods are important aspects of market structure. In Part Four of this book we discuss each of these cases for the "failure" of the competitive model in detail.

APPLICATION

Diamonds, the De Beers Cartel, and the Russian Threat

De Beers Consolidated Mines markets more than 80 percent of the uncut diamonds sold yearly in the world. De Beers owns South African mines and acts as the marketing agent for virtually all other diamond-producing and supplying nations. De Beers pays royalties out of its retail sales to these nations for the exclusive rights to market their stones. Retailers must purchase wholesale boxes of diamonds from De Beers; if they refuse, they are not necessarily invited to purchase diamonds again. De Beers is, in short, one of the world's last great cartels.

The De Beers cartel system worked well until 1979, when a new diamond pipe was discovered in Australia and a worldwide recession created massive reductions in demand for diamonds. De Beers's earnings fell from $673 million in 1979 to $183

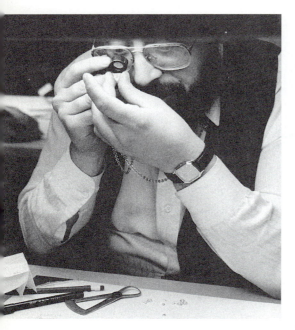

DeBeers leads the diamond cartel. Growing instability has characterized DeBeers' control over the last several decades.

million in 1982. Rather than reduce price in the face of declining demand, De Beers removed massive supplies of diamonds from the market by cutting production at its own mines to shore up the cartel price. De Beers also reduced purchases from participating nations in return for lump-sum payments. In all, De Beers added more than $1 billion worth of diamonds to its inventory between 1979 and 1982.

In 1981, Zaire pulled out of the cartel and entered into a five-year contract with three independent producers of industrial-quality diamonds, or boart. Although it was stockpiling diamonds in general, De Beers poured boart onto the market and encouraged illegal diamond smuggling by Zairian citizens. The result: Zaire's revenues and profits fell precipitously. The country was even refused loans from international agencies to upgrade its mines. In 1983, Zaire dropped the independent marketers in mid-contract. A cartel cheater was thus disciplined.

An important coup for De Beers was the securing of Australia as a member of the cartel. The two majority stockholders of Australia's huge Argyle mine had indirect ties to De Beers through a chain of stock ownership. Although there was opposition, De Beers's Australian friends helped bring Argyle within the cartel, but with some concessions: Australia is now free to market 25 percent of its industrial stones and 5 percent of its gemstones outside the cartel.

The worldwide recession of the early 1990s put new pressure on the cartel in the face of reduced demand and the desire to keep the cartel prices high.

As destructive as the threat of a global economic slowdown may appear, the event with the greatest potential for disrupting the cartel may be the dissolution of the Soviet Union. Large diamond deposits were found in Sakha, Russia's largest republic. In 1990, De Beers signed a five-year contract with Mikhail Gorbachev's government, agreeing to pay $5 billion for a mandatory sale of 95 percent of all of Russia's raw diamond production. Boris Yeltsin, however, has failed to honor the agreement and the future is (as always) uncertain.

De Beers has received uncut diamonds from Russia, but the Russians' failure to supply cut and polished stones suggests to some observers that Russia plans to establish new cutting and polishing plants in order to enter the more profitable market for "finished" diamonds. Further, it is known that the former Soviet Union stockpiled diamonds between the end of World War II and early 1990. The need for foreign exchange to aid the transition to markets and democracy in Russia is likely to prompt a sell-off of these valuable gems. De Beers continues to seek the cooperation of Moscow but has also—wisely—made deals with the regional and local governments in Sakha. De Beers is also establishing a diamond-cutting plant in Sakha.

By early 1996, the new contract was on hold due to the unwillingness of Russia to "toe the De Beers' line." While the Russian–De Beers agreement has maintained the cartel for over forty years, there has been evidence of cheating by Russia. Russian diamonds have appeared in increasing quantities at world cutting centers, in direct contravention of the cartel agreement. Though Russia's official "gem committee" (the State Committee on Precious Stones and Metals) denies it, Russia's own Interior Ministry admits that smuggling—as much as 748,000 carats of rough diamonds were sold between mid-1994 and January 1996—has been a much-used tactic. De Beers (predictably) matched the black-market price by reducing the charge on lower-quality stones by 15 percent in mid-1995. But how much cheating can the cartel take?

To make matters even worse, there are new threats from synthetic diamonds, both of industrial quality and of value in the gem market. Yellow-colored, gem-grade synthetic diamonds are being produced in and marketed by Russian interests even as De Beers is suspected of using strong-arm tactics to protect its market. Synthetics of industrial quality have been around since General Electric first "grew" synthetic diamond crystals in the 1950s. De Beers has also entered the synthetic market. But the Russians are the undisputed leaders, and the threat of Russian competition from high-quality synthetic stones, both of industrial and gem quality, is real.

De Beers apparently attempted both participation in Russian production and threats to accomplish the aims of the cartel in response to Russian competition in the later 1990s. De Beers wanted to mine diamonds in Siberia, but the deal fell through. (Russian interests must continue to be careful to avoid the flooding of the market by De Beers.) Another tactic considered by De Beers is to "brand" their diamonds by engraving a hallmark to designate quality.

De Beers is still in control of a huge segment of the diamond market, directing more than 80 percent of the $600 million industrial diamond business and 90 percent of the $5 billion annual market for jewelry-quality gems. But recessions, changing demand conditions, changing world political events, the technology and feasibility of synthetic gem production, and dissension within the diamond cartel will continue to challenge the successful operation of the De Beers cartel.

Sources: John R. Emshwiller and Neil Behrmann, "Restored Luster: How De Beers Revived World Diamond Cartel After Zaire's Pullout," *Wall Street Journal* (August 7, 1983); Vladimir Kvint, "Sorry, Mr. Oppenheimer," *Forbes* (February 15, 1993), pp. 42–43; Bill Gifford, "Pop Rocks," *The New Republic* (December 26, 1994), pp. 9–10; and Carol J. Williams, "Diamond Deal Not Forever, Russia Seems to Say," *Los Angeles Times* (December 29, 1995), p. A5.

QUESTION

Cartels are inherently unstable due to the profits that can be gained by cheating on the cartel agreement. What tactics have been used by De Beers to combat cheating by cartel members?

SUMMARY

1. Oligopoly is a market structure characterized by a few firms that recognize that their actions have an impact on one another's sales, prices, and profits. They may sell either homogeneous or differentiated products. Entry into the industry is difficult because of natural or artificial barriers.

2. When oligopolists recognize their mutual interdependence, they will engage in a variety of strategic behaviors, often trying to tacitly combine or collude. When these behaviors are successful, the market structure more closely resembles pure monopoly than pure competition, but tacit collusion does not result in all cases.

3. Game theory is an important tool for understanding oligopoly behavior because it focuses upon the variety of possible outcomes when mutual interdependence is recognized by a small number of firms selling competing products in the market.

4. The Cournot–Nash solution to the prisoner's dilemma in game theory is an important potential outcome in oligopoly markets. When the Cournot–Nash solution results from oligopoly behavior, it produces profits, outputs, and prices at levels midway between those produced under pure competition and pure monopoly.

5. Cheating appears as a dominant strategy in many games. Moreover, players may signal other players about their willingness to cooperate or to "repent" for earlier cheating. Such behavior, captured in games, helps explain a good deal of actual behavior that occurs among firms engaged in real-world competition and rivalry.

6. Cartels are formal or informal agreements among firms within an industry to restrict output or to segment the market in an effort to increase profits. The result may be similar to monopoly price and output in the industry.

7. There are potential profits for firms that cheat individually on a cartel. Cartels are therefore difficult to establish and maintain. The costs of enforcing the cartel agreement frequently jeopardize the cartel's survival.

8. Cartels can be legal or illegal. Those created and enforced by the government or those allowed to exist by government sanctions are legal. Cartels that form in the United States are illegal under antitrust laws.

KEY TERMS

oligopoly
mutual interdependence
cartel
game theory
prisoner's dilemma

dominant solution
tacit collusive solution
backward induction
cheat
market power

Cournot–Nash solution
price leadership
limit pricing
cartel enforcement

QUESTIONS FOR REVIEW AND DISCUSSION

1. What are the general characteristics of the oligopolistic market model? Compare and contrast these to the characteristics of the monopolistic competition model discussed in Chapter 10.

2. Imagine a student cartel. If your professor promised to assign a fixed number of each letter grade, regardless of class performance, is there any type of agreement that you could make with classmates to exploit this grading system? Under what circumstances (for instance, class size) would your student cartel be most likely to succeed?

3. Although it is easy to draw a hypothetical demand curve, it is difficult to determine the position of real-world demand curves. In order to maximize profits, however, managers must accurately estimate the demand for their products. In which case is this estimation more difficult—when the good in question is sold in a monopolistic market or when it is sold in an oligopolistic market? Explain.

4. Cite three personal experiences you have had with free-riding behavior.

5. Suppose that firms forming a cartel have different marginal costs. Describe, both in words and in a graph, how this situation complicates the various problems that a cartel must solve to be effective in raising prices.

6. What effect on the likelihood of collusion do the following factors have: (a) the purchase of an input in the same market (such as pigs at the stockyard); (b) long-term contracts with buyers; (c) selling to governments; (d) salespeople staying in the same motel on the road; (e) an industry trade association and price list?

7. Explain the solution to the prisoner's dilemma commonly known as the Cournot–Nash solution.

8. What is a tacit collusive solution in game theory and when might it occur?

9. How might a former cheater (who has learned her lesson) signal a competitor in a game theory situation that she is repentant and wants to cooperate again?

PROBLEMS

1. Suppose that you are one of two people hired to sell ads for a local newspaper during the summer. Your employer agrees to pay $350 per week plus a $2000 bonus to be divided by the two of you in proportion to the number of ads you sell. For example, if you sell three-fourths of the total, you get three-fourths of the bonus. Construct a simple payoff table, like the ones in Figures 11.1 and 11.2 of this chapter, in which the options for both you and your co-worker are spending little time trying to sell ads, spending some time trying to sell ads, or spending a lot of time trying to sell ads. Are there incentives for you to form a cartel? To cheat on it?

2. Suppose that you own one of two lawn care businesses in a small town. Each firm has costs (salaries, equipment, lawn chemicals, and the like). The payoff table shows the average weekly profits that you and your competitor may earn under different pricing policies. If you both charge a high price for your services, for example, you earn $1000 profit while your competitor earns $1200 profit. Use the table to answer the following questions.
   a. Why would you earn more profit than your competitor if you charge a lower price for lawn services?

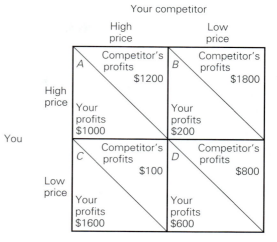

b. If you both engaged in price competition, what would be the outcome?
c. What would be the outcome if you both decided to maximize joint profits? What would be the risks?
d. If you formed a cartel, would there be an incentive to cheat? Explain.

WORKING WITH THE WEB

1. Strategic behavior becomes essential when the marketplace is not perfectly competitive. To try your hand at a game of strategy, go to http://serendip.brynmawr.edu/playground/pd.html, follow the instructions, and try your hand at some strategic behavior! Play the coin game repeatedly as instructed. Which strategy yields the best result in terms of the average number of coins you acquire? Why?

2. Licensing bodies such as the American Bar Association and the American Medical Association exist for many reasons. One of these is to create a barrier to entry into the profession. Without passing the Bar in a particular state and being licensed by the state, an individual cannot practice law. Go to www.mises.org, select "Daily Articles", and choose the link for June '98–October '98. Scroll through the list of articles until you find the article "Lawyer Cartels".
   a. According to Mr. Leef, why is the legal profession a cartel and how does it maintain its cartel status?
   b. What is the result of this cartel behavior for consumers of legal services?

P O I N T

Alfred Marshall

Joan Robinson

Alfred Marshall
and Joan
Robinson:
Perfect Versus
Imperfect
Markets

C O U N T E R P O I N T

Alfred Marshall (1842–1924) was the strong-willed son of a harsh father, who early on tried to coerce young Alfred into the ministry. Much to his parents' dismay, Marshall rejected a theological scholarship to Oxford University and entered Cambridge, where he received his M.S. in mathematics in 1865. From mathematics, Marshall veered into metaphysics. He joined a philosophy discussion group at Cambridge and lectured for almost ten years in moral science. During this period Marshall became convinced of the overriding importance of economics to individual and social action. In 1877, Marshall married Mary Paley, a former student, and moved to Bristol, where they both lectured on political economy at University College. In 1885, they returned to Cambridge, where Marshall continued his illustrious career as a lecturer in political economy.

The most important of Marshall's books was the modern bible of microeconomics, *Principles of Economics* (1890),[a] which he revised through eight editions. Many of the concepts presented in today's introductory economics courses, including the principles of perfect competition among firms, were first set down systematically by Marshall. His mathematical precision and fondness for lucid examples made the text, and economics generally, accessible and popular.

In 1903, while his work on *Principles* continued, Marshall succeeded in establishing economics as a discipline separate from moral science. He is also credited with founding the neoclassical tradition in economics—the modern version of economic principles established by Adam Smith.

Joan Robinson (1903–1983), like Alfred Marshall, spent most of her academic career at the University of Cambridge. She completed her B.A. in economics at Cambridge in 1925, the year after Marshall's death. She began a teaching career at Cambridge in 1931, at a time when Marshall's influence over the principles and methods of economics study was still great. Robinson is perhaps best known for her book *The Economics of Imperfect Competition* (1933),[b] which expands upon many of Marshall's conclusions about business organization and his theory of perfect competition.

Robinson's contributions to economics reach well beyond her theory of imperfect competition. In the mid-1930s, she and a small group of Cambridge economists helped John Maynard Keynes write his monumental *General Theory of Employment, Interest, and Money*, which ushered in a new era of macroeconomic theory. She also wrote in the areas of economic development, international trade, capital theory, and Marxian economics.

---

[a]Alfred Marshall, *Principles of Economics*, 8th ed. (London: Macmillan, 1920).

[b]Joan Robinson, *The Economics of Imperfect Competition* (London: Macmillan, 1933).

Although Robinson later questioned her own analysis of imperfect competition, her critique of Marshall's assumptions of the way the economy operates presents an interesting chapter in the development of economic thought.

The World of Perfect Competition

Although Marshall acknowledged the existence of monopolies and oligopolies, he believed that these market structures were a special case. To Marshall, the microeconomic behavior of firms and individuals was kept in constant check by the competitive nature of markets. The dynamics of free enterprise, of limitless entry to and exit from markets, enforced the norm of perfect competition among buyers and sellers. By his terms, each market is made up of sufficiently large numbers of competing firms buying and selling virtually identical products and services. No single demander or supplier of goods can affect the market price because no single firm has a large enough stake in the market. Given these conditions, the market price for goods would always gravitate to a level equal to the firm's costs of production. As a result, economic profits could not persist. Under the rigors of perfect competition, no firm would be able to rise above its equals.

To demonstrate his model of perfect competition, Marshall chose a number of illustrations, including the market for fresh fish. Marshall noted that the ordinary daily price of fish depends on intensity of demand, weather, and luck, all of which affect the size of the catch. He then introduced into this illustration a cattle plague that permanently increased the demand for fresh fish over beef. How would the competitively organized fish market react? (Remember that cold storage facilities were not readily available in Marshall's day.)

Under competitive conditions, the price per pound of fish would immediately rise. Recognizing that the price rise was not a temporary phenomenon, fishermen would respond to the increased profits (since price would now be greater than costs of production) by using their boats, fishing crews, and nets more intensively. Supply would be increased by these activities, as it would by the entry into the market of new fishing firms attracted by profits. Supply increases would ultimately bring price down to the average cost of catching fish.

Marshall's vision of perfect competition comports well with Adam Smith's theory of "the invisible hand." In fact, Marshall's theory of perfect competition describes the invisible hand at work. In his illustration, new fishing firms enter the market and old firms expand not for the benefit of customers but in hopes of earning more profits. They act only in their own self-interest but in doing so promote the interest of society. The price of fish falls to the costs of production in the long run, and more fish are provided in the market.

Perfect Competition Turned on Its Head

"It is customary," Joan Robinson wrote in *The Economics of Imperfect Competition*,"…to open with the analysis of a perfectly competitive world, and to treat monopoly as a special case….It is more proper to set out the analysis of monopoly, treating perfect competition as a special case." Beginning with these words, Robinson set out to refute Marshall's theory of perfect competition.

Modern industrialized societies, she contended, were dominated by monopolies (a single firm in a market) or oligopolies (a few large firms in a market). To a greater or lesser degree, most markets were influenced by the power of monopoly control. In other words, individual firms in these markets were large enough to affect market prices on their own. (Modern examples of imperfect competition include the automobile industry, dominated by industrial giants such as General Motors, or the fast-food industry, dominated by firms such as McDonald's.) Given these assumptions, Robinson pointed out, the prices of goods and services would not gravitate to a level equal to the firm's costs of production. Economic profits could persist, enabling dominant firms to maintain or increase their dominance.

To further illustrate her point that imperfect, rather than perfect, competition was the norm, Robinson pointed to the pervasive evidence of price discrimination in markets. Whereas Marshall contended that only one market price could prevail under perfect competition, Robinson saw many instances in which a single good or service could command several different prices in the same market. Multiple prices for the same product are possible only in a world of imperfect competition.

Challenges to Marshall's system of perfect competition by Joan Robinson and other economists have led to alterations in the theory. Modern economists stress the manner in which information affects suppliers and demanders, the consequences of potential competition and rivalry on markets, and the impact on Marshall's model of interpreting price as "full price."

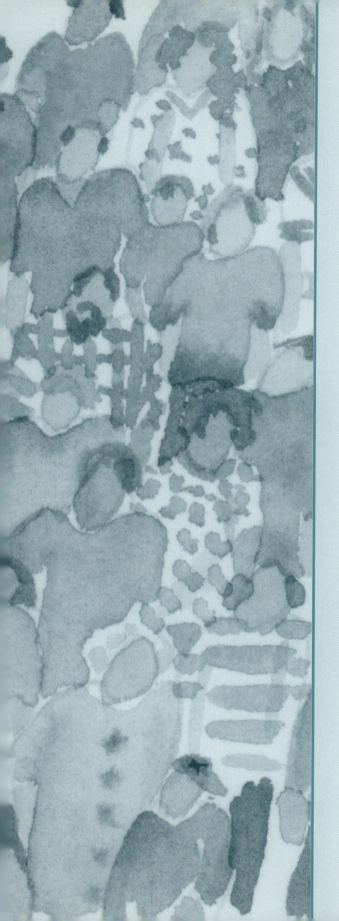

PART THREE

Input
Markets

3

Competitive Labor Markets

I n Chapter 3 we presented an overview of resource and product markets (see the circular flow model in Figure 3.1). We showed business firms as both suppliers of goods and services and demanders of inputs such as land, labor, capital, and entrepreneurship. Households were depicted both as demanders of goods and services and as suppliers of inputs. Up to this point in our study of microeconomics, we have focused on the upper part of the circular flow model and studied how the prices of final products such as psychiatric services, personal computers, and diapers are determined. We now turn to the lower part of the model to view firms as demanders or suppliers of inputs such as labor services, land, or capital. Specifically, we now inquire how input prices—wages of day laborers or engineers, lumber or machine prices—are determined. Once we know the economic process by which input values are determined, we will be able to understand better how and why people earn the incomes they do as owners of their own labor and other resources. After reading Chapter 12 you should understand

- how the demand for labor or any other input is related to its productivity and the demand for the product that the resource produces.
- the principles under which competitive firms demand labor and how income is generated by such demands.
- how human capital and its acquisition are related to individuals' wage rates and income-earning capacity.

FACTOR MARKETS: AN OVERVIEW

Factor market
A market in which the prices of productive resources (factors of production, or inputs) are determined by the interaction of firms acting as buyers with households and firms acting as suppliers of resources.

The markets in which input prices are determined are called **factor**, or resource, **markets**. The prices of factors such as wages, rent, and interest are determined through the interplay of supply and demand. Indeed, the theory of factor prices is just the familiar theory of demand and supply applied to factors of production.

We begin this chapter by presenting the marginal productivity theory of demand for one factor of production, labor. Although our example is labor, the marginal productivity theory is equally applicable to other factors of production, as we will see in Chapter 14, where we apply the theory to land and capital inputs. In the second part of this chapter, we present the theory of labor supply.

Derived Demand

Derived demand
The demand for factors of production that exists because of the demand for the products that the factors produce.

The demand for labor or any other factor of production is a **derived demand**. This term means that the demand for labor is directly related to the demand for the goods and services that the labor is used to produce. If the demand for computers increases, the derived demand for computer scientists and engineers will increase. If the demand for physical fitness increases, the derived demand for health foods and aerobics instructors will increase. If the demand for law and order increases, the derived demand for police officers will increase.

Derived demand also obeys the law of demand. All things being equal, if the price of health foods falls, more will be consumed; if the price of paper rises, fewer or shorter books will be published; if the rental prices on office space fall, more offices will be rented. So even though we call the demand for factors of production a derived demand, the law of demand applies to it in the same way that it applies to demand for final output.

Firms as Resource Price Takers

Just as there are different types of output market structures—such as competition, oligopoly, and monopoly—there are different types of resource markets. There can be perfectly competitive sellers and buyers of labor, for example. In such cases, there are large numbers of both buyers (employing firms) and sellers (workers) of a homogeneous type of labor. There can also be various types of imperfect competition in buying and selling labor, as we will learn in the next chapter. We limit the discussion in this chapter to a competitive labor market.

The following discussion of labor demand examines labor markets in which a large number of firms hire a single type of labor and a large number of people are willing to supply the labor. There are, of necessity, simplifications in our discussion. For example, we all know that labor comes in many alternative "qualities," depending on training, education, and other matters. To keep matters simple, however, we assume that labor is homogeneous. Another important simplification relates to the nature of the "wage rate." In reality, the wage that workers receive includes many factors other than the money wage. A full wage includes all nonmoney wage benefits, such as retirement plans, health insurance, vacation policy, and so on, in addition to the money wage payment. Although we mention only a wage rate in this chapter—without any elaboration of the nonwage benefits—we are referring to the full wage paid to workers.

Competitive labor market

A labor market in which the wage rate is determined by the interactions of a large number of sellers (suppliers) of labor and a large number of demanders (buyers) of labor. Neither group acts in a collusive manner.

Market demand for labor

The total quantity of labor demanded at various wage rates, other things constant. The sum of all individual firms' demands for a type of labor. The firms may or may not all be in the same industry.

Market supply of labor

The sum of all individuals' supplies of a type of labor. The total quantity of labor people will offer to the market at various wage rates, other things being equal.

In a **competitive labor market**, the wage rate is determined by the familiar forces of supply and demand. The **market demand for labor** is the sum of all firms' demand for the type of labor in question. All the firms may not be in the same industry—that is, they may not all produce the same product—but they all employ the same type of labor. For example, the demand curve in Figure 12.1a could represent the market demand for electricians. This overall demand would be found by summing the demand for electricians by all buyers of their labor, from AT&T and General Motors to construction companies, cable television companies, and even homeowners.

The **market supply of labor** is obtained by horizontally summing the supply of individual workers. As indicated by the supply curve S_m in Figure 12.1a, as the wage rate rises, a larger quantity of labor is supplied. The supply of labor to any particular occupation thus follows the familiar law of supply.

The interaction of supply and demand for labor results in an equilibrium wage W_0. Once this wage is established, the individual buyers of labor are price takers. That is, the firms must accept W_0 as the prevailing wage and may hire as many workers as they are willing and able to hire at that wage. Being perfectly competitive buyers of labor, employing firms face an infinitely elastic labor supply curve, as shown in Figure 12.1b. All buyers of any good or service who are price takers face an infinitely elastic supply curve.

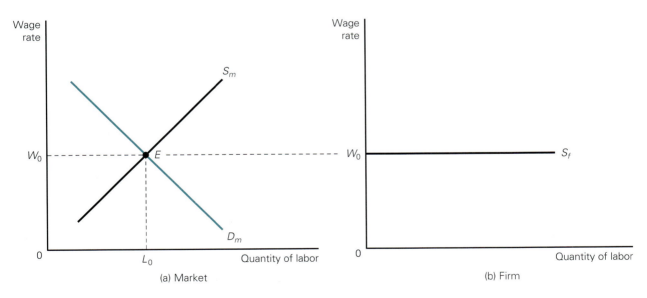

(a) Market   (b) Firm

FIGURE 12.1

The Firm as a Wage Price Taker

(a) The equilibrium wage, W_0, is determined in the competitive market by the market supply, S_m, and demand, D_m, for a particular type of labor. (b) The firm must pay wage rate W_0 for workers but is able to hire all it wants at that wage. The supply of labor to the competitive firm, S_f, is totally elastic at the prevailing wage. Note that while the scale for the wage rate is the same for both graphs, the scale for quantity of labor is smaller for the individual firm than for the market.

MARGINAL PRODUCTIVITY THEORY

We cannot say exactly how many electricians or computer programmers will be demanded within a given time period, but we can present some general rules about how the numbers of people demanded in these occupations might rise or fall. In this analysis, we reencounter many principles from earlier chapters. All apply equally to the demand for resource inputs, including labor.

The Profit-Maximizing Level of Employment

The firm hiring labor in a competitive market faces a market-determined wage. Since the equilibrium wage is established, the point of interest becomes the quantity of labor that an individual firm chooses to hire. If a firm is selling its product in a perfectly competitive product market, then how much labor will it hire at a particular wage rate?

To answer this question, let us say that the firm has many inputs, one of which is labor. Also, let the quantities of all inputs except labor be fixed. Labor, in other words, is the only variable input. (These circumstances, as you may recognize, describe a short-run situation for the firm.) To produce more output, the firm must hire more labor. The firm wishes to maximize profits and must therefore hire the profit-maximizing amount of labor.

Suppose the firm in this instance is a corn farmer who must decide whether to hire a worker to help pick and husk corn. How does the farmer make this decision? Hiring the worker will increase output, and the increase in production will be sold to obtain revenue. At the same time, hiring the worker will increase the cost of production because the farm worker must be paid. The farmer makes a profit-maximizing decision *at the margin*. If hiring the worker increases total revenue more than it increases total cost, then hiring the worker will increase profits. The farmer will always hire a worker if doing so increases profits.

Suppose the farmer is thinking about hiring a second worker. The same decision process is repeated. If the second worker adds more to revenue than to cost, then he or she will be hired. This process continues with every prospective worker. An important and familiar principle is in action: *the law of diminishing marginal returns*. As more and more of a variable input is added to a production process in which there is a fixed input, the marginal product of the variable input eventually declines. As more workers are hired, the extra output of each worker eventually falls. Since each additional worker adds less and less to total output, the additional revenues that each worker produces eventually fall below the additional cost of hiring. At some point, the farmer will stop hiring altogether. In short, the profit-maximizing farmer should hire all workers that add more to revenue than to cost but stop hiring at the point where the addition to revenue is just equal to the addition to cost.

The example of a corn farmer can also be expressed in economic terms. The extra output that each additional unit of labor adds to total output is called the **marginal product of labor** *(MP$_L$):*

Marginal product of labor (MP_L)

The additional output produced that results from hiring an additional unit of labor; change in total output divided by change in quantity of labor input used.

$$MP_L = \frac{\Delta TP}{\Delta L},$$

where MP_L is the marginal product of labor, ΔTP is the change in total product, and ΔL is a one-unit increase in labor. Adding units of the variable input to other fixed inputs will eventually lead to a decrease in the marginal product of the variable input in the short run.

Table 12.1 summarizes the hypothetical choices available to the corn farmer. The first column shows the units of labor, in number of worker-hours. The second column shows the marginal product of the workers—the amount by which total output increases as one more unit of labor is added to the production process. The first unit of labor adds 14 units of output (bushels of corn), the second adds 12 units of output, and so forth. MP_L decreases as the amount of labor increases, according to the law of diminishing marginal returns.

When the extra corn produced by each additional unit of labor is sold, the resulting increase in total revenue is called the **marginal revenue product of labor** (MRP_L):

Marginal revenue product of labor (MRP_L)
The additional revenue that results from selling the additional output produced by hiring an additional unit of labor; marginal revenue times marginal product of labor.

$$MRP_L = \frac{\Delta TR}{\Delta L},$$

where MRP_L is the mrginal revenue product of labor, ΔTR is the change in total revenue, and ΔL is the change in the amount of labor hired.

Another method of expressing MRP_L is

$$MRP_L = MR_C \times MP_L,$$

where MR_C is the marginal revenue under competitive conditions (the increase in total revenue resulting from selling one more unit of output) and MPL is the marginal product of labor.

For the firm that sells its product in a perfectly competitive market, marginal revenue is equal to the price of the product. Thus, the marginal revenue product (MRP) is simply the price (P) of the product times the marginal product (MP) of each unit. As shown in Table 12.1, the marginal revenue product of the first unit of labor is found by multiplying its marginal product, 14, by the price of the product, $2, to obtain $28. The MRP_L declines as more workers are hired because MP_L declines.

TABLE 12.1

A Marginal Revenue Product Schedule for Labor

The marginal revenue product of labor in column (4) falls as more units of labor are employed because the marginal product of labor in column (2) falls. The firm will hire additional units of labor up to the point where the extra revenue these units generate just equals the extra cost of paying for them. At this point, 6 units of labor, $MRP_L = MFC_L$.

(1) Units of Labor (worker-hours)	(2) Marginal Product of Labor MP_L (bushels of corn)	(3) Marginal Revenue $MR_C = P_C$ (dollars per bushel)	(4) Marginal Revenue Product $MRP_L = MR_C \times MP_L$	(5) Marginal Factor Cost (dollars per hour) $MFC_L = $ Wage
1	14	$2	$28	$8
2	12	2	24	8
3	10	2	20	8
4	8	2	16	8
5	6	2	12	8
6	4	2	8	8
7	2	2	4	8
8	0	2	0	8

Regardless of the economic shorthand used, the profit-maximizing firm will continue adding units of labor as long as the additional revenues the labor produces are greater than the additional costs of the labor. The firm will stop hiring when the additional revenues are less than the additional costs of hiring. The extra cost of hiring one more unit of labor is called the **marginal factor cost of labor** (MFC_L):

Marginal factor cost of labor (MFC_L)

The change in total costs associated with employing one additional unit of labor.

$$MFC_L = \frac{\Delta TC}{\Delta L},$$

where MFC_L is the marginal factor cost of labor and ΔTC is the change in total cost. Under competitive conditions, the firm may purchase all of the labor it wants at the prevailing wage rate. Each additional unit of labor in Table 12.1 has a marginal factor cost equal to the wage rate (shown as $8 on the schedule).

The profit-maximizing firm will hire labor up to the point where $MRP_L = MFC_L$. With the numbers in Table 12.1, this equation indicates that it will be most profitable for the farmer to hire 6 units of labor. Each unit from the first to the sixth adds more to revenue than to cost. By hiring 6 units, the farmer adds as much as possible to profit. However, the seventh unit adds more to cost than to revenue and therefore will not be hired.

This process should sound familiar: It is the mirror image of how the competitive firm determines its profit-maximizing output. The firm follows the same process to equate its marginal cost to marginal revenue in hiring inputs as it does in selling its output. In fact, when the firm hires the profit-maximizing quantity of labor, that amount of labor will produce the profit-maximizing level of output.

The numbers used in Table 12.1 are presented in graph form in Figure 12.2. The MP_L curve is drawn in Figure 12.2a by plotting the points from columns (1) and (2). The demand curve for the farmer's corn is shown in Figure 12.2b, where $P = \$2$. The MRP_L is found by multiplying marginal revenue by marginal product; the result is the marginal revenue product curve in Figure 12.2c.

The prevailing wage is $8, stated as MFC_L. The profit-maximizing quantity of labor is the point where the MFC_L curve crosses the MRP_L curve. At this point, the marginal revenue product of labor equals the marginal factor cost of labor.

Profit-Maximizing Rules for All Inputs

Firms employ many inputs other than labor. The profit-maximizing rule for the level of employment is the same for each resource. The corn farmer may be planning to use fertilizer, for example. If he applies 1 unit of fertilizer—a 100-pound bag—the amount of corn produced will increase. The extra corn is treated as the marginal product of the first bag of fertilizer. The extra revenue that results is the marginal revenue product, and the extra cost of the bag is the marginal factor cost. If the MRP of the fertilizer is greater than or equal to the MFC, then the farmer will purchase and use the fertilizer. The profit-maximizing amount of fertilizer is found at the point where the MRP of fertilizer is just equal to the MFC.

This rule applies to all inputs, such as tractors, seed, land, tractor drivers, and water. The profit-maximizing quantity of all inputs is the amount that makes the MRP of each input equal to the MFC of each input, or

$$\frac{MRP_1}{MFC_1} = \frac{MRP_2}{MFC_2} = \frac{MRP_3}{MFC_3} = \cdots = \frac{MRP_N}{MFC_N} = 1,$$

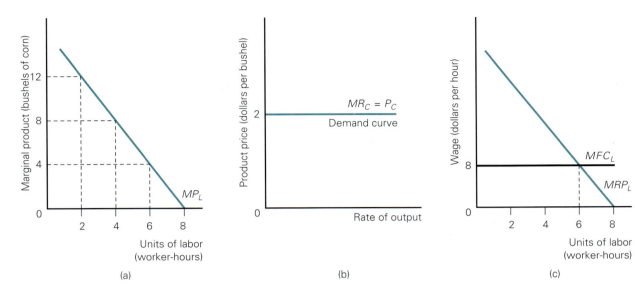

FIGURE 12.2

The Firm's Marginal Revenue Product Curve
(a) The farmer's marginal product of labor (MP_L) curve is plotted from columns (1) and (2) in Table 12.1. (b) The demand curve for the farmer's product is determined by the product price ($P_C = MR_C$ in this perfectly competitive market). (c) The marginal revenue product of labor (MRP_L) curve is found by multiplying MP_L by MR_C. The profit-maximizing firm hires labor up to the point where the marginal revenue product of labor equals marginal factor cost of labor (MFC_L). With a wage of $8 and a product price of $2, the firm will hire up to 6 units of labor.

where the subscripts 1, 2, and 3 indicate the MRP and MFC of the first, second, and third inputs, and N indicates the total number of inputs used. Each ratio of MRP to MFC is equal to 1 because the MRP of each is equal to the MFC of each. Under this condition, all inputs are employed in the profit-maximizing amounts.

THE DEMAND FOR LABOR

Marginal productivity theory gives insight into the purchasing behavior of firms. In the short run, when labor is the only variable input, the firm is willing to purchase or hire additional units up to the point at which $MRP = MFC$. The firm's marginal revenue product curve (Figure 12.2c) thus traces the relation between the price of labor (the wage rate) and the amount of labor a firm is willing to purchase. In other words, the marginal revenue product curve is also the firm's short-run demand curve for labor. Figure 12.3 illustrates this. At wage W_0 the firm chooses L_0 units of labor. A higher wage such as W_1 results in less labor hired. For each wage, the firm adjusts the level of employment to maintain the equation $MRP_L = MFC_L$. In the following sections we examine the demand for labor from several perspectives.

The Short-Run Market Demand for Labor

A single firm's demand for labor in the short run is equivalent to its marginal revenue product of labor. To obtain the overall market demand for labor in the short run, we must make some additional calculations.

Each firm will demand labor up to the point where $MRP_L = MFC_L$. Thus, at a particular wage, the market demand for labor may be shown as the sum of all the firms' MRP_L curves. Figure 12.4 shows such a curve, MRP_{L_0}. This curve represents the sum of all the firms' short-run demand curves for a particular type of labor. The curve

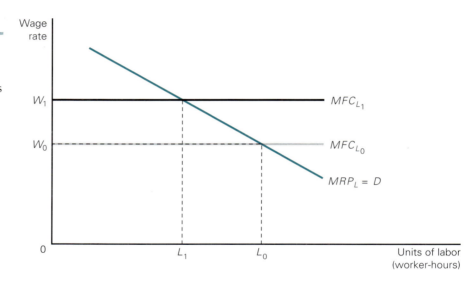

FIGURE 12.3

The Firm's Short-Run Demand for Labor

The firm hires labor up to the point where the wage is equal to the marginal revenue product of labor (MRP_L). The marginal revenue product curve shows the various quantities of labor the firm is willing to hire at all the different wage rates when labor is the only variable input.

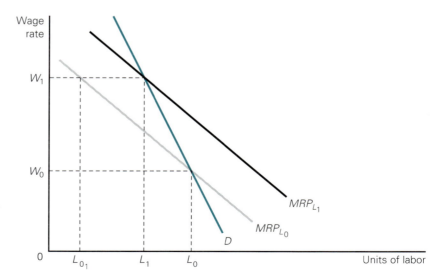

FIGURE 12.4

The Short-Run Market Demand for Labor

MRP_{L_0} represents the sum of all the firm's marginal revenue product curves for a particular occupation. When the wage for this occupation is W_0, the firms hire L_0 units of labor. If the wage rises to W_1, the firms initially hire the lower L_{0_1} units of labor. However, the increase in wages causes an increase in the price of the product. The higher product price shifts the sum of the firm's MRP_{L_0} to MRP_{L_1}. At W_1, when labor is the only variable input, the firms hire L_1 units of labor. D represents the short-run market demand curve for labor because it allows for changes in the wage rate.

labeled MRP_{L_0}, however, is not the short-run market demand curve for this type of labor, although it does establish one point on the short-run market demand curve, D.

To establish the whole demand curve, we must examine what happens when the wage rate changes. Imagine the overall demand for cornhuskers. Many farmers employ huskers at wage W_0; the total number of cornhuskers employed at W_0 is L_0. Recall that the MRP_L curve is obtained by multiplying the price of corn by the marginal product of labor. If the wage rate rises to W_1, then each firm's costs of production will rise. Initially, the employment of labor is cut back to L_{0_1}, along the original MRP_{L_0} curve. However, the increased costs of production will decrease the supply of corn and increase the equilibrium price. To obtain the new MRP_L curve (MRP_{L_1}), we multiply the marginal product of labor by the new, higher price of corn, and we sum this quantity over all the firms. The new wage, W_1, and level of employment, L_1, establish a second point on the short-run market demand curve. The short-run market demand curve, D, differs from the sum of the MRP_L curves because it allows for increases in the price of the product that result from wage increases. Note, however, that the demand curve, D, obeys the law of demand. When the wage rate rises, given other factors, less labor is ultimately employed.

The Firm's Long-Run Demand for Labor

Firm's long-run demand for labor
The relationship between all possible wage rates and quantities demanded of labor at those wage rates, given that the firm has enough time to vary the usage of all inputs.

We have so far concentrated on the short-run demand for labor, in which labor is the only variable input. In the long run, many adjustments occur when wages change. Allowed enough time, firms may vary all inputs. Also, at the industry level, not only does the price of products change directly with wages, but the number of firms changes as well.

Suppose that the market wage rate for cornhuskers increases. What happens in the long run? First, farmers will adjust to the higher price of labor by hiring fewer cornhuskers; given enough time, they may turn to substitute inputs for this type of labor, perhaps by buying combines rather than hiring human huskers. Second, the increase in the price of labor increases the farmers' costs of production. With the increase in costs, the supply of the product decreases, and its price rises. Finally, the number of firms will adjust, establishing a new equilibrium. The number of firms, in the end, is likely to decrease. When wages rise, more workers lose their jobs in the long run than in the short run; when wages fall, more workers are hired in the long run than in the short run. In other words, long-run market demand is more elastic than short-run market demand.

Changes in the Demand for Labor

Change in the demand for labor
A shift of the entire labor demand curve; caused by a change in the marginal product of labor, by a change in the demand for the product produced by the type of labor in question, or by a change in the price of some other factor of production.

What causes an increase or decrease in the demand for a particular type of labor? Why would the demand for chemical engineers suddenly increase? Or why would a restaurant suddenly hire more waiters and cooks? Such questions may be answered by examining the origins of the demand for labor and the behavior of profit-maximizing firms.

The demand for labor is derived from the demand for the product the labor produces and the marginal product of the labor itself. If either of these increases or decreases, then the demand for labor will increase or decrease in the same direction. Understanding this relation simplifies things; however, further details are of value.

1. *If the demand for the product that labor produces changes, then the demand for labor will change in the same direction.* Remember that for a competitive firm, the marginal revenue product of an input is equal to marginal revenue (the output price) times marginal product. If the demand for the good increases, then its price increases and the demand for labor (*MRP*) and all other inputs also increases. The demands for electronics technicians and computer components have increased because the demand for personal computers has increased.

   The opposite situation occurs when the demand for a product decreases. If the price of a product falls, then the demand for inputs used to produce that product falls. When the demand for American-made cars decreases, the demand for domestic autoworkers decreases (along with the demand for tires and steel).

2. *If the marginal product of labor changes, then the demand for that labor will change in the same direction.* The productivity of a particular type of labor depends to a very large extent on the firm's employment of other inputs in the production process. Additional expenditures on other inputs often increase the productivity of labor. For example, the marginal product of farm workers is influenced by the amounts of other inputs that the farmer buys, such as land, equipment, seed, fertilizer, and water. If such inputs increase the workers' productivity, their use will also increase demand for the workers' labor.

Complementary inputs

Inputs with a relation such that increased usage of one input due to a fall in its price results in increased employment of the other(s).

The relation between the quantity of nonlabor inputs and the productivity of labor can be direct or inverse. In other words, increasing the amount of one input may either increase or decrease the productivity of labor. If increased usage of one input due to a decrease in that input's price increases the marginal product of labor and thus increases the amount of labor hired at any given wage, then this input and labor are **complementary inputs**. For example, if the farmer uses more fertilizer, then cornhuskers can produce more output; their marginal product increases. Increases in inputs that complement labor will increase the demand for labor.

Substitute inputs

Inputs with a relation such that increased employment of one input due to a fall in its price results in decreased usage of the other(s).

If increased usage of one input decreases the marginal product of labor and thus decreases the amount of labor hired at any given wage, then that input is called a substitute input for labor. For cornpickers and huskers, a combine that picks and husks is a **substitute input**. If the farmer uses more combines, then the marginal product of human huskers and pickers will decrease, and so will the demand for them.

Why would a farmer suddenly choose to purchase more fertilizer or combines? A firm makes decisions on the basis of expected profits. For example, if the price of fertilizer falls, then it is in the farmer's interest to purchase more fertilizer. If the price of combines falls, then the farmer will purchase more combines. Thus, if the price of a complementary input falls, the demand for labor rises. If the price of a substitute input falls, the demand for labor decreases.

In addition to changes in the quantity of inputs, technological advances may shift the demand for labor. New production techniques may increase or decrease the demand for labor in a particular occupation. In fact, technological change generally increases the marginal product of some workers and decreases that of others. Technological change can, for example, result in robots being more adept than factory workers at performing certain tasks. As a consequence, the marginal product of factory workers falls and the demand for their labor decreases. At the same time, the marginal revenue product of workers who make robots rises as the demand for and the price of robots increases. This produces an increase in the demand for workers who make robots.

Monopoly and the Demand for Labor

We have spoken so far of demand for labor only under conditions of competition. What if the firm demanding labor enjoyed a monopoly in its output market but was still a purely competitive buyer of labor? What would the farmer's demand for labor be if he were the only producer of corn? Recall from Chapter 8 that the demand curve for the monopolist's product is downward sloping. This suggests that as the firm hires more workers and increases output, the price of the product must fall for the firm to sell the extra output. As the firm hires more labor, not only is the marginal product of labor falling but the product price is falling as well.

Even though the price of the product is falling as more output is produced, marginal revenue product, *MRP*, still describes the change in total revenue that results from hiring one more unit of labor. As before, *MRP* is equal to marginal revenue times marginal product. The difference is that the marginal revenue of the competitive seller is equal to the market price, whereas the monopolist's marginal revenue is a downward-sloping curve, derived from its demand curve.

Table 12.2 is a numerical example showing the difference between the marginal revenue product of labor under competition (MRP_C) and under monopoly conditions (MRP_m). The MRP_C is calculated as shown in Table 12.1: marginal product of labor (MP_L) multiplied by the *constant* marginal revenue of the competitive firm (MR_C). *Remember*: Under competition, marginal revenue equals the price charged, since—being a price taker—the competitive firm can sell all of its units of output at the same competitive price. This means that $MR_C = P_C$.

The marginal revenue product of labor under monopoly is found by multiplying the marginal product of labor (MP_L) by monopoly marginal revenue (MR_m).

TABLE 12.2

**Calculation of Marginal Revenue Product
Under Competition and Monopoly**

Since the marginal product of labor declines, the marginal revenue product falls with increases in labor input under both competition and monopoly in product markets. Under monopoly, MRP_m also declines because marginal revenue falls as the monopolist expands output.

(1) Units of Labor (worker-hours)	(2) Marginal Product of Labor MP_L (bushels of corn)	(3) Marginal Revenue (Competition) $MR_C = P_C$ (dollars per bushel)	(4) Marginal Revenue (Monopoly) $MR_m < P_m$	(5) Marginal Revenue Product (Competition) $MRP_C = MR_C \times MP_L$	(6) Marginal Revenue Product (Monopoly) $MRP_m = MR_m \times MP_L$
1	14	$2	$8	$28	$112
2	12	2	7	24	84
3	10	2	6	20	60
4	8	2	5	16	40
5	6	2	4	12	24
6	4	2	3	8	12
7	2	2	2	4	4
8	0	2	1	0	0

The marginal product of labor (MP_L) is the same under competition or monopoly conditions. What changes is the marginal revenue that the monopoly firm can obtain from selling more units of its product or service. The marginal revenue obtainable from selling additional units of output declines with each additional unit sold. As the monopolist sells more, he or she must reduce prices on the previous number of units sold, which means that the marginal revenue from additional sales declines more rapidly than price. In Table 12.2 this declining marginal revenue is shown in column (4). Since MR declines as more units of labor are hired (and more units of output are produced), the MRP falls more rapidly under monopoly conditions, shown in column (6), than in competitive conditions, shown in column (5).

A graphical comparison of the purely competitive firm's demand for labor and the monopolist's demand for labor is shown in Figure 12.5. The monopolist's MRP diminishes more quickly than the pure competitor's because not only is the marginal product of labor falling, but the monopolist's marginal revenue is falling as well, while the marginal revenue of the pure competitor remains constant.

A firm that enjoys a monopoly in its output market does not necessarily have any advantage in resource markets. For example, your local electric company may have exclusive rights as the only seller of electricity in your area. But this monopoly position does not imply that the electric company is the only employer of electricians, computer programmers, or bookkeepers. For these occupations, the monopoly is a purely competitive buyer of labor and must pay a competitive market wage for its labor. The marginal factor cost of labor is equal to the wage rate because the supply of labor to the firm is infinitely elastic.

In the end, the monopolist's decisions in hiring labor require the same marginal analysis as for any other firm. The firm will hire any unit of labor when its marginal revenue product is greater than its marginal factor cost and will continue to hire labor up to the point where the MRP_L is equal to MFC_L. The only difference for a monopoly firm is that its marginal revenue falls along with the labor's marginal product. The Focus "The Marginal Revenue Product of Professional Baseball Players" discusses these ideas as they relate to a special labor market.

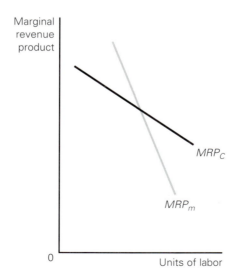

FIGURE 12.5

The Monopolist's *MRP* Versus the Competitive Firm's *MRP*

The marginal revenue product for each firm, obtained by multiplying marginal revenue by marginal product. The monopolist's marginal revenue curve is downward sloping, and the competitive firm's is equal to a given and constant product price; therefore, the monopolist's demand for labor, MRP_m, diminishes more rapidly than the competitive firm's, MRP_C.

FOCUS

The Marginal Revenue Product of Professional Baseball Players

The extra revenue that a firm obtains from hiring a worker is the marginal revenue product; if this is higher than the extra cost of the worker's wages, then the firm adds to its profits by employing the worker. Baseball players' salaries have increased sharply in the last few years, especially for superstars. Are they worth it? Are their *MRP*s greater than their wages?

Addressing this question in the 1970s, economist Gerald Scully calculated the extra revenues that team owners received from hitters and pitchers. He first found that a player's contribution to his team's win–loss record was best measured for pitchers by the percent each added to the team's strikeout-to-walk ratios and for batters by the contribution of each to the team's batting average. Using this information, Scully then estimated the total team revenue, where revenue is simply the number of tickets sold per season times the average ticket price. After adjusting for the size of the city in which the team played its home games, the age of the stadium, the team's league, and other factors affecting revenue, he calculated that every point added to the team batting average by a batter increased the team's revenue by $9504. Similarly, every .01 point added to the pitching staff's strike-out-to-walk ratio increased revenue $9297.

Once he estimated player *MRP*s, it was a straightforward calculation for Scully to determine whether the salary paid to a particular player was commensurate with the amount the player added to team revenue. For example, star hitters added from $250,000 to $383,700 to team revenues. Star pitchers contributed even more, from $321,700 to $479,000. However, during the 1968 and 1969 seasons, no player in Scully's sample was paid more than $125,000. He concluded, therefore, that players' salaries were well below their *MRP*s, with the greatest deficiency being the superstars' salaries. Scully's results help explain free agency and the huge increases in players' salaries in the 1970s, 1980s, and early 1990s. Today, numerous baseball players make more than $3 million per year. And, as salaries have grown, increasingly sophisticated attempts to measure players' marginal revenue value have been made, such as Bill James's *Baseball Abstract*.

Source: Gerald W. Scully, "Pay and Performance in Major League Baseball," *American Economic Review* 64 (December 1974), pp. 915–930.

THE SUPPLY OF LABOR

Now that we have some insight into the demand for labor, the next logical category is labor supply. We know that labor supply in competitive markets is highly elastic. But this fact does not answer two important questions: What determines the overall, or aggregate, supply of labor, and how are wage rates and labor supply interrelated?

Individual Labor Supply

Individuals in free markets are able to choose whether to offer their labor services in the market, and individuals' labor market decisions are based on the principle of utility maximization. The individual must choose between time spent in the market earning the wage that he or she may command and time spent in

Nonmarket activities
Anything an individual does while not working that directly or indirectly yields utility.

nonmarket activities, such as going to school, keeping house, tending a garden, or watching television.

Fortunately, the individual does not have to make an all-or-nothing choice. No one chooses to work twenty-four hours a day, seven days a week. People can divide their time between market and nonmarket activities. How many hours would one choose to work during an average week? This question cannot be easily answered, but we can speculate about the effect that the wage rate may have on an individual's labor supply choices.

A supply curve relates the quantity supplied of a commodity to its price. Applied to labor supply, it is a schedule that relates the quantity of work offered and different wage rates. The labor supply curve of an individual is given in Figure 12.6. The first thing to observe about this person's labor supply curve, S_i, is that below w_1 she would prefer not to work at all; she chooses all nonmarket activity. This cutoff occurs because wages below w_1 do not meet her opportunity cost; she receives more utility from nonmarket activities than she would from the income received from working. Wage w_1 may not be high enough to encourage her to forgo playing tennis, painting the house, or attending school, for example. At wages immediately above w_1, the hours of labor she supplies respond positively to increases in pay. As her wage rate rises from w_1 to w_2, the hours she is willing to supply increase accordingly, to q_2.

The value of one hour of market time (one hour spent working) is equal to the wage rate. This means that for each hour an individual chooses to enjoy nonmarket activities, he or she is forgoing an hour of pay. In other words, the opportunity cost or the price an individual must pay for an hour of leisure time is the wage rate. As the wage rate rises, the price of nonmarket time also rises. An individual's demand for nonmarket time is downward sloping, just as it is for any other good. If the wage rate rises, the individual is encouraged to opt for less nonmarket activity; that is, he or she is encouraged to substitute hours of work for hours of leisure.

FIGURE 12.6

Individual Labor Supply

The individual labor supply curve, the number of hours offered at various wages, may be positively or negatively sloped. If the substitution effect is greater than the income effect, the curve is upward sloping, as shown from w_1 to w_3. The individual substitutes hours of work for hours of nonmarket activities. As the individual's wage rises beyond w_3, his or her demand for nonmarket time increases. The income effect is greater than the substitution effect, and the curve is negatively sloped above wage rate w_3.

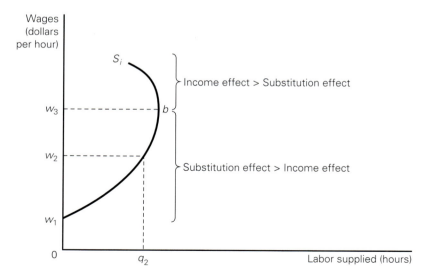

The substitution effect, however, may be offset by an income effect. As the wage rate rises, the individual's income rises. If nonmarket time is a normal good, as we might expect, then the demand for nonmarket time will increase as income rises. This type of income effect will encourage the individual to enjoy more nonmarket time and less work.

As the wage rate rises, the two effects pull the worker in opposite directions. The effect that dominates will determine whether higher wages encourage more or fewer hours of work and determine whether the labor supply curve is positively or negatively sloped. If the substitution effect is greater than the income effect, higher wages will bring more hours of labor. In Figure 12.6, the substitution effect is greater than the income effect from w_1 to w_3, so the slope is positive. However, the income effect is greater than the substitution effect at wages above w_3. In this range, higher wages bring fewer hours of labor, so the curve is negatively sloped. At point b, where the income and substitution effects are equal, the supply curve begins to bend backward.

The labor supply curves of different individuals would, in all likelihood, be shaped differently. Within a given range of wage rates, one person's labor supply curve may be positively sloped, while another person's may be negatively sloped. This could be due to differences in tastes and preferences for leisure time. The wage level that initially entices people to enter the labor market may vary across individuals for the same reason. Additionally, it would be theoretically difficult to say at which particular wage rate any one person's labor supply curve becomes backward-bending—that is, the wage rate at which the income effect becomes greater than the substitution effect.

Since the shapes of individual labor supply curves are difficult to determine, the slope of the total or aggregate labor supply curve is difficult to predict with accuracy. The aggregate labor supply curve is theoretically obtained by summing individuals' labor supply curves horizontally. The aggregate curve shows the total amount of labor supplied at all the different wages. Even though some individuals have backward-bending labor supply curves, we expect the aggregate labor supply curve to be positively sloped, as in Figure 12.7, for two reasons. First, as wages

FIGURE 12.7

The Aggregate Supply of Labor

The aggregate labor supply curve, S_A, representing the number of hours of labor supplied by all individuals, is likely to be upward sloping. As wages rise, more people join the labor force, and many people work more hours.

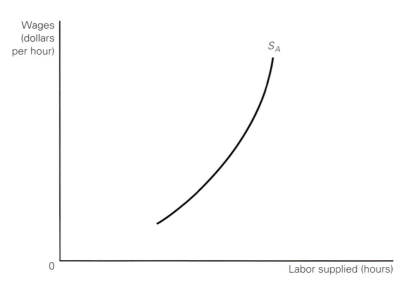

rise, many workers will work more hours. Second, as wages rise, more people will enter the labor force.

Human Capital

Some occupations, such as medicine, law, and nuclear physics, require many years of training. The fact that the wages in these skilled professions are higher than the wages of unskilled labor is not coincidental. Before people are willing to endure the years of training to become highly skilled professionals, they must be reasonably sure that their investment of time and other resources will pay off in the long run. People frequently choose to invest in some form of training to make themselves more productive and to enhance their income-earning potential. While a person is going to college, attending trade school, or gaining on-the-job training, he or she is building **human capital**.

Human capital

Any quality, characteristic, or skill an individual has that enhances the individual's productivity, such as education and job experience.

Gaining human capital requires an investment period, such as four years in college. This investment involves a large opportunity cost. A college student loses the next-best alternative when attending college. For many students, the lost opportunity is the income they would have earned if working. Figure 12.8 portrays a simplified version of two alternative lifetime income streams for an individual.

After graduating from high school at age 18, individuals have a choice. They may enter the labor market immediately and earn income stream Y_N from that time until retirement at age 65 or so. This income stream could rise through the years as the individuals acquire job-related skills, but for simplicity we let it remain constant.

Some individuals go to college. From age 18 to age 22, they do not earn steady, full-time income. The opportunity cost of going to college—that is, the income the individuals forgo by choosing not to work—is represented by the shaded area above the horizontal-axis between ages 18 and 22. In addition, they must pay the direct costs of college—tuition, books, and so on. The shaded area below the horizontal-axis between ages 18 and 22 represents the direct costs of college, a nega-

FIGURE 12.8

The Economic Costs and Benefits of College

An individual may choose to earn income Y_N from age 18 to retirement age 65. Or an individual may attend college, lose income from age 18 to 22, pay the direct cost of college, and then earn income Y_C from age 22 to retirement. The total costs of college are represented by area C, the lost income and direct costs; the benefits of college are area B, the extra income earned with a college degree. In monetary terms it pays to go to college if B is greater than C.

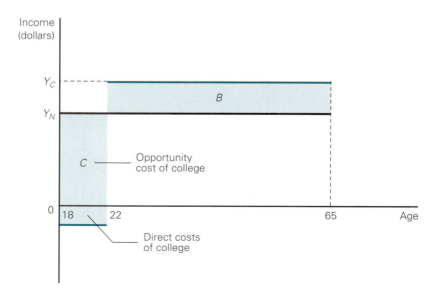

tive income. The total cost of going to college is the sum of both the opportunity cost and the direct costs of college, the entire shaded area *C*. After graduation, these individuals enter the labor market and begin earning positive income. Figure 12.8 indicates that their starting pay at age 22 after attending college is higher than it would have been had they not gone to college. They earn negative income for four years and then Y_C as a lifetime average from age 22 until retirement.

Which is the best choice? If the deciding factor is money, then the individual determines the relative values of the two income streams and chooses the higher one. One method of doing so is to compare area *C* (the investment period) with area *B*. Area *C* represents the total cost of going to college: the direct costs plus the lost income. Area *B* represents the benefits of going to college; it is the extra income earned with a college degree. If area *B* is greater than area *C*, then it pays to go to college.[1]

Some investments in human capital require more time than others and some require less time. Regardless of the length of the investment period (the number of years spent in school), if there is pure competition in the labor market and enough individuals choose the higher-income streams, then in the long run the sum total of the various income streams will be equal. That is, high school graduates will work at lower wage rates but for a greater total number of years than will college graduates. With a given retirement age for both groups, the lifetime earnings of high school graduates working more years but at a lower wage should just equal the lifetime earnings of college graduates working fewer years but at a higher wage. (This equilibrium requires that the wage rates for occupations with long investment periods be greater than the wage rates for occupations with short investment periods. The difference in wages is what equalizes the lifetime income streams.) And, of course, there may not be pure competition in the labor market. Some professions may attempt to limit entry, so as to keep their wages artificially high in the long run.

---

[1]It should be kept in mind that these values must be discounted for time, as discussed in Chapter 14.

College graduates forego income in order to add to their human capital. However, these additions, although costly, will likely pay future bonuses.

Other Equalizing Differences in Wages

A long investment period is not all that discourages individuals from entering a particular occupation. Other characteristics make it necessary for some occupations to offer higher wages to induce workers to enter. People will evaluate their alternative work possibilities in monetary and nonmonetary terms. Pay will be important, but so too will be working conditions, location, co-workers, risk, length of contract, personality of the boss, and myriad other factors. Although some of these factors are nonmonetary or psychological, this does not mean that they are not income. They are a part of workers' pay. The total compensation of a worker in a given occupation consists of the wage plus any nonmonetary aspects of the job.

The principle of equalizing differences in wages works in the following way. In a competitive labor market, laborers choose the occupation with the highest total compensation, other things equal. This brings the wage down until the total compensation for the occupation is on a par with that of other occupations. If total compensation is too low in some occupation, then people leave that occupation until the wage rises enough to equalize the total compensation. When total compensation is equalized across occupations, the competitive equilibrium is achieved. If this condition is not met, workers will move around and change jobs until it is met.

One student who spends the summer in an air-conditioned office may make a lower wage but more nonwage pay per hour than another student who spends the summer on a construction crew. As students compete for summer jobs, total pay between jobs will be equalized. This is the principle of equalizing differences at work in a competitive labor market.

The basic point is that observed wage differences across occupations may reflect differences in nonmonetary aspects of employment. Of course, labor markets may not always be competitive as we have assumed here. Some jobs may pay more and have more attractive working conditions if there are barriers to entry into the occupation. However, under competition, wage differences can exist. Forces fueled by interest groups have attempted to use the political process to impose what they regard as comparable worth in the workplace (see the Focus "Politics and 'Justice' in the Workplace: Comparable Worth" for a discussion of this phenomenon). The following are just a few of the many reasons for wage differences other than those caused by human capital differences.

- *Wages will vary directly with the disagreeableness of a job.* The more uncomfortable the job, the higher the pay will be. To induce workers to accept jobs that create discomfort—such as tarring roofs in the heat of summer—a higher monetary reward must be offered.

- *The more seasonal or irregular a job, the higher the pay will be.* To induce individuals to supply labor to irregular employments, the wage must compensate them for the likelihood of being laid off frequently. For example, construction workers often experience periods of unemployment between jobs. To have readily available workers, construction employers must pay a higher wage.

- *Jobs that require trustworthiness carry a higher wage.* Armored truck drivers, blackjack dealers, and some bank employees receive relatively high wages. One reason that such occupations pay more is that being trustworthy is both an extra burden and a form of human capital; employers must compensate such workers for their extra efforts.

FOCUS

Politics and "Justice" in the Workplace: Comparable Worth

The pay of various types of workers in a marketplace is typically assumed to be determined solely by the interaction of supply and demand. In recent years a movement has started that advocates an increased role for the government in ensuring greater equity in pay ("justice"). The aim of this movement is to ensure that the pay for different occupations reflects the comparable worth of the services provided by workers in various occupations. Advocates of comparable worth argue that the value of each type of worker can be objectively determined in terms of job qualifications and work conditions. Under their proposed system, impartial experts would rate each occupation and assign a number that reflects the worth of each particular job. A number of interest groups (women's, civil rights, and religious groups) seek the political means to end what they view as gender and racial discrimination in wages for equal skill, effort, responsibility, and working conditions—even with *different* job titles, work, or occupations.[a]

[a]A number of interest groups supported the introduction of the Fair Pay Act of 1996 in the U.S. Congress, which would have introduced the principle of comparable worth in government contracts. The legislation failed, although the demand for political solutions to labor market problems will continue.

Critics, including most economists, argue that it is impossible to assign points objectively to different occupations. The working conditions of a forest ranger are different from those of a registered nurse, but it is impossible to say which conditions are more demanding—it depends on preferences of particular workers. Physical and mental demands also differ across employments. Perhaps the most important objection is that the institution of comparable worth would rob the labor markets of signals that reflect changing demand, supply, and technological conditions in the economy. A crucial role played by labor markets is to attract new workers into growing occupations. Imposed wages could mean that, despite increases in demand, shortages in critical occupations could exist indefinitely. Comparable worth would severely restrict the ability of a market system to adjust to ever-changing conditions.

Few Americans, let alone economists, do not support the principle of "equal pay for equal work." Developing standards to make the principle operative, without creating other (sometimes unpredictable) adverse effects, is quite another matter.

- *Jobs with greater risk to health will have higher pay.* Occupations with higher than average probabilities of death or disability must compensate employees for taking a risk. People are not willing to risk lost future income because of injuries unless they can receive higher income in the present. Steelworkers who construct frames for skyscrapers must be paid more than those who work on the ground.

- *Jobs that carry the possibility of tremendous success will have a lower wage.* Acting is a good example of such a profession. Many young people aspire to be actors and are arguably attracted into acting by the sumptuous lifestyle of movie stars. Most never make it that big; the average salary of all actors is quite low. Yet some people are willing to take the plunge, feeling that they are good enough to be big winners. Attitudes toward risk are therefore important in determining relative wages. The wages for most actors will be lower because some successful actors make startlingly high pay, a possibility that induces many young people to enroll in acting school.

- *Wages will vary by region.* Wages in any region are determined by supply and demand. (For our purposes, a region may be an area within a particular country, an entire country, or several countries in close geographic proximity to each other.) However, if wages in market *A* exceed the wages in market *B*, then we expect to see labor flow from *B* to *A*. The shifting short-run supply brings wages into equilibrium. Wages fall in *A* and rise in *B*. (See the Application, "Where Do You Live? Regional Wage Differences," at the end of the chapter.)

MARGINAL PRODUCTIVITY THEORY AND INCOME DISTRIBUTION

The profit-maximizing tendency of competitive firms to set marginal revenue product (*MRP*) equal to marginal factor cost (*MFC*) leads to a wage that equals the value of a worker's marginal product. This result applies to the prices of all factors of production in competitive markets. Each resource—be it labor, land, or capital—is paid the value of its marginal product.

The marginal productivity theory of factor prices is a positive, not a normative, theory. It explains *how* factor prices are determined in markets, not how factor prices *should* be determined. It is not meant to be an ethical theory of income distribution, though it is sometimes attacked as such. It is meant as a demand and supply theory that explains the behavior of input prices and the allocation of factors of production to different employments.

It should now be clear that the theory of marginal productivity implies many things about income distribution. Where there is competitive voluntary contracting for labor services, labor's share of national income will be directly related to its marginal product. Of course, factor markets are not perfect, and various other forces affect income distribution in a society. These issues will be carefully addressed over the next several chapters. Our argument in this chapter is not that the marginal productivity theory is necessarily a good normative theory of how income should be distributed (although you might believe it is so), but rather that it provides an objective basis for understanding the economic behavior of demanders and suppliers of inputs.

APPLICATION

Where Do You Live? Regional Wage Differences

Does the "cost of living" where you live partially determine your wage rate? Why do we observe higher wages in the North than in the South or higher wages in San Francisco than in Oklahoma City? Can we expect these wage differences to persist in the long run?

Wages in any region are determined by supply and demand. However, if wages in market *A* exceed the wages in market *B*, then we expect to see labor flow from *B* to *A*. The shifting supply brings wages into equilibrium. Wages fall in *A* and rise in *B*.

The equality of wages is the result of individuals' actions. Furthermore, an individual's decision to move is based on the costs and benefits of doing so. Relocation requires resource expenditures that must be offset by extra income.

Suppose a worker could stay in location *B* and earn wage W_B or could move to location *A* and earn a higher wage W_A. The direct costs of moving are the expenses incurred in transporting the worker, her family members, and their personal belongings. There are also additional opportunity costs. The act of moving requires time, and so might finding a job in A. This is time that could have been spent earning income in B. The lost income is a cost of relocation, as shown in Figure 12.9.

At time 0 the individual must choose between earning wage W_B from T to retirement and spending time moving so as to earn wage W_A. The time T is the amount of time spent moving from B to A plus the amount of time spent seeking employment in A. The total cost of moving is the shaded area between 0 and T above and below the horizontal-axis, which represents the income forgone plus direct moving expenses. The benefit of moving—represented by the shaded area between T and retirement—is the extra income that may be earned after the move. It pays to move if the area of extra benefits is greater than the area of costs.[a]

If benefits outweigh costs, then many people will choose to move to A—the move is a good investment in human capital. However, the shifting labor supplies will increase wages in B, where workers are now scarcer, and decrease them in A. The maximum amount by which W_A can exceed W_B in the long run is the amount that forces the area of benefits to just equal the area of costs. Therefore, the lower the costs of moving, the smaller the difference in wages needs to be.

In fact, there are many reasons why we expect little variation in wages across the country within the same occupation in today's markets. First, the duration of lost income for most movers is very small. Indeed, it is quite possible to work until 5:00 p.m. on Friday in New York City and start work at 9:00 a.m. on Monday in Los Angeles. Many people will not move unless they have already found

---

[a]As in the earlier example of the economic costs and benefits of a college education, these values must be discounted for time, as explained in Chapter 14.

FIGURE 12.9

Wage Differences Across Regions

An individual must choose whether to remain in location B and earn wage W_B from time 0 to retirement or move to location A and earn wage W_A from time T to retirement. The decision to move to A necessitates costs in terms of the time T spent moving and income forgone while making the move, represented by the shaded area from 0 to T above and below the horizontal axis. After the move, the individual earns extra income represented by the shaded area from T to retirement. If this area of extra income is greater than the area of total costs of moving, the individual will choose to move.

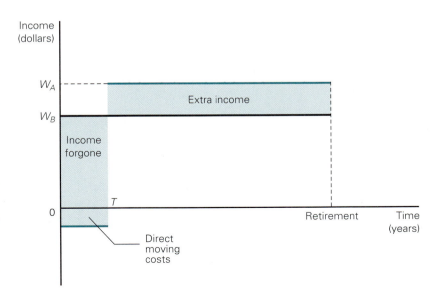

employment in the new location. If the amount of time it takes to travel across the country today were as great as it was two hundred years ago, then wage differences could be very large.

Another reason that regional differences in wages are small is that young workers have small costs and large benefits in moving. Young workers typically have small families or no families and few material possessions to move. Also, the years of receiving extra benefits are longer for young people. Thus, a smaller difference in wages can induce them to move.

Another important aspect of regional wage differences involves the demand side of the labor market. Firms will be encouraged to expand operations in areas where there are low costs of production and decrease operations where costs are high. Firms will invest more capital in low-wage area *B* and decrease investment in high-wage area *A*. Capital moves around the country just as labor does, and this movement tends to equalize wages. In fact, all resources that are mobile move to the locations that yield the resource owners the highest income.

In spite of this equalizing tendency, we observe that wages in the North are about 10 percent higher than in the South in the same occupation. Don Bellante suggests that the difference occurs only in money wages and not in real wages.[b] The cost of living in the South is about 10 percent lower than in the North. This difference in costs equalizes the real wage, just as we expect in the long run.

QUESTION

The city of Houston advertised for police men and women on Atlanta TV stations offering 30 percent (on average) higher wages than those paid by the Atlanta police department. Some personnel moved to Houston. What effect would this movement have on regional wage differences for police services between Texas and Georgia? What might we expect the average age of the migratory police workers to be?

---

[b]Don Bellante, "The North-South Differential and the Migration of Heterogeneous Labor," *American Economic Review* 69 (March 1979), pp. 166–175.

SUMMARY

1. The demand for labor is a derived demand; it is derived from the demand for the product that labor produces.

2. The demand curve for labor is a function of its marginal product and the demand for the product it produces. In the short run, demand is equivalent to marginal revenue product: $MRP_L = MP_L \times MR$.

3. The competitive firm hires the profit-maximizing amount of labor at the point where *MRP* equals the wage rate. The short-run market demand curve for labor shows the amount of

labor that firms hire when labor is the only variable input and the number of firms is constant, but it allows for changes in product price as wages change.

4. The long-run market demand curve for labor shows the amount of labor hired at different wages when all inputs are allowed to vary and firms are in long-run competitive equilibrium.

5. The demand for labor changes when the demand for the product changes or when the marginal product of labor changes.

6. The relation between the wage rate and the number of hours of labor an individual supplies depends on the substitution and income effects. If the substitution effect is greater than the income effect, then the individual's labor supply curve is positively sloped; the curve is negatively sloped if the income effect is greater than the substitution effect. The aggregate labor supply curve is the sum of individual labor supply curves and is usually positively sloped.

7. Human capital is anything an individual acquires that increases his or her productivity. In an occupation that requires human capital, the longer and more costly the investment period, the higher the wages.

8. The total compensation in all occupations in competitive markets is equalized by differences in wages. The long-run supply of labor to each occupation ensures the equilibrium difference in wages.

9. Because of changes in either supply or demand, regional wage levels may vary. However, migration of workers will tend to eliminate regional wage differences.

10. In competitive markets, resources are paid a price that is equal to their marginal product. Labor's share of the overall income distribution is related to its marginal product.

KEY TERMS

factor market
derived demand
competitive labor market
market demand for labor
market supply of labor
marginal product of labor (MP_L)

marginal revenue product of
   labor (MRP_L)
marginal factor cost of labor
   (MFC_L)
firm's long-run demand for labor
change in the demand for labor

complementary inputs
substitute inputs
nonmarket activities
human capital

QUESTIONS FOR REVIEW AND DISCUSSION

1. What derived demands will result from increased demand for each of the following goods and services: (a) automobiles, (b) candy, (c) government regulation, (d) physical fitness, (e) education?

2. Explain why an individual's supply of labor curve may bend backward at some sufficiently high wage level.

3. What does the law of diminishing marginal productivity have to do with the demand curve for labor?

4. What is the difference between the demand curve for labor of a monopolist and of a perfectly competitive firm in the output market?

5. Apply the principle of equalizing differences to explain why the relative wage of the following occupations is high or low: (a) politicians, (b) schoolteachers, (c) morticians, (d) actors, (e) brain surgeons.

6. In what sense is the marginal productivity theory of wages a positive theory? In what sense is it a normative theory?

7. What activities will frustrate the equalization of total wages across jobs in the labor market? Does this mean that there is such a thing as nonequalizing wage differences?

8. Are tractor drivers substitutes for human cotton pickers? What happens to the demand for tractor drivers if cotton pickers' wages fall?

9. Is the demand for toothpicks elastic or inelastic? What about elasticity of demand for a machine that makes toothpicks?

10. Under what conditions are labor and some other input complementary inputs?

11. Explain how the firm's marginal revenue product curve is derived. Up to what point will the profit-maximizing firm hire labor?

12. "It is simply unjust that sanitation workers earn less than most stockbrokers. They work harder and longer hours." Comment on this quotation.

PROBLEMS

1. The data in the table apply to a competitive firm.

Units of Labor	Marginal Product	Marginal Revenue	Marginal Revenue Product	Hourly Wage Rate
1	21	$1.50	$31.50	$9.00
2	18	1.50	27.00	9.00
3	15	1.50	22.50	9.00
4	12	1.50	18.00	9.00
5	9	1.50	13.50	9.00
6	6	1.50	9.00	9.00
7	3	1.50	4.50	9.00
8	0	1.50	0.00	9.00

a. What is the marginal factor cost of labor for this firm?
b. If you are the personnel manager of this firm, how many units of labor will you hire?

2. Suppose that Zina, a skilled copy editor, owns her own freelance editorial business. Further assume that she wants to earn exactly $600 per week.
a. What are the number of hours of labor that Zina is willing to supply at the (hourly) wage rates listed below?

Wage	Hours
$ 6	——
10	——
20	——
40	——
60	——
100	——

b. Draw a graph showing Zina's supply curve based on the information in part a.
c. Which is greater, Zina's substitution effect or her income effect? Why?

WORKING WITH THE WEB

1. The issue of equal pay, or comparable worth, as discussed in the Focus "Politics and 'Justice' in the Workplace: Comparable Worth," is a controversial issue and is not easily resolved. Go to www.mises.org, select "daily articles", and choose February '99. Scroll to the bottom of the list until you find the article "Women and Work". The article takes up the issue of pay equity across gender and analyzes the historical trends of men and women in the workplace.
a. What percentage of the wage differential is unexplained by some factor?
b. What is the situation for women employed in the marketing profession?

2. Regional wage differences are discussed in the Application "Where Do You Live?: Regional Wage Differences." The explanation given for regional variation in wage rates is the supply of and demand for labor. The application points out that wages tend to be higher in the North than the

South, and higher in San Francisco than Oklahoma City. First, let's look at the North–South wage differential. Go to http://www.bls.gov/oes/msa/oes_5240m.htm#b20000 and select "Professional, Paraprofessional, and Technical Occupations".
a. What is the mean annual income in Montgomery, AL, for Accountants and Auditors?
    Next, go to http://www.bls.gov/oes/msa/oes_1120m.htm and select the same category, "Professional, Paraprofessional, and Technical Occupations".
b. What is the mean annual income in Boston, MA, for Accountants and Auditors?
c. Does the data confirm that workers in the North earn more than their southern counterparts? Does the data confirm that workers in larger metropolitan areas earn more than workers in smaller areas?

Labor Unions

In the previous chapter we discussed demand and supply conditions in a competitive labor market, where the wage rates tend toward equality. Although we do see wage discrepancies in competitive markets, many of these can be attributed to circumstances such as the amount of risk a particular job involves or the amount of training it requires. We naturally expect brain surgeons to make more than dishwashers in a competitive environment because of the human capital investment brain surgeons must make to perform their services.

All labor markets, of course, are not strictly competitive. In general, factor markets can assume the same kinds of imperfect market structures that we studied in Chapters 10 and 11. The imperfection in labor markets can occur on the supply side, the demand side, or both. On the supply side, labor unions account for the largest source of imperfect competition.

In this chapter we will look at how imperfectly competitive labor markets work. Specifically, we will look at the effects of labor unions. When you finish Chapter 13 you should understand

- the history and goals of labor unions in the United States.
- how unions achieve goals such as higher wages and better working conditions for their members.
- the impact of labor unions on consumers and nonunion labor.
- some of the effects on labor when a single employer exists in an individual market.

322 CHAPTER 13 Labor Unions

TYPES OF LABOR UNIONS

Labor union
A group of individual workers organized to act collectively in an attempt to affect labor market conditions.

A **labor union** is a group of workers who organize collectively in an effort to increase their market power. By acting as a collective unit, they are able to exert a greater influence over working conditions or wages. In this sense, a labor union is similar to a cartel (discussed in Chapter 11). In a union, the sellers of labor agree not to compete among themselves but to act as a single seller of labor.

The first labor unions in the United States started as workers' guilds in the late 1700s and early 1800s. These organizations of workers within the same trade—carpenters, cordwainers (shoemakers), hatters—began meeting to set standards and prices for their output. These loosely organized trade unions were typically short-lived but were the beginnings of the American labor movement.

The Industrial Revolution brought about new opportunities for labor unions. Large manufacturing plants employed many workers with similar skills and interests who could organize at relatively low costs to pursue their common goals. Today there are three major types of labor unions: craft unions, industrial unions, and public employees' unions.

Craft Unions

Craft union
Workers with a common skill who organize to restrict the supply of labor in their trade and obtain some market power; also called a trade union.

In 1886, the American Federation of Labor (AFL) was started in an effort to organize craftspeople into local unions. **Craft unions,** which flourished in the Middle Ages, organize workers according to particular skills, regardless of the industry in which they work. Thus, there are separate guilds for electricians, carpenters, and plumbers. The main function of the guilds is to advance their members' economic well-being. When workers act as a unit, their power in the market can limit competition and raise total compensation above the competitive level. In this sense, the American Medical Association (AMA) or the American Bar Association (ABA) may be viewed as effective unions because they restrict membership in the medical and legal professions, raising professional fees above competitive levels. (See the Focus "The American Medical Association as a Union" for more along these lines.)

Trade or craft unions increase members' total compensation by decreasing the supply of skilled workers. They do so by excluding potential workers from membership. Frequently, trade unions require high initiation fees, monthly dues, and long apprenticeship programs in an effort to discourage potential entrants. Existing members enjoy the higher wage brought about by the limited supply of workers in their trade.

Trade unions are very much like cartels in the sense that supply is artificially restricted so as to command a higher price. As such, craft unions face the same problems as cartels. Just as cartel members have an incentive to cheat on the cartel price, workers outside the union who offer their labor at a wage lower than the union wage can obtain jobs at the expense of union members.

Industrial Unions

Industrial union
Workers in a given industry organized independently of their skills in an effort to obtain market power.

Large manufacturing plants first appeared during the late 1800s and early 1900s. Rather than organize individual craft unions according to different skills, all workers within the same industry would organize a single industry-wide union. In 1938, John L. Lewis formally organized the Congress of Industrial Organizations (CIO), which unified workers first at the firm level and then at the level of the industry as a whole. Contemporary examples of these **industrial unions** include autoworkers' unions and steelworkers' unions.

FOCUS

The American Medical Association as a Union

A union must be able to restrict entry and increase fees and returns in order to function successfully. The American Medical Association (AMA) functions in this fashion while having the laudable (stated) goal of protecting the health care consumer by assuring the quality of care provided. The policies and practices of medical associations may well improve quality, but they have other effects as well: They protect the health care provider from the forces of competition. The AMA might not fit the public image of a union, but it is an unassailable fact that the association employs the tactics of a union to limit competition and raise wages.

The AMA (and its affiliated and often highly specialized unions) has been enormously successful in restricting entry into the health care profession. In part, the returns to doctors and other health care providers are due to the long and arduous path to success. Those wanting to be physicians must get into and through medical school and a residency program, accredited and, to some extent, controlled by the AMA. A monopolist seeking to reduce the supply of labor would set high admission standards for those entering the market. You must have a license to practice medicine because you would face criminal sanctions if caught practicing medicine without one. Exams are given under the auspices of the AMA. All such policies are designed to reduce the supply of physicians.

"Codes of conduct" by national and state medical boards are designed to eliminate price competition among physicians. Advertising is not permitted—indeed it is designated as "unethical"—because advertising would make it possible for health care consumers to compare prices. Sanctions, such as denial of hospital privileges, are imposed on any physicians who attempt to advertise.

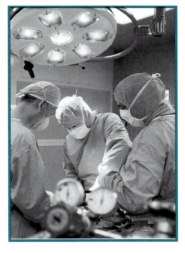

Government responded to this highly concentrated interest group long ago—in the nineteenth century, in most cases. This interest group (like the barbers and cosmetologists of Chapter 4) had criminal penalties installed for nonprescribed behavior. In addition, the government was used indirectly to support physicians. The laws regulating the market for prescription drugs effectively increase the demand for physicians. A licensed physician is necessary to write prescriptions—a necessary input in health care. Substitutes, such as midwives, nurses, or health care assistants, are heavily regulated by the states due to physician interest groups. All of these factors increase the demand for physician services.

A restriction in supply and an increase in demand lead to less competition and higher prices for health care services. However, the continuing debate over health care in the United States has not led to proposals for fostering competition among doctors. Indeed, in 1999 the AMA approved physician unions to counter the power of health maintenance organizations (HMOs). Such unions may be a step backwards. Establishing competition among physicians may be the prerequisite to solving what is called the health care crisis.

For an industrial union to be effective, it must unionize all firms in an industry. Otherwise, the lower-cost, nonunionized firms would prosper at the expense of the higher-cost, unionized firms. Thus, industrial unions often encourage membership rather than restrict it.

Public employees' union
Workers employed by federal, state, or local governments who organize in an effort to obtain market power.

Public Employees' Unions

Public employees' unions are organizations of government workers. Such unions cover a wide variety of jobs—such as fire fighting, police work, teaching, and clerical work—and include both blue-collar and white-collar workers. This sector of the union movement has been one of the fastest growing in recent years. The American Federation of State, County, and Municipal Employees (AFSCME) is now among the ten largest unions in the country. Indeed, membership in AFSCME tripled between 1968 and 1988.

The problems of public employees' unions have received a great deal of attention in recent years. Each fall finds teachers on strike for higher wages and benefits in cities across the country. The decertification of the Professional Air Traffic Controllers Union (PATCO) in the early 1980s resulted from a technically illegal strike by a public employees' union. Despite these much-publicized problems, public employees' unions continue to grow in membership relative to private sector unions. Figure 13.1 compares the percentage of union members in government with the percentage in private industries for years between 1973 and 1994.

The Decline of Union Membership in the United States

Membership in labor unions as a percentage of the total U.S. labor market grew steadily throughout the first half of the twentieth century; by 1953, about 26 percent of the workers in the United States were members of labor unions. Today, only 14 percent of all American workers belong to labor unions. Figure 13.1 shows the trends in unionization from 1973 to 1997. The composition of union member-

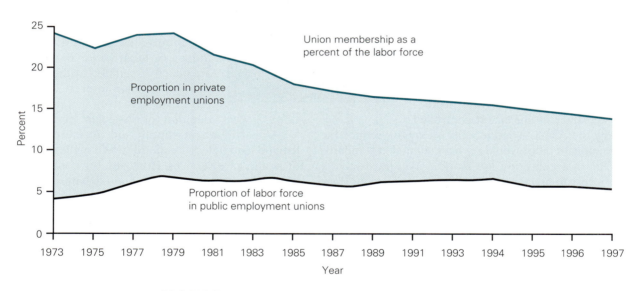

FIGURE 13.1

Trends in Union Membership
The number of workers belonging to unions as a percent of the labor force declined over the period 1973 to 1997. The percent decline was greatest in the private sector, where today only about 10 percent of private sector workers are union members. Union membership among public sector employees has remained constant at around 5 percent of the total labor force over the twenty-four-year period.
Sources: *Union Membership and Earnings Data Book* (Washington, D.C.: Bureau of National Affairs, Inc. 1995), p. 10; and *Statistical Abstract of the United States 1998* (Washington, D.C.: U.S. Government Printing Office, 1998), p. 414.

ship has changed dramatically. In 1953, less than 5 percent of union members were government employees. Today, almost half of all union members are employed by the government. These unionized government workers still represent only about 5 to 6 percent of the *total* labor force—a proportion that has remained constant over time. Such traditionally heavily unionized sectors of the economy as mining, construction, and manufacturing currently have a smaller percentage of workers represented by labor unions than does the government sector.

Several economic factors have contributed to the decline in union membership. Structural changes in the U.S. economy—brought about in part by the pressure of foreign competition—have resulted in a decline in the number of manufacturing and mining jobs relative to service sector jobs. Workers in the service sector have always been more difficult to organize because they tend to be dispersed over a large number of relatively small business firms. Another factor that has contributed to the decline in union membership is the increased participation of women in the labor force. While women have traditionally expressed stronger support for the labor union movement than have men, they have always participated in labor unions in smaller proportions than men; this reflects the concentration of women in the service sector.

UNION ACTIVITIES

Regardless of the means of organization, when workers successfully unite to act as a single seller of labor, the union gains monopoly power in its labor market. The union and its members are therefore no longer wage rate takers. There is a downward-sloping demand curve for the members' labor, and the union may seek any wage along this curve. However, the level of employment for union members is inversely related to the wage rate. Higher wages are gained at the expense of fewer jobs.

Union Goals

The ultimate goals of the union may depend on many competing objectives. Understandably, the union's elected, policy-making officials suggest that members want improved economic well-being: higher wages, more jobs, greater job security, safer jobs, more retirement pay, more fringe benefits, and so on. But relating union policy to a particular objective is difficult. For example, the union objective may be to maximize any number of options, some of which may be inconsistent—such as the utility of the union officials, the utility of members, the wage rate, the level of employment, the level of membership, the total wage income of members, the total wage income of senior members, and so on. The ramifications of pursuing three of these objectives are discussed below.

Employment For All Members   One objective of a union may be to achieve full employment—that is, a job for every member. To do so would require a wage rate that ensures that the quantity of labor demanded by firms is equal to the quantity of labor supplied by existing members. Suppose that the demand for the union's labor can be represented by curve D_L in Figure 13.2. If the amount of labor offered by the union is L_1, then wage W_1 will ensure full employment of union members.

Maximizing The Wage Bill   Although wage W_1 means that everyone in the union is working, full employment may not be the union's goal. Unions frequently have

FIGURE 13.2

The Union's Wage Goals

In setting its wage rate, a union must choose among many goals. If there is L_1 amount of laborers in a union, then wage W_1 must be chosen to achieve full employment of all members. If the elasticity of demand at W_1 is less than 1, then an increase in wages up to W_2 will increase the total wage bill while bringing about union unemployment in the amount $L_1 - L_2$. Still-higher wages such as W_3 will decrease total union income, although those union members who are working enjoy greater incomes. In trying to maximize total wages, the union may face some degree of unemployment according to this model.

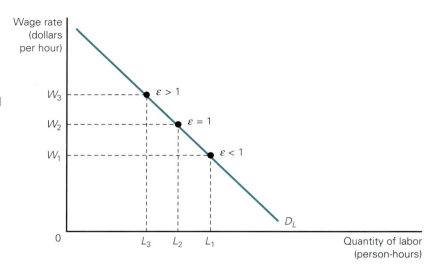

members sitting on the unemployment bench. Any wage higher than W_1 will leave some members unemployed, but there may also be some benefits to a higher wage. For example, it may increase the **total wage bill.** The total wage bill to firms hiring union workers is the wage rate times the total amount (in person-hours) of labor hired. This total wage bill is not only the total cost of labor to the firms; it is also the collective wage income of all the union members. Since workers prefer more income to less, all things being equal, the union may choose to maximize the wage bill. If the full employment wage occurs where the elasticity of demand is less than 1 (inelastic demand), then an increase in the wage will increase total union income ($W \times L$).

To understand this possibility, recall from Chapter 5 how price, total revenue, and elasticity are related. Total revenue is maximized at the price where the elasticity of demand is equal to 1. If elasticity is less than 1, then an increase in price increases total revenue; if elasticity is greater than 1, it takes a price decrease to increase total revenue. In analyzing labor demand, the total wage bill, the wage rate, and the elasticity of demand have the same relation. If the union's objective is to maximize the total union income, then the wage is set where the elasticity of demand is equal to 1.

In Figure 13.2, wage W_2 maximizes the wage bill. However, with L_1 amount of labor in the union, unemployment in the amount $L_1 - L_2$ results. This may not be a problem because the total union income ($W_2 \times L_2$) is now higher than at W_1. All members can still be better off at a higher wage if the working members provide unemployment compensation to unemployed members. On the other hand, a trade union may choose to limit union membership to L_2.

In considering attempts by unions to maximize the wage bill, it is important to interpret the wage rate as a full wage. This includes both the hourly pay and the value of fringe benefits such as hospitalization insurance, retirement benefits, and paid vacation. For many union contracts, a large portion of the full pay takes the form of fringe benefits.

Total wage bill

The total cost of labor to firms; equal to wage rate times total quantity of labor employed.

Maximizing Income for Limited Members   While wage W_2 would maximize income for the union as a whole, a higher wage such as W_3 in Figure 13.2 would increase income only for those who remain fully employed. L_3 workers would be hired, and their incomes would be higher as long as they are working the same number of hours. For example, senior members usually retain employment under a seniority system. Thus, wages above W_2 would probably increase senior members' incomes at the expense of younger members.

Union Objectives and the Elasticity of Demand

A union's ability to accomplish its goals is limited by the elasticity of demand for its members' labor. Increases in wages decrease the level of employment, but the percent decrease in employment is determined by the elasticity of demand. Unions would like to see large increases in wages with minor effects on employment; in other words, they would like the demand for their members' labor to be as inelastic as possible. The elasticity of demand for union labor is determined by many factors. Naturally changing patterns of demand and supply for the products of unions have a direct impact on elasticity and union success (see the Focus "'Services Pay' and the Restructuring of the American Economy" for an example). Unions themselves often engage in activities that decrease the elasticity of demand for union members. Such a change in elasticity of demand is shown in Figure 13.3 as a rotation of the demand curve from D_1 to D_2. Along D_2, increases in wages result in less unemployment than identical increases along D_1. The following are some familiar examples of this process.

Elasticity of Demand for the Product   The more inelastic the demand for the good or service that the unionized labor produces, the more inelastic the demand for the union's labor. While a union would like the demand for the good or service its workers produce to be inelastic, it cannot do much to decrease this elasticity. Union workers are mostly at the mercy of the market, although in some circumstances they can and do affect elasticity of demand. For example, an item's elasticity of demand is determined in part by the number and availability of substitutes. If a union can limit substitutes, then the elasticity of demand for the union workers' labor decreases. We see this happening in the automobile industry. Through the political process, U.S. autoworkers encourage import quotas, which have the effect of limiting the supply of foreign autos and decreasing the elasticity of demand for U.S.-made cars. With import quotas, increases in autoworkers' wages have less effect on employment than the same increases in wages if quotas are not imposed.

Availability of Substitute Inputs   The fewer substitute inputs for union labor, the lower the elasticity of demand for union labor. Unions would prefer no substitute inputs for their members' labor; then wage increases would have minimal effects on union employment. But there are almost always some inputs that may be substituted for union labor. Typically, nonunion labor is a good substitute. For this reason, labor unions try to form contracts with firms that maximize the use of union labor. (Closed shops—which legally bind firms to hire only union labor—are now illegal in the United States.) Unions also take direct actions to limit the amount of nonunion labor available. For example, unions support laws that restrict immigration to the United States because such laws decrease the availability of immigrant workers who could substitute for union members in the work force.

FOCUS

"Services Pay" and the Restructuring of the American Economy

Naysayers are around in all ages. When the great leap of the Industrial Revolution took hold in the eighteenth and nineteenth centuries, doom and gloom were predicted for workers in the factories as opposed to "wholesome" pursuits in farming. Agriculture and agricultural production most certainly survived, but amid ever-modernizing factories and assembly-line production. The modern "services revolution"—a technological movement of the latter part of the twentieth century—has had its critics. The deindustrialization of America, away from smokestack industries and assembly-line productions such as steel, was supposed to be replaced by low-paying, burger-flipping type jobs. Instead, high-tech positions and service jobs are paying as much as assembly-line work.

One reason for the decline in union membership (shown in Figure 13.1) is the decline in the smokestack-type production that has characterized the American economy. But this decline has been replaced by highly technical industries where unions have not made significant progress. (Public service unions, of course, have been very successful, as discussed in the text.) The critics had it that nonmanufacturing jobs created low pay and fewer fringe benefits for workers. But, for the first time in 1998, hourly earnings in services were higher than those in manufacturing (according to the Bureau of Labor Statistics). Manufacturing jobs (in 1998) were lost in the amount of 234,000 well-paying jobs, but more than one and one-half million jobs were created in high-tech industries such as computer services and telecommunications.[a]

Retailing and food-marketing jobs ("burger-flipping jobs") do not pay as well as assembly-line work, but high-tech jobs often pay workers better wages. Total returns to workers, of course, include benefits—particularly health benefits. While total (full) compensation in services is not as high as in manufacturing, it has begun to catch up. Benefits in the service industries are more flexible, however, offering employees more flexible forms of nonmonetary wages. In such industries, the competitive system, rather than labor unions, determines the provision of wages and benefits.

---

[a]Data for this focus was obtained from John Berlau, "More than Just Flipping Burgers: Service-Sector Jobs Fuel U.S. Economic Boom," *Investor's Business Daily* (March 23, 1999), pp. 1–2.

Increasing the Demand for Union Labor

Regardless of the goals of unions, the members are always in favor of an increase in the demand for their labor. With increased demand, wages, employment, or both are increased. The curve representing demand for labor shifts to the right when one of two basic things happens: an increase in the demand for the product or an increase in the marginal product of workers.

Unions can and do engage in activities that affect the demand for their members. Some of this activity is unproductive—for example, the practice of *feath-*

FIGURE 13.3

Decreasing the Elasticity of Demand for Union Labor

Unions attempt to decrease the elasticity of demand for their members' labor. For example, unions support immigration laws that retard or block the flow of competitive foreign labor into this country. The effect of such activities is represented by a rotation of the demand curve from D_1 to D_2. This rotation of the demand curve indicates that future wage increases result in smaller employment decreases. If wages rise from W_1 to W_2, employment falls only to L_2 rather than to L'_2.

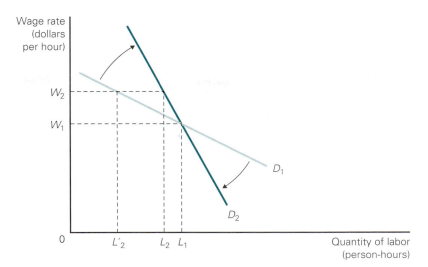

erbedding. Featherbedding is the attempt to increase demand for union labor through contractual obligations to hire what some would regard as unnecessary labor. When diesel locomotives replaced steam locomotives, firemen were no longer needed to shovel coal. Railway workers nevertheless required firemen to be hired. The union contracts of journeyman carpenters or electricians stipulate that each union member must be provided with an apprentice—regardless of need. Contracts negotiated by musicians' unions routinely require that a minimum number of players be hired—again, without regard to any reasonable expectation of need. Some of these demand-increasing activities also decrease elasticity of demand for labor.

Increasing Product Demand   Unions frequently attempt to increase the demand for the products they produce. Garment workers advertise the union label and encourage consumers, as well as union members, to buy union-made clothes. Autoworkers strongly encourage union members to buy domestically produced cars. As we have seen, unions sometimes try to influence lawmakers to decrease the supply of foreign products that are substitutes for union-made goods. Import tariffs or quotas also increase the demand for U.S. products.

Increasing Substitute Input Prices   If unions can increase the relative price of inputs that are substitutes for union labor, then the demand for union labor will increase. Unskilled nonunion workers can substitute for skilled union labor, for example. Unions have therefore supported increases in the minimum wage. As the relative price of unskilled nonunion labor rises, the demand for union labor increases.

Increasing Productivity of Members   Unions prefer that their members be very productive. If the marginal product of new members joining the union is relatively high, then the demand for all members increases. Apprenticeship programs offered by unions train new entrants in an effort to increase overall productivity. Unions also provide other services—for example, conflict resolution procedures to settle worker grievances—that may enhance worker productivity on the job.

MONOPSONY: A SINGLE EMPLOYER OF LABOR

Having examined unions' attempts to build the economic power of laborers, we now turn to the nature of the firms they face as employers. Before the Industrial Revolution, large manufacturing plants were not common. In most towns or regions there were several potential employers for most workers. As a matter of fact, most skilled craftspeople were self-employed. However, as technology changed, the benefits of mass production increased. Large manufacturing plants such as steel mills, textile mills, and coal mines became the principal employers of labor in some regions.

Monopsony

A single buyer of a resource or product; sometimes found in labor markets as the single buyer of labor.

A single buyer of a resource in a market is known as a **monopsony**. The monopsonist buyer has market power because rather than purchase all that it is willing and able to purchase at a market-determined price, the monopsony faces an upward-sloping supply curve. From along this curve it seeks the price that yields the profit-maximizing quantity of resource employment.

Consider Figure 13.4. The firm sells its product in a competitive market; its marginal revenue product or demand curve for labor is MRP_L. Since it is the only buyer of labor in the market, it faces an upward-sloping market supply curve of labor, S_L. To hire more labor, the firm must offer higher wages. Under these circumstances, the marginal factor cost of labor is no longer equal to the wage rate. The increase in total cost that results from hiring one more unit of labor is greater than the price paid for one more unit. And to attract one more unit of labor, the firm must offer a higher wage to all units of labor employed. This concept is summarized by the MFC_L curve in Figure 13.4, which lies to the left and above the supply curve of labor, S_L.

The firm will hire all units of labor that add more to revenue than to cost. Thus the monopsonist firm will maximize profit by hiring labor up to the point where MFC_L equals MRP_L. The monopsonist hires L_m amount of labor and must pay wage W_m to attract that amount of labor.

The monopsonist wage and level of employment may be compared with those of a competitive labor market under the same circumstances. If MRP_L in Figure 13.4 had been the summation of many firms' demand curves for labor, then competitive

FIGURE 13.4

Monopsony in the Labor Market

A monopsonist faces an upward-sloping supply curve of labor, S_L. It maximizes profit by hiring the amount of labor that equates its marginal factor cost (MFC_L) to its marginal revenue product for labor (MRP_L). The monopsonist's levels of employment and wage, L_m and W_m, fall below the competitive levels, L_c and W_c.

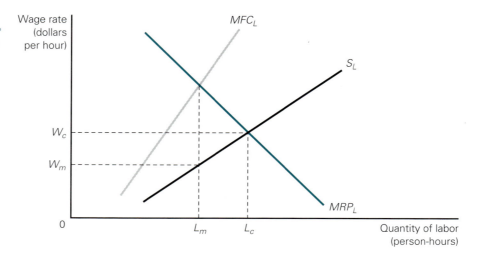

forces would have forced wages to W_c and employment to L_c. Under the same supply and MRP_L conditions, the presence of monopsony results in lower wages and lower employment.

The fact that the monopsonist pays a wage rate less than the MRP_L is known as **exploitation of labor.** If individuals are not being paid the value of their marginal product, then the monopsonist is extracting value from them. In the small regional markets of early days, monopsonists were actually exploiting the immobility of labor. As single employers, firms were able to pay lower-than-competitive wages in isolated areas because the cost of transportation was very high. It was very difficult for individuals to move around the country to work for other employers.

The more mobile an employee, the greater the number of potential employers and the more elastic the labor supply. Computers and the ability to work and transact globally from one's home are also affecting labor supply elasticity. Today, the costs of transportation are relatively low. The opportunity cost of moving from one side of the country to another or commuting to all firms within a 60-mile radius is lower today than it was a century ago, although the costs of moving may be rising along with the increase in dual-career households. It is extremely rare to find an individual who has only one potential employer. (However, see the Application "Should College Football Players Be Paid? The NCAA Monopsony" at the conclusion of this chapter for an exception.)

Bilateral Monopoly and the Need for Bargaining

If there is a monopoly in a market, then the single seller has the power to determine the price of output. If there is monopsony in a market, then the single buyer has the power to determine the price of output. But in some markets, **bilateral monopoly**—a single seller and a single buyer—could exist. In such a case, what determines the price?

The price in a bilateral monopoly market cannot be determined theoretically. No competitive forces determine a single price, and the seller has a preferred price that is higher than the buyer's preferred price. However, if the maximum price the buyer is willing to pay is greater than the minimum price the seller is willing to accept, then a bargain can be reached. Bargaining between two parties is the process by which price is determined.

Consider a labor market with bilateral monopoly. Suppose a monopsony exists in an isolated mining town with only one employer, a mining firm. The firm must rely on the town's supply of labor. As Figure 13.5 illustrates, the mining firm maximizes profit by hiring L_m workers and by paying wage W_m. The workers, though, are unhappy with wage W_m and decide to form a union. They manage to sign up workers of all skill levels throughout the community to the union, maximizing their bargaining strength.

The wage most preferred by the union is not clear. If the union's goal is to maximize the total wage bill, then it will prefer a wage such as W_u.

There is a maximum wage that the union can obtain. Any wage above the maximum would result in no union employment at all because of the high production costs that would be imposed. If wages are too high, then the monopsony may actually go out of business, turn entirely to substitutes for the union labor, or relocate in a lower-cost area. The union's ability to extract value from the firm is limited by the mobility of the firm, just as the firm's ability to extract value from the workers is limited by the mobility of the workers.

Exploitation of labor

A situation in which the wage rate paid to an input is less than the input's marginal revenue product.

Bilateral monopoly

A market in which there is only one buyer and only one seller of a resource or product.

FIGURE 13.5

Bilateral Monopoly

When a monopsonist employer chooses lower-than-competitive wage W_m and a monopoly union chooses higher-than-competitive wage W_u, the wage cannot be determined theoretically. But it can be determined by bargaining, and it will be between W_u and W_m. Although the wage is indeterminate, there is an incentive for the two parties to agree on employment level L_m because joint profits are maximized at that employment level.

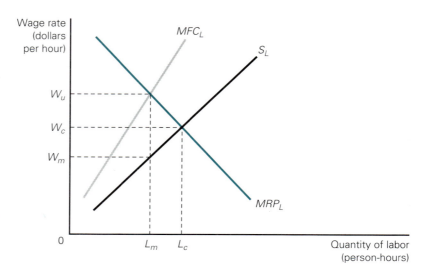

Collective bargaining

The process whereby buyers and sellers negotiate, rather than compete individually, in order to determine a wage rate.

Collective Bargaining

When labor bargains collectively with a monopsonist, the final wage will be somewhere between the wage chosen by the monopsonist (W_m in Figure 13.5) and the wage most preferred by the union (W_u in the figure). The party that comes closest to establishing its goal is the one with the best bargaining strength. In **collective bargaining,** all buyers and all sellers of labor act as a unit to enhance their bargaining power.

Bilateral monopoly brings forth the need to negotiate. The absence of competition on both sides of the market creates a situation in which neither employers nor workers are able to dictate a wage rate. Yet each year collective bargaining contracts are negotiated that cover the pay and working conditions for 6 to 9 million American workers. Unions definitely limit wage competition among their members in many markets, but are there that many monopsonies?

In some industrial unions, such as the autoworkers' union, the union representatives bargain with a single firm. Under these circumstances, a firm that employs a very large percentage of a union's members does have some monopsony power. Wages cannot be dictated by the union. On the other hand, craft unions' members are employed by many firms. Hundreds of firms in different sectors of the United States employ carpenters, for example. It might seem that a union would not have to negotiate with an employer that has no monopsony power. However, the potential employers of craft union members may form a coalition, a buyer's cartel, to negotiate with unions as a single buyer of labor. Thus, when labor bargains as a unit to gain market power, previously competitive employers would do the same. When wage contracts are determined by bargaining negotiations, there is, in effect, a bilateral monopoly in the market.

Strikes

The ability of a union to achieve higher wages depends on its bargaining strength, and its strongest weapon is the strike. When firms fail to meet labor's

Caterpillar strikers demand benefits and job security.

Strike

A collective refusal to work at the current wage or under current working conditions.

Binding arbitration

An agreement between the buyers and sellers of labor to allow a third party to determine the conditions of a work contract.

demands for a higher wage or any other demand, the union can withhold the labor services of its members. Such a refusal to work, or **strike,** can severely limit or even eliminate the firm's ability to continue production. By striking, a union withholds not only its members' labor but also that of other unions who respect the picket line. Under some circumstances, members of nonnegotiating unions also withhold their labor from the negotiating firm. A firm's failure to concede to labor's demands can therefore be very costly. Of course, conceding to higher wages is costly as well.

Yet the strike is a double-edged sword. Not only does it cost firms income, but union members lose income as well. A strike is not attractive to either party, but it is the best weapon labor has to force firms to accept the union wage. The union must decide if the lost income is worth its members' increased future income.

Similarly, firms have the power to reject employment at the union's desired wage. By doing so, a firm in effect refuses to hire labor at a particular wage or any higher wage. In a sense, the firm strikes against employing labor at too high a wage rate.

The potential costliness of a strike leads to serious bargaining by both management and labor because both sides have significant incentives to arrive at a new labor contract without a strike. In fact, negotiation is the general pattern of collective bargaining in the United States. Each year, some 120,000 labor contracts are renegotiated in collective bargaining processes. In more than 96 percent of these cases, labor and management arrive at a new agreement without recourse to a strike.

Table 13.1 provides some data about strikes since 1950. Perhaps the most relevant statistic in the table is the percentage of working time lost to strikes. As the data make clear, this figure has fallen over time and generally constitutes less than 0.05 percent of total working time, a figure far less than the time lost to worker absenteeism each year. The fact that little working time is lost to strikes means that strikes are a powerful union weapon. The threat of a strike may be sufficient to make collective bargaining work smoothly.

Sometimes, if negotiations are not successful, both parties can agree to **binding arbitration.** Such an agreement brings in a third party acceptable to labor and management to make a decision that both sides must abide by. Binding arbitration is often used for public sector union disputes because public employees usually are forbidden by law to strike. Public sector strikes in basic service activities—such as commuter transportation, garbage collection, teaching, and fire and police protection—have the potential to bring the economy to a halt. If essential services provided by government cease to be performed because of a strike, much private economic activity will cease as well.

In private sector strikes, lost output can be made up to some extent if workers work overtime after the strike is settled. Moreover, substitute products and services are available to consumers during a private sector strike. Purchasers of new cars can buy used cars or drive their present cars until an autoworkers' strike is over, for example.

TABLE 13.1

Work Stoppages Involving 1000 Workers or More, 1960–1997
As these data for selected years since 1960 show, strikes have played a steadily declining role in the lives of American workers and the U.S. economy over the last four decades.

Year	Number	Workers Involved	Idle Days	Percentage of Work Time Lost
1960	222	896	13,260	0.09
1965	268	999	15,140	0.10
1970	381	2468	52,761	0.29
1975	235	965	17,563	0.09
1980	187	795	20,844	0.09
1985	54	324	7,079	0.03
1990	44	185	5,926	0.02
1991	40	392	4,584	0.02
1992	35	364	3,989	0.01
1993	35	182	3,981	0.01
1994	45	322	5,021	0.02
1995	31	192	5,771	0.02
1996	37	273	4,887	0.02
1997	29	339	4,497	0.01

Source: Statistical Abstract of the U.S. 1998, 115th edition (Washington D.C.: U.S. Government Printing Office, 1998), p. 443.

Public Choice and Union Bargaining

The bargaining power of unions and management is affected by legislation, which in turn is affected by the political environment. Legislation can favor either management or labor in the negotiating process. Until the 1930s, the struggle between management and labor in the United States was tilted toward management. The strike was not a strong labor weapon, because employers could obtain a court order against a strike. Employees suspected of having union sympathies could be fired or roughed up by company thugs. New employees could be required to sign a "yellow-dog" contract, which forbade the employees from joining the union.

The New Deal response to the Great Depression changed all of this. The Norris–La Guardia Act (1932) and Wagner Act (1935) denied management the use of antiunion tactics and granted labor the right to organize and engage in collective bargaining in a legal framework regulated by the National Labor Relations Board (NLRB). The NLRB has five members appointed by the president for five-year terms. Its functions include ruling on unfair labor practices, settling jurisdictional disputes among unions over bargaining rights, and calling for plant elections at the request of workers. These legal changes lent a tremendous impetus to the growth of the union movement and gave unions a favorable environment for pursuing their ends.

The post–World War II era was characterized by much industrial unrest. Unions showed little self-restraint or discipline, so Congress tilted the balance

Right-to-work law

A law that prevents unions from requiring that individual workers join the union as a condition of employment by a particular firm.

between labor and management back toward management. The Taft–Hartley Act, passed in 1947, allowed states to enact **right-to-work laws,** which forbid unions from coercing workers into their ranks. It added several other constraints on union behavior, such as outlawing strikes by government workers and secondary boycotts, by which the union would set up picket lines against other suppliers of the company being struck. After the Taft–Hartley Act, charges of union corruption and ties to organized crime led to further legislation to regulate union behavior. The Landrum–Griffin Act, passed in 1959, contained various provisions to ensure that unions were honestly managed. Among other things, this law required the filing of financial reports by union officers and the auditing of union finances.

Even in the face of such restraining legislation, the labor union has assumed a position of influence and power in the U.S. economy. No longer are unions viewed as weak associations of workers fighting for a better standard of living for their members. In some respects, unions are best thought of as strong special-interest groups that are proficient at obtaining legislative favors such as protective tariffs. On the other hand, union political power is sometimes used to promote general-interest legislation. Civil rights and welfare laws, Social Security, and similar programs have been strongly supported by organized labor.

The Union as a Political Interest Group

Unions are an ideal conduit for political activity in a number of respects. Once a union is formed, it is relatively inexpensive to use the organization to do more than simply engage in collective bargaining. For example, unions can expand their efforts into the political arena fairly cheaply. For this reason unions have long been a powerful political force in the United States. Unions support and lobby for public policies that directly or indirectly benefit their members. Two simple cases illustrate this point.

First, unions are typically against free international trade. Free trade inhibits the ability of unions and domestic firms to pass along union wage demands in the form of higher prices. Not surprisingly, then, unions have been among the most outspoken critics of the North American Free Trade Agreement with Mexico and Canada.

Second, labor unions always support minimum-wage laws and increases in the minimum wage. Although union officials often use terms such as justice and fairness in explaining their position on this issue, it is worth noting that minimum-wage laws effectively protect union members from competition with lower-priced labor. Such laws raise the legal wage required to employ workers, thereby lessening the ability of some workers to compete for jobs by offering their services at lower wages. One of the effects of minimum-wage laws, therefore, is to increase the power of labor unions by restricting labor market competition. For example, a minimum-wage law will reduce regional wage differentials, making it less attractive for firms to migrate to a lower-paying area and employ nonunion labor. In such a fashion, minimum-wage laws indirectly protect union labor. Unions were strongly behind the 1996 increase in the minimum wage from $4.25 to $5.15 per hour passed by Congress and signed by President Clinton. (There is fairly constant pressure on politicians to raise the minimum wage.)

These are only two examples of the politics of unionism. As with all groups able to organize and transfer wealth, unions' political efforts are designed to increase the well-being of union members.

THE IMPACT OF UNIONS ON LABOR'S SHARE OF TOTAL INCOME

Primarily, a general increase in wages requires an increase in the productivity of workers. An increase in productivity can occur in a variety of ways. The quality of tools and other physical capital used by workers can increase, workers' skill levels can be raised through education and experience, innovation or better management can increase worker productivity, and so on. Higher real wages for all workers can be realized only if the output of goods and services in the economy is increased. It would seem to follow that unions can increase the wages of all workers only if they increase the general level of productivity in the economy. While such an impact of unions is not out of the question, it is hard to imagine how it might happen.

Who pays for the benefits that unions obtain through bargaining power, legislation, and other means? The naive answer is that, of course, employers pay, but the evidence suggests otherwise. In fact, economic analysis indicates that consumers and nonunion employees pay for the benefits that unions obtain for their members.

Consumers pay because higher union wages mean higher costs for firms that employ union labor. If these firms produce in a competitive market for their output, output prices will rise to reflect the higher cost of union labor. Basically, the same result holds if the firm that hires union labor has monopoly power, although the monopolist may bargain with the union over the level of monopoly profits earned. In either case, higher costs caused by union wages lead to higher prices. Consumers thus pay part of the tab for higher union wages.

Nonunion employees pay because higher union wages lead firms to produce less output and to substitute nonhuman capital for union labor. Both of these effects cause the level of employment in unionized industries to fall. In other words, as we saw in the models of how unions increase the relative wages of their members, these are cases where union bargaining power leads to a lower employment level for labor in the unionized industry. The workers who do not make it into the union must seek employment elsewhere in the economy. This increases the supply of labor to alternative, nonunion employments and drives down nonunion wages. Thus, nonunion employees also pay part of the tab for higher union wages.

It can be argued on the basis of economic theory that employers do not generally pay for all union gains. Consumers and nonunion employees share the burden because the price of union-made goods rises and the wage rate for nonunion labor falls. Since this effect on nonunion labor covers about three-fourths of the labor force, the resource allocation effects of unions can be substantial in the aggregate.

As international trade increases, the ability of unions and firms to affect consumer prices becomes more limited. Free trade thus hampers the market power of unions and firms and, in general, protects consumers and nonunion workers. As noted above, unions are not supportive of free trade agreements.

Table 13.2 provides some data about the behavior over time of the share of national income that goes to labor. Two ways of measuring labor's share are shown. The second column measures total employee compensation (wage and salaries) plus the employer's share of the Social Security tax as a percentage of national income. This series shows a slight upward trend since World War II, a rise that has been attributed to a decline in the number of self-employed workers over this period, primarily in agriculture.

The third column in the table adds the income of self-employed persons—such as business proprietors, lawyers, and accountants—to employee compensation. Self-

TABLE 13.2

Labor's Share of National Income

The percentage of the nation's real output that labor receives has increased slightly since World War II. This increase is attributed to a decrease in small owner-managed firms rather than to union activities.

Year	Total Employee Compensation (Including Employer Contribution for Social Insurance) (percent of national income)	Total Employee Compensation plus Self-Employment Income (percent of national income)
1960	69.0	81.1
1965	67.5	77.9
1970	73.5	83.0
1975	72.8	82.1
1980	73.7	81.6
1985	71.7	79.6
1986	72.5	80.3
1987	72.3	80.3
1988	71.7	79.8
1989	71.7	79.8
1990	72.0	80.1
1991	72.6	80.5
1992	73.0	81.5
1993	72.4	80.1
1994	71.7	80.2
1995	71.0	79.2
1996	70.5	78.9
1997	70.5	78.8
1998	71.1	79.4

Sources: U.S. Department of Commerce, *Survey of Current Business,* various issues; Council of Economic Advisers, *Economic Report of the President* (Washington, D.C.: U.S. Government Printing Office, 1999), p. 358.

employment compensation is clearly income that goes to labor. When we look at this more inclusive concept of labor's share of national income, we see that it has been virtually constant for almost forty years. Thus, even when labor union strength grew in the United States, we do not find any evidence that labor's share of national income rose. While labor unions have increased the wages of their members relative to the wages of nonunion workers, there is no evidence to suggest that they have made all workers better off in terms of their share of national income.

The fact is that higher real wages for workers can come about only through increases in worker productivity. Workers in the United States earn high wages because their productivity is high. Their wages can rise only if the output of goods and services in the American economy is increased. All things being equal, it is the level of productivity that explains real wages.

CONCLUSION

The goals of unions are easy to understand. The members want more income, greater income security, and more pleasant working conditions than the market provides. Their ability to achieve these goals is limited by many factors, including the supplies of competing inputs, the monopsony power of employers, and the political power of unions. Unions have provided their members with higher wages and better job security, but they also provide something more.

The union's role extends beyond an economic wage and employment analysis to the plant, where the union provides workers with a set of rules and representation to settle disputes with employers. This presence of the union on the job cannot be discounted as a primary source of nonpecuniary benefits to union members. Such benefits accrue to workers in the form of greater job security, a feeling of power and dignity at work, and less alienation from their work. These are important aspects of work in modern factories and offices, and the union's role in providing workplace representation is a powerful force for creating greater worker satisfaction and thus greater productivity.

There is much concern today over the meaningfulness of work. Workers are said to be alienated and bored by assembly-line types of jobs. In this respect, the role of the union as an arbitrator of workplace rules and procedures will probably become increasingly important. Workers may be willing to trade off some wage gains to obtain changes in the way their work is done. If so, unions are certain to seek more meaningful jobs and factory arrangements for workers in future labor contracts.

APPLICATION

Should College Football Players Be Paid? The NCAA Monopsony

College athletics in the United States are governed by rules established by the National Collegiate Athletic Association (NCAA), a collection of colleges and universities that compete in intercollegiate athletics. The NCAA establishes and enforces the rules under which college players can be recruited and compensated for their play. The NCAA rules are very complicated and regulate all aspects of the player's relationship with the school. The bottom line, however, is that the NCAA regulations create a collusive agreement among colleges and universities to act as a monopsony in the purchase of high school athletes' services. In other words, the NCAA has established a buyers' cartel for athletic labor.

Colleges and universities are the only buyers of high school football and basketball players. (Baseball has minor professional leagues in which high school players can work and be paid for their services; many tennis players turn professional at a young age, skipping college competition altogether.) Even though a talented college football or basketball player may generate a lot of ticket sales and television revenues for the school, NCAA rules forbid the player from being paid a wage (beyond tuition, room, board, and incidentals) equal to the marginal revenue product of the player. (Marginal revenue product is the increase in school revenues realized by having the particular athlete playing for the school.) Marginal revenue product may be small for a benchwarmer, but it can run into the millions (TV revenue, sold-out stadiums, bowl and postseason tournament revenues, bumper stickers, and so on) for the services of an All-American basketball player or a Heisman Trophy–winning football star. Instead, the player can only be given a scholarship, room and board, and certain other min-

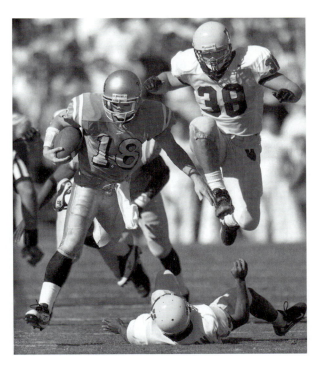

Payment of wages to college football players and other athletes, though much defended by college presidents, have a clear economic justification.

imal living allowances. Even the details of a player's summer or off-season employment are tightly regulated by the NCAA.

The NCAA system is a monopsony because (1) it is an agreement among schools to create a single system for compensating athletes, and (2) it functions so as to pay athletes less than they contribute to school athletic revenues.

Just like in an output or sellers' cartel, the NCAA agreement to hold down players' wages must be enforced. Individual schools will find it in their interest to cheat on the agreement by offering good players "illegal" inducements (cars, money) to play for them. Clearly, it is advantageous for any given school to behave in this way if all other schools follow the rules. Such a strategy will lead to the recruitment of better players, athletic success, and larger revenues. Cheaters must therefore be rooted out and punished by the NCAA. This is done in a variety of ways, such as taking away valuable bowl, tournament, and TV opportunities from violators or reducing the number of "legal" scholarships the cheating school can offer in the future.

There is no particular reason that college athletics could not be treated like any other form of student employment where the students are paid a wage for their work. What would be so bad about doing this with college football and basketball players? Colleges do not want to pay competitive market wages to their student-athletes, since this would erode their profits from athletic events. Of course, one should not downplay the ideals of amateur athletics and the amateur athlete. However, there is little economic justification for not paying the full value for the work done by student-athletes. A wage scale, for example, for college football players would bring into the open what are currently under-the-table practices, clean up the recruiting process considerably, and allow young college athletes to accrue savings.

In any event, the NCAA has established a monopsony that functions to benefit colleges and universities at the expense of student-athletes and their families (who are often from low-income and minority backgrounds). One would therefore predict that the most vocal defenders of the NCAA buyers' cartel will be college presidents. Students can easily check this prediction by soliciting the view of their president and administration on this matter; college officials will defend their position on the grounds that playing for pay would somehow corrupt the ideals of the amateur student-athlete. However, what is the difference between the basketball player and the student who works the graveyard shift at a local radio station to pay for school? Should all student jobs be banned? And what about graduate students, professors, and coaches?

QUESTIONS

Which type of schools, low-tuition or high-tuition, would you expect to violate the NCAA regulations more often? What will stadium size have to do with NCAA violations? What is the role of coaches in the NCAA cartel?

SUMMARY

1. A labor union is a group of workers in a craft, industry, or government job who organize to gain market power.

2. Labor unions attempt to improve the economic welfare of their members by increasing wages, decreasing the elasticity of demand for their services, and increasing the demand for their members' labor through a variety of activities.

3. Monopsony exists when there is a lack of competition in the employment of labor. A single buyer may force wages below the competitive level.

4. In a bilateral monopoly in a labor market, the wage is determined by the relative strength of the bargainers.

5. A union's ability to achieve its goals is in part determined by its bargaining strength. A union's ability to strike is its strongest negotiating tool.

6. It is estimated that unions have increased the wages of their members relative to nonunion workers in similar occupations.

7. Union activities have not increased all labor's share of total income. Gains made by union labor have generally been at the expense of employers, nonunion labor, and consumers.

KEY TERMS

labor union
craft union
industrial union
public employees' union

total wage bill
monopsony
exploitation of labor
bilateral monopoly

collective bargaining
strike
binding arbitration
right-to-work law

QUESTIONS FOR REVIEW AND DISCUSSION

1. How do craft unions increase wages for their members? What happens to the people who are not allowed into a craft union?

2. If industrial unions allow into the union anyone who wishes to enter, how can they increase wages? Could an industrial union in an isolated mining town increase both wages and employment?

3. Suppose the United States exports beef to Japan and imports cars from Japan. If autoworkers persuade Congress to impose a tariff on Japanese cars, what happens to the incomes of cattle ranchers and ranch hands?

4. Why do unions want to decrease the elasticity of demand for their members? How do they do so?

5. What is a monopsony? Does the existence of labor unions promote the existence of monopsonies?

6. It is frequently suggested that firms exploit women in the labor force. Monopsonists' power to exploit is based on the immobility of labor. Are women less mobile than men?

7. In the former Soviet Union, there was only one potential employer—the government. Did the former Soviet Union have the power to exploit workers? Could workers avoid exploitation?

8. Why are unions and union employers forced to negotiate wages while nonunion wages are determined without negotiation?

9. Are union wages closer to the monopsony wage or to the wage that maximizes the wage bill?

10. Suppose that a union is successful at organizing only part of the laborers in an industry. Do you predict that the union will be strong or weak? Why?

11. Why do you think unions favor minimum-wage laws?

12. How do the following affect the elasticity of demand for union labor: elasticity of demand for a product, the availability of substitutes, and union labor as a proportion of total costs?

13. What is bilateral monopoly? How is price determined in this model?

PROBLEMS

1. Suppose that all of the nurses in a particular state are employed in hospitals and nursing homes and that all earn equally competitive wages. Now suppose that some of the nurses in hospitals decide to form a union and to restrict membership in the union. Further assume that they have the legal authority of the state government to do so. As a result of these actions, nurses must be in the union to be employed in hospitals. Using supply and demand curves, show what happens to the wages in the union and nonunion nursing markets after unionization.

2. We tend to think of unions as those involving manufacturing or government services. Many professions, however, take on certain union characteristics. Consider the legal profession, for example. Entry is restricted and returns are raised. What sort of techniques and policies might lawyers and the legal profession use in order to establish and protect their "union"?

WORKING WITH THE WEB

1. Strikes are one of the most powerful tools used by unions. To get an idea of some strikes that have occurred in the past, go to http://www.igc.apc.org/strike/archive.html and scroll through the listed strikes that have been resolved. Are wages the only cause of the strikes?

2. Union membership spans a variety of occupations as well as a variety of demographic factors. Go to http://www.bls.gov/news.release/union2.nws.htm and read the summary on union statistics for 1998.
   a. What occupational group has the highest rate of union membership?
   b. Are men and women equally likely to be union members?
   c. By what percentage do union workers outpace their nonunion counterparts in terms of earnings when working full-time?
   d. What percentage of the private sector labor force is unionized? How does this compare with the unionization in the government sector?

3. Monopsony is said to exist when there is a single buyer of a resource, such as labor. A historical example of monopsony was the case of being the only employer in a town. If that was the case, workers who wished to offer their labor in exchange for a wage had no alternatives. As a result, they were paid less than the revenue they generated for the firm. A similar situation has been said to exist in Major League Baseball. To learn more, go to http://www.economicsamerica.org/econedlink/newsline/sports/app2.html.
   a. What is offered as evidence of the existence of a monopsonistic market in baseball?
   b. What is offered as an alternative system to the current draft and contract arrangement? In terms of salary, how would such a system benefit players?
   c. Does the salary data support the claim of Major League Baseball as a monopsony?

14

Capital, Land, and Entrepreneurship

T hus far, we have looked at labor and its corresponding factor payment, wages. In this chapter we look at the other factors of production, and their corresponding factor payments, including capital and interest, land and economic rent, and entrepreneurship and economic profits. As we will see, the returns to these other factors of production can also be explained by the marginal productivity theory of input prices. After reading Chapter 14 you should understand

- that the choice between consuming and saving is a key factor in producing larger quantities of goods and services.
- how the rate of interest is determined.
- the concept of economic rent and the process by which land is priced.
- the nature of entrepreneurship, including the role of entrepreneurs in any economy and the rewards entrepreneurs get.

THE ROLE OF CAPITAL

Wealthy societies consume, or use, goods and services at an ever-increasing rate. Think, for instance, of the rate at which automobiles have become available in this country. Relatively few Americans owned cars sixty years ago, and most of those proud owners were happy to keep the same car for years. Today, many of us own more than one car, and most of us change cars at least every four or five years. Since consumption is possible only through production, the basis of a wealthy society is not its ability to consume but its ability to produce, to transform raw materials into more useful goods and services through the application of human skills and physical capital such as tools and factories. Societies that are better at this transformation are able to reach higher levels of wealth and to consume more.

Roundabout Production and Capital Formation

Economic behavior is forward-looking. The availability of the food we eat today is due to the foresight of farmers in the past who undertook the appropriate productive actions. The food we will eat tomorrow depends on actions farmers take now. A simple analogy illustrates this point.

Imagine Robinson Crusoe trying to survive alone on a windswept island in the middle of the ocean. Crusoe's economy is primitive. He lives by fishing with a simple wooden spear that he found on the beach. With his spear Crusoe can catch 5 pounds of fish in about 10 hours of fishing. Suppose that one day Crusoe decides to improve his fishing technique by weaving a fishing net.

Crusoe takes a day off to build the net. His opportunity cost of building the net is the fish that he would have caught during this day by fishing with his spear. Assuming that it takes 10 hours to build the net, the opportunity cost of the net to Crusoe is 5 pounds of fish.

Crusoe's purpose in building the net is to catch more fish in the future. That is, he hopes the net will enable him to catch more than 5 pounds in 10 hours. The anticipation of more production and therefore more consumption in the future drives Crusoe to a **roundabout production** of fish.

Of course, Crusoe must have some way to support himself during the period that he stops fishing to weave the net. He provides for his needs during this time by **saving.** If he consumes 5 pounds of fish every 10 hours and it takes 10 hours to make a net, Crusoe must set aside 5 pounds of fish to support himself while making the net. To do so, he could fish extra hours for several days, or he could eat only 4 pounds each day for 5 days. The hallmark of saving is some form of current sacrifice in anticipation of a higher level of future consumption. More hours worked means fewer hours for current leisure; fewer fish eaten in the present mean fewer calories consumed. However Crusoe manages to save fish, his planned one-day abstinence from spearfishing leads to saving and to a greater yield of fish.

What is Crusoe's incentive to abstain? Suppose that with the net he can catch 25 pounds of fish in 10 hours and that the net will last indefinitely. By abstaining from spearfishing for 10 hours, at a cost of 5 pounds of fish, Crusoe is able to raise his daily catch by 20 pounds. The increase is even more significant in the long run: For an investment of a mere 5 pounds of fish, Crusoe raises his weekly catch from 35 pounds to 175 pounds, an increase of 140 pounds per week. This particular act of saving and investment of resources to produce more capital is especially profitable. Indeed, even if the net wears out every so often, Crusoe will be able to afford to take 10 hours to make a new net in anticipation of similar rates of return in the future.

This simple example has relevance to a modern economy. In a modern economy individuals specialize in their activities. They don't spend part of the day fishing and part of the day making rods and reels. But this specialization does not change any of the essential features of what is called capital formation.

The term **capital formation** refers to the process of building capital goods and adding to the capital stock in the economy. Capital goods are things such as

Roundabout production
The current production of capital goods so that greater amounts of consumption goods can be produced in the future.

Saving
The act of forgoing present consumption in order to increase future consumption.

Capital formation
An increase in the stock of capital due to roundabout production.

Capital stock

The total amount of capital goods that exists in an economy at any point in time.

machines and implements that are used to produce final goods and services. The **capital stock** of an economy is the amount of capital goods that exists at a given point in time. To increase capital stock, producers must resort to the use and production of capital goods as a means of achieving greater output in the future. Saving, or the abstinence from present consumption, is required for capital formation to take place.

Another important feature of capital is that it does not automatically reproduce itself. Instead, capital goods automatically decrease in productivity or value over time, a process known as **depreciation.** This wearing out of capital goods cannot be stopped. The capital goods or capital stock of a society must be repaired and replaced over time if the society is to continue to grow and experience high levels of consumption. This is one of the primary problems of economics: maintaining and increasing the ability to produce.

Depreciation

The wearing out of capital goods that occurs with usage over time.

Capital consumption is the opposite of capital formation. Present consumption is increased temporarily at the cost of a reduction in the future rate of consumption. Suppose that a lumber company owns trees ranging in age from 1 to 25 years. Assume that it cuts down one thousand 25-year-old trees and plants one thousand seedlings each year. As long as external circumstances do not change, this forest can yield one thousand 25-year-old trees annually. For a while, however, the yield from the forest can be increased by harvesting some of the 24-year-old trees in addition to the regular harvest, then dipping into the stock of 23-year-old trees the next year, and so on. Cut in this manner, the amount of timber harvested will increase for a while. Still, the time will come when the total output of the forest will necessarily decline. Capital in the form of younger trees has been used up to increase current output, so the future output of timber must fall. This is capital consumption.

Capital consumption

A decrease in the capital stock; occurs when the rate of depreciation is greater than the rate of capital formation.

The Rate of Interest

Saving and capital formation depend on the willingness of individuals to pass up current consumption to achieve greater consumption in the future. In other words, individuals must abstain from current consumption to provide the flow of saving that is used to produce capital goods. Economists stress that an individual's willingness to abstain from current consumption is related to his or her **rate of time preference.** Time preference is the degree of patience that an individual has in forgoing present consumption in order to save. A person with a high rate of time preference has a strong preference for current rather than future consumption. Most individuals have positive rates of time preference; that is, they prefer present to future consumption. Since people prefer to consume now rather than later, they must be paid a price, or be rewarded, for waiting. This price is called **interest.**

Rate of time preference

The percent increase in future consumption over present consumption that is necessary to just induce an individual to be indifferent between present and future consumption.

Interest

The compensation to savers for the act of saving (forgoing present consumption) or the payment made by borrowers; when measured as a percent of the amount borrowed or lent, it is referred to as an interest rate.

The concept of interest has two related meanings. In the first sense, interest refers to returns on investments. A person who saves $100 in a passbook account earns 4 percent interest on saving. A firm that invests $1000 in a new piece of machinery earns $200 more in revenue annually because of the resulting improvement in productivity. The firm's investment thus yields 20 percent interest. In these terms, interest is the amount individuals are willing to *receive* in order to sacrifice current consumption; it is a payment for their abstinence, or waiting to consume.

Interest is also the price that individuals are willing to *pay* to obtain a good or service now rather than later. A consumer who wants a car today might pay 13 percent interest for a loan from the bank. A firm that wants a new plant might pay 10 percent interest to get the necessary financing.

Interest is not just a monetary phenomenon. Whether paid or received, interest is based on the fact that people prefer to consume and invest now rather than later. Moreover, the rate of interest reflects the rate of time preference in the economy. The more impatient people are, the higher the rate of interest must be to induce them to save and to create capital goods.

Demand and Supply of Loanable Funds

The rate of interest is determined in the market for loanable funds. It is, in effect, the price of loanable funds. Like other markets, the market for loanable funds has a demand side and a supply side. (For more on the market for loanable funds, see the Application "Trading Property Rights: Stocks and Bonds" at the conclusion of this chapter.)

Demand for loanable funds
A curve or schedule that shows the various amounts individuals are willing and able to borrow at different interest rates.

The **demand for loanable funds** arises from three sources. Consumers demand loanable funds because they want to consume more now than their current incomes will permit. Loans to these individuals are called consumption loans. They are made for myriad reasons. Individuals may want to take a vacation now and pay for it on time, borrow to tide themselves over a temporary decline in income, or borrow to buy cars or household appliances.

The second source of demand for loanable funds is desire for investment loans. Investors borrow to finance the construction and use of capital goods and methods of production that are expected to be productive. Firms borrow funds to build new plants and to purchase new equipment in the expectation that such investments will increase profits.

A third source of loanable funds demand is the government. Governments at all levels—local, state, and federal—demand funds to cover deficits (when tax receipts do not cover government expenditures), to finance road construction and schools, and to service debt. This demand is added to private demands for loanable funds for consumption and investing purposes.

The sum of the demand for consumption, investment, and government loans equals the total demand for loanable funds. The law of demand applies to the demand for loanable funds just as it does to any other commodity (see Figure 14.1). The price one must pay to borrow funds for consumption or investment loans is the interest rate. According to the law of demand, the amount of funds demanded is inversely related to the interest rate. As the interest rate falls, the cost of borrowing money to finance the earlier availability of consumption and capital goods falls. Other things being equal, we thus expect to see more borrowing when the interest rate falls. At a lower rate of interest, consumers will expand current consumption, and more investment projects will appear to be profitable.

Supply of loanable funds
A curve or schedule that shows the various amounts individuals are willing and able to lend or save at different rates.

In Figure 14.1, the **supply of loanable funds,** S, is provided by savers. These are individuals or firms who are willing to consume less than their present earnings in order to set aside something for the future. As the interest rate—in this case, the return on investment—rises, more and more individuals and firms will be enticed to save; that is, they will forgo current consumption in order to consume even more in the future. Thus, the quantity supplied of loanable funds varies positively with the interest rate offered to savers.

The intersection of the demand and supply curves for loanable funds in Figure 14.1 yields an equilibrium interest rate and the equilibrium level of loanable funds. At i and Q, the market for loanable funds is in equilibrium, and the plans of borrowers are compatible with the plans of lenders. At interest rates above i,

FIGURE 14.1

FIGURE 14.1

Determination of Interest Rates

D and *S* are the demand and supply curves for loanable funds. The market for loanable funds reaches equilibrium at *i* and *Q,* where the plans of borrowers and lenders are compatible. That is, for a given interest rate, the amount that borrowers want to borrow and the amount that lenders want to lend are equal.

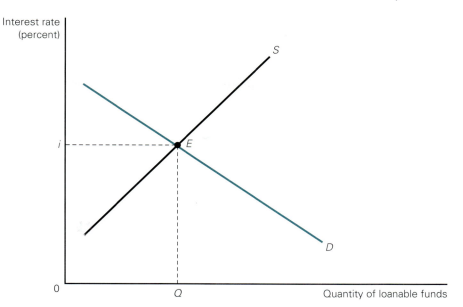

Interest rate (percent)

Quantity of loanable funds

there will be an excess supply of savings, putting pressure on the interest rate to fall. Below *i,* there will be an excess demand for loanable funds, putting pressure on the interest rate to rise. (See the Focus "Should You Be Protected from High Interest Rates? Usury and Interest Groups" for an example of the effects of controlled interest rates.)

Variations Among Interest Rates   The discussion of the supply and demand for loanable funds might suggest that there is one interest rate in the economy. In reality there is a multiplicity of interest rates: the prime interest rate given to businesses with excellent credit ratings, mortgage rates offered to home buyers, credit card rates, consumer loan rates, and so on. These interest rates tend to be different. For instance, the interest rate on government bonds is generally lower than the interest rate on corporate bonds. What are some of the reasons that interest rates differ?

Risk
The chance that a borrower will default or fail to repay a loan.

Risk   The **risk** associated with particular borrowers—their likelihood to default on repaying a loan—in part accounts for the differences in interest rates. Creditors go to great lengths to ascertain the degree of this risk, and they adjust the interest rate they charge accordingly. Loans to a government agency will carry a low interest rate because the risk of default is very low. Government can use its power to tax to repay loans. On the other hand, loans to unemployed workers will carry high interest rates because the risk of default is high.

Cost of Making Loans   The cost of making loans differs. Large loans and small loans may require the same amount of accounting and bookkeeping work. The large loan will therefore be less costly to process per dollar loaned; for this reason it will carry a lower interest rate than the small loan. This distinction means, for example, that loans to large companies will carry a lower interest rate than loans to small companies.

Time   The length of time over which a loan is made will affect the rate of interest charged. The longer the term of the loan, the more things that can go wrong for the

FOCUS

Should You Be Protected from High Interest Rates? Usury and Interest Groups

Price controls have been known to all ages and all civilizations. The Roman Emperor Diocletian invoked general price and wage controls prior to the fall of the Roman Empire. During the Middle Ages, church doctrine combined with economic policy to create civil laws related to interest-taking. The laws, called usury laws, originated as early as Greek and Roman times in the belief that an uncontrolled market produced interest rates that were "too high." The laws consisted of a legal limit on the amount of interest that lenders could charge or borrowers pay. Such laws survive today in the enactments of certain U.S. state legislatures that protect borrowers with usury or "loan shark" laws and in federal regulations that establish the maximum interest rate allowable on small savings deposits.

The mechanics of the usury laws are simple; we demonstrate them in Figure 14.2. The figure shows the free-market supply and demand for loanable funds. Market equilibrium occurs at point E, where quantity demanded equals quantity supplied (Q_E) and where the equilibrium price—the market interest rate—is i_E.

What happens when the government declares that market rate i_E is too high for the poor and that henceforth the maximum rate will be i_C, a ceiling rate below i_E? At rate i_C the quantity of loanable funds demanded, Q_D (point C in Figure 14.2), exceeds the quantity supplied, Q_S (point B). A shortage of funds, BC, develops at the ceiling interest rate because banks are unwilling to lend the quantity of funds demanded at rate i_C. The available funds, Q_S, must be rationed because of the shortage. In the absence of price rationing, the process can take other forms. Unscrupulous lenders—"loan sharks"—may charge black market rates for the limited funds. Lenders may begin demanding additional collateral or better credit standing for loans at the ceiling rate, reducing their risk and making it more difficult for less creditworthy borrowers to obtain funds. Such borrowers are often the people whom the laws were designed to protect. The poor are often compelled to acquire funds from loan sharks in such circumstances. Usury laws, like all other forms of price controls, have built-in effects that often hurt those who are supposed to be the beneficiaries.

FIGURE 14.2

Interest Rate Ceiling

When a ceiling is placed on interest rates (i_C), a shortage (BC) develops, representing the difference between the quantity of funds that lending institutions are willing and able to supply (Q_S) and the quantity of funds that borrowers demand (Q_D). Without the ceiling, the forces of supply and demand interact to create equilibrium (E) between the plans of demanders and suppliers of loanable funds.

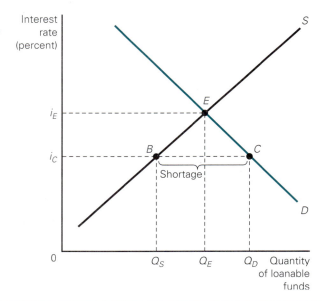

borrower. Because the risk of default rises with the length of the loan, longer-term borrowers must pay a premium for this rise. Long-term loans will carry higher interest rates than short-term loans, other things being equal. In addition to the risk factor, borrowers are willing to pay a premium for the longer availability of funds.

Nominal rate of interest
The market-determined rate of interest; usually expressed as a percentage per year of the dollar or nominal amount of the loan.

Inflation rate
The percent by which the average level of prices in an economy rises; usually expressed as a percent per year.

Real rate of interest
The nominal interest rate minus the rate of inflation; the interest measured in terms of real buying power.

Nominal and Real Rates of Interest   The **nominal rate of interest** is the interest rate set in the market for loanable funds. With inflation in the economy, the nominal rate of interest can be a misleading measure of how much borrowers pay for consumption and investment loans. Suppose that the **inflation rate,** which is the rate at which the average level of all prices in the economy rises, is 12 percent per year and that the nominal rate of interest is 17 percent. A borrower who borrows $100 will have to repay $117 in a year. However, during the year the average level of prices increases by 12 percent. The $117 paid to the lender at the end of the year will not buy the same amount of goods as the $100 made available to the borrower one year earlier. Since prices have risen by 12 percent, $100 a year ago is equivalent to $112 today. Therefore, the lender of the $100 effectively earns $5 on his or her loan ($117 minus $112), or a 5 percent real rate of return ($5 divided by $100). Thus, when the rate of inflation is factored out, the **real rate of interest** is 5 percent, or 17 percent minus 12 percent.

Lenders and borrowers will not generally be fooled by inflation. The nominal rate of interest will adjust to account for the expected inflation rate. The nominal rate of interest will include a premium to compensate lenders for the expected depreciation of the purchasing power of their principal and interest. Lenders will have to be compensated for expected inflation, or they will reduce the amount they are willing to lend. Borrowers will also recognize that they will be repaying loans with dollars of less purchasing power and will adjust the amount of interest they are willing to pay to obtain loans. In the above example, if both borrowers and lenders fully anticipate a 12 percent inflation rate, the nominal rate of interest will adjust to 17 percent. As the inflation rate changes, the nominal rate of interest will also change to reflect the level of expected inflation. The real rate of interest is the nominal rate of interest minus the expected inflation rate. In the late 1970s, the nominal rate of interest rose to over 20 percent on some types of loans, but the expected inflation rate was about 15 percent, so the real interest rate was only 5 percent.

Interest as the Return to Capital

So far we have considered interest to be the price of loanable funds. Interest may also be viewed as the return that goes to capital as a factor of production. The entrepreneur who buys a machine for $100 and makes $25 a year by using it in production earns 25 percent interest on the investment. Using this concept of interest, we can see how entrepreneurs make investment decisions.

The return earned on capital depends on the quantity of capital in use. In a world with only a few machines, the return on machines would be quite high. As the quantity of machines in use increased, the returns on the margin to each machine would decline. In Figure 14.3, the marginal return to capital is depicted as *MRC*. If a capital stock of Q_1 existed, the interest return to capital would be i_1. With a larger capital stock of Q_2, the return would fall to i_2.

To see how entrepreneurs decide how much capital to acquire, consider the marginal return to capital curve in Figure 14.3 as a demand curve. At an interest rate of i_1, entrepreneurs would prefer to hold Q_1 units of capital. If they initially had less than Q_1 units of capital, it would pay them to borrow funds at an interest

FIGURE 14.3

Return on Investment in Capital Goods

MRC shows the marginal return to capital. Because of diminishing returns, the return to capital declines as the capital stock increases. The *MRC* curve can also be viewed as the demand for capital curve, since it shows how large a capital stock entrepreneurs will want at each interest rate. If the interest rate falls from i_1 to i_2, entrepreneurs will undertake additional investment until the capital stock rises from Q_1 to Q_2.

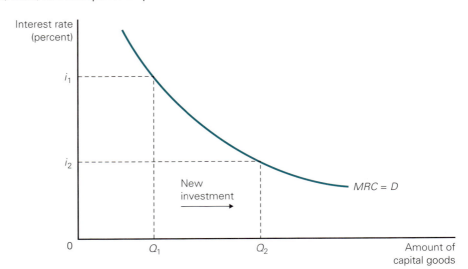

rate i_1 and use the money to obtain new capital that earned an interest rate above i_1. New capital would be acquired until the stock of capital rose to Q_1 and the return fell to i_1. Beyond that point, it no longer would be profitable to borrow money to obtain additional capital.

If the interest rate fell to i_2, firms would have an incentive to undertake new investment and increase their capital from Q_1 to Q_2 units. Other things remaining unchanged, a decline in the interest rate will lead to an increase in capital stock. A direct link exists between the market for loanable funds and the market for capital goods. An increase in the supply of loanable funds will cause the interest rate to fall, and this will lead to new investment. New investment will increase capital stock and lead to future increases in the productive capacity of the economy, causing living standards to rise.

The Nature of Returns to Owners of Capital

Individuals invest in capital goods because they expect to make a rate of return in excess of the cost of capital. The elements of this rate of return can be broken down into three categories: pure interest, risk, and profits and losses.

Pure interest

The interest associated with a risk-free loan. The interest rate that produces pure interest is called the risk-free interest rate.

Pure Interest   Capital investment yields a return called **pure interest,** the interest rate that must be paid to induce saving when the lender bears little or no risk. Think of pure interest this way: You have a sum of money, and you're trying to decide whether to invest in a piece of capital equipment or a savings account at the bank with a virtually guaranteed return of 5 percent. The 5 percent is a pure interest yield on your money; in a year you will have earned a 5 percent return on your investment in the savings account. Unless you are confident that the alternative investment in the equipment will yield at least 5 percent, there is no incentive for you to invest in it. Investments in capital equipment must pay at least the pure rate of interest, or investors will not provide funds for investments. Again, the pure rate of interest is the rate that must be paid to induce individuals to abstain from current consumption and to save.

Risk   Suppose that you are confronted with the following offer: You can have $100 for sure or you can have a 50–50 chance of receiving $200. The expected value of each alternative is the same. In the second alternative, the probability of receiving $200 is 0.50, and the probability of receiving no money is 0.50. Thus, 0.50($200) + 0.50($0) = $100. Yet the individual decision maker is not indifferent between these alternatives. The latter alternative involves risk, while the former does not. Individuals generally view the bearing of risk as a cost and have to be compensated to bear risk.

Risk has a lot to do with capital investment. There is no guarantee of a handsome rate of return on investments in capital goods. Market conditions can change, making the capital goods obsolete or making the things that the capital goods produce less popular with consumers. In other words, capital investments involve risks, so a premium must be paid to induce individual investors to bear risks on their investments. This risk premium is above and beyond the pure rate of interest.

Profits and Losses   Investors in capital goods can earn economic profits or losses. The opportunity cost of fixed capital is the price that must be paid to keep it committed to its present use. This cost consists of the pure interest and any risk premium. Yet something unexpected can happen in the economy to make the fixed capital more valuable. For example, the demand for the product produced by fixed capital may increase many times over what was expected. In such a case the owners of capital earn economic profits on their investment in addition to pure interest and a risk premium. In a competitive market, these returns will be eliminated by competition as other investors become aware of the excess returns and make capital investments of their own in the industry. Keep in mind, too, that economic profits can be negative; that is, investors in capital goods can incur large and unexpected losses.

These profits and losses are analogous to capital gains and losses to investors in the stock market. A capital gain, for example, derives from an unexpected increase in the value of a firm.

Summarizing, the rate of return to capital investment embodies three components: a pure interest return, a premium for bearing risk, and a residual component reflecting unexpected changes in the value of capital goods. Each of these components has an important allocative function in the economy. Pure interest induces people to save. The risk premium leads individuals to invest in risky but valuable ventures. Economic profits are the spur to entrepreneurship and innovation in the economy. We have more to say about profits and entrepreneurship later in this chapter.

The Present Value of Future Income

Present value
The value today of a payment to be made or received in the future; a future sum discounted by the current rate of interest.

Investment in capital goods and saving balances the needs of tomorrow with the needs of today. Economists find it useful to look at this balancing act in a precise mathematical formula called *present value*. **Present value** refers to the value today of some payment that will be received in the future. This value depends on the current rate of interest and the length of time between the present and future.

How, for instance, would the prospect of making $100 in one year or in two years compare with the prospect of making $100 now, with an interest rate of 10 percent? The $100 made now would by definition have a present value of $100. But what about the $100 made in one year? What would be the equivalent amount of money made now? That is, what amount invested now at 10 percent would be able to generate a fund of $100 in one year? The answer is $90.91 with simple interest, computed by the formula

$$PV = \frac{\text{receipts in one year}}{1 + \text{interest rate}} = \frac{\$100}{(1 + 0.10)} = \$90.91.$$

What sum invested now at 10 percent and compounded annually would produce $100 after two years? Since we are interested in the amount that would yield $100 in *two* years, we *square* the denominator of the formula we used to calculate the present value of money invested for one year:

$$PV = \frac{\$100}{(1 + 0.10)^2} = \$82.64.$$

By extension of this procedure, the present value of any amount at any time in the future can be computed. The formula for doing this is

$$PV = \frac{A_n}{(1 + r)^n},$$

where A_n is the actual amount anticipated in a particular year in the future, r is the rate of interest, and n refers to the particular year in the future.

Note two aspects of present value computations. First, the lower the rate of interest used in making these computations, the higher will be the present value attributed to any given amount of income to be made in the future. Table 14.1 illustrates this point clearly. The present value of $100 one year from now is approximately $97.10 at a 3 percent interest rate and approximately $89.30 at a 12 percent interest rate. Second, the present value of a given amount to be received in the future declines as the date of receipt advances farther into the future. In Table 14.1, for any given interest rate the present value of $100 is less the farther it is to be received in the future. To see this relation, simply read down any column in the table. The point is that the present value of future revenues or costs is inversely related to the rate of interest and the distance of the date in the future when payment will be received.

The Benefits of Capital Formation

Saving means abstaining from consumption now in the expectation of being able to consume more in the future. Saving thus provides the resources needed to increase the stock of capital goods in the economy. A large stock of capital goods raises the rate of consumption that can be sustained in the future. Saving clearly benefits the saver, but it also benefits those who do not save. Indeed, the benefits from saving are diffused throughout the whole economy. Most of us benefit from advances in computer technology, though few of us contributed to the saving that made such advances possible.

Saving and capital formation also lead to higher wages and incomes for workers. In a competitive economy wages are a function of the productivity of workers, and this productivity is in turn a function of the amount and quality of the equip-

TABLE 14.1

The Present Value of $100 at Various Years in the Future
The farther in the future the $100 is received, reading vertically down the table at any interest rate, the less it is worth now. Reading horizontally across the table, the higher the interest rate, the less is the value of $100 at any year in the future.

Years in the Future	3%	5%	7%	10%	12%
1	$97.10	$92.50	$93.50	$90.90	$89.30
2	94.30	90.70	87.30	82.60	79.70
3	91.50	86.40	81.60	75.10	71.10
4	88.80	82.30	76.30	68.30	63.60
5	86.30	78.40	71.30	62.00	56.70
6	83.70	74.60	66.60	56.40	50.70
7	81.30	71.10	62.30	51.30	45.20
8	78.90	67.70	58.20	46.60	40.40
9	76.60	64.50	54.40	42.40	36.00
10	74.40	61.40	50.80	38.50	32.20
.	.	.	.	.	.
.	.	.	.	.	.
15	64.20	48.10	36.20	23.90	18.30
.	.	.	.	.	.
20	55.40	37.70	25.80	14.80	10.40
.	.	.	.	.	.
30	41.20	23.10	13.10	5.73	3.34
.	.	.	.	.	.
40	30.70	14.20	6.70	2.21	1.07
.	.	.	.	.	.
50	22.80	8.70	2.13	.85	.35

ment and tools that workers use. A worker with a tractor is far more productive than a worker with a mule-drawn plow. Since more productive workers are paid more, some of the benefits from capital formation are spread to workers who did not necessarily contribute to the saving that made the capital formation possible.

Indeed, those who save and who build capital goods are among the chief benefactors of society. The reverse is also true: Policies that reduce the incentive to save and to produce capital goods, while appearing to harm the suppliers of saving and the owners of capital goods, actually hurt all of us.

THE CONCEPT OF ECONOMIC RENT

Rent
A payment to a factor of production in excess of the factor's opportunity cost.

A farmer pays rent to a landowner for the use of an acre of land. A student leases an apartment and pays rent to the landlord each month. A sales representative rents a car to call on customers in a distant city. These examples use the word *rent* in its most familiar sense—payment for the use of something. For the economist **rent** refers to the portion of the payment to any factor of production—land, labor, or capital—that is over and above the factor's opportunity cost. It is the amount a factor is paid that is greater than the forgone value of its next most productive use. Nearly every factor you can name has alternative uses. Farmland could be used as the site of an industrial park. An engineer could be put to use typing correspondence.

Pure economic rent
The total payment to a factor of production whose supply curve is perfectly inelastic.

Economists originally introduced the concept of rent in discussing the nature of the returns to landowners. A **pure economic rent** is the payment to a factor of production that has a perfectly inelastic supply curve. In such a case the price of the resource is determined solely by the level of demand for its services because supply is fixed and does not change as price changes. Land in the aggregate is the classic example of a resource whose supply is given and whose return is characterized as a pure economic rent.

LAND RENTS

How is land priced? The obvious answer is that the price of land is determined where its demand and supply curves intersect. While this is correct, there are some special aspects of the price-determination process in the case of land. These aspects concern how the supply curve of land is defined. Although the focus of our discussion will be the supply of land, keep in mind the role of the demand curve for land. As you learned in Chapter 12, this demand curve is based on the marginal productivity of land. In this regard the demand curve for land is the same as the demand curve for any factor of production—it is based on the expected marginal revenue product of land as a factor of production. When land is rented, rent is paid to the landowner. The greater the demand for land, the larger the rent will be. In equilibrium, where the quantity demanded and the quantity supplied of land are equal, the rent to the landowner is equal to the marginal revenue product of the land to the renter.

Aggregate supply of land
The total amount of land available for use by the entire economy.

A distinction must be made between the fixed supply of land and its potential allocation to varying uses. In Figure 14.4a the supply curve of land is drawn for all land, or the **aggregate supply of land.** The curve is drawn as a vertical line, indicating that land in the aggregate is in fixed supply. In general, the amount of land on earth is given by nature and cannot be changed. Actually, common sense tells us that the assumption of a perfectly inelastic supply of land is not completely true. The supply of usable land can be increased through reclamation of swamps and marshes or reduced through erosion. Nonetheless, it is a useful approximation to think of the aggregate supply curve of land as perfectly inelastic, as drawn in Figure 14.4a.

What are the economic implications of this vertical supply curve for all land? First, the perfectly inelastic nature of the supply of land in the aggregate means that the quantity supplied of land is unresponsive to price. Whether land is priced at $1 per acre per year or $1 million per acre per year, the quantity supplied of land in the aggregate will not change. Because the quantity of land—Q in Figure 14.4a—is fixed, the rental price of land will be determined solely by the level of demand.

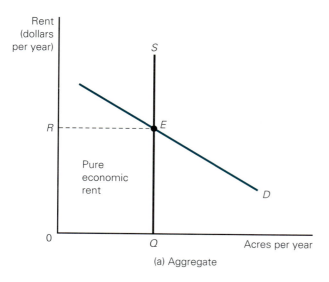

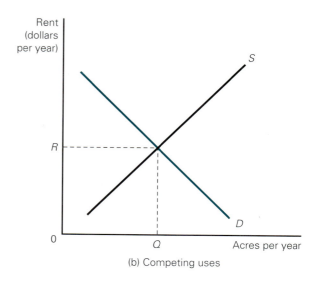

(a) Aggregate

(b) Competing uses

FIGURE 14.4

Pure Economic Rent and the Supply of Land

(a) The supply curve for land in the aggregate is perfectly inelastic with respect to rent, which means that the return to land in the aggregate is a pure economic rent. (b) The supply curve of land to competing uses appears as it is normally drawn—sloping upward to the right. This slope reflects the fact that land has competing uses and hence that the price of using land or rent plays an important role in determining the uses to which land is put.

Thus, the equilibrium level of rent on the vertical axis depends on where the demand curve for land intersects the fixed supply curve.

The return to land in the aggregate is labeled a pure economic rent. To understand this concept, recall that economic rent is defined as a payment in excess of the opportunity cost of a factor of production. Recall also that a factor's opportunity cost is reflected in its supply schedule because a supply schedule indicates what it takes to bid resources away from their next-best alternative use. A vertical supply curve such as in Figure 14.4a means that land in the aggregate has no opportunity cost; nothing is given up for its supply, for it has no alternative uses. Very simply, this means that the whole return to land in the aggregate is a pure economic rent. In Figure 14.4a, land garners $REQ0$ in pure rent.

The concept of pure economic rent is normally associated with the supply curve of all land. However, it is possible that other resources will exhibit a range of their supply curve that is perfectly inelastic and that they therefore stand to earn pure economic rents. This characteristic may be true of uniquely talented performers (superstars) in the worlds of sport and art, for example.

The Supply of Land to Alternative Uses

Since the return to land in the aggregate is a pure economic rent, a price does not have to be paid to call forth a supply of land. If rent does not have to be paid to call forth a supply of land, then why pay it? Or why not tax all rents away as an unearned surplus to landowners? The attractiveness of such a tax is apparent—it raises the revenue without affecting the available supply of land. In Figure 14.4a, for example, a tax equal to the area of pure rents, $REQ0$, would leave the supply of land unaffected at Q.

In 1879, in his book *Progress and Poverty,* Henry George proposed a single tax of 10 percent on land rent on just these grounds. George argued for a single tax on land because he felt that landowners contributed nothing to the land's productivity. Rising land values were determined by general economic growth and by increases in the demand for land. Thus, a tax on land would not affect the amount of land available to the economy and would prevent landowners from getting rich from windfall profits while nonlandowners remained poor. (Windfall profits could occur to lucky landowners with favorable and unexpected changes in economic conditions.) Moreover, George thought a single tax on land rents could finance all the government of his day, eliminating the need for other types of taxes.

George's proposal rests on the assumption of a perfectly inelastic supply curve of land. He was essentially assuming that land has no alternative uses. But this assumption concerns land only in the aggregate. While land in the aggregate has a vertical supply curve, the supply of land to alternative uses does not. Consider what happens, for example, as a city expands. Farmland is converted to sites for houses and shopping centers, as people bid for the right to use the land in other ways. The market process reallocates the land from less valued to more highly valued uses, from farmland to city land.

The supply curve of land for particular uses slopes upward to the right, as shown in Figure 14.4b. To rent land for a particular use, one must bid it away from competing uses. As more desirable land is rented, the rental rate rises. With a normally sloped supply curve, the rental price paid for land serves to allocate land to competing uses. Those who value the use of a parcel of land more highly will offer higher rents than others. In this sense, rent functions like any other price in signaling the intentions of buyers and sellers in the market for land.

The proper distinction to keep in mind is that while the supply curve of land in the aggregate is approximately vertical, the supply curve of land to alternative uses is positively sloped. Since the latter concept of the supply of land is far more relevant to real-world situations than the former, a proposal such as Henry George's could do much damage to the economy. It was never implemented, although George was a popular politician and twice ran for mayor of New York City.

Whether land is viewed in the aggregate or as a resource of varying desirability and alternative uses, rent does serve a function: It rations land among available bidders.

PROFITS AND THE ALLOCATION OF RESOURCES

Profits are a residual return to those individuals in the economy who provide economic foresight and leadership in an uncertain environment. Profits play an instrumental role in the way the competitive price system works to allocate resources to their most highly valued uses.

Profit Data

For individual firms, industries, or the economy as a whole, profits are not computed directly but are determined by what is left over from revenues after payments have been made to land, labor, and capital. It is in this sense that the profit earner is referred to as the *residual claimant*. This view of profits as a residual contrasts sharply with the common but misguided notion that employees and other input suppliers are paid only after the entrepreneur has secured profits.

Have levels of profits earned in the economy as a whole grown over the years? Table 14.2 traces after-tax corporate profits and nonfarm proprietors' income for selected years between 1970 and 1998. Corporate profits as a percentage of national income (NI) ranged between 3.9 percent of NI in 1985 and 7.4 in 1997. In contrast, nonfarm proprietors' income exhibits a strong constant trend as a percent of NI, showing little change from year to year. Overall, the data in Table 14.2 fail to confirm the widely held perception that profits and proprietors' income have been rapidly growing over time, at least as a percentage of national income.

Rate of Return on Capital

Rate of return on invested capital

Profits earned during a period of time divided by the value of invested capital; usually measured as a percent per year.

The profit data given in Table 14.2 are not directly relevant to the decisions of firms concerning investments in plant and equipment. What matters for such purposes is not the absolute level of profits but the economic **rate of return on invested capital.** That is, at the margin it will pay to buy an additional dollar's worth of equipment only if the firm expects to earn more than a dollar from the sale of the resulting output from the equipment.

TABLE 14.2

Corporate Profits and Nonfarm Proprietors' Income, 1970–1998

Corporate profits have remained quite steady as a percentage of NI (between 3.9 and 7.4 percent) since 1970. Nonfarm proprietors' income has exhibited steady growth but has remained fairly constant as a percentage of NI.

	CORPORATE PROFITS		NONFARM PROPRIETORS' INCOME	
Year	**After Tax (billions)**	**Percent of National Income**	**After Tax (billions)**	**Percent of National Income**
1970	44	5.2	65.4	7.8
1975	89.5	6.9	97.7	7.5
1980	156.6	7.0	164.4	7.3
1985	133.4	3.9	245	7.2
1990	231.2	5.0	338.6	7.3
1991	240.8	5.0	347.2	7.3
1992	263.4	5.3	386.7	7.8
1993	300.2	5.7	418.4	7.9
1994	348.5	6.2	434.7	7.8
1995	424.6	7.2	465.6	7.9
1996	454.1	7.3	488.8	7.8
1997	488.3	7.4	515.8	7.7
1998*	479.4	6.9	543.9	7.8

*Average of first 3 quarters of 1998.

Source: Economic Report of the President (Washington, D.C.: U.S. Government Printing Office, 1999), p. 358.

The economic rate of return on capital may be approximated with accounting data by dividing the amount of stock or capital valued at its current replacement cost into profits earned during the year. Historical data indicate that after-tax rates of return on capital have fallen over time. The average annual rate of return between 1955 and 1969 was 10.1 percent, with the highest rates occurring during the 1960s. By contrast, the average annual rate of return on capital between 1970 and 1998 was approximately 8 percent. This decline in rates of return has two important implications. The first involves incentives to make capital investments. For investments in capital to be profitable, not only must the rate of return be positive, but the rate of return on capital must exceed the expected return on alternative investments. Since a larger number of competing uses of funds—buying bonds, for example— become attractive as the rate of return on capital falls, the available data suggest that incentives to invest in plants and equipment during the 1970s were lower than in earlier years. Second, the data provide further evidence that the popular view of large and ever-increasing corporate profitability is mistaken.

Accounting Versus Economic Profits

Accounting profit

Total revenue minus total explicit payments for inputs or out-of-pocket costs.

Economic profit

Total revenue minus total opportunity costs of production.

As noted in Chapter 7, **accounting profits** tend to overstate the level of **economic profits** because accountants by necessity take a less theoretical view of costs than do economists. Accountants count as costs only those business expenditures involving direct money outlays—wages and salaries, raw materials purchased, rental payments on land and buildings, borrowing costs, advertising expenses, and so forth. Economists identify costs as *all* opportunities forgone, explicit or implicit. If you are self-employed, for example, you must count what you could earn working for somebody else as a cost of your operation. Accounting profits thus generally overstate economic profits because they understate economic costs.

ENTREPRENEURSHIP

Entrepeneur

An individual who perceives profit opportunities, organizes resources into productive ventures, and bears the uncertain status of residual claimant of the resulting risky economic outcome.

Assuming that economic profits can be measured, what role do they play in the economic process? Economic profits are the return to a particular factor of production, entrepreneurship. As such, profits are the residual income accruing to the **entrepreneur** as a return on the services he or she brings to the productive process. These services include technical abilities in organizing the other factors of production into combinations appropriate for the efficient manufacture of goods. More important, though, is the entrepreneur's alertness to the existence of potential profit opportunities in the economy. In this sense, entrepreneurship consists of linking markets by perceiving the opportunity to buy resources at a lower total cost than the revenue obtainable from the sale of output, or by recognizing that sellers in one market are offering to sell output at a price lower than buyers in another market are willing to pay.

Put another way, entrepreneurship consists of offering the most attractive opportunities to other market participants—perceiving unfulfilled demands, offering higher prices to sellers or lower prices to buyers, improving existing goods or making them more cheaply, finding more effective means of communicating to consumers the availability and attributes of goods. In all of these activities, the entrepreneur takes advantage of opportunities that exist because of the initial ignorance of other market participants. But as a result of the entrepreneur's actions, markets move closer to the prices and quantities emerging in equilibrium, the plans of buyers and sellers more closely dovetail, and the knowledge of economic data held by market participants is increased.

In addition to alertness and organizational skills, the entrepreneur brings to the production process a willingness to act in the presence of uncertainty. (We distinguish risk from uncertainty in that risk involves events that occur with known probabilities—the toss of a coin, for example—while uncertainty entails outcomes whose probabilities cannot be specified with precision—for example, war or peace and long-run weather forecasts.) There is no guarantee that perceived profit opportunities will materialize. Because it takes time between the purchase of inputs and the sale of output—between the expenditures on resources and the receipt of revenue—intervening events may reveal the entrepreneur's plans to be either over-ambitious or underambitious when evaluated with the advantage of hindsight. Entrepreneurs, then, bear responsibility for incorrect anticipations. Profits can be viewed as a return for bearing both risk and uncertainty.

Entrepreneurs and Information: The Austrian View

Economists who work in the tradition of the Austrian economic theorists of the late 1800s are referred to as the modern Austrian school of economics. The modern Austrians include Friedrich A. von Hayek, who won the Nobel Prize in economics in 1974, and Israel Kirzner.

The traditional view of the entrepreneur as a person who discovers and bears the risks of profit opportunities has been expanded in the modern Austrian view.[1] In this view, the entrepreneur must also design and sell particular commodities or particular groups of commodities. Most products and services, such as dishwashing detergent and automobiles, are sold in a variety of qualities, locations, and with a variety of financial terms and warranties. For example, generic and brand name detergents are often found side by side in supermarkets. The entrepreneur not only must perceive profit opportunities in producing and selling such items but also must develop and fit the *characteristics* of each product or service to a targeted group of consumers. The entrepreneur must discover what consumers are willing to buy and inform them about the wares available for purchase.

One very important aspect of the modern Austrian view of competition is that it is a *rivalrous process,* which contrasts with the traditional view of competition as a static *situation* (as presented in Chapter 8). The traditional model, which often assumed homogeneous products with perfect knowledge of consumers' demand curves, gives the economist an exact account of the course of economic events with the aid of scientific generalizations. But the traditional model of competition has some limitations. Concentrating on some of these limitations, the modern Austrians view competition as the businessperson's rivalry against competitors for a prize. Assuming freedom of entry and *non*homogeneous products and services, the Austrian view is one of perpetual disequilibrium. Economic profits are created and destroyed perpetually, and products and product qualities change continually as an integral part of the process. In this view, entrepreneurs are constantly experimenting with different products and informing consumers about these differences.

---

[1] The Austrian view of the entrepreneur's role in the competitive process is detailed in Israel Kirzner, *Competition and Entrepreneurship* (Chicago: University of Chicago Press, 1973) and in Friedrich A. von Hayek (winner of the 1974 Nobel Prize), "The Nonsequitur of the Dependence Effect," in E. Mansfield, ed., *Microeconomics: Selected Readings* (New York: W. W. Norton and Co., 1979). See also Robert F. Hebert and Albert Link, *The Entrepreneur* (Boston: D. C. Heath, 1988).

If consumers received perfect information, there would be no reason to inform them about new products or services, let alone about different qualities of existing products or services. Having perfect information about products or services amounts to having innate wants for products or services. If tastes in music were innate, for example, no amount of advertising by an entrepreneurial promoter could convince someone predisposed to classical music to attend a country music concert. Economists such as Hayek argued that very few human wants, except for food, shelter, clothing, and sex, are innate. Human wants, personality, and opinions are shaped by a cultural environment, and one element in this environment is advertising. An entrepreneur may, in a free market, attempt to devise products and affect their consumption, but consumers will also be informed about competing products. The success of an individual entrepreneur will depend on the actions of other producers and many other factors that affect consumers of any particular product. The main point is that consumers cannot react without information. To argue that some tastes and desires are unimportant or irrelevant when compared with desires for food, shelter, and clothing would be to ignore much of cultural history, in Hayek's view.

One role of the entrepreneur, then, is to develop, design, and sell products in the market process. Part of this entrepreneurial role is the ability to advertise products and product qualities. The costs of *selling* output by informing customers of goods and services through advertising and other means are, in other words, part and parcel of entrepreneurship. When the entrepreneur successfully discovers consumer tastes and preferences, and when he or she molds products and services to meet these desires, consumer utility and welfare are enhanced.

The entrepreneur is a prime actor in the economic process. Entrepreneurs develop products, organize production, and provide necessary capital; they are alert to profit opportunities, willing to act in uncertain conditions, and can inform consumers and potential consumers about the product. Profits are simply a payment to another factor of production, but they are different from the other factors in that the entrepreneur is paid last, claiming the residual after the other factors have been compensated. Profits spur entrepreneurial activity in the economy and thereby encourage the whole competitive process.

This completes our discussion of factor pricing and the associated returns to each factor. Hopefully, at this point the unity of microeconomics is apparent. Demand and supply conditions determine prices and quantities in all markets, and the principles that guide individual behavior across these markets are the same. Opportunity cost matters, choices are made at the margin, and individual behavior is purposeful and rational. We started our study of microeconomics in Chapter 1 by emphasizing these points, and now the student is in a position to understand why they are so very important.

APPLICATION

Trading Property Rights: Stocks and Bonds

Most daily newspapers list the previous day's closing prices of stocks and bonds. These listings show how the market for loanable funds works, coordinating the supply of funds, primarily held by investors and investor groups, with the demand for funds, primarily the desire by corporations to raise capital for future production. Figure 14.5 explains how to read newspaper stock listings.

Corporations have two primary means of raising capital: selling shares of stock or issuing bonds. By selling shares of stock, a corporation is effectively selling prop-

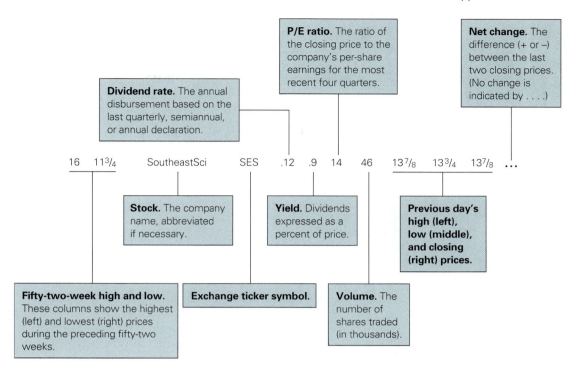

P/E ratio. The ratio of the closing price to the company's per-share earnings for the most recent four quarters.

Net change. The difference (+ or –) between the last two closing prices. (No change is indicated by . . . .)

Dividend rate. The annual disbursement based on the last quarterly, semiannual, or annual declaration.

16   11³/₄   SoutheastSci   SES   .12   .9   14   46   13⁷/₈   13³/₄   13⁷/₈   ...

Stock. The company name, abbreviated if necessary.

Yield. Dividends expressed as a percent of price.

Previous day's high (left), low (middle), and closing (right) prices.

Fifty-two-week high and low. These columns show the highest (left) and lowest (right) prices during the preceding fifty-two weeks.

Exchange ticker symbol.

Volume. The number of shares traded (in thousands).

FIGURE 14.5

Sample New York Stock Exchange Listing

Most daily newspapers carry complete listings of transactions on the New York Stock Exchange. This sample listing for the stock of a hypothetical company, Southeast Scientific Company, is accompanied by explanatory notes.

erty rights to itself: When you buy a share of stock, you are trading property rights over one asset (money or other assets) and acquiring property rights over a portion of the firm. The shareholders of a corporation are its owners. Each share of stock permits its holder one vote at meetings that determine the firm's future management. In this way, corporate policy is directed by the will of the holders of the majority of the firm's shares—whether one or many individuals. Shareholders do not make operating decisions for the firm, but they are legally responsible for hiring the managers—the board of directors—who do. When shareholders are pleased with the existing management of the firm, they usually assign their votes to the management, which then acts as a proxy for the shareholders in voting on corporate policy.

The stock market is an organized exchange where corporate shares are bought and sold. In the stock market the prices of shares issued by different firms reflect the market's estimate of the future profitability of the firms in question. From the shareholders' standpoint, investing in the stock market means bearing the risk resulting from the uncertain prospects of any given firm. A share of the stock's future value is not guaranteed and can rise or fall with the firm's fortunes, or because of general market conditions such as interest rates.

Corporations and governments also issue another type of obligation—bonds. Unlike shares of stock, bonds do not confer ownership rights; they simply

An investor considers his options with the New York Stock Exchange (on Wall Street in New York City) in the background.

represent IOUs. The firm or government body agrees to pay the bondholder a fixed sum (the principal that represents the loan to the firm) either on a specific date or in installments over a specified period. Most bonds pay, in addition, a fixed return per year, usually expressed as a percentage of the face value of the bond. For example, a corporation may issue a $10,000 bond (which, if sold, represents a $10,000 loan to the corporation for some specified period) at an interest rate of 5 percent. This bond would pay the holder $500 per year until maturity, when the entire $10,000 is returned to the investor.

Although bonds tend to be issued for long terms (thirty-eight years in the case of some U.S. Treasury bonds), bonds are commonly bought and sold prior to the date of maturity. The bond market is like the stock market; it represents an organized exchange specializing in the buying and selling of bonds.

Interest rates affect the prices of shares of stock indirectly by their impact on the activities and hence the profitability of firms, but interest rates bear a direct relation to the price of bonds. Take, for example, a bond issued with a face value of $10,000 that pays an annual rate of interest of 6 percent. Until maturity, whoever holds the bond is entitled to $600 annually. Suppose, however, that the market interest rate rises to 10 percent. Purchasers of newly issued $10,000 bonds can earn $1000 annually, other things equal. What happens to the price of the 6 percent bonds? Their market value must fall to reflect the new, higher interest rate. No one, in other words, would invest in a bond paying less than 10 percent, since they can earn 10 percent on newly issued bonds. The price of the 6 percent bond must fall to $6000 to reflect the new, higher rate of 10 percent. Individuals will not buy the original bonds unless their price falls so as to produce a 10 percent return on a given investment ($600/$6000). The bond will still pay $10,000 at maturity (the firm must pay back what it borrowed), but the sales value of the bond right now is $6000.

The general point to remember is that the price of a bond varies inversely with the interest rate. When the interest rate rises, the price of a bond falls; when the interest rate falls, the price of a bond rises.

It is worth noting that firms can hold back part of their earnings as an additional source of investment capital. Modern corporations routinely retain a part of their earnings rather than paying all of it out to stockholders.

QUESTIONS

What do you think would be the stock market's reaction to an unexpected rise in interest rates? What would your response be as an investor?

SUMMARY

1. Wealth can be defined as a high level of sustainable consumption in an economy. The elements of a wealthy society are production, resources, knowledge, capital, technology, and institutions.

2. Time preference is a measure of an individual's concern for present versus future consumption.

3. Interest is the price that individuals must be paid for waiting to consume later; it also is the price that individuals are willing to pay in order to consume now rather than later.

4. The rate of interest is determined in the market for loanable funds by the demand and supply of loanable funds.

5. In reality, there is a multiplicity of interest rates—such as prime rates, government rates, and credit card rates—determined by the degree of risk, cost, and time allowed for payment. Because it takes the rate of inflation into account, the real rate of interest is lower than the nominal rate of interest.

6. The returns to capital are composed of pure interest, a risk premium, and economic profits or losses.

7. An economic rent is a return in excess of the opportunity cost of an owner of a resource.

8. Land in the aggregate is fixed and has a perfectly inelastic supply curve. Its entire return is a pure economic rent determined by the level of demand for land as a factor of production.

9. The supply of land to competing uses is not fixed. Land must be bid away from competing uses, so the supply curve of land to a specific use is upward sloping.

10. Proposals to tax land rents away would be costly to the economy. Land is like any other factor of production. It has alternative uses, and it is used in the production process by entrepreneurs and firms up to the point where its marginal revenue product equals its marginal cost.

11. Economic profits are a residual that the entrepreneur receives after the other factors of production have been paid. Profits can be positive or negative (or zero). The receivers of profits are called residual claimants. Although the absolute level of profits in the economy has grown over time, the rate of return on capital has not. It has declined in recent years. The rate of return on capital is the crucial determinant of firm profitability.

12. Accounting profits differ from economic profits. Typically, accounting procedures understate economic costs and thus overstate economic profits.

13. Profits are the force in the economy that leads to entrepreneurship. They are a return to decision making under conditions of risk and uncertainty. The most basic characteristic of entrepreneurs is that they are alert to economic opportunities.

KEY TERMS

roundabout production
saving
capital formation
capital stock
depreciation
capital consumption
rate of time preference
interest

demand for loanable funds
supply of loanable funds
risk
nominal rate of interest
inflation rate
real rate of interest
pure interest
present value

rent
pure economic rent
aggregate supply of land
rate of return on invested capital
accounting profits
economic profits
entrepreneur

QUESTIONS FOR REVIEW AND DISCUSSION

1. Suppose that you are thinking about investing in a personal computer and laser printer. Your costs will be $2500 and the equipment will last four years. You expect to earn $900 a year typing papers part-time with the computer. The bank will lend you the money at 19 percent interest. Should you buy the computer and printer? What if the bank's interest rate was 12 percent?

2. Why is the concept of time preference important in the discussion of interest rates? Explain.

3. How would the following events affect the prime rate of interest in the United States?
   a. The threat of war in Central America
   b. An increase in the inflation rate
   c. The discovery of massive domestic oil resources
   d. Greater impatience in the general population
   e. Capricious government intervention in the economy

4. At what point in the production process do residual claimants receive their return? Can their return be negative?

5. What are the essential things that an entrepreneur does?

6. There is a fixed supply of oil in the world. Is the return to oil producers therefore a pure economic rent? Explain carefully.

7. Evaluate the following statement: Land rent should be completely taxed away.

8. Suppose that all of your earnings were a rent. What implications would this situation have for your behavior in the workplace? Would you be cantankerous with your superiors or docile and easy to get along with? Why?

9. Are you earning economic rents as a college student? (Hint: Suppose your college raises tuition.)

PROBLEMS

1. Identify the present value of a stream of payments of $150 per year for the next seven years if the interest rate is 10 percent. (Use Table 14.1 for this problem.)

2. Suppose that Enrique, an entrepreneur, has determined that land yields the following marginal revenue product per year:

Acres	MRP
1	21,000
2	16,400
3	10,600
4	8,400
5	6,200
6	3,600
7	1,720
8	480

If Enrique can employ as many acres as he chooses at a rent payment of $6200 per acre per year, how many will he employ? Why? Present your conclusion in graphical form.

WORKING WITH THE WEB

In this chapter, you have been introduced to the Austrian school of economics. To learn more about the Austrian school, go to www.mises.org, select "daily articles", and choose November '98. Scroll through the articles until you find "The Austrian Tradition". This is a bit lengthy but contains good information about the differences between the Austrian school and other schools of economic thought. Use this article to answer the first two questions that follow.

1. According to the Austrian school, how do entrepreneurship, private property, and government intervention fit into its view of the economy?

2. The "third virtue" of Austrian economics is the theory of entrepreneurship. According to Mises, why is everyone considered an entrepreneur?

3. One difference between the Austrian school and the neoclassical school of economics is that the former views competition as a process while the latter views competition as a static situation. Economist Thomas DiLorenzo maintains that the static view of competition has contributed to the attack on Microsoft. Go to , select "daily aricles", and choose June '98–October '98. Scroll through the articles until you find "Static Analysis". What is DiLorenzo's point regarding market dominance, given that Microsoft stands accused of being a monopolist?

Income Distribution, Poverty, and Health Care

I n studying income distribution, economists look at how personal or family earnings are measured and divided among members of society. They try to see how various factors such as individual choice and effort, education, experience, and discrimination influence the distribution of income. Also, they pay close attention to the effects of various government policies on income distribution. Economists generally have strong personal views concerning the equity of various income distributions. However, recognizing that their views are value judgments, economists tend to focus on other aspects of redistribution proposals. In particular, they pay much attention to efficiency aspects of various proposals to redistribute income. Although it is tempting to imagine that programs such as tax reform simply transfer income from those who need it less to those who need it more without side effects, redistribution never works so simply. Inevitably, some individuals will incur costs to avoid paying higher taxes, while others will adjust their circumstances to qualify for new subsidies. Due to such activity, it almost always ends up costing some groups in society more than a dollar for each dollar that is transferred to other groups. Economists therefore are aware that any program to redistribute income involves a trade-off between equity and efficiency.

Many contemporary public policy issues are distributional issues. Health care and poverty are two examples. Health care costs in the United States are soaring, and many Americans do not have health insurance. Poverty persists in many parts of the United States. Any government program that attempts to reduce poverty or to reform the health care system will involve income distribution. After reading Chapter 15 you should understand

- some of the differences between economic efficiency and social equity as they relate to income distribution.

- the meaning of income inequality and how it is measured.
- patterns and characteristics of income distribution in the United States, especially those related to poverty and discrimination.
- modern policy programs and proposals relating to distribution, poverty, and health care in contemporary society.

THE INDIVIDUAL AND INCOME DISTRIBUTION

The economic question of why some individuals are rich and others are poor has many facets. Individuals accumulate income from their labor and entrepreneurial skills, from the ownership of assets such as stocks and bonds and land, or from the receipt of cash or government subsidies called transfer payments. At the same time, most individuals pay a certain portion of income through taxes. We will analyze each factor of **individual income** briefly.

Individual income
The earnings individuals receive from their labor, from their assets, and from government transfer payments, minus their tax payments.

Labor income
The payments an individual receives from supplying work time; equal to the wage rate times the number of hours supplied.

Labor Income

Labor income—income received from supplying labor—is the wage rate received multiplied by the number of hours worked. The supply of labor is by far the largest source of individual income. The supply of labor ordinarily varies according to wage rates, but individuals also differ in their choice of work hours over leisure hours, and wages themselves vary for a number of reasons.

Choices of Work Versus Leisure   Different people with the same skills will often supply different quantities of labor at identical wage rates. The same wage rate affects people differently because they can make choices about the trade-off between work and leisure. Harpo, who has the same skills as Gummo, chooses to play his harp six hours a day for no pay and to work two hours a day for pay. Gummo chooses work and income over leisure, working twelve or fourteen hours a day.

What else accounts for differences in attitudes toward work? No human being is a machine who can supply labor without limit. At higher and higher wage rates and longer and longer hours worked, we all become leisure lovers (see Chapter 12 on this point). As we choose more work, the costs of losing more and more leisure rise and the rewards of earning more income fall.

Differences in Wage Rates   Wage rates vary widely among occupations. The wage rate you earn is largely a function of the human capital you have built up through education and investments in other skills. Human capital has a lot to do with whether you are rich or poor. Level of schooling attained (a college degree, a high school diploma) is a ticket to enter some occupations. Given government-enforced regulations of the American Medical Association, entry into the physicians' market without a medical degree would almost certainly land you in jail.

Luck also plays a role in the wage rate. At the beginning of the energy crisis in the early 1970s, those entering the labor market with degrees in petroleum engineering received much higher wages than under previous conditions. (The situation was short-lived, since more and more college students were attracted to petroleum engineering by high wages, and, as usual, supply expanded and wages fell.)

Individuals' or families' incomes are also determined by their stage in the life cycle. Law students at Harvard, Stanford, or the University of Michigan may be poor now—students everywhere tend to be poor now—but they will not always be poor. Income or earnings tend to rise throughout the period of the active work life. Earnings increase at a fairly rapid pace in early to middle work life. In the latter portion of the work life, earnings still tend to increase, but at a slower pace. After retirement, earnings generally decrease. Other factors also influence the wage rate an individual receives. Without question, race and sex discrimination have historically affected wage rates. We look at this matter in more detail later in the chapter.

Income from Savings and Other Assets

Asset income

Earnings from interest on savings, from capital investments, and from land; all result from forgone consumption in the past.

The other major source of income is the return from savings or other assets one owns or has accumulated. Motives for the sacrifice of current consumption are numerous: security, expected future gaps in income, education, retirement, large consumer expenditures, and so forth. In any case, the sacrifice of current consumption for future consumption is rewarded by an interest return or **asset income.**

Many people save for future generations. Some current income earners set aside assets for their children's later use, which brings us to another major source of income. Inheritance of money or other assets is related to the luck of having had wealthy parents. Historically, free societies have permitted inheritance and protected the rights of income owners to bequeath gifts at death or while still alive. Most societies have nevertheless taxed the recipients of inheritance on the grounds that such wealth was not due to their own productivity.

The returns from both savings and other wealth and asset accumulations also depend on one's skill at investing. Returns on all sorts of investments—monetary, real capital, or land—are determined by the costs of investing and the incentives to maximize income from investments.

Taxes and Transfer Payments

Ex ante distribution

The distribution of income before government transfer payments and taxes are accounted for.

Ex post distribution

The distribution of income after government transfer payments and taxes are accounted for.

Transfer payment

A resource received by an individual from government that is not directly or explicitly paid for by that individual; it may be in the form of money or goods and services such as education or health care.

A final source of income is government tax collections and benefit distributions. Economists distinguish between the *ex ante* **distribution** of income, the before tax and transfer payments distribution, and the *ex post* **distribution,** or after tax and transfer payments distribution. We all receive benefits from government, and we all pay taxes in one form or another. National defense, roads, and the local public swimming pool are some of the benefits; property taxes, sales taxes, and income taxes are some of the costs.

Most individuals are either net taxpayers or net benefit receivers. In other words, the determination of how rich or poor we are *ex post* depends partly on our position with regard to taxes and benefits. The receipt of government services and **transfer payments**—such as direct welfare payments, food stamps, subsidized public housing, Social Security, and unemployment compensation—must be added to privately earned income. Transfer payments are money or real goods or services transferred by government from one group in society (taxpayers) to other groups (transfer recipients). Tax payments of all kinds must likewise be subtracted to help explain *ex post* why we, as individuals, are rich or poor. Most government statistics on income distribution reveal only *ex ante* money distributions of family or household income, but economists have attempted to make some *ex post* calculations as well.

HOW IS INCOME INEQUALITY MEASURED?

Family income
The total of all incomes from all sources except transfers received by members of a household.

The money income of families (often termed *households*), or **family income,** is calculated annually by the U.S. Bureau of the Census. Table 15.1 shows family income in the United States for selected years between 1970 and 1996. Total family income is broken down into the percentage received by each fifth of the total number of families over these years, ranked from the lowest, or poorest, fifth to the highest, or richest, fifth. (A fifth of a total distribution is called a quintile.) In addition, Table 15.1 gives the percentage of total money income earned by the top 5 percent of income earners between 1970 and 1996.

Interpretation of Money Distribution Data

The data in Table 15.1 reveal something very interesting: *the distribution of reported money income did not change significantly between 1970 and 1996,* although in recent years the disparity in income distribution appears to have widened. Reading horizontally across the table, we see that the shares for each quintile stayed roughly the same. The lowest quintile received about 5 percent

TABLE 15.1

Money Income of Families, Percent of Aggregate Income: 1970–1996

These data show an amazing uniformity in pretax income distribution over more than twenty-five years. Special care must be used in interpreting the data, however, since noncash transfers by government also affect income distribution.

PERCENT OF AGGREGATE INCOME

Families by Quintile	1970	1975	1979	1984	1987	1991	1996
1. Lowest fifth	5.4	5.4	5.3	4.7	4.6	4.5	4.2
2. Second fifth	12.2	11.8	11.6	11.0	10.8	10.7	10.0
3. Middle fifth	17.6	17.6	17.5	17.0	16.9	16.5	15.8
4. Fourth fifth	23.8	24.1	24.1	24.4	24.1	24.1	23.1
5. Highest fifth	40.9	41.1	41.6	42.9	43.7	44.2	46.8
Highest 5%	15.6	15.5	15.7	16.0	16.9	17.1	20.3

Sources: U.S. Department of Commerce, Bureau of the Census, Current Population Reports—Consumer Income, *Money Income of Households, Families, and Persons in the United States 1984* (Washington, D.C.: U.S. Government Printing Office, 1986), p. 37. 1998 Update, Department of Commerce, Bureau of Census Web Site.

of aggregate income, and its share is declining, while the highest quintile consistently got over 40 percent. Further, the share of the highest quintile has been rising, as has the share of the top 5 percent of income earners. Before accepting these figures at face value, we should note some limitations of the data in Table 15.1.

1. Money income statistics reported by the Bureau of the Census do not conform to the economist's definition of income. Income, in the economist's sense, is what an individual accumulates from labor, assets, or transfer payments minus what is paid in taxes. By contrast, the Census Bureau's statistics on income ignore transfer payments, all assets such as capital gains, and income and payroll taxes.

2. The government statistics report family, not individual, income. Therefore, an increase in the number of family units, income remaining the same, will alter the reported income distribution. In the period 1960–1998, the number of family units increased significantly through later marriages, high divorce rates, and the increasing independence of the elderly. The government's statistics do not take this increase into account.

Given these two deficiencies in the Census data, conclusions about the distribution of economic welfare should be deferred until the raw statistics are refined. Before actually making some of these refinements, we turn to the tools economists use to deal with income distribution.

The Lorenz Curve

Lorenz curve

A curve plotting the actual cumulative distribution of income in percentages; usually compared with a curve showing a perfectly even distribution of income.

Economists have developed a number of useful methods for describing and analyzing income distribution. The **Lorenz curve,** the primary tool for measuring income distribution, was developed in 1905 by M. O. Lorenz. A Lorenz curve plots the relation between the percentage of families receiving income and the cumulative percentage of aggregate family income. To gain an understanding of the Lorenz curve, consider a hypothetical income distribution for a hypothetical country in the year 2020, as shown in Table 15.2. Table 15.2 tells us that the lowest 20 percent of family income earners in this country receive only 5 percent of total income. The next 20 percent of families get 15 percent. Therefore, the lowest 40 percent receives a cumulative share of 20 percent. The middle 20 percent get 20 percent of total income, indicating that the lowest 60 percent of income earners receives only 40 percent of total income. Obviously, 100 percent of income recipients receive a cumulative total of 100 percent of income.

The data in Table 15.2 may be translated into graphical form. The vertical axis of Figure 15.1 represents the cumulative percentage of family income, and the horizontal axis shows the percentage of income-earning families. If all families earned equal incomes, the Lorenz curve would be a straight line. Ten percent of all families would earn 10 percent of income; 80 percent of families would earn 80 percent; and so on. Such a curve would actually be a diagonal cutting the square in half, as represented by the line of perfect equality in Figure 15.1.

A Lorenz curve may be constructed from the hypothetical data of Table 15.2. Point A in Figure 15.1 corresponds to point A in Table 15.2—it is the intersection

TABLE 15.2

Hypothetical Income Data for the Year 2020

The second column shows the percent share of total income received by each quintile of families in this hypothetical country; the third column adds these shares cumulatively. For instance, since the lowest fifth receives only 5 percent of total income and the second fifth receives 15 percent, together these lowest two-fifths receive a cumulative share of only 20 percent of total income. The lowest four-fifths receive a cumulative share of 65 percent. Data from the third column are plotted on a Lorenz curve in Figure 15.1.

	AGGREGATE INCOME	
All Families by Quintile	**Percent Share (year 2020)**	**Cumulative Percent Share (year 2020)**
A. Lowest fifth	5	5
B. Second fifth	15	20
C. Middle fifth	20	40
D. Fourth fifth	25	65
E. Highest fifth	35	100

FIGURE 15.1

A Hypothetical Lorenz Curve for the Year 2020

The Lorenz curve shows the cumulative percentage of family income earned by percentages of families. The Lorenz curve indicates that 40 percent of families earned only 20 percent of total income, while 80 percent earned a cumulative 65 percent. This distribution is unequal and falls short of the line of perfect equality. The shaded area in the diagram indicates the degree of income inequality. The farther the Lorenz curve moves away from the line of perfect equality, the less equal is the income distribution.

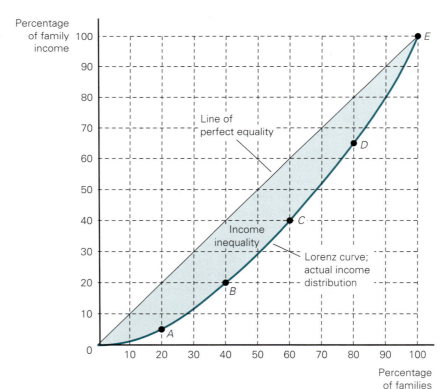

of the lowest 20 percent of families and their cumulative share of total income. Point *D* in Figure 15.1 shows that 80 percent of families (the fourth fifth in Table 15.2) received 65 percent of total income. The combination of points *A, B, C, D,* and *E* forms a Lorenz curve.

The distance of the Lorenz curve from the line of perfect equality is a measure of income inequality. The shaded area of Figure 15.1 is a measure of the degree of income inequality for our hypothetical society. Should the shaded area become larger, or more bowed, money income would be more unevenly distributed. A smaller area or a flatter curve would signal a more equal income distribution.

INCOME DISTRIBUTION IN THE UNITED STATES

We have already looked at family income distribution for selected years between 1970 and 1996. We now construct Lorenz curves with the data for the years 1970 and 1996. In Table 15.3, the cumulative percent share of all families by quintiles is calculated from the simple shares for 1970 and 1996. In 1970, for example, the lowest 60 percent of families received 35.2 percent of total income; their share had dropped to 30.0 percent in 1996.

Lorenz curves are calculated for these two years in Figure 15.2. Money income distribution has changed very little over the period, as shown by the differences between the Lorenz curves. For the lowest and the fourth quintiles of income

TABLE 15.3

Share and Cumulative Share in Income Distribution of All Families, 1970 and 1996

The data show changes in income distribution. The second fifth lost about 2.2 percent of its share between these two years, while the highest 20 percent gained about 6 percent. The middle fifth lost about 1.8 percent.

Quintile	Percent Share 1970	Percent Cumulative Share 1970	Percent Share 1996	Percent Cumulative Share 1996
Lowest fifth	5.4	5.4	4.2	4.2
Second fifth	12.2	17.6	10.0	14.2
Middle fifth	17.6	35.2	15.8	30.0
Fourth fifth	23.8	59.0	23.1	53.1
Highest fifth	40.9	100.0	46.8	100.0

Sources: U.S. Department of Commerce, Bureau of the Census, Current Population Reports—Consumer Income, *Money Income of Households, Families, and Persons in the United States: 1991* (Washington D.C.: U.S. Government Printing Office, 1999), p. B-11. 1999 Statistical Update, U.S. Department of Commerce Web Site.

Note: Data do not sum due to rounding.

FIGURE 15.2

Lorenz Curves for 1970 and 1996

The Lorenz curves of income distribution for 1970 and 1996 show little change in before-tax income distribution in the United States.

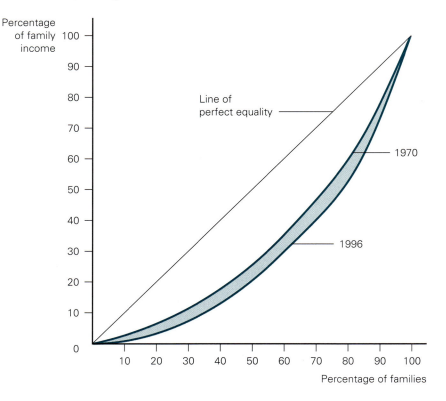

receivers, the distribution of income remained about the same. In between these two quintiles, income shares declined. The share of the highest quintile rose.

What can we conclude from this money income data? Has overall distribution become more unequal over the period 1970–1996? Have the lowest 60 percent of income recipients on balance become worse off? Have the rich gotten slightly richer?

The answers to these questions lie in the taxes and transfers that are not reported in the *ex ante* money income statistics from which the Lorenz curves of Figure 15.2 were constructed. Consider what happens to income distribution when adjustments are made for such things as income and payroll taxes, capital gains, in-kind transfers, money transfer or welfare payments, and other factors.

Adjustments to Money Income

Adjusted income
An individual's income after all taxes and all government transfer payments are accounted for.

Two important factors related to money income data must be considered before any conclusions are drawn about recent trends in income distribution in the United States. First, the data in Tables 15.1 and 15.3 do not account for payroll and income taxes. Since the U.S. income tax system is progressive, meaning that the higher-income recipients pay higher tax rates, the **adjusted income** distribution is affected in the direction of greater equality.

TABLE 15.4

Distribution of Adjusted Income in 1990

Adjusted income distribution statistics for any single year require the addition of such items as in-kind transfer benefits and the subtraction of income and payroll taxes. In a 1976 article Edgar K. Browning calculated the distribution resulting from these adjustments using data for 1972. Browning showed that when adjusted and unadjusted figures are compared, the adjusted distribution is considerably more equal. The following table compares the adjusted with the unadjusted income distribution for a more recent year.

HOUSEHOLDS BY QUINTILE (SHOWN IN BILLIONS OF DOLLARS)

Income Item	Lowest	Second	Third	Fourth	Highest	Total
Unadjusted money income	39.5	276.5	543.9	864.5	1772.4	3461.4
Plus						
Benefits in kind, capital gains, potential additional earnings, and other adjustments	167.4	104.7	55.0	33.7	30.3	391.1
Minus						
Income and payroll taxes	1.3	29.0	89.3	166.8	445.7	696.7
Equals						
Adjusted money income total	205.6	352.2	509.6	731.4	1357.0	3155.8
Adjusted percent distribution	6.5%	11.2%	16.1%	23.2%	43.0%	100%
Unadjusted percent distribution	1.1%	7.9%	15.5%	24.7%	50.7%	100%

Sources: Edgar K. Browning, "The Trend Toward Equality in the Distribution of Net Income," *Southern Economic Journal* 43 (July 1976), p. 914; Council of Economic Advisers, *Economic Report of the President* (Washington, D.C.: Government Printing Office, 1992); and Bureau of the Census, *Money Income of Households, Families, and Persons in the United States: 1991* (Washington, D.C.: U.S. Government Printing Office, 1992).

In-kind transfer payments

Transfer payments that take the form of goods and services such as public housing, veterans' hospitals, or a mass transit system.

A second important set of items that is not included in the raw money income statistics is transfer payments. These include **in-kind transfers** of benefits other than money—such as food stamps, public housing, Medicare, Medicaid, and other subsidies received largely by lower-income groups—in addition to money transfers or welfare payments. Such in-kind subsidies also tend to equalize income distribution across the various classes.

Economist Edgar K. Browning has attempted to develop a measure of income that conforms more closely to the definition of income used by economists. Browning estimated the effects of compensation for taxes, welfare transfers, transfers (benefits other than money), and other factors for the year 1972. In Table 15.4 we report similar calculations for a more recent year, 1990. The table shows the distribution of money income in 1990 in billions of dollars, with adjustments for in-kind transfers and other factors added in and with income and payroll taxes subtracted from the raw money income data.

Consider the additions to money income shown in Table 15.4. In-kind benefits are received largely by the poorest classes in society, whereas capital gains on stocks, bonds, and houses—which are not reflected in money income data—are six to seven times greater for the highest quintile of income recipients than for the lowest.

After these items are added to money income, taxes must be subtracted to obtain an estimate of net income. In the United States the largest burden of income tax—in both percent terms and total amount—falls on those in the highest quintile. In 1990, as the income and payroll taxes line in Table 15.4 shows, this group paid about $159.3 billion more in income taxes than all other income earners combined.

What is the net result of these adjustments to money income? Table 15.4 reports the results in terms of total income adjustment and in unadjusted and adjusted percent distribution. Total income rises for each class after additions to and subtractions from money income are made. But the important point is that the percent distribution among the quintiles is affected. The poorest 60 percent of income recipients all receive increased shares, with the lowest 20 percent receiving a 5.4 percent increase in adjusted income.

The effects indicated in the data of Table 15.4 are summarized in Figure 15.3 as Lorenz curves. Figure 15.3 shows a set of three Lorenz curves for 1990. The most bowed curve is the unadjusted distribution of money income. Figure 15.3 also shows a Lorenz curve that is adjusted for payroll and income taxes. The tax adjustment makes the curve less bowed and moves income distribution closer to the line of perfect equality. This shift indicates that a progressive tax system does effect greater

FIGURE 15.3

Lorenz Curve Including Income Adjustments

When taxes are subtracted from before-tax money income and in-kind transfers and other factors are added, the Lorenz curve moves closer to the line of perfect equality.

Source: Figure based on conclusions of Browning, "The Trend Toward Equality in the Distribution of Net Income." *Southern Economic Journal* 43 (July 1976), pp. 912–923 and Table 4.

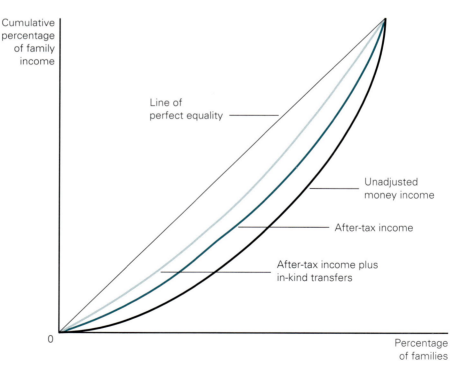

equality in income distribution. The inclusion of in-kind transfers and other adjustments pushes income distribution to still-greater equality, as the third Lorenz curve shows. These curves indicate the importance of social programs such as Medicare, food stamps, and public housing in creating greater income equality across the various segments of society.

Factors Affecting Income Distribution

Recently, considerable attention has been focused on data that indicate that the share of total unadjusted income earned by the poorest quintile of families has declined sharply since 1970. At that time, the poorest fifth of all families earned about 5.4 percent of *unadjusted* income. By 1996, this figure had fallen to about 4.2 percent. In attempting to explain the decline, a number of factors have been considered. Some observers attribute the decline to reductions in spending on government social programs. Others have placed the blame on foreign competition, which, in their view, has displaced American workers from high-paying jobs in manufacturing to low-paying jobs in the service sector. There are many reasons explaining low earnings, including the increase in single-parent families (see the Focus "Divorce, Single-Parent Families, and Income Distribution"), the age distribution of the population, and the degree of income mobility in the economy.

Age Distribution and Income

Another useful factor in understanding income distribution is the age structure of the income-receiving population. Take your own situation as an example. Perhaps you are a college student with a part-time job. If so, you are now probably part of the poorest quintile of the population in calculated annual income distribution. But you are not likely to be poor forever. Education and training alone will give you an edge in earning income later. At any point in time, the relative mean income of heads of households tends to peak between ages 45 and 55. Therefore, annual income figures will either overstate or understate multiyear inequality in income distribution, depending on the age structure of the population.

If the population is heavily populated by young people in the college age group, annual data will overstate actual lifetime or multiyear inequality in income distribution. There is in fact less inequality over multiyear distributions in the United States than there appears to be in any given year. Economists' estimates vary on how much more equal income distribution is over the long run, but all agree that there is more equality when age distribution is considered.

Rags to Riches Mobility

Economic mobility
The movement of individuals among income ranges.

Economic mobility—movements up or down in the quintiles of income distribution—also influences the question of how seriously annual data should be taken. How, for example, do we know that a family in the poorest quintile of income receivers in 1965 was not in the richest quintile in 2000, or vice versa? The answer

FOCUS

Divorce, Single-Parent Families, and Income Distribution

One factor that has received relatively little attention is the growing divorce rate and the resulting increase in the number of single-parent families. Families in the top quintile have always differed from those in the bottom quintile in terms of age, education, and the number of employed adults. In 1970, about 95 percent of families in the top quintile were husband–wife units, and this figure has changed little since then. What has changed is the percentage of high-income families with an employed wife—it has risen from 50 percent to about 70 percent. As a consequence, the total income of top quintile families has risen sharply. In contrast, the growing divorce rate has brought about a sharp decline in the percentage of husband–wife families in the lowest quintile—from 70 percent to about 50 percent today. Divorce transforms one family into two—usually

resulting in a drop in income for at least one of the two, if not both. If income statistics are reported on a per family basis, the increasing numbers of low-income single-parent families will lead to increases in income inequality. Data from the U.S. Department of the Census are indeed self-explanatory in this regard. In 1996 (the last year for which data are available), the median income of married couples was $49,707. For male-headed households, with wives not present, median income was $31,600, and for female-headed households, with husbands not present, median income was $19,111.[a]

Divorce and single-parenting have a clear and discernable effect on poverty.

––––––––––––––
[a]See *Statistical Abstract of the United States 1998* (Washington, D.C.: U.S. Government Printing Office, 1989), p. 473.

is that we do not know. To the extent that there is upward (and downward) mobility among income classes, greater equality is achieved over time.

Most studies indicate that there is a high degree of mobility in the United States, especially in the lower quintiles, but there are important statistical problems with identifying mobility over long-run periods. Such problems also extend to measuring age distribution factors and multiyear inequality. While it is safe to say that age distribution factors and economic mobility undoubtedly *reduce* income inequality over time, economists and policy-makers do not yet have the data or the wherewithal to judge the exact amount of the reduction.

CHARACTERISTICS OF INCOME DISTRIBUTION: POVERTY AND DISCRIMINATION

The data in population surveys and Census reports reveal a great deal about ourselves as a nation. Consider the total and average incomes of white, African Amer-

Mean income

A measure of average income; can be computed as per capita, per family, or per earner of income.

Per capita income

Average income per person; the total income of a population divided by the number of people in the population.

Poverty

A substandard level of income.

ican, and Hispanic families for 1997. The **mean**—or average—**income** of white families was about $18,000 greater than that of both African American and Hispanic families. (If **per capita income**—income per person—were compared for white, African American, and Hispanic families, the differences would be even more striking because white families are, on average, smaller than African American and Hispanic families.) Some of these differences are undoubtedly the consequence of differences in education, training, and experience, but some of the differences result from economic discrimination.

Although the numbers change from year to year, the pattern of income distribution continues to show that there are striking differences among the mean incomes of white, black, and Hispanic families, not all of which can be accounted for by differences in age, education, or family size.

Poverty

Poverty and economic discrimination are interrelated within our economic system. First we will define poverty; then we will examine various contributing factors to poverty in the United States.

Poverty can be defined as the condition of relatively lower incomes for some individuals or groups compared with others in a society. Defined this way, poverty will always be with us. As long as the Lorenz curve for unadjusted income is not diagonal—in other words, as long as there is not perfect income equality—some families will be better off than others.

Government measures of poverty are based on a poverty index devised by the Social Security Administration in 1964 and modified by a Federal Interagency Committee in 1969. (Indeed, Social Security was designed as a plan to protect the poor. See the Application "Does Social Security Protect the Poor?" at the end of this chapter.) This is an attempt to define poverty in absolute terms. The index delineates a poverty level according to such factors as size of family, rate of inflation, number of children under age 18, and place of residence. Accepting this official definition, we can observe changes in the incidence of poverty over time to different types of families.

Even when measured in absolute rather than relative terms, much poverty still exists in the United States. Many of the poorest families in our society are living in conditions below those that most Americans would deem to be acceptable. Table 15.5 provides an overall profile for various types of families for selected years between 1959 and 1996. In 1959, the number of persons living below the poverty line was almost 40 million, or more than 22 percent of all persons in this country. By 1996, the poor had fallen in number to below 37 million, or 13.7 percent of the population; but this progress is somewhat misleading: In 1979, the number of persons living below the poverty line was 26.1 million, or 11.7 percent of the population. Overall, then, there has been an increase in poverty since 1979.

Although the number of African Americans living in poverty fell more than 25 percent between 1959 and 1996, the incidence of poverty among African American families has remained high since 1979, falling only during the prosperous 1990s. Unemployment rates for Hispanic families have remained at about twice the national average. A third demographic group for which poverty rates have remained high is families headed by single women. In 1996, 40 percent of

TABLE 15.5

Poverty by Family Status, Race, and Sex of Householder, 1959–1996
While poverty has declined in absolute numbers and in percentage terms over time, the relative positions of African Americans and female householders are still a matter of concern.

Family Status, Race, and Sex of Householder	NUMBER BELOW POVERTY LEVEL (MILLIONS)					PERCENT OF PERSONS BELOW POVERTY LEVEL				
	1959	1969	1979	1987	1996	1959	1969	1979	1987	1996
All persons	39.5	24.2	26.1	32.5	36.5	22.4	12.1	11.7	13.5	13.7
White	28.5	16.7	17.2	21.4	24.6	18.1	9.5	9.5	10.5	11.2
African American	9.9	7.1	8.1	9.7	9.7	55.1	32.2	31.0	33.1	28.4
Hispanic	(NA)	(NA)	2.9	5.5	8.7	(NA)	(NA)	21.6	28.2	29.4

Sources: U.S. Department of Commerce, Bureau of the Census, Current Population Records—Consumer Income, *Money Income and Poverty Status of Families and Persons in the United States: 1984* (Washington, D.C.: U.S. Government Printing Office.,1986), pp. 20–24: *Statistical Abstract of the United States* (Washington, D.C.: U.S. Government Printing Office, 1998). p. 447. (1998 Statistical Update, U.S. Department of Commerce Web Site.)

such families were living in poverty, and over one-half of all poor families were headed by women.

Race and Sex Discrimination in Wages

The overall statistics on poverty since the 1960s do show improvement, but the undeniable fact is that there are poor among us and that poverty is often related to race, sex, and family status. What are the reasons for the facts of poverty? Factors are many and often interwoven. Some people are unlucky. Others are not able-bodied; they are simply unable to work. But these factors cannot explain the existence of all poverty.

Lower incomes also exist for clearly identifiable economic reasons. The poor tend to have lower skills and lower stocks of human capital. These lower stocks of human capital are the result of less education and lower job-related training. Lower productivity means unemployment and lower wages, lower wages mean lower incomes, and lower incomes mean poverty. Environmental factors may make poverty a vicious cycle: Children of the poor often receive less education and training. Moreover, many wage and income differences are the result of outright race and sex discrimination. In particular, current differences in training and education may be related to past and present economic discrimination.

We must be careful to distinguish between social discrimination and economic discrimination that leads to significantly lower wages and income, although the two are often related. Groups such as Jews, gays, and the handicapped may meet with social discrimination in seeking housing and club memberships but be little affected by economic discrimination.

Economic wage discrimination

A situation in which individuals in the same occupation who have the same productive abilities are paid different wage rates by a given employer. The wage-rate differences are based on race, sex, religion, or national origin rather than on productive differences.

Economic wage discrimination exists when individuals of equal ability and productivity in the same occupation earn different wage rates. Thus, while the median income of African Americans is only 60 percent of that of whites (in all income classes), empirical studies show that about half of this difference is related to educational, productivity, and job-training differences. The remaining half is the apparent result of economic discrimination or other unidentified factors.

Economists do not pretend to know the causes of discrimination. Nonetheless, economic discrimination involves costs to those who discriminate as well as to those against whom discrimination is practiced. An employer who refuses to hire women or African Americans of equal productivity to men or whites is discriminating. If the wages of the preferred groups are driven up by these actions, employers must pay a premium for their labor services. In a competitive system, discriminating firms will be at a disadvantage in the marketplace. Employers who do not discriminate in hiring can acquire equally productive labor at lower wage rates, eventually driving discriminating competitors out of business.

Consumer-initiated discrimination

Wage discrimination arising from consumers' preferences for goods or services produced by individuals of a certain sex, race, religion, or national origin. Consumers must pay a premium in the form of higher prices or lower quality to exercise such discrimination.

Even if employers do not discriminate, consumers may. In a competitive system, **consumer-initiated discrimination** is costly to the discriminator as well as to those discriminated against. Consumers who will deal only with whites or men (avoiding, say, African American or female lawyers, doctors, or interior designers) must pay a premium for their prejudice. Prices of goods and services of favored sellers will be higher than prices for the same goods or services available to those who do not discriminate. In sum, the competitive system makes it costly for employers or consumers to discriminate. This economic deterrent has failed to eradicate discrimination in our economy, however, as have government regulations explicitly forbidding discrimination.

Alleviating Poverty: The 1996 Revolution in Welfare

Welfare programs center on the relative needs of the poor. In-kind benefits such as food stamps, Medicare, housing subsidies, and outright money transfers (such as Aid to Families with Dependent Children) have been, for more than six decades, allotted to the poor on the basis of a government agency's determination of need. Passed as a "safety net" during the Great Depression of the 1930s, federal guarantees of welfare benefits were supposed to be a temporary stopgap for those that found themselves in poverty. These programs became increasingly "federalized" with the federal government mandating benefits to the poor, although benefits did vary from state to state and among local governments.

Without questioning the need or the existence of poverty, economists have for many years analyzed the costs of fairly and accurately administering these programs. But more important, economists are concerned with the effects of such programs on the incentives of the poor. While there will always be those who for health or other reasons cannot work, the strongly federalized welfare system historically discriminated against most of the poor in one respect: It has tended to discourage any effort on the part of the poor to better themselves by earning income in addition to their subsidy and perhaps acquiring job training in the process. The specter of third and fourth generation (often fatherless) families on welfare payments mandated by the federal government created an enormous groundswell for change.

In November 1988, the first major welfare reform legislation in fifty-three years, the Family Support Act of 1988, was signed into law. As a major revision in the rules affecting the approximately 11 million people receiving Aid to Families with Dependent Children (AFDC), the program attempted to institute economic incentives into the welfare system. It was specifically addressed to the problem created by the tremendous increase in the number of households headed by women. In particular the Act created a system whereby working did not disqualify the welfare recipient from receiving assistance.

But this change in the Act was clearly not enough to have a significant effect on those on welfare and in poverty. In 1996, the government embraced one of the largest "social experiments" concerning poverty since federally mandated welfare assistance was passed during the presidency of Franklin D. Roosevelt. Congress passed and President Clinton signed the Personal Responsibility and Work Opportunity Act in August 1996, ending the sixty-one-year guarantee that families and poor children are entitled to federal benefits. This historic piece of legislation returns to states the authority to establish many of the rules and regulations concerning qualifications for welfare. Each state receives a set amount of money for welfare payments with the option of spending more out-of-state funds. Each state must maintain its welfare disbursements at 75 percent of the total amount spent in 1994, however.

In principle, the entire incentive structure will change for those in poverty and receiving welfare. In addition to the change in terms of responsibility for welfare, some of the major provisions of the bill:

- Require that states cut off welfare benefits after an individual has collected for five years;
- Provide no cash benefits to unmarried teenage parents unless states decide to provide benefits to teen mothers who remain in school and live with an adult;
- Mandate that all able-bodied adults work after two years on welfare. Refusal to work would mean a cut-off of benefits, although states could make "hardship" exemptions for 20 percent of the recipients;
- Allow nonworking, childless adults to qualify for food stamps for six months during a three-year period for only three months at a time. Students remain eligible for school lunch programs so long as they are legally eligible for free public education;
- Cut off those convicted of drug felonies from food stamps and cash assistance (pregnant women and those in drug treatment are excepted);
- Permit state officials to deny Medicaid benefits to adults who fail to work and who have lost benefits, although health benefits would be guaranteed to families on welfare, continuing for one year after individuals go to work;
- Exclude illegal immigrants from most benefits and future legal immigrants (noncitizens) for their first five years in the United States.

Economists, generally, have hailed these reforms as a step in the right direction of providing incentives for individuals and families to remove themselves from poverty. Although critics have complained that children are not adequately protected under this system, supporters see the new welfare rules as the only way to provide compassion for poor children and their families. The short-term preliminary evidence on welfare reform (between the 1996 Act and 1998) is quite positive.[1] Welfare caseloads fell dramatically, with most states experiencing double-digit reductions. But we must be very careful in interpreting these stark reductions in the welfare rolls. Welfare rolls are known normally to fluctuate with the business cycle. As the unemployment rates goes down, so does the welfare participation rate. We should expect fewer people and families to be on the rolls over the highly prosperous 1990s.

Surely, welfare reform at the federal and state levels has had a positive effect on poverty and labor force participation, but the real question is "how much?" When the (inevitable) business cycle turns downward, will families and individuals continue to be employed in the economy or will they experience long-term unemployment, putting pressure on private charities? A number of years must pass before these important questions will be answered. Clearly, there was very little defense of the system as it existed, either from politicians or from society at large. The new system means that states, not the federal government, will compete and lead to the evolution of innovative policies to deal with the problems of poverty and welfare assistance.

HEALTH CARE: AN ONGOING PROBLEM

The provision of health care is closely related to the issues of income distribution and poverty. Consider the fact that infant mortality rates in the United States are higher among people living in poverty than among people in higher-income groups or the fact that people in higher-income groups tend to live longer than people in lower-income groups. Health care is thus intimately linked to issues of income distribution.

The U.S. Health Care System

Despite some obvious inequities in the provision of health care, surveys indicated that most Americans were generally satisfied with the level of health care benefits they were receiving during the 1990s. What conditions, then, led to the widespread belief among Americans around that time that an overhaul of the U.S. health care system had become essential? First, there was the matter of soaring health costs. Between 1985 and 1995, spending on health care grew at a faster rate than the overall economy. In fact, health costs grew faster than GDP in all but one of the 32 years prior to 1993, and there was every reason to believe that the trend would continue. Health care expenditures, which accounted for 6 percent of GDP in 1965, swallowed up more than 14 percent of GDP in 1995. Some experts suggested in the early 1990s that inaction on health care matters would cause health care's share of GDP to increase to 17 percent by the year 2000 and 37 percent by 2030, although the rise in health care costs moderated the second half of the 1990s.

---

[1] For additional information on this issue, see the *Economic Report of the President 1998* (Washington, D.C.: U.S. Government Printing Office, 1998), pp. 117–120.

FOCUS

Should You Buy Health Insurance?

In 1996, by some estimates, approximately 15 percent of all persons in the United States (41 million) were without any form of health insurance *at any given time.* Access to health insurance is considered a major indicator of access to health care for individuals and families. Consequently, reducing the number of uninsured persons is a common goal of most proposals to reform the health care system in the United States.

By itself, however, the 41 million figure for the uninsured population may not be very helpful in understanding access to health care. Over time, there are changes in the composition of the uninsured population, a process called churning. In other words, most of the uninsured are uninsured for relatively brief periods of time—usually when they are between jobs.

The uninsured tend to use fewer health care services than the insured, and as a result may have a poorer health status than the insured population. However, while the uninsured may use fewer health care services, they nevertheless generally do receive some health care. Some of the uninsured pay for these services out of their own pockets; some receive care from clinics that receive public subsidies; and some get care from providers who are subsidizing their care through increased charges to their paying customers. By law, the condition of anyone who checks into a hospital emergency room must be at least stabilized. Much of hospitals' uncompensated care was financed by shifting the cost to patients with insurance.

A sizeable portion of the uninsured population is not poor. Forty percent of uninsured households have incomes of $20,000 or more; 22 percent have incomes of $30,000 or more; and 13 percent have incomes of $40,000 or more. Most uninsured individuals are in the middle (and healthier) years of life (18–54). Many of these families choose to "self-insure." In other words, they plan to pay for necessary health care costs as they arise.

Does the purchase of some level of health insurance make sense for you? Economists can only guess at the incentives involved. If an individual is young, healthy, risk-loving, and earning a small income, no insurance or a minimum amount rationally may be chosen. Older, less healthy, risk-averse, and high-income individuals rationally would make other choices. Difficulties are introduced into the system when portability and the prospects of a catastrophe are considered. Basically, the purchase of insurance depends on a number of individual factors, not least of which is your attitude toward risk.

Sources: Madeleine Smith, *Health Insurance Coverage: Characteristics of the Insured and Uninsured Populations* (Washington, D.C.: Library of Congress, Congressional Research Service, August 19, 1991); Joseph L. Bast, Richard C. Rue, and Stuart A. Westbury, Jr., *Why We Spend Too Much on Health Care* (Chicago: The Heartland Institute, 1992); and *Statistical Abstract of the United States 1998* (Washington, D.C.: U.S. Government Printing Office, 1998), p. 125.

While expenditures on health care (as a percentage of total expenditures) have remained fairly constant over the 1990s, dissatisfaction with the state of the health insurance industry in the United States has prompted calls for change. As many as 41 million Americans—15 percent of the population—are uninsured, and another 37 million "underinsured." This number may be seriously misleading, however, and it may well be rational behavior for some Americans to remain uninsured (for more details, see the Focus "Should You Buy Health Insurance?"). The high cost of health insurance was a significant factor in the large size of the uninsured population in the 1990s, but many observers also pointed to the linkage of health insurance and employment and the virtually unlimited ability of insurers to "dump" people with serious illnesses or who pose serious risks.

Health Care Reform: Some Models

Bill Clinton's pledge to do something about reforming the U.S. health care system was partly responsible for his victory over George Bush in the 1992 presidential election. Indeed, shortly after taking office, Clinton appointed a health care task force (chaired by the First Lady, Hillary Rodham Clinton) and charged its members with developing a reform plan. Deciding how to fix the system proved to be an enormously complicated job, and the Clintons' efforts at reform were rebuffed by Congress in 1994. The issue is not over, however, and it is useful to reflect upon some of the things that we learned from this historic debate over health care reform. For one thing, there is more than one way to structure a health care system. One method is the Canadian system of universal health insurance. This single-paper system is what is termed "socialized medicine" in that all essential medical services are provided equally for everyone at government (that is, taxpayers') expense. Americans have apparently rejected this system. But the issue of rising health care costs remains on the minds of voters and politicians. Some reform, therefore, is to be expected. Some of the alternative systems and the means of financing them must be considered.

Managed Competition   Whereas the Canadian model provides a large role for government, most managed competition or "managed care" proposals are a hybrid of free market forces and government intervention. At the heart of all managed competition proposals are organizations called health insurance purchasing cooperatives (HIPCs) or health alliances. Some proposals envision the cooperatives as privately run consumer advocacy groups. Each HIPC would function as a kind of medical "farmer's market," where buyers and sellers of benefit packages that meet or exceed the federal government's standard package would be brought together to conduct transactions. The appeal of the HIPCs is that they provide a way for health providers to spread the costs and risks associated with universal coverage over a vast pool of individuals. In other words, the number of individuals in each pool would be large enough that providers could afford to charge everyone in the pool an average, or community, rate, thereby eliminating the need for cost adjustments based on individuals' medical histories. Additionally, the sheer size of the HIPCs—millions of individuals would belong to each cooperative—would give them tremendous bargaining strength with health providers. Each HIPC, therefore, would be able to negotiate for the highest-quality, lowest-cost medical services being offered.

The most extreme managed care proposals include some regulatory powers for the health alliances. Some reformers have advocated establishing a global health budget—or a cap on all health expenditures, public and private—in order to curb rising costs. There have also been calls for limiting the amount by which health insurance premiums can be increased each year. If these two proposals were enacted, the health alliances would be charged with enforcing the associated regulations. It is worth noting that a configuration in which the cooperatives have regulatory powers closely resembles the Canadian system.

Another wrinkle in health care policy concerns the role of health care providers such as health maintenance organizations (HMOs). These organizations substitute for insurance policies and offer the individual a range of medical services for a fee. However, HMOs employ a particular form of medicine. The patient,

FOCUS

Who Pays the Bill for Patients' Rights?

Can your insurance company deny you necessary medical treatment? What rights do you have as a patient, and how much do they cost? Health maintenance organizations (HMOs) now cover more than 60 percent of the American population and reduce costs by better organizing health care. They introduce new efficiencies and reduce the use of expensive medical treatments when less costly ones are available.

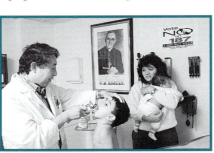

In response to outrage over the withholding of certain medical treatments and restrictions on consumers' choice of doctors, politicians of both stripes are promoting patients' bills of rights at both the state and federal levels. This legislation typically provides for independent arbitration between patients and their health plans, holds health plans accountable for injuries caused by the restriction of treatments, and protects doctors who report abuses of the health plan companies for which they work.

President Clinton's proposal contains rights such as access to accurate, easily understood information, choice of health care providers, access to emergency services, participation in treatment decisions, and grievances and appeals processes. While many of the provisions are common sense and are already a part of standard medical services, mandating them across the board will have costly economic effects. By mandating that HMOs must cover a broader range of expensive treatments, these new rights will force all ratepayers to buy unwanted coverage like the mandates in some states that require coverage for such things as hair transplants and massage therapy. The bill of rights will therefore result in higher premiums, make health insurance less affordable, and enrich lawyers. It has been estimated that as many as 600,000 people would no longer be covered by health insurance if the patients' bill of rights is passed.

Rights are not for free. Scarcity still plays a role. Guaranteeing high-quality medical care comes at a price that consumers must pay and prices health insurance beyond the reach of more Americans. Alternative policies, or simply letting competition work in this new industry, may provide improvement in health plans at a lower cost.

---

for example, is guaranteed a doctor's services, but not the services of a particular doctor. Also, HMOs limit benefits and treatments in some respects. For such reasons, HMOs are under political attack, and there are presently calls for legislation respecting patients' rights in dealing with HMOs. (For more information, see the Focus "Who Pays the Bill for Patients' Rights?")

Tax-Code Changes   Some observers blame many of the problems that created the crisis in health care on the U.S. tax code. Medical care and health insurance provided by employers as part of an employee's wage package are exempt from federal taxes. Therefore, employees have an incentive to take a larger share of their total compensation in the form of health care than they would if health care were subject to federal taxes. Removing the exemption would create an incentive for employees to bargain with their employers for more take-home pay and less health care. (A similar idea—taxing benefits that go beyond some government-defined list of core benefits—is popular with people who doubt that any attempt to create a new health care system overnight will succeed.) With the proper incentives, employees might even decide to provide for their own health care by dealing directly with providers or by buying health insurance on their own. When employees rely on employers to finance their health care, they have little incentive to monitor costs. Because the recipients of health care are in the best position to monitor costs, tying health care to employment and one's compensation package is not the most efficient approach. Whether or not individuals know enough about health care to judge the best plan for their family's needs is a matter of debate. Some observers feel that most people would be better off letting a government agency make the choice for them. Others argue that individuals usually make well-informed choices when they are provided with strong economic incentives.

Deregulation   The provision of health care in the United States has always been influenced by government regulatory policies, tax subsidies, and various price and output policies. Government owns and operates medical facilities and purchases vast amounts of medical sector output at prices it helps to set. Virtually all aspects of the supply and demand of the health care market are affected by government. Some observers argue that government actions distort market price signals and that large government spending programs do a poor job of controlling rising medical costs. One possible reform, therefore, would eliminate existing government health insurance programs (Medicare and Medicaid) and require that every family have a major medical insurance policy, which the family would purchase in a competitive insurance market. In most cases, each family would pay for its own insurance coverage and would receive a reduction in taxes in return from the government. Special provisions might be made for lower-income families or for families unable to qualify for private insurance at reasonable rates.

Obviously, providing even a modest package of health benefits to every American is an enormously expensive—and complex—undertaking. Working out the details relating to the structure of a universal-coverage scheme may actually be easier than finding a formula for financing the program. Even among President Clinton's advisers there were numerous disagreements over alternative schemes for financing the administration's proposed reforms.

Health reforms relating to the "portability" of health insurance were passed in 1996. The Health Insurance Reform Act (also called the Kassebaum–Kennedy Act) aimed at making it easier for people to renew or acquire health insurance coverage despite "preexisting conditions" or health status, particularly when they lose or change their jobs. These new rules apply to all employment-based health plans and prohibits these plans from denying or limiting coverage for more than twelve months for most "preexisting" medical problems. Further, the Kassebaum–Kennedy legislation guarantees group-to-individual coverage portability for those individuals who leave group coverage. The bill also permits an "experiment" whereby a sample of 750,000 individuals may opt for "medical savings accounts" or voluntary purchasing pools offering insurance contracts (although Kassebaum–Kennedy puts rate restrictions on the latter).

Some economists are skeptical of the value of the Kassebaum–Kennedy "reforms." A number of economists point to one critical problem—the matter of insurance rates. Rates have been based on risk assessments for certain conditions—high-risk individuals have been "redlined" or charged higher rates to reflect the higher risk. Under the 1996 legislation, the government mandates that individuals be covered, but does not put rate restrictions on this coverage. Under such circumstances, rates will rise, and healthy people will subsidize the higher costs to those with higher health risks. It is not difficult, from a public choice–interest group perspective, to understand the popularity of such legislation.

The debate about health care reform is part of a larger debate about the proper role of government. Some people advocate more direct government involvement and finance to set things right, while others advocate the use of the tax system to provide individuals with the financial wherewithal to make their own decisions about health care. Time will tell which approach wins out.

THE JUSTICE OF INCOME DISTRIBUTION

Justice itself is not part of the positive economist's vocabulary, but the effects of concepts of justice are within the economist's purview. More than a century ago, the classical economist John Stuart Mill observed that two kinds of equality are involved in questions of distribution: *ex ante* equality and *ex post* equality. *Ex ante* equality is a situation where "all start fair"—where, through educational opportunities, the absence of discrimination, social and economic mobility, and so on, every individual is given an opportunity to maximize his or her potential. *Ex ante* equality is equivalent to equality of opportunity. *Ex post* equality is a guarantee that through redistributive policies all end up at the same place. While Mill championed *ex ante* equality, he believed that differing incentives, innate talents, luck, and so on meant there would be differences in income distribution in the end. To guarantee all citizens *ex post* equality would stultify incentives, which are the very core of economic progress. Enforced *ex post* equality would surely shrink the total economic pie.

Modern economists concerned with income distribution face the same problem. The trick is to evaluate the contemporary system and to propose means that provide that all start fair but that do not force redistributions that significantly reduce incentives to produce.

APPLICATION

Does Social Security Protect the Poor?

The Social Security Act was passed during the Great Depression era of the 1930s as part of President Franklin D. Roosevelt's New Deal policies. The central program of Social Security is government-guaranteed supplemental retirement benefits paid for by Social Security taxes (some of which come out of your paycheck under the heading F.I.C.A.). Protecting the poor against severe hardship is a primary justification for forcing virtually everyone into the Social Security system.

In order to help the poor and lower-income worker, Social Security was designed with a scale of "progressive benefits," where those with lower wage rates receive a higher percentage of their average monthly income in Social Security benefits than do average and high-wage earners. Low-wage workers get a Social Security retirement benefit check equal to approximately 58 percent of their pre-retirement income, while average income earners receive 43 percent and high-wage workers get back only about 25 percent. The system would seem to benefit the poor and lower-income groups.

Despite its bias toward helping the poor, there are many reasons that Social Security does not benefit low-wage workers or protect people from poverty. Today, more than 10 percent of senior citizens live in poverty, with nearly 20 percent of elderly widows and 30 percent of elderly African Americans living below the poverty line. It seems that there is little that can be done to increase these benefits, because the system is expecting a shortfall in revenues during the first half of the twenty-first century. Absent reform, this long-predicted crisis in Social Security could ultimately necessitate up to a 25 percent cut in benefits to close the gap between the system's revenues and its expenses. Such a big cut in benefits would be particularly painful to low-income groups that are already below or just above the poverty line.

The system of progressive benefits that is supposed to benefit low-wage workers is offset by the regressive nature of the Social Security tax. The total Social Security tax is now the equivalent of more than 15 percent of wages. This tax applies to the first $62,000 in annual income, so that the poor and middle-income workers pay the tax on all their income, but high-income earners stop paying the tax after they reach that limit. Social Security, therefore, not only takes a high percentage of income from the poor, it takes a higher proportion of income from low-wage earners.

Studies have also shown that the progressive scale of Social Security benefits may be completely offset, if not reversed, by differences in life expectancy. Low-wage individuals tend to die younger than high-wage individuals, and therefore they collect fewer retirement checks from Social Security. Men in the highest income bracket live three years longer than men in the lowest income bracket and therefore receive, on average, thirty-six more checks from Social Security.

Differences in income and longevity also result in different benefits for African Americans and whites. The life expectancy of a black man born today is 66 years—a fact that translates into only one year of benefits in exchange for decades of taxes. African American males who reach age sixty-five are expected to live an additional fourteen years, but this is two years and twenty-four checks less than the average white male. The Rand Corporation estimated that Social Security is a $10,000 per person transfer from blacks to whites.

Low-wage workers also tend to work more years than high-wage workers, who often attend college and graduate school. A high-school dropout would work and pay Social Security taxes for nearly fifty years before being eligible for full Social Security benefits, but someone who went to graduate school might work less than forty years. Because Social Security benefits are based on a maximum of thirty-five years of earnings, the additional years above thirty-five mean the individual pays more taxes that are not compensated for by higher benefits.

Finally, Social Security taxes are so high now that low-wage workers accumulate little or no private savings over their lifetime. Private savings help supplement Social Security income to raise individuals above the poverty level. Unlike Social Security, private savings can be passed down to future generations. For all these reasons, Social Security appears to be a bad deal for low-wage workers.

Private investing yields a much better return than Social Security. Consider private investment as an alternative to Social Security. If a couple who dropped out of high school both worked at full-time minimum-wage jobs, the total Social Security taxes on their labor (including Medicare taxes) would exceed 15 percent, or more than $250 per month. If they invested $250 per month in a tax-free mutual fund account that invested in conservative stocks and bonds with an average return of 7 percent, they would have a nest egg of more than $1.2 million when they retired at age sixty-five. If the money was invested in a more aggressive stock fund that averaged 11 percent, their nest egg would amount to more than $5 million dollars.

Without spending any of the principal, the couple would have an annual retirement income of $84,000 in the case of the conservative investment and $550,000 per year in the case of the aggressive investment. Not only would our couple live much better than if they had to live off of Social Security, but they would have a substantial inheritance to give to future generations. It may seem implausible that families would save 15 percent of their income, but the Japanese save at an even higher rate. Our government could provide tax incentives to encourage people to save more.

In addition to the poor returns that the current and future Social Security recipients receive, the two main economic problems with Social Security are that the taxes discourage work and employment and the benefits discourage savings. Reverting to a private system in which the government provided incentives to save and allowed people to keep all of their investment returns would permit individuals, especially low-income individuals, a way to accumulate wealth and break the cycle of poverty. Experiments in partial privatization of Social Security in the South American country of Chile and Galveston County, Texas, have thus far proven successful and popular with citizens.

QUESTIONS

Has Social Security fulfilled its promise? Why might low-income individuals oppose a return to private investing and other reforms of Social Security?

Source: A reference for the material in this Application is Carrie Lips, "The Working Poor and Social Security Privatization," (Washington, D.C.: Cato Institute), September 29, 1998.

SUMMARY

1. Economists deal with positive, not normative, aspects of income distribution. The economist does not normally deal with questions of justice or fairness, but focuses instead on the facts of income distribution and on the possible effects of alternative welfare programs.

2. Money income distributions differ for a number of reasons: Some persons choose leisure over work and income, while others earn lower incomes because of bad luck, poor health, lower educational opportunities and productivity, and race or sex discrimination.

3. A Lorenz curve is one measure of income inequality. Ordinarily, the more bowed the Lorenz curve, the more inequality there is in a society's income distribution.

4. Lorenz curves showing money income distribution for a given year overstate actual inequality when in-kind benefits, income and payroll taxes, and other factors are considered. Age distribution of the population and income mobility also create greater long-term equality in income distribution.

5. Poverty and economic discrimination are interrelated features of our economic system. Economic discrimination exists when individuals of equal productivity are paid different wages on the basis of sex or racial differences.

6. Economic discrimination exists against African Americans and women in our society; only half of the difference between African American–white and male–female earnings is related to productivity differences.

7. Economic discrimination cannot be practiced by employers or consumers without costs in a competitive environment. Government-sanctioned regulations and restrictions on competitors appear to account for a large amount of observed economic discrimination in the United States.

8. In 1996 Congress passed and President Clinton signed the Personal Responsibility and Work Opportunity Act. This legislation returns authority over welfare programs to the states and sets time limits and work requirements for welfare recipients.

9. Spending on health care has been growing faster than the overall economy for more than thirty years. Numerous reform measures have been proposed, most of which are designed to curb rising costs while guaranteeing every American a standard package of health benefits. In 1996 Congress passed and President Clinton signed legislation implementing health care reform, stressing the portability of insurance across jobs, access to health insurance for those with preexisting conditions, and medical savings accounts.

KEY TERMS

individual income
labor income
asset income
ex ante distribution
ex post distribution
transfer payment

family income
Lorenz curve
adjusted income
in-kind transfer payments
economic mobility
mean income

per capita income
poverty
economic wage discrimination
consumer-initiated discrimination

QUESTIONS FOR REVIEW AND DISCUSSION

1. What are the components of an individual's income? Which of these are matters of choice by the individual?

2. How does an individual obtain asset income?

3. What does a Lorenz curve show? What does it mean if the Lorenz curve moves closer through time to the line of perfect equality?

4. What is the difference between income as measured by government and adjusted income as reported by some economists?

5. What is economic wage discrimination? Give an example of wage discrimination that fits the description.

6. Why do young people have lower incomes than older people?

7. If every married couple in the United States obtained a divorce, would the Lorenz curve move away from the line of perfect equality? Would this alteration change the actual distribution of income?

8. Suppose all people were born with the same amount of natural abilities and the same amount of inherited money wealth. Under these circumstances, what would the sources of income differences be?

9. Is a perfectly equal distribution of income necessarily desirable? Why or why not?

10. What conditions led to the widespread dissatisfaction with the U.S. health care system that developed in the early 1990s? Discuss two possible solutions to the health care problem and indicate which you would prefer to see implemented. Explain your selection.

11. There are constraints to public solution of the retirement problem. Devise a possible solution to the problems posed by the Social Security crisis.

PROBLEM

The table shows the distribution of family income in the small nation of Microvia before taxes and transfer payments.

Quintile	Household Income	Adjusted Income
Lowest	$10,000	———
Second	$20,000	———
Third	$30,000	———
Fourth	$40,000	———
Highest	$50,000	———

a. Suppose that the Microvian government enacts a transfer payment that gives $5000 to every household that earns less than $20,000. Also suppose that it enacts a progressive income tax with no taxes for households that earn $20,000 or less, a 10 percent tax on household income of $30,000, a 15 percent tax on household income of $40,000, and a 20 percent tax on household income of

$50,000. Fill in the blanks in the table to show household income after it is adjusted for the transfer payments and income taxes.

b. Complete the following table using the data provided for income and adjusted income in the first table.

Quintile	Percent of Income	Cumulative Percent	Percent of Adjusted Income	Cumulative Percent of Adjusted Income
Lowest	———	———	———	———
Second	———	———	———	———
Third	———	———	———	———
Fourth	———	———	———	———
Highest	———	———	———	———

c. Draw the Lorenz curves for the unadjusted and adjusted income distributions you have calculated.

WORKING WITH THE WEB

1. The Application "Does Social Security Protect the Poor?" discusses a variety of problems that exist with the current Social Security system as well as with proposed changes to the system, such as privatization. In San Diego, city employees are exempt from Social Security and instead are required to invest in a defined contribution plan. Go to http://www.socialsecurity.org and read the article "Social Security Differences" by J. T. Young, which was the "Daily Comment" for June 25, 1999.

   Analyze the case of the San Diego employee who invests 3.1% of their $32,000 salary compared with the expected returns if this individual participates in Social Security. Under which plan is this person better off?

2. To see the reality of the impact of privatization, return to http://www.socialsecurity.org and choose the link that allows you to calculate what you would gain from privatization. Or, if you prefer, the direct link is http://www.socialsecurity.org/calc/calculator.html. Click on the button "Estimate Social Security." Assume you were born in 1975 and that your current earnings are $50,000. Leave the other settings unchanged (i.e., they should read retirement age 67, Salary Scale 5%, Inflation 3%, Bond Return 6%, Bond/Stock 50%/50%, Stock Return 10%, Social Security Pct You Expect to Receive 100%).

   a. In nominal 2042 dollars, what is your annual retirement income under Social Security?

   b. In nominal 2042 dollars, what is your annual retirement income if you have invested aggressively in a stock fund?

   c. Is there any private investment alternative (i.e., bond fund, mixed fund, or stock fund) that leaves you worse off than the annual income expected under Social Security?

3. The Cato Institute offers a plan for an alternative to Social Security. Go to http://www.socialsecurity.org/alternative.html and read "Cato's Social Security Alternative."

   a. Does Cato advocate eliminating Social Security entirely?

   b. How does the level of investment differ between Social Security and Cato's proposed plan?

Thomas Malthus

POINT

Gary Becker

Thomas Malthus
and Gary Becker:
The Economics of
Population Growth

COUNTERPOINT

T homas Malthus (1766–1834) was born in Surrey, England, during the Industrial Revolution. It was widely believed at the time that the effects of industrialization, such as increased trade and specialization of labor, would eventually improve the quality of human life. When anarchist and pamphleteer William Godwin published his utopian outlook for society in his book *Political Justice* in 1793, an argument developed between Malthus and his father. Malthus's father was inclined to agree with Godwin's views, but the younger Malthus believed that society was caught in a trap in which population would increase more rapidly than the food supply, leaving the standard of living at a subsistence level at best. In 1798, the same year he became a minister of the Church of England, Malthus published his views of population and the economy in his treatise *An Essay on the Principle of Population.* It was this pessimistic treatise on the future of humanity that led essayist Thomas Carlyle to label economics "the dismal science."

Malthus went on to become the first professor of political economy in England at the East India College in 1805. His work on population influenced his friend and critic David Ricardo as well as Charles Darwin.

Gary Becker (b. 1930), currently University Professor of Economics at the University of Chicago, gained international recognition for his work in applying microeconomic theory to areas such as marriage, crime, and prejudice. His book *The Economics of Discrimination* (1971) introduced prejudice and discrimination as forces that can be analyzed and measured in their effect on the economy. In *The Economics of Human Behavior* (1976), Becker argues that all human behavior, even selection of a marriage partner, is based on economics.

In 1965, Becker authored *Human Capital,* his famous treatise on the concept of human capital. In *Human Capital,* Becker treats the individual as a "firm" that makes investment decisions (such as education or on-the-job training) on the basis of rate of return. Soon after the book's publication, Becker was awarded the John Bates Clark medal by the American Economic Association for excellence in research by an economist under the age of 40. In 1992, Becker was awarded the Nobel Prize in economic science.

The Check of Misery

Malthus's theory of population growth is strongly pessimistic. In *An Essay on the Principle of Population,* Malthus wrote that the world's population will increase at a rate that will ultimately test the limits of our available food supply and other subsistence goods. As the supply of food increases through additional labor and agriculture, population will increase as well, with the result that per capita income—the fruits of labor—will never exceed bare subsistence standards for the population as a whole. The threat of widespread famine will persist indefinitely. Only the lucky will survive.

An alternative way of stating Malthus's proposition is that children are what economists call normal goods, demand for which rises and falls in response to changes in income. Any increase in income to parents will increase their demand for children, other things being equal. At the point when an additional child will actually reduce living standards below subsistence—a point Malthus called the "check of misery"—parents will cease reproducing.

Given this gloomy scenario, it is not surprising that Malthus, a parson, would urge "moral restraints" on parents. Such restraints included abstinence and postponing marriage. It is interesting to speculate about whether Malthus would urge modern forms of birth control. The morality of contraceptive use, forced sterilization, and abortion is one of the burning issues of our times.

Malthus's theory of population growth seems today most applicable to the exploding populations of China, Mexico, Bangladesh, and other developing countries. In the industrialized nations, including the United States, the last century has seen actual declines in average family size, while average family incomes have risen well above the level of bare subsistence. Many economists, including Gary Becker, have sought reasons that the theory has not, fortunately, held true.

The Price of Children

Becker's theory of human capital helps explain both the power and the limits of the Malthusian theory. For Becker, the choice of whether to reproduce has a second rationale, one beyond a simple change in income. Parents' demand for children will be influenced not only by changes in income but also by the relative "price" of children. This price is partly the direct costs of raising the child, but it also includes the opportunity costs that additional children represent. As the parents' income increases, the opportunity cost of children will also tend to increase. In other words, the sacrifices borne by increasing the size of a family will increase with income. To take one example, if an executive forsakes a high-paying job to stay home with the children so that his or her spouse can pursue a career, the cost of that decision is the wages and income the executive receives now and the higher income he or she could expect to receive in the future.

As the costs of children increase, the quantity demanded will decrease, other things being equal. As a result, parents may substitute quality for quantity in their decisions to raise children. Instead of feeding an additional child, parents might decide to spend additional income on housing, education, or any of a host of goods that improve living standards for the children they already have.

Becker's approach to the costs of children helps explain why parents in developed countries, with relatively high incomes, have fewer, better-educated children than parents in developing countries with relatively low incomes. In less-developed, largely subsistence agricultural countries, children represent direct labor inputs—even small children can do useful work on a subsistence farm—thus lowering the price of children. Where the price of children is lower, we expect to see more children produced, other things being equal. Thus we see the law of demand at work.

According to Becker, then, Malthus failed to take into account relative prices in his theory of population. While rats or horses may tend to breed up to the limit imposed by the available food supply, the behavior of human beings will also reflect the influence of opportunity costs and the rational choices such costs inspire.

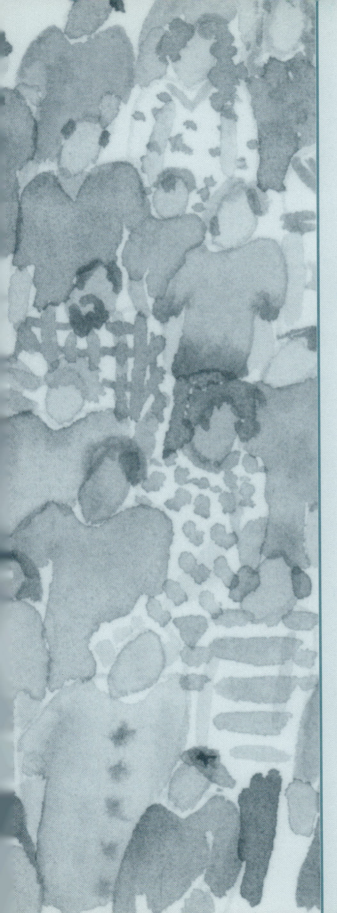

PART FOUR

Applied Microeconomics and Public Choice

4

Antitrust, Regulation, and Public Policy

O ur market economy has grown in ways that Adam Smith could never have imagined. Smith believed that market forces, operating under a laissez-faire form of government, would eventually bring us to a point of perfect competition among firms, what Smith termed "a nation of shopkeepers." Our economy, however, has followed a different path, and its market structures range from nearly pure competition to nearly complete monopoly

Public policy in the area of monopoly is two-pronged. Some policies are designed to restore and maintain competition where viable competition can exist. These **antitrust policies** control business practices such as anticompetitive mergers, cartels, price discrimination, and deceptive advertising. **Regulatory policies,** on the other hand, establish and manage the behavior of firms and industries where competition cannot exist or where positive goals—for example, health and safety—are pursued. Here, the government imposes on natural monopolies and other businesses rules and regulations that substitute for competition and undesirable behavior in markets. After you read Chapter 16 you should know

- how economists recognize and measure monopoly power in the economy.
- how government has dealt with monopoly and large-scale enterprise through antitrust and regulatory policies.
- how regulation may have *created* more monopoly power than it has dispersed.
- whether deregulation of natural monopolies helps economic efficiency and enhances consumer welfare.

Antitrust policies
Regulations established by laws and government agencies that attempt to preserve business competition.

Regulatory policies
Administrative or legal attempts to influence the behavior of firms or industries when competitive goals cannot be realized or when positive goals are to be pursued.

Concentration ratios
A measure of the degree to which the largest firms in an industry account for total industry assets, sales, or some other factor.

MEASURING INDUSTRIAL CONCENTRATION

Economists have devised several methods of detecting the existence of monopolies—all of which assumed that the number of firms in an industry indicates the degree of competition present. We examine a rough estimate of the degree of concentration of market power within an industry—industry concentration ratios.

Industry Concentration Ratios

A method of looking at business structure is to calculate **concentration ratios** (*CR*) for various industries. Concentration ratios are determined by ranking firms within an industry from largest to smallest and then calculating the share of some aggregate factor such as sales, employment, or assets held by the largest four or eight firms. Sales is the most common factor used in these calculations.

Figured by this method, the concentration ratio will lie between 0 and 100. If an industry is totally monopolized, one firm will have 100 percent of industry sales, or *CR* = 100. If an industry has several firms but the four largest have 50 percent of the market sales, then *CR* = 50. If a very large number of companies each have a very small market share, then *CR* will be close to zero, suggesting the existence of competition.

Table 16.1 displays four-firm and eight-firm concentration ratios for a small sample of manufacturing industries. Some industries are very highly concentrated. In 1992, for example, the top eight producers of electric lamps accounted for 94 percent of industry shipments, indicating that the remaining lamp manufacturers were very small businesses indeed. In contrast, the eight largest firms supplying ready-mix concrete had only an 11 percent share of total sales in 1992, suggesting that this industry is made up of a large number of relatively small companies. (The system for calculating ratios in particular industries has been undergoing significant change in the mid to late 1990s. Data later than 1992 is not directly comparable to that for 1992 or earlier.)

Table 16.1 also reveals trends in concentration. Concentration ratios that have risen over the years indicate that the leading firms have grown relative to other industry members, either by internal expansion, merger, or decreases in the number of other firms. Declining concentration ratios imply that more and more competitors have made successful inroads into the industry and thereby reduced the dominance by leading firms. While examples of each pattern appear in the table, in general concentration ratios remain fairly stable.

One problem with using concentration ratios to determine the degree of competition in an industry is that the data can obscure quite vigorous competition. Since the ratios do not identify individual firms, the concentration ratio can remain stable over time even though the leading firms rapidly turn over. For example, if the first and fourth companies in meat packing change places, the four-firm concentration ratio would remain unchanged. Additionally, concentration ratios usually ignore the impact of foreign firms that sell goods and services in a country on that country's industry structure. Concentration ratios calculated solely from the assets or sales of domestic firms will understate the degree of competition in an industry when domestic firms in the industry face stiff foreign competition. This understatement is clearest for such product categories as motor vehicles or radios and TVs (see Table 16.1).

A further difficulty with the concentration ratios in Table 16.1 is that they are based on the Commerce Department's Standard Industrial Classification (SIC) groups. The SIC codes group firms that produce similar products, but these codes

TABLE 16.1

Selected Concentration Ratios in Manufacturing

Concentration ratios measure the share of sales held by the largest four or eight firms in an industry. The data shown here represent a selected group of manufacturing industries for the years 1963, 1982, 1987, and 1992. In some industries—such as men's and boy's suits—the concentration ratio increased through the years, suggesting that the largest firms obtained a larger share of total industry output. In some cases—such as jewelry and precious metals—the ratio fell, suggesting a more competitive situation.

CONCENTRATION RATIOS

	1963 Four-Firm	1963 Eight-Firm	1982 Four-Firm	1982 Eight-Firm	1987 Four-Firm	1987 Eight-Firm	1992 Four-Firm	1992 Eight-Firm
Meat packing	31	42	29	43	32	50	50	66
Fluid milk	23	30	16	27	21	32	22	30
Cereal breakfast foods	86	96	86	97	87	99	85	98
Distilled liquor	58	74	46	68	53	75	62	82
Roasted coffee	52	68	65	76	66	78	66	75
Cigarettes	80	100	–	–	92	–	93	–
Men's and boy's suits and coats	14	23	25	37	34	47	39	50
Women's and misses' dresses	6	9	6	10	6	10	11	17
Mobile homes	–	–	24	39	30	44	35	50
Pulp mills	48	72	45	70	44	69	48	75
Book publishing	20	33	17	30	24	38	23	38
Pharmaceutical preparations	22	38	26	42	22	36	26	42
Petroleum refining	34	56	28	48	32	52	30	49
Flat glass	94	99+	85	97	82	–	81	–
Ready-mix concrete	4	7	6	9	8	11	6	11
Blast furnaces and steel mills	48	67	42	64	44	63	37	58
Metal cans	74	85	50	68	54	70	56	74
Electric lamps	92	96	91	96	91	94	86	94
Radio and TV receiving sets	41	62	49	70	39	59	41	53
Motor vehicles, car bodies	–	–	92	97	90	95	84	91
Jewelry, precious metals	26	33	16	22	12	18	16	21
Pens and mechanical pencils	48	60	41	62	49	65	49	73

Sources: U.S. Department of Commerce, Bureau of the Census, *Census of Manufacturers* (Washington, D.C.: U.S. Government Printing Office, 1977); U.S. Department of Commerce, Bureau of the Census, *Concentration Ratios in Manufacturing* (Washington, D.C.: U.S. Government Printing Office, 1982, 1987). Update by Census Bureau Website http://WWW.Census.GOV/, March 1996.

do not account for substitutability by buyers. For example, plastic panes may frequently be substituted for flat glass, but the SIC codes compare glass manufacturers only with other glass manufacturers. Thus, the concentration ratios do not show the competition among groups that results from actual market structures. Also, the SIC categories include sales data for the entire nation and therefore do not give information about concentration levels in different geographic regions; concentration in particular regions may be greater than that for the nation as a whole.

PUBLIC POLICY: ANTITRUST

Purely competitive industries represent the ideal in market performance. In industries characterized by imperfect competition, the ideal is not obtained—profits may be greater than normal, production costs are not necessarily minimized, and welfare losses can occur. If these losses to society are significant, then there is a call for social action in the form of government regulation of some businesses' activities.

Public solutions to the monopoly problem take four basic forms.

1. Antitrust laws basically designed to prevent the creation of monopolies.
2. Price regulations designed to allow the existence of monopolies but to control their prices and profits.
3. Government ownership that removes the firm from the private sector and thus places its performance directly in the hands of the public.
4. Laissez-faire policy that allows the market to determine the fate and performance of firms with no government interference.

Antitrust Law

Predatory pricing
The temporary pricing of goods or services below cost in order to reduce or eliminate competition.

The late 1800s was a time of great change in the American economy. A significant merger wave led to the creation of very large firms with nationwide operations—the first modern corporations. Some of these firms engaged in questionable business practices, such as **predatory pricing** (the act of selling goods below cost as a method of destroying competitors), price fixing, and collusion.

Antitrust policies are aimed at preventing firms from engaging in such anticompetitive activities. During the 1870s and 1880s, an antitrust movement sprang up, primarily among American farmers. Facing falling prices for their products and stable prices for the goods they bought, they became fearful that monopolies or trusts were wielding unwarranted economic power. Through organizations such as the National Grange and the National Anti-Monopoly Cheap Freight League, the farmers successfully influenced the two major political parties to add antimonopoly planks to their 1888 election platforms. Antitrust legislation was enacted soon after, with subsequent revisions to strengthen the government's ability to fight monopolistic practices in court.

Sherman Antitrust Act   The Sherman Antitrust Act of 1890, the first antimonopoly law passed by Congress, provided that "every contract, combination in the form of trust or otherwise, or conspiracy, in restraint of trade or commerce among the several states, or with foreign nations, is hereby declared to be illegal. . . ." The

Sherman Act also declared "every person who shall monopolize, or attempt to monopolize. . .[is] guilty of a misdemeanor, and subject to fine or imprisonment." The statute did not spell out what would constitute an illegal restraint of trade. Its main purpose was to place the antitrust issue under federal law and to provide a means of penalizing monopoly whenever it was discovered.

Clayton Antitrust Act   Believing that the Sherman act was ineffective in preventing monopoly, Congress passed the Clayton Act in 1914. The Clayton act enumerated some specific restraints of trade that could be challenged if their effects lessened competition substantially or created a monopoly. These included (1) price discrimination—selling the same product to different customers at different prices not related to cost differences; (2) tying arrangements—making the sale of one good contingent on the purchase of some other goods; (3) interlocking directorates—the same person's serving on the boards of competing companies; and (4) exclusive dealing—selling to a retailer only on the condition that the firm not carry rival products.

Federal Trade Commission Act   Section 5 of the Federal Trade Commission (FTC) Act, also passed by Congress in 1914, contains the broadest statutory language, declaring illegal "unfair methods of competition in commerce." The act established a five-member commission independent of the executive branch, with the idea that the FTC would be a repository of economic and antitrust expertise not available to the federal courts.

The Federal Trade Commission building, where mergers and "unfair" methods of competition in commerce are considered.

Other Antitrust Statutes   The Clayton Act has been amended twice. In 1936, the Robinson–Patman Act revised the provisions relating to price discrimination and added language prohibiting predatory pricing. In 1950, the Celler–Kefauver Act closed a Clayton Act loophole relating to mergers through the acquisition of physical assets.

The FTC Act has been revised even more often. First, in 1938 the Wheeler–Lea Act added "unfair or deceptive acts or practices in commerce" to the behavior declared illegal. In the late 1970s, the Hart–Scott–Rodino Antitrust Improvement Act established a premerger notification system by which firms contemplating a merger would notify the FTC and the Department of Justice prior to consummating the acquisition.

Antitrust Agencies

The United States has a dual system of antitrust enforcement whereby two government agencies—the Federal Trade Commission and the Justice Department's

Antitrust Division—share responsibility for policing the antitrust laws. Both agencies can enforce the Clayton Act, and, since 1948, the FTC has had the power to bring charges against behavior that violates the Sherman Act.

In addition to the two government agencies, complaints charging Sherman and Clayton antitrust violations can be brought by private parties. Private plaintiffs can sue for treble damages; that is, guilty defendants can be required to pay penalties of up to three times the value of the actual injury caused by their illegal conduct. Because private suits offer such potentially large rewards for successful plaintiffs, in any given year the number of private antitrust actions is many times greater than the number of cases brought by government.

Enforcement of Antitrust Policies

Antitrust policies are carried out in the courtroom. Antitrust officials, policy-makers, and court officials face difficulties in distinguishing between behavior that is a conscious intent of firms to decrease competition and behavior that is the result of firms' responding to external changes. For this reason, the Justice Department and the FTC treat every market situation as unique. Before either agency takes action in altering market activities, it examines the individual firms and their activities. Firms judged to be in violation of antitrust laws may be ordered to stop their anticompetitive practices or to divest themselves of some of their assets by splitting a monopoly into several smaller competing firms. Sound economic theory is not always well represented in these court decisions. We will consider some specific cases that have been tried and the consequences of the decisions.

Cartel Policies   In 1927, the Supreme Court held that price-fixing conspiracies were per se illegal under the Sherman Act, even though the act did not specifically prohibit price fixing.[1] That is, attempts by competitors to fix prices would be found illegal regardless of the level of the fixed price.

The case involved the activities of the Sanitary Potters Association (SPA), a Trenton, New Jersey, trade association, whose twenty-three member firms produced 82 percent of the U.S. output of bathroom sinks, tubs, and commodes. The SPA published price lists that included suggested discounts and surcharges for six geographic regions; members following the SPA lists charged identical prices.

The question addressed by the Supreme Court was whether a lower court judge was correct in directing the jury not to consider the reasonableness of the particular prices charged. The Court held that "uniform price-fixing by those controlling in any substantial manner a trade or business in interstate commerce is prohibited by the Sherman Law, despite the reasonableness of the particular prices agreed upon."[2] Economic theory would support the Court's decision. If a large percentage of the firms in an industry agree on price, then it is likely that price competition has been abolished.

---

[1]*United States v. Trenton Potteries Co.*, 273 U.S. 395 (1927).
[2]See Phillip Areeda, *Antitrust Analysis: Problems, Text, Cases,* 3rd ed. (Boston: Little, Brown, 1981), p. 165.

Merger
The combining of the ownership of two firms' assets, which results in a single firm.

Merger Policy   One way that concentration ratios may rise is through **mergers.** If there are only a few firms in an industry, the combination of two or more firms into one may decrease the degree of competition. However, the types of mergers vary and thus their effect on the market varies. There are three basic types of mergers: horizontal, vertical, and conglomerate. Each type is distinguished by the relation between the products produced by the merging firms.

A horizontal merger occurs when the merger partners produce the same product. Examples include mergers between two beer producers, two manufacturers of glass containers, two retail grocery stores, and so forth. Horizontal mergers may decrease competition because they have the direct effect of raising industry concentration ratios and moving the affected market closer to monopoly.

Mergers are characterized as vertical if the product of one firm serves as an input for the other firm—that is, if the merging companies are at different stages of a production process. A vertical merger would occur if a company producing crude oil acquired a petroleum refinery, if a steel producer purchased iron ore deposits, or if an automobile manufacturer acquired a string of retail car dealerships. Vertical mergers do not raise industry concentration levels and are usually motivated by the prospect of lower costs. Accordingly, vertical mergers do not normally decrease competition.

Conglomerate mergers occur when the products of the firms are unrelated—when an insurance company buys a firm that produces bread or when a cigarette producer merges with a soft drink company. The usual explanation for such mergers is that they are motivated by a desire to spread the risks associated with economic ups and downs across products. However, spreading risks can be accomplished much more simply by, for example, purchasing shares of a variety of businesses. Rather, conglomerate mergers can better be explained by the desire to diffuse managerial expertise across firms. That is, if an efficient corporate management team believes that its executive talents can be profitably applied to some other firm, it will have an incentive to acquire another company regardless of the product produced by the other firm. Since conglomerate mergers do not raise industry concentration levels, they do not generally decrease competition.

As we noted earlier, the Clayton Act, as amended by the Celler–Kefauver Act, seeks to limit corporate acquisitions that "tend to create a monopoly." Under the Hart–Scott–Rodino premerger notification system, large firms contemplating a merger are required to apprise both the FTC and the Justice Department's Antitrust Division of their intentions. The agency chosen to handle the merger must decide whether to challenge it by seeking a preliminary injunction in federal court or to allow the merger to proceed without opposition.

An important aspect of merger law enforcement is the use of guidelines to establish which particular acquisitions will be challenged. For example, vertical and conglomerate mergers are not often challenged, but horizontal mergers that significantly decrease competition are. The merger guidelines issued by the Justice Department contain numerical standards that identify markets thought to be "unconcentrated" or "concentrated" prior to a merger. The guidelines set limits on the amount that concentration will be allowed to rise in each case before antitrust action is initiated. Concentration ratios were established for this purpose in 1968.

In 1966, before these measures were in use, the Supreme Court considered the legality of a merger between two Los Angeles retail grocery chains, Von's Grocery Company and Shopping Bag Food Stores.[3] At the time of the acquisition, 1960, Von's was the third largest grocery chain in Los Angeles; Shopping Bag was the sixth largest. Together, the two grocery retailers accounted for only 7.5 percent of sales in the Los Angeles area, however. Despite the relatively small market shares involved in the merger, the Court held that Von's had violated the Clayton Act. The decision placed great weight on the fact that the number of owners operating single grocery stores in Los Angeles had declined from 5365 in 1950 to 3818 in 1961. This decline, the Court alleged, indicated a trend toward concentration.

If the number of firms in an industry is declining because of technological changes, economic theory suggests that the optimal size of firms is increasing. This change will naturally lead to an increase in concentration. According to economic theory, therefore, the merger probably should not have been prevented, especially since the two firms constituted such a small percentage of the market.

Price Discrimination   Charges of price discrimination may also require subtle distinctions. In a private suit, the Utah Pie Company charged Continental Baking Company,[4] Carnation Company, and Pet Milk Company with price discrimination in the sale of frozen pies. Utah Pie, located in Salt Lake City, alleged that its three California-based competitors sold pies shipped to Salt Lake City at prices below those charged for pies sold nearer their own plants.

The evidence before the Supreme Court pointed to a highly competitive pie market in Salt Lake City. The price discrimination evidence appeared superficially correct in the sense that, given the cost of transportation, one would not expect the prices of the California firms to be lower in Salt Lake City. Accordingly, the Supreme Court found in favor of Utah Pie.

Some feel that the Court's decision does not square with some of the facts, however. For one thing, it can be argued that the prices charged by Utah Pie were consistently lower than the prices of its rivals throughout the price discrimination episode. Second, Pet Milk Company suffered substantial losses on its Salt Lake City sales. Third, Utah Pie consistently increased its sales volume and continued to make a profit while facing the alleged anticompetitive practices of its rivals. Finally, prior to the entry of Continental, Carnation, and Pet, Utah Pie enjoyed a 67 percent market share in Salt Lake City, and while the new competition cost Utah Pie a portion of its market, at the end of the price discrimination period the Salt Lake City firm still accounted for 45 percent of the pies sold in the area. It appears to some observers that Utah Pie could have been using the antitrust policy to eliminate price competition and to gain a larger share of the market.

---

[3] *United States* v. *Von's Grocery Co.*, 384 U.S. 270 (1966).
[4] *Utah Pie Co.* v. *Continental Baking Co.*, 386 U.S. 685, 699 (1967).

Pure Monopoly and Antitrust Cases   Antitrust policies have also been applied to pure monopolies. The Aluminum Company of America (Alcoa) was involved in antitrust litigation as early as 1912 on allegations that it had violated the Sherman Act by, among other charges, monopolizing deposits of bauxite (the crucial ore in aluminum production), conspiring with foreign aluminum firms to fix world prices, and entering into exclusive contracts with power companies guaranteeing that the power companies would not supply electricity to any other aluminum producers. In 1945, the U.S. Court of Appeals for the Second Circuit finally rendered its decision on charges brought by the government that Alcoa had monopolized the production and sale of virgin aluminum ingot.

The appeals court decision, written by Judge Learned Hand, is one of the most celebrated in American antitrust history.[5] Judge Hand, in overturning a lower court decision favoring Alcoa, wrote that even though Alcoa's monopoly was "thrust upon it" and the firm "stimulated demand and opened new uses for the metal," the firm would not increase production in anticipation of increases in demand. He contended that Alcoa prevented new firms from entering by increasing its capacity as demand increased and that because of Alcoa's lower cost, no new firms could effectively compete.

Although the court found Alcoa guilty, it refused to dissolve "an aggregation which has for so long demonstrated its efficiency." The "problem" of lack of competition in the aluminum industry was solved at the end of World War II, when the government sold to Reynolds Metals and Kaiser Aluminum the aluminum production plants it had set up for the war effort.

Multinational Firms

The economies of the world are becoming increasingly interdependent. Events outside our borders have an important impact on our economy—so much so that the U.S. economy should be viewed as but one component in the global economy. This global setting has important implications for U.S. antitrust and regulatory policies.

Many firms in the global economy operate as multinational corporations. These firms operate simultaneously in a number of countries. Many business arrangements fall under the heading of the multinational corporation. Firms may locate production facilities abroad to obtain lower labor and production costs; Ford Motor Company, for example, has production facilities in Mexico. Other firms, such as RCA, make arrangements with foreign suppliers to produce products abroad for sale in the United States under the American firms' respective brand names.

Globalization of business firms and increased international competition will make the U.S. economy more competitive. If U.S. producers have high costs, they

---

[5]*United States* v. *Aluminum Co. of America*, 148 F.2d (2nd Cir. 1945).

will lose market share to foreign competitors. The huge increase in the number of imported cars in the United States since the 1960s aptly illustrates this point. Similarly, the presence of excess profits in the U.S. economy will attract the entry of foreign competitors. To some extent, then, international competition is a substitute for U.S. antitrust policy.

The proliferation of multinational firms is not without its troubling aspects, however. Multinational firms owe allegiance to no particular country; they can operate wherever they please, holding out the prospect of jobs and incomes to competing countries for promises of a less strict regulatory and antitrust environment. Moreover, these large firms may find it easier to collude and to behave monopolistically across international markets. In short, multinational firms may be better equipped to undermine competition.

Multinational firms are a mixed economic blessing. Their impact on competition must be assessed on a case-by-case basis. However, one cannot adequately assess the role of competition and competitive policy in the U.S. economy without considering these firms.

An Economic View of Antitrust Cases

How well enforcement of the antitrust laws agrees with economic principles is a complex question with no simple answers. On the basis of our brief sketch of laws, agencies, and court interpretations, we can draw the rough conclusion that economic theory has not made a large impression on legal thinking.

In particular, the courts seem to equate the degree of competition with the number of firms in an industry and to seek to protect competition by protecting competitors. This focus on the number of firms in an industry ignores the other dimensions of competition (number of buyers, entry and exit conditions, degree of product homogeneity, number of close substitute goods, and so forth). More important, the numbers game neglects the possibility that firms can grow relative to their rivals not because they use unfair methods of competition or expand by buying out their competitors but because they can serve consumers better at lower cost. Modern technology has fostered similar antitrust cases—cases where monopolization might be the result of success (see the Focus "The Microsoft Case: Is It Monopoly, or Is It Envy?").

PUBLIC POLICY: REGULATION

Natural monopoly
A combination of market demand and cost conditions that results in only one firm in an industry being able to produce output profitably; occurs when decreasing long-run average costs exist up to the level of total industry demand.

Antitrust policies are basically designed to maintain competition when competition can exist. Therefore, the antitrust policies are not very effective when a natural monopoly exists. A **natural monopoly** occurs where conditions in the market lead to a situation when only one firm is able to produce profitably. How does the public avoid the potential problems of monopoly when only one firm can survive in an industry? Price regulation is offered as a solution to some of the problems that can arise under these circumstances. Governments may attempt to regulate prices to keep them low for consumers' sake or may even establish agencies controlling the activities of specific industries. Like

FOCUS

The Microsoft Case: Is It Monopoly, or Is It Envy?

No antitrust case in recent memory has generated as much interest as *United States* v. *Microsoft*. The Department of Justice (DOJ) filed the case on behalf of the "people," alleging that Bill Gates's company is a monopoly with the wherewithal to restrain trade. The issue is the bundling (selling together) of the Internet Explorer web browser with Microsoft's Windows operating system. The allegation is that such bundling—selling Windows packaged with the Explorer—gives Explorer an "unfair" advantage in the market.

This high-profile case has created (actually uncovered) a debate that will rage long after the case is (politically) settled in the courts. The case raises critical economic issues. How, for example, can we tell if high and/or growing market share is due to monopoly or simply to success in the market? No one debates the fact that Microsoft has been wildly successful. When Microsoft entered the combined Windows–Explorer market, Netscape was the chief competitor to the Explorer web browser. Netscape then had a high market share. Furthermore, prices for web browsers fell only *after* Microsoft introduced its Explorer.[a] That is, of

course, not what one would expect if Microsoft were establishing a monopoly (remember that a monopolist will reduce output and raise price).

Other important issues are raised by the case. In industries such as high-tech PC development, there is a trade-off between standardization (such as bundling the net browser with the operating system) and technological innovation. There is, for example, every indication that the bundled product is the way consumers want to buy these products. (The DOJ, in July 1994, permitted the company to develop "integrated products" given, of course, that it did not force consumers to buy them.)

Most basically, perhaps, antitrust authorities are acting not on what *has* happened in the PC market, but on what *might* happen. The DOJ's case against Microsoft appears to revolve critically on what the company may do if and when it outcompetes its rivals. Many, but by no means all, economists are skeptical that technological innovation can be better run by the courts (government) than by the market. Competition is not comfortable. The DOJ appears to argue that Microsoft's success is "unfair" to the competition. History contains many examples of arbitrary punitive action against the successful and the "politically incorrect." Such may well be the case with the *United States* v. *Microsoft*.

[a]For additional insight, see Barry Fagin, "The Case Against the Case Against Microsoft" (Competitive Enterprise Institute, April 1999).

antitrust litigation, however, these regulatory efforts may have unwanted economic effects.

Regulatory Agencies

Broadly, regulation is any administrative or legal attempt to influence markets for goods and services. Government at any level can create regulation, which takes the form of subsidies to businesses, municipal zoning commissions, rate regulation of telephone and electricity services, legal support of occupational licensing, or any other attempt to intervene in markets.

TABLE 16.2

Major U.S. Regulatory Agencies
A great deal of industry regulation was passed in the 1930s, including that related to telephone service, pipelines, and broadcasting. More recent regulation has centered on health, safety, and the environment.

Agency	Year Established	Jurisdiction
	Economic Regulation	
Interstate Commerce Commission (ICC)	1887	Interstate railroads (1887)
		Interstate trucks (1935)
		Interstate water carriers (1940)
		Interstate telephone (1910–1934)
		Interstate oil pipelines (1906–1977)
State regulatory commissions	35 states 1907–1920; 50 states by 1973	Local electricity (46 states by 1973) Local gas (47 states in 1973) Local telephone (48 states in 1973)
Federal Communications Commission (FCC)	1934	Interstate telephone (1934)
		Broadcasting (1934)
		Cable television (1968)
		Cable television prices and services (1992)
Federal Power Commission (FPC)	1935	Interstate wholesale electricity (1935)
		Interstate natural gas pipelines (1938)
		Field price of natural gas sold in interstate commerce (1954)
Federal Energy Regulatory Commission (FERC)	1977	Oil pipelines (1977)
		Interstate gas and gas pipelines (1978)
Federal Maritime Commission (FMC)	1936	Ocean shipping (1936)
Civil Aeronautics Board (CAB)	1938	Interstate airlines (1938)
Postal Rate Commission	1970	Established classes of mail and rates for these classes; set fees for other services (1970)
Federal Energy Administration (FEA)	1973	Petroleum prices and allocation (1973)
Energy Regulatory Administration (ERA)	1974	
Copyright Royalty Tribunal	1976	Copyright material (1976)

In the United States, regulation by administrative tribunals, or commissions, is a compromise between outright government ownership and free market functioning. Since legislative bodies (Congress, state legislatures, city councils) are ill-equipped to directly regulate industries themselves, the regulatory commissions they set up deal with monopolistic imperfections such as natural monopoly. The first such commission at the federal level was the Interstate Commerce Commission, which was established to regulate the rates and practices of interstate railroads (see Table 16.2). The

TABLE 16.2 (*Continued*)

Agency	Year Established	Jurisdiction
Environmental, Safety, and Health Regulation		
Food and Drug Administration (FDA)	1906	Safety of food, drugs (1906), and cosmetics (1938) Effectiveness of drugs (1962)
Animal and Plant Health Inspection Service	1907	Meat and poultry packing plants (1907)
Federal Trade Commission (FTC)	1914	False and misleading advertising (mainly after 1938)
Securities and Exchange Commission (SEC)	1934	Public security issues and security exchanges (1934) Public utility holding companies (1935)
Civil Aeronautics Board (CAB)	1938	Airline safety (1938) (flight standards program only)
Federal Aviation Administration (FAA)	1958	
Atomic Energy Commission (AEC)	1947	Licensing of nuclear power plants (1947)
Nuclear Regulatory Commission (NRC)	1975	
National Highway Traffic Safety Administration (NHTSA)	1970	Automobile safety (1970), automobile fuel economy (1975)
Occupational Safety and Health Administration (OSHA)	1971	Industrial safety and health (1971)
Environmental Protection Agency (EPA)	1972	Air, water, and noise pollution (various environmental laws were enforced by several agencies 1963–1972)
Consumer Product Safety Commission	1972	Safety of consumer products (1972)
Mine Enforcement Safety Administration (MESA)	1973	Safety and health in mining, especially coal mines (1973)
Mine Safety and Health Administration	1978	

ICC (finally eliminated in 1995) and all other administrative commissions at all levels of government extend the legislative power of government with members appointed by the administrative branch (the president, governors, mayors, or city councils) and confirmed by the legislative branch.

Within the limits set forth by the respective legislative bodies that create them, commissions do a good deal of rule making and "quasi-judicial" decision making. On some major points of law, commission decisions may be brought before state or federal courts, but the regulatory commissions regulate industries or services for the most part autonomously.

What are the industries and services that have been subjected to commission regulation in the United States? As you can see from Table 16.2, electricity, gas, and telephone services followed the railroads into regulation early in this century. A surge of new federal regulations in the 1930s brought interstate commerce in electricity, natural gas, broadcasting, telephone, ocean shipping, airlines, and securities issuance under the regulatory umbrella. This period produced the

Securities and Exchange Commission (SEC), the Federal Communications Commission (FCC), and the Food and Drug Administration (FDA), among others. Recent federal regulatory activity has focused on such matters as industrial health and safety, automobile safety and fuel economy, air and water pollution, and the safety of consumer products. When state and municipal regulations—of occupations, zoning, rents, sanitation, highway safety, funeral homes, milk producers—are added to federal regulations, practically no area of the economy remains untouched by regulation.

The Purpose of Regulation

Economists hold varying interpretations of how and why regulatory policies emerge. In a natural monopoly, the market fails to provide goods and services in quantities and at prices that would prevail under competitive conditions. However, there are many regulations in businesses and professions where the market does seem to provide goods and services at competitive prices and quantities. Why, for example, are physicians, lawyers, nurses, and hairstylists subject to extensive regulations?

Public interest theory of regulation

Maintains that regulations are contrived so as to promote the public interest by correcting market failures and improving economic efficiency.

Some economists argue that regulation promotes the public interest by correcting market failures and improving economic efficiency. This is the **public interest theory of regulation.** Other groups of economists believe that in many cases regulatory agencies are captured by the industry or profession they are supposed to regulate. This is the **capture,** or **interest group, theory of regulation,** wherein groups interested in the suppression of competition lobby legislatures and press regulatory agencies to obtain particular goals. Electricians, carpenters, barbers, and construction firms typically lobby at local or municipal levels for "standards restrictions" that limit entry into their lines of work. Physicians, lawyers, veterinarians, nurses, and architects have engaged in similar efforts at the state and federal levels. Such occupational licensing has important economic effects—notably, to restrict entry into the profession and carefully limit competition. Unions, of course, have similar effects. On a larger scale, some economists argue that whole industries have at times "captured" the agencies that regulate them: namely, railroads, the trucking industry, television networks, airlines, and coastal water transportation.

Capture, or interest group, theory of regulation

Argues that regulations are constructed so as to further the interests of the existing firms within a particular industry.

Regulatory agencies are said to be captured when an industry or a subset of firms within an industry can influence agency activity to the benefit of the industry. This might be accomplished by agency employment of industry partisans or "experts," by hiring agency staff within the industry after their agency tenure, or by other means. Administrative bodies are appointed to balance the benefits and costs of imposing regulations. Regulations always benefit some industry members or some consumers and impose costs on others. Legislators frequently must weigh the benefits they receive from proponents of regulation (in terms of votes, money, and other perquisites) against the costs they incur from imposing regulation (also in terms of votes and support). Proponents of the capture theory argue that this process redistributes wealth based on politicians' self-interest. They argue, further, that consumers, who do not have a large *pro rata* stake in legislation and regulation, often get shortchanged. The stronger interests of industry tend to dominate.

Price Regulation   Public utilities—such as firms that provide local electricity, telephone, gas, and water services—are often considered natural monopolies because their provision is usually associated with economies of scale. Figure 16.1 illustrates the relation between demand for and cost of these services.

With no regulation, a firm holding a natural monopoly chooses the profit-maximizing price and output P_m and Q_m, which result in profits. If the local government chooses to regulate the firm to eliminate profits, it may force the firm to charge a price that just covers its average cost of production.

This price regulation is achieved through an agreement between the firm and the local government—the government allows the firm to exist as the sole provider of services, and in return, the firm agrees not to allow profits to rise above a normal rate of return and also agrees to meet the total demand for the product. The resulting price and output, P_{AC} and Q_{AC}, occur where the industry demand crosses the average cost curve. Economic profits are zero, since price equals average cost.

This **average cost pricing** is indeed a very popular form of price regulation. It seems to eliminate one of the problems of regulating a monopoly. However, it does not result in the optimal level of output. Many economists believe that price should instead be set equal to marginal cost, in what is called **marginal cost pricing.** The

Average cost pricing

A regulatory policy that causes a firm to charge a price equal to average cost, inducing the firm to produce an output such that economic profits are zero.

Marginal cost pricing

A regulatory policy that forces a firm to charge a price equal to marginal cost, resulting in a socially optimal allocation of resources.

FIGURE 16.1

Two Forms of Price Regulation

An unregulated natural monopoly might charge the profit-maximizing price P_m, at which it would sell the quantity Q_m. With average cost price regulation, the price would be set equal to the firm's average cost, P_{AC}, increasing the quantity sold to Q_{AC}. Marginal cost pricing would result in even lower price and higher quantity: Price P_{MC} and output Q_{MC} result where the demand curve intersects the marginal cost curve. But such a policy would force the firm to operate at a loss, for the marginal cost is lower than the firm's average cost of production.

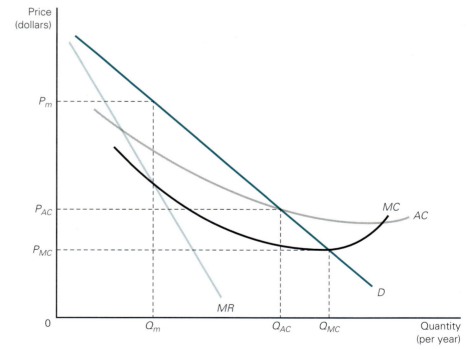

price and output that result from the intersection of the demand curve and the marginal cost curve, P_{MC} and Q_{MC}, are optimal. That is, when price equals marginal cost, the benefit to society of one more unit of output is just equal to the extra cost of that unit. However, as in the case shown in Figure 16.1, marginal cost pricing may result in losses for the firm. One of the basic problems of price regulation is that natural monopolies cannot be forced into the ideal competitive solution where $P = AC = MC$. Since marginal cost pricing may result in losses, average cost pricing may be the preferred form of price regulation.

Another problem with price regulation is that when firms are forced to earn only a normal rate of return, their incentive to achieve efficiency is diminished. Maintaining low costs of production is not rewarded with higher profits. For this reason we may see public utilities allowing costs to rise.

In spite of the potential problems of price regulation, direct control of industry prices became popular in the late nineteenth century. It was believed that government regulation beyond antitrust legislation could promote more efficient behavior than could market forces.

Problems with Price Regulation   Direct regulation of prices to achieve economic efficiency and to improve consumer welfare often proves to be self-defeating. When rates are inflexible over a period of time, surpluses or shortages are likely to occur with changes in demand or cost. The inability of a board of commissioners to accurately predict market forces can cause great inefficiencies in some regulated markets.

In an attempt to establish prices that reflect costs, state and federal regulatory agencies have resorted, with regard to telephone and electric rates especially, to **rate of return (*ROR*) regulation.** Instead of setting the prices charged by utilities, regulators attempt to control prices and output *indirectly,* by placing maximum allowable rates of return on capital and other investments. Rate of return regulation is a direct attempt by state and federal regulatory commissions to limit to competitive levels the aggregate return that a utility makes on its operations. In calculating the allowable rate of return for a utility firm, a commission must estimate what a "competitive" rate would be for a comparable firm in the marketplace. For example, if an electric utility is earning 14 percent on its investment in capital and the allowable rate (computed from returns to similar businesses) is 11 percent, the regulatory commission will order price reductions to increase the welfare of the utility's consumers. Calculations of an allowable or competitive return will differ among various commissions and jurisdictions for a number of reasons, including regional differences in costs and technology. Unfortunately, rate of return regulation may induce regulated firms to behave inefficiently. If the allowable rate of return exceeds the firm's cost of acquiring capital, the firm may overinvest in capital to increase the basis for its allowable return. Consumers might have to pay higher prices to support this overinvestment.

Product Quality and Price Regulation   To add to the problems of price regulation, it is impossible to regulate *all* dimensions of a market. For many years, the Civil Aeronautics Board regulated airline rates as well as entry into the airline ser-

Rate of return regulation

A cap imposed by a regulatory commission on the allowable percentage that a utility can earn on its capital invested.

vices market, but the CAB did not regulate service quality. Since regulated airlines could not compete on the basis of nominal price, they competed by constantly changing and improving quality. Costs rose because of better meals, better in-flight service and more flights for more departure–arrival time choices, even though planes were seldom filled to capacity. Costs increased to equal (and sometimes exceed) the regulated rates imposed by the CAB. Deregulation of rigid rates—in this case, their elimination—was necessary for the survival of some airlines, and the policy was supported by many competing carriers. Presently, in the era of deregulation, airlines have better control over nominal rate schedules and are able to offer consumers many alternative price–quality "packages" of airline services. Deregulation, the relaxation or elimination of legal price or entry controls on firms or industries, is discussed later in this chapter.

What if the Monopoly Is Not "Natural"?   Many modern economists have questioned the usefulness of regulation. In part, doubts about regulation are related to concerns that many markets may be mislabeled "natural monopolies." That is, they may not experience the constantly downward-sloping average cost curve shown in Figure 16.1.

The important issue for public policy is whether and to what degree a firm can sustain its monopoly power. If a monopoly can completely forestall entry in the absence of regulation, it is a **sustainable monopoly.** Such a firm is able to restrict output and, therefore, to reduce economic welfare; the firm might properly be the subject of regulation. On the other hand, if entry into any of the firm's markets is viable, the market is said to be characterized by **contestability.** If the firm's cost curves are U-shaped over the range of demand, unlike those in Figure 16.1 which slope downward over the range of demand, the need for regulation does not exist; market forces will ultimately generate competitive results. With a U-shaped cost curve, the average or unit cost of producing the good or service does not decline over the entire range of demand. If one firm can satisfy all demanders at lower and lower unit costs, entry by other firms is, if not impossible, far less likely. (See the Focus "Airline Deregulation: Success Story or Consumer Nightmare?" later in this chapter for a discussion that relates this point to the airline industry.)

Sustainable monopoly

A monopoly that can forestall the entry of competitors in the absence of regulation.

Contestability

Characteristic of a market in which the entry of competitors is possible.

Health and Safety Regulation

As Table 16.2 reveals, much of the recent economic regulation deals with product safety and safety in the workplace. Here, we briefly consider the issue of safety in the workplace.

If employers are not liable to employees for accidents that result from unsafe work conditions, employers may have an incentive to scrimp on safety; safety equipment tends to be expensive. This does not mean, however, that employers will have no economic incentive to provide safety. The employer whose place of work is unusually dangerous will be at a competitive disadvantage in recruiting workers and must compensate by offering higher wages. The issue, then, is the degree of safety provided.

Theoretically, there are several ways employers could be induced to improve safety. The government could subsidize installation of safety procedures and equipment, but this would burden taxpayers. Alternatively, tax penalties could be imposed on employers with bad safety records. Or the liability for accidents due to negligence could be placed solely on the employer; this solution would require changes in current workers' compensation laws, which limit the employer's liability.

Most modern health and safety regulations do not employ any of these methods. The Occupational Safety and Health Administration (OSHA) instead relies on a system of standards for safe behavior, and the burden of maintaining these standards is on businesses. While health and safety standards have changed the behavior of business firms, they are costly to enforce because each place of business must be inspected regularly by an OSHA employee. In addition, there is reason to believe that there are much cheaper ways to provide equal levels of safety.

To comply with government standards, for example, employers might be required to provide hard hats for each employee—even though employees have little use for hard hats and generally refuse to wear them. If, instead, employers were provided with incentives to improve safety records (either by fines or by strict assignment of liability), they would have an incentive to spend money wisely to reduce accidents.

Government Ownership

Socialization

Government ownership and operation of a firm or industry.

An alternative to antitrust policy or regulation is government ownership, or **socialization,** of firms. When monopolies exist and their performance is less than socially optimal, government may choose to own and operate the firm in the interests of the public. We see this happen occasionally, more often at the state or local level than at the national level. For example, many public utilities such as electric services, water, and natural gas are owned and operated by local governments.

Socialization of firms is a solution to the monopoly problem, but is it an efficient solution? Ideally, the firm should approximate the competitive equilibrium. It should minimize its costs of production and charge a price equal to marginal cost. However, the performance of the firm depends on its managers. The managers must operate within the bounds allowed by the politicians who employ them, the voters, and the buyers of their services.

The efficiency of publicly owned firms is questioned by many economists. Many suggest that there is a lack of incentive for efficiency because there are no residual claimants. That is, no one may receive any profits acquired by the socialized firm, so managers have no reason to ensure low costs of operation or product quality.

To judge the efficiency of publicly owned firms, it is possible under some circumstances to compare their price, costs, and quality of service with those of privately owned firms in the same industry. For example, we can compare a locally owned electric firm's price and service to a privately owned electric firm's price and service. Many industries—such as education, medical care, telecommunications, television, garbage services, and employment agencies—have both privately owned and publicly owned firms. However, in most situations we must compare government-owned firms with government-regulated firms, as in the case of electricity.

The U.S. Postal Service is a socialized firm that we cannot compare directly with a private firm, for the government prohibits the delivery of first-class mail by anyone except the U.S. Postal Service. However, there are many firms wishing to enter the mail delivery market, and occasionally they do so illegally. The suggestion that private firms could make a profit at the same price whereas the U.S. Postal System does not is an indication that the Postal Service is run inefficiently. Indeed, many government-owned firms must be subsidized by tax dollars.

Despite its lack of incentives for efficiency, socialization is still considered by some supporters to be an appealing alternative to trust-busting or regulation in monopoly-prone industries. The price of medical services has been rising, and socialized medicine has been offered as a solution. AT&T (American Telephone and Telegraph) was divested through an antitrust case, but an alternative could have been to socialize telephone services. The possible consequences of such actions can be predicted by observing the prices and quality of services of similar industries that have been socialized in other countries.

When government seeks to improve the efficiency of certain businesses, it may not be necessary for the government to regulate or operate the facility itself. As a compromise, the government may acquire the property rights to supply the good or service and then franchise, or lease, the right out to private businesses. Cities as diverse as New York City and Scottsdale, Arizona, use this system of **franchise bidding** to provide garbage collection, fire protection, and other public services. The practice, first formalized by the utilitarian philosopher Jeremy Bentham and his associate Edwin Chadwick, has been employed in European cities for centuries. (See the Focus "Franchising Funerals in Nineteenth-Century London and Paris.")

Franchise bidding

The privatization of traditionally governmental responsibilities via a bidding process.

Laissez-Faire

Antitrust policies, regulations, and government ownership are not the only alternatives to the monopoly problem. Under many circumstances, the forces of the market are capable—given enough time—of eliminating the undesirable performances of monopolies, cartels, and trusts. Over a long enough period of time, for example, entry and new competition will emerge, perhaps through technological innovation, to challenge existing monopolies. Leaving an industry alone is called **laissez-faire** (allow to do) policy.

Laissez-faire

A public policy of not regulating to any degree or interfering with market activities (from the French, meaning, roughly, "allow to do").

THE MOVEMENT TO DEREGULATION

In addition to simply leaving monopolized industries alone, a laissez-faire policy might dictate removing previous regulations—a process called **deregulation.** Firms in regulated industries often attempt to use regulatory agencies to promote the firms' profits. Government regulation has often protected the very companies that antitrust laws and regulations are intended to suppress. In particular, regulatory limits on the entry

Deregulation

The removal of some or all government regulations from a previously regulated industry in an effort to improve the allocation of resources.

FOCUS

Franchising Funerals in Nineteenth-Century London and Paris

Franchising is often presented as an alternative both to government ownership or operation and to more traditional forms of regulation. The most ardent proponent of franchising was nineteenth-century English social reformer Sir Edwin Chadwick (1800–1890). Practically no industry escaped Chadwick's scrutiny. Chadwick wanted the government to take over property rights to sell the good or service (milk, beer, police services, prisons) and then auction the rights to private businesses as a franchise wherever waste or inefficiencies were found.

Consider Chadwick's case for franchising funerals in London. He estimated that between 600 and 700 undertakers in London performed over 100 funerals per day. Therefore, about six undertakers competed for each funeral. Though the market situation appeared to be noncollusive and roughly competitive, Chadwick alleged that the funeral suppliers acted as monopolies. They could charge exorbitant prices because demanders were faced with high information and search costs when shopping for a funeral supplier. Such high costs, moreover, encouraged home funerals, which led to health and sanitary hazards—all the more reason to make funeral supply a fit object of franchising.

Parliament ignored Chadwick's proposals, but Munich, Frankfurt, Berlin, and Paris implemented his principle. Chadwick estimated the total cost of 28,000 interments in Paris at £80,000 in 1843, while the estimated cost of 45,000 interments in London under open competition was £626,000. Under the Paris rate system, Chadwick estimated that London funerals would have cost £166,000, a savings of £460,000, which would be directly attributable to uniform rates within the various classes of services. Thus, in Chadwick's logic, monopoly power created by high information costs could be eliminated by franchising.[a]

How good was Chadwick's case? In the first place, it is doubtful whether funeral service directors, then or now, have significant monopoly power. At the time of bereavement, most individuals rely on recommendations by friends and family when selecting a funeral home. (Most funeral homes today allow you to plan ahead.) Experience and reputation are important in the business, and long-standing firms represent high or acceptable quality levels.

Franchising funeral services by contract would entail—whenever implemented, even today—policing, enforcing, and contracting costs. If you lose the franchise, what happens to the "horses and carriages" and how would they be transferred? How long will the contract run? What happens if costs or demand change within the period of the contract, forcing losses on the funeral suppliers or abnormal profits? What happens to private property? Chadwick's proposals would apply whenever "waste" occurs in markets. It would apply not only in natural monopoly (or regular monopoly) situations, but also when *competitive markets* are in *disequilibrium,* as may have been the situation in the funeral example Chadwick describes. Chadwick failed to recognize that a real-world competitive system always operates with some friction.

---

[a]Edwin Chadwick, "Results of Different Principles of Legislation and Administration in Europe; of Competition for the Field, as Compared with Competition Within the Field of Service," *Royal Statistical Society Journal* 22 (1859), pp. 389–390; or see Robert B. Ekelund, Jr., and George S. Ford, "Nineteenth Century Urban Market Failure? Chadwick on Funeral Industry Regulation," *Journal of Regulatory Economics* 12 (July 1997), pp. 27–52.

of new firms into an industry and on the prices charged by existing companies can give the existing firms a degree of market power they could not otherwise achieve.

That regulation is more costly to society in many cases than the benefits it produces was first perceived by economists in the 1960s and early 1970s. Nobel Prize–winner George Stigler demonstrated that state electric utility regulation had done little to reduce prices and price discrimination and to suppress monopoly returns in that industry.[6] Glaring inefficiencies and misallocations of resources on railroads and airlines also brought the public's attention to the problem. During the Carter and Reagan administrations, portions of the transportation, banking, telecommunications, and natural gas industries were deregulated. Table 16.3 shows the major deregulation decisions since 1968.

Technology, moreover, erodes monopoly power created by the government, ultimately necessitating deregulation. Such has been the case with modern telecommunications. The simple fact is that the invention of coaxial cable and fiber optics, not to mention the establishment of the Internet (and net communications, advertising, entertainment, etc.) made competition more feasible in some communications markets. Thus, deregulation has ensued, often with mixed results. Monopolists will not willingly give up the monopolies created for them by prior government regulations. The Application at the conclusion of this chapter, "The Telecommunications Act of 1996: Good Intentions Meet Market Realities," delves at some length into this issue.

Two examples of deregulation have occurred in the interstate trucking and airline industries. Until 1980, the Interstate Commerce Commission severely restricted entry of new firms into the trucking industry, as well as price competition among firms. The Motor Carrier Act of 1980 decreased the ICC's ability to restrict new entry. Since that time, the number of firms has increased by several thousand, and prices have fallen 20 percent. (The ICC was finally eliminated in 1995.) In the airline industry, the Civil Aeronautics Board set passenger fares and restricted entry until the Airline Deregulation Act in 1978. From then until the CAB's demise in late 1984, the CAB's ability to restrict price competition and entry was severely limited. Deregulation results in the airline industry have been similar to those in trucking. The number of firms has increased and prices have fallen. Since deregulation, some trucking and airline firms have also gone bankrupt—exactly what one would expect of inefficient firms facing competition. (For an analysis of the successes and problems of airline deregulation, see the Focus "Airline Deregulation: Success Story or Consumer Nightmare?")

The negative impact of deregulation can be quite severe. When banks and savings and loan institutions (S&Ls) were deregulated in the 1980s, the system of federally insuring deposits up to $100,000 remained in effect. This encouraged the owners and directors of S&Ls to undertake very risky investments, many of which subsequently failed. The federal government has had to bail out many failed S&Ls by reimbursing depositors. The government bailout has been an extremely expensive program, but it would not have been necessary if S&Ls had been required to provide their own deposit insurance. The problem was not the deregulation of the banking industry; rather, it was the way the banking industry was deregulated.

Moreover, the privatization and deregulation of industry is a hallmark of economies across the world. The transitional economies in the former Soviet Union and Eastern Europe have been selling off state-run enterprises to private

---

[6]George J. Stigler and Claire Friedland, "What Can Regulators Regulate? The Case of Electricity," *Journal of Law and Economics* 5 (1962), pp. 1–15.

TABLE 16.3

Major Deregulation Decisions Since 1968

Deregulation of the communications, transportation, and financial services industries is an ongoing process and has taken place in both Democratic and Republican administrations.

1968	The Supreme Court permits non-AT&T equipment to be connected to the Bell system.
1969	MCI is permitted to connect its long-distance network with local phone systems.
1970	Interest rates are deregulated on bank deposits of $100,000 or more.
1972	The Federal Communications Commission (FCC) establishes a domestic satellite open skies policy.
1975	The Securities and Exchange Commission ends fixed brokerage fees for stock market transactions.
	Rate bureaus for railroads and trucking firms are prohibited from protesting independent rate filings.
1976	The Railroad Revitalization and Regulatory Reform Act of 1976 partially deregulates railroads and makes rate setting more cost-based.
1977	Deregulation of air cargo gives airlines more freedom in pricing.
1978	Congress partially decontrols natural gas.
	The Occupational Safety and Health Administration revokes 928 "nit-picking" rules.
	The Civil Aeronautics Board is phased out, eliminating controls over airline entry and prices.
	The Environmental Protection Agency permits emissions trading.
1980	The FCC removes most federal regulation of cable TV and of equipment in consumers' premises.
	The Motor Carrier Act eliminates barriers for new entries and permits operators to establish fares and routes with little oversight by the Interstate Commerce Commission.
	The Depository Institutions law phases out interest rate ceilings and permits savings and loans and banks to offer interest-bearing checking accounts.
	The Staggers Rail Act enables railroads to adjust rates without government approval and enter into contracts with shippers.
1981	President Reagan decontrols crude oil prices and petroleum allocations.
	The FCC removes many radio regulations.
1982	A new bus regulatory statute allows intercity bus companies to change routes and fares.
	The Garn-St. Germain Act allows savings and loans to make more commercial and consumer loans and removes interest rate differentials between banks and savings and loans.
1984	As part of an antitrust settlement, AT&T agrees to divest local operating companies.
	Individual ocean shipping companies are allowed to offer lower rates and better service than shipping "conferences."
1986	Trading of airport landing rights allowed.
1987	Sale of Conrail.
	The FCC eliminates fairness doctrine.
1989	Natural Gas Wellhead Decontrol Act.
1992	Energy Policy Act modified to allow for the creation of a new class of independent power producer free from corporate and geographic restrictions imposed by current law.
1995	Interstate Commerce Commission is dissolved.
1996	Telecommunications Act sets standards for the deregulation of local phone service, cable rates, radio and television provision, and many other features of telecommunications.
1999	Cable rates fully deregulated.
1999	Maritime agreements between shippers and ocean carriers deregulated, allowing short- and long-term contracts between parties to be held in private.

Sources: Dennis W. Carlton and Jeffrey M. Perloff, *Industrial Organization* (Glenview, Illinois: Scott, Foresman, 1990), Chapter 23; Murray Weidenbaum, *The Benefits of Deregulation* (Contemporary Issues Series 25, Center for the Study of American Business, Washington University, December 1987); Tenpao Lee, C. Phillip Baumel, and Patricia Harris, "Market Structure, Conduct and Performance of the Class I Railroad Industry, 1971–1984," *Transportation Journal* 26 (1987), pp. 54–66; and Robert N. Hahn, "Regulation: Past, Present, and Future," *Harvard Journal of Law and Public Policy* 13 (Winter 1990), p. 183, and author update.

FOCUS

Airline Deregulation: Success Story or Consumer Nightmare?

The airline industry has undergone enormous changes since the Airline Deregulation Act of 1978. Both fares and route patterns have been deregulated, determined by airline management and the marketplace. Most economists would argue that airline deregulation provided and continues to provide enormous generalized welfare benefits to consumers. However, deregulation has not been a total success. Problems include (possible) monopoly pricing in specific ("hub") markets,[a] a confusing fare structure, and crowding at airports. In order to gauge the benefits and costs of deregulation, it is necessary to understand the market structure of the industry before and after regulation.

When airfares were controlled, nonprice competition in the form of higher quality meals, better service, and greater frequency of flights caused costs to rise. Airline routes were established under regulation in north–south and east–west patterns, imitating railroad corridors established in the nineteenth century.

Since deregulation, many airline passengers have grown accustomed to the availability of relatively cheap restricted fares. Price discrimination does exist, however, with business travelers—who cannot always plan ahead or travel only on certain days—paying significantly higher fares than tourists. All travelers have had to adjust to a radically different route structure since deregulation. Most airlines have replaced their pre-deregulation linear routes with a hub and spoke system. This flexible system feeds traffic through medium and small cities (spokes) to one of several regional hubs. The implementation of this system has resulted in much bet-

ter coordination of flights, lower costs, and much less inconvenience to airline passengers (the necessity of changing airlines and making several intermediate stops having been sharply reduced for most travelers). New computer reservation systems—which also provide consumers with car rental and other services in addition to ticketing and boarding passes—and new marketing plans (for example, frequent-flier programs) have also increased consumer welfare and enhanced the cost efficiency and managerial effectiveness of airline operations.

In addition to changing fare and route structures, the airline industry has been characterized by mergers, bankruptcies, and price wars since the early 1980s. Those companies that were able to gain strategic advantages in the highly competitive market (companies such as American, Delta, and United) have prospered. Most of the other carriers have been punished by the market, and some, such as Eastern and Pan Am, were driven out of business.

When an airline establishes a hub, the airline usually comes to dominate service to the hub city. For example, Delta dominates the Atlanta market and American dominates the Dallas market. There is some evidence that travelers in hub cities pay fares that are slightly higher than fares elsewhere, but, on average, fares have fallen significantly since deregulation. (It appears that consumers do in fact prefer lower-priced, no-frills service.) Some travelers—especially business travelers—may complain about high unrestricted fares, but many of these same travelers have probably also benefited from "supersaver" fares or from frequent-flier programs. Overcrowding is an occasional problem at certain airports—particularly hub airports—but this is to be expected when airfares are as affordable as bus and train fares, as has often been the case in recent years. Overcrowding is also, for many people, a small price to pay for cheaper fares. All in all, consumers have enjoyed dramatic gains from deregulation.

---

[a]Some economists dispute the fact that monopoly is created at hub cities. See Andrew N. Kleit and Steward G. Maynes, "Airline Networks as Joint Goods: Implications for Competition Policy," *Journal of Regulatory Economics* 4 (June 1992), pp. 175–186.

bidders, with some success. Privatization and deregulation of industry are part and parcel of the same phenomenon. They represent a return to reliance on private "incentives" and markets to allocate resources and spark economic recovery and growth.

CONCLUSION

We have examined several forms of public policy that are aimed at preventing poor market performance. Each of these—antitrust, regulation, socialization, and laissez-faire—has its merits, but no public policy can achieve the efficiency generated by a competitive market. When imperfect competition exists, our best solutions are themselves imperfect.

Not only are our best solutions theoretically imperfect, but actual government policies appear to be schizophrenic. One action attempts to increase competition and reduce profits, while other actions promote monopolies and their profits. The reason for these contradictions is that public policies are formulated in a political arena and not by impartial economic theorists or forces. An understanding of public choice theory—to be explored in Chapter 18—can tell us more about public policy in monopolized industries.

APPLICATION

The Telecommunications Act of 1996: Good Intentions Meet Market Realities

Trumpets blared as President Clinton signed the new Telecommunications Act into law on February 12, 1996. The purposes of the Act were explicit—". . . to provide for a pro-competitive, de-regulatory national policy framework" to take into account the astonishingly rapid technological development in most areas of modern telecommunications. Bright promises of enhanced competition, lower prices, and expanded choices in the provision of all telecommunications services raised great expectations on the part of consumers everywhere.

But surprises were in store. Despite the best of stated intentions, the Telecom Act has done very little to establish market competition in many areas of modern telecommunications. How are consumers getting the short end of the stick? Here are only a few ways.

Local Phone Service

Local exchange companies (both Bell and non-Bell) retain their monopolies over local phone communications despite the Act's stated intention that competition prevail in these markets. The government effectively deregulated long-distance phone service fifteen years ago, and rates have fallen by half with the new competition. Why not the same for local rates? The problem is that the local companies are attached to their monopolies. With the help of state public service commissions (PSCs) around the country, they have maintained local monopoly control. Kicking and screaming and with lawyers in tow, they have kept competition out of local phone markets by effectively preventing potential competitors from gaining access to their local exchange operations (which the Telecom Act envisioned). These hold-ups have taken many forms, including the attempt to charge outrageous rates for renting facilities. Merely leasing resale facilities does not, moreover, amount to the establishment of viable competition.

Payphones

Used a pay phone lately? If so, you probably have noted that local pay phone providers, most prominently local Bells, have upped the rate to call for a cab. These rates were "deregulated" by the Act and are administered by your local PSC. The intention was to provide more pay phones at competitive rates. The problem is that the owner of the property on which the phone sits is free to charge "monopoly" rates for use of the location. Translated, that means that you, the consumer, are paying *higher* rates to property owners with the "deregulation."

Credit Card Calls

Use of credit cards from a pay phone is also costing you more. The FCC decided that local exchange carriers (again mostly local Bells) should be compensated for 800 and credit card calls made from payphones. The problem is that the rate that your long-distance carrier must pay to use the facilities is far higher than a competitive rate. Guess who pays for these monopoly-priced long-distance calls? These so-called "pass-throughs" are charges passed right on to you, the consumer.

Cable Rates

Noticed your cable bill rising lately? They have risen by about 21 percent across the country in 1997. "Deregulation" of cable meant that prices of cable were not to be regulated at the local level, but by the Federal Communications Commission. This is just what the cable companies wanted. Out of sight, out of mind. It is far harder for you to get a response from a Washington agency than from City Hall. The cable companies still have their local monopolies. The result: higher *and rising* cable rates for basic service despite threats to effectively re-regulate rates by Congress. Cable companies claim that costly new services have been added to the consumer's menu, although recent research shows that the welfare decrease caused by the increase in price is just matched by the additional welfare to consumers from a new channel.[a] Whether new and higher-quality cable services compensate for the higher prices may determine whether re-regulation of rates will occur.

---

[a]See T. Randolph Beard, Robert B. Ekelund, Jr., George S. Ford, and Richard S. Saba, "Price-Quality Tradeoffs and Welfare Effects in Cable Television Markets," (Manuscript, Auburn University, 1999).

Radio and TV Markets

The structure of radio and over-the-air TV markets, once forcefully fragmented to a great extent, is now characterized by increasing levels of concentration. The Telecommunications Act contained provisions that allowed greater concentration of ownership of broadcast media resources. This new concentration, created in recognition that new efficiencies might be had by additional local and national ownership concentration, has caused genuine concerns about the creation of market power—in, for example, the potential ability of communications firms to charge monopoly rates to local and national advertisers. The Department of Justice has disallowed some media mergers on such grounds. The evidence, however, is that efficiency rather than market power characterizes media mergers, at least in radio.[b] The hope is that emerging new information and entertainment technologies may create close substitutes for radio and television advertising outlets, such as those appearing on the Internet.

Has the Telecommunications Act of 1996 yet fulfilled its promises? In certain areas of telecommunications the answer is clearly "no." Competition has not materialized between local Bells and cable companies; between long-distance providers and local Bells; and among computer service providers, phone, and cable operations. At least a modicum of technology exists to accommodate myriad kinds of new competition. Local Bells are engaged in some serious foot-dragging with local competition. Delay benefits these companies because they want to enter the long-distance market without paying the dues of letting long-distance carriers into their local markets. Baby Bells want a piece of the lucrative long-distance trade rather than tinker with less remunerative local cable competition. Cable companies do not want to lose their local monopolies, either, and they have been fighting effective regulation tooth and nail. Meanwhile, consumers continue to pay unnecessarily high prices for service.

Despite the problems, it is probably not wise to engage in re-regulation in the many areas of telecommunications. Positive experience with deregulation and competition in other formerly regulated markets over the past two decades clearly argues against such a myopic interpretation. Huge consumer benefits realized in airlines, trucking, banking, long distance, and so on provide ample testimony to the general soundness of moving from a government-controlled monopoly to a market-controlled competitive environment. But competition was evolving in these markets *before* full deregulation.

In the case of telecommunications, technology should be given a chance to work through the stubborn actors in the monopoly play. In local exchange phone services, however, there is little or no actual competition in place, and the market-disciplining force of potential competition is weak at best. As a result, deregulation is premature and will only lead (as it already has) to monopoly pricing and preemptive practices that actually *delay* the advent of meaningful competition. In effect, the Telecommunications Act raises hopes that, in today's market

---

[b]See Robert B. Ekelund, Jr., George S. Ford, and Thomas Koutsky, "Market Power in Radio Markets: An Empirical Analysis of Local and National Concentration," *Journal of Law and Economics* (April 2000).

environment, simply cannot be met. *Government can encourage competition, but it cannot create it.*

The Act and its enforcers failed to recognize the important realities of the affected markets—the most important being the incentives of both regulators and regulatees to resist its implementation. Government *created* much of the monopoly in telecommunications. Reorienting markets of this magnitude takes time. Politicians and regulators should recognize, however, that consumers' patience is wearing thin. Technology may come to consumers' rescue, but technology must, of course, work through all-too-fallible human institutions.

QUESTIONS

To what extent do you believe the problems of telecommunications deregulation to be of a "short-term" nature? Do you believe re-regulation is the answer in such markets as cable television? Why or why not?

SUMMARY

1. Antitrust laws are basically designed to promote and maintain competition in the economy.

2. Industry concentration ratios change through time because the optimal number of firms changes as demand and cost conditions change.

3. The number of firms in an industry is determined by the number of firms of optimal size that industry demand is able to support. A natural monopoly exists when industry demand is sufficient to support only one firm of optimal size in an industry.

4. Mergers are the combination of two or more firms in an industry into a single firm. Mergers may decrease competition or enhance competitive efficiency. The latter effect may result from technological innovations that reduce the number of firms required in an industry for economic efficiency.

5. Price regulation allows the existence of monopoly but attempts to decrease the social loss by imposing a particular pricing policy. However, price regulation may decrease the firm's incentive to maintain efficiency. Regulation of competitive industries has resulted in government-managed cartels.

6. Government ownership as an alternative to monopoly can prevent higher-than-normal profits. However, a government-owned business is not forced by the market to maintain efficiency.

7. Franchise bidding is an attempt to assure that competitive prices will be charged without destroying incentives for efficiency.

8. Economic regulation has the potential to achieve results in the public interest. However, economic groups that are harmed by or that could benefit from regulation have an incentive to capture the regulatory process and frustrate regulations conceived in the public interest.

9. Since regulation is inevitably imperfect, the existence of a less-than-perfect unregulated market does not necessarily justify regulation.

10. A laissez-faire system is an alternative to active public policy. Under some circumstances this policy to leave the market alone is clearly preferable.

KEY TERMS

antitrust policies	public interest theory of regulation	sustainable monopoly
regulatory policies	capture (interest group) theory	contestability
concentration ratios	of regulation	socialization
predatory pricing	average cost pricing	franchise bidding
merger	marginal cost pricing	laissez-faire
natural monopoly	rate of return regulation	deregulation

QUESTIONS FOR REVIEW AND DISCUSSION

1. Why does government sometimes act, through regulation, to enforce a cartel? Why do voters and consumers put up with such programs and policies? What effect would deregulation have on such an industry?

2. Blue laws outlaw Sunday sales in a given locality. From the point of view of economic regulation, explain who gains and who loses from such legislation.

3. How does rate of return, or profit, regulation affect firm behavior? Does this regulation promote production efficiency? Do we achieve the optimal output with average cost pricing?

4. Are local television companies natural monopolies? How could the answer be determined? If they are, would they want to be regulated?

5. Can public policy change an industry characterized as a natural monopoly into a competitive industry that results in competitive equilibrium?

6. Suppose that your university decided to have its cafeterias operated under a franchise bidding arrangement. Could the university assure that the franchisee maintained adequate standards in the food served? Might the franchisee actually improve the quality of food served? Explain.

7. States uniformly require teachers of primary and secondary schools to be licensed, but they do not require the licensure of college professors. Between students and professors, which group do you think would be more likely to make demands for the licensure of professors? What does your answer say about your confidence in the capture theory of regulation versus the public interest theory?

8. Businesses and workers often have conflicting interests about worker safety. Can you think of some safety standard that both workers and businesspersons would oppose? One that they both would support?

9. Some economists argue that there is a trade-off between safety regulations and employment in a particular industry. Is it likely that tighter safety standards in, say, the textile industry will lead to fewer textile jobs? Explain.

PROBLEMS

1. Look back at the concentration ratios for the jewelry and precious metals industry in Table 16.1. Has this industry become more or less concentrated through time? Does an increase in concentration always imply an increase in monopoly power? Why or why not? How might consumers actually benefit from an industry becoming more concentrated?

2. How do public choice and interest group politics affect regulation? Pick a particular area of business and explain the interests that might support or reject government regulation. Why might these interests be effective or ineffective in obtaining regulations?

WORKING WITH THE WEB

1. The Focus "The Microsoft Case: Is It Monopoly, or Is It Envy?" in this chapter reviews the Department of Justice's antitrust case against Microsoft. You learned earlier in the text that monopolists are price searchers; that is, they search for the price that maximizes profit. They also create artificial scarcity by restricting output. Hence, compared with a competitive market, monopolists offer less output for sale and do so at higher prices. Go to http://www.cei.org/MonoReader.asp?ID=702 and choose the link "Full Text Available in PDF."

   Read Fagin's paper on the Microsoft case, "The Case Against the Case Against Microsoft."

   a. Which antitrust Act is Microsoft accused of violating?

   b. The Focus article notes that web browser prices fell after the introduction of Microsoft's Internet Explorer. What price did Microsoft charge for Internet Explorer? Is this indicative of monopoly behavior?

   c. Typically, once a monopolist has "locked in" its consumers, it is likely to increase its price. Microsoft has many users, given that the Windows operating system is the most common system on computers today. In this respect, a large proportion of Microsoft customers can be considered locked in. Has Microsoft increased the prices of its software and operating system upgrades over time to take advantage of its captive customer base?

2. Another Focus in the chapter addresses the pros and cons of airline deregulation, noting that on balance, consumers have gained from deregulation. Recently, however, there has been a push for government regulation of airlines in the form of a "passenger bill of rights" as airlines increasingly overbook flights, cancel flights, or have delays without providing adequate information to passengers. For example, in January 1999, thousands of Northwest Airlines passengers were stranded due to a snowstorm and many were stuck on the runway for up to nine hours! Go to http://www.freep.com/news/airtravel/qair182.htm and read the article about the proposed changes offered by the airlines.

   a. Why did Congress feel pressured to act on behalf of consumers?

   b. What does the proposal promise passengers in the event their luggage is "mishandled"?

   c. Upon making a reservation, in the past some airlines required immediate payment. What does the new proposal suggest regarding payment terms?

   d. How will customers who searched the Internet for the lowest plane fares likely be affected by the proposed changes?

CHAPTER 17

Natural Resources, the Environment, and Public Goods

C oncerns about the use of scarce, perhaps even vanishing, natural resources and about environmental issues are commonplace in today's headlines. Global warming, the ozone layer, the rain forest, endangered species, urban pollution, soil erosion, and other natural resource and environmental topics raise concerns on every front. The costs of addressing such issues and who pays these costs are also of concern to the interested groups. User fees, higher automobile prices, bans on urban barbecuing, international competitiveness, and the like animate the activities of those who must pay for the use of environmental assets.

Natural resources and the environment represent challenging issues for the application of economic principles. Not the least of the reasons for this is that markets sometimes work well in pricing natural resources and environmental assets, and sometimes they fail miserably. As we shall see, markets are excellent devices for pricing renewable and nonrenewable resources and for ensuring a steady supply of these commodities when property rights are well defined among resource owners. However, in the case of the environment, markets sometimes fail to achieve desirable economic results. That is, markets can fail to provide goods and services in the right quantities at the right prices. Market failure with respect to environmental and natural resources often arises from problems of incomplete or nonexistent ownership rights to basic resources. Owners of private property bear directly the economic results of the use of property and are therefore motivated to use resources efficiently. In contrast, when property is held or used by everybody in common, users do not bear the full costs of its use. Common ownership creates a conflict between the pursuit of self-interest and the common good.

We also consider another role for government in this chapter as the provider of certain goods and services that markets would fail to produce in the correct amounts, if at all (e.g., national defense). These goods are called public goods, and their existence represents another potential role for government in a market economy.

In this chapter we review the economics of natural and environmental resources and the approach to market failures, including the failure of markets to provide certain public goods. To improve on situations of market failure, we must carefully weigh the costs and benefits of alternative policies. After reading Chapter 17 you should understand

- how the markets for nonrenewable (oil) and renewable (forests) resources work.
- how common ownership of property creates an incentive problem with respect to the management (or lack of it) of natural resources, and how the definition of property rights can overcome this problem.
- the nature of market failure and how market failures such as pollution and overfishing can be corrected.
- how market failure may have international implications through the creation of global problems.
- how the legal system—specifically, assignment of rights to use property—might be used in market failure situations.
- the nature of public goods and their relation to market failure.

Our analysis begins with a discussion of how the market for nonrenewable and renewable resources works in terms of the familiar concepts of demand and supply. We then present an analysis of the problem of commonly owned resources. We consider two concrete cases from the U.S. economy: the common stock of fish in international waters, and the oil pool. The discussion then turns to global environmental problems: acid rain and global warming.

NATURAL RESOURCES

Natural resources
All those renewable and nonrenewable resources that are given to an economy or society.

Nonrenewable natural resources
Resources that exist in finite quantities.

Renewable natural resources
Those resources that may be reproduced through time if not exhausted by unwise policies.

Natural resources are those resources that come to an economy or society from nature. Some societies are endowed with abundant natural resources, while others have few and have to trade for those that they desire to use. Natural resources fall into two broad groups.

First, there are **nonrenewable natural resources**. These are resources that exist in finite quantities. There is, for example, only so much oil, coal, bauxite, natural gas, and iron ore in the world. When we consume some of these resources today, there is automatically less available for consumption tomorrow.

There are also **renewable natural resources** which include plant and animal life such as forests and fish. Renewable resources can be used over and over again, provided that we do not exhaust them through unwise policies. A key problem with renewable resources, as we shall discuss in this chapter, is to provide the proper economic incentives to those who supply renewable resources so as to ensure that these resources are not depleted in the present at the expense of our future well-being.

The prices and quantities used of natural resources are determined in markets for these goods. By understanding how these markets work, we take the first step to a fuller appreciation of what the appropriate policies are for conserving both renewable and nonrenewable natural resources.

The Market for Nonrenewable Resources

We begin with the market for nonrenewable resources; we use oil as our example. The demand for oil is derived in the same way as that for any factor of production. The demander uses oil in production according to the marginal revenue product of oil. In other words, the demand for oil depends on its contribution to firm revenues (see the discussion in Chapter 12), and this is the basis on which the demand curve for oil (D_{market}) in Figure 17.1 is drawn.

The derivation of the supply curve of oil involves a couple of steps. There is a fixed (finite) supply of oil in the world. There is only so much oil, and no more. Thus the aggregate supply curve of oil is totally inelastic. The total supply of oil depends on the total amount in existence. If we use oil this year, there will automatically be less for use next year. This means that the relevant concept of supply in this case is how much oil do we extract and offer for sale *today* as opposed to *tomorrow*. This supply curve of oil (S_{today}) is given in Figure 17.1, and it shows the positive relationship between the price of oil and the amount that producers are willing to supply (discover, refine, and so on) today or this year. As price rises, producers are willing to extract and sell more of the fixed resource of oil today. As in any other market, the price and output of oil are determined by the intersection of the supply and demand curves in Figure 17.1, which represents a market equilibrium outcome in the oil market ($14 and 100 million barrels).

FIGURE 17.1

The Market for Nonrenewable Resources

The current price of a nonrenewable resource is set at $14, where the quantity demanded and quantity supplied of oil are equal. The supply curve of oil is the amount that producers are willing to sell at current prices, or S_{today}. The fact that we consume 100 million barrels of oil today means that there will be less oil available to consume in the future and that oil in the future will carry a higher price. These effects are represented by the shift to $S_{tomorrow}$ in the figure.

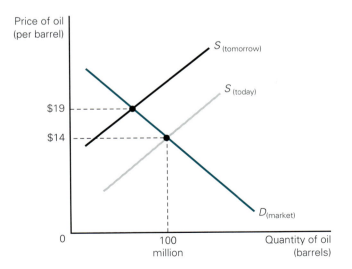

Remember that the oil we consume today cannot be consumed tomorrow. This effect is illustrated in Figure 17.1, where the supply curve of oil has shifted to the left (decreased) to $S_{tomorrow}$. Today's consumption means less oil is available for consumption tomorrow; moreover, the oil tomorrow will be more costly to find and extract for sale. This is why the supply curve of oil decreases. Producers have already discovered and produced the lowest-cost oil, and as we consume that oil, future oil becomes more costly to find and to produce. Over time, then, there will be a tendency for the price of this or any other nonrenewable resource to rise. The price of such resources should be higher tomorrow than today because of the forces of supply and demand depicted in Figure 17.1.

This rise in the price of oil means two things. First, the higher price means that, by the law of demand, users will be driven to reduce their consumption of oil and economize on its use. This helps society spread out the available stock of oil in the most effective way possible. Only those consumers who place the largest marginal values on the use of oil will bid for and use oil. Second, the higher price of this valuable input will spur entrepreneurs to seek new sources of oil and innovators to seek cheaper ways of extracting oil and alternative ways to power the world than oil. This is because the invention of an effective alternative power source to oil would make such individuals wealthy. There is, of course, no guarantee that innovation will help the world avoid the ultimate resource scarcity of oil dictated by nature, but history is replete with examples of such ingenuity. (See the Focus "The Economics of Doomsday.")

Oil field owners will decide what to do with their oil based on profit maximization, just as the owners of any other resource will do. If they make more money by pumping oil and selling it, then that is what they will do. If not, they will keep the oil in the ground. In general, if the returns to investments in the economy are high, they will pump and sell the oil and invest in these other high-yielding investments. Thus, the rate of oil supplied today will be a function of the interest rate. As interest rates rise, oil field owners will pump more oil because the return to holding oil in the ground has fallen.

Pumping more now, however, raises the future price of oil, counteracting the incentive to pump more now. Equilibrium is reached where the marginal return from pumping oil now is just offset by the marginal return to pumping oil tomorrow. In this way, private owners will conserve the fixed resource in just the right way over time, pumping and selling when it is in their interest and holding and selling tomorrow when it pays to do so. With private ownership, we get the optimal rate of extraction of a finite resource over time.

The Market for Renewable Resources

Renewable resources can reproduce themselves. The problem that an economy faces in this case is to be sure that the owner of a renewable resource, such as a forest, has an incentive to renew the resource at a rate that is coincident with what is best for the economy as a whole. In other words, what rate of replenishment do we want?

Forest owners could cut down and sell all their trees today, and then we would be without the products produced by trees (e.g., lumber to build homes) for a while. The increase in trees produced today means a decrease in trees produced tomor-

FOCUS

The Economics of Doomsday

Predictions of a global environmental collapse may be just the latest in a string of disaster scenarios relating to natural resources that now dates back more than 10,000 years. Below are some of the more prominent examples of important doomsday predictions:

- Global warming—1990s (the earth will heat up and be covered by water);
- Water crisis—1980 to 1982 (only 18 percent of America will have a drinkable water supply);
- New Ice Age—1970s (pollution brings about new Ice Age);
- The energy crisis—1970s (the world is running out of oil);
- The timber famine—1900 to 1930 (the world is running out of trees);
- The first oil crisis—mid-1800s (the world is running out of whale oil);
- The English energy crisis—1550–1650 (the world is running out of trees);
- Greek timber crisis—seventh century A.D. (the world is running out of wood);
- Greek Bronze crisis—1000 B.C. (bronze is becoming very expensive); and
- Early food crisis—8000 B.C. (there is a growing scarcity of food for hunter-gatherers).

History has shown that these doomsday predictions never come to pass. In the face of increased scarcity, people adapted, used substitutes, and invented new technology. In response to the early food crisis, for example, people switched from being hunter-gatherers to farming and domesticating animals; and they improved their diet and standard of living as a result. The scarcity of bronze encouraged people to switch to iron, which turned out to be more abundant and more useful. The scarcity of whale oil resulted in a switch to petroleum. Energy and wood crises encouraged people to conserve and to adopt new technologies.

Economists also have had their own doomsday predictions. For example, economist Robert Malthus's population theory held that population would outpace food production, and the world would be faced with an ongoing food shortage and famine. While this theory is still popular today, history has demonstrated that food production has grown with population and that famines are short-lived phenomena mostly due to war, not population growth.

Modern doomsday predictions about global warming and new Ice Ages should be put in the context that human beings have shown the ability to conserve, adapt, and invent new technologies and have in many cases emerged better as a result of the challenge.

Source: Charles Maurice and Charles W. Smithson, *The Doomsday Myth: 10,000 Years of Economic Crisis* (Stanford, Calif.: Hoover Institute Press, 1984).

row, so that the forest owner's decision lowers the price of wood products today and raises it tomorrow. The tree farmer's decision of what to do, just like the owner of the oil, depends on the interest rate. If the interest rate rises, the tree farmer will convert trees into cash in order to earn the higher interest rate. Thus, rising interest rates are associated with increased present consumption of renewable resources, and falling interest rates are associated with more future consumption.

Counteracting this tendency is the fact that as the tree farmer cuts down more trees today, the current price of trees falls and the future price of trees rises. Just like the nonrenewable case of oil, these adjustments go on until the market allocates trees to their highest-valued uses now and in the future.

So long as we depend on markets to produce and allocate nonrenewable and renewable natural resources, the result obtained will be that natural resources, even ones that are limited in supply, are properly allocated between present and future uses. This result, however, depends critically on the presence of clearly defined property rights among the owners of natural resources. If this condition does not hold, private production of natural resources can lead to problems, as we see in the next section.

THE ECONOMICS OF COMMON PROPERTY

Common ownership
An arrangement whereby the property rights to a resource are nonexistent or poorly defined; by default, anyone may use or consume the resource.

The fundamental economic disadvantage of **common ownership**—the right to the use of a resource by anyone or by competing users—is the lack of incentive to invest in the productivity of the common property. Rather, each person with access to the resource has an incentive to exploit it and neglect the effects of his or her actions on the resource's productivity. This principle applies both to renewable resources, such as fish, and nonrenewable resources, such as oil.

Fishing in International Waters

In international waters anyone may acquire exclusive ownership of a fish by catching it, and no one has rights to the fish until it is caught. This system causes each fisherman to ignore the effect of the well-known biological law that the cur-

Ocean fisheries present a common-pool problem whereby each individual has little incentive to conserve present stocks of fish.

rent stock of a species of fish determines its reproduction rate. Thus, fish harvested today reduce today's stock and thereby affect the size of tomorrow's stock and tomorrow's harvesting costs and revenues. Overfishing results because no single fisherman has an incentive to act on this bioeconomic relation. If all fishermen would cooperate to restrain themselves now, tomorrow's stock would be larger and future harvesting cheaper and more profitable. However, under competitive conditions, each individual knows that if he or she abstains now, rivals will not, and the effect of abstention is lost. Further, the reduction in future costs would accrue to everyone, not just to the abstainer. Hence each person has little reason to abstain, since the major effect is to lower others' future costs at some immediate present cost to the abstainer.

Sole ownership removes this dilemma. If only one person is fishing, he or she need not worry that rivals will not abstain. (Of course, groups such as tribes of indigenous people can also be sole owners, but the group must be able to control the behavior of its members with respect to the resource.) When there is more than one owner, all parties involved could negotiate an agreement to abstain, and all would benefit. The fact that such agreements are not usually successfully negotiated is due to the costs of dealing with all current and potential people who will fish and the difficulty of ensuring that all abstain as agreed.

Another method of dealing with this dilemma is government regulation. Such regulation usually sets an annual catch quota. To allocate the quota, regulators rely on restrictions on technology or simply close the season when the quota is taken. Both means create difficult enforcement problems and potential economic waste. If the season is closed when the quota is taken, for example, excess profits are dissipated in competition among fishermen to buy bigger, faster boats and thus get a larger share of the quota. The season progressively shrinks, and resources stand idle or are devoted to inferior employments.

Thus, fishing in international waters presents a devilish problem of negotiating international agreements, and there is widespread evidence of the depletion and possible extinction of a major source of food supply for the world.

Drilling for Oil

Oil presents another version of the same common ownership dilemma (see Figure 17.2). Unlike fish, oil is nonrenewable. However, oil does move about, so pumping one well lowers the entire reserve and affects the pressure below other wells. These characteristics create a problem when more than one person has rights to the same oil reserve. For example, if the land above a reserve of oil is owned by two people, each has the right to drill for oil. But the only way to own the oil is to pump it to the surface. Oil in the ground belongs to the landowner only when that person pumps it to the surface. Herein lies the crucial lack of private ownership rights to oil reserves.

It may be more economically efficient to exploit an oil reserve with a single well than with two wells—not only because it costs more to drill two wells than one, but also because the existence of one well interferes with the other's technical ability to pump. If one person owned the property rights to all the oil, he or she would probably use only a single well. Likewise, if two landowners with rights to

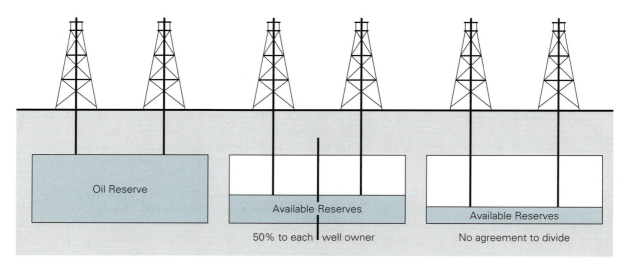

FIGURE 17.2

The Problem of Common Ownership in Oil Drilling
If a fixed reserve of oil is owned in common and the co-owners cannot agree to share
the reserves, then each owner will likely try to pump as much oil as possible from
the reserve. Doing so reduces the available reserves at a rate disadvantageous to both owners.

a common oil pool negotiate, both can be made better off by agreeing to split the
proceeds of a single well rather than both drilling.

If they cannot negotiate, perhaps because of legal restrictions, or if a larger
number of owners causes difficulties in communication, each may go ahead and
drill. Once two wells are in production, there is an economically efficient rate of
pumping for each well that a single owner would adopt to maximize his or her
wealth. Nevertheless, if the two owners cannot agree on efficient exploitation, each
will be tempted to pump oil at too high a rate, a tendency reinforced by the fear
that the other is doing the same thing. In fact, even if negotiations are successful,
it may be costly to monitor each other's pumping, and the agreement might dissolve in mutual cheating. The costs of negotiating and enforcement probably rise
in proportion to the numbers of owners, as do the incentives for each to overpump
because others are likely to do so.

The problems of market failure and common property resources encountered in modern society are not unique to contemporary modes of production,
nor are they based on greed. There is evidence that overexploitation of resources
was a common feature of primitive peoples. For example, the Anasazi Indians of
the Southwest developed settlements in Chaco Canyon, Arizona, but failed to
manage the forest product resources in the vicinity by replanting or employing
conservation techniques. As a result, according to one account, the community's
size and progress were limited and it was ultimately abandoned. The woolly mammoth disappeared from the North American continent as a result of rapid population growth and the absence of private property rights thousands of years

ago.[1] In New Zealand, scientists have linked the disappearance of the moa, a huge flightless bird, to overzealous exploitation by natives in search of food. The problems of market failure are not the result of good or bad behavior, so blaming any population, ancient or modern, is unproductive. The lesson regarding common property resources is straightforward: What belongs to everyone belongs to no one; the deterioration and rapid exploitation of common property resources are clear implications of economic theory.

International Pollution Problems: Acid Rain and Global Warming

Market failure can occur on a global level. Pollution in many forms is a particularly persistent side effect of "progress." As more countries have become developed, the problems associated with pollution have grown in scope. Pollution stems from by-products of the production and consumption of goods and services. The problem, basically, is this: Gaseous by-products of industrial and agricultural production, such as carbon dioxide, methane, nitrous oxide, ozone, and chlorofluorocarbons, have collected in the atmosphere. At best, the collection of these gases has become undesirable; it may be, however, that our failure to control pollution in the past will have catastrophic effects now and in the future.

We know that the residue of the gaseous by-products of production returns to earth as acid rain. Acid rain kills trees, streams, even whole lakes. Besides damaging the ecosystem, acid rain speeds the deterioration of bridges and buildings. Even worse, many scientists warn of a "greenhouse effect," or global warming, which could have drastic effects on weather, food production, sea levels, and the environment. The warming effect could be an increase of between three and nine degrees Fahrenheit in mean temperature by the mid-twenty-first century. This seemingly minor temperature change would have dramatic effects. Melting glaciers would raise the level of the seas, causing whole islands to disappear and altering coastlines everywhere. Shifts in regional weather patterns, brought about in part by warmer sea water, would bring drought to some areas and greater than normal rainfall to others, with profound implications for agricultural production. The ozone layer in the upper atmosphere is also being depleted by gaseous by-products. Holes in the ozone layer caused by pollution let in rays of the sun that encourage skin cancer, eye diseases, and immune system deficiencies.

Naturally, these problems have caused a great deal of debate among scientists, politicians, producers, and consumers. While the extent of the problem is hotly disputed, no one denies that a market failure of some magnitude does exist. In other words, the socially optimal amount of some good—in this case, clean air—is not being produced. Incomplete or nonexistent property rights to air have resulted in the failure of individuals, acting in their own self-interest, to conserve this resource.

---

[1]On these fascinating issues see two articles by Jared Diamond, "The American Blitzkrieg: A Mammoth Undertaking," *Discover* (June 1987) and "The Golden Age That Never Was," *Discover* (December 1988).

FOCUS

The Kyoto Treaty: Who Benefits from Global Warming?

A conference on global warming was held in Kyoto, Japan, in December 1997; from this, the "Kyoto Treaty" was developed. It calls on thirty-eight developed countries to cut the emission of greenhouse gases to 95 percent of their 1990 level by the year 2010. Economists have examined important aspects of this treaty, which has yet to be ratified.

Will the Kyoto Treaty reduce pollution? Most nations are exempt from the restrictions, and these "developing" nations have done the least to clean up their environments and are predicted to greatly expand their pollution over time. Also, countries facing restrictions will be allowed to buy the right to pollute or could move their high-pollution activities to nonrestricted countries.

How much will the treaty cost, and who will pay? The treaty is potentially very expensive. The United States would have to reduce emissions by 7 percent of 1990 levels, but that will mean a 40 percent cut in 2010 levels. The price of energy and electricity would have to rise dramatically; coal prices and energy-intensive production processes would be hurt the most. The treaty is expected to be expensive to the United States relative to other countries and particularly harmful to poor, coal-producing states like West Virginia and Alabama.

Who will benefit from the treaty? Other than environmental groups, who are the moral crusaders for a cleaner environment, it is difficult to identify the true beneficiaries. However, economics does allow us to identify the nations, industries, and companies that expect to benefit from the treaty and push for its implementation.

Countries that are unrestricted by the treaty support it, because they will be able to sell their unused rights to pollute. Other countries hope the treaty will raise their competitors' costs and thus earn them a greater share in world markets. Certain industries, such as natural gas, also expect to benefit from higher prices as producers switch from coal to natural gas. Finally, firms in the alternative energy business such as Archer-Daniels-Midland already receive a $300 million subsidy for producing ethanol as a substitute for gasoline, and the treaty both protects and will probably increase the amount of the subsidy. Economics shows that an unusual coalition of nations, environmental groups, and major corporations expect to benefit from "global warming" and, more importantly, provides a more realistic view of the effects of regulations such as the Kyoto Treaty.

Information for this Focus was drawn from Bruce Yandle, "Bootleggers, Baptists, and Global Warming" (Political Economy Research Center, 1998).

Identifying the problem is simpler than solving it, however. (See the Focus "The Kyoto Treaty: Who Benefits from Global Warming?") Because pollution controls—such as automobile emissions standards or requirements that smokestacks be outfitted with scrubbers—are not free, resistance by producers and consumers to new and more severe regulations can be expected. Strong resistance is likely when the suggested solutions entail huge costs, particularly when the scientific evidence is in dispute. Further, the global nature of market failure and the potentially discriminatory effects of radical temperature change have not encouraged international cooperation. Some regions and countries may actually benefit from potential temperature changes. Countries whose pollution causes acid rain may not

Externality
Benefits or costs of an individual's activity that the individual does not receive or bear.

Negative externality
A situation that arises when an individual or other economic entity imposes costs on others without compensating them.

Positive externality
A situation that arises when an individual or other economic entity creates benefits for others without receiving any compensation in return.

themselves bear the costs due to prevailing wind patterns in the atmosphere. Air pollution is a most complex common ownership problem. Everyone agrees that world governments should do something, but there is much disagreement on what should be done and on who should bear the costs.

EXTERNALITY THEORY

Under certain circumstances, an individual's pursuit of his or her self-interest results in costs or benefits to others. This kind of market failure is called an **externality**; the costs and benefits are external to the individual who caused them. Obviously, any economic entity can create an externality, including firms, government agencies, and individuals.

Negative and Positive Externalities

A common example of an externality is a factory's emission of smoke as a by-product of production. If the factory is able to avoid responsibility for the consequences of its smoke—such as the expenses for painting soot-covered buildings nearby or laundering sooty clothes—the output of the factory will be excessive, in that the value of additional output is less than the additional costs of the additional output plus the damage. If the factory were held responsible for the damage done by its smoke, its costs would rise, its product would become more expensive, and it would produce less. This example illustrates a **negative externality,** a situation in which production entails costs for others, such as those living near a factory. Other potential examples of negative externalities are the exhaust emissions of automobiles, a neighbor's excessively loud stereo, low-flying jet airplanes landing at an airport, drunk drivers, the contamination of underground water by toxic chemical dumps, and so on.

A positive externality is created when bee-keeper's bees pollinate the apple blossoms in an orchard, making the orchard more productive.

Positive externalities are benefits accruing without costs to the beneficiaries. Suppose a beekeeper and the owner of an apple orchard have adjoining land. The beekeeper's bees fly into the orchard and pollinate the apple blossoms, making the orchard more productive. If the beekeeper were to reap the consequences of the increased value of the orchard, the yield on his investment in bees would rise, and he would raise more bees. But as it is, his bees' social service is provided free. For both illustrations, the point is identical: Externalities arise when one person's activities affect the well-being of others, either positively or negatively. Some other examples of positive externalities are the reductions in contagious diseases that result from widespread inoculation and the clothes homeless people receive from charitable organizations.

Determining the Need for Government Intervention

To promote general economic well-being through a more socially efficient allocation of resources, an ideal government would intervene to encourage the production of goods that generate positive externalities and retard the production of goods that yield negative externalities. These inducements to alter production may be indirect in that they focus on the side effects of production, but they nonetheless work to change the amounts of output produced, which generated the externalities to begin with. Consider the externalities associated with the previously mentioned factory and bees. Government might intervene to reduce the amount of smoke emitted by the factory or to increase the number of bees kept by the beekeeper. Intervention is not always called for, however. Individuals might settle such matters privately.

To enhance the bees' contribution to the orchard's productivity, the orchard owner could contract with the beekeeper to supply more bees.[2] Alternatively, the orchard owner could raise his own bees. As long as the beekeeper's marginal costs of raising additional bees are less than the value the bees contribute to the orchard owner, it will be possible for both parties to reach an agreement that will leave each better off. Such private contracting in effect eliminates the apple–bee externality and makes public intervention unnecessary.

In addition to the possibility of private settlements, a second consideration when determining the need for government intervention in externalities is whether the externality is irrelevant or relevant. Externalities are trivial when the situation is not worth anybody's effort to do anything about it. The world is full of trivial externalities. You may not like the way a friend dresses, but not enough to say anything about it. Some people's unfailingly gracious and friendly behavior creates external benefits, and yet they are rarely complimented or rewarded for such behavior. The same goes for an attractive lawn. Neighbors reap external benefits from a well-kept lawn, but not so much that they would offer a subsidy to support the yard work.

Externalities are termed irrelevant when the externality generates insufficient demand by the affected party to change the situation. Your neighbor's messy yard may disturb your sense of propriety. You would be willing to pay her $50 a year to clean up the mess, but her price to clean it up is $600 a year. In this event her yard will not be cleaned up, and the externality will persist. The messy yard is a nuisance but not enough of a nuisance to cause sufficient demand to get the yard cleaned up. In principle, the best thing to do with an irrelevant externality is to leave it alone because it costs more than it is worth to correct the problem.

---

[2]See Steven N. S. Cheung, "The Fable of the Bees: An Economic Investigation," *Journal of Law and Economics* 16 (April 1973), pp. 35–52.

A relevant externality creates sufficient demand on the part of those affected by it to change the situation. Suppose that your neighbor is willing to clean up her messy yard for $10. You are willing to pay as much as $50. In this case you can make an effective offer to correct the externality and reach a deal with your neighbor. With relevant externalities, it is worthwhile to correct the situation because the benefits of correction exceed the costs.

Correcting Relevant Externalities

Economic theory suggests that correction of relevant externalities can be approached in a number of different ways. In general, these can be categorized as defining property rights, taxing negative externalities or subsidizing positive ones, selling rights to create an externality, and establishing regulatory controls.

Establishing Ownership Rights   Externality problems generally persist because of the presence of some element of common ownership. The beekeeper's and the apple grower's ownership rights are clearly established and easily transferable. In such a situation it will be in the interest of both parties to conclude an agreement that places resources in their most highly valued uses. But in the case of the polluting factory, does the factory have the right to use the air as it pleases, or do the people in the surrounding community have the right to clean air? Air-use rights are indefinite and nontransferable: It is generally impossible for people to buy and sell rights to the use of air. In this case, there is no reason to believe that the pursuit of individual interest will promote the use of air in its most highly valued manner.

The establishment of ownership, then, is one way of eliminating problems associated with externalities. Since nonownership is a source of market failure, the creation of ownership is a means of correcting market failure. (See the Application "Can Economic Incentives Save the Elephant and Other Endangered Species?" at the conclusion of this chapter.)

An important analysis of the economics of establishing ownership rights was first introduced by R. H. Coase, who was awarded the Nobel Prize in economics in 1991 for this work.[3] Coase posed the question: Does the legal assignment of property rights to one party or the other in an externality relationship make any difference to the observed market outcome? To keep the analysis simple, Coase assumed that the costs of bargaining and transacting among the parties were zero.

We will apply the Coase analysis to an example of air pollution—a factory belching smoke over a nearby community. Figure 17.3 illustrates the analysis. Firm output per unit of time is given along the horizontal axis. The marginal benefits (MB) to the firm of producing this output are given in dollar terms on the vertical axis. For the sake of this analysis, marginal benefits can be thought of as the net profits of producing additional units of output. The MB schedule therefore declines

---

[3]R. H. Coase, "The Problem of Social Cost," *Journal of Law and Economics* 3 (October 1960), pp. 1–44.

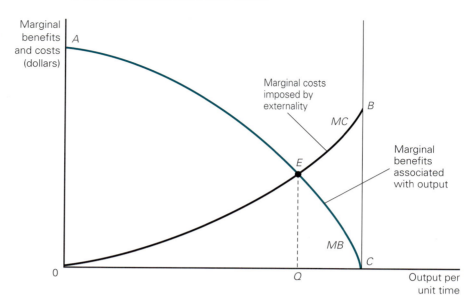

FIGURE 17.3

The Coase Theorem

In this graph depicting the Coase theorem, *MC* represents the externality imposed by the firm's pollution, and *MB* represents the profits to the firm from producing various levels of output (*Q*). The Coase theorem states that regardless of who is assigned ownership rights to the air, costless bargaining between the parties will result in the same market outcome at *Q*.

with increases in output because the rate of return on additional production generally declines (see Chapter 7). The marginal cost (*MC*) curve represents the externality caused by the firm's production and is also given in dollar terms along the vertical axis. The *MC* function measures the additional cost created at each output level by additional smoke. (Assuming that the amount of smoke the firm produces is directly related to its rate of output, more production will cause more smoke.) The *MC* curve rises as output increases.

Now we apply Coase's analysis. As an experiment, we give the ownership right to clean air to the homeowners in the surrounding neighborhood. Assuming that bargaining costs nothing, we can predict what will happen with the help of Figure 17.3. For rates of output up to *Q*, we observe that *MB* > *MC*. The firm's profits on additional units are greater than the additional pollution costs borne by the neighborhood; this means that the firm would be willing to buy and the neighborhood would be willing to sell the right of using the air to produce these units. Since the total cost of the externality caused by this output is represented by the area under the *MC* curve, 0*EQ*, a bargain can be struck between the firm and the neighborhood to produce *Q* by agreement on how to divide the surplus marginal benefit, *AE*0. Beyond *Q*, *MC* > *MB*. A bargain to produce these units cannot be reached between the firm and the neighborhood because the firm would not be willing to bid enough to obtain the right to produce these units. So *Q*, where *MB* = *MC*, is the equilibrium outcome when the neighborhood is given the transferable right to use of the air.

Suppose that a judge decided instead to award the firm the right to use the air as it chooses. What happens in this case? We go through the same analysis, but now we see that the neighborhood must pay the firm to produce less output. For up to *Q* units of output, *MB* > *MC*, which means that the neighborhood cannot offer a large enough sum of money to induce the firm to reduce its output and its smoke. Beyond Q, the situation is changed: The firm would be willing to accept an offer of money to reduce its output. Beyond Q, the smoke causes $EBCQ$ in damage to the neighborhood, and the benefits to the firm of this output are only ECQ. The neighborhood is therefore willing to make it worthwhile to the firm to reduce pollution to the point where $MB = MC$ at Q.

Coase theorem

States that the amount of an externality-generating activity will be the same regardless of the assignment of property rights if the bargaining costs are small.

Provided that we have been logical, we have shown a simple but powerful result: No matter who has the legal right to the use of the air, the amount of pollution is the same. When the firm must pay to pollute, it produces Q. When the firm has the unfettered right to pollute, it produces Q. This is the central insight offered by the **Coase theorem**: In a world in which bargaining costs nothing, the assignment of legal liability *does not matter*. A certain equilibrium level of output and its resulting level of pollution will exist regardless of whether firms or consumers own the air.[4] Under the stated conditions of the Coase theorem, government intervention—in the form of pollution guidelines, tax penalties, and the like—cannot improve upon a settlement negotiated by those parties who are directly involved with the externality problem. Note also that the efficient solution in this case implies the presence of a positive amount of pollution. It is rarely going to be efficient to set pollution at zero.

The Coase theorem provides a benchmark for analyzing externality problems. It shows what would happen in a world of zero bargaining and transaction costs. Many real-world externality problems can be analyzed with the Coase theorem, as long as the bargaining and transaction costs are low.

Nevertheless, using the establishment of ownership to correct externalities cannot always be relied upon to eliminate the difficulties of market failure because it may be exceedingly difficult, if not impossible, to establish ownership in some instances. Many externality problems do not fit the assumption of zero or low transaction and bargaining costs. In the factory smoke example, the neighbors of the plant are likely to be numerous, difficult to organize, and diffuse in their interests with respect to the air pollution problem. The widely dispersed sufferers of the smoke damage would face insuperable costs if they had to organize to purchase the agreement of the factory to reduce its emissions. If the firm had the right to pollute, it is not likely that the neighborhood could overcome these problems, get organized, and offer the firm money to cut pollution back to Q in Figure 17.3. Looked at the other way around, if the neighborhood owned the air space, the firm would find it costly to track down all homeowners and arrange for the purchase of their consent to produce up to output Q.

No matter who held the right to use of the air, bargaining costs would be high, and the likelihood is that nothing would be done to correct the situation. If the neighborhood owned the property rights, for example, some homeowners would seek to hold out for a larger payment from the firm. This would jeopardize the

---

[4]The Coase theorem also marked the beginning of a new field in economics called *law and economics,* which studies the impact of legal rules and institutions on the economy; the Coase theorem, for example, analyzes the role of legal liability assignment in an externality problem. Many law schools have specialized fields in law and economics, and much of the literature in this area is published by the *Journal of Law and Economics* and the *Journal of Legal Studies.*

possibility of a bargained agreement. The costs of defining and enforcing a system of ownership can be so high that some system of taxation or administrative control would be more effective than reliance on the definition of property rights and any contractual arrangements.

Taxing or Subsidizing Externalities   A seemingly simple way of dealing with externalities is to tax activities such as pollution that create negative externalities and to subsidize activities such as beekeeping that create positive externalities. Many complexities surround such a simple-sounding prescription, however. How could a negative externalities tax be levied? Against the product the factory produces? Against the amount of smoke it emits? Either solution might create burdens on the industry and on consumers that are not necessary in cleaning up the environment. Similarly, how would a subsidy for positive externalities be worked out? Based on the honey produced by the beekeeper? Based on the number of bees kept? Despite such complexities, the essential idea of taxing the negative externality and subsidizing the positive has a rich tradition in economic theory.[5]

To understand the effects of taxation, consider the pollution problem in terms of output decisions facing individual firms. In deciding what output to produce, the competitive firm compares marginal cost and marginal revenue. Marginal cost in this context means **marginal private costs** (MPC), the extra costs that the firm must pay to increase its output. These costs do not include externalities. By definition, an externality imposes costs on others that are not reflected in the private costs of the firm. The full costs to society of an increase in the firm's operations are summarized as **marginal social costs** (MSC). MSC are equal to MPC plus the externality costs (E): $MSC = MPC + E$. When there is no externality ($E = 0$), then $MSC = MPC$.

This analysis can be applied to the competitive industry. Consider the situation depicted in Figure 17.4. These are the same types of graphs that we used in Chapter 8. Figure 17.4b shows that an industry is initially in equilibrium at E_1, where industry demand (D) and supply (S_1) intersect. Under these conditions the firm (Figure 17.4a) reacts as a price taker to P_1 and sets its MPC curve equal to P_1 ($= d_1 = MR_1$). The competitive firm, acting on the basis of marginal private costs, produces q_1 units of output.

Notice, however, that the firm's MSC curve lies above the MPC curve at all levels of output; for example, it exceeds MPC by ab at q_1 units of output. The MSC curve traces the externality that the firm's operations impose, such as the amount of damage that the firm's air pollution causes in the surrounding neighborhood.

What can government do to improve the situation? Basically, government must get the firm to behave as if its marginal cost curve is MSC, not MPC. In this way the competitive firm would equate MSC to price, and the externality would be "internalized" in the firm's output decision; that is, the firm will produce the output where $MSC = P$, which is the correct output from society's point of view. (As

Marginal private cost

The change in total costs that only the firm bears when output changes by one unit.

Marginal social cost

The change in total cost borne by the economy as a whole (the firm plus all others, or society) that results from a one-unit change in the firm's output.

---

[5]The tax-subsidy approach to externalities is often called Pigovian, after A. C. Pigou, author of the *Economics of Welfare* (London: Macmillan, 1920).

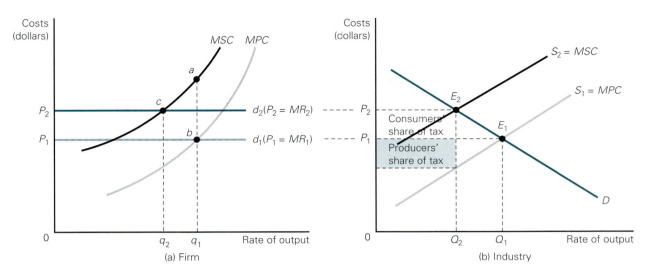

FIGURE 17.4

The Effects of a Tax on an Externality

(a) A pollution excise tax of *ab* per unit is placed on the output of the firm to correct the externality. The marginal private costs facing the firm are given by *MPC*, and marginal social costs are given by *MSC*. The tax raises the *MPC* curve to become identical with the *MSC* curve. In such a way the firm is made to account for the externality in its decision about how much output to produce. (b) At the industry level, the pollution tax reduces industry supply to S_2, and the pollution tax is paid by both consumers and producers, though the proportions need not be equal as depicted in Figure 17.4b.

we saw with the Coase theorem, the socially optimal level of pollution is not zero. At some point, clean air costs more than it is worth.)

This solution can be obtained by imposing a tax on the industry's output that reflects the degree to which *MSC* and *MPC* diverge. Such a tax is illustrated in Figure 17.4 as an excise tax imposed on the firm of *ab* per unit. The impact of the pollution tax is to shift the marginal cost curve of the firm from *MPC* to *MSC*. This change is reflected at the industry level by a shift in the industry supply curve from S_1 to S_2. The tax forces the competitive firm to account for the externality in choosing its output level. It thus chooses the socially efficient output level where $MSC = P_2$, or where marginal social costs are equal to marginal private benefits.

Who pays the pollution tax? Part of the tax will be paid by producers and part by consumers. Consumers will face a higher price for the industry's output, but the price will not rise by the amount of the tax. The producer thus absorbs some of the pollution tax. (See the earlier discussion of the incidence of an excise tax in Chapter 5.)

Selling Rights   A simple alternative to the tax example is to establish a market for externality rights such as the right to pollute. In this approach, government sets an allowable level of pollution and sells the right to pollute. In theory, this market works like any other market. Those who value the pollution rights most highly will buy and hold them. Firms will make decisions about whether it is less costly to install pollution-control equipment or to buy pollution rights. Government does not tell industry how to clean up the air. Instead, it sets the allowable level of pollution and lets firms decide how to control their pollution. This marketlike approach to pollution control has the virtue of ensuring that the acceptable level of pollution is reached at least cost. In fact, the Bush administration started such a program for the smokestack emissions of public utilities in 1990. Under this program, utilities are allowed to trade pollution rights.

Difficulties arise in such a scheme, however. Indeed, whether it chooses to tax pollution or sell pollution rights, government must somehow estimate what the "optimal" level of pollution is. The relevant knowledge in this case is economic rather than technical; the government's interest is less in determining the damage done by varying degrees of air pollution than it is in determining the values individuals attach to the different degrees of damage. Such knowledge is not easy to come by. Moreover, both a tax scheme and a pollution rights scheme must be monitored and enforced by government. Without such actions, tax evasion and pollution without permit will be serious problems.

Setting Regulations   In the past, government has most often not adopted an economic approach to control externalities such as pollution. More typically, government has sought to control pollution and other externality problems through direct regulation of industry. In the case of pollution, regulation generally consists of detailed rules about the technology that firms must adopt to control pollution. Firms in certain pollution-prone industries must install special pollution-control equipment as a condition of being able to stay in the industry. This is a practical way to control pollution. Each firm must clean up its emissions in the prescribed manner. In contrast to the pollution-rights approach, however, direct regulation does not allow firms to choose the most efficient means of staying below the allowable level of pollution. Firms cannot choose to pollute or not pollute or select among different types of pollution-control technologies. They must follow the rules laid down by government.

Each approach to the problem of externality control that we have discussed—the establishment of property rights, taxation or subsidy, selling of rights, and direct regulation—has costs and benefits in different applications. In some cases, the establishment of property rights may resolve the externality. Selling pollution permits may work to control air pollution by public utilities. In other cases, like automobile pollution, some form of government taxation or regulation may be used to control the externality of pollution. No approach will yield a perfect solution to these problems.

Public Choice, Politics, and Externalities   The attempted solution to real-world externality problems often directly involves the political process. Solutions dictated by political forces do not necessarily produce economic efficiency. Consider, for example, the attempt to save several species of Gulf Coast sea turtles, particularly the Kemps Ridley turtle. Some environmentalists—a clear "interest group"—claim a major reason for the disappearance of the turtles is that many are killed in shrimpers' nets. This alleged externality has been at the center of a protracted debate involving fishermen, environmental groups, state governments, federal agencies, and legislators. Over the years, environmentalists have supported a technological solution to the problem—the use of turtle exclusion devices to be attached to shrimpers' nets. Sewn into shrimp nets, the cagelike devices are designed to permit accidentally snagged turtles to escape. Fishermen—another interest group—charge that the devices are ineffective and, more important, that they reduce the shrimp catch by up to 20 percent.

The debate became politicized, with some U.S. senators and representatives from coastal states arguing that the proposed devices would put unnecessary financial hardship on shrimpers. Most state legislators and state fishery commissions opposed mandatory use of the devices. The National Marine Fisheries Service (an agency of the Department of Commerce) has enforced implementation of the device, although Congress initially disapproved of the agency's spending federal money to enforce the proposed regulations. High costs of government enforcement due to the large number of shrimpers has meant spotty implementation of the exclusionary devices. Meanwhile, the turtle population continues to decline.

PUBLIC GOODS THEORY

As we discussed in Chapter 4, government affects the economic well-being of a society in two essential ways. Government provides and maintains a system of laws to protect and enforce property rights and to permit the free flow of goods through markets. And government provides various goods and services that are not ordinarily provided through the free market system. Public goods thus represent another example of potential market failure.

Public good

A good such that, once produced, one individual's consumption of the good does not reduce or exclude the ability of other individuals to consume the good.

These government-provided goods and services fall into the broader category of **public goods** —goods such as national defense that, once provided to one person, are available to all on a noncompeting or nonrivalrous basis. It is difficult or impossible to exclude anyone from the use of a public good, and its use by one person does not prevent its use by another. A nuclear submarine, for example, provides national defense as a public good for all members of a society. One member's consumption of national defense does not preclude another's consumption. The use of a lighthouse beam by one ship does not stop other ships from using the same beam. The consumption of a public good by one consumer does not impose an opportunity cost on other consumers; all can consume the public good at the same time.

A private good is consumed exclusively by the person who buys it. Its consumption by one individual precludes consumption by others. When Benny eats a cheeseburger, Barbara cannot eat the same cheeseburger. The concern here is not with the fact that Benny bought the cheeseburger and owns it (in the sense that he has legal title to it). The concern is with a technical characteristic of consumption—that when one person is consuming a private good, it cannot be simultaneously consumed by other people. The consumption of a private good carries an opportunity cost: Consumption of the same good is denied to other consumers.

A mixed good embodies attributes of both private and public goods. A parade, for example, would seem to be a pure public good. Two people can watch it at the same time without interfering with each other's consumption. If the crowd gets large enough, however, the parade can become more of a private good because congestion detracts from each person's view. In other words, rather than being equally available to all, consumption becomes rivalrous; some people's consumption of the parade detracts and may even prevent other people's consumption. We say then that the parade is a mixed good. It has characteristics of both private and public goods.

Public Provision of Public Goods

How can a free market system provide national defense? Once a defense system is provided, it is equally available to all consumers or citizens. Since individuals cannot be excluded from the benefits of military defense, who would voluntarily contribute to its provision? Most individuals would hold back in the expectation that someone else would provide the necessary funds, and then they would reap the benefits of military defense for free.

Lighthouses provide another illustration of market failure to provide public goods. A lighthouse's beam is available to all ships passing by, regardless of whether a particular ship pays for the light. Since it is difficult or impossible to exclude non-payers from using the beam, individual shipowners probably will not contribute to the lighthouse, even though it provides an obviously valuable service for all shippers. To overcome this market failure, government assumes responsibility for the lighthouse. Through its power to tax, government can raise enough revenue to build and maintain the lighthouse.[6]

Public health services also illustrate the need for government to overcome market failure to provide a public good. At certain times when the public health seems in danger, such as the swine flu outbreak in the late 1970s, the government provides inoculations against disease. Individuals who are inoculated protect themselves against the disease. Their inoculation also protects those who are not inoculated. As more and more people are inoculated, the sources of contagion for the disease are reduced, so person A's inoculation reduces the odds that B and C, who have not been inoculated, will catch the disease. Persons B and C theoretically owe A something for the protection, but would they pay for it? Obviously not, since they cannot be excluded from A's protection. Government's providing such a public health service is a way of overcoming the market failure in this case.

Not all goods provided to a number of people at once require government provision. In some cases, the costs of excluding noncontributors are low enough that private firms will produce goods enjoyed cooperatively by many people. For

---

[6]While the lighthouse has long served as an archetype of a public good, the private provision of lighthouses is an historical fact. See R. H. Coase, "The Lighthouse in Economics," *Journal of Law and Economics* 17 (October 1974), pp. 357–376.

example, a movie, a football game, and a concert are goods that are jointly provided to many consumers at once. In this respect these goods are like the lighthouse and national defense. The difference is that it is feasible for the producers of these goods to exclude those who do not pay for their provision, and so they can be supplied by private producers within the free market.

Free Riders

Sellers of private goods can exclude nonpayers from using the goods by charging a price for their use. Once a public good is produced, however, it is equally available to all consumers, regardless of whether they contribute to its production or not. Individuals who do not contribute to production and yet enjoy the benefits of goods are called **free riders.**

The problem facing producers of public goods is that free-riding behavior makes it difficult to discover the true preferences of consumers of a public good. Individuals will not reveal their true preferences for public goods because it is not in their self-interest to do so. For example, if a neighborhood tried to organize a crime-watch group, many neighbors might not contribute but would still appreciate any protection provided, thus concealing their true preferences for the service. On the other hand, some who do not contribute voluntarily might be totally disinterested in the service. The possibility of free riding makes it difficult to determine the true level of demand for the public good.

If everyone free rides and no one contributes to the production of public goods, then everyone will be worse off as a result. No public goods will be produced, even though each individual would like some provision of public goods. Herein lies a rationale for government provision of public goods. Government has the power of coercion and taxation, and it can force consumers to contribute to the production of public goods. Citizens cannot refuse to pay taxes and thus contribute to the costs of public sector output. When the cost of excluding nonpayers is high, government can produce public goods through tax finance.

Pricing Public Goods

Should a price be charged for use of public goods? In a sense, the correct price of a public good is zero. Take the example of a bridge. Once the bridge is built, the marginal cost of one more car going over it is approximately zero. If we follow the rule in Chapter 8 for optimal pricing, we should set price equal to marginal cost. Since the marginal cost of an additional bridge crossing is effectively zero, price should be zero according to the $P = MC$ rule. According to this logic, public goods should be free.

This rationale is fine as far as it goes, but it does not go far enough. In rationing the use of the good among demanders, zero is the correct price. Except for cases of congestion, a public good presents no rationing problem; by definition, additional individuals can consume a public good at zero marginal cost. But rationing is not the only function of price. A second important function of price is to achieve the right quantity of the public good by relating quantity to demand.

Free rider

An individual who receives the benefit of consuming a public good or service without paying for it.

FIGURE 17.5

Sharing the Costs of Defense

MC is the marginal cost curve for production of military protection under an alliance. D_A and D_B are the individual country demand curves for national defense. The appropriate "prices" for national defense for each country are P_A and P_B. $D_A + D_B$ is the vertical sum of D_A and D_B. Optimal output for the alliance is QT where $D_A + D_B = MC$.

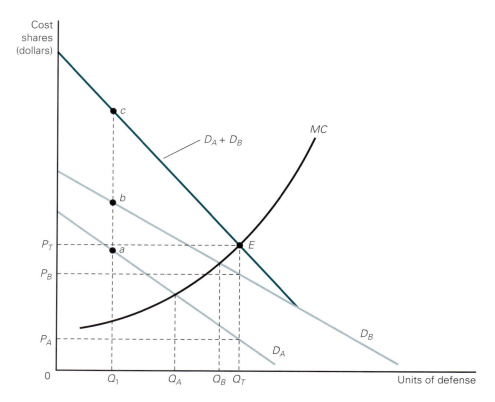

Without information about what people are willing to pay to cross the bridge, authorities are left in the dark about the desired amount of bridge construction to undertake. After all, public goods involve the expenditure of scarce resources, and prices for public goods help public officials develop information about the demand for these goods.

How then should a price be set for a public good? Suppose a defense alliance is formed by two countries, *A* and *B*.[7] The alliance provides for a common defense policy through a treaty agreement. National defense is a public good for the alliance, and the problem facing the two countries is how to reach an agreement on the amount of national defense to be produced by the alliance. Figure 17.5 illustrates the problem.

We assume that each country faces the same marginal cost curve (*MC*) for providing a common defense. *MC* rises because additional scarce resources devoted to defense come at an increasing cost to the two countries.

Each country has a demand curve for national defense, D_A and D_B. The consumption of private goods is mutually exclusive. When *A* gets a unit of a private

---

[7]See Mancur Olson and Richard Zeckhauser, "An Economic Theory of Alliances," *Review of Economics and Statistics* 47 (August 1966), pp. 266–279.

good, there is one less unit available for B to consume. In Chapter 3, this condition meant that to derive a market demand curve for a private good, the demand curves of individual consumers had to be summed horizontally. National defense, however, is not a private good. It is a public good, and this makes the nature of the "demand curves" in Figure 17.5 quite different.

Consumption of a public good is not mutually exclusive among consumers. All the units along the horizontal axis in Figure 17.5 are equally available to both demanders for simultaneous consumption. Both A and B receive benefits from, for example, Q_1 units of military protection. Thus, the total protection benefits offered by Q_1 to A and B are equal to the vertical sum of their demand prices for this quantity or output. At Q_1 the benefit that each country places on alliance protection is read vertically off its demand curve. A derives aQ_1, B derives bQ_1, and both countries together place a value of cQ_1 (equal to $aQ_1 + bQ_1$) on Q_1 units of alliance output.

This point applies to all public goods. The **market demand curve for a public good** is obtained by vertically summing all individuals' demand curves. The demand curves are summed vertically rather than horizontally because all demanders can consume any given unit of output along the horizontal axis at the same time. In Figure 17.5, then, market demand is given by $D_A + D_B$, which is the vertical sum of D_A and D_B.

At points along the horizontal axis less than Q_T, marginal benefit exceeds marginal cost ($D_A + D_B > MC$), and production will be expanded. At points beyond Q_T, marginal benefit is less than marginal cost ($D_A + D_B < MC$), and production will be cut back. Equilibrium output is at E, where $D_A + D_B = MC$. The equilibrium defense output in the alliance is Q_T, and the alliance defense budget is $P_T \times Q_T$.

How should this budget be divided between the two countries? One way to apportion the costs is in proportion to the benefits received. P_B represents the benefit that accrues to country B from consuming Q_T units of defense, and P_A is the benefit that country A receives from consuming the same amount. Country B pays more because it benefits more from alliance output. Country B, for example, may be larger, with more income, capital, and population to defend.

This is an idealized presentation of alliance behavior. For example, what happened to the concept of free riding? Basically, we ignored it to depict a perfect outcome for the alliance. But free riding will be a thorn in the alliance's side. Look at the individual equilibrium positions of the two countries in Figure 17.5. Given the marginal cost of providing defense, the small country prefers Q_A as its defense output; the large country prefers Q_B. When the treaty to form the alliance is signed, A gains access to the benefits of B's production. B's production more than satisfies A's demand for national defense. In group alliances, small countries like A will therefore have strong incentives to reduce their defense spending and to free ride on the defense expenditures of larger countries such as B. This tendency will lead to much bargaining and many debates about contributions to alliance output, with the large countries complaining about the efforts and contributions of the small countries. The problem of free riding will be more pronounced the more countries there are in the alliance.

Market demand curve for a public good

Obtained by summing vertically, instead of horizontally, all individuals' demands for the public good. Vertical summation is used because consumption is noncompeting.

A ROLE FOR GOVERNMENT

The presence of common-resource problems and other externalities and public goods means that government has an important and productive role to play in the economy. Externalities lead to a regulatory role for government. Public goods imply a role for government as a direct producer of some goods and services. If properly undertaken, government activities will serve to enhance the productivity of the private sector by providing police protection, a system of property rights and their enforcement, a court system, national defense, and other goods and services that might otherwise not be provided by purely private markets.

APPLICATION

Can Economic Incentives Save the Elephant and Other Endangered Species?

The property rights structure (common or private) that evolves or is chosen in an economy has much to do with the scarcity of a particular resource. Common ownership—the right of anyone to use resources in unrestricted quantities—has a powerful impact on the incentives of individuals to neglect conservation. Property rights systems begin to change at the point when increases in demand for a resource held in common begin to exceed the supply of that resource. In the case of renewable resources such as timber, lobsters, shrimp, or fish, overfishing or timber stripping can have negative effects on future harvests. In many cases, however, it is possible to save a resource by altering property rights. This has enormous implications for various endangered species. Consider the endangered African elephant.

Children of all ages love elephants, as any zookeeper will tell you. Unfortunately, an externality in the form of a common pool problem has created a growing (and justified) fear of extinction of the African species. Data suggest a continent-wide decrease in the number of elephants by 30 percent in only 8 years (from 1.2 million in 1981 to 760,000 in 1988). In particular countries the decline is indeed shocking. In the Sudan, the decline between 1979 and 1989 was from 134,000 to 40,000 animals. In Zaire, over the same period, the decline was from 377,700 elephants to 85,000.[a]

Biological characteristics of elephants (such as a long gestation period) are undoubtedly part of the problem. But there is an externality created by the common pool—that which belongs to no one will soon be gone. Besides much pleasure to the zoo visitor, the elephant produces hide, meat, and, most importantly, valuable ivory. Ivory poaching has become a way of life and a means to prosperity for many Africans. Good intentions and help from outside agencies have not been enough in most countries to protect the elephant on its way to extinction. An ivory ban, honored by most nations, has been implemented by world conservation organizations, again with every good intention. But an ivory ban may not do the trick when economic incentives are considered.

An ivory ban, if it is not totally enforced and honored around the world, may in fact hasten the demise of the elephant, at least according to some economists.[b] Although the ban may temporarily alleviate pressures on elephant populations, it will also (if not very effectively) drive the price of ivory up, encouraging more intense poaching and improved poaching technology. The total ban on ivory sales,

---

[a]See Phillip Shabecoff, "Seeing Disaster, Groups Ask Ban on Ivory Import," *New York Times* (June 2, 1989), p. 19.
[b]See Michelle McKeever, "The Economics of Conservation: African Elephants and the Ivory Trade" (Auburn University thesis, 1991).

although laudable in intent, does nothing to eliminate the poacher. Goodwill and enforcement monies, especially in poor Central and East African countries, may be at a premium insofar as the security of the elephant is concerned.

Southern African nations such as Zimbabwe and Botswana have launched innovative solutions that take economic factors and incentives into account. These countries have calculated the biologically optimal number of elephants in particular habitats, used property-rights assignments, and permitted the limited and scientific harvesting of elephant ivory to finance wildlife conservation programs. Hunting rights are given to farmers who harvest elephants themselves or sell the rights to others. (Elephants themselves create negative externalities by competing with farmers for land and crops in some regions.) Incentives to create picture safaris are also being implemented. Populations grew from 1981 to 1989 by 38,000 elephants in Botswana and by 2000 in Zimbabwe.[c] By 1999 elephant populations in southern Africa were burgeoning, reaching an estimated 200,000.[d] All these elephants have created an enormous debate between villagers, whose water supplies and crops are endangered by the animals, and wildlife preservation interests. (An average adult elephant eats 650 pounds of vegetation and drinks 40 gallons of water a day, reducing or endangering many other species in the process.) In 1989 the United Nations banned the ivory trade, but in a controversial decision, a UN panel gave permission for a one-time auction of ivory from Namibia, Zimbabwe, and Botswana to Japanese buyers. Tusks were those of elephants who died naturally or were culled from oversized herds, and funds were to go to conservation efforts in theses poor countries.

Outside of these Southern African countries, elephant populations have been in decline. Saving the elephant from a common-pool disaster may require a variety of solutions. One policy, currently in play, is to relocate elephants from areas of high population to those countries where they are endangered. In Zimbabwe, with a population of more than 70,000, elephants have become a problem for farmers and ranchers. Here they are captured and moved to areas such as Angola and Mozambique, where they are endangered. These practices and the use of economic incentives and biological considerations are surely part of any rational approach to such problems.

Of course, the application of economic and property-rights theory to endangered species will not work in all cases. There are special problems, for example, with migratory populations and with species for which an "economic value" is small or nonexistent. But the application of legal rights may work in many instances, as in the case of alligators, with economic and/or social benefits for all concerned interests.

QUESTIONS

The sidewalks, landscaped grounds, swimming pools, and social facilities typically found in condominium developments are common areas—that is, they belong to everyone in the development. How are such areas usually maintained? What do you predict would happen if the individual owners were responsible for the upkeep of common areas?

---

[c] Data from "Saving the Elephant," *Economist* (July 1, 1989), p. 16.
[d] Information from "Ivory Tusks Auction Gives Activists an Uneasy Feeling," *Orlando Sentinel* (April 4, 1999), p. A-11.

SUMMARY

1. Dependence on markets to produce and allocate nonrenewable and renewable natural resources will mean that such resources are properly allocated between present and future uses.

2. Market failure occurs when the private market system fails to allocate resources in an optimal or ideal fashion. Externalities and public goods are two categories of market failure.

3. Owners of private property bear the economic results of its use. When property is held in common, users do not bear the full costs of its use. Common or undefined ownership creates a conflict between the pursuit of self-interest and the common good. The implication is that common resources will be overused and exploited. Creating ownership is one way to correct market failure.

4. An externality occurs when an economic unit does not bear all the value consequences of its actions. Externalities can be positive or negative, trivial, irrelevant, or relevant. A relevant externality creates an effective demand to correct the externality.

5. The Coase theorem assumes that in a world of zero transactions and bargaining costs, the amount of an externality such as pollution will be the same no matter who has legal liability for it.

6. Where transaction and bargaining costs are high, other routes to externality control become feasible. A per-unit pollution tax would force a firm to act as if its marginal cost curve were identical to its marginal cost curve plus the cost of the externality, or the marginal social cost curve. Other approaches include establishment of a market for pollution rights and direct regulation of firm technology.

7. Public goods are goods that are nonrivalrous in consumption, with high costs of excluding nonpayers. Whereas a private good is consumed exclusively by one individual, a public good can be simultaneously consumed by all consumers. A mixed good has characteristics of private and public goods.

8. To "free ride" means to reap the benefits of a public good without bearing its costs. If everyone free rides, no public good is produced by the private sector, even though each individual values its production. Such behavior means that public goods typically have to be produced by government through its power to tax.

9. Public goods are not free; they cost real resources. In terms of rationing a public good among consumers, a zero price is the correct price because additional consumers can consume a public good at near-zero marginal cost. However, a zero price for a public good offers no guidance for public officials about how much of a public good to produce. There is thus a trade-off regarding the pricing of public goods.

10. Individual demand curves for public goods are summed vertically to arrive at total demand for a public good. Optimal output of a public good occurs where the vertically summed individual demand curves intersect the marginal cost curve. Optimal prices for this output are read off the individual demand curves.

KEY TERMS

natural resources
nonrenewable natural resources
renewable natural resources
common ownership
externality

negative externality
positive externality
Coase theorem
marginal private cost
marginal social cost

public good
free rider
market demand curve for a
   public good

QUESTIONS FOR REVIEW AND DISCUSSION

1. Are whales an example of a common property resource? If so, what sort of behavior would you predict among whale hunters?

2. What is an externality? Name the various types of externalities. Why is an externality considered a type of market failure?

3. Suppose that pollution is controlled with a pollution tax on polluting firms. Who will pay the tax? Firms? Consumers?

4. Define a public good. What is the difference between a private good and a public good? How will individuals behave when asked how much they will contribute toward payment for a public good? What does this mean for the nature of the demand curves for public goods?

5. Evaluate the following statement: Museums should be free.

6. Are all public goods produced by government? If not, name some goods that fit the definition of a public good that are produced by private producers.

7. Explain the importance of private property rights in preventing the kinds of market failure that are typically associated with common ownership.

8. Explain the Coase theorem and tell how it could solve externality problems in a world with zero transaction and bargaining costs.

9. Because real-world transaction costs are not zero, taxes or subsidies are sometimes used to eliminate externalities. Explain how taxation eliminates an externality such as pollution.

10. Explain what is meant by noncompeting consumption for a public good.

PROBLEMS

1. Suppose that the government of a hypothetical city has decided to add ten new programs to local schools, each with a cost of $100,000. Each group of voting citizens must share equally in the tax to pay for the new programs. The table shows the dollar value of the benefits that each of eight citizen groups receives from the programs.

Group of Individuals	Benefits
A	$ 80,000
B	140,000
C	160,000
D	60,000
E	40,000
F	180,000
G	120,000
H	110,000

a. If each group gets only one vote and if each group votes on its *pro rata* net benefit from the public good, will the city schools get the new programs?

b. On the basis of the total benefits and total costs, should the programs be provided?

c. Why do most local governments provide primary and secondary education for "free" as public goods? Is such "free" provision necessarily optimal? Explain.

2. "The market and technology work in mysterious ways. The Internet, for example, may ultimately have profound effects on the environment." Explain briefly.

WORKING WITH THE WEB

1. As explained in the chapter, when common ownership of a resource exists, it typically is overutilized. The case of ocean fishing is one example of the common ownership problem, where in this case, overfishing results. As a result, many commercially important fish species have been depleted. Go to http://seawifs.gsfc.nasa.gov/OCEAN_PLANET/HTML/peril_overfishing.html. There is a brief introduction to the problem of overfishing followed by an overview of the status of many fish species, ranging from depleted (the worst case) to abundant (the best case).
   a. Other than the damage to the fish population, what other perils exist as a consequence of overfishing?
   b. Who enforces fisheries law?
   c. According to the web site statistics, is it a good time to be a northern Atlantic (either northeast or northwest) fisherman? Explain.
   d. Go to http://www.wh.whoi.edu/sos/spsyn/pg/cod.html and read a bit about the cod species. What are some of the regulations in effect to prevent elimination of the species?

2. The link between private property rights and environmental protection is demonstrated in South Carolina, where island property owners take it upon themselves to preserve beaches and other island attributes rather than rely on or promote government–sponsored beach erosion programs. Go to http://www.perc.org/june99.pdf and download the file to your hard drive. (This file is in Adobe Acrobat format. If you do not already have the Adobe Acrobat Reader, go to http://www.adobe.com and

find out how to download it for free.) Open the file and look for the article called "Preserving Beaches" on page 7.
   a. What is the value to oceanfront property owners of increasing the beach width from 322 to 472 feet? Is there any value to inland residents?
   b. As the article describes, the beach protection programs are short-lived and must be undertaken repeatedly to maintain the wider beaches that protect the island and the property on the island. How is it determined whether or not a protection program should be undertaken? Is the method efficient from an economic perspective?

3. The Coase theorem is one way to resolve an externality problem. An alternative solution might be obtained via a system of taxes and subsidies. The Coase theorem, however, relies on the assignment of property rights to achieve an efficient solution. Go to http://www.reason-mag.com/9701/int.coase.html to read an interview with Ronald Coase conducted by economist Thomas Hazlett in *Reason* magazine.
   a. In describing the Coase theorem in his own words, what determines the "best" use of a resource?
   b. Pollution is often used as an example of a negative externality, as in your text. According to Coase, why is pollution both a negative and a positive?
   c. What is Coase's opinion of government regulation? Does he have an example of a good regulation?

Public
Choice

Democratic governments act through a unique set of institutional arrangements, such as majority voting, representative democracy, political parties, bureaucracies, and special-interest groups. The theory of **public choice** attempts to use economics to understand and to evaluate how governments operate. We have already discussed public choice issues in some detail in this book. We have examined why people vote, how government price controls affect markets, how politicians act to supply regulation to industries, the behavior of countries in defense alliances, along with other examples of public choice at work. In fact, this book is permeated with examples and discussions of public choice. In order to gain more perspective on public choice issues and to expand our consideration of the theory of public choice, this chapter discusses some of the key elements of public choice analysis.

The fundamental premise of public choice is that political decision makers (voters, politicians, bureaucrats) and private decision makers (consumers, market intermediaries, producers) behave similarly: They follow the dictates of rational self-interest. In fact, political and economic decision makers are often one and the same person—consumer and voter. The individual who buys the family groceries also votes in an election. If the premise of public choice is correct, we can learn a lot about such issues as why people take the time and trouble to vote by applying the same logic to the voting decision that we have applied to the grocery-buying decision. As we do so, keep in mind that the institutions and constraints facing political decision makers are different from those facing private decision makers. For example, the benefits of buying groceries are fairly obvious, but what are the benefits of voting? We will be careful to specify such differences between private and public choices throughout our analysis.

Public choice
The economic analysis of political decision making, politics, and the democratic process.

Normative public choice
Economic analysis that determines shortcomings and failures of the political process and suggests improvements.

Positive public choice
Economic analysis of political decision making and other political behavior that aims to understand, explain, and predict such behavior.

Public choice, like the rest of economics, has both a normative and a positive side. **Normative public choice** involves judgments about the desirability of certain political situations. In the design of voting procedures, for example, how does majority rule compare with other voting rules in reflecting the true preferences of voters? Is there a better voting rule or process through which to make political decisions? Normative public choice looks at the way political institutions work from the standpoint of how we might make them work better.

Positive public choice seeks to explain actual political behavior. Why do high-income individuals vote more often than low-income individuals? How do committees and legislatures work? What is the impact of special-interest groups on government? In this chapter we will examine both normative and positive aspects of public choice after first exploring how self-interest affects decision making. When you finish Chapter 18 you should understand

- some of the consequences of treating government decision makers as rationally self-interested individuals.
- how the process of voting may not lead to optimal choices by individual voters.
- how self-interested groups affect government.
- the nature of bureaucratic behavior and its relation to government growth.

SELF-INTEREST AND POLITICS

The public choice approach to politics is based on the idea that political actors are no different from anyone else: They behave in predictable ways and seek to obtain their goals efficiently.

Proprietary
Relating to private ownership and profit motivation; individuals directly bear the consequences of their decisions.

Nonproprietary
Relating to nonprivate ownership; entails motivations other than strictly profit motivations; individuals do not always or fully bear the consequences of their decisions.

Nevertheless, market behavior and political behavior differ in the constraints facing decision makers. The market is a **proprietary** setting—one in which individuals bear the economic consequences of their decisions, which either enhance or decrease their wealth. In the market economy, a firm that produces a new product stands to make profits or losses depending on the quality of its efforts. The political arena is a **nonproprietary** setting—one in which individuals do not always bear the full economic consequences of their decisions. For example, the political entrepreneur who comes up with a new political program does not bear the full costs of the program if it is a failure and does not reap all the benefits if it is a success. Behavior will therefore differ in market and in political settings, not so much because the goals of behavior are different but because the constraints on behavior are different.

We can distinguish the economic constraints at work in a market or proprietary setting and in a political or nonproprietary setting by analyzing the roles of agents and principals in each case. In both settings the agent, whether a firm or a politician, agrees to perform a service for the principal, whether a consumer or a voter. Because the agent and the principal are both self-interested, the agent will not always act in the interest of the principal, particularly if the agent's behavior is costly to monitor.

The agent–principal problem has been analyzed primarily in a private setting. For example, the corporate manager is an agent, and stockholders are principals.

How do the stockholders get the manager to act in their interest? They do so primarily through economic incentives. Managers of private firms have incentives to control costs in their firms because increased costs cause a decrease in the firm's profitability. Stockholders, through such mechanisms as stock options and takeover bids, can discipline managerial behavior toward maximizing wealth.

Managers of political "firms," or bureaucracies, do not face a similar incentive to control costs. They cannot personally recoup any cost savings that they achieve for their agencies, and the means available to voters to curtail poor performance by political managers are minimal and costly to implement. This does not mean that public officials can do anything that they want to do. Like any other economic actors, they are constrained by costs and rewards.

The main point about the agent–principal problem is that political agents face different constraints on their behavior than do private agents because political principals face different incentives to control the behavior of the agents. This difference is the focus of public choice analysis.

PUBLIC CHOICE ANALYSIS OF MAJORITY VOTING

Normative public choice theory analyzes the performance of political institutions in serving voters. In this section we illustrate the usefulness of this approach by examining the process of voting by majority rule.[1]

In a democracy, public choices are typically based on a majority vote: If candidate A wins even one vote more than candidate B, then candidate A is elected to office. Particularly when more than two choices are available, majority rule does not always accurately reflect voter preferences.

Imagine a three-person nominating committee that must choose from among three alternatives—Smith, Jones, and Tobin—the nominee for club president. Each committee member ranks the three candidates in order of preference (first, second, third), and the winner is to be selected by majority vote (two out of three committee members in favor). Table 18.1 shows the rankings of the three candidates by the committee members (A, B, and C). Member A, for example, prefers Smith to Jones and Jones to Tobin. Note that each member has consistent preferences; that is, each member is able to rank the three candidates in order of preference.

Now let the voting begin. To find the preferred nominee, the committee pairs each candidate against one of the other two until a winner is found. Suppose they start with Smith against Jones. Who wins? A votes for Smith, B votes for Smith (B prefers Tobin overall, but between Smith and Jones prefers Smith), and C votes for Jones. Smith wins by a majority vote of 2 to 1. Can Smith now beat Tobin? A votes for Smith, B votes for Tobin, and C votes for Tobin. Tobin wins that round.

---

[1] The origins of this analysis can be found in Kenneth Arrow's *Social Choice and Individual Values* (New York: Wiley, 1951) and in Duncan Black's *The Theory of Committees and Elections* (London: Cambridge University Press, 1958). Arrow won the Nobel Prize in economics in 1972.

TABLE 18.1

A Voting Problem

The committee must choose among Smith, Jones, and Tobin. The candidate receiving a simple majority (two votes) wins. When each candidate is paired against another (Smith versus Jones, Jones versus Tobin, Tobin versus Smith), no clear winner emerges. Smith beats Jones, Tobin beats Smith, but Jones beats Tobin. This is a problem of simple majority voting with two candidates at a time. Individual voters can clearly rank candidates, but majorities cannot. Majority voting in this case leads to a repetitive cycle of winners.

Committee Member	Smith	Jones	Tobin
A	1	2	3
B	2	3	1
C	3	1	2

Now, how does Tobin fare against Jones? Since Smith previously beat Jones, we would also expect Tobin to dominate Jones because Tobin dominated Smith. But notice what happens: A votes for Jones, B votes for Tobin, and C votes for Jones. This time, Jones wins! Thus in three rounds of voting, a different candidate wins each round.

The committee's stalemate points up a problem with majority voting. Under majority voting each individual voter can have consistent preferences among multiple candidates or issues, and yet voting on candidates two at a time can lead to inconsistent collective choices. In other words, individuals can make clear choices among Smith, Jones, and Tobin, but majorities cannot. Majorities will choose Smith over Jones, Tobin over Smith, Jones over Tobin, and on and on in a repetitive voting cycle until a way is found to stop the voting. Either Smith, Jones, or Tobin will win when the voting is stopped, but only because the voting stopped at a particular point, not because one candidate is a clear winner over the other two.

This simple proof strikes at the rationality of majority voting procedures. Although individual choices will be clear and rational, majority choices will be inconsistent and cyclical. Where does such a paradoxical result lead us? First, it leads us to look for a better voting procedure than simple majority rule when voting on two issues or candidates at a time. (See the Application "Registering Minority Votes," which discusses a proposal for "point" voting to protect minority interests, at the conclusion of this chapter.) Second, the problem of voting cycles is mitigated to some extent by the institutions of democracy. Our legislatures and committees do not cycle endlessly among alternative proposals without reaching a decision. Votes are taken and decisions are made. Attempts to reach agreement do not go on forever. Powerful committee chairpersons, for example, can call for votes on legislation and see to it that the legislature produces new laws. While such legislative procedures do not solve the problem of inconsistent choices in majority voting, they do keep the tendency toward voting cycles in check.

PUBLIC CHOICE ANALYSIS OF POLITICS

Positive public choice analysis is like positive economics: It consists of the development of models of political behavior that can be subjected to empirical testing. In this section, we present some positive propositions about government and political behavior that seem to be supported by evidence from the world around us.

Political Competition

Have you ever wondered why by election time the two major parties' candidates sound like Tweedledum and Tweedledee, and you cannot see any difference in the views espoused by either? Perhaps more important, why do we have only two major political parties in the United States? The following model helps us answer these and other questions about political competition in a democratic setting.

Assume that voter preferences on issues can be distributed along an imaginary spectrum running from radical left (perhaps the Socialist Workers) to radical right (perhaps the John Birch Society), as in Figure 18.1. Further assume that voters vote for the candidate closest to their ideological position. The normal distribution of voters holding different ideological positions is split down the middle by M. The total area under the curve in Figure 18.1 represents 100 percent of the voters. We call the voter at M the median voter. If either candidate in a two-party race adopts a middle-of-the-road position such as M's position, he or she is guaranteed at least a tie in the election; he or she will receive at least 50 percent of the vote, since 50 percent of the votes lie to the left of M and 50 percent lie to the right. If the other party's candidate adopts any other position, such as R, he or she will get less than 50 percent of the vote. Remember: Voters follow the rule of voting for the candidate closest to their ideological position;

FIGURE 18.1

Ideological Distribution of Voters

The distribution of voters in this example is single-peaked, ranging from radical left to radical right. M represents voters at the middle, or median, of the distribution. The total area under the curve represents 100 percent of the votes. Two-party political competition leads to middle-of-the-road positions, similar to those held by voters at M. Points a and b represent ideological positions midway between points L and M and points R and M, respectively.

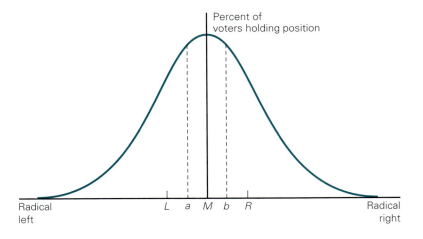

Percent of voters holding position

Radical left L a M b R Radical right

fewer than half the voters in Figure 18.1 are closest to *R*. With one candidate at *R* and one at *M*, the candidate at R receives the percentage of total votes to the right of the line at *b*, while the candidate at *M* receives the larger percentage equal to the area under the curve to the left of *b*. Point *b* represents the ideological stance midway between *M* and *R*. The best strategy for each candidate is to adopt position *M* and hope that random error (pulling the wrong lever) by voters will make him or her a winner. *M*, the median position, is the vote-maximizing position for both candidates; by election time, therefore, both candidates are virtual carbon copies of each other.

This model of political competition is oversimplified, but it does offer some insights into political behavior. Where the distribution of voter preferences is single-peaked, as at *M* in Figure 18.1, there are strong tendencies toward median outcomes. This holds true for virtually any type of collective decision process, from a committee consensus to a public election. Middle-of-the-road policies are vote-maximizing; therefore, we expect middle-of-the-road candidates and policies to be winners. In addition, the analysis underlying Figure 18.1 gives some clues as to why we have only two major parties in the United States. If parties can enter on either the left or right flank of parties at *M*, such entry jeopardizes control of government by the center parties. We can expect that the *M*-type parties will do their best to place barriers to entry in the way of noncenter parties, such as making it costly and difficult for a new party to get on the election ballot.

Finally, this discussion assumes that parties know what the distribution of voters is. If there is uncertainty or lack of information about what voters want, then political parties will have to spend resources and take risks to better understand voter desires. Individuals may also have that incentive (see the Focus "Can You Buy an Election?"). Uncertainty about the distribution of voters explains why political parties commission polls, spend money on campaigns and advertisements, and engage in a host of activities to try to attract voters.

Logrolling

Logrolling
The exchange of votes by legislators, usually in order to gain support for particular legislation.

Positive public choice also takes into account the behavior of officials once they are in office. A typical political behavior is **logrolling,** a term used to describe the process of vote trading. Representatives in a legislature are constantly making deals with one another. One wants a dam in his district; the other wants a new courthouse in hers. They agree to trade votes on issues: You vote for my dam; I'll vote for your courthouse.

There are many beneficial aspects of logrolling. Mainly, it enables representatives to register the intensity of their preferences across issues. For example, a minority representative who feels strongly about animal rights can trade his votes on issues about which he does not feel so intensely for support on the animal rights issue. Logrolling also helps mitigate the problem of indifferent majorities winning over intense minorities. In essence, logrolling, or vote trading, is a form of exchange, and economists usually view exchange as a productive and efficiency-enhancing process.

FOCUS

Can You Buy an Election?

Recent elections have seen billionaire candidates like Steve Forbes and Ross Perot entering national elections and a near-epidemic of abuses of campaign finance regulations, most notably allegations of Chinese influence on U.S. elections. As a result, campaign finance reform has been a hot topic in Washington, but little has been done.

Economists view campaign donations as a means to an end. You need money to carry on a modern political campaign, but victory goes to the candidate with the most voter support, not to the one with the biggest bucks. Donations help purchase election experts, pollsters, equipment, campaign literature, and television advertisements, but they are no guarantee of success.

Steve Forbes and Ross Perot, for example, spent millions of dollars but did not win; in fact, they did not even come close. Other wealthy candidates for Senate and House also have fared poorly in recent elections. It appears that rich people cannot purchase office. It is also the case that the candidate with the most money does not always win. Well-funded candidates can and do beat candidates with larger campaign war chests on a regular basis, and sometimes poorly funded candidates such as Jesse Ventura beat well-known and well-funded opponents.

Is too much money spent on politics? Spending by candidates in congressional races alone is approaching a total of $1 billion per election. However, even if you took spending by all candidates from local, state, and federal races during an election year, the total spending would only be around $10 per eligible voter. As a nation we spend much more on goods such as ice cream, lottery tickets, and Barbie dolls. These goods are in some sense trivial when compared with the impact of politics on our lives.

Another argument against most proposed campaign finance reforms is that campaign contributions are protected by the First Amendment to the Constitution as a form of political free speech. Donors are simply" voicing" their support for the candidate of their choice, just as campaign volunteers and those that write letters to the editor do.

Regulation of campaign finance is also a tricky constitutional and practical matter. Third-party candidates, who do not have the expert staffs and extensive donor lists of the major parties, consider current regulations unfair and burdensome. Recent elections have shown that major-party candidates can evade regulations by raising "soft money," which is donated to their political parties but used to support their campaign. Interest groups can avoid spending limits by producing their own "issue ads" that indirectly support their candidate. It seems that regulation produces a new set of problems for the electoral process.

We must be careful, though, in assessing logrolling. Its general efficiency depends on the political setting. Most legislatures, for example, are formed on the basis of geographic representation, under which a representative's constituents have one thing in common: They all reside in the same area. Any bill the representative can get through the legislature that benefits the members of her district should win votes at election time. In effect, a geographically based system provides the legislator with incentives to represent local interests in the national legislature at the expense of broader national issues.

Most individuals in a community share an interest in the vitality of the community's economy. In many instances, a bloc of voters from a single voting district may receive income from a single firm or industry, as in a company town or in geographically concentrated industries like the steel, automobile, lumber, defense, and regional agricultural industries. When economic activity is concentrated, representatives can win political support by serving the economic interests of their respective home districts. Tariffs, industry- and company-oriented tax concessions and subsidies, local public works projects, and defense contracts are all examples of issues that often are decided, in part, on the basis of their economic impact on certain regions.

Representatives therefore trade their support on national issues, such as air pollution control, for support on amendments or separate bills that serve their local interests. National legislation often becomes a vehicle for local support, and the result is pork-barrel legislation that carries rich rewards for specific locales. Logrolling, which attempts to redistribute income toward certain regions and industries, generally does not lead to a more productive economy. Rather, it leads to legislation such as individual industry tariffs, unnecessary and costly public works legislation, and special-interest tax "reform" bills. This form of logrolling at the national level is unproductive not because it reveals relative intensities of preferences on national issues, but because in its most blatant forms it reveals relative intensities of preference on essentially local issues. When restricted to national issues, however, logrolling can be a beneficial means for revealing voter preferences. For example, the voters of one senator's state may prefer more foreign aid for Latin America, while the voters in another's state may strongly favor increasing Social Security benefits to the elderly. The necessary legislation for both issues may be passed with the exchange of the senators' votes, thereby indirectly promoting voters' preferences.

Voting

In Chapter 6 we discussed whether voting was rational. Simply put, one voter out of many has very little impact on any election. Therefore, even if the marginal costs of voting—the time it takes to register and go to the polls—are very low, it may be too costly for the average voter to vote. The voter is rational; he or she will vote when the marginal benefits exceed the marginal costs of voting. If an election is predicted to be close, the marginal benefit of voting will rise, and voter turnout will rise.

In this section we examine the act of voting in more detail by discussing some of the relevant differences between the market and voting as means to allocate resources. We compare consumer behavior within market institutions and voter behavior within political institutions.

1. *In markets, consumers make marginal choices; in politics, voters must evaluate package deals.* When you buy carrots or hot dogs, you can buy one more or one less; that is, you engage in marginal decision making. When you vote for a politician or a party, you vote not for a single issue but for a package or a platform—a form of all-or-none decision making. Politicians do not offer voters a little more or a little less of this or that public program. They offer package deals.

Political decisions at the national level take place within the Congress of the United States.

This feature of voter choice makes voting complex and costly. Moreover, when people are forced to make package choices, they are likely to end up choosing a lot of items that they really do not want in order to get a few things that they do want.

2. *Elections generally involve the choice of numerous candidates and issues.* In addition to the packaged nature of political choice, the voter has to make a variety of choices at the same time; many candidates and issues are on the ballot. To some extent, this is efficient. It is better to vote on many things at once than to vote on a lot of individual matters in separate elections. Clearly, economies of scale accrue in voting. But having numerous candidates and issues on the ballot also leads to greater complexity and cost in voter choice.

3. *Consumption is frequent and repetitive; voting is infrequent and irregular.* The consumer goes grocery shopping weekly or daily; the voter votes every year or every two or four years. This infrequency makes it more difficult for the voter to find reliable policies and candidates. Imagine how the grocery-buying decision would be altered if you bought groceries once a year. Your ability to discard bad products and try new ones would be reduced dramatically.

4. *The primary difference between voting and the market, deriving from the preceding three factors, is that voters have little incentive to be informed.* Voting is

more complicated than market choice. This means that voters have little incentive to gather information about their public choices. In market choice, consumers have direct and strong incentives to gather information and to search for useful, reliable products. In public choice, voters have difficulty evaluating candidates and issues. The costs of being informed are high. How can the average voter hope to obtain the information needed to make rational decisions about proposals for dams, foreign aid, welfare, relations with China, the money supply, jobs, and so on? Voters are quite rationally uninformed about such matters; they estimate that the costs exceed the benefits of being fully informed. Indeed, they may free ride by not gathering information, not voting, and letting those who do vote make the choices for them. If the choices of other voters happen to be beneficial to nonvoters, the nonvoters benefit without bearing any of the costs. This behavior leads to a fifth and final implication.

5. *Since voters are not well informed, the information transmitted to politicians by elections is not very useful in helping politicians determine what voters want.* Politicians predictably have great difficulty assessing the implications of an election with respect to what voters want them to do. Politicians who are good at reading the public's pulse will survive and be reelected. Nevertheless, the transmission of information is not direct. In markets, if consumers want more carrots, they can effectively transmit this information to producers and get more carrots. In voting, if consumers want more domestic spending and less defense spending, it is costly and hard to make this preference known to politicians.

Interest Groups

Interest groups
Collections of individuals with one or more common characteristics, such as occupation, who seek collectively to affect legislation or government policy so as to benefit members of the group.

As we discussed in Chapter 4, the behavior of **interest groups** helps explain a significant amount of government activity. To see how interest groups affect government policy, consider the process by which a group of florists might organize to advance their interests.

Organization is the most fundamental difficulty facing the florists. The individual florist has every incentive to remain outside the interest group. Why? Because the success of the group at some objective—say, raising prices—will "spill over" to the florist who "free rides" and obtains benefits without paying a fee. Free-riding behavior makes the formation of interest groups difficult but by no means impossible. Interest groups seek ways to limit the benefits of their activities to members only for such reasons.

Assume that the florists organize. Representatives of the florist group go to the state legislature and use all means at their disposal to obtain a legally sanctioned florists' cartel. The cartel's primary purpose is protection; that is, to protect florists from new competition by creating entry barriers into the florist business. This entry control allows florists to price their wares above the costs of production. Government is petitioned to increase the wealth of florists, but at the expense of flower product demanders. The florists are, in effect, demanders of a wealth transfer from the state.

If the organized florists are the demanders of the wealth transfer, who are the potential suppliers? Flower consumers are the suppliers of the transfer. These consumers do not find it worthwhile to organize and to resist having their wealth taken away by the florist-demanders. Of course, this is a nontraditional concept of supply, but it is a clear supply concept. Consumers of flowers and florist services—the suppliers of wealth—do not find it in their interest to spend money to protest the florists' proposals. The cost would exceed the benefit. It may cost the individual (average) consumer $200 to defeat the florists' plan to bring about a $20 cost savings. Why spend $200 to save $20?

This example describes a "demand" and a "supply" of wealth transfers in the case of florists. (It is exactly analogous to the case described for barbers in Chapter 4.) What are the features of the market for wealth transfers? Politicians are brokers in this market and in the **market for legislation.** Politicians in effect pair up demanders and suppliers of wealth transfers. A miscalculation—a transfer of too much or too little wealth—will mean that they will be replaced at the next election by more efficient brokers.

Results for the florists are described in Figure 18.2. Assume that florists begin as a purely competitive industry, producing Q_c flower arrangements per year at a price of P_c. Due to the establishment of their interest group, the legislature is persuaded to grant them cartel status. Persuasion of the legislature is facilitated because the consumers who are harmed by the cartel do not find it worthwhile to protest to the legislators. Florists are the only ones to be heard, and perhaps by putting their arguments for a cartel in public-interest terms ("inferior flowers must be driven from the market," "there's chaos in the market for flowers," and so on), they carry the day with the legislature.

The legislators assess the costs and benefits of creating a flower cartel. In Figure 18.2, the florists seek P_gABP_c in cartel profits at the expense of consumers'

Market for legislation

The interaction between interest groups acting as demanders of legislation beneficial to the group and legislators acting as suppliers of legislation; legislation generally entails some type of wealth transfer.

FIGURE 18.2

How an Interest Group's Demands Are Met

P_c is the competitive price that the industry charges, and P_g is the price established by the group after it is granted cartel status. After the cartel is formed, it stands to gain P_gABP_c in profit from consumers, and consumers stand to lose ACB in welfare. In some cases, the former wealth transfer dominates the latter welfare loss, and a law is passed sanctioning the cartel.

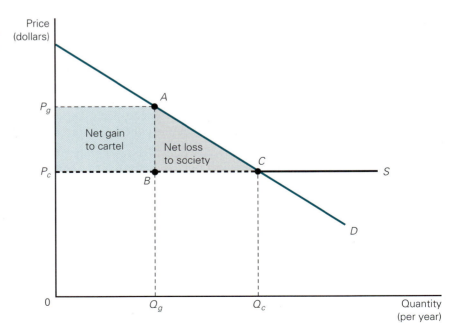

welfare; flower consumers also incur an additional loss equal to *ACB*. (Area *ACB* represents the welfare loss due to monopoly discussed in both Chapter 4 and Chapter 9. The per capita gains to florists, who are a relatively small number of producers, exceed the per capita costs to the more numerous flower consumers. The result: The legislature passes a law giving the florists a cartel (and, perhaps, the florists make campaign contributions to the legislators who supported their cartel bill).

However, this discussion is highly stylized. Interest groups do not always work as producers versus consumers. Technically, any group can organize and act as an interest group. There are labor unions; women's rights groups; religious groups; trade associations; and organizations for doctors, lawyers, hunters, environmentalists, and farmers. Moreover, not all of these groups are small. Many large groups, such as farmers, are effectively organized as an interest group. And not all interest groups seek money transfers from government; some seek increases in utility or satisfaction from the passage of a particular public policy. However, the basic point is that you can begin to explain why a certain law is passed if you try to answer two questions: Who wins? and Who loses? The Focus "Economics of the Birds and the Bees" presents an example of how the demands of interest groups result in government subsidies that are not justified on economic grounds.

Bureaucracy

Bureaus

The arms of government that serve to implement and enforce legislation and to administer programs created by legislation.

While legislatures enact laws and authorize levels of public spending, the actual implementation of those laws is delegated to a variety of agencies, commonly referred to as **bureaus.** Created by the legislature, bureaus are generally supportive of the legislature's interests. Bureau employees generally fare better as the bureaus' budgets expand because, among other things, opportunities for promotion expand and, with them, salaries. At the same time, legislators have strong interests in the enactment of legislation that will be implemented by bureaus. Consequently, bureaus and the legislative committees with which they deal generally have similar interests.

As organizations engaged in the supply of services, public bureaus differ from private firms in two important respects. These differences in turn lead to important differences between the conduct of bureaus and the conduct of firms.[2]

1. Bureaus derive revenue from legislative appropriations, which in turn come from tax collections. By contrast, firms derive revenue from the voluntary buying decisions of customers.

2. There are no transferable ownership rights in public bureaus. In bureaus, there is no status comparable to that of stockholders, the residual recipients of dif-

---

[2] See, for example, Ludwig von Mises, *Bureaucracy* (New Haven, Conn.: Yale University Press, 1944); Gordon Tullock, *The Politics of Bureaucracy* (Washington, D.C.: Public Affairs Press, 1965); Anthony Downs, *Inside Bureaucracy* (Boston: Little, Brown, 1967); and William A. Niskanen, *Bureaucracy and Representative Government* (Chicago: Aldine-Atherton, 1971).

FOCUS

Economics of the Birds and the Bees

Everyone knows that birds, bees, butterflies, and a host of other creatures are important for the pollination of plants, including an estimated $10 billion worth of crops per year. For example, bees pollinate fruit and nut trees and thus provide a positive externality to the owner of orchards.

The problem arises if not enough bees are available in nature. Fruit and nut production will be reduced. Economists used the example of the bees and apple orchards as a prime example of this type of market failure—low bee populations and reduced pollination. In 1952, the federal government responded to bee and orchard interest groups. An interest rate subsidy was established for beekeepers to increase the number of beekeepers and to foster the joint production of bees (honey) and fruit farming. The subsidy affects 3000 to 5000 beekeepers in about a half-dozen states.

Economist Steven Cheung examined the market for bees and found that the case for government subsidies was a "fable" and that elaborate and effective contracts between beekeepers and farmers were routine and effective in overcoming the supposed market failure.[a] Cheung found that some plants produce much nectar but did not require pollination, that other crops require bees for pollination but produce little surplus nectar for honey, and still other crops yield high amounts of nectar and require pollination. He found that the contracts and rental fees for bees reflected both pollination requirements and nectar production.

In 1990, the General Accounting Office of Congress agreed that the subsidy was unnecessary and that fruit and nut growers who needed bees could buy or rent them. There was no market failure; there was a failure to examine the market. In 1993, the $16 million subsidy to beekeepers was eliminated.

---

[a]Steven N. S. Cheung, "The Fable of the Bees: An Economic Investigation," *Journal of Law and Economics* 16 (1973), pp. 11–33.

---

ferences between revenues and expenses. Although there may be profits in the operation of bureaus, these profits do not show up as residual income to residual claimants or owners. Rather than being converted to personal use, any differences between revenue and expense disappear through added expenditures. For example, at the end of each fiscal year in Washington, bureaus with funds left over try to find ways to spend the funds—which helps explain why many large research grants are made at the end of the fiscal year.

The difference in incentives between private and public decision making yields many familiar results. It is often more difficult to register a car or get a passport than it is to buy an automobile or plane ticket. It is more difficult to buy alcoholic beverages from a state-franchised liquor store than from a private firm. Under government operation, a bureau's hours of operation are usually shorter than those of private businesses and, hence, less convenient to customers. There is also a reluctance on the part of bureaus to accept checks and credit cards.

Without the profit-maximizing incentives of private business, there are numerous ways that the indirect appropriation of excess funds through higher expenditures can take place within bureaus. Different public bureaus face different opportunities for appropriating profits. A public hospital, for instance, may overinvest in equipment that is underutilized. A highway department may award contracts without competitive bidding and pay higher prices than necessary. Since excess funds cannot be appropriated directly, they are appropriated indirectly, as these funds are dissipated through expenditures.

One main difference between a private firm and a public bureau lies in the identification of the customer. For private firms, the people who use the good or service are the customers whose continued favor is essential for the firm's success. The public bureau's customers, however, are not the people who queue up for space at a public campground or who try to get efficient service at the motor vehicle department. Although the bureau provides services to those people, the public bureau's customer actually is the legislature because it is responsible for the bureau's existence through legislation and funding. To remain in existence and to be successful, the bureau must please the legislature.

To some extent, of course, the legislature reflects the interests of citizens. But we must distinguish between the special interests of particular citizens and the interests of citizens in general. In cases where a bureau's performance pursues special interests, those special interests may represent a quite different set of people from those who use the bureau's service. For legislation to reward some special interests, it must penalize other, general interests. The often poor performance of public bureaus is another feature of a special-interest approach to government; this performance may not be so poor viewed from the perspective of the bureau's true customers—the special interests that benefit from the legislation.

CONSTITUTIONAL POLITICAL ECONOMY

A normative branch of public choice theory is called constitutional economics or political economy. This is an important area of analysis that takes us beyond the world of ordinary, everyday politics. That is, in a constitutional democracy there are two levels of political decision making: day-to-day decisions about running the government, which are made under given rules and procedures, and decisions about the rules and procedures themselves. The first level of decision making takes place under given political constraints. The second involves the choice of the constraints themselves, which amounts to selecting a constitution or the set of rules under which day-to-day government operates. For example, the choice of whether to employ simply majority voting or some other system would be a constitutional choice, while voting on current issues with the chosen voting system would be part of the day-to-day process of running the government.

Constitutional decision making
The process of choosing which set of rules (voting rules, for example) society will adopt for its use.

Public choice theory can be applied to an analysis of **constitutional decision making.**[3] As an illustration, we will analyze the choice of a voting rule for the legislature. We assume that the constitutional decision makers are unbiased and impartial (a large assumption). Figure 18.3 illustrates the analysis.

---

[3] This analysis was first developed by James M. Buchanan, the Nobel laureate in economics for 1986, and Gordon Tullock, *The Calculus of Consent* (Ann Arbor: University of Michigan Press, 1962).

FIGURE 18.3

Constitutional Choice

Curves D and E represent the expected costs facing the constitutional decision maker. D represents the costs of collective decision making; as the number of voters increases, D increases at an increasing rate. E is the cost of a decision rule requiring less than unanimity. Summing the two curves ($D + E$) and taking the minimum point gives the optimal voting rule chosen by the constitutional decision maker. N_1 represents the optimal number of individuals in the society of N persons who must agree before a collective decision is made. N_1 may be any number. Here it is a simple majority, $(N/2) + 1$.

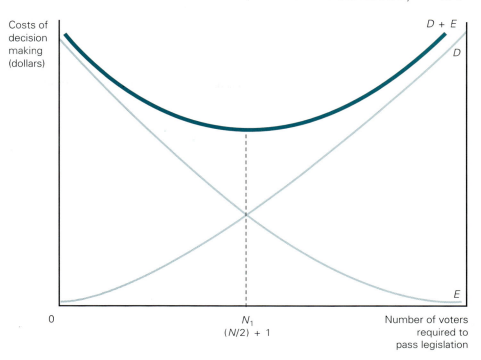

Costs of decision making (dollars)

$D + E$

D

E

N_1
$(N/2) + 1$

Number of voters required to pass legislation

The horizontal axis measures a number of people N, all the members of a hypothetical society; N can also be thought of as all the voters in the society. The vertical axis is a measure in dollars of the expected costs of the various voting rules that could be selected for the society. Examples of these costs will be presented shortly.

Constitutional decision makers face the following problem: How do they choose the voting rule that minimizes the expected cost of collective decision making in this society? The answer to the question can be found by examining the D curve and the E curve in Figure 18.3. The D curve measures the costs of collective decision making. As the voting rule is made more inclusive—requiring, for example, a two-thirds vote rather than a simple majority for approval or defeat of an issue—the costs of reaching collective decisions increase. In fact, as more people are required for agreement, the D curve increases at an increasing rate. This is a logical result in any group decision process. More people require more discussion, larger meetings, more bargaining, and so on. Agreement is more costly to obtain in a larger group.

The E curve reflects the potential costs that a collective decision can impose on the individual affected by the decision. If very few people are required to agree on a measure, agreement will occur more frequently, and E-type costs will be high. In other words, a small number of people could get together and pass measures that benefit them at the expense of other voters. If a unanimity rule prevails, however, requiring that all members of the legislature must agree before a tax can be passed, then *E*-type costs to any individual will be zero. Under these conditions, no collective decision can be made unless every voter consents. Unanimity means that one person can block a collective decision.

We have, then, the two major categories of costs related to the choice of a voting rule by constitutional decision makers. The minimum of the two costs can be found by vertically summing the *D* and *E* functions and picking the minimum point on that curve. This occurs at N_1 in Figure 18.3. In this society, the two types of voting costs are minimized where N_1 persons are required to agree before a collective decision is made. N_1 may be any number. It may, for example, be a simple majority voting rule—$(N/2) + 1$ in Figure 18.3—or it may be a stricter voting rule in which more than a simple majority agreement is required before a collective decision is made. Though stricter voting rules involve higher *D*-type costs, the prospect of lower *E*-type costs could easily make stricter voting rules an important route to the improvement of collective decision procedures. What would happen, for example, if every proposal for a public expenditure had to carry with it a proposal for the taxes to finance it and, moreover, to pass the legislature with a majority of seven-eighths?

Constitutional political economy thus examines the rules and procedures of politics in an effort to improve the way societies make their public choices. As such, this type of work by economists and political scientists is critical and important.

The theory of public choice represents an expansion of normal economic analysis into the realm of politics. This area of research will undoubtedly attract the attention of economic researchers in the future. Hopefully, work in this area will enhance our understanding of how the political process works and how it can be made to better serve the interests of the average citizen.

APPLICATION

Registering Minority Votes

We explored the problems of *majority* voting in this chapter. What about the interests of *minorities*? How do they fare under majority rule?

Imagine the simplest of all democratic processes: a local referendum to increase the property tax by a relatively small amount and to use the funds to build a new school. This situation can easily lend itself to a problem of neglected minority interests. For example, a majority of voters may not have children and may be slightly opposed to the measure because of the small tax increase that accompanies it. The parents of school-age children may be intensely in favor of the tax–school package because of the poor condition of the existing school. Despite their strong concern, the parents lose to a relatively indifferent majority in the defeat of the referendum. Conversely, one could envisage a situation in which the parents are in the majority, the proposed tax increase is substantial, the present school is in good condition, and the nonparents feel tyrannized by the passage of the tax–school referendum because it promises more costs than benefits for them. In one person/one vote majority rule, unless all voters have an equal expected gain or loss from the outcome of an issue, voting may not accurately reflect the underlying intensities of voter preferences.

To clarify the example further, look at the distribution of potential gains for two voters over a set of issues, shown graphically in Figure 18.4. The height of each curve is a measure of the potential gain to a voter from a favorable outcome on a

FIGURE 18.4

The Minority Voting Problem

Utility curves A and B measure the intensity of preference of two voters or two groups of voters across issues. The B group feels more strongly about each issue than the A group. A one person/one vote majority rule does not register this different intensity of feeling in voting outcomes. Point voting, when each voter is given a certain number of votes to allocate among all issues, may be a solution to this problem.

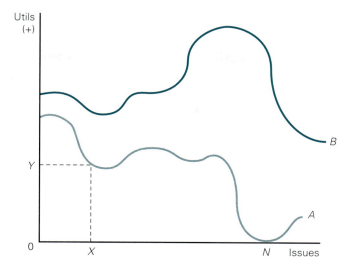

particular issue (a favorable outcome may represent either the passage of a desired bill or defeat of an undesired bill). To avoid the problem of minority interest under majority rule, each voter must have exactly the same utility curve. For example, all voters must experience a Y gain from the outcome on issue X. If 51 percent of the voters have a utility curve like A and 49 percent have a curve like B, the A's will win on every issue even if the B's feel more strongly in each case. Majority rule is disadvantageous to minorities in this case and does not lead to voting outcomes that reflect the preferences of all the voters.

The problem is that no mechanism exists by which minorities and majorities can vote according to their differing intensities of feelings on issues. When voters have only one vote per issue, this vote represents a different underlying amount of gain or loss to majority and minority voters.

Suppose, however, that instead of having one vote on each issue, each voter is given 1000 votes and is asked to allocate them in proportion to his or her preferences over a wide number of issues. If issue J provides 7 times as much benefit as issue K, the voter allocates 7 times as many votes to it. Voting would consist of each voter's filling out a form indicating how the 1000 votes are to be assigned to each issue and whether the voter casts them for or against each issue. The issues would be decided by totaling the votes over all voters and passing all the issues that receive more yes votes than no votes.

This *point voting system* gives accurate information about the relative intensities of each voter's preferences over the various issues and makes it unnecessary for all voters to have the same utility curve. Stated in economic terms, point voting reveals individuals' marginal rates of substitution among issues, analogous to marginal rates of substitution among private goods. In other words, point voting for public issues is like the process of consumer equilibrium discussed in Chapter 6. The consumer allocates his or her fixed number of dollar votes in such a way as to establish equal marginal rates of substitution across goods. Point voting provides the voter with the opportunity to do the same with public issues.

Point voting is a possible solution to the problem that minority interests are not registered under one person/one vote majority rule. No voting system is perfect, however. The voting scheme that accurately reflects the preferences of all voters in final voting outcomes has yet to be invented. One of the key jobs of the public choice analyst is therefore to analyze voting systems and seek improvements in them.

QUESTION

It is well known that different cities provide different levels of public goods such as education, street repair, police and fire services, and so on. Individual citizens, however, do not value different "packages" of public goods in the same manner. One response to the situation is to move to other cities when those other cities offer a more satisfactory package. Describe conditions of local public goods supply under which you might prefer one city over another.

Source: Dennis C. Mueller, Robert D. Tollison, and Thomas D. Willett, "Solving the Intensity Problem in Representative Democracy," in Ryan C. Amacher, Robert D. Tollison, and Thomas D. Willett, *The Economic Approach to Public Policy* (Ithaca, N.Y.: Cornell University Press, 1976), pp. 444–473.

SUMMARY

1. Public choice analysis is the study of government with the tools of economics. It treats government decision makers like private decision makers—as rationally self-interested actors.

2. Public choice theorists assume that government officials maximize their individual interests, not the "public interest." In the process, they face different constraints than private decision makers, and so they behave differently.

3. Normative public choice analysis evaluates the effectiveness with which political institutions represent the preferences of voters, focusing on the evaluation of voting rules.

4. Voting on issues two at a time by majority rule can lead to a voting cycle where there is no clear winner, even though each individual voter knows clearly which candidate he or she prefers.

5. Positive public choice analysis seeks to present testable theories of government behavior. It is analogous to positive economics applied to politics.

6. In political competition the median voter is the controlling force. Parties and candidates compete by taking middle-of-the-road positions.

7. Logrolling, or vote trading, reveals relative intensities of preference across issues. When combined with geographic representation, however, logrolling can lead to an overexpansion of local public projects.

8. Voting and the market are two different means of allocating resources. For a variety of reasons, voters have little incentive to be informed in making voting decisions. As a result, voting is an imperfect mechanism for allocating resources.

9. Interest groups seek wealth transfers from government. Successful interest groups win transfers at the expense of general efficiency in the economy.

10. Bureaucracy is the production and management side of government. Unlike private production, government production takes place in a not-for-profit environment. As a consequence, bureaucrats behave differently from private decision makers.

11. Constitutional political economy represents a branch of public choice that describes the process of choosing sets of rules, such as voting rules, that society adopts to use in making collective decisions.

KEY TERMS

public choice
normative public choice
positive public choice
proprietary

nonproprietary
logrolling
interest groups
market for legislation

bureaus
constitutional decision making

QUESTIONS FOR REVIEW AND DISCUSSION

1. What is a voting cycle? What conditions cause a voting cycle?

2. What is logrolling? What are the benefits and costs of logrolling?

3. Name three differences between voting and the market as mechanisms for allocating resources.

4. What is the difference between a public bureau and a private firm as a productive unit?

5. Discuss three experiences you have had in dealing with government that can be explained by the not-for-profit nature of government production.

6. Suppose that the size of government is declining relative to the size of the economy. Apply public choice theory to explain how this might happen.

7. Using the median voter model of voter preferences discussed in the chapter, explain why Democratic presidential candidates are more liberal in the primaries than in the general election.

8. Why do we not observe voting cycles in the U.S. House of Representatives?

9. In public choice theory, what is the fundamental assumption regarding the behavior of politicians and bureaucrats?

10. What is the primary problem with majority voting? Explain.

11. What role do interest groups play in the market for legislation? What do they hope to gain from the legislative process?

PROBLEM

Suppose that ten members of a large family jointly own a vacation home. The family is trying to decide whether to build a swimming pool on the property. Building and maintaining the pool will cost $3000 per year, and each family member must pay an equal amount to cover the expenses of the pool. The table shows the dollar value of the benefits that each family member would receive each year from the pool.

a. Find the annual cost per person of the pool and then determine the net benefits or costs of the pool per year for each family member.

b. If each family member's vote is determined by his or her net benefits or costs, which family members will vote for the pool and which family members will vote against the pool? Will the pool be built?

c. When the total costs and benefits are considered, does this project represent an efficient use of resources?

Family Member	Annual Benefits
A	$450
B	0
C	65
D	400
E	350
F	150
G	0
H	650
I	385
J	420

WORKING WITH THE WEB

1. The issue of campaign funding is a controversial one, as described in the Focus "Can You Buy an Election?" Go to http://www.pbs.org/wgbh/pages/frontline/president to read more about the issue and select the link "The Money Charts."
   a. Which candidate in the 1996 election raised the most money? Where did billionaire candidate Steve Forbes land on the money list?
   b. Which industries put most of their support behind Texas Senator Phil Gramm?
   c. Which industry had the largest amount of campaign contributions to a candidate? Which candidate was the recipient of this generosity?
   d. What special-interest group was the largest contributor to the Democratic National Committee? Which group was the largest contributor to the Republican National Committee?
   e. At this point, we all know Democratic candidate Bill Clinton won the election. Did the Democratic National Committee have a greater level of donations than the Republican National Committee? Does this imply the election was bought?

2. The impact of interest groups in politics is well known. Clearly, different interest groups seek different benefits from government, ranging from money transfers to favorable legislation. To see the influence of Political Action Committees (PACs) in campaign funding in 1997–1998, go to http://www.opensecrets.org/pacs. At this site you will find a listing of the various PACs. Under each category, summary as well as complete statistics are listed.
   a. The tobacco industry was under heavy criticism in 1998. The link for the tobacco PACs can be found under "Agriculture." How did the level of contributions from tobacco PACs vary across Democrats and Republicans? Why do you think the tobacco PACs contributed in this manner?
   b. Another industry that has strong PACs on each side of the issue is the gun industry, where there are both gun control advocates and gun rights advocates. Review the statistics of the Gun Control PAC as well as the Gun Rights PAC (both appear under the heading "Ideological/Single Issue"). Which PAC contributed more to candidates in 1997–1998? What is the largest single PAC (in terms of total financial contribution) within both the Gun Control and Gun Rights PACs?

3. Which single PAC in the Computer Equipment & Services category was the largest contributor in 1997–1998? In light of what you learned in Chapter 16 as well as what you have learned in the current chapter about interest groups and the public choice approach to politics, is this surprising?

Ronald Coase

A. C. Pigou
and
Ronald Coase:
Solving
the Problem
of Social Costs

A. C. Pigou

Arthur Cecil Pigou (1877–1959), an English economist, succeeded Alfred Marshall in the chair of political economy at Cambridge University in 1908. Like Marshall, Pigou had been drawn to economics because of its social importance. Both men were deeply interested in improving the living standards of the poor. Both had great faith in the power of economics to improve the welfare of all members of society. Pigou and Marshall disagreed, however, on the proper role of government. Like his neoclassical peers, Marshall advocated laissez-faire policies, whereas Pigou felt that government's power to tax and redistribute wealth among all members of society was a crucial ingredient of general economic prosperity.

Pigou held his prestigious position at Cambridge for more than thirty-five years. During this period he wrote several books, including *Wealth and Welfare, The Economics of Welfare,* and *The Theory of Unemployment.* His students at Cambridge included Joan Robinson and John Maynard Keynes. Pigou continued to be productive after his retirement from Cambridge in 1943. For many, his death in 1959 marked the end of the English neoclassical tradition in economics, a tradition begun in the 1870s.

Ronald Coase (b. 1910) has earned international recognition for his papers "The Nature of the Firm" (*Economica,* November 1937) and "The Problem of Social Cost" (*Journal of Law and Economics,* October 1960). Modern theories of the firm and of externalities owe much to the work of this English-born economist. Coase's novel economic analysis of institutions, particularly the law of business, has helped spawn a new area of economic inquiry, much of which has challenged traditional views of how government and government regulations affect the behavior of firms. Coase has written extensively on utilities, broadcasting, and other government-regulated monopolies. He is generally critical of the effects of regulatory law, believing that solutions to market failure can and do exist outside of government intervention. Coase was awarded the Nobel Prize in economics in 1991. He is professor emeritus of economics at the University of Chicago. He has held posts at the University of Buffalo and the University of Virginia.

Taxing the Smoke

Pigou pioneered the modern microeconomic theories of externalities and market failure. In *The Economics of Welfare* he distinguished between private costs of production—the operating and maintenance costs of producers—and social costs of production—the expense or damage to society that results from the producer's activity. There are many possible illustrations of social costs. A nuclear power plant's social costs include the potential danger of radiation to the surrounding community. A railroad's social costs might include the danger of fire caused by sparks from its wheels. Pigou's own example of private and social costs is a smoke-belching factory. The factory owner's private costs derive mainly from the people and machines that make up the factory. The social costs of the factory derive from the smoke the factory produces as a by-product of its operation. The smoke from the factory soils clothing and property nearby, creates a noxious odor, and poses a health risk to the community.

Pigou pointed out that there is nothing in the economic forces of market supply and demand to prevent the factory owner from continuing and even increasing the pollution. Since the market, in essence, permits the owner to shift part of the costs (the smoke) onto others, the owner will likely protect this advantage.

Pigou also sought to prove that market failure resulted in inefficient resource allocation. According to Pigou's theory, the factory owner will try to manage production so that the marginal private costs of the factory equal the price of the product. Pigou pointed out that by doing so, however, the owner is not responding to the true costs of production. Since the owner's private costs are less than the full (private plus social) costs of production, the owner will produce "too much" output. If, however, the owner managed production so that private plus social costs equaled price, the excess output would be eliminated, and all resources would be allocated according to their true opportunity cost.

To remedy the inequities and inefficiencies of market failure, Pigou proposed a tax on polluters and other sources of social costs. In the case of a smoke-belching factory, the tax would depend on the amount of smoke produced and would force the owner to restrict pollution to the point at which the benefits of production were equal to its true costs. Such a tax would also restrict output. In this way, both producers and consumers would share the costs of the tax.

Assigning Liability

In his 1960 article "The Problem of Social Cost," Ronald Coase challenged Pigou's major assumption that social costs always move in one direction—from producer to society. In fact, Coase argued, the issue of social costs poses potential harm to both parties. On the one hand, society may be harmed by the unwanted by-products of production, and on the other hand, producers may be harmed by society's attempt to correct the market failure through taxation. In terms of Pigou's example, should the factory owner be allowed to pollute the local community, or should the local community be allowed to drive up the factory's costs of production by forcing it to cease polluting? The issue is especially pertinent today in the debate over acid rain and toxic waste.

Coase argued that an efficient solution to the problem of social costs would involve negotiation between the polluter and those affected by the pollution. If it were possible for both sides to negotiate, then a market might be created between them. The two sides could "trade" for the right to the pollution: Either the factory would pay the local community for the right to pollute or the community would pay the factory not to pollute. Coase showed that the actual outcome of such negotiations would be the same regardless of which side had the "right" to use the atmosphere as it saw fit.

In the real world, such negotiations between parties help solve a variety of potential social cost problems. For example, restaurant customers have influenced restaurants to segregate smokers from nonsmokers, eliminating the social cost of tobacco smoke. Home buyers shopping for a house near an airport can negotiate for a lower price to offset the social cost of airplane noise.

Often, both sides in the dispute face enormous transaction costs to enter such negotiations. A community, for instance, might find it very costly to organize into a bargaining unit with a nearby factory. The millions of people affected by acid rain and the hundreds of producers responsible for the pollution could hardly transact freely. In such instances Coase suggested that the parties look to the courts, not the legislature, for a solution. Courts could determine the relative costs involved and could assign liability, or responsibility, to the party whose costs of adjusting to the social cost are lower.

For example, who should be responsible for injuries and death resulting from the use of defective products? For a long time, the rule of *caveat emptor,* or "let the buyer beware," prevailed in the courts, and the consumer was fully responsible for the safe use of products. Such a rule worked reasonably well in times when products were relatively simple in design and use. However, as products become more complex, consumers may not be able to judge their safety and reliability. As a result, the courts have gradually increased the range of cases in which producers are held liable for shoddy and dangerous merchandise. This shift in the legal posture of the courts is an illustration of the Coase idea at work: The legal system alters liability assignment in response to the relative costs of adjusting to social costs.

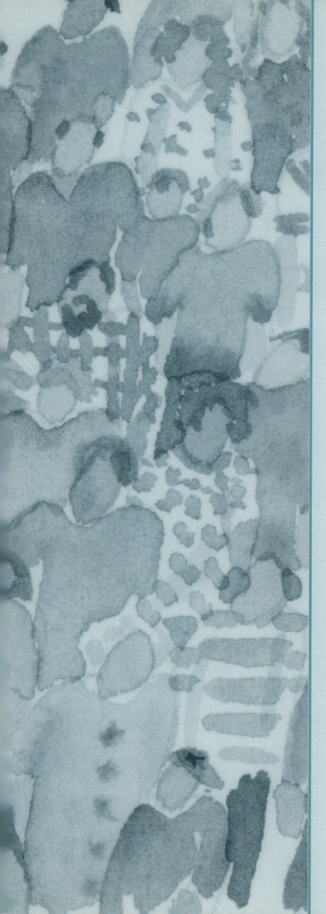

PART FIVE

The Fundamentals of Macroeconomics

5

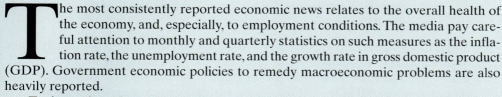

Contemporary Macroeconomics

The most consistently reported economic news relates to the overall health of the economy, and, especially, to employment conditions. The media pay careful attention to monthly and quarterly statistics on such measures as the inflation rate, the unemployment rate, and the growth rate in gross domestic product (GDP). Government economic policies to remedy macroeconomic problems are also heavily reported.

Topics such as the real rate of growth in the economy may seem abstract and distant, but they do have an immediate and lasting impact on individual economic well-being. Economists have spent more than 200 years seeking to understand how conditions in the macroeconomy—the economy as a whole—shape our lives.

Think for a moment about how the major macroeconomic issues—inflation, unemployment, and growth—are likely to influence your future. Will economic conditions affect your ability to repay your college loan? Will you enter the job market during a time of high unemployment? Will your hopes for a high-paying job, a comfortable home, a promising future for your children be realized? How will government deficits or surpluses affect your future economic welfare? The study of macroeconomics can better equip you to plan for the future. This chapter presents an overview of basic macroeconomic policy goals and introduces much of the terminology employed by macroeconomists. When you complete Chapter 19 you should understand

- the overall goals of macroeconomic policy and the trade-offs among goals.
- the nature of unemployment and inflation, and their effects on economic growth.

- how, in general terms, fiscal and monetary policies are used to achieve the goals of macroeconomic policy.
- the essential tools of aggregate demand and aggregate supply that economists use to analyze the macroeconomy.

THE GOALS OF MACROECONOMICS

In Chapter 1 we defined *macroeconomics* as the analysis of the economy as a whole. When working with macroeconomic theory, the focus is on what economists call aggregate quantities. Macroeconomics concerns not just one market but all markets; not just one price change but all price changes; not just one firm's employees but all employment.

As with any discipline, the field of macroeconomics is made up of many specialized areas, competing theories, and ongoing debates. Consistent throughout macroeconomics, however, is a shared set of goals. Both macroeconomists and the politicians who heed (or disregard) their advice are interested in achieving three separate, sometimes conflicting, objectives: full employment, price stability, and economic growth. Indeed, economists are at the ready as advisers in how government might achieve these goals (see the Application "One-Handed Economists: The President's Council of Economic Advisers" at the conclusion of this chapter). We discuss each of these goals separately, but you will soon see that they are closely intertwined.

The Full-Employment Goal

Full employment is a primary goal of any economic society for obvious reasons. The more fully resources are employed, the greater the levels of output of goods and services, and the higher the prosperity.

Social Concern over Unemployment   Not only does high unemployment threaten to bring poverty to millions of citizens, but it also can lead to political upheaval. During the Great Depression of the 1930s, for example, signs of social and political unrest appeared in the United States. Farmers marched on Washington, D.C., makeshift camps of the poor and out-of-work dotted the nation's cities, and mass migrations of the jobless from the Dust Bowl of the Midwest to the Promised Land of California took place. When World War II mobilized the economy, full employment was restored before serious political and social upheaval could erupt.

Other nations of the world have experienced similar upheavals. Consider the frequent changes of government and political systems in developing nations, where poverty—much of it caused by widespread unemployment—is rampant. Increased crime and even violent revolution can result from failure to attain the macroeconomic goal of full employment.

The purely human costs of unemployment on individuals, families, and society itself can be devastating. Unemployment is a primary cause of poverty, dislocations of families, and, in extreme cases, homelessness. It puts extraordinary pressure on social and welfare services that are funded with taxes. More important, unemployment represents resources *not used* to produce goods and services— perhaps the ultimate inefficiency.

In recognition of the social and political implications of unemployment, the U.S. government passed the Employment Act of 1946 on the heels of the Depression and World War II. The act recognized and enshrined maximum employment as a macroeconomic goal of the federal government. The meaning of the term *maximum employment* has been modified in the intervening years, but policy-makers still respect the intent, if not the letter, of the law. Unemployment rates of 10 percent and more, for example, which characterized the U.S. economy in 1982 and 1983, brought great concern to the U.S. Congress and to the Reagan administration. In 1992, unemployment rates of around 8 percent were a factor in the defeat of President George Bush by Bill Clinton. By 1999, the unemployment rate was hovering below 5 percent.

In all nations, the goal of full employment is critical. Social programs such as unemployment compensation and food stamps ease the burden of unemployment, but they cannot substitute for the economic benefits of full employment.

Defining the Levels of Employment and Unemployment

Some unemployment in specific markets is always expected. In a dynamic economy, demand grows for some goods and services and declines for others. In recent years, for example, the demand for high-technology outputs such as microcomputers, lasers, and fiber optics has outpaced demand for the products of heavy industry, and temporary unemployment in heavy industries such as steel and machine tools has been very high. Some workers may develop new skills, however, and temporarily unemployed resources may flow into new areas of production.

From a macroeconomic perspective, there is little reason to be concerned with the temporary periods of unemployment that workers in specific fields experience as the economy undergoes change. In such cases, **unemployed** workers generally remain out of work for relatively brief periods of time before they succeed in obtaining another job. However, there is reason for concern when numerous workers in many different industries simultaneously become unemployed. When this happens, output levels fall far below potential, and families of the unemployed workers experience real hardship over extended periods of time. For this reason, the federal government keeps close tabs on the **unemployment rate** each month.

The labor force is therefore defined as the total of employed and unemployed persons. To calculate the unemployment rate, the number of unemployed persons is divided by the total labor force. Table 19.1 presents data on the unemployment rate, the number of unemployed workers, and the size of the labor force for the period 1975–1998. The Bureau of Labor Statistics also breaks down the unemployment rate into rates for various demographic groups to show the *differing rates* of unemployment for particular groups in the economy. Figure 19.1 shows the total unemployment rate in the U.S. economy for the period 1960–1998 and the corresponding unemployment rates by race, sex, and age. Some facts about the composition of the unemployment rate are apparent: (1) Minority groups have experienced a higher unemployment rate than whites, (2) teenagers in the 16–19 age group have experienced a higher unemployment rate than any other age group, and (3) women over 20 years of age have generally experienced higher unemployment rates than men of the same age.

Despite the presence of unemployment, **full employment** remains a political goal. As we have seen, the Employment Act of 1946 charged the federal government with the responsibility of promoting maximum employment. In 1978, Congress passed the Full Employment and Balanced Growth Act, which committed the government to full employment, defined as an unemployment rate of 4 percent. The goals of the act have been modified (unemployment allowed upward) in the intervening years.

Unemployed
A labor-force status characterized by an individual who is actively seeking employment but is not working.

Unemployment rate
The percentage of the labor force without jobs.

Full employment
A situation in which unemployment exists only because of normal market adjustments to changing demand or supply or to outmoded skills of workers; also a numerical federal government goal for the unemployment rate.

TABLE 19.1

Unemployment, the Unemployment Rate, and the National Labor Force, 1975–1998

The number of unemployed persons, along with the unemployment rate, varies over time. Both the total number and the rate decreased between 1992 and 1995.

Year	Unemployment Rate (percent)	Unemployment (thousands of persons)	Civilian Labor Force (thousands of persons)[a]
1975	8.5	7,929	93,775
1976	7.7	7,406	96,158
1977	7.1	6,991	99,009
1978	6.1	6,202	102,251
1979	5.8	6,137	104,962
1980	7.1	7,637	106,940
1981	7.6	8,273	108,670
1982	9.7	10,678	110,204
1983	9.6	10,717	111,550
1984	7.5	8,539	113,544
1985	7.2	8,312	115,461
1986	7.0	8,237	117,834
1987	6.2	7,425	119,865
1988	5.5	6,701	121,669
1989	5.3	6,528	123,869
1990	5.5	6,874	124,787
1991	6.7	8,426	125,303
1992	7.4	9,384	126,982
1993	6.8	8,734	128,040
1994	6.1	7,996	131,056
1995	5.6	7,404	132,304
1996	5.4	7,236	133,943
1997	4.9	6,739	136,297
1998	4.5	6,210	137,673

Source: Council of Economic Advisers, *Economic Report of the President* (Washington, D.C.: U.S. Government Printing Office, 1999), pp. 368, 376, 378.

[a]Age 16 and over

Natural rate of unemployment

A theoretical concept; the unemployment rate that coexists with macroeconomic stability or labor-market equilibrium in the long run.

How can full employment be defined as allowing for any unemployment? Some economists feel that there is a **natural rate of unemployment** (or employment), the rate that would exist under long-run equilibrium conditions because of the time needed for adjustments in the labor market, the lag in matching vacancies and workers, the costs of hiring and firing and of changing jobs, regulations affecting structural changes in labor markets, and so forth. Market forces and institutions, not individuals, determine the natural rate of unemployment at any given time. The actual rate of unemployment can be compared with the theoretical con-

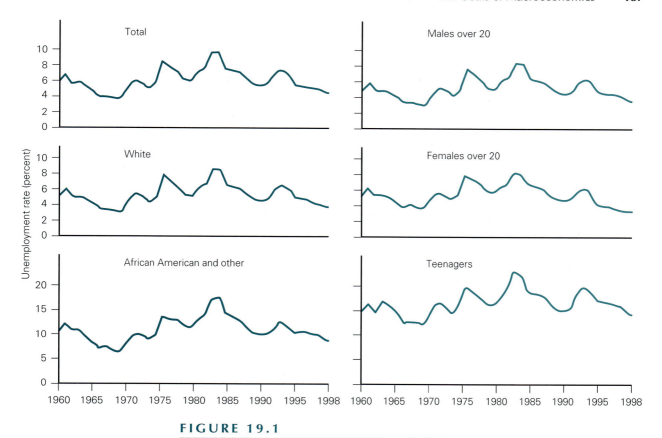

FIGURE 19.1

Unemployment Rates, 1960–1998
The unemployment rate (the number of persons unemployed divided by the labor force) rises and falls with other economic activity. However, African Americans and teenagers consistently have higher rates of unemployment than other groups.

cept of the natural rate, as in Figure 19.2. Note that the actual unemployment rate has fluctuated around the natural rate, with cycles of business activity producing unemployment below the natural rate in some periods and above the rate in other periods. In the most direct sense, macroeconomics deals with why the actual rate of unemployment differs from the natural rate and with what might cause the natural rate to change over time.

Economists debate, sometimes hotly, what the appropriate level of full employment is. In fact, the unemployment rate has fallen only twice below 5 percent since 1973 (in 1997 and 1998), and many economists now think that the "full-employment" unemployment rate should be in the 5–7 percent range, a range close to the theoretical concept of the natural rate of unemployment.

Price stability
A situation of no inflation or deflation in the economy; no change in the overall level of prices of goods, services, and resources.

The Goal of Price Stability

The second major macroeconomic goal is **price stability**—the absence of inflation or deflation in the overall level of prices. Inflation is a process of price level increases that take place over time. Inflation can be stable and predictable or

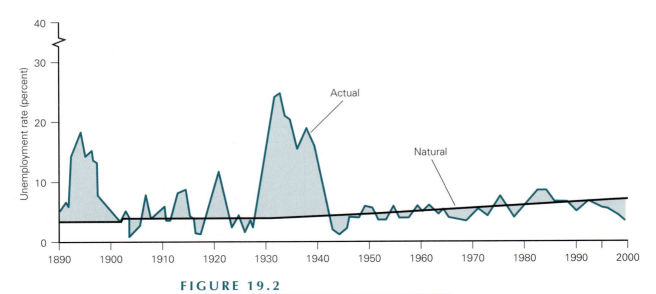

FIGURE 19.2

Rate of Unemployment, 1890–1998

The actual rate of unemployment has fluctuated widely since 1890. The unemployment rate rose to dangerous levels during the 1930s but has stayed within narrower limits since World War II. The actual unemployment rate has fluctuated around the natural rate of unemployment, a theoretical concept that depends on the situations and institutions surrounding the demand and supply of labor.

unstable and unanticipated—in either case, bringing higher costs to consumers and producers, and to buyers and sellers. Inflation is far more disruptive when it arrives unannounced, however.

Inflation is not simply a rise in the price of gasoline or chicken. Rather, inflation is a macroeconomic situation characterized by sustained and continuous increases in the overall level or average of all prices. One way to measure inflation is to look at the average of prices for some representative collection, or market basket, of goods and services that people buy. An increase in this average, or general, level of prices over some given time period (a month or a year) indicates the presence of inflation in the economy.

Suppose that food was the only good people bought. A 2 percent increase in the average level of food prices during the month of March means that the consumer must spend $1.02 at the end of March to buy the same market basket of food items that $1.00 would purchase in February. Never mind that bacon prices actually fell in March and that potato chip prices rose by 10 percent. Inflation is measured by considering the average prices of some representative bundle of goods at some given level—such as the retail, wholesale, or producer level.

If the cost of some market basket of goods and services was, say, $200 in one month and $210 in the next month, then prices in general would have risen by 5 percent during the month. When the change in prices over any period of time (a month here) is expressed as a percentage, the number calculated is called the **inflation rate.** The inflation rate is the speed at which prices in general are increasing. In this example, the inflation rate calculated is 5 percent per month. If prices continued to increase at the same speed for an entire year, the inflation rate would be

Inflation rate

The percentage change in the average level of prices over a period of time; the speed at which prices in general are rising.

80 percent per year (5 percent per month compounded for 12 months). A statistic calculated by the federal government's Bureau of Labor Statistics, called the consumer price index (CPI), is used to measure the overall average level of prices in the United States. By calculating the percentage changes in the CPI, the inflation rate in the U.S. economy can be measured. (The CPI will be explained and discussed fully in Chapter 20.)

Deflation
Sustained decreases in the average level of prices.

Deflation is a decrease in the general price level. Since World War II, price instability has been due to inflation rather than deflation. During the 1970s, for example, the United States experienced double-digit inflation rates reaching almost 14 percent per year in 1980.

Certainly we have plenty of evidence that inflation can get out of hand. Like severe unemployment, runaway inflation can wreak havoc in a society, causing social and political disintegration. A classic example occurred in post–World War I Germany when the inflation rate was as high as thousands of percentage points *per day.* Eventually, the German mark was worth more as paper—it was actually used as wallpaper—than as money. As a result, goods disappeared from markets and people starved. Looking farther back in time, economic historians claim to have evidence that runaway inflation was partly responsible for the breakdown of the Roman Empire's economic and political institutions.

Many of the costs of inflation and deflation can be traced to the inability of various economic institutions to adjust quickly to unanticipated price changes. When inflation is fully anticipated, adjustments can be made in personal savings for education, retirement, or vacations; tax codes; and financial contracts. But when inflation is unanticipated, adjustments become costly and difficult. People who live on fixed incomes—many of them elderly and poor to begin with—are particularly hard hit by inflation, as we will see in Chapter 29.

Historically, inflation has been a problem in the United States during postwar periods. Even then, as Figure 19.3 shows, the inflation rate has seldom risen above 10 percent per year. In the period of inflation following the Vietnam War, the inflation rate rose to 13.5 percent in 1980, before falling sharply. Other countries have had much worse inflation problems in recent years. For example, the inflation rate in Argentina and Brazil reached annual levels in excess of 1000 percent during the 1980s. In Bolivia, the annual inflation rate exceeded 20,000 percent in 1985. In the 1980s, Mexico had inflation rates in excess of 150 percent but has since adopted policies that sharply reduced the inflation rate, to less than 25 percent per year. Inflation in the United States has remained generally low in the 1990s, approximating 3 percent in 1995 and only 1.6 percent in 1998.

Even when the rate of inflation stands at relatively modest levels, it can pose problems for the economy. First of all, inflation has peculiar redistributive effects. That is, it enhances some people's real incomes at the expense of others'. **Real income** is the quantity of goods and services that can be bought with an individual's **nominal,** or money, **income.** In other words, real income is the real purchasing power of one's nominal income. For example, if a person was earning $10,000 per year in 1975 and continued to do so in 2000, a modest inflation rate of 6 percent per year from 1975 to 2000 would mean that the person's real income, or purchasing power, would have fallen by well over 50 percent, even though his nominal income remained the same. This loss of real income is all too familiar to people on fixed money incomes—those on fixed pension plans, for example. When prices of the goods and services consumed by these groups rise, but their nominal incomes remain the same or do not rise as fast as prices, the real income of these consumers

Real income
The purchasing power of money income; the quantity of goods and services that money income can buy.

Nominal income
Income measured in terms of money, not in terms of what the money can buy.

FIGURE 19.3

The Rate of Inflation, 1960–1998

The inflation rate is measured by calculating the yearly percentage change in the consumer price index. Inflation rates varied greatly over the period 1960–1998, although the trend since 1960 has been toward a higher average rate of inflation. Notice, however, the downward trend in the inflation rate since 1980.

Source: Council of Economic Advisers, *Economic Report of the President* (Washington, D.C.: U.S. Government Printing Office, 1999), p. 399.

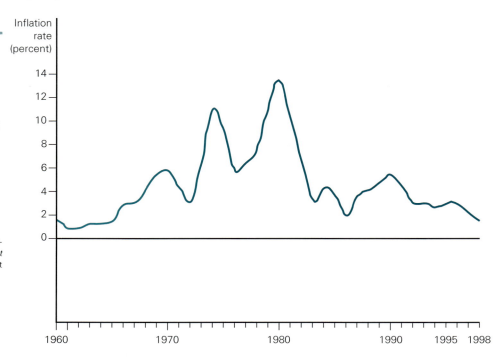

falls. Naturally, consumers whose income is rising at a faster rate than prices are better off during inflationary periods. Under such circumstances, arbitrary redistributions take place, with those on fixed incomes bearing the costs.

Uncertainty about future prices also results from price instability. Debtors and creditors, for instance, must guess at future prices and charge or pay interest rates that may or may not cover the real change in the value of money. Inflation also disrupts decisions of producers and consumers. Consumers' expectations about future prices and future real incomes are especially important. Consumers may adjust to their expectations, buying today if they expect prices to push higher tomorrow or if they think that inflation will reduce purchasing power in the future. (Likewise, if consumers expect deflation at some point in the future—far less likely, given U.S. experience—they would be more likely to postpone purchases, especially of durable goods.) While fully expected inflation may cause some transaction costs, unanticipated inflation and an unstable, unpredictable inflation rate greatly disrupt the plans of buyers and sellers. Before 1981, consumers also faced the possibility of real income erosion due to the tax structure. When nominal income increased as a result of attempts to maintain real income, income earners were forced into higher tax brackets. This "bracket creep" occurred because tax rates have been levied on money income received, not on real income earned. **Tax indexation** is one way to curb this detrimental effect of inflation. Under tax indexation, the federal tax tables are tied to the inflation rate. Tax indexation was first implemented in 1981, was preserved in the Tax Reform Act of 1986, and continues in the 1990s.

Producers are also profoundly affected by unanticipated inflation. With uncertainty about inflation, producers may withhold output of goods and services from the market. Under extreme uncertainty, the plans of investors and business entre-

Tax indexation

The basing of income taxes on real income instead of nominal income.

preneurs can be badly upset, causing postponement or abandonment of projects that enhance employment and economic growth. High, unpredictable rates of inflation help explain the low rates of capital formation and slow economic growth in some developing nations.

The Objective of Economic Growth

Economic growth

A sustained increase in the overall productive capacity of an economy over time.

The third major macroeconomic issue is growth in the economy. **Economic growth** refers to any increase in the productive capacities of the economy, whether as a result of an increase in the labor supply, an increase in the productivity of labor (the output per worker), or a net increase in the quality or quantity of the nation's capital stock, the wherewithal of production.

The labor supply grows through increases in population, immigration, or the number of people willing to work. Increased productivity of labor in output per worker is achieved through improvements in education and human capital or through a higher quantity and quality of capital stock supplied to labor. Writers and secretaries, for instance, may increase their productivity by switching from typewriters to word processing systems. Additions to the nation's capital stock are made through new investment in capital goods—word processors in offices, machines in factories. This investment arises from another macroeconomic variable, private saving. To save, individuals must forgo present consumption. Under favorable economic conditions, when the two goals of price level stability and full employment are achieved, any given rate of private saving is more likely to generate more new investment, capital formation, and economic growth than would otherwise be the case.

Gross domestic product (GDP)

A measure of the final goods and services produced by a country with resources located within that country.

Real economic growth, measured in terms of change in **gross domestic product (GDP),** has averaged about 3 percent per year in the United States over the past hundred years. However, this rate of growth has slowed somewhat in the last two decades. Another related problem in recent U.S. experience has been slowed growth in productivity—a reduction in growth of the ratio of total output to the number of employed workers. While the reasons for a slowdown in productivity growth are complex—as are the relations between economic growth and changes in productivity—one major problem has been a reduced rate of technological development in the United States. Reduced productivity may translate into much slower economic growth in the future and a lessened standard of living for Americans.

Nominal GDP

The total production of final goods and services within a country measured in monetary units that have not been adjusted for changes in the price level.

Real GDP

The total production of final goods and services within a country measured in monetary units that have been adjusted for changes in the price level.

The effects of these slower growth rates are not immediately apparent. However, the cumulative effect of a slower growth rate can become staggeringly large in just a generation. For example, if a country's rate of growth is 8 percent per year instead of 10 percent per year, real GDP will be only half as large within 36 years as it would have been at the slightly higher annual rate. Except for the period of the Great Depression, for over 100 years each generation of Americans has had reason to believe that it would have a markedly higher standard of living than the preceding generation. If U.S. productivity and economic growth fall to low levels, this expectation may no longer be realistic for many Americans. Figure 19.4 shows two measures of aggregate economic growth between 1960 and 1998. One line measures **nominal GDP;** the other line, **real GDP.** Nominal GDP for each of the years is measured in terms of prices that prevail in that year. Therefore, increases in nominal GDP can be caused either by increases in output or by increases in prices. Real GDP is a measure of the economy's output adjusted for general price level changes. The measures of real GDP in Figure 19.4 reflect the quantities of

FIGURE 19.4

Real and Nominal GDP
The black line shows the rising level of nominal GDP. Most of this increase is caused by rising prices. The colored line shows the trend in real GDP by removing the effects of inflation on prices. Real GDP, in other words, rises less rapidly in terms of constant 1992 dollars.
Source: Council of Economic Advisers, *Economic Report of the President* (Washington, D.C.: U.S. Government Printing Office, 1999), pp. 326, 328.

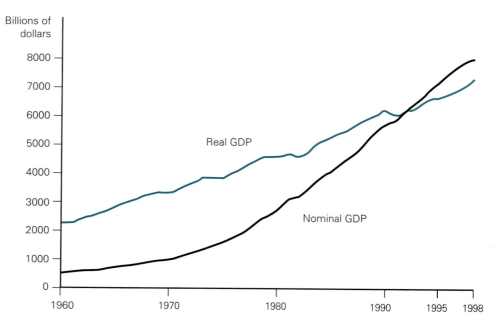

goods that are produced in the various years in constant dollars, or in prices that existed in some given year (1992 in Figure 19.4).

The distinction between real GDP and nominal GDP is important: Price changes cloud the picture of the value of output over time. Nominal GDP can increase between any two years even if production levels fall, because the effect of rising prices can offset the effect of reduced production on nominal GDP. Therefore, we focus on real GDP, not nominal GDP, in measuring the rate of economic growth.

Global Objectives

A final goal of U.S. macroeconomic policy is to maximize domestic economic well-being through international trade. As noted in Chapter 2, international output can be maximized by employing the principles of specialization, comparative advantage, and trade. Under these principles, one macroeconomic goal—for the United States or for any other country—is to achieve balance between exports and imports. A huge and growing volume of trade will maximize domestic production for exports, increase domestic employment of labor, and create demands for all other resource inputs, including capital and land.

The United States is a relative newcomer on the trade scene. Countries such as Switzerland, the United Kingdom, France, and Germany have a great deal of experience with international trading arrangements. The vast size of the United States makes its involvement in trade of great significance, but until recently, the international sector (imports and exports) made up a relatively small portion of total economic activity in the United States. Only thirty years ago, less than 4 percent of all of the goods purchased by Americans were imported. In 1998, about 10 percent of all goods purchased by Americans were imported. Many more goods, including automobiles and computers, contain imported components.

Media coverage of trade "deals," free trade agreements, and the value of the dollar in relation to other currencies all suggest that trade relations have become important to the average American. Changes in technology, capital investments, and resource prices are constantly altering trade patterns. One goal of macroeconomic policy in the United States is to take maximum advantage of trade opportunities within an overall system of balanced world trade relations.

STABILITY, GROWTH, AND BUSINESS CYCLES

Economic stabilization

A situation in which the price level and the unemployment rate vary from desired levels only temporarily and by small amounts.

The overall goal of macroeconomic policy is to achieve **economic stabilization.** By stabilization, we do not mean *no* economic growth. Instead, the term describes an environment in which price changes (resulting either from inflation or from deflation) are moderate and in which the unemployment rate differs little from the full-employment level. In such an environment, the prices of individual goods will change, leading to changes in employment levels, as existing industries grow and contract and as new industries arise. However, neither a persistent change in the price level nor excessive unemployment will upset overall consumption and production and disrupt economic growth under stabilization.

Economic stability thus means the achievement of full employment under inflationless or near inflationless conditions to attain maximum economic growth in the present and future. Stabilization is a tall order in a modern economy, where economic activity is subject to fluctuations. These fluctuations, called **business cycles,** are the result of severe variations in the plans of buyers and sellers beyond those variations necessary for changes and improvements in production and consumption.

Business cycles

Recurrent, systematic fluctuations in the level of business activity; usually measured by changes in the level, or rate of growth, of real GDP over time.

Business cycles are made up of, at one extreme, peaks and, at the other extreme, recessions or depressions. At the peak of a business cycle, the economy is expanding rapidly, with employment at or near capacity. In a recession or depression, resources—especially human resources—are grossly underused. In the expansionary phase of a cycle, increased demand for goods and services causes rapidly increasing demand for all resources, putting pressure on the supplies of labor, capital, and raw materials. One signal that the economy is in the expansionary phase is that business inventories are rapidly being depleted. This period of a business cycle is often characterized by increased inflation, as business activity and employment expand. After the peak of the cycle, the economy enters a contractionary phase. As production of goods exceeds demand for them, inventories build up— one signal of contraction. This phase is characterized by stable or falling prices, excess production capacities, and unemployment. When depression or recession is reached, the economy experiences negative real economic growth rates and stagnation. When recovery is relatively quick in arriving, the period of stagnation is termed a *recession*. A *depression* is a longer, more damaging period of stagnation. Eventually, however, growing demand for goods and services will pull the economy out of any slump. Figure 19.5 shows cycles of business activity as measured by real GDP growth rates since 1960. Figure 19.6 illustrates a typical business cycle.

The goals of macroeconomic policy are to even out or counterbalance the opposing forces of the business cycle. Such policy is therefore called countercyclical policy. Its role is to counter the business cycle to produce inflationless economic growth with full employment. The role of macroeconomic and monetary theory is to understand the causes of changes in business activity—that is, the causes of the business cycle.

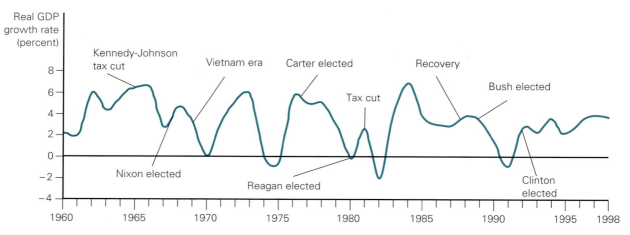

FIGURE 19.5

Cycles of Real Annual Growth Rate in GDP, 1960–1998

Periods of economic expansion and contraction have varied a great deal in this century. Note the roller-coaster path since 1960, punctuated by sharp recessions in 1974–1975, 1980, 1981–1982, and 1990–1991.

Source: Council of Economic Advisers, *Economic Report of the President* (Washington, D.C.: U.S. Government Printing Office, 1996), p. 283.

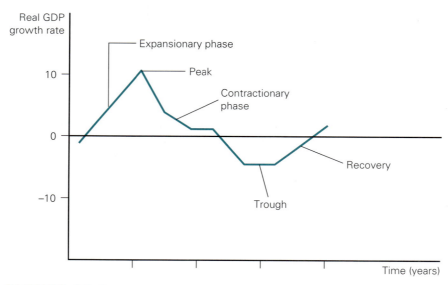

FIGURE 19.6

A Typical Business Cycle

Business cycles vary in length and intensity. A typical cycle includes an expansionary phase of rising business activity and growth, a peak of activity, a contractionary phase of falling activity, and a low point, usually referred to as a trough.

THE COSTS OF BUSINESS CYCLES

Business cycles have received much attention from economists and politicians because they entail genuine economic costs. When the economy goes into a recession or depression, the production of goods and services falls, causing living standards to fall. It may seem that these reductions in living standards are only temporary and that rapid increases in production during the recovery stage of the business cycle will counteract them. However, much of the lost production can never be regained. An economic downturn results in unemployment of economic resources of all types. Plants are closed down, farmland may lie idle, and workers with all types of labor skills remain out of work. Although all of the idle resources may become employed when the economy recovers, the lost production cannot be regained; a worker unemployed for a year cannot make up for lost production during the ensuing year. Production that is lost due to idle resources is production that is lost forever.

The second way in which business cycles reduce living standards is by depleting the capital stock. At any point in time, a society's ability to produce goods and services depends crucially on the size of its capital stock. As we saw in Chapter 2, a society's production possibilities curve is shifted rightward when capital accumulates and leftward when the capital stock declines. During an economic recession or depression, existing capital continues to depreciate, which lowers the capital stock. In a normal business environment, business firms have an incentive to replace and even add to depreciating plant and equipment; in a recession, firms are less likely to replace depreciating capital. Sales are so low that existing firms have idle capital and little incentive to replace equipment that becomes worn out. As a consequence, business downturns tend to erode the stock of productive capital and to reduce future production ability.

It is more difficult to predict how a downturn in the business cycle will affect the stock of human capital. In a recession, individuals have conflicting incentives to invest in human capital—that is, in education or on-the-job training. On the one hand, additional training or education may seem like a waste of time—why study to become a welder if there are no jobs for welders? On the other hand, unemployed persons may choose to get education or training because the opportunity cost of their time is low. If individuals consider their current level of training and skills inadequate, schooling may be a hope for a better life.

Government may step in to prevent the stock of human capital from declining. This is precisely what happened in the United States (and elsewhere) during the Great Depression of the 1930s. Programs such as the PWA and the WPA hired unemployed workers to construct bridges, highways, and public buildings. In doing so, they provided job skills for workers (human capital) and improved the nation's infrastructure. Despite these programs, the United States entered World War II with a greatly reduced stock of capital goods, which hampered U.S. military mobilization at the outset of the war.

The economic disadvantages of business cycles are not necessarily limited to the costs associated with high unemployment. There is also evidence that business cycles are a cause of inflation. During economic "booms," when demand for goods and services grows rapidly, bottlenecks in the production process are likely to arise. Rapid economic growth often frustrates the economy's ability to quickly match unemployed workers with job openings; the newly created jobs may arise in geographic areas or in industries with relatively few unemployed workers. The consequence of production bottlenecks is that wages and prices are bid up, causing inflation.

The alternative—and much happier—state of affairs is a long period of prosperity. The 1990s, after 1992, appears to have been such a period, as the tables and figures of this chapter show. Some economists and politicians appear to believe that booms will last forever, but as always, history is an excellent teacher. Irving Fisher, a leading American economist, declared in 1929 that America had entered a period of "perpetual prosperity" just before the stock market crashed and ushered in the Great Depression. Keynesian economists declared the business cycle dead during the great boom of the 1960s, just before a period of stagnation and inflation ("stagflation") of the 1970s. Likewise, after averting the stock market crashes in the late 1980s economists declared the business cycle a thing of the past, just before the recession of the early 1990s. Politicians and economists have been wrong before, and there are good reasons to deny that the business cycle is over after the prosperity of the 1990s (see the Focus "The Boom of the 1990s: Is the Business Cycle Dead?").

AGGREGATE DEMAND, AGGREGATE SUPPLY, AND MACROECONOMIC POLICY

Identifying goals is only the first step. Questions abound: How can full employment be reached? How can inflation be tamed? How can real economic growth be sustained? Questions such as these require both theoretical and political answers. In this section we briefly introduce two of the most important macroeconomic theoretical tools—aggregate demand and aggregate supply—and the two most important types of macroeconomic policy.

Aggregate Demand and Aggregate Supply

Aggregate demand
The total spending that occurs in an economy at various price levels during a specified period of time.

In examining macroeconomic phenomena, it is often useful to conceive of aggregate demand and aggregate supply curves. In the abstract, **aggregate demand** represents all components of expenditure on domestically produced goods and services. Like an ordinary demand curve, which shows the quantity of a particular good or service that buyers as a group are willing to purchase at each possible price, an aggregate demand curve shows the value of all goods and services that buyers (domestic consumers, business firms, government agencies, foreign buyers) are willing to purchase at each price level over a specific period of time. Similarly, the **aggregate supply** curve shows the time-specific value of all goods and services that producers as a group are willing to offer for sale at each possible price level. In drawing an aggregate demand or supply curve, price level is measured on the vertical axis, and aggregate output is measured on the horizontal axis. Typical aggregate demand and supply curves are depicted in Figure 19.7.

Aggregate supply
The total output that will be produced by an economy at various price levels during a specified period of time.

Although the analogy between demand and supply in an individual market (such as the market for CDs) and the aggregate demand and supply of all goods and services is not perfect, the concepts are similar. Both the demand curve for an individual product and the aggregate demand curve are negatively sloped; as price declines, quantity of goods and services demanded rises. Several factors lead to

FOCUS

The Boom of the 1990s: Is the Business Cycle Dead?

The 1990s witnessed one of the longest periods of continuous economic prosperity in American history. With the exception of the recession in the early 1990s, America has been experiencing positive economic growth since the recession of the early 1980s—an unprecedented period of prosperity.

Two important indicators of economic prosperity beside Gross Domestic Product (GDP) are unemployment and the stock market. Unemployment rates have fallen substantially since the 1970s and the recession of the early 1980s, and they have even fallen below what economists used to consider the natural rate of unemployment. The stock market has likewise skyrocketed, with the Dow Jones Industrial Average of stock prices rising from around 1000 in 1982 to above 10,000 in 1999.

What are the factors that account for such economic growth? How has the United States achieved this consistent growth and this remarkable economic stability? Many now believe that the business cycle, with its period booms and busts, is dead.

It is unlikely that the business cycle has passed away. Although the current cycle is subdued, it would be unwise and premature to conclude that cycles will no longer be a part of our economy. Indeed, one is reminded of the telegram that Mark Twain, upon reading his obituary erroneously published in a London newspaper in 1897, sent to the Associated Press: "The reports of my death are greatly exaggerated."

Several factors are known to have contributed to recent economic growth, including the supply-side tax cuts during the Reagan administration and deregulation of important industries like trucking, airlines, and long-distance telephone services. The downfall of communism and freer international trade have also enhanced competition and economic growth. However, economic growth does not ensure economic stability if the economy experiences high levels of inflation and interest rates.

The combination of falling interest rates and reduced inflation have no doubt contributed to economic growth, economic stability, and booming stock markets. Alan Greenspan, the Chairman of the Federal Reserve Board (Fed) during this period, has been given much credit for lower interest rates and inflation. Greenspan is an "inflation hawk" promoting a tighter monetary policy, allowing the market to determine interest rates, and using his monetary tools only in times of market panics, such as the stock market crash of 1987.

One reason to believe that the business cycle is not dead is that Greenspan cannot remain Chairman of the Fed forever. Second, other leading industrial nations like Japan and Germany also experienced long periods of prosperity but now are mired in long recessions. Predicting the timing of business cycles is extremely difficult, but all past predictions about the death of the business cycle have been wrong. Ironically, it seems that the best indication of impending economic bust is the rising chant of politicians and their economic advisers that they have tamed the economy and made the business cycle extinct.

larger aggregate demand at lower price levels. One of the most obvious is an increase in export sales to foreign buyers. A decrease in prices in this country is likely to make American goods more attractive to foreign buyers, causing the foreign component of aggregate demand to rise. Spending by domestic buyers is also likely to increase, for reasons we will detail in Chapter 24.

Like a typical supply curve in an individual market, the aggregate supply curve shown in Figure 19.7 is positively sloped. Producers as a group are revealed in Figure 19.7 to be willing to supply larger quantities of goods and services at higher price levels, presumably because higher price levels yield higher rates of profit. A detailed discussion of the forces underlying aggregate supply will also be presented in Chapter 24.

FIGURE 19.7

Aggregate Demand and Aggregate Supply Curves

Like the demand and supply curves for a single good, the aggregate demand and aggregate supply curves for all goods and services determine a price level and a level of output for all goods produced and consumed. Equilibrium is achieved at the point where aggregate demand equals aggregate supply.

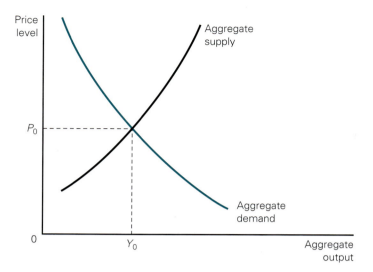

Equilibrium occurs where aggregate demand equals aggregate supply. This occurs at a price level of P_0 and an output level of Y_0 in Figure 19.7. At price levels above P_0, aggregate supply of goods and services exceeds aggregate demand. This surplus of goods and services in aggregate supply exerts downward pressure on prices, causing the price level to fall to P_0. At price levels below P_0, aggregate demand is greater than aggregate supply. General shortages of goods and services cause prices to rise, driving the price level up to the equilibrium at P_0.

Aggregate demand and supply curves are useful for examining the issues of unemployment, price stability, and economic growth. Depending on the positions of aggregate demand and supply, the equilibrium level of output can be at high or low levels. Unemployment becomes a serious problem when the equilibrium level of production is too low, causing many workers to lose their jobs.

To consider the goal of price stability, it is necessary to consider shifts in aggregate demand and supply over time. Such shifts can lead to price instability— changes in the equilibrium price level above or below P_0 in Figure 19.7. Price stability occurs if neither of the curves shifts or if both shift rightward or leftward at the same rate. However, suppose that aggregate demand increases more rapidly than does aggregate supply. In this case, the economy will experience inflation, as the price level rises to an equilibrium level above P_0. Similarly, the economy would experience deflation if aggregate supply rose relative to aggregate demand.

Comparisons of the equilibrium level of output at different points in time provide a picture of economic growth. Shifts to the right in either aggregate demand or aggregate supply will cause economic growth, the pace depending on the rate at which aggregate demand or supply increases.

MACROECONOMIC ISSUES: CAN GOALS BE MET IN A WORLD OF POLITICS?

Unfortunately, policies to achieve full employment, price stability, and economic growth often fail. One explanation for this is that macroeconomic policies that might work beautifully in isolation sometimes can conflict with each other. For example, policies that shift aggregate demand rightward to attain full employment will tend to cause price increases rather than price stability. Also, certain policies to contain inflation will increase unemployment. In such cases, decision makers are faced with a **policy trade-off;** they are forced to decide which of the economic goals is more important to attain.

Additional problems in implementing macroeconomic policy arise from political considerations. Certain policy changes, such as reductions in government spending or tax increases, are politically unpopular. Therefore, such policies tend not to be implemented or tend to be delayed, even when economically desirable.

Can Discretionary Macroeconomic Policy Work?

A more fundamental macroeconomic issue relates to the advisability of using **discretionary policies** (monetary or fiscal adjustments in the economy). Some economists question whether the economy can be managed at all by fallible public officials who possess imperfect information. **Fiscal policy**—taxing and spending policy—is controlled by Congress and the president. **Monetary policy**—control over the growth in the money stock—is controlled by the politically appointed Federal Reserve Board. The issue is whether these groups could ever know enough about the economy or react quickly enough to disturbances to direct and control the economy in discretionary fashion. If mistakes are possible, could not discretionary policies create so much uncertainty and confusion that they might sometimes have the opposite effects to those intended?

Some contemporary macroeconomists believe that, for reasons such as conflicting goals and imperfect information, discretionary fiscal and monetary policies have built-in side effects that make them worse than useless. These economists call for the use of policy rules such as predetermined growth in the money supply and balanced federal budgets instead of discretionary control of the macroeconomy. Rules and balanced budgets would, in the view of some, take policy out of error-prone human hands, leading to more certain expectations among consumers, producers, and investors in the economy.

Underlying a faith in establishing rules rather than discretion in enacting policy is the belief, held by early classical economists and upheld by their followers today, that the economy, if left undisturbed by government, will automatically achieve the goals of full employment, price stability, and maximum economic growth. Much of the policy controversy discussed in ensuing chapters centers on issues such as these. Can discretionary policy work? How automatic are free market forces in achieving macroeconomic goals? Are rules preferable to continual alterations in fiscal and monetary policies?

Demand-Side Versus Supply-Side Policies

Most contemporary macroeconomic theory and policy, originating in the 1930s in the writing of John Maynard Keynes, is directed toward manipulating aggregate demand, either in discretionary fashion or with rules designed to produce full employment, price stability, and growth. This approach is now referred to as **demand-side policy.**

Some economists, notably those associated with the Reagan administration, have focused instead on some of the factors related to output response or to aggregate supply changes. As noted earlier, output response is largely determined by factors related to resource supply and to investment and capital accumulation. **Supply-side policy** emphasizes the possible effects of taxes on work effort, labor supply, and investment. High tax burdens on consumer-workers and on investors

---

Policy trade-off

A situation in which a policy that promotes the attainment of one macroeconomic goal necessarily implies that the attainment of another macroeconomic objective becomes more difficult.

Discretionary policy

A policy or change in policy that is determined by choices or decisions of policy-makers.

Fiscal policy

The use of government spending and taxation to effect changes in aggregate economic variables.

Monetary policy

The use of money supply changes to effect changes in aggregate economic variables.

Demand-side policy

Fiscal or monetary policy intended to alter the overall level of spending, or aggregate demand.

Supply-side policy

Fiscal or monetary policy intended to alter the incentives to produce output; policies designed to shift the aggregate supply curve to the right.

mean that the economy's output response is constricted. A lower output response creates rigidities in the economy, limiting the attainment of macroeconomic goals. Indeed, one of the goals of most tax reform proposals of the 1980s was to stimulate output by lowering the federal income tax rates individuals and businesses face. Institutional changes surrounding the work decision—such as an increase in the number of women in the work force—plus government social programs and minimum-wage laws may also play a role in influencing aggregate supply. A focus on aggregate supply should not be taken to mean that aggregate demand theory or policy is unimportant. As we will see, both aggregate demand and aggregate supply play critical roles in explaining success or failure in obtaining macroeconomic goals.

In any discussion of macroeconomic policy, some allowance must be made for the possibility that policy-makers will not make the "right" response—that is, the fiscal or monetary policy change consistent with accepted economic theory. Experience tells us that in the world of interest-group politics, economic considerations are not always uppermost in the minds of policy-makers. There is every reason to believe that, like everyone else, elected politicians are self-interested individuals. What is it that the self-interested politician seeks to maximize? Is it the public interest or job security (the probability of future reelection by voters)? Many economists believe it is the latter, so they recognize that knowledge of economic theory on the part of government policy-makers does not guarantee justifiable decisions. Political motives, in other words, frequently dominate fiscal policy decisions and in fact, may actually create a business cycle (see the Focus "Is There a Political Business Cycle?").

FOCUS

Is There a Political Business Cycle?

Some economists have suggested that there is a political business cycle. Incumbent politicians pursue economic policies that promote their reelection, and, as a consequence, the economy goes through a business cycle every four years. In an attempt to enhance their reelection prospects, incumbent politicians promote expansionary policies prior to election day—tax cuts, increased government spending, and greater money supply growth. These policies have politically popular consequences in the short run: lower unemployment and interest rates, along with growth in real output of goods and services. Immediately after the election, the politicians reverse course. To limit the higher inflation rates that the reelection strategy fosters, they raise taxes and cut spending, and money supply growth is reduced. The result of these political moves is a business cycle whose length is roughly equal to the interval between elections.

Important objections have been raised to this idea. The model is said to be naive because it assumes that voters in a presidential election care only about inflation and unemployment. The critics note, correctly, that election results turn on a variety of issues, including foreign relations, income distribution, "family values," and the personalities of the candidates. Timing is also a problem—politicians cannot easily predict how particular policies might affect the economy or when. But the most important issue is whether voters can be systematically fooled. If individuals are actually short-sighted, then the political business cycle hypothesis would seem to be plausible. If people can actually and rationally predict the effects of politics, the political gain the incumbent politician had hoped for would vanish or be diminished.

There have been a number of attempts to test for various aspects of the political business cycle theory. Many of these tests consist of searches for patterns in unemployment rates or other macroeconomic variables during the periods surrounding congressional or presidential elections. The results are so far inconclusive, and there is evidence on both sides of this issue. But the idea continues to intrigue economists.

MODERN MACROECONOMICS: A MIXED APPROACH

Our brief look at the issues surrounding the attainment of macroeconomic goals suggests that modern economists can lay claim to a practical understanding of the basic functioning of the aggregate economy. Still, economists often take different policy positions based on alternative outcomes—and different magnitudes of outcomes—predicted by different theories. No single theory tells us everything we want to know. Rather, there are a number of theoretical approaches that may be viewed as alternative or complementary to each other in explaining developments in the macroeconomy. And, of course, one should never minimize the role of "politics" in macroeconomic analysis.

APPLICATION

One-Handed Economists: The President's Council of Economic Advisers

President Harry S. Truman is reputed to have once remarked that he would have been willing to pay a princely sum for a one-handed economist. After the Council of Economic Advisers (CEA) gave their economic policy recommendations, Truman bemoaned, his economists would always end up saying, "But on the other hand. . . ."

What is the Council of Economic Advisers, and what exactly does it do? The CEA was established as an office in the executive branch of the federal government by the Employment Act of 1946. The CAE's basic duties are to supply the president with economic analysis and advice in order to assist in the development and implementation of national economic policy. Outstanding economists such as James Tobin, a Nobel laureate (1981) appointed by President John F. Kennedy, have served as members of the CEA.

The CEA consists of three members who are appointed by the president, with approval of the Senate, one of whom serves as chair of the CEA. The professional staff of the CEA is made up of eleven senior and six junior economists, as well as a statistician. The staff economists specialize in fields of expertise such as macroeconomics, international finance, labor, public finance, taxation, monetary policy, regulation, and agriculture. In most cases, the senior staff economists are on leave of absence from major universities, research institutions, or other government agencies.

By far, the CEA's most important duties are to provide the president with sound economic analysis concerning areas where policy decisions, either legislative or regulatory, are to be made. These areas include, of course, the broad area of national macroeconomic policy. Along with assisting the president in formulating macroeconomic policy, the CEA also participates in designing the necessary programs through which such policy is carried out. Forecasts and projections of critical macroeconomic variables such as the deficit, inflation, real GNP growth, and foreign exchange rates are all prepared by the CEA. In addition, the CEA has prepared economic analyses of such microeconomic issues as farm credit, airline and trucking deregulation, banking deregulation, space shuttle pricing, immigration, and antitrust legislation.

At the end of each January, the CEA submits an annual report to the president. This report, together with the president's own report, is then transmitted to Congress. These are then published yearly as the *Economic Report of the President.* The *Report* is an informative analysis of recent economic events and current problems, and it is also one of the better sources of economic statistics. Data on everything from budget deficits to farm income to unemployment are reported here, some information going as far back as 1929. The CEA also is responsible for data contained in a more up-to-date monthly publication called *Economic Indicators.*

Members of the CEA do not decide on policy. That is the duty of the president and Congress. Moreover, the president and Congress also have plenty of other economic advice. These include two very important economic institutions: the U.S. Secretary of the Treasury—a top manager of the nation's economy—and the Chairman of the Federal Reserve Board—the nation's top banker and controller of interest rates and the money supply. During the Clinton administration, these latter advisers, Robert Rubin and Alan Greenspan, respectively, assumed the most important roles in dealing with economic problems. Despite the relative power of these individuals under particular administrations, the CEA is in a position to strongly influence economic policy. The CEA chair and members are usually chosen on the basis of shared philosophy with the president. For example, President George Bush selected Stanford University economist Michael Boskin, a moderate, and President Bill Clinton chose Laura Tyson and (later) Janet Yellen, liberals of the University of California at Berkeley, to chair their CEA. Like all other advisers, CEA members influence decision making by force of personality, reputation, and personal relationship with the president.

QUESTION

If you were a faculty member at your university, what *economic* factors would enter your decision to accept or turn down a position offered to you on the CEA? Remember that the salary of a CEA member is generally less than what the appointee could earn at a university.

SUMMARY

1. Whereas microeconomics is concerned with the functioning of supply and demand in specific markets, macroeconomics studies the effects on inflation, unemployment, and economic growth of the interplay of aggregate demand and aggregate supply.

2. The overall goal of macroeconomic theory and policy is economic stabilization. Specifically, macroeconomic policy aims at an inflationless and fully employed economy with maximum economic growth. Some unemployment is expected in any fluid, dynamic economy, as individuals change jobs and other resources adapt to changing market conditions.

3. Inflation and unemployment are the enemies of economic growth because they create an environment within which private saving and new investment are reduced. A reduction in new investment means lower capital formation and reduced growth prospects.

4. Runaway inflation can have disastrous social and economic effects in an economy. Redistributions of real income from those on fixed incomes, often the poor and the elderly, extreme variations in buyers' and sellers' plans, and arbitrary increases in taxes required by government are among the problems created by inflation.

5. A business cycle is a recurrent but not predictable fluctuation in GDP. No two business cycles are exactly alike.

6. The four phases of a business cycle are expansion, peak, recession, and trough.

7. Trade-offs may exist in the pursuit of economic goals, such as decreased inflation and increased unemployment.

8. Fiscal policy and monetary policy are the two major means for manipulating aggregate demand and aggregate supply. Fiscal policy is the alteration in tax or spending activities by government. Monetary policy is control of the money supply and interest rates.

9. Economists have differing opinions about whether discretionary macroeconomic policy is stabilizing or destabilizing in promoting economic goals. In the view of some economists, rules should be substituted for authority in the quest for economic stabilization.

10. Supply-side economists have shifted attention to the factors affecting output response in the economy, such as the effect of taxation on work effort, new investment, and labor productivity.

KEY TERMS

unemployed
unemployment rate
full employment
natural rate of unemployment
price stability
inflation rate
deflation
real income

nominal income
tax indexation
economic growth
gross domestic product (GDP)
nominal GDP
real GDP
economic stabilization
business cycles

aggregate demand
aggregate supply
policy trade-off
discretionary policy
fiscal policy
monetary policy
demand-side policy
supply-side policy

QUESTIONS FOR REVIEW AND DISCUSSION

1. What is price stability? Is a constant rate of inflation at 10 percent less harmful than an inflation rate that randomly fluctuates between 2 percent and 8 percent?

2. What are the three major goals of macroeconomic policy? Which of these goals are most politicians least concerned about achieving? Why?

3. Why do economists disagree on macroeconomic policies? Does this imply that economists do not understand macroeconomics?

4. What is discretionary-demand management policy? Can discretionary fiscal policy eliminate swings in the business cycle?

5. Suppose that the economy is experiencing less than full employment. Utilizing the aggregate demand and aggregate supply theory developed in this chapter, explain the possible trade-offs that would have to be made to attain full employment.

6. What is necessary to achieve economic growth? Do inflation and unemployment hinder this process?

7. Can discretionary-demand management cause aggregate supply problems? What other trade-offs exist for policy-makers?

8. Which do you suppose is better for the economy, an increase in aggregate demand or an increase in aggregate supply? What is the difference?

9. Why is the unemployment rate a less than perfect measure of the overall condition of the economy?

10. If the actual rate of unemployment exceeds the natural rate of unemployment, what happens to the production possibilities frontier?

11. What are some of the problems associated with unanticipated inflation?

12. "The 1990s has seen a remarkable and constant period of economic prosperity and growth. The study of macroeconomics is therefore superfluous." Comment.

WORKING WITH THE WEB

1. Go to the Bureau of Economic Analysis web site, http://www.bea.doc.gov. Under the heading "National," click on GDP and related data. In the row for time-series estimates, you will find "Summary data, 1929–97, from the *Survey of Current Business*." Click on the HTML link under "tables" and locate the table for present real gross domestic product and its components, in chained dollars (Table 2A).

   a. In the postwar period (after 1953), find the years where GDP has decreased. When GDP decreases, how do personal consumption expenditures, gross domestic investment, and government spending change?

   b. Generally speaking, how has the share of government spending in GDP (i.e., government spending divided by GDP) changed over this period?

2. The economic fluctuations that occur during the business cycle are often cited as causal factors for a wide variety of social ills. One such social ill is crime. Find http://www.bestplaces.net and do the following exercise.

   Record the property crime rate (property crimes per 100,000 persons) to the unemployment rate for these California cities: Los Angeles, San Francisco, Bakersfield, Fresno, San Diego, Sacramento, Santa Barbara, Redding, San Jose, and Anaheim. After you collect this data, it may help to draw a graph (e.g., a scatter plot). Label the vertical axis as the crime rate and the horizontal axis as the unemployment rate.

   a. What relationship (e.g., a positive or negative relationship) do you observe when comparing the property crime and unemployment rates of these ten cities?

   b. If the relationship you observed was a positive one, then does this prove that high unemployment rates cause high property crime rates?

CHAPTER

20

Measuring
The
Macroeconomy

I n Chapter 19 we presented recent data on the American economy, including statistics on gross domestic product, unemployment, and inflation. In this chapter we
look at these measures in more detail, examining the components of GDP, the relation between GDP and national income, and the methods through which economists derive these aggregate data. We also look at the methods for measuring inflation
in the economy and at how a price index is compiled. Statistics such as GDP and the
rate of inflation are the bread and butter of macroeconomic study and of policy debate.
Price changes are revealed monthly and real GDP performance is revealed quarterly.
Consumers and businesses, not to mention many world markets, react to each announcement of the data. When you complete Chapter 20 you should recognize

- what aggregate measures of economic well-being include (and what they do not
  include).
- why no measure of an economy's progress is perfect and why all measures must
  be qualified.
- the methods upon which economists and statisticians build the national income
  accounts.
- how price changes and inflation or deflation relate to aggregate measures of economic progress.

AGGREGATE ACCOUNTING AND THE CONCEPT OF GDP

Economists have long been interested in aggregate economic statistics, but it was not until the 1930s in both the United States and Great Britain that economists and government agencies began to collect such data. At that time, Congress instructed the Department of Commerce to assemble and report on the national accounts. Modern **national income accounting,** or the statistical measurement of the nation's economic performance, was officially born. These principles were, in large measure, the legacy of two Nobel Prize–winning economists—Simon Kuznets in the United States and Sir Richard Stone in Great Britain.

By now, you are familiar with one of the most common national income aggregates: **gross domestic product (GDP).** A more comprehensive national income statistic is **gross national product (GNP).** GNP is the total market value of all final goods and services produced over a given period in the United States. It is perhaps more helpful to define GNP as the total market value of final goods and services owned by U.S. residents. This is an important distinction in that there are foreign-owned U.S. factories and American-owned foreign factories. GDP measures total production of U.S. factories regardless of the nationalities of their owners. GNP adds to GDP the net investment income (profits) received by American owners of foreign factories. When Americans receive more income from their overseas investments than foreigners receive from their investments in the United States, GNP exceeds GDP. When the reverse is true, GDP exceeds GNP.

As we shall see in more detail later, the word *gross* means that the total market value of all goods produced in the domestic economy, including the production of capital goods, is included in GDP. GDP therefore does not account for the wear and tear on physical assets—called depreciation—that takes place during a given period. The word *product* refers to the market value of final goods and services. We are able to calculate the sum of the money or market values of different goods and services because businesses keep records of their receipts for tax purposes.

Two other elements of the definition are important. First, only sales of **final goods** and services are counted in GDP. To do otherwise would be to double-count. The value of McDonald's or Burger King's purchases of raw meat would be added to consumers' purchases of hamburgers and thus be double-counted if all purchases of goods and services sold in the domestic economy were used to calculate GDP.

A second point involves the time period. GDP ordinarily refers to final sales over the period of a year. GDP and other national income accounts, such as GNP, are measures of what economists call *flows*. Flows are processes taking place through time and, as such, are measured per unit of time. GDP is the total output of an economy *per year*. A stock, such as the capital stock of an economy, is the total amount of something in existence at a point in time. Additionally, economists also discuss the rates at which variables such as GDP are changing. These growth rates are measured by calculating percentage changes of the variables from one period to the next.

What GDP Does Not Count

Official statistics on GDP are far from perfect. The most serious shortcoming is that they fail to include the value of certain types of production. Goods and services

---

National income accounting
The process of statistically measuring the nation's aggregate economic performance.

Gross domestic product (GDP)
A measure of the final goods and services produced by a country with resources located within that country.

Gross national product (GNP)
The value, measured at market prices, of all final goods and services produced in an economy in one year.

Final goods
Goods sold to the final consumers of the goods.

produced for home consumption are omitted, for example. This category includes such activities as backyard vegetable gardens, do-it-yourself home repair, and the myriad services provided by homemakers. Since the value of such goods and services is so hard to estimate, national income accountants omit the value of this kind of production in their calculations of GDP.

A second category that does not appear in official GDP estimates is the underground economy. Various goods and many services, such as yard work or maid service, are paid for in cash and are not reported for tax purposes. Also, some firms avoid paying taxes by not recording all sales. GDP accountants elect to omit such transactions because it is so difficult to estimate their magnitude. (See the Application "Beating the IRS: How Big Is the Underground Economy?" at the end of this chapter.)

The third major category of omitted production is illegal goods and services. As you know, profits from illegal drug sales run into the billions worldwide each year. These transactions are omitted from official statistics—again, because the magnitude of drug sales is difficult to judge, but also because there is a reluctance to view the production of illegal goods as an addition to national income.

Such glaring omissions caution against making sweeping statements about international comparisons of GDP. In developing countries, a huge percentage of all production may be produced by the large rural population for home consumption. In other countries, a majority of all production may be sold in the underground economy. Official GDP statistics understate actual levels of production in all economies, though not necessarily to the same degree. Official statistics showing the GDP of the United Kingdom to be slightly larger than the GDP of Italy are not conclusive evidence that actual production is larger in the United Kingdom. It may simply be that a smaller proportion of Italian production is included in GDP statistics.

Other transactions are excluded from GDP calculations because they do not represent purchases of current goods or services. For example, the purchase of stock or other securities is not included because it represents a transfer of assets and not production of goods or services. Similarly, real estate transactions involving old homes are not counted. However, any fees paid to stockbrokers or real estate agents would be included, since they represent payment for current services.

GDP as a Measure of Economic Welfare

Measure of economic welfare (MEW)
A concept of social and economic well-being that accounts for the production of all goods and services, not just those transacted for in markets.

It is tempting to use readily available GDP statistics to measure economic welfare. Even if the problem of uncounted production were solved, however, GDP still would not accurately measure worldwide economic welfare. Raw GDP statistics do not include pollution and congestion costs, which go hand in hand with economic growth in most developed countries. Also, the average work week in industrial countries has declined markedly in this century, but GDP statistics do not capture the value of increases in leisure time. Actually, GDP never was intended to be a measure of economic welfare. GDP is a measure of production—without any indication of who gets the goods and services produced or what the goods and services are. GDP is indifferent between the provision of handguns or health care. Nonetheless, some economists have attempted to compute a **measure of economic welfare (MEW)** based on GDP statistics.

NATIONAL INCOME ACCOUNTING

We have thus far spoken only of the market value of goods, but aggregate value in the economy can actually be derived either by summing all expenditures for final goods or by summing all income received. Now, we will explain why these constructs yield identical results and the factors to take into account to arrive at identical sums.

The Circular Flow of Economic Activity

Flow of expenditures

Total spending of consumers, businesses, and government on final goods and services during any given time period.

Flow of earnings

Total income received by resource suppliers during any given time period.

National income (GDP) can be measured in two ways: the flow of expenditures approach and the flow of earnings, or income, approach. The **flow of expenditures** approach looks at national income as the total amount spent on final goods and services. The **flow of earnings,** or income, approach looks at national income as the amount earned by factors of production (land, labor, capital, and the entrepreneur).

Logically, the two approaches have to yield the same figure for national income: All income earned by all factors in the production of goods and services is spent on those goods and services. Figure 20.1 is a circular flow diagram for an economy with only two sectors—a household, or consumer, sector and a firm, or business, sector. In the inner loop of the upper part of the diagram, firms (suppliers) produce goods for sale to consumers (demanders). The flow of goods to households is matched by a return flow of expenditures, indicated by the outer flow line. Businesses use the revenue from final sales to cover their costs of operation.

The inner part of the lower loop shows businesses or firms (demanders) employing factors of production from the household sector (suppliers). The factors of production are paid incomes that reflect their productivity in producing final output. Firm revenues are exhausted by factor payments because any left-over, or residual, portion accrues to the entrepreneur or owners of the firm in the form of profit, which is a type of income.

The upper and lower loops of the circular flow diagram illustrate the identity of the two approaches to measuring national income. The revenues from producing final goods and services are transformed into payments to cover the costs of producing the output. Total revenues from producing goods break down into profits, wage payments, interest, and land rent. By necessity, the dollar value of the expenditure flow on goods and services equals the dollar value of the income, or earning, flow to the factors of production. The important point is that national income can be measured with either approach, and the results will be identical. The flow of expenditures approach is formally identical to the flow of earnings, or income, approach.

Leakages and Injections: Some Complications

Before using these equivalent approaches to national income, consider some complications. The simple case described by Figure 20.1 excludes such features as saving and other important sectors of the economy such as government or the foreign sector. Without them, the flow of income to factors of production matches the flow of expenditures on final goods and services to firms. But since the excluded features and sectors are part of the economy, Figure 20.1 does not account for certain leakages out of and injections into the simple flow of expenditures and receipts. A leakage occurs when spending is diverted from the income stream. Household or business saving is a leakage from the expenditure stream. When processed

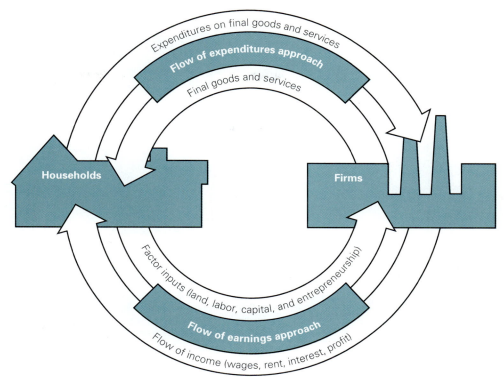

FIGURE 20.1

The Circular Flow of Economic Activity

The circular flow diagram is portrayed with only a business and a household sector. The upper loop is the flow of final output and expenditures on final output. The lower loop is the flow of input factors of production and the return flow of factor incomes. By definition, the value of the upper and lower loops must be equal. Therefore, GDP as measured by the flow of expenditures approach and GDP as measured by the flow of earnings approach must be identical.

through banks and other financial institutions or intermediaries, such saving becomes investment, an injection or addition to the expenditures flow.

Likewise, government expenditures are injections into the simple flow of expenditures, since the government, like households and businesses, makes expenditures on goods and services. Government transfers income to recipients through welfare and other programs as well. All such expenditures are injections into the circular flow. Financing such expenditures, however, requires the taxation of households and businesses. Taxation represents a leakage from the expenditure stream of the private economy.

The U.S. economy is also heavily involved in international trade and exchange, but the simple flows shown in Figure 20.1 do not include exports and imports. Exports—the sale abroad of goods and services produced in the United States—are an injection into the circular flow of expenditures and income, while imports—expenditures on goods and services produced abroad—are leakages from the simple income–expenditure flow.

In short, the simple income–expenditure model of Figure 20.1 does not account for certain leakages and injections. Government expenditures and exports must

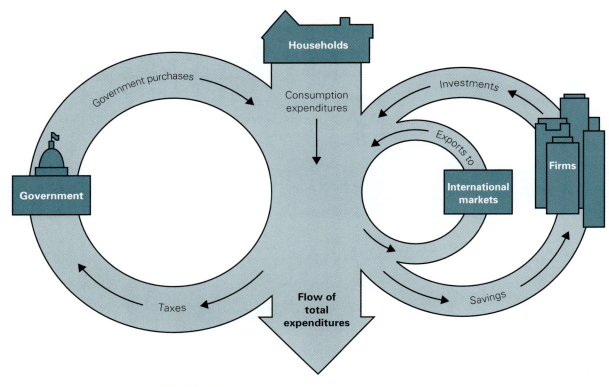

FIGURE 20.2

Leakages from and Injections into the Circular Flow
The simple two-sector economy portrayed in Figure 20.1 does not include the leakages represented by savings, taxation, and imports and injections represented by investment, government purchases, and exports. When these additional concepts are included, economists speak of a four-sector economy, including firms, households, government, and international markets.

be counted as injections into the expenditure stream. Likewise, household and business savings, along with government taxes and imports, are leakages from the simple circular flow of economic activity (see Figure 20.2).

The Flow of Expenditures Approach

National income accounting puts into practice the principles of the simple, two-sector circular flow diagram as amended by injections and leakages. The national income accountants apply the flow of expenditures approach to measuring GDP by breaking the economy down into four sectors: household, business, government, and foreign. Individuals in the economy are assigned among the four sectors, and GDP is estimated by adding the amount spent on final output by individuals in each sector. Table 20.1 gives the 1998 data on spending in each sector. Figure 20.3 compares the flow of expenditures with the flow of earnings.

Personal consumption expenditures (C)
Total spending by households on final goods and services.

Personal Consumption Expenditures   Expenditures by individuals and nonprofit institutions are called **personal consumption expenditures (C).** These expenditures

TABLE 20.1

Gross Domestic Product, 1998: The Flow of Expenditures

Total expenditures in the economy are broken down into four basic groups: private consumption expenditures; private domestic investment expenditures by businesses; government expenditures; and net exports (foreign purchases of U.S. goods minus U.S. purchases of foreign goods).

	Expenditures (billions of dollars)	
Personal consumption expenditures (C)		
Durable goods	724.7	
Nondurable goods	1662.4	
Services	3420.8	
Total		5,807.9
Gross private domestic investment (I)		
Fixed investment	1307.8	
Change in business inventories	59.3	
Total		1367.1
Government purchases (G)		
Federal	520.6	
State and local	966.5	
Total		1487.1
Exports and imports of goods and services		
Exports (X)	959.0	
Imports (M)	1110.2	
Net total ($X - M$)		-151.2
Total expenditures on GDP		8551.0

Source: Council of Economic Advisers, *Economic Report of the President* (Washington, D.C.: U.S. Government Printing Office, 1999), pp. 340–341.

are broken down into spending on durable goods, on nondurable goods, and on services. Durable goods are items such as refrigerators that are expected to last for more than three years. Nondurable goods are such things as food and clothes that are not expected to last for more than three years. Services are intangible items such as travel, car repair, entertainment, and medical care. Personal consumption expenditures represent the largest expenditure component of GDP ($5807.9 billion in 1995).

Gross private domestic investment (I)

Total spending by private businesses on final goods, including capital goods and inventories.

Gross Private Domestic Investment   Expenditures on final output by private business firms (including resource-owning households) are called **gross private domestic investment (I).** Investment expenditures include spending on capital goods such as machinery and warehouses, new residential construction, improvements to existing houses, farm investments, and inventories. These expenditures were $1367.1 billion in 1998. The qualifier *gross* is used because these expenditures include spending on new plant and equipment as well as on the replacement of worn-out plant and equipment. Business inventories are an investment in the holding of

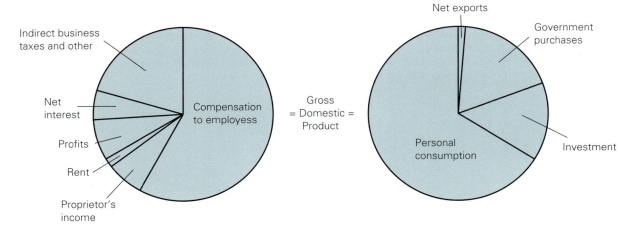

FIGURE 20.3

Total Expenditures Equal Total Income Plus Adjustments
In any given year, total expenditures, composed of consumption, investment, government purchases, and net foreign spending, must equal the income to the factors of production plus corrections. This income is composed of wages, rents, interest, proprietor's income, and corporate profits. The flow of total expenditures must equal the flow of total earnings.

finished goods, semifinished goods, or raw materials by business firms. Investment in business inventories can vary greatly; that is, inventories can be built up or drawn down. For example, firms often draw down the level of their inventories in a period when business is bad, such as a recession. They hold fewer goods in inventory in the anticipation of decreased demand for the goods by consumers. Conversely, businesses will add to inventories in anticipation of sales increases and prosperous times. Investment, for example, appears to have played a key role in the boom of the 1990s (see the Focus "Business Investment Leads the 1990s Boom").

Government purchases (G)
Total spending by federal, state, and local governments on final goods and services.

Net exports (X − M)
Total spending by foreigners on domestically produced goods and services minus total spending by domestic residents on foreign produced goods and services.

Exports (X)
Total spending by foreigners on domestically produced goods and services.

Imports (M)
Total spending by domestic residents on foreign produced goods and services.

Government Purchases   The third component in the expenditure approach to GDP is **government purchases (G)** of final goods and services at the federal, state, and local levels. Government spending was $1487.1 billion in 1998. Government transfer payments, such as Social Security and veterans' benefits, are not included in this figure because such payments are not made to individuals for current productive activities.

Net Exports   The final category of spending in the expenditure approach to GDP is **net exports (X − M). Exports (X)** are domestic goods purchased by foreigners. **Imports (M)** are foreign goods purchased by U.S. citizens. The purpose of GDP accounting is to measure current production in the economy. Thus, we must add the value of domestic goods purchased by foreigners and subtract the value of foreign goods purchased by Americans in calculating GDP by the expenditures approach. In other words,

$$\text{Net exports} = \text{Total exports } (X) - \text{Total imports } (M).$$

FOCUS

Business Investment Leads the 1990s Boom

The role of private business investment in creating the basis for prosperity can hardly be overestimated. The boom of the 1990s is a prime example. Figure 20.4 compares the average role of investment in the post–World War II expansions (in lighter shade) with that in the expansion and prosperity of the 1990s (in black).[a] Total business fixed investment is divided into producers' durable equipment and nonresidential structures. Clearly, the dominant influence of investment derives from outlays for producers' durable equipment, which increased at a real annual rate of over 10 percent and contributed twice as strongly to GDP growth over the 1990s as in the average postwar boom. This effect has dominated investments in nonresidential structures (primarily "buildings").

Four keys to this incredible investment boom are not hard to find.

- Robust real output growth (see Figure 19.4 for example) and sales obviously stimulate growth in capital stock. (Note, of course, that higher investment growth also stimulates income growth.)

---

[a]Data and figure from the *Economic Report of the President* (Washington, D.C.: U.S. Government Printing Office, 1999), pp. 69–73.

- A second factor is the significantly higher profit rates that occurred over the period of the 1990s. Compared with the 1980s peak of profits at about 9 percent, for example, profits represented almost 12 percent of national income in 1998.

- A third factor is the availability of funding through higher savings in the 1990s. With the balanced budgets (or less "imbalanced" budgets) of the late 1990s, less Federal borrowing has been necessary, leaving a larger amount of loanable funds to private investment (also signaling lower interest rates).

- Finally, a fourth factor spurring private investment, particularly in equipment, is the highly significant drop in the price of computers. Over the first three quarters of 1998 alone, for example, the price of computers dropped 30 percent (after 25 percent drops in 1996 and 1997). Real computer spending in 1999 was about twelve times as large as in the late 1980s.

The important result of this boom in investment has been economic prosperity, accompanied by low unemployment and a decline in the rate of inflation. Small wonder that economists pay so much attention to investment as an indicator of economic health!

FIGURE 20.4

Contribution of Business Investment to GDP Growth

Investment in equipment rather than buildings accounts for a much higher share of real GDP in the 1990s than has been the case in earlier postwar booms. Total business fixed investment is the sum of producers' durable equipment and expenditures on nonresidential structures.

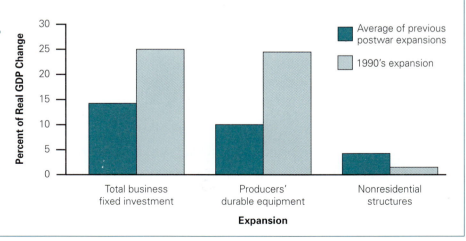

Net exports can be negative or positive. Obviously, if we spend more on imports than we sell in exports, net exports are going to be negative. In 1998, net exports were negative. We imported more than we exported by $151.2 billion.

The flow of expenditures approach to measuring GDP is quite simple:

GDP = Personal consumption expenditures (*C*)
  + Gross private domestic investment (*I*)
  + Government purchases (*G*)
  + Net exports (*X* − *M*),

or

$$GDP = C + I + G + (X - M).$$

By this method, GDP was $8551.0 billion in 1998, as shown in Table 20.1. Keep in mind that the expenditures approach is the national income accounting measure of the upper loop in the circular flow model of economic activity.

The Flow of Earnings Approach

The flow of earnings approach should give us the same value for GDP as does the expenditures approach. Table 20.2 gives the categories used in the flow of earnings approach. (Refer also to Figure 20.3.)

National income (NI)

Total earnings of resource suppliers during a given period of time.

National Income The most inclusive figure in the flow of earnings approach to GDP is specifically called **national income (NI).** NI is determined by adding the

TABLE 20.2

Gross Domestic Product, 1998: The Flow of Earnings

GDP can be calculated by summing the incomes received by suppliers of resources. Labor income, interest income, rental income, and profits are all summed—with adjustments for in-direct business taxes and depreciation—to obtain the same level of GDP as found by the expenditures approach.

	Earnings (billions of dollars)
1. Compensation of employees	4981.0
2. Proprietors' income	577.2
3. Rental income of persons	162.2
4. Corporate profits	824.6
5. Net interest	449.3
National income (total of 1–5)	6994.7
6. Indirect business taxes and other adjustments	606.4
7. Capital consumption allowances (depreciation)	908.0
Gross domestic product (GDP)	8511.0

Source: U.S. Department of Commerce, Bureau of Economic Analysis, www.bea.doc.gov/bea.

Note: GDP is in nominal 1998 dollars.

income earned by factors of production (land, labor, capital, and entrepreneur-ship) used to produce final goods and services during a given period. Table 20.2 shows national income of $6994.7 billion for 1998, the sum of income items 1 through 5: compensation of employees, proprietors' income, rental income of persons, corporate profits, and net interest.

- *Compensation of Employees.*   Compensation of employees is the largest component of national income. It is the sum of wages and salaries paid to employees plus employer contributions to Social Security and employee benefit plans. In 1998, this category amounted to $4981.0 billion.

- *Proprietors' Income.*   Proprietors' income is the net income earned by sole proprietorships and partnerships. Both proprietorships and partnerships are mainly small businesses that are not incorporated. This income in 1998 was $577.2 billion.

- *Rental Income of Persons.*   Rental income of persons is the income of individuals from renting property, such as a house or a car, as well as returns to individuals who hold patents, copyrights, and rights to natural resources, such as an oil or timber lease. National income accountants also estimate a rental value to owner-occupied houses. In other words, home ownership is treated like a business that produces a service sold to the owner. All of these forms of rental income yielded earnings of $162.2 billion in 1998.

- *Corporate Profits.*   Corporate profits are the net income of private corporations, including profits on foreign operations. The total of corporate profits was $824.6 billion in 1998.

- *Net Interest.*   Net interest consists of the interest received by U.S. households and governments minus the interest paid by these households and governments. Net interest was $449.3 billion in 1998.

From National Income to Gross Domestic Product   The figure for national income in Table 20.2—the sum of income items 1 through 5—does not equal the 1998 figure for gross domestic product in Table 20.1 figured by the flow of expenditures approach. Yet we know by the principle of the circular flow model that both approaches to measuring GDP must yield the same result. The problem is that there are two items—items included in total expenditures that are not income to anyone—that must be added to national income to obtain GDP. Let us examine these adjustments.

- *Indirect Business Taxes and Other Adjustments.*   Indirect business taxes and other adjustments ($606.4 billion in Table 20.2) must be added to national income to determine GDP because such taxes are part of the total expenditures on goods and services but are not received by anyone as income. These include sales and excise taxes paid by purchasers of goods and services; property taxes; business transfer payments such as corporate donations to charitable institutions; government subsidies; and other minor statistical adjustments.

- *Capital Consumption Allowances.*   Capital consumption allowances, or depreciation, are an adjustment made for the wearing out of capital goods such as plant and equipment during the current production period. Capital consumption allowances, like indirect business taxes, enter the flow of earnings approach to calculating GDP even though they do not truly represent earnings. They do represent, however, part of the resource cost of producing

GDP. Depreciation is not an expenditure on final output. For this reason, these items are included in the flow of earnings calculation of GDP. In Table 20.2, depreciation is equal to $908.0 billion. With adjustments for indirect business taxes and capital consumption allowances, GDP figured by the flow of earnings approach is $8511.0 billion, the same estimate derived from the flow of expenditures approach given in Table 20.1. Using the flow of earnings method of accounting, GDP is, in short, the sum of returns to the factors of production (wages, proprietors' income, rents, interest, and corporate profits) plus indirect business taxes and depreciation.

THE MEASUREMENT OF PRICE CHANGES

Was GDP in 1998 greater than in 1980? To answer this question, we might simply compare GDP for 1980 and 1998. Yet changes in prices make such comparisons difficult. Think of a simple world in which only chocolate fudge is produced. The fact that total expenditures on fudge rose from $5 million in 1980 to $10 million in 1998 tells us very little. Total expenditures will increase if (a) more fudge is produced, (b) the price of fudge rises, or (c) both (a) and (b) happen at the same time. The same facts hold for changes in GDP. GDP can change over time because total output increases, prices increase, or both happen at the same time. Thus, because we are interested in comparing differences in aggregate output over time when using national income statistics, a means has to be found to adjust GDP data for changes in prices. (The more difficult issue of changes in the type and quality of goods over time is treated in the Focus "Should You Trust GDP as an Economic Measure?") The **price level** is the average of the prices of all goods and services. It is not to be confused with relative prices, which show the price of one good in terms of another.

Price level

The average of the prices of all goods and services in the economy; used for calculating the inflation rate and for converting nominal into real values.

Price index

A statistic used to calculate the price level and the rate of inflation.

Economists and national income statisticians approach the problem of detecting price level changes by constructing a **price index.** All indexes use a base year, against which subsequent changes in prices are measured. Any price index compares the average level of prices at a given point in time (be it today or 1947) to the average level of prices at some specific point in the past (the base year or period). If the ratio is greater than 1, then prices in general are greater at the time for which the index is calculated than they were in the base year. If the ratio is less than 1, then prices are generally lower than in the base period. (The consumer price index formula is multiplied by 100.)

Price indexes serve two very important functions. Above all, they give us a measure of what is happening to the overall level of prices. By calculating the percentage change in a price index, the inflation rate over any given time period is measured. Additionally, a price index can be used to convert nominal variables, such as GDP, to real variables. Suppose the price index is based in 1982. Dividing nominal GDP in 1998 by the price index in 1998 (based in 1982) gives a measure of the total output of the economy in 1998 measured in 1982 prices. This allows more accurate comparisons of GDP between years, comparisons that are not biased by price changes. This gives a more accurate picture of how aggregate output changes over time. Almost all nominal variables can be converted to real variables by dividing by a price index. Government statistics calculate several indexes for the American economy.

FOCUS

Comparisons of GDP over time are even more complicated than controlling for price changes with a price index. Such comparisons are fundamentally difficult because entrepreneurs introduce new and improved goods and services to the economy. For example, how useful is it to compare GDP in 1890 with GDP in 2000? The United States at these two time periods comprised two different economies. In 2000, there are cars, fast-food restaurants, televisions, computers, and liver transplants. These goods and services did not exist in 1890. On the other hand, there was a great deal of open land, a relatively low crime rate, and little or no acid rain in 1890.

The goods available to consumers—that is, the final outputs of the economy—change over time. Even someone with a lot of money in 1890 could not have purchased what the average middle-income family purchases today. The point is simple but profound. An economy changes across time, and comparisons of GDP therefore lose much of their relevance.

So, while we know that the U.S. economy has grown remarkably over its history, the fact that the bundle of goods available to consumers has changed over time makes the measurement of this growth difficult. For example, real GDP per capita in 1999 was more than twice what it was in 1960. Does this mean that workers in the United States produced roughly twice the amount in 1999 as those in 1960? The problem is that GDP cannot give a clear answer to this type of question. (Remember: A change in GDP does not necessarily measure a change in welfare.) The goods produced in each period have changed. We do not now produce more of the same goods produced in 1960, or even in 1998. Our capacity to produce goods and services has increased, no doubt, but the exact amount of this growth is not measured by the growth of real GDP.

The farther apart in time that comparisons of GDP are made, the more severe is the problem caused by the differences in economies in the two periods. However, even over a short period, GDP comparisons are difficult because of changes in the quality of existing goods. In a span of a little more than ten years, consumers in the United States have gained access to improved goods such as cable television and more efficient computers. Do these improvements in quality mean growth in the value of the economy? If so, how could it possibly be measured? These complications indicate that GDP comparisons over time are useful, but not perfect.

Finally, exactly the same point can be made about the difficulty of comparisons of GDP across countries. Countries obviously produce different bundles of goods, and for the reasons just given, international comparisons of GDP are difficult and subject to interpretation. Different tastes for goods and services likely exist across countries, further complicating simple GDP comparisons intended to reflect differences in economic well-being. None of this argues that comparisons of GDP are meaningless. The point is that such comparisons should be made carefully and conclusions drawn about economic growth only after a careful study of all the relevant information about the economy or economies concerned. A healthy bit of skepticism should accompany all statistics!

The Consumer Price Index

Consumer price index (CPI)

A price index that uses the prices of goods and services consumers generally buy to calculate the price level and the rate of inflation.

The **consumer price index (CPI)** measures price changes in a typical market basket of goods purchased by urban wage earners and clerical workers. This "market basket" was developed from a survey of about 20,000 families, who provided information on their buying habits. The market basket includes food, housing (rental costs), apparel, transportation, health and recreation, and miscellaneous services.

To measure price changes in the market basket, the Bureau of Labor Statistics at the Department of Labor collects data every month from a wide variety of retail stores and service establishments. The CPI is issued monthly, and its base period is 1982–1984. Current prices are compared with average base-period prices. In the CPI, 1982–1984 = 100.

The Implicit Price Deflator

Implicit price deflator
A price index that uses the most comprehensive set of prices to calculate the level of prices and the rate of inflation facing households, businesses, and government; also called the GDP deflator.

Another major index is the **implicit price deflator,** often called the GDP deflator. This index goes to the heart of the problem of measuring price changes over time. As we have seen, it is impossible to add the different outputs of goods over time. Rather, we add the dollar amounts spent on commodities. But since both prices and quantities of commodities can change over time, the comparison of GDP at different points in time is difficult. Remember that the economist is interested in measuring the economy's real output. Therefore, the GDP statistician must be careful to distinguish current or nominal GDP, which is evaluated in current dollars, from real or constant GDP, which is evaluated in constant dollars. The implicit price deflator is a means to convert nominal GDP values into real GDP values.

The GDP deflator is similar to the CPI in that it is a price index. However, the GDP deflator is a broader index of prices than the CPI. The CPI pertains only to goods and services purchased by consumers; the implicit price deflator also takes into account goods and services generally consumed by producers and government. A major weakness of price indexes is the noncompatibility of base years. Government agencies that collect and publish various statistics often change the base year used, causing potential confusion. Nominal GDP is converted to real GDP by use of the GDP deflator—that is, by dividing nominal GDP by a constant GDP value for the same base-year prices. For example, Table 20.3 reveals that the GDP deflator was 1.127 in 1998. This number tells us that, on average, prices were 12.7 percent higher in 1998 than in 1992 (1992 being the base year). Nominal GDP for 1998, $8511.0 billion, divided by the GDP deflator for 1992 gives the real GDP for 1998: $7551.9 billion (8511.0/1.127). This number indicates what the value of GDP would have been in 1998 if prices had not changed since 1992. Thus, it measures the value of the output of goods and services in 1998 in terms of 1992 prices.

Table 20.3 shows GDP both in constant-dollar and current-dollar (or nominal) terms, using the varying price deflator for GDP for the period 1975–1998. One interesting aspect of these data is that between 1979 and 1980, 1981 and 1982, and 1990 and 1991, GDP in current terms was rising while real GDP was falling. In other words, growth in the GDP was due to inflation in prices rather than to increases in output. The proper measure of the real performance of the economy is the movement of real GDP over time.

We have talked a great deal in this chapter about the deficiencies of various measures of economic health. It should now be clear that no single measure of unemployment, inflation, or economic growth is a perfect indicator of economic well-being. Despite their limitations, however, such measures are useful: They form the basis for an understanding of the effects of macroeconomic and monetary policies.

TABLE 20.3

Nominal GDP, GDP Deflator, and Real GDP, 1975–1998

The GDP deflator is used to convert nominal GDP into real GDP. By dividing any year's GDP by that year's GDP deflator, one can estimate real GDP in terms of 1992 dollars.

Year	Nominal GDP (billions of dollars)	GDP Deflator (1992 = 1)	Constant GDP (billions of 1992 dollars)
1975	1630.6	0.422	3865.1
1976	1819.0	0.446	4081.1
1977	2026.9	0.475	4279.3
1978	2291.4	0.509	4493.7
1979	2557.5	0.553	4624.0
1980	2784.2	0.604	4611.9
1981	3115.9	0.661	4724.9
1982	3242.1	0.702	4623.6
1983	3514.5	0.732	4810.0
1984	3902.4	0.759	5138.2
1985	4180.7	0.786	5329.5
1986	4422.2	0.806	5489.9
1987	4692.3	0.831	5648.4
1988	5049.6	0.861	5862.9
1989	5438.7	0.897	6060.4
1990	5743.8	0.936	6138.7
1991	5916.7	0.973	6079.0
1992	6244.4	1.000	6244.4
1993	6550.2	1.026	6383.8
1994	6931.4	1.050	6604.2
1995	7269.6	1.075	6761.7
1996	7661.6	1.095	6994.8
1997	8110.9	1.115	7269.8
1998	8511.0	1.127	7551.9

Source: Council of Economic Advisers, *Economic Report of the President* (Washington, D.C.: U.S. Government Printing Office, 1999), pp. 326, 328, 330.

APPLICATION

Beating the IRS: How Big Is the Underground Economy?

The underground economy refers to all the transactions between individuals and firms that are not officially recorded in the government's national income accounts. Unrecorded transactions are not limited to illicit transactions such as gambling, prostitution, and the drug trade. They also include the summer yard work that children and teenagers do for pay, babysitting and daytime child-care services that are paid for in cash and not reported to the Internal Revenue Service (IRS), the many kinds of barter transactions that occur, and a multitude of other exchanges that take place in economies that simply do not get entered on the official books.

The exact size of the underground economy is unknown but estimates range up to 25 percent of GDP.

One factor responsible for the existence of the underground economy is the income tax and all other taxes levied at all levels of government. Individuals act in their own self-interest, and some will choose to evade paying a portion of their taxes in order to increase their wealth. Some professionals simply do not declare all their earned income on their income tax forms. Waiters and waitresses occasionally underestimate their tips to the tax authorities. One result is that the value of these services does not enter the government's official income accounts. Nonetheless, the services these people perform make the economy wealthier and should be reflected in GDP. Quite often these unreported transactions are purely cash transactions. Checks or credit cards leave a paper trail, whereas cash is much harder for income tax auditors to trace.

Income tax rates have traditionally played a major role in determining the extent and size of the underground economy. When people barter or swap goods and services, the value of the transaction goes unreported in GDP but still enhances the barterer's economic welfare. When the relevant tax rates that individuals face are lower, the incentive to barter is diminished, and the underground economy will shrink in size. Indeed, this was one of the reasons that the top federal income tax rate was lowered in the late 1980s. (In 1991 and, more significantly, in 1993, the top marginal rate was raised; however, other taxes at all levels—including Social Security taxes—have also been rising in recent years.)

A third explanation for the existence of the underground economy is that artificial entry barriers exist in many occupations. Factors such as a person's age, immigrant status, union status, or other legal requirements may prevent employment in the regular economy. Illegal aliens may work as domestics for unreported income in order to avoid detection and deportation. Hundreds of "gypsy cabs" operate in New York City; these private automobiles that ferry passengers about the city are driven by people unable to obtain a license for an official taxicab. Other people work in the underground economy because they can earn larger incomes than they could by working in the official economy.

Just how big is the underground economy? No one knows for sure, and economists have used various techniques to estimate its size. One method is to compare Department of Commerce data on GDP to the IRS's income data. Another approach looks at government data concerning the proportion of the population that is officially reported as employed. This figure can be compared with the number that could reasonably be expected in calculating the size of underground income earned. A third method tracks the total amount of cash, including the amount in "large" bills, circulating in an economy and compares it with total checking accounts and credit purchases. Unusually large amounts of cash or numbers of large bills indicate a large underground economy.

Estimates on the size of the underground economy in the United States for the late 1970s range from 4 to 25 percent of GDP. If 10 percent of all economic activity were hidden from official view in 2000, then underground GDP would total well over $500 billion. While this is large in absolute terms, some have estimated Italy's underground economy to amount to about 35 to 40 percent of that country's official GDP. Japan, however, appears to produce only about 1 to 2 percent of its total output in an underground economy. Clearly, such factors as tax rates, cultural attitudes, laws, and resources devoted to uncovering the underground economy will influence the extent of such activity across countries.

QUESTIONS

What measures can government take to reduce the size of the underground economy? Explain how underground markets may actually be more efficient than legal markets.

SUMMARY

1. National income accounting is concerned with the measurement of the aggregate performance of the economy.
2. Gross domestic product (GDP) is the market value of all the final goods and services produced in an economy during a given period. It includes only currently produced goods and services, and it excludes such items as illegal transactions and household production.
3. GDP is not a measure of economic welfare. It does not count social costs such as pollution, which lower economic welfare, or such goods as leisure, which raise economic welfare.
4. Gross domestic product can be computed in two ways: by adding expenditures on final goods and services produced during a given period or by adding the earnings or incomes of the factors of production used to produce final goods and services during the period. The two approaches, subject to a statistical discrepancy, yield the same result for GDP:

The Flow of Expenditures Approach

personal consumption expenditures	gross private domestic investment	government purchases of final goods and services	net exports	
(C)	+ (I)	+ (G)	+ ($X - M$)	= GDP

The Flow of Earnings Approach

wages	+	proprietors' income	+	rents	+	net interest	+	corporate profits
+		indirect business taxes		+		depreciation	=	GDP

The flow of expenditures approach focuses on buyers' evaluations of goods produced during a year. The flow of earnings approach concentrates on the cost of production of goods and services. The circular flow of economic activity, therefore, ensures that the two approaches are identical. That is,

$$\text{Dollar spending on final outputs} = \text{GDP} = \text{Dollar costs of producing final outputs.}$$

5. To compare GDP in different time periods, some method must be used to control for price changes. The government uses indexes, including the consumer price index and the implicit price deflator for GDP.

KEY TERMS

national income accounting
gross domestic product (GDP)
gross national product (GNP)
final goods
measure of economic welfare
(MEW)
flow of expenditures

flow of earnings
personal consumption
expenditures (C)
gross private domestic
investment (I)
government purchases (G)
net exports (X − M)

exports (X)
imports (M)
national income (NI)
price level
price index
consumer price index (CPI)
implicit price deflator

QUESTIONS FOR REVIEW AND DISCUSSION

1. Why does GDP count only the production of final goods and services? Why aren't intermediate goods and services counted?

2. List three reasons GDP should not be considered an overall indicator of society's well-being.

3. What are the three approaches used to estimate GDP?

4. American society has become more urbanized and industrialized since 1930. Other things being equal, do you think this means that our measurement of GDP is more or less precise? Why?

5. What is GDP in constant dollars? How is it calculated?

6. Why might GDP be a misleading statistic with which to compare the economy of the United States with that of China?

7. Which of the following are counted in the calculation of this year's GDP: (a) the services provided by a homemaker; (b) the wage paid to a maid; (c) Sam's purchase of an antique desk; (d) Joan's purchase of ten shares of stock; (e) Social Security checks received by the elderly; (f) Social Security taxes paid by workers?

8. In the former Soviet Union, black markets supplied final goods and services that the central government did not provide in adequate quantities. Were these final goods and services counted as part of the Soviet Union's GDP?

9. How are leakages transformed into injections?

10. Using the flow of expenditures approach, why are trade deficits detrimental to the economy?

11. If fewer final goods and services are produced this year than were produced last year, can GDP increase during the same time period? How?

12. Explain the differences between the consumer price index and the implicit price deflator.

PROBLEMS

1. Suppose that nominal GDP in 1998 totals $8475 billion and rises to $12.5 trillion ten years later. If the GDP deflator for 1998 is 1.85 and for 2008 is 2.75, in what year is real GDP greater? By how much?

2. Consider the following information for the country Alpha. During the past year, consumption expenditures increased by $13.5 billion, gross private domestic investment increased by $5.8 billion, and government purchases declined by $10.4 billion. In addition, the country experienced a trade deficit of $2.9 billion. Did Alpha's GDP increase or decrease? By how much?

WORKING WITH THE WEB

1. The size of the underground economy is a relevant issue within the context of measuring GDP, and yet as the chapter implies it is difficult to measure. One method mentioned in this chapter's Application is to consider the growth of "large" bills in circulation. A discussion of this topic can be found through the web site of the National Center for Policy Analysis (http://www.ncpa.org).

   When you arrive at the site, do a search for the document by entering the words "Analysis 273." You should see a link for the report "Brief Analysis 273: The Underground Economy." Click on this link, read the article, and answer the following question.

   Based on the growth of $100 bills as a percentage of the value of all outstanding U.S. currency, explain whether the underground economy appears to be growing or shrinking.

2. The Federal Reserve Bank of Minneapolis has an inflation calculator at their web site (http://woodrow.mpls.frb.fed.us/economy/calc/cpihome.html). This calculator allows you to find out the value of money from any year between 1913 and 1998.

   a. What is the value of $100 worth of goods purchased in 1920 in each of the following years: 1930, 1940, 1950, 1960, 1970, 1980, and 1990 (these years should be entered in the second "box" where a year must be recorded, while 1920 should be entered in the first "box")?

   b. Do you observe deflation or inflation between 1920 and any of these years?

Classical Macroeconomic Theory

Measuring the rise and fall of macroeconomic variables such as the rate of inflation, GDP, and unemployment is only a first step toward understanding why these economic indicators fluctuate and what measures, if any, are needed to maintain stability and growth.

The next three chapters survey some of the major theoretical tools of macroeconomics to discover the conditions under which the economy can achieve stability and growth. We concentrate on both aggregate demand—the spending side of the economy—and aggregate supply—the producing side of the economy. This chapter and Chapter 22 develop economic principles pertaining to aggregate demand. Chapters 23 and 24 deal with the interaction of aggregate demand and aggregate supply.

Some simplifications are necessary to understand how aggregate demand and supply interact to sustain full employment, economic growth, and low levels of inflation. This chapter and the next concentrate on two views of consumer and business spending—the private or nongovernment part of aggregate spending. The first view is the classical notion of a self-regulating aggregate economy; the second is the perspective of John Maynard Keynes, who focused attention on how spending changes cause prosperity and depression. To simplify our development of aggregate demand and supply theories, we only briefly cover here important but complicating variables such as the money supply. We defer our in-depth analysis of money until Part Six.

The classical view sees the economy as self-regulating, without need of large-scale government intervention. A full appreciation of the classical view is the starting point for understanding how and why Keynes and others modified macroeconomic theory. When you complete Chapter 21 you should understand

- why the classical writers had faith that a nonregulated economy could fully employ all resources in the long run.
- the four essential components of the classical view that the economy would function at or near full employment over time.
- the basic classical view that government intervention should be minimized in the private economy.
- how classical macroeconomic theories and their policies interrelate.

CLASSICAL THEORY

Will the economy remain as close as possible to its production possibilities frontier? Will it manage to keep all resources, human and nonhuman, fully employed? More fundamentally, will the economy automatically produce full employment, a maximum GDP, and price stability? If not, what actions are necessary to maintain these important goals?

Classical macroeconomic theory

A view of the macroeconomy as being self-adjusting and capable of generating full employment and maximum output in the long run without government intervention; dominant from the late eighteenth century through the early twentieth century.

Historically, economists have given many different answers to these difficult questions. **Classical macroeconomic theory** stems from Adam Smith's pioneering work, *An Inquiry into the Nature and Causes of the Wealth of Nations*, published in 1776. Smith, and those who followed in the classical tradition, believed that given laissez-faire government policies and enough time, the economy would achieve the goals of price stability, full employment, and economic growth through its own ability to correct short-run unemployment and inflation. In other words, the classical theorists believed that unemployment and inflation were temporary phenomena. In the long run (a period of time that is hard to specify), the economy would remain close to or on its production possibilities frontier and enjoy a stable level of prices. The theory that grew from Smith's faith in a self-adjusting market mechanism was the work of many economists who wrote at different times in response to different conditions. The following simplified discussion of classical macroeconomics is a composite of various individual contributions. First, consider the classical engine of economic growth.

The Classical Blueprint for Economic Growth

Classical process of economic growth

A process based on the division of labor, but also involving increases in saving, investment, capital accumulation, and, ultimately, growth in real GDP.

The classical economists were writing at a time of rapid technological advance. Attitudes toward the Industrial Revolution—the catchphrase for the technological advances of the eighteenth and early nineteenth centuries—undoubtedly colored the classical economists' conception of how the economy works and grows. The **classical process of economic growth** conceives of a circular flow of human activities leading to growth in per capita output and economic well-being for the average citizen of the economy. The circular flow of this classical process of economic growth—like the one considered in Chapter 20—focuses on the real factors and activities leading to economic growth.

Division of labor

An economic principle whereby individuals specialize in the production of a single good, service, or task, thereby increasing overall productivity and economic efficiency.

The heart of Adam Smith's view of economic progress is the natural tendency for society to divide tasks. The **division of labor** in producing output creates enormous advantages for society. A modern assembly line or fast-food production by McDonald's are excellent examples of the division of labor. Given enough time, a single worker could certainly build an automobile from scratch. Only the hobbyist would approach car building this way, however. Adam Smith hit on the critical idea (from observation) that the division of tasks (in the context of automobile manufacturing, fitting parts, welding motor parts, installing windshields, and the like) educates workers in some critically important ways. The repetition of specific tasks in production leads to increased skill and dexterity in every worker, thereby increasing human capital and productivity. The repetition of specific tasks also fosters invention and creativity in workers—an advantage encouraged by the narrow focus of the individual's attention on particular tasks. Moreover, while training and retraining for specific tasks takes time, on balance the application of the division of labor saves time in that workers need not move from task to task.

Figure 21.1 shows, in simplified form, how the division of labor leads to the growth of real output as it works its way through production processes in an economy. As the circular flow progresses, increased real GDP creates higher real wages and higher per capita incomes. Higher wages and incomes permit individuals to consume and save more annually. But, as we will see in more detail later in the chapter, saving by some individuals is translated directly into investment by other individuals. At low interest rates, individuals want to invest more, and savers want to save less. High rates encourage savers and discourage investors. There is a point at which the desires of savers and of investors are in equilibrium.

The process depicted in Figure 21.1 is continuous; there is no starting point. Each element is equally important to the process, and each can serve as the "first step." For ease in understanding, however, we may think of the process as beginning with increased demand (consumption) for goods. The saving of consumers permits, through the link to investment, additional capital accumulation. An increase in the (net) capital stock raises the productivity of both labor and natural resources, permitting more division of labor. The result of greater application of capital and enhanced division of labor is higher real GDP. Wages rise, as do per capita incomes, leading to more consumption, saving, and investment. The process continues until, in Adam Smith's words, the extent of the market is reached—that is, until domestic and international markets are saturated with goods and services.

It is worthwhile to remember that, in this simple process, savings are translated *automatically* into the exceptionally important mechanism of investment. Through investment, capital is accumulated. Capital—broadly defined to include factories, machinery, tools, and human skills—is a force for growth because it permits and facilitates the division of labor. Increased capital accumulation, as shown in the circular

FIGURE 21.1

The Classical Process of Economic Growth

Enhanced division of labor in the classical growth process leads directly to increased output of goods and services. The division of labor is directly fueled by capital accumulation in the circular flow.

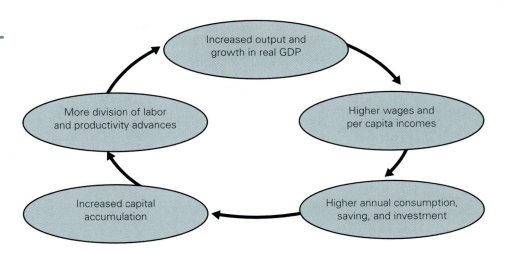

flow of Figure 21.1, allows increased division of labor and, along with it, increased *productivity of labor and capital.* Using Smith's words again, the "wealth of a nation"—GDP—is the annual product of the raw materials, land, and labor of a society, assisted, critically, by the accumulation of capital goods and the division of labor.

Many of the classical economists' predecessors equated the accumulation of gold and other precious metals with the wealth of a nation. Instead, according to the classical economists, human capital and resource development, assisted by growing capital and the division of labor, produced the wealth of the nation and contained the keys to economic growth. The division of labor gives rise to increased output and economic growth. Higher per capita wages and incomes result from increased real output. Higher incomes produce higher consumption and savings. Additional savings lead to additional investment in capital and in capital accumulation. Capital accumulation enhances and facilitates a greater division of labor, and the process continues.

Limits to Growth   The process depicted in Figure 21.1 is neither instantaneous nor limitless. As we already mentioned, the growth process may be limited by the "extent of the market." Profitable investment outlets may dry up as demand, both foreign and domestic, for goods and services becomes saturated. The classicals knew that the economy's maximum attainable output is limited by its actual supply of human and nonhuman resources, the state of technology, productivity, and population. The classical view of the macroeconomy was a **long-run equilibrium** conception. In other words, classical theory was concerned with how an economy adjusts to some hypothetical equilibrium given some actual supply of resources, level of population, technology, or state of specialization.

The classicals believed that mechanisms within the economy were self-adjusting—in other words, that mechanisms automatically brought full employment in the long run. Full employment of resources in the long run is, of course, tantamount to being on the economy's production possibilities curve (see Figure 21.2a). Society's choice between capital and consumer goods in the present has an effect on future economic growth. In the classical context, a choice of more capital goods relative to consumer goods means more investment and capital accumulation, which produces a greater division of labor and more rapid future economic growth. The point to remember, however, is that the attainment of any point such as A on PP_0 in Figure 21.2a is the result of self-adjusting forces in the economy in the long run. The exact point chosen on any production possibilities curve also depends on society's relative demands for present and future consumption. The society that chooses more capital goods at the expense of consumer goods will enjoy more future growth potential. The society that chooses more consumer goods in the present will enjoy more goods and services now but will have less growth potential.

Points such as A on PP_0 in Figure 21.2a also imply that all resources are fully employed in the economy. At the risk of getting a little ahead of ourselves, we should note that later economists, including Keynes, challenged the belief that automatic, self-adjusting forces could be relied upon to get the economy to points such as A on PP_0. They believed that certain short-run factors, such as wage and interest-rate inflexibility, inhibited the classical mechanism. For now, just keep in mind that points such as A in Figure 21.2a are attained only after adjustments take place in the long run and full employment is reached in the entire economy.

Economic Growth and Aggregate Supply   Economic growth, as summarized by a production possibilities model, may also be related to the aggregate (economy-

Classical long-run equilibrium

The hypothetical adjustment of an economy to full employment given an actual supply of resources, population, technology, and degree of specialization.

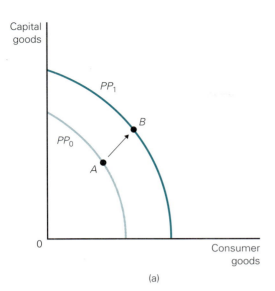

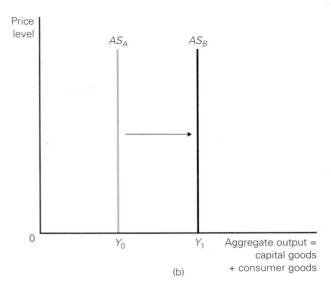

(a)

(b)

FIGURE 21.2

Production Possibilities and the Aggregate Supply Curve

In the long-run adjustment mechanism of classical economics, attainment of points such as A on production possibilities curve PP_0 of Figure 21.2a translates to a vertical aggregate supply curve such as AS_A and output level Y_0 in Figure 21.2b. In the classical model, there is no unemployment in the long run. Technological advances or discovery of new resources could be part of the long-run economy-wide adjustments that shift the production possibilities frontier and aggregate supply curve rightward.

wide) supply curve developed in Chapter 19. If production possibilities curve PP_0 is drawn under assumptions of constant technology, possibilities for the division of labor and economic growth are limited. The attainment of point A in Figure 21.2a may be viewed as equivalent to a level of income, Y_0, that defines the aggregate supply curve AS_A in Figure 21.2b. At any given moment, then, the growth process is limited by, among other things, the state of technology. The maximum amount of output that can be had out of the economy, irrespective of the price level, is designated AS_A or Y_0. Note that the vertical supply curve of Figure 21.2b differs from the upward-sloping aggregate supply curve in Chapter 19 because the attainment of any point on production possibilities curve PP_0 means that consumer and capital goods production is maximized. The upward-sloping aggregate supply curve indicates that some unemployment of resources exists—in other words, that the outer limits of the production possibilities curve have not been reached.

A change in technology or the augmentation of resources (perhaps through international trade or through resource discoveries) would shift the production possibilities curve rightward. Attainment of a new equilibrium point such as B in Figure 21.2a through long-run, economy-wide adjustments would shift the aggregate supply curve rightward. All points on new production possibilities frontier PP_1 contain higher total production of consumer and capital goods than on PP_0. In terms of Figure 21.2b, aggregate supply shifts to AS_B at output level Y_1. In short, the aggregate supply curve of any economy is based on the "possibilities" of attaining maximum production. A vertical aggregate supply curve means that society has reached the production possibilities curve of the economy.

Aggregate Demand, Aggregate Supply, and the Macroeconomic Problem

The aggregate demand and supply apparatus developed in Chapter 19 may be used to show possible policy choices facing economic decision makers. The impact of any change in aggregate demand created by fiscal or monetary policy will depend on the shape of the aggregate supply curve and on the initial point of intersection. The shape of the aggregate supply curve depends on the state of the economy—that is, on prevailing economic conditions. Consider Figure 21.3. The conditions described in this chapter—full employment of resources, an economy on its production possibilities frontier—are represented by the vertical portion of the aggregate supply curve in Figure 21.3 (the portion labeled "classical case"). When all available resources are employed, an individual producer can expand production only by bidding resources away from other competing producers. Under these con-

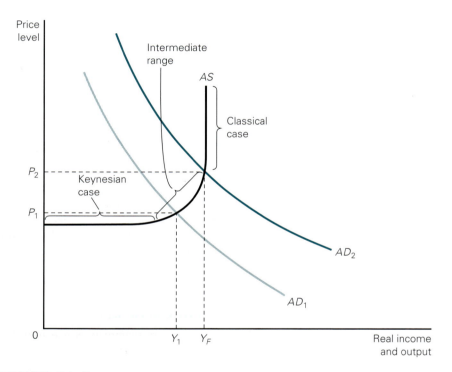

FIGURE 21.3

Aggregate Demand, Aggregate Supply, and Policy Choices

The effects of changes in aggregate demand on prices and output will be determined by the shape of the aggregate supply curve. Given economic depression and widespread unemployment (the Keynesian case), an increase in demand will increase real income with no increase in the price level. With fully employed resources (the classical case), an identical increase in aggregate demand will simply cause inflation with no increase in income. In the classical case, output cannot increase in real terms; it can, however, increase in nominal terms—an outcome called *inflation*. In the intermediate case, both the price level and real income respond somewhat to aggregate demand increases, such as a shift from AD_1 to AD_2.

ditions, any increase in aggregate demand will drive the price level up without increasing overall production.

Suppose, however, that the economy is merely producing fairly close to capacity. Under these conditions the aggregate supply curve will be steeply sloped, as depicted in Figure 21.3 by the portion of the curve labeled "intermediate range." In this case, any attempt to increase production leads to shortages of certain resources. The average cost of many productions of goods and services will rise with an increase in aggregate demand, as shown by the shift from AD_1 to AD_2 in Figure 21.3. Such an increase will inevitably increase prices from P_1 to P_2. Note, however, that aggregate output of goods and services, measured as real output on the horizontal axis of Figure 21.3, will rise from Y_1 to Y_F.

The existence of an intermediate case implies the existence of economic conditions that are the opposite of those represented by the vertical portion of the aggregate supply curve. Indeed, the horizontal portion of the aggregate supply curve, labeled "Keynesian case," represents a situation in which there are large quantities of unemployed resources available for work. (This portion of the aggregate supply is named for John Maynard Keynes, who paid a great deal of attention to the situation of massive unemployment in the economy.) When the economy is operating far below its capacity in this manner, production can increase without causing much of an increase in input prices. Not only is it possible to employ more labor without wage increases, all other kinds of resources (machinery, land, and capital) are readily available. Firms can hire more inputs without having to compete with other firms for them, thereby avoiding increased resource prices and higher average production costs. Small increases in aggregate demand would lead to large increases in national output.

The simple apparatus of aggregate demand and aggregate supply can show us the alternatives facing the economy, but a fuller understanding of economic policy can only be had with a closer analysis of each policy position. Keynesian and other newer views will be developed in future chapters. In this chapter we investigate how the classicals arrived at two startling conclusions: (1) that the aggregate supply curve was vertical and (2) that a self-adjusting mechanism virtually guaranteed that the economy would always tend toward full employment and full production in the long run if left unassisted by outside forces such as government.

Cornerstones of Classical Macroeconomic Theory

Classical economic theory primarily concerned itself with how economies grow and prosper. Imbedded within the elements of economic progress they described, however, is a theory of the macroeconomy. Taken as a group, the classicals developed an exact theory of how the economy adjusts in the long run to reach a point on the production possibilities or aggregate supply curve. The classical economist's belief that the economy self-adjusts in response to short-run disturbances and produces full employment and economic growth without government interference rests on four cornerstones:

1. Say's law;
2. Interest rate flexibility;
3. Price–wage flexibility; and
4. The quantity theory of money.

The first three cornerstones deal with the flexibility of the macroeconomy in maintaining full employment. The fourth concerns the determination of the price level and the control of inflation.

Say's law

A proposition of the classical economists that the production of goods and services will generate incomes sufficiently large that those goods and services will be purchased.

Say's Law   **Say's law** is an economic proposition first attributed to Jean-Baptiste Say (1767–1832). According to Say's law, diagrammed in Figure 21.4, the act of supplying goods, or total real output, is the equal but opposite side of demanding goods, or total real expenditures. Say's law implies that full employment is a permanent, built-in feature of the macroeconomy. Resource unemployment is impossible because the act of producing goods is the same act as demanding goods. In other words, supply creates its own demand.

Say believed that in a money economy the aggregate demand for goods and services is financed through the earning of income, as in the circular flow diagram in Figure 20.1. How do productive factors earn wages, rents, interests, and profits? They do so by producing goods and services. In this system, as in a barter system, the act of producing specific goods and services results in the demand for other goods and services.

According to Say, supply creates its own demand, since the income generated in the act of producing (or supplying) goods would always be used to buy (or demand) goods of equal value. Say's law may seem perfectly sensible, but what happens when consumers choose to save part of their income? The act of saving—the sacrifice of present consumption for larger future consumption—disrupts the perfect balance between income and output.

Saving is a leakage, or withdrawal, from the circular flow of income and spending. If this withdrawal from spending is not matched by an injection—another form of spending to compensate for the saving withdrawal—underconsumption and unemployment result, and Say's law does not work. Investment spending is one form of injection into the circular flow to make up for a savings leakage. But how do private savings—the leakage—and investment—the injection—become linked? Can Say's law be vindicated? The answer, the classical economists thought, lay in the mechanism of interest rates.

FIGURE 21.4

Say's Law

In the circular flow of income and output, the act of supplying goods and services is necessarily equal to the act of demanding goods and services.

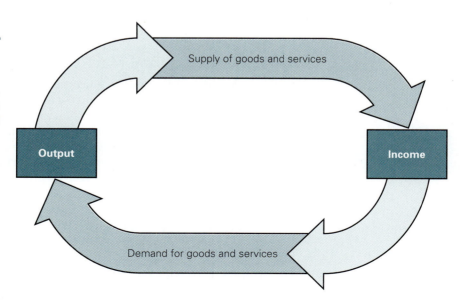

Interest Rate Flexibility　People save, or postpone current consumption, because of a reward for doing so. Interest paid on savings is their reward, enabling savers to consume more goods later. This important relation may be expressed

$$S = s(r),$$

Real rate of interest

The nominal interest rate minus the inflation rate; the interest rate that measures the true incentives and costs that savers and investors face.

or saving (S) is a function of the real rate of interest (r). The rate of interest is both the percentage that savers earn annually on their savings and the percentage that borrowers must pay to use funds deposited in savings institutions. The **real rate of interest** is the nominal rate of interest minus the annual rate of inflation. The real rate reflects the fundamental forces of saving and investment in the economy.

Classical economists believed that saving was positively related to the real interest rate: A rise in the interest rate increased the amount saved. For example, when the real interest rate increases from r_0 to r_1, depicted in Figure 21.5, consumer-savers in the economy are encouraged to save more for future consumption. The higher the interest rate, the less you must sacrifice today in order to increase consumption by a given amount in the future for a new car, a college education, a new house. A high interest rate encourages savers to devote greater amounts to saving out of current income because future goods become *cheaper* relative to current consumption. Any increase in attitudes encouraging saving would cause the S curve in Figure 21.5 to shift to the right, indicating more saving at all rates of interest. If attitudes toward thrift become discouraged, of course, the whole curve would shift to the left.

Keep in mind that increases in saving are accompanied by simultaneous decreases in current consumption. In other words, according to the classical model, aggregate demand falls by the amount that saving increases. Will an increase in saving mean that aggregate supply will not call forth enough aggregate demand? Will goods remain on shelves, inventories pile up, and thousands of workers be laid off? To both of these questions, the classical economists answered no—with the qualification that the economy must be allowed to reestablish its equilibrium. Not only does the interest rate paid to savers determine their choices, but the interest rate charged on loans determines the behavior of investors. Investment is a

FIGURE 21.5

The Classical Concept of Saving

Saving and interest rates are positively related. As the real rate of interest rises, from r_0 to r_1, the level of saving in the economy rises from S_0 to S_1. An increase in the amount saved means that present consumption, or demand, is diminished by an equal amount.

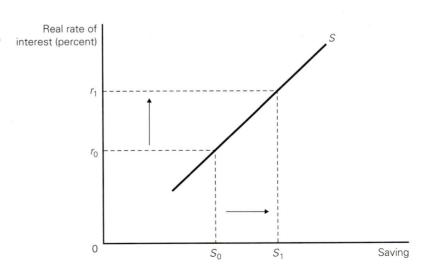

FIGURE 21.6

The Classical Concept of Investment

The amount invested (I) and the real rate of interest (r) are negatively related, given a constant rate of return on investment in capital goods. As the rate of interest falls from r_0 to r_1, businesses invest more in capital goods. The increase in investment expenditures from I_0 to I_1 represents a net increase in demand.

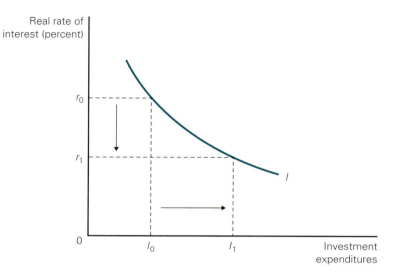

flow of expenditures to repair or replace capital goods or to make additions to the capital stock of the nation. Investment spending, just like consumption spending, generates income and employment.

In classical theory, a lower rate of interest makes more investment projects—such as expenditures for warehouses and machinery—profitable. Since interest payments factor into the cost of new investment, higher interest rates make new investment more costly, other things being equal. Investments become more attractive when the interest rate falls. The interest rate may be thought of as the price of loanable funds to investors. As this price (the interest rate) rises, investors are discouraged from engaging in new investment projects. As it falls, investors spend more on capital goods. Technically, this relation can be expressed as

$$I = i(r),$$

or investment (I) is a function of the real rate of interest (r). However, unlike the relation between saving and interest, investment and the real rate of interest are negatively related. Rises in r cause declines in the amount of I, and reductions in r provoke increases in the amount of I.

This inverse relation is depicted in Figure 21.6. As the real rate of interest declines, the investment spending represented by curve I increases. Conversely, when the rate of interest rises, fewer and fewer investment projects become profitable, and investment spending declines. Increases in the productivity of capital—through inventions or improvements in technology—would increase the level of investment at every rate of interest, shifting the whole curve to the right.

According to the classical system, saving and investment are balanced by means of the interest rate. Figure 21.7 reproduces the saving and investment curves already discussed. An initial economy-wide equilibrium is established where saving equals investment at interest rate r_0. At interest rate r_0, in other words, the amount that individuals in society wish to direct from consumption to savings is S_0. Real interest rate r_0 is the savers' reward for their thrift. At interest rate r_0, moreover, investors find I_0 worth of investment projects to be profitable—no more, no less. Given curves S and I, no other interest rate is compatible with equilibrium.

FIGURE 21.7

The Relation Between Rate of Interest, Saving, and Investment in the Classical System

Initial equilibrium E_0 is established at interest rate r_0 with saving and invest-ment curves S and I. An increase in thrift will cause the saving function to shift rightward from S to S_1, low-ering the rate of interest from r_0 to r_1. As the interest rate declines, the amount of investment spending increases. Reduction in the amount of consumption spending brought about by increased saving is there-fore accompanied by a counterbalancing increase in the amount of invest-ment spending.

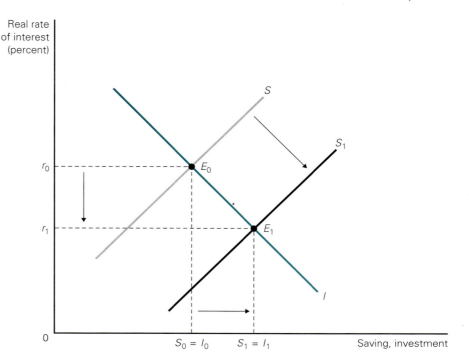

Why? Because an interest rate lower than r_0 would create a shortage of invest-ment funds, and one higher than r_0 would mean a surplus of funds. In the former case, according to the laws of supply and demand, investors' demand would force the interest rate up to r_0; in the case of a surplus of funds, savers' demand would force the interest rate down to r_0. To put the matter formally, macroeconomic equi-librium requires that the amount of saving equal the amount of investment, or, in terms of the preceding equations, that

$$S = I.$$

What happens if the whole saving curve or investment curve shifts, reflecting a sudden change in society's underlying attitudes toward thrift (increased saving for retirement or expectations of hard times) or a technological breakthrough that increases the productivity of investments? Suppose, for example, that individuals wish to save more at every rate of interest, shifting the saving function rightward from S to S_1 in Figure 21.7. A surplus of saving develops at interest rate r_0, forcing the rate of interest down. As the rate falls, investors take advantage of new, prof-itable investments. Finally, at the new equilibrium interest rate, r_1, a new higher quantity of savings, S_1, equals a new, higher level of investment expenditures, I_1.

If Say's law is true, all leakages from the income stream must be replaced by injections. According to classical economics, increases in saving (leakage) are replaced by increases in investment (injection) through the mechanism of the real rate of interest. Aggregate demand for goods and services would fall short of aggre-gate supply were it not for the mechanism of interest rates. In other words, the clas-sical economists believed that Say's law is valid if the interest rate is able to adjust freely upward or downward without regulations or restrictions. Consumption spending plus investment expenditures will be sufficient to purchase all of the output produced by the economy.

Price–Wage Flexibility The validity of Say's law requires another cornerstone of classical thought: **price–wage flexibility.** To understand this second concept, suppose that future economic conditions appear very uncertain. There might be expectations of war, of a coming depression, or even of an overall decrease in prices. In response to this uncertainty, individuals seek greater immediate economic security. A drastic increase in saving at such a time of crisis will have the effect of lowering the interest rate; the price of loanable funds is reduced to investors, encouraging more investment and additions to the capital stock and making up the difference for the reduction in consumption. But in the event of a sudden surge of saving, investors might not be able or willing to adjust their spending quickly enough to make up the difference in total spending. Aggregate demand would be insufficient to carry off the aggregate supply of goods and services, and Say's law (temporarily) would not hold; supply would not be creating its own demand. Unemployment would increase disastrously, leaving the economy vulnerable to collapse. According to classical theory, however, any such reduction in demand would also provoke another mechanism—price–wage adjustment.

With a (temporary) reduction in total spending, prices and wages would be expected to fall in the economy in proportion to the size of the reduction. As the prices of shoes, computer software, hair stylings, and all other goods and services decline, additional quantities of goods will be demanded, and all excess production will quickly be bought up by consumers. Wages of laborers and the prices of all raw materials and other inputs will also decline, encouraging their employment by businesses. Nominal wages and the price level (for commodities) will both decline, helping to preserve the purchasing power of the new, lower nominal incomes. The flexibility of prices and wages in a competitive market helps guarantee full employment, even in the event of a sharp and protracted reduction in aggregate demand.

It must be emphasized that the classical cornerstone of price–wage flexibility applies when aggregate demand is insufficient to maintain full employment for *any* reason. Natural disasters and wars were thought to pose no threat to full employment in the long run, as long as prices and wages were allowed to adjust. The purely competitive market system—an assumption of classical economists— is the fail-safe mechanism through which unemployment over long periods of time was thought to be impossible. For the system to operate properly, of course, there could be no restrictions on prices (such as price controls) or wages (such as minimum wage) in either product or resource markets.

The Quantity Theory of Money In the long run, real GDP and employment would be maximized in a laissez-faire economy. Thrift, the productivity of capital investment, and Say's law guaranteed maximum output in the classical economist's theoretical system. The price level and the nominal wage level were explained in the classical system by a theory that, in the long run, viewed output and employment as independent of the money supply—the **quantity theory of money.** The quantity theory of money simply states that, in the long run, there is a clear and proportional relation between the money supply and the price level in the economy.

While we postpone a detailed discussion of money and prices until later, it is useful at this point to understand some of the principles that underlie the formation of prices and inflation. The classical economists (like modern economists)

Price–wage flexibility
An economic principle whereby prices and wages can fluctuate with changing economic conditions; thus the economy will be self-adjusting toward full employment even in response to shocks in supply and demand.

Quantity theory of money
A theory stating that in the long run with output and velocity fixed, changes in the money supply cause proportional changes in the price level.

used certain relationships in the real world to explain and predict how the price level is formed. They began their argument by noting that the following relationship existed:

Money supply × Velocity = The price level × Real GDP.

In symbols,

$$MV = PY,$$

where

M = the money supply, consisting of currency in the hands of the public plus all checkable deposits (all checkbook money) used in transactions by the public (in the U.S. monetary system, M is determined by the Federal Reserve System, an agency of the federal government);

V = velocity, or the average number of times a unit of money changes hands per year (or other time period) in financing the purchase of real output by the public;

P = the price level of all output (goods and services); and

Y = the final real output of goods and services produced and sold in the economy over some time period. (Y, in other words, is real GDP.)

If money is defined as currency plus checkable deposits held by the public, the public, at any given time, will hold a certain portion of their wealth in the form of money, in addition to houses, goods, and other types of assets. They will demand money (currency and checkable deposits) to facilitate transactions as a proportion of their total income. For example, if income in the economy was $9 trillion in 2000 and the public demanded one-third of this amount to facilitate all transactions in the economy, the average dollar exchanged hands or "turned over" three times in the economy in 2000. This means that **velocity** (necessary to facilitate the purchase of yearly GDP) was 3. The classical economists thought that this proportion was a constant over specific time frames, such as a year, and that velocity changed slowly due to (slow-changing) institutions in the economy.

If we consider the above equation and believe, along with the classical economists, that money serves individuals only as a medium of exchange, we may understand that increases in the *supply* of money will cause the price level to rise in the same proportion. That is, by assuming velocity and real GDP are constant, the equation $MV = PY$ becomes an expression of the quantity theory of money. If the money supply, M, were to double, the equation indicates that the price level, P, also would double. More money in the hands of individuals means that too much is being held to facilitate their level of goods and services transactions. What will people do? They will increase their demands for these goods and services by offering larger amounts of money for them. But recall from the other three foundations of the classical system that *real* output of these goods and services is always (over the long run) at a maximum. When no more goods can be obtained, prices must rise. If the velocity of money, which is another way of expressing individuals' money demand behavior, is constant, and if real income is already at a maximum, the only possible effect of an increase in the money supply is to cause an increase in the price level.

If resources were for any reason unemployed in the short run, and if, as this implies, real output (real GDP) were not at a maximum, increases in M with constant velocity would imply that real output and employment could be brought to

Velocity

The average number of times a unit of money changes hands per year in financing the purchases of GDP.

a maximum. New spending created by increases in M would increase society's real output of goods and services and employ the resources necessary to produce them. This means that velocity is a key to understanding why increases in the money stock could be used in a short-run situation of unemployment to return the economy to full employment. The classical economists assumed that the public's money demand (which determined velocity) was stable and did not change when the money supply was altered. Thus, the strict quantity theory relationship—for example, a doubling of M causing a doubling of P—held only in the long run, when real output and employment were at a maximum and velocity was constant.

Throughout the nineteenth century and into the twentieth, the size of the money supply was, in the main, determined by gold and silver stocks. The discovery (or hoarding) of precious metals had a profound impact on the price level at any time (and on the rates of inflation or deflation). In the modern U.S. system, the money supply is independent of the amount of gold or silver in the economy. It is controlled by the Federal Reserve System, an agency of the federal government. The Federal Reserve directs the money supply by regulating lending and other activities of banks in our economy. All of these matters will be carefully discussed in later chapters, but for now it is useful to remember that the classical writers thought that resources were fully employed and real output was maximized in the normal state of the world.

CLASSICAL THEORY AND POLICY: THE MEANING OF A SELF-ADJUSTING ECONOMY

The cornerstones of classical macroeconomic theory imply that self-adjusting forces in the economy will guarantee full employment. Long-run unemployment is simply not possible if the economy functions as the theory predicts. Consider the meaning of the **classical self-adjustment mechanism** in a real-world context.

Classical self-adjustment mechanism

The theory that, through Say's law, full employment will be reached given interest rate flexibility and price–wage flexibility.

The classical economists knew that adjustments due to supply "shocks" such as rapid technological change or new inventions, weather conditions, or wars were not instantaneous. Suppose, for example, that a drought occurs. A sharply reduced supply of grain and other foodstuffs means that the price of food will rise (given downward-sloping demand). But given the logic of the quantity theory of money, the prices of other goods that are consumed in the economy must fall! Adjustments of nominal prices in all of the various markets of the economy will be accompanied by changes in the nominal wage rates associated with each production. While all of these prices and wages are changing, the economic system will be in disequilibrium, with temporary surpluses and shortages of some goods and with excess demand for or supplies of labor in various markets. Unemployment of labor and other resources, as a temporary *and necessary* phenomenon, will take place, a fact the classical economists freely acknowledged. If wages and/or prices were "sticky"—that is, if they were not allowed to rise—unemployment would be more persistent. A critical question is: How long will the economy have to endure this temporary phenomenon in actual time? Two months? One year? Ten years?

While never directly answering this question, the classical economists did offer some important insights, based on the understanding that any interference by government or private coalitions would make the problem of adjustment worse. In other words, although natural and unfettered market forces would not restore equilibrium instantaneously, reliance on market forces was the best choice in an imperfect world. The setting of wage or price controls of any kind, such as minimum wages or union-controlled wage rates, would only impede flexibility in the marketplace. Market forces would eventually conquer the controls, extending the time period for adjustment. Unemployment would last longer if wages, prices, and interest rates were not permitted to adjust through unregulated market forces. The long run over which the market will adjust to changing underlying conditions in the economy (a drought, perhaps, or technological changes) was an indeterminate period of time that was minimized by the absence of controls in the economy. Many modern economists believe that the logic and principles of the classical system are the appropriate way to deal with contemporary institutional change in our economy. (See, for example, the Focus "Other Things Also Matter: Technology and Growth in the Twenty-First Century.")

John Maynard Keynes took exception to classical economic theory's conception of the nature of actual conditions in the economy—specifically, the issue of how rigid or flexible prices and wages are in the real world. The logic of classical economics led to the conclusion that market forces, in and of themselves, are the best means of providing adjustments in prices, wages, employment, and output. All

FOCUS

Other Things Also Matter: Technology and Growth in the Twenty-First Century

The self-adjusting economy, as posited by the classicals and discussed in detail in the text, encompassed a belief that free market adjustments were the surest bet to bring order and renewed prosperity *when* changes occur in the economy. (No system, of course, is free of adjustment costs.) The ill effects of "shocks," such as plagues or hurricanes, would be minimized. But other crucial changes in institutions or technology also matter to any economy. Institutions matter, in short, and the classical economists recognized this feature of all economies.

Technology is a critically important aspect of the world we now live in, as it was in earlier ages. The invention of mechanical devices—steam power and electric power, for example—had enormous effects on economic growth and development. These effects were felt through stimulated productivity, production, income, and profit generation and through economic exchange. Furthermore, these changes took time. The shift from a primarily agriculturally based economy to the economy of the machine age (commonly called the Industrial Revolution) took centuries. Productivity increases after electric power (invented before the turn of the

nineteenth century) also took time to stimulate big gains in productivity (not felt until well into the twentieth century).

Does the same "time lapse" apply to the computer revolution and other massive advances in communications and biology? The rapidly advancing technology and falling prices of computers (and such innovations as fiber optics and genetic engineering) may just be beginning to have their effects on our economy. Adaptation of businesses and individuals to this new technology takes time. Businesses must adapt to the information age to take greatest advantage of the new technology.

The classical macroeconomic perspective on this kind of institutional change is, as much as possible, to permit free markets to implement change. Encouragement of industry by deregulation, promoting full flexibility of prices, interest rates, and wages, and a minimum of government intervention would be the classicals' recipe for full implementation of these new technologies that will, ultimately, power economic growth in the twenty-first century. Their view of the world did not end in the nineteenth century. Properly implemented, it could be a blueprint for the future as well.

adjustments take time, of course, but in the classical view free market adjustments minimize the time necessary for full employment of resources to take place.

Classical Policies for Rapid Self-Adjustment

The classical economic policy recommendations fit hand in glove with the theoretical cornerstones. If the logic of their system required full flexibility of prices, wages, and interest rates—as well as the encouragement of industry—then their economic policy had to promote free markets. On practically every point of economic policy, the classicals supported economic freedom. Consider some of the chief tenets of their economic policy. (The Application "How Classical Economics Affects You" considers similarities between classical economic policy prescriptions and recent economic policy in the United States.)

Balance the Budget   Classical economists emphasized the need for a balanced government budget for a number of reasons. If government is allowed to spend more than it receives in taxes, the government will be forced to compete with investors to borrow available funds. Such competition will tend to increase real interest rates, choking off private investment, capital formation, and economic growth. Financing deficits by printing money—an attractive option when governments have access to the presses—would have equally bad effects on the private economy. As we will discuss in Chapter 28, increases in the money supply can create inflation, which is tantamount to a tax on the private sector.

Keep Government Small   High levels of taxes necessary to finance big government reduce incentives to private saving from which new investments are made. Big government, in the classical view, short-circuits the mainspring to progress. Moreover, large-scale government includes domestic or international regulations that tend to reduce trade, productivity, and consumers' well-being. In the classical laissez-faire view, the government should be restricted to providing national defense, a legal system, and a few other functions.

Laissez-Faire   Capitalism requires well-defined property rights. The classical economists underscored this belief by promoting policies that encouraged individual ownership and increased incentives to save and invest. These were primarily "hands-off" policies, or laissez-faire. The theory is that most regulation in the workplace, business, and in financial markets should be dismantled; also, all newly proposed regulations should be viewed with extreme skepticism. The classicals also adhered to the belief that much regulation was inspired by interest groups who wanted to capture the political process for their own gain. A good example of this is the factory legislation of early nineteenth-century England, which, supposedly, was passed to protect children from exploitation. (See the Focus "The Factory Acts and the Macroeconomy of Nineteenth-Century England.") Any laws or regulations that reduced saving, investment, or capital formation—domestic or international—were opposed by classicals.

Free Foreign Trade   The self-adjusting macroeconomy and economic growth were also believed to be fostered by international free trade. The free-trade philosophy espoused by nearly all classical economists brought about calls for the elimination of all barriers to free exchange, such as tariffs and quotas. A major strand of classical economic policy, then, was the removal or reduction of all impediments to both internal and external trade—anything, in other words, in the way of the gains from specialization and comparative advantage.

FOCUS

The Factory Acts and the Macroeconomy of Nineteenth-Century England

In general, policy recommendations of the classical economists were based on the notion of a self-adjusting economy. The vehemence of the classical economist Nassau Senior's (1790–1864) objections to factory legislation is not unusual.

The Factory Acts, enacted between 1833 and 1850, were a series of restrictions on the employment of women and children in the British textile industry. Senior's key reason for opposing the Factory Acts rested on the impact on the macroeconomy of legislatively mandated reductions in work hours and labor participation in the textile industry. Senior interviewed mill owners on the matter of the proposed restrictions, quoting one as having said, "When a laborer lays down his spade, he renders useless, for that period, a capital worth eighteen pence. When one of our people leaves the mill, he renders useless a capital that has cost 100 pounds."[a] In other words, restrictions on labor contracts idled capital and reduced the marginal efficiency of capital, thereby reducing the efficiency of resource allocation. Senior knew that a legislated

reduction in the efficiency of capital would lower the rate of return on capital investment in the textile industry below that which could be earned outside the industry. Higher-cost producers would leave the industry, reducing employment and granting a competitive advantage to foreign producers not subject to legislated restrictions on work hours and labor participation.

Senior's point, shared by most classical economists, was that regulations that had negative effects on investment, capital formation, and domestic employment were detrimental to maximizing society's total income. A modern parallel of this argument is the U.S. Environmental Protection Agency's regulations on the sulfur content of coal. This legislation has adversely affected the demand for coal extracted in Appalachia by coal demanders such as electrical utilities in the northeastern United States. The response of these utilities has been to import coal (of lower sulfur content) from western Canada (through the Panama Canal) and from Latin American countries. Economists, of course, do not dispute the fact that clean air has value or that some humanitarian purpose might have been accomplished by the Factory Acts. Rather, they point out that rules and regulations have costs—costs that are often ultimately reflected in the self-adjusting character of the economy and in the economy's attainable output and income potential.

[a]Nassau W. Senior, *Selected Writings on Economics* (New York: Augustus Kelley, 1966), p. 14. Also see Nassau W. Senior, *Industrial Efficiency and Social Economy*, vol. 2 (New York: Henry Holt, 1928), p. 309; and Gary M. Anderson, Robert B. Ekelund, Jr., And Robert D. Tollison, "Nassau Senior As Economic Consultant: The Factory Acts Reconsidered," *Economica* 56 (February 1989), pp. 71–81.

Classical Theory and Policy: Summary

The classical cornerstones of macroeconomic theory were part of a long-run view of economic activity. Yet the classical writers never stated the actual time period needed for the economy to self-adjust. They merely emphasized that any short-run government tinkering with the private economy in either a macroeconomic or a microeconomic sense would have negative long-run effects. In their view, the best long-run economic hope for all members of society—laborers, households, consumers, businesspeople, investors, savers—was to let unfettered market forces work in the private economy, unassisted by government.

Recessions, depressions, or periods of high unemployment caused by massive shifts in consumption spending, natural disasters, or wars all could wreak short-run havoc and temporary unemployment in the economy, as all classical economists knew. Society's members, however, would all be better off to suffer the temporary consequences rather than demand that government intervene. In the classical view, nearly all short-run actions of government in the aggregate economy only made problems worse, prolonged recessions or depressions, and created built-in instabilities in the macroeconomic system. Capitalism was not perfect, but society's inability to endure the short-run pains of recession and unemployment (reflected in demands for government to *do something*) meant that there would be greater economic pain in the long run.

APPLICATION

How Classical Economics Affects You

Undeniable parallels exist between classical and modern macroeconomic theory and policy. In theory, many modern macroeconomists, including the monetarists and new classical economists (see Chapters 28 and 29) hold to the classical idea that government intervention in markets will, at best, do little good and could reduce output potential in the economy. While modern theories of economic functioning are much more complex than the classical theory, they share the underlying premise that maximum output results from free market functioning with minimal government interference.

Especially on the campaign trail, Democrats and Republicans alike often appear to be in agreement with classical economists. Virtually all presidential candidates in 1996 pledged to make efforts to balance the federal budget and to reduce the federal debt. (As noted in the text, classical writers and policy-makers insisted on balanced budgets because government borrowing tends to crowd out private saving and investment.) Judged by their records rather than by their rhetoric, however, Reagan and Bush would be regarded as disappointments by classical economists. Federal budget deficits ranged from $150 billion to over $250 billion throughout the 1980s. In 1992 the federal deficit reached an all-time high—$290.4 billion—but it has come down since then. In a dramatic reversal, a budget surplus of $69.2 billion was reached in 1998 with projected surpluses of $79.3 and $117.3 billion in 1999 and 2000, respectively. (The federal debt, however, was a record high of $5.5 *trillion* in 1998.) Recent attempts to develop these surpluses, despite the huge debt, would be looked upon favorably by classical economists.

It is interesting to contrast recent events with the more draconian policies of politicians in the classical era. Consider the policies of William Gladstone, who was appointed vice president of the Board of Trade in England under the Conservative government of Prime Minister Robert Peel in 1841. Gladstone aimed to eliminate as much government intervention in the private sector as possible. To this end, he removed import tariffs (a form of excise tax on imported goods and a major source of government revenues) from all but 15 of the 400 products subject to the tariffs. Gladstone's tariff reductions resulted in a temporary government deficit. To balance the budget, Gladstone called for a 10 percent income tax. The income tax rate was reduced in subsequent years, before being eliminated altogether. In other words, the income tax was a temporary measure and disappeared after its aims had been achieved.

Tariff reductions (and eliminations), one of the most treasured policy prescriptions of the classicals to promote economic growth, have also been part of contemporary macroeconomic policy. The United States, Canada, and Mexico have eliminated most of the existing trade barriers among the three nations and have become the world's largest free trade zone. The classical economists would clearly approve in spite of what are regarded as short-term financial and other problems within the Mexican economy! Modern economists, along with their classical counterparts, support *worldwide* reductions in tariff and nontariff barriers to trade. Consumers of all participating nations in a free trade zone and consumers of other nations (if trade agreements can be made between zones) will gain from increased specialization and trade. (Chapters 2 and 31 explain in detail how specialization, comparative advantage, and trade increase net economic welfare.)

Deregulation—a classical tenet—has also characterized recent political administrations. President Jimmy Carter's administration (1976–1980) achieved significant deregulation in the economy—for example, in the airline industry. President Ronald Reagan's original economic proposals emphasized less total government spending and lower taxes to increase private saving and investment, although lower total spending proved to be infeasible politically. Reagan was more successful in continuing the trend toward deregulation, notably in the transportation and communications industries.

In general, Reagan's policies had a long-run orientation. Certainly, the Reagan administration's so-called trickle-down theory (the idea that prosperity follows a downward course from increased industry to the poor) is consistent with the tenets of classical macroeconomics. In the 1992 and 1996 campaigns, "trickle-down" economics was ridiculed by Bill Clinton, who argued that more government subsidies and spending are required to ensure jobs, growth, and prosperity. Clinton's campaigns focused on distinctly nonclassical themes: higher taxes on the "wealthy"; increased government spending on "infrastructure," such as highways, bridges, and public works; and government job creation reminiscent of the Depression-era Works Progress Administration. At times, however, Clinton has sounded a more classical tone, calling for limitations on welfare, support of freer trade, and a balanced budget.

Today, the role of government in the U.S. economy is so pervasive that even marginal changes are considered radical. The Reagan–Bush policies aimed at lowering the financial base of the federal government were less successful than those aimed at deregulating some critical industries and transferring control over resources from the public to the private sector and from federal to state and local governments. The so-called "Republican Revolution" inaugurated with the takeover of Congress in the midterm elections of 1994 aimed at the decentralization of government championed by the classical economists. At the local level, shrinking tax revenues have made returning garbage collection, ambulance services, and many social services to the private sector more attractive. If nothing else, the return to private operation of such activities fits into the classical idea that government should only be responsible for those desired activities that private enterprise cannot perform, will not undertake, or does not do sufficiently well.

The projected "decentralization" of the economy, as contained in the 1994 Republican Revolution, has not been realized, however. The size of government has continued to grow despite budget balance (advocated by both Republicans and Democrats). The classical economists would most certainly judge the *absolute size* of U.S. government (approximately 40 percent of GDP for all government levels) as clearly excessive. Neither Republicans nor Democrats have shown any willingness to deal with this critical issue.

QUESTION

Which recent U.S. economic policies reflect the principles of the classical macroeconomists? Which policies deviate from these principles?

SUMMARY

1. The classical blueprint for economic growth consists of progressive extensions of the division of labor, private saving and investment, and capital accumulation.

2. Economic growth in any economy is limited by, among other things, the economy's actual supply of human and nonhuman resources, the state of technology, productivity, and population.

3. Given the factors that limit growth at any one point in time, the best the economy can attain is a point on the production possibilities curve. The point of attainable possibilities corresponds to a vertical aggregate supply curve for the economy.

4. Classical macroeconomics consists of four cornerstones: Say's law, price–wage flexibility, interest rate flexibility, and the quantity theory of money. From these foundations, classical economists concluded that the economy would self-adjust to reach a full-employment level of production and income.

5. Say's law states that the act of supplying goods creates an automatic demand for the goods. The act of saving or hoarding does not mean that overproduction will occur. If prices and wages are flexible downward, price and wage declines will ensure that all units of production will be sold. Further, the linkage between the rate of interest and sav-ing and investment guarantees that what is removed from the income stream (saving) will be returned in a different form of spending (investment). The quantity theory of money indicates that the price level is proportional to the nominal money supply and suggests an avenue by which prices change when the money supply changes.

6. Classical economic policy, in the main, reflected the classical economists' theoretical view of the macroeconomy. Consequently, they supported policies that promoted the flexibility of prices, wages, and interest rates in the face of ever-changing conditions.

7. In the classical view, maximum price and wage flexibility would be promoted by the reduction both of internal and external regulations and by minimal government involvement in the economy and a balanced budget.

8. Classical macroeconomic theory was a long-run theory that emphasized the self-adjusting character of the economy as the least-cost means for arriving at the economy's production possibilities curve. In the classical view, all economies must go through adjustments, and the best way to let all markets adjust is through reduction or elimination of government interference.

KEY TERMS

classical macroeconomic theory
classical process of economic
   growth
division of labor

classical long-run equilibrium
Say's law
real rate of interest
price–wage flexibility

quantity theory of money
velocity
classical self-adjustment
   mechanism

QUESTIONS FOR REVIEW AND DISCUSSION

1. According to Say's law, under what circumstances would the quantity of goods demanded be less than the quantity of goods supplied?

2. Will people be willing to save money when the real rate of interest is equal to zero? What is the real rate of interest on a passbook savings account if the inflation rate is 7 percent and the bank pays 5 percent interest?

3. According to the classical view, why does an increase in savings not decrease the total level of spending? Would this be true if interest rates were not flexible?

4. What is the importance of price and wage flexibility under the classical system? What would be the consequence of rigid wages or prices if the macroeconomic system were disturbed by, say, poor grain crops?

5. Does the self-adjusting mechanism of classical economics indeed guarantee full employment of labor and other resources at all times? (Remember the distinction between the short run and the long run.)

6. How were classical macroeconomic theories and economic policy recommendations related?

7. Why did classical economists recommend small balanced budgets for government? Why did they suggest that large budget deficits would lead to lagging economic growth?

8. Why did the classical economists oppose regulations on business behavior? What did laissez-faire mean to classical economists?

9. How do flexible interest rates ensure that Say's law will hold even when consumers engage in saving?

10. If the money supply doubles while velocity and real GDP remain constant, will the economy experience inflation or deflation and to what degree?

11. In the classical framework, how does division of labor lead to growth in real GDP?

12. List three factors that limit economic growth according to classical theory.

13. In your opinion, would the classical economists approve of the degree to which our government and economy are related?

14. How, generally, do technological changes affect the overall health of the economy? How would classical economists treat the introduction of new inventions such as the computer?

WORKING WITH THE WEB

1. This chapter discusses price–wage flexibility as one of the cornerstones of classical economic thought. Go to the web site for two (mail order) catalog-producing companies: L. L. Bean (http://www.llbean.com), and J. C. Penney (http://www.jcpenney.com). It's common knowledge that catalogs are one way in which companies provide information about their prices. Depending on the type of business, this can also be done with menus, advertisements, and so on. As you visit the web

sites above, find the links to their catalogs and then note how often the new catalogs are produced and distributed.

With the rise of the Internet, there are a growing number of on-line catalog companies. Check the web sites of two different on-line catalog companies, Eastbay (http://www.eastbay.com) and Value America (http://www.valueamerica.com), and observe how they make their pricing information available.

Although the Internet clearly introduces possibilities for technological advance, the Internet may also have another effect on the economy that relates to the cornerstones of classical economic thought. Using the examples above, how has the Internet made the world more like that assumed by classical macroeconomists?

2. Go to the Economic Time Series Page (http://www.Economagic.com). Click on the link for "Most Requested Series." You will need to locate several different data links. When you arrive at each linked data page, you will need to produce a graph (which you can print out). For each data category, a graph can be produced by following this process: (a) click on the data link you want; (b) when you arrive at the next page, click on link for "GIF graph" below the green banner (next, you will see a chart, but will need to change it); (c) set the appropriate options for the chart ("Starting Year" and "Transformations on Right Scale"); and (d) click on the button for "Make Chart."

a. Reread the section that describes how M and P relate within the quantity theory of money. Using the steps described above, create a chart for "M2 Money Stock, SA" and one for "Consumer Price Index." Click on the transformation (on right scale) buttons for both that say "Period-to-period percentage change at annual rates." Does the quantity theory appear to hold between 1970 and 1999?

b. Reread the section on self-adjustment. This process has implications for the severity of unemployment. Using the steps described above, create a chart for "Unemployment Rate" for the years 1970–1999, but make no transformation (on right scale). Does self-adjustment appear to occur?

C H A P T E R

22

Keynesian Macroeconomics

Classical economic theory, the topic of the previous chapter, dominated the economic debate until the early twentieth century, when a series of catastrophic events sorely tested economists' faith in a self-adjusting economy and the validity of Say's law. After the unevenly prosperous 1920s, the United States and the rest of the world fell into the deepest and most prolonged depression in modern history.

In September 1929, the market for stocks and other securities began to fail. On what has come to be known as Black Thursday, October 24, 1929, stock prices plummeted and thousands of investors lost hundreds of millions of dollars' worth of securities. The stock market crash was the most public indicator of steep declines in industrial production, real income, and civilian employment. For more than a decade, between 1929 and 1940, industrial production in the United States failed to exceed its 1929 level. Real economic output (expressed in 1982 dollars) was about $700 billion in 1929, a level unmatched until 1939. Most important, civilian unemployment rose to more than 30 percent by 1933.

The exact causes of the Great Depression are still a matter of debate among macroeconomists, but the prolonged economic chaos is a matter of fact. The Depression and the unemployment that accompanied it brought ruin for millions of Americans and similar hardships around the world. The classical self-adjusting macroeconomic system did not appear to work. In this chapter we present the theory of John Maynard Keynes, which was a reaction to the apparent failure of the macroeconomic system to adjust to the problems of the Depression. Modern macroeconomists, whether of a classical or a Keynesian stripe, all believe that the economy adjusts to some natural rate of full employment *in the long run.* Keynes and his modern followers part company with classical thinkers on how to achieve full employment without inflation over *shorter periods of time.* Thus, an understanding of basic Keynesian theory is absolutely necessary in order

547

to appreciate the forces underlying economic fluctuations in our modern economy. After reading Chapter 22 you should understand:

- Keynes's criticisms of the self-adjusting classical principles of macroeconomics.
- how total private expenditures by consumers and businesses form the basis for Keynes's model of income determination.
- how the impact of spending changes on income described by Keynes is important in explaining cycles of business and economic activity.
- how foreign trade and government act as components of spending in the economy.
- how government spending and taxation in a Keynesian system are called upon to alleviate downturns and to modify inflationary pressures in the private economy.

KEYNES AND THE CLASSICALS

Economists were among the first to recognize that the catastrophic events of the Great Depression appeared to overwhelm theory. John Maynard Keynes (1883–1946) was particularly vocal. In open letters to President Franklin D. Roosevelt, published in the *New York Times,* Keynes advocated the use of government spending and taxation policies to supplement private spending as a cure for the ailing economy. (Roosevelt, clinging to more traditional thinking, heeded Keynes's advice guardedly and hesitantly.) Keynes was firmly convinced that, contrary to classical theory, private market forces would not be sufficient to regain full-employment equilibrium in the depressed economy. He dismissed the long-run self-adjustment theory of the classical economists with scorn. As he said in another context, "In the long run we are all dead." The economy could be stuck at some equilibrium characterized by high levels of unemployment for an extended period of time, as it seemed to be in the early 1930s.

Since the classical theory, in Keynes's view, did not offer rescue from the Depression, Keynes sought a better model from which to interpret events. In 1936, Keynes published his *General Theory of Employment, Interest and Money,* which established a new theory of how the economy functions—a new macroeconomics. In proposing this theory, Keynes had to counter the foundations of the classical macroeconomic system.

Recall that Say's law states that supply creates its own demand if savings (a leakage) can be transformed into investment expenditures (a compensating injection) through a flexible interest rate and if prices and wages are flexible when aggregate demand is exceeded by aggregate production. Keynes took exception to Say's law and to the two other cornerstones that support it—the belief that price–wage flexibility and interest rate flexibility will cure any temporary disruptions in the economy.

First, Keynes argued that saving and investment are determined by a host of forces in the economy in addition to the rate of interest. In Keynes's view, savers and investors are different groups with different sets of motivations and interests. Savers, he thought, are more responsive to their amount of personal disposable income than to the rate of interest in deciding how much to save.

Similarly, investment was not very responsive to the short-run interest rate, in Keynes's view. Much investment, especially in large projects, takes place over long periods. Once investment decisions are made, the investment is autonomous, unrelated to the interest rate or other variables. The point is that the different motivations of savers and investors mean that saving and investment plans could become unlinked. A flexible interest rate, responsive to the desires of savers and investors, would not guarantee that the saving leakage would automatically be turned into the investment injection. There was no built-in assurance that savings would equal investment at a full-employment, growth-maximizing level of economic activity.

Second, Keynes argued that in reality the internal structure of the economy was not competitive enough to permit prices and wages to fall in response to insufficient aggregate demand. To Keynes, the existence of monopoly and union pressures in the economy had to be taken into account. If demand fell off, monopolies would let output fall rather than accept price reductions. Workers, moreover, would refuse to take cuts in their money wages, thereby creating unemployment and layoffs by businesses. Even if workers did take money wage cuts, the reduction in income would further reduce the demand for goods and services, probably reducing output and employment even more. The conclusion: *Classical self-adjusting mechanisms in the private economy would not lift us out of a depression.*

THE INCOME–EXPENDITURES MODEL

Keynes believed that a prolonged depression proves that the economy can establish equilibrium at less than full employment. The classical economists, as we have seen, placed their confidence in a flexible price system—flexible prices, wages, and interest rates—as the self-adjusting mechanism that would assure full employment when aggregate demand got out of kilter with aggregate supply.

Income–expenditures model

A theory suggesting that private expenditures are basically determined by the level of national income and that these expenditures in turn determine the levels of output and employment in the economy.

Keynes argued instead that aggregate demand and economic activity in general were determined by income and by changes in income. He thereby developed an **income–expenditures model** of macroeconomics. Keynes focused on aggregate demand or spending because he viewed rapid aggregate demand changes as the villain in recessions and depressions. Keynes believed that aggregate supply factors—large-scale changes in productivity, such as new technology and inventions and changing incentives to work and produce—changed slowly and could therefore be neglected when considering short-run macroeconomic problems. (Aggregate supply factors will be considered in Chapter 23.) In the short run, the time period most relevant to Keynesian macroeconomics, the economy's production or supply of goods and services is seen to react passively to changes in total expenditures.

Private Consumption Expenditures

The classical writers, as we saw earlier, placed primary emphasis on the real rate of interest in determining the relation between savings (income reserved for future consumption) and expenditures (income used in current consumption). One of Keynes's basic criticisms of classical theory was that the rate of interest could not always enable us to predict how much of current income an individual would choose to save or to spend. Keynes believed that current income was the most reliable and predictable determinant of consumption expenditures. Private saving, the residual of income after consumption, was also a function of, or was explained by, income. The simple Keynesian model of consumption and saving, in other words, does not account for any factors other than current income. Let's consider how these relations between consumption and income and between saving and income might be expressed and analyzed.

Consumption and Saving Functions

Keynes constructed consumption and saving functions and schedules based on income. The consumption function and the saving function can be expressed simply as

$$C = C(Y) \quad \text{and} \quad S = S(Y).$$

In other words, consumption (C) is a function of income (Y), and saving (S) is a function of income, which simply means that consumption and saving are related to income in some way. Both consumption and saving, as we will see, are positive functions of income, meaning that an income increase will increase both consumption and saving, and an income decrease will decrease both consumption and saving.

Planned consumption and saving relations can also be regarded as schedules. A consumption–income schedule shows the amount that households would desire or plan to consume at every level of income. Likewise, a saving–income schedule shows the desired or planned level of saving that households would undertake at various levels of income.

In the basic Keynesian model, income can be disposed of by households in only two ways: They may consume it or save it. This observation means that

$$Y = C + S,$$

and it also means that consumption and saving are related in a unique way.

Numerous studies have attempted to relate saving and consumption to family income. The evidence provided by these studies shows that as income increases, families increase both saving and consumption.

Macroeconomists are often interested in knowing how consumption or saving will change with a change in income. The two concepts that give us this answer are the marginal propensity to consume and the marginal propensity to save. The **marginal propensity to consume (MPC)** is defined as the ratio of the change in consumption (ΔC) to the change in income (ΔY) that causes the change in consumption, or

$$MPC = \frac{\Delta C}{\Delta Y} = \frac{\text{Change in consumption}}{\text{Change in income}}.$$

Marginal propensity to consume (MPC)
The percentage of an additional dollar of income that is spent on consumption; change in consumption divided by change in income.

Marginal propensity to save (MPS)
The percentage of an additional dollar of income that is saved; change in saving divided by change in income.

The **marginal propensity to save (MPS)** is the ratio of a change in saving (ΔS) to a change in income that causes the change in saving, or

$$MPS = \frac{\Delta S}{\Delta Y} = \frac{\text{Change in saving}}{\text{Change in income}}.$$

Since households in the simple Keynesian model dispose of income only by consuming or saving, any change in income will be completely exhausted by the resulting changes in consumption and saving. Because the MPC measures the change in consumption resulting from a change in income and the MPS measures the change in saving arising from the same change in income, the MPC plus the MPS must add up to 1:

$$MPC + MPS = 1.$$

Average propensity to consume (APC)

The percentage of a particular level of income that is spent on consumption; total consumption divided by total income.

Average propensity to save (APS)

The percentage of total income that is saved; total saving during any given period divided by total income in the same period.

Economists are also interested in how much, on average, households consume and save at various income levels. The **average propensity to consume (APC)** is the proportion of income consumed at any income level, or C/Y. Likewise, the **average propensity to save (APS)** is the ratio of saving to income at any level of income, or S/Y. Since consumption and saving are the only two ways that households can dispose of income, a unique relation exists between the APC and the APS:

$$1 = \frac{\text{Consumption}}{\text{Income}} + \frac{\text{Saving}}{\text{Income}}, \text{ or } 1 = APC + APS.$$

The Keynesian Model of the Private Economy

The features of actual household consumption and saving behavior can be translated into a theoretical model of consumption and spending for the entire economy—how the country as a whole would choose to spend or save at different levels of national income. To make this model easier to comprehend—with no important loss in accuracy—we will assume that the consumption–income and saving–income relations are in the form of straight lines. This assumption means that the MPC and the MPS are constant. No matter what the level of income, the MPC will be the same number. If, for example, the MPC were 0.8 at the $100 billion level of income, it would be 0.8 at the $300 billion and the $750 billion levels also. The same relationship holds for the MPS. This simplifying assumption does no damage to our conclusions, and it greatly facilitates understanding of these crucial ideas.

Hypothetical information about economy-wide consumption and saving is given in Table 22.1. The hypothetical data of Table 22.1 show, in billions of dollars, what private consumption and private saving would be at alternative levels of income. Consider, for instance, a year in which national income is $100 billion. How would

TABLE 22.1

Hypothetical Consumption and Saving Data for the Economy

The economy consumes and saves more as income increases. Further, the average propensity to consume declines and the average propensity to save rises with increases in income. For the sake of simplicity, the MPC and the MPS are assumed to be constant.

National Income (billions of dollars) (Y)	Planned Consumption Expenditures (billions of dollars) (C)	Planned Savings (billions of dollars) (S)	Average Propensity to Consume (APC = C ÷ Y)	Marginal Propensity to Consume (MPC = ΔC ÷ ΔY)	Average Propensity to Save (APS = S ÷ Y)	Marginal Propensity to Save (MPS = ΔS ÷ ΔY)
0	40	-40	—	0.8	—	0.2
100	120	-20	1.2	0.8	-0.2	0.2
200	200	0	1.0	0.8	0	0.2
300	280	20	0.93	0.8	0.7	0.2
400	360	40	0.90	0.8	0.10	0.2
500	440	60	0.88	0.8	0.12	0.2
600	520	80	0.87	0.8	0.13	0.2
700	600	100	0.86	0.8	0.14	0.2

Dissaving

Occurs when consumption is greater than income; the use of previous years' savings or borrowing to finance consumption expenditures that are greater than current income.

Autonomous consumption

Consumption expenditures that are independent of the level of income.

households plan to divide this income between purchases of consumption goods and saving? Consumption expenditures at a $100 billion level of national income would exceed income by $20 billion. This −$20 billion would be **dissavings.** To consume $120 billion at an income level of $100 billion, in other words, households would have to draw down $20 billion in previous savings. A special interpretation is given to dissaving at a zero income level. Note that all households would consume at the level of $40 billion even if no income were earned; this $40 billion is independent of income. Such **autonomous consumption** expenditures are independent of income. At levels of income higher than zero, consumption expenditures increase until they are equal to income. If national income were $200 billion, all income would be devoted to consumption. At income levels higher than $200 billion, consumption expenditures fall short of current income, and the remainder is devoted to saving.

Consumption and the 45-Degree Line   An important method for understanding how consumption is related to income is to compare historical consumption levels with a hypothetical relation in which consumption spending is always equal to income. When consumption spending always equals income, graphing the two variables yields a straight 45-degree line like that in Figure 22.1. The positive slope of

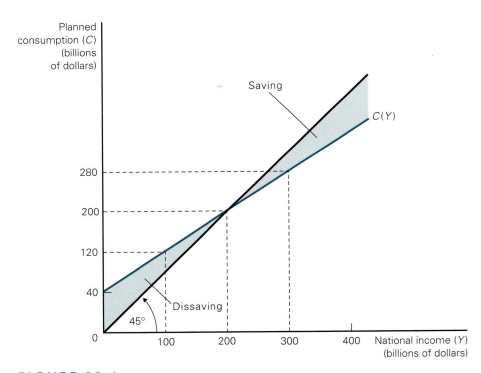

FIGURE 22.1

The Level of Consumption as a Function of the Level of Income

The consumption function, $C(Y)$, shows that the level of consumption expenditures rises as income rises. When income is $100 billion, consumption spending is $120 billion; when income is $200 billion, consumption is $200 billion; and when income is $300 billion, consumption is $280 billion. Along the hypothetical 45-degree line, consumption expenditures are exactly equal to income. The degree to which consumption differs from income indicates dissaving and saving by society as a whole. In this example, consumption spending is equal to income only at the $200 billion income level. Along the consumption function and above the 45-degree line, society dissaves; along the consumption function and below the 45-degree line, positive saving takes place.

the consumption schedule graphed in Figure 22.1, $C(Y)$, reflects Keynes's basic notion that the larger our income, the larger will be our consumption expenditures.

Examine Figure 22.1, on which national income levels are displayed on the horizontal axis and consumption expenditures on the vertical axis. At every point on the 45-degree line in Figure 22.1, total spending—in this case, consumption spending—*equals* total income. The extent to which actual consumption levels for particular periods differ vertically from this 45-degree line indicates the degree to which consumption does not equal income. Points along the **consumption function** above the 45-degree line indicate dissavings; points below it indicate savings. In Figure 22.1, actual consumption is equal to income only at the $200 billion income level. At a national income below this break-even point, society would go into debt or dip into past savings; above it, society would save some of its income.

Consumption function

The positive relationship between levels of consumption expenditures and levels of income, holding all other relevant factors that determine consumption constant.

The Consumption Schedule   Household consumption is the major factor in total spending, spending that creates jobs and production in the economy. Macroeconomists are therefore very interested in how much planned household consumption will change with changes in national income. The value of the marginal propensity to consume tells us how much more will be consumed out of an additional dollar—or an additional 100 billion dollars—in national income.

The marginal propensity to consume is of course different for different individuals and for different groups in society. Some of us are more likely than others to spend every dollar we have. In this example, we simplify the variations by choosing an *MPC* value of 0.8 for society as a whole and by holding this value constant across varying national income levels. In Figure 22.2, an increase in national income from $300 billion to $400 billion will increase the level of planned consumption spending from $280 billion to $360 billion, an increase of $80 billion. Likewise, an increase from $400 billion to $500 billion will cause planned consumption spending to increase by another $80 billion. The *MPC* is, therefore, the ratio 80/100 or 80 percent or 0.8, as indicated in Table 22.1.

FIGURE 22.2

Marginal Propensity to Consume

Along a straight-line consumption function, $C(Y)$, the *MPC* is constant. In this graph, *MPC* = 0.8. Each time income rises by $100 billion, the level of consumption rises $80 billion. Or, for every $1 increase in income, consumers increase expenditures by $0.80.

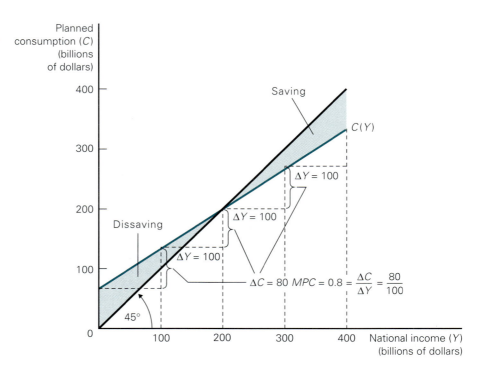

Saving function
The positive relationship between levels of current saving and levels of income, holding constant all other relevant factors that determine saving.

Though the actual relation of the *MPC* to national income is a matter of debate, we know that the average propensity to consume changes as income levels change. In general, as income rises, the *APC*, or the ratio of consumption to income, falls. At a $300 billion income level, for instance, consumption expenditures are $280 billion and the *APC* equals 280/300, or 0.93. On average, the population would be spending 93 percent of its income. But if national income rose to $600 billion, households would spend only 87 percent of their income (520/600).

The Saving Schedule   Like consumption, saving is a positive function of income. That is, the more income we have, the more we save; the lower our income, the less we are able to save. In the hypothetical **saving function** in Figure 22.3, at a national income level of $400 billion, desired saving is $40 billion. In fact, saving becomes positive rather than negative at all levels of income greater than $200 billion in this example.

The marginal and average propensity to save are also illustrated in Figure 22.3. Remember, the *MPS* is the ratio of a change in saving to a change in income. As shown in Figure 22.3, incremental changes of $100 billion change saving by $20 billion, so

$$MPS = 20/100 = 0.2.$$

The average propensity to save is the ratio of savings to income at any level of income. The *APS* rises as income rises, as you can see in Table 22.1, from which the data in Figure 22.3 are taken.

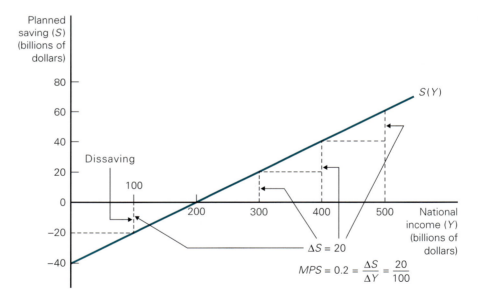

FIGURE 22.3

A Saving Function
The saving function, *S*(*Y*), shows that the desired or planned saving is positively related to the level of national income. At a low level of income (below $200 billion), there is dissaving. As the level of income rises from $200 billion to $300 billion, the level of saving rises from $0 billion to $20 billion. At *Y* = 400, *S* = 40, and at *Y* = 500, *S* = 60. The figure also illustrates the marginal propensity to save. Along a straight-line saving function, the *MPS* is constant. Here the *MPS* is equal to 0.2. For each increase in income of $100 billion, the level of saving increases by $20 billion.

Assuming the straight-line consumption and saving functions and the use of all income as either saving or spending,

$$1 = MPC + MPS \qquad \text{and} \qquad 1 = APC + APS,$$

or

$$MPS = 1 - MPC \qquad \text{and} \qquad APS = 1 - APC.$$

The values of MPC, MPS, APC, and APS are very important for economic policy. A high MPC means that increases in income will generate a large amount of additional private spending. A low value for the MPC (or, exactly the same thing, a high MPS) means that increases in income will generate only small increases in consumption. (Keep in mind that the values of MPC and MPS given in Figures 22.2 and 22.3 are based on hypothetical data.) These features of the consumption function will have an extremely important impact on the model of total expenditures developed in the following chapters.

Nonincome Factors Influencing Consumption and Saving

Although Keynes's basic argument involved the effects of income levels, income is not the only factor affecting consumption expenditures. A host of nonincome factors also determine the amount of planned consumption spending by all households. If any nonincome determinant of consumption spending changes, the entire consumption function shifts upward or downward. The amount of planned consumption changes at every income level when a nonincome element affects consumption changes. In contrast, a change in income simply changes the amount of income consumed, expressed graphically as a movement along a given consumption function.

In Figure 22.4, assuming an initial consumption function $C_0(Y)$, a change in any nonincome factor affecting consumption will shift the consumption schedule either upward to $C_2(Y)$ or downward to $C_1(Y)$. (The break-even level of income, where consumption spending equals income—on the graph, the point where the consumption function intersects the 45-degree line—also changes: to Y_2 with consumption C_2 or to Y_1 with consumption C_1.) By contrast, if income increases from Y_0 to Y_2, planned consumption increases along consumption function $C_0(Y)$ from point A to point F.

What are the nonincome factors that may affect consumption? Such factors are numerous, but the most important nonincome factors are thought to be (accumulated) wealth, the price *level*, price and income expectations, credit and the interest rate, taxation, age, and geographic location and population. Consumption and saving patterns will also change over your lifetime, some of them induced by government policies (see the Application "Mortgaging Your Future: The Government and Your Incentive to Save" at the end of this chapter).

Naturally, people consume on the basis of a previously accumulated stock of wealth. As the price level changes and the money value of items in that stock of wealth changes (the money value of your house or your Andrew Wyeth drawing), your consumption will change—even though your income does not. Feeling wealthier will affect your spending in a positive direction. Price level changes also produce changes in the *real* value of money or bonds (denominated in money terms). A doubling of the price *level* (not the price of, say, broccoli) will cut the purchasing power of these assets in half, and consumption spending will fall.

FIGURE 22.4

Shifts in the Consumption Function

Any change in nonincome f actors affecting consumption spending will shift the consumption function, $C_0(Y)$, either upward or downward. An increase in consumption means that planned consumption spending rises for every level of income (from A to B); a decrease in spending creates a fall from A to D in the figure. By contrast, a change in income, all other factors being equal, moves consumers along a given consumption function. For example, increasing national income from Y_0 to Y_2 would move consumption from point A to point F in the figure.

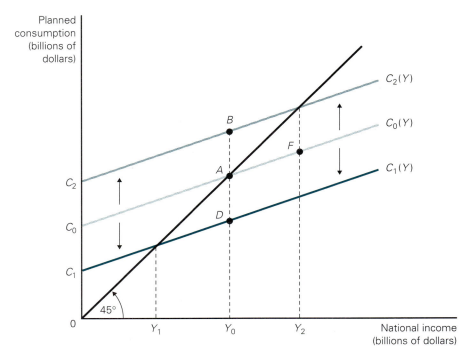

Expectations of higher or lower prices or incomes will also affect consumption spending. For example, an expectation of higher prices in the future will ordinarily increase current consumption. Moreover, as interest rates rise or fall—other things such as credit terms being equal—consumers will reduce or increase their present consumption expenditures. Taxation and government transfers also have direct effects on spending. Higher income taxes will reduce consumption and saving, whereas increases in Social Security benefits will increase spending and saving. Finally, population, age distribution, and geographic location all have an impact on consumption and saving. Middle-aged individuals are more likely to save—that is, they tend to save a greater proportion of their income—than are the young and the old. Urban dwellers, other things equal, tend to spend more of their incomes than rural families; a declining rural population will tend to increase overall consumption.

A change in *any* nonincome factor will shift the consumption function either upward or downward. A single consumption function, however, is constructed by holding all of the factors constant and by varying income. (How well does the data on actual consumption fit Keynes's theory? The answer to that question can be found in the Focus "Keynes's Key Insight: Consumption Is a Function of Income.")

Investment Expenditures

Investment spending

Expenditures made by businesses on capital goods plus any change (positive or negative) in business inventories.

So far, we have looked at household consumption and its relation to income. Private spending in the economy also includes investment spending. In a macroeconomic context, **investment spending** means spending by the private sector—mainly businesses—on capital goods. Public investment in goods such as schools, water reclamation projects, or dams is not included in private investment expenditures.

FOCUS

Keynes's Key Insight: Consumption Is a Function of Income

Unlike the classical economists, John Maynard Keynes believed that consumption was a direct and predictable function of income (given, of course, nonincome determinants such as those discussed in the text). How well, and in what way, does this notion stand up to the actual data?

Data on consumption and income are replicated in Figure 22.5 in such a manner that the two categories may be compared for the period 1972–1998 (in constant 1992 dollars). Here we abstract from the impact of taxes on income. Consumption spending (shown on the vertical axis in Figure 22.5) in the

United States remains at about 60 percent of gross domestic product (depicted on the horizontal axis).

From even a casual examination of the data, it would appear that Keynes was exactly right: There appears to be a clear and predictable relation between income and consumption. As income rises, consumption rises; as income falls, consumption falls. But we must look a little more closely at the data. It appears, as later followers of Keynes argued, that although consumption rises with increases in income, it does not increase at the same rate as the rise in income. The same is true of declines in income

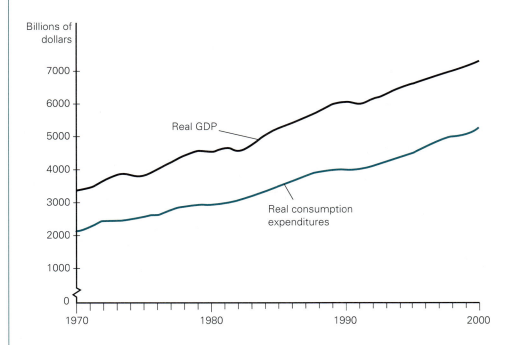

FIGURE 22.5

Consumption and Income in Real Terms, 1970–1998

Just as Keynes predicted, real consumption expenditures are related to real income, although the correspondence is not perfect. Specifically, consumption rises as income rises, but not at the same rate.

Source: Council of Economic Advisers, *Economic Report of the President* (Washington, D.C.: U.S. Government Printing Office, 1996), p. 282.

continued

continued

such as the 1982 and 1990–91 recessions, for example). People reduce consumption during recessions (periods of income declines), but not at the same rate as the reduction in their incomes. Consumers will save when incomes are disproportionately high and "dissave" (spend out of savings) when incomes are disproportionately low.

There are a number of explanations for the latter phenomenon. Consumption may, in effect, be "conditioned" by increases in income so that we become accustomed to high levels of consumption spending. When income falls, we dissave in order to maintain that higher level of spending. Alternatively, we may consume in the present on the basis of some idea of our expected permanent income over our entire lifetime. According to the second theory, consumption in the present is conditioned by today's value of income received in the future. Some medical, law, or MBA students buy Infinitis, Porsches, and fine wardrobes. These people are dissaving out of current income, but they may also be seen to be consuming in response to expected income over their life cycles. Whatever the explanation for longer-term effects on consumption, however, it is clear that Keynes was on the mark with his major insight into macroeconomic theory: Current consumption does depend in an important manner on current income.

Public investment expenditures are categorized as government spending and will be covered later in this chapter. Private investment refers to the national income category gross private domestic investment, defined previously as including fixed investment in plant and equipment, all private sector residential and nonresidential construction, and changes in business inventories (increases or decreases in stocks of finished goods, semifinished goods, or raw materials).

Clearly, there are two effects on the capital stock of the nation at any given time: Some of it is being used up or depreciated, and new net investment is creating additions to it. Businesses usually replace their worn-out capital stock and add to their stock of capital with new investments. Keynes argued that in the short run, investment expenditures could be viewed as autonomous—that is, independent of the level of income, profit expectations, the interest rate, and all of the other factors possibly affecting investment. The idea that investment could be autonomous in the short run stems from the fact that most investment expenditures in any current period have been determined by past investment decisions.

Businesses, in fact, make investment decisions from a long-run perspective. The building of new plants and the installation of sophisticated equipment typically take a number of years to complete. During the investment period, planned investment expenditures are often carried out regardless of current business conditions. Planned investment expenditures are those that businesses desire to undertake. (Planned investment expenditures may not be the same as actual expenditures, as we will see later in this chapter.) These investment expenditures are then independent of the level of income.

Autonomous investment

Investment expenditures that are independent of the level of income.

The concept of **autonomous investment** spending can be analyzed within the framework of the simple Keynesian model of private spending. If I stands for investment spending by businesses, autonomous investment is simply described as some constant level, I_0, or

$$I = I_0,$$

where the subscript 0 means that expenditures are constant at some specified level—$20 billion, $50 billion, $100 billion—during a given period. This means that investment is independent of whatever the level of income happens to be.

Long-Run Factors Affecting Investment   While investment is considered autonomous in the Keynesian context, it is subject to a number of factors over a longer period of time, including the rate of interest, the cost of capital, and current and expected sales.

- *Rate of Interest and the Cost of Capital.*   Ultimately, profitability—or expectation of future profits—determines the amount of investment that businesses will undertake. Profitability is, in simple terms, the difference between a firm's revenues and its costs.

    The cost of capital investment depends heavily on the rate of interest. Whether a business uses its own internal funds or borrows to make an investment, it incurs an opportunity cost in the form of interest lost. An increase in the interest rate, other things being equal, will reduce the amount of investment; a reduction in the interest rate will increase investment. The cost of the capital equipment itself is also important in determining the amount of desired investment. An increase in costs, other things being equal, reduces the amount of investment.

- *Current Sales and Expected Sales.*   The other side of the profitability of business investment is sales. If a large capacity to produce already exists, an increase in current sales will not encourage new investment expenditures very much. If businesses are operating close to the limits of their ability to produce, an increase in current sales will cause current investment spending to rise.

    Expectations are also a central feature of Keynes's theory of investment. Sales expectations require estimates of future business conditions and tend to vary greatly and quickly over time. Optimism concerning future sales and business conditions will mean increases in capital investment in the present. Pessimism will have the opposite effect.

As we will see in later chapters, the volatility of profit expectations is a principal cause in the creation of unstable income levels, unemployment, and cycles of business activity. Before turning to these issues, however, we must first understand how income equilibrium is defined in a purely private economy.

PRIVATE INCOME–EXPENDITURES EQUILIBRIUM

The classical economists argued that full employment would be achieved automatically simply through the activity of supplying goods in an essentially private economy, an economy theoretically free of government intervention. Should difficulties in adjustment to this full-employment equilibrium take place, prices, wages, and interest rates would change to bring the aggregate output of goods in line with aggregate expenditures.

For reasons already outlined, Keynes did not agree that wages, prices, or interest rates would change in any predictable way to bring the demand for goods in line with the supply of goods. How could a depression economy reach equilibrium with high unemployment? Keynes argued that levels of private spending (consumption and investment) determine the output of goods produced in the economy. In other words, businesses react to any level of total expenditures by producing the quantities demanded. If households want more kitchen appliances, they are produced; if businesses demand less computer software, less is produced.

TABLE 22.2

Planned Total Expenditures Determine Total Output and Equilibrium Income

For equilibrium in the private economy, planned total expenditures, $C + I$, must equal total income or output, Y. In this example, equilibrium is reached at a national income (or output) level of $300 billion. At national incomes less than $300 billion, total expenditures exceed total income. At national incomes higher than $300 billion, total expenditures are less than total income.

	National Income or Output (Y)	Planned Consumption Expenditures (C)	Planned Investment Expenditures ($I = I_0$)	Desired or Planned Total Expenditures ($C + I_0$)	Difference Between Total Expenditures and Total Output ($C + I_0 - Y$)
	100	120	20	140	+40
	200	200	20	220	+20
Equilibrium	300	280	20	300	0
	400	360	20	380	-20
	500	440	20	460	-40

Since it obviously takes more or less labor and other resources to produce more or less total output, the level of employment is also affected.

Keynes's theory of output and income determination can be expressed in symbolic terms using the tools of private spending analysis developed previously. All of our previous consumption, investment, and income figures are reproduced in Table 22.2. Total expenditures, shown in the fourth column, are equal to the sum of consumption and investment expenditures. Recall that planned consumption depends directly on the level of national income, reported in column (1). According to the circular flow model, the first column represents both the total output of goods and services in the economy as well as national income. Total planned expenditures may be greater or less than total production or output. The amount by which income or output exceeds planned expenditures is shown in the last column.

As Table 22.2 shows (and we have already suggested), there is a difference between planned expenditures and actual expenditures. Unless we are speaking of equilibrium income and spending, all references to consumption, saving, and investment are schedules of intentions or desires. Only one of these will be realized and that is the *equilibrium* value for these variables. Hereafter we typically omit the adjective "planned" or "desired" in front of consumption or saving, but the adjective "equilibrium" always refers to actual values.

At an income level of $100 billion, for example, total expenditures are greater than total output by $40 billion. This situation is possible only if businesses draw down on inventories of goods. Producers react to such a situation by producing greater quantities of goods and services, thus generating additional income to workers and to the other factors of production. The resulting increases in income will change consumption plans. At incomes higher than $100 billion, households will spend greater amounts on goods and services, indicated in the second column of Table 22.2 and Figure 22.6, which merely reproduces the information of Table 22.2 graphically. (Note in Figure 22.6 that investment is added vertically to the consumption function at an autonomous level of $20 billion in order to obtain the $C + I$ line.)

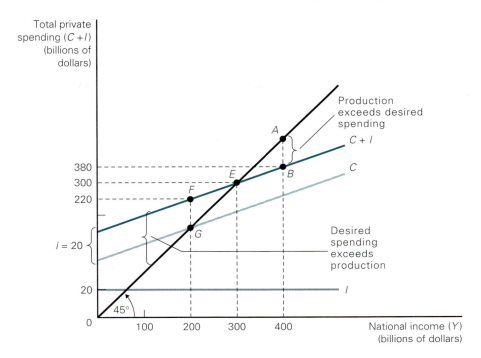

FIGURE 22.6

Private Sector Equilibrium

The equilibrium level of income exists when total private expenditures are just great enough to purchase the total output of the economy. At equilibrium, expenditures and output will meet at the point along the 45-degree line where they are exactly equal. At income level $Y = 300$, the economy is at equilibrium, E. At an income or output level of 400, desired total private expenditures at point B are insufficient to purchase the total output generated at point A. Inventories of goods will pile up, causing reductions in the rate of output and a lowering of income. These reductions will take place until income and output again equal the equilibrium level of 300. At this level, total expenditures equal total output produced in the economy. The opposite is true for income and output levels that are less than the equilibrium level.

Equilibrium level of national income

In the income–expenditures model, the level of income at which total private expenditures equal total output.

A new, higher level of output produced and income received at $200 billion creates higher total spending, but there is still an excess of total expenditures over output (amount FG in Figure 22.6). Inventories continue to be drawn down and production stepped up until an **equilibrium level of national income** of $300 billion is reached. Only at this level of income will production plans be in line with the plans of households and businesses to consume and invest.

What would happen at an income level greater than $300 billion, say $400 billion? If an income level of $400 billion were temporarily established, total output would temporarily exceed total expenditures by $20 billion, or AB in Figure 22.6. Unwanted inventories of goods would pile up unsold, and producers would cut back the rate of production. Since a cutback in production would reduce income, consumption plans of households would be revised downward. Equilibrium would again be achieved when the level of income dropped to $300 billion.

It is always worth remembering that the simple Keynesian model of total private spending is a short-run model. Prices, wages, and interest rates do not adjust as they do in long-run classical theory. The only factors that are adjusting are the real quantities of goods and services produced in the economy.

Unlike the classical economists, who believed that the economy would self-adjust until full employment was reached, Keynes thought that the economy could adjust to an equilibrium level with widespread unemployment. In terms of the situation depicted in Figure 22.6, the $300 billion level of income is not necessarily the full-employment level of income. Moreover, fluctuations between unemployment and inflation would normally be experienced if the private economy was left to itself. This unfortunate state of affairs, in Keynes's view, either was permanent or would last a long time. In either case, some action was demanded in the economy. That action, as we will see, formed the basis for a role for the government.

FLUCTUATIONS IN THE PRIVATE SECTOR

Before turning to the role of government in the Keynesian macroeconomic system, consider the source of fluctuations in the economy. In the Keynesian model, output and income can increase or decrease in response to any change in the components of total expenditures. For example, if autonomous consumption or investment increases, income will increase. If the economy-wide marginal propensity to consume increases, income will increase.

To see how changes in these factors actually affect income and output, consider an increase in autonomous investment spending. Recall that autonomous investment spending is independent of income and depends instead on factors such as the cost of capital, expected sales, and business profits. What happens to income when investment spending increases? In the example illustrated in Figure 22.7, the initial level of income of $300 billion is determined by the private spending level $C + I_0$. Assume that investment spending then increases by $20 billion because of an increase in expected future profits. The total spending curve shifts upward to $C + I_1$ by the amount $\Delta I = \$20$ billion. Desired spending then exceeds the output

FIGURE 22.7

The Effects of an Increase in Investment Expenditures

When the level of autonomous investment increases by $20 billion, from $60 billion to $80 billion (*AB*) in the figure, and the marginal propensity to consume is 0.8, equilibrium income rises by $100 billion—in this case, from $300 billion to $400 billion. The multiplier effect causes the level of income to rise by more than the amount of the increase in investment.

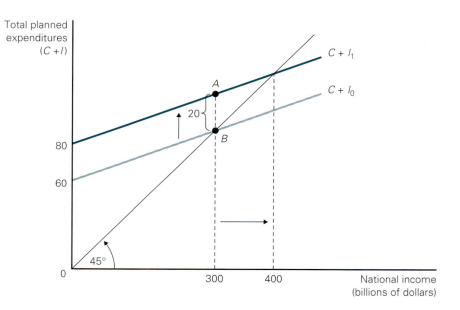

of goods and services by $20 billion (distance *AB* in Figure 22.7). To meet the demand, inventories are drawn down, producers step up the rate of output, and income rises. The question is: What effect does a $20 billion increase in autonomous investment spending have on equilibrium income? Does income increase by $20 billion exactly or by a greater or lesser amount? As you may have noticed in Figure 22.7, income increases by $100 billion with an investment spending increase of $20 billion. Why does such a relatively small increase in investment result in such a relatively large increase in income?

Instability in the Economy: The Expenditure Multiplier

The answer to this question is given by the value of the multiplier, a number found by dividing the change in income by the change in autonomous spending that caused the change in income. In Figure 22.7, we are looking at a change in autonomous investment spending. Thus the **investment multiplier** is found by dividing $100 billion by $20 billion or, if k_I represents the investment multiplier,

Investment multiplier
The multiple by which equilibrium income will change given a change in autonomous investment expenditure; 1/*MPS*.

$$k_I = \Delta Y/\Delta I = 100/20 = 5.$$

If autonomous investment spending increases by ΔI, or $20 billion, the initial expenditure first generates an addition to income of $20 billion ($\Delta Y$) because expenditures on investment goods create returns (or income) to resources. However, the process does not end here, for all resource owners, laborers, holders of capital or land, and so on, are consumer-savers. New income will cause the consumer-saver to spend some and to save the rest. The *MPC*—the marginal propensity to consume—and the *MPS*—the marginal propensity to save—will always add up to 1 out of total income. (What is consumed is not saved; what is saved is not consumed.) Consumption expenditures on goods and services, then, create additional income out of which another set of income recipients spend a portion and save the rest. In this process, the initial increase of $20 billion is multiplied at each stage.

The same principle applies to the autonomous portion of consumption spending. The **autonomous consumption multiplier** applies to the autonomous portion of consumption, that portion of consumption spending independent of income and determined instead by variables such as thrift attitudes and the rate of interest on savings.

Autonomous consumption multiplier
The multiple by which equilibrium income will change given a change in autonomous consumption expenditure; 1/*MPS*.

If autonomous consumption increases, income also increases by some multiple. If, for example, the autonomous component of consumption increases from $40 billion to $50 billion in a society with a marginal propensity to save of 0.2, equilibrium income would rise to $450 billion from its previous level of $400 billion. The change in income can be expressed as follows:

$$\frac{\Delta \text{ Autonomous consumption}}{MPS} = \frac{\$10 \text{ billion}}{0.2} = \$50 \text{ billion.}$$

Thus the autonomous consumption multiplier, like the investment multiplier, is the reciprocal of the *MPS* (in this example, 1/0.2 = 5). The higher the *MPC* (or, what is the same, the lower the *MPS*), the higher the consumption multiplier and the higher the income change from a given change in autonomous expenditures.

The value of the multiplier is determined by the *MPC* or *MPS*. A quick method of determining the multiplier, therefore, is to divide 1 by the *MPS*: $k_I = 1/(1 - MPC) = 1/MPS$. Using an *MPC* of 0.8, $k_I = 1/(1 - 0.8) = 1/0.2 = 5$. Any change in income caused by a change in an autonomous expenditure may then be determined by multiplying the autonomous expenditure change by the multiplier or, in the example, $\Delta Y = k \Delta I = (1/MPS) \times (\Delta I) = 5 \times \$20$ billion $= \$100$ billion.

A change in the *MPS*, which also means a change in the *MPC*, will obviously alter the value of *k,* the multiplier. The multiplier is the reciprocal of the *MPS*. If the *MPS* is 0.1, the multiplier is 10. Under these circumstances, a $20 billion injection of autonomous expenditures would increase income by $200 billion. Or, if Americans saved one-half of every additional dollar received in income, the multiplier would take on a value of 2. (On a piece of scratch paper, demonstrate to yourself why this is so.) In this case, a $20 billion increase in investment spending would raise equilibrium income by $40 billion.

To summarize, income will rise or fall by an amount greater than the expenditure change because of a multiplier process. The multiplier, which is simply the reciprocal of the *MPS,* magnifies the change in autonomous expenditures that creates the change in equilibrium income. Stated another way, changes in equilibrium income are calculated by applying the multiplier to changes in autonomous expenditures.

These concepts are of importance for practical policy-making. The most significant effect of the multiplier is that very small changes in spending may be greatly magnified in resulting income and employment changes. For example, a small change in private spending could precipitate a relatively large economic contraction or reduction in employment and business activity. As we will see later in this chapter, Keynes recommended that government's fiscal actions be used to counteract the instabilities generated by the multiplier effects of private spending on GDP, employment, economic growth, and inflation.

CONTRACTIONARY AND EXPANSIONARY GAPS

Failure of the private economy to provide stable growth and predictable, stable levels of full employment led to Keynes's fundamental criticism of classical economics. Though Keynes himself did not discuss a business cycle, in his view the private economy was erratic and subject to long-run periods of large-scale unemployment and low production levels. The contractionary phase of the cycle would engender more and greater pessimism about future business conditions, keeping the economy in a contractionary phase of the cycle for a very long period of time. Only accident, not dependable market forces as the classical economists had maintained, would produce a stable equilibrium at full employment with no inflation.

Contractionary gap
The amount by which total planned expenditures at the level of full-employment income fall short of the level required to generate full-employment income; also called a recessionary gap.

Expansionary gap
The amount by which total planned expenditures at the level of full-employment income exceed the level required to generate full-employment income without inflation; also called an inflationary gap.

For our more familiar income–expenditures approach to the macroeconomy, Keynes envisioned the economy as reaching, and remaining in, either a contractionary gap or an expansionary gap. A **contractionary gap** (sometimes called a recessionary gap) exists when equilibrium output is less than full-employment output. This occurs when the level of total expenditures that would exist at full employment is insufficient to purchase total output. Inventories pile up, and the level of output adjusts to a lower equilibrium level as businesses cut back production. An **expansionary gap** (sometimes called an inflationary gap), the opposite situation, means that total private expenditures exceed those expenditures necessary to produce a full-employment level of income without inflation. Excess expenditures, in other words, put pressure on the employment of resources. Since the economy cannot push output beyond its production possibilities frontier, inflation is created.

GOVERNMENT SPENDING AND TAXATION

Keynes believed that the invisible hand—those forces that would return the economy to full-employment equilibrium without inflation—was seriously arthritic. Even if such forces on private spending did exist, in Keynes's opinion they would probably be unendurably slow in restoring equilibrium. Keynes argued that society should not have to endure contractionary or expansionary gaps of long duration. Since automatic forces were unreliable, he saw discretionary government interventions as necessary. Keynes felt that macroeconomic management should be entrusted to the central government, which theoretically has the ability to adjust aggregate spending in line with national economic goals by the use of its two major budget weapons: government spending and taxation. Changes in one or both of these areas constitute fiscal policy, the object of which is the manipulation of total spending in the economy.

Government Expenditures

In the context of the basic Keynesian income–expenditures model, government spending (G) is an addition to total private spending, represented graphically by raising the $C + I$ curve to account for the new source of spending.

Once a government sector is incorporated into the model, the equilibrium production level is that at which output is equal to consumption (demand from households) plus investment (demand from businesses) plus government spending on goods and services (demand from the government sector). Previously, we had operated under the assumption that the level of government purchase of goods and services was zero. Then, total spending consisted of household spending (consumption) plus business spending (investment).

Government spending can take many forms and have many (sometimes conflicting) objectives. For example, in one sense the government behaves like a business, purchasing inputs used in its daily operations, such as labor, machinery, and buildings. In another sense, the government acts like a consumer, purchasing products for its own use, such as missile systems, tanks, ammunition, and airplanes. An extensive and controversial type of government spending does not result in the outright purchase of goods and services: namely, transfer payments that redistribute income among various groups in society—from rich to poor, from able to disabled, from healthy to sick, from employed to unemployed. These transfer payments are not included in our definition of government purchases of goods and services; government spending, which we will designate as G, thus includes only purchases of goods and services.

Keep in mind that a government's decision about how much to spend is somewhat different from private decisions to consume or invest. A major difference is that the government is a not-for-profit sector of the economy. Its decisions are often not motivated by private profit or economic efficiency. Furthermore, its spending is not constrained by its income in tax receipts. Congress can, and often does, spend far more than it raises in the form of taxes, issuing government bonds or creating money to cover the difference. Because government spending is not constrained by government tax collections, enormous budget deficits have built up in recent years, causing much concern among the electorate and in Congress. It is dangerous to ignore the consequences of budget deficits, but in the first approach we will do so to keep the model simple.

Autonomous government expenditures

Government expenditures that are independent of the level of income.

To further simplify the analysis, we will assume that government expenditures to purchase goods and services actually are **autonomous government expenditures;** in other words, they do not depend in any predetermined way on national income. Thus we may write, as we did previously for investment, $G = G_0$ to indicate that government expenditures are independent of income. Total spending can now be redefined as follows:

$$C + I + G_0 = \text{Total expenditures.}$$

Graphically, the addition of autonomous government spending, G, results in a parallel upward shift of the total spending function. In Figure 22.8, the $C_0 + I_0 + G_0$ curve is higher than the $C_0 + I_0$ curve at each level of national income by whatever amount of G_0 the government decides to spend. Notice that the addition of government spending to the total expenditures curve has the effect of moving the total spending curve to an intersection point higher up the 45-degree line. In other words, government expenditure, taken by itself, is expansionary; it leads to a higher level of equilibrium income.

The Effects of Taxation

To introduce the concept and effect of government spending, we merely acknowledged the impact of an injection of new spending on the macroeconomy. In fact, government spending decisions are rarely made in a budgetary vacuum. Decisions about taxes—both their level and their structure—often accompany decisions concerning government spending. We will disregard changes in tax structure and con-

FIGURE 22.8

Effects of Government Expenditures on Total Spending

The introduction of government spending increases total spending and the equilibrium level of income. With government spending of G_0 added to autonomous consumption and investment, $C_0 + I_0$, total income rises from Y_0 to Y_1.

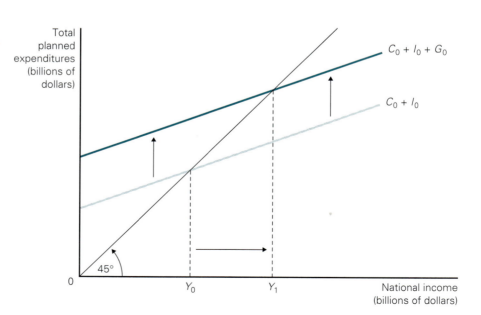

centrate on the effects on output and employment of changes in the level of taxes. Taxes represent a leakage from the income–expenditures flow. In this respect they are like savings and for analytical purposes can be treated in the same way as savings. (You might think of taxes as "public saving" in conjunction with the private decision to withhold from spending a part of national income.)

In order to concentrate on the effect that taxation has on equilibrium output, assume that the type of tax the government levies is a **lump-sum tax,** whose effect is straightforward: Every income earner is taxed the same amount, say $100. Each dollar increase in lump-sum tax revenue collected by the government results in a dollar lost from household and disposable income. An increase in the lump-sum tax therefore shifts the consumption curve downward, but the curve does not shift downward by the full amount of the tax because the saving schedule is also shifted downward. If MPC equals 0.8 and MPS equals 0.2, then every dollar increase in the lump-sum tax will reduce consumption by 80 cents and reduce saving by 20 cents. The downward shifts in the consumption schedule will be parallel; a lump-sum tax means that the tax amount is the same regardless of the level of income. Figure 22.9 shows the shifts in the consumption curve resulting from the imposition of a lump-sum tax.

The effect of a tax increase, taken by itself, is contractionary. It causes a reduction in aggregate income and output. This point is readily seen in Figure 22.9, where the effect of the tax is to reduce national income equilibrium from Y_0 to Y_1.

Lump-sum tax

A fixed level of total taxes; total taxes do not change as the level of income changes.

INTERNATIONAL TRADE AND THE GLOBAL ECONOMY

Thus far, we have operated under the assumption that all goods produced in the United States are sold here and that all goods purchased by American households, business firms, and government agencies are made in the United States. There was a time when the foreign sector could be ignored without sacrificing believability; the United States used to be relatively self-sufficient. Now, any realistic economic model must include a foreign sector. Fortunately, incorporating a foreign sector into our basic Keynesian model is easy to do. First, the notion of equilibrium income must be modified slightly. With foreign trade, equilibrium occurs when domestic production of goods and services is equal to total spending for those goods and services, including spending by foreign buyers. In other words, **exports** (X), defined as spending by foreign households, business firms, or government agencies on goods produced in the United States, must be added to C, I, and G as a component of total spending. At the same time, the model must be altered to take imports into account. A portion of consumption spending, business spending, and government spending may be on goods produced abroad, and such expenditures do not represent demand for domestically produced goods. Therefore, if we define **imports** (M) as total spending on foreign goods, we must subtract M from total spending. Total spending, then, is equal to $C + I + G + (X - M)$, and the equilibrium level of national income is that level at which Y is equal to $C + I + G + (X - M)$.

The concept of a foreign trade component of total domestic spending is intuitive. The import of cashmere sweaters by consumers, computer chips by business investors, or titanium by the U.S. government replaces domestic spending by these groups and represents increased demands for *foreign* producers. Increased demand by U.S. consumers, investors, and by the U.S. government generates

Exports

Expenditures by foreigners on domestically produced goods.

Imports

Expenditures by domestic residents on goods produced in foreign countries.

FIGURE 22.9

Effects of a Lump-Sum Tax on Aggregate Household Spending and Saving

A lump-sum tax decreases both consumption and saving. The decrease in consumption from C_0 to C_1 is determined by the MPC. If MPC = 0.8, a lump-sum tax reduces consumption by 80 percent of each tax dollar paid. A lump-sum tax reduces equilibrium income—in this case, represented by the shift from income level Y_0 to Y_1.

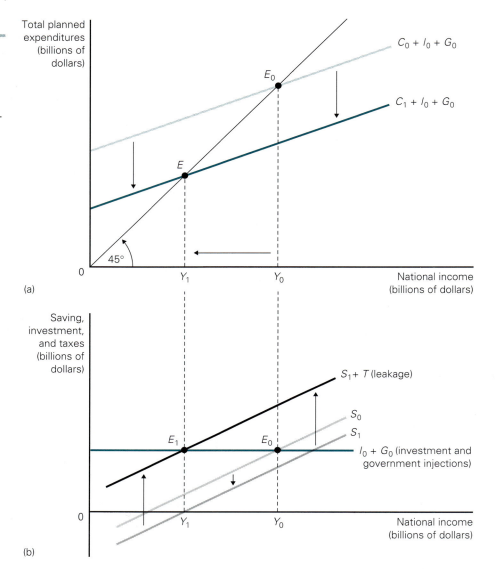

income in foreign countries. On the other hand, exports of American wheat, machinery, and airplanes represent demand for domestic products. These components of total spending (both positive and negative) must be compared before we can determine whether the trade sector contributes to or detracts from total expenditures in the United States. When imports exceed exports, total spending declines at home. The opposite occurs when our exports of goods and services exceed our purchases abroad.

In recent years, the United States has been a net importer of goods and services to the tune of over $100 billion per year. This means that Americans collectively spent over $100 billion more on goods and services produced abroad than foreigners spent on U.S. products. In terms of the Keynesian model, this means that total domestic expenditure on all goods and services was billions of dollars less than it would have been had our exports equaled our imports. This international trade deficit has a number of implications for the U.S. economy, but we postpone a more complete discussion of foreign trade and its effects until Chapters 30 and 31, where both real and financial aspects of international transactions are considered.

COUNTERCYCLICAL FISCAL POLICIES

Countercyclical fiscal policy

Changes in government expenditures or taxes that are designed to reverse changes in private expenditures or savings that produce unemployment or inflation.

Having reached an understanding of how the presence of a government sector influences the economy, we now move the discussion toward a fuller understanding of the Keynesian prescriptions for **countercyclical fiscal policy.** Fiscal policy, as we have already noted, means budget actions: government expenditure changes, tax changes, or a combination of the two. To say that a policy is countercyclical means that the policy seeks to correct whatever phase of the business cycle—contractionary or expansionary—the economy happens to be in. In a recession, for example, total spending, output, and employment are below the full-employment equilibrium level. In such circumstances, countercyclical fiscal policy would seek to raise the level of total expenditures to the full-employment level. During inflation, a countercyclical fiscal policy must try to induce a lower level of total spending. But knowing the appropriate direction of budgetary changes does not guarantee that the exact equilibrium target will be achieved. To do that, policy must be guided by knowledge of the relevant expenditure multipliers. Expenditure multipliers play a major role in the following analysis. Any autonomous expenditure is subject to the multiplier process; thus it is possible to identify consumption multipliers, investment multipliers, government spending multipliers, export multipliers, import multipliers, and so on.

Fiscal Policy to Deal with a Recession

To see how fiscal policies are used to change the direction of the business cycle, let us first suppose that the economy is in a recession. Imagine that government economic policy-makers have determined that the actual level of aggregate income-output is $50 billion below the full-employment level. In Figure 22.10, the government's problem can be seen as that of moving the economy from an income level of $2.50 trillion to one of $2.55 trillion (an increase of $50 billion). What is required in this case is an increase in G or a decrease in T, either of which would lead to an increase in total spending, $C + I + G + (X - M)$. If government simply increases G by $50 billion, it will overshoot the desired target because the new additional expenditure of $50 billion will be multiplied through various rounds of spending into a much larger increase. What, then, is the appropriate fiscal stimulus?

The answer depends on the size of the contractionary gap, whether households or businesses are the ultimate recipients of government expenditures, and the value of the relevant multiplier. In the following analysis, assume (1) that only households will receive the government expenditures and (2) that MPC equals 0.8. Under these conditions we can determine the size of the contractionary gap, $AB,$ and design a fiscal policy to eliminate it.

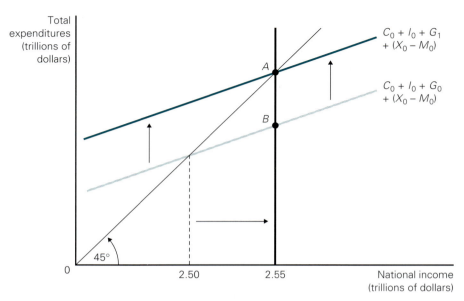

FIGURE 22.10

Government Spending to Eliminate a Contractionary Gap in Income

If total spending, $C_0 + I_0 + G_0 + (X_0 - M_0)$, is not great enough to achieve full employ-ment, then an increase in government expenditures may restore full employment. In this example, initial expenditures, $C_0 + I_0 + G_0 + (X_0 - M_0)$, are insufficient to create a full-employment level of income. Government expenditures are increased to $C_0 + I_0 + G_1 + (X_0 - M_0)$, and, through a multiplier process, the contractionary gap, AB, is eliminated.

Since we know the value of MPC, we can compute the consumption multi-plier (the only relevant multiplier in this case):

$$k = \frac{1}{1 - MPC} = \frac{1}{0.2} = 5.$$

We know the size of the income gap ($50 billion), and we know that whatever increase in government spending occurs will be multiplied by 5. Therefore, we can determine the size of the contractionary gap, AB, by the formula

$$\text{Contractionary gap} = \frac{\text{Income gap}}{k} = \frac{\$50 \text{ billion}}{5} = \$10 \text{ billion}.$$

In this case, an increase in total expenditures of $10 billion will, via the multiplier, produce an increase in aggregate income of $50 billion, thereby moving the econ-omy to its full-employment equilibrium level.

There are two ways that fiscal policy could produce the additional $10 billion expenditure. The most direct way is to increase government expenditures, G, by $10 billion. We assume that this direct injection to the spending stream is not subject to any leakages. Therefore, the full $10 billion enters the expenditure flow at once.

An indirect way to accomplish the same thing is to cut taxes to stimulate con-sumption spending, as shown in Figure 22.11. Remember, however, that tax changes

FIGURE 22.11

Taxation to Eliminate a Contractionary Gap

If total spending, $C_0 + I_0 + G_0 + (X_0 - M_0)$, is not great enough to achieve full employment, then total expenditures may be increased by a tax cut. In this example, if taxes fall, then consumption increases from C_0 to C_1 to achieve full employment. A tax cut increases the disposable income of consumers, causing them to spend more.

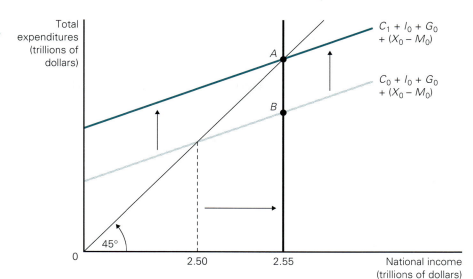

do not produce expenditure changes of the same dollar amount because taxes are paid partly at the expense of consumption and partly at the expense of saving. Against a contractionary gap of $10 billion, a lump-sum tax cut of $10 billion will only induce additional consumption of $8 billion ($MPC \times \Delta T$). To raise consumption spending by $10 billion requires in this instance a tax cut of more than $10 billion to offset the increase of saving that occurs when household disposable income increases. A lump-sum tax cut of $12.5 billion, given that $MPC = 0.8$, would be required to raise aggregate consumption by $10 billion and thereby eliminate the $10 billion contractionary gap.

Government expenditure changes are more direct and more powerful, dollar for dollar, than tax changes of the same amount. This must be kept in mind when expenditures and taxes are changed simultaneously.

Fiscal Policy to Deal with Inflation

Once full employment is reached, further increases in total spending will tend to drive the price level upward, creating an expansionary gap. An expansionary gap develops because raw materials, labor, and inputs of all kinds become increasingly scarce. GDP, the economy's output, can be pushed only so far by excessive spending and only at the cost of causing inflation to accelerate. The reverse of a given policy that works in one phase of the business cycle works for the opposite phase of the cycle. If the economy is characterized by inflation and full (or "overfull") employment, the appropriate fiscal response would be a decrease in government expenditures or an increase in taxes.

An expansionary gap, as discussed earlier, is the difference between the existing level of total spending and the desired level. The trick is to bring the actual level of total expenditure, $C + I + G + (X_0 - M_0)$, in line with the desired full-employment level. As in the case of contractionary gaps, the correction can be achieved in one of two ways: either a change of government expenditures or a change of taxes.

Assume that the economy is operating at a level of nominal output-income too high for full employment. (We are talking about the effects of inflation, so the concepts of real and nominal come into play.) In what sense could the nominal level of income be too high? "More is better than less" when it comes to economic output, but there are two factors to consider. First, by definition, aggregate real output in the macroeconomy cannot increase after full employment has been reached, because the economy is already at a point on its production possibilities frontier. Second, income measures beyond the full-employment level mean that a constant amount of goods and services is valued at higher unit prices, showing the effect of inflation. When the newspapers say that the economy is "overheating," they mean that a lower level of national income is preferred to the present higher one. Too high a level of total spending produces inflation.

The problem posed by inflation, then, is how to reduce the level of nominal income by some amount, say by $50 billion. With a multiplier of 5, a reduction in spending of one-fifth the observed income gap will produce the desired effect. This result can be achieved by cutting government expenditures by $10 billion, leaving taxes unchanged. It can also be achieved by leaving government expenditures unchanged and raising lump-sum taxes by $12.5 billion (to reduce the consumption component of aggregate demand by $10 billion). The mechanics of these changes are exactly the reverse of those used in the contractionary-recessionary situation. Changes in taxes or government expenditures therefore composed Keynes's arsenal of methods for counteracting contractionary or inflationary swings of the business cycle.

The actual potential of Keynesian fiscal policy to deal with recession or inflation may, in reality, be severely limited. We must never forget that G and T are enacted within a political process. Within this process, other goals—such as balancing the budget—may receive priority. (See the Focus "How the Political System Helps Create Deficits.")

Keynesian Economics in Historical Context

Was Keynes right about the ability of government to use countercyclical fiscal policies to counteract extreme phases of the business cycle? Although the policy and theoretical issues are complex, it is probably the case that certain theoretical and political effects unforeseen by Keynes have inhibited the ability of government to control the business cycle and thereby guarantee continuous inflation-free levels of full employment and maximum economic growth.

Keynes was primarily concerned with the economic and human costs of economic depression (or, if you prefer, an extreme contractionary phase of the business cycle). His advice, though not fully implemented in Western democracies during the Great Depression of the 1930s and early 1940s, was at least partially responsible for the increased economic role of government at the time and, perhaps, for the absence of prolonged and serious depressions after World War II. But problems other than depression have been paramount in the U.S. economy since the late 1960s—particularly high rates of inflation combined with slowed economic growth and large budget deficits. Keynesian economics was not explicitly designed to deal with these problems.

How could actual fiscal policy have caused these problems? The use of Keynesian countercyclical fiscal policy means that balancing government expenditures and receipts—a balanced budget—takes on secondary importance. The cumula-

FOCUS

How the Political System Helps Create Deficits

In Keynesian macroeconomic theory, surpluses are called for in an overheated inflationary economy, and deficits are called for when recession or depression (slow economic growth, low and falling employment rates) occur. The implication is that Congress and the president are able to read the economic tea leaves and are actually willing and able to raise or lower government spending and/or taxation at the appropriate time to ensure future economic growth and low unemployment rates.

The federal budget is *supposed* to be balanced over the business cycle according to the Keynesian theory. Unfortunately, things have not worked out that way. Aside from the technical problems of judging the timing of economic cycles, lags in recognizing problems, and lags in implementing policies, political realities often hinder policy effectiveness. Self-interested politicians want to be reelected. Politicians who are under a reelection constraint will work very hard to improve their net chances of winning the next election. This means that policies whose lobbies and supporters can deliver the largest vote totals (and possibly other perks) have the best chance of being enacted. Similarly, other policies will not be enacted (unpopular tax increases, for instance) because there are insufficient incentives or even disincentives for politicians seeking reelection. Some call this process democracy in action. However that may be, the result has been a bias toward deficit spending at the federal level and an abridgement of Keynesian principles of discretionary fiscal policy.

Deficits occur when government expenditures exceed government income from taxation in any given fiscal year. The national debt is the sum at a certain point in time of all prior deficits. During the 1980s and early 1990s, huge deficits were incurred by the federal government, although they moderated after 1992, and a budget surplus was achieved in 1998. These deficits pushed the projected national debt to right at $5.7 *trillion* in 2000. The point to be made is that these deficits were not primarily the product of conscious discretionary—that is, Keynesian—action to eliminate contractionary gaps. They were simply inevitable given the nature of the democratic political process.

The behavior of politicians with regard to the supply of deficits is understandable, but why would some voters reveal a preference for deficit finance? Those who earn little or no income and who receive large net benefits from the government have little incentive to demand restraint from politicians. Since taxes fall disproportionately on *human* capital in the form of income taxes in the United States, some voters have an incentive to support deficit finance over direct pay-as-you-go taxation to finance the activities of the federal government. In effect, these voters are electing to pass part of the burden of financing government expenditures on to succeeding generations of taxpayers.

The plain fact is that politicians want to get reelected; and some voters would like to pass the bill for present enjoyment on to future generations. The economic effects of deficits (which will be discussed at length in Chapter 25) are less clear. What is obvious is that the lack of effective budget constraints on members of Congress and the president or on the financing process means that democracies have built-in tendencies to run deficits.

---

tive effect of unbalanced budgets is ignored in this approach. As we have seen, antirecessionary fiscal policy requires raising government expenditures or reducing taxes, either of which tends to produce a budget deficit. For reasons that will be explained more fully in Chapter 25, the history of fiscal policy in the United States has been one in which, since World War II, annual deficits have outnumbered annual surpluses by a margin of almost 20 to one, a policy that Keynes probably would not have supported. A deficit implies that government expenditures exceed revenues, further implying the need for creation of money and credit. Credit creation, in turn, has implications in the money markets of the macroeconomy. The most important of these implications is inflation.

Public works projects, such as the construction of this powerhouse and dam, are examples of how governments act as consumers. Keynes advocated such projects as a means of artificially stimulating the economy.

A major deficiency of the income–expenditures model we have employed to this point is that it excludes monetary variables, particularly prices. Therefore, it does not tell all of the macroeconomic story. Prices affect both consumption and investment spending, which in turn affect macroeconomic activity. In other words, simple Keynesian economics leaves us ill-equipped to analyze adequately more recent macroeconomic experience with unemployment and inflation. A more complete macroeconomic theory of total expenditures, one including prices and other monetary factors, will help us better understand today's macroeconomic problems. This expanded theory will be presented in Chapters 23 and 24.

APPLICATION

Mortgaging Your Future: The Government and Your Incentive to Save

A great challenge facing the United States is reversing the decline in the national saving rate. This concern is based on the notion that the level of a country's savings determines how much it has to invest in new plant and equipment. A decline in the saving rate therefore leads to less investment, which in turn reduces the ability of the economy to produce goods and services.

Although there is some controversy concerning the importance of the saving rate as a determinant of economic growth, two things are clear: The saving rate in the United States has declined sharply over the last twenty years, and this decline has brought the U.S. saving rate to a level far below that of other major economic powers (although it is worth noting that there are variations in the ways other countries measure savings). In 1973, Americans were saving about 10 percent of their disposable income; this percentage fell to under 3 percent in 1987. Since then, the trend has reversed somewhat, and the saving rate reached 4 percent by 1998.

In explaining the difference between the saving rate in the United States and in other countries, much attention has been paid to the way that interest income is taxed in the United States. In the United States, interest earnings are taxable income. If a family has accumulated, say, $20,000 in savings that yields 9 percent interest, the $1800 in annual interest is an addition to taxable income. Assuming the family to be middle income, each additional dollar of taxable income will lead to an increase of $0.28 in federal taxes owed by the family. In addition, this family probably would pay about $0.05 in state taxes for each additional dollar in interest earnings. When state and federal taxes are combined, $600 of the $1800 earned in interest will go to pay taxes—in effect reducing the interest rate to 6 percent. By taxing interest income, the tax system in this country reduces the returns to saving and presumably causes the saving rate to be lower than it otherwise would be.

In addition to discouraging saving, the U.S. tax system subsidizes borrowing. If a family in this country borrows $100,000 to buy a new home, any interest that the family pays is tax-deductible. Assuming mortgage interest payments of $9000 per year on the loan, this debt enables the family to reduce taxable income by $9000, which lowers state and federal taxes by about $3000. In effect, the loan costs the family only 6 percent in interest. Until recently, all interest paid on consumer loans was tax-deductible. However, this deduction has been phased out, explaining in part the recent upturn in savings. Nonetheless, U.S. tax policy still reduces the return to saving.

What is the impact of a low saving rate for the U.S. economy? Other things being equal, anything that reduces the private saving rate will have a tendency to reduce private investment over time. (Other policies, such as the taxing of capital gains, also reduce individual investment.) One of the key factors in determining the level of private investment is the cost of making new investments in capital, equipment, labor training programs, and research and development. One of the major components in that cost is the rate of interest. A reduction in private savings for any reason will increase the rate of interest and raise the cost of new investment in the economy. Since, as Keynes noted, private investment (and investment volatility) is a prime determinant of the level of income over the short (and long) run, policies affecting private investment—such as taxes on savings and subsidies to borrowing—are of great importance to economic and employment growth.

In addition to tax policies and to the natural inclination of individuals to value the present more than the future (which helps explain why higher interest rates in the present yield more present savings), other more subtle long-run factors affect the saving rate. While the consumption stream is roughly constant or slightly rising over time, the average individual's income flow is much lower in early age and in old age than in middle age. This means that individuals (and households) consume more of the value of their (expected) lifetime income flow in early age and in old age and less in middle age. When birth rates are constant, this poses no problem for a country's savings. But significant changes in the age distribution of the population may have important impacts on the distribution of long-term savings.[a] In the United States, the aging of the "baby-boomers"—the large group born between the end of World War II and 1964—may well have a negative impact on private saving and investment.

Finally, we need to mention how, until recently, trends in finance have tended to reduce private investment. Government borrowing has resulted from high federal deficits in the public accounts (when current government spending exceeds tax revenues). In order to finance all of its activities the government must in effect compete with private businesses for private savings. As we have seen, a lower supply of private savings tends to drive up interest rates. Increased government

---

[a]This feature of saving and consumption is called the "life-cycle" saving hypothesis.

demands have the same effect, which means that politically determined spending and tax policies at the federal level will have huge implications for economic growth rates in the economy.

The movement to so-called surpluses in the federal budget, projected at least for several years through the year 2000, will ease the absorption of savings into the government sector. It is problematic, however, whether such surpluses will last long into the future. Long-running budget deficits, piled up over the postwar years in the United States, will continue to have an effect on saving. The resulting debt (estimated at $5.7 *trillion* in 2000)—and the necessary payments of interest, or "service," on the debt—are certain to play a major role in capital formation, economic growth, and growth in employment in the U.S. economy well into the twenty-first century.

QUESTIONS

What could the federal government do to encourage private saving? What does a low saving rate imply about the future prospects of the U.S. economy?

SUMMARY

1. In the 1930s, John Maynard Keynes criticized classical theory as being an inadequate description of events in the real world. He based macroeconomics on a model of total expenditures. In the simple private sector model, consumption and investment spending determine equilibrium output and income.

2. Keynes argued that consumption was primarily a function of current income and that the marginal and average propensities to consume were related to income in a stable and predictable manner. Investment, the other kind of private spending, was related to expectations and to a number of factors but could, in the short run, be considered autonomous of income.

3. The income–expenditures model of equilibrium output-income determination employs Keynes's arguments concerning the relationship of certain macroeconomic variables. The level of consumption spending is positively related to the level of income. The marginal propensity to save (MPS) measures the change in saving that results from a $1 change in income. Other factors, such as the price level, wealth, and taxation, help determine consumption and saving. Investment spending is assumed to be autonomous.

4. In the income–expenditures approach, the equilibrium level of income exists when total expenditure equals total income or output in the economy ($Y = C + I$). Whenever total expenditure does not equal total income or whenever desired saving does not equal desired investment, unintended investment in the form of inventory change exists. The unintended investment will drive income or output toward its equilibrium level. However, the equilibrium level of income may not be a level of income at which full employment occurs.

5. A multiplier is calculated by dividing a change in income by the change in autonomous expenditures that caused the change in income. The multiplier is the reciprocal of the marginal propensity to save, or $1/MPS$. A multiplier may be applied to any change in autonomous expenditures. For example, if the autonomous portion of consumption expenditures increases, income changes by the value of the expenditures multiplied by the reciprocal of the MPS.

6. Fiscal policy consists of budgetary action taken by the central government. More specifically, fiscal policy means action to adjust either the level of taxes or the level of government expenditures to achieve a stable level of growth.

7. An increase in government expenditures, *G*, or a decrease in taxes, *T*, is expansionary. A decrease in government expenditures or an increase in taxes is contractionary. Insofar as tax changes affect private spending only indirectly, a tax change is less effective than the same dollar amount of change in government expenditures. Output effects from changes in *G* or *T* are multiplied. Although the value of the consumption multiplier (1/*MPS*) is the same in both cases, the output effects are different because a $1 change in taxes affects consumption less than a $1 change in government expenditures does.

8. Exports and imports also have an impact on total expenditures. When imports exceed exports, total spending declines in the United States. Total spending increases when exports to other countries exceed our imports from abroad.

9. Keynes's macroeconomic theory and his remedies for macroeconomic ills, while probably appropriate for periods of contraction and widespread unemployment, omitted crucial monetary variables, especially prices, from primary consideration. More inclusive theories are able to explain inflation and other contemporary macroeconomic problems.

KEY TERMS

income–expenditures model
marginal propensity to consume (*MPC*)
marginal propensity to save (*MPS*)
average propensity to consume (*APC*)
average propensity to save (*APS*)
dissaving
autonomous consumption

consumption function
saving function
investment spending
autonomous investment
equilibrium level of national income
investment multiplier
autonomous consumption multiplier

contractionary gap
expansionary gap
autonomous government expenditures
lump-sum tax
exports
imports
countercyclical fiscal policy

QUESTIONS FOR REVIEW AND DISCUSSION

1. How does Keynes's view of saving differ from the classical view of saving? How does Keynes's view of wage–price flexibility differ from the classical view?

2. Define marginal propensity to consume and average propensity to consume. What is the essential difference between the two?

3. If the *MPC* is 0.75 and national income increases by $200 billion, then by how much will consumption expenditures increase?

4. Can you think of any nonincome factors not listed in the text that might affect consumption decisions?

5. What is autonomous investment spending? Does it change as the level of income changes?

6. When does equilibrium occur in the income–expenditures model? What adjusts to obtain equilibrium?

7. Define the consumption function and explain its relationship to the 45-degree line.

8. Juan spends an additional $20 a week in response to a $30 per week raise. What is Juan's *MPC*? His *MPS*?

9. What effect does a $30 billion decrease in autonomous investment have on total expenditures when the *MPC* is 0.9?

10. What is the essential implication of the investment multiplier? What is multiplied when autonomous investment changes?

12. What was Keynes's basic dispute with the classical economists? What were his recommendations for smoothing out the business cycle?

13. What fiscal policy would Keynes recommend for large-scale unemployment? What would he recommend for inflation?

14. What effect does a lump-sum tax of $20 billion have on total expenditures if the *MPC* is 0.9? Would it have a greater effect if the *MPC* were 0.8?

15. Describe a contractionary gap and an expansionary gap and show each graphically.

16. What happens to the level of national income if consumption increases by $20 billion, investment increases by $5 billion, government expenditures decrease by $10 billion, and net exports increase by $15 billion?

PROBLEMS

1. Consider a basic income–expenditures model (with no government sector and where $Y = C + I$) in which Y is real national income, C is real consumption expenditures, and I is real autonomous investment expenditures. Let $C = \$40$ billion $+ (MPC)Y$ and let $I = I_0$. If $I_0 = \$50$ billion and $MPC = 0.5$, compute the equilibrium levels of national income, Y; consumption, C; and saving, S.

2. Suppose that an increase in national income from $200 billion to $350 billion increases consumption expenditures from $180 billion to $255 billion, or by $75 billion. Given this data, calculate the marginal propensity to consume and the average propensity to consume before and after the change in national income.

3. Suppose that in private sector equilibrium, consumption expenditures are $50 billion and that investment expenditures are $10 billion. What is the *APC*? The *APS*? If the *MPC* is 0.75 and consumption expenditures increase by $40 billion as a result of an increase in income, what happens to the level of savings?

4. Suppose that total expenditures are $250 billion short of the full-employment level of income and that $MPC = 0.7$. In the Keynesian framework, by how much would government expenditures have to increase to bring the economy to full employment?

5. Suppose that a wave of optimism spreads through the business community, causing autonomous investment to increase by $60 million. As a result, the equilibrium level of national income increases by $500 million. Find k, the *MPS*, and the *MPC*.

6. Assume that a consumption function is given as $C = 400 + 0.80Y$. Let all of the other variables be autonomous as follows: $I_0 = 80$, $G_0 = 120$, $X_0 = 75$, and $M_0 = 60$. Determine the equilibrium level of income.

WORKING WITH THE WEB

1. Go to The Dismal Scientist web site (http://www.dismal.com). You should see a row at the top with a series of links. Click on the first link, "economy." On the next page, locate the box on the left side of the screen called "Economic Releases," and click on the link for "Consumers." You should see a table with recent consumer-related information. Find the row for consumption, and click on that link (i.e., the word consumption). If you've lived a good life, you should finally see a box entitled "Additional Data" on the left side of the screen. Click on the link for "Income and Consumption Overview."

    The savings rate is also the average propensity to save, a concept that is discussed in this chapter (you can also read about this if you go to the link for Definitions on this page).

    a. What do you observe about the savings rate during 1998 and 1999?
    b. Using concepts from the chapter, explain your findings in part (a).

       Go to the bottom of the page and expand the graph to include the last three years of data (the control for this is just below the graph).
    c. Describe the general relationship you observe between income and consumption.

       Go to the link (in the left-side box) for "Consumption by Category." You should arrive at more data in a table and graph, showing that consumption includes durable, nondurable, and service-related goods.
    d. Do you expect each of the consumption categories to have the same relationship to income that you found in part (c)?

2. The typical Keynesian discussion tends to center on the need for fiscal policy (i.e., government expenditure and taxation). The Ludwig Von Mises web site (http://www.mises.org) has a collection of articles that discuss the role of government from a more libertarian perspective. Go to this web site and find the link for "Daily Articles." Once you've clicked on this link, click again on the link that includes articles from January '99. Go to the article, "Public and Private" (note: after going to the Daily Articles page, you can also search for this article by using the title, "Public and Private").

    Read this article and then explain why we cannot necessarily infer much about the government's role in the economy by observing the government's level of expenditure.

3. Keynesian economics is viewed as supporting the discretionary use of fiscal policy (i.e., government expenditure and taxation). Multiplier analysis describes how these changes in government expenditure and taxation affect the economy (i.e., output or income). When we assume that investment expenditure is autonomous, however, we ignore the possibility that changes in government expenditure may affect other variables, like interest rates. For example, an increase in government expenditure alone may cause interest rates to rise, which in turn causes nonautonomous investment expenditure to change.

    Go to the Economagic web site (http://www.Economagic.com) and, by going through the link for "Most Requested Series," find the data for Bank Prime Loan Rate. While on this second page, do a search. Next, enter the keyword phrase "Fixed investment" and locate two data titles: "Real Private Residential Fixed Investment" and "Real Private Nonresidential Fixed Investment" (both in chained 1992 dollars).

    Create a graph for all three sets of data (after clicking on the link to either page of data, click on the link for "GIF Chart" on the green banner) over the time period 1982–1999. Does this particular interest rate (the prime rate) have an observable relationship with both types of investment?

Aggregate Demand and Aggregate Supply

After World War II, a moderate inflation rate in the United States held off a doubling of the price level for twenty-five years. Less than ten years later, however, the price level doubled again. The acceleration of the inflation rate slowed between 1981 and 1999, but many economists believe there is a prospect of higher inflation in the future. By international standards, the United States has an enviable record of avoiding inflation. Peru, Mexico, and Brazil have experienced annual inflation rates in excess of 100 percent in recent years. In each case, runaway inflation devastated the country's economy. Such experiences should teach us the importance of avoiding economic policies that lead to excessive inflation.

When we began our discussion of macroeconomics in Chapter 19, we included price stability in our list of primary macroeconomic goals. (The other two were full employment and economic growth.) Subsequent chapters developed a model that explained how the level of national income was determined. This model was used to explain unemployment and inadequate economic growth. However, in that model the price level remained unchanged; the model did not address the problems of inflation and deflation. This chapter develops a model of aggregate demand and aggregate supply in which the interaction of these two forces determines both the level of national income and the price level. We will show how shifts in either aggregate demand or in aggregate supply can cause inflation or deflation. After you complete Chapter 23 you should understand

- how price level changes cause changes in total real expenditures by consumers and businesses.
- how the aggregate demand curve relates national income and output to price level changes.

- how the aggregate supply curve is constructed, and how its shape is determined by production and capacity levels.
- how shifts in aggregate demand and supply affect output and price levels.

PRICE CHANGES AND AGGREGATE DEMAND

We have defined the function $C + I + G + (X - M)$ as total expenditures. But an important distinction must be made between total expenditures and aggregate demand once the price level is explicitly recognized. The term *aggregate demand* refers to the relation between the price level of all output and the total quantity of all goods and services demanded. In other words, from here on, as we discuss contractionary and expansionary phases in the economy and proper macroeconomic policies to remedy such phases, we will be tying total real expenditures to a specific price level, a composite index of all prices in the economy. We will then vary the price level to see how such changes affect equilibrium output or income, since price level changes will affect total real expenditures.

Price Changes and Changes in Purchasing Power

Chapter 22 defined the difference between nominal, or money, income—the income we receive in dollar terms—and real income—the purchasing power of those dollars. In times of inflation, nominal incomes may increase, yet real incomes may remain the same or even fall. For example, if you receive a 5 percent raise in a year in which the annual rate of inflation is 6 percent, you have actually lost ground in terms of the goods and services your salary can purchase. Since inflation erodes the purchasing power of each dollar received, real income, or income adjusted for changes in the price level, is a more accurate measure of how the economy is performing.

Inflation affects more than income, unfortunately. It also affects wealth. The term *income* is usually taken to mean the sum of weekly, monthly, or annual earnings. **Wealth,** on the other hand, is the sum of all assets. Income is a flow variable; wealth is a stock variable. Flow variables are measured per unit of time. Speed, for example, is a flow variable—it is measured in meters per second or miles per hour. By contrast, weight is an example of a stock variable; it is defined independently of time. It is meaningful to say that someone weighs 120 pounds without making any reference to time.

Wealth may be pecuniary (dollar-denominated, such as a savings account) or nonpecuniary (non-dollar-denominated, such as a house, auto, or Persian rug). The distinction between pecuniary and nonpecuniary wealth is important, because the value of each type of wealth is affected differently by changes in the price level. Compare a $10,000 Persian rug with a $10,000 deposit in a savings account. When the price level doubles under 100 percent inflation, what happens to the real value of these two kinds of wealth? Dollar-denominated assets such as the $10,000 deposit in a savings account or a bond with a face value of $10,000 have a fixed dollar value. With a 100 percent increase in the price level, the value of a dollar-denominated asset has been cut in half, in terms of purchasing power. However, the higher price level implies that the nominal value of all non-dollar-denominated assets, including the Persian rug, has increased, assuming that prices of collectibles keep pace with the general price level. But the rug is still a rug: In real terms it is worth as much as it was before. It would now fetch $20,000 in the marketplace

Wealth

The total value of monetary plus nonmonetary assets in existence at a point in time; a stock variable.

instead of $10,000, but the higher dollar amount would merely purchase the same amount of goods and services as $10,000 would have previously. In other words, the real value of many nonpecuniary assets (real estate, paintings, jewels) is unaffected by changes in the price level.

Now contemplate the unfortunate effects of the same degree of inflation on the $10,000 savings deposit. Except in the unlikely case that the interest rate has kept pace with the 100 percent rate of inflation, the real value of the deposit will have declined. Assuming no interest rate change, the same $10,000 that would have purchased $10,000 worth of goods and services before inflation will purchase only $5000 worth of goods and services now. In other words, price level changes bring about changes in the real value, or purchasing power, of pecuniary assets.

The Real Balance Effect

As inflation erodes the purchasing power of the money in our bank accounts and of our holdings of other dollar-denominated assets, we have to economize—buy fewer books, try to keep the old car running instead of buying an expensive new one. This change in consumption behavior that results from a change in the price level is sometimes called the **real balance effect.**

Real balance effect

The effect on investment and consumption spending of a change in the price level that alters the real value of pecuniary assets.

If we let MS stand for society's entire stock of pecuniary, or dollar-denominated, assets and P for the aggregate price level, then the value of real balances can be expressed as MS/P. The level of real household consumption expenditures will be determined by the value of real balances as well as by the level of disposable income.

The relation between consumption and real money balances is positive, just as the relation between consumption and income is positive. If prices fall, assuming that MS remains the same, the value of real balances rises and consumers experience an enhanced wealth effect; that is, their money assets will purchase more goods and services than before. Thus, consumption will rise in response to greater real wealth. Graphically, the consumption function will shift upward, establishing a higher equilibrium level of output and employment. Conversely, if prices rise, the value of real balances declines, the consumption curve subsequently falls, and lower output and employment result. Changes in real balances are capable of inducing the same kinds of changes in total expenditures as fiscal policy manipulations (ΔG and ΔT).

We have already encountered this important concept. Recall that classical economists before Keynes generally believed the wage–price flexibility would automatically bring about total expenditure changes that would correct the cyclical swings of the macroeconomy. The logic behind this self-correcting view was as follows: If the economy slides into a recession and unemployment occurs, labor markets will be faced with an excess supply of workers. In competitive labor markets, this excess of workers will create downward pressure on wages. As wages fall, so will the unit costs of production; prices will therefore decline as well. The general decline in prices will sooner or later raise the real value of money balances, thus inducing consumers to spend more. The increased spending will thereby stimulate output and employment, lifting the economy out of the recession. In a similar fashion, the presence of inflation will eventually lead to a reduction in real balances and a consequent decline in total spending, thereby eliminating the inflationary tendencies. For the classical economists, the real balance effect on consumption helped explain the self-adjusting nature of the economy.

This important process can be fixed more precisely in graphical terms. In Figure 23.1, three total spending functions are shown for three alternative price levels. Given some price level P_0 and some constant level of pecuniary assets in the economy, real balances will produce some level of consumption, C_0. Consumption function C_0 and given levels of investment, government, and net foreign expenditures, I, G, $(X - M)$, produce an equilibrium level of real income Y_0.

What happens in the event of a price decline? A price reduction will increase the real value of pecuniary balances, causing an increase in the consumption component of total spending. In Figure 23.1, the original total spending function shifts upward to $C_1 + I + G + (X - M)$ at the new, lower price level. This new, higher total expenditures function is associated with a higher level of equilibrium income, Y_1. By the same reasoning, a rise in the price level above the initial level brings a reduction in equilibrium income to Y_2.

The Interest Rate Effect

We have seen that changes in the price level affect the purchasing power of our pecuniary assets and equilibrium income. Price level changes also affect income through the mechanism of interest rates.

Interest rates are always in the news. Consumers are highly interested in whether interest rates are high or low, rising or falling. Interest rates to some extent determine the purchasing decisions made by consumers—whether to buy a new car or to mortgage the purchase of a new home. Interest rates also influence the decisions of businesses. Businesses watch interest rate levels when deciding

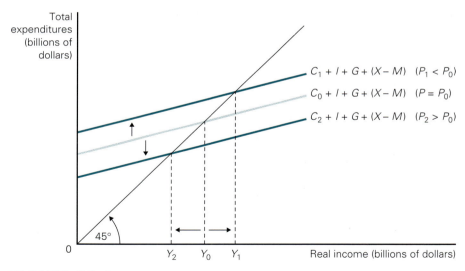

FIGURE 23.1

How Price Level Changes Alter Consumption Spending and Real Income

Any change in the price level, from the initial level P_0, will create a real balance effect on consumption, shifting the total spending curve upward or downward. A lower price level, P_1, is associated with a higher level of equilibrium real income, Y_1, and the total spending curve shifts upward to $C_1 + I + G + (X - M)$. A price level P_2 higher than the initial price level would, for similar reasons, be associated with a lower level of equilibrium income, Y_2, and a spending curve that shifts downward to $C_2 + I + G + (X - M)$.

whether to make capital investments—build a warehouse, acquire new machinery, expand their inventories.

In general, interest rates depend on changes in the price level. When the price level rises, interest rates tend to rise; when the price level falls, interest rates tend to fall. As with all other goods, individuals will want to hold equilibrium quantities of real money—balances for transactions, for investments, or simply as a precautionary ("rainy day") measure. In other words, people are interested in the real value, or purchasing power, of their money balances, not in their nominal holdings of money. The value of dollar-denominated assets is inversely related to the price level, since these assets are fixed in money terms. The real supply of money is also altered by price level changes. The purchasing power of each dollar we hold rises when the price level falls and declines when the price level rises. In part, interest rates are the product of the demand for real money balances and their supply in real terms. Thus, as the real supply of these balances increases with reductions in the price level, the interest rate tends to fall. And, as the real supply of money balances declines with increases in the price level, the interest rate tends to rise. It is important to recognize that these interest rate changes affect the investment and consumption components of expenditures.

Figure 23.2 shows the effect of changes in the price level on interest rates. Investors react to these changes because the interest rate change alters the cost and profitability of investment projects; consumers react by changing expenditure plans, especially for durable goods (such as refrigerators or homes). These changes in expenditures in turn cause changes in income and employment. As prices rise (and the value of real money falls), output and real income decline; as prices fall, output and real income increase.

The **interest rate effect** can be viewed in the income–expenditures model depicted in Figure 23.3. With the price at some initial level, P_0, total expenditures equal $C + I_0 + G + (X - M)$. A decrease in the aggregate price level to P_1 will lower interest rates. Other things being equal, lower interest rates will lower the cost of all new investment projects. The consequent effect in the total expenditures

Interest rate effect

The effect on investment spending that results from a change in the interest rate produced by a change in the price level.

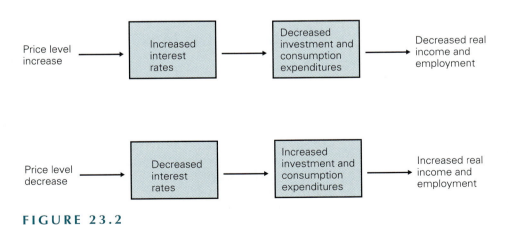

FIGURE 23.2

The Interest Rate Effect

An increase in the price level may be related to a decrease in real income and employment via the process of investment and consumption spending. Conversely, a decrease in the price level can lead to an increase in income. The lower half of the diagram shows that declines in the price level tend to lower the interest rate and expand investment and consumption expenditures. Increased production and jobs result.

FIGURE 23.3

The Price Level and Investment Spending

Decreases in the price level from P_0 to P_1 lower interest rates and increase investment from I_0 to I_1. The higher level of investment increases real income from Y_0 to Y_1. Increases in the price level to P_2 increase interest rates and decrease investment to I_2 and income to Y_2.

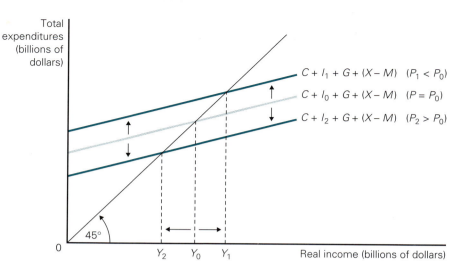

model is to raise the investment function, thus stimulating the economy to a higher level of output and employment, Y_1.

Conversely, higher aggregate price levels tend to drive up interest rates. Now all new investment projects will be more costly than before, so a decline in the investment schedule can be predicted. In Figure 23.3, the total expenditure schedule will shift downward to $C + I_2 + G + (X - M)$ and establish a lower level of income at Y_2.

To summarize, changes in the aggregate price level are likely to affect aggregate consumption (the real balance effect and the interest rate effect) and aggregate investment (the interest rate effect). The macroeconomy, viewed realistically, is a complex structure of relations in which the level of total expenditures is determined by the aggregate levels of income, wealth, and prices.

AGGREGATE DEMAND

Aggregate demand curve

Graphical relation showing the different levels of national income that exist at different price levels.

In Chapter 4, we saw that all demand functions relating prices and quantity demanded are downward sloping. This also applies to the **aggregate demand curve,** which captures the relation between the aggregate price level and real national income. The aggregate demand curve basically tells us that as the price level falls in the macroeconomy, other things being equal, households and businesses tend to buy more. Conversely, as the price level rises, other things being equal, households and businesses tend to decrease their spending. Again, a contrast between microeconomic supply and demand relations and the macroeconomic concepts is instructive. Recall from Chapter 3 that the demand curve for a particular good or service slopes downward because a price decrease for some good—say, football tickets—alters its *relative* price compared with all other goods. A lower relative price causes the student to substitute football tickets for all other goods in her budget; this substitution explains the negative slope of the demand curve. The negative slope of aggregate demand in macroeconomic theory does not depend on changes in relative prices but on changes in the price level—a relation that can be shown with the Keynesian income–expenditures model.

FIGURE 23.4

Derivation of Aggregate Demand from Total Expenditures

A decrease in the price level from P_0 to P_1 creates an increase in consumption and investment spending. (a) A decrease from P_0 to P_1 increases real income from Y_0 to Y_1. Increases in the price level decrease C and I, so real income falls from Y_0 to Y_2. (b) The price and income combinations trace out the aggregate demand curve: Greater quantities of goods and services are demanded at lower prices.

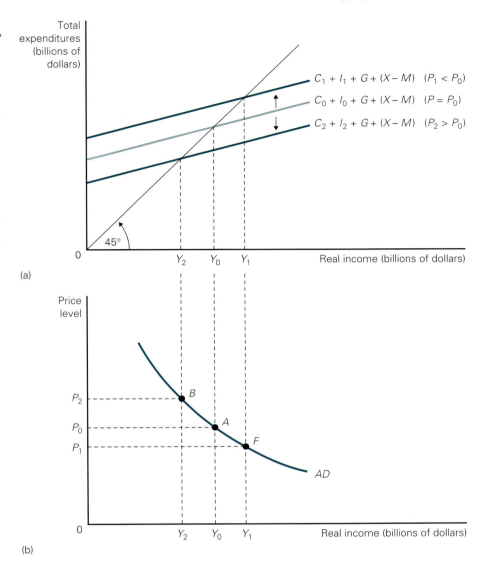

(a)

(b)

Deriving the Aggregate Demand Curve

Examine Figure 23.4, in which the macroeconomy is assumed to be in equilibrium at Y_0. The $C_0 + I_0 + G + (X - M)$ curve in Figure 23.4a is constructed for a given price level, P_0 in Figure 23.4b. Starting from this point, we can hypothetically vary the price level up and down in Figure 23.4b and observe the corresponding income level produced. Matching pairs of P and Y will trace out the aggregate demand curve. For example, assume the price level falls from P_0 to P_1. The effect of this price decline will be to raise household consumption (the real balance effect) and to raise business investment (the interest rate effect). Thus, total expenditures will shift upward, establishing a higher income level at Y_1. A lower price level, P_1, therefore, matches a higher level of real income, Y_1. This matched pair of variables is plotted in Figure 23.4b as point F.

We can continue the conceptual experiment by raising the price level from P_0 to P_2. Inflation causes the consumption function to shift downward (the interest rate effect), moving the equilibrium income to Y_2. The combination (P_2, Y_2) is shown in Figure 23.4b as point B. The aggregate demand curve (AD) is the locus of all points generated in the manner of points B, A, and F. The curve is downward sloping, as stated at the beginning of this section.

The Shape of the Aggregate Demand Curve

Both the real balance effect and the interest rate effect cause the level of aggregate demand to increase as the price level falls and to decrease as the price level rises. The shape of the aggregate demand curve depends on the magnitude of the two effects. If in Figure 23.4 a price level reduction from P_0 to P_1 causes a large increase in consumer wealth (perhaps because consumers have large holdings of dollar-denominated stocks), the total spending function will shift upward by a large amount. This in turn will result in a level of aggregate demand much greater at a price level P_1 than at P_0. Accordingly, income level Y_1 will lie far to the right of Y_0, causing the aggregate demand curve to be flat. On the other hand, if consumers have few dollar-denominated assets, a fall in the price level will have little effect on total spending and the aggregate demand curve will be steep. In a similar fashion, the stronger the interest rate effect, the flatter the aggregate demand curve.

The shape of the aggregate demand curve is important. With flat aggregate demand curves, shifts in aggregate supply will primarily affect the level of output, having little impact on the equilibrium price level. With steep aggregate demand curves, a shift in aggregate supply will have a large impact on price level but little impact on the level of production.

Shifts in the Aggregate Demand Curve

In tracing out the relation between the aggregate price level and the aggregate level of income, certain variables other than price are assumed constant. These constants are numerous. They involve all of those things that shift the demand function either rightward or leftward. The following list of factors that are capable of shifting aggregate demand is representative but not exhaustive:

- household consumption (C): autonomous component
- business investment (I): autonomous component
- government expenditures (G)
- saving (S): autonomous component
- net exports ($X - M$)
- the money stock (MS)
- taxes (T)

A change in any of these factors will result in a different level of national income at the same level of prices. Graphically, a change in any of these factors will create a rightward or leftward shift in the aggregate demand function. Table 23.1 summarizes the effects on aggregate demand for each change listed, and Figure 23.5 shows the shifts graphically.

To test our understanding of the principles involved, assume some change in total expenditures, such as an increase in the net export balance. Spending increases at every price level, creating higher real income for every possible price level. In

TABLE 23.1

Shifts in the Aggregate Demand Function

A change in any of the listed variables will shift the aggregate demand function rightward or leftward, depending on whether the variable increases (↑) or decreases (↓).

Rightward Shift	Leftward Shift
Autonomous consumption ↑	Autonomous consumption ↓
Autonomous investment ↑	Autonomous investment ↓
Government expenditures ↑	Government expenditures ↓
Net exports $(X - M)$ ↑	Net exports $(X - M)$ ↓
The money supply ↑	The money supply ↓
Saving ↓	Saving ↑
Taxes ↓	Taxes ↑

Figure 23.5, the aggregate demand curve shifts to the right from AD_0 to AD_1, illustrating that the real income at each price level increases. The same effect would occur with an increase in consumption (a reduction in saving), investment expenditures, or government expenditures.

Leftward shifts in the aggregate demand curve are likewise caused by both private sector and government-controlled factors. Reductions in consumption (increases in saving), investment, or net exports would cause a leftward shift in the aggregate demand curve, from AD_0 to AD_2 in Figure 23.5, for example. An increase in taxes or a reduction in government spending would also shift the function leftward. These shifts occur due to a reduction in spending at every possible price level, meaning that the level of real income associated with any given price level falls.

FIGURE 23.5

Shifts in Aggregate Demand

Any change in a nonprice factor affecting total expenditures will shift the aggregate demand curve rightward or leftward. An increase in savings, for example, will reduce total expenditures and aggregate demand at each price level, causing a leftward shift from AD_0 to AD_2. A decrease in taxes or an increase in government expenditures will shift the curve rightward from AD_0 to AD_1, reflecting greater spending on goods and services at every price level.

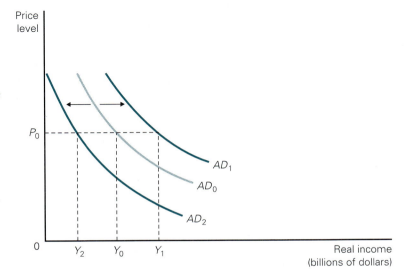

As we have seen, many economic variables are capable of altering aggregate demand in the macroeconomy, thereby also altering the equilibrium levels of output, income, and employment. Some of these variables—such as household consumption and business investment—are determined by millions of decentralized, individual decisions. Others are determined by highly centralized government directives—decisions such as the appropriate level of government expenditures and taxes and the money supply. Among the latter decisions are various policy actions to combat the ups and downs of the business cycle.

The point of discretionary budget policies—manipulating taxes or government spending—is to stimulate the economy during periods of economic contraction and unemployment and to cool down the economy during periods of rapid expansion and inflation. Such efforts by the government to steer the economy are known as **discretionary fiscal policies.**

Discretionary fiscal policies
Government policy actions that attempt to influence aggregate demand.

Before we can discuss the possible effects of fiscal policy on aggregate demand, however, we must look at aggregate supply, the other major force determining the quantity of goods and services produced in the economy. We cannot determine the actual quantity of output produced through demand factors alone; we must also know what all businesses in the economy are willing to produce at alternative price levels.

AGGREGATE SUPPLY

Although higher price levels reduce the level of aggregate demand, they tend to have the opposite effect on aggregate supply. When producers receive higher prices for output, their profits rise, giving them an incentive to increase production. Furthermore, when producers attempt to increase production levels, they use existing resources more intensively, which drives up production costs. Producers are forced to charge higher prices to recover increased costs. The **aggregate supply curve** traces the relation between the price level and the aggregate level of production.

Aggregate supply curve
A graph showing the different levels of aggregate output produced at different price levels.

The Shape of the Aggregate Supply Curve

As noted in Chapter 21, the shape of the aggregate supply curve depends on the state of the economy. When the economy is operating far below capacity with large quantities of unemployed resources, production can be increased without having much effect on input prices. Not only is it possible to employ workers of nearly all types, but productive inputs such as land and machinery are also readily available. This means that firms can hire more inputs without having to compete for them and that output can be expanded without much of an increase in average production costs. Therefore, small increases in the price level will lead to large increases in the level of production. This portion of the aggregate supply curve is called the Keynesian range, reflecting Keynes's concentration on large-scale unemployment in an economy.

When the economy is producing fairly close to capacity, the aggregate supply curve will be much steeper. In this range, attempts to increase production lead to shortages of certain inputs. Average production costs will rise, as firms are forced to pay more for scarce inputs. While it is possible to expand production, additional output can only be obtained at substantially higher price levels.

In the classical range—named for the classical economists, who described a full-employment economy—resources are fully employed and the economy is producing at some point on the production possibilities frontier. Since all available resources are employed, an individual producer can expand production only by bidding resources away from competing producers. The effect is to drive the price level up without increasing overall production. In this range, the aggregate supply curve becomes vertical.

Shifts and "Shocks" in the Aggregate Supply Curve

In drawing an aggregate supply curve, certain variables other than price level are held constant. Should any of these variables change, the entire aggregate supply curve will shift. A complete list of variables that *might* cause aggregate supply to shift would be lengthy, but a relatively small number of variables have the greatest impact on aggregate supply—in particular, productive resource supply, technology, tax rates, and freedom to respond to economic incentives. Table 23.2 shows the effects of changes in these four factors.

Resource supply often affects aggregate supply in obvious ways. For example, the discovery of new energy resources will cause energy prices to fall and productive capacity to rise; at all price levels, firms will have an economic incentive to increase output. Increases in resource availability, then, shift the aggregate supply curve to the right; decreases cause a leftward shift. (Sudden changes in resource or capital supply are sometimes called supply "shocks.") Now consider a less obvious example—the recent criticism of the educational system in the United States and the many proposals for educational reform. Proponents of reform argue that improved education is necessary for the country to remain competitive in world markets. In terms of aggregate demand and supply, this proposal is an economic policy to increase the stock of human capital and, therefore, aggregate supply. (For an analysis of the effects of a decrease in the supply of both human and nonhuman resources, see the Focus "Black Death and Black Gold: Aggregate Supply Shifts in Ancient and Modern History.")

An improvement in technology affects aggregate supply in a way similar to an increase in resource availability. It also reduces production costs and increases the economy's capacity, shifting the aggregate supply curve to the right.

To understand how a change in tax rates affects the aggregate supply curve, it is necessary to keep in mind that in a free society aggregate supply is determined by the willingness of producers to produce, not just by the ability to produce. With high marginal tax rates, producers must pay a substantial portion of their incomes

TABLE 23.2

Shifts in the Aggregate Supply Function

Any change in any of the factors listed in the table will cause aggregate supply to shift. These supply shifts are called shocks if they occur quickly and without warning.

Rightward Shift	Leftward Shift
Technological advance	Destruction of capital
Increase in human resources	Decrease in human resources
Increase in natural resources	Decrease in natural resources
Decrease in taxes	Increase in taxes

FOCUS

Black Death and Black Gold: Aggregate Supply Shifts in Ancient and Modern History

A change in the supply of a resource or the level of technology will cause the production possibilities of an economy to expand and the economy's aggregate supply curve to shift. Supplies of resources, both human and nonhuman, can change dramatically in a number of ways. Here we consider two supply shocks—the first resulting from a natural disaster and the second resulting from the deliberate actions of humans.

One of the greatest natural disasters ever visited upon the Western world was the bubonic plague—the so-called Black Death. Between 1347 and 1350, rats infested with plague-ridden fleas spread death throughout Europe; between 33 percent and 65 percent of the population perished. Since labor had been cheap and plentiful relative to other resources before the plague, agricultural methods had been oriented to the large untrained labor supply. The scarceness of labor following the plague (even with fewer mouths to feed) meant that society had to devote a large portion of its resources to food and other consumption goods in order to survive. This situation is represented in Figure 23.6

by the sudden leftward shift in the aggregate supply curve (from AS_0 to AS_1).

For our second example we consider a more recent case. In the late 1970s, the Organization of Petroleum Exporting Countries tried to hold Western economies hostage by reducing oil supplies (and increasing prices). Labor and other productive factors suddenly had less energy to work with, which led to a reduction in the productive effects of labor and other resources. The final result: a reduced demand for labor. OPEC thus caused a shift in aggregate supply, shown as a shift from AS_0 to AS_1 in Figure 23.6.

Fortunately, both of these stories have relatively happy endings. Relatively expensive labor, brought about by the general population reduction in the fourteenth century, meant that businesses economized or rationed labor by trying to substitute capital and other resources for labor. In the process, many labor-saving devices—including some that made use of water power—were invented. Later, steam power supplemented or replaced water power. The Black Death may have ultimately

FIGURE 23.6

Reductions in Human and Nonhuman Resources Shift the Aggregate Supply Curve Leftward

Reductions in population due to the Black Death and in oil and energy due to the OPEC cartel both caused a sudden leftward shift in the aggregate supply curve. As the economy "recovers," the aggregate supply curve shifts again to the right.

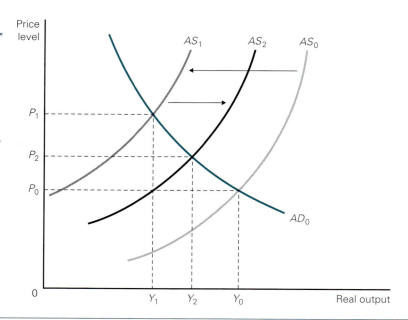

continued

sparked progress in European technology. The aggregate supply curve certainly shifted rightward over time (as from AS_1 to AS_2 in Figure 23.6).

Similarly, the 1980s witnessed a reversal of the OPEC supply shocks of the 1970s. Due in part to price cutting by OPEC members and an inability to maintain and police output restrictions, the cartel lost much of its power. As a result, U.S. producers and consumers had access to more oil at lower prices, a situation represented by the rightward shift in aggregate supply from AS_1 to AS_2 in Figure 23.6. To the extent that the formation of OPEC con-

tributed to the inflationary and recessionary trends of the 1970s, its partial dissolution fostered lower inflation rates and higher output levels in the 1980s.

The critical point is this: An economy will tend to respond to supply shocks by developing alternative methods and resources. New resource development, such as solar energy, and alternative production techniques reduced the impact of the initial OPEC-induced supply shifts. Improvements in agricultural technology and methods following the Black Death paved the way for the advances that characterized the Industrial Revolution.

in the form of taxes, and this reduces the incentive to produce. Workers in high tax brackets may choose to work shorter hours or to retire earlier. Reductions in tax rates remove disincentives to work and shift the aggregate supply rightward. Similarly, many economists believe that certain governmental regulations form a barrier between individuals and the business activities in which they have economic incentives to engage. Removal of regulations would increase the incentive to produce and cause aggregate supply to shift to the right. Much of the deregulation policy initiated during the Carter and Reagan administrations attempted to increase aggregate supply by reducing government red tape and, in Reagan's case, taxes. Since the Reagan administration, however, deregulation has taken a backseat to other concerns, such as deficit reduction and health care reform.

THE EQUILIBRIUM LEVEL OF PRICES AND PRODUCTION

Because both the aggregate demand curve and the aggregate supply curve are plotted with real output on the horizontal axis and the price level on the vertical axis, both curves can be plotted on the same graph. In Figure 23.7a, we see that AD_0 and AS_0 intersect at price level P_0 and output level Y_0. At any price level above P_0, the quantity of goods producers are willing to supply will exceed the quantity demanded by households, business firms, and so on. The excess demand for goods will cause prices to fall and drive the price level down to the equilibrium level, P_0. Aggregate demand and aggregate supply jointly determine the level of prices and output. Furthermore, any change in the equilibrium price level or output level can be viewed as being caused by a shift in either aggregate demand or supply. If, in Figure 23.7a, the aggregate demand curve were to shift to AD_1 because of a change in one of the variables affecting aggregate demand, both the price level and the level of production would increase—to P_1 and Y_1, respectively. As depicted in Figure 23.7a, an increase in aggregate supply would lead to an increase in equilibrium output and a decrease in the equilibrium price level. Decreases in aggregate supply have the opposite effects. Economists have even noted the possibility (especially over the 1970s and 1980s) of "stagflation"—a combination of effects that

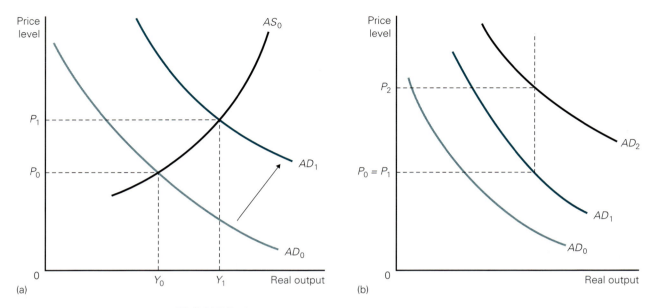

(a)

(b)

FIGURE 23.7

Equilibrium Price and Output Levels

(a) With aggregate supply AS_0 and aggregate demand AD_0, the equilibrium price level will be P_0 and the equilibrium level of output will be Y_0. A change in any of the variables affecting aggregate demand that leads to increased aggregate demand shifts the curve rightward—in this case, to AD_1. This increase in aggregate demand increases the equilibrium price level to P_1 and raises the equilibrium level of real output to Y_1. In (b), both classical and Keynesian ranges of the aggregate supply curve are depicted. An increase in aggregate demand from AD_0 to AD_1 results in an increase in output without a rise in the price level. An increase from AD_1 to AD_2 increases the price level without having any effect on the full-employment level of income.

could produce both unemployment and inflation simultaneously. (See the Focus "Stagflation: Gone but Not Forgotten.")

Consider, however, the situations described as "Keynesian" or "classical"—perhaps less theoretical and more like the conditions of our economy in the late 1990s. Figure 23.7b shows an aggregate supply curve with both a Keynesian range and a classical range. In the former, increases in aggregate demand from AD_0 to AD_1 have a unique impact on output—increasing it—with no increases in inflation. In the classical range, when the economy is at full employment, increases in aggregate demand from AD_1 to AD_2 will only increase inflation, having no effect on employment. (For an example of aggregate demand–aggregate supply analysis, see the Application "From Outhouse to Penthouse: First Recession Then Boom, Boom, Boom in the 1990s" at the end of this chapter.) The former case, as the data from Chapters 19 and 20 reveal, may have approximated the economy in the late 1990s. With employment below 5 percent in 1997 and 1998 and inflation under control (by some calculation, prices were actually falling in some sectors), one might depict the situation as described by AD_1 in Figure 23.7b. The trick, of course, was and is to maintain high employment levels without inflation or increases in the price level. This takes us out of the realm of pure economic theory and into a

FOCUS

Stagflation: Gone but Not Forgotten

Aggregate demand and supply theory has an obvious advantage over the Keynesian total expenditures approach in explaining price inflation. Aggregate demand and supply theory helps predict what effects fiscal policy will have on prices. Assuming that the aggregate supply curve is in the intermediate or "upward-sloping" range, aggregate demand changes will either increase prices along with increasing output and employment or they will decrease prices with accompanying decreases in jobs and production. In other words, there may be a built-in trade-off between inflation and employment. But consider another possibility—stagflation, inflation accompanied by unemployment or stagnation. This condition appears to have existed in the United States between 1969 and 1970, 1971 and 1972, 1973 and 1974, 1975 and 1976, and most dramatically in terms of the inflation part, between 1979 and 1981. Could stagflation happen again?

Stagflation can be analyzed in terms of demand and supply curves such as those developed in this chapter. In Figure 23.8, point A represents a recessionary level of output and employment in the economy. In response to high unemployment, government increases spending or decreases taxes in an effort to shift the aggregate demand curve rightward from AD_0 to AD_1. Prices rise, creating inflation, but output and employment also increase. Now assume that some other component of private expenditures—consumption, investment, or exports—decreases, causing a shift leftward in the aggregate demand curve from AD_1 to AD_2.

The result is that prices fall along with output to point F. But what if union or monopoly pressures mean that prices are too "sticky" to fall at all in response to the decreased demand? In this case, prices remain at high levels, and the full impact of the demand decrease falls on employment and output. Production falls as the economy stagnates, but inflationary pressures do not diminish. In terms of Figure 23.8, the economy would move to point C rather than to point F. Thus inflation and joblessness might go hand in hand.

While there are other interpretations of stagflation, the problem illustrates the usefulness of a macroeconomic theory—aggregate demand and supply analysis—that includes prices. In the post-Keynesian period, attention has focused on price inflation as well as on employment in considering aggregate demand management as a means for fine-tuning the economy. The fact that stagflation poses a possible lack of trade-off between inflation and unemployment illustrates some of the problems associated with the use of fiscal policy to control demand and to stabilize the economy.

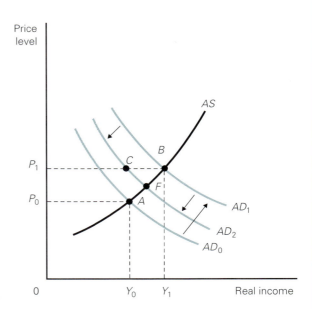

FIGURE 23.8

Aggregate Demand Shifts and Stagflation

The phenomenon of stagflation is produced by an increase in aggregate demand from AD_0 to AD_1 caused by some fiscal action (government spending increase or a tax reduction) and a reduction in some component of private spending (autonomous investment, consumption, or exports). Prices, however, are sticky and fail to fall with the demand reduction (from AD_1 to AD_2), creating stagflation—inflation and unemployment at the same time.

consideration of economic policy. However, it is only through an understanding of the factors that determine aggregate demand and aggregate supply (and, consequently, national income and the price level) that the problems of unemployment and inadequate economic growth can be addressed. Specific government policies—those designed to shift either the aggregate demand curve or the aggregate supply curve—are the subject of Chapter 24.

APPLICATION

From Outhouse to Penthouse: First Recession Then Boom, Boom, Boom in the 1990s

Aggregate demand and aggregate supply provide a means of analyzing the macroeconomy, although the analysis must always be integrated with real-world events. Consider the 1990s, which started off with a whimper and ended with a big bang as far as economic well-being is concerned.

Flash back to the beginning of the decade. The U.S. economy experienced agonizingly slow growth between 1989 and 1992. Officially, a recession occurs when real GDP declines (as a percentage change from the preceding period) for two successive quarters. This happened in the third and fourth quarters of 1990 (−1.6 percent and −3.9 percent, respectively). Between the second quarter of 1989 and the third quarter of 1992, economic growth measured in terms of percentage change in GDP never exceeded 3 percent. Coupled with massive layoffs and increasing unemployment, conditions were extremely unsettling, if not catastrophic, to many Americans. The annual growth rate in U.S. GDP was only 1.2 percent in 1990 and was actually negative in 1991 (−0.9 percent). (See GDP growth rates in Figure 23.9.)

What is the explanation for the disappointing state of affairs in the U.S. economy in the early 1990s? As usual, the explanation and analysis of this period of slow or negative growth are not simple and must be approached with a great deal of caution. But, as usual, the tools of aggregate demand and supply are most helpful in organizing our thoughts about the economy. Consider the changes in two stages: (a) the 1990–1992 sluggish–recession period, and (b) the 1992–2000 boom period.

DOG DAYS: 1990–1992

First, there are certain long-term factors to consider in analyzing the 1990s economy. These factors affect the availability (and price) of both very generalized inputs (such as energy) and technology. When the supply of any resource or the level of technology increases, the production possibilities of the economy expand and aggregate supply increases. Two of the factors that have had profound effects on the U.S. economy since the 1970s are the supply and price of oil and the changing nature of production in the United States. We really cannot understand the early recession and the subsequent boom of the 1990s without consideration of these longer-term effects.

In the 1970s, the Organization of Petroleum Exporting Countries (OPEC) decreased the amount of oil available for the production of goods and services in the United States, tending to shift the aggregate supply curve leftward. An opposite shift (rightward) resulted from the technological advances made over the past three decades. The very nature of technology in our economy has changed as cleaner substitutes for domestic energy have developed, as computers and other

FIGURE 23.9

The Growth Rate of GDP, 1960–2000

Growth rates of GDP have varied over the past four decades. Compared with the sharp downturn of 1982, the long, slow "recessionary" period of 1990–1992 was relatively mild. One of the two longest continuous boom periods in U.S. history occurred between 1992 and 2000.

Source: Council of Economic Advisers, *Economic Report of the President* (Washington, D.C.: U.S. Government Printing Office, 1999), p. 331 (rates for 1999 and 2000 are projections).

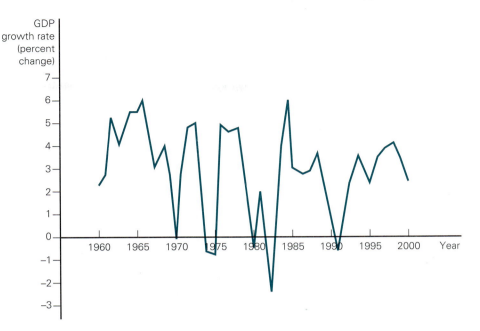

digital-based technology have replaced heavy industry, and as the service sector has grown in importance relative to the manufacturing sector. This technological transition has not been accomplished without economic adjustments that have affected long-term aggregate supply. As OPEC lost control of the price and availability of energy and as the economy has adjusted to new technology and production, the aggregate supply has shifted rightward, a situation that has had price-and-wage-moderating and growth-generating effects on the economy.

A number of intermediate-term factors are important in explaining current conditions. High rates of growth in the Japanese and German economies after World War II have been accompanied by self-sufficient production in Japan and Germany, which has caused a reversal of trade patterns with the United States. Declining exports and increasing imports into the United States in the 1980s and 1990s led to large trade deficits and to leftward shifts in aggregate demand. Moreover, huge federal budget deficits began to build up during the 1980s and into the 1990s. Taken by themselves, the deficits would have had an expansionary effect on aggregate demand. But the financing of these deficits withdrew private savings from an economy that did not save much, causing an upward bias in interest rates and reducing private consumption and investment (a leftward shift in aggregate demand).

A number of critical short-run factors were injected into this mix of influences on macroeconomic performance. As mentioned in the text, tax changes play a large role in determining aggregate demand. Marginal tax rates were reduced in both 1981 and 1986—with demand-increasing effects. The Bush administration increased taxes (primarily excise taxes, payroll taxes, and Social Security taxes), which had the effect of reducing aggregate demand. Moreover, overbuilding in commercial real estate, overinvestment in oil and gas resources, and investment in very risky ventures (together, no doubt, with inappropriate government regulations) caused a massive wave of bank and savings and loan bankruptcies in the late 1980s and early 1990s. These factors weighed more heavily in certain regions (Texas, the

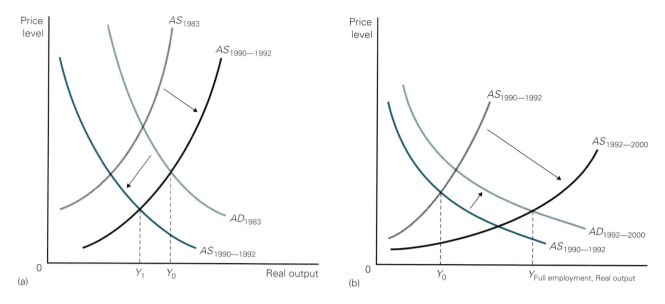

FIGURE 23.10

Aggregate Demand and Supply Shifts in the 1980s and 1990s
(a) The OPEC cartel's impact on aggregate supply began to wane in the early 1980s, which in part explains the rightward shift of the supply curve. A lack of consumer confidence was partly responsible for the leftward shift in aggregate demand. (b) Both aggregate demand and supply shifted rightward to produce the boom of the 1990s (1992–2000). Restoration of consumer confidence and the diffusion of new computer and other technologies are partial explanations for the boom.

Northeast, and California) than in others. Eventually, however, high unemployment rates in these pockets of the economy spilled over into other areas. Between 1989 and 1992, economic confidence on the part of both producer-seller-employers and worker-consumers fell—a factor that also suppressed aggregate demand.

With appropriate assumptions, the 1990–1991 recession and the sluggish recovery throughout 1992 may be depicted by the aggregate demand and supply curves shown in Figure 23.10a. By 1983, the aggregate supply curve was beginning to recover from the OPEC oil shock of the 1970s. Lower taxes, new technology, less regulation, and increased immigration (more labor) undoubtedly increased aggregate supply further during the 1980s (say, to $AS_{1990-1992}$). A decrease in aggregate demand, however, was a critical factor in explaining the dip in income growth and the higher unemployment rates experienced between 1990 and 1992. Surprisingly, after the United States' victory over Iraq in the Persian Gulf War in 1991, consumer confidence in the United States waned, causing a leftward shift in aggregate demand to $AD_{1990-1992}$.

THE GO-GO 1990S: 1992–2000

The higher unemployment and lower (even negative) growth rate had a stark effect on consumers. *Despite* lower interest rates and a low inflation rate, a crisis in consumer confidence had occurred. This was probably due to such factors as the massive layoffs that resulted from corporate "downsizing," the threats to the financial system, larger budget deficits, and dollar devaluations in financial markets. This economic malaise helped lead to the election in 1992 of President Bill Clinton, who argued (with clear correctness), "it's the economy, stupid."

The turnaround in the U.S. economy since 1992 has been nothing short of dramatic. By January 1999, the S&P 500 (Standard and Poor's stock index) quadrupled from its bottom in October of 1990. In 1997 and 1998, the unemployment rate was *below* 5 percent—the lowest in decades. The huge deficit of the 1980s and 1990s (through 1997) turned to a surplus of $69.2 billion in 1998. Meanwhile, inflation was tamed to a reported rate of only 1.6 percent in 1998. (Some economists even believe that the economy is undergoing a *de*flationary period.) Most able-bodied individuals who wanted a job in the late 1990s had one. The boom, moreover, affected all segments of society (although there is debate about relative increases in economic well-being).

In purely static terms, this happy state of affairs may be described as in Figure 23.10b. Starting from aggregate demand and supply curves in 1992, we clearly observe shifts in both demand and supply. Demand shifted rightward from $AD_{1990-1992}$ to $AD_{1992-2000}$. Likewise, aggregate supply shifted rightward from $AS_{1990-1992}$ to $AS_{1992-2000}$. Real output has clearly grown, which would result from either or both demand and supply shifts. But note that, as in the microeconomic curves of Chapter 3, a rightward shift in aggregate demand would have a price-increasing effect whereas a rightward shift in supply would cause prices to decrease. For the price level to moderate (suggesting a lower inflation rate), aggregate supply must have shifted rightward by an even greater amount than aggregate demand.

The *effects* are clear. The exact *causes* are much harder to discern. There are many candidates. Any explanation including long-term effects must discuss the continued cheap supply of energy to fuel the economy, as mentioned above. (Over the latter 1990s, for example, the *real* price of gasoline reached three-decade lows.) But, perhaps even more significantly, there has been the diffusion of job-creating new technologies. The shift to a "service" economy intensified in the latter 1990s, creating both demand and supply effects. Lowered computer prices fueled the introduction and integration of computer technology into businesses. New investments in computer technologies helped fire up aggregate demand, reduced information and transaction costs generated by business and private computers, and helped shift supply rightward.

Policy changes, moreover, are not to be neglected in any explanation of the 1990s boom. Deregulation of telecommunications (furthered by the Telecommunications Act of 1996), transportation, and electric power undoubtedly stirred competitive forces, leading to efficiencies in the economy. Welfare reform (supported by both Republicans and Democrats) helped streamline and energize the American labor force, ultimately creating both demand-side and supply-side effects. Labor productivity also rose over the late 1990s, due in part to new technology.

The move to balance the budget also had an enormous effect on business and consumer confidence. The growing surpluses in the 1990s meant that the federal government reduced borrowing in the private sector, leaving more savings for private investment purposes.

Individuals, not least, had a huge impact on orchestrating the record peacetime growth of the 1990s—close to the all-time record of the 1960s. That inflation hawk, Alan Greenspan, maintained close control over the money supply and interest rates. Low interest rates helped power both the investment and consumption components of aggregate demand. These factors, plus consumer confidence levels at record highs, help explain the rightward shift in the aggregate demand curve (from $AD_{1990-1992}$ to $AD_{1992-2000}$).

Even an extremely abbreviated analysis of the recession and boom of the 1990s reveals that macroeconomic events are not simple phenomena. Only rarely can the macroeconomist link specific causes to specific effects. However, aggregate demand and aggregate supply analysis helps us isolate the effects of long-run factors relating to resources and technology; economic conditions in the global economy; the tax, spending, and regulatory policies of government (at all levels); and "consumer confidence," all of which are interconnected in the real world.

QUESTION

How would a sharp increase in U.S. exports vis-à-vis the rest of the world affect the macroeconomy?

SUMMARY

1. The simple income–expenditures model is limited because it ignores monetary variables and price changes. These factors have become increasingly important since the late 1960s because of inflation.

2. Price level changes affect household consumption by changing the real value of money balances held by consumers. This real balance effect means that price increases will decrease consumption spending and that price decreases will increase consumption spending. These spending changes affect the level of real income and employment, meaning that price changes may be related to the aggregate demand for output.

3. Price changes also alter business investment expenditures via the mechanism of interest rates. Investment spending will increase with declines in interest rates and decrease with increases in interest rates. The interest rate effect means that real income and employment are negatively related to prices through investment spending.

4. The aggregate demand function relates national income and output to changes in the price level;

it is a downward-sloping function, like the demand curves discussed in Chapter 4.

5. Changes in both private and public nonprice variables (autonomous consumption, imports, government spending, taxation) cause the aggregate demand curve to shift rightward or leftward.

6. The aggregate supply curve relates the production of goods and services to the price level. It is a positively sloped function because higher prices increase the incentive to produce goods.

7. The shape of the aggregate supply curve depends on the level of production. At production levels that are low relative to capacity, the aggregate supply curve will be flat; its slope will increase until it becomes vertical as the production level reaches capacity.

8. The interaction of aggregate demand and aggregate supply determines the equilibrium level of output and the equilibrium price level, much like demand and supply for a particular good determine its equilibrium price and quantity.

KEY TERMS

wealth
real balance effect

interest rate effect
aggregate demand curve

discretionary fiscal policies
aggregate supply curve

QUESTIONS FOR REVIEW AND DISCUSSION

1. What macroeconomic goal does the simple Keynesian model of aggregate demand ignore? Why was this goal disregarded in the years immediately following World War II?

2. What effect does an increase in the price level have on the interest rate and, therefore, on the level of investment? Is this change in investment an example of the real balance effect?

3. Suppose that relatively small changes in the interest rate lead to large changes in business investment. Does this have any effect on the shape of the aggregate demand curve?

4. Moving from one point to another along the aggregate demand curve, what happens to exports? To government spending?

5. Can you think of two specific changes that would lead to a rightward shift of the aggregate demand curve? Two that would lead to a decrease?

6. As price level rises, what is likely to happen to business profits? To production levels?

7. Is it possible to solve major macroeconomic problems by inducing the aggregate supply curve to shift to the left?

8. If the government wanted to reduce the price level, would a reduction in aggregate demand be necessary?

9. What variable is likely to affect both aggregate demand and aggregate supply?

10. Under what circumstances is an increase in aggregate demand most likely to cause inflation? Least likely?

11. What is the real balance effect? Assuming the stock of money (MS) to be constant, what happens to the value of real balances if the price level in the economy increases? How does this affect people's wealth?

12. If the level of imports into the United States rises while the level of U.S. exports remains the same, what is the impact on aggregate demand?

13. What impact, if any, do you think time has on the shape of the aggregate supply curve?

14. If the economy is operating on the production possibilities frontier, what impact will an increase in the money supply have on economic output?

15. The 1990s were magical for the macroeconomist. Inflation was low, growth in GDP was steady, and unemployment was the lowest in almost thirty years. Present at least two central explanations for this phenomenon.

PROBLEM

Use the data in the following table for parts a and b.

a. Graph aggregate demand curves AD_1, AD_2, and AD_3 and aggregate supply curve AS. Indicate the equilibrium price level and output for each aggregate demand curve.

b. Describe the prices and outputs that identify the Keynesian, intermediate, and classical ranges of the aggregate supply curve in part a.

AD_1		AD_2		AD_3		AS	
P	Q	P	Q	P	Q	P	Q
60	45	60	120	60	190	90	0
70	40	70	110	70	180	90	10
80	35	80	100	80	170	90	20
90	30	90	90	90	160	90	30
100	25	100	80	100	150	100	40
110	20	110	70	110	140	110	50
120	15	120	60	120	130	120	60
130	12	130	50	130	120	130	70
140	10	140	40	140	110	140	80
150	8	150	30	150	100	150	90
160	6	160	20	160	90	160	90
170	4	170	15	170	80	170	90
180	2	180	10	180	70	180	90
190	1	190	5	190	60	190	90

WORKING WITH THE WEB

1. One explanation for the slope of the aggregate demand curve is that the curve embodies the interest rate effect. This effect corresponds with an assumed positive relationship between the price level (or inflation) and interest rates. You will attempt to verify that relationship in this question.

   Go to the Central Bank of Israel's web site (http://www.bankisrael.gov.il) and locate data on Interest rates and Inflation. When you arrive at the site, click on "English" (unless you know Hebrew), then "Publications and Data," and lastly "Main Israeli economic data." Within the list of tables, find the interest rate table (it should be Table A-6). Check also the graph at http://www.bankisrael.gov.il///fig/3-86.htm, which illustrates the trends in inflation, inflationary expectations, and interest rates.

   a. What relationship do you observe between inflation and interest rates?

   b. How would you explain this relationship?

2. The Bureau of Labor Statistics (BLS) is responsible for producing series of data on unemployment, productivity, prices, and so on. Like many government agencies, the BLS maintains a web site link for its most requested series. Go to the BLS most requested series page directly (http://stats.bls.gov/top20.html) or indirectly (go to http://www.bls.gov and click on the "Data link, then on the "Most Requested Series" link).

   Click on the link for "Major Sector Multifactor Productivity Index" and create a table for Multifactor Productivity (in manufacturing) that covers the years 1991–1996.

   a. How has this measure of productivity changed between 1991 and 1996?

   b. If no other variables changed during this time, how would the change in productivity that you observed directly affect aggregate demand and/or aggregate supply?

   Go back to the most requested series page and click on the link for "Local Area Unemployment Statistics." Find your favorite state in the United States, click on its link, and create a table for the state's labor force that includes all of 1998.

   c. Comparing January to December (1998), how has the size of the labor force changed?

   d. If no other variables changed during this time, how would the change in the labor force that you observed directly affect aggregate demand and/or aggregate supply?

Fiscal Policy and the Supply Side: Using the Tools

ontemporary macroeconomic theory and policy contain a large measure of both the classical and the Keynesian world views. The major Keynesian prescription uses policies designed to manipulate aggregate demand to correct imbalances of employment and income growth in the economy. But in the debate over policy today, more and more attention is being paid to the concerns first expressed by Adam Smith and other classical economists. Labor productivity and capital accumulation were major concerns of the classical writers—the supply side of the economy. Supply-side economics, popular early in the Reagan administration, is based on the idea that overreliance on aggregate demand management, in the form of taxation and spending policies, has had ill effects on the growth of aggregate supply and has fostered economic instability. This chapter considers the relation between aggregate demand and aggregate supply from both of these policy perspectives. When you complete Chapter 24 you will have insight into

- the role of government spending and taxing policies (fiscal policy) in Keynesian and new classical views of macroeconomics.
- using discretionary tools to affect the business cycle.
- how changes in fundamental factors affect the supply side of the economy and aggregate output and income.
- the interaction between policies designed to affect aggregate demand and the institutions and mechanisms that underlie aggregate supply.

POLICIES DESIGNED TO SHIFT AGGREGATE DEMAND

In large part, macroeconomic policy is an attempt to correct perceived failures in the private laissez-faire economy. When markets do not adjust automatically or adjust too slowly to correct imbalances in employment or economic growth, macroeconomic policies such as changes in taxes, government spending, or supply-side stimulation may be used as correctives. To assess the effects of macroeconomic policies, however, it is necessary to understand both the classical and Keynesian views of how the economy functions to correct imbalances.

Classical and Keynesian Perspectives

The classical economists had a long-run perspective on adjustments in the economy. Prices and wages were assumed to be flexible when there was an excess demand for or excess supply of labor in the labor market. These adjustments were not given a "clock time"; rather, classical theory assumed instantaneous adjustments. The result was a vertical supply curve.

This classical supply curve can be matched with an aggregate demand curve, as in Figure 24.1. The simplicity of the classical argument is revealed when aggregate demand is either increased or decreased from an initial equilibrium. Suppose, as in Figure 24.1, that the economy experiences a reduction in aggregate demand due to a fall-off in some component of private spending—the autonomous component of consumption, investment, or expenditures on exports. This reduction of aggregate demand is shown as a shift in the demand function from AD_0 to AD_1.

Equilibrium was established initially at E_0, where the economy was producing full-employment output (experiencing the natural rate of unemployment) at price level P_0. With the decrease in aggregate demand, we can think of the economy as moving to point A, where supply ceases to create its own demand. Demand is insufficient to purchase Y_F worth of output at price level P_0. Contraction of production and employment temporarily sets in, since prices (and money wages) will not totally and immediately adjust downward. Once prices start to fall from P_0 to P_1, additional spending will increase output back to the full-employment level. As noted in

FIGURE 24.1

The Classical Long-Run Self-Adjustment Mechanism

In the classical view, when aggregate demand decreases, as from AD_0 to AD_1, the level of output temporarily falls from Y_F to Y_0, causing the level of employment to fall as well. The price level then falls from P_0 to P_1, and output rises back to Y_F. With flexible wages and prices, the economy returns to full employment.

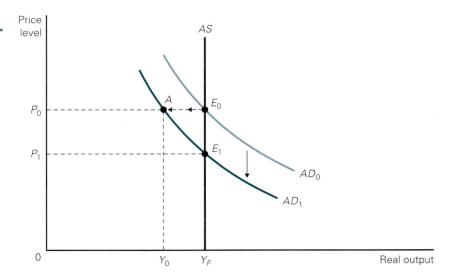

Chapter 23, falling prices will increase consumption spending and investment spending through increases in real balances and decreases in the rate of interest.

When spending declines, unemployment is initially created. But in the classical version of events, wages also decline, so that all laborers seeking work find work, but at a lower nominal wage. In terms of Figure 24.1, prices and wages fall, so the economy rapidly ends up at a new full-employment equilibrium, E_1 at Y_F, but at a lower price level, P_1. In fact, the key to understanding the basically non-interventionist policies of the classical writers in macroeconomic affairs is the point that price, wage, and interest rate adjustments take place very rapidly.

Economists who adhere to modern versions of classical principles are called new classical economists. Keynesians and the new classical theorists differ on many policy issues. One of the central differences rests on the time required for automatic macroeconomic adjustment to take place. This difference is conceptualized in Figure 24.2. Once more, assume that autonomous consumption, investment, or export expenditures decline, causing the aggregate demand curve to shift from AD_0 to AD_1. Demand is again insufficient to purchase the full-employment output Y_F and to sustain full employment at price level P_0. In this case, the economy is in disequilibrium; aggregate supply, represented by point E_0, exceeds aggregate demand at point A for price level P_0. The degree and speed of wage and price level flexibility determines how quickly the economy will adjust to the excess supply at price level P_0. In the classical view, prices will quickly adjust downward to point B, but Keynesians believe that downward adjustments in prices and wages can be slow, unpredictable, and "sticky." Either drop—to A or to B—creates a certain amount of **demand deficiency unemployment,** unemployment that results whenever aggregate demand is insufficient to purchase the quantity of goods and services produced under full employment. Whether Keynesian principles were ever "tried" or not is debatable (see the Focus "Did Keynesian Economics and World War II Save Us from the Depression?").

Under rigid Keynesian assumptions, prices and money wages are totally inflexible, meaning that the economy would move to point A with a relatively large amount of demand deficiency unemployment. Demand deficiency unemployment

Demand deficiency unemployment

A short-run situation in which the level of employment is less than if the full-employment level of output were produced; arises when aggregate demand is insufficient to purchase the full-employment output given the price level.

FIGURE 24.2

Demand Deficiency Unemployment: Short-Run Keynesian and New Classical Views

If aggregate demand falls from AD_0 to AD_1, unemployment will result. If prices and wages do not adjust at all, the short-run Keynesian view, a movement from point E_0 to point A takes place. The economy will produce a level of output equal to Y_1. The difference in employment levels at Y_F and Y_1 is the measure of demand deficiency unemployment. In the classical view, prices will adjust quickly to point B. Demand deficiency unemployment will be less—the difference between unemployment levels Y_F and Y_0.

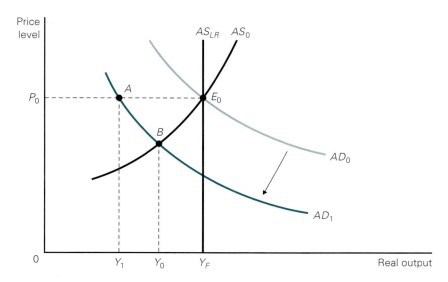

FOCUS

Did Keynesian Economics and World War II Save Us from the Depression?

Keynes developed his famous theory in the midst of the Great Depression of the 1930s. Conventional wisdom has it that his ideas somehow "saved" Americans—especially through wartime spending on World War II—from continued economic ills. Was this the case?

In spite of monetary reforms, massive public works projects such as the WPA (Works Progress Administration), and new government regulations, the U.S. economy continued to falter throughout the 1930s. What appeared to be prosperity began to return as Americans anticipated more direct participation in World War II and as the government began to reorient production to war goods. The increases in government spending that occurred before and after the war are often served up by historians and others as a prime example of Keynesian economics at work, but not according to recent research into the so-called prosperity of the 1940s and into the theoretical explanation for it.

Economist Robert Higgs argues that both the economic measurement of the business cycle and the Keynesian "spin" given it for the 1940s are seriously flawed.[a] Higgs argues that the prosperity of the war years was an illusion. While there was no *official* unemployment, a full two-fifths of the labor

force was not being used to produce consumer goods or even goods that would increase U.S. capacity to produce consumer goods after the war was over. The index of real personal consumption per capita rose only two percentage points from 1939 to 1944. Business profits and the stock market prices lagged during the war years.

The United States became a command economy, as virtually all economies do in war. This means that massive reallocations of resources from private production to war goods was accomplished through artificial means such as price controls and quantity restrictions on consumer and other goods. The command economy performed well at turning out war goods and munitions, but it worked only because authoritarian controls made it work.

Not only do the data not tell the correct story of the so-called wartime prosperity, Higgs argues, but World War II itself did not *cause* the postwar boom in America. In Keynesian terms, the war did not create investments that would later be turned into income- and consumption-generative activities through a "multiplier." Rather, expectations were transformed and financial wealth was built up in America during World War II. These laid the groundwork for the genuine spurt of prosperity experienced in the second half of the 1940s, and in the decades that followed. World War II and "Keynesian principles" were not responsible for postwar prosperity.

[a]Robert Higgs, "Wartime Prosperity? A Reassessment of the U.S. Economy in the 1940s," *Journal of Economic History* 52 (March 1992), pp. 41–60.

is measured as employment at the full-employment output, Y_F, minus the employment that will exist if the economy produces a level of output equal to Y_1. If prices and wages were somewhat flexible over a short period of time, however, a movement from E_0 to a point such as B on the short-run aggregate supply curve AS_0 would result. In this case, demand deficiency unemployment would equal the level of employment at Y_F minus the level of employment at Y_0.

Short-run unemployment of labor and reductions in real output are a fact of life both for modern Keynesians and for new classical theorists. But they differ widely in the kind of policies they would recommend. Keynesians favor the use of discretionary fiscal policy—the use of government expenditures and taxation or, to a lesser degree, discretionary monetary policy—to force the aggregate demand rightward from AD_1 back to AD_0 in Figure 24.2. According to Keynesian analysis, the economy is quasi-permanently stuck at point *B*, where unemployment exists. Government must do something about it.

By contrast, new classical economists believe that attempts to manipulate aggregate demand are doomed to fail. They feel that the discretionary actions of government—through fiscal and monetary policy—are unsettling and disruptive; they heighten fears about inflation and the economy in general, making the restoration of equilibrium even more difficult to achieve. New classical economists would prefer that government refrain from countercyclical fiscal policies except under certain conditions. Building on the simple concepts just outlined, we can describe some important aspects of the nature and practice of fiscal policy.

Fiscal Policy and Demand Management

Ordinarily, the economy's aggregate supply curve is positively sloped, meaning that, like the supply curves of individual products, higher levels for all output are associated with higher levels of production. The positively sloped aggregate supply curve is midway between traditional classical assumptions and rigid Keynesian assumptions about the speed of price and wage adjustments to changes in the aggregate economy. In Figure 24.3, such a supply curve is reproduced along with the negatively sloped aggregate demand curve.

Equilibrium output occurs initially at the intersection of the aggregate demand curve AD_0 and the aggregate supply curve AS along the ordinary, upward-sloping intermediate range of the supply curve. A level of real output or income is produced within the economy in the amount of Y_0 at a price level P_0. However, aggregate demand level AD_0 is insufficient to provide a level of full-employment output Y_F. What kind of macroeconomic policy would be called for? For fiscal policy, the government would attempt to stimulate spending by reducing taxes and thereby increasing consumption, by increasing government spending, or by stimulating consumption and investment spending (see the Focus "Politics and Fiscal Policy: How Brave Are Politicians Anyway?"). Demand management consists of manipulation

FIGURE 24.3

Fiscal Policy Shifts the Aggregate Demand Curve to Combat Recession

Assuming a positively sloped aggregate supply curve, *AS*, an increase in government spending or a decrease in taxes will shift the aggregate demand curve rightward from AD_0 to AD_1. The increase causes prices to rise as real income and employment rise to the full-employment level.

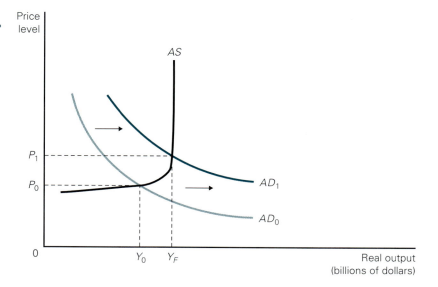

FOCUS

Politics and Fiscal Policy: How Brave Are Politicians Anyway?

In any discussion of government economic policy, some allowance must be made for the possibility that policy-makers will not make the "right" response—that is, the policy change consistent with accepted countercyclical economic theory. Experience tells us that in the world of interest-group politics, economic considerations are not always uppermost in the minds of policy-makers. There is every reason to believe that, like everyone else, elected politicians are self-interested individuals. What is it that the self-interested politician seeks to maximize? Is it the public interest or job security (the probability of future reelection by voters)? Many economists believe it is the latter, so they recognize that knowledge of economic theory on the part of government policy-makers does not guarantee justifiable decisions. Political motives, in other words, frequently dominate fiscal policy decisions.

Consider the accepted "cure" for inflation, according to economic theory. In the Keynesian view, the appropriate fiscal response is a cut in government expenditures, an increase in taxes, or some combination of the two. But how many elected officials have the courage to vote for a tax increase in an election year? By the same token, reductions in government expenditures are politically unpopular with interest groups that receive these expenditures. What are politicians to do? If they wish to curry favor with the electorate—and what politician doesn't?—they will vote against unpopular fiscal measures, even though such measures may be sound countercyclical actions. Proof of this principle is the fact that the United States has incurred budget deficits in all but three years since World War II. If economic theory had dictated the deficits, their existence would imply that the U.S. economy has been in a quasi-perpetual state of recession, with Congress continually trying to spend us out of the slump. We know that this has not been the case. For many of the postwar years, Congress has actually pursued procyclical rather than countercyclical policy because

politicians were unwilling to pay the political price for an unpopular though analytically sound economic policy.

One possible solution to this dilemma is to reduce the degree of autonomy that politicians have over fiscal policy; to take decisions out of their hands to a degree by placing fiscal constraints on the executive branch and the Congress. One such fiscal constraint is a balanced budget rule imposed by a constitutional amendment. This would prevent Congress and the president from spending amounts larger than tax revenues allow. In other words, it would prevent them from creating budget deficits. While a legal balanced budget requirement (or the pegging of government expenditures to a percent of GDP) could be procyclical, some argue that there would be less inflationary bias than under the current political system. Some type of constraint, the argument goes, would force Congress and the president to choose more carefully how to spend a more limited source of funds. A legal fiscal constraint may prevent, during periods of inflation, pork-barrel spending legislation; it might remove some of the built-in incentives politicians have to cast economically unsound votes.

The "bravery" of politicians has been severely tested as boom conditions appeared in the economy in the late 1990s. Budget surpluses—at least those including the Social Security trust fund receipts—appeared in the economy for the first time in almost three decades. A legal fiscal constraint might take various forms. The surplus might be used to pay off the accumulated 5.7 to 6 *trillion* dollar debt, it might be returned to individuals through tax relief, it might be used to shore up a failing Social Security system, or it might be spent on new government projects. Without a constraint, the built-in incentives of politicians are to spend the surplus or to otherwise dispose of it in a manner that will further *their* political interests. Tax relief and lower levels of government spending become problematic.

of these politically controlled variables (the tax system and government spending) to shift AD_0 to AD_1, or to move demand in the opposite direction to combat rapid expansion and inflation. Fine-tuning the economy by shifting aggregate demand either rightward (to stimulate economic activity) or leftward (to cool down economic activity), the government thus manages aggregate demand to achieve economic goals of full employment and maximum economic growth.

Many government policies other than tax or spending changes and practices affect aggregate demand. Federal policies relating to international trade, for example, can affect aggregate demand. As noted in Chapter 22, *net* foreign spending—the difference between exports and imports—is a component of aggregate demand. Anything that affects either imports or exports, such as the erection or elimination of trade barriers, will shift the aggregate demand curve either to the right or to the left. Trade agreements with Japan to limit the American importation of automobiles or computer components will, for example, increase domestic aggregate demand by increasing *net* foreign spending (exports *minus* imports). Likewise, policies that encourage exports of American products will shift the aggregate demand curve rightward.

Demand and Supply Interaction

Figure 24.3 shows a situation in which an increase in aggregate demand and an increase in real income and employment are accompanied by an increase in the price level. This is not always the case. Whether or not prices will rise with increases in aggregate demand depends on the shape of the aggregate supply curve, as we discussed in Chapters 19 and 23.

The economy performs within its production possibilities frontier when there is widespread unemployment of resources. An increase in aggregate demand through government fiscal policies will have the effect of increasing real output and employment *without* creating inflation by raising prices. Why? Widespread resource availability permits increased real output without putting pressure on resources and output prices. This situation is close to the one Keynes described for the Depression of the 1930s and 1940s. Under these extreme conditions, fiscal policy could achieve increases in output and employment without inflation.

The opposite extreme is also possible. When resources are fully and most efficiently employed, the economy is operating at or very near the production possibilities frontier. Given the state of technology, resources, and institutions, there is some maximum possible amount of real output and employment. If the economy is at this maximum point, the aggregate supply curve is vertical. With a vertical supply curve, an increase in aggregate demand created by monetary or fiscal policies will be inflationary. Demand management is unnecessary in the classical case because, as we saw in Chapter 20, the economy is self-adjusting and will produce full employment and maximum output automatically. Economists who adhere to classical principles or to modern versions of them argue that discretionary demand management by government is unnecessary and possibly harmful to the economy.

Between the two extremes lies an intermediate case. Increases in aggregate demand will put some pressure on prices along with causing some increase in real national income and employment. This situation was depicted in Figure 24.3. An increase in demand will create some increase in prices, but real output and employment will also rise. However, shortages will develop in some resource markets, creating production bottlenecks and price increases. As the economy approaches full employment and the production possibilities frontier, prices will ordinarily rise at a faster rate and output increases will be smaller and smaller as resource shortages become more acute.

In sum, the effectiveness of managing demand by monetary or fiscal means depends in part on the shape of the aggregate supply curve. In the Keynesian case, reflecting depression conditions, demand changes will have their full impact on real income and employment with no effect on prices. In the classical case, demand management is virtually useless in affecting employment or output: Its sole effects are on the price level. The intermediate case contains elements of both Keynesian and classical conclusions. Aggregate demand changes will change real output and employment as well as the price level. The government's ability to adjust spending and aggregate demand to contractionary or expansionary gaps—to control unemployment and inflation and to promote economic growth—is therefore partially limited by the shape of the aggregate supply curve.

Possible Limits to Discretionary Demand Management

In addition to extreme shapes of the supply curve, demand management by the government may be limited in its effectiveness by the realities of private decision making. About two-thirds of annual total expenditures in the economy come from the private sector—households and businesses. The private sector may have an ability to spend roughly equivalent to its income and wealth, and its desire to spend is not subject to direct government control. Thus it is possible for any governmental policy designed to accelerate or decelerate total expenditures to be thwarted by cumulative individual decisions to reduce or increase spending. In the context of the simple Keynesian model, for example, an increase in government spending could be partially or totally offset by a decrease in some autonomous component of private expenditures. By and large, the limits of discretionary demand management are related to expectations in the private economy and to the supply behavior of workers and other resource suppliers in the economy.

AGGREGATE SUPPLY POLICIES

Policies affecting the aggregate demand for goods and services in the U.S. economy are only one important part of macroeconomic policy. Beginning in the 1970s, academic economists began investigating the possibility that prolonged use of demand management might adversely affect aggregate supply. Many economists, for example, investigated the effects of tax rates on work incentives, the labor supply, and productivity. Some economists believe that tax rates, tax rate changes, and unpredictable changes in government spending affect the aggregate supply curve and thus employment and prices. Others emphasize the impact of institutional factors, such as minimum-wage laws and income maintenance programs, on raising the natural rate of unemployment. This means that discretionary aggregate demand changes brought about by altering tax rates (as well as legislatively mandated institutional changes) might be partially offset by adverse shifts in aggregate supply. In that event, macroeconomic policy might be self-defeating.

Aggregate Supply and Resource Employment

As we stressed in Chapter 23, aggregate supply in the economy is related to the cost and availability of resources, especially labor resources. To classical economists, **full employment** meant that everyone who wanted a job had one; in other words, there was no excess demand for labor. In this view, the real wage established by the interaction of supply and demand for labor is the full-employment wage. Some unemployed workers would work for wages higher than the equilibrium real wage, but they are not considered unemployed because they voluntarily take themselves out of the labor force. All who would accept lower than equilibrium real wages are employed.

Full employment

To the classical economist, a situation in which all workers willing and able to work at the current market real wage rate are employed.

Today, economists prefer to talk of a natural rate of employment or unemployment. A certain amount of unemployment is expected in an economy at any given time. Because of changing demand conditions, resources constantly shift among producers. As we explained in Chapter 19, a certain rate of unemployment arises from "friction" in the economic system, although the precise rate has changed over time and is a topic of debate among economists.

The **natural rate of unemployment** is easier to define than to measure: It is the rate of unemployment that exists when all unemployment is either frictional or structural unemployment. These two types of unemployment primarily result when there is imperfect labor market information, when job search requires time, and when there is no match between the skill and location requirements of job openings and those of unemployed workers. The natural rate of unemployment stems from fundamental market and institutional changes that affect the decisions of workers to supply and employers to demand labor. Specifically, changes in minimum-wage laws, tax laws (especially income tax laws), and the availability and scope of retirement benefits affect workers' incentives to supply labor and thus the natural rate of unemployment. Another important factor is the increased participation rate of women in the labor force since the 1960s.

Natural rate of unemployment

The rate of unemployment due to frictional unemployment plus structural unemployment; the rate of unemployment that will exist when expectations of inflation reflect actual inflationary conditions and all short-run macroeconomic adjustments have been made.

The business environment also affects the natural rate of unemployment on the demand side of resource markets. Taxes and tax laws affect business investments in capital and resources, including labor resources. Changes in tax laws or business regulations will affect the natural rate of unemployment in the economy.

Once these institutional factors are accounted for, the natural rate of unemployment may be interpreted as the rate of unemployment that occurs when full employment exists. This implies that the level of full-employment real output, Y_F, will be produced when the natural rate of unemployment exists. Any change in the institutional factors that affects either the supply of or the demand for resources will shift the aggregate supply curve either rightward or leftward. Supply-side economics, therefore, attempts to shift the aggregate supply curve rightward by changing policies and institutions that reduce the natural rate of unemployment. A rightward shift, for example, would enhance economic growth in terms of actual employment of resources and higher output.

The effects of supply-side or aggregate supply shifts may be shown utilizing the aggregate demand–aggregate supply apparatus from previous chapters. In Figure 24.4, long-run vertical aggregate supply curves are shown with an aggregate demand curve AD_0. Assume that initial equilibrium is associated with the intersection of the aggregate demand curve, AD_0, and aggregate supply curve AS_0. If the full-employment level of income produced by this intersection, Y_{F_0}, is insufficient, policy-makers might choose policies to increase income and employment growth.

FIGURE 24.4

The Effects of Increases in Aggregate Supply
If government policies such as tax cuts and deregulation reduce the natural rate of unemployment, the aggregate supply curve will shift rightward—in this case, from AS_0 to AS_1 to AS_2. As a consequence, the price level will fall (below P_0) and real output will rise, from Y_{F_0} to Y_{F_2}.

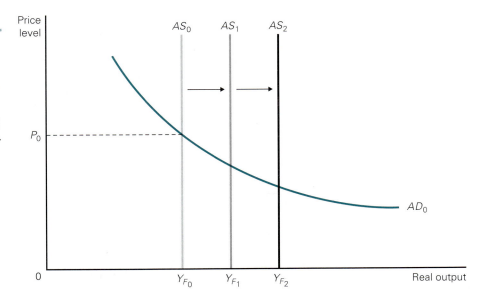

Policies that affect the natural rate of unemployment and aggregate supply will shift the aggregate supply curve rightward to new equilibrium positions. Two of these positions are shown in Figure 24.4. Tax reductions or deregulation in labor or product markets will decrease the natural rate of unemployment and increase the equilibrium income potential in the economy. In terms of Figure 24.4, policies designed to increase aggregate supply would increase the output potential of the economy from Y_{F_0} to Y_{F_1} or Y_{F_2}. These supply-side policies have been the concern of politicians and policy-makers in Congress for a number of years.

Supply-Side Economic Policies

Macroeconomic policy since the mid-1970s has been shaped by the recognition that excessive and prolonged use of demand management might have adverse effects on the economy. Some economists and policy-makers believe that discretionary aggregate demand changes have produced offsetting shifts in aggregate supply. Specifically, they contend that certain fiscal and legislative measures, particularly tax measures and regulatory changes, alter incentives. Do businesses and workers respond to tax decreases by increasing investment in and production of goods and services? The Reagan administration made **supply-side economics**—the attempt to stimulate real production by providing new incentives to workers and businesses—a hallmark of its economic policy. In this section we consider the nature of some supply-side policies.

Supply-side economics
Policies designed to stimulate production by altering incentives of producers; policies designed to shift the aggregate supply curve to the right.

Policies to Increase Work Effort and Savings   Americans tend to save a smaller portion of their incomes compared with income earners in most other industrialized countries. However, Americans are not simply spendthrifts who live only for the present: We have been encouraged by the design of fiscal policies to borrow more and save less. Interest income from savings is taxed as ordinary income, while for many years interest *payments* were tax deductible. Under present law, interest earnings are still taxed as ordinary income, although deducting interest payments on loans for consumer goods purchases is no longer allowed. (Interest on home mortgages and home equity loans remains deductible.)

Policies enacted during the 1980s were directed at upgrading American saving and work habits, especially among low-income groups. Interest rate restrictions paid to small savers by banks and other financial institutions were loosened or removed, thereby encouraging private saving. The largest income tax cuts in recent history were passed in 1981 and 1986 to increase both saving and work incentives. Individual Retirement Accounts (IRAs), which allowed income earners to shelter some income from taxes for retirement purposes, were also instituted in the early 1980s. IRAs clearly encourage private saving, especially among lower- and middle-class income earners.

These efforts continued into the 1990s with the development of new forms of individual retirement accounts and savings accounts for specific purposes. The so-called Roth IRA, which came into existence in 1997, is a means of paying taxes on savings "up front" with fewer requirements for disbursements and tax-free income after retirement or for one's inheritors. In addition, Congress has come up with plans that support or encourage savings for particular problems or activities such as medical care or education. Partly because of these policies, gross private personal savings increased slightly between 1986 and 2000. Tax increases passed during the Clinton administration (in 1992 and 1993), developed as part of a deficit-reduction plan, naturally dampened these incentives. The saving rate in the United States (of around 4 percent of GDP) still markedly contrasts to the savings rate of 10 percent in a number of developed nations (including Japan).

Policies to Encourage Business Investment   Higher saving rates usually translate into higher investment rates by businesses. Institutional restrictions, such as high capital gains taxes and output-lowering regulations, have hampered productive investment in the past (and continue to do so today). Capital gains taxes are taxes on profits from the sale of stocks, real estate, and other investments. Prior to the Tax Reform Act of 1986, capital gains were taxed at a *lower* rate than ordinary income to encourage productive investment by small and large investors alike. (Purchasing stocks and bonds is similar to saving in that both allow businesses to make investments.) These investments are an essential vehicle for creating higher employment and output growth. Because such investments actually help create jobs, many economists believe that a reduction in the capital gains tax is justified.

The Tax Reform Act of 1986 increased the capital gains tax by treating capital gains from investments as ordinary income. That is, after 1986, capital gains were taxed at the same rates as earned income (15, 28, or 33 percent, and now up to 40 percent with surtax). Critics of this action claim that it had a chilling effect on investment—reducing the aggregate supply curve of the economy and thereby reducing economic growth potential. Institutional rigidities—in this case, a tax on investment—may have a negative impact on aggregate supply and on economic performance. In partial response to this negative effect, Congress passed in 1997 a reduction in the capital gains tax to 20 percent. The full effects of this reduction were not felt until 1998 and beyond, and the investment boom of the late 1990s was (at least partially) the result.

Deregulation of Markets   Red tape and unnecessary regulations hamper economic performance in markets for goods and services or inputs, including labor.

In the late 1970s, the federal government took steps to deregulate several industries, including the banking and financial services industry. The financial system that has emerged is more flexible and efficient, although the result has been tempered by widespread bankruptcies in the savings and loan industry, which may or may not be the result of deregulation.

Partial deregulation of transportation, including airlines, railroads, and interstate trucking, began under President Carter and continued through the Reagan administration. Deregulation of these industries gave consumers lower prices, larger output, and greater choice of services. Elimination of institutional restrictions on businesses by government agencies, including the Occupational Safety and Health Administration (OSHA), increased the productivity of business capital and encouraged new investment during the 1980s. Some changes in labor markets were also supply-oriented. For instance, modification of the minimum-wage law included a general increase in the minimum hourly wage but permitted the hiring of teenagers in need of job experience at lower-than-minimum wages for a limited "training period." The intended effects were enhanced aggregate supply and improved long-run labor productivity.

There are indications that such institutional changes have produced a more efficient use of resources, but this is not to say that all supply-oriented changes have been beneficial. Because of federal deposit insurance, taxpayers have had to bail out the savings and loan industry—at a cost of several hundred billion dollars. The reprieve that business had from stricter and ill-formed rules and regulations from OSHA, the EPA, the Food and Drug Administration, and other government agencies was basically rescinded under the Clinton administration. Many environmental regulations—rules that did not undergo economic cost–benefit analysis—were foisted on business and industry. The failure to use economic principles in the development of these regulations undoubtedly slowed private investment and economic growth below what it would have been otherwise (though the economy *did* experience positive and significant growth over this period).

Trade Policies and the Supply Side   Protectionism has contradictory and self-defeating effects on the economy. The imposition of import tariffs or other trade restrictions may temporarily benefit the economy by providing a temporary increase in aggregate demand. However, the imposition of tariffs or other less formal trade restrictions will simultaneously reduce the long-run growth potential of the economy by reducing competition for domestic firms, input availability, and aggregate supply. While formal tariffs and quotas on goods and services are presently low (see Chapter 31), foreign cartels such as OPEC and "voluntary" trade agreements to restrict importation of foreign products or raw materials, which are more plentiful, have the same effects. As shown in a Focus in Chapter 23, the OPEC cartel created a negative supply shock in the U.S. economy in the 1970s, although its effects have been mitigated somewhat since. Likewise, import restrictions on imports to protect domestic industries such as the computer and textile industries reduce aggregate supply and the growth potential of the economy. Because it removed many of the restrictions on trade among the United States, Canada, and Mexico, the North American Free Trade Agreement (NAFTA) will enhance the growth potential of all three countries for several generations. Actual and potential changes in trade restrictions have an enormous impact on macroeconomic well-being and affect both aggregate supply and aggregate demand (see the Application "The Impact of Freer Trade on Macroeconomic Health" at the conclusion of this chapter).

The Impact of Supply-Side Policies

The results of supply-side policies enacted since the late 1970s have so far been mixed. A recession in the early 1980s, possibly precipitated by inflation-control measures, dampened enthusiasm for some such policies, although growth rates in real output and employment rose in 1983 and 1984. The economic growth rate in terms of real GNP was at a two-decade high in 1984 (6.8 percent); the rate has slowed to a little over 3 percent per year since 1984. Unemployment rates fell steadily after 1984. In 1988, Americans experienced the lowest unemployment rate (around 5 percent) since 1972. Inflation was brought down from 18 percent in 1979 to a little more than 6 percent in 1983 and has remained below that level—often significantly lower—since.

Many believe that the recession of 1990–1991 was the product of supply-side policies gone bad. Defenders of supply-side economics often blame the recession on the tax increase supported by Congress and President Bush in 1990. The 1990 budget compromise may have had demand-decreasing effects, but the causes of the downturn and slow recovery are likely complex and varied. Consumer perceptions and confidence undoubtedly played a major role. It is widely believed that President Bush's inaction—his decision not to invoke discretionary fiscal policy (which might have had growth-reducing long-term effects)—cost him the 1992 election. It is important to note that, albeit weakly, the economy did recover on its own. President Clinton raised taxes in 1992, and his era in government has been associated with lower deficits. Although all Americans have not shared equally, the period of the late 1990s was one of unrestrained prosperity. The United States opened the year 2000 with an economic growth rate between 3 and 4 percent, with inflation in check (at around 2 percent), and with record lows in unemployment (below 5 percent). Rarely do very short-term changes create such conditions. Supply-side policies such as deregulation and institutional factors such as the diminution of military expenditures due to a cessation of the Cold War undoubtedly played a part in the new prosperity.

DEMAND AND SUPPLY INTERACTION: PROBLEMS AND PROSPECTS

By the early 1980s, the ill effects of decades of countercyclical demand policies on aggregate supply were apparent to many economists. From the perspective of these economists, government at all levels tended to overspend and the increased taxation or inflationary tendencies created by deficit finance constrained work effort and private business investment. Aggregate demand policies by government may have worked faster than supply policies to alter inflation or unemployment, but their negative long-run effects on the economy's aggregate output of goods and services could no longer be ignored. Many economists now feel that quick-fix aggregate demand policies do not get at the long-run problems of economic growth and productivity. Aggregate supply policies—especially those relating to labor productivity, long-run business investment, and institutional change—will be more effective, but they also take more time. In this view, demand policies should receive consideration, but supply issues should be raised to equal importance.

Unfortunately, demand- and supply-side policies are enacted within a political process that often prevents or hampers coordination of macroeconomic policy goals. During the 1980s, tax cuts were enacted—a reasonable supply-side policy to enhance work effort, saving, and productivity. But at the same time, government expenditures were not reduced enough to cover increasing deficits in the federal accounts. These huge federal deficits were tantamount to an enormous Keynesian demand-side boost in total expenditures, which might explain the economic growth and general prosperity of the 1980s. But the federal deficit leads to uncertainty in private markets, which has a negative impact both on aggregate demand and aggregate supply. The deficit signals to potential savers and investors that inflation and/or government competition for private funds might soon be on the way. Deficits, then, have a dual impact: They increase the government portion of aggregate expenditures while reducing private expenditures through the creation of adverse expectations. Deficit reduction is an obvious macroeconomic good. However, as the bitter, highly partisan fight over the Clinton administration's $496 billion deficit-reduction plan demonstrated in the summer of 1993, it is difficult to achieve. The "Republican Revolution" based on their 1994 "Contract with America"—aimed at reduced spending and budget balance—was another bitter conflict that ended in federal government "shutdowns" in 1995 and 1996.

The prosperity of the late 1990s, discussed above (and in the Application in Chapter 23), did create higher tax receipts and (relatively) small budget surpluses. Whether such surpluses will grow and continue will depend on a number of factors. The aggregate demand and supply apparatus developed in this and the previous chapter will help us analyze price level and income changes created through fiscal policy. But fiscal policy is, of necessity, created in the context of the U.S. political system. Incontrovertibly, politics sometimes overrides the "public interest" in high growth, low unemployment, and low inflation. There is, moreover, scant evidence that the "era of big government" is over with respect to the macroeconomy.

APPLICATION

The Impact of Freer Trade on Macroeconomic Health

World trade totaled $8.5 trillion in 1994, up from $1.6 trillion in 1974. In the United States, exports now account for more than 10 percent of GDP—double the percentage of 20 years ago. These magnitudes illustrate the enormous potential trade has for increasing aggregate supply and demand in the United States over the long run. Aggregate supply will increase (shift rightward) whenever labor productivity rises, which is precisely what happens with a more efficient (lower cost) allocation of labor created by more open trade. Freer trade will also result in a rightward shift in aggregate demand if net foreign spending (exports minus imports) rises after trade restrictions are reduced or lifted.

Economists since David Ricardo (1772–1823) have emphasized the importance of economy-wide specialization and trade for economic growth in the macroeconomy. But special interests—industries and labor groups who gain from protection in the form of quotas or tariffs—have at times freely used the political process to reduce the volume of trade and to increase artificially the price of domestic wares to consumers. Such activities have reduced both aggregate supply and demand in the U.S. economy over time.

As Table 24.1 shows, the most protectionist legislation enacted in this century was the Smoot–Hawley Act, passed in 1930 at the onset of the Great Depression. Since that time, the trend has been toward freer trade. Tariffs have been systematically lowered, creating more exports and jobs. The trend, however, has been toward multilateral tariff reductions—those involving many countries.

Chiefly responsible for the modern liberalization of trade have been the multilateral trade negotiations conducted under the General Agreement on Tariffs and Trade (GATT), which was both an international charter designed to set out

TABLE 24.1

Major Trade Legislation in the United States

Since the end of the nineteenth century, trade legislation in the United States has promoted both protectionism and freer trade. Since the Depression era, and especially after the initial GATT agreement in 1947, legislation has generally moved in the direction of freer trade.

Legislation	Year	Type
Dingley Act	1897	Protectionist
Payne–Aldrich Act	1909	
Underwood Act	1913	Freer trade
Fordney–McCumber Act	1922	Protectionist
Smoot–Hawley Act	1930	Very protectionist
Reciprocal Trade Agreement Act	1934	Freer trade
(renewed eleven times between		
1934 and 1962)		
GATT negotiations:		
Geneva	1947	
Annecy	1949	
Torquay	1950–1951	
Dillon-Round	1956–1961	
Trade Expansion Act	1962	Freer trade
GATT Kennedy Round	1964–1967	
Trade Act of 1974	1974	Freer trade
GATT Tokyo Round	1974–1979	
Trade Agreement Act	1979	Freer trade
GATT Uruguay Round	1986–1994	
New GATT Agreement		Freer trade
Omnibus Trade Bill	1988	Protectionist
North American Free Trade Association (NAFTA)	1994	Freer trade
Helms–Burton Law	1996	Protectionist
Clinton–Labor–Clothing Agreement	1997	Protectionist

SOURCE: Peter Moser, *The Political Economy of the GATT* (St. Gallen: Verlag Ruegger, 1990), p. 62, and authors.

the rules of conduct in international trade (the General Agreement) as well as an international organization for oversight of the agreement and management of multilateral trade negotiations (the General Secretariat). Responsibilities for settling trade disputes and overseeing multilateral trade agreements shifted to the World Trade Organization (WTO) in January 1995. Founded in 1947, the GATT currently has ninety-three member countries who account for over 80 percent of world trade. Another thirty-one countries have agreed to abide by the rules of GATT. The General Agreement has provided a forum for multilateral talks aimed at expanding trade by encouraging member countries to lower trade barriers and to eliminate discriminatory treatment.

Beginning in 1947 with the first round set in Geneva, there have been eight rounds of such negotiations, the most recent being the Uruguay Round. The formal negotiating process, involving representatives from 108 countries, began in late 1986 and concluded when the Final Act was signed in Morocco in April 1994 and ratified in the United States on December 8, 1994. The focus of this most recent round was not the reduction of tariffs but rather issues such as nontariff barriers, intellectual property rights, trade in services, trade in agriculture, and the functioning of the GATT system.

It has always been the case that groups favoring tariff protection—most notably, large manufacturers and labor unions—have been both vocal and politically influential. In fact, protectionism in the past has warped resources to particular production processes as tariff protection became enshrined in law. Society earns a huge net benefit from free trade, but those benefits are spread among hundreds of millions of consumers whose individual share of these benefits is small. As a result, the interests of consumers—unlike the interests of groups such as textile manufacturers in the United States—are, almost always, underrepresented in congresses and parliaments around the world.

It has been suggested that no industry is farther from the ideal of free trade than farming. The price tag of the taxes and higher prices that consumers around the world currently pay to support farmers has been estimated at $300 billion per year. The net welfare loss caused by the farm policies of industrial nations—the amount that exceeds the transfer of income to farmers—is thought to be approximately $100 billion per year. Especially in the European Community, recent efforts to reduce agricultural subsidies have been met with fierce resistance by farmers. The complex and emotional issue of agricultural subsidies and trade barriers proved to be a challenge for GATT negotiators.

GATT negotiators also confronted a well-organized environmental movement. Environmentalists have attacked both the North American Free Trade Agreement (NAFTA) and GATT (1994) on the grounds that freer trade promotes greater environmental hazards and costs along with economic growth. Many environmentalists are strongly opposed to agreements that limit national sovereignty because they fear that the relatively strong environmental measures currently in place in certain countries could be diluted.

GATT has also been threatened at times by the actions of participating nations. In the United States, for example, the Omnibus Trade Bill of 1988 contained the "Super 301" clause which was intended to automatize the process of retaliating against foreign trade practices deemed "unfair" by U.S. industries by threatening them with higher tariffs unless they altered their trade policies (this provision expired in 1990). This process has been likened to "prying open foreign markets with a crowbar." Such detours on the route toward trade liberalization directly undermine the foundation that has been set by the GATT.

Several studies concur that the increase in global real income from the Uruguay Round's full implementation in 2005 will be about 1 percent of the world's 1992 GDP. Merchandise trade is predicted to grow by more than 12 percent ($745 billion in 1992 dollars) over what would have occurred in the absence of such agreements. Some studies estimate the gains to less-developed coun-

The GATT agreement is projected to increase world merchandise trade by three-quarters of a trillion dollars by the year 2005.

tries from this stimulation of world trade to total $78 billion in 1992 dollars by the year 2005. Obviously, protectionist policies adopted unilaterally by GATT nations could significantly threaten the welfare- and productivity-enhancing capabilities of such agreements. In macroeconomic terms, freer trade—through multilateral agreements—is key to achieving dramatic long-term rightward shifts in both aggregate supply and aggregate demand.

QUESTIONS

Using graphs, show how trade liberalization through tariff and quota reductions might affect aggregate supply and demand (income and the price level) over time. If protectionist policies are known to have deleterious effects on economic growth and productivity, why do they remain so politically popular?

Sources: U.S. Bureau of the Census, *U.S. International Trade in Goods and Services,* series FT-900(94); Jadish Bhagwati, "It's the Process, Stupid," *The Economist* (March 27, 1993), p. 69; and IMF, *World Economic Outlook 1994,* pp. 84–87.

SUMMARY

1. The interplay of aggregate supply and aggregate demand, in the long-run perspective of classical economists, produces full employment and economic growth at stable prices. Fiscal policy as a discretionary tool of government is largely unnecessary in the context of classical supply and demand interactions.

2. The Keynesian view of macroeconomics is that concerted discretionary policy is necessary to alleviate imbalances in aggregate demand and supply, since the private economy cannot produce an equilibrium at full employment with output growth.

3. Fiscal policy is the taxing and spending power of government. It can affect aggregate demand by increasing total government spending in the economy or by stimulating private consumption and investment spending (via tax cuts, for example). In the event of inflation, fiscal policy may also be used to reduce aggregate demand—that is, it can be contractionary as well as expansionary.

4. Policies other than tax and spending changes can also affect aggregate demand in the economy. Since net foreign spending is a component of aggregate demand, any policy change that affects imports or exports will shift the aggregate demand curve rightward or leftward.

5. The effects of fiscal policy by government depend on the shape of the aggregate supply curve. In the Keynesian range, demand increases cause increases in real income but not in prices; in the classical range, demand increases are inflationary, with no increase in income and employment; in the intermediate range, both prices and real income increase with increases in demand.

6. Supply-side economics is based on the idea that overreliance on aggregate demand management, in the form of tax policy, has had ill effects on the aggregate supply side of the economy.

7. Aggregate supply is related to the cost and availability of resources in the economy, especially labor resources. It is also related to the natural rate of unemployment, which exists when all unemployment is either frictional or structural in nature.

8. The natural rate of unemployment depends on the institutions surrounding decisions to supply or demand labor. These institutions include but are not limited to tax policies on work and investment, the amount of government regulation, and trade policies.

9. Supply-side policies are designed to enhance work incentives, to increase productive investment, to eliminate regulations on businesses and workers, and to reduce formal or informal trade barriers.

10. Macroeconomic policies relating to both aggregate demand and aggregate supply have been hampered by the existence of huge federal deficits.

KEY TERMS

demand deficiency
  unemployment

full employment
natural rate of unemployment

supply-side economics

QUESTIONS FOR REVIEW AND DISCUSSION

1. Discuss the classical long-run adjustment mechanism with regard to a decrease in aggregate demand.

2. What is demand deficiency unemployment? How do short-run Keynesian and new classical views of this situation differ?

3. What, exactly, is demand management?

4. Why do modern Keynesians favor discretionary fiscal policies to address short-run unemployment problems?

5. In general, why do new classical or supply-side economists oppose demand management to address short-run problems of unemployment?

6. How would the elimination of all trade barriers with Japan affect aggregate demand and aggregate supply in the United States?

7. Suppose that demand management policies are effective in reducing aggregate demand. How will the price level be affected? Does your

answer depend on the shape of the aggregate supply curve?

8. Define the natural rate of unemployment. How do market and institutional changes affect the natural rate?

9. How do policies related to saving and business investment affect output growth and employment in the economy?

10. Does the political process ever prevent or hamper the achievement of macroeconomic policy goals? How?

11. What are the three portions of the aggregate supply curve? How do increases in aggregate demand affect the price level in these different ranges?

12. During World War II, a large portion of the population left the work force in order to fight overseas. What impact would such an exodus have on the aggregate supply curve?

PROBLEM

Hurricane Andrew had devastating effects on local economies in Florida and Louisiana in the fall of 1992. Hurricane Opal blasted through North Florida in 1995. San Francisco experienced similar problems following the earthquake of 1989. Massive flooding along the Mississippi River in the summer of 1993 wiped out crops, homes, and businesses and disrupted transportation in the Midwest. Many billions of dollars of damages resulted from these natural disasters. Use graphs to show the short-run and long-run supply-side effects of such catastrophes.

WORKING WITH THE WEB

1. Go to the Virtual Economy Homepage (http://ve.ifs.org.uk). This resource helps you determine the effects of different government policies on variables like output, output growth, inflation, and so on. The setting is the U.K. economy, and so the monetary values are denominated in British Pounds (£).

   It may help to survey the site and read all relevant information provided through the various links. When you are done doing this, return to the "home" location given above. Find the "4ᵗʰ Floor, The Model" link near the bottom of the page. Go through this link to a page that allows you to choose whether to work with the easy version (Selected variables form) or the hard version (All variables form). For this question, use the easy version.

   Using principles from the chapter, discuss the effect of each policy change listed below. Report the general results (use the accompanying graphs or tables) for changes in GDP, unemployment, and inflation. A straightforward way of reporting your results is to compare what you got (after economic reforms—the red line) to what each variable would have been without your changes (before economic reforms—the blue line). Also, remember to reset the model after each part below.

   a. Increase the Basic Tax Rate from 23 percent to 30 percent.
   b. Increase Government Current Spending by 10 percent.
   c. Decrease the V.A.T. tax from 17.5 percent to 10 percent.

2. The Liberty Search web site (http://www.libertysearch.com) provides links to numerous articles that reflect a libertarian perspective. You will need to visit this web site to read an article on "supply side economics" by Stephen Moore. When you arrive at the site, click on the link to "economics" and then to "supply side." You should see a link to an article entitled "Are Supply-Siders All Washed Up?" Click on this link, read the article, and answer the questions below.

   [Note: an alternative route is to visit the Cato Institute site (http://www.cato.org) and use the search engine at the bottom of the page. By entering the words "supply siders," the article should appear as a link. If you want to do some additional background reading on this topic, go to Encyclopedia.com at http://www.encyclopedia.com. Using the phrase "supply side," your word search should take you to a link called "supply-side economics."]

   a. The article mentions the "tax increase of 1993." Does this phrase refer to an increase in tax rates or an increase in tax receipts?
   b. Use information from both the article and chapter to explain how tax rates changed between 1982 and 1989, and why tax receipts would grow during this period.

CHAPTER 25

Taxes, Deficits, and the Debt

In Chapter 24, we examined how fiscal policy could shift aggregate demand and supply curves to attain important macroeconomic goals. While fiscal policy may be a recommended stabilizing device, political pressures have led systematically to pervasive deficit spending in the second half of the twentieth century. Between 1960 and 2000, the U.S. government ran surpluses in only three years—1969, 1998, and 1999. Deficits exceeded $200 billion several times during the 1980s and topped $300 billion in 1991. Despite political promises to balance the budget and recent surpluses, the national debt has risen more than tenfold since 1960, to almost $6 trillion in 2000. The practice of fiscal policy involves the subject of public finance, or the role of government expenditures, taxation, and debt in the economy. Each of these areas of government policy is important and to some extent controversial. For example, the public, politicians, and economists are anxious about the effects of deficits and debt. This chapter examines the political foundation of federal deficits and debt. After reading Chapter 25 you should understand

- the proposed effects and the results of fiscal policy.
- features of government finance that automatically help control business cycles of recession and inflation.
- basic principles of public finance, especially as related to taxation.
- why deficits and debt concern economists and the public.

623

FISCAL POLICY IN PRACTICE

Fiscal policy is often difficult to implement—primarily because it must work through a political process. Inherent in this process are impediments to the smooth functioning of discretionary fiscal policy. It is often difficult to forecast economic downturns accurately or to implement appropriate fiscal policies in a timely fashion. In addition, political motives often cause politicians to favor certain fiscal measures.

Governments continually levy taxes and make expenditures on a variety of goods and services, and all taxes and expenditures have fiscal effects. But most government taxes and expenditures appear in the budget no matter what the particular phase of the business cycle happens to be. The *level* of these tax receipts and expenditures varies with phases of unemployment and inflation in the economy, however, and these changes, called **automatic stabilizers,** are a part of fiscal policy.

Tax Structures

Automatic stabilizers
Taxes and government expenditures whose levels do not depend on decisions by policy-makers for change but instead change countercyclically in response to changes in the level of economic activity.

Before explaining the role of automatic stabilizers, we briefly consider three types of tax structure. (Although we use the example of income taxes here, these concepts can be applied to other kinds of taxes as well.)

Proportional income tax
A tax that is a fixed percentage of income for all levels of income.

Proportional Taxes   A tax that requires individuals to pay a constant percentage of income in taxes is a **proportional income tax.** If the proportion is 10 percent, a taxpayer earning $50,000 per year would pay $5000 (or 10 percent) in taxes. If a taxpayer earned $5000, his or her tax bill would be $500 (or 10 percent). Some states, such as Michigan, Illinois, and Indiana, levy a proportional income tax (with deductions and exemptions allowed). Much of the current discussion of the so-called flat tax proposal involves the idea of proportional income taxation.

Progressive income tax
A tax that is a percentage of income and that varies directly with the level of income.

Progressive Taxes   A **progressive income tax** requires that a larger percentage of income be paid in taxes as income rises. If the tax structure is based on this principle, an individual with a $15,000 income may pay only 5 percent of income in taxes, whereas an individual with a $30,000 income may pay 15 percent. The federal income tax system is based on the principle of progressive taxation.

Regressive income tax
A tax that is a percentage of income and that varies inversely with the level of income.

Regressive Taxes   With a **regressive income tax,** a lower percentage of income is paid in taxes as income rises. An individual with a $15,000 income may pay 10 percent in taxes, whereas an individual with a $30,000 income may pay 8 percent in taxes. While a regressive tax results in a lower percentage of income paid in taxes as income rises, people with higher incomes may pay higher taxes in absolute amounts. State and local sales taxes are good examples of regressive taxes, as are the more selective excise taxes on tobacco and alcohol.

How Much Is Discretion? How Much Is Automatic?

Prior to 1986, the personal income tax code in the United States was highly progressive (as opposed to proportional or regressive). The advantage of a progressive structure is that it can act as a built-in stabilizer against inflation and recession in the economy. As money income rises—pushing the economy against its production possibilities frontier and fully employing resources—rising money incomes would push people into higher and higher income tax brackets. This, in turn, would withdraw some inflation-producing consumption expenditures from the economy.

(This effect assumes that government does not spend the increased tax revenues.) As income falls, the total tax bill of individuals declines with lower and lower tax rates placed on declining incomes, causing unemployment-reducing purchasing power to be automatically injected into the economy. (In this case, the tax bill will also fall with a proportional tax, but it will fall faster with a progressive tax.)

Certain types of government expenditures, such as transfer payments from entitlement (aid) programs, also constitute an automatic stabilizer in the economy. Social Security payments, Aid to Families with Dependent Children, food stamps, unemployment compensation, and other such income security programs automatically inject purchasing power into the poorer and older segments of the economy in case of recession and unemployment. At federal, state, and local levels—but especially at the federal level of government—larger amounts of support flow through these programs during periods of unemployment, and smaller amounts are paid out during periods of fuller employment (and often inflation). For example, the eligibility period for receiving unemployment benefits was extended several times during and after the 1990–1991 recession. Thus, both the tax structure and expenditure programs can be designed and set in place to act as moderating influences on adverse swings in the business cycle of unemployment and inflation.

What, then, is discretionary fiscal policy? If the Congress (with the help of the president) has previously decided the rules under which individuals will receive transfer payments and the rules under which individuals will be taxed, what is left to discretion? One obvious answer is that setting up the automatic stabilizers is itself an act of discretion. The U.S. tax system underwent significant changes in 1986 and in 1993. The Tax Reform Act of 1986 changed the automatic tax stabilizers that were part of the previous tax system, reducing the number of **marginal tax rates** from more than a dozen to two. (A third rate was added in 1991.) The Clinton administration's 1993 economic plan added two new marginal rates for upper-income Americans. Marginal income tax rates by 2000 included taxation at 15, 28, and 33 percent, with surtax rates rising to 40 percent of income (a surtax is a tax levied when income rises above a certain amount). (The marginal tax rate is the percentage rate that applies to some additional amount of taxable income; it is figured by dividing the change in taxes by the change in taxable income.) Welfare or entitlement program eligibility also may be changed periodically by Congress, as was recently the case when President Clinton signed welfare reform into law in 1996, and this has an impact on the countercyclical effectiveness of automatic stabilizers.

At any point in time, some expenditures (and tax sources) are controllable and some are not. Approximately 25 to 35 percent of federal expenditures are fully discretionary—that is, not tied to ongoing, in-place programs such as Social Security, unemployment compensation and other income security programs, and interest payments on the federal debt. The bulk of these fully discretionary expenditures includes a large portion of national defense expenditures, public works programs, and appropriations to federal agencies and to state and local levels of government. Without question, Congress has the power and the responsibility to set up all tax and expenditure programs over the long run, but once many of these programs are set, room for short-run discretion is narrowed considerably. Over the short run, discretionary fiscal policy in the hands of Congress and the president is limited by the conditions attached to automatic stabilizers already in place. Some expenditures in the short run are controllable; some are uncontrollable.

Marginal tax rate

The tax rate, in percentage terms, that applies to additional taxable income; additional taxes divided by the additional income taxed.

Fiscal Policy and the Budget

Budget surplus

The amount by which government's tax revenues exceed government's expenditures in a year.

Budget deficit

The amount by which government's expenditures exceed government's tax revenues in a year.

Cyclically balanced budget

A long-term view of the budget, in which surpluses generated during expansions match deficits created during recessions over a period of years.

Federal debt

The total value of federal government bonds outstanding; arises from both current and past budget deficits.

As we have seen, discretionary fiscal policy suggests **budget surpluses** during periods of inflation and **budget deficits** over periods of unemployment and recession. While some classical economists advised strict balance in government accounts, the Keynesians argued that the budget should be balanced over the business cycle. A **cyclically balanced budget** in theory requires that budget surpluses run during periods of inflation match budget deficits run during periods of economic distress and unemployment. That is, economic contractions demand budget deficits that expand aggregate demand, and inflation demands a surplus in the federal accounts to reduce total spending on goods and services.

Unfortunately, the fiscal process has not worked exactly in this fashion over the past three decades. Deficits, which are supposed to be cyclically counterbalanced by surpluses, have been run by the federal government in all but three of the years since 1960. These deficits have fiscal ramifications of their own. As we will see later in this chapter, a pileup of deficits since 1960 pushed the **federal debt** to almost $6 trillion in 2000. It is most unlikely that such debt will bankrupt the United States, since the federal government has the power to tax and (unlike any individual or other unit of government) to create money. Economists do worry about other effects of deficits and debt, however. Such effects include adverse impacts on private spending in the present and potential reductions in economic growth and production possibilities in the future.

The Federal Budget: Process and Problems

Currently, federal government spending (including transfer payments) makes up nearly 25 percent of the United States's approximately $6 trillion GDP. The budget submitted to Congress by President Reagan in January of 1987 was the first ever to exceed $1 trillion, and the size of the federal budget has increased every year since. Clearly, expenditures of such magnitude will affect aggregate demand. The process by which the level of federal government expenditures is determined each year is complicated. These expenditures are not simply set by the president and implemented immediately; they must be proposed, debated, and approved in a complex budget process.

In 1974, the Congress and President passed the Congressional Budget and Impoundment Control Act. The stipulations set out in this act are still in effect today. The major effects of the 1974 act are to deny the president the authority to refuse to spend congressionally appropriated funds and to establish a specific timetable for all the steps of the budgetary process (see Table 25.1). The act also established the Congressional Budget Office (CBO) to specialize in budgetary analysis for the Congress. The GAO by this time had acquired so many other duties, and federal budgets had become so very large and complicated, that Congress felt better economic analysis of federal spending could be provided by an office for which this was the sole task.

Though the reforms established by the 1974 act were intended to make the budget process more efficient and streamlined, they had the opposite effect. Deadlines are seldom reached, deficits have ballooned, and, frequently, special temporary budgets have been approved to prevent the government from running out of money and ceasing operations. A number of proposals have been suggested for overcoming these problems.

TABLE 25.1

Timetable for the Congressional Budget Process

To pass a federal budget for government expenditures, the Congressional Budget and Impoundment Control Act of 1974 requires that these specific legal actions be taken by the president and Congress each year. The act also sets deadlines for each step.

Deadline	Action to Be Completed	Deadline	Action to Be Completed
November 10	President submits current services budget	Seventh day after Labor Day	Congress completes action on bills and resolutions providing new budget
Fifteenth day after Congress meets	President submits budget	September 15	Congress completes action on second required concurrent resolution on the budget
March 15	Committees submit reports to budget committees	September 25	Congress completes action on reconciliation bill or resolution, or both, implementing second required concurrent resolution
April 1	CBO submits report to budget committees	October 1	Fiscal year begins
April 15	Budget committees report first concurrent resolutions to their houses		
May 15	Committees report bills and resolutions authorizing new budget authority; Congress completes action on first concurrent resolution on budget		

Among the most popular is the line-item veto, a power given to most state governors. This would allow the president to veto specific parts, or line items, of budgets passed by Congress. A major problem with the budget process, as some see it, has been that the president faces an all-or-nothing situation. Prior to 1996 the budget passed by Congress had to be accepted intact or vetoed. That provided an incentive to attach special-interest spending bills, known as riders, to major spending bills. The line-item veto was scheduled to go into effect in 1997, but it did not survive a constitutional challenge in the Supreme Court. Congress was not permitted to abdicate to the president its constitutional authority to originate and determine government spending.

Other proposals include implementing a two-year (instead of a one-year) budget and dividing the budget into a current expense budget and a capital budget. With a two-year budget, Congress would go through the budget process only once every two years, rather than annually. Since the budget process has become a costly, drawn-out affair, this proposal has some merit. Dividing the budget into a capital budget for public goods, investment outlay (for example, highways), and a current expense budget for yearly operating expenses also may provide for greater fiscal flexibility as well as greater opportunity for the president and Congress to agree on federal expenditures.

PUBLIC FINANCE

Government expenditures obviously require some means, such as taxation, to finance them. When government finances the production of public goods or services—a local sewer system, a research program looking into the cause of acid rain, a nuclear warhead, a presidential limousine—it uses taxes to help pay the bill. In the United States, about 82,000 governmental bodies at federal, state, county, city, school district, municipal, and township levels have the power to establish taxes. As we saw in Chapter 3, the market fails to provide the optimal amounts of public goods such as national defense, police and fire protection, and education. In response, federal, state, and local governments traditionally have taken an active role in providing or influencing the production of such goods and services. In macroeconomic stabilization, government expenditures and taxation (especially at the federal level) take on new roles and new significance. Since the impact of fiscal policy is felt in the economy through government expenditures and taxation, it is important to understand some of the history and foundations of **public finance,** which is the study of government expenditures and revenue-collecting activities. Each and every government expenditure, along with the various tax schemes to finance it, has fiscal effects in terms of helping or hindering economic stabilization.

Public finance

The study of how governments at the federal, state, and local levels tax and spend.

Government Expenditures

There are two basic types of government expenditures: (1) direct purchases of goods and services and (2) transfer payments, which are the redistribution of income from one group of people to another. Direct purchases involve spending on items such as defense, fire and police protection, and wages and salaries of government employees. Transfer payments include such expenditures as Social Security payments, Aid to Families with Dependent Children, and unemployment insurance.

The size of all government expenditures, adjusted for inflation, is shown in Table 25.2 for selected years from 1960 to 1998. Total government expenditures have increased dramatically since 1960 and are expected to rise even higher. These expenditures are ultimately determined by legislative decision, but about 70 to 80 percent are part of ongoing programs such as funds for police protection, water and sewer services (at the local level), military salaries, welfare entitlement programs, Social Security, and interest on the federal debt.

Trends in Government Expenditures   In Table 25.2, total expenditures are broken down into federal government expenditures and state and local government expenditures. Federal expenditures (which include grants-in-aid—cash distributions—to state and local governments) exceed state and local expenditures by a fairly constant proportion. Up to the early 1900s, local government expenditures exceeded the sum of federal and state expenditures. The Reagan administration attempted to return the provision and financing of many government goods and services to state and local entities, which caused many state and local governments to reorient their fiscal activities. This policy was dubbed the "New Federalism" because it sought a return to the fiscal system that existed prior to the 1930s in the United States.

Per household and per capita government expenditures at all levels have increased in the last few decades. Not only has the absolute level of expenditures increased, but the level of government expenditures as a percentage of GDP has simultaneously increased. Government expenditures at all levels increased from 21.3 percent of GDP in 1950 to 23 percent in 1960, 28 percent in 1970, and 32 percent in

TABLE 25.2

Real Government Expenditures, 1960–1998 (in billions of 1998 dollars)
All government expenditures increased during the period 1960–1998, with real state and local expenditures increasing at about the same rate as real federal expenditures. This increase was not simply due to population growth; per capita real expenditures nearly tripled between 1960 and 1998.

Year	Total Government	Federal Government	State and Local Government	Total Expenditures Per Capita (dollars per capita)
1960	590.0	435.1	186.5	$3265.7
1965	763.3	554.1	259.0	3928.4
1970	1085.9	775.2	401.1	5295.6
1975	1381.8	996.8	531.6	6398.1
1980	1574.8	1166.0	575.0	6915.5
1985	1887.5	1401.8	630.0	7915.0
1990	2174.2	1550.7	783.3	8698.4
1991	2206.1	1561.7	822.5	8732.4
1992	2333.7	1671.7	856.5	9138.0
1993	2363.6	1679.7	888.5	9158.1
1994	2381.2	1678.9	916.5	9137.2
1995	2426.7	1718.2	931.2	9225.6
1996	2474.7	1748.7	951.8	9322.5
1997	2507.8	1763.3	972.4	9361.1
1998	2542.5	1769.2	1005.0	9406.6

Source: Council of Economic Advisers, *Economic Report of the President* (Washington, D.C.: U. S. Government Printing Office, 1999), pp. 330, 367, 424.

Note: Federal grants-in-aid to state and local governments are counted in both "Federal Expenditures" and "State and Local Expenditures." The "Total Government" and "Total Expenditures per Capita" data do not double-count these expenditures. Dollar figures converted to 1998 dollars by the authors using the GDP implicit price deflator.

1986; the percentage declined slightly in the late 1980s before beginning to increase again at the present (see Figure 25.1).

Since the 1950s, federal government expenditures have increased most in the area of transfer payments, a trend that was sharply reinforced in the 1960s under the Great Society policies of the Lyndon Johnson administration. These Great Society policies expanded the welfare system, setting such expenditures at a sharply increasing rate of growth. As shown in Figure 25.2, the trend in federal expenditures on national defense declined as the percentage of outlays on social programs rose. Figure 25.2 also shows that the trend in these two broad expenditure classes reversed slightly under the Reagan administration, which emphasized defense readiness and military parity, or equality, with the Soviet Union.

The post–Cold War era has, as expected, seen a downsizing of the military. Further, massive welfare reforms at both the federal and state level during the Clinton administration have reoriented (if not reduced) welfare and transfer payments. Further, despite promises to end "big government as we know it" by President

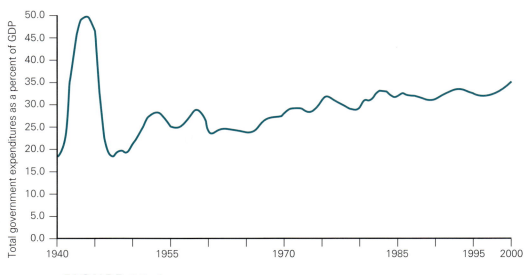

FIGURE 25.1

Government Expenditures as a Percent of GDP, 1960–1998
Government expenditures at all levels have grown to over 30 percent of GDP, although they have fluctuated widely—especially during wartime; note for example the huge increase during the World War II era due to increased defense spending.

Source: Council of Economic Advisers, *Economic Report of the President* (Washington, D.C.: U.S. Government Printing Office, 1979 and 1999), pp. 282, 371.

Clinton and a philosophical ground in less government by the Republican Congress (between 1994 and 2000), government has grown in both nominal and real terms. In 1998, every man, woman, and child in America contributed $9406 on average to government at all levels (see Table 25.2).

Direct purchases of goods and services by the federal government also have increased in absolute terms but have decreased as a percentage of total expenditures. Direct purchases at state and local levels exceed those of the federal government. Such a result is not surprising when you consider the programs offered. Most streets, roads, and highways, police and fire protection, hospitals, education, and sewage and garbage disposal are provided by state and local governments. Indeed, state and local governments probably have a greater fiscal influence on our daily lives than does the federal government.

Discretionary Policy and the Level of Government Spending   Aspects of government finance at the various levels are critical to understanding the expenditure side of discretionary fiscal policy. Unquestionably, the expenditures of states, counties, townships, and cities have an impact on cycles of inflation and unemployment. Emphasis on the effectiveness of discretionary fiscal policy must be placed on *federal* policies, however, and the reason is not hard to understand. State and local governments, in most cases, *must* rely on tax sources to finance government expenditures. Most states and lower units of government, for example, are constitutionally forced to balance their budgets. (The predicament of states is this: A state cannot use its fiscal policy to help the country out of a recession,

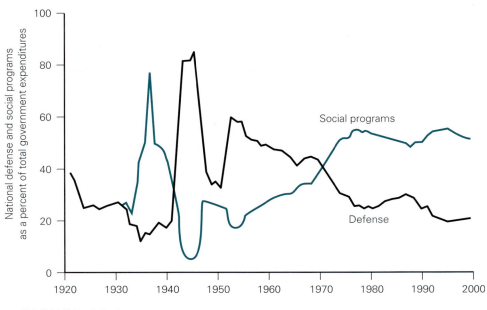

FIGURE 25.2

Defense and Social Programs as a Percent of Government Expenditures, 1920–1998

Expenditures in these two categories of government finance have fluctuated through time. In percentage terms, social programs have grown dramatically since the mid-1950s and the Great Society programs of the 1960s, while defense has generally declined since 1950.

Source: Council of Economic Advisers, *Economic Report of the President* (Washington, D.C.: U.S. Government Printing Office, 1993), p. 441.

and it is difficult for a state to recover from a recession while the country is in one.) Although some governmental entities may borrow (largely through bond sales) to finance longer-term projects and budget deficits, their ability to sustain large debt is limited. Unlike the federal government, they do not have the power to print money and to engage in massive levels of debt. The result is that budget policy at the state and lower levels of government tends to be procyclical in character—expenditures are reduced on the downswing due to reduced tax collections and increased on the upswing when tax revenues are rising. In periods of economic distress and widespread unemployment, for example, these levels of government are forced to cut back on all kinds of goods, purchases, and services. For example, the weakening of OPEC in the early 1980s and the consequent fall in oil prices caused recessions and reduced tax revenues in the oil-producing states of Texas, Louisiana, and Oklahoma. These states' response was, at least in the short run, to reduce expenditures on goods and services, such as road repair, public education, and county and city services of all types. This response is said to be procyclical rather than countercyclical in character because discretionary policy would call for increased government expenditures and/or reduced taxes in the face of recession and unemployment. Indeed, the fact that state and local fiscal policy tends to be procyclical in nature is itself important for the conduct of discretionary policy at the federal level.

Tax Revenues

Bonds

Financial instruments that create future obligations on the part of the issuers to make principal repayments and interest payments.

The two basic methods of financing public expenditures are taxing and borrowing. State and local governments usually borrow, as we have stated, by selling **bonds** to finance special projects such as highways, schools, or hospitals, but their access to such funds is limited by their ability to meet future obligations—that is, by their financial soundness and the faith that they will be able to pay off debt in the future. The federal government has come to use borrowing as a routine means of financing its burgeoning deficit, a practice that might eventually create economic problems of its own. Nevertheless, the largest portion of government expenditures is still financed by taxes. As shown in Figure 25.3a, the largest single source of federal tax revenues is the personal income tax, followed closely by Social Security taxes.

Property taxes and sales taxes are the two largest contributors to combined state and local government revenues. Figure 25.3b shows that sales taxes account for a larger percentage of tax revenues of state and local governments than any other tax. One thing is not apparent from Figure 25.3b: Property tax revenues have not been rising as rapidly as sales and income tax revenues. This indicates that property owners are being taxed relatively less over time than other groups.

Equitable Taxation: Theories About Who Should Pay Given government's need for tax revenues, how should taxes be levied among the people? While voter-taxpayer resistance to specific forms of taxation is always a factor to consider since incumbent politicians must face voters after tax increases, the issue of tax equity is also important. Our society attempts to find an equitable way of distributing the tax burden, but there are no easy formulas for determining what is truly equitable. Theoretically, there are two basic methods by which we may determine who should

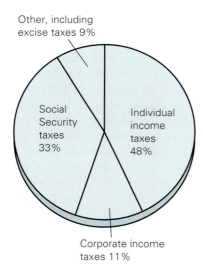
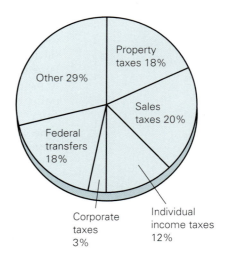

FIGURE 25.3

Distribution of Government Revenue

Income taxes are the largest source of federal revenue. State and local governments receive most of their revenue from sales and property taxes.

be taxed and by how much: the benefit principle and the ability-to-pay principle. While these principles are not directly concerned with the impact of discretionary fiscal policy, they are worth mentioning briefly here.

Benefit principle

A method of determining individuals' tax burdens on the basis of the beneficiaries of the expenditures that are financed by taxes; an example is a gasoline tax.

Many taxes arise from the **benefit principle,** which means simply that individuals who receive the most benefits from government goods and services should pay the most for their production. Public transport facilities such as buses or subways, publicly owned electrical, water, and gas utilities, and toll roads charge users for the services provided. Many goods, such as national defense, interstate highways, and some educational facilities, provide indirect benefits to citizens that are not easily calculated. Some individuals receiving government benefits cannot always afford to pay an equitable share of taxes, even if the benefits they receive could be calculated exactly. For these reasons, most taxes are based on the ability-to-pay principle.

Ability-to-pay principle

A method of determining individuals' tax burdens on the basis of those most capable of paying taxes.

According to the **ability-to-pay principle** of taxation, those who are more able to pay should pay more taxes than those less able to pay. Under this principle, levels of an individual's income, wealth, or expenditures are measures frequently used for determining the level of tax obligation. There is general agreement that the wealthy should pay more taxes than the poor, but the question of how much more is not easily resolved.

FEDERAL TAXATION, TAX REFORM, AND FISCAL POLICY

All taxation at federal, state, and local levels alike has a direct impact on the overall economy through its effect on individuals. The very *fact* of taxation means that income is withdrawn from the private sector of the economy, reducing aggregate demand. On the other side, the very *fact* that governments at all levels spend means that governments affect aggregate demand. A *change* in government spending or taxation also will have effects on economic stabilization, *whether or not the effects are intended.*

When examining discretionary fiscal policy, however, we may provisionally ignore taxing and spending systems that are procyclical in nature and concentrate instead on those types of expenditures and taxes that may be used intentionally to affect aggregate demand. State and local spending and taxing policies certainly affect the economy. But such taxes and expenditures may be downplayed when discussing discretionary changes in fiscal accounts because they tend to be procyclical in nature. Likewise, some taxes collected at the federal level, such as Social Security taxes, will clearly affect aggregate demand in the economy. But they are not, in the usual case, the taxes used to conduct discretionary policy in dealing with cyclical swings in unemployment and inflation.

Income and Corporate Taxes

Federal taxes on both individuals and on corporations were significantly altered in 1913 with the passage of the Sixteenth Amendment. This amendment allowed the federal government to levy income taxes on U.S. citizens. After its inception, the income tax system grew rapidly in size and complexity.

Beginning in 1966, the issue of tax reform was uppermost in political rhetoric. In 1976, President Carter called the U.S. tax system "a disgrace to the human race" due to its confusing and complex provisions. The major criticism of the tax system was the number and kinds of items allowed both individuals and corporations as

Investment tax credit

A percentage or amount of new investment expenditure that is directly subtracted from the investor's tax bill in calculating total taxes.

deductions from income. Rather than viewing the tax system as primarily a means of generating revenue, federal taxation was used for a number of other purposes. Special breaks were given to individuals and to corporations, for example, for investment purposes. The **investment tax credit** was instituted (in the early 1960s) on the principle that the tax code should encourage industrial modernization. Accelerated depreciation of business investments also was featured for the same purpose. Other deductions for both individuals and businesses were introduced, creating a tax code of incredible complexity and inequity.

Most economists believed that the tax code was inequitable and that it established counterproductive incentives for individuals and businesses. Tax "shelters" were sought and used to generate income losses to deduct from regular reportable income. The availability of tax shelters led to investments that generated loss potential rather than economic growth, which in turn weakened the economy. High marginal tax rates, moreover, may have caused individuals to work less or to work in the underground (untaxed) economy. Further, huge quantities of resources were employed in finding loopholes (tax provisions that generated tax-lowering deductions) in the tax laws.

Tax Changes in 1986 and 1993   In the largest tax overhaul since World War II, Congress passed the Tax Reform Act of 1986. One major thrust of the reform was to scale down individual and corporate tax rates and to reduce tax complexity. (Figure 25.4 summarizes tax rates from 1913 to 1993.) Initially, two tax brackets replaced the fourteen in place previously, and a maximum marginal tax rate of 28 percent replaced the old top rate of 50 percent. (For a time, a 5 percent surcharge was applied to certain income groups, effectively creating a maximum rate of 33 percent.) Another major accomplishment of the act was the reduction and standardization of exemptions. While both individual and corporate rates fell as a result of the 1986 law, more income was taxable, as many deductions were eliminated.

The Tax Reform Act of 1986 was also designed to provide more equity. Partly as a result of increased personal exemptions, millions of low-income families were

FIGURE 25.4

Summary of Individual and Corporate Tax Rates, 1913–1998

Individual and corporate tax rates have varied widely since 1913, with individual rates reaching a maximum marginal rate of 90 percent. The Omnibus Budget Reconciliation Act of 1993 set the maximum marginal rate on individuals at 39.6 percent and the maximum marginal rate on corporations at 35 percent.

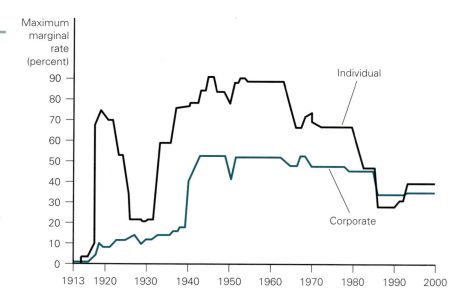

completely removed from the tax rolls. In addition, the elimination of many tax loopholes forced more well-to-do Americans to pay their fair share of taxes.

The Omnibus Budget Reconciliation Act of 1993, the official name of the Clinton administration's deficit-reduction package, went a long way toward reversing the simplification of the U.S. tax system that was achieved in 1986. This piece of legislation added a marginal rate of 36 percent for individuals with incomes in excess of $115,000 and couples with more than $140,000 in annual taxable income. (Taxable income is the amount of income left over after subtracting personal exemptions and itemized deductions such as casualty losses and mortgage interest.) A new 10 percent surcharge on taxable income above $250,000 meant that the maximum marginal rate in 1998 was effectively 39.6 percent.

In addition to changing the personal income tax structure, the 1993 budget bill increased the corporate tax rate from 34 percent to 35 percent and raised the federal excise tax on gasoline. Another significant change was the repeal of the so-called "luxury tax" on purchases of boats, aircraft, jewelry, and furs, which was enacted during the Bush administration (the tax on purchases of luxury cars—those with a sticker price of $30,000 or more—remained in place, however).

Flat tax

A single tax rate levied on all income.

A Flat Tax?   Today, the talk in the air is about a **flat tax,** a proposal that would radically simplify the federal tax system. There are several different flat tax proposals, but essentially the flat tax envisions a tax return that can be filled out on the back of a postcard. This system would feature *one* tax rate for all income levels and for *all* income. In other words, how much did you make last year? Multiply it by, say, 17 percent, and send it in. There would be no deductions or other complications. The debate over such proposals has been intense. Proponents argue that it will stimulate economic growth and compliance with the tax laws. Opponents suggest that it is not fair and that it is a tax break for the wealthy. Taxpayers seem to love the idea of simpler taxes; tax preparers, such as H & R Block, are dead set against such proposals. It is difficult to tell at this point what the political fate of the flat tax will be. (The Focus "Fat Chance for Flat Taxes" explores the pros and cons of this proposal and the prospects for such fiscal change.)

DEFICITS, DEBTS, AND FISCAL POLICY

High deficits in the 1980s and 1990s alarmed voters, economists, and politicians. Just what are the effects of huge deficits and the growing federal debt they have created?

Deficits and the Recent Surplus

As we have shown, deficits are created when government expenditures exceed revenues from taxation. Figure 25.5 provides a disturbing portrait of the emerging deficit situation. Since local and state governments tend to have balanced budgets, the overall government deficit is created primarily at the federal level. Large deficits were a feature of federal finance since 1960, but their magnitude began to grow in the mid-1970s. In the 1980s, federal deficits showed explosive growth, reaching over $200 billion in 1985 and 1986. Between 1990 and 1994, these gargantuan deficits continued at levels over $200 billion (reaching $290 billion in 1993). Deficits of these magnitudes did not emerge overnight. The fiscal pressures of the Vietnam War, the social programs of the Great Society of the 1960s, the modernization of national defense by the Reagan administration, and so on—all added to the contemporary *debt* problem.

FOCUS

Fat Chance for Flat Taxes

A powerful undercurrent in America is calling for tax reform. The average American works from January 1 to the middle of May just to pay federal taxes and then spends a good part of the following April trying to figure out tax rules and forms. Reports of IRS agents intimidating taxpayers and IRS help lines offering incorrect information have only added fuel to the tax reform movement.

In response, several reform proposals have come forward. Billionaire publisher and presidential candidate, Steve Forbes, supports the flat tax, which in its purest form would tax all income at the same rate and eliminate all tax deductions and exemptions. Taxes would be withheld from your paycheck, and there would be no tax forms to fill out. The flat tax would reduce the tax rate for most citizens but would increase taxes on those who take full advantage of tax deductions, such as for purchasing a house.

The other major proposal is to institute a national sales tax. Championed by Representative Bill Archer of Texas, this tax would eliminate the income tax altogether and replace it with a sales tax on purchases. This reform would leave Americans with larger take-home pay, but increase the price of the goods and services they buy by as much as 20 percent or more.

The benefit of the flat income tax would be fewer resources wasted in filling out income tax forms and the removal of distortions from our spending decisions (such as buying a bigger house just to take advantage of the tax deduction). The national sales tax would also eliminate paperwork and reduce distortions, though by taxing only consumption it adds the incentive for people to save and invest, a distortion that many economists concerned with the low saving rate in America support.

Despite the tangible economic benefits, real tax reform is unlikely. Special-interest groups have an incentive to protect their breaks in the current tax code. Accountants, tax attorneys, and taxpayers with large deductions do not want the system radically reformed. The average American taxpayer would like less paperwork, but neither of the two major reforms promises any substantial tax cuts. Finally, Congress does not want to eliminate the tax code because interest in changing the tax code generates large amounts of campaign donations. Their actions forecast the true chances of real reform. In the last major revision of the tax code in 1998, Congress provided special tax breaks to certain groups, added to the number of different tax forms, and increased the length of the tax code.

Since 1995, deficits have moderated (see Figure 25.5). A surplus was experienced in 1998 (the first since 1969), and surpluses are projected through the year 2000. While these surpluses are most welcome relief for fiscal soundness and for the pressures that government deficits have put on private savings, there is some skepticism about the government's calculations and even more about whether politicians will maintain fiscal responsibility. (For discussion concerning these and other features of surpluses, see the Application "Do Budget Surpluses Mean Less Government?" at the end of this chapter.) There would be no deficit problem if Congress and presidential administrations were willing to tax in order to pay for government goods. Their unwillingness to do so means that resulting deficits, or additions to the total federal debt, must be finance.

Deficits, Fiscal Policy, and Crowding Out

How else could the federal government finance a deficit in its accounts? Since the federal government is allowed to print money, it could simply create money to

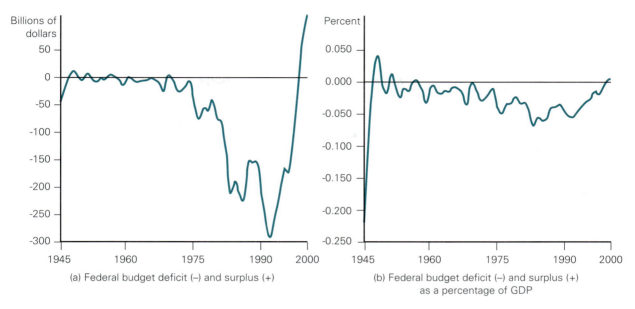

(a) Federal budget deficit (–) and surplus (+)

(b) Federal budget deficit (–) and surplus (+) as a percentage of GDP

FIGURE 25.5

Deficits Over Time and as a Percentage of GDP

While the size of the federal deficit has grown over time, the deficit as a percent of GDP has remained fairly stable. This result is not surprising, since GDP is growing also.

Source: Council of Economic Advisers, *Economic Report of the President* (Washington, D.C.: U.S. Government Printing Office, 1999), p. 419.

finance the shortfall between expenditures and receipts. The creation of money, discussed in the next few chapters, would erode the purchasing power of individuals' money holdings. The effect would approximate taxation, since resources are shifted to government from the private sector without the explicit consent of the governed.

The federal deficit is financed primarily through the sale of bonds to both individuals and privately owned commercial banks. Predictably, increases in the supply of bonds resulting from deficit financing lower bond prices. As the price of a bond declines, however, its interest rate rises. Thus, increases in the supply of bonds raise interest rates and channel private saving from private investment into government expenditures. When bonds are sold directly to individuals (EE or HH savings bonds, Treasury bills and notes, and such) or to commercial banks, pressure is placed on private investment if additional funds are not saved. This phenomenon, known as **crowding out,** means that, depending on the reaction of savers and investors to the rise in interest rates, government borrowing may crowd out private investment. If private investment is discouraged, the rise in the interest rate may reduce the long-term growth prospects of the economy—unless individuals react to the increased deficit by saving more for future generations.

The high interest rates that result from government deficits may also lead to another type of crowding out—the displacement of domestically produced goods by foreign goods. As we will explain in more detail in Chapter 31, high interest rates in the United States make U.S. dollars attractive to foreign investors. This

Crowding out

The competitive pressure exerted on private investment by government expenditures.

increase in demand for the dollar causes its price to rise in world markets; that is, the amount of a foreign currency that can be obtained for one dollar increases. For example, instead of getting 90 yen for a dollar, high interest rates in the United States may make it possible to obtain 100 yen. As a consequence, foreign goods become cheaper to Americans, but American goods become more expensive to foreign buyers. This leads to an increase in U.S. imports and a decrease in U.S. exports—both of which cause aggregate demand to shift to the left. In this way, an increase in the government's budget deficit crowds out private spending by both domestic and foreign buyers.

Often when the Treasury finances a government deficit, the Federal Reserve attempts to prevent interest rates from rising by simultaneously buying bonds on the open market. This might temporarily keep interest rates down and prevent crowding out, but it causes the money supply to rise, which ultimately leads to inflation and higher interest rates.

Internally held debt

The amount of a country's total federal debt that is owned by the country's various governments, businesses, and individuals.

Externally held debt

The amount of a country's total federal debt that is owned by foreign governments, businesses, and individuals.

Deficits and the Federal Debt

Large deficits have created a total federal debt of more than $5.5 trillion in 1998. In order to assess its importance, it is instructive to see who owns the debt.

Table 25.3 shows the composition of debt ownership in 1998. Ownership of the federal debt is dispersed among private individuals, banks, and foreigners. Most of the debt is thus **internally held debt,** with a sizable portion held by individuals and banks outside the United States. (The importance of this **externally held debt**—claims or IOUs against U.S. resources by foreigners—is discussed in the Focus "Who Bears the Burden of the Debt?")

TABLE 25.3

Ownership of the Federal Debt in 1998

The federal debt is owned, or held, by various groups. This table shows the distribution of ownership of the federal debt in 1998. All numbers are in billions of dollars.

Type of Holder	Amount (billions of dollars)	
Total federal debt:	5518.7	
Total U.S. government ownership	2217.7	
(U.S. government agencies and the Federal Reserve)		
Total private ownership:	3301.0	
Commercial banks		260.0
Corporations		271.4
Insurance Companies		188.0
Individuals		352.3
Foreign ownership		1217.2
Other, including state and local governments		1012.1

Source: Council of Economic Advisors, *Economic Report of the President* (Washington, D.C.: U.S. Government Printing Office, 1999), pp. 429, 430. Figures are for September 1998.

FOCUS

Who Bears the Burden of the Debt?

Deficits occur when government expenditures exceed the taxes necessary to finance them. When the government borrows to finance these deficits, debt is created. The federal government has created debt from the very beginnings of the nation. Likewise, the debate over such policies is an ancient one among economists, politicians, and voters. In the nineteenth century and for part of the twentieth, sizable debt was issued before and during wartime, with repayment effected through taxation after war's end. Modern times have witnessed the explosion of bond-financed deficits and a federal debt reaching more than $5.5 trillion in 1998. Does the sheer size of the debt forebode disaster? Are we burdening our children, grandchildren, and more remote descendants with the disastrous prospect of having to pay our debts back?

As a way to begin answering these questions, we again point out that it is most unlikely that the federal government of the United States will ever have to declare bankruptcy. Since the federal government is permitted (by the Constitution) to print money, the debt could be covered, if necessary and perhaps with ill consequences, in this fashion. Further, since the rate of growth in GDP exceeds the growth rate of the debt, the economy is (in a real sense of productivity) able to "stand" the growth in the debt. But problems associated with bankruptcy are not what economists contemplate when discussing the burden of the debt.

Economists usually think in intergenerational terms when discussing the possible effects of debt. They are concerned with whether government debt is borne solely or only partly by present or future generations. One idea prevalent in the post-Keynesian period is that "we owe the debt to ourselves" and that, therefore, it is not a problem to be very concerned about. A simplified version of this view,

attributed to economist Abba Lerner, asks the questions, "Who owns the debt?" and "Who owes the debt?" Since the answer in both cases is "Americans," Lerner concluded that we owe the debt to ourselves.[a] While some of our children will inherit debt through taxation, others (or the same individuals) also will inherit claims (government bonds) to offset these debts.

However, a number of matters arise when we consider Lerner's proposition. In the first place, what if foreign individuals and governments hold some of our debt? Over $1.2 trillion of the U.S. debt was so held in 1998. These foreign-held bonds represent real claims against the resources and output of the United States.

Another important matter is that the issue of debt by the federal government may have distributional effects over time. Bonds are usually purchased by high-income groups in our economy, but taxes are paid by all income ranges. Total economic well-being may be affected when a burden is placed on some Americans to the benefit of other Americans. Depending on propensities to consume, total private expenditures may be biased downward when debt is repaid from overall taxation to the upper-income groups over time.

Then there is the necessity of paying interest on the bonds that make up the debt. Unless there is a declaration of bankruptcy, interest payments must be paid. They are, as Social Security has become, an untouchable area of the federal budget. During periods of high interest rates, this burden can become especially acute, putting demands on the tax system or on new debt finance. (In 1998,

---

[a] Abba P. Lerner, "The Burden of the National Debt," in *Income, Employment, and Public Policy* (New York: W. W. Norton and Company, 1948).

continued

these interest payments were over $225 billion, a significant part of the total federal budget.)

Nobel laureate James M. Buchanan argues that the effects taxation and debt have on present and future generations are *not* equivalent due to the fact that interest payments place a burden on present and future taxpayers.[b] When debt is created, buyers and sellers engage in voluntary exchange

and therefore cannot be made worse off. But when it becomes necessary to pay interest on government bonds, taxation is required, and it is not voluntary. Future generations, therefore, do bear at least a portion of the burden of the debt.

Economists disagree over the question of where the burden of debt should be placed. The issue of whether our grandchildren will bear a portion of the burden of present government expenditures is an open one, but at least some effects of debt are passed on.

[b]James M. Buchanan, *Public Principles of Public Debt* (Homewood, Ill.: Richard D. Irwin, 1958).

The Effects of the Federal Debt

Many economists, citizens, and politicians argue that the growing federal debt is a grave present and future problem for the economy and for economic growth. Their concerns relate to (1) the supposed relation between the size of the debt, inflation, and interest rates and (2) the possible burden of the debt on present and future generations.

Debt, Inflation, and Interest Rates   Depending on how government debt is financed, it tends either to raise interest rates or to cause inflation. When the U.S. Treasury places bonds up for sale, it has no control over who the purchaser will be—that depends on who is willing to pay the most for the bonds. When the highest bidders are individuals, business firms, or financial institutions, the deficit will drive up interest rates by the amount necessary to attract these buyers. At other times, the bonds will be purchased by the Federal Reserve, the central banking authority in the United States. (The details of such purchases will be made much clearer in Chapter 26.) Purchase by the Federal Reserve tends to keep interest rates down (at least in the short run), but it can lead to higher inflation in the future. (Again, Chapters 26 and 27 will make it clear why this is likely.) The upshot is that financing the deficit inevitably leads to higher interest rates, inflation, or both—something to consider when such deficits are recommended.

Are Deficits and Debt a Burden on Future Generations?   Economists are divided on the issue of whether the federal debt is a burden on future generations. The preponderance of opinion is that it is not, although the issue is far from settled.

How can this opinion be justified? First, the U.S. government will go bankrupt only if the government cannot meet all the debt claims that it issues. This is unlikely. If economic growth and the tax receipts that it brings continue at vigorous levels, the government will have no trouble meeting its obligations.

Other troublesome features of a large public debt are more subtle. Economic growth may be retarded if deficit and debt crowd out private investment expenditures. If private sector expenditures are directed to more efficient and cost-effective investments, as they are under the revised tax system, productive expenditures might be crowded out by possibly less-productive government expenditures through government bond sales.

Ownership of the debt, moreover, might create other problems. A portion of the debt is owned by middle- to high-income families, although pension funds, which tend to be owned by low- to middle-income families, are also invested heavily in government bonds and notes. To the extent that future generations must finance present debt through tax payments, the burden of the debt will fall upon *all* future taxpayers. In other words, that portion of the debt owned by upper-income groups will be paid for by all income groups in society in the future; some income will be intergenerationally redistributed from poor to rich.

Debt Management, Interest Payments, and Fiscal Policy   Discretionary fiscal policy may be influenced in several ways by the existence of the large federal debt. In 1995, almost 15 percent of total federal expenditures was composed of interest payments on the federal debt. A growing proportion of interest payments to total federal expenditures creates a growing problem with both the size of the annual deficit and the ability of Congress to manipulate expenditures and taxes to control periodic swings in the business cycle. At times, growing interest payments may help create larger deficits, which, in turn, create larger debt, and so on. In other words, it is possible that the debt is self-perpetuating.

Can the Federal Deficits and Debt Be Controlled?

While it is easy to become unduly alarmed over deficits and the mounting federal debt, some real problems do exist. Economic growth and income distribution may be influenced in undesirable ways by growing debt and the problems (such as interest payments) that accompany it. Moreover, if discretionary fiscal policy is destabilizing, as some economists argue, efforts to balance the budget may bring some stability to the economy.

In late 1985, the U.S. Congress passed the Balanced Budget and Emergency Deficit Reduction Control Act (or Gramm–Rudman–Hollings) in an attempt to deal with growing deficits and debt. Gramm–Rudman–Hollings was supposed to "prorate," or automatically reduce, federal government expenditures when Congress did not come within preset deficit guidelines for the period 1986–1991. In the end, however, various political and legal challenges rendered the act ineffective at controlling deficits. In the early 1990s, the issue of deficit reduction rose to a position near the top of the national political agenda. In the 1992 presidential campaign, independent candidate Ross Perot focused on the issue and garnered nearly one-fifth of the vote. Perot's strong showing and postelection popularity suggested that many Americans were concerned about the effects of the federal government's huge budget deficits on their lives. In the spring of 1993, the Clinton administration responded to the growing concern about the federal debt by unveiling a controversial deficit-reduction plan. Opponents faulted the plan for relying too heavily on higher taxes and not enough on spending cuts. Still, by the narrowest of margins, a modified version of the Clinton plan gained congressional approval in the summer of 1993. All parties agreed, however, that this action represented only the first step in bringing the government's deficits under control. In 1995 and 1996 the Republican-led Congress pushed hard for a seven-year program to balance the budget—one that includes reductions in the rate of growth in many cherished programs including Medicare and Medicaid. The sheer size of the deficit and debt make some kind of actions to bring it under control inevitable. The implication of deficit-reduction efforts are far-reaching: The entire question of whether discretionary fiscal policy can be effective in controlling unemployment and inflation is intimately bound to tax, spending, and budget policies, as well as to constraints at the federal level of government.

Today, the argument has become not whether to balance the budget, but how? Some prefer a balanced budget amendment and others discretionary tax increases and expenditure reductions. This is an historic argument over the role and size of government in the economy, the outcome of which is not yet determined.

APPLICATION

Do Budget Surpluses Mean Less Government?

After nearly four decades of "runaway" deficit spending by the federal government, President Clinton and the Congress proudly declared an unexpected budget surplus in 1998 along with projections for even greater surpluses in coming years. In fact, long-term forecasts project a total of more than $1 trillion in budget surpluses before deficits return in the next century.

Has Washington really learned its lesson of fiscal responsibility? Will the national debt finally be paid off? Or will Americans get a tax cut? If you received a large windfall of money, would you pay off your debt, invest the money in your future, or just spend it?

What politicians do with the budget surplus has important economic consequences. There are three possible courses of action. Tax rates could be cut—a move that would provide incentives to produce and leave more money in individuals' pockets. Keynesians might suggest that the money could also be used to reduce the national debt, which has increased to almost $6 trillion dollars. This would have the effect of reducing interest rates and encouraging investment. Finally, government could simply increase its own spending. This would mean more bombs, more welfare, and higher salaries for government employees.

The evidence suggests that our government has chosen a combination of these options, but that the distribution of the surplus money on tax cuts, deficit reduction, and spending increases has changed over time. A study prepared for the Joint Economic Committee examined the federal budget over the last 208 years. Surpluses have actually outnumbered deficits, 108 to 100, but there have been only nine surpluses during the 52 years since World War II.

The study breaks the historical record into four roughly equal periods and takes war years and the size of the national debt into account. Over our entire history, a dollar of surplus translated to 37 cents of new spending, but in the modern era, 73 cents of a dollar of surplus is translated into increased spending. In other words, if we have a $100 billion surplus this year, politicians will spend $73 billion more in next year's budget and provide only $27 billion for tax and debt reduction. Table 25.4 shows how a dollar of surplus in one year affected the spending, deficit reduction, and

TABLE 25.4

How Surpluses Have Been Spent in the Past

A dollar of budget surplus will result in a combination of tax cuts, debt reduction, and spending increases in next year's budget. The table shows how the federal government has spent previous surpluses over our entire history and over four 50-year intervals.

$1 of surplus =	1792–1998	1800–1849	1850–1899	1900–1949	1950–1998
Tax cuts	14¢	63¢	22¢	10¢	5¢
Debt reduction	49¢	26¢	48¢	31¢	21¢
New spending	37¢	11¢	30¢	59¢	73¢

tax cuts in the next year during the four historical periods. The evidence shows that surpluses were used to cut taxes and reduce government debt in the nineteenth century, but have been used almost exclusively to increase spending in the twentieth century.

Why have these spending patterns changed? The investigators "suspect it is because the political environment in which budget policy is formulated has changed. The marginal political benefits from government spending have risen with the emergence of interest group politics." They conclude that the "prospects of maintaining budget surpluses are small," and the resulting increased government spending "should be viewed with concern" because of the "abundant evidence that increases in government spending as a percent of total output are accompanied by lower rates of economic growth."[a]

When the Cold War ended with the downfall of the Soviet Union, there was much talk about a "peace dividend" whereby Americans would receive a tax cut resulting from reduced military spending. This did not come to pass. Likewise, welfare reform did not result in reduced welfare budgets and tax cuts. Historical evidence indicates that the budget surplus will also not result in much tax and debt reduction, but will be spent mostly on increased government.

[a]Richard K. Vedder and Lowell E. Gallaway, "Budget Surpluses, Deficits and Government Spending," Joint Economic Committee, United States Congress, December 1998. Quotes are from pp. 11, 13, and 14.

SUMMARY

1. Fiscal policy is the intentional manipulation of government expenditures and receipts to control cycles of unemployment and inflation in the economy. Its role is to help provide, along with monetary policy, stable growth in the economy without inflation.

2. While from a Keynesian perspective budgets are to be balanced over the business cycle, perennial deficits have been a feature of federal finance for more than thirty years. The mounting debt that these yearly deficits have produced has been a cause of concern.

3. Automatic stabilizers exist within the framework of government finance, wherein the levels of tax receipts and expenditures vary with rising and falling incomes in the economy, although they do not replace discretionary actions on the part of the president and Congress. They are not sufficient to produce a cyclically balanced budget.

4. Taxing and spending policies of states, counties, townships, and cities have an impact on cycles of inflation and employment, but these entities have a limited ability to engage in deficit finance. Budgets at these levels tend to be balanced and procyclical in character.

5. There are two basic principles of taxation: the benefit principle and the ability-to-pay principle, where those who are more able to pay actually pay more in taxes.

6. With a progressive tax, individuals pay a larger percentage of their income in taxes as their income rises. A proportional tax takes a constant percentage of income for taxes. A regressive tax takes a smaller percentage of income as income rises.

7. The Tax Reform Act of 1986 simplified many aspects of the tax structure, including reducing the number of income tax brackets and reducing the complexity of tax deductions. More recent changes have, in general, made the tax system more complex.

8. Many economists and politicians warn that allowing the federal debt to grow as it did throughout the 1980s and early 1990s will have serious consequences for economic growth and the distribution of income.

KEY TERMS

automatic stabilizers
proportional income tax
progressive income tax
regressive income tax
marginal tax rate
budget surplus

budget deficit
cyclically balanced budget
federal debt
public finance
bonds
benefit principle

ability-to-pay principle
investment tax credit
flat tax
crowding out
internally held debt
externally held debt

QUESTIONS FOR REVIEW AND DISCUSSION

1. Mention and discuss three automatic or uncontrollable expenditures in the federal budget. How large are controllable or alterable federal expenditures relative to those that are less easy to change?

2. Name the principles of discretionary budget policy.

3. If the federal government had both a capital budget and a current-expenses budget, which budget would contain federal spending on education?

4. Name and discuss two important trends in spending at the federal level and at the state and local levels of government.

5. What is public finance? Are the principles of public finance the same as those of personal finance? If not, how do they differ?

6. Clearly distinguish between progressive and regressive taxation, giving examples of each.

7. What are some of the economic advantages to society of the Tax Reform Act of 1986 over the previously existing tax code?

8. Economist Abba Lerner once observed that we owe the federal debt to "ourselves." Explain whether you agree or disagree with this proposition, and why.

9. How would you control deficits and debt at the federal level? Is a constitutional amendment the answer? Why or why not?

10. How do classical and Keynesian views on balanced budgets differ?

11. What are the methods used for financing government expenditures? How do state and local governments differ from the federal government in their reliance on these methods?

12. Politicians usually claim that they strive for "fairness" in determining the nation's tax structure. The concept of "fairness" usually implies taxing the wealthy at a much higher rate than the poor—in other words, imposing a progressive tax. Analyze excise taxes on tobacco and alcohol on the basis of fairness.

13. Do you think the ability-to-pay principle or the benefit principle is more appropriate for the following government expenditures?
    a. national defense
    b. fire protection
    c. public schooling
    d. drug enforcement
    e. foreign aid
    f. health care

14. What are the chances for real tax reform and simplification of the tax system, for example, through the imposition of a flat tax?

PROBLEMS

1. George and James are two taxpayers with different incomes. George's annual income is $65,000; James earns $40,000 per year. The amounts each taxpayer would owe under three different income tax proposals are given below. Calculate the tax rates for each taxpayer and tell whether the tax would be proportional, progressive, or regressive.

a. George—$5200; James—$3200
b. George—$8450; James—$2400
c. George—$4550; James—$4800

2. Suppose that the table shows the country of Macroland's annual fiscal standing for six recent years. Assume that interest payments on the debt are covered by government expenditures and that budget surpluses are used to retire the debt. (Amounts shown are in billions of dollars.)

Year	Government Expenditures	Tax Revenues	Deficit (−) or Surplus (+)	Debt
1	$1800	$1800	$——	$ 0
2	1180	1780	——	——
3	2200	——	−1500	——
4	——	2100	——	500
5	——	2400	+100	——
6	2500	2600	——	——

a. Calculate the missing data.
b. What factors might affect government expenditures and tax receipts from year to year?

WORKING WITH THE WEB

1. The Bureau of the Public Debt maintains a web site at http://www.publicdebt.treas.gov. Go to the third (middle) paragraph and click on the link that says, "The Public Debt." After arriving at the next "page," The Public Debt Online page (http://www.publicdebt.treas.gov/opd/opd.htm), consider the following questions.

   Under the boldfaced heading "Facts and Figures," follow the link for "Historical Public Debt Outstanding—Annual" and answer the following questions.
   a. Between 1791 and 1986, when is the outstanding public debt at its smallest level?

      Return to the Public Debt Online page mentioned above, at http://www.publicdebt.treas.gov/opd/opd.htm, and look for the link to Frequently Asked Questions. Read this document and answer the following questions.
   b. What causes the public debt to decrease?
   c. Does anyone make personal contributions to reduce the outstanding public debt?

2. In 1999, there was a lot of political discussion about our supposed government budget surplus. Go to the Congressional Budget Office site at http://www.cbo.gov. When you arrive at the initial page, you should see a link for "The Economic and Budget Outlook: Fiscal Years 2000–2009." Click on this link. Look for the link in Chapter 2 that says, "The Budget Outlook."

Click on this link, read the document, and answer these questions.
   (Note: If you do not see the original link, then it is possible to locate this document by doing a word search with the phrase "Economic and Budget Outlook.")
   a. Did we have a budget surplus in 1998?
   b. What is the difference between an on-budget and off-budget expenditure?
   c. In the chapter on Inflation, the consumer price index was discussed. How does the "accuracy" of the consumer price index relate to the government's budget?

An Integrative Question for Chapters 24 and 25

3. The National Budget Simulator (http://garnet.berkeley.edu:3333/budget/budget.html) provides an opportunity to better understand the process of balancing the budget. Go to the site, and play the Short Version of the simulator. Decrease all "tax expenditures" by 10 percent (leave "spending" unchanged), and report and explain your result.

   Remember that a cut in tax expenditures involves eliminating "tax loopholes," which implies that a tax-expenditure cut is similar to a tax-rate decrease.

Joseph A. Schumpeter

POINT

John Maynard Keynes

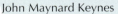

John Maynard Keynes and Joseph Schumpeter: Intervention or Innovation?

COUNTERPOINT

John Maynard Keynes (1883–1946) was the son of John Neville Keynes, a famous logician and writer on economic method. Educated at Eton and later at King's College, Cambridge, the younger Keynes developed interests in literature, mathematics, and, later, economics. One of his teachers at Cambridge, the neoclassical economist Alfred Marshall, strongly urged Keynes to become an economist.

As an undergraduate, Keynes became an integral part of a small coterie of British intellectuals known as the Bloomsbury Group. Its members included novelist Virginia Woolf and biographer and literary critic Lytton Strachey. The group provided Keynes with an arena for intellectual debate, but he still had to decide on a career.

After a brief stint in a civil service job in London, Keynes returned to Cambridge and became editor of the prestigious *Economic Journal,* a post he held for thirty-three years. He joined the British treasury in 1915 as a monetary expert and became a key figure representing Britain at the Versailles Peace Conference at the end of World War I. In 1919, he wrote *The Economic Consequences of the Peace,* a condemnation of the Versailles Treaty, which brought him international recognition. He went on to write a *Treatise on Probability* (1921) and to amass a personal fortune in the risky game of speculating in foreign exchange markets.

In the late 1920s, Keynes's interest turned increasingly to the theory and practice of macroeconomics. His productivity was enormous: Major works of the period include the *Treatise on Money* (1930), *Essays in Persuasion* (1931), and *Essays in Biography* (1933). In 1936, Keynes published the work for which he is most famous, *The General Theory of Employment, Interest, and Money.* In this book, Keynes rejected the idea of automatic adjustment in the economy and maintained that public policy and government expenditure are required for the prevention of economic stagnation and excessive unemployment. During World War II, Keynes negotiated lend-lease programs and was a leading figure in plans to restore the international monetary system. He died of a heart attack soon after the war ended.

Joseph A. Schumpeter (1883–1950) and Keynes were born only a few months apart. Schumpeter was raised in a provincial town in Austria (then Austria-Hungary) and studied law at the University of Vienna, where he also attended seminars on economics led by Carl Menger and Frederick von Weiser, two founders of the neoclassical Austrian school of economics. Schumpeter practiced law briefly before deciding to devote himself to economics. At the age of twenty-eight he produced a brilliant doctoral dissertation, *The Theory of Economic Development* (1911), which brought him recognition as a first-rank theorist. After World War I, Schumpeter served as Austria's minister of finance. Throughout the 1920s, he lectured throughout Europe. In 1932, he emigrated to America and

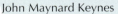

became the senior economics faculty member at Harvard, where he remained until his death.

Schumpeter stands out as an extremely innovative thinker. He rejected many contemporary approaches to macroeconomic theory partly because they were based on pure mathematical insight. Schumpeter preferred to base his theory of economic change on the creative force of the individual, whose social, historical, and psychological dimensions are largely ignored by strict mathematical formulas. Schumpeter is also known for his broadly historical views of the discipline itself, which are presented in the posthumously published *History of Economic Analysis* (1954). Another work, *Capitalism, Socialism, and Democracy* (1942), is famous for its prediction that capitalism will eventually destroy itself, not because of its failures (as a Marxist would contend) but because of its successes.

Fine-Tuning the Engine of Demand

Keynes's central work, *The General Theory of Employment, Interest, and Money,* shared one important characteristic with the work of economist Alfred Marshall: a love for abstraction. Robert Heilbroner calls the *General Theory* "an endless desert of economics, algebra, and abstraction, with trackless wastes of the differential calculus, and only an oasis here and there of delightfully refreshing prose."[a] Beneath the calculus, however, were ideas capable of influencing an entire generation of economists and affecting the economic fortunes of millions of people.

Keynes's great insight rested upon his central abstraction, aggregate demand—in shorthand, $C + I + G + (X - M)$. Unlike his classical and neoclassical predecessors, Keynes believed that insufficient demand, or spending, by consumers would leave the economy in disequilibrium, stagnating permanently below full employment. Accordingly, Keynes focused on means to increase demand through government policies and interventions in the economy.

In Keynesian terms, the economy is inherently unstable yet manageable. Guided by economic variables such as national income and business investment, government policy-makers can rely on fiscal measures to increase or decrease aggregate demand in amounts sufficient to restore equilibrium. Individ-

ual, or microeconomic, decisions to spend, invest, or save would predictably follow whatever course the fiscal and monetary planners design.

Despite the increased role he recommended for government, Keynes was mistrustful of overreliance on central planning. He wrote the following in response to criticisms by economist Friedrich Hayek that an overplanned economy represents tyranny: "Moderate planning will be safe enough if those carrying it out are rightly oriented in their own minds and hearts to the moral issue [of tyranny]."[b]

Creative Destruction

Whereas Keynes could be said to honor the economist's role in rescuing a stagnant economy, Schumpeter honored the entrepreneur's role. In many respects Keynes viewed the economy from above, from the heights of abstraction. Schumpeter looked from below, from the vantage point of individuals whose risk-taking and profit-seeking behavior spurred innovations and new growth opportunities. Accordingly, Schumpeter looked for ways to ensure free enterprise, not manage it.

To Schumpeter, the tendency of an economy to fall below levels of full employment resulted from shrinking opportunities for profits. As breakthroughs in technology or production occur, inspiring new investment and greater opportunities for profit, the economy generates growth. Schumpeter called the process *creative destruction* of profit opportunities, the continual rebirth of production frontiers.

Schumpeter naturally argued against government intervention and central control of the economy. He was much more mistrustful of the results of fiscal management than Keynes and felt that governmental tyranny would be its inevitable result. The first victim of such tyranny, in Schumpeter's mind, would be the entrepreneurial spirit. As Schumpeter summarized the matter: "The problem that is usually being visualized is how capitalism administers existing structures, whereas the relevant problem is how it creates and destroys them."[c]

---

[a] Robert Heilbroner, *The Worldly Philosophers,* rev. ed. (New York: Simon & Schuster, 1961), p. 235.

[b] Heilbroner, p. 244.

[c] Joseph A. Schumpeter, *Capitalism, Socialism, and Democracy,* 3rd ed. (New York: Harper & Row, 1950), p. 81. Also see the excellent article by Peter Drucker, "Schumpeter and Keynes," *Forbes* (May 23, 1983), pp. 124–128, on which some of the themes of this section are based.

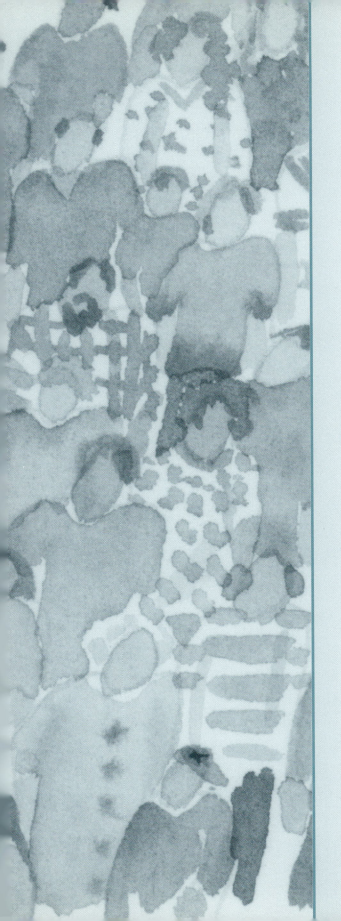

PART SIX

Money

6

Money,
Banking,
and the
Federal
Reserve

A s suggested in our discussion of macroeconomic theory, money is a vital factor in our economy. This chapter and the following explore the nature of
money and its economic role. We look at how economists define money, how
money functions within the economy, and the reasons people hold and use
money. Further, we see how money is related to the banking system and how the banking system itself is regulated by the government.

Money and monetary control are intimately related to the major goals of economic
stabilization. Conversely, lack of monetary control can contribute to a society's economic
downfall. Before we delve into these issues, our goal in the present chapter is to lay the
groundwork for an understanding of the role of money.

Economics is interested in the nature of money and its role in our individual and
collective lives. When you complete Chapter 26 you should understand

- the definition of money and the role of commercial banking and other financial
  institutions in the monetary system of the United States.
- the structure and basic economic functions of the Federal Reserve System.
- how money is created through the banking system.
- how the Federal Reserve System controls money creation.

FUNCTIONS OF MONEY

Barter economy

An economy in which money is not used to facilitate exchange between individuals and firms; goods trade directly for other goods.

To understand the essential functions of money, try to imagine what a society would be like without it. Without the use of money all goods or services would be traded for other goods or services—a **barter economy** would exist. A visit to a psychiatrist, for example, would require a trade of some good or service for an hour on the couch. Suppose that you are the psychiatrist and three potential clients are waiting for your services, each with his or her own item of specialization to trade. Sam offers four hours of typing services, Bill offers three Persian kittens, and Judy, a farmer, offers one fully dressed hog. Will the demanders of psychiatric services be able to trade with you?

Double coincidence of wants

A situation in trading in which each party to the trade has what the other wants and wants what the other has.

The result would depend on whether you, the psychiatrist, demand those goods or services in exchange for your own skills and on whether a price—a certain quantity of pork or kittens or typing services per hour of psychiatry—could be agreed on. In other words, a **double coincidence of wants**—a cat breeder wanting psychiatry and a psychiatrist wanting cats—would be required for a mutually beneficial exchange to take place. It may be that, although not a cat lover yourself, you know someone who would be willing to exchange cassette tapes for Persian cats. In that event, a more complicated set of exchanges might be arranged. But these sorts of trades would require either luck or a great deal of information gathering. Transaction costs—the costs of getting buyers and sellers together for mutually advantageous exchanges—are astronomical in a barter economy. Many mutually beneficial transactions in a money economy could never take place in a barter economy due to high transaction costs.

It is not surprising that where barter is practiced, specialization and trade tend to be at relatively low levels. The high transaction costs associated with barter inhibit specialization and trade. A modern free-trade economy could not be founded on a system of barter because of the system's limiting effects. Money emerged to overcome these limitations.

Money as a Medium of Exchange

Medium of exchange

An item that is generally acceptable as payment for goods and services.

The evolution of money as a **medium of exchange,** or means of payment, came about from the desire to avoid the transaction costs associated with barter and to achieve greater economic efficiency. The need for a coincidence of wants between traders is avoided by the introduction of money. Once money is generally accepted as a means of payment, hog or kitten owners sell their output in hog and kitten markets. They are willing to accept money in exchange for their products or services because they know that psychiatrists and sellers of all other items they consume are willing to do likewise. No longer is the psychiatrist required to search out demanders for psychiatric services who are simultaneously suppliers of goods or services that the psychiatrist demands. Use of money as a means of exchange fosters specialization and economic efficiency.

A huge variety of commodities have, throughout history, served as money. These commodities have included horses, cowrie shells, elephants, stone wheels, cigarettes, colored beads, slaves, gold and other precious metals, cows, paper, and feathers. Obviously, the best commodity monies have been scarce relative to demands for them. (See the Focus "The Stone Money of Yap" for an example of how a rather bizarre material serves as money.) Gold is perhaps the most familiar

FOCUS

The Stone Money of Yap

Yap is a tiny, thirty-seven-square-mile island in the South Pacific about 500 miles southwest of Guam. In the past, like many other areas of the world, the Yapese used commodity monies in order to facilitate trade among themselves and with the occasional foreign trader. Unlike most parts of the world today, commodity money still plays a major role in expediting exchange among the Yapese. Such items as *yar* (pearl shell), *gau* (shell bead necklaces), *mbul* (woven mats), and bottles of beer all serve the citizens of Yap in making trades. U.S. dollars also circulate in Yap and are widely used in daily commerce.[a]

In Yap, however, one commodity has served people as a money for some 2000 years and continues to do so today. A *rai* is a circular limestone with a hole in the center, much like the shape of an ordinary washer. They range in size and weight from a few inches across and weighing several ounces to twelve feet across and weighing more than a thousand pounds. Some *rai* are so large that they require a pole placed through the center of the stone and ten people in order for the money to be carried by hand.

Until the twentieth century, the stone money of Yap was used in many types of transactions, ranging from everyday trade to paying for tribal feasts and financing island wars. Today its use has dwindled but has not disappeared. *Rai* have been used in modern times as partial payment for house construction and for some large purchases such as land transactions. Its use also seems rooted deep within the Yapese culture and traditions. Yapese men still offer payments with *rai* for the right to marry to the fathers of prospective brides. An offer of dollars would be considered bad manners and an insult. The stone money also is used in making payments that settle disputes that have arisen among the islanders. It is by no means merely ceremonial, however. *Rai* still trade for many goods and services. This is, of course, the major reason that *rai* still actually functions as a money rather than being a mere historical artifact.

Limestone money is used in the island of Yap.

The exchange value of any particular stone is unusually determined. Size is not the only factor determining what any particular stone will command in the Yapese marketplace. The age of the stone seems to matter most. The first *rai* were transported to Yap from the neighboring island of Palau by raft. Generally, these are the most valuable in terms of their command over goods. In the 1870s, a shipwrecked sailor transported a large number of *rai* to the island. Today, these stones are worth about half as much as the earlier ones. Currently, there are about 6500 stones used as money in Yap.

The stones have, at first glance, some characteristics that a good commodity money would not possess. For example, *rai* are not easily transported. The Yap islanders avoid this nuisance by simply assigning ownership rights to the stones. The stones therefore need not be physically moved in facilitating exchange; only the ownership rights are

[a]*Sources:* Materials for this Focus have been assembled from Art Pine, "Fixed Assets, or: Why a Loan in Yap Is Hard to Roll Over," *Wall Street Journal* (March 29, 1984); and Cora Lee C. Gilliland, *The Stone Money of Yap: A Numismatic Survey* (Washington, D.C.: Smithsonian Institution Press, 1975).

continued

continued

transferred. Divisibility does pose a problem sometimes, which is the reason that other commodity monies have developed in Yap and the *rai* are used today in a limited range of transactions.

There are advantages, though, that go along with the stone money. The money is easily identified. Counterfeit *rai* do not pose a problem, nor do pickpockets. They are also fairly stable in supply as well as relatively scarce. Perhaps most important, they have served as a means of preserving the culture and customs of the Yapese. In fact, as a goodwill gesture, a representative from Yap has even offered a *rai* to the United States government as a contribution to help reduce the budget deficit.

Commodity money
An item that serves as a medium of exchange and that is also a good itself.

commodity money. The opportunity cost of using gold as money is particularly important. Most societies have valued gold highly as decoration, as an object of possession, and, more recently, in industrial or medical uses such as dentistry. Gold that is used for money cannot simultaneously be used to produce jewelry or to serve any other purpose. The value of gold in nonmoney uses is precisely the value given up when gold is used as money. When this opportunity cost rises above the value of gold in use as a medium of exchange, gold will be converted—coins melted down—to the uses of higher value.

Two problems—the opportunity cost of using commodities as money and instabilities in the exchange value of the commodity used as money—contributed to the emergence of fiat money. **Fiat money** is paper (or some other inexpensive, low-cost item such as lead or nickel) that is certified by government decree, or fiat, to be money. Dollars, pesos, rubles, and yen are all fiat money. Fiat money is not backed by a commodity such as gold; that is, it is not freely and perfectly convertible into that commodity. A system of paper backed by a commodity functions exactly the same as commodity money: The commodity must be stored for instant convertibility, thereby incurring an opportunity cost.

Fiat money
Money, usually paper, that is made acceptable in exchange by law; usually not backed by any commodity such as gold.

Even though fiat money is not backed by a commodity, governments have various ways of giving the money a generally accepted value as a medium of exchange. Fiat money sponsored by government is issued under closely enforced monopoly restrictions by the state. As long as the state does not allow the quantity of fiat money to grow too rapidly, the public generally remains willing to accept the money. Each individual remains confident that any fiat currency received will be accepted by others as payment for goods and services. The government contributes to the general acceptability of fiat money by declaring that debts are forgiven if the creditor refuses to accept fiat money as payment and by accepting fiat money as payment for taxes.

In the United States, responsibility for issuing government fiat resides with the Department of the Treasury.

Money as a Unit of Account

Money transactions are preferred to barter partly because money reduces the cost of economic transactions. Suppose that a leathersmith in a small-scale barter economy produces tanned leather in exchange for blankets, gunpowder, food, alcohol, and metal traps. Without money serving as a unit of account, the leathersmith (and anyone else who trades) must calculate relative prices of goods in terms of other goods in order to make rational trades. To allocate exchanges rationally, the leathersmith must consult separate markets to find out the leather price of blankets, of food, and so on. Each trader must do the same. As the number of traders and the number of goods rises, the number of calculations rises exponentially.

Unit of account
A standard measure, such as the dollar, that is used to express the values of goods and services; a function of money.

The use of money as a **unit of account** helps solve such problems. When money is introduced, all goods are valued in a common measure. Thus, if Jane knows that leather coats cost $4 each and that alcohol costs $2 a bottle, she will also automatically know that her can of gunpowder, worth $8, will trade for two leather coats or four bottles of alcohol or any other combination of goods equaling $8. The function of money as a unit of account means that the number of mental calculations required to determine the relative prices of all traded goods is vastly reduced.

Money as a Store of Value

Store of value
The ability to own wealth in the form of some item, such as money; a function of money.

Individuals who want to save must store wealth, and one way to store it is in the form of money. Money's role as a **store of value** is its least exclusive function. Virtually all commodities, including furniture, houses, stamps, Pekinese puppies, and money, serve as temporary storehouses of wealth or value. But there are better and worse keepers of value. Commodities such as perishable foods are used up relatively quickly. Other commodities, such as land, precious metals, works of art, or buildings, tend to change value relatively slowly.

Liquidity
The ease with which any asset or commodity can be converted into money with little or no risk of loss to the holder.

While any commodity is a store of value, not all commodities are instantly salable. The salability of commodities is called **liquidity,** the ease or rapidity with which any commodity can be converted into a medium of exchange. Money is the most liquid asset—the one most readily accepted in exchange for other goods and services. All other commodities take varying amounts of time to be converted into money. When cash is needed, land or warehouses cannot easily be converted into cash, but stocks and bonds (which are not money) can. Land is therefore less liquid than stocks and bonds. Money has its own advantages and disadvantages as a store of value. It may retain its value over long periods, but during periods of inflation it may be a poor store of value.

THE OFFICIAL DEFINITION OF MONEY

Now that we have gained some understanding of money by examining its various functions, we can define more carefully what we mean by the word *money*. Of the various functions that money serves, its use as a medium of exchange is of greatest economic importance. Therefore, our definition of **money** is along these lines: Money is anything that is generally acceptable as a medium of exchange. Since coins and currency and checkbook money are widely accepted for payment, they must be considered money. To these, we want to add all close substitutes. Since how close a substitute certain assets are to currency is a matter of judgment, various official definitions of the money supply have emerged.

Money
Anything that is generally acceptable as a medium of exchange.

Transactions accounts
Demand deposits or other checkable accounts that allow the transfer of funds by writing a check.

Possible confusion caused by the terminology surrounding checkbook money can be avoided by remembering that any accounts from which payments or funds transfers may be made are called **transactions accounts.** These include all demand deposits and checkable deposits managed by banks and other financial

Demand deposits

A type of transactions account with virtually no restrictions as to the size, timing, or number of checks that can be written on the account.

Checkable deposits

Demand deposits plus other types of transactions accounts that pay interest but that may carry some restrictions on use, including minimum balance and limits on the number of checks that can be written per month.

institutions. **Demand deposits** are those transactions accounts against which an unlimited number of checks may ordinarily be written. **Checkable deposits** often carry restrictions on transferability—a maximum number of checks may be written per month without penalty, for example. Both demand deposits and checkable deposits are "checkable" in the sense that either may be utilized as a medium of exchange.

Though the "general acceptability" definition is reasonably clear-cut, a number of assets, such as noncheckable savings accounts, may have important effects on the behavior of investors and consumers and, therefore, on the economy. These less-liquid assets, sometimes called "near-monies," are therefore included in some statistical compilations. Thus the nation's money supply is officially measured in a number of ways.

Two major measures of money developed by the Federal Reserve System, the nation's central bank, are described in Table 26.1. Notice that the M-1 measure corresponds to the definition of general acceptability. M-1 is composed of coins and currency in the public's hands and checkable deposits at many financial institutions including commercial banks, savings institutions, and credit unions. M-1 also includes interest-earning accounts on which the owner may write checks. Travelers' checks and money market accounts upon which checks may be written are also included in this most basic measure of money.

The M-2 measure of the money supply—one that has gained popularity in studies of the impact of money—includes M-1 plus a number of less liquid assets. These include small savings deposits (ordinarily more liquid than larger deposits) and some money market mutual funds (see Table 26.1). The M-2 measure includes those items that closely determine behavior of money holders on the basis of liquidity. Other measures are available for other purposes.[1]

You may be wondering why credit card balances have not been included in any of our definitions of the money supply. After all, if money is viewed as *anything* that is generally acceptable as a medium of exchange, credit card balances should qualify. Having $500 in unused credit card balances is as useful in making purchases as having $500 in a checkable account. Albeit indirectly, unused credit card balances are included in each of our money supply definitions. One component of M-1 (and therefore of the other money supply measures) is deposits in checkable accounts. Credit cards operate this way: The issuing company maintains checkable balances that are transferred to the merchant's account whenever the merchant accepts one of the company's cards as payment. It would be double-counting to include both these deposits and the unused balances held by cardholders.

Definitions of *money* and *near-monies* evolve with new developments, such as the recent emergence of checkable accounts at nonbank financial institutions such as credit unions. Various items in the Federal Reserve System's definitions are lumped together because they are more alike than other possible groupings. Each definition has its own strengths and weaknesses as a tool for measuring the nation's money stock. M-2, for example, may be used in analyzing economic problems where a broad view of liquidity is appropriate.

---

[1] The Federal Reserve arranges measures from M-1 to L in order of decreasing liquidity. Small savings deposits, included in M-2, are ordinarily more liquid than large-denomination time deposits, included in M-3, since convertibility of the latter into cash often requires advance warning to the financial institution. U.S. government securities, included in measure L but not in M-3, are less liquid still, and so on.

TABLE 26.1

Measures of the Money Stock, May 1999

Federal Reserve System classifications of money stock range from M-1 to L (only M-1 and M-2 are illustrated here), in order of decreasing liquidity. The most liquid measure is M-1, which includes currency in the public's hands, most checkable and demand deposits at financial institutions, and travelers' checks. Although L is many times greater than M-1, economists often identify money as only assets that are generally accepted as a medium of exchange—that is, M-1.

Measure	Components	Definitions	Amount (billions of dollars)
M-1	Currency, including coins and paper money held outside banks		
	Checkable and demand deposits at commercial banks, savings institutions, and credit unions		
	NOW and super-NOW accounts	NOW (negotiable order of withdrawal) account: Interest-earning account on which owner may write checks; super-NOW account; NOW account with higher interest and additional restrictions on withdrawals.	
	ATS accounts	ATS (automatic transfer savings) account: Interest-earning account, the contents of which are automatically transferred to an individual's checking account when the checking account falls to a minimum level.	
	Travelers' checks		
	Checkable money market accounts		1104.3
M-2	M-1		
	Savings deposits and small-denomination time deposits in both commercial banks and savings institutions		
	Certain money market mutual funds	Money market mutual funds: Investment funds managed by banks or investment companies whereby investors' money is pooled and used to buy or sell bonds or other interest-earning investments; investors generally can write checks against their fund balances under some restrictions.	
	Overnight Eurodollars	Overnight Eurodollars: Short-term dollar-denominated deposits held in foreign banks.	
	Overnight repurchase agreements	Overnight repurchase agreements: Overnight loans of idle funds, in which Treasury bills serve as collateral.	4507.4

Source: Federal Reserve Statistical Release (June 1999) at www.bog.fnb.us/release.

MONEY AND THE BANKING SYSTEM

Basically banks perform two essential functions: They accept deposits and make loans. Early goldsmith-warehousers originated the practice. Gold "warehouses" developed, often run by people whose job it was to certify the gold or silver content of coins and to stamp the coins accordingly. These warehouses were a primitive though essentially complete form of the modern bank. Goldsmiths stored the precious metal for traders, issuing a receipt representing the quantity of gold on deposit. These warehouse receipts, which were claims to gold, soon became acceptable as the medium of exchange in both local and international commerce.

A second major role of commercial banks is to make loans, a profitable but sometimes dangerous practice that was also devised by early bankers. In the beginning, the warehouser undoubtedly earned some income solely by guarding the deposited gold and charging a fee for risk and insurance. The warehouser's receipts were backed by 100 percent of the deposited gold. Soon, however, the primitive banker recognized that not all depositors presented receipts for payment at the same time. On the average, perhaps half the receipt holders demanded their gold during any given day or week. The ever-present profit motive took over. Gold (or gold receipts) could be lent to borrowers at some rate of interest, as long as some "safe" percentage of gold holdings was kept in reserve for conversion on demand. In this way, a **fractional reserve banking system,** in which banks maintain only a fraction of cash reserves against deposits, was born. The early goldsmiths issued more receipts than the actual value of gold in their vault. They kept a fraction of gold reserves in their vaults against the likelihood that depositors would demand their specie (gold and silver). The rest was lent at interest, creating another source of profit.

In performing the banking functions of accepting deposits and making loans, early goldsmith-bankers also encountered dangers similar to those inherent in modern fractional reserve banking. Lending too much money for profit—that is, underestimating the fraction of total gold reserves demanded by depositors at any given time—brought disaster. Bank runs occurred when customers became fearful that the goldsmith's deposits were not safe and immediately sought to withdraw their funds.

Two points related to early banking are central to understanding modern banking systems: (1) The practice of lending at interest in a fractional reserve system meant that goldsmiths could actually alter the money supply, expanding it by lending, reducing it by calling in loans; and (2) goldsmiths could place all deposits and banks in jeopardy by misjudging the fraction of depositors' liabilities that would be presented for payment at one time. The first matter—multiple expansion and contraction of checkable deposits by commercial banks in a modern fractional reserve system—is the next subject of this chapter. The second issue—the safety of the banking system and its regulation by the Federal Reserve System—is treated later in this chapter. First, we take a brief overview of the contemporary banking system.

The U.S. Banking and Financial System

There are currently about 9000 commercial banks in the United States. A **commercial bank** is a privately owned but publicly regulated financial institution whose primary role is accepting checkable deposits and making business and consumer loans. For years, there was a clear distinction between commercial banks

Fractional reserve banking system
A banking system in which banks hold only some percentage of deposits as reserves.

Commercial bank
Chartered financial institution that accepts deposits of various types, especially demand deposits, and that makes commercial and consumer loans.

and other financial institutions: Only banks could issue checkable accounts. However, during the 1970s, other financial institutions found ways to circumvent rules preventing them from offering checking privileges. Since then, regulations have been changed so that checking services can now be offered by the 12,000 credit unions and the 1200 savings and loans in this country. Since 1980, regulatory changes have brought these nonbank institutions increasingly under the control of the Federal Reserve System. Today, the primary difference between banks and nonbanks lies in the types of loans in which they specialize. (Actually, functions of other institutions can take on the character of banks: see the Focus "Can a Pub Become a Bank? The Modern Case of Ireland.") However, it is still informative to focus on commercial banks in discussing the role of financial institutions in money and money creation.

Both the individual states and the federal government charter, or license, privately owned commercial banks. National bank charters are issued by the Comptroller of the Currency (an official of the U.S. Treasury Department), while state banking commissions or similar bodies issue state bank charters. By law, all national banks must belong to the Federal Reserve System, whereas state banks may elect membership in "the Fed" subject to the approval of the **Federal Reserve System.** The basic role of the Federal Reserve System, a system of banks organized by geographic region, is to regulate member banks and other financial institutions. About two-thirds of all banks do not belong to the Federal Reserve System, but as we will see, this limited membership does not prevent the Federal Reserve System from overseeing and regulating the activities of all banks.

The **Federal Deposit Insurance Corporation (FDIC)** provides the commercial banks with insurance in case of default for a fee expressed in percentage terms. (Other financial institutions have similar government-sponsored insurance agencies.) Such insurance serves to add depositor confidence (up to $100,000 per deposit) against the possibility that imprudent bank managers may bring their institution to illiquidity or insolvency. It also greatly adds confidence in the banking system, which reduces the "panics" or runs on banks that characterized earlier banking in the United States.

Statistics on commercial bank assets and liabilities provide an idea of the overall importance of the commercial banking system in our economy. Table 26.2 shows the balance sheet (total assets equal total liabilities plus net worth) of all domestically chartered commercial banking institutions in the United States in February of 1999.

A glance at Table 26.2 reveals that the major functions of the U.S. commercial banking system—accepting deposits and making loans—are identical to those of the early gold warehousers. Modern U.S. banking follows the same tradition, but it is far more complex in that many financial instruments—variants of the early bankers' warehouse receipts—have evolved. Regulations to prevent problems in the banking system have also evolved; in the United States the Federal Reserve System, which was created by the Federal Reserve Act of 1913, makes and enforces such regulations.

Assets   Many of the assets and liabilities of the commercial banking system are self-explanatory, but some require comment. As shown in Table 26.2, total commercial bank cash assets in February 1999 were $259.7 billion. This total includes vault cash, cash items in process of collection, demand balances due from other depository institutions, and deposits due from other Federal Reserve Banks.

Federal Reserve System

The central bank of the United States; regulates financial institutions and establishes and conducts monetary policy.

Federal Deposit Insurance Corporation (FDIC)

A government institution that provides commercial banks with insurance against default and protects bank customers up to $100,000 per deposit.

FOCUS

Can a Pub Become a Bank? The Modern Case of Ireland

The proportion of hand-to-hand currency relative to checkbook money is low in most advanced societies. Historically, Americans' use of currency is only one-third the amount of checkable deposits, although the ratio does change over time. Other countries have even lower ratios of currency to demand deposits. Ireland's ratio, for example, was 18 percent in 1966, 15 percent in 1970, and 14 percent in 1976. But Ireland is unique in that its banks close frequently and for longer periods of time than banks of any other relatively advanced nation in the world. In fact, Irish banks closed for varying periods during 1966, 1970, and 1976 because of industrial disputes. For almost seven months (May 1–November 17) during 1970, citizens of the Republic of Ireland were deprived of the services of the Associated Banks, their branches, and their clearing facilities, which controlled virtually all of Ireland's demand deposits. Without 85 percent of its money supply, could Irish society function? Did the Irish resort to barter and the reduced economic activity associated with barter? In 1979, economist Antoin E. Murphy of Trinity College, Dublin, presented some intriguing evidence on all of the bank closures, especially the long 1970 closure.[a]

Money did not totally disappear after the bank closures. Irish currency and coin continued to circulate, and some major companies were provided with account facilities and clearing services by North American and non-Associated banks. The Central Bank of Ireland transferred currency to government departments at the beginning of the closure to pay wages and salaries of government employees and to continue welfare payments, but at the end of the closure there was only a net addition of 4 million pounds to the currency supply.

The increased demand for currency was partially offset by the summer tourist trade. Currency freely circulates in Ireland, and from April to November currency in circulation grew from £5 million to about £40 million. The North American and non-Associated banks provided some demand deposit transac-

tions with means of alternative payment, but the aid was very limited because these banks had no branch facilities and were physically incapable of handling the volume of new business. By the end of May most of these banks refused to handle new accounts. In November 1970, according to Murphy's estimate, there was a total of £52 million in new demand deposits to facilitate consumers' money demands. This was less than one-twelfth of the closed Associated Banks' demand deposit accounts! How, then, did the Irish manage to transact?

People simply continued writing checks against pre-closure deposits and against checks received from other parties. During the bank closure, checks were written not against known accounts, but against the value of other uncleared checks along with the check receiver's assessment of the writer's creditworthiness. In such circumstances, default risk increased. Further, there was uncertainty about when the banks would reopen. Credit was therefore undated.

In this situation, a personalized transaction system substituted for an institutionalized one. The nature of the Irish economy helped. A high degree of personal contact exists in the Irish population of about 3 million. Where personal information was lacking, credit information often existed at the 12,000 retail shops and at the more than 11,000 pubs in the Republic. One pub exists in Ireland for every 190 citizens over eighteen years of age. A pub keeper does not serve ale to a customer for years, as Murphy put it, "without discovering something of his liquid resources." Thus, pubs and shops provided goods, services, and currency for their customers against undated checks. They in fact formed the nexus of a substitute banking system.

Economic activity actually grew over the period at a somewhat reduced rate. There were no significant differences in retail sales and no significant deflationary trends. The important point is that information was the key to the emergence of a substitute medium of exchange. The Irish economy did not collapse or even cease growing when deprived of over 80 percent of its money. It simply and naturally fell back on old forms of transacting or invented new and alternative ones.

---

[a]Antoin E. Murphy, "Money in an Economy Without Banks: The Case of Ireland," *Manchester School of Economics and Social Studies* 46–47 (1978–1979), pp. 41–50.

TABLE 26.2

The Balance Sheet of all Commercial Banks, February 1999

The aggregate balance sheet of all commercial banks highlights the major assets and liabilities of commercial banks. Major assets are cash and income-earning loans and securities. Major liabilities include demand and savings deposits (transaction and nontransaction deposits). Double-entry bookkeeping guarantees that total assets equal total liabilities plus capital or net worth.

Total Assets (billions of dollars)		Total Liabilities and Capital (billions of dollars)	
Total Cash	259.7	Deposits	3342.3
		Transaction	656.7
Securities	1207.3	Nontransaction	2685.6
U.S. Government Securities	793.6		
Other securities	413.7	Borrowings	1969.8
Loans	3300.7	Net due to related foreign	
Commercial and Industrial	942.1	offices	226.5
Real Estate	1331.4		
Consumer	504.3	Other liabilities	324.9
Other	522.9		
Interbank loans	221.9		
		Residual	
Other assets	340.5	(assets less liabilities)	417.9
Total assets	5271.6	Total liabilities	4853.7

Source: *Federal Reserve Bulletin* (May 1999), p. A15.

Securities held by commercial banks constitute the second largest asset group. In February of 1999, commercial banks held $1207.3 billion in securities. U.S. government securities made up a full 70 percent of the banks' security portfolio.

Loans to industrial and nonindustrial consumers constitute the largest asset of the commercial banking system. The commercial banking system had outstanding loans of $3300.7 billion in February of 1999. Loans for real estate and commercial and industrial uses make up more than half the total dollar amount loaned by commercial banks. Consumer loans, for that new car or high definition TV, amounted to $504.3 billion.

Liabilities   The major liabilities of commercial banks are deposits of several kinds. Transaction deposits are checkbook money—generally accepted orders by one business or individual depositor to pay another. Recall that such checkable deposits are included in M-1 and are therefore money as we have defined it. Savings and time deposits include passbook savings accounts; these are included in Table 26.2 under the heading Nontransaction Deposits. Most time deposits require notification of intended withdrawal or invoke interest penalties for early withdrawal. If savings accounts are checkable, or instantly transferable to checkable deposits, they are money in the M-1 sense.

The borrowing category includes borrowings from other banks, financial institutions, or the Federal Reserve System. Commercial banks often borrow from each other and from the Federal Reserve to invest in interest-earning assets such as loans or securities.

The Federal Reserve System

The Federal Reserve System is the basic regulatory agency in the business of commercial banking and other financial intermediaries.[2] The Federal Reserve System has two essential functions. One is the older function of serving as a lender of last resort to commercial banks and other lending institutions—to respond quickly and adequately to bank runs, panics, or liquidity crises by providing currency or specie to meet withdrawals. The other, more modern function is to control the money supply to affect the business cycle and economic activity—to produce significant short-run effects on the rates of employment, inflation, and real income growth. This latter function developed slowly and has come into prominence only since the Great Depression of the 1930s, but it is now the major purpose of the Federal Reserve System. The Federal Reserve also conducts other service functions such as issuing currency and holding deposits of the federal government and its agencies.

Structure   The structure of the Federal Reserve System is shown in Figure 26.1. The Federal Reserve System is composed of two basic units: the 12 Federal

---

[2]It should be noted that the Federal Reserve System shares some regulatory responsibilities with the U.S. Treasury Department's office of the Comptroller of the Currency and also with the Federal Deposit Insurance Corporation (discussed in the text).

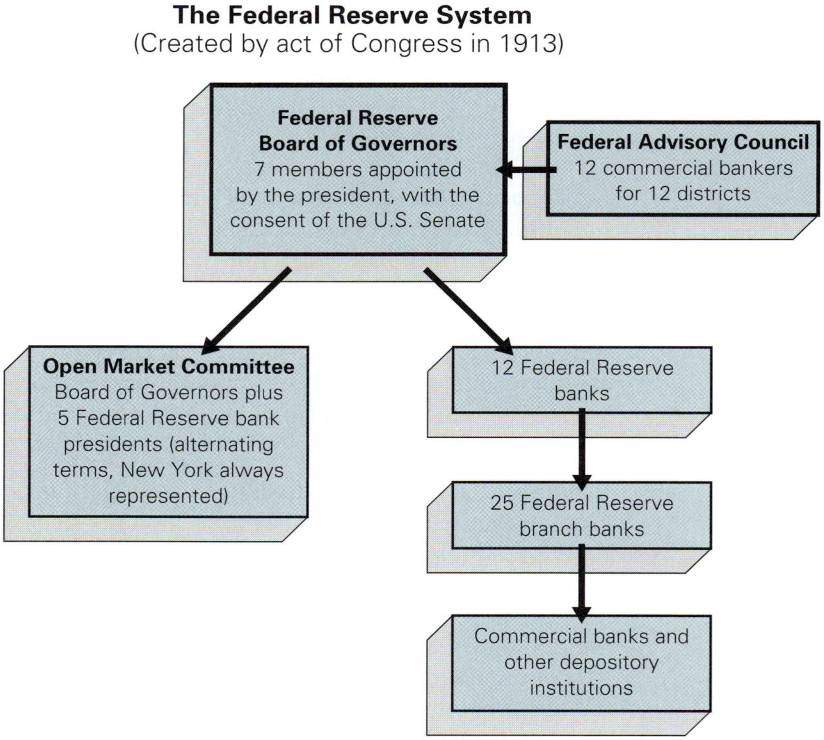

FIGURE 26.1

The Federal Reserve and Commercial Banking Systems

The commercial banking system and other institutions issuing checkable deposits are regulated and controlled by the Federal Reserve System, which is composed of 12 Federal Reserve banks and 25 branch banks. Monetary control is exercised through the Board of Governors and the Federal Open Market Committee in Washington, D.C. The seven members of the board, including its chair, are appointed by the president, subject to Senate approval.

The Federal Reserve System
(Created by act of Congress in 1913)

Federal Reserve Board of Governors
7 members appointed by the president, with the consent of the U.S. Senate

Federal Advisory Council
12 commercial bankers for 12 districts

Open Market Committee
Board of Governors plus 5 Federal Reserve bank presidents (alternating terms, New York always represented)

12 Federal Reserve banks

25 Federal Reserve branch banks

Commercial banks and other depository institutions

Reserve banks in different regions of the country and the central node of power, the Board of Governors in Washington, D.C. The Board of Governors consists of seven members appointed by the president, with six governors serving staggered fourteen-year terms; the chair of the board serves a four-year term. The board in general and the chair of the board in particular establish national monetary policy.

The **Federal Open Market Committee (FOMC)** consists of the seven members of the board plus five Federal Reserve bank presidents; the president of the New York bank is always on the committee because of the amount of major financial activity that takes place in New York City. Virtually all monetary policy is carried out by the board and the Open Market Committee. The board must approve any changes in regulations that directly affect the supply of money.

In contrast to the centralization of power and action in the hands of the board and the FOMC, the actual structure of the Federal Reserve System is elaborate and decentralized. The system is organized into 12 districts with one Federal Reserve bank and a varying number of branch banks for each district. The Federal Reserve bank for the sixth district is in Atlanta, for example, and branch banks for that district are in Miami, Jacksonville, New Orleans, Birmingham, and Nashville. The Federal Reserve banks and their branches are geographically dispersed to service and inspect member banks and other depository institutions in their areas.

Membership   Membership in the Federal Reserve System has fluctuated over the years. Assets and deposits of member banks declined between the mid-1960s and 1980, especially during the late 1970s. The major reason for this decline was the increasing regulatory cost of belonging to the federal system in contrast to looser regulations over banks at the state level. Shifts therefore occurred from national bank charters to state charters. In response, Congress gave the Federal Reserve System sweeping new powers over all banks and over nonbank depository institutions with the passage of the Depository Institutions Deregulation and Monetary Control Act of 1980. The Financial Institutions Reform, Recovery, and Enforcement Act of 1989 gave the Federal Reserve System additional regulatory powers over both banks and nonbanks. Despite declining membership in the Federal Reserve System, the system directly controls all checkable deposits in all U.S. financial institutions, the largest component of the money supply. This control enables the Federal Reserve System to control the overall money supply and greatly influence the course of economic growth.

HOW BANKS CREATE MONEY

The *fractional reserve banking system*—in which banks keep only a percentage of funds deposited with them available for withdrawals—is a vital aspect of banking behavior regulated by the Federal Reserve System. Why? Because banks are profit-maximizing institutions and will wish to make money by lending money. But, by making loans, banks expand checkable deposits and therefore the money supply.

Cash assets of commercial banks held in their own vaults or at the district Federal Reserve bank are called **cash reserves.** The Federal Reserve specifies that banks and other deposit-issuing institutions must keep a certain percentage of their cash reserves on hand or with a Federal Reserve bank at all times. These

Federal Open Market Committee (FOMC)

A committee of the Federal Reserve System made up of the seven members of the Board of Governors of the Federal Reserve System and five presidents of Federal Reserve district banks; directs open market operations (buying and selling of securities) for the system.

Cash reserves

Commercial banks' and other depository institutions' holdings of vault cash or deposits at the Federal Reserve district banks.

Required reserves

Reserves against checkable deposits that banks and other depository institutions are required by the Federal Reserve to keep in the form of cash reserves; equal to the required reserve ratio times checkable deposits; also called legal reserves.

Reserve ratio

The percentage of checkable deposits that banks and other depository institutions hold as reserves.

Excess reserves

Total reserves minus required reserves.

required reserves, sometimes called legal reserves, can be expressed as a percentage of checkable deposits or as a **reserve ratio:**

$$RR = r \times D,$$

where r is the reserve ratio, D is the amount of demand deposit liabilities, and RR is the amount of required reserves for demand deposits. (Different reserve ratios apply to the various kinds of savings and time deposits.) If, for example, the deposit liabilities at a commercial bank are $1,000,000 and r is 10 percent, or 0.10, required reserves equal $100,000. If r is 5 percent, 0.05, required reserves are $50,000.

Depending on business conditions or expected loan demand, the bank may well decide to hold more than the required percentage of deposits as cash reserves. The total quantity of cash reserves held by a bank or the banking system consists of required reserves and excess reserves. **Excess reserves** are cash reserves over and above those reserves required by the Federal Reserve. If total reserves were $1,000,000, the required reserve ratio were 10 percent, and deposit liabilities were $1,000,000, excess reserves would total $900,000 ($1,000,000 − $100,000 = $900,000). Some of these excess reserves could be desirable for the bank; for one thing, they provide an extra cushion against the possibility of default—that is, the possibility that the bank will be unable to meet its depositors' demands for cash. Some excess, however, may be undesirable, for the bank is holding funds that it could use to earn profits through loans or purchases of securities. Generally, banks try to minimize the amount of excess reserves they keep on hand.

The ability of a single commercial bank to lend and create new checkable deposits (thereby increasing the money supply) is strictly limited by the amount of excess reserves it has. Why? This is because the deposits created can be "checked away" to other banks. But this limitation does *not* apply to the banking system *as a whole.*

Money Expansion in the Multibank System

The process of money creation within the banking system is not mysterious at all. Consider some simplifying assumptions. First, we assume that the entire banking system is initially fully committed with loans. There are initially no excess reserves in the system. Second, all borrowers at all commercial banks are assumed to want their loans in demand deposits rather than in currency. Third, as in the previous balance sheets, savings deposits are assumed not to exist. Fourth, we assume that banks are solely profit maximizers and do not wish to hold any excess cash reserves. In other words, banks do not hold any reserves in excess of legally required reserves. Finally, to simplify matters even further, we assume that in each transaction, the bank granting a loan lends its entire excess reserves to a single borrower who places the loan in another bank, which then does the same thing. We assume that excess reserves work their way through the banking system in this simplified manner.

Initially, we assume that Cut and Shoot National Bank and all other commercial banks are fully committed with loans. Suppose that Monica, a wealthy miser, deposits $1 million in cash in Cut and Shoot National Bank. The bank acquires cash reserve assets and demand deposit liabilities (to Monica) of $1 million. Cut and Shoot is now in a position to lend dollar for dollar with its excess reserves. Given the assumptions described previously and a legal required reserve ratio of 10 percent, excess reserves exist in the amount of $900,000: $R − rD = $1,000,000 − (0.10 \times $1,000,000) = $900,000. With total reserves in the bank of $1 million, required reserves are $100,000.

Cut and Shoot finds a borrower, Jonathan, for the entire amount of its excess reserves. The asset category Loans is enhanced by $900,000, as are deposits of a like amount. Jonathan, however, does not let his demand deposit lie idle. He has been in debt to Yvonne of Altoona State Bank on a business deal and wishes to pay back $900,000 of the debt. Jonathan writes a check to Yvonne, who deposits it in her bank. When Jonathan's check is cleared through the Federal Reserve System's clearing-house, Cut and Shoot loses cash reserves of $900,000 and Jonathan's deposit liabilities of the same amount. Simultaneously, Altoona State Bank gains cash reserves and deposit liabilities of $900,000. Cut and Shoot is left with an interest-earning asset (the loan to Jonathan), but its cash reserves have been checked away to another bank. At a 10 percent legal reserve ratio, Cut and Shoot is fully committed with loans.

Not so at Altoona State Bank. After Yvonne's deposit, Altoona State Bank has excess reserves in the amount of $810,000 [$900,000 − (0.10 × $900,000)]. These reserves may be lent to provide income for the bank. A borrower, Chris, wants the entire proceeds of the loan in the form of a demand deposit so that he can pay off a debt to Susan, a creditor who lives in Buffalo. Susan accepts Chris's check and deposits it in her bank (Buffalo Bank and Trust). After Chris's deposit is checked away to Buffalo, Altoona State Bank loses deposit liabilities of $810,000 and cash reserves of the same amount. Altoona State Bank is fully committed with loans when it holds $90,000 in legally required reserves against Yvonne's deposit of $900,000.

Excess reserves make their way through the entire banking system in this manner. Each individual bank can lend only an amount that is within its excess reserves, but part of these reserves become excess to some other bank in the system. Given our assumptions about the continuous movement of excess reserves through the system, the money creation process stops only when there are no more excess reserves within the commercial banking system. Table 26.3 summarizes this process.

TABLE 26.3

Creating Money as Excess Reserves Work Their Way Through the Banking System

The money multiplier, the reciprocal of the required reserve ratio, determines the amount by which the money supply can increase. With a required reserve ratio of 10 percent and initial excess reserves of $9,000,000, demand deposits and the money supply can be increased by $9 million.

Bank	Reserves and Deposits Acquired	Required Reserves	Excess Reserves	Bank Loans	Increase in Demand Deposits	Increase in Money Supply
Cut and Shoot	1000	100	900	900	900	900
Altoona State	900	90	810	810	810	810
Buffalo Bank and Trust	810	81	729	729	729	729
/	/	/	/	/	/	/
/	/	/	/	/	/	/
/	/	/	/	/	/	/
All other banks	7290	729	6561	6561	6561	6561
Totals	10,000	1000	9000	9000	9000	9000

Note: All numbers are in thousands of dollars.

The initial $1 million deposit of cash creates $9 million worth of new loans and deposits. As the individual commercial banks make loans, they are accepting something from borrowers that is not money—a private note payable to the bank—and are providing the borrower with a demand deposit that is money. Individual banks can only lend dollar for dollar with excess reserves because they face the possibility of losing both cash reserves and deposits, but reserves and deposits cannot be lost to the multibank system as a whole. Therefore, we may think of this system as closed. **Deposit expansion** is the total amount of money created above some initial amount of excess reserves.[3]

Money is expanded on the basis of excess reserves, and **money expansion** takes place at the same rate as the expansion of loans and deposits. In fact, money expansion is equivalent to demand deposit expansion. The process of money expansion can also work in reverse. In other words, contraction of the money supply is possible within the fractional reserve commercial banking system.

Deposit expansion
The total amount of additional money or checkable deposits created by some given amount of excess reserves.

Money expansion
The increase in the money supply created by some given amount of excess reserves.

Money Supply Leakages

The money expansion process within the commercial banking system is limited by two important "leakages" from the system: cash withdrawals and idle reserves. In the example described in the previous section, if a depositor had withdrawn cash from his or her account in the Cut and Shoot Bank, a chain of deposit destruction could have been brought about. While the act of currency withdrawal by itself does not initially alter the money supply, the bank's cash reserves—the raw material that it draws on to make loans—would be depleted.

A normal demand for cash is to be expected, even in a modern system of electronic transfers and at-home computerized bill payment. Currency and coin are still necessary to accommodate day-to-day transactions—coins for a candy bar or soda from a machine or currency to pay for a subway ride or lunch. If this currency leakage continues to circulate and the cash does not find its way back into banks—a likely event—the deposit- and money-creating potential of the banking system is reduced.

A second "leakage" is the idle reserves that banks might wish to hold, especially during periods of high economic uncertainty. Banks are privately owned, profit-maximizing institutions, but they also tend to be prudent. As we indicated earlier, a bank totally committed with loans will fall below its legal required reserve if so much as $1 in cash reserves is withdrawn. Banks will not ordinarily let this happen because of the resulting embarrassment and possible repercussions from the Federal Reserve System or from other lenders or clients. Commercial banks therefore usually hold an additional amount in cash reserves. It should be clear that any holding of idle reserves by commercial banks further reduces the possibilities of money and deposit expansion. In other words, the holding of idle reserves, like the currency drain, acts as a brake to increases in the money supply as well as a cushion against decreases.

---

[3]The total amount of deposits that can be supported by cash reserves can be conveniently expressed as $D = R(1/r)$, where D is the total amount of deposits and demand deposit money created, R is the total amount of cash reserves, and r is the required reserve ratio. The reciprocal of the reserve ratio $(1/r)$ is sometimes referred to as the simple money multiplier—the number multiplied by reserves to obtain total deposit expansion. In the example of the multibank system, the money multiplier is 10 ($1/0.10 = 10$). The lower the required reserve ratio, the larger the money multiplier; the higher the ratio, the smaller the multiplier. For example, a value of 20 percent for r would reduce the value of the multiplier to 5 ($1/0.20 = 5$).

By now you may suspect a deeper theme to money creation and destruction than the simple mechanical exercises of this chapter. Another actor in addition to the commercial banks and the public lurks backstage. The Federal Reserve System pulls the strings that control deposit and money expansion within the commercial banking system. We have only indirectly hinted at the tools of the Federal Reserve in manipulating the money stock.

Government Regulations

Banks are for-profit, privately owned institutions, but they are also regulated by government. Their major function of creating or destroying money is of the highest importance to economic society. The regulatory umbrella over the entire banking system includes a multiplicity of state and, particularly, federal regulations. These regulations have not always been totally effective. Some regulations over the financial system have sometimes been insufficient to stem particular problems in particular financial institutions (see the Application "Modernizing Financial Services" at the end of this chapter). The maintenance of legally required reserves is but one of the Federal Reserve System's regulations. Indeed, the U.S. constitutional authority to print and control money is carried out through the Federal Reserve System.

HOW THE FEDERAL RESERVE CONTROLS MONEY CREATION

Basically, the Federal Reserve achieves control over the money supply by manipulating member institutions' reserves. As noted above, banks can lend by a multiple of their excess reserves, thereby expanding or contracting the money supply. By increasing assets, either through new loans to member institutions or by purchasing securities from members, the Federal Reserve makes additional reserve funds available to member banks.

While increases in Federal Reserve assets increase bank reserves, increases in liabilities other than commercial bank reserves reduce the banks' reserves. Increases in the Federal Reserve's stock of securities would increase bank reserves, for example, while decreases in loans to banks would decrease reserves. The difference between the value of the factors increasing bank reserves and those decreasing reserves is called **reserve bank credit** outstanding. This statistic is deemed so important that it is reported on a weekly basis in the *Federal Reserve Bulletin*. Changes are often viewed as an indicator of whether the Federal Reserve is increasing bank reserves (and therefore increasing the money supply) or limiting bank reserves (and therefore decreasing the money supply).

The Federal Reserve attempts to control the money supply by controlling the **monetary base,** the sum of banks' reserves (including the reserve in their own vaults as well as the reserves deposited with the Federal Reserve) and currency in the hands of the public. Controlling the monetary base is the object of Federal Reserve control because of the direct relation between the monetary base and M-1, the money supply. Naturally, the public decides how much currency it wishes to hold relative to demand deposits. To control the money supply, then, the Federal Reserve must control bank reserves—the stuff of demand deposit money creation—and adjust for the changes in currency holdings of the public, which also affect the ability of banks to create money.

Reserve bank credit
The total value of loans and securities owned or held by the Federal Reserve System. Changes in reserve bank credit affect member institutions' reserves.

Monetary base
The sum of depository institutions' reserves plus currency held by the public.

Currency withdrawals limit the amount of money that commercial banks can create. Sharp increases or decreases in the public's currency demands could have far-reaching effects on the total quantity of bank reserves in the system and thus on the ability of such reserves to support a certain total money supply. Factors such as currency withdrawals are said to be outside the system's control, which does not mean, however, that the Federal Reserve cannot estimate and predict them. It does mean that overall Federal Reserve control of reserves and the money supply is a complicated business.

METHODS OF FEDERAL RESERVE CONTROL

The Federal Reserve can control the money supply in a number of ways. Some methods, such as open market operations (discussed below), affect the monetary base directly. Others, such as changes in the reserve requirement, affect the ability of depository institutions to lend and affect the monetary base indirectly. The major tools of the Federal Reserve, sometimes called **credit controls,** are the following:

Credit controls

The method or tools that the Federal Reserve System uses in efforts to control the monetary base and the money supply, including reserve requirements, open market operations, the discount rate, and other selective credit controls.

1. Open market purchases and sales of securities;
2. Changes in the discount rate; and
3. Alterations in the reserve requirement.

Open Market Operations

Open market operations

The purchase or sale of securities by the Federal Reserve System in order to affect the monetary base and the money supply; the major tool of monetary policy.

The most important and flexible tool available to the Federal Reserve in its attempt to control the monetary base is **open market operations**—the buying and selling of securities on the open market. The Federal Reserve uses this tool daily to directly affect member banks' reserves. Again, when the Federal Reserve increases its securities holdings by purchasing government-issued bonds, the reserves of banks are increased. With increased reserves, banks have greater capacity to lend money, which leads to an increased money supply. When the Federal Reserve sells its securities, the reserves of banks are decreased and the money supply contracts. Open market operations are used to correct short-run, predictable fluctuations in the money supply or to expand or contract the money supply over longer periods. If, for example, the Federal Reserve purchases government securities directly from the portfolio of commercial banks, the bank acquires reserve assets and loses securities assets in an equal amount. The bank will want to turn these reserves into interest-earning assets (loans), a process that creates deposits and expands the money supply. If the Federal Reserve purchases securities from nonbank individuals, the result is essentially the same: An individual receives the proceeds of the sale in a check and then deposits the check in a commercial bank, thereby providing the banking system new reserves on which to lend.

The Role of the Federal Open Market Committee (FOMC)   The Federal Open Market Committee is the principal operating arm of the Federal Reserve System. It is responsible for Federal Reserve Board decisions to buy or sell securities. This committee ordinarily meets every three or four weeks to set trading policies, which are kept secret to avoid upsetting the plans of buyers and sellers. In these sensitive, closed-door sessions, the FOMC considers such factors as the inflation rate, the economy's growth or real income (GDP or GNP), the unemployment picture, the size of excess reserves and borrowings from the Federal Reserve, probable currency drains, and the international balance of payments. It then decides on a monetary base, or reserve target, and a federal funds rate target to shoot for.

Federal funds rate
A market-determined interest rate on loans and borrowings of bank reserves among commercial banks and other depository institutions.

The **federal funds rate** is the interest rate commercial banks charge on overnight and short-run loans to other banks. Banks often lend excess reserves overnight and short term in order to earn interest returns; the rate is basically determined by the supply of and demand for these reserves. The key point here, however, is that the Federal Reserve attempts to influence this rate by altering the supply and demand for reserves through open market operations. When the Federal Reserve targets changes in the federal funds rate, it is attempting, in effect, to change all interest rates, such as the prime interest rate and mortgage rates.

After the FOMC decides how it would like to alter reserves, the money supply, and the federal funds rate, the decision is transmitted to the open market account manager, an officer of the Federal Reserve Bank of New York. This individual, who controls the open market desk at the New York Federal Reserve and deals directly with commercial securities and investment houses on Wall Street, then implements the intentions of the FOMC. According to 1979 rule changes, the account manager has only narrow latitude in affecting monetary aggregates (such as bank reserves, the monetary base, and the money supply), but the account manager is still given a specific target for the federal funds rate.

As of June 1999, the Federal Reserve System held $486 billion worth of securities on its balance sheet. In any given month, billions of dollars' worth of securities are bought and sold by the Fed. Let's see how these open market transactions affect the condition of the banking system, expanding or contracting the money supply. There are two open market channels through which the Federal Reserve can affect bank reserves and the money supply: It can deal directly with banks or with the nonbank public.

Purchase of Securities from Banks   First consider a Federal Reserve purchase of securities (bonds, notes, or bills) from commercial banks. The effects of a $5 billion purchase are summarized in Table 26.4, which shows only changes in accounts. The Federal Reserve acquires $5 billion in assets (+ securities) but creates a new

TABLE 26.4

Purchase of Securities from Banks
When the Federal Reserve purchases securities from commercial banks or other depository institutions, it provides them with reserves on which the banks may make new loans, increasing the money supply. The Federal Reserve's purchase of $5 billion in securities from commercial banks changes those assets from a securities entry to a reserves entry in the commercial banks' aggregate balance sheet.

FEDERAL RESERVE SYSTEM		COMMERCIAL BANKS	
Assets (billions of dollars)	Liabilities and Capital Accounts (billions of dollars)	Assets (billions of dollars)	Liabilities and Capital Accounts (billions of dollars)
+ Securities 5	+ Reserves 5	- Securities 5	
		+ Reserves 5	

reserve liability to the banks to pay for the securities in exactly the same amount
(+ reserves). On the other hand, the commercial banks lose a securities asset on
the asset side of their balance sheet but gain an asset—reserves—of equivalent
amount. The crucial point is that the monetary base rises as excess reserves—those
above required reserves—are created in the banking system. Banks cannot lend
on the basis of securities, but they can lend on the basis of excess reserves. After
the Federal Reserve's purchase of securities, these excess reserves are ready to be
lent. Given a specific reserve requirement, the banking system's desired reserve
holdings, and a desired ratio of currency to deposits on the part of the public, money
creation may proceed apace. In theory, as the Federal Reserve buys securities and
as the banks begin supplying new loan funds, interest rates tend to fall initially,
encouraging consumers and investors to borrow. (A securities sale would have the
opposite effect.) In reality, the monetary expansion also depends on general business conditions and expectations for the future.

Purchase of Securities from the Public   Another method by which the Federal
Reserve conducts open market operations pumps demand deposits in or out of
the monetary system directly. Suppose that rather than purchasing $5 billion worth
of securities from commercial banks, the Federal Reserve buys them directly from
the nonbank public. The results of such a purchase are summarized in the balance
sheets of Table 26.5.

When the Federal Reserve buys securities from the public and pays for them
with, in effect, checks written on itself, the public gains demand deposit assets and
loses securities assets in equal amounts. Note that the commercial banks gain new

TABLE 26.5

Purchase of Securities from the Public

When the Federal Reserve buys securities from the public and the public deposits the
proceeds in banks, the public gains demand deposit money and commercial banks
acquire new reserves. Banks may then lend additional money on the basis of their excess
reserves.

FEDERAL RESERVE SYSTEM BALANCE SHEET

Assets (billions of dollars)		Liabilities and Capital Accounts (billions of dollars)	
+ Securities	5	+ Reserves	5

PUBLIC BALANCE SHEET

Assets (billions of dollars)		Liabilities and Capital Accounts (billions of dollars)	
– Securities	5		
+ Demand deposits	5		

COMMERCIAL BANKS' BALANCE SHEET

Assets (billions of dollars)		Liabilities and Capital Accounts (billions of dollars)	
+ Reserves	5	+ Demand deposits	5

reserve assets and new deposit liabilities of $5 billion if the public deposits all of its proceeds from the sale into banks. In such a case, the money supply is increased directly by $5 billion by the very act of the public sale. Monetary expansion will depend on banks' desired idle reserves, the legal reserve ratio, the public's desired currency holdings, and, more broadly, general economic conditions. The extent of monetary expansion due to a securities purchase does not depend on the seller of securities to the Federal Reserve—commercial banks or the public.

These open market operations take place daily and are the most flexible and efficient tool in the Federal Reserve's arsenal. But how can the Federal Reserve be sure that banks or the public will be willing to sell or buy securities on demand? Simple supply and demand analysis provides the answer. When the Federal Reserve sells securities, it increases the supply of securities on the open market in quantities large enough to affect the interest rate. When the Federal Reserve buys securities, demand for them is increased. An increase in supply lowers the price and increases the interest return on securities, making security holdings an attractive investment for banks or the public. Likewise, when the Federal Reserve places an order to buy on the open market, the demand increase causes security prices to rise and the interest return from holding them to fall. Selling securities to the Federal Reserve then becomes attractive to banks and the public because of the possible capital gains from selling and because of the reduced yield from holding the securities. Supply and demand conditions thus assure the Federal Reserve that there will be a response to its actions in the open market.

Who gets the interest return on the large quantity of securities held by the Federal Reserve? The Federal Reserve itself does. Congress permits the Federal Reserve to use this income to finance its operations. Historically, the Federal Reserve has been able to pay its own way out of its earning assets. Excess income is turned over to the U.S. Treasury. Remember, however, that the Federal Reserve is not supposed to be in business to make profits but to control the money supply for purposes of economic stabilization. The same is true of the other earning assets on the Federal Reserve balance sheet, such as loans to depository institutions. Like securities, these assets are used to affect monetary policy and are not for profit.

Loans to Banks: The Discount Rate

Discount rate

The interest rate charged by the Federal Reserve to depository institutions on loans of reserves from the Federal Reserve.

The process of lending to banks at some interest rate, called a **discount rate,** is the oldest function of a central bank. The discount rate is an interest rate (expressed as a percentage) charged by the Federal Reserve to depository institutions for loans backed up by some form of collateral—securities, notes, or commercial paper. This loan process was originally related to the status of a central bank as a lender of last resort—an institution that provided liquidity and currency to the banking system in times of sudden currency demands. Many of these bank crises or panics took place in the United States prior to the establishment of the Federal Reserve System in 1913. Yet modern banks are not immune to crises. In 1984, the massive Continental Illinois National Bank and Trust Company of Chicago, the nation's largest business and industrial lender, narrowly avoided closing its doors. The Federal Deposit Insurance Corporation (FDIC) and the Federal Reserve came to the rescue, the latter through loans and through the discounting of notes for the bank. More recently, banks and savings and loans have been closed by the authorities (but with full payments to depositors).

Initially, the discount rate was perceived to be the Federal Reserve System's major tool to avert crises. In modern times, loans to member banks and other financial institutions have performed another function as well—to control expansions and reductions in money and credit. Several discount rates are charged by the Federal Reserve depending on the kind of collateral put up by the banks and the purpose and duration of the loans. The rate for short-run or seasonal credit is lower than that for extended credit to institutions whose loans extend beyond 150 days. These differential rates reflect the Federal Reserve's policy toward banks' motivations for borrowing. A commercial bank may borrow because of seasonal cash drains, to cover very short-run deficiencies in legal reserves, or because it sees the Federal Reserve discount loans as a source of profit. If there is a wide spread between the discount rate paid for borrowing excess reserves at the Federal Reserve and the interest rate banks receive on lending out these excess reserves, banks may seek to borrow from the Federal Reserve to enhance their profits. The Federal Reserve discourages borrowing for this reason by charging higher rates for longer-run credit. In fact, the Federal Reserve may stop this sort of borrowing entirely. Whatever the reason for borrowing, lending by the Federal Reserve swells the quantity of reserves at the disposal of the banking system.

The Federal Reserve has several ways of encouraging or discouraging borrowing: (1) it alters the rate or rates charged; (2) it changes the form of collateral required; and (3) it always retains the option to lend or not to lend. Loans to depository institutions and acceptances (another form of short-run lending with different collateral required) make up a relatively small percentage of the Federal Reserve's financial transactions compared with open market operations. But the ultimate importance of the discount rate hinges not so much on the quantity of loans as on the information the rate conveys concerning the intentions of the Federal Reserve. Commercial and consumer interest rates, such as the prime rate (the rate that banks charge to their lowest-risk commercial borrowers), tend to anticipate or follow the discount rate. Along with the Federal Reserve's changing monetary base targets, the discount rate is seen by the banking and business community as one indicator of whether the Federal Reserve is following an expansionary or contractionary monetary policy. A higher rate indicates a tightening of credit and a contractionary policy. A lower rate indicates the reverse. The stock market, for one, is apt to react sharply to changes in the Federal Reserve discount rate. Thus, while the discount rate is not the major mechanism of Federal Reserve control over the monetary base, it is often considered the principal messenger of the Federal Reserve's policy intentions.

Changing the Reserve Requirement

Changing the legal reserve requirement is potentially the most powerful tool at the disposal of the Federal Reserve, but it is seldom used. To understand this seeming contradiction, remember that an alteration in the legal reserve ratio affects the ability of any given amount of excess reserves to support new money, and it increases or decreases the amount of excess reserves held by depository institutions.

Reserve requirements limit the profitability of banking and depository institutions and so are regarded as a necessary evil by the financial system. Table 26.6 provides a summary of reserve requirements in force in June 1999. Changes in the requirements (especially increases) can cause massive disruptions and large-scale adjustments in the portfolios of member banks and other institutions required to

TABLE 26.6

Contemporary Reserve Requirements of Depository Institutions

Reserve requirements have been made uniform for all institutions issuing demand, savings, or time deposits. The total amount of reserves required for an individual bank or savings and loan, for example, depends on the type and amount of deposits issued by the institution.

Net Transactions Accounts	Nonpersonal Time Deposits
3% up to 46.5 million	0% on less than $1\frac{1}{2}$ years maturity
10% over 46.5 million	0% on more than $1\frac{1}{2}$ years maturity

Source: Federal Reserve Bulletin (May 1999), p. A4.

hold legal reserves. Even small changes might create financial crises for some institutions, depending on their profitability. When banks are fully committed with loans—that is, have low amounts of excess reserves—an increase of only one-quarter or one-half percent in the legal reserve could reduce lending and money creation by billions of dollars, creating tight money and possibly bank failures. The Federal Reserve is therefore reluctant to make sudden large changes in the reserve requirement. Open market operations are far more flexible in operation and predictable in effect. The reserve requirement will always be a part of monetary control, but it will likely be used sparingly.

　　The Federal Reserve has other means for affecting the monetary base—including attempts to simply *persuade* banks that some course of action is desirable or undesirable.[4] But the Federal Reserve is always on sounder ground if it can affect the nature of banks' portfolios directly. Table 26.7 summarizes the Federal Reserve's major tools for money control and their likely effects.

MONETARY CONTROL: RESERVES, THE MONETARY BASE, AND THE MONEY SUPPLY

We have seen that the Federal Reserve has numerous means of altering the stock of reserves and the monetary base. It remains to be shown how the monetary base—the sum of bank-held reserves and currency in circulation—is related to the money supply. In February 1998, for example, the U.S. monetary base was $520 billion, while the M-1 measure of the money supply was $1.09 trillion. These figures indicate a money supply on the order of two times the value of the monetary base. The **M-1 money multiplier** is the number by which the monetary base is multiplied to obtain the M-1 measure of the money supply. This number can change over both short-run and long-run periods. We must understand why and how it changes, because the very ability of the Federal Reserve to control the money supply through the monetary base depends on the predictability of the money multiplier.

M-1 money multiplier
The multiple by which the money supply will change given a change in the monetary base.

----

[4]This kind of policy is called moral suasion. The Fed also possesses controls over the margin requirement—the percentage of the total price of a stock that must be paid in cash when borrowing money for stock market transactions. The latter rate changes infrequently, and has been 50 percent since 1974.

TABLE 26.7

Major Federal Reserve Controls and Their Probable Effects

Alterations in any one of the three major credit controls of the Federal Reserve will affect the monetary base of the financial system, bank reserves, and the money supply.

			EFFECTS			
Federal Reserve System Tools	**Bank Reserves**	**Money Supply**	**Monetary Base**	**Excess Reserves**	**Money Multiplier**	**Currency**
Open market operations:						
Federal Reserve buys bonds	Increase	Increases	Increases	Increase	Remains same	Increases
Federal Reserve sells bonds	Decrease	Decreases	Decreases	Decrease	Remains same	Decreases
Discount rate:						
Raise rate	Decrease	Decreases	Decreases	Decrease	Remains same	Decreases
Lower rate	Increase	Increases	Increases	Increase	Remains same	Increases
Reserve requirement:						
Raise requirement	Decrease	Decreases	Remains same	Decrease	Decreases	Decreases
Lower requirement	Increase	Increases	Remains same	Increase	Increases	Increases

How the Money Stock Is Determined by the Fed

To understand the forces determining the money stock, M-1, we must consider the role of the money multiplier. In simplified terms, the money stock is

$$\text{M-1} = \text{Monetary base} \times \text{M-1 money multiplier.}$$

We have already seen that the Federal Reserve controls the monetary base by pumping reserves into or withdrawing them from the banking system through its credit control powers. But recall that bank reserves are only one part of the monetary base. Currency in public circulation is the other part of the monetary base, and currency holdings by the public are determined by the desires of the public. An individual may, at his or her discretion, convert demand deposits into cash by writing a check at the bank or some other place that cashes checks. The individual's decision to hold cash has an impact on the banking system's ability to expand the money supply. It would reduce the money-expanding capabilities of the system if an individual made a permanent decision to hold more cash than checkbook money.

The actual money multiplier is determined by a number of factors. We have seen that the reserve requirement is one important determinant, but there are others. As we have implied, determination of the money multiplier must take into account the desires of the public to hold currency and a host of other factors. The actual value of the money multiplier is often difficult to predict in the short run, but it is clearly an element in being able to calculate the money supply accurately. The monetary base—controllable by the Federal Reserve in general—is only one factor in determining the money supply.

Federal Reserve Controls

In practice, it is often difficult to tell what the Federal Reserve is attempting to control—the money supply or interest rates. Although the Board of Governors of the Federal Reserve has at various times in the past stated clear objectives concerning the *size* of the money supply or the *level* of interest rates, the board has often failed to hit its targets. These failures have raised the question of whether the Fed is able to control the money supply or—through controlling the money supply—interest rates.

Any change in the money supply is caused by either a change in the monetary base or in the money multiplier; if these remain the same, the money supply in the preceding example will remain at a level of $1.09 trillion. Can the Fed control the size of the monetary base? The answer to this question is yes, though with some difficulty. As we discussed earlier, the monetary base changes when the Fed engages in open market operations or when banks borrow additional reserves from the Fed or repay loans previously taken from the Fed. Since the Fed is in total control of open market operations, it can regulate any changes in the monetary base that originate from this source. However, the Fed has only indirect control over bank borrowing at the discount window. For example, the Fed may lower the discount rate to discourage banks from reducing their borrowed reserves, but the Fed cannot prohibit banks from repaying these loans, thereby reducing the monetary base. While this complicates the Fed's control over the monetary base, it does not make control impossible. If banks insist on repaying a certain amount (say $2 billion) in borrowed reserves, the Fed can counter this by purchasing exactly $2 billion in bonds on the open market. In this manner, the Fed can control the overall size of the monetary base regardless of independent action by banks.

Independent actions by banks or by the public can cause the money supply to change—perhaps in a way not desired by the Fed. However, by making appropriate changes in the required reserve ratio, the discount rate, or in open market operations, the Fed can offset these undesired changes in the money supply—which is another way of saying that the Fed does exercise some control over the money supply.

Despite short-run alterations in the money multiplier, the Federal Reserve is perfectly able to control the money supply within fairly narrow bounds by following monetary aggregate targets. The question that concerns macroeconomists is whether any discretionary control over the money stock would be adequate medicine for the macroeconomic ills of inflation, unemployment, and lagging growth in GDP. We further analyze this critical question in Chapter 27.

APPLICATION

Modernizing Financial Services

The 1930s were a watershed in the metamorphosis of the financial system. Between 1920 and 1933, massive bank closings (both banks that belonged to the Federal Reserve System and those that did not) led to numerous bank reforms in the post-1930s era. These reforms included

- a deposit insurance requirement of member banks and the provision of insurance facilities for nonbank financial intermediaries (such as savings and loans);
- tighter regulation of bank holding companies;

- maximum interest rates on time and savings deposits by commercial banks, later expanded to savings and loans (S&Ls) by the Federal Home Loan Bank in 1966; and
- an absolute prohibition of the payment of interest rates on demand desposits.

Clearly, the stated intent of such rules and regulations was to provide safety and soundness to the financial markets, markets of great diversity and specialization. Traditionally, for example, for most of the post-1930s era, banks specialized in "selling" demand deposits and making shorter-term loans, whereas "thrifts" such as saving and loan institutions sold long-term home mortgages and were repositories of saving and time deposits (which were noncheckable).

For a time, several decades or more, these Depression-inspired regulations appeared to achieve their stated intent. But fundamental market and institutional forces would not stay still, and change was afoot in the financial services markets. Changes in consumer-borne transactions costs, in the technology of delivering financial services, and, above all, in real-world economic and financial markets created conflicts between market behavior and the rigidity of financial regulation. In particular, the drive up in interest rates during the 1970s had profound effects. Those effects were simple. When you could earn 8 or 10 percent interest, why keep so much money in checking accounts (paying no interest by law) or savings accounts (with a legal interest maximum of 5.5 percent to depositors at savings and loans)?

Since interest rates could not be paid on demand deposits at banks and since demand deposits could not, by regulation, be issued by savings and loans, a process called financial disintermediation took place—savers and investors could purchase market securities (for example, corporate securities) directly by bypassing intermediaries. During the 1970s customers were being regaled to make deposits with financial institutions with promises of radios, dishes, travel, toasters, TV sets, and myriad other goodies. A substantial movement of funds away from home-lending purposes created a challenge to the economic stability of the whole economic system. With the help of the Depository Institutions Deregulation Act of 1980 and other legislation, huge changes in the direction of freer markets were facilitated. Interest rates could be paid on demand deposits, the distinction between savings and demand deposits was blurred, and banks and nonbanks became more alike.

Unfortunately, these changes, particularly those relating to savings and loans, had a number of unforeseen and even tragic effects. As a consequence of the "deregulation," S&Ls began offering higher interest rates to attract depositors. Further, nearly all of the S&Ls in the country were members of the Federal Savings and Loan Insurance Corporate (FSLIC), a government agency that insured deposits at member S&Ls. Member savings and loans were charged an insurance fee equal to one-twelfth of one percent of their deposits for insurance coverage protecting all depositors against loss on accounts containing up to $40,000. In paying higher interest on deposits, the S&Ls put themselves in the position of having to generate higher interest rates on their loans in order to turn a profit. As a consequence, they turned from loans to local customers for the purpose of financing homes and autos to loans to high-risk ventures and to investors willing to borrow at high interest rates. Inexperience in making these kinds of loans was one of the factors that eventually led to insolvency in massive parts of the system. Such mismanagement was greatly encouraged by the existence of cheap FSLIC insurance for depositors. When you are insured, say for auto collision, you are somewhat less careful about fender-benders and other minor accidents. This so-called "moral hazard" afflicted the managers of the S&Ls, meaning that they were less careful about loan security than if they were responsible for the full amount of their liabilities.

The subsequent S&L bankruptcy debacle over the late 1980s and the 1990s is well known. The American taxpayer was forced—due in large part to *government regulatory ineptness*—to bail out the S&Ls to the tune of at least half a *trillion* dollars. (Relatively little of the money has been recovered from the owner-managers of the institutions.) Low interest rates over the 1990s, perhaps more than anything else, have contributed greatly to the low failure rates in the S&Ls over the same period.

New regulations have generally returned the financial system to relative soundness, but an ever-changing marketplace with ever-changing technologies has created the impetus for further evolution. Important commercial competitors such as securities and insurance firms—not subject to the same financial regulations as banks and S&Ls—are viable competitors to depository institutions for capital. In the wake of the S&L disaster, Congress in 1989 passed the Financial Institutions Reform, Recovery, and Enforcement Act (FIRREA), which has had the effect of forcing consolidation within the banking and S&L industries. The number of banks has shrunk from about 15,000 to about 9000 in 1999, with S&Ls being reduced from more than 5000 to about 1200.

What has motivated these changes? The quest for capital has led banks and other depository institutions to attempt to penetrate markets by providing convenient and efficient services to customers. (Such new services are, of course, costly.) This has led to wholesale mergers and acquisitions within the banking industry, as mentioned above, and calls for expanded roles for banks in Congress. In 1999 reform legislation was introduced in the U.S. Senate that would unshackle banking from the 1930s legislation that prohibited entrance into financial securities markets.[a] A Senate bill, the Financial Services Modernization Act (S.R. 900), advocates that new financial activities should be conducted by holding company affiliates of national banks rather than under operating subsidiaries of banks themselves. The reasoning is simple and convincing—bank holding companies are regulated by the Federal Reserve, an institution with more independence from political pressures than may be exerted by the executive branch of government (the president). The Comptroller of the Currency, which is directed by politicized administrations, regulates national banks. The FDIC, moreover, applies a federal insurance guarantee to banks (not to holding companies and nonbank entities). This would limit the federal guarantee and, quite possibly, the exposure of taxpayers to improper activities created by moral hazard.

The fate of this particular legislation is uncertain. What is certain is that financial institutions (including banks) will continue to evolve. While financial services are somewhat different products from shoes or computers, their efficient survival

---

[a]We are grateful to Senator Phil Gramm (R–Tex.), chairman of the Senate Banking Committee, for discussions and information concerning proposed banking reform.

must depend critically on market forces. As long as these institutions are malleable in the sense of an unfettered ability to react to changes in technology, transaction costs, and consumer tastes and desires, they will be able to provide extremely important services to the checking, savings, and investing public. But a large part of government regulation of the industry over the twentieth century has tended to restrict the ability of these institutions to provide and introduce new financial products efficiently. A minimum regulation to promote safety appears to be the most practical response to the demand for safety and security of banking.

QUESTIONS

What do you think explains the observed reduction in the number of banks—that is, a wave of merger consolidation of banking systems over the 1990s? Do mergers and consolidation in banking necessarily mean that the banking industry is becoming more monopolized?

SUMMARY

1. Money was invented to avoid the transaction and information costs of barter, which required a coincidence of wants among traders and imposed limits on the division of labor and specialization.

2. Money serves as a medium of exchange, a unit of account, and a store of value. Money's most important function is its general acceptability among traders as a means of exchange or payment.

3. Money has a number of alternative official definitions, but the one most commonly used by economists is the classification M-1, which consists of all currency and coins in circulation and all checkable deposits at banks and other financial institutions, and M-2, which adds small saving and time deposits and certain money market mutual funds.

4. The Federal Reserve System was formed in 1913 to regulate and control the banking system. Its functions are to prevent bank collapse, to control the money supply to help promote full employment and economic growth, and to prevent inflation.

5. Fiat money is paper or other low-cost money that is nonconvertible to gold or other commodities. Fiat money is certified by governments, and its general acceptability is fostered by its acceptance by the government as payment for taxes.

6. The structure of the Federal Reserve System includes 12 geographically dispersed Federal Reserve banks and 25 branch banks to serve the commercial banking and financial system. Decision-making power rests with the Board of Governors and the Federal Open Market Committee, both located in Washington, D.C.

7. Through double-entry bookkeeping, the deposit of cash by an individual or business means that the bank's cash assets are counterbalanced by a corresponding amount of demand deposit liabilities.

8. The Federal Reserve System requires that all banks and financial institutions accepting checkable deposits hold a certain percentage, called the required reserve ratio, of cash reserves against deposit liabilities.

9. An individual commercial bank can lend dollar for dollar with its excess reserves. The commercial banking system can lend and create money by a multiple of its excess reserves. The multiple of excess reserves by which the banking system can create money is called the money multiplier. Deposits and the money supply will expand or contract by an amount equal to the multiplier times the change in excess reserves.

10. The monetary base is the sum of banking system reserves and currency in the hands of the public. The Federal Reserve attempts to control the monetary base, which is the basis of expansions and contractions in the money supply.

11. The monetary base is controlled by the Federal Reserve's use of major credit controls: open market operations, loans or discounts to commercial banks, and changes in the required reserve ratio.

12. Purchases of securities from commercial banks or the public, lowering of the discount rate, and lowering of the required reserve ratio all have the effect of increasing bank reserves. Sales of securities, raising of the interest or discount rate charged to banks for loans, and increases in the required reserve ratio decrease bank reserves and the monetary base.

13. Federal Reserve control over the money supply is made trickier by changes in the money multiplier. A change in the money multiplier may be caused, in both the short run and the long run, by changing desires on the part of the public to hold currency relative to demand deposits.

KEY TERMS

barter economy
double coincidence of wants
medium of exchange
commodity money
fiat money
unit of account
store of value
liquidity
money
transactions accounts
demand deposits

checkable deposits
fractional reserve banking system
commercial bank
Federal Reserve System
Federal Deposit Insurance
 Corporation (FDIC)
Federal Open Market
 Committee (FOMC)
cash reserves
required reserves
reserve ratio

excess reserves
deposit expansion
money expansion
reserve bank credit
monetary base
credit controls
open market operation
federal funds rate
discount rate
M-1 money multiplier

QUESTIONS FOR REVIEW AND DISCUSSION

1. Explain why a money system of exchange is better than a barter system.

2. For money to lower the costs of transactions and to perform its other functions well, it must have certain physical characteristics. List and explain the desirable physical characteristics and also explain why paper makes better money than M&Ms or stamps.

3. Define money and then discuss why each of the following is not considered money: IRAs, savings accounts, certificates of deposit, and gold.

4. What is the major feature that distinguishes M-1 from M-2?

5. What are the options for a bank if it finds that its actual reserves have fallen below its required reserves?

6. By how much can a single bank increase the money supply from a deposit of $1 million of new cash? By how much can the entire banking system increase the money supply from such an injection?

7. If a bank purchases U.S. government securities from the Federal Reserve, does this purchase increase the money supply? Does the money supply change if an individual purchases a government bond from the Federal Reserve?

8. If $2 million were stolen from a bank's vault, would this theft increase or decrease the money supply?

9. "Banks do not like to hold excess reserves." Is this statement true? Explain.

10. How does the Federal Reserve System control the money supply through the banking industry? What tools does the Federal Reserve use? How does it control the money supply without using the banking system?

11. What is the monetary base? Is this the same thing as the money supply?

12. Discuss the following statement: The Federal Reserve can control the minimum amount of reserves that the banking system holds but not the maximum amount.

13. If the statement in question 12 is true, does it mean that the Federal Reserve can limit increases in the money supply but cannot stop the money supply from falling?

14. In terms of the money supply, how do Federal Reserve purchases of securities from the non-bank public differ from purchases from the banking system?

15. "The Federal Reserve is just a big cartel that is operated by the government to make greater profits for the banking industry." Give some arguments that may support this view and some that may refute it.

PROBLEM

Use the following table showing the various components of a hypothetical money supply for the United States to answer the questions.

Component	Amount (in billions)
Paper currency	$301
Coins	9
Checkable deposits at commercial banks	980
NOW accounts	2
Savings deposits	624
Large-denomination time deposits	853
U.S. savings bonds	441
ATS accounts	3
Money-market mutual funds	260
Commercial paper	35
Traveler's checks	28
Short-term government securities	98
Eurodollar deposits held by U.S. individuals	30

a. What is the total amount of cash in the economy?

b. Using the M-1 measure, what is the value of the money supply?

c. Using the M-2 measure, what is the value of the money supply?

WORKING WITH THE WEB

1. The chapter points out that all money serves as both an asset and a means of facilitating exchange. How individual types of money come to fill this role is an interesting story. One of the Focus areas within the chapter discusses the stone money used on the Island of Yap.

   Yap's stone money is discussed on the web at http://www.maxrules.com/yap.html, and in two documents within the Federated States of Micronesia site (http://www.fm): http://www.fm/naturesway and http://www.fm/yap.htm.

a. Discuss whether Yap's stone money represents a fiat money or a commodity money.

A neighboring island, Palau, has developed a unique monetary unit as well. Go to the Micronesia Center (http://www.micronesia center.com) and read the excerpt "The Native Money of Palau."

b. Does this native money perform each of the functions of money cited in the chapter?

2. The Federal Reserve Board maintains a web site at http://www.federalreserve.gov that features an abundance of materials relating to monetary policy, economic data, and discussions of the Federal Reserve system itself.

Go to this site and click on the link for "Publications." Next, find the link for "Federal Reserve Bulletin Articles" and click on that. Locate the April 1999 article entitled "Highlights of Domestic Open Market Operations during 1998."

Read the summary paragraph below the title (you may also want to download the article and read it—to do so read the instructions about reading files in pdf format at http://www.federalreserve.gov/faq.htm).

a. When the Federal Open Market Committee (FOMC) wants to achieve its short-term objective for open market operations, the FOMC uses open market operations to keep a specific variable at its "target rate." What variable is this?

b. Explain the process that the FOMC uses to keep this variable at its target rate.

Go back to the Publications page mentioned above. Click on the link for "Federal Reserve Brochures," and then on the link for "The Structure of the Federal Reserve System." Read this document and answer the following question.

c. Fiscal policy is implemented through legislation that must pass through both the executive and legislative branches of government. When it comes to implementation, what advantages does monetary policy appear to have over fiscal policy?

3. The two primary components of M1 are currency and demand deposit accounts. Has the relative importance of holding money as currency versus holding money in a demand deposit account changed over time?

Answer this question by doing the following. Go to the Federal Reserve Board's web site (http://www.federalreserve.gov). Click on the link for "Research and Data" and then again on the link for "Statistics: Releases and Historical Data." Under the heading "Weekly Releases" you will see a link for Table H.6, "Money Stock and Debt Measures." Click on the link for "Historical data."

Using Table 1, locate the level of M1 from January 1960 and from January 1998 (use the seasonally adjusted column for M1). Using Table 2, locate the levels of currency and demand deposits from these same two years in January.

Dividing currency by M1, and then demand deposits by M1, allows you to find the percentage (or share) of M1 held as currency, and the percentage held as demand deposits. Think of these share calculations as revealing the relative importance of each component, and then answer the question above.

Money and Inflation

Money clearly matters. The Federal Reserve Board announces weekly changes in M-1, the nation's basic money supply, and that announcement—which can suggest the possibility of loose or tight credit in the future—creates optimism or pessimism along Wall Street. Investors react by buying or selling stock. Buyers and sellers of home mortgages and all other financial instruments also anxiously observe the weekly changes in M-1 in an attempt to predict changes in interest rates and the future profitability of their financial investments.

The main reason for all of the attention paid to M-1 is the relationship between M-1 and price inflation. Inflation has been perhaps most aptly described as "too much money chasing too few goods," and although economists have constructed elaborate theories to explain inflation, it is still best understood in these simple terms. When the production of real output (bananas or personal computers or hair stylings) does not grow as fast as the money supply, inflation sooner or later is the result. And most people readily understand that when their nominal money income does not grow at the same rate that prices increase, they are worse off.

In this chapter we take a brief look at monetary theories, specifically at the relation between the money supply and the price level. After reading Chapter 27 you should understand

- the three components of the demand for money and their importance for monetary theory and policy.
- how classical, Keynesian, and modern monetarist writers interpret the relation between money, prices, and the real output of goods and services in the economy.

- who wins and who loses from inflation.
- some of the causes of and cures for inflation.

THE DEMAND FOR MONEY

How do economists explain the relation between M-1 and inflation? Economists argue that, like the value of other goods, the value of money—the price level of all output—depends on its demand and supply. However, when discussing how money supply and demand interact to determine the price level, we need to be particularly careful with the terms we use. When economists talk about the demand for money, they are implicitly talking about **real money demand.** Real money demand is a demand to hold or own purchasing power in the form of money (cash and checkable deposits), not just the demand to hold pieces of paper. Thus, real money demand should always be interpreted as a purchasing-power concept. (The purchasing power of a dollar changes with alterations in the price level.) The money supply, though, is a nominal variable unrelated to purchasing power. When economists speak of the supply of money, they simply mean the total current number of dollars that the amount of cash plus checkable deposits in the economy add up to. Throughout the remainder of this chapter, we will use these meanings for money demand and supply.

We have seen that the Federal Reserve controls the nominal money supply, but the Federal Reserve does not control real money demand. People in their roles as money holders determine what real money demand is and what specific quantity of real money they wish to hold. Economists have singled out three reasons or motives for holding purchasing power in the form of money—in other words, for the existence of real money demand. These motives, which may exist simultaneously, are described as the transactions, precautionary, and speculative demands for money.

Real money demand

Demand on the part of individuals and businesses to hold purchasing power in the form of cash and checkable deposits.

Transactions Demand

People hold or demand money, the medium of exchange, as a simple means of carrying out transactions—to buy chewing gum, dinner at a fancy restaurant, or a personal computer. Businesses demand money to pay for labor, materials, and other inputs. The amount of real money holdings that accommodates transactions of businesses and consumers is referred to as the **transactions demand** for money.

The transactions demand for money is related to the real income of consumers and businesses. As real incomes rise, the demand for more and more money to carry out transactions also rises. For example, a family with an income of $30,000 will have a greater transactions demand for money than a family with an income of only $15,000. This general relation is true of the economy as a whole as well. As real income rises throughout the economy, the transactions demand for money will also increase.

Transactions demand

Money demand that arises from the desire of businesses and consumers to facilitate exchange with the use of money.

Precautionary Demand

A second reason for holding money is the "rainy day" motive. People usually want to keep some money readily available to meet unforeseen emergencies such as illness or car repair. Likewise, firms generally exercise caution in how much money they hold.

Precautionary demand

Money demand that arises from the desire of businesses and consumers to hold money in order to facilitate unexpected purchases.

The **precautionary demand** for money is simply the amount of money that households and firms want to hold to meet unforeseen events. Ordinarily, the amount of money that people wish to hold against unforeseen contingencies rises with income. Precautionary demands may therefore be included with transactions demands as being directly related to income.

Speculative Demand

Speculative motive or demand

Money demand arising from the uncertainty of future interest rates and the fact that people can substitute between holding money and holding bonds.

A final explanation for money demand is the **speculative motive or demand.** Like precautionary demand, the speculative motive for holding money is based on uncertainty: Some individuals will want to hold money to speculate in the markets for bonds or other liquid assets whose price and interest rate vary. These speculators have to choose between holding money and holding interest-bearing bonds. To make the choice, they consider the present interest rate and the degree of uncertainty about future conditions.

To money holders, the nominal interest rate is the opportunity cost of holding money. It is the return we give up by holding money and not investing it in some other asset (a savings account, a checking account, a share of a firm's stock, or a bond) that would yield interest. Holding money means keeping or owning some quantity of cash and/or checkable deposits over a period of time. Economists theorize that high interest rates make people want to hold bonds. The price of a bond and its interest yield are inversely related; high interest rates mean relatively low bond prices, and vice versa. When interest rates are high, bonds are a good deal for two reasons. One obvious reason is the high interest return; in addition, if the price of bonds rises in the future, bond holders would experience a capital gain. A capital gain occurs when bond buyers purchase bonds at a low price and then bond prices increase. In the event of rising bond prices—which occurs with falling interest rates—selling bonds becomes more attractive. With high bond prices and low interest rates, people generally prefer to hold more money and fewer bonds. Conversely, low bond prices and high interest rates mean that people will hold less money and more bonds.

The speculative motive for holding money means that real money demand is inversely related to the interest rate. As the interest rate rises, bonds are a more attractive asset, and the real quantity of money demanded declines. As the interest rate falls, bonds are less attractive and money is more attractive.

Figure 27.1 graphically expresses the preceding ideas. The curve labeled L_S is the speculative demand for money (L is demand for money, or "liquidity"). At any time, money holders have formed some expectations about what interest rates and therefore bond prices will be in the future. Given expectations about future bond prices and interest rates, a present interest rate of r_0 means that the real quantity of money demanded for speculative purchases is L_{S_0}. A lower interest rate, such as r_1, means that actual bond prices rise and, as discussed above, the amount of money that individuals will want to hold for speculative reasons will rise. In Figure 27.1, the real quantity of speculative balances demanded rises to L_{S_1}.

The speculative demand for money is concerned with *liquidity preference*—how liquid people want to be. The speculative motive for holding money also forms

FIGURE 27.1

The Speculative Demand for Money

Individuals hold money for speculative purposes—that is, to take advantage of good deals in the bond market. A low interest rate, r_1, means relatively high bond prices and increased real money holdings. A higher interest rate, r_0, indicates higher bond holdings and lower holdings of money for speculative purposes, L_{S_0}.

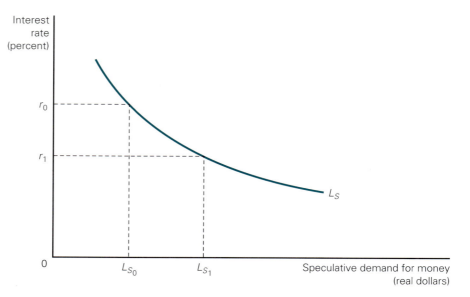

the basis of the **liquidity preference theory,** which states that the rate of interest is determined by overall money demand and supply. As we will see later in this chapter, this theory implies that economic activity, including price changes, flows from changes in the rate of interest.

Liquidity preference theory
A theory stating that the interest rate is determined by the interaction of real money demand and supply, and that interest rate changes due to real money demand or supply changes produce changes in real economic activity.

THE QUANTITY THEORY OF MONEY

One of the essential ingredients of classical economic theory and policy, developed toward the end of the eighteenth century, was the **quantity theory of money.** This theory maintains that there is a direct and predictable relation between the money supply, M-1, and prices, given a constant transactions demand for money. If the number of real dollars demanded to carry out everyday transactions (referred to by the classical economists as the income velocity) remains constant, then an increase in the nominal money supply will increase prices.

Quantity theory of money
A hypothesis suggesting a predictable positive relationship between the money supply and the price level—specifically, that money supply changes cause price level changes.

The Simple Quantity Theory

In economic shorthand, the simple quantity theory is written

$$MV = PQ,$$

where M = the nominal money supply, M-1, consisting of currency in the hands of the public and checkable deposits;

V = the **income velocity,** or the average number of times dollars (the medium of exchange expressed in M-1) are used per year (or week or month) to finance the final purchase of goods and services;

P = the price level of all goods and services; and

Q = the final real output of all goods and services produced and sold in the economy over some period (a year, a month, a week).

Income velocity
The average number of times that a unit of money (a dollar) is used, or changes hands, in purchasing nominal GDP.

One of the oldest commonsense macroeconomic propositions is that inflation is "too much money chasing too few goods." The quantity theory explains why that is true. First note that, in general, V and Q were assumed to be constant and predictable. Income velocity—the turnover of money—was thought to be relatively constant over the short run and predictable over the long run. Although the velocity of money, or its average turnover time, for money holders varied from individual to individual, its average remained constant and stable for all money holders taken together.

Why didn't early quantity theorists worry about the level of Q, the final output of real goods and services? They simply assumed that real output was at a maximum. In fairness to these early theorists, we should point out that theirs was a long-run view. Economic disasters created by financial panics, wars, famines, supply shocks, or other disruptions were certainly as much a part of their world as ours, as were beneficial economic events such as inventions and improvements in technology and labor productivity. These events obviously caused reductions or increases in real output. Early monetary theorists such as Adam Smith, David Ricardo, Alfred Marshall, and Irving Fisher neither were unattuned to real-world events nor were they fools. They knew that there would always be short-run fluctuations in output and in the employment of resources—what economists call business cycles. Adjustments were always taking place. The classical economists assumed that output and therefore income were at a maximum because they believed there is a persistent tendency to have economy-wide full employment of resources, implying maximum Q.

The significance of assuming V and Q to be constant or predictable is that the quantity theory of money becomes a theory of cause and effect. Money supply is the cause; prices are the effect. In a modern context, if velocity and real income are constant, increases in M-1 will increase prices; decreases in M-1 will decrease prices. But by how much do prices increase with increases in M-1? And, more pointedly, how exactly do "too many dollars" end up "chasing too few goods"? A feature of the relation between money and prices assumed by many early economists answers both questions.

Money and Relative Prices

Neutrality of money
A proposition stating that in the long run the relative prices of goods and services are not affected by changes in the money supply.

Early economists advanced a proposition called the **neutrality of money,** which means that the relative prices of all goods and services (how many computer games trade for concert tickets, for example) are independent of the overall price level.

The neutrality of money can be easily understood with a simple example. Suppose that, starting from some stable equilibrium money supply that produces an equilibrium price level—that is, where money demand equals money supply—the money supply is suddenly doubled. That is, we wake one morning to find that the banks will redeem every \$1 bill with \$2 and will double the value of all of our checkable deposits. The quantity theory predicts what will happen:

$$MV = PQ,$$

so

$$2MV = 2PQ.$$

If consumers' tastes remain the same, the price level will exactly double in the long run when the excess balances created by a doubling of the money supply are spent, but relative prices of goods and services will not change.

What does this mean in practical terms? At first, individuals perceive the increase in their money holdings to be a bonanza. Their new real money holdings exceed their real demand for money. What do they do to restore a balance between money demand and supply? They spend their excess money holdings in the attempt to acquire more goods. If their tastes do not change, their relative expenditures on shoes, candy, and gasoline do not change. But there are no more goods to be had. The neutrality of money assumes that changes in the money supply do not have significant effects on real variables such as employment and output; the economy is already at a full-employment level of real output. The only effect of these increased money expenditures is to drive all prices up. The price level doubles, but relative prices remain unchanged if money is neutral. Once the price level has doubled in response to the doubling of the nominal money supply, people find themselves with the same real holdings of money. Their attempts to spend excess real money stop because there no longer is excess real money. The process ends with the price level exactly doubled but no change in relative prices.

Thus, if money is neutral, relative prices are independent of the price level and of the nominal prices of all goods and services traded in the economy. Neutrality means that money is the oil of trade, not the wheel of trade.

The Simple Quantity Theory: Transmission Mechanism

The aggregate supply curve is vertical at full employment. If we now designate Y as real output of goods and services, Y_f represents the full employment of all resources. An increase in the money supply from M_0 to M_1 has the effect of shifting the aggregate demand curve rightward from AD_0 to AD_1. In the classical view of the macroeconomy, an increase in the money supply (assuming full employment at Y_f) has *no* effect on real output; for a time, the real supply of money is greater than the demand for it. People attempt to purchase more goods and services, but these attempts are thwarted by the fact that full employment exists. The result is a rise in the price level, as shown in Figure 27.2, from P_0 to P_1. At the new point of

FIGURE 27.2

The Classical Transmission from Money to Prices

An increase in the money supply has no effect on any "real" variables in the economic system, such as real output or income. In the long run, prices rise as aggregate demand shifts upward from AD_0 to AD_1.

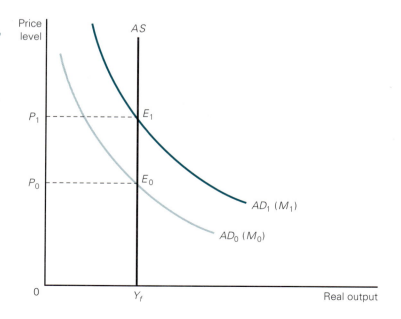

equilibrium—E_1 in Figure 27.2—money demanders are again holding actual balances equal to their desired balances. In the classical transmission mechanism, the only impact of a change in the money supply in the long run is to cause an increase in the price level. (The interesting question of how illegal money production, or counterfeiting, affects inflation is discussed in the Focus "Counterfeiting and the Quantity Theory of Money" on p. 691).

SPECULATIVE MONEY DEMAND AND PRICES: KEYNES'S PERSPECTIVE

We now consider a second important theory about the relation between money supply and prices. The classical economists, as we have seen, emphasized the transactions and precautionary motives for holding money and related money demand solely to real income. John Maynard Keynes emphasized a third motivation for holding money—to speculate in bond and other asset markets where price and interest rates vary. Recall also that this speculative demand for money varies inversely with interest rates: When interest rates rise, the quantity of money demanded for speculative purposes declines, and vice versa.

The Importance of Speculative Demand

In the Keynesian view of macroeconomics, speculative demand plays a special and important role. Assuming that transactions and precautionary demands are satisfied, the rate of interest is the product of the demand for speculative balances and their supply. This is called the liquidity preference theory of money and interest. More important, *economic activity is determined by changes in the rate of interest.*

The importance of the speculative demand for money becomes apparent when we examine the effects of increases in the money supply on the rate of interest and of changes in the rate of interest on economic activity. Figure 27.3a shows that the rate of interest is a product of the interplay of speculative balances demanded, L_S (reproduced from Figure 27.1) and the supply of money devoted to speculation, M_S. (Transactions and precautionary money demands are assumed to be satisfied.) The interplay of speculative demand and supply produces an equilibrium interest rate r_0 when supply is M_{S_0}. As Figure 27.3a shows, an increase in the supply of money available for speculative purposes—in this case, to M_{S_1}—drives interest rates down. The higher bond prices that result from lower interest rates cause asset holders to opt for fewer bonds and more speculative money balances. In other words, lower interest rates create a preference for the liquid asset, money, over the less-liquid asset, bonds.

The key to understanding the importance of speculative demand is to observe that investment and consumption might be affected by changes in the interest rate, as the classical economists had suggested. As discussed in Chapter 21, a rise in the interest rate reduces desired investment and increases desired saving, whereas a fall in the interest rate has the effect of increasing both investment and consumption. In the classical approach, lower interest rates ordinarily mean higher spending, higher output, and higher employment. In the event of unemployed resources, monetary policy—altering the quantity of money—could be used to lower interest rates, to increase consumption and investment spending, and to help bring the economy back to full-employment equilibrium if it ever veered from that level.

Keynes rejected the classical assessment. He did not believe that interest rate reductions would necessarily have much impact on investment and consumption. In his view, consumption and investment were largely insensitive to interest rate changes,

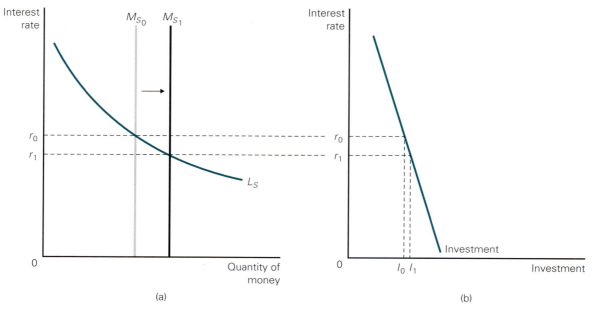

FIGURE 27.3

Money Supply, Interest Rates, and Investment Spending
In the Keynesian framework, an increase in the money supply for speculative balances
may succeed in lowering the interest rate (a), which may increase investment spending in
the economy (b). Keynes thought these events unlikely in a depression economy, however.

being autonomous or more responsive to changes in income. In Figure 27.3b, increases
in the money supply from M_{S_0} to M_{S_1} produce a small reduction in the rate of interest from r_0 to r_1. These reductions in the interest rate may have an impact on investment, but this effect depends on the responsiveness of investment to changes in the
interest rate. Keynes believed that individuals would be hesitant to invest in bonds
(or in durable consumption goods—big-ticket items) in periods of economic distress.
Uncertainty about economic conditions would cause people to hold money even
though bond prices were falling (making bonds "a good deal"). Likewise, businesses
would exercise extreme caution about investments in new capital in the midst of recessions or depressions. In short, investment would not be very responsive to reductions
in the interest rate. Figures 27.3a and 27.3b show that interest rate reductions would
increase investment only slightly, from I_0 to I_1. Monetary policy, in Keynes's view,
would not be a very effective way to nudge the economy toward full employment.

Money and Prices: The Keynesian Transmission Mechanism

What does Keynes's view mean for the short-run relation between the money supply and prices? The addition of speculative demand to the transactions and precautionary demand for money short-circuits the cause-and-effect relation between
the money supply and prices. Increases in the money supply may have little or no
effect on the price level if the spending generated by an interest rate decrease is
small or nonexistent.

FOCUS

Counterfeiting and the Quantity Theory of Money

Throughout history, counterfeiting has been a critical economic problem for both governments and private money issuers. Successful counterfeiting obviously takes the control over the quantity of money from the money producer. In order to increase costs to counterfeiters, governments have taken extraordinary measures over the years to make their currency and coin unique. Benjamin Franklin had some unusual suggestions for making early U.S. currency difficult to counterfeit: Reproduce an actual leaf with a unique and intricate pattern of veins and intentionally misspell words on the currency. Modern producers of money use unique papers, ink, design, and printing techniques to foil would-be counterfeiters.

The counterfeiting operations depicted in movies and on television usually consist of one or two small-time criminals printing small bills on a basement printing press. Therefore, most people have probably never considered the possibility that nations can use counterfeiting to wage economic warfare on each other. Because one of the principal advantages of using money is to help eliminate the transactions costs of barter, successful counterfeiting can quickly reduce an economy to the most primitive forms of exchange. As exchange breaks down, so does production and specialization. Goods are hoarded in anticipation of still higher prices; chaos reigns.

Many examples of such economic warfare may be cited. Both sides in the U.S. Civil War made stabs at replicating the other side's currency. The United States and allied governments were reported to have made attempts to disrupt the currency system of Nazi Germany. There are contemporary examples as well. For example, it was alleged in the early 1990s that the government of Iran was printing and circulating (through Syria) U.S. $100 bills in an attempt to ease its budget deficit and to disrupt U.S. foreign exchange markets abroad. Counterfeit bills of excellent quality appeared outside the U.S. banking system in European markets. The same bills, often making up as much as 30 percent of given deposits of laundered drug money *within* the U.S. banking system, apparently slipped by commercial banks and the Federal Reserve System's sorting equipment as well. Western nations got into the act and apparently printed and introduced into Iraq's economy vast quantities of Iraqi currency. New U.S. $100 bills were introduced into circulation in 1996 and new $50 and $20 bills in 1998 with newer safeguards against counterfeiting. Other new bills are to follow. But warfare will continue.

Currency warfare is evidence that virtually all governments have an implicit understanding, however crude, of the quantity theory of money. Counterfeiting obviously creates "runaway" inflation—any overzealous use of the printing press does—and unrestrained increases in the money supply can eventually reduce an economy to primitive economic conditions and negative economic growth.

Keynes's view of the transmission from money to prices is depicted in Figure 27.4. *If* increases in M-1 actually do cause interest rates to fall and *if* the fall in interest rates causes investment and consumption to increase, total expenditures would increase and aggregate demand would shift rightward. As we have seen, Keynes believed that in the presence of uncertainty about economic conditions money holders, consumers, and investors would hold on to speculative money balances and postpone purchases of consumer and investment goods. We show these effects with a minimal increase in aggregate demand and small increases in real output in the economy for a change in the money supply from M_0 to M_1 in Figure 27.4. Clearly, the Keynesian prescription for economic recovery had to rely on other factors affecting total spending and aggregate demand—namely, increases in government spending and/or reductions in taxes.

FIGURE 27.4

The Keynesian Transmission Mechanism

Keynes did not have much faith that monetary expansion could increase real output and employment during recessions or depressions. As the money supply increases, investors (and consumers) *might* increase spending *if* the interest rate actually falls. Aggregate demand increases, however, would likely be insignificant.

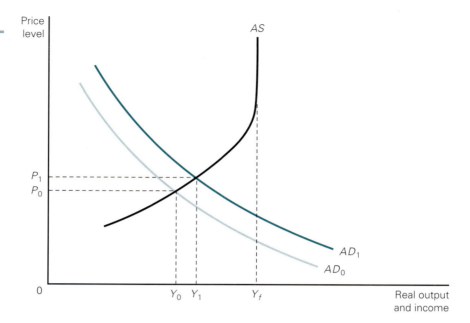

MODERN MONETARISM AND INFLATION

Recall that inflation is a rate of increase in prices, not a simple rise in the price level. In a static framework, it is sometimes convenient to say, as we did using the simple quantity theory, that a doubling of M produces a doubling of P and to identify this once-and-for-all change as inflation. In a dynamic real-world setting, however, the money supply is constantly being increased or decreased by the Federal Reserve Board at some rate per week, month, or year. Likewise, prices are rising or falling at some rate. Real income is also changing, by values typically expressed in terms of growth rates such as 3 percent per year, although in the present simple discussion of the inflation process we assume a constant income growth rate. To arrive at the modern conception of inflation, therefore, we must adapt the static quantity theory to a dynamic setting.

The Process of Inflation

The simple process of inflation is best understood by starting from a dynamic equilibrium position in the economy. In this initial position, the economy is characterized by the following conditions.

Rate of monetary expansion

The annual percentage by which the nominal money supply is changing.

1. There is a constant **rate of monetary expansion** (whether 3 percent or 50 percent growth in the money stock, M-1, per year—the actual percentage is not important as long as it is constant).

2. Expected and actual inflation rates are equal, and further, market participants will expect the inflation rate to be exactly what it has been in the present and recent past.

3. The nominal rate of interest equals the real rate of interest plus the constant inflation rate. Since the inflation rate has been constant in the most recent past

experience, the inflation rate (and therefore the nominal rate of interest) is expected to be the same in the future.

4. People are actually holding real cash balances equivalent to their desired holdings of money balances. The quantity demanded of money is equal to the quantity supplied of money in real terms.

5. Real income or real GDP is growing at a constant rate.

If we numerically express the percentage rates of change of the items in the quantity theory, we can calculate a rate of change in prices. If, for example, the monetary expansion rate, which we now designate with a dot on top of M, or $\dot{M}$, is 12 percent, and the constant growth rate in real income, $\dot{Q}$, is 4 percent, and velocity V is constant ($\dot{V}$ is thus zero), the inflation rate $\dot{P}$ is easily calculated. The dynamic quantity theory becomes

$$\dot{M} + \dot{V} = \dot{P} + \dot{Q},$$

or, given the hypothetical numbers,

$$12\% + 0\% = \dot{P} + 4\%,$$

$$\dot{P} = 12\% - 4\% = 8\% \text{ inflation rate.}$$

The inflation rate is thus calculated as 8 percent.

The exercise of casting the quantity theory into rates of change might seem mechanical so far, but it is invaluable in providing a simple understanding of inflation as a process. To initiate the inflation process we need simply to suppose that the Federal Reserve, through its powers over the monetary base, suddenly increases the rate of monetary expansion from 12 percent to 15 percent. Further, the Federal Reserve maintains the rate of monetary expansion at 15 percent from that point forward and forever.

Figure 27.5 illustrates what happens. The new, higher growth rate in the money supply initially creates disequilibrium among money holders. After the expansion, but before prices begin rising faster, money demanders find themselves holding more real money balances than they want to hold. Consumers and businesses will attempt to rid themselves of these excess balances by spending more on all goods and services.

What, however, is the long-term impact of the increased spending on real income and employment? Because output and employment were already growing at a constant full-employment rate, the attempt to purchase more goods will only drive up prices and money income more rapidly. Thus the actual inflation rate begins to rise. Because it takes time for higher actual inflation rates to be translated into expectations of higher inflation, higher expected inflation rates will lag behind the actual rate.

It is easy to predict what will happen next. Since the nominal interest rate equals the real interest rate (which we assume to remain constant) plus the expected inflation rate, nominal rates begin to climb. This rise in the nominal rate affects the desired real holdings of money. Since the real demand of money is partially a function of the nominal interest rate (the opportunity cost of holding money), the higher interest rate generated by higher inflation expectations leads to lower desired money holdings. This effect reinforces the attempt of money holders to rid themselves of cash balances. That is, the higher nominal rate further fans the rise in the inflation rate.

FIGURE 27.5

How the Fire of Inflation Gets Fanned

The process of inflation begins with an increased rate of M-1 expansion by the Federal Reserve. Excess money holdings are spent, creating higher actual inflation and higher expected inflation. Higher expected inflation causes higher market interest rates, further increasing spending and inflation. The process continues until the Federal Reserve stabilizes the rate of growth in M-1.

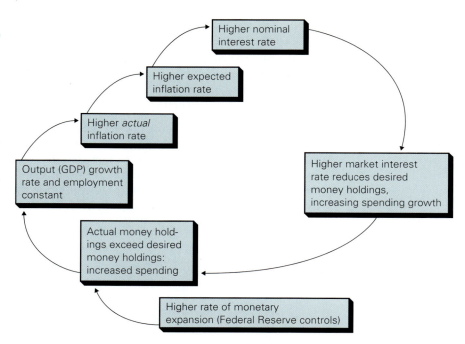

When does the process stop? When is a dynamic equilibrium reattained? The process will stop only if the Federal Reserve sticks to a constant rate of monetary expansion (15 percent in our example). The process of increasing inflation rates will continue only if the Federal Reserve continues to increase the rate of money creation. If the Federal Reserve holds the rate to 15 percent, for example, equilibrium will be reattained at a new constant inflation rate, a new nominal interest rate, and a new rate of price expectations equal to the actual inflation rate. In the numerical terms of our example, equilibrium will take place when

$$\dot{M} + \dot{V} = \dot{P} + \dot{Q},$$

or

$$15\% + 0\% = 11\% + 4\%.$$

Here, inflation is 11%. Prices must rise, in other words, so that *actual* real money holdings are equivalent to *desired* real money holdings. Spending and the inflation rate will rise until real money demand equals money supply. This process goes on continuously (see the Focus "From Truman to Clinton: Fifty Years of Price Changes").

Some Preliminary Lessons About Inflation

Monetarism

A theory that centers on money supply growth, real money demand, nominal and real interest rates, and inflationary expectations in explaining the process of inflation or deflation.

The preceding explanation of inflation is a central tenet in an economic school of thought called **monetarism.** The monetarist view of inflation contains certain explicit and implicit lessons. First and foremost, monetarists argue that inflation is

FOCUS

From Truman to Clinton: Fifty Years of Price Changes

Inflation renders historical comparisons of prices and values misleading. The great Babe Ruth made a salary of $90,000 in 1933, while today the average baseball player salary is well over one million dollars. A house purchased in California after World War II is now worth about one million dollars today. In the early 1800s, President Thomas Jefferson made the Louisiana Purchase, which included more than half the land west of the Mississippi River, for $15 million dollars.

Economists use price indexes in an attempt to gauge the value or purchasing power of money over time. These price indexes reflect the average price level changes from one time period to the next. In Table 27.1, the prices of goods during the presidency of Harry Truman are compared with current prices using the consumer price index (CPI). The CPI measures changes in inflation over time and helps us compare prices from one time period to the next. Over the last fifty years, prices are now 6.93 times as high as they were when Harry Truman was inaugurated.

However, not all prices change in the same manner. The inflation-adjusted prices of groceries such as flour, coffee, and eggs have *fallen*, along with movie tickets and home appliances such as washing machines. The inflation-adjusted price of eggs has declined by 75 percent. The prices of wool suits and mufflers have stayed roughly the same, while the price of Coca-Cola has risen. The inflation-adjusted price of first-class postage stamps from the Post Office has risen the most—an increase of 136 percent after adjusting for inflation. If we adjust Babe Ruth's salary of $90,000, it would exceed one million current dollars but would nevertheless fall far short of the $10 million that some current superstars take home.

TABLE 27.1

Prices of Selected Goods in 1949 and 1999

The actual price of most goods in this sample has declined when Truman-era dollars are translated into Clinton-era dollars. A big exception is postage stamps.

Item	1949 Price (Truman dollars)	Equivalent Number of Clinton Dollars	1999 Price (Clinton dollars)
Flour (10 lb)	$0.83	$5.75	$3.39
Eight O'Clock coffee (1 lb)	$1.15	$7.96	$3.29
Lean ground beef (1 lb)	$0.45	$3.12	$2.49
Dozen eggs (large)	$0.57	$3.95	$0.99
Coca-Cola (12 oz)	$0.05	$0.35	$0.50
Wool suit	$39.75	$275.49	$295.00
Muffler	$4.95	$34.30	$29.95
Movie ticket (adult)	$1.32	$9.15	$6.00
Washing machine (Hotpoint)	$119.95	$831.25	$299.00
Postage stamp (first class)	$0.02	$0.14	$0.33

always a monetary phenomenon. Economists Milton Friedman and Anna Schwartz have supported this proposition with massive hundred-year empirical studies of the quantity theory in the United States and England.[1] The villain in the monetarists' inflation scenario is expansionist policies pursued by the monetary authority that controls the money stock.

In the monetarist version of events, for example, high interest rates do not cause inflation; rather, they are the *result* of inflation. What we did not mention in our simplified treatment is that one short-lived initial effect of the Federal Reserve's monetary expansion is a temporary decline in market interest rates. Of course, the market rates begin to rise as expectations of higher inflation take hold of borrowers and lenders. Observers and politicians often make the mistake of arguing that the money stock growth rate should be expanded to lower the interest rates. As we have seen, however, the monetarists show that such a shortsighted policy will have the opposite effect: Increasing the rate of expansion of the money supply will soon raise nominal interest rates. Higher interest rates follow higher inflation rates, but higher monetary expansion is necessary for both events to occur.

Many people also think that inflation is self-generating. Higher nominal interest rates do affect desired money balances and spending. But in the monetarist view, this process must come to an end if the central bank holds the money expansion to a constant rate. It may, of course, take time for inflationary expectations to adjust between consumers and producers, borrowers and lenders, and employers and employees, but when the market adjusts, a dynamic equilibrium will be attained.

It is very important to note that an increased rate of monetary expansion *will* have some short-run effects on the economy. Specifically, the Federal Reserve can temporarily lower both the nominal and the real rates of interest, thereby creating a *temporary* surge in total spending. This might have short-term effects on output and employment as well if employment is not growing at a full-employment rate (or if overfull employment is a temporary possibility). If the economy is at or near full employment, however, the inevitable result in the monetarist view is a higher rate of inflation. A contemporary school of macroeconomics called *rational expectations theory* goes one step further than monetarism on the matter of even the short-run possibility of monetary policy having any real effects on the economy. As discussed in Chapter 28, rational expectations theory is based on the belief that monetary policy can have no effects on real output or employment because all of the effects of policy are fully anticipated by market participants.

INFLATION

Several measures of inflation are used in the real world to guide policy-making. Both a consumer price index and a producer price index are calculated by the Bureau of Labor Statistics. A third major index is the implicit price deflator, which is a means of converting nominal GDP values into real GDP values. No matter what measure is used, the presence of higher indexes over time indicates a rising price level. Actual U.S. inflation rates between 1960 and 1998 are shown in Table 27.2.

---

[1]See Milton Friedman and Anna J. Schwartz, *A Monetary History of the United States* (Princeton, N.J.: Princeton University Press, 1963).

TABLE 27.2

Two Measures of Inflation, 1960-1998

Two popular measures of inflation used in the United States are the implicit price deflator, a means for converting nominal GDP into real values, and the consumer price index, which bases the inflation rate on price changes in some hypothetical market basket of consumer goods. The numbers given for both indexes are annual rates.

	INFLATION RATE AS MEASURED BY			INFLATION RATE AS MEASURED BY	
Year	Implicit Price Deflator	Consumer Price Index	Year	Implicit Price Deflator	Consumer Price Index
1960	1.5	1.7	1980	9.2	13.5
1961	1.3	1.0	1981	9.2	10.3
1962	1.3	1.0	1982	6.3	6.2
1963	1.2	1.3	1983	4.2	3.2
1964	1.5	1.3	1984	3.9	4.3
1965	2.0	1.6	1985	3.3	3.6
1966	2.9	2.9	1986	2.7	1.9
1967	3.1	3.1	1987	3.1	3.6
1968	4.3	4.2	1988	3.7	4.1
1969	4.7	5.5	1989	4.2	4.8
1970	5.4	5.7	1990	4.3	5.4
1971	5.2	4.4	1991	4.0	4.2
1972	4.3	3.2	1992	2.8	3.0
1973	5.7	6.2	1993	2.6	3.0
1974	8.7	11.0	1994	2.4	2.6
1975	9.6	9.1	1995	2.3	2.8
1976	5.6	5.8	1996	1.9	3.0
1977	6.3	6.5	1997	1.9	2.3
1978	7.7	7.6	1998	0.9	1.6
1979	8.5	11.3			

Source: Council of Economic Advisers, *Economic Report of the President* (Washington, D.C.: U.S. Government Printing Office, 1999), pp. 331,399.

The Effects of Inflation

The statistical presence of inflation in the economy tells us little about the costs and other distortions it inflicts there. Runaway inflation of 80 or 2000 percent per month or per year, such as that sometimes experienced in war-torn or developing countries with low or severely restricted stocks of goods and services, can reduce an economy to barter or cause it to collapse altogether. Milder inflation—3 to 15 percent per year—also creates economic costs in any advanced economy. The full effects of increases in inflation rates may take some time to be fully realized, so inflation has both short- and long-run effects.

Inflation, Fixed Incomes, and Assets   The most publicized effect of inflation is the redistributive impact it has between specific groups in society. Inflation affects those who can least afford to pay for it—the sick, the poor, and especially the elderly and others on fixed incomes—through erosions of purchasing power. Congress, in recent years of inflation, indexed or "tied" Social Security and other welfare benefits to a price level index, thereby alleviating some of the problems inflation causes for the retired or the aged. Nevertheless, inflation is a constant threat to the most economically vulnerable groups in society.

Inflation also adversely affects holders of assets denominated in nominal, or money, terms as opposed to real terms. Suppose you purchase a house—a real asset—and hold it for five years, over which time the price level doubles because of inflation. What happens to the nominal value of your investment? Excluding the real factors of natural appreciation and depreciation that might take place over the five years (resulting from the location, deterioration of property, and so on), the money value of your house should closely follow the inflation rate over the period, doubling at the end of the five years.

While the value of real assets tends to follow inflation, the value of money-denominated assets may not. Suppose that you lend a friend $10,000, to be paid at the end of a five-year period, and that your friend issues you a promissory note attesting to the loan. Again suppose that the price level doubles over the five-year span because of inflation. Aside from any interest paid by your friend, what has happened to the real value of your asset? Although the nominal value of the note remains at $10,000, the real value is only half of what it was at the beginning of the five-year period. You will now be able to purchase only half the goods and services that you could have bought before you made the loan. Capital gains or losses—changes in real value—are always associated with holding any kind of asset in the face of unanticipated inflation. Real assets generally gain in value, whereas money assets—those expressed in fixed money terms—generally lose value. Naturally, all of these occurrences are reversed when deflation is considered. Only rarely has deflation been a problem in the United States, but with very low inflation rates in the late 1990s, some economists feel a threat (see the Focus "Deflation: Malignant or Benign?").

Disruptive Expectations   A second major effect of inflation is that it distorts expectations of inflation, wage rates, and interest rates. When the inflation rate is not perfectly anticipated, workers and employers, buyers and sellers of goods and services, and borrowers and lenders will be uncertain of future real values. Since these transactors will generally make mistakes in forecasting the effects of inflation in specific markets, there will be continuous and unanticipated transfers of wealth among workers and employers, buyers and sellers, borrowers and lenders.

Escalator clauses

Provisions of labor contracts that tie changes in nominal wages to changes in some price index.

Market participants try to protect themselves, of course. Workers belonging to labor unions often bargain for **escalator clauses** in their contracts, provisions that tie future wages to some index of the price level as a hedge against inflation.

Inflation and expectations of the rate of inflation also affect nominal interest rates. When the inflation rate fluctuates, so do expectations of inflation as well as nominal and real interest rates. These changes can have severe effects on the economic well-being of various groups and individuals in the economy by altering the real value of indebtedness. In the late 1970s, for example, unexpected infla-

FOCUS

Deflation: Malignant or Benign?

Inflation in the United States and many other industrial nations has declined from double-digit rates in the 1970s and 1980s to the single-digit levels in the 1990s. Inflation in the United States as measured by the consumer price index was only 1.6 percent in 1998.

This decline in the problem of inflation is hailed as a great achievement in economic policy, but it has led many economists and central bankers, especially those who believe in the Phillips curve, or an inverse relation between unemployment and inflation (see Chapter 29 for an extended discussion), to turn their attention and concern to the potential problems of deflation. It is well known, for example, that deflation accompanied the Depression of 1921, the Great Depression of the 1930s, and many of the banking panics and crashes of the 1800s.

Deflation, however, need not be a recipe for economic disaster. There are two types of deflation. The malignant form of deflation involves sharp and severe decreases in prices and is associated with economic depression and liquidation of stock markets, such as occurred during America's Great Depression. In contrast, the benign form of deflation is mild and is associated with economic growth and widespread prosperity.[a]

For example, America was highly prosperous during the nineteenth century when we were on the classical gold standard (i.e., when gold coins served as the medium of exchange). During this period, Americans experienced this mild or benign form of deflation because it was a period when the economy tended to grow slightly faster than the supply of gold. This increased the purchasing power of gold and caused a deflation of prices for goods and services. Deflation of this form contributes to economic growth for several reasons. First, it is beneficial to savers and bondholders and thus helps stimulate savings. Second, it helps to spread the benefits of increased productivity and increased labor, because the nominal wages of labor gain increased purchasing power over time. Most importantly, mild deflation, like zero or low inflation, provides the business confidence that monetary stability brings.

Scientifically viewed, even malignant deflation is often simply a necessary component of the business cycle. As the great economic historian of business cycles, Clement Juglar, makes clear, the causes of business cycles occur prior to the panic of crash, and the effects, such as deflation, occur afterward. His analysis would suggest that policy-makers be more concerned with the causes of business cycles and excessive financial speculation than with the aftereffects.[b]

[a]George Selgim, *Less than Zero: The Case for a Falling Price Level in a Growing Economy* (London: Institute of Economic Affairs Occasional Paper, 1997).

[b]Clement Juglar, *A Brief History of Panics and Their Periodic Occurrence in the United States* (New York: G. P. Putnam's Sons, 1916).

tion worked to the benefit of many homeowners by substantially reducing the real value of their mortgage payments, the real value of the indebtedness incurred when they borrowed money to buy houses. Of course, there is the other side of this coin. Lenders were being paid back, in real terms, much less from homeowners than they had originally agreed to. (This problem was later lessened by adjustable rate mortgages, or ARMs.) The presence of volatile inflation and interest rates not only transfers wealth among groups in society, but also will serve to make credit markets function less efficiently. Consider how unexpected inflation may affect individuals.

Who Wins, Who Loses from Unexpected Inflation?   Just as price changes for a particular commodity can benefit one group and simultaneously harm another, the financial positions of debtors and creditors also can be modified by unexpected changes in the inflation rate. Expectations of the future inflation rate are built into nominal or money rates of interest. The nominal rate of interest at the time money is borrowed or lent not only reflects the real interest rate, but also the inflation rate that the borrower and lender expect will persist over the term of the loan. If, after the loan is made, the rate of inflation that actually occurs turns out to be different from that expected, the purchasing power of the interest and principal repayments turns out to be different from what both parties to the loan expected it to be. The result is an unexpected wealth transfer between the debtor and the creditor. The direction of the transfer depends on whether inflation was "overanticipated" or "underanticipated."

Consider the case of underanticipated inflation—when the rate of inflation that exists turns out to be higher than the rate the debtor and creditor expected when the loan was made. Assume that a student wishes to borrow $3000 from a rich aunt for one year to finance college expenditures. Both agree that the real interest rate on this family loan will be 0 percent. Suppose that both expect no inflation—an inflation rate of 0 percent—over the year. The student then promises (a loan contract) to repay $3000 at the end of the year. Since both parties to this agreement expect no inflation over the course of the year, they expect the $3000 repayment to have the same purchasing power at the end of the year that the $3000 loan had at the beginning of the year. The promise (or the loan contract) is to repay $3000 nominal dollars. The expectation implicit in the loan agreement is that the $3000 nominal dollars will purchase the same amount of goods and services at the end of the year as they were able to purchase at the beginning of the year.

At the end of the year, suppose that the price level had doubled; that is, suppose that the inflation rate had been 100 percent. The student would be obligated to pay back $3000, but each dollar would purchase only one-half as much as it did at the beginning of the year. In essence, the student would pay back only $1500 constant-purchasing-power dollars. The inflation rate was actually 100 percent, but the debtor and creditor expected 0 percent. Hence, inflation was underanticipated, and as a result, a wealth transfer of $1500 constant-purchasing-power dollars from the creditor (the rich aunt) to the debtor (the student) has taken place.

The direction of the wealth transfer is not always from creditors to debtors, however. It is quite possible for it to be in the opposite direction. Consider the fictitious student loan discussed above. Suppose, though, that both parties expect a 100 percent inflation rate over the year. The student will agree to pay back $6000 at the end of the year because it is expected that each dollar paid back will be worth half as much as each dollar borrowed. A constant-purchasing-power payback of 3000 beginning-of-the-year dollars is expected. If the actual inflation rate during the year turns out to be 0 percent, who wins? The rich aunt expected a purchasing-power repayment of $3000 ($6000, but at a doubled level of prices). But with zero inflation, she will receive 6000 nominal dollars that have a purchasing power of 6000 beginning-of-the-year dollars. The wealth transfer here goes from the student (debtor) to the rich aunt (creditor) because both overanticipated inflation when the loan was made.

Inflation as a Tax   Inflation also levies two different kinds of "taxes" on people, taxes that are not directly imposed through the traditional democratic process of taxation by legislation. The first of these is the **pure inflation tax.** No one fills out an inflation tax form and writes a check, but the pure inflation tax is nonetheless very real. The taxpayers are those individuals and businesses who hold money. Anyone who holds money over, say, a month will see the purchasing power of that money decline due to inflation. The amount by which the purchasing power of an individual's money holdings declines is the pure inflation tax.

Pure inflation tax

The reduction in purchasing power of an individual's nominal money holdings due to inflation.

A second way in which inflation acts as a tax is more direct. In many countries, including the United States, a progressive income tax exists. Higher tax rates are applied to higher incomes. When the tax rate that a person is subject to depends on the person's nominal income, inflation pushes people into higher tax brackets even though their real incomes have not changed or have even fallen. The individual ends up paying a larger fraction of income in income taxes solely because of inflation, not because of any increase in real income or any direct change in the tax laws.

This phenomenon, sometimes called "bracket creep," became prevalent in the United States during the inflationary years of the 1970s. In 1981, however, the Congress voted to include **tax indexation** as a feature of the federal income tax code. Beginning in 1985, tax indexation eliminated bracket creep due to inflation by adjusting the income tax brackets yearly to account for any inflation that has occurred during the year. This makes the U.S. income tax a tax on real, rather than nominal or money, income.

Tax indexation

Periodic adjustment of the tax brackets of a progressive income tax so as to base taxes on real, not nominal, income; eliminates bracket creep and increased income taxes due solely to inflation.

The degree of inflation, both expected and unexpected, is also heavily influenced by politics. Inflation may be particularly affected by the degree of independence that the central bank of a country has from the political apparatus. In general, the more independent and further removed control over the money supply is from political manipulations, the lower the degree of inflation and, hence, the lower the tax on citizens. (See the Application "Fed Independence, Politics, and Inflation" at the end of this chapter.)

THEORIES OF INFLATION

Theories about the cause of inflation can be broadly divided into two categories: cost-push and demand-pull. In brief, **cost-push inflation** results from monopoly or union power pushing prices up. Either unions may respond to rising monopoly output prices by demanding higher wages or monopolists may respond to union demands for higher wages by raising prices. A variant of the cost-push explanation is the supply shock theory of inflation, which explains inflation as the result of a sudden increase in production costs caused by some resource scarcity, such as that created by OPEC or by crop failure.

Cost-push inflation

Increases in the price level caused by monopoly and/or union power or by shocks to the economy that reduce aggregate supply.

Demand-pull inflation is an increase in prices that results from increases in expenditures on goods and services. When actual holdings of cash balances exceed consumers' and investors' desired holdings, they begin to spend. Such spending drives prices upward until they rise enough to reduce actual real money holdings to desired real holdings. In other words, increases in demand pull prices up.

Demand-pull inflation

Increases in the price level caused by increases in aggregate demand.

Monetarists adhere to the demand-pull explanation of inflation. In their view, long-run inflation is the result of the Federal Reserve's pumping the money supply above the level necessary to keep its growth in line with the growth in the public's desired real holdings of money. Most Keynesians view inflation as a combined result of demand-side and supply-side forces in the economy.

Cost-Push Theories of Inflation

Cost-push explanations place the blame for inflation on pressures from monopolies or unions or from sudden shortages of natural resources. Two theories of how these factors can cause inflation are the monopoly power/wage–price spiral argument and the supply, or resource, shock explanation.

The Monopoly Power/Wage–Price Spiral Theory   Some economists argue that one cause of inflation is that the prices of goods and services are pushed up by monopoly power. There are two variants of this argument, depending on the source of monopoly power—monopolies in product markets or monopolies, such as labor unions, in resource markets. Concentration of monopoly power in input or output markets causes rigid constraints on the ability of prices and wages to move downward in response to falling aggregate demand. Output monopolies are able to resist cutting prices by controlling output—by supplying lower quantities in an effort to maintain their revenues. Rather than accept lower wages, input monopolies such as giant labor unions curtail labor's supply in an effort to counteract falling demand for labor. The rigidities imposed by output and input monopolies mean that prices and wages are not freely adaptive to changes in demand. When aggregate demand falls, the result is lower output and employment rather than falling prices and wages.

Another version of this argument is that, at any point in time, the price demands of monopolies or the wage demands of unions will create a **wage–price spiral** of inflation. If monopolies can set prices and make higher prices stick, the wage demands of unions will escalate; erosions of real purchasing power will cause union members to demand higher nominal wages. Either increased monopoly price demands or union wage demands will reduce the short-run aggregate supply of output, because both market activities have the short-run effect of temporarily reducing the hiring of labor.

Any wage–price spiral must ultimately be **accommodated** by the Federal Reserve. Unless the Federal Reserve validates price and wage increases by increasing M-1, unemployment and reduced output will occur. Monetary and fiscal authorities may stand their ground, forcing unions and monopolies to endure unemployment until prices and wages fall and the economy is brought back to equilibrium at full employment. Or the Fed may accommodate cost-push pressures by increasing the money stock, thereby validating inflation. At most, argue critics of the wage–price spiral, unions and monopolies can force a once-and-for-all increase in nominal wages and prices—unless the Federal Reserve accommodates these pressures in the economy. The rise in prices will not be continuous—that is, inflationary—unless the Federal Reserve permits it to be so.

The Supply Shock Theory of Inflation   Another cost-push explanation of inflation is related to **supply shocks**—natural or artificial reductions in the supply of

Wage–price spiral
The process whereby increased prices of final goods cause increased wage rates and other resource prices, which in turn result in still-higher prices of final goods; for the spiral to continue, the money supply must continually increase or real output must continually fall.

Accommodation of cost-push inflation
Increases in the money supply designed to offset a decrease in aggregate supply caused by monopoly or union action or by an aggregate supply shock; increased aggregate demand results, preventing decreases in real output.

Supply shock inflation
Price level increases stemming from a decrease in aggregate supply; decreased aggregate supply usually occurs because of sudden increased scarcity of essential resources.

an input to a production process. The United States also experienced oil price shocks in the 1970s, when the OPEC nations progressively monopolized the oil export industry and raised prices. Since oil-based energy was an important input in U.S. manufacturing and other uses, some observers argued that increases in costs were passed on to consumers in the form of higher prices. OPEC's price demands were seen as ushering in a higher rate of inflation. (Between 1974 and 1980, the average inflation rate was approximately 9 percent.)

In determining who was to blame for the inflation of the 1970s, then, some economists might begin with the oil sheiks. Others believe that the supply shock scenario just described would have been impossible without the cooperation of the Federal Reserve's expansionary monetary policy. After all, not every OPEC-dependent country suffered the same inflationary consequences. Switzerland, for example, whose central bank followed a much more conservative policy than that pursued by the Fed, seemed to suffer less from the OPEC supply shock than the United States.

Demand-Pull Theories of Inflation

The theories we have discussed so far—monopoly power, wage–price, and supply shock—focus on the supply side of inflation. These theories predict inflation on the basis of shifts in the aggregate supply curve.

Inflation, of course, also has roots in the demand side of the economy. Any rightward shift in the aggregate demand curve, given an upward-sloping supply curve, will create or increase inflationary pressures. Monetary expansion on the part of the Federal Reserve will shift the aggregate demand curve and drive the price level up. (The effects of demand shifts depend on the shape of the aggregate supply curve.) Other factors that can shift the aggregate demand curve include increased government spending, investment spending, and consumer demand.

Money-Supply Growth and Inflation   Monetarists and other economists believe there is a direct relation between expansionary monetary policy on the part of the Federal Reserve and inflation. In other words, inflation—a continuously rising price level—cannot take place without a continuously rising money supply.

This demand-pull theory of inflation is based on an updated version of the quantity theory of money. Briefly stated, the monetarist demand-pull model assumes that monetary expansion on the part of the Federal Reserve will merely increase the cash holdings of individuals without affecting output. If individuals rid themselves of excess money holdings by spending, but output is constant, then prices will go up. Price increases will fuel expectations of higher prices as well as higher nominal interest rates. Higher interest rates will increase pressure on the Federal Reserve to increase the money supply, and so on. Monetarists believe that this cycle of inflation can be halted only when the Federal Reserve maintains a steady growth rate in the money supply. Such a policy will stabilize money demand, price expectations, and interest rates and permit steady growth in output.

Inflation and the Deficit   Politicians are fond of blaming high inflation on growing government deficits. Economists, however, are less sure of the effects of deficits on the inflation rate. For one thing, deficits are not always caused by increasing government expenditures. They may also result from decreasing revenues. Therefore, the deficit may be increasing at a time when the economy is in a recession and prices are not under inflationary pressure. Deficits can affect inflation, however, if the government finances them in certain ways. When the government borrows money from the Federal Reserve System, it spurs growth in the money supply, setting off the inflationary spiral. Reserves and deposits are added to the banking system with no withdrawals, which would have occurred with taxation. When the government borrows from private sources, it contributes to higher interest rates, another source of inflationary pressure.

CURES FOR INFLATION

Solutions to inflation—policies that might bring about price stability—are always being hotly debated. Just as there is no single agreed-upon cause for inflation, there is no single accepted cure. When policy-makers attempt to resolve the inflation problem, moreover, they may bring about other, perhaps worse, consequences. Many blame the Federal Reserve's anti-inflationary policy of 1979–1980 for the severe recession that followed almost immediately. Strategies to combat inflation can be placed in two broad categories: nondiscretionary policies and discretionary policies.

Nondiscretionary Cures

Those who believe that inflation is directly attributable to monetary expansion urge restraint on the Federal Reserve. This restraint may take several forms. Monetarists urge that the Federal Reserve avoid policies that disrupt the price expectations of the public. Sudden expansions or contractions of the money supply, for example, usher in cycles of rising and falling prices. Such changes affect future prices and interest rates and require future discretionary actions. The roller-coaster path of high inflation followed by debilitating recessions is not caused by a destabilized economy but by a destabilizing stop-and-go policy on the part of the Federal Reserve. Monetarists urge that the Federal Reserve adopt a money supply growth rule. Such a rule, they believe, can allow the economy to reach a proper, long-run equilibrium rate of GDP growth with stable prices.

Discretionary Cures

Discretionary policies to combat inflation are varied. The first step in proper policy-making is accurate diagnosis: Is the inflation a supply-side or a demand-side phenomenon? If the inflation is caused by excessive demand, the proper fiscal cures involve budget cuts or higher taxes to dampen the growth in expenditures. Such policies are obviously not very popular with politicians or voters, so inflation-fighting measures are often left to the Federal Reserve. The Federal Reserve's proper monetary policies include reductions in M-1 growth rates and higher interest rates. Both actions tend to choke off consumption spending and investment, reducing the pressure on prices (and meanwhile risking a recession).

Policies to combat inflation caused by supply factors such as monopoly or union pressures and the wage–price spiral are also varied. We briefly look at one such policy: price and wage controls.

Price and Wage Controls   Gain Without Pain? Under price and wage controls, price and wage increases are forbidden by Congress, with penalties for noncompliance. Direct price and wage controls are a familiar, staple policy of governments. From the time of the Roman emperor Diocletian (and probably earlier), governments have tried to put a ceiling on price levels by legal means or by the use of price and wage "guidelines," with means of enforcement ranging from fines to death by firing squad. The most notable experiment with the price and wage controls in the United States occurred during the Nixon administration. Two basic beliefs underlie the modern advocacy of price and wage controls: (1) Structural rigidities—monopolies and unions—are the cause of inflation, and (2) fiscal and monetary policies are at times insufficient for dealing with the inflation problem.

Price and wage controls usually fail because they cannot be enforced or because they are too costly to enforce. Black markets develop in both output and input markets where there is excess demand for goods or input services (see Chapter 4). Rationing output through coupons and other devices usually fails to overcome these problems. After the OPEC oil crisis, the Carter administration initiated plans for an emergency rationing program for gasoline. The program sparked much controversy and was eventually dropped.

Most economists are opposed to price and wage controls because they distort production and economic relations between transactors in the market. If the government is successful as an enforcer of controls, which is itself a costly and difficult job, short-run price expectations may be somewhat stabilized, helping to contain inflationary pressures. Most often, however, a simultaneous and politically popular increase in monetary expansion takes place along with the price and wage controls, turning expectations in the other direction and creating more difficulties. Many economists believe that announced and concrete action on the part of government to control money and fiscal growth has proved to be of greater benefit in containing and stabilizing expectations and, therefore, inflation. Most economists believe that wage and price controls attack the symptoms of inflation but not the cause.

APPLICATION

Fed Independence, Politics, and Inflation

The Federal Reserve System was created by Congress in 1913 to administer and manage the money supply as directed in the Constitution. As an agency of Congress, the Federal Reserve Board represents or is an extension of Congress, but Congress set up the Federal Reserve to be quasi-independent—that is, at some distance from the control of the president and from direct congressional involvement. For example, Federal Reserve Board members other than the chair are appointed for fourteen-year terms by the president, which means that they can remain on the job regardless of which party controls the White House. The chair is also appointed as a member of the Board for a fourteen-year term. The appointment as chair lasts four years but may be renewed. Independence is also reflected in the fact that the Federal Reserve does not depend on congressional and administrative budget appropriations. The Federal Reserve finances all of its own operations, mainly through interest earned on government bonds.

Is the Federal Reserve too independent? Should it be brought under closer scrutiny of Congress or the president, or is its current position appropriate to its intended function? Critics argue that the loose connection between the president and the Federal Reserve System creates discoordination between fiscal and monetary policy. Monetary policy, in this view, should be under the direct control of the executive branch of government so that it is tied closely to the democratic wishes of voters. Such criticism is usually heard during periods of high interest rates and tight money.

Defenders of quasi-independence claim that control of the money supply and other aspects of monetary policy should be insulated from politics. Defenders of the Fed argue that quasi-independence permits monetary policy-makers to have a longer-run perspective, to be able to see beyond the next election. They point out that the Federal Reserve is a creation of Congress and that it can be abolished at any time by an act of Congress.

The Federal Reserve Board chair is required to present periodic reports to Congress, relating to the management of money measures and interest rates. To go beyond this level of accountability, some say, might tempt politicians into inflating the money supply to cover budget deficits, unwise government spending, or political ambition.

Table 27.3 provides evidence that central bank independence has beneficial effects in keeping inflation low. The World Bank has calculated (with an index expressed as a percent) the "legal" independence of central banks from political control, the turnover of central bankers at each central bank, and inflation rates between 1980 and 1989 for various nations.[a] Table 27.3 shows the relation between the World Bank's index of legal independence and the inflation rates in twenty-one industrial countries. While *legal* independence may differ from actual independence (especially in developing economies), the study concludes (a) that legal independence is a significant determinant of price stability in industrial nations and (b) that the turnover rates of central bank governors (not shown here) are significant in explaining the inflation rates of developing countries over the 1980s. Germany, for example, has had very low inflation rates since World War II, and its central bank (the *Bundesbank*) operates essentially unfettered by elected politicians. All but one of the countries in Table 27.3 with more central bank independence than the United States—Denmark—had lower inflation rates than the United States had over the 1980s. Thus it is reasonable to conclude

[a]*World Bank Policy Research Bulletin* (November–December 1992), vol. 3, no. 5, pp. 1–6. For further details see Alex Cukierman, Steven B. Webb, and Bilin Neyapti, "Measuring the Independence of Central Banks and Its Effect on Policy Outcomes," *World Bank Economic Review* 6 (1992), pp. 353–398.

TABLE 27.3

Degree of Central Bank Independence and Inflation

In the table, a measure of the legal degree of central bank independence in twenty-one countries is shown with the average inflation rates in those countries. In general, during the period 1980–1989, the greater the degree of independence, the lower the inflation rate.

Economy	Legal Central Bank Independence (index)	Average Annual Inflation Rate (index)
Germany, Fed. Rep of	0.69	3
Switzerland	0.64	3
Austria	0.61	4
Denmark	0.50	7
United States	0.48	5
Canada	0.45	6
Ireland	0.44	9
Netherlands	0.42	3
Australia	0.36	8
Iceland	0.34	32
Luxembourg	0.33	5
Sweden	0.29	8
Finland	0.28	7
United Kingdom	0.27	7
Italy	0.25	11
New Zealand	0.24	12
France	0.24	7
Spain	0.23	10
Japan	0.18	3
Norway	0.17	8
Belgium	0.17	5

Source: *World Bank Policy Research Bulletin* (November-December 1992), vol. 3, no. 5, p. 4.

that more independence from normal politics may result in better performance by central bankers.

QUESTION

It has been illustrated that countries with central banks operating independently of government typically have lower inflation rates than other countries. Why do you suppose a government would want to control a nation's central bank?

SUMMARY

1. There are three basic demands for money: transactions demands, precautionary demands, and speculative demands in the bond or securities market.

2. Transactions and precautionary demands are directly related to income. An increase in income, for example, would cause an individual to hold a proportionately greater amount of money for transactions and precautionary purposes.

3. The public also holds money to speculate on the bond market. Expectations of higher bond prices (lower interest returns) would mean that individuals would choose to hold money rather than bonds, whereas lower bond prices (higher interest returns) would mean that individuals would prefer to hold bonds rather than money. Speculative money demands are therefore inversely related to the interest rate.

4. The simple quantity theory of money is a macroeconomic theory of how the price level is formed. When transactions demands are considered proportional to income, velocity is assumed constant. Since real output and income are also assumed to be at a maximum, increases in money supply, M-1, cause proportionate increases in the price level.

5. The monetarists view inflation as a dynamic process originating with higher rates of M-1 expansion by the Federal Reserve System. Increased spending leads to higher actual and expected inflation rates (real GDP being constant) and therefore to higher nominal interest rates. Higher nominal interest rates lead to lower money demand, more spending, and more inflation.

6. In the monetarist explanation of inflation, the inflationary process does not end until the Federal Reserve stabilizes growth of the money supply.

7. Inflation is a process of price increases. Inflation redistributes income in society away from those on fixed incomes and those holding dollar-denominated assets. Inflation also disrupts expectations and amounts to a tax that is imposed without having been voted on.

8. Nonmonetary theories of inflation focus on structural problems in the economy such as the existence of or increases in monopoly and union power. In this view, unreasonable demands can create a wage–price spiral that can be stopped only through government intervention or through price and wage controls.

9. Monetarists argue that the ultimate cause of inflation is monetary expansion in excess of the economy's ability to produce goods and services. They feel that only rules pertaining to the conduct of both fiscal and monetary policy can create stability in the macroeconomy.

KEY TERMS

real money demand
transactions demand
precautionary demand
speculative motive or demand
liquidity preference theory
quantity theory of money
income velocity

neutrality of money
rate of monetary expansion
monetarism
escalator clauses
pure inflation tax
tax indexation
cost-push inflation

demand-pull inflation
wage–price spiral
accommodation of cost-push
    inflation
supply shock inflation

QUESTIONS FOR REVIEW AND DISCUSSION

1. Why do people hold money? What effect does the level of income have on the amount of money people hold?

2. What is the cost of holding money? If bond prices fall, does the cost of holding money rise or fall?

3. What is the quantity theory of money? How is it related to the neutrality of money?

4. What is the income velocity of money, V? How does V relate to the transactions demand for money?

5. If the rate of growth of the money supply is equal to 10 percent, the velocity of money is constant, and real output is falling by 2 percent, what will be the rate of inflation according to monetarist theory?

6. What effect does an increase in the rate of monetary expansion have on the total level of spending? The actual rate of inflation? The expected rate of inflation?

7. According to monetarists, what causes inflation? How is inflation stopped?

8. How does inflation decrease individuals' wealth? How can people protect themselves from inflation?

9. In what sense is inflation a tax? Do government tax revenues increase when inflation occurs?

10. How might monopolies or unions cause inflation? Can monopolies cause inflation without the assistance of monetary expansion?

11. Why do wage and price controls fail to stop inflation when monetary expansion continues?

12. A number of economists in the late 1990s predicted deflation for the American economy. Would deflation be good or bad for the economy of the early twenty-first century? Present arguments for both sides.

PROBLEMS

1. Suppose that the rate of monetary expansion is 10 percent per year, the growth rate in real income is 3 percent, and velocity is constant. Calculate the inflation rate using the dynamic quantity theory. Now suppose that the rate of monetary expansion rises to 15 percent per year, all else remaining the same. What is the rate of inflation? Clearly explain the process by which the increase in monetary expansion changes the inflation rate.

2. The following table represents the prices and quantities of all the goods produced and purchased in an economy in a year.

Good	Price	Quantity
Tape rentals	$4.50	240
Shoes	$8.00	220
Shirts	$6.50	300
Pants	$7.00	350
Sardines	$1.20	750
Tequila	$3.00	400

Given the information in the table, what is the nominal GDP, the real output, and the price level? If the money supply equals $3.80, then what is the velocity of money? If the money supply rises to $5.70 and money is neutral, then what happens to the price level and the quantities of the goods produced?

WORKING WITH THE WEB

1. Return to the chapter's discussion of velocity. As the chapter implies, one of the early points of contention between monetarist and Keynesian economists was over the stability of velocity. Go to the Economagic (time series) web site at http://www.Economagic.com and locate data for nominal GDP and M1 by going to the link that connects you with data at the St. Louis Federal Reserve. The M1 data is connected with the data series entitled "M1 Money Stock; SA," and the nominal GDP data is connected with the data series entitled "Gross Domestic Product in Current Dollars."

   Use the equation of exchange to calculate velocity for each quarter (i.e., three months) in 1960 and 1998. Note that the GDP data is given in quarters but that the M1 data is given in months. When using the M1 data in your calculation, assume that the first quarter corresponds with month 3, the second quarter with month 6, and so on.
   a. After calculating velocity for each quarter in 1960 and in 1998, interpret your results.
   b. What explanation can you offer for the change between these two periods?
   c. Does this change imply that monetarists are wrong, and Keynesians right?

2. The JSTOR web site (http://www.jstor.org) has archived older versions of several well-known economics journals. Go to this site and browse through the economics journals until you locate the *Journal of Political Economy*. When you find the listings for this journal, go to volume 89 (1981), issue 6, and read the "Miscellany" piece by Martin S. Feldstein (pp. 1266–1269).

   This piece humorously addresses the initial impact of Nobel laureate Milton Friedman on the paradigm of Keynesian economics. What three monetarist views from the chapter are cited in Feldstein's piece?

3. Locate Rachel Hellerstein's Winter 1997 article "The Impact of Inflation" at the Federal Reserve Bank of Boston web site (http://www.bos.frb.org). When you arrive at the Boston Fed site, click on "Publications" and then page down to the link for the "Regional Review." You will find the article in the list of articles that follow. Alternatively, you can do a search using the term "hell97" (which is part of the article's web address).

   Read the article, paying special attention to the results of the survey by Robert Schiller and the discussion at the end of the article on "Money and Morals."
   a. Explain why the article states that "most Americans seem to believe in a 'lagged wage–price' model of the economy."
   b. What reasons does the article give in arguing that inflation affects the moral fabric of an economic system?

Milton Friedman

James Tobin

Milton Friedman (b. 1912) is best known for his strong and eloquent defense of capitalism and the free market, for his support of monetarism, and for his arguments against government intervention in the economy.

Born in Brooklyn, New York, Friedman was the son of immigrant parents. His mother was a seamstress; his father, the owner of a small retail dry goods store. When his father died, 15-year-old Friedman and his mother were left with very little money. The teenager showed great aptitude in mathematics in high school and won a scholarship to Rutgers University in 1929. While a student at Rutgers, Friedman waited tables to support himself, passed exams to become an accountant, and then became increasingly interested in economics. His professor, Arthur Burns, who later became chairman of the Federal Reserve Board, taught him the importance of empirical research in economics, and another professor, Homer Jones, encouraged Friedman to apply for a scholarship to graduate school at the University of Chicago. Friedman went on to receive his M.A. from Chicago and, in 1946, a Ph.D. from Columbia University. During the 1930s he worked as a statistician for the National Bureau of Economic Research, and in 1938 he married economist Rose Director, a fellow graduate student at the University of Chicago. Friedman taught economics at Chicago until his retirement in 1977, when he moved his scholarly base to the Hoover Institute at Stanford University. Friedman was the winner of the Nobel Memorial Prize in Economics in 1976.

In *Capitalism and Freedom* (1962), Friedman argues that market forces are sufficient in both individual and aggregate markets to direct resources and to establish steady growth in the economy. Government fiscal policies, Friedman believes, often bring about results contrary to those that policy-makers intend and disrupt planned expenditures in the private sector. In his classic work *A Monetary History of the United States* (1963), coauthored by Anna Schwartz, Friedman claims that money velocity—related to the demand for money—is stable enough to make the money supply an excellent barometer of inflation, output, and economic growth. His views provided the basis for modern monetarist theory.

James Tobin (b. 1918), winner of the 1981 Nobel Memorial Prize in Economics, grew up during the Depression with an awareness that many of the world's problems were economic in origin. He made the decision to become an economist while taking an introductory economics course during his sophomore year at Harvard University in 1936. One of his major influences at that time was his teacher, Spencer Pollard, who suggested he read Keynes's *The General Theory,* which had just been published. According to Tobin, *The General Theory* "was a difficult book, but when you are 19 you don't know what's difficult and what's not. You just plow into it."

Describing himself as a "very, very, shy, noncompetitive individual" during his undergraduate years, Tobin went on to obtain his Ph.D. from Harvard in 1947 and was appointed Sterling Professor of Economics at Yale University in 1957. He faithfully carried Keynesian principles into the public policy arena when he was appointed to President John F. Kennedy's Council of Economic Advisers in 1961. He was one of the architects of the Kennedy–Johnson tax cut of 1964 and has consistently advocated a loose rein on the money supply. He has also played a key role in the recent effort to join Keynesian macroeconomics and neoclassical microeconomics.

Tobin received the Nobel Prize primarily for his analysis of portfolio selection and financial markets. He was president of the American Economic Association in 1971 and continues to support modern activist economic policies.

Keeping Watch Over the Money Supply

Friedman and Tobin certainly represent different views on monetary and fiscal policies. For Friedman, control of the money supply is the main determinant of economic stability. For his part, Tobin emphasizes the effects of government spending, taxation, and stable interest rates on economic performance. Juxtaposed, the views of each man illustrate the difference between monetarist and Keynesian approaches to the economy.

Are money supply fluctuations a cause or an effect of changes in real income? This question may be impossible to answer definitely, but Milton Friedman has consistently argued that money supply growth is the best barometer we have of economic expansion and contraction. Friedman cites a variety of statistics to back his claim. For example, since the turn of the century, fluctuations in rates of growth in real GNP have strongly coincided with annual growth rates in the nation's money supply. Prior to recession and depression, the money supply growth rate has fallen dramatically; prior to expansions and a booming inflationary economy, the money supply growth rate has shown marked increases.

To explain this statistical marriage of money supply and economic activity, Friedman argues that money velocity is a stable variable. Therefore, interest rates, which may go up or down in response to government

spending, do not contribute to economic fluctuations as many economists believe. They are merely a sideshow to the growth patterns in the money supply.

If Friedman's premise is correct, then the government's attempts to fine-tune the economy through spending and taxation policies are largely misdirected. For the sake of stability, Friedman argues, government should concern itself with a stable growth rate in the money supply. By doing so, he believes, the roller-coaster ride of business cycles, of temporary boom followed by temporary bust, can be leveled out and the economy can achieve consistent, measured growth for the future.

There are many complicated issues surrounding Friedman's proposal. For instance, can government officials afford to sit idly by in times of high unemployment, believing that over the long run a stable monetary policy will rescue the economy? Experience in the 1960s and 1970s suggests that Friedman's proposal is perhaps politically unfeasible. A second issue involves the definition of money supply. For Friedman, the only significant money supply definition is M-1—currency plus demand deposits. Recently, however, changes in the banking system have created uncertainties over what exactly constitutes money in the traditional sense of M-1. If the Federal Reserve policy-makers cannot rely on a firm definition of the money supply, efforts to control its growth may be frustrating or even futile. Friedman strongly believes that the concept of M-1, for all its apparent weaknesses, is the Federal Reserve's best measure of money supply. Larger aggregates, such as M-2 or M-3, are far beyond the control of the Federal Reserve System.

Fiscal Activism and Stable Interest Rates

For James Tobin, the issue of what determines ups and downs in the economy is not nearly so straightforward. In essence, Tobin believes that consumption and investment activity are the true determinants of economic performance. Controlling or directing such activity, however, is much more complicated than simply monitoring the money supply. On the one hand, it involves spending and taxation policies to counterbalance the rise and fall of aggregate demand. On the other hand, it involves monetary policies to keep interest rates at acceptable levels.

Unlike Friedman, Tobin believes that the velocity of money is unstable. If this assumption is correct, then interest rates are much more important in economic policy than M-1 growth rates because interest rates determine the shifting demand between different kinds of money assets, leading to greater or lesser consumption and investment activity. Tobin argues that the "strict monetarist regime" he believes to have been in effect at the Federal Reserve between 1979 and 1982 was a failure. He blames the recession and high unemployment between 1981 and 1983 on the Fed's attempt to place limits on M-1 growth.[a] Rather than

---

[a]For details on Tobin's position, see his "Monetarism: An Ebbing Tide?" *The Economist* (April 27, 1985), pp. 23–25.

target M-1 or the money base, the Fed, according to Tobin, should target broader economic aggregates such as the growth rate in nominal GDP and adjust its monetary policy according to its best estimate of where the economy is headed. (Friedman disputes the idea that monetarism has ever been tried by the Federal Reserve System.)

Tobin's position not only admits the need for politicians to do something in times of high unemployment, but it argues for such action. His activist stance, however, can be a two-edged sword. Spending policies can adversely affect interest rates, and therefore fiscal and monetary policies can conflict with one another. The current debate over high government deficits reflects this conflict, for many economists argue that growing deficits drive up interest rates.

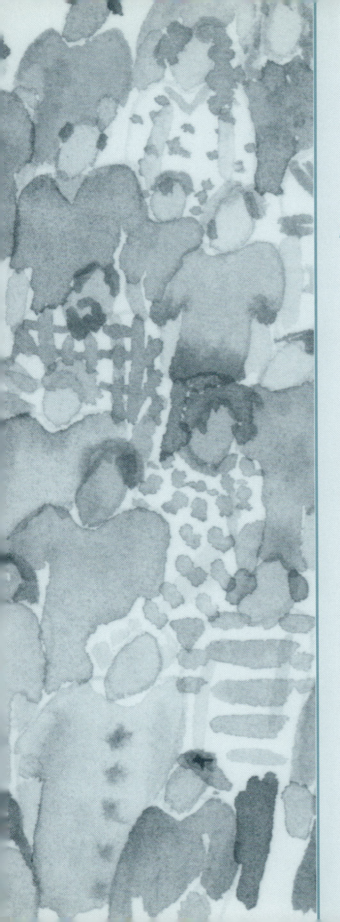

PART SEVEN

Macroeconomic Policy and Economic Growth

Macroeconomic Theory and Policy

As we have seen in previous chapters, economists find it hard to agree on where the economy is heading and what, if anything, should be done about altering its course. How many times have you heard different predictions of future macroeconomic events by government economic advisers, academics, and business economists? Economists often are equally at odds over the proper policy to correct or sustain economic forces. These differences over policy often arise from differences in theory, particularly differing opinions regarding the inherent stability of the economy. Earlier we discussed how specific theories of the economy, such as early classical theory and Keynesian theory, have led to quite different policy prescriptions. In the view of most economists, these older theories have not fully explained events or predicted accurately. Over the past two decades new theories have arisen that build upon older ideas and that are currently being tested. After reading Chapter 28 you should understand

- how macroeconomic policy prescriptions designed to alleviate inflationary or unemployment situations depend on theories about how the economy functions.
- how new Keynesians and new classical writers—those who lean toward monetarist or "rational expectationist" theories—view fiscal and monetary policy.
- some of the elements in the debate among macroeconomists on the issues of discretionary versus nondiscretionary policies.

717

POLICY ALTERNATIVES

The purpose of macroeconomic policy is to ensure economic stability—full employment, price stability, and steady growth. There are, of course, various interpretations of exactly what full employment, price stability, and steady growth mean in percentage terms, but most economists and policy-makers would agree, for instance, that persistent unemployment rates of 12 or 14 percent or inflation rates of 15 or 20 percent are unacceptable. Likewise, most economists and observers would agree that unemployment rates of 5 to 7 percent, inflation rates of 2 to 4 percent, and real GDP growth rates of 3 percent are "in the ballpark" as acceptable macroeconomic policy goals. These ballpark figures are about the right percentages for a well-functioning economy.

In previous chapters on macroeconomic and monetary theory, we saw that there are a number of interacting monetary and nonmonetary factors that affect prices, real income, and employment. Figure 28.1 summarizes these various forces. As the figure shows, the nonmonetary factors are consumption, investment, real interest rates, and net foreign trade expenditures on the private side and government spending and taxation on the public side. The monetary factors are money supply and money demand.

A subset of these variables can be manipulated through discretionary government policy. Fiscal policy—manipulation of government spending or taxation by Congress and the president—is one means of ensuring overall stability. Monetary policy—actions of the Federal Reserve Board to alter the money supply or interest rates—is another means of achieving macroeconomic goals. Table 28.1 summarizes these two types of policy.

FIGURE 28.1

Determinants of Price Stability, Full Employment, and Economic Growth

Both monetary and nonmonetary variables determine whether the goals of economic policy are achieved. Of these determinants only government spending, taxation, and the money supply may be directly altered in discretionary fashion (also see Figure 28.2).

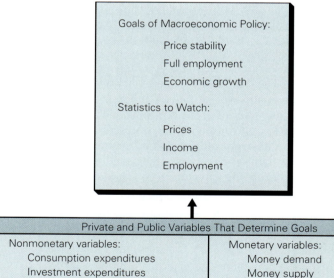

Goals of Macroeconomic Policy:

Price stability

Full employment

Economic growth

Statistics to Watch:

Prices

Income

Employment

Private and Public Variables That Determine Goals

Nonmonetary variables:
Consumption expenditures
Investment expenditures
Real interest rates
Government spending and taxation
Net foreign trade

Monetary variables:
Money demand
Money supply

TABLE 28.1

Types of Macroeconomics Policies
Fiscal policy is controlled by the president and Congress. Monetary policy is directed by the Federal Reserve Board.

Type of Policy	Scope	Tools
Fiscal policy	Changes in government taxation, spending	Alterations in income tax rate or other tax rates
		Changes in government spending on goods and services or for transfer payments
Monetary policy	Changes in money supply, interest rates	Open market operations
		Changes in discount rates
		Changes in reserve requirements

Fiscal and monetary policies differ according to the amount of time each takes to implement, the magnitude of their effects, and the direction of their effects. For example, by using one of its specific tools the Federal Reserve can act to alter the money supply when there is a perceived employment downturn or inflation upsurge, but Congress usually requires a bit more time to enact fiscal correctives. Fiscal policies, moreover, may have more immediate effects on the economy, but the effects of monetary policies may be longer lasting. In the following sections, we consider different views of these possible effects.

NEW KEYNESIAN THEORY AND POLICY

Early Keynesian economics, developed in the 1930s and 1940s, was a product of the era in which it was born: It was primarily oriented toward the problems of depression and unemployment. New Keynesians retain a belief that the economy, left to itself, is unable to adjust to falling aggregate demand and to restore the equilibrium level of income and full employment. In this view, fundamental instabilities pervade the economic system. In the broadest sense, the role of policy is to overcome the forces of instability in the economy.

An Unstable Economy

Sharp fluctuations in GDP, unemployment, and inflation can occur for a variety of reasons. Investment spending can initiate cycles of rising and falling business activity. Supply shocks, caused by natural disasters or international upheaval, can disrupt domestic markets. Autonomous consumer spending, magnified by the multiplier, can drive GDP and unemployment up or down.

Our analysis of aggregate demand shifts in Chapter 24 helps illustrate graphically the effects of such disturbances. Figure 28.2 shows aggregate demand and aggregate supply of a hypothetical economy. Along curve AD_0, the economy reaches full employment, Y_f. Assume, however, that investment spending, in

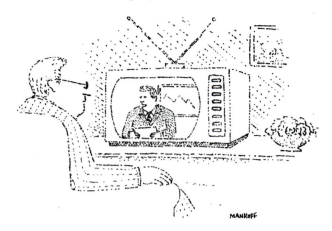

**"On Wall Street today, news of lower interest rates sent the stock market up,
but then the expectation that these rates would be inflationary
sent the market down, until the realization that lower rates
might stimulate the sluggish economy pushed the market up,
before it ultimately went down on fears that an overheated economy
would lead to a reimposition of higher interest rates. "**

response to a sudden change in profit expectations, drops. As a result, unemployment increases and real output falls. Figure 28.2 shows the effect: a shift in aggregate demand from AD_0 to AD_1 and a fall in income from Y_f to Y_1. The gap in employment caused by the shift in aggregate demand is usually referred to as demand-deficiency unemployment. With resources idle and a gap in demand, policy-makers must wrestle with these two questions: Will the economy be able to

FIGURE 28.2

The Keynesian Stand on Demand-Deficiency Unemployment

A decrease in real expenditures causes aggregate demand curve AD_0 to shift downward to AD_1, also causing a shift from full employment, Y_f, to Y_1. This gap in income caused by a shift in aggregate demand produces demand-deficiency unemployment. Keynesians suggest that this unemployment can be eliminated through the use of fiscal policy, returning aggregate demand, income, and employment to their original levels.

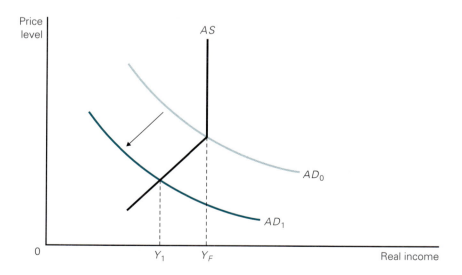

self-correct the deficiency? and How long will it take to do so? In the long run, as we have noted, theory predicts that prices and wages will fall in response to a shift in aggregate demand. But what about the short run? Can the economy or the unemployed afford to wait for natural market forces to restore full employment?

Countercyclical Fiscal Policy

In the Keynesian view, time is at the heart of the problem and, to Keynes, the short run could last a long time. While the economy might be self-correcting in the long run, the adjustment would be painful and time-consuming. In the short run, prices and wages would not fall sufficiently to restore full employment. Unnecessary economic disruption—in product and labor markets—would occur if the economy were allowed to establish its own natural rate of income and employment growth. The Keynesians' recommended cure for macroeconomic problems is to apply countercyclical fiscal policy. Proper macroeconomic policy in the event of recession and unemployment is to run budget deficits—that is, to keep government expenditures greater than tax revenues. And, though the advice has seldom been taken, inflation calls for budget surpluses—that is, for tax receipts to exceed government expenditures.

Table 28.2 simplifies and summarizes the Keynesian position. During recession or depression, Congress, the administration, and state and local governments should increase spending and/or reduce taxes. Inflation calls for the opposite policies.

Naturally, the real world has proved more complex than this simple Keynesian proposal. Surpluses have been run only three times in the thirty years since 1969. According to Keynesian prescription, the fiscal signal of high unemployment should signal deficits. Huge U.S. deficits experienced over this period, leading to multi-trillion-dollar debt, were certainly not keyed to unemployment. (The Application "Should Permanent Budget Balance Be Forced on Congress?" at the end of this chapter deals with the politics of budgets.) Moreover, at times the

TABLE 28.2

Keynesian Prescriptions to Control the Business Cycle
In the fiscal arena, budget deficits should be employed to cure unemployment and lagging economic growth, while inflation should be controlled by budget surpluses. Throughout all phases of the cycle, stable interest rates should be maintained by the Federal Reserve in money markets.

	KEYNESIAN CORRECTIVE	
Economic Problem	**Fiscal Policy**	**Monetary Policy**
Recession (high unemployment and slow income growth)	Budget deficits ($G > T$) (government spending greater than taxation)	Increase M-1 and keep interest rates low and stable
Inflation	Budget surpluses ($G < T$) (taxation greater than government spending)	Reduce M-1

economy has contained inflation and unemployment simultaneously (called "stagflation"). Keynes offered no prescription for such situations. Then, there are states of the economy that are characterized by an "even keel"—low inflation, low unemployment, and stable growth. The latter occurred during the late 1990s with so-called surpluses being run in the federal budget. (Whether or not these were actually surpluses is a matter of debate—see the Focus "When Surpluses Are Really Deficits.") But as a simplified theoretical proposition, Keynesian economics is a discretionary policy calling for deficits in economic downturns and surpluses, in periods of prosperity.

Keynesian Monetary Policy

Note in Table 28.2 that monetary policy is also included in the Keynesian approach to economic instability. Most Keynesians advocate that the Federal Reserve Board respond to inflationary or recessionary pressures in the economy by keeping order in financial markets. That is, the Federal Reserve should use its discretionary power over the M-1 money supply to stabilize interest rates, which, left unchecked, can rise to levels that discourage or even choke off private spending.

FOCUS

When Surpluses Are Really Deficits

Federal budget deficits were a key economic topic of the 1980s and 1990s, until the government announced an unexpected budget surplus in 1998 and predicted more budget surpluses for some years to come. After decades of failing to balance the budget, how was this accomplished?

Closing the gap between revenues and expenditures was produced not by spending cuts, but by a booming economy and higher tax revenue. With unemployment rates at historically low levels, income taxes and Social Security taxes as well as other taxes and fees have been at much higher levels than expected. Social Security taxes in particular have grown significantly and, rather than being invested in a true trust fund, this money has helped fill the Treasury's coffers. In other words, Uncle Sam is borrowing less from the public and borrowing more from Social Security taxes.

Several other trust funds are used for the same purpose. You pay a tax on every airline ticket you buy, and the money is supposed to pay for new airports, better facilities, improved service mechanisms, and new safety technology. If Washington decides not to spend all the money, the excess can be counted to reduce the reported level of the deficit. This "robbing of trust funds" allows Washington to turn large deficits into smaller ones and small surpluses into larger ones.

In 1997, the Social Security trust funds increased by $75 billion, of which $35 billion represented excess Social Security taxes and therefore a contribution to reduce the deficit (the other $40 billion was interest, which is both an expense and receipt for the U.S. Treasury). In 1998, the Social Security trust fund increased by $106.9 billion, of which $57.6 billion represented excess taxes and a contribution to increasing the surplus. In 1999, President Clinton announced a $99 billion surplus and surpluses totaling more than $1 trillion over the next fifteen years. It is most likely that future surpluses in the Social Security trust funds will be borrowed to create those surpluses in the federal budget.

As outlined in the discussion of the liquidity preference curve and the speculative demand for money in Chapter 27, the Federal Reserve might be unable to increase or decrease interest rates at will. Changes in the money supply can affect interest rates, but only if money demanders cooperate. If, for example, money demanders want to hold additional balances for speculative purposes due to dim expectations about bond prices or about the economy in general, an addition to the money supply will not have much effect on interest rates. Alternatively, if the Federal Reserve wanted to increase interest rates by lowering the supply of money, individuals might simply reduce their holdings of money for speculative purposes in roughly equal proportions, which again would result in little or no change in interest rates. Further, any change in interest rates—large or small—might not translate into changes in consumption or investment spending if expectations are that future investment profitability and economic conditions will not be good.

The use of an interest rate target, therefore, is an unpredictable method of changing total spending because the Federal Reserve is constrained by the liquidity preference curve. Because speculative demands for money are based on expectations, liquidity preference is likely to change without much notice. The role of the Federal Reserve, therefore, is to attempt to maintain order in financial markets and, if possible, to keep interest rates low to encourage consumption and investment spending.

Direct Versus Indirect Policy   Given recurring short-run instabilities in the economy, Keynesians consider fiscal policy a more direct and more immediately effective tool to manage aggregate demand than monetary policy. In the Keynesian model, there is no solid link between changes in M-1 and changes in aggregate demand. If M-1 increases, the larger holdings of money by individuals and businesses might not all be spent on more goods and services; some of these funds will be channeled into speculative holdings.

Problems with M-1   In addition, the money supply is less suited to discretionary policy. The Federal Reserve is sometimes unable to keep interest rates within specified targets by manipulating M-1. One reason for this problem is the recent emergence of close money substitutes such as money market mutual funds (a type of checkable deposit not included in M-1), which have tended to blur the definition of M-1 money. Without a reliable measure of the money supply, the Federal Reserve is potentially unsure of the effects of its M-1 policy.

For these reasons and others, Keynesians believe that tax and spending policies can give policy-makers greater discretionary control over the business cycle than can monetary policies. The effects of monetary adjustments, especially on interest rates, are a second, unpredictable line of defense to ensure economic stability.

More important, perhaps, than the issue of whether fiscal or monetary policy is the preferred tool of policy-makers is the issue of whether such policy does what it is supposed to do—correct the instabilities caused by shifts in aggregate demand. Keynesians obviously believe that ignoring such instabilities in the short run would inflict greater potential harm on the economy. As we will see, however, not all economists believe that countercyclical discretionary policy is the best way to ensure stability.

NEW CLASSICAL ECONOMICS: MONETARIST THEORY AND POLICY

New classical economics (NCE) is an alternative view of the macroeconomy that predicts that, in the extreme, monetary policy will have no effect on real magnitudes of output and employment and that fiscal policy will not have the effects on output and employment that Keynes had predicted. It combines elements of a number of older theories—classical, supply-side, monetarist—to produce a theory of market behavior based on perceptions and learning by market participants. Much of new classical economics is based on the assumption of rational expectations—the assumption that rational market participants (investors, consumers, taxpayers) learn to anticipate the effects of monetary and fiscal policy changes and act to neutralize them. Because new classical economics takes monetarism one step further, let us again consider the monetarist policy position, aspects of which were treated in Chapter 27. The monetarist, like the classical economist but unlike the Keynesian, views the economy as inherently stable.

A Self-Stabilizing Economy

Figure 28.3 analyzes demand-deficiency unemployment from the monetarist perspective. Assume there is a reduction in autonomous consumption or investment, shifting the original aggregate demand curve from AD_0 to AD_1. The reduction in autonomous spending is accompanied by an increase in consumers' and

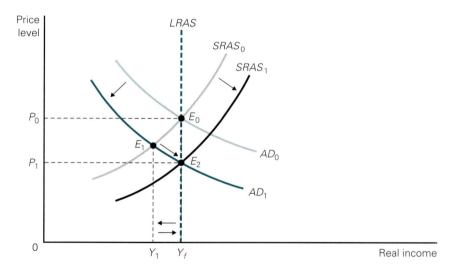

FIGURE 28.3

Monetarist Policy on Demand-Deficiency Unemployment
According to monetarist theory, the economy will self-adjust to the natural rate of unemployment, Y_f, in the event of a decline in aggregate demand. Price and nominal wage reductions occur when aggregate demand declines from AD_0 to AD_1, creating increased real balances, which in turn increase consumption and investment spending. Such price reductions also create, through adaptive expectations, rightward shifts in short-run aggregate supply from $SRAS_0$ to $SRAS_1$. The economy finally readjusts to the full-employment level of output, Y_f, at equilibrium E_2 with lower price level P_1.

businesses' holdings of real money balances. Initially, the economy is in equilibrium at point E_0. The price level is P_0, and the full-employment level of output, Y_f, is being produced. The rate of unemployment in the economy is the natural rate of unemployment that will exist when Y_f is produced. In the short run, the drop in aggregate demand moves the economy to a new equilibrium at point E_1, where the level of real income produced is Y_1—less than the full-employment level of income. The rate of unemployment is higher than the natural rate of unemployment, or, what is the same thing, the level of employment is less than full employment. Then the economy self-adjusts to a new long-run equilibrium at E_2. Real income rises back to Y_f. The level of employment returns to the full-employment level, and of course, the rate of unemployment falls back to the natural rate of unemployment.

Errors in Real Wage Perceptions

How might we explain the important process of movement from E_0 to E_1 and then from E_1 to E_2? When aggregate demand falls from AD_0 to AD_1, the level of prices and, to a lesser degree, nominal wages also fall. Employers correctly perceive an increase in real wages and respond by reducing the amount of labor employed. Although the price level has fallen somewhat, workers' price expectations have yet to adjust downward. They still perceive the price level as being P_0. This means that workers believe their real wage has fallen. They will consequently reduce their labor supply. The economy will move along the short-run aggregate supply $SRAS_0$ to point E_1, and real income will fall to Y_1. Temporarily, unemployment exists in the economy equal to the level of employment associated with real output level Y_f minus that associated with output level Y_1. This unemployment is demand-deficiency unemployment.

From the monetarist perspective, the demand-deficiency unemployment that occurs when the economy produces Y_1 cannot exist permanently. In the monetarist view of the macroeconomy, dynamic forces are at work assuring a return to the full employment of resources at some new equilibrium, E_2. If we assume that no fiscal or monetary actions are undertaken by Congress or the Federal Reserve to deal with unemployment, two sets of automatic changes will dominate. First, falling prices will affect the aggregate demand for goods and services through the real balance effect. A decline in the price level will increase real holdings of money, leading to increased consumption and, through lower interest rates brought about by the increased real money supply, to increased investment.

A second effect will act on the short-run aggregate supply curve. When workers' expectations adapt to the lower price levels, their perceptions of the real wage they receive will change. Specifically, they will adapt their expectations to falling actual prices, which signal an increase rather than a decrease in real wages. Time is required, in short, for workers to perceive the actual decline in prices. They will begin to supply more, not less, labor at every wage level. This adaptation in expectations has the effect of shifting the short-run aggregate supply curve rightward from $SRAS_0$ to $SRAS_1$.

Given pressures on prices, where will equilibrium finally reemerge? Downward pressure on nominal wages and prices will exist as long as there is unemployment in the system. As price expectations adjust to lower price levels, the $SRAS$ curve shifts rightward because of unemployed workers' desires to regain work even at lower nominal wages. After effects from the drop in prices have taken place and after expectations have finally adjusted to the lower prices, equilibrium will reemerge at E_2. The economy moves along aggregate demand curve AD_1, and the relevant short-run supply function will be $SRAS_1$. Due to the initial decrease in consumption and investment spending, prices will fall to P_1, a level to which both employers and workers will again adjust.

In the monetarist view, the interplay between price changes and aggregate demand and between price–wage changes and short-run aggregate supply is sufficient to return the economy to full employment at E_2. However, the monetarist result hinges crucially on the *absence* of interventions by Congress or the Federal Reserve. In the monetarist view, such interventions interfere with the adjustment of price level expectations. As a result, they complicate and prolong the adjustment process.

Destabilizing Effects of Fiscal and Monetary Policies

Monetarists adhere to the belief that the market economy will stabilize at full employment. But alternating periods of recession and inflation have been, and continue to be, a feature of market economies. How do monetarists explain the facts of instability?

Like Keynesians, monetarists admit that shifts in aggregate demand can cause waves, or cycles, of unemployment and inflation. Monetarists, however, believe that the primary cause of aggregate demand shifts is not the movement of investment or consumption spending but the actions of government fiscal and monetary policy-makers. According to monetarists, the destabilizing element in the macroeconomy is the shifting expectations of market participants—laborers, businesspeople, consumers, and producers—created by erratic alterations in government expenditures, taxation, and the money supply.

The Effects of Financing Government Expenditures   In the monetarist view, increases in government expenditures—one of the primary tools of fiscal policy—come at the expense of private expenditures. If government spending is financed through taxation, private consumption and investment spending are reduced by the amount of the tax. If government spending is financed through borrowing in private markets, the government's demand for loanable funds will likely raise real interest rates; higher interest rates will tend to choke off investment, depending on the responsiveness of investors to the increase. This competition for private funds is termed the crowding-out effect. If government spending is financed through the selling of Treasury bonds to the Federal Reserve, the result is potentially inflationary (Chapters 26 and 27 explain why this is so). In sum, the effects of financing government expenditures may offset any gain those expenditures offer a demand-deficient economy. In addition, such policies may create destabilizing effects.

Lags in Fiscal Policy   Another problem with fiscal policy often cited by monetarists concerns legislative frailties. Given the nature of public policy and the competing demands of political interest, fiscal policy-makers are often slow to recognize and act on economic distress signals. **Recognition lags** are the time it takes the president and Congress to identify impending or existing economic conditions. Predicting economic events is both a science and an art. But an even larger

Recognition lag

The amount of time it takes policy-makers to realize that a destabilizing economic event has occurred.

problem for economic policy-makers is that time-consuming data analysis is required before experts can comment conclusively on the health of the economy. All during the 1992 presidential campaign, for example, President Bush kept insisting that the economy was growing at a satisfactory rate—or would be very soon. Bill Clinton argued that the economy needed fiscal stimulus to get moving again after the recession of 1990–1991. Before the election, both the anecdotal evidence—people's perceptions—and the government's statistics tended to support Clinton's position. In December 1992, however, one month after Bush's defeat, the government released figures showing a growth rate in GDP of 4.6 percent for the third quarter of 1992—very respectable indeed, but too late to help Bush's reelection bid. Meanwhile, President Clinton's economic stimulus plan was defeated in Congress, largely on the basis of the 4.6 percent rate of growth in GDP for the third quarter of 1992. As it turns out, such stimulus might well have caused inflation since it would have added to the stimulus and growth experienced over the mid to late 1990s.

Administrative lag

The amount of time between recognition of a destabilizing economic event and the implementation of a policy designed to correct it.

In addition to the difficulties of recognizing a problem in time, there are administrative lags with fiscal policy. **Administrative lags** are the length of time between politicians' recognition of a business cycle problem and their enactment of legislation to correct the problem. (The lag is even more properly called a decision lag—the time it takes to decide what to do.)

Once fiscal policy is enacted, it also takes time for its full impact to be realized—an impact lag, if you will. Estimates vary, but it is thought that tax or spending changes may take from one to two years to have their full impact on income and employment. Recognition and administrative lags make monetarists dubious about the effectiveness of fiscal policy. The unpredictability of how long it may take even well-intentioned fiscal policy to have an effect means that market participants' expectations about prices and future incomes are thrown into uncertainty in the meantime.

Effects of Monetary Policy   Discretionary monetary policy has its own problems in the monetarist view. Like fiscal policy, the attempt to control the money supply in countercyclical fashion is also subject to recognition and administrative lags. In the case of monetary policy, it is the quasi-independent Federal Reserve Board and its Federal Open Market Committee, not politicians, who must recognize macroeconomic problems and then enact and administer a change in policies affecting interest rates or the money supply. While problems of recognizing signs of recession or anticipating unemployment or assessing inflationary pressures may be as great as with fiscal policy, they are somewhat easier to handle because of the small number of Federal Reserve Board or Open Market Committee members. Concerted discretionary recognition and action is probably quicker than with the larger numbers of participants in the fiscal policy setting.

Despite the quicker response, the time between enactment of monetary policy and when it takes effect is as unpredictable as the time related to fiscal manipulations. Some economists believe that the lag between growth in the money supply and the rate of inflation is at least two years long. Critics also argue that even the best-intentioned fiscal policy is unable to address certain

FOCUS

Homelessness and Unemployment: The Limits of Discretionary Policy

Economists have identified two major types of unemployment: frictional and structural. Frictional unemployment—movement from job to job or from one kind of job to another—is a perfectly natural and necessary part of any market economy that has efficiency as its goal. With structural unemployment, adjustments to new kinds of work either never take place or take place very slowly. The unemployment that has resulted from the shift from coal to other (cleaner) types of energy is a case in point. Whether discretionary fiscal policies ever could have an impact on this type of "hard-core" unemployment is doubtful.

During the 1980s, another form of hard-core unemployment—utter homelessness—became a part of the lexicon of America's social ills. Although "street people" are found in virtually every major urban area in the United States, relatively little is known about the homeless. Estimates of their numbers ranged from 0.5 million to 1 million in 1993. Sociologists believe that about one-third of the homeless are afflicted with severe mental conditions and that more than 50 percent are addicted to drugs or alcohol. A relatively small proportion of the homeless are single mothers. Most of the homeless are virtually unemployed, meaning that they represent an opportunity cost of forgone production for the United States.

Economists have been unable to pinpoint the exact causes of homelessness, although several studies suggest that certain factors appear to be consistently important. There is some evidence that homelessness is positively related to local rent levels, rent controls, and unemployment rates.[a] Homelessness appears to be negatively related to higher levels of public spending on alcohol, drug, and mental health rehabilitation but not to increased federal expenditures on housing. This last point warrants some elaboration, for if true, it means that homelessness is not per se a housing problem!

How could homelessness not be a housing problem? Most observers would agree that areas such as New York, San Francisco, and Washington, D.C., harbor a large percentage of the nation's homeless.[b] These metropolitan areas also tend to provide high-quality resources to homeless persons. Therefore, many of the best resource opportunities for the homeless are found in areas where the opportunity of finding affordable housing is greatly reduced—large urban centers. In other words, the homeless are drawn to those areas in which they are least likely to find affordable housing. Many big cities have rent controls, which, as economic theory predicts, create a variety of local housing problems—including shortages. Local zoning restrictions and urban "renewal" projects may also create housing shortages in major metropolitan areas. There is no doubt that a lack of housing is a symptom of homelessness; a lack of housing may well not be a cause of homelessness, however.

Hard-core unemployment does not respond well, if at all, to aggregate fiscal or monetary policies. A tax cut or an aggregate spending increase will likely not affect hard-core unemployment or homelessness very much. More likely to have an impact are specific policies, such as providing subsidies to larger numbers of halfway houses for recovering addicts across the country. Employment problems—the province of macroeconomic policymakers—are not monolithic. Institutional considerations and rational analysis must be applied when designing policies that attempt to bolster employment or economic growth.

[a]See William Harris Troutman, John D. Jackson, and Robert B. Ekelund, Jr., "Public Policy, Perverse Incentives, and the Homeless Problem," *Public Choice* 98 (1999), pp. 195–212.

[b]William Tucker, "How Housing Regulations Cause Homelessness," *The Public Interest* (Winter 1991), pp. 78–88.

kinds of economic problems (see the Focus "Homelessness and Unemployment: The Limits of Discretionary Policy").

The monetarist conclusion is that, on balance, discretionary fiscal and monetary policy will not be able to control swings of the business cycle. Indeed, in some regard, business cycle alterations are caused by destabilizing attempts to control cycles of inflation and unemployment. Stop-and-go policies that accelerate, decelerate, or otherwise interfere with private saving and spending are seen as the primary causes of aggregate demand instability, leading to prolonged recession and unemployment. The solution to the problems created by discretionary political or quasi-political attempts to control the business cycle is to establish rules through which fiscal and monetary policy is carried out.

In general, monetarists advocate that both fiscal and monetary policy be taken out of the hands of discretionary authorities—Congress, the president, and the Federal Reserve Board. Indeed, monetarists advocate the use of a **monetary rule** that would replace stop-and-go Federal Reserve policies with a constant growth rate in the money stock. On the fiscal side, monetarists argue, government's budget should be balanced at all levels—local, state, and federal—through fiscal restraint or through a balanced budget amendment. (For a discussion of the pros and cons of a Balanced Budget Amendment to the Constitution, see the Application at the end of the chapter.) Along with balanced budgets, the monetarists and other economists urge that government regulations supporting monopoly be eliminated or modified. Deregulation in some industries and some occupations would create greater price and wage flexibility. Greater price and wage flexibility would in turn encourage a faster adjustment to both demand-deficiency unemployment and to inflation when the economy is disturbed.

Monetary rule

A monetary policy consisting of a fixed rate of growth of the money supply.

NEW CLASSICAL ECONOMICS: RATIONAL EXPECTATIONS

Some of the new classical economists are concerned with the ability of the economy to adjust to the policy actions of Congress or the Federal Reserve. In the opinion of traditional classical writers such as A. C. Pigou, market participants (buyers, sellers, consumers, investors) could not be consistently manipulated by government. Their "rationality" was based on an assumption of perfect information, although classical models did not formally take rationality into account. We have seen, however, that "adaptive" expectations are central to the monetarist view of the effects of policy. What is the difference between the monetarist conception and the newer theory of rational expectations?

The adaptive expectations theory holds that market participants form expectations about the future course of the inflation rate by tracking past rates of inflation. To use a simple example, suppose that people expect inflation this year to be what it was last year. If it was 10 percent last year, people expect it to be 10 percent this year, but if the inflation rate turns out to be 5 percent this year, people adapt and expect it to be 5 percent next year. At each period the public adjusts its expectations according to the differences between the actual inflation rate and the predicted inflation rate. It takes time and many readjustments of expectations for people to become convinced that any inflation rate (be it 6 percent or 106 percent) is permanent.

The Rational Expectations Hypothesis

Rational expectations theory
A theory of behavior that assumes that people make efficient use of all past and present relevant information in forming expectations; implies that people's reactions to policy may neutralize the intended effects of the policy.

Over the past two decades, a group of new classical economists has developed a new theory of expectations to challenge and amend the adaptive expectations hypothesis. It was founded on a pioneering contribution by economist John Muth in 1961.[1] Although much of this work—called **rational expectations theory**—is extremely technical, the major thrust of the idea is simple, straightforward, and intuitively appealing. According to the rational expectations view, people are rational in the sense that they make use of both past and present relevant information in forming expectations of the future. Here, information includes not only the current values of important policy variables such as government expenditure and money growth; it also includes knowledge of the structure of the relationships among variables such as that between the inflation rate and the nominal interest rates. It suggests that, after some learning, individuals begin to understand some of the fundamental workings of the economy. For example, they will learn through experience that increases in the rate of monetary expansion by the Federal Reserve are generally followed by increases in the inflation rate, which are then followed by higher nominal interest rates. Knowing something of the basic structure of the economy as well as the current values of key policy variables, individuals will be able to form expectations of likely future outcomes in the economy.

Does this mean that market participants will always be correct in their anticipations? In a world filled with uncertainty, outcomes will depend on an enormous number of random occurrences. Individuals will not always be right in their expectations about future economic events, but they will be correct on average.

If people can anticipate discretionary policy and its effects, they are in a position to neutralize the purpose of the policy. For example, if the Federal Reserve Board increases M-1 to increase employment but workers and firms perfectly anticipate the resulting increase in prices, then workers will instantly demand a proportionately higher nominal wage. Firms, anticipating higher nominal revenues, would be willing to pay the higher nominal wage, thus leaving the real wage and the level of unemployment unaffected. In this contest, policy-makers are pitted against market participants; policy-makers will not win continuously, and they certainly will not win over time. Policy-makers may attempt to surprise the public, but they cannot do so forever. People catch on to, say, the effects of federal deficits on inflation, anticipate the change, and neutralize or counteract the effects of the change. In the long run, when a model of macroeconomic behavior is learned and

---

[1]See John Muth, "Rational Expectations and the Theory of Price Movements," *Econometrica* (July 1961), pp. 315–335. Other innovators in this area include macroeconomists Thomas J. Sargent, Neil Wallace, and Robert E. Lucas; see Thomas J. Sargent, "Rational Expectations, the Real Rate of Interest, and the Natural Rate of Unemployment," *Brookings Papers in Economic Activity* 2 (1973), pp. 429–472; Thomas J. Sargent and Neil Wallace, "Rational Expectations and the Theory of Economic Policy," *Journal of Monetary Economics* (April 1976), pp. 169–184; and Robert E. Lucas, "An Equilibrium Model of the Business Cycle," *Journal of Political Economy* (December 1975), pp. 1113–1144. Lucas won the Nobel Prize in Economics in 1995 for this work.

actions are correctly anticipated, fiscal or monetary policy is totally ineffective in producing intended alterations on the demand side of the economy. Paradoxically, to have any purposeful effect, fiscal and monetary policy would have to be random. If it is not—if policy-makers act in any systematic manner—learned behavior over time will neutralize the policy.

At base, the theory of rational expectations reinforces the classical-monetarist position: The private economy, while not perfect in providing full employment and maximum income at all times, is superior to fiscal and monetary authorities in providing a relatively stable economy. But rational expectations theory goes further and proposes that over time the effects of fiscal and monetary manipulations can be fully anticipated and therefore neutralized. Policies related to aggregate demand will either have no effect or in the longer run will actually produce reductions in aggregate supply. In short, there is little or no room for discretionary macroeconomic policy.

NEW KEYNESIAN CRITICISMS OF NEW CLASSICAL ECONOMICS

The rational expectations approach to policy has generated an enormous amount of interest. Much of the contemporary research has been devoted to the question of whether or not and under what conditions the policy-neutral implications of new classical economics hold. A good deal of sophisticated econometric testing has left open the answer to the question: Does discretionary policy work? Until testing yields consistent results, the matter of policy neutrality and the theoretical foundations of the new classical economics will form a lively debate between the rational expectationists and those with differing theoretical perspectives. Chief among the critics of new classical economics are the new Keynesians.

While many new Keynesians see value in more sophisticated theories of expectations, they retain a belief in the efficacy of discretionary government action in the economy. Policy, to the new Keynesians, is nonneutral and necessary in an economy that is inherently and endogenously unstable over nontrivial time periods. The basic dispute is over the form of the expectational assumptions of the rational expectationists and over the related issue of the efficiency of market functioning.

New Keynesians (and others) object that the new classical economics requires market participants to be more sophisticated than they really are in their abilities to predict. How might we expect buyers of VCRs and sellers of rental properties to utilize intricate and sophisticated theories of economic functioning in order to accurately predict prices, outputs, interest rates, or any other economic variable into the future and to act quickly and accurately on the prediction in the present?

Rational expectationists counter with the point that market participants are correct, *but only on average* and only after a "learning" period. If, in other words, policy itself is not random (which would be a peculiar manner of conducting it), those who consistently come up with inaccurate predictions would be severely punished in the market through losses on exchanges. Acting in their own self-interest, market participants would attempt to learn the probable effects of policy. Armies of economists in the "think tank" or "prediction service" business are hired by market participants to help them learn or to give them rational information about the future. It would be strange, indeed, for market participants not to react in this manner.

Importantly, new Keynesians argue that rational expectations theory fails to explain prolonged periods of unemployment and depression. New Keynesians regard the economy as inherently unstable (especially with regard to investment spending) and characterized by institutionalized sticky prices and wages (from monopolies and other imperfections in both product and labor markets). Rational expectationists do *not* believe, as the old classical writers did, that full production and employment *always* characterize the economic system. Unanticipated policy and price surprises cause real variables such as employment and income to diverge from their natural rates. Once market participants discover the "true" nature of the policy change, expectations catch up with actual economic magnitudes (such as prices) and the economy returns to the rational expectations equilibrium. An important question is: How long does this process take?

New Keynesians point to events such as the Great Depression of the 1930s, with its prolonged periods of unemployment and reduced growth rates in real GDP or GNP, as proof that market participants do not react in the manner described by the rational expectationists. To restate the question, even if expectations are "rational" and even if they eventually return the economy to the natural or full-employment level of output and employment, aren't the sacrifices unacceptable?

The question is, of course, a good one. The actual situation of the 1930s economy has proved difficult to gauge. New Keynesians believe that factors such as reduced aggregate demand and sticky nominal wages and prices due to effective rigidities in both product and labor markets are the essential explanation for the prolonged depression of the 1930s. Rational expectationists counter by arguing that that depression was prolonged, if not fostered, by wrongheaded government policies. Price changes failed to clear product and labor markets due to the *continuous* and *persistent* policy and institutional changes by the government. Discouragement of business investment and unanticipated policy "surprises" were the result of the government's increased participation in the private market system. Blame for the origins and length of the Great Depression is also placed at the door of the Federal Reserve System, which failed to perceive and correct for the precipitous decline in the real stock of money during the period.

The debate between the new Keynesian and the rational expectationist views of the proper role of policy will, of course, continue. Whether discretionary policy or "rules" give the best results will not be decided by theory or opinion, but by facts, illuminated by econometric testing.

THE MAJOR POLICY POSITIONS: A SUMMARY

We have now evaluated three major policy positions based on three theories of the functioning of the aggregate economy. Some theoretical or policy views are contrasting and some are complementary, as Table 28.3 reveals.

New Keynesians hold that the private economy is inherently unstable and unable to correct itself during periods of inflation and unemployment. In their

TABLE 28.3

Alternative Positions on Macroeconomic and Monetary Policy
A simplified menu of economic policy choices includes various recommended roles for fiscal and monetary policy. The new Keynesian position places primary emphasis on fiscal policy, while the monetarist defends a rule for monetary policy and balance in the budget. The rational expectations theory predicts that, over the long run, neither fiscal nor monetary policy will have a positive effect on the aggregate economy.

Policy Position	Role of Monetary Policy	Predicted Effects of Monetary Policy	Role of Fiscal Policy	Predicted Effects of Fiscal Policy
New Keynesian	Maintain orderly and low interest rates through discretionary adjustments in money supply	Possible destabilizing effects on interest rates if Federal Reserve only attempts to control money supply	Primary tool of macroeconomic stabilization; discretionary changes in government spending and taxation	Discretionary fiscal policy capable of ensuring full employment
Monetarist	Maintain a 3–5% growth rate in M-1	Discretionary policy will destabilize decision making in private markets; monetary rule will stabilize expectations	Provide stable environment for private economy through balanced budgets	Discretionary policy will bring erratic effects on income, employment, and prices; such policy creates an unstable economy
Rational expectations theory	Same as monetarist	In the long run, rational expectations will neutralize discretionary policy	Same as monetarist	Possible adverse long-run aggregate supply effects

view, government should take a primary role in managing fiscal and monetary policy for economic stabilization. Of the two major arms of policy, new Keynesians advocate discretionary fiscal policy as the primary weapon in controlling unemployment and inflation. Fiscal policies, they believe, have direct effects on spending in the private economy, whereas monetary policy (control of the money stock) has only indirect results. Monetary policy should maintain the order or stability of interest rates, keeping them low or moderate.

Monetarists and rational expectationists view the economy as essentially stable and self-correcting. Both views envision the private decisions of laborers, employers, money demanders, and consumer-savers and investors as producing a natural equilibrium constituting some natural rate of output and employment (or unemployment). In the monetarist view of this process, discretionary policy of any sort produces instabilities in private markets that distort, exaggerate, or accentuate any natural changes. In the monetarist view, discretionary fiscal or monetary policy contributes to instability in the private economy. That is, discretionary policy (consciously taken direct government action) either creates inflation and unemployment of itself or has erratic effects on the private economy's ability to establish economic stability. The solution: Conduct monetary and fiscal policy so as to minimize disturbances of private market participants' expectations and decisions. In the monetarist's policy views, such stability can be achieved by invoking a monetary rule, such as fixing the money supply growth rate, and insisting on balanced government budgets.

In the rational expectations variant of macroeconomic theory, the recommended role of fiscal and monetary policy is identical to that espoused by monetarists. Differences between these two positions lie rather in the rational expectationists' view of the probable effects of monetary and fiscal policy. As market participants gain sufficient information about the effects of economic policy through time, policy can have no effects on the private economy. Participants learn the effects of anticipated policy and act more and more quickly to counteract them. The rational expectations approach might be regarded as an extreme view within the monetarist position.

The important point is that *macroeconomists have not reached a consensus on exactly how the macroeconomy works.* Under such circumstances we expect to see a variety of policy views, as Table 28.3 shows. One of the problems with establishing a consensus among macroeconomists is the difficulty of proving one view with a statistical test that all would accept. The economist, like the meteorologist, is faced with a kaleidoscope of ever-changing conditions; hard-and-fast answers are difficult to come by.

APPLICATION

Should Permanent Budget Balance Be Forced on Congress?

A great deal of fanfare accompanied the "balancing of the budget" and the "running of a surplus" in 1998 (with budget surpluses projected several years into the future). Whether the surplus is actually a surplus (and not another deficit) is a matter of whether so-called "trust funds" are counted (see the Focus "When Surpluses Are Really Deficits" in this chapter). These events, corresponding to a period of high income growth and high tax collections at the federal level, have lowered the decibels on calls for imposing budget balance on Congress. Considering the political nature of fiscal policy, however, it is likely that deficits will reemerge in the future.

Prior to the favorable economic conditions of the late 1990s, there was much grassroots support for a constitutional amendment to balance the budget. Since 1977, thirty-two states (two short of the required number) have called for a constitutional convention to consider such an amendment. In addition, such an amendment was part of the House Republicans Contract with America in the 1994 elections, and the House passed such an amendment in 1995. The vote on the amendment fell one vote short in the Senate. So the country may be on the verge of passing a balanced budget amendment to the Constitution (a feature of many state constitutions). And, indeed, support for a constitutional amendment persists, fueled by frustration and anxiety over Congress' (and the president's) seeming inability to do anything about budget deficits.

Why not simply balance the budget in seven (or some other number) of years, as suggested in the political ruckus created in later 1995 and early 1996 between President Clinton and Congress? The real problem is that no future Congress is bound by the decisions of any past Congress. Why should future Congresses (or presidents) feel obliged to make the hard cuts that budget balancing must bring without huge increases in taxes? In so many of the proposals to balance the budget without a constitutional amendment, all of the pain of cuts in domestic welfare and other entitlement programs is pushed to the future. Budget agreements without legal constraints have all the solidity of quicksand.

The federal government has a clear record. In 1982 tax hikes were passed to relieve deficit pressures. They did not have that effect. Congress tried again in 1985 with the Gramm–Rudman–Hollings Deficit Reduction Act. It was soon avoided by Congress. Gramm–Rudman II was necessitated in 1987 because politicians would not live by the rules of the first one. Again, no effect. A bipartisan tax increase was designed to reduce the deficit in 1990 with no impact. Finally, in 1993, the Clinton tax hikes were designed to reduce deficits. Projections of the future (including the Clinton administration's) are politically motivated and have had a poor track record.

The problem is that budget agreements or tax increases will never balance the budget so long as politicians cater to the wishes of particular constituencies in order to be reelected. Further, as mentioned above, there is no reason for one Congress to respect the laws or appropriations passed by Congresses of the past. Thus, those who argue for a balanced budget amendment stress that a legal constraint rather than simply a congressional–administration agreement would be required to bring budgets into balance.

Why is a balanced budget amendment so critical to the future of America? The answer is complex, but many believe budget balance to be the linchpin of the future of American democracy. There are the obvious economic reasons for putting absolute limits on aggregate spending and taxation. Budget balance and eventual debt reduction will bring stability to financial markets, lowering interest rates, increasing investment, and benefiting all Americans regardless of age, sex, ethnicity, and income class.

Budget balance is easy to achieve from a "philosophical" perspective, but is far more difficult when particular expenditures are threatened with elimination.

But there are reasons that some advocate a legal budget rule for the federal government—a return to a self-enforcing and self-sustaining "federalism" in our government that protects individual rights and economic growth. The key to this kind of federalism is a hierarchy and balance of power between national and state-local governments, with "regulation" (including taxation) primarily determined at the *lower* levels of government.

This balance underwent revision in only two instances in American history—after the Civil War and in the wake of the Great Depression. The lifting of the constraints on federal government growth in relation to lower levels of government—accepted in the norms of society after the 1930s—has resulted in an unrestrained federal government in terms of functions and effects in this view. Budget and debt problems are only a manifestation of this secular shift in the federal system. Incursions on the property rights of lower-level governments and on individual citizens through federal mandate are another. A balanced budget amendment would put a halt to or strictly limit such activity on the part of the federal government.

QUESTION

There has been much talk in recent years favoring a constitutional amendment to balance the federal budget. Given this, why do we still not have a balanced budget amendment at the federal level?

SUMMARY

1. Macroeconomic policies—those prescribed to solve macroeconomic problems such as inflation and unemployment—rest on alternative versions of macroeconomic theory.

2. The tools of policy-makers include changes in taxes, government spending, and the money supply to effect changes in total spending.

3. The new Keynesians argue that fiscal policies—government spending and taxation policies—have direct and predictable effects on the private economy. Discretionary fiscal policies should be used to cure economic problems such as demand-deficiency unemployment and inflation. Money supply changes may affect spending indirectly through their impact on interest rates.

4. Monetarists advocate a stable, nondiscretionary fiscal and monetary approach to economic stabilization. Monetarists assert that lags in the recognition of economic problems on the part of both fiscal and monetary authorities, as well as lags between policy implementation and the effects of policies, are potentially disruptive in controlling the macroeconomy. Monetarists advocate a balanced budget on the fiscal side and a rule fixing money supply growth for the Federal Reserve's conduct of monetary policy.

5. Rational expectations theorists argue that, rather than ignore useful information, market participants use all learned information to predict the outcome of policy-makers' discretionary decisions. Decision makers with rational expectations are not always right, but they learn through time and are able to predict outcomes over the long run. The result is that when the discretionary decisions of policy-makers are perfectly anticipated, monetary and fiscal policy will have no effect on aggregate demand. Unanticipated policy or events will have short-run effects, which are eventually overcome through natural adjustments. Fiscal demand-side policies, moreover, may result in long-run adverse shifts in aggregate supply.

KEY TERMS

recognition lag
administrative lag

monetary rule
rational expectations theory

QUESTIONS FOR REVIEW AND DISCUSSION

1. Explain how fiscal and monetary policies differ with respect to the amount of time necessary to implement them and the amount of time required for their full force to be realized.

2. Under what conditions is Keynesian fiscal policy most effective? What fiscal policies are called for during times of recession? During inflation?

3. What role do the monetary authorities play in Keynesian policies? In the monetarists' view, what is the proper role of the monetary authorities?

4. According to monetarists, what variables adjust to maintain full employment? What effect do discretionary demand management policies have on the economy?

5. According to monetarists, what effect does increased government spending have on aggregate demand? What effect do recognition and

administrative lags have on the cycles of inflation and unemployment?

6. Why do monetarists suggest that monetary rules be followed rather than discretionary policies?

7. According to the rational expectations view, what are the probable effects of discretionary monetary and fiscal policies?

8. What theoretical conditions would have to exist before discretionary fiscal or monetary policies could completely eliminate the cyclical swings in inflation and unemployment?

9. How would Keynesian economics (and Keynesian economists) approach the situation of predicted budget surpluses (as those anticipated in the late 1990s)? Would debt reduction be a part of the policy mix?

PROBLEM

The figure represents aggregate demand and aggregate supply for some hypothetical economy Keynesland. Initially, the Keynesland economy is operating on aggregate demand curve AD_0 and short-run aggregate supply $SRAS_0$ at point A. Suppose that Keynesland's central bank increases the money supply, resulting in a shift in the aggregate demand curve to AD_1.

a. Describe what happens in the economy in the Keynesian view. What policy would a Keynesian recommend to eliminate the problem created by the increased aggregate demand in the economy? Explain.

b. Describe what happens in the economy in the monetarist view. What policy would a monetarist recommend? Explain.

c. Describe what happens in the economy in the rational expectations view. What policy would a rational expectationist recommend? Explain.

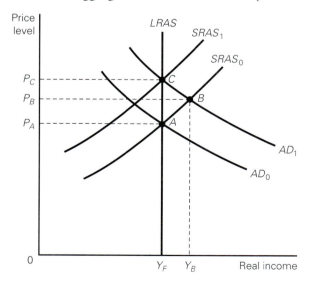

WORKING WITH THE WEB

1. Oftentimes, an institution reflects the beliefs of its high-level officials. Due to its proximity to the University of Minnesota, the Minneapolis Fed is thought to reflect a viewpoint that is predominantly Rational Expectations. The supposed founder of the Rational Expectations macroeconomic school of thought is Robert E. Lucas. A commemorative article by David Fettig about his work, entitled "A Time to Learn New Things," is provided at the Minneapolis Fed's web site (http://woodrow.mpls.frb.fed.us). Do a search for this article using the phrase "time to learn new things." You will see a link for "Robert Lucas original Rational Expectations paper." Click on this link and read the article.

   a. Robert Lucas made an important contribution toward analyzing government policy. What was that important contribution?

   b. Based on the article, what effect would Lucas predict from government pursuing an expansionary monetary policy?

2. A lengthy argument opposing passage of the Balanced Budget Amendment is found at the web site of MIT economist Jeremy Irons (http://www.mit.edu:8001/people/irons/bba/bba.html). Locate this page, and go through the various links before answering the questions below.

   a. What effect would a Balanced Budget Amendment have on the business cycle?

   b. Considering how a Balanced Budget Amendment would interact with the economy's automatic stabilizers, some claim that this amendment creates an incentive for smaller government. Why would this be true?

3. Go to the web site of the San Francisco Federal Reserve Bank (http://www.frbsf.org) and click on the "Inside the FRBSF" link. Click on "Publications & Resources," and then the link for "U.S. Monetary Policy Q&A." Look at the section discussing "How does monetary policy affect the U.S. economy?"

   a. Based on the article, how long does monetary policy take to affect inflation and output/unemployment?

   b. How close is the author's world to the one assumed by Rational Expectations economists?

Global Economic Growth and Development

A full-employment economy without inflation is the major goal of macroeconomic policy. But achievement of this goal does not necessarily mean that an economy is growing over the long run. Full employment and price stability surely affect long-run economic growth prospects, but factors such as population, natural resources, capital growth, and improvements in technology also determine the economy's future.

Long-run growth has been the key to the United States' prosperity. The **standard of living,** usually defined as the quantity of real goods and services that the average citizen is able to consume per year, has risen by an average of 2 to 3 percent per year for more than 150 years in America. Other nations have not experienced such good fortune. Many developing nations in Asia, Africa, and Latin America, for example, are stymied in their growth prospects because of a lack of productive labor or capital equipment or because population is growing as fast as or faster than output of real goods and services.

Unfortunately, there is some evidence of a slowdown in long-run growth rates in the United States. Is the slowdown in U.S. growth temporary or is it a permanent state of affairs resulting from the fixed or dwindling supplies of some of our natural resources? Will future generations of Americans suffer the effects of a shrinking economy, or are there economic policies that might ensure steady prosperity? In a global economy, what impact do political institutions—especially those found in developing countries—have on international trade and worldwide economic growth? This chapter attempts to provide insight into such questions. After reading Chapter 29 you should understand

• how economic growth is defined and some of the factors that lead to growth.

Standard of living
The real value of the quantity of goods and services consumed by the average member of the economy.

- how aggregate demand and labor productivity are key elements in explaining economic growth.
- some of the features of U.S. economic growth, past and present.
- problems of economic growth in a global context, especially in the developing world.
- the role of international trade in U.S. and global economic growth.

THE MEANING OF ECONOMIC GROWTH

Economic growth
Increases in real GDP or real per capita GDP over time.

Economic growth actually has two definitions. It may simply refer to increases in real GDP, the value of the annual output of final goods and services in the economy adjusted for inflation. While this measure certainly tells us whether overall economic performance has improved, it does not tell us much about whether the average citizen is better or worse off than at some previous time.

Real per capita GDP
Real GDP divided by the population size; real output per person in the economy.

An increase in **real per capita GDP** is a more accurate measure of economic growth. If real GDP increases by 4 percent over some period and population increases by 2 percent, real economic growth per capita has taken place. By contrast, a population increase of 6 percent with 4 percent growth in real output means that the average citizen is worse off, that economic decline has occurred in per capita terms.

Both measures are useful for understanding growth processes. For example, a statement that Mexico's real GDP grew at a rate of 3 percent last year tells us that some of the prerequisites for growth exist in Mexico. Likewise, to say that per capita GDP grew at only 1 percent last year indicates that Mexico may be having population problems, since per capita income growth depends on population growth. Both measures, however, are merely statistical concepts; economists generally recognize that neither measure, no matter how useful for comparison purposes, can tell us definitively about the quality of life or the distribution of wealth in a society.

The Causes of Growth

The causes of economic growth are complex. We have already pinpointed some of the important short-run requirements of economic growth: Adequate employment of productive resources, price stability, efficient allocation of resources, and other such conditions generally ensure a rising standard of living.

To sustain long-run growth in real GDP, however, an economy must enjoy steady growth in population, natural resources, productivity of labor and resources, capital formation, human capital, and technological improvement, encouraged by a free market environment and free trade policies.

Population Population may be detrimental to growth in real per capita GDP in many modern nations, especially developing nations, but under certain conditions, an expanding population may be essential to growth. During the industrialization of the United States in the nineteenth century, rapid population growth, much of it achieved by immigration, fueled a phenomenal economic growth rate. On the supply side, growth in population and labor supply led to increased efficiency in production through higher productivity in the use of machinery and natural resources. Mass production such as assembly-line techniques greatly improved the productivity of labor through increased specialization. On the demand side, higher population led to increased demand for all goods and services, making possible mass production and greater consumption. Population growth is therefore an ingredient in growth, but increases in population by themselves are insufficient for sustained economic growth. As we will see later in this chapter, rampant or unrestrained population increases may retard, halt, or even reverse any progress in per capita GDP.

Natural Resources   Every society is endowed with some quantity of land and natural resources such as fresh water, forests, and minerals. The United States, the former Soviet Union, and China, for example, have large quantities of both. Possession of land and natural resources may make growth easier, but it will not guarantee growth; nor will lack of natural resources prevent growth. Japan has a small quantity of land and natural resources, yet Japan's post–World War II growth rate has been greater than that of most other countries.

By themselves, natural resources are valueless. They must be developed by labor and capital. Improvements in technology, moreover, may make resources more productive—as in fertilizing land—or even contribute to the development and invention of new resources. It is a common misconception that the quantity of certain natural resources is absolutely fixed in supply. For example, as technology develops, it becomes possible to tap oil reserves at previously unreachable depths. New technology also may create opportunities to extract oil profitably from shale. Should the supply of oil ever begin to run short, new technology would likely bring alternative fuel sources to the market. Technological change continuously alters the relative scarcity of natural resources.

Productivity of Labor   Economic growth is very closely tied to the **productivity of labor**—how much output per hour, week, and so on, results from labor input. Labor's productivity depends on a number of factors, including the quantity (population size) and quality (degree of education and skill) of the labor supply, the stock of capital and other resources each laborer has to work with, and the technology available for production. Educational development and on-the-job training of laborers—growth in human capital—is a rather obvious requirement for productivity increases, but productivity increases are also closely linked to capital formation and technology.

Productivity of labor
Output per worker over any given period of time.

Capital Formation and Infrastructure   A fourth ingredient of economic growth is growth in the size and quality of the capital stock—productive assets like buildings, machinery, and equipment used in production and the infrastructure, the roads, bridges, and communications systems used in moving goods and disseminating information. Clearly, investments in infrastructure involving improvements in transportation and communications reduce transactions costs (broadly considered) and increase the volume of utility-producing exchange. Further, labor productivity—output per worker—is enhanced when the stock of capital available grows faster than the labor supply. When capital is growing faster than the labor supply, capital is said to be deepening. **Capital deepening** has occurred throughout most of the economic history of the United States. In contrast, many countries experience rapid population growth and little capital accumulation, which causes labor productivity to fall and adversely affects the growth potential of these countries.

Increases in capital stock are costly, however. Resources, including time, must be sacrificed to produce capital goods that are not directly consumable, so capital growth requires saving or abstention from current consumption. For new investments in machinery, buildings, and equipment to grow, society's ability to save

Capital deepening
Increases in the total stock of capital in conjunction with increases in the ratio of the capital stock to the labor force; occurs when the capital stock grows at a faster rate than the labor force.

must grow. The reward for saving is greater future growth in either consumable goods or in more capital stock. In the latter sense, economic growth is cumulative: It feeds on itself by using capital to produce more capital.

Improvements in Technology   Technological growth and invention—improvements in the methods by which goods and services are produced and sold—is another key to economic growth. The Industrial Revolution of the eighteenth and nineteenth centuries in Europe and the United States ushered in the age of mechanization, increasing the productivity of labor and natural resources. The result has been the highest standard of living for the greatest number of people in the recorded history of humanity. Such living standards would have been impossible to achieve without the invention of items such as the steam engine, the spinning jenny, assembly-line production, and indoor plumbing. Who could have imagined thirty years ago, for example, that a high-speed digital computer no larger than a breadbox would be within the reach of the average American to calculate income taxes, store recipes, to surf the Internet, or play games on? Technology and invention have been responsible for nothing less than the modern world. Some observers believe that technology will soon banish work as we know it (see the Focus "Is Work Obsolete?").

The Market Environment   Most Western economists believe that the market environment surrounding the growth in, among other things, natural resources, labor productivity, and capital formation is a large contributing factor to economic growth. A competitive market system, many believe, encourages invention and rapid innovation. Those holding this view generally argue that free trade policies also enhance a country's ability to grow economically; such policies enable the country to specialize in the production of the goods and services at which it is most efficient. However, Japan's experience shows that growth can also occur in a restrictive environment; despite the Japanese government's elaborate system of barriers to internal and external trade, the country has achieved a remarkable record of economic growth since 1950 (see the Focus "The Japanese Economy: Model for Growth and Development?" on p. 746).

The Production Possibilities Frontier Revisited

All of the fundamental elements of long-run economic growth may be summarized in terms of a production possibilities frontier. A production possibilities frontier, as explained in Chapter 2, shows the choices available to society in producing two goods, given a fixed quantity of resources—labor, capital, and natural resources—and assuming a given state of technology. If society is positioned on the production frontier, it is fully employing and efficiently allocating all resources and utilizing technology to its best advantage. However, most societies, even highly efficient ones, are at times positioned inside the frontier because of unemployment or underemployment of resources. Societies cannot advance beyond the frontier because of absolute limits at any given time in the quantity and quality of resources.

Figure 29.1 shows production possibilities frontiers for two economic societies—country X and country Y, respectively—both of which must choose production levels for consumption goods and capital goods. Each country is assumed to possess a similar resource base and the same technology. Country X's initial choice between capital goods and consumer goods is labeled A in Figure 29.1a;

FOCUS

Is Work Obsolete?

Many self-described futurists predict a world in which most of the population will not have to work for a living. They point to a number of Western European countries that have experienced double-digit unemployment rates for decades at a time without significant social disturbances or turmoil. Like others before them, those who foresee a largely jobless society base their predictions on new labor-saving technology.

One scenario has computers and robots making human labor unnecessary. The elimination of work would begin in heavy industries—such as automaking—and eventually spread to other industries, creating a leisure class. In this view, putting citizens "on the dole" would be cheaper than paying them to work in unproductive jobs.

Futurist Alvin Toffler and his "third wave" paint a similar picture. He sees knowledge as the key to a laborless society because it is *the* factor of production that can be replicated at zero cost and substituted for all other factors of production, like land and labor. For example, "just in time" inventory is knowledge about inventory requirements substituted for large inventory warehouse facilities that require much land, labor, and capital to build.

Economists are understandably leery about such futuristic predictions about work-free societies and "leisure classes." During the Great Depression, when a high percentage of the world labor force was unemployed, economist John Maynard Keynes worried about such problems as the satiation of demand and feared that capitalism had produced a supply of goods far in excess of demand. Here technological developments such as the assembly line and improved information via the invention of the phone, radio, and television would make labor and capital increasingly unnecessary.

Critics claim that society can only move now in two directions. One is to provide welfare to encourage people not to work. The European model provides such welfare on a limited basis, but the problem with such a model is that the more incentive given to individuals to get "in the wagon" the less incentive people have to "pull the wagon," and the overall economy slows down and stagnates. On a mass scale such welfare is socialism, and everyone, including most futurists, agrees that socialism does not "work."

The other view, and the one emphasized by most economists, is that labor-saving technologies—computers, robots, and information—do not change the necessity to work; they change the conditions of work. In this view, labor becomes less physical and repetitive and is more personal and creative. The long trend of economic development has also meant that many people work fewer hours, and this trend can also be expected to continue. The economic prediction about the future is that people will continue to work, but in jobs such as real estate agents, movie producers, designers, and university professors where work is more "leisurely."

---

country Y's choice in Figure 29.1b is labeled B. Country X has devoted a higher proportion of its resources to capital goods production in year 1 than has country Y. The net result—and the key to understanding the principles underlying economic growth—is that country X's choice results in a higher production possibilities frontier in some future year, say, year 2. In year 2, societies X and Y will again choose some capital–consumer goods combination on a new frontier, but if both countries remain fully employed, country X's economy will have grown to a higher level of output and presumably to a higher level of real GDP per capita.

Economic growth, in other words, is determined by society's choice of future goods over present goods. This fact does not mean that the capital stock is the only element in growth. Capital combines with labor and natural resources to increase society's growth possibilities, even with a constant state of technology.

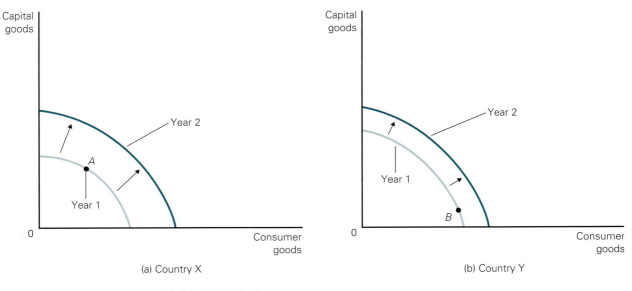

(a) Country X   (b) Country Y

FIGURE 29.1

Economic Growth and the Production Possibilities Frontier
Growth is assumed to result from increases in the stock of capital goods. (a) If one economy forgoes a relatively larger amount of consumption goods than another economy in
order to obtain more capital goods, then its production possibilities frontier will shift outward by a larger amount. (b) Country Y's preference for consumer goods in year 1 results
in significantly less growth by year 2.

Comparative Growth Rates

Economies grow at different rates. Diminishing marginal returns when one or more
resources are fixed or growing slowly is a major aspect of theories featuring limits to growth. For instance, bottlenecks may be predicted when all arable land and
freshwater resources in a country are already being used intensively for food production. Whether the limits to long-run economic growth are absolute or relative,
it is clear that growth is an extremely complex matter. Further, it is clearly the case
that even small differences in growth rates matter a great deal over time.

Table 29.1 presents actual average growth rates in real GDP between 1990
and 1998 for seven nations. The growth rates varied from 2.4 percent (United States
and Germany) to 1.3 (in Italy).

In the rest of Table 29.1, we consider what would happen if each of the nine
economies continued to grow at the actual average 1990–1998 rate. We begin in
2000, and, for the sake of simplicity, assume that each country has a GDP of $500
billion in that year. After five years of about 2.4 percent growth per year, Germany's GDP would be $803 billion, or about 13 percent higher than the French
GDP of $700 billion. It should be clear from Table 29.1 that relatively small dif-
ferences in the growth rates of two countries will produce huge differences in real
income in the not-too-distant future.

A warning about the determinants of growth in different nations: Many cultural and institutional factors heavily influence actual growth rates. Significantly
different growth rates even in highly developed nations may ultimately be
explained only in terms of a particular society's cultural, governmental, and insti-

TABLE 29.1

Cumulative Effects of GDP Growth

Different growth rates applied to the same hypothetical GDP in 2000 will produce dramatic changes in real GDP in the future. GDP will double in twenty years with an approximate growth rate of 3.5 percent per year.

Country	Average Growth Rate of Real GDP, 1990–1998 (annual percent change)	Hypothetical Real GDP, 2000 (billions of dollars)	Projected Real GDP, 2005 (billions of dollars)	Projected Real GDP, 2010 (billions of dollars)	Projected Real GDP, 2015 (billions of dollars)	Projected Real GDP, 2020 (billions of dollars)
United States	2.4	500	563	634	714	803
Canada	1.8	500	547	598	653	714
Japan	1.6	500	541	586	634	687
France	1.7	500	544	592	644	700
Germany[a]	2.4	500	563	634	714	803
Italy	1.3	500	533	569	607	647
United Kingdom	1.7	500	544	592	644	700

Source: Council of Economic Advisers, *Economic Report of the President* (Washington, D.C.: U.S. Government Printing Office, 1999), p. 454.

[a]Former West Germany

tutional structures, areas where the economist may not be able to analyze key differences. To understand the economic development of any nation, we must look to cultural and institutional factors, as well as the quantifiable features of growth.

GROWTH AND MODERN MACROECONOMIC THEORY

Modern economic theory has much to say on the issue of growth. Foremost in current analysis is the importance of capital formation and improvements in technology. According to modern analysis, growth potential also depends on the ability of an economy to absorb growth.

The Demand Side of Growth

Growth absorption

Increases in total spending sufficient to purchase additional output generated by increases in productive capacity.

Growth absorption means keeping up with the expanding productive capacity of the economy through increasing total expenditures. Recall that aggregate demand must always be sufficient to create full employment at any point in time. The same must hold true to create full employment and maximum economic growth over time.

Figure 29.2 shows total expenditures on the vertical axis and the output capacity of the economy over time on the horizontal axis. Along the 45-degree line, total expenditures equal the total output capacity of the economy. A central requirement for sustainable economic growth is that total expenditures, private and public, must keep the economy on or near this 45-degree line through time; otherwise, unemployment and slower growth will result. If output capacity is Y_0 in the year 2000, total expenditures must be at the level of TE_0 to achieve maximum income and income growth. A given level of net investment and capital formation in 2000

FOCUS

The Japanese Economy: Model for Growth and Development?

Japan's industrial revolution began in the early twentieth century, and by the time of World War II, Japan was a leading industrial power. But after the war, the Japanese economy was in shambles; its people were poor, and its production processes were primitive. Japan was essentially a developing country.

The growth and development of the Japanese economy since 1950 has been astonishing. Between 1950 and 1993, real GDP per capita in Japan rose by a factor of twenty-four (from $843 to $20,523). In 1993, Japanese GDP per capita was about 85 percent of that of the United States; in 1950 it had been only 12.7 percent. Today the Japanese economy ranks with those of most European nations in terms of per capita GDP.

To put the Japanese economy in perspective, it must be noted that Japan is 10 percent

smaller than California, has only about half the population of the United States, and of the major industrial countries is the poorest in nonhuman natural resources, importing virtually its entire supply of raw materials. Finally, Japan is one of the most densely populated countries on earth. Yet, despite these obvious disadvantages, Japan has an enviable development record.

Japan has a capitalist market economy characterized by an industrial policy and extensive import restrictions. The term *industrial policy* refers to government-led industrial consortiums, health care plans, worker training, and tax policies. Despite such heavy and direct government involvement in the economy, virtually all productive resources are privately owned and operated. Lifetime employment contracts are still common in the case of larger firms, which partly explains the absence of national labor unions. Local unions in Japan, moreover, do not exert much power over labor allocation. The high degree of economic efficiency

observed in Japan has been achieved in an atmosphere virtually free of labor market rigidity.

Two features of the Japanese economy are probably most responsible for Japan's rapid growth: historically low marginal and absolute tax rates and high rates of saving and investment.

During the period 1960–1979, almost one-third of Japan's GDP was allocated to investment—a considerably larger fraction than could be found in other developed countries. Japan still saves a far greater percentage of its GDP than the United States—18 percent compared with 4 percent in 1992. The Japanese government increases investment by taxing businesses and capital gains at low rates and exempting from taxation capital gains derived from sales of securities. In contrast, the Clinton administration increased the top corporate tax rate in 1993 and kept the capital gains tax very high.

Another ingredient in Japan's amazing growth is worth mentioning—its unabashed copying of technology developed in the West. Extremely successful in this area, the Japanese have invested heavily in research and development. Approximately 3 percent of its GDP in the 1990s is devoted to research.

The Japanese economy experienced a sharp downturn in the 1990s (with a *negative* growth rate, −2.5 percent, in 1998 according to the International Monetary Fund). Nevertheless, perhaps due to labor policies, the unemployment rate was only about 4 percent in 1998. Many believe that new government involvement in the economy, including new taxes and the government's industrial policy, is to blame for the economic slowdown. The work ethic is another matter, as many young Japanese do not share their parents' work ethic. Yet there were

continued

continued

signs, including a rebounding stock market in 1999, that the Japanese economy would turn around. Private initiative and relatively low government involvement created one of the great success stories of economic development in the twentieth century. It remains to be seen whether the quest for "security" and higher levels of government in the

Japanese economy will turn success into another cautionary tale.

Sources: Steve Lohn, "The Japanese Challenge: Can They Achieve Technological Supremacy?" *New York Times Magazine* (July 8, 1984); Paul Sperry, "Must We Copy Our Competitors?" and "Is the Grass Greener Abroad?" *Investor's Business Daily* (April 13–14, 1993), pp. 1–2; and *Economic Report of the President* (Washington, D.C.: U.S. Government Printing Office, 1999), pp. 453–454.

creates a larger output capacity in 2010, Y_1, which in turn requires a rise in total expenditures in 2010 to realize the growth potential of the economy in 2010.

Ensuring adequate aggregate demand for maximum growth is one of the goals of short-run macroeconomic theory. New Keynesians argue that the economy should be managed in discretionary countercyclical fashion to keep aggregate demand at full-employment levels. Monetarists and new classical economists argue that adequate growth in aggregate demand can be achieved only through stable rules for Congress and for the Federal Reserve System. However one looks at the matter, policies to ensure adequate aggregate demand are essential in maintaining a sustained high rate of economic growth.

The Supply Side of Growth

The other facet of economic growth involves the factors that enhance or enlarge the productive capacities of the economy. All of the factors—capital growth, technological improvements, growth in natural resources—discussed earlier in this chapter create supply increases. We call these *supply-side* factors because they have the effect of shifting the aggregate supply curve of real output to the right.

FIGURE 29.2

Growth in Total Expenditures Required for Economic Growth

In this simple model, increases in total expenditures must keep up with expanding resources and population to bring about maximum economic growth from an output capacity of Y_0 in the year 2000 to Y_1 in 2010; the aggregate demand curve must shift from TE_0 to TE_1 by 2010 to keep resources fully employed. Total output equals total expenditures along the 45-degree line.

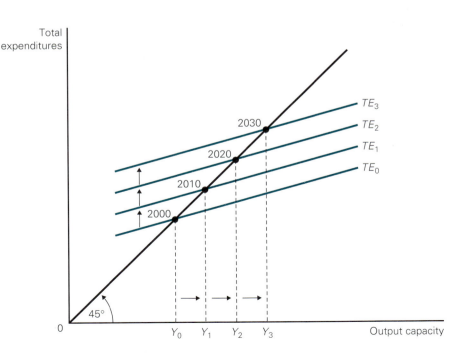

FIGURE 29.3

Economic Growth and Rightward Shifts in Long-Run Aggregate Supply

Over time, the level of technology or the supply of resources may increase, shifting the long-run aggregate supply curve to the right and increasing full-employment income.

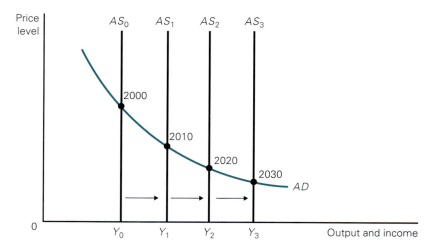

In Figure 29.3, we assume that the economy's demand for goods and services will be sufficient to absorb the increased output of goods and services made possible by growth. The question we ask instead is: What factor or factors underlie rightward shifts in the aggregate supply curve? The long-run supply of goods and services is influenced by certain variables—capital accumulation, the productivity of labor, taxation, and so on. For purposes of discussion, however, there are two major economic factors to watch in predicting the growth rate in the productive capacities of any economy:

1. Growth in private saving and investment, which leads to capital formation; and
2. Growth in the number of laborers, in laborers' participation in the work force, and in labor's productivity.

Any variable, policy, or institutional factor that affects these two factors will affect economic growth through its effect on the long-run aggregate supply curve.

Does Growth Cause Inflation?

The belief in the existence of a trade-off between growth and inflation has long been a driving force in economic policy. According to this view, unemployment can be fought with a higher rate of inflation, and inflation can be reduced but only at the expense of higher unemployment. However, U.S. economic performance, especially in the 1990s when both inflation and unemployment were low, undermines belief in this trade-off.

In 1958, British economist A. W. Phillips published an important paper in which he used actual data to show that there may be a ping-pong trade-off between inflation and unemployment.[1] (Actually, Irving Fisher was the first to notice the inverse relation between inflation rates and unemployment rates.[2]) Phillips's data are

---

[1]See A. W. Phillips, "Relation Between Unemployment and the Rate of Change of Money Wage Rates in the United Kingdom, 1861–1957," *Economica* 25 (November 1958), pp. 283–299.
[2]See Irving Fisher, "A Statistical Relation Between Unemployment and Price Changes," *International Labor Review* (June 1926), pp. 785–792. Reprinted posthumously as "I Discovered the Phillips Curve," *Journal of Political Economy* 81 (March–April 1973), pp. 496–502.

based on money wage rates; because they follow the inflation rate, money wage changes may serve as a proxy for inflation. Phillips's data showed an almost hundred-year (i.e., long-run) inverse relation between inflation and unemployment for the United Kingdom. The data also indicated that the cost of less unemployment is higher inflation rates or, conversely, that the cost of lowering the inflation rate is a higher unemployment rate.

Phillips's study caused a great stir among macroeconomists, because an inverse relation between unemployment rates and inflation means that the long-run aggregate supply curve is positively sloped, not a vertical line. In other words, higher levels of output and employment are invariably associated with higher price levels. This means that long-run income and employment growth must come at the expense of inflation. If Phillips is correct, the promise of achieving one economic goal means that another economic goal must be forgone and policy-makers must choose between problems in a no-win trade-off.

Phillips curve

A graph showing the relation between the rate of inflation and the unemployment rate.

The **Phillips curve** is a graph showing the relation between the rate of inflation and the unemployment rate. Figure 29.4 depicts the hypothetical relation between unemployment and inflation that was suggested by Phillips. The inflation rate is depicted along the vertical axis and the unemployment is shown along the horizontal axis. The Phillips curve is negatively sloped, indicating an inverse relationship between inflation and unemployment. Phillips's basic argument is straightforward. A reduction in unemployment comes at the expense of higher inflation. Inflation is a necessary evil.

University of Chicago economist Milton Friedman argued that the Phillips curve was just an illusion. Inflation would fool business into thinking that the demand for their products was increasing and hire more workers. However, business would eventually wise up to the fact that they were experiencing inflation, that their own costs were rising, and that they had not experienced a real increase in demand. The stagflation of the 1970s, when both inflation and unemployment rates were high, was enough evidence to convince most economists that there was no Phillips curve in the long run, although some still maintained that it held true in the short run.

FIGURE 29.4

A Hypothetical Phillips Curve Relating Inflation and Unemployment

According to A. W. Phillips, there is an inverse relation between the inflation rate and the rate of unemployment. At an inflation rate of 16 percent, the unemployment rate is 4 percent. If the inflation rate falls to 14 percent, unemployment rises to 5 percent. At zero inflation, unemployment is very high.

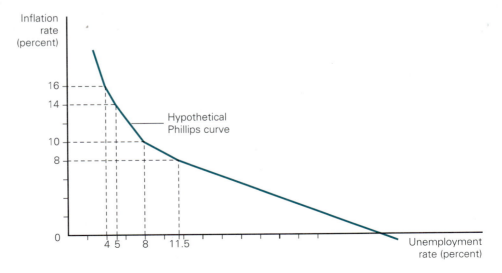

The historical evidence demonstrates that there is not a stable relationship between inflation and unemployment. During the 1970s we had high rates of inflation and unemployment, while in the 1990s the American economy experienced low rates of both inflation and unemployment. In other years, the Phillips trade-off appears to hold. Basic economics holds the key to this statistical puzzle.

A high rate of economic growth (i.e., low unemployment) cannot by itself cause inflation. Inflation is a monetary phenomenon and is caused by too much money chasing too few goods. In fact, if the money supply is stable, economic growth is consistent with falling prices (i.e., deflation) because the same amount of money is chasing an ever-increasing supply of goods. Prices fall rather than rise, and the purchasing power of your money increases over time. The United States experienced this in the second half of the nineteenth century when the economy witnessed high rates of economic growth while on the gold standard, which held the supply of money relatively stable.

While monetary policy may still be able to "stimulate" the economy in the short run, the evidence suggests that policy-makers concerned about the long-run health of the economy should disregard the Phillips curve and maintain monetary stability without fear about higher unemployment and should pursue policies that promote economic growth, such as tax cuts, without concern over inflation.

RECENT U.S. ECONOMIC GROWTH AND PRODUCTIVITY

The various growth rates in real GDP in industrialized nations shown in Table 29.1 have numerous causes. Short-run economic stabilization—the ability of an economy to provide full employment of resources—will naturally affect long-run growth prospects. But the supply-side features of economic growth are of greatest importance in explaining U.S. growth trends.

Capital Formation

Capital formation
The process whereby the stock of capital in an economy increases.

A measure of **capital formation** is net investment as a percentage of GDP. This measure is the fraction of total output being put into new plant and equipment, and it is an indicator of the future productivity of the economy. Over the past two decades, it has ranged from 4 to 5 percent. Net investment falls during (and prior to) recessions, reducing future productivity (as it did in 1991), and it also presages periods of prosperity. Since 1992, for example, and up until 2000 real net private investment in the U.S. economy rose markedly (to the range of 6 to 7 percent in the late 1990s). Such investments have set the stage for growth in the twenty-first century (see the Focus "Business Investment Leads the 1990s Boom" in Chapter 20 for additional discussion).

Saving

Personal savings are the primary source of new investment and capital formation in the United States. However, corporations also engage in saving when they retain earnings, as do governments when they run government surpluses. In recent years, foreign capital has flowed into the United States, providing an additional source of savings. Figure 29.5 shows that while, historically, Americans have saved about 7 percent of their disposable income, the rate in the late 1970s and for most of the 1980s was lower—at times, significantly so.

The dip in personal savings coincided with an era of enormous government deficits up to the mid-1990s. To finance these deficits, the government has been forced to compete with private investors. Accumulated savings drained to finance government deficits greatly reduce the funds that are available for private capital formation.

The low savings rate is a cause for concern as the U.S. economy approaches the twenty-first century. One problem is that savings income (interest earnings) are taxed at the rate of ordinary income in the United States, a fact that contrasts with many developed countries. The low and declining rates experienced in the 1990s are not an encouraging sign for vigorous growth in the future.

Productivity

The declines in net investment and saving combined to reduce U.S. productivity in the early 1980s (see Table 29.2). After 1982, total output and output per hour rose dramatically; the 7.9 percent rate of output growth in 1984 was the highest since 1950. Since 1984, the growth rate has moderated somewhat, and while the rate remains much higher than it was in the late 1970s and early 1980s, productivity growth remains low compared with what it has been throughout most of U.S. history.

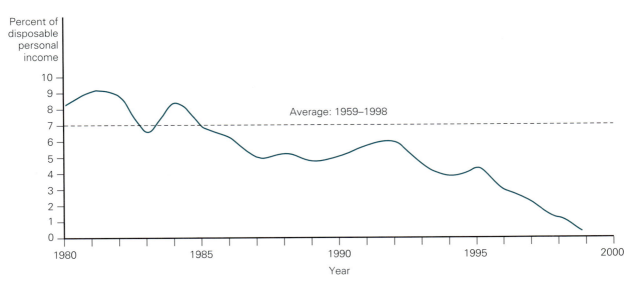

FIGURE 29.5

Personal Saving Rate in 1980–1998

The personal saving rate stood at about one-half of 1 percent in 1998. This rate is well below the average savings rate of about 7 percent for the period 1959 to 1998.

Source: Council of Economic Advisers, *Economic Report of the President* (Washington, D.C.: U.S. Government Printing Office, 1996), p. 310.

TABLE 29.2

Output and Productivity Growth Rates in Nonfarm Business Sector, 1980-1998

The output growth rate fluctuated throughout the 1980s and into the 1990s, with growth in productivity (output per hour) lagging stubbornly behind.

GROWTH RATES (PERCENT)

	Output per hour	Output
1980	-0.4	-1.2
1981	1.1	1.9
1982	-0.8	-3.2
1983	4.2	6.1
1984	1.7	7.9
1985	1.0	3.6
1986	2.6	3.4
1987	-0.2	3.0
1988	0.8	4.1
1989	0.6	3.2
1990	0.5	0.7
1991	0.7	-1.8
1992	3.1	3.0
1993	0.1	3.0
1994	0.5	3.9
1995	0.6	3.0
1996	2.4	4.1
1997	1.4	4.5
1998	2.3	4.3
1980–1998 (average)	1.2	2.8

Source: Council of Economic Advisers, *Economic Report of the President* (Washington, D.C.: U.S. Government Printing Office, 1999), p. 385.

Small differences in productivity growth rates and in the rates of investment and capital formation that cause them may seem inconsequential. Over the long run, however, they are critical to growth. As the Council of Economic Advisers pointed out in 1983,

> The consequences of reduced productivity growth for our standard of living over the long run are greater than those of any other current economic problem. In 1981 the American economy produced approximately $12,780 worth of output per capita. Had productivity growth continued at the 1948–67 rate during the 14 years subsequent to 1967, output per capita would have reached $16,128 in 1981, 26 percent higher than the actual value.[3]

---

[3]Council of Economic Advisers, *Economic Report of the President* (Washington, D.C.: U.S. Government Printing Office, 1983), p. 13.

Small changes in productivity, investment, and capital formation growth rates can have a major impact on overall economic growth. Increasing the annual productivity growth rate by only 2 percentage points, for example, would more than double the standard of living in terms of goods and services by the year 2020.

The somewhat disappointing picture of growth in the U.S. economy in recent years has many interrelated causes. Unfortunately, economists have not been able to pinpoint the exact causes of the slowdown. Even if they could, however, economists and policy-makers alike would be unlikely to agree on a plan to reverse the trend.

The long-range (over the last two decades) slowdown in labor productivity has been attributed to, among other things, lower research and development expenditures; a transition to a high-technology economy; higher energy prices; swings in the business cycle; increased regulation affecting saving, investment, and labor markets; changing composition of the labor force; and changing attitudes of workers. Discrimination against private capital formation has taken a number of forms, including tax policies, destabilizing inflation created by expansionist monetary policies, and the competition for investment funds by the federal government through government budget deficits.

The recent upturn in all of the major economic indicators (low unemployment, low inflation, and high growth rates in the late 1990s) bodes well for the future. Especially encouraging is the rise in productivity measured as output per hour (see Table 29.2) to the range of about 2 percent between 1996 and 1998. Increases in business investment, particularly in new and technologically superior equipment, have accompanied these productivity increases. There is therefore cause for cautious optimism concerning the high-growth prospects for the future U.S. economy.

ECONOMIC GROWTH AND ECONOMIC DEVELOPMENT

Economic development
The process through which an economy achieves long-run economic growth; involves capital formation, the development of markets, productivity growth, and the improvement of entrepreneurial ability and labor skills.

Why do some economies grow at brisk rates while others grow slowly, if at all, in terms of per capita income? To better understand growth prospects for the United States in the future, it is instructive to study the process of economic development. In economic terms, development is not quite the same as growth. Economic growth usually refers to the increase in per capita GDP in an economy; **economic development** is the process of capital formation, improvement in entrepreneurial and labor skills, and growth in economic productivity that causes rates of economic growth to rise. The U.S. economy provides a model of successful economic development, in that the United States has succeeded at combining a growing population with high and sustained rates of economic growth. In 1776, however, the United States was in many respects an underdeveloped economy. The transition from a low state of development to a high one occurred rapidly during the nineteenth century. The critical question is whether the United States can maintain high levels of growth in the future, and the experiences of some developing nations may be instructive.

In the modern world, the developed nations are the relatively rich economies, and the developing nations are the relatively poor economies. Many developing countries are relatively stagnant economically, while others are gaining rapidly in terms of per capita income, productivity, and output. Most developing nations are experiencing high rates of population growth. Why do they differ in growth experience? It appears that the form of economic institutions plays an important role in determining the extent to which economies, both developed and developing, grow.

The Characteristics of Developing Countries

Developing countries

Countries with relatively low levels of per capita real GDP; generally characterized by a large subsistence agricultural sector, low saving rates, and high population growth.

Most countries of the world are considered less-developed countries, or **developing countries;** three-quarters of the world's population lives in developing countries. But there is an amazing amount of diversity among these countries; the only thing they have in common is their less-developed status. Economically, what characteristics are associated with the low development rates of less-developed countries?

There is general agreement, in describing less-developed countries, that certain fundamental features stand out: low per capita income, a dominant agricultural-household sector, relatively low savings rates, and rapid population growth. Most critically, however, are the relatively poor institutional structures within these countries, including the absence of market structures and inefficient or ineffective assignments of property rights.

A less-developed country is a poor country in the sense that its per capita GDP is low. Compared with poverty in developed countries, poverty in less-developed countries is more severe. In many less-developed countries, the plight of the lowest income group has not changed dramatically in hundreds of years. The second defining characteristic of less-developed countries is a dominant agricultural-household sector. In a way, this is merely another way of saying that less-developed countries are poor—a large proportion of their population is engaged in subsistence agriculture. Nearly two-thirds of the labor force of the low-income countries of Asia, Africa, and South America are employed in agriculture. In contrast, only 2 percent of the U.S. labor force is employed in agriculture. The size of the household (or nonmarket) sector in less-developed countries is generally much larger than in developed nations. Most households in less-developed countries are engaged in subsistence production in the sense that they raise their own food, make their own clothes, and construct their own homes. The degree of specialization in production in these economies is limited compared with the more-developed economies. With the degree of specialization limited and a large amount of time devoted to subsistence production, the opportunities for welfare-enhancing exchange and trade with others in the society becomes relatively limited as well.

The other two characteristic features found in most less-developed countries (although there are important exceptions) are low saving rates and high rates of population growth. Many poor economies have low saving rates because saving is very difficult (or even impossible) when income is at or near the subsistence level. Low saving rates mean that very little income is set aside each year for investment in capital goods for increased production. This inability to save, in turn, contributes to continuing low rates of development. The term sometimes used for this problem is the **vicious circle of poverty.**

Vicious circle of poverty

An attempt to explain why some countries remain less developed that centers on low savings and investment as the cause of low real incomes, which in turn lead to low saving and investment rates.

Rapid population growth is another condition commonly associated with less-developed countries. The population of the poor countries of Asia, Africa, and South America has been expanding at an average rate of about 2.5 percent per year. At this rate, the populations of these nations double every twenty-five or thirty years. In contrast, the populations of developed nations grow less than 1 percent per year on average. The difference is often taken to mean that rapid population growth is a major contributor to low rates of development because such growth imposes an increasing burden on the limited resources of less-developed countries. The more people, the greater the need to provide education, health care, and other basic services—which require resources that would otherwise be available for capital investment. To the extent that rapid population growth repre-

An identifying characteristic of developing countries is the dominance of the agricultural sector.

sents more mouths to feed, per capita income will decline as population grows, other things being equal.

Like wealth and poverty, development and underdevelopment are relative concepts. In 1750, England was probably the richest and most-developed country in the world, but by modern standards mid-eighteenth-century England was relatively poor and undeveloped. (We must never forget that all past great nations have undergone decline over time. See the Focus "Is 'Star Wars' in Our Future?") Moreover, we cannot judge reliably whether any given country should be counted as a developed or less-developed economy on the basis of secondary characteristics—such things as the rate of population growth, degree of literacy, or degree of industrialization. There are, for example, some developed countries that have high rates of population growth and a lesser degree of industrialization than do some less-developed countries. A more reliable way to distinguish quantitatively between the developed and less-developed countries is by per capita income—that is, the level of a country's GDP divided by its population. On these grounds, according to calculations by the World Bank, per capita income in the industrial market economies in 1998 was estimated to be on the order of twelve times greater than that in less-developed countries. Not all developing countries are experiencing slow growth, however, and economic institutions may provide some explanations for the differences.

Property Rights Arrangements and Economic Growth

Can differences in economic institutions be pinpointed as a major cause of underdevelopment and slow growth? It is often pointed out that economists are not able to bring societies into the laboratory and use the experimental method to test their theories. While this is certainly true, economists are able to observe the effects of different economic institutions on economic performance.

Considering countries "in transition" from communist-style organizations to markets is instructive. A history of capitalism, together with a gutsy return to market capitalism, are the probable reasons that the countries of Central and Eastern Europe progressed from a negative growth rate of −10.0 percent in 1991 to a positive growth rate of 1.6 percent in 1995 to a very respectable 3.4 percent rate in 1998. These differences in institutions may go far in explaining why the Russian economy, mired in bureaucracy and controls almost a decade after communism's end, experienced negative growth in all but one year of the period 1991–1998.[4]

[4]Data from the Council of Economic Advisers, *Economic Report of the President* (Washington, D.C.: U.S. Government Printing Office, 1999), p. 454.

FOCUS

Is "Star Wars" in Our Future?

History is full of examples of the rise of successful societies that experience peace, economic prosperity, and cultural development. However, as time passes, these successful nations become larger, more bureaucratic, and warlike. Eventually, the entire system collapses and the empire dissolves.

This was the case with ancient Egypt, Greece, and Rome. It was also the case with modern France and Great Britain, which at one time ruled possessions around the world during the eighteenth, nineteenth, and twentieth centuries. The same might even be said of the Soviet Union, which controlled much of Europe and Asia before it collapsed in 1989, leaving the United States as the sole superpower.

George Lucas's *Star Wars* world paints a similar picture of the future. Here a once prosperous and peaceful Republic degenerates into a bureaucratic and rent-seeking "democracy," which eventually is displaced by the "evil empire." In the end, of course, the Empire always loses. An interesting and controversial theory of economic growth, developed by the late economist Mancur Olson, may help us understand the life and death of nations.[a]

In Olson's view, economic growth and development depend on the "age" of a nation and the bureaucratic control that government has over society. New or younger societies have an advantage over older societies because they have fewer efficiency-reducing organizations like labor unions, regulatory bureaucracies, and business organizations that have special privileges from government. These special-interest groups obtain concentrated benefits, such as monopoly privileges, at the expense of large, unorganized groups such as "consumers" or "taxpayers" that do not have the incentive to organize and fight to repeal such privileges. Over time, these special-interest groups and their special privileges build up, and society (and its economy) begins to die a death of a thousand cuts.

Olson's thesis helps explain the high growth rates in Japan and Germany after World War II. Normally when war destroys capital and kills people, the economy is worse off. However, when war destroys the government, society can be "born again" without all the "red tape" of the old regime. Olsen uses this approach to explain why the South and Western States have experienced higher rates of economic development than in the older states of the Northeast and Midwest. These long-settled areas have had more time to accumulate special-interest organizations, such as labor unions, which are concentrated in the Northeast.[b]

---

[a]Mancur Olson, *The Rise and Decline of Nations: Economic Growth, Staflation, and Social Rigidities* (New Haven, Conn.: Yale University Press, 1982).

[b]Mancur Olson, "The South Will Fall Again: The South as Leader and Laggard in Economic Growth," *Southern Economic Journal* 49 (April 1983), pp. 917–932.

Consider some countries that, despite their common culture, similar climates, and common ethnic–religious origin, have taken radically different routes to economic development. This comparative analysis will shed some light on the causes of underdevelopment and growth.

Mainland China, Hong Kong, and Taiwan   Until fairly recently, the People's Republic of China (mainland China) had one of the strictest, and least flexible, systems of central economic planning anywhere in the world. Unlike some other communist countries, for example, China before the late 1970s apparently did not have a legally sanctioned private sector in the economy; in other words, economic activity was even more tightly controlled by the state than in the Soviet Union.

China apparently also had very little in the way of an underground economy; in the Soviet Union, the black market helped restore some degree of flexibility to the centrally planned system. Therefore, prereform China can serve as a good example of the effect of communist institutions on economic development.

It is instructive to compare the level of economic development in China in 1980—before most of the current economic reforms had been instituted—with development in the neighboring countries of Taiwan and Hong Kong. In 1998, GDP per capita in mainland China was about $2000. Although the people of Taiwan and Hong Kong are ethnically identical to the people on the Chinese mainland, Taiwan and Hong Kong have market economies, with relatively small public sectors. In fact, both countries have considerably less government regulation than the United States. Of the two, Taiwan has the greater endowment of natural resources. Hong Kong is very poor in natural resources; it has little level land for agriculture and must import both food and water from the mainland. Yet each of these economies has enjoyed successful economic development. Estimated 1998 GDP per capita for Taiwan was $13,000; for Hong Kong, $21,000. The standard of living in each economy is high and visibly improving. Largely unrestricted by government, entrepreneurship thrives. Although China's per capita GDP still lags far behind those in Taiwan and Hong Kong, the extensive market reforms undertaken in China since 1980 are allowing the huge population of China to enjoy the development advantages of markets, too.

The Two Koreas   The experiences of North Korea and South Korea—neighboring countries with vastly different institutions—offer additional evidence that differences in social, political, and economic institutions may be a major cause of differences in economic development and growth.

The two Koreas were one nation for hundreds of years. When the two separated in 1950, they adopted diametrically opposed paths to economic development. The Democratic People's Republic of (North) Korea has adhered strictly to the central planning model. It has one of the world's most highly socialized and centrally planned economies. All industrial enterprises are either directly owned by the state or are cooperatives owned indirectly by the state. Agriculture is carried out on either collective or state farms. Following the old Soviet model, the central planning system has allocated priority to investment in heavy industry at the expense of the consumer and agricultural sectors. Despite this emphasis, the performance of the industrial sector has been disappointing. Productivity is low, and virtually all plants and equipment are obsolete, although North Korea has recently begun to purchase Western equipment and technology, including complete plants. Nominal per capita income in 1998 was approximately $1500 per year. There is little variety in consumer goods, and quality is uniformly low. Shortages are common, and standing in long lines to purchase basic necessities is a way of life. Consumer durables such as appliances are usually unavailable.

Although the land, climate, and people of South Korea are similar to those of North Korea, there are dramatic differences between the two countries. The Republic of (South) Korea has an economy based on private enterprise and a market economy. In a little over twenty years, South Korea transformed itself from an economy dominated by subsistence agriculture (which is characteristic of most poor nations) to a modern economy with an emphasis on light industry. A thriving export market has led to South Korea's surge of development, and exports increased annually between 1974 and 1998. This growth reflects, in part, the improving quality of its exports, including finished goods such as Hyundai automobiles and trucks and Reebok shoes. The standard of living is among the highest in modern Asia; per capita income for South Koreans in 1998 was about $10,000, with a diverse array of high-quality consumer goods available. Interestingly, South Korea has only 10 to 20 percent of the Korean peninsula's deposits of mineral resources.

Such real-world examples suggest that different systems of property rights and incentive structures play a vital role in relative economic development. In other words, economists believe that many differences in economic development between North and South Korea can be explained on the grounds of different institutions. These institutional differences, especially those relating to political controls or to regulation of markets and economic processes, are often more important than the endowment of resources in determining economic progress.

Development and Trade Liberalization   At times, developing countries have made the task of development more difficult by following ill-advised policies designed to restrict the flow of foreign trade. Such policies prevent the international economy from taking full advantage of the law of comparative advantage, thereby reducing global economic efficiency. Perhaps worst of all, the developing countries that have adopted restrictions on foreign trade have usually reduced the rate of growth of their own economies in the process. Recently, however, many developing countries have modified their trade policies in the direction of greater liberalization.

A major aim of recent trade reforms has been the elimination of quantitative restrictions (for example, trade quotas) in such countries as China, Colombia, Gambia, Ghana, Indonesia, and Mexico. At the same time, many developing countries have replaced quantitative restrictions on trade with tariffs. This makes the degree of protection "transparent," which allows voters to easily see how a protectionist trade policy increases the costs they must pay for imported consumer goods. As a result, tariffs have already been substantially reduced in many countries, and political pressure is building for further reduction. Falling tariffs in developing countries are leading to more international trade and greater economic efficiency in the use of resources.

Trade reform tends to increase economic efficiency by increasing competition in domestic markets and by reducing distortions in the prices of traded versus non-traded goods. One measure of the degree of openness in a country's trade policy is the ratio of average exports and imports to GDP. Table 29.3 shows that the rate of economic growth in seventy-four developing countries tended to increase with the degree of openness in trade policies.

Even when the size of the economy and other factors that affect growth—such as the investment rate, terms of trade, and domestic inflation—are taken into account, there is a statistically significant relationship between the degree of openness and growth. In Asia, for example, an increase in the degree of openness of 10 percent is associated with an increase of nearly 1 percent in the growth rate. In other parts of the world, especially in Africa, the correlation between openness and growth is not as strong, however. It may be that the relatively greater flexibility of the Asian economies—the direct result of rapid capital formation in the last twenty years—allows resources to flow more rapidly into expanding sectors.

TABLE 29.3

Developing Countries: The Degree of Openness and Economic Performance

Developing countries can use the law of comparative advantage to accelerate their rates of economic development. Countries with relatively open foreign-trade policies experience higher rates of economic growth and lower rates of inflation than countries with restrictive trade policies, although they may have slightly lower investment rates.

	Number of Countries	Growth (in percent per year)	Inflation (in percent per year)	Investment (in percent of GDP)
Average Degree of Openness[a]				
Less than 25	28	3.5	244.6	24.8
25 to 40	23	5.2	50.7	24.3
More than 40	23	5.7	5.0	20.9
Openness by Exports[b]				
Less than 25	38	3.5	247.6	24.7
25 to 40	16	5.3	14.4	23.4
More than 40	20	6.2	3.1	22.0

[a]Defined as the average of exports and imports as percent of GDP.

[b]Defined as exports as percent of GDP.

LOOKING AHEAD: EXPLAINING ECONOMIC GROWTH AND DEVELOPMENT

Why do economies, developed and less developed, grow at different rates? Why do many, but not all, less developed countries have difficulty matching the levels of development found in Europe, Japan, and North America? In terms of economic growth, how will the United States fare, comparatively, in the global economy in coming years? We explore these controversial issues in the following sections.

U.S. Growth

Careful studies of the sources of growth (such as those done by the late Edward Denison) suggest the complexities involved in trying to identify causes of growth and then trying to stimulate them. Factor growth and, with it, technological change—the importance of which was downplayed in classical economics—are the two essential causes of growth. The long-run benefits and the possible short-run costs of rapid technological change have received a great deal of attention from politicians, economists, and the media in recent years, creating a rather muddy picture.

It is clear that the United States is experiencing a transformation from traditional smokestack industries (coal, steel, heavy machinery) to high-technology industries (computers, communications). The political blame for much of this economic change has been placed on foreign competition. The United States is no longer a self-sufficient economy; it imports more than twice as many goods now as in 1970, with a trade deficit in 1998 of about $243 billion. Total U. S. imports for 1998 were over $900 billion.

The two major reasons for heightened foreign competition are the lower wage rates and the swift spread of technology to foreign countries. Labor costs in South Korea and Taiwan are about one-fifth those in the United States. Japan, relying greatly on automation, uses approximately six times as many industrial robots as the United States. Some economists and business leaders fear that more automation in the United States will lead to higher unemployment, while other economists feel there will be a shift into other jobs. (Most believe the latter.)

New jobs are being created in the service industries. According to Labor Department statistics, about 22 million people were employed in manufacturing industries in 1997, while more than 54 million people were employed in **service industries**—those offering teaching, health care, financial services, and food service, for example. McDonald's now employs more workers than USX (formerly U.S. Steel).

Service industries

Those industries whose major, or sole, output is a consumer service, such as banking, entertainment, and health care.

The United States is not alone in its transition from heavy industry to high-technology and service industries. European industrial nations are also having difficulty with changing economies. Even Japan is experiencing some decline in heavy industry, but Japan, unlike Western countries, encourages changes in the economy. Japanese companies diversify greatly in areas of production. One company produces products ranging from foodstuffs to nuclear power plants. This diversity allows workers whose jobs become unnecessary to move into other branches of production within the same company, but it requires large-scale retraining programs within the companies.

Rather than following the Japanese model, politicians, businesspeople, and workers in the United States have demanded protection for the old smokestack industries against foreign competition. During the late 1970s and through the mid-1980s, the United States experienced its worst outbreak of protectionism (the establishment of legal artificial trade barriers and restrictions such as tariffs and import quotas) since the 1930s. The United States has tried to reduce imports and place quotas on autos, steel, and many other products, as we will see in Chapter 30. However, trade restrictions could well do more harm than good to the United States. The United States now exports more than twice the quantity of products it exported in 1980, and retaliation (in the form of trade restrictions on U.S. goods set in place by foreign governments) by other nations in response to U.S. restrictions is always a possibility. Such reactions inevitably reduce economic growth and well-being among all traders. The fate of U.S. growth may ultimately lie in successful implementation of free-trade agreements, especially the North American Free Trade Agreement and those negotiated under the General Agreement on Tariffs and Trade.

Contrary to popular belief, the United States has not fallen behind its major competitors in terms of economic growth. According to the Organization for Economic Cooperation and Development, average unemployment in 1998 was 4.5 percent in the United States, 9.7 percent in Europe, and 8.3 percent in Canada. Inflation was also lower in the United States (1.6 percent) than in all of the OECD countries (3.7 percent). Per capita GDP in the United States for 1997 was $29,326, compared with $23,761 in Canada, $18,698 in Europe, and $24,574 in Japan.

Some economists believe that rigid government regulation in other countries—including industrial policies consisting of government-directed technology, targeted investment strategies (favorable or unfavorable tax treatment), and mandated job training and health insurance programs—has retarded economic growth. Many international businesses, especially German and Japanese firms, have located in the United States because costs are lower here. Institutions matter to employment and economic growth, and government policies in both developed and less-developed countries affect institutions. The very size of government may have an enormous impact on growth (see the Application "Are Growth and Freedom Related?" at the end of this chapter).

U.S. Growth and Global Development

Clearly, the causes for economic growth in nations around the world are complex. For developing nations, there are special problems, such as the "vicious circle of poverty" and high population rates. But it appears that neither of these problems has prevented economic development in Hong Kong, Taiwan, and South Korea. These nations have developed rapidly by attracting foreign investment, not relying primarily on foreign aid.

The level of technology in most developing countries is low. But this is an effect, not a cause, of low levels of development. Poor countries are unable to afford the sophisticated equipment and techniques found in rich countries. The technology itself—inventions, and new processes and techniques—is widely available to less-developed countries as is the knowledge necessary to improve productivity. What less-developed countries lack are the property rights arrangements and institutions that reward economic efficiency, consumer choice, and entrepreneurship—the things that make the acquisition of technical knowledge worthwhile.

There is a lesson for the United States in the experiences of developing nations. It is not likely that the United States will meet the challenge of economic growth by increasing restrictions and regulations on competition or on capital formation. Rather, the United States can sustain growth only by adapting to new technology through competition and human capital development. The management of change in a complex economy is a difficult matter. It often amounts to a balancing of the present interests of workers and other resource suppliers against the overall interests of consumers and economic growth. American prosperity is clearly the result of earlier technological challenges that were met head-on within the context of vigorous and open competition, with due regard for the temporary distortions that new trade and technology might create.

APPLICATION

Are Growth and Freedom Related?

One of the hottest and longest debates in economic science has been the issue of economic growth and what is the best path of achieving it—the market and freedom, or government with its power to "rationally" direct resources. Adam Smith, in his *Inquiry into the Nature and Causes of the Wealth of Nations,* concluded that it was the invisible hand of market freedom that produced economic growth and wealth. Despite Smith's finding and the recent collapse of Soviet-style communism, the debate continues and government continues to grow.

The connection between economic freedom and economic growth is based on the idea that freedom allows people to pursue their self-interest, and in pursuing individual self-interest they also promote the general interest of society. Individuals increase their incomes by putting their own resources to work at their most valuable uses. As individual incomes increase, the income and wealth of society increases. The case against economic freedom is based on the idea that society must transfer resources to government in order to provide for public goods and to better rationalize the allocation of resources. Critics of economic freedom claim that even if such transfers do not increase economic growth, they do enhance living standards by providing goods such as art, scientific research, health care, and infrastructure that would otherwise not be provided. Critics of government reply that increased government imposes a higher excess burden of taxation, that government is less productive when it expands into new areas like health care, that government involvement inhibits entrepreneurship, and that government redistribution of income and regulation encourages people to pursue wealth-transfer activities rather than wealth-creating activities.

In the spirit of Adam Smith's *Inquiry,* economists have examined the connection between freedom and prosperity using statistical techniques to compare nations around the world with one another. The conclusion of these studies confirms Smith's original conclusion that economic freedom promotes economic growth and the general interests of society.

Several recent studies have examined the relationship between the size of government and the rate of economic growth. Using data on countries around the world over the last several decades, these studies have universally found that the size of government is negatively related to economic growth. That is, when the size of government is large, economic growth is generally low, but when government is small, economic growth rates are higher. For example, the United States has government expenditure equal to about 35 percent of GDP, and this is a small percentage relative to other countries. In contrast, government expenditures in Sweden consume two-thirds of GDP. In recent years, economic growth in the United States has surpassed that of Sweden by a significant amount.

The same result holds true when all countries are examined. When government is small compared with the overall size of the economy, the average annual increase in GDP exceeds 5 percent, but when government exceeds 50 percent of the overall economy, economic growth generally stagnates at 2 percent or less. The difference between big government/low growth countries and small government/high growth countries adds up over time. In small government countries, income doubles about every decade, but in big government countries, income may not double during your entire lifetime.

Japan is a good example of how the size of government affects economic growth. In the 1960s, the Japanese government represented only a small fraction of GDP; over this period, the average annual growth rate exceeded 10 percent. Since then, the Japanese government has grown enormously and now represents a higher percentage of GDP than in the United States. Not surprisingly, as the government grew in Japan, the rate of economic growth rate dipped into the single digits in the 1970s and 1980s and has been anemic in the 1990s. Former big government/slow growth economies such as Ireland, New Zealand, and the United Kingdom have all reduced government spending as a percentage of GDP, and economic growth has been revitalized as a result. Statistical analysis confirms that it is economic freedom that causes economic growth.[a]

Other statistical tests indicate that economic freedom is responsible for higher levels of prosperity in both industrialized and nonindustrialized countries. Prosperity is found to stimulate additional economic freedoms and, indirectly, additional political freedom, so that the best recipe for economic growth is economic freedom.[b]

QUESTION

America is composed of fifty states. If you compared the ten fastest-growing states with the ten slowest-growing states, what major differences between the two groups would you expect to find?

---

[a]Wenbo Wu and Otto A. Davis, "The Two Freedoms, Economic Growth and Development: An Empirical Study," *Public Choice* 100 (July 1999), pp. 39–64.

[b]W. Ken Farr, Richard A. Lord, and J. Larry Wolfenbarger, "Economic Freedom, Political Freedom, and Economic Well-Being: A Causality Analysis," *Cato Journal* 18 (Fall 1998), pp. 247–262.

SUMMARY

1. Economic growth is defined as growth in real GDP or in real GDP per capita.

2. The causes of economic growth are complex, but they certainly include growth in population, labor productivity, capital accumulation, and technology.

3. Economic growth requires increases not only in the productive capacity in the economy but also in aggregate demand, which must keep pace with increases in potential output.

4. The Phillips curve relation suggests that there is a trade-off between inflation and employment, but economic experience over the 1990s casts doubt on the suggested inverse relation.

5. An essential feature of slower U.S. economic growth in the 1980s was the decline in the growth rate of the productivity of labor—in output per worker. Though numerous factors caused the decline, the major factor appears to be a reduction in capital formation.

6. A lower saving rate, which has led to a lower growth rate in investment expenditures, is a major factor in explaining the lower rate of capital formation in the United States.

7. The United States is faced with a high-technology challenge to economic growth—a movement away from heavy industries such as steel, automobiles, and shipbuilding to industries based on electronics and other advanced technologies and to service industries. America's response to this challenge will determine growth prospects for many decades to come.

8. The less-developed countries of the world are characterized by low per capita income, large and growing populations, low saving and investment rates, and slow economic growth.

9. The vicious circle of poverty refers to the fact that there is little saving in a poor economy and, therefore, little chance for future development. Economies are thus said to be poor tomorrow because they are poor today. This idea has some merit in explaining underdevelopment, but it must be applied carefully.

10. Institutions matter to economic growth and development, as illustrated by the experiences of economies such as Hong Kong, Taiwan, and South Korea.

KEY TERMS

standard of living	capital deepening	economic development
economic growth	growth absorption	developing countries
real per capita GDP	Phillips curve	vicious circle of poverty
productivity of labor	capital formation	service industries

QUESTIONS FOR REVIEW AND DISCUSSION

1. What is the difference between growth in real GDP and growth in real GDP per capita? Would it be accurate to suggest that the percent change in real GDP per capita is equal to the percent change in real GDP minus the percent change in the population?

2. Would it be accurate to suggest that a developing country with an abundance of natural resources has the potential for a high growth rate? What must occur in such countries before a high rate of growth can occur?

3. What is the cost of capital? What happens to real GDP per capita when the number of machines increases?

4. What changes occurred during the Industrial Revolution that resulted in large increases in real GDP per capita? Are similar changes necessary to obtain growth in developing countries?

5. Explain what economic growth means in terms of production possibilities curves. What causes this growth? Is this identical to increases in aggregate supply?

6. Suppose that 1000 tractors were added to a nation's stock of capital every year. Would total farm output rise by the same amount every year? Why or why not?

7. If growth causes an increase in aggregate supply, what must happen to the price level to achieve the higher level of output? Does this suggest that increases in aggregate demand must accompany increases in aggregate supply to maintain price level stability and full employment?

8. What has happened to the rate of growth in real GDP per capita in the United States since the late 1960s? What has caused or accompanied this trend?

9. If you had to choose between price and employment stability and sustained growth in real GDP per capita, which would you choose?

10. What are the primary characteristics of a less-developed economy?

11. Evaluate the following statement: Less-developed countries are poor today because they were poor yesterday.

12. Evaluate the following statement: To achieve economic growth, an economy requires lots of resources, including land, and a low rate of population growth.

13. Some economists, for example, A. W. Phillips, believe that there can be an inverse relationship between inflation and growth. Briefly analyze this position, recognizing that the U.S. economy in the 1990s was typified by low inflation and high levels of employment and growth.

PROBLEM

Draw a production possibilities curve for the economy of Macronesia for the year 2000. Place consumer goods on one axis and capital goods on the other. Suppose that in 2000 net investment of $20 billion in new capital occurs, with no change in technology levels or in any other resources.

    a. Show the new production possibilities curve for 2001.

    b. If additional (new) net investment of $20 billion occurs in 2000, 2001, and 2002 with no change in the level of technology or other resources, what happens to the production possibilities curve for 2001, 2002, and 2003? Why?

    c. Do your results change if the initial and subsequent net investment increases are in government infrastructure spending financed by taxation? Explain.

WORKING WITH THE WEB

1. Find the CIA World Fact Book (http://www.odci.gov/cia/publications/factbook) and look up data for the following countries: Argentina, Brazil, China, India, Iran, Jordan, Mexico, South Korea, and Thailand. Locate data on GDP per capita, life expectancy at birth, and literacy (total population).

    a. What relationship exists between literacy and GDP per capita?

    b. Assume that changes in literacy lead to changes in GDP per capita, in a process similar to what you might expect from analysis using a production possibilities frontier. Within the context of this graph, explain and interpret your findings from part (a).

    c. Do you observe a relationship between the variables for life expectancy and GDP per capita?

    d. Provide a general interpretation of your findings from part (c).

2. In a paper presented at the San Francisco Federal Reserve Bank's home page, read one author's discussion of recent U.S. growth. Use either of the following two approaches to find the article "Supply Shocks and the Conduct of Monetary Policy." Locate the article, read it, and then discuss this author's beliefs about the factor(s) behind U.S. growth in the late 1990s.

    The first approach is to proceed through a series of links. Go to http://www.frbsf.org and select the link for "Economics Research." On the next page, use the menu under "Publications and Resources" to select "Economic Letter." Page down to the link to the "Supply Shocks" article (dated July 2, 1999). The second approach is to go directly to the article by entering the following address: http://www.frbsf.org/econrsrch/wklyltr/wklyltr99/el99-21.html.

3. One area of discussion at the United Nations Conference on Trade and Development site (UNCTAD) concerns lesser-developed nations. Go to this site (http://www.unctad.org) and after clicking the appropriate language, select "Least Developed Countries" from the menu below the heading "UNCTAD PROJECT SUBSITES."

    a. What are some of the criteria used in determining whether a nation is an LDC?

    b. Between 1968 and 1994, has the number of LDCs increased or decreased?

Robert E. Lucas, Jr.

Paul Samuelson

POINT

COUNTERPOINT

Paul Samuelson and Robert Lucas: Do We Need Discretion or Discipline in Policy?

Paul Samuelson (b. 1915) "has done more than any other contemporary economist to raise the level of scientific analysis in economic theory." So announced the Swedish Academy of Sciences in 1970, when Samuelson became the first American recipient of the Nobel Prize in economics. Although he has been called on frequently by presidents and Congress for his advice on economic matters, Samuelson has never held an official policy role in any administration. He has worked principally in the service of his profession: as a professor of economics at M.I.T., as president of the American Economic Association, and as a frequent contributor to journals and magazines. Born in Gary, Indiana, Samuelson received his Ph.D. in economics from Harvard in 1941. His doctoral dissertation, *Foundations of Economic Analysis,* was published in 1947 and became one of the definitive technical treatises on neoclassical economics. Today, Samuelson is one of the most widely respected Keynesian economists.

Robert E. Lucas, Jr. (b. 1937), credited with introducing rational expectations theory into macroeconomics, has helped change the way economists view the role of macroeconomic policy. Born in Yakima, Washington, Lucas received his Ph.D. in economics in 1964 from the University of Chicago, where he gained a firm background in Keynesian economics. One of the texts he found particularly influential at that time was Samuelson's *Foundations of Economic Analysis.*

After graduate training, Lucas became increasingly disillusioned with Keynesian interpretations of the macroeconomy. His article "Econometric Testing of the Natural Rate Hypothesis," published in 1972, is one of many that discuss the implications of rational expectations theory. This theory assumes that people will make economic decisions based on their knowledge of economic policy, their past experiences, and their expectations of future events. In theory, such rational behavior can distort or even neutralize the effects of well-publicized fiscal and monetary policies. According to Lucas, he and his early followers were initially regarded as "very far out" by colleagues for their nontraditional views. However, appreciation of rational expectations theory earned Lucas the Nobel Prize in 1995. Lucas has held academic posts at Carnegie-Mellon University, the Ford Foundation, and the University of Chicago, where he currently teaches.

The Case for Activism

In 1964, the unemployment rate stood at 5.2 percent and GDP was $638 billion. The economy was near the end of a bitter recessionary period. Government policy advisers, following Keynesian theory, called for direct intervention in the form of a massive tax cut. Congress responded by passing the 1964 Revenue Act, which slashed personal income taxes by almost 20 percent and corporate taxes by almost 8 percent.

The tax cut, aided by a surge in the money supply, ushered in several boom years. Over the next four years, GDP grew over 11 percent and unemployment dropped to 3.8 percent. Policy activists cite the 1964 tax cut as evidence of the usefulness of well-planned fiscal and monetary actions. Although the evidence since the 1960s has been less clear-cut, the case for activism rests on the assumption that the economy cannot easily readjust to full employment without some form of countercyclical policy, whether in the form of monetary growth, monetary restraint, fiscal cutbacks, or fiscal spending. The fiscal actions are generally preferred by activists because they can exert a direct impact on the flow of expenditures. Monetary policy works more slowly and less directly on expenditures, through the mechanism of interest rates.

Defending the need for activism, Samuelson and other economists focus on the terrible social costs of economic downturns and sudden shocks to the system. Left to correct itself, a shrinking economy could inflict insufferable damage on millions of people before prices and aggregate demand readjust to full-employment levels.

The record of policy activism gives some support for this view. Since World War II, the United States has suffered several recessions, but depressions seem to be a thing of the past. "Another depression on the order of the 1930s just doesn't seem possible," says Samuelson. The government nowadays "will do what it has to do" to avert economic disorder. "There's no longer the sense that we must somehow sweat these things out."[a]

Although activist policy has eased the severity of business cycles, it has not found a means to avoid them altogether. Indeed, there are many who argue that the economy's boom-and-recession pattern since World War II has been more the effect of discretionary policy than the cause. Also, there are many economists who point to the accelerating inflation suffered over these years and the failure of government to apply the appropriate countercyclical fiscal medicine: budget surpluses.

The Case Against Activism

For Robert Lucas, attempts to unbend the business cycle through discretionary, countercyclical policy are

---

[a]Quoted in "Economists Don't See Threats to Economy Portending Depression," *Wall Street Journal* (October 12, 1984), p. 1.

based on some unexamined assumptions. For such a policy to work, individuals and firms must respond cooperatively; when the government tries to close a recessionary gap, they must respond as if such actions will have no effect on prices.

Lucas believes that expectations about prices will always direct behavior, whether one is speaking in microeconomic or macroeconomic terms. If individuals and firms believe that government policy will drive up prices, they will act to protect themselves: Wage earners will demand higher wages, investors will seek higher interest rates, and so on. When such expectations are considered, Lucas deems most countercyclical policy to be futile and counterproductive. For instance, if policy-makers try to reduce unemployment through deficit spending, wage earners who have experienced the effects of such spending in the past will anticipate higher inflation. They will naturally try to keep the wages they have and to increase them. In the face of such demands, employers will find it more and more difficult to hire additional labor, and unemployment will remain despite the increase in aggregate demand. Rather than bend the recessionary cycle, the policy-makers will have managed to foster inflationary pressures, perhaps ushering in high unemployment and high inflation.

The checkered performance of macroeconomic policy in the early 1980s provided Lucas plenty of ammunition to blame discretionary policy for a variety of economic ills. To Lucas, appropriate macroeconomic policy would try neither to fool nor to ignore the expectations of individuals and firms. Instead, Lucas calls for some fixed limits for policy that recognize the long-run patterns of growth in the economy, which have been in the range of 3 to 4 percent for GDP over the past 100 years. He also advocates a monetary rule that would keep the growth rate of the money supply to approximately 3 percent.

Many economists find the rational expectations model extreme in its assumptions. How is it, they ask, that citizens can adopt an accurate set of expectations about the effects of policy when even competent observers of the economy are often misjudging the rate or even direction of economic change? Moreover, what happens when fiscal or monetary policies are overwhelmed by a supply shock? Will government then be required to overcome the instability? Questions such as these have brought lively debate over the future course of activism in policy.

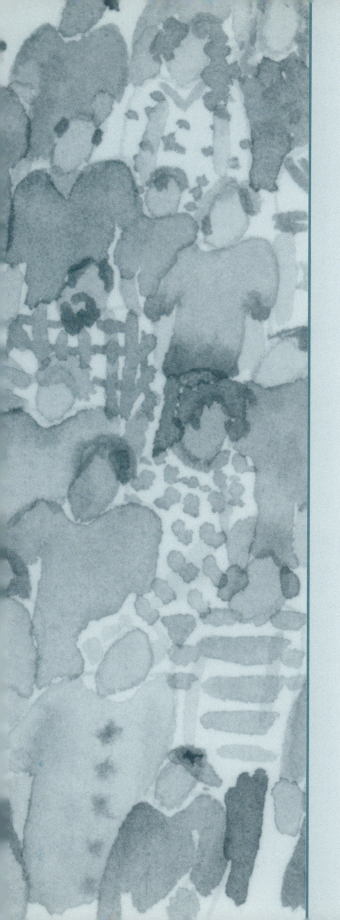

International Trade and the Global Economy

International Trade

We do not often stop to ponder all the ways in which imported goods enrich our lives and improve the material well-being of all nations of the world. On a typical day, for example, an American student's consumption patterns are clearly global. She awakes on sheets made in England and prepares breakfast on a hot plate made in Taiwan. Donning a cotton dress made in India and shoes made in Mexico, she catches the morning news on a TV with components manufactured in Japan. She drives to campus in a Japanese-made car.

The desirability of a diverse array of available goods and services and the interrelation of the U.S. economy with the economies of other nations present us with issues and problems we have left mostly unexamined until now. The issue of the competitiveness of U.S. firms in world markets may have directly affected you or your family. The large foreign trade deficit that arose in the 1980s and 1990s spawned much debate in business, labor, and government circles on the desirability of a new U.S. trade policy with countries such as Japan, Canada, and Mexico. Large swings in the value of the U.S. dollar overseas can alter not only vacation plans but consumption patterns and employment as well.

New technology has enabled nations to become more economically interdependent. In a sense, the whole world is now an economic system. Our entire study of economics has highlighted the role of global factors in U.S. economic functioning. In particular, we have emphasized the impact of free markets and trade on U.S. competitiveness and economic growth and on global development. In this chapter and the next, we focus closely

In many ways, importing automobiles from Japan into the U.S. economy in exchange for corn is no different from residents of Hawaii and California trading pineapples for oranges.

on international trade and finance in order to make clearer the role the United States plays in the global economy. We will demonstrate that the familiar concepts of supply and demand and production possibilities are extremely useful in discussing international trade (Chapter 30) and the financial system that supports it (Chapter 31).

International economics is composed of both microeconomic and macroeconomic elements. This chapter focuses on the microeconomics of trade. After reading Chapter 30 you should understand

- the reasons for and the advantages of specialization and trade.
- the factors that determine actual amounts and directions of trade between countries.
- how artificial interferences with trade, such as tariffs and quotas, affect the prices and quantities of goods and services sold in importing countries.
- how historical and contemporary trade policies and international integration, such as that contemplated by Western European nations, affect world trade.

THE IMPORTANCE OF INTERNATIONAL TRADE

Specialization
An economic entity's (an individual's or a nation's) producing only one good or service, or the performance of a single task in a production process by an individual.

All nations have particular talents and resources; like individuals, whole nations can specialize in one or many activities. For example, the islands of the Caribbean have abundant sunshine and good weather year round, and so these islands specialize in tourism. **Specialization** enables nations to emphasize the activities at which they are most efficient and at the same time gain certain advantages through trade.

Examples of international specialization and trade abound. France has a favorable climate and specialized land for wine growing, so it exports wine to Colombia and the United States and imports Colombian coffee and U.S. machinery. Likewise, both Colombia and the United States specialize and trade products that best utilize their qualities and quantities of resources.

National Involvement in International Trade

The overall magnitude of international trade and countries' shares in this trade can be measured in a variety of ways.

Table 30.1 lists the foreign trade of eleven nations as a percentage of gross domestic product for 1996/1997; the percentages vary widely. Exports accounted for 30 percent of Germany's total output but less than 10 percent of Argentina's output. Imports were about one-fourth to one-third of the real consumption of such countries as South Africa, Germany, Sweden, and Switzerland.

Percentage figures do not tell the whole story, of course. In absolute terms the United States was the world's largest trader in both exports and imports in 1997. The value of merchandise exports totaled $625 billion, and the value of merchandise imports was over $822 billion. (The values of both exports and imports have doubled in a generation.) The United States trades with virtually every nation of the world, the primary sources of imports being Canada and Japan (both with about 19 percent in 1997). The main destinations of U.S. exports in 1997 were Canada, Japan, and Western Europe. In terms of products, the three main U.S. imports are

TABLE 30.1

Exports and Imports as a Percentage of GDP in 1996/1997

Country	Exports as a Percentage of GDP	Imports as a Percentage of GDP
United States	7.7	10.2
United Kingdom	21.6	22.8
Switzerland	57.5	50.2
Sweden	48.0	38.0
Japan	13.7	11.0
Italy	20.2	15.3
Germany	30.0	26.2
Canada	31.7	30.0
Argentina	7.2	8.7
South Africa	11.6	10.4
Venezuela	11.2	6.0

Source: Central Intelligence Agency, *World Factbook* (1998) at www.odci.gov/cia/publications.

crude oil, motor vehicles, and food, and the three main exports are machinery, motor vehicles, and grain.

The United States is far and away the biggest exporter of products in the world, although exports were only 10.2 percent of GDP in 1996/1997. Some countries' economies—Venezuela, Germany, and Switzerland, to name just three—depend very heavily on exports; economic business cycles in other (importing) countries can have a dramatic effect on these countries' macroeconomies.

Why Trade Is Important: Comparative Advantage

The reason for all this trading is that all nations benefit from some degree of specialization and trade. Suppose two nations produce computer components and food with an equal expenditure of time and resources. Trade between the two countries will likely emerge because each can specialize at what it does better—emphasizing the production at which it is more efficient—and trade with the other country for the other good. As we will see, both countries will be better off because specialization and trade lead to increases in production and therefore to increases in the attainable consumption levels of both goods in both countries.

Comparative advantage
An economic entity's (an individual's or a nation's) ability to produce a good at a lower marginal opportunity cost than some other entity.

According to the principle of **comparative advantage,** countries will specialize in producing those goods and services in which they have relatively lower opportunity costs than their trading partners. For example, a hilly, rocky country will not be able to raise as many sheep per acre as a country with fertile grasslands, but the rocky land cannot support any production other than sheep raising, whereas the grassland will support more lucrative cattle production. Even though the grassland is absolutely more productive at raising both sheep and cattle, the rocky land has a comparative advantage in sheep growing because the opportunities forgone are very small. The rocky country will therefore tend to specialize in sheep; the grassy country, in cattle.

Consider the simplicity and power of the idea that each country produces those products that it can produce with relatively greater efficiency—that is, at a lower relative opportunity cost. Countries that have relatively lower opportunity costs of producing certain goods and services have a strong incentive to produce those goods and services. The large amounts of fertile U.S. farmland combined with advanced farm technology have made the American farmer the most productive in the world. America has a clear comparative advantage in certain farm products and raw materials. America's skilled labor force and high rate of technological advance through huge investments in private and public research and development have helped make the United States relatively efficient in producing highly sophisticated machinery and equipment. Trading partners of the United States, especially Japan, have specialized in routinized productions such as automobiles and steel. Energy regulations and increased demand have forced the United States to import immense quantities of petroleum. The pattern of U.S. imports and exports therefore shows the process of economic specialization and comparative advantage at work. (For an example of the idea of comparative advantage, see the Application "NAFTA: Free Trade or Free-for-All?" at the end of this chapter.)

Production Possibilities Before Specialization To demonstrate more precisely how all trading partners benefit by exercising their comparative advantages, we must look at what happens in each country before and after specialization and trade. Suppose that both the United States and Japan, in isolation, produce just two goods: computer components and food. Further assume that the production possibilities schedules facing the United States and Japan are depicted in Table 30.2, which gives the alternative combinations of food and computer components that could be produced in the United States and Japan if resources are fully employed. The United States, for example, may choose to produce 60 units of food and no computer components, 40 units of food and 10 units of computer components, 20 units of each, or 30 units of computer components and no food. With fully employed resources, Japan may choose between 45 units of computer components and no food at one end of the production spectrum and no computer components with 30 units of food at the other, or combinations between these extremes, as shown in Table 30.2.

These production alternatives are merely the trade-offs that are implicit in the countries' production possibilities curves. For the United States, the extreme choice is between producing 60 units of food (F) or 30 units of computer components (CC). That is, if the United States produces 60F, it will have to forgo 30CC. Within the United States, then, the opportunity cost of producing 1F will be ½ a unit of CC. Alternatively, the cost to the United States of producing 30CC is 60F, or 1CC costs 2F. In summary, within the United States,

60F costs 30CC to produce, or

1F costs ½CC to produce, or

1CC costs 2F to produce.

TABLE 30.2

U.S. and Japanese Production Possibilities Schedules for Food and Computer Components

Within the United States, 2 units of food cost 1 unit of computer components. Within Japan, ⅔ unit of food costs 1 unit of computer components. The relative opportunity cost of food production is lower in the United States, and the relative opportunity cost of computer component production is lower in Japan.

PRODUCTION POSSIBILITIES (AT FULL EMPLOYMENT)

	1	2	3	4
United States				
Food	0	20	40	60
Computer components	30	20	10	0
Japan				
Food	0	10	20	30
Computer components	45	30	15	0

These costs measure how many units of food must be given up to obtain a unit of computer components, or how many units of computer components must be given up to get an additional unit of food. In either case, what is being measured is the relative opportunity cost of producing food or computer components in the United States—that is, what must be given up to increase the production of food or computer components.

Exactly the same analysis can be applied to Japan. For Japan, the production possibilities schedule indicates that, in the extreme, either 45 units of computer components and no food or 30 units of food and no computer components can be produced. The opportunity cost of producing 1F in Japan is then 1½CC. Likewise, 1CC costs ⅔ a unit of F. In Japan, the opportunity cost of production is summarized as

30F costs 45CC to produce, or

1F costs 1½CC to produce, or

1CC costs ⅔F to produce.

Therefore, in this example, the United States has a comparative advantage in producing food and Japan has a comparative advantage in producing computer components. Do you see why?

Gains from Specialization and Trade   The concepts of production possibilities and opportunity costs provide a perspective for understanding the benefits of trade. Continuing our example of trade between the United States and Japan, first look at the U.S. and Japanese production possibilities curves in Figure 30.1. Notice that these production possibilities curves are straight lines. In practical terms, this means that resources can be transformed from food production to computer component production at constant opportunity cost, that resources are perfectly adaptable to one production process or the other in both economies. The simplicity of this assumption does not compromise the argument for specialization and trade.

The important part of the argument for gains from specialization turns on the pretrade opportunity costs of producing the two goods that face Japan and the United States. Before trade, consumers in the United States must sacrifice 2 units of food to produce 1 unit of computer components, while Japanese consumers must sacrifice only ⅔ unit of food to produce the same amount of computer components. Or American consumers must sacrifice ½ unit of computer components to obtain 1 unit of food, while their Japanese counterparts must give up 1½ units of computer components to get 1 unit of food. Thus, Japan is the least-cost producer of CC, and the United States is the least-cost producer of F. This is not the end of the story, however!

Both countries can gain from trade. Since the United States produces food at an opportunity cost of ½CC and Japan produces computer components at an opportunity cost of ⅔F, we know that the Americans would gain if trade gave them more than ½CC for 1 unit of food, and the Japanese would gain from more than ⅔F for a single unit of computer components. These differences in relative opportunity costs of producing food and computer components yield a basis for specialization and trade between the two countries.

Terms of trade

The number of units of one good that exchange in the market for one unit of some other good; a relative price.

At what price will trade take place? The **terms of trade**—the ratio at which two goods can be traded for each other—will settle somewhere between the relative opportunity cost ratios for each country. For example, terms acceptable to

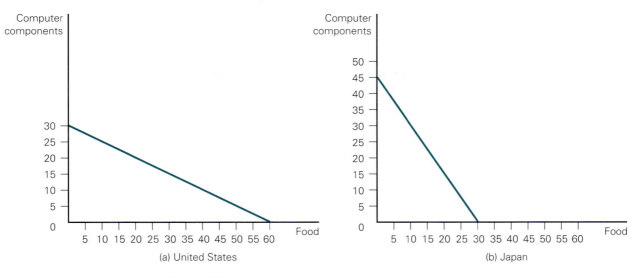

FIGURE 30.1

Prespecialization Production Possibilities Curves

The straight-line production possibilities curves for the United States and Japan indicate that resources can be transferred from computer component production into food production at constant opportunity cost. The different slopes of the two curves indicate that different opportunity costs provide the basis for both countries to benefit from specialization and trade. The United States has a comparative advantage in food production, whereas Japan is relatively more efficient at producing computer components.

both Japan and the United States will fall between $\frac{2}{3}F = 1CC$ (Japan) and $2F = 1CC$ (United States). We might say that the two countries bargain to set the terms of trade, and the bargaining range is determined by each country's internal opportunity cost trade-off. Let us assume that the terms of trade settle at 1 unit of food for 1 unit of computer components, or $1F = 1CC$.

Figure 30.2 illustrates the potential outcomes of this agreement in terms of the production possibilities curves and each country's posttrade **consumption possibilities curve.** If the countries choose to specialize totally according to comparative advantage, the United States produces 60 units of food and Japan produces 45 units of computer components. Each country can now trade for the product it no longer produces; each country is no longer restricted to consuming a combination of goods on its production possibilities curve. Without trade, a country is restricted to consuming whatever it produces. In the absence of trade, its production possibilities curve and its consumption possibilities curve would be one and the same.

With trade, however, each country's consumption opportunities are determined by how much of its specialized output is produced and the terms of trade. A country's consumption possibilities curve shows all the possible combinations of the two goods that could be consumed if production were specialized (according

Consumption possibilities curve

All the possible combinations of two goods that could be consumed by first specializing according to comparative advantage and then trading at the terms of trade.

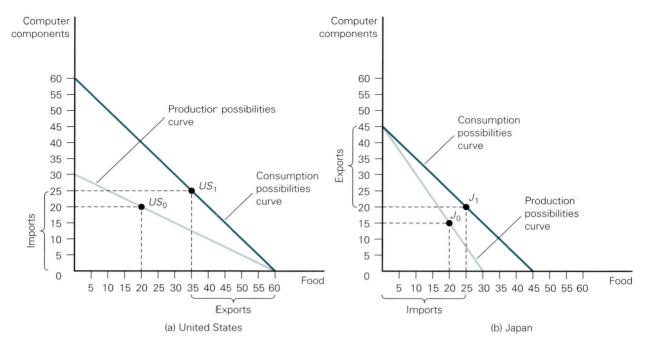

FIGURE 30.2

Production and Consumption Possibilities Curves
The United States specializes in food, producing 60 units; Japan specializes in computer components, producing 45 units. Once trade can take place at the terms of trade of 1F for 1CC, the consumption possibilities curves become relevant. The United States exports 25F and imports 25CC, increasing its consumption (over the pretrade situation) of food by 15 units and computer components by 5 units. Japan exports 25CC and imports 25F, increasing its consumption (over the pretrade situation) of food by 5 units and computer components by 5 units.

to comparative advantage) and trade could take place at the given terms of trade. Of course, only one combination can actually be consumed, so the consumption possibilities curve should be viewed as a menu of alternatives open to the country. The consumption possibilities curve with trade will always lie beyond the production possibilities curve, indicating that specialization and trade will leave the country economically better off. Remember, without trade, the country's consumption and production opportunities are identical.

Given that each country specializes and can now trade (at a price or terms of trade of 1F = 1CC) for the product it no longer produces, the consumption possibilities curves in Figure 30.2 become relevant. In contrast to a domestic opportunity cost of 60F for 30CC, the United States now enjoys a situation in which production of 60F could be traded for 60CC. (Naturally, Japan's resource base will not allow production of 60CC—only a maximum of 45CC.) Japan enjoys a similar expansion of consumption opportunities with specialization and trade. By specializing and trading, both countries are made economically better off. Each has the ability, with trade, to consume a bundle of goods beyond its production possibilities curve. This would be impossible, given each country's resources and technology, without trade. Specialization does not even have to be complete for the two countries to gain from trade. We have used the example of complete specialization here for simplicity.

If we assume that U.S. consumers originally consumed the bundle of food and computer components labeled US_0 in Figure 30.2a, we can note the improvement in their well-being by considering a new, posttrade consumption bundle, US_1, on their consumption possibilities curve. More of both goods are consumed after specialization and trade. A similar conclusion arises for Japan if we compare hypothetical pre- and postspecialization and trade consumption bundles, J_0 and J_1, respectively. Specialization and trade enlarge the consumption possibilities of the trading nations so that both countries can consume more of both goods after trade occurs.

Note that trade between the United States and Japan in this example takes place according to the principle of comparative advantage. Figure 30.3 shows the explicit pattern of trade. The United States exports food (25 units) because it has a comparative advantage over Japan in food production. This is so because 1F costs the United States only ½CC to produce, whereas 1F would cost Japan 1½CC to produce. Japan exports computer components for the same reason. It has a comparative advantage in producing them over the United States. Each country imports the good for which it is at a comparative disadvantage—that is, the good for which its trading partner possesses a comparative advantage. Gains from trade accrue to producers and consumers. In this example, American consumers of computer components benefit from the lower prices made available by imports, while American food producers benefit by obtaining a price for the food they export higher than the price they could obtain by selling it in the United States—which is not to suggest that no one is harmed by free trade. U.S. food consumers must pay higher food prices as a result of the decision to export some U.S. production. Similarly, U.S. producers of

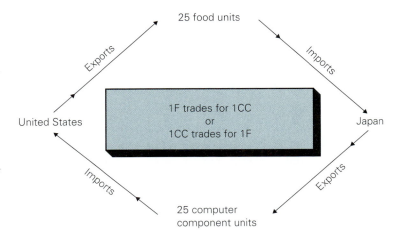

FIGURE 30.3

**The Pattern of
U.S.–Japan Trade**

Japan has a comparative advantage in computer component production; the United States, in food production. This means that Japan will export computer components and import food, whereas the United States will export food and import computer components. The terms of trade, 1F for 1CC in this example, must be between the two countries' opportunity costs of production.

computer components are harmed when Japanese suppliers enter the market and cause prices to fall. On balance, however, gains from free trade exceed losses; free trade leads to improved standards of living in both countries.

Our discussion has been based on a simple example of how the principle of comparative advantage works. In discussing two-good trade between Japan and the United States, we assumed that each country was absolutely more efficient than the other at producing one of the two goods. What if one country is absolutely more efficient in producing both goods? Suppose that productivity in the United States tripled—production of computer components increasing to 90 units and production of food increasing to 180 units. U.S. production capacity in this case would outpace Japan two to one in computer components and six to one in food. Nonetheless, the opportunity cost to the United States of producing each computer component would still be 2 units of food, which is higher than Japan's opportunity cost. It would still be mutually advantageous for the United States to specialize in food and to obtain computer components from Japan through trade. Remember, the argument for free trade is based on the principle of *comparative* advantage. Trade between two countries is mutually beneficial whenever the countries bear different opportunity costs of producing goods. This is true even if one of the countries is absolutely more productive at producing both goods.

Tariffs and Quotas

Tariff
A tax or levy on imported goods.

Quota
A restriction or limit on the quantity of an imported good.

Despite the advantages of specialization and trade, certain barriers to trade exist in the real world. Some are natural costs of exchanges, such as negotiating and transportation costs, and cannot be avoided. Other barriers to trade are artificial contrivances of governments designed to raise revenues or protect domestic producers from foreign competition. The major examples of artificial trade barriers are tariffs and quotas. A **tariff,** or import duty, is simply a tax levied on particular imported goods. For example, the United States imposes a tariff on imported shoes and steel. A **quota** is a partial or absolute limitation on the quantity of a particular good that can be imported. For example, until 1972, the United States imposed a quota on the importation of foreign oil and permitted oil refiners to import only the allowed amount of oil. Both tariffs and quotas reduce the extent of specialization and trade and, therefore, the gains that consumers obtain from free trade. Both raise the prices of imported and domestically produced goods and restrict imports. In these respects, tariffs and quotas are similar.

THE EFFECTS OF ARTIFICIAL TRADE BARRIERS

Free trade
The exchange of goods between countries without the presence of artificial trade barriers such as tariffs and quotas.

With very few exceptions (to be discussed later in the chapter), **free trade**—trade without artificial barriers—leads to maximum economic welfare among nations. Free trade and specialization expand consumption possibilities and deliver goods to consumers at the lowest possible costs. Yet given all the benefits of free trade, the world does not often seem to allow it to work, at least not completely. The reason is that some parties are harmed by free trade. Pressures are brought to bear on governments by producer groups for protection from foreign competition. Sometimes these groups win political favors, such as tariffs or quotas, to reduce the competitive threat. In this section we use economic theory to show how these interferences with free trade reduce the overall economic welfare of a country.

Welfare Loss from Tariffs

Consider the effects of a protective tariff on the society as a whole, using a hypothetical market for television sets. Figure 30.4 represents the domestic market for TV sets, including the domestic supply of the product and the U.S. demand. Prior to the imposition of a tariff, American consumers buy Q_4 units at the world price P_w. Of this quantity purchased, Q_1 are sold by domestic manufacturers and Q_1Q_4 are imported from abroad.

Assume that a tariff is imposed in the amount t, causing the price of TVs to American consumers to rise to P_{w+t}. (For clarity, we have assumed that the foreign TV supply curve is horizontal. A totally elastic supply curve would exist if TV production in the world was a constant-cost industry.) American TV producers gain additional profits or producer surplus in the amount represented by $P_{w+t}E_2E_1P_w$ because of the increased domestic output permitted by the higher price. Imports are reduced to Q_2Q_3, and the total number of sets sold decreases to Q_3. Consumers lose total benefits in the amount of $P_{w+t}E_3E_4P_w$. At the same time, the tariff on imported TV sets creates government revenues. These revenues are composed of the per unit amount of the tariff multiplied by the units of TV sets imported after the tariff is imposed (area E_2E_3AB in Figure 30.4).

FIGURE 30.4

The Effects of a Tariff

Gains in producer profits and government revenue do not equal consumer losses from tariff-imposition. Net consumer losses are shown in the shaded triangles in the figure. Before a tariff on TV sets, consumers purchase Q_4 units at price P_w. The tariff causes the price to rise to P_{w+t}, imports to decrease from Q_1Q_4 to Q_2Q_3, and the total number of TVs sold to decrease to Q_3. Consumers' total loss is represented by $P_{w+t}E_3E_4P_w$ but producers gain $P_{w+t}E_2E_1P_w$, and government tariff revenues are E_2E_3AB. The net loss to society is therefore the sum of the areas E_2BE_1 and E_3E_4A.

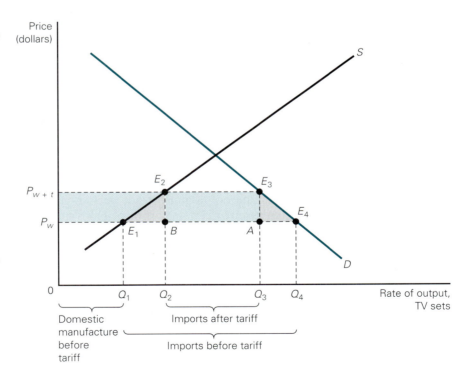

Economists typically assume that the government revenue is used in a manner that produces benefits equivalent to those lost by consumers of TV sets. However, the tariff causes a net loss in benefits to society, of which TV consumers are a part, represented by the sum of the two areas E_2BE_1 and E_3E_4A. The sum of these triangles represents a loss that is not counterbalanced by the sum of producers' gains and government revenue resulting from the tariff. Economists call this loss a **welfare loss to society** due to the imposition of a tariff.

Welfare loss to society
The net loss to an economy resulting from the imposition of an artificial trade barrier.

Why Are Tariffs Imposed?

If tariffs create a welfare loss to society, why are they imposed? Certainly tariff revenue to the federal government is minuscule when compared with other sources of government revenue.

The source of tariff protection is to be found in the urgings of "merchants and manufacturers" as well as from labor in domestic import-competing industries. Consumers of TV sets and of any goods that actually bear a tariff could conceivably convince both producers and the government not to impose tariffs because, as we have shown, consumers lose more than producers and government gain from tariffs. Practically, however, the world does not work this way. Consumers, the gainers from free trade, are widely dispersed and costly to organize in any fight for free trade. Interest in fighting a tariff or quota is also apt to be low among consumers because their *pro rata,* or proportionate, share of losses from artificial barriers to trade is generally small. To an individual consumer, for example, the tariff is a small proportion of the total price of an automobile. The incentive to organize and fight protective tariffs is therefore small.

Not so for producers. The *pro rata* share of the effects of tariff protection is much higher among manufacturers, for they are far fewer in number than consumers. Manufacturers thus have stronger incentives than consumers to form an interest group, and, being fewer in number, their costs of organizing are lower. For such reasons, the consumer interest in free trade is often thwarted.

Nontariff Barriers to Trade

Nontariff trade barriers
Alternative (to tariffs and quotas) means of restricting trade; examples include domestic content legislation and health and safety regulations.

Historically, tariffs and quotas have been the most important types of artificial trade restrictions. In recent years, other types of restrictive practices, which are generally called **nontariff trade barriers** (NTBs), have taken on increased importance. Examples of nontariff trade barriers include domestic content legislation (laws that require a certain portion of goods sold in a country to be produced there) as well as safety or health regulations designed to discriminate against foreign products. NTBs have grown rapidly in recent years because many countries have enacted trade legislation that forbids tariffs or quotas; NTBs represent an alternative form of protectionism. The use of NTBs varies greatly among countries. In the United States, NTBs exist for about 25 percent of imported goods. The corresponding percentage for Japan is about 12 percent. Within the European Community, percentages vary but average about 20 percent.

Although it is difficult to determine the specific effects of nontariff trade barriers, the general effects are quite similar to those of tariffs. Figure 30.4 shows how a tariff artificially raises the price of imported goods and causes the quantity of imports to fall. NTBs have similar effects. If, for example, the United States were to enact legislation requiring that cars sold in this country have a 50 percent domestic content, the Japanese could continue exporting cars to the United States only if at least half of the parts and the assembly were American. The cost of compliance would be higher production costs to the Japanese, but it would be very difficult to determine how much costs would rise. The effect therefore would be identical to the imposition of some specific tariff. Without knowing by how much this legislation would increase production costs, it would be impossible to determine what an equivalent tariff would be.

Nontariff trade barriers have become a major issue in the United States, particularly with regard to the economic unification of Europe. There is some concern that the European Community will implement technical standards that discriminate against foreign firms. Some observers have suggested that U.S. exports to Europe would fall sharply as a result of any such barriers. Although it is impossible to predict what economic policies the European Community will pursue, the complete economic unification of Europe is sure to present certain advantages to U.S. exporters. For one thing, U.S. firms will no longer have to contend with different NTBs in each of the European countries. Also, it will no longer be necessary for U.S. companies to produce a different product for each country in order to meet different standards.

A Quota Is a Quota Is a Tariff

Quota agreements between two countries to voluntarily limit exports from one country to the other have become a popular alternative to tariff controls. One form of quota agreement is called the Voluntary Export Restraint (VER). In 1990, for example, President Bush used the device to restrict imported steel through 1992. The Clinton administration continued to use threats of unilateral import restrictions in trade talks with particular nations. But a precedent for these actions had been established during the Reagan administration with VERs on automobiles.

On April 1, 1981, an international trade agreement between the governments of Japan and the United States was put into effect. Under the VERs, the government of Japan would prevent Japanese automakers from exporting as many cars as they would like to the U.S. market. Japanese car manufacturers were restricted to shipping only 1.68 million cars to the U.S. market per year from 1981 to 1984. What was the economic effect of the VERs on U.S. automobile producers and consumers?

To answer this question, we must first recognize that this "voluntary" restraint was nothing more than a quota of 1.68 million cars. The U.S. government effectively restricted imports from Japan to a level of 1.68 million cars. The next question to answer is: What effect did the imposition of an import quota have on the domestic U.S. market for automobiles?

Figure 30.5 will help answer this question. In Figure 30.5, P_W is the price of a car in the United States before imposition of a quota. Domestic producers sell Q_1 cars, and imports equal Q_4 minus Q_1 autos. Once the quota, equal to Q_3 minus Q_2, is imposed, how does the domestic market move to a new equilibrium? Recall that an equilibrium price is one at which quantity demanded equals quantity supplied. Part of quantity supplied is supplied by foreign producers, the amount of the quota in this case. To find what equilibrium price will be under the quota, we need only find a price at which the horizontal distance between the demand and supply curves equals the quota. At price P_{W+Q}, domestic output, Q_2, plus the quota, Q_3 minus Q_2, equals total quantity demanded, Q_3. Thus, at price P_{W+Q}, quantity demanded equals total quantity supplied. P_{W+Q} will then be the domestic price of a car if a quota of Q_3 minus Q_2 is imposed.

Figures 30.4 and 30.5 are similar in many respects, because tariffs and quotas are similar in many respects. They both raise domestic price and reduce imports, but the tariff works initially by affecting price and letting quantity adjust, whereas the quota directly affects quantity with the result that prices adjust. Whichever method is used to restrict trade, higher domestic prices and fewer imports result.

There are some differences between tariffs and quotas, however. In Figure 30.5, if a tariff had driven domestic price up to P_{W+Q}, the U.S. government would have collected tariff revenue in the amount of area E_2E_3AB. However, under the VERs, no tariff revenue was collected from Japanese automakers. In fact, the United States government merely allowed the Japanese government and Japanese automakers to decide for themselves which companies would fill the quota of 1.68 million units. With the import rights left specifically unassigned (and not charged for) by the U.S. government, the area E_2E_3AB became revenue to Japanese producers (and their U.S. dealers) rather than tariff revenue for the United States. This is one of the

---

FIGURE 30.5

The Effect of a Quota on the Domestic Market

When the quota is imposed, it is still necessary for quantity demanded to equal quantity supplied for the domestic market to be in equilibrium. Only at price P_{W+Q} will total quantity demanded, Q_3, equal total quantity supplied. Total quantity supplied equals quantity supplied domestically, Q_2, plus imports, Q_3 minus Q_2. The quota raises price, increases domestic producers' profits, and produces welfare losses—just as a tariff does.

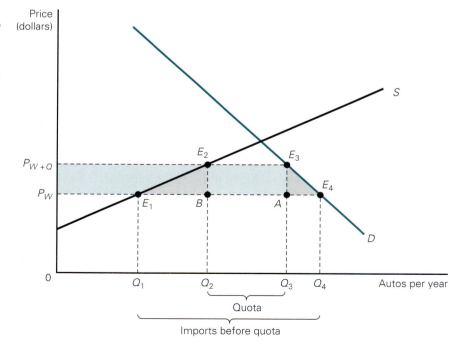

wealth transfers, from American consumers to Japanese producers, of a quota designed in this fashion. (For a further discussion of "voluntary" export restraints, see the Focus "Autos, Peanuts, and Politics: How Quotas Affect You.")

THE CASE FOR PROTECTION

Throughout history, numerous arguments have emerged in defense of protection from free trade. Most of these arguments are but thin veils for producers' interests. All the arguments—both the well-constructed and the questionable ones—deserve scrutiny.

National Interest Arguments for Protection

The two oldest and best-formed arguments in defense of protection and against free trade are the national defense argument and the "infant industries" argument. Both arguments contain a grain of truth, but each should be closely scrutinized before serving as a base for protectionist policies.

FOCUS

Autos, Peanuts, and Politics: How Quotas Affect You

Quotas, like tariffs, raise the prices of the products you buy. While trade has been liberalized through the reduction of tariffs—and through free trade zones such as NAFTA—quotas may be even more insidious at increasing the prices of consumer goods in the United States. Consider some examples. Economist Robert Crandall of the Brookings Institution in Washington, D.C., studied the Reagan administration's VERs in an attempt to gauge the economic effects on consumers and producers of automobiles.[a] He estimated that in 1984 the price of a Japanese car sold in the United States was about $2500 more than it would have been without the VERs. Additionally, the higher prices of Japanese imports allowed U.S. automakers to charge about $1000 more per car than they would have been able to in the absence of quotas. The stock-holders of U.S. auto companies and the employees of these companies clearly benefited from the VERs. Crandall also estimates that American auto consumers paid approximately $16 billion more for cars in 1984–1985 than they would have in the absence of the quotas.

Quota and tariff concessions to special interests who pressured politicians for favors were a part of the Bush and Clinton administrations' trade policy. For example, the United States Department of Agriculture (USDA) estimates that peanuts cost $491 per metric ton to produce in the state of Georgia, although the world market price is about $300 per ton. The USDA peanut price support program permits U.S. farmers to sell peanuts in the U.S. market for more than $600 per ton. American consumers pay more because there is a virtual ban on the importation of peanuts. Quotas may benefit producers, but they definitely injure consumers and economic welfare.

[a]Robert W. Crandall, "Detroit Rode Quotas to Prosperity," *Wall Street Journal* (January 29, 1986), p. 30.

National Defense   The oldest argument for protection—and the one with super-ficially the best justification—is that such restrictions are necessary for national defense. As military technology has changed, steel, gunpowder, manganese, ura-nium, and a host of other inputs have all been commodities essential to making war and they have all been the subject of tariffs and quotas to keep domestic pro-duction of these commodities strong.

The logic of protection for defense is clear: Since the ultimate function of gov-ernment is national defense, any possible threat to national defense, such as the unavailability of some resource during a crisis, must be avoided. A loss in con-sumers' benefits from protection is thus justified for a greater benefit—the avail-ability of essential materials to be prepared for war. Artificial barriers to trade in these materials are used to protect domestic industries considered essential for national defense.

The national defense argument is plausible for some industries and some prod-ucts, but consider that cheese, fruit, and watch manufacturers and other, non-defense-related industries have all resorted to the argument. History seems to prove that patriotism is the last and best refuge of a producer seeking protection from foreign competition. The national defense argument has seen double duty as an argument for maintaining unprofitable routes on railroads and protecting truck, air, and railroad companies by setting legalized cartel rates. The telephone indus-try was long protected on similar grounds.

The imposition of tariffs and quotas is not the only way to handle the national defense issue. A tariff is nothing but a hidden subsidy or cash grant to domestic producers. Thus, if an industry is to be protected for national defense reasons, an explicit subsidy may be more effective than tariff protection. That way, the national defense issue is made clear, and voters know how much defense actually costs them. If, for example, it is deemed vital to national security that the United States have a certain capacity to produce iron and steel, an alternative public policy would be to subsidize domestic iron and steel producers rather than to protect them against foreign competition with a tariff or quota.

Protection of Infant Industries   Possibly the most frequently heard argument for protection, especially in developing nations, is the so-called **infant industries** argu-ment. The infant industries argument is related to the idea of economies of scale. Economies of scale exist when, as plant size increases up to a point, long-run unit costs decline. This occurs because individual workers become more proficient at narrowly defined tasks, and machines are more closely tailored to individual processes. Scale economies may also occur because both workers and managers "learn by doing" and acquire more experience as output grows. Often, moreover, production of certain manufactured goods results in an enormous initial setup cost. As firm and industry output grow larger, these setup costs are spread over larger and larger numbers of units produced. A number of developing nations use this economies of scale or infant industries argument today in their quest for unilat-eral tariff protection. One-crop economies, whose foreign earnings are heavily dependent on a single export, seek to use an umbrella of protectionist policies to buy time for diversification.

As much as one might be concerned for the economic plight of poor nations, great care must be exercised in applying the infant industry argument to them. At best, the argument is one for allowing domestic industry to gain a foothold in inter-

Infant industry
A new or developing domestic industry whose unit production costs are higher than those of established firms in the same industry in other countries.

national competition. Protection for any reason, as we have seen, means lost benefits for consumers. Obviously, any gains from ultimate independence must be balanced against the costs of lost consumer benefits over the period of protection.

A final question that should be applied to the infant industries argument concerns the vagueness of the goal of removing protection when the industry "grows up." It is hardly legitimate to apply the infant industries argument to the present-day steel industry in the United States and Western Europe, but the argument is still being used. Entrenched protectionist interests will always attempt to prolong the "infancy" of any industry. The dangers of giving protectionists a general legal foothold negate any merit the argument might have in limited and specific cases.

Industry Arguments for Protection

A number of other arguments for protection crop up from time to time, usually put forward by domestic firms and industries seeking protection for protection's sake. We characterize these arguments as wrong because they are assaults on the very principle that gains may be realized from trade. They are all variations on the theme that special-interest groups deserve protection from international competition.

The "Cheap Foreign Labor" Argument   A common argument for tariff or quota protection is that labor or some other resource is cheaper abroad, enabling foreign manufacturers to sell goods at lower prices than U.S. manufacturers. This argument is usually heard from producers and workers who fear displacement by imports and foreign competition. Most recently, it has been the argument used by Ross Perot, Pat Buchanan, and others to urge the defeat of the North American Free Trade Agreement. Opponents of NAFTA claim that a massive loss of jobs will result as U.S. firms relocate to take advantage of lower-cost labor in Mexico.

While the argument may be correct—foreign producers may be more efficient combiners of resources—this truth in no way denies the benefits to free trade. The *absolute* level of wages in any other country does not matter. As we have seen, gains from trade derive from *comparative* advantage. Indeed, the request for protection from cheap labor turns the gains from trade position on its head: The reason for trade becomes a reason to limit or restrict trade. Open trade is beneficial precisely because resources may be cheaper or combined more efficiently elsewhere. The opening or extension of trade creates a temporary disruption of markets, including the unemployment of resources. To impose tariffs or quotas on the grounds that some groups of U.S. laborers are temporarily thrown out of work or that some U.S. stockholders are losing wealth is to subsidize special interests at a greater cost to all U.S. consumers of the subsidized product or service. Moreover, the domestic economy may actually gain from the movement of domestic resources into new fields of comparative advantage. For example, resources released from domestic steel production may be reallocated to computer production.

Side issues arise in the cheap foreign labor argument. One common complaint is that foreign governments subsidize the production of exported goods to shore up their domestic industries and prevent unemployment. This complaint is used as a plea for protection from cheaper imports. But to argue for tariffs on these grounds is to look a gift horse in the mouth. The benefits from trade are independent of the reasons that imports are cheaper. If governments choose to subsidize their exports, they in effect tax their own citizens to benefit foreign consumers.

Dumping

The selling of goods in foreign markets at prices lower than those charged in domestic markets.

Dumping, selling goods abroad at a lower price than in the home market, is also related to the cheap foreign labor argument for protection. The practice, an example of price discrimination, means that foreign buyers gain greater benefits from consuming the commodity or service than domestic consumers. In practice, it is often difficult to determine whether goods are being dumped. As defined by U.S. trade policies, dumping occurs when a foreign producer sells in the American market either below costs or at a price below that charged to the foreign producer's domestic customers. In real-world cases, then, a producer could be selling to his or her own customers at monopoly rates and be prohibited from selling to American consumers at lower rates (even though they more than cover costs). Such restrictions, if enforced by trade authorities, work against American consumers.

Special interests in the favored country often complain that dumping constitutes "unfair competition," but the argument for free trade remains intact nonetheless. Consumers in the favored nations are able to purchase goods at lower prices, and overall welfare in the consuming country is enhanced.

It should not matter why foreign prices are low, as long as the foreign supplier who is dumping goods in U.S. markets has no monopoly power. If the producers of Japanese television sets undersell U.S. producers with an eye to putting them out of business and subsequently raising price to a monopoly level, dumping does pose an issue for public concern. More often, "dumping" by foreign producers is a reflection of their lower costs of production and puts competitive pressure on U.S. producers.

The "Buy American" Argument   The "buy American" argument, a call to patriotism, is based on the notion that Americans will be better off by keeping their money at home. More specifically, "buy American" means that imports should be restricted so that high costs or inefficient producers and their employees may be protected from foreign competition.

This well-known argument is fallacious on several counts. First, it asks consumers to pay higher prices for goods and services than are available to them through trade, thereby negating the potential expansion of trade benefits. Second, when money is kept at home, foreign consumers are less able to purchase domestic exports, reducing the welfare of domestic export producers and their workers and other input suppliers.

"Terms of Trade" Advantage   A final argument applies to countries that have monopoly power in international markets. It suggests that a country employ its power to increase its share of the gains from international trade. Thus, if the United States is the world's largest supplier of computers, putting restrictions on computer exports will drive up the price of computers in the international market. Although the United States will then sell fewer computers, it will get a higher price per computer and possibly higher computer sales revenues. In effect, by restricting computer exports, the United States would alter the terms of trade in international transactions in its favor.

Terms of trade argument

Defending the use of artificial trade barriers, combined with monopoly or monopsony power in international markets, in order to produce an improvement in a country's terms of trade.

The **terms of trade argument** suggests that countries exercise monopoly and monopsony power where possible. Doing so is a means for a country to increase its revenues from international trade. The argument founders, however, on a simple point: the possibility of retaliation by other countries. If all countries seek terms of trade advantages, the trading nations of the world *collectively* may be made worse off. The exercise of monopoly or monopsony power to improve the terms of trade for all countries could mean a shrinking of total world production for exports. This negates the gains from comparative advantage and from the division of labor and reduces specialization within nations.

Perhaps the greatest flaw in all arguments for protection lies in the implicit assumption that other nations will lose export markets and will not retaliate. It is improbable that a country could win permanent terms of trade advantages on a unilateral basis while its trading partners sit idly by. U.S. history is peppered with examples of tariff wars. One of the fiercest tariff wars in history took place in the midst of the Great Depression of the 1930s, discussed in the next section. Tariffs or other forms of trade barrier retaliation can only create a reduction in world-wide economic welfare and massive and inefficient allocations of resources. Whatever the initial reasons for protective tariffs, consumers ultimately suffer the costs.

Clearly, the reduction or removal of tariffs or quotas benefits consumers as a whole, producing a *net* benefit to society. But against these gains must be set the losses that occur to laborers (and other input suppliers) in businesses and industries that no longer are protected. Many economists support *temporary* retraining and assistance programs for workers and industries that suffer hardship as a result of freer trade. Further, despite contemporary arguments for "fairness" in trade, economists as a whole continue to emphasize the benefits of free and open trade whenever prices are lower for imports (see the Focus "'Fair Trade' and Protectionism: The Steel Industry").

FOCUS

"Fair Trade" and Protectionism: The Steel Industry

Often one hears of "fair trade" rather than "free trade" in the ongoing debate over protection. Sometimes "fair" trade, advocated by particular interest groups (businesses, labor, etc.) means simply that these groups want only trade policies that will benefit them—consumers be damned. The "fair trade" argument, however, has other variants, variants that appear to provide "fairness." Two of these arguments are the "dumping" issue (discussed in the text) and the "unfair" subsidy issue.

The subsidy issue is often raised because many governments around the world, in common with the United States, subsidize particular areas in their respective economies. These subsidized commodities, such as certain agricultural products within the European Union, then find their way into international markets where, sometimes, they underprice domestically produced products. The point is that consumers benefit from these price reductions, no matter the source. Arguments for free trade are sound, no matter the source of lower prices. Consumers benefit more than producers lose.

Such arguments are, of course, the source of interest-group demands for protection. The dumping ("fair trade") argument was used, for example, in demands for U.S. steel industry protection in the late 1990s. The surge of steel imports led steel laborers and certain domestic manufacturers to demand a limit to steel imports to 25 percent of the U.S. market. President Clinton nevertheless sided with free traders in the U.S. Senate, and the bill was killed in June of 1999 despite a mixed record on free trade of the Clinton administration. The support from both parties was also mixed, with senators from steel-producing states voting for protection. Likewise, the demand for trade restrictions was mixed in that large domestic steel producers who enlarged their inventories from abroad were silent on the issue. Free trade won in this instance, but all kinds of "fairness" pretexts are raised against it. The next time someone argues for restrictions in the name of "fair trade," ask yourself "fair to whom?"

U.S. TARIFF POLICY

U.S. tariff history has been punctuated by cycles of less-restricted and more-restricted trade, with a move toward free trade in the past fifty years that may be more apparent than real. The average tariff rates for the years between 1821 (the year of the first good statistics) and 2000 are shown in Figure 30.6, along with some highlights of our tariff history. In the twentieth century, import duties as a percentage of the value of all imports subject to duty have ranged from almost 60 percent in the early 1930s to about 3 percent in 2000.

Why has the average tariff fluctuated so widely during U.S. history? Before turning to a specific analysis of changing conditions, one broad issue will help us answer the question. With the minor exception of tariffs imposed for revenues to fight wars or to apply foreign policy pressures, the average tariff has varied with business conditions, falling in periods of prosperity and rising during prolonged recessions or depressions. During periods of rising prosperity, manufacturers and workers displaced by free trade find little political support for the imposition of tariffs. When general business conditions turn downward, creating reduced demand for products and increased unemployment, the cry for protection grows louder in the political arena.

Early Tariff Policy

Tariffs were a major source of revenue for our republic in its early years, as they are for some developing countries today. Post-1820 tariffs tended to vary with business conditions, rising during recessions and falling during more prosperous periods of business activity. On the eve of the Civil War, tariff revenues stood at about 19 percent of the value of imports, the lowest level in American history up to that time. In 1861, Congress passed the Morrill tariff under the pretext of generating much-needed revenue for the Union treasury. Whatever the initial intention, the Morrill tariff set off a wave of protectionism in U.S. policy that lasted until the second decade of the twentieth century. Tariffs declined dramatically during the Wilson administration, standing at only 16 percent in 1920.

The dramatic downturn in the economy beginning in the late 1920s had a stark and lingering effect on protectionism in the United States. Manufacturing and commercial interests, coinciding with a willing political climate, produced the Smoot–Hawley Act of 1930, which legislated the highest peace-time tariff in U.S. history. Average tariff levels were raised to almost 60 percent of the value of imports, setting off a frenzy of protectionist retaliations in other nations. The result of what was perceived as American self-interest was falling real incomes, sharply reduced consumer welfare, and a deepened and prolonged depression in the major world-trading countries.

Modern Tariff Policy

Contemporary tariff policy may be viewed as an attempt to overcome the disastrous effects of protectionism embodied in the Smoot–Hawley Act. The first Roo-

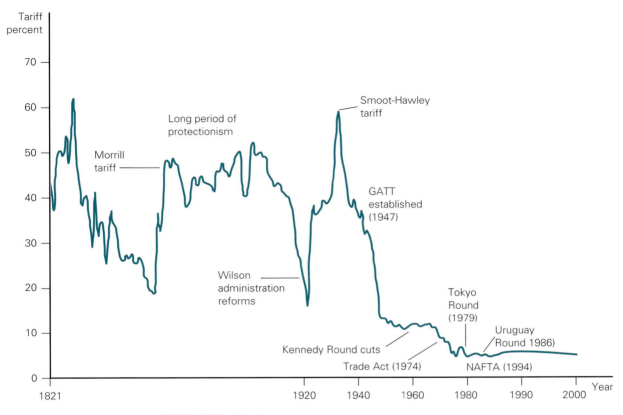

FIGURE 30.6

Level of Tariffs

The United States today has lower tariffs, as measured by the ratio of tariff fees collected to the value of imports, than at any other time in its history. Since the establishment of the General Agreement on Tariffs and Trade (GATT) in 1947, tariffs have followed a downward trend.
Source: U.S. Bureau of the Census, *Historical Statistics, Colonial Times to 1970* (Washington, D.C.: U.S. Government Printing Office, 1975), p. 888; U.S. Bureau of the Census, *Statistical Abstract of the United States, 1995* (Washington, D.C.: U.S. Government Printing Office, 1995), p. 824; and author's calculations.

sevelt administration, under the aegis of Secretary of State Cordell Hull, acted swiftly to counteract the protectionism of the Smoot–Hawley tariff. In 1934, the Reciprocal Trade Agreements Act was passed, giving the president power to negotiate bilateral tariff reductions of up to 50 percent with other countries. This act was the important first step in establishing the character of modern U.S. tariff policy. It established a framework within which free trade is envisioned as a policy goal and to a large extent it stripped Congress of its tariff-making power (but not the power to set nontariff barriers). While Congress could legally remove the tariff-setting powers of the president, these powers have been renewed and strengthened a number of times since 1934.

In the post–World War II era, the powers of the president have been expanded to include multilateral negotiations for tariff reductions—that is, negotiations with many nations simultaneously. A manifestation of America's multilateral policy was its support of the General Agreement on Tariffs and Trade (GATT) in 1947. GATT sets rules and conditions for tariff reductions and oversees bargaining with all participating nations simultaneously. Modern U.S. trade policies evolve through GATT, and tremendous gains and an expansion of world trade have occurred since the first GATT talks. Moreover, Congress has expressed some willingness to move toward free trade. In 1962, a Trade Expansion Act was passed, permitting the president to negotiate tariff reductions on all commodities simultaneously rather than commodity by commodity. This act led to the so-called Kennedy Round of tariff reductions (1964–1967), which produced huge concessions on manufactured and industrial products, with special concessions for developing countries. Subsequent GATT rounds have produced additional tariff reductions. A new GATT tariff agreement was reached in 1994 with the so-called Uruguay Round. The World Trade Organization (WTO) was then charged with implementing the provisions of the GATT agreement. Its role is to help negotiate trade agreements and generally reduce tariffs within the member nations. (One sticky point has been the exclusion of China from the WTO—see the Focus "China and the World Trade Organization").

Where Does the United States Stand in the Battle for Free Trade?

Given the rhetoric of recent U.S. administrations and changes in U.S. tariff policy, one can be forgiven for concluding that the United States unabashedly supports free trade. Beyond a doubt, there has been movement toward free trade in recent years. The United States has forcefully worked toward lowering tariffs worldwide in a series of GATT negotiations and, through these same channels, has actively supported measures to free up trade in agricultural products. In addition, the United States and its largest trading partner, Canada, removed all trade barriers between the two countries in 1989, the first step in the creation of a combined North American market (including Mexico) under the North American Free Trade Agreement which went into effect on January 1, 1994. Finally, the disintegration of the Soviet bloc made longstanding trade and finance restrictions against Eastern European countries obsolete—virtually overnight.

The United States is a long way from having completely free trade, however. With three exceptions—Canada, Mexico, and Israel—no country escapes having certain of its imports taxed by the United States. The U.S. tariff policy for the European Community is uncertain, but creation of a free trade zone with the member countries appears unlikely.

In terms of nontariff barriers, the United States has been moving away from a policy of free trade. Since the authority to enforce laws against dumping was transferred to the Department of Commerce in 1980, the number of dumping cases has risen sharply. In the last ten years, the United States initiated about 30 percent of all the antidumping cases worldwide—a percentage exceeded only by Australia. The United States has applied pressure on other countries to enter into "voluntary" agreements to limit exports of various products to the United States. In addi-

FOCUS

China and the World Trade Organization

What is a "world" trade organization when China, the world's most populous nation, is not included? This is the question that advocates of China's inclusion in the World Trade Organization (WTO) have been asking. Opponents suggest that China is guilty of civil rights abuses and unfair trading practices and should not be included.

The stakes are high, with China's foreign trade growing from $20 billion in 1978 to nearly one-third of a trillion dollars in just twenty years. China is the fastest-growing market for American products, totaling $35 billion in 1998. Americans have also benefited greatly from cheap imports such as textiles; however, critics charge that America's trade deficit with China has zoomed to $57 billion in 1998, second only to that with Japan.

The WTO is charged with enforcing the Uruguay Round of the General Agreement on Tariffs and Trade (GATT). The purpose of GATT is to negotiate multilateral agreements between member nations to reduce tariffs and to increase international trade. GATT has been successful in reducing tariff rates, although some critics charge that these reductions have taken too many years to achieve. The WTO will oversee the implementation of the scheduled reduction in tariffs negotiated during the Uruguay Round and help resolve trade disputes between nations.

Nontariff barriers to trade are a big area of dispute. For example, European nations have, in effect, "protected" their local farmers by preventing imports they claim do not meet local regulations that prohibit the use of certain hormones in cattle or pesticides on crops. Such restrictions have been used to keep U.S. beef and Central American bananas out of European markets, but these restrictions could be considered violations of the Uruguay Round by WTO officials.

China has been trying to obtain membership in WTO and GATT for over thirteen years, leading one Chinese official to complain that the negotiation process has "made black hair turn gray." China seeks entry to gain better access to foreign markets, to play a role in future negotiations, and to achieve full status as a major economic power in world trade. China must get permission from the United States and other WTO members to enter the organization.

American interests have several concerns about Chinese membership in WTO, including alleged widespread civil rights abuses in China. Another area of concern is the protection of intellectual property rights, because China has "pirated" rights to products such as music and computer software on a large scale for many years. There are other sources of tension between the two countries such as illegal campaign donations by the Chinese, stealing of nuclear bomb secrets, Chinese military threats against Taiwan, and the United States' accidental bombing of a Chinese embassy. However, one of the largest obstacles is Chinese barriers to imports. The Chinese government still controls large sectors of the economy and can prevent imports without tariff restrictions. China also has import regulations, import quotas, and both indirect and direct subsidies to industries that put foreign competitors at a disadvantage. These nontariff barriers to trade are a big reason for China's delayed entry into the WTO.

tion to the well-known agreement with Japan to limit the number of cars sold in the United States, voluntary export agreements have been negotiated with other countries to limit the amounts of textiles, steel, and various agricultural products that enter the United States. In short, the United States is actively protectionist in its use of nontariff barriers to trade.

The dramatic reduction in tariffs over the last half of this century, as revealed in Figure 30.6, is thus grossly misleading. As long as interest groups (steel, auto, agricultural, etc.) are effective in persuading enough members of Congress to obtain protection, free trade will be subverted. In terms of nontariff barriers, the United States has been moving away from a policy of free trade. At the dawn of the twenty-first century, all sorts of nontariff qualifications are being used as the pretext for "fair" versus "free" trade. It is important to remember that it does not matter *why* prices are lower for goods and services purchased from abroad; the gains to American consumers from free trade are real, nevertheless.

APPLICATION

NAFTA: Free Trade or Free-for-All?

The North American Free Trade Agreement (NAFTA) passed the U.S. House in a close vote (234 to 200) and went into effect January 1, 1994. What is a free trade zone, and what are the benefits of NAFTA for the United States? NAFTA provides for the phased elimination of tariff and most nontariff barriers to regional trade within ten years, although a few "import-sensitive" products will have a fifteen-year transition period. Tariffs are basically taxes on imports, so lowering tariffs will lower the costs of imports. Nontariff barriers include measures such as quotas, the elimination of which will have the effect of increasing trade among the member nations. Along with trade creation, free trade zones, by vastly increasing the size of the market, increase competitive pressures which, in turn, lead to greater efficiency in production and lower prices for consumers.

In reality, NAFTA is not without its shortcomings. On the U.S. side of the issue, complaints have arisen that Mexico has not moved fast enough in particular areas— express-mail delivery, tires, and wine—to open up its markets to U.S. imports as required under the agreement. For example, United Parcel Service (UPS) has cried "foul" with respect to Mexico's restriction that delivery vehicles be no bigger than four tons, a regulation that the firm argues makes it much less efficient and, hence, less competitive in that market. Mexican officials, facing domestic unrest due to a sharp recession in the economy, have acknowledged their fear of political retaliation from domestic delivery services if these restrictions are lifted.

The ability of special interests to influence the political process became apparent in the bitter debate which occurred over the ratification of NAFTA in the U.S. Congress. Industries and their employees who will benefit from increased specialization and growth in the volume of trade had every incentive to support the agreement through the political process. However, some industries and workers will be displaced in the move toward freer trade and could, therefore, be expected to oppose the agreement. A fierce opponent of NAFTA was organized labor in the United States, including the AFL-CIO, arguing that "cheap Mexican labor" would take high-paying union jobs as a result of reductions in tariffs on automobiles, textiles, and other goods. This claim denies the operation of the principle of comparative advantage in directing trade and specialization. Mexico will specialize according to its own comparative advantage in low-tech, low-pay industries due to a relative abundance of low-skill labor. As such industries move south, valuable resources will be freed up in the U.S. economy for investment in high-tech, high-pay industries, where our nation enjoys a comparative advantage arising from a relative abundance of high-skill labor.

It is important to keep the advantages of free trade firmly in mind. The increased value to consumers resulting from higher outputs and lower prices in all three nations will dwarf the costs to certain workers and particular industries with the free trade area. Some studies estimate that the agreement has created about 170,000 new jobs in its first five years of implementation. Job creation resulting from NAFTA has occurred in new, more efficient industries. The challenge for the United States is to help displaced workers make the transition to new jobs. Over the long term, the primary impact of increased trade will be higher incomes made possible by greater efficiency and faster growth. Efficiency in the United States, Canadian, and Mexican economies will be boosted by the tendency of each to export those goods and services in which it enjoys a comparative advantage.

QUESTIONS

If the economic case for free trade is so strong, why did so many politicians fight the ratification of NAFTA? What implications do protectionist demands hold for the future and effectiveness of such free trade agreements?

SUMMARY

1. All individuals possess talents that give them advantages in trade. Nations, like individuals, benefit from specialization and trade. Nations trade not resources, but rather the products and services created with resources. Differing resource endowments are the basis for trade in products because products are ordinarily more mobile than the resources that produce them.

2. Specialization and trade may take place between countries of vastly differing degrees of economic development. The reason for this is the law of comparative advantage, which states that trade is possible when the relative opportunity cost of producing two goods differs between two countries.

3. Specialization according to the law of comparative advantage permits the production possibilities and hence the rate of sustainable consumption of nations to expand. That is, the parties to trade may obtain more of both traded goods after specialization and trade.

4. There are both natural and artificial barriers to trade. Natural barriers are all exchange costs, including transportation costs of moving goods from one country to another. Artificial barriers include taxes on imports of goods, or tariffs, and limitations or prohibitions on imported items, or quotas.

5. Tariffs on imports increase the profits of domestic producers and the revenue of government, but consumers lose more than producers and governments gain. This net welfare loss is the reason most economists oppose protectionist policies.

6. Quotas have similar effects on markets as tariffs, except that the revenue goes not to government but to producer groups.

7. Although tariffs and quotas carry a net loss to society, they are imposed whenever domestic producer-competitors are strong enough to supply gains to politicians. Consumer groups may oppose tariffs but are seldom well enough organized or vocal enough to oppose them successfully.

8. Two substantive arguments are made for protection: the national defense and infant industries arguments. Most economists, however, question the adequacy of these arguments in actual operation. Other arguments—such as "cheap foreign labor" or "buy American"—are regarded by most economists as only thinly veiled protectionist fallacies.

9. U.S. trade policies have historically waxed and waned with prosperity and depression, becoming more protectionist during economic downturns. Although import tariffs have been reduced dramatically in the past fifty years, freer trade has not necessarily resulted. Protectionism lives on in the form of quotas and nontariff trade barriers.

KEY TERMS

specialization	tariff	nontariff trade barriers
comparative advantage	quota	infant industry
terms of trade	free trade	dumping
consumption possibilities curve	welfare loss to society	terms of trade argument

QUESTIONS FOR REVIEW AND DISCUSSION

1. Evaluate and discuss the following statement: Trade across international boundaries is essentially the same as trade across interstate boundaries.

2. How can two countries simultaneously gain from trade? Under what circumstances can two countries not gain from trade?

3. What is the difference between natural barriers and artificial barriers to trade? Was the development of the Panama Canal an artificial encouragement of trade?

4. What does a tariff do to the terms of trade? Are consumers in both countries hurt by a tariff?

5. How are tariffs and quotas similar? How are they different? Would consumers prefer one of these barriers to the other?

6. Who is hurt by a tariff? Who is helped? Who encourages government to impose tariffs?

7. What is the purpose of protective tariffs? Who or what is protected?

8. Evaluate the following statement: Tariffs discourage the movement of goods between countries; therefore, they encourage the movement of resources such as capital and labor between countries.

9. What are the effects of trade on a country's consumption possibilities? After trade, what is the relationship between the consumption and production possibilities curves and what does this imply for the country?

10. What are nontariff trade barriers? Compare the effects of nontariff barriers and the effects of tariffs.

11. What is the difference between "free trade" and "fair trade"?

12. Should China and other countries charged with "human rights" abuses be admitted to organizations whose object is the free trade of goods and services?

PROBLEMS

Nations Alpha and Beta have the following production possibilities for goods X and Y.

Alpha	X	0	3	6	9
	Y	12	8	4	0
Beta	X	0	4	8	12
	Y	15	10	5	0

1. Draw the production possibilities curves for both countries. What does 1 X cost in Alpha before trade? What does 1 Y cost in Beta? If these countries traded, which would export X and which would export Y?

2. If some country Omega can produce 100 units of X with all its resources or 60 units of Y, how much does 1 unit of Y cost? If another country, Gamma, can produce 60 X or 40 Y, what does 1 unit of X cost in Gamma? Which country has a comparative advantage in the production of X?

WORKING WITH THE WEB

1. Go to the following web sites to collect information on U.S.–Canada trade:
   - U.S. State Department's Country Reports: http://www.state.gov/www/issues/economic/trade_reports
   - Statistics Canada: http://www.statcan.ca/english/ Pgdb/Economy/intern.htm

   At the State Department site, access the 1998 Trade report for Canada.
   a. In 1998, what was Canada's percentage of total merchandise exports and imports with the United States?
   b. Why do you think that the United States is such a large trading partner with Canada?

   At the Statistics Canada site, access the (by product) tables for exports and imports.
   c. What were Canada's three largest exports and imports in 1998?
   d. Assume that your response in part (c) predominantly reflects U.S.–Canada trade. Explain whether your findings are consistent with what you would expect from the theory of comparative advantage.

2. One of the best starting points on any data search is the Resources for Economists on the Internet site (http://rfe.wustl.edu/EconFAQ.html). Go to this site, click on the link for "Data," and then click on the subsequent link for "U.S. Macro and Regional Data." Locate the link to the web site for the "Bureau of Economic Analysis" and go there (the web address should be http://www.bea.doc.gov). Once at the BEA site, select the link for "Data" under the heading "International." Go down a few rows, click on "Exports and Imports, Monthly," and look at the tables presented on this page.
   a. The table presents data for the United States. Compare exports and imports of goods and services, and report your findings.
   b. Make a comparative advantage argument supporting your findings in part (a).

3. Go to the Economagic web site (http://www.Economagic.com) and locate data on the government's budget surplus/deficit and the current account for goods and services (trade account). The St. Louis Fed has one of the largest databases there,

so click on this link. Page down until you find "Federal Government Surplus or Deficit (–) (NIPA); annual" and "Balance of Payments: Balance on Current Account; SA" (alternatively, you can use the appropriate Data Headings to find this data).

Create a graph for both data series that covers the time period 1960–1999. To create a graph, you will need to be on the data page you want to graph. Click on the link for "GIF chart," and then set the time period when the next page appears (note that the existing graph only covers the last several years). Make a graph for each series of data (Government Budget and Current Account).

a. Do you observe a relationship between the two series? Explain.

b. Should the Government Budget be related to the Current Account in a typical Keynesian model of the economy?

International Finance

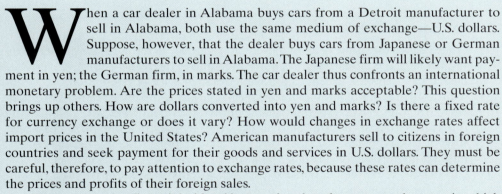

When a car dealer in Alabama buys cars from a Detroit manufacturer to sell in Alabama, both use the same medium of exchange—U.S. dollars. Suppose, however, that the dealer buys cars from Japanese or German manufacturers to sell in Alabama. The Japanese firm will likely want payment in yen; the German firm, in marks. The car dealer thus confronts an international monetary problem. Are the prices stated in yen and marks acceptable? This question brings up others. How are dollars converted into yen and marks? Is there a fixed rate for currency exchange or does it vary? How would changes in exchange rates affect import prices in the United States? American manufacturers sell to citizens in foreign countries and seek payment for their goods and services in U.S. dollars. They must be careful, therefore, to pay attention to exchange rates, because these rates can determine the prices and profits of their foreign sales.

The monetary, or financial, side of international trade concerns the ways in which countries pay for the goods and services they exchange. In this chapter we examine many aspects of the relations among the currencies of the world, relations that reflect a kaleidoscope of changing conditions in each country, from interest rates and inflation rates to exports and imports of goods and capital. When you finish Chapter 31 you should understand

- how international trade takes place when transactions must be made in terms of other countries' currencies.
- how currency transactions are determined when governments fix their respective currencies' value and when the market determines the relative value of currencies.

- how macroeconomic fiscal and monetary policies both affect and are affected by foreign trade and international exchange rates.
- the meaning of the balance of payments, its relation to exchange rates, and its importance for economic growth.

THE FOREIGN EXCHANGE MARKET

Foreign exchange

The monies of countries that are used to facilitate international trade in goods, services, and financial assets.

International sellers and buyers usually prefer to deal in the currency of their own country. American sellers prefer U.S. dollars for their products, and Japanese sellers prefer yen. The currency of another country that is required to make payment in an international transaction is called **foreign exchange.** Foreign exchange is bought and sold in **foreign exchange markets**—typically, large brokers and banks scattered about the globe.

Foreign exchange markets

The interaction of the suppliers and demanders of foreign exchange, through which exchange rates are determined in a flexible exchange rate system.

Sometimes consumers demand foreign exchange; for example, when American travelers arrive at a foreign airport, they often exchange dollars for the local currency. Large firms dealing in international transactions simply keep bank deposits in foreign currencies to cover their foreign transactions. An American importer of French wine will likely pay for its purchases by writing checks on an American bank that holds an account in a French bank. The American bank will use the importer's dollars to purchase the francs needed for payment.

The demand for foreign exchange arises because a country's residents want to buy foreign goods. Conversely, the supply of foreign exchange arises because foreign customers want to buy U.S. goods. For example, we have a demand for francs by the U.S. importer who wishes to purchase French wine and a supply of francs by French customers who wish to purchase U.S. personal computers.

Exchange Rates

Exchange rate

The (relative) price of one national currency in terms of another national currency.

An **exchange rate** is the price of one country's money in terms of some other country's money. It is a relative price, much the same as the relative price concept discussed in Chapter 4, except that it is the relative price of one national currency expressed in terms of another national currency. Like the relative prices of goods, exchange rates can be expressed in one of two equivalent ways. We can talk about one concert ticket "costing" five pizzas, or we can say that one pizza costs one-fifth of a concert ticket. Either way, the relative price of one good in terms of another good (one concert ticket in terms of pizzas or one pizza in terms of concert tickets) is expressed. Which expression we choose is simply a matter of preference or convenience.

So it is with exchange rates. Because they are relative prices of one money in terms of another money, the way we choose to express the exchange rate is a matter of preference and convenience. For example, in April 1999, one U.S. dollar traded on the foreign exchange market for about six French francs (ff), the national currency of France. One U.S. dollar costs about six French francs to buy, or one U.S. dollar sold for about six French francs. This exchange rate is the relative price of the U.S. dollar in terms of French francs. Alternatively, it would be just as accurate to say that one French franc costs, or would buy, about 17 cents. This would

The worldwide volume of trade on foreign exchange markets exceeds $500 billion per day.

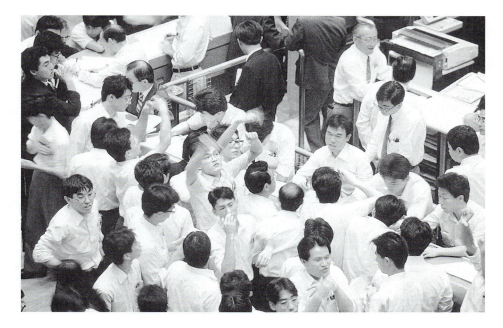

be the relative price of the French franc in terms of the U.S. dollar. One is nothing more than the inverse, or reciprocal, of the other. Exchange rates are often expressed both ways. An American in France must use French francs to make purchases. Starting out the vacation, the traveler may have a budget, say $500, that she wishes to spend on meals. By using the U.S. dollar in terms of French francs exchange rate (6 per dollar), she can calculate that she will have 3000 ff (6 ff per dollar × $500) to spend on meals in France. Once in France, if our tourist pays 100 ff for a lunch, she may wish to know how many dollars the lunch cost. A quick calculation using the French franc in terms of the U.S. dollar exchange rate will provide a good estimate ($0.17 per ff × 100 ff = $17).

Of equal importance are changes in exchange rates, for such changes can alter the prices of imports and exports. Suppose that a bottle of French wine sells for 100 ff. Ignoring transportation costs and any tariffs, with a dollar–franc exchange rate of $0.17 per French franc, the wine will cost $17 in the United States. But suppose the exchange rate were to change to $0.25 per French franc. The same bottle of wine would still cost 100 ff in France, but its cost in the United States would rise to $25. Changes in the exchange rate alter the prices of foreign goods in home markets and of domestic goods in foreign markets.

Just as tourists must pay attention to exchange rates in order to make plans and informed decisions, so must businesses and governments. International trade, like interpersonal trade, requires the use of money. The prices of these monies relative to one another are important economic variables. A sudden change in an exchange rate can alter the actual values of any business transaction, making it more or less profitable than at first thought. Such changes

Knowledge of current exchange rates is crucial to tourists traveling in foreign countries.

influence business decisions and can alter the volume of international trade. At issue, then, is what determines exchange rates. Why, in 1999, did a dollar buy (cost) about six French francs and not four or ten French francs? What has caused the U.S. dollar price of French francs, or for that matter German marks, English pounds, Japanese yen, Mexican pesos, or any other country's money, to change from day to day, month to month, and year to year?

Naturally, the existence of multiple currencies has costs. When you take a trip to Europe, for example, exchanging dollars (or some other currency) for national monetary units takes time and resources. The same is, of course, true for businesses exchanging goods and services. Thus, a common currency reduces transaction costs of all kinds. This is the aim of the new common currency for Europe, scheduled to go into effect in 2002 (see the Focus "The Euro, Europe's New Money").

Exchange Rate Systems

Exchange rates, like any other price, are determined in markets by the forces of supply and demand. However, exactly who suppliers and demanders are, and under what constraints the market operates, determines the type of system within which the exchange rate will be determined. One type, the **flexible, or floating, exchange rate system,** is a system whereby the exchange rate is determined solely by the interaction of private demanders and suppliers of foreign exchange. This is the type of system most major trading countries employ today to determine the world market value of their respective currencies. Of course, government fiscal and monetary policies can help determine the exchange rate under such a system by influencing the behavior of private market participants. But government policies usually are not specifically designed to influence the exchange rate directly.

A second system of exchange rate determination is called a **fixed exchange rate system.** A fixed exchange rate system was in existence from the late 1940s until 1971. A few countries today still fix the value of their currencies on world markets in terms of U.S. dollars. Under a fixed exchange rate system, government intervenes directly in the foreign exchange market, either as a buyer or as a seller, in order to fix the exchange rate at some level. Some European countries combine elements of both the fixed- and flexible-rate systems. The values of these

Flexible, or floating, exchange rate system
An international monetary arrangement in which exchange rates are determined by private suppliers and demanders without government intervention.

Fixed exchange rate system
An international monetary arrangement in which exchange rates are set by the government, which then must intervene in the foreign exchange market in order to maintain the pegged exchange rate.

FOCUS

The Euro, Europe's New Money

European nations have been attempting to better integrate their economies since after World War II and the signing of the Treaty of Rome in 1957. The general plan has been to reduce trade barriers and other restrictions that impede the flow of goods across borders in the spirit of the old dictum "if goods don't cross borders, armies will." An important part of economic integration is the establishment of a common currency.

On January 4, 1999, the Euro was launched as a common money of Europe. The Euro replaces the European Currency Unit (ECU), which was used only as a unit of account between European central banks. The idea behind the new currency is that individuals and businesses will be able to use the currency all over Europe, as well as have their accounts denominated in Euros. The situation will be analogous to that of America, where we can spend dollars in all fifty states. The distribution of paper and coin money begins on January 1, 2002, and will consist of eight denominations of bills and eight coins (national currencies will cease to function as legal tender on July 1, 2002).

The value of the Euro is based on a weighted average of the values of the currencies of the eleven participating countries of Europe's Economic and Monetary Union, the EMU. The currencies of large economies like Germany and France carry a larger weight than those of smaller economies like Austria

and Finland. Possessing a Euro will be like having a basket of European currencies all rolled into one.

An important condition of the Maastricht Treaty, which laid the groundwork for the Euro, is that the exchange rate between the eleven national currencies will be irrevocably fixed. This means that the nations will have to keep the value of their currencies in line with all the other members. Fixed exchange rates for paper currencies have been difficult, if not impossible, to achieve in the past; hence as preconditions for membership, nations must meet strict requirements to maintain low inflation, interest rates, budget deficits, and national debt, and they must grant their central banks full independence.

The European Central Bank (ECB) will control the fate of the Euro after the national currencies have ceased to exist. The ECB has been designed with full independence and been given the sole task of maintaining price level stability with inflation at less than 2 percent per year. Detractors feel that the system will collapse politically, while critics fear the loss of national sovereignty and the inflation potential of the ECB if it loses its independence. If successful, this experiment would rid Europe of high inflation, encourage fiscal responsibility among member nations, and speed up economic growth in the stagnant economies of Europe. Could the Euro become Europe's economic hero?

European currencies are fixed relative to one another, but all float against the U.S. dollar.

Since 1973, the exchange rate system determining the relative prices of national currencies has been a blend of these two systems. By and large, the flexible-rate system is in use for the currencies of the United States and other major industrial countries. No country, however, allows its exchange rate to float freely all the time. Wide swings in the exchange rate are controlled by government intervention in the foreign exchange market. For this reason, the present international monetary system is called a **managed flexible-rate system.** In the next two sections we analyze how floating exchange rates and fixed exchange rates work.

Managed flexible-rate system
Primarily a flexible exchange rate system, but with occasional government purchases or sales of foreign exchange intended to influence the exchange rate.

FLEXIBLE EXCHANGE RATES

As we pointed out earlier, U.S. demand for foreign currency arises because U.S. citizens wish to buy foreign products, travel in foreign countries, invest in foreign companies, and carry on other international activities. The supply of foreign currencies to the United States arises because foreigners want to buy U.S. goods, travel in the United States, send their children to school in the United States, invest in this country, and so on. All of these forces of supply and demand affect the exchange rate between the U.S. dollar and other currencies. In effect, they form the basis of the supply and demand schedules in the foreign exchange markets.

Exchange Rates Between Two Countries

We begin our analysis with a simple model of the determination of floating, or flexible, exchange rates. For simplicity, we assume that international trade takes place only between two countries, the United States and Switzerland. The U.S. demand for foreign exchange is thus a demand for Swiss francs; the supply of foreign exchange is a supply of Swiss francs.

Supply, Demand, and the Market for Foreign Exchange Before beginning our analysis of the factors that determine and change exchange rates, some preliminaries are in order. The exchange rate is determined in the foreign exchange market; it is the relative price of one money in terms of another. As we have indicated, the actions of both the Americans and the Swiss are manifested in this market. But any action on the part of residents of one country is mirrored in the actions of residents of the other. Swiss exports are American imports, and vice versa. This means that technically we would want to look at both the supply and demand of dollars and the supply and demand of Swiss francs to the foreign exchange market in order to examine exchange rate determination. But because the dollar–franc exchange rate is just the inverse of the franc–dollar exchange rate (so that changes in one are mirrored by changes in the other), and because Swiss imports are American exports, we can simplify matters. We need only examine the supply and demand for either francs or dollars on the foreign exchange market in order to discuss exchange rate determination. We will look at the supply and demand for Swiss francs, the foreign exchange in our discussion.

Figure 31.1 depicts the supply and demand for foreign exchange, Swiss francs. What establishes the supply and demand for francs on the foreign exchange mar-

FIGURE 31.1

A Two-Country Foreign Exchange Market

The exchange rate—in this case, the dollar price of one Swiss franc—is measured on the vertical axis. The quantity of francs is measured on the horizontal axis. The equilibrium exchange rate is $0.75 per Swiss franc, because this is the only exchange rate that equates quantity demanded with quantity supplied. At the exchange rate of $0.90 per franc, there exists a surplus of francs, and the exchange rate will fall. At the $0.50 exchange rate, a shortage of francs on the foreign exchange market exists, which will drive the exchange rate back to $0.75.

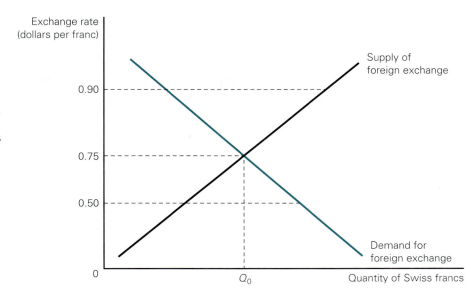

ket? Consider the demand for franc foreign exchange first. American importers of Swiss goods must pay Swiss producers with francs. Thus, American imports from Switzerland are the basis of foreign exchange demand. The demand for foreign exchange slopes downward because, other things constant, a higher exchange rate (more dollars per franc) implies higher import prices, fewer imports, and a smaller quantity demanded (by Americans) of foreign exchange.

The supply of foreign exchange arises from Swiss import activity and, therefore, American export activity. Swiss importers must pay for goods produced in the United States (American exports) with dollars. In order to obtain dollars, they must buy them with francs in the foreign exchange market. The supply of foreign exchange originates with Swiss imports or, what is the same thing, American exports. It is upward-sloping because, other factors considered, a rise in the dollar price of the franc (the exchange rate measured on the vertical axis) means that one franc now buys more dollars, making American goods cheaper to the Swiss. This implies an increase in the desire of the Swiss to import from the United States. They will then offer more francs for sale at the higher exchange rate to obtain additional dollars. The additional dollars are then used to purchase the larger quantity of imports.

The equilibrium exchange rate, like any other price, is one that equates quantity demanded with quantity supplied. In Figure 31.1, this equilibrium exchange rate is $0.75 per Swiss franc. Suppose that the exchange rate were below equilibrium, at $0.50 per franc. The quantity demanded of foreign exchange would then exceed the quantity supplied of foreign exchange. There would be a shortage of francs on the foreign exchange market. As in any other market, a shortage in the foreign exchange market will tend to drive price back toward equilibrium.

Given the fundamental economic factors determining exports and imports in both countries, an exchange rate below the equilibrium exchange rate ($0.50 per franc in Figure 31.1) creates a situation in which Americans wish to import much more from Switzerland than the Swiss wish to sell. At this exchange rate, Swiss goods are "too cheap" to Americans because the dollar price of the franc is "too low." On the other side of the coin, American goods are "too expensive" to the Swiss. Swiss imports are too low, and thus the quantity supplied of foreign exchange is also too low. To stimulate the quantity of Swiss imports and increase the quantity supplied of foreign exchange, as well as to reduce the quantity of U.S. imports and reduce the quantity demanded of foreign exchange, an increase in the exchange rate is necessary. The movement to equilibrium from $0.50 to $0.75 results from the bidding up of the dollar price of francs by American consumers eager to obtain Swiss goods. (Americans demand Swiss francs and *simultaneously* supply U.S. dollars.) The actions of American consumers tend to elevate the price of Swiss francs in terms of dollars, returning the dollar–franc market to equilibrium. Naturally, the rise in the dollar price of francs reduces the quantity demanded of Swiss goods and services by Americans as equilibrium is approached. (The Swiss are willing to supply the additional francs because of the higher price of their currency expressed in dollars.)

Likewise, the exchange rate of $0.90 per franc is too high for equilibrium, creating a surplus of foreign exchange. At $0.90 per franc, Swiss products are very expensive for Americans and American products are relatively inexpensive to the Swiss. As the Swiss demand dollars to get American goods, the price of dollars in terms of francs rises and the price of francs in terms of dollars falls. Simultaneously, with Americans wanting to import less than the Swiss wish to export to the United States, a surplus of franc foreign exchange exists. A fall in the dollar price of the franc will increase American imports and the quantity demanded of foreign exchange. This same fall will also make American goods more expensive in Switzerland, reduce imports, and thus reduce the quantity supplied of francs to the foreign exchange market. Equilibrium is restored, as shown in Figure 31.1, when the dollar price of francs returns to $0.75.

Changes in Flexible Exchange Rates

The foreign exchange market is like any other market studied in economics. Supply and demand determine price, and surpluses and shortages of foreign exchange will move the exchange rate toward its equilibrium value. We now examine why the supply of or demand for foreign exchange might change, producing a change in the equilibrium exchange rate in a flexible exchange rate system.

Appreciation and Depreciation   The dollar price of the Swiss franc, or any other currency, fluctuates from day to day and even minute to minute. Trying to explain every small fluctuation in the exchange rate would be a fruitless exercise. However, broad and significant changes in exchange rates have occurred since the collapse of the fixed-rate system and subsequent inception of the managed flexible-rate system in 1973. The late 1970s and the early 1990s were periods of dollar **depreciation.** A depreciation of a country's currency on world markets means that the equilibrium exchange rate has changed such that it requires more of the currency to purchase other money. An increase in the equilibrium dollar price of the Swiss franc from $0.75 to $0.90 constitutes a depreciation of the dol-

Depreciation

A decrease in the equilibrium exchange market value of a country's currency in a flexible-rate system; an increase in the number of units of a country's money required to purchase one unit of a foreign country's money.

lar. It takes more dollars to buy a franc than previously, or equivalently, one dollar buys fewer francs. Another term used frequently by the financial press to describe a depreciation is a "weakening" of the currency on the foreign exchange market. The early 1980s was a period of dollar **appreciation.** An appreciation is the opposite of a depreciation; less of the money is required to buy other monies on the foreign exchange market. A fall in the equilibrium exchange rate from $0.75 to $0.50 per franc signifies a dollar appreciation (and a franc depreciation). A currency that has appreciated is said to have "strengthened" on world currency markets or is a "strong" currency. The basic reasons and fundamental causes of currency appreciations and deprecations are addressed in the following sections.

Appreciation

An increase in the equilibrium exchange market value of a country's currency in a flexible-rate system; a decrease in the number of units of a country's money required to purchase one unit of a foreign country's money.

Price Levels, Money Supplies, and Inflation Rates

One factor that can cause the exchange rate to change is a shift in the price level of either country. Suppose that the price level in the United States were to increase by 20 percent while the general level of prices in Switzerland was stable. Figure 31.2a depicts the effects this would have on the foreign exchange market and the exchange rate. Other things equal, higher U.S. prices would reduce Swiss import demand for American goods.

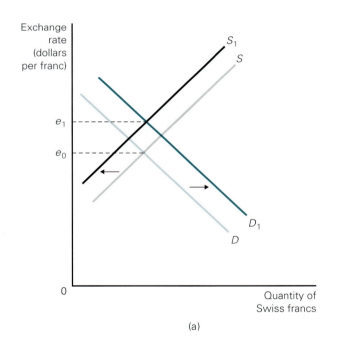

(a)

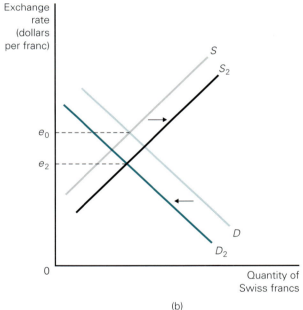

(b)

FIGURE 31.2

Price Level Changes in the Flexible Exchange Rate System

S and D are the initial foreign supply and demand curves. In Figure 31.2a, an increase in the U.S. price level, holding the Swiss price level constant, causes the supply of foreign exchange to shift to S_1, while the demand for foreign exchange shifts to D_1. This causes the Swiss franc to appreciate from e_0 to e_1. This can also be described as a depreciation of the dollar. If the Swiss price level increased while the price level in the United States remained unchanged, the supply and demand curves would shift to S_2 and D_2 in Figure 31.2b. This would cause the exchange rate to fall from e_0 to e_2.

This would, in turn, cause a decrease in the supply of foreign exchange, shown as a shift of the supply curve of francs from S to S_1. The rise in the prices of U.S. goods also would make Swiss goods relatively more attractive to Americans. American import demand would increase, and the demand for foreign exchange also would then increase. In Figure 31.2a, the demand for foreign exchange shifts from D to D_1.

The effect is to increase the dollar price of the franc. The equilibrium exchange rate rises from e_0 to e_1, or the dollar depreciates on the foreign exchange market. Of course, one could also say that the franc has appreciated. Had the price level in Switzerland risen by 20 percent with the price level in the United States constant, just the opposite would have occurred. Swiss goods would have become more expensive to Americans, reducing American import demand and the demand for foreign exchange from D to D_2 in Figure 31.2b. Swiss import demand would increase as American goods become cheaper in Switzerland, causing the supply of foreign exchange to increase from S to S_2. The equilibrium exchange rate would fall from e_0 to e_2, and a dollar appreciation (franc depreciation) would have taken place.

Real Income, Exports, and Imports   Other factors also can cause a currency to appreciate or depreciate on world currency markets. Consider the effect of an expansion in the Swiss economy that results in an increase in Swiss real income. As Swiss real income increases, the demand for imports from the United States also increases. More francs are supplied to the foreign exchange market at any given exchange rate, and the supply of foreign exchange increases. In Figure 31.3, the foreign exchange supply curve shifts from S to S_1 and the equilibrium exchange rate falls from e_0 to e_1. The increase in Swiss real income has caused the dollar to appreciate on the foreign exchange market or, equivalently, the franc to depreciate.

FIGURE 31.3

Real Income Changes and the Exchange Rate

An increase in real income in Switzerland has the effect of shifting the supply of foreign exchange from S to S_1. This appreciates the dollar in the foreign exchange market, causing the exchange rate to fall from e_0 to e_1. Should U.S. real income rise, the effect will be to increase the demand for foreign exchange to D_1 and depreciate the dollar, moving the exchange rate from e_0 to e_2.

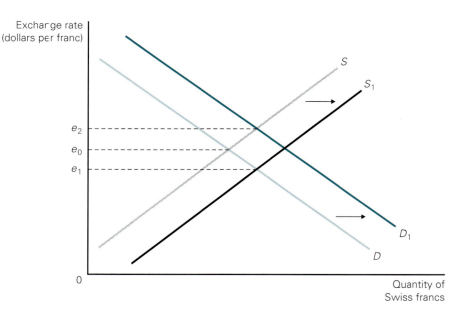

Should real income in the United States rise, the dollar would depreciate on the foreign exchange market. Larger U.S. real income would cause a desire for greater imports from Switzerland. The demand for francs would increase in Figure 31.3 from D to D_1. Given the initial supply of foreign exchange, S, the rise in U.S. real income causes a depreciation of the dollar (appreciation of the franc) on the foreign exchange market. In this case, the exchange rate rises from e_0 to e_2.[1]

Changes in factors that directly affect exports and imports can also cause changes in exchange rates. Should consumer tastes in the United States change in favor of goods produced at home, for example, the demand for foreign exchange would decrease, causing an appreciation of the dollar. Government policies aimed at restricting imports or encouraging exports tend to reduce the demand for foreign exchange and appreciate the country's currency on world markets.

Interest Rates   So far, we have discussed the supply of foreign exchange as arising from the desires of foreigners to buy goods and services produced in the United States. But foreigners purchase real estate and financial assets in the United States as well; for instance, Rockefeller Center in New York was purchased by Japanese investors. Stocks and bonds issued by U.S. businesses and governments (state, local, and federal) are other, less-publicized examples of such purchases by foreign businesspeople. Both such examples are foreign investments in the United States. Just as the purchase of U.S. goods by foreigners creates a supply of foreign exchange, so does the purchase of financial assets or real assets such as automobile or computer assembly plants. Likewise, U.S. citizens purchase the financial assets of other countries, adding to the demand for foreign exchange.

An increased desire on the part of the Swiss to invest in the United States, to buy more U.S. financial or real assets, signals an increased supply of foreign exchange. More francs are supplied to the foreign exchange market to purchase the dollars necessary to buy U.S. assets. In Figure 31.4, the supply of foreign exchange increases from S to S_1 and the exchange rate falls from e_0 to e_1. What would cause this to happen?

Investors everywhere look at many different variables in deciding how to allocate their investment funds among particular firms, industries, or countries. Such factors as risk, liquidity, and the degree of political stability are all important. However, a primary factor that goes into any investment decision is the real rate of interest those funds earn.

The real interest rate, recall, is the rate of interest earned adjusted for inflation. Suppose that the real interest rate in the United States rose. That would make U.S. financial assets more attractive to own and would increase the demand by foreigners to purchase U.S. financial assets. This increase in the U.S. real interest rate would have caused the increase in the supply of francs to the foreign exchange market depicted in Figure 31.4. The effect of a rise in the real interest rate in the United States is dollar appreciation, or, in terms of Figure 31.4, a decline in the dollar price of the Swiss franc on the foreign exchange market from e_0 to e_1.

---

[1]We are assuming that as real income rises, the money supply increases enough to accommodate the extra demand for money.

FIGURE 31.4

Real Interest Rate Effects on the Exchange Rate

When the U.S. real interest rate rises the Swiss wish to invest more in the United States, to buy more financial assets. The supply of foreign exchange increases to S_1, and the exchange rate falls to e_1. Higher U.S. real interest rates cause dollar appreciation. When the real interest rate in Switzerland rises, Americans wish to buy more Swiss securities, and the demand for foreign exchange increases. The exchange rate moves from e_0 to e_2, and the dollar depreciates.

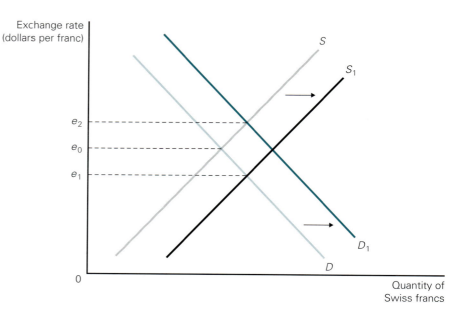

Alternatively, should the real interest rate increase in Switzerland, the demand for francs on the part of Americans would increase, from D to D_1 in Figure 31.4. Given the supply of franc foreign exchange of S, the exchange rate would rise to e_2. An increased Swiss real interest rate causes the dollar to depreciate, or the franc to appreciate, on the foreign exchange market.

FIXED EXCHANGE RATES

As we have seen, a system of flexible exchange rates allows the foreign exchange market to determine the prices at which currency will change hands. By contrast, a fixed exchange rate system does not allow exchange rates to float in a free market. Government intervenes in the foreign exchange market to fix or "manage" the international price of its currency. Once fixed exchange rates are established, governments stand ready to protect the rates through intervention in the foreign exchange market.

The Operation of a Fixed Exchange Rate System

Undervalued

A term describing the foreign exchange market value of a country's money that occurs when the number of units of a country's money that purchases one unit of a foreign currency is greater than the equilibrium exchange rate.

Although the United States and Switzerland no longer trade on the basis of a fixed exchange rate, imagine what would happen if they did. Figure 31.5 illustrates what happens when a fixed exchange rate between francs and dollars does not happen to correspond to ever-shifting market conditions. If the current market equilibrium rate is e_0, but the U.S. government seeks to maintain an exchange rate of e_1, the official or fixed rate is above the equilibrium rate. In this case, the dollar is said to be undervalued relative to the Swiss franc. The dollar is **undervalued** because

FIGURE 31.5

Fixed Exchange Rates Above and Below Equilibrium

If the government sets an exchange rate below equilibrium, such as e_2, a shortage of foreign exchange develops, and the central bank must continuously sell foreign exchange from its exchange reserves to keep the rate at e_2. If the rate is set at e_1, a surplus of foreign exchange is created, and the central bank must continuously buy foreign exchange, adding to its exchange reserves, in order to maintain the fixed rate.

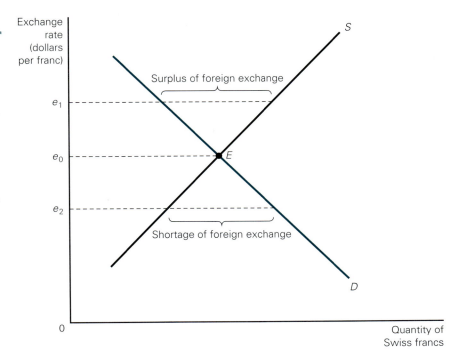

Overvalued

A term describing the foreign exchange market value of a country's money that occurs when the number of units of a country's money that purchases one unit of a foreign currency is less than the equilibrium exchange rate.

Foreign exchange market intervention

Purchases or sales of foreign exchange by government, usually a central bank, with the goal of maintaining a fixed exchange rate or influencing the exchange rate in a flexible-rate system.

Foreign exchange reserves

The stock of a foreign exchange held by a central bank that is available for use in exchange market intervention.

at exchange rate e_1 each dollar will buy fewer francs than it would at the lower equilibrium exchange rate, e_0. Of course, if the dollar is undervalued, then the franc is overvalued. Similarly, if the government were to fix the exchange rate at e_2, each dollar would purchase more francs than it would at the equilibrium exchange rate, e_0. In this case, the dollar (franc) would be **overvalued** (undervalued).

Suppose that the government decides to fix the price of its currency in the foreign exchange market at e_1. To do this, the central bank must continuously engage in **foreign exchange market intervention.**

When the government fixes the exchange rate at e_1, even though fundamental foreign exchange market forces dictate an equilibrium exchange rate of e_0, a surplus of francs on the foreign exchange market is created. At the high dollar price of the franc, quantity supplied of francs will exceed quantity demanded. Without exchange market intervention, as described earlier, the exchange rate would fall back to its equilibrium value, e_0. The central bank can prevent this fall, and maintain exchange rate e_1 only if it intervenes in the exchange market by buying up the franc surplus. The buying of francs, in this case, by the central bank builds up the central bank's **foreign exchange reserves,** its holding of foreign currencies. Such an intervention is not a one-time affair. Each month or year that the exchange rate is fixed above its equilibrium value, the central bank must purchase the surplus of francs in order to maintain the fixed rate. Fixing the rate above equilibrium tends to make a country's exports cheaper and its imports more expensive. Hence, such a policy may be used by governments in an attempt to reduce imports and encourage exports.

Sometimes central banks fix the exchange rate below the market equilibrium exchange rate, such as rate e_2 in Figure 31.5. This creates a shortage of foreign exchange, since quantity demanded at exchange rate e_2 is greater than quantity supplied. Again, without continuous exchange market intervention, the exchange rate would move back toward its equilibrium level, e_0. In this case, foreign exchange market intervention takes the form of sales of foreign currency (Swiss francs) from the central bank's foreign currency reserves. Setting such an exchange rate, one that deliberately overvalues the country's currency in world markets, is not a policy that most countries could pursue indefinitely. Sooner or later the central bank would run out of reserves and be unable to support the fixed exchange rate. Fixing the exchange rate below equilibrium tends to encourage imports and discourage exports.

Fixed Exchange Rates

The fixed exchange rate set by government can stray significantly from the equilibrium exchange rate. A country will therefore experience persistent problems in international trade; namely, it will confront persistent surpluses or deficits in its foreign trade. In the balance of trade between exports and imports, a country whose exports have greater value than its imports is said to have a **balance of trade surplus;** one whose imports' value exceeds its exports' value has a **balance of trade deficit.** What are the options under a fixed-rate system for alleviating such situations?

Changes in Domestic Macroeconomic Policy   Consider first the example of Figure 31.5, where the dollar price of the franc is maintained at e_1 while the equilibrium price is e_0. The dollar is undervalued, and the United States experiences a balance of trade surplus, while Switzerland runs a persistent deficit, importing more than it exports. The Swiss will demand that something be done.

One option is to change domestic macroeconomic policies in the two countries. Suppose the United States allows its money supply to rise and Switzerland lets its money supply fall. In the United States the increase in money supply will lead to higher prices and costs. In Switzerland the opposite effects will occur: There will be lower prices and costs. Thus, U.S. exports will fall because they are now relatively more expensive on world markets, and U.S. imports will rise because foreign goods are now cheaper and income is higher. In Switzerland exports will rise because Swiss goods are now relatively cheaper, and imports will decline because U.S. goods are more expensive and Swiss GDP has fallen. The basic tendency in both countries, then, is toward adjustments that erase the surplus of exports over imports in the United States and the corresponding deficit in Switzerland.

An important point emerges from this discussion. In a fixed exchange rate system, where the government chooses to defend the fixed rate at all costs, imbalances in foreign trade must be resolved through macroeconomic adjustment of entire domestic economies. To keep one price—the foreign exchange rate—fixed, the United States and Switzerland manipulate the level of all the other prices in their economies. A flexible-rate system, by contrast, changes one price—the foreign exchange rate—to resolve balance of trade problems.

Balance of trade surplus

Occurs when the value of a nation's exports exceeds the value of a nation's imports; also called a trade surplus.

Balance of trade deficit

Occurs when the value of a nation's exports is less than the value of a nation's imports; also called a trade deficit.

Devaluation and Revaluation   The second option facing two fixed-rate countries with a trade imbalance is to change the official exchange rate. In this way, the two governments can avoid costly manipulation of their domestic economies to restore foreign trade equilibrium. There are two possible changes in this regard.

Devaluation

An official change in a country's exchange rate in a fixed-rate system; the number of units of a country's money that purchases one unit of another country's currency is increased by the government.

One is **devaluation** of one country's currency. When the dollar is overvalued (e_2 per franc in Figure 31.5), the United States suffers a trade deficit and Switzerland a trade surplus. With Switzerland's agreement, the United States can lower the official exchange value of its currency. In this case, we say that a devaluation has occurred. In terms of Figure 31.5, this means that the dollar price of francs is moved upward, closer to its equilibrium value. This change in the exchange rate changes the relative prices of each country's imports and exports so as to help erase the U.S. deficit and the Swiss surplus without each country's having to resort to costly deflation and inflation of its domestic economy.

Where the official rate is above the equilibrium rate (such as e_1 per franc in Figure 31.5), the opposite process can be applied. In this case, the United States has a trade surplus and Switzerland a deficit. The two countries can support this exchange rate if the United States buys francs or if Switzerland sells dollars or some combination of both. However, to avoid inflation in the United States and deflation in Switzerland to correct the balance of trade situation, the two countries might agree to revalue the dollar. A **revaluation** occurs when the official price of a currency is raised. This means that the dollar price of francs would move downward in Figure 31.5, closer to its equilibrium value. The value of the dollar is thus raised, or revalued, and the corresponding value of the franc is lowered, or devalued.

Revaluation

An official change in a country's exchange rate in a fixed-rate system; the number of units of a country's money that purchases one unit of another country's currency is decreased by the government.

Adjustments in official exchange rates seem less costly than the manipulation of whole economies. However, as we will see later, such adjustments are not always easy to accomplish. The Swiss may reap advantages from a balance of trade surplus and may resist efforts to devalue the dollar or to implement a domestic economic policy that chips away at their surplus. Complex international negotiations are inherent in a fixed-rate system.

Changes in Trade Policy   A third option for resolving balance of trade difficulties under a fixed-rate system is for a deficit country to erect barriers to international trade. Tariffs, quotas, and other barriers to the free movement of people and goods across international borders can be established to try to solve a trade problem. This is not an option that would find much favor among economists, however. As detailed in Chapter 30, such impediments to international trade cost the worldwide economy economic efficiency and gains from specialization.

Instead of erecting trade barriers, another policy is pressuring trading partners to abolish current import restrictions. This strategy has been advocated as a means of reducing the persistent trade deficit between the United States and Japan.

Both floating and fixed exchange rate systems have been used in the past. The most economically powerful countries presently operate essentially on a floating system and have done so since 1973. Before that, starting shortly after World War II, a fixed exchange rate system governed international monetary relations. We will discuss the historical evolution of the international monetary system later in the chapter.

MACROECONOMIC POLICY, EXCHANGE RATES, AND TRADE BALANCE

Foreign trade can have dramatic effects on a government's macroeconomic policy. We consider briefly how monetary policy and fiscal policy are affected by foreign trade.

Monetary Policy

The link between the foreign exchange market and monetary policy depends on whether trade takes place under a system of fixed or floating exchange rates. In the former case, the central bank fixes the exchange rate and allows the money supply to be determined by the economic system; in the latter case, the central bank lets the exchange rate be determined in the market for foreign exchange and manipulates the domestic supply of money.

The Case of Fixed Exchange Rates
To support a fixed exchange rate, the central bank must be prepared to buy and sell whatever foreign exchange is necessary to keep the exchange rate at the fixed level. Suppose that there is a surplus in the balance of trade: At the current exchange rate, the quantity of foreign exchange supplied by exporters exceeds the amount of foreign exchange demanded by importers. In this case, the central bank must purchase foreign exchange by an amount equal to the excess supply to eliminate the tendency for the exchange rate to fall. The central bank purchases foreign exchange by printing more domestic currency, and this increase in the supply of money sets forces in motion that tend to restore equilibrium. Other things being equal, domestic prices rise with a larger money supply, and these higher prices will discourage exports and encourage imports, thus diminishing the trade surplus. In the case of a trade deficit, the central bank will be selling foreign exchange (in effect decreasing domestic currency) to keep the exchange rate from rising. This action will lower the domestic money supply, and the accompanying lower domestic prices will tend to discourage imports and encourage exports. The important point is that to fix one price—the exchange rate—the central bank must give up other money supply controls and allow all other prices to adjust. (The fixed exchange rate system operates like the old gold standard, which is described in the Focus "Should We Return to a Gold Standard?")

The Case of Flexible Exchange Rates
If the government is using a flexible exchange rate system, the central bank can use its domestic monetary policy tools, allowing the exchange rate to be determined by the market. Starting from equilibrium, an increase in the domestic money supply tends to raise prices, and these higher prices tend to encourage imports and discourage exports. Thus, there is a trade deficit (an excess demand for foreign exchange) at the old exchange rate. For individuals to be willing to supply the extra foreign exchange to finance these trade movements, the exchange rate must rise by whatever amount is necessary to eliminate the excess demand. The result of an increase in the domestic money supply is therefore a rise in the exchange rate by exactly the same proportion.

FOCUS

Should We Return to a Gold Standard?

The relatively high inflation rates experienced by the United States during the late 1970s and early 1980s led to a variety of proposals for a return to a gold standard. Proponents of the gold standard argued that linking the nominal money supply to gold would prevent large increases and decreases in the money supply that lead to inflations and deflations. Congress established a U.S. Gold Commission to study the question, and the members not only debated the desirability of again tying the dollar to gold but also considered how to implement a new gold standard.

Proponents of a return to the gold standard argue that the Federal Reserve has neither the willingness nor the ability to follow monetary policies that promote price stability and that some constraint on excessive monetary expansionism is necessary. What are the advantages and disadvantages of gold-backed dollars?

Under a gold standard, currency is freely convertible into gold at some fixed rate, such as $35 per ounce, which was for many years the official U.S. price of gold. Thus, a nation's currency supply is directly related to its supply of gold. The supply of currency can be expanded relative to the supply of gold only by devaluing the dollar in terms of gold—that is, by raising gold's dollar price. A gold standard therefore enforces monetary discipline. In the absence of devaluation, the currency supply can be increased only at a rate equal to the increase in the output of gold, an expansion that has occurred historically at about 1.5 to 2 percent annually. Such a

monetary policy would foster price stability with little or no inflation in the economy.

There are several major drawbacks to a gold standard. Real resources are tied up in money production—gold must be mined, stored, and transported. Also, the supply of gold is relatively inelastic. Expansion in the demand for money as economic growth occurs will generate downward pressure on the general price level. If the supply of gold rises more slowly than the demand, a gold standard will bring about persistent deflation. Discovery of new gold sources or improvements in the technology used to extract gold from existing mines would likely bring about rapid inflation.

Despite the problems, some economists point to the enormous success of a gold standard in promoting sound money and economic growth. It would be difficult to imagine bigger economic success stories than Great Britain between 1717 and 1914 or the United States between 1834 and 1914. Both nations were on the gold standard over these periods (except for brief wartime interludes).

In the United States, the Federal Reserve System has amply demonstrated its willingness to gradually reduce the inflation rate during the 1980s and 1990s. This would appear to take some of the steam out of the argument for a return to the gold standard. But gold standard advocates point out that the Fed's work could easily be undone at any time with a greater degree of political participation in directing the decisions of the U.S. central bank.

Fiscal Policy

The effects of a government's fiscal policy initiatives on exchange rates depend largely on how the changes in government spending are financed. If we assume, for simplicity, that all increases in government expenditures are financed by borrowing, then expansionary fiscal policies stimulate aggregate demand, including the demand for imports on the one hand, and raise government borrowing on the other. The increased demand puts upward pressure on the exchange rate because of the additional foreign currencies required to finance the increased imports. But the increased government borrowing tends to raise interest rates, attracting foreign capital and placing downward pressure on the exchange rate. The net change in the exchange rate resulting from the expansionary policy depends on which of the two effects dominates.

Similarly, contractionary fiscal policies may raise or lower the exchange rate. A lower level of government spending will reduce aggregate demand, reduce the demand for imports, and, at the same time, lower government borrowing. The lower import demand will tend to lower the exchange rate by fostering an excess supply of foreign currencies. But with less government borrowing, interest rates tend to fall. Capital outflows increase, putting upward pressure on exchange rates. Again, the net change of the exchange rate depends on which event—the fall-off in imports or the decline in interest rates—has greater effect.

THE BALANCE OF PAYMENTS

Balance of payments
An official accounting record of all the foreign transactions of a nation's residents, businesses, and governments.

Countries keep track of the flow of international trade and periodically publish a report of their transactions, called the **balance of payments.** The balance of payments is essentially an accounting record of a nation's foreign business. It contains information about the level of exports, imports, foreign investment, and the transactions of government such as purchases and sales of foreign currencies.

The balance of payments, as an accounting statement, is kept according to the principles of double-entry bookkeeping. The concept of double-entry bookkeeping is simple: Each entry on the credit side of the ledger implies an equal entry on the debit side. Thus, each international transaction creates both a debit (−) and a credit (+) item in the balance of payments ledger.

There is a simple rule to follow in classifying debits and credits: Any foreign transaction that leads to a demand for foreign currencies (or a supply of dollars) is treated as a debit, or a minus, item. The act of importing is a debit entry in the balance of payments. Any foreign transaction that leads to a demand for dollars (or a supply of foreign currency) is entered as a credit, or a plus, item. The act of exporting is a credit entry in the balance of payments.

Suppose that a U.S. firm exports computers to France, and the French importer of the computers pays for the purchase with an IOU. The French IOU is entered on the credit side in U.S. balance of payments bookkeeping because the French importer must ultimately demand dollars to pay off its IOU to the U.S. firm. The sale of computers is entered on the debit side as the offsetting part of the transaction. The U.S. firm must give up a computer in return for the French importer's payment. Since each transaction implies an equal debit and credit, the balance of payments must always balance. In this respect, the balance of payment is like any other accounting balance sheet.

Of course, although the total balance of payments of a country must always balance (debits minus credits equal zero), its component parts need not balance. For example, the imports and exports of specific merchandise such as automobiles do not have to balance. But overall, surpluses in one part of the balance of payments must be canceled out by deficits in other parts. This is not to say, of course, that countries do not experience balance of payments problems. Problems arise, as we will see, from persistent surpluses or deficits in the component parts of the balance of payments.

Exports and Imports: The Balance of Trade

Table 31.1 presents the data on the U.S. balance of payments for 1997. Items 1 and 2 represent exports and imports of goods and services. The difference between the sums of these aspects of the balance of payments—exports contrasted with imports—is the balance of trade. Note that trade in merchandise is only one facet of this balance. Merchandise trade figures are the result of a country's international trade in physical goods, such as books, cars, planes, and computers—the visible exports and imports. The data in Table 31.1 show that in 1997 merchandise exports (1a) were less than merchandise imports (2a) by

TABLE 31.1

U.S. Balance of Payments, 1997

U.S. exports enter the balance of payments with plus signs because buyers of these exports must pay U.S. firms with dollars. Dollars thus flow into the United States and are recorded as a plus, or credit, in the balance of payments. U.S. imports receive a minus sign, indicating that to pay for foreign goods U.S. buyers must supply dollars to foreign countries. Dollars thus flow out of the United States, and imports are then treated as a minus, or a debit, in the balance of payments. Similarly, outflows of U.S. capital and inflows of foreign capital are treated as debits and credits, respectively. To classify an item as a debit or a credit, think of whether dollars are leaving or entering the country. If they are leaving, the item is a debit; if they are entering, the item is a credit.

Item	Amount (billions of dollars)
1. Exports of goods and services	1179
a. Merchandise, excluding military	679
b. Services and other	500
2. Imports of goods and services	-1295
a. Merchandise, excluding military	-877
b. Services and other	-418
3. Unilateral transfers	-37
4. U.S. assets abroad, net (capital outflow)	-479
5. Foreign assets in U.S., net (capital inflow)	733
6. Statistical discrepancy	-100
7. Total	0

Source: U.S. Bureau of the Census, *Statistical Abstract of the United States, 1998* (Washington, D.C.: U.S. Government Printing Office, 1998), pp. 786–787.

$198 billion. This figure is sometimes called the merchandise trade balance and is equal to merchandise exports minus merchandise imports. If the figure is positive, there is a merchandise trade surplus. It was negative in 1997, so there was a merchandise trade deficit.

Many imports and exports are invisible. U.S. citizens and firms supply various services to foreigners, such as transportation, insurance, and telecommunications. Payments are received for these services just as in the case of visible exports. Items 1b and 2b represent invisible exports and imports in the balance of payments. When both visible and invisible exports and imports are considered in Table 31.1, U.S. exports were still substantially less than U.S. imports, yielding a trade deficit of $116 billion.

Net Transfers Abroad

Net unilateral transfers abroad are one-way money payments from the United States to foreigners or United States citizens living abroad. Included in this category are such items as foreign aid and pension checks to retired U.S. citizens living abroad. Nothing tangible comes back to the United States for these transfers, but they do give rise to a demand for foreign exchange. They thus are entered as a debit item in the balance of payments. In 1997, the United States made $37 billion worth of such transfers.

Current Account Balance

The balance on current account is equal to exports of goods and services minus imports of goods and services minus net unilateral transfers abroad. The United States had a deficit on current account in 1997 of $153 billion.

Net Capital Movements

When U.S. residents purchase foreign stocks and bonds, they obtain a claim to foreign capital (buildings, factories, future foreign government payments, and so forth). Funds that would otherwise be invested in the United States are exported, or, to put it another way, capital is exported. When foreign citizens purchase the stocks and bonds of U.S. businesses and governments, foreign capital is imported into the United States. In 1997 capital outflows were $479 billion, whereas capital inflows were $733 billion.

Note what happens in bookkeeping terms when capital flows into and out of a country. Capital outflows are treated as a debit item in the balance of payments because they constitute a payment; they give rise to a demand for foreign exchange with which to make foreign investment. Capital inflows are a credit item because they consist of receipts by U.S. residents from foreigners; they generate a supply of foreign exchange necessary to obtain dollars with which to purchase U.S. financial assets.

Statistical Discrepancy

Item 6 in Table 31.1 is called statistical discrepancy, an accounting fudge factor. When all the data were collected and debits and credits computed, the credits outweighed the debits by $100 billion. The negative statistical discrepancy is added to make the balance of payments balance by compensating for imperfections in data gathering. (Some debits have apparently gone unrecorded in computing the balance of payments. These could include hidden imports or unrecorded capital outflows. Most experts think that the former is the source of most of the discrepancy, which can be quite large.)

The Balance of Payments and the Value of the Dollar

The last entry in Table 31.1 is zero, indicating that the balance of payments must balance. This is the way any double-entry accounting system works. The balance of payments, however, is an aggregate record of a country's international payments for one year. Behind this record are the myriad transactions of U.S. citizens and firms with foreign citizens and firms. These transactions determine how the U.S. dollar fares in the foreign exchange market.

THE EVOLUTION OF INTERNATIONAL MONETARY INSTITUTIONS

Major world trading nations today rely on floating exchange rates. These governments will occasionally intervene in the foreign exchange market when exchange rate changes are significant, but generally currency prices are free to adjust according to the forces of supply and demand. We briefly review the developments over the past hundred years that led the major trading nations to adopt floating exchange rates in 1973.

The Decline of the Gold Standard

Gold standard
An international monetary system in which currencies are redeemable in gold at fixed rates or prices.

In the period before World War I, dating back to the 1870s, most currencies in the world economy were tied to gold. This means that each country was prepared to redeem its currency at a fixed price in gold to both its own citizens and foreigners. The United States, for example, stood ready to exchange an ounce of gold for $20.67 over this period. In addition, countries on the **gold standard** linked their money supplies to their holdings of gold bullion.

The gold standard worked reasonably well in eliminating balance of trade surpluses and deficits over the period 1870–1914. Nonetheless, for a variety of reasons the gold standard broke down after World War I. There were attempts to return to the gold standard in the 1920s, but the shock to the international economy caused by the Great Depression in the 1930s brought the gold system down once and for all.

Bretton Woods and the Postwar System

Bretton Woods System
The fixed exchange rate system established among Western countries after World War II.

Not until after World War II were the problems of the international monetary system addressed in a concerted way. Negotiators for the free-world countries met in Bretton Woods, New Hampshire, in 1944 to develop a new international monetary order. The **Bretton Woods System,** which was in place for almost thirty years, was

International Monetary Fund (IMF)

An international organization, established along with the Bretton Woods system, designed to assist in the efficient functioning of the Bretton Woods fixed exchange rate system.

characterized by fixed exchange rates and an international central bank, called the **International Monetary Fund (IMF),** to oversee the new system.

We have already discussed the economics of fixed exchange rates. The basic idea of the Bretton Woods system was that, over time, countries would obtain or pay for their imports with their exports. There might be temporary periods over which a country might wish to run a trade deficit to obtain more imports than its current level of exports allowed it to obtain. Under the Bretton Woods system, it could do so by borrowing international reserves from the IMF. Over time, the country was expected to return to a trade surplus and pay back the earlier loan of reserves.

The IMF was the bank that held the reserves that allowed the system to operate in this way. When the IMF was formed, each member country was required to contribute reserves of its currency to the bank. The bank thus accumulated substantial holdings of dollars, marks, francs, pesos, and so on, and when member nations ran into balance of trade deficits, the bank would lend them reserves. Each time a loan was made, the debtor nation was encouraged to reform its economic policies to avoid future deficits. Sound economic management might also lead to a trade surplus and a source of funds to repay the IMF loan.

The Bretton Woods system sounds fine in principle, and indeed it functioned tolerably well for a number of years. However, as we saw earlier, fixing the price of a currency is like fixing the price of any other good or service—it is very likely to cause surpluses and shortages in the market. As the conditions affecting imports and exports across countries change, the demand and supply of currencies will shift. Countries can find themselves with overvalued fixed exchange rates, which means that they will face persistent balance of trade deficits. Under the IMF system, the deficit country could draw on its IMF reserves to settle the deficits, but it could not do this forever because it would exhaust its reserves. Chronic deficit countries with overvalued exchange rates were thus said to be in fundamental disequilibrium.

In our discussion of the theory of fixed exchange rates, we reviewed the various courses of action that a country in fundamental disequilibrium could take. First, it could devalue its currency as a step toward restoring equilibrium in its balance of trade. Once its currency was devalued, the exchange rate would again be fixed and defended. Second, the country could attempt to improve its trade balance by imposing tariff and quota barriers to imports and perhaps by subsidizing exports. In other words, the country could move away from free trade to balance its imports and exports. Third, the country could behave as if it were on the gold standard. This would mean adopting restrictive monetary and fiscal policies designed to promote domestic deflation and high interest rates in the hope that such changes would restore the balance of trade to equilibrium. This, of course, is a problematic course of action for any country. For example, if the country's unemployment rate were already high, it is hard to believe that the nation's leaders would be sufficiently disciplined to undertake a deflationary course of action.

Speculation by buyers and sellers of currencies also undermines a fixed exchange rate system. Suppose Great Britain is running chronic trade deficits, and everyone, including speculators, expects that the pound will be devalued (even

Speculation

The buying and selling of currencies on the foreign exchange market with the intent of profiting from possible devaluation or revaluation in a fixed-rate system or from possible future movements in the exchange rate in a flexible-rate system.

though British central bankers will deny such rumors vehemently). In effect, speculators are in a no-lose position. Will they continue to hold pounds? Clearly, they will not; pounds are about to become less valuable relative to other currencies. Speculators will sell their pounds for other currencies, increasing the supply of pounds to the foreign exchange market and putting additional downward pressure on the pound. By selling the weak currency and buying a strong currency, speculators make it difficult for authorities to find a new fixed value for the pound. This is why speculation in a fixed exchange rate system is often termed destabilizing.

In the early period of the Bretton Woods system, the United States ran a large trade deficit, and this deficit provided a means of supplying dollar reserves to the rest of the world. It was thought that this deficit was a temporary problem that would soon be replaced by a U.S. trade surplus. This was the premise of the Bretton Woods system. Yet the dollar was overvalued, and the U.S. deficits continued and grew larger into the 1950s and 1960s. The United States was in a difficult position. It was hard for it to devalue the dollar because the dollar was held by virtually every nation as an international reserve asset. A U.S. devaluation would have decreased the wealth of all those countries holding dollars. Several times, the United States tried to impose a restrictive macroeconomic policy to correct its balance of trade. However, when unemployment rose as a consequence, such policies were rapidly abandoned, as political pressures were brought to bear on policy-makers. U.S. deficits continued to grow, and foreign holdings of dollars rose.

Speculators entered again. Many holders of dollars became concerned about what the United States was going to do. There were various runs on the U.S. gold stock, as dollars were traded in by foreigners. In 1950, the United States had 509 million ounces of gold; by 1968, this stock had fallen to 296 million ounces. Confidence in the dollar fell further, and the stage was set for a drastic change in the international monetary system.

The Current International Monetary System

The present international monetary system was born in 1971. In the face of continuing large trade deficits and mounting speculation against the dollar, President Nixon broke the link between the dollar and gold in August 1971. No longer would the United States stand ready to exchange gold for dollars at $35 an ounce. In effect, the dollar was set free to fluctuate and seek its own level in the foreign exchange market. As a result, the overvalued dollar depreciated substantially against other major currencies. There were interim attempts to fix the price of the dollar again, but they failed. By early 1973, all the major currencies were floating.

The international monetary system that has been in effect since 1973 is a managed flexible-rate system. Exchange rates are allowed to seek their free market values, as long as fluctuations are within an acceptable range. If fluctuations fall outside this range, governments may intervene with their reserve holdings to dampen the fluctuations in their currencies. Thus, exchange rates are not completely free; government intervention in the foreign exchange market will be forthcoming if a country's currency falls dramatically in value. In 1978, for example, the dollar fell sharply, and the Carter administration intervened to restrict this decline with international reserves and loans from West Germany and Japan. The central banks of major trading countries also have stepped up intervention activity since September of 1985. It should be remembered, though, that under the managed flexible-rate system, the ranges within which governments consider exchange rate fluctuations acceptable are not well defined as a matter of policy. As a result, it is difficult to tell how far a nation's currency would have to appreciate or depreciate before central bank interventions would occur.

Although the new system abandoned fixed exchange rates, it did not abandon the IMF, which still exists as an international monetary organization. The role of the IMF under the managed flexible-rate system is still evolving, and to this point it has consisted of helping countries that have persistent balance of payments problems by giving them loans and policy advice about how to conduct domestic macroeconomic policy to overcome these problems. The World Bank, which is part of the IMF system set up by the Bretton Woods agreement, has also played an increasing role in the new system. This sister institution of the IMF makes long-run development loans to poor countries. The whole system came under close scrutiny when the Asian financial structure was mortally threatened in 1997. The financial "meltdown" in Asia created worldwide financial problems (see the Application "The Asian Economic Crisis" at the end of this chapter).

Advantages of the Current System   Despite the recent crisis, the consensus view seems to be that the new system has worked very well under difficult circumstances. The following are the major advantages of the flexible-rate system.

1. It allows countries to pursue independent monetary policies. If a country wants to inflate its economy, it can do so by letting its exchange rate depreciate, thereby maintaining its position in international markets without sacrificing its preferred monetary policy.

2. Under the fixed-rate system, a country sometimes had to deflate its economy to solve a balance of trade deficit. With floating rates it only has to let its exchange rate depreciate. Clearly, it is easier to change one price than to change all prices to resolve balance of trade difficulties.

3. The current exchange rate system has proven capable of handling large economic disturbances. When the OPEC countries dramatically raised the price of oil in 1973–1974, the world economy experienced a tremendous shock. The greatest achievement of the flexible-rate system is the way it handled this shock. Oil-importing countries developed large trade deficits; huge trade surpluses built up in OPEC countries. These deficits and surpluses were accommodated by floating rates. Moreover, the huge oil revenues of the OPEC countries were recycled into Western investments. Though exchange rates changed significantly over the period, the new system weathered the storm and got the job done.

Disadvantages of the Current System   The flexible-rate system is not, however, without its critics. Some of the major disadvantages of the current system are discussed in this section.

1. Some observers point out that flexible rates can be very volatile, and this volatility creates considerable uncertainty for international trade. Thus, exchange rate flexibility leads to conditions that can retard the amount of international trade and therefore the degree of specialization in the world economy.

2. A second criticism of floating rates is that they promote increased world inflation rates. Under a fixed-rate system, countries experience a balance of trade deficit if they inflate their respective economies. This link is severed under a flexible-rate system. Hence, domestic political authorities can more easily give in to interests that benefit from inflation.

3. Some countries that have relied primarily on adjustments in exchange rates to resolve trade imbalance problems have found that the solution has been a long time in coming. For example, despite depreciation of the dollar, the U.S. trade deficit with Japan has persisted for years, causing some observers to conclude that dollar depreciation never will solve the problem.

In sum, there are pros and cons with respect to the present international monetary system, but in general the system seems to have worked well over a difficult period in the international economy. Growing problems in the international payments system, however, call for the prospect of further reform of the system.

APPLICATION

The Asian Economic Crisis

In January 1997, a Korean steel conglomerate collapsed, unable to make payments on its heavy debt. In February, a company in Thailand missed its foreign debt payments, and in March another Korean steel conglomerate failed. At the time, the International Monetary Fund (IMF) was confidently proclaiming that there was no reason for the crisis to develop any further. Looking back, we can see clearly now that these were the first signs of the economic crisis in Asia that would devastate local economies, cause violence and political upheaval, and spread economic woes throughout the world.

The summer of 1997 was one of currency meltdown. In Thailand, the Philippines, Malaysia, and Indonesia, the value of currency declined as traders in international monetary markets sold the declining currencies. Local leaders blamed international speculators, such as George Soros, for their problems. Hong Kong, Singapore, and Vietnam all took steps to help stabilize their currencies. Thailand called on the help of the IMF and agreed to financial reforms and budget austerity measures in exchange for a $16 billion bailout package.

As the economic troubles spread throughout Asia and began to have economic ramifications around the globe, violence erupted in Indonesia in May of 1998 in conjunction with the collapse of the long-ruling Suharto regime. Citizens protested and rioted, and the military was called upon to restore order. This social upheaval was the result of the combination of growing unemployment and the skyrocketing prices that resulted from the downfall of the currency. The effect was to further undermine confidence in the currencies and economies of the region.

As the region sank into economic depression and with the regional economic powerhouse, Japan, already stuck in a long recession, Asia began spreading economic problems throughout the world. (Some analysts called it the "Asian contagion.") Asia imports a great deal of food, fuel, and raw materials from around the world to feed its populations and factories. When incomes and production declined, world markets were affected. Agricultural exports from Argentina, Australia, Canada, and New Zealand were all affected by lower prices and less demand for their exports. Oil and mineral exporters such as Chile, Ecuador, Mexico, Peru, Russia, and Venezuela all suffered greatly from lower prices for oil and minerals, their main source of foreign exchange earnings. Stock markets in all these countries fell sharply while unemployment grew. In the United States, certain sectors of the economy such as farming and steel were affected, but falling import prices and expanding technology cushioned the blow to the macroeconomy, and unemployment remained at record low levels. Foreigners were holding dollars and investing in U.S. stock markets, keeping the value of the dollar strong and stock prices firm.

The Asian world had been turned upside down. For the last quarter century, eastern Asia had been the fastest growing region of the world and had gone through an industrial revolution. Led by Japan, the "Pacific Rim" countries such as South Korea, Taiwan, Thailand, Malaysia, Indonesia, Hong Kong, Singapore, the Philippines, and, most recently, Vietnam were considered models of economic development. They were often labeled the "Asian Tigers" because their economic growth and prosperity seemed unstoppable. In fact, income growth was much more rapid in Asia than during previous "industrial revolutions" (see Table 31.2).

What caused this crisis? Most of the traditional causes of financial debacle, such as high inflation, budget deficits, slow growth, and low savings rates were not present. Indeed, the Asian Tigers had a remarkable record of "managing" their

TABLE 31.2

Industrial Revolutions and How Long It Took to Double Income
It took industrial revolutions in the United Kingdom and the United States nearly half a century to double per capita income, but it took South Korea and China only about a decade to achieve the same result.

Country	Beginning of Industrial Revolution	Number of Years to Double Income
United Kingdom	1780	58
United States	1839	47
Japan	1885	35
South Korea	1966	11
China	1977	10

Source: Council of Economic Advisers, *Economic Report of the President* (Washington, D.C.: U.S. Government Printing Office, 1999), p. 227.

macroeconomies. Upon closer examination, this "management" turned out to be "crony capitalism" in which corruption was a major factor in how resources, specifically loans and credits, were allocated. Major companies were granted virtually unlimited credit on favorable terms, were provided with lucrative government contracts, and received special privileges from their governments.

The expansion of credit led to a construction and real estate boom throughout the region. Stock markets rose, but so did debt. Companies were highly leveraged, and as the amount of fixed capital grew, the return on capital shrank and turned negative as the currency crisis and depression hit. The Asian crisis and its "contagion" is a classic case of a rapid and artificial expansion of credit and bad investment that eventually leads to the pain of bankruptcy, liquidation, and even social upheaval.

QUESTIONS

In addition to Thailand, the IMF has provided large bailout packages of loans and guarantees to countries like Mexico, Russia, and Yugoslavia. What effects do these bailouts have? Do you think they encourage countries to act more or less financially responsible?

SUMMARY

1. Foreign exchange is the currency of another country that is needed to make payment in an international transaction.
2. Foreign exchange can be obtained in the worldwide foreign exchange market. The demand for foreign exchange arises from the desire to buy foreign goods. The supply of foreign exchange arises from the desire of citizens of one country to buy the goods of another country.
3. A foreign exchange rate is the price of one currency in terms of another. A currency's value appreciates when its purchasing power in terms of other currencies rises. It depreciates when its purchasing power falls.
4. The demand for foreign currency depends largely on income and relative price levels in the trading countries.
5. Under a floating, or flexible, exchange rate system, a country allows its exchange rate to be set by the forces of supply and demand in the foreign exchange market. Flexible exchange rates change in response to changes in countries' money supplies, price levels, inflation rates, real interest rates, and fundamental factors such as technology, consumer rates, and government export and import policies. Under a flexible-rate system, exchange rate movements act to alleviate balance of trade surpluses and deficits.
6. Under a fixed exchange rate system, governments intervene in the foreign exchange market to set and defend the value of their currency. When a country's currency is overvalued relative to the equilibrium rate, the country will run a balance of trade deficit. It can seek to cure this deficit by deflating the domestic economy, establishing trade barriers, or devaluing its currency to a new, lower, fixed rate of exchange. When the fixed exchange rate is below its equilibrium value, a country will experience a balance of trade surplus and will sometimes revalue its currency upward.
7. An important difference between floating- and fixed-rate systems is that the former changes one price to maintain equilibrium in the balance of

trade, while the latter changes all prices in the economy to maintain a fixed exchange rate.

8. The balance of payments is a record of the international transactions of a country's economy. It follows the principles of double-entry bookkeeping and must therefore always balance in an accounting sense. Transactions that give rise to a demand for foreign exchange are entered as debits; transactions that give rise to a supply of foreign exchange are treated as credits.

9. The modern history of the international monetary system began with the gold standard, followed by a system of fixed exchange rates managed by the International Monetary Fund. The present international monetary system is a managed floating-rate system. Exchange rates are set by supply and demand, but governments can and have intervened if exchange rate movements are too large.

KEY TERMS

foreign exchange
foreign exchange markets
exchange rate
flexible (floating) exchange
    rate system
fixed exchange rate system
managed flexible-rate system
depreciation

appreciation
undervalued
overvalued
foreign exchange market
    intervention
foreign exchange reserves
balance of trade surplus
balance of trade deficit

devaluation
revaluation
balance of payments
gold standard
Bretton Woods System
International Monetary Fund
    (IMF)
speculation

QUESTIONS FOR REVIEW AND DISCUSSION

1. Suppose that the British pound is worth $1.50, and that $1 is worth about 6.5 Swedish krona. How much would a Jaguar automobile cost in U.S. dollars if the British price is 20,000 pounds? How much would a Volvo cost in U.S. dollars if the Swedish price is 84,000 krona?

2. Suppose that the United States and Sweden are on a floating exchange rate system. Explain whether the following events would cause the Swedish krona to appreciate or depreciate.

a. U.S. interest rates rise above Swedish interest rates.

b. American tourism to Sweden increases.

c. Americans fall in love with a newly designed Volvo, and Volvo sales in the United States skyrocket.

d. The U.S. government puts a quota on Volvo imports.

e. The Swedish inflation rate rises relative to the U.S. rate.

f. The United States closes a military installation in Sweden at the urging of the Swedish government.

3. How would you treat the following items in the balance of payments? In other words, would you enter them as debits or credits?

a. An American travels to Canada.

b. A U.S. wine importer buys wine from Italy.

c. A California wine grower sells wine to England.

d. An Austrian corporation pays dividends to American stockholders.

e. General Motors pays dividends to French investors.

f. Several Japanese visit Hawaii on an American cruise ship.

g. A Swedish citizen invests in a U.S. company based in Houston.

4. Explain why capital inflows are a credit entry in the balance of payments and capital outflows are a debit entry.

5. When we say that the fixed exchange rate system requires that all prices but one be changed to overcome a balance of trade deficit, what do we mean?

6. What are the primary advantages and disadvantages of the present international monetary system?

7. Use the following exchange rate tables to answer the questions:

U.S. DOLLAR PER CURRENCY UNIT

	Thursday	Wednesday
Swiss franc	0.7978	0.8003
Italian lira	0.0006480	0.0006474

CURRENCY PER U.S. DOLLAR

	Thursday	Wednesday
Swiss franc	1.2535	1.2495
Italian lira	1543.30	1544.55

a. Did the Swiss franc rise or fall from Wednesday to Thursday?

b. Did the Italian lira rise or fall from Wednesday to Thursday?

c. What happened to the dollar value of the franc?

d. What happened to the dollar value of the lira?

PROBLEM

What happens to the floating exchange rate of a country that has a higher inflation rate than other countries? Show your answer graphically.

WORKING WITH THE WEB

1. Go to the Virtual Economy web site at http://ve.ifs.org.uk. Find the link to "4th Floor, The Model" near the bottom of the page. On the next screen, click on the link "Selected variables form." This site allows you to determine the impact on the U.K. economy from general changes in fiscal policy. Make any changes mentioned below, and then submit those changes by clicking on the "Run Model" button.

    a. What is the effect on the current account ratio and exchange rate from raising the Basic (Income) Tax Rate from £23 per year to £30 per year?

    b. Explain the reason for the changes you described above.

2. Locate the paper entitled "The Crisis in Emerging Financial Markets" by going to the Brookings Institution home page at http://www.brook.edu. After doing a search with the phrase "crisis in emerging financial markets," click on the appropriate link (the web address of this paper should be http://www.brook.edu/pa/conferencereport/cr3/cr3.htm).

    An interesting alternative site houses a video lecture series that addresses this question as well. Go to the Center for Economic Studies home-page at http://www.lrz-muenchen.de/~ces and click on "Video Lectures." Ruediger Dornbusch's lecture is particularly good (to view the lecture you will need to download the program Windows Media Player, which is available at the bottom of the page).

    How did capital mobility play a role in the Asian financial crisis?

3. The IMF was involved in bailing out the economies of Russia, Mexico, and various Asian nations during the 1990s. Go to the Hoover Institution's homepage at http://www-hoover.stanford.edu and do a word search with the phrase "Adios IMF." You should see a link entitled "Uncommon Knowledge, show #320" (alternatively, you can select the link on the initial homepage for "Uncommon Knowledge" and locate show #320).

    When reading the article (note that you can also view it or listen, using the appropriate software), you will find that the discussants take issue with IMF bailouts.

    In terms of how these bailouts affect the risk and return associated with investing in these nations, how might these bailouts affect future capital flows to countries like Mexico?

Peter Tamas Bauer

P. T. Bauer
and Gunnar
Myrdal:
Third World
Development
and Trade

Gunnar Myrdal

Peter Tamas Bauer (b. 1915) is a distinguished critic of development theory. Bauer's studies of the rubber industry and West African trade paved the way for his works on development—*Dissent on Development* (1972) and *Reality and Rhetoric: Studies in the Economics of Development* (1984). Bauer struck his central theme concerning economic development in earlier works: Economic growth, Bauer argued, is the product of voluntary responses and efficient domestic and international markets—not of state intervention or central planning by governments.

Born in Hungary, Bauer was a fellow of Gonville and Caius College at Cambridge (England) between 1946 and 1960 and again from 1968 to 1984. He was also professor of economics in the University of London at the London School of Economics from 1960 until his retirement in 1983. While in these academic posts, Bauer launched attacks on the conventional wisdom regarding economic development, including theories relating to the widening gap of income differences within and between countries, the vicious circle of poverty, the operation of marketing boards and commodity agreements in developing countries, and the operation of foreign aid. Principally, Bauer targeted the economic development theories of Gunnar Myrdal.

Gunnar Myrdal (1898–1987), sociologist and economist, was a joint recipient of the Nobel Memorial Prize in economics with Friedrich A. von Hayek in 1974. Myrdal is best known for his work on racial discrimination and social problems. His most famous work, *An American Dilemma: The Negro Problem and Modern Democracy,* began as a study commissioned by the Carnegie Corporation in 1938 and had an enormous impact on American attitudes toward integration. His later works explored trade and economic development: *The Political Element in the Development of Economic Theory* (1935) focused on the philosophical foundations of classical free trade doctrine to the problems of economic development.

Myrdal was born in the Gustaf parish of Sweden. He studied law as an undergraduate at the University of Stockholm and received his Ph.D. in law from the university in 1927. In 1924, he married Alva Reimer, with whom he researched and wrote a study of Sweden's decreasing population, which was published in 1934. After graduation, Myrdal taught economics, traveled abroad, and served the government of Sweden both as a representative of the Social Democratic party and as cabinet minister. In 1947, he was appointed executive secretary of the United Nations Economic Commission for Europe, a position he retained for the next ten years. In 1960, he became a professor of international economics at the University of Stockholm.

829

What Is the Problem?

Both Bauer and Myrdal pursued answers to timeless questions regarding the economic development of Third World nations. Does free trade promote or impede economic development in poor nations? Which is more conducive to economic growth and progress in developing nations—central planning or free markets? What is the nature and what are the effects of economic aid from industrialized nations to poor and developing nations of the world?

Bauer and Myrdal occupy opposite ends of the philosophical spectrum; they could not agree on what the problem of economic development is, much less any solution. Myrdal, for example, would center the investigation around the causes of poverty, while Bauer would have economists investigate the causes of prosperity and development. In other words, the burden of any theory of development is either to explain how certain nations and people got rich (Bauer) or why certain nations remained poor (Myrdal).

Not only are Myrdal and Bauer worlds apart on the definition of the problem of development, they stand apart on the philosophical nature of equality and power. Of great importance here is the concept of "equality," which both economists support, but in vastly different forms. As an important modern commentator on their views has remarked, "Whether Myrdal or Bauer is more in favor of equality depends entirely on whether equality is conceived as equality of economic results or equality of political process. Myrdal clearly believes more in equality of economic results—and Bauer equally clearly prefers equality of social processes."[a] In other words, the goal of economic development, in Myrdal's view, is to promote economic equality—similar levels of development and equitable income distributions—between rich and poor nations. Economic power exemplified by concentrations of monopoly power, Myrdal believed, is the root cause of inequalities. Bauer, on the other hand, believes that economic development requires that social processes and access to economic activity be open to all and be free and unfettered. In Bauer's view, power restricts the choices of others, most often exemplified by government planning and regulation.

The rich, according to Bauer, most often get that way by expanding the choices and opportunities of others.

Trade, Central Planning, and Economic Aid

Not surprisingly, the philosophical differences between Bauer and Myrdal show very different views of key elements in economic development. Here we consider only three of these key elements.

Trade

In Myrdal's view, the principle of comparative advantage and free trade works in favor of rich nations and keeps poor nations locked within a vicious cycle of poverty. The low saving rates of poor countries mean low investment, which means low economic growth, which means low savings, and so on. To Myrdal, trade with other countries does not unlock this vicious cycle. In *Rich Lands and Poor: The Road to World Prosperity* (1957), he writes, "The forces in the market tend to increase, rather than to decrease, the inequalities between regions." Myrdal points to the so-called banana republics, underdeveloped nations that specialize in one product. In Myrdal's view, such overspecialization leaves a country vulnerable to changes in demand and puts its economy in continuous peril. He suggests that tariffs and subsidies would provide the impetus for developing nations to diversify production and to reduce dependence on one or a few exports.

In Bauer's analysis of trade, these views are wrongheaded and counterproductive. In the first place, Bauer denies that there is a vicious cycle of poverty in underdeveloped countries. Saving and investment take place even where people are poor and illiterate. In his classic study of the rubber industry, Bauer showed that very rapid growth was possible as a consequence of voluntary responses by peasants to expanded opportunities and contacts of developed countries in the West.[b] Further, Bauer argued that

---

[a]Thomas Sowell, *A Conflict of Visions* (New York: William Morrow and Company, 1987), p. 159.

[b]A. A. Walters, "Peter Tamas Bauer," *The New Palgrave: A Dictionary of Economics,* edited by John Eatwell, Murray Milgate, and Peter Newman (London: The Macmillan Press Limited, 1987), vol. I, p. 207. For further information on Myrdal, see Paul Streeten, "Gunnar Myrdal," *The New Palgrave,* vol. III, pp. 581–583.

trade restrictions and attempts to substitute domestic production for goods that can be obtained more cheaply abroad were a certain path to welfare reductions and to lower growth and development. Development could be maximized only with free interaction between *all* trading nations.

Central Planning and Aid

Myrdal urged central planning as an extension of his belief that unequal distribution of power and property was the principal obstacle to equitable economic growth. Institutional planning, production goals, and price planning are all parts of the system that Myrdal urged on developing nations as prerequisites to growth and changing attitudes. He had faith that, with enough information and competent managers, planning would be superior to any other method of achieving growth and human development. Further, he believed the role of industrialized countries was to provide aid to poor nations.

Sentiments expressed by Bauer more than two decades ago have a very contemporary feel. Bauer pointed out then that planning, if it works at all, does not maximize an economy's opportunities. All investment undertaken for political motives is wasted. Bauer likewise criticized foreign aid as intergovernmental grants of taxpayers' money. While such aid augments resources in recipient countries, Bauer believes there is no reason to expect that, in the hands of politicians, bureaucrats, and administrators, it will be put to productive uses. With few exceptions, foreign aid promotes centralized and closely controlled economies (factors that choke growth), and it sometimes generates resentment and suspicion toward the donor.[c] Of far greater effect is aid provided on a commercial basis, direct foreign investment in developing nations, and—of ultimate importance in Bauer's view—free and open trade between rich nations and poor.

---

[c]For more on economic aid, see P. T. Bauer, *Dissent on Development: Studies and Debates in Development Economics* (Cambridge, Mass.: Harvard University Press, 1972), pp. 114–135.

GLOSSARY

A

ability-to-pay principle A method of determining individuals' tax burdens on the basis of those most capable of paying taxes.

accommodation of cost-push inflation Increases in the money supply designed to offset a decrease in aggregate supply caused by monopoly or union action or by an aggregate supply shock; increased aggregate demand results, preventing decreases in real output.

accounting costs Actual money expenditures associated with any activity; payments a firm actually makes to resource suppliers; out-of-pocket costs or explicit costs.

accounting profit The amount by which total revenues exceed total accounting, or explicit, costs; total revenue minus total explicit payments for inputs or out-of-pocket costs.

adjusted income An individual's income after all taxes and all government transfer payments are accounted for.

administrative lag The amount of time between recognition of a destabilizing economic event and the implementation of a policy designed to correct it.

advertising Any communication or information that firms offer consumers to increase demand for a product.

aggregate demand The total spending that occurs in an economy at various price levels during a specified period of time.

aggregate demand curve Graphical relation showing the different levels of national income that exist at different price levels.

aggregate supply The total output that will be produced by an economy at various price levels during a specified period of time.

aggregate supply curve A graph showing the different levels of aggregate output produced at different price levels.

aggregate supply of land The total amount of land available for use by the entire economy.

allocative efficiency A situation in which the socially optimal amount of a good or service is produced in an industry; the socially optimal amount depends on the tastes and preferences of society and on the opportunity cost of the resources used to produce the good or service.

antitrust policies Regulations established by laws and government agencies that attempt to preserve business competition.

appreciation An increase in the equilibrium exchange market value of a country's currency in a flexible-rate system; a decrease in the number of units of a country's money required to purchase one unit of a foreign country's money.

arc elasticity A measure of the average elasticity between two points on the demand curve.

artificial barriers to trade Restrictions created by the government that inhibit or prevent trade; includes import quotas and tariffs.

asset income Earnings from interest on savings, from capital investments, and from land; all result from forgone consumption in the past.

automatic stabilizers Taxes and government expenditures whose levels do not depend on decisions by policymakers for change but instead change countercyclically in response to changes in the level of economic activity.

autonomous consumption Consumption expenditures that are independent of the level of income.

autonomous consumption multiplier The multiple by which equilibrium income will change given a change in autonomous consumption expenditure; $1/MPS$.

autonomous government expenditures Government expenditures that are independent of the level of income.

autonomous investment Investment expenditures that are independent of the level of income.

average cost pricing A regulatory policy that causes a firm to charge a price equal to average cost, inducing the firm to produce

an output such that economic profits are zero.

average fixed cost Total fixed costs divided by the level of output.

average product Total output divided by the number of units of the variable input used to produce the total output; output produced per unit of variable input used.

average propensity to consume (APC) The percentage of a particular level of income that is spent on consumption; total consumption divided by total income.

average propensity to save (APS) The percentage of total income that is saved; total saving during any given period divided by total income in the same period.

average total cost Total costs divided by the level of output.

average variable cost Total variable costs divided by the level of output.

B

backward induction The incentive each player has to cheat in the last period of the game; exists because there are no future periods left to play in which possible consequences from cheating could occur.

balance of payments An official accounting record of all the foreign transactions of a nation's residents, businesses, and governments.

balance of trade deficit Occurs when the value of a nation's exports is less than the value of a nation's imports; also called a trade deficit.

balance of trade surplus Occurs when the value of a nation's exports exceeds the value of a nation's imports; also called a trade surplus.

barter Direct exchange of one good or service for another without the use of money.

barter economy An economy in which money is not used to facilitate exchange between individuals and firms; goods trade directly for other goods.

benefit principle A method of determining individuals' tax burdens on the basis of

833

the beneficiaries of the expenditures that are financed by taxes; an example is a gasoline tax.

bilateral monopoly   A market in which there is only one buyer and only one seller of a resource or product.

binding arbitration   An agreement between the buyers and sellers of labor to allow a third party to determine the conditions of a work contract.

bonds   Financial instruments that create future obligations on the part of the issuers to make principal repayments and interest payments.

Bretton Woods system   The fixed exchange rate system established among Western countries after World War II.

budget deficit   The amount by which government's expenditures exceed government's tax revenues in a year.

budget surplus   The amount by which government's tax revenues exceed government's expenditures in a year.

bureaus   The arms of government that serve to implement and enforce legislation and to administer programs created by legislation.

business cycles   Recurrent, systematic fluctuations in the level of business activity; usually measured by changes in the level, or rate of growth, of real GDP over time.

C

capital consumption   A decrease in the capital stock; occurs when the rate of depreciation is greater than the rate of capital formation.

capital deepening   Increases in the total stock of capital in conjunction with increases in the ratio of the capital stock to the labor force; occurs when the capital stock grows at a faster rate than the labor force.

capital formation   An increase in the stock of capital due to roundabout production; the process whereby the stock of capital in an economy increases.

capital stock   The amount of nonhuman resources available in the economy. These include tools, land, machinery, equipment, and so on; the total amount of capital goods that exists in an economy at any point in time.

capture, or interest group, theory of regulation   Argues that regulations are con-

structed so as to further the interests of the existing firms within a particular industry.

cartel   An alliance of firms that act collusively to reduce output and increase price in an industry in order to increase profits.

cartel enforcement   Attempts by members of the cartel to prevent other members from cheating and thus destroying economic profit potential.

cash reserves   Commercial banks' and other depository institutions' holdings of vault cash or deposits at the Federal Reserve district banks.

ceteris paribus   The Latin phrase for "all other things held constant."

change in demand   A shift of the entire demand curve to the right or left.

change in quantity demanded   A change in the amount of a good a consumer is willing and able to purchase that is caused by a change in the price of the good or service.

change in quantity supplied   A change in the amount of a good a producer is willing and able to produce and sell that is caused by a change in the price of the good or service.

change in supply   A shift of the entire supply curve to the right or left.

change in the demand for labor   A shift of the entire labor demand curve; caused by a change in the marginal product of labor, by a change in the demand for the product produced by the type of labor in question, or by a change in the price of some other factor of production.

cheating   The act of violating a collusive agreement; may result in an increase in short-run economic profits to the firm that cheats, followed by zero economic profits in the long run.

checkable deposits   Demand deposits plus other types of transactions accounts that pay interest but that may carry some restrictions on use, including minimum balance and limits on the number of checks that can be written per month.

choices at the margin   Decisions based on the additional benefits and costs of small changes in a particular activity.

classical long-run equilibrium   The hypothetical adjustment of an economy to full employment given an actual supply of resources, population, technology, and degree of specialization.

classical macroeconomic theory   A view of the macroeconomy as being self-adjusting and capable of generating full employment and maximum output in the long run without government intervention; dominant from the late eighteenth century through the early twentieth century.

classical process of economic growth   A process based on the division of labor, but also involving increases in saving, investment, capital accumulation, and, ultimately, growth in real GDP.

classical self-adjustment mechanism   The theory that, through Say's law, full employment will be reached given interest rate flexibility and price-wage flexibility.

Coase theorem   States that the amount of an externality-generating activity will be the same regardless of the assignment of property rights if the bargaining costs are small.

collective bargaining   The process whereby buyers and sellers negotiate, rather than compete individually, in order to determine a wage rate.

commodity money   An item that serves as a medium of exchange and that is also a good itself.

common ownership   An arrangement whereby the property rights to a resource are nonexistent or poorly defined; by default, anyone may use or consume the resource.

comparative advantage   An economic entity's (an individual's or a nation's) ability to produce a good at a lower marginal opportunity cost than some other entity.

competition   A market which functions under two conditions—no collusion among sellers or buyers (which occurs with a large number of buyers and sellers) and freedom to enter and exit the market. Competition results in prices equal to the costs of production plus a normal profit for sellers.

competitive labor market   A labor market in which the wage rate is determined by the interactions of a large number of sellers (suppliers) of labor and a large number of demanders (buyers) of labor. Neither group acts in a collusive manner.

complementary inputs   Inputs with a relation such that increased usage of one input due to a fall in its price results in increased employment of the other(s).

complements   Products that are related such that an increase in the price of one will decrease the demand for the other or a decrease in the price of one will increase the demand for the other; two goods whose cross elasticity of demand is negative; $\varepsilon_c < 0$.

concentration ratios   A measure of the degree to which the largest firms in an industry account for total industry assets, sales, or some other factor.

constant returns to scale   As plant size either increases or decreases, long-run average total cost does not change.

constant-cost industry   An industry in which the minimum *LRATC* of production does not change as the number of firms in the industry changes; expansion (contraction) of the number of firms does not bid up (down) input prices; long-run industry supply is horizontal.

constitutional decision making   The process of choosing which set of rules (voting rules, for example) society will adopt for its use.

consumer equilibrium   A situation in which a consumer chooses quantities of goods that maximize total utility given a budget constraint; equilibrium implies that the per-dollar marginal utility obtained from the last unit of each good consumed is equal for all goods.

consumer price index (CPI)   A price index that uses the prices of goods and services consumers generally buy to calculate the price level and the rate of inflation.

consumer-initiated discrimination   Wage discrimination arising from consumers' preferences for goods or services produced by individuals of a certain sex, race, religion, or national origin. Consumers must pay a premium in the form of higher prices or lower quality to exercise such discrimination.

consumers' surplus   The difference between what consumers are willing to pay for a given quantity of a good or service (the total consumer valuation) and what they have to pay (their total expenditure).

consumption function   The positive relationship between levels of consumption expenditures and levels of income, holding all other relevant factors that determine consumption constant.

consumption possibilities curve   All the possible combinations of two goods that could be consumed by first specializing according to comparative advantage and then trading at the terms of trade.

contestability   Characteristic of a market in which the entry of competitors is possible.

contractionary gap   The amount by which total planned expenditures at the level of full-employment income fall short of the level required to generate full-employment income; also called a recessionary gap.

contrived scarcity   A situation in which a monopoly produces an output below what a competitive industry would produce; the contrived scarcity results in price and profits above competitive levels.

cost-push inflation   Increases in the price level caused by monopoly and/or union power or by shocks to the economy that reduce aggregate supply.

costs   An implication of scarcity; the necessary sacrifices associated with making any choice.

countercyclical fiscal policy   Changes in government expenditures or taxes that are designed to reverse changes in private expenditures or savings that produce unemployment or inflation.

Cournot-Nash solution   The likely outcome of a one-shot game or a game with a known end point; in this case, both firms cheat, thus bringing profits below the joint profit-maximizing level.

craft union   Workers with a common skill who organize to restrict the supply of labor in their trade and obtain some market power; also called a trade union.

credit controls   The method or tools that the Federal Reserve System uses in efforts to control the monetary base and the money supply, including reserve requirements, open market operations, the discount rate, and other selective credit controls.

cross elasticity of demand   Measures buyers' relative responsiveness to a change in the price of one good in terms of the change in the quantity demanded of another good; the percent change in the quantity demanded of one good divided by the percent change in the price of another good.

crowding out   The competitive pressure exerted on private investment by government expenditures.

cyclically balanced budget   A long-term view of the budget, in which surpluses generated during expansions match deficits created during recessions over a period of years.

D

decreasing-cost industry   An industry in which the long-run industry supply is downward-sloping; expansion (contraction) of the number of firms bids down (up) input prices; minimum *LRATC* of production falls as the number of firms in the industry increases.

deflation   Sustained decreases in the average level of prices.

demand curve   A graphic representation of the quantities of a product that people are willing and able to purchase at all possible prices.

demand deficiency unemployment   A short-run situation in which the level of employment is less than if the full-employment level of output were produced; arises when aggregate demand is insufficient to purchase the full-employment output given the price level.

demand deposits   A type of transactions account with virtually no restrictions as to the size, timing, or number of checks that can be written on the account.

demand elasticity coefficient   The numerical representation of the price elasticity of demand: $\varepsilon_d = (\Delta Q/Q) \div (\Delta P/P)$.

demand for loanable funds   A curve or schedule that shows the various amounts individuals are willing and able to borrow at different interest rates.

demand-pull inflation   Increases in the price level caused by increases in aggregate demand.

demand-side policy   Fiscal or monetary policy intended to alter the overall level of spending, or aggregate demand.

deposit expansion   The total amount of additional money or checkable deposits created by some given amount of excess reserves.

depreciation   The wearing out of capital goods that occurs with usage over time; a decrease in the equilibrium exchange market value of a country's currency in a flexible-rate system; an increase in the number of units of a country's money required to purchase one unit of a foreign country's money.

deregulation   The removal of some or all government regulations from a previously regulated industry in an effort to improve the allocation of resources.

derived demand   The demand for factors of production that exists because of the demand for the products that the factors produce.

devaluation   An official change in a country's exchange rate in a fixed-rate system; the number of units of a country's money that purchases one unit of another country's currency is increased by the government.

developing countries   Countries with relatively low levels of per capita real GDP; generally characterized by a large subsistence agriculture sector, low saving rates, and high population growth.

diamond-water paradox   Adam Smith's belief that water and diamonds did not follow the same theory of value—a paradox confusing total and marginal utility that is unlocked by the principle of diminishing marginal utility.

differentiated product   A product with features that make it distinct, in consumers' eyes, from close substitutes.

discount rate   The interest rate charged by the Federal Reserve to depository institutions on loans of reserves from the Federal Reserve.

discretionary fiscal policies   Government policy actions that attempt to influence aggregate demand.

discretionary policy   A policy or change in policy that is determined by choices or decisions of policymakers.

diseconomies of scale   A situation in which, beyond a point, the long-run average total cost of producing output increases as plant size increases.

disposable personal income   Personal income minus taxes; income available to spend.

dissaving   Occurs when consumption is greater than income; the use of previous years' savings or borrowing to finance consumption expenditures that are greater than current income.

division of labor   An economic principle whereby individuals specialize in the production of a single good, service, or task, thus increasing overall productivity and economic efficiency; the result of specialization.

dominant solution   A situation in game theory in which each player has the same best choice no matter what course of action other players may choose.

double coincidence of wants   A situation in trading in which each party to the trade has what the other wants and wants what the other has.

dumping   The selling of goods in foreign markets at prices lower than those charged in domestic markets.

dynamic efficiency   A condition summarized in the idea that monopolies may, over time, be more innovative and efficient than competitive firms at developing new products and new production techniques.

E

economic development   The process through which an economy achieves long-run economic growth; involves capital formation, the development of markets, productivity growth, and the improvement of entrepreneurial ability and labor skills.

economic efficiency   The allocation of resources that allows maximum benefit to be achieved at minimum cost.

economic goods and services   Goods and services that are scarce.

economic growth   A sustained on permanent increase in the overall productive capacity of an economy over time; increases in real GDP or real per capita GDP over time.

economic mobility   The movement of individuals among income ranges.

economic profit   The amount by which total revenues exceed total opportunity cost; total revenue minus total opportunity costs of production.

economic stabilization   A situation in which the price level and the unemployment rate vary from desired levels only temporarily and by small amounts.

economic system   The part of the social system determining what, how, and for whom goods and services are produced.

economic wage discrimination   A situation in which individuals in the same occupation who have the same productive abilities are paid different wage rates by a given employer. The wage-rate differences are based on race, sex, religion, or national origin rather than on productive differences.

economic welfare   The value society places on goods and services consumed.

economies of scale   A situation in which long-run unit costs *(LRATC)* decline as plant output increases.

elastic demand   A situation in which buyers are relatively responsive to price changes; the percent change in quantity demanded is greater than the percent change in price: $\varepsilon_d > 1$.

elasticity   A measure of the relative responsiveness of one variable to a change in another variable; the percentage change in a dependent variable divided by the percentage change in the independent variable.

elasticity of supply   A measure of producers' or workers' relative responsiveness to price or wage changes; the percent change in quantity supplied divided by the percent change in the price or wage rate.

entrepreneur   An individual who perceives profit opportunities, organizes resources into productive ventures, and bears the uncertain status of residual claimant of the resulting risky economic outcome.

equilibrium price   The price at which quantity demanded is equal to quantity supplied; other things being equal, there is no tendency for this price to change.

escalator clauses   Provisions of labor contracts that tie changes in nominal wages to changes in some price index.

***ex ante* distribution**   The distribution of income before government transfer payments and taxes are accounted for.

***ex post* distribution**   The distribution of income after government transfer payments and taxes are accounted for.

excess capacity   A situation in which industry output is not produced at minimum average total cost. The output actually produced is less than the output that would minimize average total cost.

excess reserves   Total reserves minus required reserves.

exchange costs   The opportunity costs of the resources used in making trades; includes transaction costs, transportation costs, and artificial barriers to trade.

exchange rate   The (relative) price of one national currency in terms of another national currency.

expansionary gap   The amount by which total planned expenditures at the level of full-employment income exceed the level required to generate full-employment income without inflation; also called an inflationary gap.

explicit costs   Accounting costs.

exploitation of labor   A situation in which the wage rate paid to an input is less than the input's marginal revenue product.

exports (X) Total spending by foreigners on domestically produced goods and services.

external costs The opportunity costs of production that are not borne, or paid, by producers.

externality Benefits or costs of an individual's activity that the individual does not receive or bear.

externally held debt The amount of a country's total federal debt that is owned by foreign governments, businesses, and individuals.

F

factor market A market in which the prices of productive resources (factors of production, or inputs) are determined by the interaction of firms acting as buyers with households and firms acting as suppliers of resources.

factors affecting demand Anything other than price, such as consumer income and preferences, that determines the amount of a product or service that consumers are willing and able to purchase.

factors affecting supply Anything other than price, such as technology or input costs, that determines the amount of a product or service that sellers are willing and able to offer for sale.

family income The total of all incomes from all sources except transfers received by members of a household.

federal debt The total value of federal government bonds outstanding; arises from both current and past budget deficits.

Federal Deposit Insurance Corporation (FDIC) A government institution that provides commercial banks with insurance against default and protects bank customers up to $100,000 per deposit.

federal funds rate A market-determined interest rate on loans and borrowings of bank reserves among commercial banks and other depository institutions.

Federal Open Market Committee (FOMC) A committee of the Federal Reserve System made up of the seven members of the Board of Governors of the Federal Reserve System and five presidents of Federal Reserve district banks; directs open market operations

(buying and selling of securities) for the system.

Federal Reserve System The central bank of the United States; regulates financial institutions and establishes and conducts monetary policy.

fiat money Money, usually paper, that is made acceptable in exchange by law; usually not backed by any commodity such as gold.

final goods Goods sold to the final consumers of the goods.

firm An economic institution that purchases, organizes, and assembles resources to produce goods and services.

firm coordination The process that directs the flow of resources into the production of a particular good or service through the forces of management organization within the firm.

firm's long-run demand for labor The relationship between all possible wage rates and quantities demanded of labor at those wage rates, given that the firm has enough time to vary the usage of all inputs.

fiscal policy The use of government spending and taxation to effect changes in aggregate economic variables.

fixed costs The costs of inputs that cannot be varied in the short run.

fixed exchange rate system An international monetary arrangement in which exchange rates are set by the government, which then must intervene in the foreign exchange market in order to maintain the pegged exchange rate.

fixed input A factor of production whose level of usage cannot be changed in the short run.

fixed plant A given amount of equipment and size of production facilities with which the firm can use variable inputs in the short run.

flat tax A single tax rate levied on all income.

flexible, or floating, exchange rate system An international monetary arrangement in which exchange rates are determined by private suppliers and demanders without government intervention.

flow of earnings Total income received by resource suppliers during any given time period.

flow of expenditures Total spending of consumers, businesses, and government on

final goods and services during any given time period.

foreign exchange The monies of countries that are used to facilitate international trade in goods, services, and financial assets.

foreign exchange market intervention Purchases or sales of foreign exchange by government, usually a central bank, with the goal of maintaining a fixed exchange rate or influencing the exchange rate in a flexible-rate system.

foreign exchange markets The interaction of the suppliers and demanders of foreign exchange, through which exchange rates are determined in a flexible exchange rate system.

foreign exchange reserves The stock of a foreign exchange held by a central bank that is available for use in exchange market intervention.

fractional reserve banking system A banking system in which banks hold only some percentage of deposits as reserves.

franchise bidding The privatization of traditionally governmental responsibilities via a bidding process.

free enterprise Economic freedom to produce and sell or purchase and consume goods without government intervention.

free goods and services Things that are available in sufficient amounts and provide all that people want at zero cost.

free rider An individual who receives the benefit of consuming a public good or service without paying for it.

free trade The exchange of goods between countries without the presence of artificial trade barriers such as tariffs and quotas.

full employment A situation in which unemployment exists only because of normal market adjustments to changing demand or supply or to outmoded skills of workers; also a numerical federal government goal for the unemployment rate; to the classical economist, a situation in which all workers willing and able to work at the current market real wage rate are employed.

full price The total opportunity cost to an individual of obtaining a good; includes money price and all other costs, such as transportation costs or waiting costs.

G

game theory A theory involving decision making in an atmosphere of mutual interdependence and imperfect information.

gold standard An international monetary system in which currencies are redeemable in gold at fixed rates or prices.

goods All tangible things that satisfy people's wants and desires.

government license A legal right granted by state, local, or federal governments to enter an occupation or industry.

government purchases (G) Total spending by federal, state, and local governments on final goods and services.

gross domestic product (GDP) A measure of the final goods and services produced by a country with resources located within that country.

gross national product (GNP) The value, measured at market prices, of all final goods and services produced in an economy in one year. gross private domestic investment (I) Total spending by private businesses on final goods, including capital goods and inventories.

gross private domestic investment (I) Total spending by private businesses on final goods, including capital goods and inventories. (p. 496)

growth absorption Increases in total spending sufficient to purchase additional output generated by increases in productive capacity.

H

historical costs Costs measured by the cost of a resource at the time the resource was purchased.

homogeneous product A good or service for which the consumer is indifferent as to which firm produces it; each firm's product is a perfect substitute for other firms' products in the eyes of the consumer.

human capital Any quality, characteristic, or skill an individual has that enhances the individual's productivity, such as education and job experience.

human resources All forms of labor and skill used to produce goods and services.

I

imperfect competition Market models, such as oligopoly, cartels, monopoly, and monopolistic competition, in which individual sellers' actions influence price.

implicit costs Nonpecuniary costs associated with the consumption of a good or service; the opportunity costs of resources used in production for which no explicit payments are made.

implicit price deflator A price index that uses the most comprehensive set of prices to calculate the level of prices and the rate of inflation facing households, businesses, and government; also called the GDP deflator.

imports (M) Total spending by domestic residents on foreign-produced goods and services.

in-kind transfer payments Transfer payments that take the form of goods and services such as public housing, veterans' hospitals, or a mass transit system.

income effect The change in the quantity demanded of a good that results from a change in real income.

income elasticity of demand A measure of consumers' relative responsiveness to income changes; the percent change in quantity demanded divided by the percent change in income, holding price constant.

income velocity The average number of times that a unit of money (a dollar) is used, or changes hands, in purchasing nominal GDP.

income-expenditures model A theory suggesting that private expenditures are basically determined by the level of national income and that these expenditures in turn determine the levels of output and employment in the economy.

increasing returns to scale As plant size increases, long-run average total cost decreases.

increasing-cost industry An industry in which the expansion (contraction) of the number of firms bids up (down) input prices; minimum LRATC of production changes as the number of firms in the industry changes; long-run industry supply is upward-sloping to the right.

individual income The earnings individuals receive from their labor, from their assets, and from government transfer payments, minus their tax payments.

industrial union Workers in a given industry organized independently of their skills in an effort to obtain market power.

inelastic demand A situation in which buyers are relatively unresponsive to price changes; the percent change in quantity demanded is less than the percent change in price: $\varepsilon_d < 1$.

infant industry A new or developing domestic industry whose unit production costs are higher than those of established firms in the same industry in other countries.

inferior good A good that a consumer chooses to purchase in smaller quantities as income rises or in larger amounts as income falls.

inflation A sustained increase in the general level of prices; inflation reduces the purchasing power of money.

inflation rate The percent by which the average level of prices in an economy rises; usually expressed as a percent per year.

information A scarce and important element in the process of economic exchange and growth.

institutions The sum total of the traditions, mores, laws, and governmental structures of an economy.

interest The compensation to savers for the act of saving (forgoing present consumption) or the payment made by borrowers; when measured as a percent of the amount borrowed or lent, it is referred to as an interest rate.

interest groups Collections of individuals with one or more common characteristics, such as occupation, who seek collectively to affect legislation or government policy so as to benefit members of the group.

interest rate effect The effect on investment spending that results from a change in the interest rate produced by a change in the price level.

internally held debt The amount of a country's total federal debt that is owned by the country's various governments, businesses, and individuals.

International Monetary Fund An international organization, established along with the Bretton Woods system, designed to assist in the efficient functioning of the Bretton Woods fixed exchange rate system.

investment multiplier The multiple by which equilibrium income will change given a change in autonomous investment expenditure;1/MPS.

investment spending   Expenditures made by businesses on capital goods plus any change (positive or negative) in business inventories.

investment tax credit   A percentage or amount of new investment expenditure that is directly subtracted from the investor's tax bill in calculating total taxes.

L

labor income   The payments an individual receives from supplying work time; equal to the wage rate times the number of hours supplied.

labor union   A group of individual workers organized to act collectively in an attempt to affect labor market conditions.

laissez-faire   A public policy of not regulating to any degree or interfering with market activities (from the French, meaning, roughly, "allow to do").

law of demand   The price of a product or service and the amount purchased are inversely related. If price rises, then quantity demanded falls; if price falls, quantity demanded increases, all other things held constant.

law of diminishing marginal returns   A situation in which adding more and more of a variable input to a fixed plant results in smaller and smaller amounts of additional output produced.

law of increasing costs   As more scarce resources are used to produce additional units of one good, production of another good falls by larger and larger amounts.

law of one price   In perfect markets, the market forces of supply and demand produce a single, equilibrium price for a good or service.

law of supply   The price of a product or service and the amount that producers are willing and able to offer for sale are positively related. If price rises, then quantity supplied rises; if price decreases, then quantity supplied decreases.

legal barriers to entry   Government actions that prohibit other firms or individuals from producing particular products or entering particular occupations or industries; such barriers take the form of legal franchises, licenses, and patents.

limit pricing   A pricing policy consisting of temporarily setting a price lower than

the short-run profit-maximizing price in order to deter entry and maximize profits in the long run.

liquidity   The ease with which any asset or commodity can be converted into money with little or no risk of loss to the holder.

liquidity preference theory   A theory stating that the interest rate is determined by the interaction of real money demand and supply, and that interest rate changes due to real money demand or supply changes produce changes in real economic activity.

logrolling   The exchange of votes by legislators, usually in order to gain support for particular legislation.

long run   An amount of time sufficiently long that all input usage levels can be varied.

long-run average total cost   The lowest per-unit cost of producing any level of output when the usage of all inputs can be varied.

long-run competitive equilibrium   A market situation in which economic profits are zero for all firms; each firm produces output at minimum average total cost.

long-run industry supply   The quantities of a product that all firms in an industry are willing and able to offer for sale at various prices when the number of firms and the scale of operations of each firm are allowed to adjust.

long-run marginal cost   The additional cost of producing an additional unit of output when all inputs, including plant size, can be varied.

Lorenz curve   A curve plotting the actual cumulative distribution of income in percentages; usually compared to a curve showing a perfectly even distribution of income.

lump-sum tax   A fixed level of total taxes; total taxes do not change as the level of income changes.

M

M-1 money multiplier   The multiple by which the money supply will change given a change in the monetary base.

macroeconomics   Analysis of the behavior of an economy as a whole.

managed flexible-rate system   Primarily a flexible exchange rate system, but with occasional government purchases or sales of foreign exchange intended to influence the exchange rate.

manager   An individual who organizes and monitors resources within a firm to produce a good or service.

margin   The difference between costs or benefits in an existing situation and after a proposed change.

marginal analysis   Looking at changes in the costs and benefits of a change from the status quo to a proposed new situation. These marginal changes in the costs and benefits are the basis for rational economic choice.

marginal cost   The additional cost of producing one more unit of output; the change in total cost divided by the change in output.

marginal cost pricing   A regulatory policy that forces a firm to charge a price equal to marginal cost, resulting in a socially optimal allocation of resources.

marginal factor cost of labor (MFC$_L$)   The change in total costs associated with employing one additional unit of labor.

marginal opportunity production cost   The number of units of one good that do not get produced when one additional unit of another good is produced.

marginal private benefit curve   A curve, equivalent to a demand curve, which represents the value that consumers place on marginal units of the good or service.

marginal private cost   The change in total costs that only the firm bears when output changes by one unit.

marginal private cost curve   A curve showing the marginal or additional cost to society—the opportunity cost of scarce resources—of producing additional units of a good or service.

marginal product   The additional output produced by employing one additional unit of a variable input.

marginal product of labor (MP$_L$)   The additional output produced that results from hiring an additional unit of labor; change in total output divided by change in quantity of labor input used.

marginal propensity to consume (MPC)   The percentage of an additional dollar of income that is spent on consumption; change in consumption divided by change in income.

marginal propensity to save (MPS)   The percentage of an additional dollar of income that is saved; change in saving divided by change in income.

marginal revenue   The change in total revenue resulting from the sale of one additional unit of output; the change in total revenue divided by the change in output.

marginal revenue product of labor (MRP$_L$)   The additional revenue that results from selling the additional output produced by hiring an additional unit of labor; marginal revenue times marginal product of labor.

marginal social cost   The change in total cost borne by the economy as a whole (the firm plus all others, or society) that results from a one-unit change in the firm's output.

marginal tax rate   The tax rate, in percentage terms, that applies to additional taxable income; additional taxes divided by the additional income taxed.

marginal utility   The amount by which total utility changes when consumption of a good or service changes by one unit; calculated by dividing the change in total utility by the change in quantity consumed.

market   A collection of buyers and sellers exchanging resources, goods, or services; prices tend toward equality in a market through the continuous exchange between suppliers and demanders.

market coordination   The process that directs the flow of resources into the production of goods and services through the price signaling mechanism.

market demand   The total amount consumers are willing and able to purchase of a product at all possible prices, obtained by summing the quantities demanded at each price over all buyers.

market demand curve for a public good   Obtained by summing vertically, instead of horizontally, all individuals' demands for the public good. Vertical summation is used because consumption is noncompeting.

market demand for labor   The total quantity of labor demanded at various wage rates, other things constant. The sum of all individual firms' demands for a type of labor. The firms may or may not all be in the same industry.

market failure   A situation in which the socially optimal (most economically efficient) amount of a good or service does not get produced by the private market; usually stems from unclear property rights assignments.

market for legislation   The interaction between interest groups acting as demanders of legislation beneficial to the group and legislators acting as suppliers of legislation; legislation generally entails some type of wealth transfer.

market power   A situation in which an established firm has influence over price and profit levels due to barriers impeding the entry of rival firms.

market supply   The total amount producers are willing and able to offer for sale of a product at all possible prices, obtained by summing the quantities supplied at each price over all producers.

market supply of labor   The sum of all individuals' supplies of a type of labor. The total quantity of labor people will offer to the market at various wage rates, other things being equal.

mean income   A measure of average income; can be computed as per capita, per family, or per earner of income.

measure of economic welfare (MEW)   A concept of social and economic well-being that accounts for the production of all goods and services, not just those transacted for in markets.

medium of exchange   An item that is generally acceptable as payment for goods and services.

merger   The combining of the ownership of two firms' assets, which results in a single firm.

microeconomics   Analysis of the behavior of individual decision-making units, including individuals, households, and business firms.

model   A simplified abstraction of the real world that approximates reality and makes problems easier to analyze; also called a theory.

monetarism   A theory that centers on money supply growth, real money demand, nominal and real interest rates, and inflationary expectations in explaining the process of inflation or deflation.

monetary base   The sum of depository institutions' reserves plus currency held by the public.

monetary policy   The use of money supply changes to effect changes in aggregate economic variables.

monetary rule   A monetary policy consisting of a fixed rate of growth of the money supply.

money   A generally accepted medium of exchange.

money expansion   The increase in the money supply created by some given amount of excess reserves.

money price   The dollar price that sellers receive from buyers; a price expressed in terms of money, not in terms of an amount of another good.

monopolistic competition   A market model with freedom of entry and exit and firms producing similar but differentiated products.

monopsony   A single buyer of a resource or product; sometimes found in labor markets as the single buyer of labor.

mutual interdependence   A relation among firms in which the decisions and actions of one firm have a significant impact on the decisions, actions, and profits of other firms.

N

national income (NI)   Total earnings of resource suppliers during a given period of time.

national income accounting   The process of statistically measuring the nation's aggregate economic performance.

natural monopoly   A monopoly in which the relation between industry demand and cost structure makes it possible for only one firm to exist in the industry; occurs when decreasing long-run average costs exist up to the level of total industry demand.

natural rate of unemployment   A theoretical concept; the unemployment rate that coexists with macroeconomic stability or labor-market equilibrium in the long run; the rate of unemployment due to frictional unemployment plus structural unemployment that will exist when expectations of inflation reflect actual inflationary conditions and all short-run macroeconomic adjustments have been made.

natural resources   All those renewable and nonrenewable resources that are given to an economy or society.

negative externality   A situation that arises when an individual or other economic entity imposes costs on others without compensating them.

net exports (X - M)   Total spending by foreigners on domestically produced goods and services minus total spending by domestic residents on foreign produced goods and services.

neutrality of money   A proposition stating that in the long run the relative prices of goods and services are not affected by changes in the money supply.

nominal GDP   The total production of final goods and services within a country measured in monetary units that have not been adjusted for changes in the price level.

nominal income   Income measured in terms of money, not in terms of what the money can buy.

nominal rate of interest   The market-determined rate of interest; usually expressed as a percentage per year of the dollar or nominal amount of the loan.

nonhuman resources   All resources other than human resources, such as machines and land.

nonmarket activities   Anything an individual does while not working that directly or indirectly yields utility.

nonprice competition   Any means other than pricing decisions that firms use to sell output.

nonproprietary   Relating to nonprivate ownership; entails motivations other than strictly profit motivations; individuals do not always or fully bear the consequences of their decisions.

nonrenewable natural resources Resources that exist in finite quantities.

nontariff trade barriers   Alternative (to tariffs and quotas) means of restricting trade; examples include domestic content legislation and health and safety regulations.

normal good   A good that a consumer chooses to purchase in smaller (larger) amounts as income falls (rises).

normative economics   Value judgments based on moral principles or preferences about how economic life should be.

normative public choice   Economic analysis that determines shortcomings and failures of the political process and suggests improvements.

O

oligopoly   Market models characterized by a few firms producing either homogeneous or differentiated products, with entry of new firms very difficult or prevented.

open market operations   The purchase or sale of securities by the Federal Reserve

System in order to affect the monetary base and the money supply; the major tool of monetary policy.

opportunity cost   The highest-valued alternative forgone in making any choice.

opportunity cost of capital   The return that could be received from the next-best alternative investment.

opportunity costs of production   The opportunity costs of resources used to produce goods and services.

overvalued   A term describing the foreign exchange market value of a country's money; occurs when the number of units of a country's money that purchases one unit of a foreign currency is less than the equilibrium exchange rate.

P

patent   A monopoly right granted by government to an inventor for a product or process; valid for 17 years in the United States.

per capita income   Average income per person; the total income of a population divided by the number of people in the population.

perfect information   A situation that arises when information about prices and products is costless to obtain; complete knowledge about the market.

perfect market   A market in which there are enough buyers and sellers that no single buyer or seller can influence price.

personal consumption expenditures (C) Total spending by households on final goods and services.

Phillips Curve   A graph showing the relation between the rate of inflation and the unemployment rate.

policy trade-off   A situation in which a policy that promotes the attainment of one macroeconomic goal necessarily implies that the attainment of another macroeconomic objective becomes more difficult.

positive economics   Observations, explanations, or predictions about economic life; scientific economics.

positive externality   A situation that arises when an individual or other economic entity creates benefits for others without receiving any compensation in return.

positive public choice   Economic analysis of political decision making and other political behavior that aims to understand, explain, and predict such behavior.

poverty   A substandard level of income.

precautionary demand   Money demand that arises from the desire of businesses and consumers to hold money in order to facilitate unexpected purchases.

predatory pricing   The temporary pricing of goods or services below cost in order to reduce or eliminate competition.

present value   The value today of a payment to be made or received in the future; a future sum discounted by the current rate of interest.

price ceiling   A form of regulation in which a maximum legal price is established by government above which exchange between buyers and sellers is illegal.

price control   The setting, by government, of a price in a market different from the equilibrium price.

price discrimination   The practice of charging one buyer or group of buyers a different price than that charged to others. The price difference is not due to differences in the cost of supplying the two groups.

price elasticity of demand   A measure of buyers' relative responsiveness to a price change; the percentage change in quantity demanded divided by the percentage change in price.

price floor   A form of regulation in which a minimum legal price is established by government below which exchange between buyers and sellers is illegal.

price index   A statistic used to calculate the price level and the rate of inflation.

price leadership   A market where a single firm sets industry price, with the remaining firms charging what the price leader charges. Industry price changes are initiated by the leader.

price level   The average of the prices of all goods and services in the economy; used for calculating the inflation rate and for converting nominal into real values.

price searcher   A firm that is able to choose a profit-maximizing price from a range of prices rather than have price imposed by market conditions and competition; such a firm faces a downward-sloping demand curve.

price stability   A situation of no inflation or deflation in the economy; no change in the overall level of prices of goods, services, and resources.

price taker   An individual seller who faces a single market price and is able to sell as much as desired at that price.

price-wage flexibility   An economic principle whereby prices and wages can fluctuate with changing economic conditions; thus the economy will be self-adjusting toward full employment even in response to shocks in supply and demand.

prices   The market-established opportunity costs of goods and services obtained through exchange.

principle of diminishing marginal utility   The more of a good or service being consumed, the smaller is the marginal utility obtained by consuming one additional unit of the good or service, all other factors equal.

prisoner's dilemma   A scenario that illustrates the mutual interdependence of decision making; the basis for game theory.

private choice   Choices made through the private (non-governmental) markets.

private costs   The opportunity costs of production that are borne, or paid, by producers.

private property   Property that an individual (as opposed to a government) holds the right to control.

producers' surplus   The difference between the total revenue to producers from selling a given quantity of a good or service and the total cost to them and to society of using the scarce resources in that particular production.

production possibilities frontier   The curve that graphs all the possible combinations of two goods that an economic entity can produce given the available technology, the amount of productive resources available, and the fact that these resources are fully utilized.

productive efficiency   A condition in which total industry output is produced at the lowest possible opportunity cost of resources.

productivity of labor   Output per worker over any given period of time.

products market   The forces created by buyers and sellers that establish the prices and quantities exchanged of goods and services.

profit-maximizing price   The price associated with the quantity sold at which the difference between total revenue and total cost is greatest; the price associated with the quantity sold at which marginal revenue equals marginal cost.

profits   The amount by which total revenue exceeds total opportunity cost of production.

progressive income tax   A tax that is a percentage of income and that varies directly with the level of income.

property rights   Any legal and/or enforceable rights to the use of resources of any kind.

proportional income tax   A tax that is a fixed percentage of income for all levels of income.

proprietary   Relating to private ownership and profit motivation; individuals directly bear the consequences of their decisions.

public choice   The economic analysis of political decision making, politics, and the democratic process.

public employees' union   Workers employed by federal, state, or local governments who organize in an effort to obtain market power.

public finance   The study of how governments at the federal, state, and local levels tax and spend.

public franchise   A firm or industry's exclusive, government-granted right to produce and sell a good or service.

public good   A good such that, once produced, one individual's consumption of the good does not reduce or exclude the ability of other individuals to consume the good.

public interest theory of regulation   Maintains that regulations are contrived so as to promote the public interest by correcting market failures and improving economic efficiency.

pure capitalism   An economic system in which most resources are owned, and most relevant decisions are made, by private individuals.

pure communism   An economic system in which most productive resources, both human and nonhuman, are publicly owned.

pure economic rent   The total payment to a factor of production whose supply curve is perfectly inelastic.

pure inflation tax   The reduction in purchasing power of an individual's nominal money holdings due to inflation.

pure interest   The interest associated with a risk-free loan. The interest rate that produces pure interest is called the risk-free interest rate.

pure monopoly   An industry in which a single firm produces a product that has no close substitutes and in which entry of new firms cannot occur.

purely competitive market   The interaction of a large number of buyers and sellers under the condition that entry and exit are not restricted.

Q

quantity demanded   The amount of any good or service consumers are willing and able to purchase at all various prices.

quantity supplied   The amount of any good or service that producers are willing and able to produce and sell at some specific price.

quantity theory of money   A theory stating that in the long run with output and velocity fixed, changes in the money supply cause proportional changes in the price level.

quota   A restriction or limit on the quantity of an imported good.

R

rate of monetary expansion   The annual percentage by which the nominal money supply is changing.

rate of return on invested capital   Profits earned during a period of time divided by the value of invested capital; usually measured as a percent per year.

rate of return regulation   A cap imposed by a regulatory commission on the allowable percentage that a utility can earn on its capital invested.

rate of time preference   The percent increase in future consumption over present consumption that is necessary to just induce an individual to be indifferent between present and future consumption.

rational expectations theory   A theory of behavior that assumes that people make efficient use of all past and present relevant information in forming expectations; implies that people's reactions to policy may neutralize the intended effects of the policy.

rational self-interest   The view of human behavior espoused by economists. Given circumstances and preferences, people weigh the costs and benefits of choices in order to do the best they can for themselves.

rationing   The allocation of goods among consumers with the use of prices. The equilibrium price rations the limited amount of a good produced by the most willing and able suppliers, or sellers, to the most willing and able demanders, or buyers.

real balance effect   The effect on investment and consumption spending of a change in the price level that alters the real value of pecuniary assets.

real GDP   The total production of final goods and services within a country measured in monetary units that have been adjusted for changes in the price level.

real income   The buying power of a consumer's budget; determined by the consumer's money income and the prices of goods and services; the quantity of goods and services that money income can buy.

real money demand   Demand on the part of individuals and businesses to hold purchasing power in the form of cash and checkable deposits.

real per capita GDP   Real GDP divided by the population size; real output per person in the economy.

real rate of interest   The nominal interest rate minus the inflation rate; the interest rate that measures the true incentives and costs that savers and investors face; the interest measured in terms of real buying power.

recognition lag   The amount of time it takes policymakers to realize that a destabilizing economic event has occurred.

regressive income tax   A tax that is a percentage of income and that varies inversely with the level of income.

regulatory policies   Administrative or legal attempts to influence the behavior of firms or industries when competitive goals cannot be realized or when positive goals are to be pursued.

relative price   The price ratio or "tradeoff" in consumption between one product (or service) and another product (or service) or between one good and other goods taken as a whole.

renewable natural resources   Those resources that may be reproduced through time if not exhausted by unwise policies.

rent   A payment to a factor of production in excess of the factor's opportunity cost.

required reserves   Reserves against checkable deposits that banks and other depository institutions are required by the Federal Reserve to keep in the form of cash reserves; equal to the required reserve ratio times checkable deposits; also called legal reserves.

reserve bank credit   The total value of loans and securities owned or held by the Federal Reserve System. Changes in reserve bank credit affect member institutions' reserves.

reserve ratio   The percentage of checkable deposits that banks and other depository institutions hold as reserves.

resources   Those things used to produce goods and services. These include land, machines, energy, and human labor and ingenuity. Resources are also called factors of production.

resources market   The forces created by buyers and sellers that establish the prices and quantities exchanged of resources such as land, labor services, and capital.

revaluation   An official change in a country's exchange rate in a fixed-rate system; the number of units of a country's money that purchases one unit of another country's currency is decreased by the government.

right-to-work law   A law that prevents unions from requiring that individual workers join the union as a condition of employment by a particular firm.

risk   The chance that a borrower will default or fail to repay a loan.

roundabout production   The current production of capital goods so that greater amounts of consumption goods can be produced in the future.

S

saving   The act of forgoing present consumption in order to increase future consumption.

saving function   The positive relationship between levels of current saving and levels of income, holding constant all other relevant factors that determine saving.

Say's law   A proposition of the classical economists that the production of goods and services will generate incomes sufficiently large that those goods and services will be purchased.

scarcity   The condition whereby the resources, goods, and services available to individuals and society are limited relative to the wants and desires for them.

service industries   Those industries whose major, or sole, output is a consumer service, such as banking, entertainment, and health care.

services   All forms of intangible but useful activities that are valued by people.

short run   An amount of time insufficient to allow the usage of all inputs to vary.

short-run firm supply curve   That portion of a firm's marginal cost curve above the minimum point on the average variable cost curve.

short-run industry supply curve   The horizontal sum of all existing firms' short-run supply curves.

shortage   The amount by which quantity demanded exceeds quantity supplied at a price below the equilibrium price.

shutdown   A loss-minimizing procedure in which the firm stops production to eliminate all variable costs, although it must still pay fixed costs.

social costs   The opportunity costs of all resources used in the production of goods and services; the sum of private and external costs.

socialism   An economic system in which most nonhuman productive resources are owned by the state.

socialization   Government ownership and operation of a firm or industry.

specialization   An economic entity's (an individual's or a nation's) producing only one good or service, or the performance of a single task in a production process by an individual.

speculation   The buying and selling of currencies on the foreign exchange market with the intent of profiting from possible devaluation or revaluation in a fixed-rate system or from possible future movements in the exchange rate in a flexible-rate system.

speculative motive or demand   Money demand arising from the uncertainty of future interest rates and the fact that people can substitute between holding money and holding bonds.

standard of living   The real value of the quantity of goods and services consumed by the average member of the economy.

static inefficiency A condition associated with the welfare loss due to the presence of a monopoly. The loss can be summarized as the production of too little output sold at too high a price.

store of value The ability to own wealth in the form of some item, such as money; a function of money.

strike A collective refusal to work at the current wage or under current working conditions.

substitute inputs Inputs with a relation such that increased employment of one input due to a fall in its price results in decreased usage of the other(s).

substitutes Products that are related such that an increase in the price of one will increase the demand for the other or a decrease in the price of one will decrease the demand for the other; two goods whose cross elasticity of demand is positive; $\varepsilon_c > 0$.

substitution effect The change in the quantity demanded of a good that results only from a change in the relative price of the good.

sunk costs Previously incurred, irretrievable costs of a currently owned resource.

supply curve A graphic representation of the quantities of a product or service that producers are willing and able to sell at all possible prices.

supply of loanable funds A curve or schedule that shows the various amounts individuals are willing and able to lend or save at different rates.

supply shock inflation Price level increases stemming from a decrease in aggregate supply; decreased aggregate supply usually occurs because of sudden increased scarcity of essential resources.

supply-side economics Policies designed to stimulate production by altering incentives of producers; policies designed to shift the aggregate supply curve to the right.

supply-side policy Fiscal or monetary policy intended to alter the incentives to produce output; policies designed to shift aggregate supply.

surplus The amount by which quantity supplied exceeds quantity demanded at a price above the equilibrium price.

sustainable monopoly A monopoly that can forestall the entry of competitors in the absence of regulation.

T

tacit collusive solution A possible outcome in game theory when, given an indefinite time horizon and no formal communication, rivals recognize that it is in their best interest to act so that joint profits are maximized.

tangency solution A long-run equilibrium situation in which the firm's downward-sloping demand curve is tangent to its *LRATC* curve; zero economic profits are earned.

tariff A tax or levy on imported goods.

tax indexation Periodic adjustment of the tax brackets of a progressive income tax so as to base taxes on real, not nominal, income; eliminates bracket creep and increased income taxes due solely to inflation.

technology Knowledge of production methods associated with producing a particular good.

terms of trade The number of units of one good that exchange in the market for one unit of some other good; a relative price. Although not expressed in terms of money, it is a price nonetheless.

terms of trade argument Defending the use of artificial trade barriers combined with monopoly or monopsony power in international markets in order to produce an improvement in a country's terms of trade.

total consumer valuation The total amount that consumers are willing to pay for a given quantity of a good or service rather than go without it.

total cost of production The total opportunity cost of all resources used in production; the sum of all explicit and implicit production costs.

total costs All the costs of a firm's operations; total variable costs plus total fixed costs.

total expenditures The total amount spent by consumers on a good or service; calculated as equilibrium price times equilibrium quantity.

total product The total amount of output produced.

total revenues Total receipts of businesses; always equal to total expenditures by consumers; calculated as market price multiplied by the amount of output sold; the dollar value of sales.

total utility The total amount of satisfaction derived from consuming any given quantity of a good or service.

total wage bill The total cost of labor to firms; equal to wage rate times total quantity of labor employed.

transaction costs The opportunity costs of the resources directly associated with trade; includes time costs, brokers' fees, and so on.

transactions accounts Demand deposits or other checkable accounts that allow the transfer of funds by writing a check.

transactions demand Money demand that arises from the desire of businesses and consumers to facilitate exchange with the use of money.

transfer payment A resource received by an individual from government that is not directly or explicitly paid for by that individual; it may be in the form of money or goods and services such as education or health care.

transportation costs The value of resources used in the transportation of goods that finalize any trade.

U

undervalued A term describing the foreign exchange market value of a country's money; occurs when the number of units of a country's money that purchases one unit of a foreign currency is greater than the equilibrium exchange rate.

unemployment of resources A situation in which some human and/or nonhuman resources that can be used in production are not used.

unemployment rate The percentage of the labor force without jobs.

unit elasticity of demand A condition where the percent change in quantity demanded is equal to the percent change in price: $\varepsilon_d = 1$.

unit of account A standard measure, such as the dollar, that is used to express the values of goods and services; a function of money.

utility A measure of the satisfaction that the consumption of goods or services yields an individual.

V

variable costs The costs of inputs whose usage levels can be changed in the short run. Variable costs change as output changes.

variable input   A factor of production whose level of usage may be changed in the short run.

velocity   The average number of times a unit of money changes hands per year in financing the purchases of GDP.

vicious circle of poverty   An attempt to explain why some countries remain less developed that centers on low savings and investment as the cause of low real incomes, which in turn lead to low saving and investment rates.

W

wage-price spiral   The process whereby increased prices of final goods cause increased wage rates and other resource prices, which in turn result in still-higher prices of final goods; for the spiral to continue, the money supply must continually increase or real output must continually fall.

wealth   The total value of monetary plus nonmonetary assets in existence at a point in time; a stock variable.

welfare loss due to monopoly   The consumers' surplus lost by consumers and not gained by the monopolist that results from a monopoly producing a less-than-competitive amount of output and charging a greater-than-competitive price; also called deadweight cost.

welfare loss to society   The net loss to an economy resulting from the imposition of an artificial trade barrier; government revenues plus producer gains minus consumer losses.

Z

zero economic profits   A condition in which total revenue equals total opportunity cost of production. Firms earn a normal rate of return and $P = MR = LRMC = LRATC$.

CREDITS

INDEX